Mini
**Cambridge-Eichborn
German Dictionary**

Mini Cambridge-Eichborn German Dictionary

Business and Economics

English–German
German–English

Cambridge University Press
Cambridge
London New York New Rochelle
Melbourne Sydney

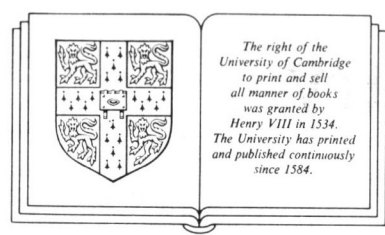

The right of the
University of Cambridge
to print and sell
all manner of books
was granted by
Henry VIII in 1534.
The University has printed
and published continuously
since 1584.

Published by the Press Syndicate of the University of Cambridge
The Pitt Building, Trumpington Street, Cambridge CB2 1RP
32 East 57th Street, New York, NY 10022, USA
10 Stamford Road, Oakleigh, Melbourne 3166, Australia

First published 1985

Printed in West Germany at Mohndruck Gütersloh

British Library cataloguing in publication data

Mini Cambridge-Eichborn German dictionary.
  1. German language – Dictionaries – English
  2. English language – Dictionaries – German
  433'.21   PF3640

ISBN 0 521 27718 3

This, the most compact of the family of
Cambridge-Eichborn German dictionaries
is intended for students and professionals in
the fields of economics, business and
accountancy.

It has been condensed very carefully from
the lexicon of the *Shorter Cambridge-
Eichborn German Dictionary* so that
significant topics are still well covered.

Abbreviations

a	=	adjective
Br.	=	chiefly used in Great Britain
fam.	=	familiar
fig.	=	figurative
o.s.	=	oneself
s.o.	=	someone
sl.	=	slang
US	=	chiefly used in the USA

Repetition sign

Entry words in bold type when repeated in the paragraph are substituted by a repetition mark (~).

Italics

A word printed in italics indicates the particular field of meaning, within which the head word is used.

Spelling

Where the American spelling differs from the British, words have been printed as follows:
catalog(ue), hono(u)r, instal(l)ment, program(me), wag(g)on.

A

A 1*(US)* erstklassig, ausgezeichnet, prima.
abandon *(v.) (balance sheet)* ausbuchen, *(customs)* abandonnieren;
~ **an option** Optionsrecht aufgeben.
abandoned ship Wrack.
abandonment *(accounting)* Ausbuchung, *(customs)* Zollabandonnierung;
~ **of the gold standard** Abgang vom Goldstandard;
~ **clause** Abandonklausel.
abate *(v.) (decrease)* abnehmen, geringer werden, *(price)* herabsetzen, ermäßigen, mindern;
~ **a fee** Gebühr niederschlagen; ~ **a tax** Steuer erlassen.
abatement *(accounting)* [Bilanz]berichtigung, *(discount)* Abschlag, [Preis]nachlaß, *(duty)* Zollerlaß;
~ **of income tax** Steuernachlaß.
ability | **to earn a livelihood** Erwerbsfähigkeit;
~ **to pay** Zahlungs-, Leistungsfähigkeit, Solvenz.
able | **to earn one's livelihood** arbeits-, erwerbsfähig;
~ **to meet competition** konkurrenzfähig.
abolish *(v.)* | **a post** Stelle streichen; ~ **a tax** Steuer abschaffen (beseitigen).
aboliton | **of debts** Schuldenannulierung; ~ **of resale price maintenance** Aufhebung der Preisbindung.
absconding debtor unbekannt verzogener Schuldner.
absentee Abwesender, Nichterschienener;
~ **rate** *(workers)* Abwesenheitssatz.
absolute unbeschränkt, absolut, bedingungslos, *(unmixed)* unvermischt, unverdünnt;
~ **assignment** Forderungsabtretung; ~ **bill of sale** unbedingter Lieferschein; ~ **indorsement** unbeschränktes Giro.
absorb *(v.) (carrier)* Frachtnachlaß gewähren, *(prices)* auffangen, *(stocks)* aufnehmen;
~ **buying power** Kaufkraft abschöpfen; ~ **part of the cost increase** Kostenerhöhungen teilweise selbst tragen; ~ **losses** Verluste auffangen; ~ **its full share of overhead** voll zur Deckung des Gemeinkostenanteils beitragen.
absorbing company *(merger)* aufnehmende Gesellschaft.
absorption *(carrier)* Frachtnachlaß, *(prices)* Auffangen;
cost ~ Kostenübernahme;
~ **of charges** Gebührenübernahme; ~ **of liquidity** Liquiditätsabschöpfung, entzug;
~ **account** Wertberichtigungskonto; ~ **costing** Kostenaufteilungsverfahren.
abstract | **of account** Konto, Rechnungsauszug; ~ **of balance sheet** Bilanzauszug;
~ **service** *(US)* Ausschnittsdienst.
abundance Ergiebigkeit, Überfluß, Fülle, Menge;
~ **of money** Geldschwemme;
~ **economy** Überflußgesellschaft.
abuse of monopoly Mißbrauch einer Monopolstellung.
accelerated | **allowance** erhöhte Abschreibung; ~ **course** Schnellkurs.

accelerating premium progressive Leistungsprämie.
acceleration clause *(instal(l)ment contract)* Fälligkeitsklausel.
accept *(v.)* | **a bill** Wechsel akzeptieren; ~ **[delivery of] goods** Waren[lieferung] abnehmen; ~ **the treasurer's account** Schatzmeister entlasten.
acceptance Auf, Annahme, *(bill of exchange)* Akzept, Akzeptierung, *(marine insurance)* Entgegennahme der Abandonerklärung;
accommodation ~ Gefälligkeitsakzept; **blank** ~ Blankoakzept; **qualified** ~ Annahme unter Vorbehalt;
~ **of a bid** *(auction sale)* Zuschlag; ~ **supra protest** Interventionsakzept;
to hono(u)r (meet) an ~ Akzept einlösen;
~ **bill** Dokumentenwechsel; ~ **credit** Akzept-, Trassierungs-, Rembourskredit; ~ **house** Diskontbank; ~ **maturity tickler** Wechselverfallbuch.
acceptor Akzeptant, Wechselverbundener.
access to capital Zugang zum Kapitalmarkt.
accession rate Einstellungsquote.
accessory | **advertising** begleitende Werbeaktion; ~ **charges (expenses)** Nebenausgaben.
accident *(casualty)* Unglücks-, Unfall;
industrial ~ Betriebsunfall; **nonoccupational (off-the-job)** ~ Unfall außerhalb der Arbeitszeit;
~ **annuity** Unfallrente; ~ **branch** *(insurance)* Gefahrenklasse.
accommodate *(v.)* unterbringen, bewirten;
~ **s. o. with small change** jem. mit Kleingeld aushelfen; ~ **a client** einem Kunden einen Dienst erweisen.
accommodation *(favo(u)r)* Gefallen, Gefälligkeit, *(loan)* finanzielle Unterstützung, *(lodgement, US)* Unterbringung;
single-room ~ Einzelzimmerreservierung;
~ **of a railway carriage** Laderaum eines Waggons;
to supply bank ~ bankmäßige Geschäfte besorgen;
~ **acceptance** Gefälligkeitsakzept; ~ **address** Hilfs-, Deck-, Gefälligkeitsadresse; ~ **allowance** Wohnungsgeldzuschuß; ~ **bill** Keller-, Gefälligkeitswechsel.
accord *(v.)* **a commission** Provision gewähren.
account Soll und Haben, Konto, (~ *stated)* Kontobestätigung, *(advertising agency)* Kunden-, Werbeetat, *(bill)* Rechnung, *(financial statement)* Jahresabschluß, *(invoice)* Faktura;
for ~ **and risk** auf Rechnung und Gefahr; **for one's own** ~ auf Eigenrechnung; **when opening an** ~ bei Kontoeröffnung;
~ **payee only** *(check)* nur zur Verrechnung;
advance ~ Vorschußkonto; **blocked** ~ Sperrguthaben; **bull** ~ Hausseposition; **checking** ~ *(US)* Girokonto; **dead** ~ umsatzloses Konto; **expense** ~ Spesenkonto; **impersonal** ~ *(Br.)* Sachkonto; **loose-leaf** ~**s** Loseblattbuchhaltung; **national** ~

volkswirtschaftliche Gesamtrechnung; **our ~** *(US, balance sheet)* Nostroguthaben; **~s payable** *(US, balance sheet)* Kreditoren, Lieferantenschulden; **profit and loss ~** Gewinn- und Verlustrechnung; **property ~** Liegenschaftskonto; **aging ~s receivable** *(US)* Debitorenaufstellung nach Fälligkeit; **~ stated** bestätigter Kontoauszug; **sundry ~s** Konto pro Diverse; **valuation ~** Wertberichtigungskonto; **~s agreed upon** festgestellter Rechnungsabschluß; **~ of customs** Zollrechnung;

~ *(v.)* *(give an account)* Rechnung ablegen, abrechnen *(place to account)* buchen; **~ for one's expenses** seine Spesen abrechnen; **to balance an ~** Konto saldieren; **to block an ~** Guthaben sperren; **to carry to new ~** auf neue Rechnung übertragen; **to cook the ~s** bei der Kontenführung Unregelmäßigkeiten begehen; **to handle an ~** Werbeetat verantwortlich bearbeiten; **to make up one's ~s** Jahresabschluß machen; **to operate on own ~** auf eigene Rechnung betreiben; **to pass to the credit of an ~** Konto kreditieren (gutschreiben); **~ carrying charges** Kontospesen; **~ day** *(stock exchange)* Abrechnungstag; **~ executive** *(advertising)* Kontakter; **~ receivable financing** *(US)* Finanzierung durch Abtretung der Debitoren; **proforma ~ sales** fingierte Verkaufsrechnung; **~ turnover** Kontoumsatz; **~ year** Rechnungs-, Wirtschaftsjahr.

accountable rechenschaftspflichtig; **~ event** Buchungsvorgang; **~ warrant** Auszahlungsanweisung.

accountability *(employee)* Haftung des Erfüllungsgehilfen, *(liability)* Haftpflicht, *(liability to give account)* Rechnungslegungspflicht.

accountant Rechnungsführer, Bilanzbuchhalter, -prüfer, bilanzsicherer Buchhalter. **certified public ~** *(US)* öffentlich zugelassener Wirtschaftsprüfer; **chartered ~** *(Br.)* geprüfter Bücherrevisor, Wirtschaftsprüfer; **~'s certificate** Prüfungsbescheinigung.

accounting *(bookkeeping)* Buchführung, -haltung, *(internal auditing)* Revisionswesen; **cost ~** betriebliches Rechnungswesen; **job order cost ~** Stückerfolgsrechnung; **manufacturing ~** Betriebsbuchhaltung; **national income ~** volkswirtschaftliche Erfolgsrechnung; **~ for units** Stück-, Einheitsrechnung; **~ dollar** Verrechnungsdollar; **~ entity** selbständig bilanzierendes Unternehmen; **General ~ Office** *(US)* Bundesrechnungshof; **~ period** Rechnungsabschnitt, Buchungszeitraum; **~ principles** Bilanzierungsrichtlinien; **~ year** Rechnungsjahr.

accredit *(v.)* Akkreditiv einräumen.

accrual | **s** *(balance sheet)* Zugänge; **depreciation ~s** entstandene Abschreibungen; **~ of interest** Auflaufen von Zinsen.

accrued aufgelaufen, angewachsen, entstanden; **~ holiday remuneration** einklagbare Ferienver-

gütung; **~ aufgelaufene Zinsen; ~ rent** Mietrückstände; **~ taxes** *(balance sheet)* Steuerschulden; **~ wages** Lohnrückstände.

accruing fällig werdend, entstehend.

accumulated | **charges** aufgelaufene Kosten; **~ demand** Nachfrageballung; **~ depreciation on fixed assets** *(balance sheet)* Wertberichtigung auf Posten des Anlagevermögens; **~ income** Unternehmensertrag, nicht verteilter Gewinn, Gewinnvortrag; **~ value** Endwert.

accumulation *(of capital)* Kapitalansammlung, *(of interest)* Auflaufen, *(life insurance)* Gewinnansammlung; **~ of an annuity** Endwert einer Annuität; **~ of reserves** Reservenbildung; **~ of savings** Spareinlagenzunahme.

achievement quotient Leistungsquotient.

acid test *(balance sheet)* Liquiditätsprüfung; **~ ratio** *(US)* Flüssigkeitsverhältnis, Liquiditätsgrad, Kennziffer.

acknowledgement Anerkenntis, *(of account)* Richtigbefund; **~ of order** Auftragsbestätigung; **~ of receipt of payment** Zahlungsbestätigung.

acquire *(v.)* | **a controlling interest in a concern** Kapitalmehrheit eines Unternehmens erwerben; **~ a customer** Kunden gewinnen.

acquisiton Erwerb, Anschaffung, Ankauf; **original ~** Ersterwerb; **~ agreement** Übernahmevertrag; **~ commission** Abschlußprovision; **~ value** Anschaffungswert.

acre produce Ertrag pro Morgen.

across-the-board increase genereller Lohnanstieg (Preisanstieg).

act Werk, *(deed)* Urkunde, Schriftstück; **Bankrupty ~** *(Br.)* Konkursordnung; **~ of bankruptcy** Konkursvoraussetzung; **~ of hono(u)r** Ehreneintritt, Notadresse; **to commit an ~ of bankruptcy** Konkursvergehen begehen.

acting diensttuend, *(managing)* geschäftsführend; **~ manager** *(Br.)* geschäftsführendes Vorstandsmitglied.

action Tätigkeit, *(lawsuit)* Klage, Prozeß, Rechtsstreit; **~ report** Tätigkeitsbericht.

active tätig, *(market)* lebhaft, *(share)* gängig; **~ account** Konto mit häufigen Umsätzen; **~ bonds** *(Br.)* festverzinsliche Obligationen; **~ capital** flüssiges Kapital; **~ commerce** *(export)* Aktivhandel; **~ debts** Außenstände; **~ demand** lebhafte Nachfrage; **~ owner (partner,** *Br.)* tätiger Teilhaber; **~ shares** gängige Aktien; **~ side** *(balance sheet)* Aktivseite; **~ trade balance** aktive Handelsbilanz.

activity Tätigkeit, *(functions)* Aufgabengebiet; **nonbanking ~** bankfremde Geschäfte.

actual | **amount** Effektiv-, Istbestand; **~ assets** Reinvermögen; **~ cash value** Versicherungswert; **~ costs** Selbst-, Ist-, Herstellungskosten; **~ hours** tatsächliche Arbeitsstunden; **~ total loss** tatsächlicher Gesamtverlust.

actuarial versicherungstechnisch, -statistisch;
~ **value** Versicherungswert.
actuary Versicherungsstatistiker.
ad *(abbr. for advertisement, US)* Anzeige, Inserat;
four-colo(u)r- ~ Vierfarbanzeige;
~ **placements** Stellenanzeigen.
add *(v.)* hinzurechnen, zuzahlen, nachschießen;
~ **the interest to the capital** Zinsen zum Kapital
schlagen.
addition Zusammenrechnung, *(balance sheet)* Zugang [beim Sachanlagevermögen], *(employees)*
Zugänge, *(thing added)* Zugabe;
~s **and improvements** Wertveränderungen; ~ **to
reserve** Zuführung zum Reservefonds.
additional | **amount** Zuschußbetrag; ~ **annuity** Zu-
satzrente; ~ **care** besondere Vorsicht; ~ **charges**
Aufschlag, ~ **comsumption** Mehrverbrauch; ~
dividend Zusatzdividende, Bonus; ~ **duty** Steuerzuschlag, *(customs)* Zollaufschlag; ~ **income** Ne-
beneinkommen; ~ **insurance** Nachversicherung;
~ **price** Preisaufschlag.
address Adresse, *(letter)* Anschrift, *(superscription of
letter)* Anrede;
abbreviated ~ Telegrammadresse; **business** ~ Ge-
schäftsanschrift; **cable** ~ Drahtanschrift;
~ **in case of emergency** *(bill of exchange)* Notadresse;
~ **label** Adressenzettel.
addressed bill Domizilwechsel.
addressing machine Adressiermaschine.
adhesive envelope gummierter Briefumschlag.
adjacent owner Anlieger.
adjourn *(v.)* **a general meeting** Generalversammlung
vertagen.
adjournment | **of a meeting** Sitzungsunterbrechung;
~ **of a petition in bankruptcy** Aufschub eines Konkursantrages.
adjudge *(v.) (award)* (zuerkennen, zuteilen);
~ **s. o. a. bankrupt** Konkursverfahren über jds.
Vermögen eröffnen; ~ **damages** Schadenersatz zu-
sprechen.
adjudicate *(v.)* zuteilen, zuschlagen;
~ **s. o. [to be] bankrupt** über j. den Konkurs verhängen; ~ **a claim** Forderung anerkennen.
adjudicated bankrupt Gemeinschuldner.
adjudication *(at auction)* Zuschlag[serteilung];
~ **in bankruptcy** Konkursverhängung.
adjunct account Hilfskonto.
adjust *(v.) (balance)* ausgleichen, abwickeln, [Ver-
sicherungs]ansprüche regulieren, *(income tax)*
fortschreiben;
~ **accounts** Konten bereinigen; ~ **the average**
Versicherungsschaden durch Besichtigung feststellen; ~ **an entry** Buchung berichtigen.
adjusted berichtigt, bereinigt;
~ **for price** preisbereinigt;
~ **costs** auf den Tageswert umgerechnete Kosten;
~ **gross income** *(US)* steuerpflichtiges Bruttoeinkommen.
adjuster, adjustor Schadenssachverständiger.

adjustment *(balancing)* Regulierung, Wertberichtigung;
average ~ Havarie-, Seeschadensberechnung; **currency** ~ Währungsangleichung; **end-of-year** ~
Rechnungsabgrenzung;
~ **of accounts** Kontenabstimmung, -glattstellung;
~ **of damages** Schadensregulierung; ~ **of real-
estate value** Fortschreibung des Grundstücks-
wertes;
~ **account** Berichtigungskonto; ~ **[income] bond**
(US) Besserungsschein; ~ **measures** Ausgleichs-
maßnahmen.
administer *(v.)* verwalten, *(price)* regulieren.
administered price Richtpreis.
administration Verwaltung, Verwaltungsapparat;
wage and salary ~ Lohn- und Gehaltswesen;
~ **of a bankrupt's estate** Konkursverwaltung; ~ **of
the National Debt** Staatsschuldenverwaltung.
administrative | **body** Verwaltungsgremium; ~ **fine**
Zwangsgeld.
administrator Verwalter, Verweser.
~ **in bankruptcy** *(Br.)* Konkursverwalter.
admission Zugeständnis, Einräumung;
duty-free ~ Zulassung zur zollfreien Einfuhr;
~ **free** Eintritt frei;
~ **of securities** Zulassung von Effekten zum Börsenhandel;
~ **tax** *(US)* Vergnügungssteuer.
admit *(v.)* ein-, zulassen;
~ **a claim** Forderung anerkennen; ~ **for quotation
on the stock exchange** zum Börsenhandel zulassen.
admitted zulässig, *(acknowledged)* anerkannt;
~ **[net] assets** von der Versicherungsgesellschaft
anerkanntes Vermögen.
admonitory letter Mahnbrief.
advance Erhöhung, *(auction sale)* Mehrgebot, *(budget)* Vorgriff, *(earnest money)* Handgeld, *(loan)*
Kredit, *(payment beforehand)* Vorschuß[zahlung],
Anzahlung, *(stock exchange)* Aufwärtsbewegung;
cash ~ Barvorschuß; **collateral** ~ Effektenlombard; **salary** ~ Gehaltsvorschuß;
~ **on the succeeding budget** Haushaltsvorgriff; ~
to a new high Steigerung auf einen neuen Höchstkurs; ~ **for travel(l)ing** Reisekostenvorschuß;
~ *(v.)* steigen, anziehen, *(building society)* zuteilen, *(lend)* [aus]leihen, [ver]borgen;
~ **the price (rate)** *(stock exchange)* Kurs hinauf-
setzen;
to close with small ~s *(stock exchange)* mit kleinen
Kursaufbesserungen schließen; **to score an** ~ **of 5
points** Kursgewinn von 5 Punkten verzeichnen;
~ **account** Vorschußkonto; ~ **booking** [Karten]-
vorverkauf, Vorausbestellung; ~ **commitment**
Kreditzusage; ~ **order** Vor[aus]bestellung; ~ **quota** Vorgriffskontingent.
advanced | **capital** Einlage; ~ **cost of living** gestiegener
Lebenshaltungsindex; ~ **member** *(building society,
Br.)* zugeteilter Bausparer; ~ **tax payment** Steuer-
vorauszahlung.
advancement Vorschuß[zahlung].

advancing | **market** Markt mit steigendem Preisniveau; ~ **prices** steigende Preise (Kurse).

adventure *(carrier)* Versand auf eigene Rechnung, *(hazardous enterprise)* gewagtes Unternehmen, *(risk)* Risiko, Wagnis;
gross ~ Bodmerei; **marine** ~ Seerisiko.

adverse | **balance** Verlustsaldo, ~ **budget** unausgeglichener Haushalt.

advertise, advertize *(v.)* werben, Werbung betreiben, Reklame machen, *(in newspaper)* inserieren;
~ **a vacancy** freie Stelle ausschreiben.

advertisement, advertizement Reklame, Werbung, Anzeige, Annonce;
classified ~ nach Branchen geordnete Inserate; **editorialized** ~ redaktionell gestaltete Anzeige; **original** ~ Einführungsreklame; **reader** ~ Textanzeige;
~ **for deposits** *(Br.)* Einlagenwerbung; ~ **in short story** feuilletonistische Anzeige;
to run an ~ **only once** Einzelinserat aufgeben;
~ **canvasser** Anzeigenakquisiteur; ~ **money** Beträge aus der Werbewirtschaft; **rate** *(Br.)* Anzeigentarif.

advertiser, advertizer Inserent, Werbungtreibender;
industrial ~ Anzeigenblatt der Wirtschaft.

advertising, advertizing Reklame, Werbung;
association ~ Gemeinschaftswerbung; **corporate [image]** ~ Firmen-, Prestigewerbung; **direct mail** ~ Postwurfsendung; **institutional** ~ Prestigewerbung; **launch** ~ *(US)* Einführungswerbung; **mailorder** ~ Versandhausreklame; **point-of-purchase** ~ Werbung innerhalb des Ladens; **stopgap** ~ Füllanzeige; **tie-in** ~ eingeblendete Reklame; **tie-up** ~ kombinierte Werbeaktion;
~ **adviser** Werbeberater; ~ **agency** Werbeagentur, Anzeigenannahme; ~ **aids** Werbematerial; ~ **approach** Aufhänger; ~ **block** Anzeigenklischee; ~ **card** Annoncentarif; ~ **copy** Werbetext; ~ **film** Werbefilm; ~ **medium** Werbeträger; ~ **motto** Slogan; ~ **page plan** Anzeigenspiegel; ~ **rate** Anzeigentarif; ~ **rate card (book)** Anzeigenpreisliste.

advice Empfehlung, Rat, *(notice)* Anzeige, Benachrichtigung;
credit ~ Gutschrift[saufgabe], **debit** ~ Lastschrift; **shipping** ~ Versandanzeige;
~ **in due course** Aufgabe folgt; ~ **of delivery** Rückschein; ~ **of fate** Bezahltmeldung.

advise *(v.)* anzeigen, avisieren;`
~ **a client** Mandant beraten.

advisory board Beratungsgremium.

affiliate Zweig-, Konzern-, Tochtergesellschaft, Filiale, Zweigorganisation;
~ *(v.)* angliedern.

affiliated angeschlossen;
~ **company (corporation,** *US)* Konzern-, Tochtergesellschaft.

affluent society Überflußgesellschaft.

affreight *(v.)* Frachtschiff heuern (chartern).

affreightment Schiffsfrachtvertrag.

afloat zirkulierend, *(debts)* ohne Schulden;
to keep bills ~ Wechsel im Umlauf haben.

afterhours *(stock exchange)* Nachbörse.

afterservice for customers Werkstätten- und Pflegedienst.

agate | **line** *(US, advertising)* Anzeigenmaß; ~ **rate** *(advertising)* Zeilenpreis.

age Lebensalter, *(full age)* Mündigkeit;
pensionable ~ Pensionierungsgrenze;
~ *(v.)* **accounts** Konten nach ihrer Fälligkeit aufgliedern;
~ **allowance** *(taxation)* Altersfreibetrag; ~ **relief** *(taxation)* altersbedingte Einkommensteuervergünstigung.

agency Tätigkeit, *(US, authority)* [Verwaltungs]behörde, Dienststelle, *(business of agent)* Agentur, Vertretung, *(place of business)* Geschäftsstelle, Büro;
chief ~ Generalvertretung; **commission** ~ Kommissionsgeschäft; **employment** ~ Stellvermittlung; **mercantile** ~ Auskunftei; **real estate** ~ Immobilienbüro; **travel** ~ Reisebüro, -agentur;
~ **coupled with an interest** Provisionsvertretung;
~ **account** Filialkonto; ~ **agreement** Geschäftsbesorgungs-, Agenturvertrag; **on an** ~ **basis** kommissionsweise; ~ **service** Dienstleistungsgeschäft; ~ **work** Vertretertätigkeit.

agenda Tagesordnung, Verhandlungsgegenstände;
to adopt the ~ Tagesordnung annehmen.

agent *(go-between)* Zwischenhändler, Vermittler, Makler, Agent, Vertreter, Geschäftsführer [im Sinne des Bürgerlichen Gesetzbuches];
bargaining ~ Tarifvertragsbevollmächtigter; **closing** ~ Abschlußagent; **general** ~ Generalvertreter, -bevollmächtigter; **house** ~ Immobilienmakler; **insurance** ~ Versicherungsvertreter; **shipping** ~ Schiffsmakler, *(US)* Verlader, Spediteur;
~**s in the field** auswärtige Vertretung;
to act as ~ in fremdem Namen handeln;
~**'s business** Kommissionshandel.

aggregate | **amount** Gesamtbetrag; ~ **mortality table** *(insurance)* Aggregattafel; ~ **wage tax** Lohnsummensteuer.

aggressive | **portion** *(investment trust, US)* risikoreicherer Teil; ~ **sales manager** draufgängerischer Verkaufsleiter.

aging | **accounts receivable** überfällige Außenstände; ~ **schedule** Fälligkeitstabelle.

agio Agio, Aufgeld, *(brokerage)* Maklergeschäft.

agiotage Aktienspekulation.

agree *(v.)* vereinbaren, übereinkommen;
~ **accounts** Konten abstimmen; ~ **about [upon] a price** Preisvereinbarung treffen.

agreed | **price** abgemachter Preis; ~~**value clause** Abschätzungsklausel.

agreement Übereinkommen, -einkunft, Vereinbarung, Abkommen;
barter ~ Tauschhandelsabkommen; **covering** ~ Mantelvertrag; **marketing** ~ Marktabsprache; **master** ~ Mustertarifvertrag; **pocket** ~ Revers; **trade** ~ Handelsabkommen; **working** ~ Interessengemeinschaft;

~ **with one's creditors** Akkord, Vergleich; ~ **by the piece** Stückakkord; ~ **country** Verrechnungsland.

agricultural | **bloc** *(parl.)* grüne Front; ~ **enterprise** landwirtschaftlicher Betrieb; ~ **marketing** Absatz landwirtschaftlicher Erzeugnisse.

aid Hilfe, Beistand, Unterstützung, *(politics)* Entwicklungshilfe; **grant-in-** ~ Staatszuschuß; **short-term interim** ~ kurzfristige Zwischenfinanzierung.

aided recall Gedächtnisstütze, Erinnerungshilfe; ~ **survey** *(insurance)* Fragebogen mit vorgedruckten Antworten.

air | **cargo** Luftfracht; ~ **carrier** Lufttransportgesellschaft; ~ **consignment note** *(Br.)* Luftfrachtbegleitschein; ~ **express** Lufteilgut, -expreßfracht; ~ **fare** Flugschein; ~ **fee** Luftpostzuschlag; ~ **shipment** Luftfrachtsendung; ~ **terminal** Großflughafen, Flughafenabfertigungsgebäude; ~ **ticket** Flugkarte, -schein.

airbill Luftfrachtbrief.

aircraft Flugzeug, Luftfahrzeug; ~ **business** Flugzeugindustrie; ~ **insurance** Flugzeug-, Luftfahrtversicherung.

airfield Flugplatz, -hafen.

airfreight Luftfracht; ~ **service** Frachtluftverkehr.

airline Flug[verkehrs]linie, Flugstrecke, *(company)* Flug-, Luftverkehrsgesellschaft, -linie; **commercial** ~ Linienfluggesellschaft; **nonscheduled** ~ Chartergesellschaft; ~ **company** (corporation, *US*) Luftverkehrsgesellschaft; **[scheduled]** ~ **service** [fahrplanmäßiger] Luftverkehrsdienst.

airliner Passagier-, Linien-, Verkehrsflugzeug; **commercial** ~ Linienflugzeug.

airmail Luft-, Flugpost; ~ **fee** Luftpostgebühr.

airplane *(US)* Flugzeug; **company** ~ Betriebsflugzeug.

airport [Verkehrs]flughafen, Flugplatz; **customs-free** ~ Freiflughafen; **to serve an** ~ **commercially** Flugplatz mit Linienflugzeugen anfliegen; ~ **restaurant** Flughafenrestaurant; ~ **service charge** Fluggastgebühr; ~ **terminal** Flughafenabfertigungsgebäude.

airway Fluglinie, -strecke, -route, -straße, Luftverkehrslinie.

alien | **corporation** *(US)* ausländische Gesellschaft; ~ **employee** Gast-, Fremdarbeiter.

alienate *(v.)* veräußern, übertragen; ~ **capital** Kapital abziehen; ~ **customers** Kunden abwerben.

alimentation of an account Dotierung eines Kontos.

alimony Unterhaltsbeitrag; ~ **payment** Unterhaltszahlung.

all | **-at-one price** Einheitspreis; ~ **-cargo service** durchgehende Gepäckabfertigung; ~ **-commodity rate** Stücktarif; ~ **-expense tour** *(US, trip)* voll-

bezahlte Besichtigungsreise; ~ **-in insurance** Einheits-, Globalversicherung; ~ **-night service** durchgehender Betrieb; ~ **sales final** kein Umtausch; ~ **-time high** absoluter Höchststand.

allocate *(v.)* zuwenden, zuweisen, zuteilen, umlegen, bestimmen, *(adjudicate)* zuschlagen, vergeben, *(intergovernmental control)* rationieren; ~ **an account** Konto dotieren; ~ **an amount to the reserve fund** Betrag dem Reservefonds zuführen; ~ **export quotas** Export kontingentieren.

allocated goods rationierte Waren.

allocation Zuwendung, *(of an account)* Dotierung, *(adjudication)* Zuschlag[serteilung], *(quota)* Kontingent, Quote; **foreign exchange** ~ Devisenzuteilung; ~ **of contract** Auftragsvergabe; ~ **of funds** Geldbewilligung; ~ **of shares** Aktienzuteilung; ~ **by tenders** Vergabe im Submissionswege.

allot *(v.)* zuweisen, *(lottery)* durch Los zuteilen, verlosen, *(shares)* repartieren; ~ **to the highest bidder** dem Meistbietenden zuschlagen.

allotment Zuerkennung, Zuschlag, *(allocation)* Zuweisung, -teilung, *(lottery)* Verlosung, *(of shares)* Aktienzuteilung; ~ **of pay** teilweiser Gehaltsverzicht; ~ **certificate** *(US)* Zuteilungsanzeige; ~ **ticket** Lohnzahlungsanweisung.

allottee Bezugsberechtigter, Zeichner.

allow zulassen, *(deduct)* in Abzug bringen, anrechnen; ~ **a bill to be protested** Wechsel zu Protest gehen lassen; ~ **a debtor time to pay** einem Schuldner Zahlungsfrist gewähren; ~ **4 % interest on deposits** Einlagen mit 4 % verzinsen; ~ **one's daughter a stipend** seiner Tochter Nadelgeld zukommen lassen; ~ **for [the] tare** Tara vergüten.

allowable zulässig, abzugsfähig.

allowance *(allotment)* Zuteilung, *(board expenses)* Kostgeld, *(discount)* Abzug, Abstrich, Rabatt, [Preis]ermäßigung, *(for entertainment)* Aufwandsentschädigung, *(taxation, Br.)* Steuerfreibetrag, *(weight)* Gutgewicht; **age** ~ *(Br.)* Altersfreibetrag; **annual** ~ *(Br.)* jährliche Absetzung für Abnutzung; **capital** ~ *(Br.)* *steuerlich zulässige Abschreibungen;* **child** ~ *(US)* Steuerfreibetrag für Kinder; **cost-of-living** ~ Lebenshaltungszuschuß; **duty-free** ~ Zollfreibetrag; **earned-income** ~ *(Br.)* Freibetrag für Einkünfte aus freiberuflicher Tätigkeit; **free baggage** ~ *(US)* Freigepäcksgrenze; **initial** ~ *(taxation, Br.)* erhöhte Sonderabschreibung; **mil(e)age** ~ Kilometergeld; **overtime** ~ Überstundenvergütung; **repairs** ~ 7b-Abschreibung; **separation** ~ Trennungszulage; **travel(l)ing** ~ Spesensatz; ~ **for board** Beköstigungsgeld; ~ **for cost of living** Teuerungszulage; ~ **for depreciation** Entwertungsrücklage; ~ **for doubtful (bad) debts** Rückstellung für Dubiose; ~ **for professional expenditure** Abzüge für Werbungskosten; ~ **of items in an account**

Rückstellung für einzelne Rechnungsposten; ~ **in kind** Deputat, Sachbezüge, -leistungen; ~ **for wear and tear** Absetzung für Abnutzung;
to make ~ *(accounting)* Rücklage bilden, *(grant reduction)* [vom Preis] nachlassen, Rabatt geben; **to stop s. one's** ~ jem. den Unterhaltszuschuß sperren.

allround price Pauschal-, Gesamtpreis.

alteration *(company)* Satzungsänderung;
~ **of a check** Scheckfälschung.

alternative tarif Ausweichfrachtsatz.

amelioration Bodenverbesserung, *(prices)* Preissteigerung.

amendment of a charter Konzessionsänderung.

amenity value *(real estate)* Annehmlichkeitswert.

American | **envelope** Versandtasche; ~ **plan** *(US)* Vollpensionssystem.

amortization [Schulden]tilgung, Amortisation;
~ **charges** Abschreibungslasten; ~ **fund** Tilgungsstock; ~ **loan** Amortisationsanleihe; ~ **mortgage** Amortisationshypothek; ~ **schedule** Tilgungsplan.

amortize *(v.)* tilgen, amortisieren, *(depreciate)* abschreiben;
~ **costs over a period of 3 years** Unkosten über 3 Jahre verteilen.

amount *(accounting)* Kapital und Zinsen;
good for any ~ gut für jeden Betrag;
actual ~ Ist-, Effektivbestand; ~ **brought in** *(bookkeeping)* Vortrag aus vorjährigem Rechnungsjahr;
~ **covered** *(insurance)* von der Versicherung gedeckter Betrag; **face** ~ Nennbetrag; **fractional** ~ *(stock exchange)* Spitzenbetrag; **guaranteed** ~ Haftsumme; **invoiced** ~ Rechnungsbetrag; **uncovered** ~ offener Posten;
~ **of** [**ordinary**] **annuity due** Endwert einer (vor[nach]schüssigen) Rente; ~ **carried over** Übertrag; ~ **of depreciation earned** verdiente Abschreibung; ~ **due at maturity** Fälligkeitsbetrag; ~ **of production** Produktionsmenge; ~ **of stock** Kapitalanteil;
to bring an ~ **up to round figures** Betrag nach oben abrunden.

ample means (resources) reichliche Mittel.

analyse *(v.)* **a balance sheet** Bilanz zergliedern.

analysis | **of an account** Kontenaufgliederung; ~ **of the market** Marktanalyse; ~ **of the cost price** Selbstkostenberechnung.

ancillary | **industries** Zulieferindustrie; ~ **workers** Hilfspersonal.

announce *(v.)* **shares** Aktien auflegen.

announcement Ankündigung, Bekanntmachung, Veröffentlichung, *(broadcasting)* kurze Werbeeinblendung;
~ **campaign** Einführungskampagne.

annual | **accounts** Jahresrechnung; ~ **audit** Jahresabschlußprüfung; ~ **depreciation** jährliche Abschreibung auf das Anlagevermögen; ~ **general meeting** *(Br.)* Hauptversammlung; ~ **increment** *(salary)* jährliche Gehaltssteigerung; ~ **report (return)** *(Br.)* Tätigkeits-, Jahresbericht, -abschluß; **gross** ~ **value** *(Br.)* Bruttojahresertrag.

annuity [Jahres]rente, Jahreseinkommen, *(annual payment)* Jahreszahlung, *(Br.)* Staatspapier, Annuität;
~ **certain** Zeitrente; **deferred** [**life**] ~ Anwartschaftsrente; **ordinary** ~ nachschüssige Rente; **survivorship** ~ Überlebensrente;
to buy an ~ sich in eine Rentenversicherung einkaufen; **to transfer the cash value into an** ~ Kapitalwert in eine Rente umwandeln;
~ **bond** Rententitel; ~ **contract** [Leib]rentenvertrag; ~ **holder** Rentenempfänger; ~ **insurance** Rentenversicherung; ~ [**benefit**] **payment** Rentenzahlung; ~ **policy** Rentenversicherungspolice.

answer Antwort, Bescheid;
in ~ **to a request** in Erledigung eines Gesuchs;
~ *(v.)* **a bill of exchange** Wechsel einlösen; ~ **by return of post** umgehend [be]antworten.

answerable for damages schadenersatzpflichtig.

answering service telefonischer Auftragsdienst.

antedate *(v.)* **a check** Scheck zurück-, vordatieren.

anticipate *(v.)* | **a bill** Wechsel vor Verfall einlösen; ~ **one's salary** Vorschuß nehmen.

anticipated | **interest** Antizipadozinsen; ~ **requirements** voraussichtlicher Bedarf.

anticipation Vorwegnahme, Vorgriff, *(extra cash discount)* [Bar]rabatt, *(rebatement)* Kleinhandelsrabatt bei frühzeitiger Warenlieferung;
~ **of property** Vorausverfügung über Vermögenserträge; ~ **test** Konjunkturbefragung.

anticipatory *(patent)* neuheitsschädlich;
~ **expenditure** [Ausgaben im] Vorgriff.

anticyclical | **measures** marktkonforme Mittel; ~ **program(me)** Konjunkturprogramm.

antitrust gesellschafts-, kartellfeindlich;
~ **action** *(US)* Kartellklage.

apart einzeln, getrennt, abgesondert;
to set ~ *(bankruptcy proceedings)* absondern.

apartment *(US)* [Miet]wohnung, Etagenwohnung, Etage, Appartment, Zimmerflucht, *(room, Br.)* Zimmer;
condominimum ~ *(US)* Eigentumswohnung; **higher-bracket** ~ Wohnung für gehobene Ansprüche;
to let furnished ~s möbliert vermieten;
~ **block** Wohnblock; ~ **building** *(Br.)* Mietshaus, Wohngebäude, Appartment-, Mehrfamilienhaus; ~ **rent** [Wohnungs]miete.

apparel manufacture *(US)* Konfektionsindustrie.

appeal *(customers)* Anklang, Anziehungskraft;
mass-emotional ~ auf Massenwirkung gerichtete Werbung;
~ *(v.)* **for funds** um Mittel werben.

appear | *(v.)* **on the debit side of the balance sheet** auf der Passivseite der Bilanz erscheinen; ~ **in the gazette** *(Br.)* in der Konkursliste erscheinen.

applicant Bewerber, Antragsteller, *(issue of shares)* Zeichner, *(job)* Stellungsuchender, Stellenbewerber;
~ **for insurance** Versicherungsnehmer; ~ **for shares** *(Br.)* Aktienzeichner.

application *(appropriation)* Konkretisierung, *(insurance)* Versicherungsaufnahmeantrag, *(for a position)* Bewerbung, Stellengesuch, Bewerbungsschreiben;
loan ~ Kreditantrag;
~ **for adjournment** Vertagungsantrag; ~ **for admission** Zulassungsgesuch, ~ **with full career details** Bewerbung mit vollständigem Lebenslauf; ~ **of funds** Mittelverwendung; ~ **of payments** Zweckbestimmung von Zahlungen; ~ **of proceeds** Verwendung des Gegenwertes; ~ **for shares** *(Br.)* Aktienzeichnung;
to file an ~ Gesuch einreichen; **to make** ~ **for shares** *(Br.)* Aktien zeichnen;
~ **backlogs** nicht bearbeitete Anträge; ~ **blank** Bewerbungs-, Anmeldeformular; ~ **call** erste Einzahlung [auf Aktien]; ~ **form** Antragsformular, -vordruck, *(Br., deposit receipt)* Einzahlungsformular, *(shares, Br.)* Bezugsrechtsformular.

applied | **art** Gebrauchsgraphik; ~ **cost** verrechnete Gemeinkosten; ~ **political economy** angewandte Volkswirtschaft.

apply *(v.)* **for** *(position)* sich bewerben um; ~ **for a credit line** Kreditantrag stellen; ~ **payments to the reduction of interest** Zahlungen zur Verkürzung der Zinsrückstände verwenden.

appoint *(v.)* | **an agent** Vertreter bestellen; ~ **a committee** Ausschuß einsetzen; ~ **a meeting** Versammlungstermin festlegen.

appointed for life auf Lebenszeit angestellt.

appointee *(US)* Kandidat, *(beneficiary)* Nutznießer.

appointment *(appropriation of money)* Zweckbestimmung, *(engagement)* Verabredung, *(nomination)* Ernennung, Einsetzung, Bestallung;
probationary ~ Probeanstellung;
~ **of an agent** Vertreterbestellung; ~**s of an office** Amtseinkünfte, Sporteln;
~**s board** *(Br.)* Büro für die Vermittlung von Führungskräften; ~ **book** Terminkalender.

apportion | *(v.)* **the costs** Kosten umlegen; ~ **losses evenly over the year** Verluste gleichmäßig über das ganze Jahr verteilen.

apportionment *(shares)* Repartierung;
~ **of contract** Sukzessivlieferungsvertrag; ~ **of indirect cost** Gemeinkostenumlage.

appraisal [Ab]schätzung, Bewertung, Wertbestimmung;
condemnation ~ Enteignungstaxe;
~ **of damage** Schadensabschätzung; ~ **of investment** Anlagenbewertung;
~ **profile** Bewertungsskala.

appraise *(v.)* abschätzen, bewerten, taxieren.

appraised value Schätz[ungs]wert.

appraisement *(valuation)* [Ab]schätzung, Taxierung, *(value)* Taxwert;
official ~ Bewertung durch Sachverständige.

appraiser Schätzer, Taxator, *(insurance)* Schadensabschätzer;
general ~ *(US)* Zollsachverständiger.

appreciate *(v.)* *(improve)* sich im Wert verbessern,

(raise in value) Wert erhöhen, *(rise in value)* im Wert steigen, Wertsteigerung erfahren, *(valuate)* bewerten, taxieren, [ab]schätzen.

appreciation *(balance sheet)* Aufwertung von Anlagen, *(investment fund)* Wertzuwachs, *(rise in value)* Wertzuwachs;
~ **in prices** Kurs-, Preissteigerung.

apprehensive period *(insurance)* Zeitspanne erhöhter Gefahr.

apprentice Volontär, Eleve, Lehrling, Lehrjunge;
~ **age** Lehrlingsjahre; ~ **program(me)** [Lehrlings]-ausbildungsprogramm.

apprenticeship [kaufmännische] Lehre, Lehrzeit;
to serve one's ~ in der Lehre sein;
~ **agreement** Lehrlingsvertrag.

approach Auffahrt, Zugang, *(advertising)* Aufhänger, Blickfänger im Anzeigentextanfang.

appropriation *(bankruptcy proceedings)* Aussonderung, *(US, funds set apart)* Bereitstellungsfonds, *(setting apart of funds)* Bereitstellung, Zuweisung;
budgetary ~**s** Ansätze des Haushaltsplans; **discretionary** ~**s** *(US)* freie Rücklagen; **legal** ~**s** *(US)* gesetzliche Rücklagen;
~ **of unascertained goods** Konkretisierung einer Gattungsschuld; ~ **of money to a debt** Verrechnung auf die Schuldsumme; ~ **of profit** Gewinnverwendung; ~ **of surplus** *(US)* Rücklagen-, Reservenbildung;
~ **account** Rückstellungskonto.

approval Zustimmung, *(of account)* Richtigbefund;
~ **of the acts of directors** Entlastung des Vorstands; ~ **of the balance sheet** Bilanzverabschiedung;
~ **sale** Kauf auf Probe.

approve *(v.)* **an account** Richtigkeit einer Rechnung anerkennen.

approved | **bill** anerkannter Wechsel; ~ **indorsed notes** zusätzlich girierte Solawechsel.

approximate | **amount** ungefährer Wert; ~ **calculation** Kostenüberschlag; ~ **value** Annäherungswert.

apron Talon.

arbitrage Arbitrage, *(arbitration)* Schiedsspruch;
compound ~ Mehrfacharbitrage; **interest** ~ Zinsarbitrage; **stock** ~ Effektenarbitrage;
~ **dealer** Arbitragehändler.

arbitral award Schiedsspruch.

arbitrary willkürlich, eigenmächtig, *(discretionary)* in das Ermessen gestellt;
~ **assessment** auf Schätzungen beruhende Veranlagung; ~ **method of profit distribution** *(insurance)* mechanisches Dividendensystem; ~ **price** willkürlicher Preis.

arbitrate *(v.)* [durch Schiedsspruch] schlichten, *(stock exchange)* durch Kursvergleich feststellen.

arbitration Schlichtungs-, Schiedsverfahren;
compound ~ Mehrfacharbitrage; **stock** ~ Effektenarbitrage;
~ **agency** Schlichtungsstelle.

arbitrator Schiedsrichter, -mann, Schlichter;
~ **of average** Dispacheur.

area Fläche, Raum *(region)* Region, Bezirk, [Geltungs]gebiet, *(tel.)* Gebührenzone;
big-city ~ Großstadtgebiet; **built-up** ~ geschlossene Ortschaft; **depressed (distressed)** ~ Notstandsgebiet; **development** ~ *(Br.)* Fördergebiet; **postal** ~ Postzustellungsbezirk; **trading** ~ Wirtschaftsraum; **undeveloped** ~ noch nicht erschlossenes Gelände;
~ **of assessment** Steuerbezirk; ~ **under cultivation** Anbaufläche;
~ **agreement** *(bargaining)* Regionalabkommen; ~ **-development program(me)** Notstandsgebietsplan; ~ **headquarters** Bezirksgeschäftsstelle; ~ **pricing** Zonentarif.
armament | **industry** Rüstungsindustrie; ~ **plant** Rüstungsbetrieb.
arrange *(v.) (agree upon)* vereinbaren, verabreden; ~ **with creditors** Gläubigervergleich schließen; ~ **an insurance** Versicherung[svertrag] abschließen.
arrangement *(agreement)* Ab-, Übereinkommen, *(compromise)* [Gläubiger]vergleich; **blocking** ~ Stillhalteabkommen; **financial** ~s Zahlungsvereinbarungen; ~ **of claims** Rangfolge von Konkursforderungen; ~ **for an extension of time** Zahlungsabkommen.
arrears [Zahlungs]rückstände; **rent** ~ rückständige Miete; ~s **on interest** Verzugszinsen; ~ **of wages** Lohnrückstand; **to be in** ~ **with one's correspondence** Briefschulden haben.
arrest of goods Warenbeschlagnahme.
arrival | **of goods** Warenzufuhr; **await** ~ *(post)* nicht nachsenden!; ~**book** Fremdenbuch; ~ **draft** *(US)* Tratte mit beigefügten Verschiffungsdokumenten.
art, applied Kunstgewerbe; **finished** ~ reproduktionsreife Vorlage; ~ **director** Atelierleiter; ~ **paper** Kunstdruckpapier.
article *(agreement)* Vertrag, *(clause)* Klausel, Bestimmung, Paragraph, Absatz, *(commodity)* Artikel, Ware;
branded ~s Markenartikel; **high-class** ~ Qualitätsware; **knockdown** ~ Massenware; **price-maintained** ~ Waren mit gleichbleibenden Preisen;
~ **of average quality** Durchschnittsware; ~ **of every-day use** täglicher Gebrauchsartikel;
~ *(v.) (bind as apprentice)* in die Lehre geben; ~ **a seaman for a voyage** Seemann für eine Reise anheuern;
to have an ~ **in stock** Artikel führen.
articles Satzung, *(goods)* Güter, Waren;
factory-produced ~ Fabrikware; **mass-produced** ~ Massenartikel, -ware; **ship's** ~s Heuervertrag; ~ **of apprenticeshup** Lehrvertrag; ~ **of association** *(Br.)* Gesellschaftsvertrag, Satzung; ~ **of incorporation** *(US)* Gründungsurkunde (Satzung) einer AG; ~ **of high quality** Qualitätsware; ~ **of quick sale** Artikel mit hoher Umschlagsgeschwindigkeit;
to serve one's ~ seine Lehrjahre durchmachen.

ascertain *(v.)* | **a balance** Saldo vergleichen; ~ **the costs** Kosten ermitteln; ~ **a price** Preis festsetzen.
ascertained damages festgestellter Schaden.
ascertainment | **of costs** Kostenerfassung; ~ **of price** Preisfestsetzung; ~ **of profits** Gewinnfeststellung; ~ **error** *(statistics)* Erhebungsfehler.
asked gefragt, gesucht, *(stock exchange)* Brief; **at the best possible** ~ bestens; ~ **and bid** *(stock exchange)* Brief und Geld; ~ **price** *(stock exchange)* Briefkurs.
assay Metallprobe, -analyse; ~ *(v.)* Feingehalt feststellen; ~ **office bar** amtlich auf Feingehalt geprüfter Goldbarren; ~ **value** Münzwert.
assemble einberufen, *(fit together)* zusammensetzen, montieren.
assembly Versammlung, Zusammenkunft, *(fitting together)* Zusammenbau, Montage, *(production unit)* Fertigungseinheit.
~ **cost system** Kostenrechnung für Montagebetrieb; ~ **automated** ~ automatische Montageeinrichtungen.
assembly line laufendes Band, Montagebahn, Fließband.
assembly-line production Fließbandfertigung.
assembly | **plant** Montagewerk; ~ **schedule** Montageplan; ~ **work** Montagearbeit.
assess *(v.) (charge with a tax)* besteuern, [steuerlich] veranlagen, *(value)* [steuerlich] bewerten, einschätzen, taxieren;
~ **separately** *(income-tax return)* steuerlich getrennt veranlagen;
~ **a building** Einheitswert feststellen; ~ **a fine** Bußgeld festsetzen; ~ **property for improvements** Einheitswert eines Grundstücks neu feststellen.
assessable taxierbar, *(liable to duty)* abgabesteuerpflichtig, steuerbar;
~ **stock** *(US)* nachschußpflichtige Aktien.
assessed | **rental** steuerlicher Mietwert; ~ **valuation** Abschätzung zu Steuerzwecken; ~ **value** Einheits-, Steuerwert.
assessment Steuerbetrag, [Steuer]veranlagung, *(appraisal)* Einschätzung, *(capital stock)* Nachzahlungsveranlagung, *(contribution, US)* Umlage, Beitrag, *(duty)* Steuer, Abgabe, *(ship)* Havarieaufmachung, *(valuation of property)* Grundstücksbewertung;
additional ~ Nachveranlagung; **rating** ~ Einschätzung der Kreditfähigkeit;
~**of damage** Schadenfeststellung;
to apply for a separate ~ um getrennte Steuerveranlagung einkommen;
~ **costs** Veranlagungskosten; ~ **district** Steuer[veranlagungs]bezirk; ~ **notice** Steuerbescheid.
assessor Beisitzer, Steuerschätzer, Taxator; **loss** ~ Schadensabschätzer.
asset *(balance sheet)* Aktivposten, Haben; **to discard an** ~ [Betriebs]anlage außer Betrieb setzen.
assets *(balance sheet)* Aktiva, Deckungsforderun-

gen, *(insolvence)* [Konkurs]masse, *(of merchant)* Betriebsvermögen, *(property)* Vermögenskomplex, -bestand, Güter und Rechte; **active** ~ produktives Betriebsvermögen; **admitted** ~ *(insurance law)* anerkannte Versicherungsansprüche; **bankruptcy** ~ Konkursmasse; **concealed** ~ verschleierte Vermögenswerte; **dead** ~ unproduktive Anlagen; **floating (fluid,** *US)* ~ Betriebsmittel, Umlaufvermögen; **limited-life** ~ kurzfristige Anlagegüter; **liquid** ~ *(accounting)* flüssige (liquide) Mittel, *(US, balance sheet)* Umlaufvermögen; **nominal** ~ Buchwerte; **permanent** ~ Anlagevermögen; **short-life** ~ kurzlebige Wirtschaftsgüter; **watered** ~ Wirtschaftsgüter mit überhöhtem Buchwert; **working** ~ Betriebskapital; ~ **in kind brought in** Sacheinlage; ~ **and liabilities** Aktiva und Passiva; **to carry as** ~ [in der Bilanz] aktivieren.

asset | account Bestandskonto; ~ **-creating** vermögenswirksam; ~ **and liability statement** Gewinn-und Verlustrechnung; ~ **valuation reserve** Wertberichtigung.

assign *(v.) (allot)* anweisen, zuweisen, *(transfer)* übertragen, -eignen; ~ **in blank** blanko übertragen.

assignee Zessionar, Forderungsübernehmer; ~ **for the benefit of creditors** zugunsten der Gläubiger bestellter Pfleger (Treuhänder).

assignment *(allotment)* Zu-, Anweisung, Zuteilung, *(transfer)* Zession, Übertragung; **general** ~ Vermögensübertragung zugunsten der Gläubiger; ~ **of accounts receivable** Diskontierung von Buchforderungen, Debitoren-, Forderungsabtretung; ~ **for the benefit of creditors** außerkonkursliche Abwicklung zugunsten der Gläubiger; ~ **of property** Vermögensübertragung; ~ **of a share in partnership** Abtretung eines Gesellschafteranteils.

assistance Unterstützung, Hilfe; **national** ~ *(Br.)* Fürsorge[unterstützung], Sozialhilfe; **public (social)** ~ *(US)* Sozialhilfe, Fürsorge[unterstützung].

assistant Mitarbeiter, Gehilfe, Hilfskraft, -person; **shop** ~ Verkäufer, Ladenangestellter; ~ **auditor** Hilfsrevisor; ~ **director** stellvertretender Direktor;

assisted person *(Br.)* Fürsorgeempfänger.

associate Gesellschafter, Teilhaber; ~ *(v.)* **o. s. with s. o. in an undertaking** jds. Teilhaber in einem Unternehmen werden.

associated | buying office gemeinsames Einkaufsbüro; ~ **company** *(Br.)* Konzern-, Beteiligungsgesellschaft; ~ **overseas territories** assoziierte überseeische Gebiete; ~ **trademarks** Sortiments-, Serienmarken.

association *(EC)* Assoziierung, *(corporation)* Gesellschaft, *(society)* Genossenschaft, Verband; **building and loan** ~ Bausparkasse; **industrial** ~ *(US)* Wirtschaftsverband; **professional** ~ Berufsgenossenschaft; **vocational** ~ Fachverband;

~ **of creditors** Gläubigervereinigung; ~ **of trademarks** Verbindung von Warenzeichen; ~ **advertising** Gemeinschaftswerbung; ~ **agreement** Tarifvereinbarung, *(Common Market)* Assoziatsabkommen.

assort *(v.)* | **a cargo** Ladung zusammenstellen; ~ **a stock of goods** mit einem Warensortiment ausstatten.

assortment Sortiment, Auswahl, Kollektion.

assume *(v.)* **all risks** volles Risiko übernehmen.

assumption of risk Risikoübernahme.

assurance *(life insurance, Br.)* [Lebens]versicherung; **convertible term** ~ *(Br.)* Risikoumtauschversicherung; **industrial** ~ *(Br.)* Kleinlebensversicherung; ~ **payable at death** *(Br.)* Todesfallversicherung.

assure *(v.) (life insurance, Br.)* versichern, *(property)* auflassen; ~ **s. one's life** *(Br.)* j. in eine Lebensversicherung einkaufen; ~ **s. one's position** jds. Stellung festigen.

assurer *(Br.)* Assekurant, Versicherungsträger.

astray | freight Stückgutfracht; ~ **waybill** Stückgutbegleitschein.

attach an account *(v.) (US)* Konto pfänden.

attached business value Verkehrswert.

attachment Arrest, Beschlagnahme, Pfändung; **economic** ~ wirtschaftliche Angliederung; ~ **of earnings** *(Br.)* Lohnpfändung aus Unterhaltsklage; ~ **of risk** *(insurance)* Risikobeginn.

attend *(v.)* | **to the collection of a bill** Inkasso eines Wechsels besorgen; ~ **to an order** Auftrag ausführen.

attendance *(at meetings)* Besucherzahl, *(service)* Bedienung, Aufwartung; ~ **on the stock exchange** Börsenbesuch.

attention Aufmerksamkeit, Beachtung, *(care)* Wartung, Pflege; ~ **of** zu Händen von; **for your kind** ~ zur gefälligen Kenntnisnahme; ~ **of a conscientious businessman** Sorgfalt eines gewissenhaften Kaufmanns; ~ **value** Werbe-, Zugkraft, Reklamewirkung.

attest *(v.)* | **a copy of record** Abschrift beglaubigen.

attic flat ausgebaute Mansardenwohnung.

attraction *(advertising)* Zugkraft.

attractive price günstiger Preis.

attribute *(v.)* **profits** Gewinne [steuerlich] zurechnen.

auction [öffentliche] Versteigerung, Auktion; **mock** ~ Scheinauktion; **to put up at** *(US)* **(to,** *Br.)* ~ öffentlich versteigern, meistbietend verkaufen; ~ **bill** Versteigerungsliste; ~ **company** Versteigerungsfirma; ~ **day** Versteigerungstermin; ~ **fees** Auktionsgebühren, Versteigerungskosten; ~ **mart** Auktionslokal; ~ **price** Auktions-, Versteigerungspreis; ~ **sale** Auktion, Versteigerung.

auctioneer Auktionator, öffentlicher Versteigerer.

audience Audienz, Empfang, *(readers)* Hörer-, Lesekreis; **high-income** ~ wohlsituiertes Publikum; **viewing** ~ Fernsehpublikum;

~ **analysis** Hörer-, Zuschauer-, Leseranalyse; ~ **builder** zugkräftige Sendung (Werbung); ~ **research** Leser- und Höreranalyse.

audit [amtliche] Rechnungsprüfung, Buch-, Bilanzprüfung, Revision, *(rent)* Mietabrechnung, *(statement of accounts)* Bilanz;
cash ~ Kassenrevision, **desk** ~ Buchprüfung auf Grund mitgenommener Belege; **external** ~ Buchprüfung durch [betriebsfremde] Berufsprüfer; **voucher** ~ Belegprüfung;
~ **for credit purpose** Kreditprüfung; ~ **of personnel** *(US)* Personalbeurteilung;
~ *(v.)* **an abstract of account** Kontoauszug vergleichen;
~ **a balance sheet** Bilanz prüfen;
~ **certificate** Revisionsbericht; **internal** ~ **department** Innenrevision; ~ **fees** Prüfungsgebühren; ~ **period** Prüfungszeitraum; ~ **year** Revisionsjahr.

audited balance sheet geprüfte Bilanz.

auditing Rechnungsprüfung, Revision[swesen];
~ **above local level** überörtliche Revision;
~ **company** Revisionsgesellschaft, ~ **expert** Buchsachverständiger, Prüfer, Revisor; ~ **order** Revisions-, Prüfungsauftrag.

auditor Buch-, Kassen-, Rechnungsprüfer, Buchsachverständiger, Wirtschaftsprüfer, *(firm)* Treuhandgesellschaft;
official ~ Revisionsbeamter; **professional (public)** ~ öffentlicher Bücherrevisor, Wirtschaftsprüfer;
to have the ~s in Betriebsprüfung haben;
~'s **certificate** Prüfungs-, Revisionsbericht.

austerity program(me) Sparprogramm der öffentlichen Hand, Not-, Sanierungsprogramm.

autarchy Autarkie.

authority *(expert)* Sachverständiger, Fachmann, *(government agency)* [Verwaltungs]behörde, *(delegated power)* Vertretungsmacht, Bevollmächtigung;
approving ~ Genehmigungsbehörde;
~ **to act** Vertretungsbefugnis; ~ **to collect debts** Inkassovollmacht; ~ **to contract** Abschlußvollmacht; ~ **to pay** *(banking)* Einlösungsermächtigung; ~ **to sign** Unterschriftsvollmacht;
to be invested with full ~ mit Vollmacht versehen sein.

authorization Ermächtigung, Genehmigung;
~ **to fill in a blank** Blankettausfüllungsbefugnis;
~ **to pay** Auszahlungsermächtigung;
~ **form** Vollmachtsformular; ~ **request** Behördenanforderung.

authorize *(v.)* bevollmächtigen, Vollmacht erteilen, ermächtigen, autorisieren;
~ **the sale of effects** Effektenverkaufsauftrag erteilen.

authorized befugt, verfügungsberechtigt, ermächtigt, bevollmächtigt, beauftragt, autorisiert;
to be ~ **to negotiate** Verhandlungsvollmacht haben;

~ **agent** Bevollmächtigter; ~ **capital** *(Br.)* [stock, US] Stamm-, Grundkapital; ~ **dealer** Vertragshändler; ~ **version** maßgebende Fassung.

auto | **assembly** Automontage; ~ **court** Motel; ~ **dealership** Autovertretung; ~ **insurance** Kraftfahrzeugversicherung; ~ **sales** Umsätze der Autoindustrie; ~ **trial** Kfz-Abnahme.

automatic | **basement** Ausverkaufsabteilung; ~ **currency** elastische Währung; ~ **selling** Automatenverkauf; ~ **telephone** Selbst[wähl]anschluß; ~ **telephone answering service** Fernsprechauftragsdienst; ~ **wage adjustment** automatische Lohnregulierung.

automobile | **insurance** *(US)* Kraftfahrzeugversicherung; ~ **public liability** Kraftfahrzeughaftung.

auxiliary | **account** Hilfskonto; ~ **advertising** Zusatzwerbung; ~ **book** Kladde.

availability *(broadcasting)* noch verfügbare Werbezeit, *(ticket)* Gültigkeit;
~ **date** *(US, banking)* Wert[stellung], Valuta.

available | **in all sizes** in allen Größen lieferbar;
~ **assets** jederzeit greifbare Aktiva; ~ **funds** liquide Mittel; ~ **surplus** *(balance sheet)* nicht zweckgebundener Gewinn.

avails *(US)* Ertrag.

aval Wechselbürgschaft, Aval.

average Durchschnitt, Mittelwert, *(ship)* Havarie, Seeschaden, *(statistics)* arithmetisches Mittel;
free from ~ nicht gegen Havarie versichert; **general (gross)** ~ große Havarie; **particular (simple)** ~ besondere (einfache) Havarie;
~ *(v.)* **down** *(stock exchange)* Durchschnittskosten vermindern;
to adjust the ~ Havarie aufmachen;
~ **adjuster** Dispacheur, Havarievertreter; ~ **adjustment** Havarieberechnung; ~ **book** Durchschnittssaldenlist; ~ **burden rate** Durchschnittsgemeinkostensatz; ~ **due date** mittlerer Zahlungstermin; ~ **life** durchschnittliche Nutzungsdauer; ~ **net assets** Nettovermögen; ~ **price level** Gesamtpreisindex; ~ **sort** Mittelsorte; ~ **stock** durchschnittlicher Lagerbestand.

aviation Luftfahrt, Flugwesen, Fliegerei;
~ **industry** Flugzeugindustrie; ~ **insurance** Flugzeug-, Luftfahrtversicherung.

avoidance | **of bankruptcy proceedings** Konkursabwendung; ~ **of taxes** Steuerumgehung.

avoirdupois [weight] Handelsgewicht.

award Zuerkennung, Zubilligung, *(arbitration)* Schiedsspruch;
~ **of a contract** Auftragsvergabe;
~ *(v.)* **a contract** [Fabrikations-, Lieferungs]auftrag (Zuschlag) erteilen; ~ **a prize** prämieren;
to offer an ~ Belohnung aussetzen.

awarded damages zuerkannter Schadenersatz.

awarding of contracts Auftragszuteilung.

axe *(v.)* **expenditure** Ausgaben beschneiden;
to get the ~ *(US, coll.)* entlassen werden.

B

b *(trade)* Güteklasse B. zweite Qualität.
baby | **bonds** *(US)* kleingestückelte Schuldverschreibungen; ~ **car** Kleinwagen.
back *(bill of exchange)* Rückseite, *(Br., stock exchange)* Prolongationsgebühr;
~ *(v.)* **the currency** Währung stützen; ~ **out of a bargain** sich aus einem Geschäft zurückziehen; **to be** ~ **in one's rent** mit seiner Miete im Rückstand sein; **to be a little high** ~ *(stocks)* stark zurückgefallen sein;
~ *(a.) (overdue)* rückständig, im Rückstand; ~ **charges** Rückspesen; ~ **-to-** ~ **credit** *(US)* Gegenakkreditiv; ~ **interest** Zinsrückstände; ~ **taxes** Steuerrückstände.
backbone *(business)* Stammpersonal.
backed | **bill** avalierter Wechsel; ~ **note** abgestempelter Ladeschein.
backer Wechselbürge.
background Vorgeschichte, Werdegang; **financial** ~ finanzieller Rückhalt.
backing Hilfe, Stütze, Unterstützung, *(bank notes)* Deckung, *(bill of exchange)* Giro, Indossament, *(stock exchange)* Stützungskäufe.
backletter *(US)* Ungültigkeitsvereinbarung.
backlog *(of orders, US)* unerledigter Auftragsbestand;
~ **demand** Bedarfsreserven.
backup *(delivery)* Wartezeit;
~ **of goods** Warenanhäufung.
backwardation *(Br.)* Deport, Kursabschlag, *(Br., stock exchange)* Prolongationsgebühr;
~ **business** *(Br.)* Deport-, Kostgeschäft; ~ **rate** *(Br.)* Prolongationsgebühr.
bad | **bargain** schlechtes Geschäft; ~ **check** ungedeckter Scheck; ~ **claim** unbegründeter Anspruch; ~ **coin** falsche (schlechte) Münze; ~ **debtor** zahlungsunfähiger Schuldner; ~ **-faith taker** bösgläubiger Erwerber.
bag Sack, *(Br.)* Geldbeutel, Börse;
to hold the ~ *(US)* auf seiner Ware sitzenbleiben.
baggage *(US)* [Reise]gepäck;
checked ~ aufgegebenes Gepäck; **excess** ~ Mehrgepäck, gebührenpflichtiges Gepäck; ~ **check** Gepäckschein; ~ **checkroom** Gepäckaufbewahrung; ~ **counter** Gepäckaufgabe; ~ **locker** Handgepäckschließfach; **self-claim** ~ **system** Gepäckselbstbedienung.
bagman *(Br.)* Handlungsreisender.
bail Bürge, *(security)* Bürgschaft, Kaution;
~ *(v.)* Bürgschaft leisten, bürgen, *(deposit)* [Waren] hinterlegen;
~ **bond** Bürgschaftsschein.
bailee Verwahrer, Gewahrsamsinhaber, Depositar, Pfandgläubiger, *(trustee)* Treuhänder.
bailment Bürgschafts-, Kautionsleistung;
gratuitous ~ unentgeltlicher Hinterlegungsvertrag.

bait *(advertising)* Lockartikel, Köder.
balance Bilanz, *(difference between Cr. and De.)* Rechnungs-, [Konten]saldo, Saldoauszug;
adjusted trial ~ berichtigte Rohbilanz; **adverse** ~ passive Bilanz; ~ **brought (carried) forward** Saldovortrag, Vortrag auf neue Rechnung; **credit** ~ Guthaben; **debit** ~ Soll-, Debetsaldo, Verlustabschluß;
~**s with home and foreign bankers** Nostroguthaben bei in- und ausländischen Bankfirmen; ~ **in favo(u)r** Saldoguthaben; **favo(u)rable** ~ **of trade** aktive Handelsbilanz; ~ **of trade in goods and services** Waren- und Dienstleistungsbilanz;
~ *(v.)* saldieren, abschließen;
~ **the books** Bilanz ziehen; ~ **the budget** Etat ausgleichen;
to carry a ~ **forward [to new account]** Saldo auf neue Rechnung vortragen; **to show in the** ~ in der Bilanz aufführen; **to strike a** ~ Saldo feststellen, Bilanz ziehen;
~ **clerk** Bilanzbuchhalter; ~ **deficit** Verlustabschluß; ~ **ledger** Saldenliste.
balance of payments Zahlungsbilanz;
~ **adjustment** Zahlungsbilanzausgleich; ~ **burden** Zahlungsbilanzverpflichtung; ~ **deficit** Zahlungsbilanzdefizit.
balance sheet Bilanz, Rechnungsabschluß;
audited ~ geprüfte Bilanz; **consolidated** ~ konsolidierter Jahresabschluß;
to make the ~**s public** Bilanzziffern veröffentlichen;
~ **date** Bilanz[ierungsstich]tag; **[consolidated]** ~ **item** [konsolidierter Bilanzposten].
balanced budget ausgeglichener Etat.
balancing | **of accounts** Bücher-, Rechnungsabschluß; ~ **entry** Ausgleichsposten, Gegenbuchung.
bale Ballen;
~ **goods** Ballengut.
balloon *(v.) (stock exchange, US)* Börsenpapiere künstlich in die Höhe treiben.
ballyhoo laute Reklame, Werberummel.
band *(advertising)* Streifenanzeige, *(exchange system)* Bandbreite;
~ **conveyor** Transport-, Fließband.
bank Bank[haus], Bankgeschäft, *(typewriter)* Tastatur;
clearing ~ Abrechnungsstelle; **deposit** ~ Depositenbank; **Federal Reserve** ~ *(US)* [etwa] Landeszentralbank; **investment** ~ Emissionsbank; **jointstock** ~ *(Br.)* Aktienbank; **labor** ~ *(US)* Gemeinwirtschaftsbank; **mutual savings** ~ *(US)* Genossenschaftsbank; **post-office savings** ~ *(Br.)* Postsparkasse; **works savings** ~ Betriebssparkasse; **International** ~ **for Reconstruction and Development** Weltbank; ~ **for International Settlements** Bank für Internationalen Zahlungsausgleich;
~ *(v.)* Banktätigkeit ausüben, Bankgeschäfte machen;

to be deeply in hock to the ~s stark bei den Banken verschuldet; to have an account with a ~ Konto bei einer Bank unterhalten; to run on a ~ Ansturm auf die Bankschalter machen.

bank | account bankkonto, -guthaben; ~ accountant Bankbuchhalter; ~ annuities (Br.) Staatspapiere, Konsols; ~ bill Banknote, (bill of exchange) Bankwechsel, (US) Kassenanweisung; ~ cashier Kassierer; ~ charter Bankprivileg; ~ cheque (Br.) (check, US) Bankscheck, -anweisung; ≗ Commissioner (US) Bankaufsichtsbehörde; ~ credit card Kreditkarte; ~ debt to trade debt mit den Bankschulden hinter den Lieferantenschulden zurücktreten; ~ depositor Einleger; ~ discount [Bank]diskont; ~ failure Bankkrach; ~ holdings Bankguthaben; ~ holiday (Br.) Bankfeiertag; ~ messenger Kassenbote; ~ money order Bankanweisung; ~ note Banknote, Kassenschein; ~ rate policy (Br.) Diskontpolitik; ~ reconciliation statement Kontoabrechnung; ~ shutdown Bankenschließung; ~ statement Bankauszug, (balance sheet) Bankbilanz.

bankable bankfähig, diskontierbar.

bankbook Einzahlungs-, Kontobuch.

banker Bankier, Bankverbindung, Zahlstelle.

banker's | acceptance credit Akzeptkredit; ~ commission Bankprovision; ~ order (Br.) Bank-, Dauerauftrag.

banking Bankwesen, -geschäft, Kreditgewerbe; ~ account Bankkonto; ~ business Bankgeschäft, -gewerbe; ~ committee Bankenenquête; ~ hours Schalterstunden; ~ regulations staatliche Ordnung des Kreditwesens; ~ support Bankenintervention.

bankroll (US) Bündel Banknoten.

bankrupt, [adjudicated] Konkurs-, Gemeinschuldner, Insolvent, Bankrotteur; involuntary ~ Zwangsgemeinschuldner; to adjudge s. o. a ~ j. bankrott erklären; to discharge a ~ Konkursverfahren aufheben.

bankruptcy Bankrott, Konkurs[verfahren]; to file a petition in ~ Antrag auf Konkurseröffnung stellen; to lodge a proof in ~ Konkursforderung anmelden; ~ commissioner Konkursrichter; to initiate ~ proceedings Konkursverfahren einleiten.

banner (Br. advertising) Werbespruchband, Streifanzeige, (headline) Balkenüberschrift; ~ profit einmaliger Gewinn.

bar (ingots) Barren; ~ gold Barrengold.

bargain Geschäft, Abschluß, Kaufvertrag, (cheap purchase) Gelegenheitskauf, Sonderangebot, Spottpreis, (stock exchange, Br.) einzelner [Geschäfts]abschluß, Börsengeschäft; into the ~ als Zugabe, gratis, obendrein; ~s done (stock exchange) gehandelte Kurse; losing ~ Verlustabschluß; optimal ~ Prämiengeschäft; ~ (v.) feilschen, schachern, handeln; ~ away mit Verlust verkaufen;

to rescind a ~ von einem Geschäft zurücktreten; ~ basement Ausverkaufsabteilung im Erdgeschoß; ~- basement prices Niedrigpreise, (stock exchange) gewinnbringende Anfangskurse; to be on the ~ counter (stock exchange) billig angeboten sein; ~ hunting (stock exchange) Effektenspekulation; ~ level niedrigst kalkulierbarer Preis; ~ price Ausverkaufspreis.

bargaining Handeln, Feilschen, (collective agreement) Tarifabschluß; industry-wide ~ Manteltarifvertragsverhandlungen; to be on the ~ cards im Verhandlungsspielraum liegen; ~ unit Tarifgruppe.

barometer stocks (US) Standardwerte.

barren money totes Kapital.

barter Tausch[geschäft], -handel; ~ (v.) Tauschhandel treiben, handeln; ~ exchange Kompensationsverkehr; ~ transaction Kompensationsgeschäft.

base Basis, Grundlage, (statistics) Bezugs-, Grundwert, (taxation) Steuerobjekt; ~ (a.) (debased) unecht, falsch; ~ coin (US) Scheidemünze, (Br.) falsche Münze; to form a ~ pattern (marketing) Widerstandslinie aufbauen; ~ pay Grundgehalt, (guaranteed rate) garantiertes Grundgehalt; ~ price Einkaufspreis; ~ salary Grundgehalt; ~ year Basisjahr, (statistics) Vergleichsjahr.

basic | abatement Steuerfreibetrag; ~ expenditure bleibende Unkosten; ~ hourly rate Ecklohn; ~ industry Schlüssel-, Grundstoffindustrie; ~ inventory Anfangsinventur; ~ piece rate Stücklohn; ~ rate Grundtarif; ~ value Einheitswert eines Grundstücks.

basing point system (US) Preisberechnungsverfahren auf einheitlicher Frachtbasis.

basis Basis, (securities) Rendite; adjusted ~ bereinigte Besteuerungsgrundlage; cost ~ Bewertungsgrundlage; ~ of allocation Verteilungsschlüssel; ~ of exchange Umtauschverhältnis; to operate on a nonprofit ~ gemeinnützig arbeiten.

basket (economics) Warenkorb.

bear (stock exchange) Baissespekulant, Baissier; ~ (v.) auf Baisse spekulieren; to go a ~ auf Baisse spekulieren; ~ (a.) (market) flau, lustlos, (prices) fallend; ~ account (Br.) Baisseposition; ~ transaction Baissegeschäft.

bearer Überbringer, (holder) [Wechsel]inhaber; ~ bond Inhaberobligation; ~ share Inhaberaktie.

bearish (stock exchange) baissetendenziös; ~ covering Deckungskäufe der Kontermine; ~ tendency (tone) Baissetendenz, -strömung.

behindhand im Rückstand.

belt conveyor Förderband.

benefical | enjoyment Nießbrauchrecht; ~ improvement Schönheitsreparaturen; ~ ownership wirtschaftliches Eigentum.

beneficiary Begünstigter, *(insurance)* Versicherungsnehmer, Leistungsberechtigter;
   primary ~ Rentenempfänger;
   ~ **association** Unterstützungsverein.

benefit Vergünstigung, Vorteil, *(insurance)* Versicherungsleistung, *(pecuniary aid)* Unterstützung, Beihilfe, Zuschuß;
   for the public ~ im öffentlichen Interesse; **in pecuniary** ~ in gewinnsüchtiger Absicht;
   death ~ Sterbegeld; **disablement** ~ Versehrten-, Invalidenrente; **immediate** ~ *(insurance)* sofortiger Versicherungsschutz; **maternity** ~ Wochengeld; **package** ~ tarifliche Sondervergütung; **severance** ~ Trennungsgeld;
   ~ *(v.)* begünstigen, Nutzen bringen, nützen;
   ~ **by the exchange** Kursgewinne mitnehmen;
   ~ **association** Unterstützungsverein; ~ **fund** Unterstützungsfonds; ~ **pension** Ruhegehaltsbezüge; ~ **plan** Sozialzulagensystem; ~ **society** *(Br.)* Hilfskasse.

benevolent association Wohltätigkeitsverein.

berth *(position, Br.)* Stelle, *(ship)* Ankerplatz, *(sleeper)* Schlafwagenplatz, Koje;
   to load a ship on the ~ Schiff mit Stückgut befrachten;
   ~ **cargo** Stückgutladung; ~ **freighting** Stückgutfrachtgeschäft.

best, at *(price)* bestens, bestmöglich;
   ~ **quality** erste Sorte, feinste Qualität; ~ **seller** Verkaufsschlager.

betterment tax Wertzuwachssteuer.

beverage industries Getränkeindustrie.

bid [Lieferungs]angebot, Offerte, *(at auction)* Gebot, *(stock exchange)* geboten, Geld;
   feigned ~ Scheingebot; **maximum** ~ Höchstgebot; ~**s and offers** *(stock exchange)* Brief und Geld;
   ~ *(v.)* **on government contracts** sich an staatlichen Ausschreibungen beteiligen;
   to invite ~**s** *(US)* Auftrag ausschreiben;
   ~ **bond** *(US)* Bietungsgarantie; ~ **price** *(stock exchange)* Geldkurs.

bidder Ausschreibungsbeteiligter;
   successful ~ Auftragnehmer;
   to allot to the highest ~ dem Meistbietenden zuschlagen.

bidding Gebot, Bieten;
   to lose out on a ~ bei einer Auftragszuteilung leer ausgehen;
   ~ **period** Ausschreibungsfrist; ~ **price** Erstangebot.

big | **business** *(US)* Großunternehmen; ~ **-income earner** Großverdiener; ~ **ticket** teurer Verkaufsartikel.

bill *(US, abstract of account)* Kontoauszug, *(account)* Rechnung, Faktura, Nota, *(US, bank note)* Banknote, *(bill of exchange)* Wechsel, *(certificate)* Schein, Bescheinigung, *(poster)* Anschlag[zettel];
   accommodation ~ Gefäligkeits-, Freundschaftswechsel; **auction** ~ Auktionsliste; **blank** ~ Blanko-
wechsel; **bogus** ~ Kellerwechsel; **demand** ~ Sichtwechsel; **discountable** ~ disksontfähiger Wechsel; **dishono(u)red** protestierter Wechsel; **domiciled** ~ Domizilwechsel; **eligible** ~ landeszentralbankfähiger Wechsel; **fine** ~ *(Br.)* Primawechsel, erstklassiger Handelswechsel; **hand** ~ Schuldschein, *(bill of exchange)* eigener (trockener) Wechsel;
   ~ **payable to order** Orderpapier; ~**s payable** *(US, balance sheet)* Wechselverpflichtungen; **renewal** ~ Prolongationswechsel; **shipping** ~ Konnossement, Frachtbrief, Ladeschein; **trade** ~ Warenwechsel;
   ~ **of charges** *(US)* Gebührenrechnung; ~ **of clearance** Zollfertigungsschein; ~ **for collection** Inkassowechsel; ~ **of consignment** Frachtbrief; ~ **after date** Datowechsel; ~ **on deposit** Pensionswechsel; ~**s eligible for discount** Diskontmaterial; ~ **of entry** Zolldeklaration.

bill of exchange Wechsel, Tratte;
   ~ **against documents** Wechsel gegen Dokumente.

bill | **of exchequer** Schatzanweisung; ~**s in hand** Wechselbestand, -portefeuille; ~ **of health** *(ship)* Gesundheitsattest.

bill of lading Seefrachtbrief, Konnossement, *(US)* Frachtbrief, Ladeschein;
   grouped ~ Sammelkonnossement; **shipped** ~ Bordkonnossement.

bill | **of parcels** spezifizierte Warenrechnung; ~ **of quantities** Baukostenvoranschlag; ~ **of sale** Verpfändungsurkunde; ~**s in a set** Satz, Wechsel; ~ **of sight** Zollerlaubnisschein; ~ **of specie** Sortenzettel, Bordereau, Stückverzeichnis;
   ~ *(v.)* in Rechnung stellen, fakturieren, *(poster)* Zettel ankleben, plakatieren;
   to accept a ~ Wechsel akzeptieren; **to back a** ~ Wechselbürgschaft leisten; **to compute a** ~ Verfallstag eines Wechsels berechnen; **to discount a** ~ Wechsel diskontieren; **to furnish a** ~ **with a stamp** Wechsel verstempeln; **to leave a** ~ **unpaid** Wechsel nicht honorieren; **to make a** ~ **payable** Wechsel zahlbar stellen; **to note a** ~ Wechselprotest erheben; **to protest a** ~ Wechselprotest einlegen; **to run up a** ~ anschreiben lassen; **to trade in** ~**s** Wechselreiterei betreiben;
   ~ **board** Anschlagtafel; ~ **broker** *(Br.)* Wechselmakler; ~ **brokerage** Wechselcourtage, ~ **case** *(Br.)* Wechselportefeuille; ~ **discount** *(Br.)* Wechseldiskont; ~ **form** Wechselvordruck; ~ **jobber** Wechselreiter; ~ **protest** Wechselprotest.

billboard *(US)* Anschlagtafel.

billed order angekündigte Kommissionsware.

billfold *(US)* Brief-, Geldscheintasche.

billhead Rechnungsvordruck.

billing Fakturieren;
   ~ **clerk** Fakturist.

billposter Plakat-, Zettelankleber.

billposting Plakatanschlag, Plakatierung.

binder Aktendeckel, *(insurance, US)* Deckungszusage.

binding | **agreement** unwiderrufliches Abkommen; ~ **offer** freibleibendes Angebot.

black *(balance sheet)* Gewinnzone, -bereich;
to show up in ~ **on the balance sheet** sich auf der Aktivseite der Bilanz niederschlagen;
~ **-coated worker** *(Br.)* Büroangestellter; ~ **list** *(bankruptcy)* Insolventenliste.
black market Schwarzmarkt;
~ **operations** Schwarzhandel[sgeschäft].
black | marketeer Schwarzhändler; ~ **rent** ungesetzliche Miete.
blackleg *(strike, Br.)* Streikbrecher.
blank *(lottery)* Niete, *(printed form)* Formular, Vordruck;
~ *(a.)* leer, *(form of bill)* unausgefertigt, *(unfilled space)* unausgefüllt;
to accept in ~ blanko akzeptieren; **to sign in** ~ *(document)* blanko unterschreiben;
~ **acceptance** Blankoakzept; ~ **bill** Wechselblankett; **to give s. o. a.** ~ **check** jem. unbegrenzte Vollmachten erteilen; ~ **form** Blankoformular, Blankett; ~ **policy** Generalpolice.
blanket pauschale Kostenangabe;
~ *(v.)* **the entire market** ganzen Markt erfassen;
~ **insurance** Kollektivversicherung; ~ **price** Einheits-, Pauschalpreis; ~ **rate** Pauschaltarif.
bleed *(advertising)* Anschnitt;
~ *(a.)* druckangeschnitten; ~ **premium** Anschnittzuschlag.
blind | advertisement Blindanzeige; ~ **-alley job** Beruf ohne Aufstiegsmöglichkeiten; ~ **entry** Pro-memoria-Buchung.
blitz-training Schnellkurs.
block Block, *(of buildings, US)* Häuserkomplex;
in ~**s** in Bausch und Bogen;
currency ~ Währungsblock;
~**of securities** Effektenpaket;
~ *(v.)* **an account** Guthaben (Konto) sperren;
~ **booking** *(advertising)* Gesamtauftrag; ~ **policy** Generalpolice; ~ **slip** *(check book)* Kupon; ~ **trade** *(stock market)* Pakethandel.
blockade | [by sea] Blockade;
economic ~ Wirtschaftsblockade.
blockbuster *(US)* Kassenschlager.
blocked gesperrt, blockiert, *(capital)* eingefroren;
~ **account** Sperrkonto; ~ **currency** nicht frei konvertierbare und transferierbare Währung.
blocking | of account Kontensperre;
~ **arrangement** Stillhalteabkommen.
blowup Vergrößerung, *(advertising)* Riesenformat, *(smash, US)* Pleite.
blue | chips *(US, stock exchange)* Standard-, Spitzenwerte; ~**collar people** *(US)* Fabrikarbeiter; ~ **-ribbon task force** hochdotierter Arbeitsstab.
blueprint Lichtpause, *(fig.)* Planung, Entwurf;
~ **stage** Entwurfsstadium.
blurb Reklamestreifen.
board *(billboard)* Anschlagtafel, *(board money)* Pension, Kostgeld, *(directors of a company)* Vorstand, *(governmental department)* Ministerialabteilung, Dienststelle, *(US)* Börse;
bound in ~**s** steif broschiert, kartoniert; **on the** ~ *(stock exchange)* *(US)* börsenfähig;

executive *(US)* ~ geschäftsführender Ausschuß; ~ **partial** ~ Halbpension; **rationing** ~ Bewirtschaftsstelle;
~ **and lodging** volle Pension, Kost- und Logis;
~ **of Audit** *(US)* Landesrechnungshof; ~ **of creditors** Gläubigerausschuß; ~ **of directors** Verwaltungsrat nach angelsächsischem Recht, *(acting board)* Firmenvorstand; ~ **of Exchequer** *(Br.)* Finanzministerium; ~ **of Governors** *(International Monetary Fund)* Direktorium; ~ **of management** Vorstand, Direktorium; ~ **of Trade** *(Br.)* Wirtschafts-, Handelsministerium, *(US)* Handelskammer;
~ *(v.)* *(provide with meals)* ver-, beköstigen;
to be represented on the ~ im Aufsichtsrat [vertreten] sein; **to take goods on** ~ Waren an Bord nehmen;
~ **approval** Vorstandsgenehmigung; ~ **chairman** Vorstandsvorsitzender; ~ **lot** *(US, stock exchange)* handelsfähige Nominalgröße; ~ **room** Sitzungsraum, *(stock exchange)* Börsensaal.
boarder Pensionär, Kostgänger.
boarding money Kostgeld.
boardinghouse Gasthaus, [Fremden]pension.
body *(advertisement)* Haupttext, *(number of persons)* Gremium;
advisory ~ beratendes Organ;
~ **of creditors** Gläubigerausschuß; ~ **of a letter** eigentlicher Briefinhalt;
to treat as a ~ **corporate for tax purposes** steuerlich wie eine juristische Person behandeln.
bogus | bill Kellerwechsel; ~ **check** *(US)* gefälschter Scheck; ~ **company** Schwindelfirma; ~ **transactions** Scheingeschäft.
boil *(v.)* **over** *(business cycle)* überschäumen.
bona fide gutgläubig, *(genuine)* echt, solide;
~ **capital** aus verkäuflichen Waren bestehendes Kapital; ~ **creditor** gutgläubiger Forderungsinhaber; ~ **offer** solides Angebot.
bonanza *(US)* unerwartet großer Gewinn;
~ **period of industrial development** wirtschaftliche Blütezeit; ~ **year** Erfolgsjahr.
bond *(customs, Br.)* Zollniederlagen, -lager, *(debenture)* [öffentliche] Schuldverschreibung, festverzinsliches Wertpapier, Obligation, Pfandbrief;
in ~ unter zollamtlichem Verschluß; **out of** ~ verzollt, ab Zollager;
average ~ Havarieschein; **baby** ~**s** Kleinobligationen; **business corporation** ~ Industrieobligation; **construction** ~ Kaution des Bauunternehmers; **convertible** ~**s** *(US)* Wandelschuldverschreibungen; **coupon** ~**s** Inhaberschuldverschreibungen; **Exchequer** ~ *(Br.)* langfristige Schatzanweisungen; **fidelity** ~ Garantieschein; **high-yield** ~**s** hochverzinsliche Obligationen; **investment** ~**s** Anlagepapiere; **local** ~ *(Br.)* Kommunalschuldverschreibung; **lottery** ~ Auslosungsanleihe; **master** ~ Unternehmerkaution; **municipal** ~ *(US)* Kommunalschuldverschreibung; **other** ~**s** *(balance sheet)* sonstige Verbindlichkeiten; **passive** ~ zins-

lose Schuldverschreibung; **preference** ~ Vorzugsobligation; **registered** ~ Namensobligation; **special assessments** ~ Anliegerbeiträge; **tax** ~ *(US)* Steuergutschein; **tax-exempt** ~s ertragsteuerfreie Obligationen; **treasury** ~s Schatzanweisungen;

~s **and other interests** *(balance sheet)* Beteiligungen und Wertpapiere; ~s **with attractive tax features** mit attraktiven Steuervorteilen ausgestattete Obligationen;

~ *(v.)* unter Zollverschluß nehmen, *(debenture)* Schuldverschreibung ausstellen;

~ s. o. Kaution für j. stellen lassen;

to be in ~ im Zollverschluß liegen; **to issue** ~s Pfandbriefe ausgeben; **to take out of** ~ ausklarieren;

~ **broker** *(US)* Fondsmakler; ~ **capital** Anleihekapital; ~ **creditor** Pfandbriefgläubiger; **to spread** ~ **discount over the years** das Disagio eines Pfandbriefs über die Jahre verteilen; ~ **issue** Pfandbriefausgabe; ~ **market** Pfandbriefmarkt; ~ **yieldings** Pfandbriefrendite.

bonded unter Zollverschluß, *(pledged)* verpfändet; ~ **debt** fundierte Schuld; ~ **goods** zollpflichtige Waren; ~ **port** [Zoll]freihafen; ~ **warehouse** Transitlager.

bondholder Obligationär, Pfandbriefinhaber.

bonding warehouse Lagerhaus für unverzollte Waren.

bonus *(compensation for a loan)* Kreditprovision, *(douceur)* Bestechungsgeld, *(extra dividend)* Superdividende, *(gratuity)* Tantieme, *(increase in salary)* Gehaltszulage, *(insurance)* Dividende, *(premium)* Prämie, *(salesman)* Umsatztantieme, *(share of profits)* Gewinnbonus, *(subsidy to industry)* Subvention;

Christmas ~ Weihnachtsgratifikation; **cost-of-living** ~ Teuerungszulage; **hazard** ~ Gefahrenzulage; **incentive** ~ Leistungszulage; **no-claim** ~ Prämie für unfallfreies Fahren;

~ **on shares** Gratisaktie;

~ **arrangement** Tantiemenvereinbarung; ~ **issue** Ausgabe von Gratisaktien; ~ **share (stock,** *US)* Genuß, Gratisaktie; **to work on a** ~ **system** auf Prämienbasis arbeiten.

book Kassen-, Geschäftsbuch;

bargain ~ Schlußnotenregister; **slovenly kept** ~s unordentlich geführte Bücher; **loose-leaf** ~ Buch in Loseblattform; **order** ~ Auftragsbuch; **savings bank** ~ Sparkassenbuch;

~ **of arrivals** Fremdenbuch; ~ **of [printed] forms** Formularsammlung; ~ **of rates** Zolltarif;

~ *(v.)* buchen, anschreiben, aufzeichnen;

~ **in advance** im voraus buchen; ~ **a long-distance call** Ferngespräch anmelden; ~ **an omitted item** Posten nachtragen; ~ **an order** Auftrag annehmen; ~ **a sleeper** Schlafwagenkarte lösen; ~ **space** Anzeigenraum in Auftrag geben;

to audit the ~s Bücher revidieren; **to be deep in the** ~s hohe Schulden haben; **to shut the** ~s Unternehmen aufgeben;

~ **account** Kontokorrentkonto; **assigned** ~ accounts *(US)* abgetretene Buchforderungen; ~ **claim** Buchforderung; ~ **cost** Buchwert; ~ **entry** Buchung; **to send by** ~ **post** *(Br.)* unter Kreuzband verschicken; ~ **value** Bilanz-, Buchwert, *(net worth)* Nettowert eines Unternehmens.

booked besetzt, belegt, *(registered)* gebucht.

booking Buchung, Bestellung;

advance ~ Vorverkauf; **heavy** ~s umfangreiche Vorbestellungen; **onto** ~ *(airport)* Anschlußbuchung;

~ **clerk** *(Br.)* Schalterbeamter, Fahrkartenverkäufer; ~ **item** Buchungsposten; ~ **order** Bestellzettel.

bookkeeper Buchhalter, Rechnungsführer.

bookkeeping Buchführung, -haltung;

columnar ~ amerikanische Buchführung; **factory** ~ Betriebsbuchhaltung;

~ **by double (single) entry** doppelte (einfache) Buchführung;

~ **loss** Buchverlust; ~ **voucher** Buchhaltungsbeleg.

booklet Werbebroschüre, -faltblatt, Prospekt.

boom geschäftliche Blütezeit, wirtschaftlicher Aufschwung, [Hoch]konjunktur;

backlog ~ Aufholkonjunktur; **stock-market** ~ Aktienhausse;

~ **in capital investment** Investitionsgüterkonjunktur;

~ *(v.)* rapiden Aufschwung nehmen, *(business)* konjunkturellen Auftrieb haben;

to be on the dark side of the ~ im Konjunkturschatten liegen; **to curb the** ~ Hochkonjunktur bremsen;

~ **market** Haussemarkt; ~ **years** Zeiten wirtschaftlicher Blüte.

booming | demand Nachfragekonjunktur; ~ **economy** glänzende Konjunktur, Hochkonjunktur; ~ **recovery** konjunkturelle Erholung.

boomlet Kleinkonjunktur.

boomtime konjunkturelle Blütezeit.

boost *(US coll.)* Preistreiberei, -steigerung;

~ **in taxes** Steueranstieg;

~ *(v.)* **business** Wirtschaft ankurbeln; ~ **a company into the black** Unternehmen in die Gewinnzone führen.

booster Preistreiber.

booth Verkaufs-, Schau-, Jahrmarktsbude;

fund-raising ~ Sammelstelle für Geldspenden.

borrow *(v.)* borgen, entnehmen, [ent]leihen;

~ **heavily on a short-term basis** sich kurzfristig erheblich verschulden; ~ **for the purchase of land** Grundstücksankauf finanzieren.

borrowed capital Fremd-, Leih-, Kreditkapital.

borrower Darlehns-, Kreditnehmer;

first-class ~ erste Adresse.

borrowing *(loan)* Schuld-, Kreditaufnahme;

treasury ~ Steuergutscheinausgabe;

~ **on accounts receivable** *(US)* Kreditaufnahme durch Abtretung von Debitoren;

~ **demand** Geldbedarf; ~ **power** *(director)* Kreditaufnahmebefugnis.

boss Betriebsleiter, Chef.

both-to-blame *(law of insurance)* beiderseitiges Verschulden.

bottleneck in production Engpaß in der Produktion.

bottom *(stock exchange)* Tiefpunkt;
~ **(v.)** **[out]** *(market)* Widerstandslinie aufbauen; ~ **price** Tiefstpreis, niedrigster Preis, *(stock exchange)* Tiefst-Kurs; ~ **quality** schlechteste Qualität.

bottomry Bodmerei[geld], Schiffsverpfändung;
to advance money on ~ Geld auf Bodmerei geben; ~ **bond** Bodmereibrief, Schiffswechsel; ~ **interest** Bodmerei, -prämie.

bought | **by auction** ersteigert;
~ **book** Einkaufsbuch; ~ **note** Kaufnote, Schlußschein.

bouncer *(cheque)* ungedeckter Scheck.

bounty Subvention, Ausfuhrprämie;
~-**fed** subventioniert.

box *(advertisment)* Kästchen, *(luggage, Br.)* Reisekoffer, *(post office, US)* Schließfach, Safe; ~ **letter** postlagernder Brief; ~ **number advertisment** Kennzifferanzeige.

box office Vorverkaufsstelle;
~ **draw** *(US)* Kassenmagnet.

box | **rent** *(US)* Schließfachmiete; ~ **wag(g)on** *(Br.)* Güterwaggon.

boxcar *(US)* Güterwaggon.

boxed for export in Seeverpackung.

boycott Boykott[verfahren].

bracket Schicht, *(loan)* Tranche, *(taxation)* Steuerklasse, Einkommensstufe;
salary ~ Besoldungsgruppe; **wage** ~ Lohnstufe; **to be in the higher income** ~s zu den wohlhabenden Leuten zählen.

brain trust *(US)* Beraterstab, Gehirntrust, hochqualifizierte Expertengruppe.

branch *(banking)* Neben-, Zweigstelle, Filiale *(of business establishment)* Zweiggeschäft, -stelle, -niederlassung;
manufacturing ~ Fabrikationszweig; ~ **of industry** Gewerbe; ~ **account** Filialkonto; ~ **business** Zweiggeschäft.

brand Sorte, Marke, Klasse, *(quality)* Qualität, *(trademark)* Güte-, Waren-, Fabrikzeichen;
house ~ Firmenzeichen; **top-selling** ~ Spitzenerzeugnis der Markenindustrie; ~ *(v.)* zum Markenartikel entwickeln; ~ **advertising** Markenartikelwerbung; ~ **image** Markenbild, Werbestil; ~ **manager** Markenbetreuer; ~-**new** fabrik-, funkelnagelneu.

breach *(infringement)* Übertretung, Verstoß;
free from ~ **and damages** frei von Bruch und Beschädigung; ~ **of professional etiquette** satndeswidriges Verhalten; ~ **of warranty** Gewährleistungsbruch.

bread | **line** *(fig.)* Existenzminimum; ~ **ticket (US)** Essensbon.

bread and butter notwendiger Lebensunterhalt.

breadearner, breadwinner Ernährer.

break Bruchstelle, *(labo(u)r)* Arbeitspause, *(radio)* Sendeunterbrechung für Werbedurchsagen, *(stock exchange, US)* Kurseinbruch;
~ **(v.)** **(go bankrupt)** bankrott machen; ~ **far below the previous low level** weit unter den letzten Tiefststand fallen; ~ **bulk** mit Entladen anfangen; ~ **a code** entschlüsseln; ~ **down** *(analyse, US)* aufgliedern, -schlüsseln; ~ **up** entflechten, *(safe deposit)* aufbrechen, *(ship)* verschrotten, abwracken.

break even *(US)* Geschäftsabschluß ohne Gewinn und Verlust;
~ *(v.)* Rentabilitätsschwelle erreichen; ~ **analysis** Deckungsbeitragsrechnung; ~ **chart** Rentabilitätabelle, Gewinnschwellendiagramm; ~ **rent** Ertragsmiete.

break-in period Einarbeitungszeit.

breakage Bruch[schaden], Refaktie.

breakdown Zusammenbruch, *(analysis)* Analyse, Aufschlüsselung, -gliederung;
~ **of costs** Kostenaufgliederung; ~ **of machinery** Maschinenausfall; ~ **gang** Unfallkolonne, Abschleppmannschaft; ~ **value** *(securities)* Substanzwert.

breaking | **up cartels** Entkartellisierung; ~ **bulk** Löschen der Ladung.

breakup | **price** Abbruchpreis; ~ **value** Altmaterial-, Abbruchswert.

bring *(v.)* **forward** auf neue Rechnung vortragen.

brisk *(business)* lebhaft, flott;
~ **sale** glatter Absatz.

broad market aufnahmefähiger Markt.

broadcast Rundfunk[übertragung], Radiosendung;
delayed ~ Bandaufzeichnung; **sponsored** ~ *(US)* Patronatssendung; ~ **advertising** Werbefunk.

broadcasting | **of news** Nachrichtendurchsage;
~ **business** Rundfunkindustrie; ~ **network** Sendegruppe; ~ **station** Rundfunkstation, -anstalt.

broaden *(v.)* **its line of products** sein Produktionsprogramm ausweiten.

broadsheet Plakat, Prospekt-, Flugblatt.

broadside [großer] Faltprospekt, Schautafel.

brochure Druck-, Flugschrift, Broschüre.

broke *(sl)* pleite, abgebrannt, blank.

broken kaputt, *(bankrupt)* bankrott, ruiniert;
~ **down by** aufgeschlüsselt nach; ~ **account** *(Br.)* umsatzloses Konto; ~ **money** Kleingeld; ~ **time** Verdienstausfall.

broker [Börsen-, Waren-, Wechsel-, Handels-]makler, *(go-between)* Mittelsmann;
bill ~ Wechselmakler, *(money* ~*)* Geldvermittler; **bond** ~ Fondsmakler; **curb[stone]** ~ *(US)* Freiverkehrsmakler; **customs** ~ Zollagent; **exchange** ~ Kurs-, Börsenmakler; **insurance** ~ Versicherungsagent; **real-estate** ~ *(US)* Immobilienmakler.

broker's | **commission** Maklerprovision; ~ **memorandum (note)** Schlußnote, -schein, -zettel.

brokerage Maklergeschäft, -gebühr, Courtage;
buying ~ Einkaufsprovision;

~ **account** Courtagerechnung; ~ **concern** Maklerfirma, -büro.
brought forward Vortrag, Übertrag.
bubble company Schwindelgesellschaft.
buck slip interne Aktennotiz.
bucket shop *(US)* Winkelbörse.
budget Haushalt[splan], Staatshaushalt, Etat, *(cost of living)* Lebenshaltungskosten;
adverse ~ Haushaltsdefizit; **balanced** ~ ausgeglichener Haushalt; **direct labo(u)r** ~ Arbeitskräftebedarf; **workmen's** ~ Arbeiterhaushalt;
~ *(v.) (US)* Haushaltsplan aufstellen;
to balance the ~ Etat (Haushalt) ausgleichen; **to open the** ~ Haushaltsrede halten; **to put the** ~ **in the red** Haushaltsdefizit herbeiführen; **to trim fat from one's** ~ übersetzten Etat (Haushalt) kürzen;
~ **accounting** Soll-, Plankostenrechnung; ~ **bill** *(US)* Haushaltsvorlage; ~ **costs** Soll-, Plankosten; ~ **grant** bewilligte Haushaltsmittel; **to hold the** ~ **line** festgesetzten Etat nicht überschreiten; **~-priced** preisgünstig, *(advertising)* realistisch kalkuliert; ~ **savings** Etatseinsparungen; ~ **year** Budgetjahr.
budgetary haushaltsmäßig, -rechtlich, etatsmäßig;
~ **accounting** Finanzplanung; ~ **appropriations** bewilligte Haushaltsmittel; **industrial** ~ **control** finanzielle Betriebsplanung; ~ **estimate** Etats-, Haushaltsvoranschlag.
budgeted production Produktionsplanung.
budgeteer Haushaltsexperte, -spezialist.
budgeting Haushaltsaufstellung, Etatisierung.
build *(v.)* **one's business in a country** sich in einem Land absatzmäßig verankern.
build up | an inventory Lager aufstocken; ~ **a lot of loan demand** erheblichen Kreditbedarf auslösen; ~ **reserves** Reserven ansammeln.
builder's estimate Baukostenvoranschlag.
building Gebäude, Bauwerk;
high-rent ~ hochverzinsliches Renditeobjekt; **prefabricated** ~ Fertigbau;
~s less depreciation *(balance sheet)* Gebäude nach Abschreibungen;
~ **account** Gebäudekonto; ~ **boom** Baukonjunktur; ~ **business** Bauwirtschaft; ~ **contractor** Bauunternehmen; ~ **ground** Bauplatz, -stelle; ~ **lease** *(Br.)* Erbbauvertrag; **home ~ and loan association** *(US)* Bausparkasse; ~ **slump** rückläufige Baukonjunktur; ~ **society** *(Br.)* Bausparkasse.
buildup of stocks Lageraufbau.
built-in flexibility *(economic policy)* eingebaute Flexibilität.
bulge *(US)* plötzliches Anziehen der Effektenkurse.
bulk *(cargo)* unverpackte [Schiffs]ladung;
to get the ~ **of one's income by way of commission** Hauptteil seines Einkommens im Provisionswege verdienen; **to lose the** ~ **of one's goods** fast sein ganzes Vermögen verlieren;
~ **article** Massenartikel, -gut; ~ **cargo** Waggonladung, Schüttgut; ~ **consumer** Großverbraucher; ~ **mail** Postwurfsendung, Massendrucksachen; **~-**

order price Pauschalbezugspreis; ~ **rate** *(Br.)* Mengenrabatt; ~ **sampling** Stichprobenentnahme; ~ **shipment** Sturzgütersendung; ~ **tour** Pauschalreise.
bulky | cargo sperrige Ladung; ~ **goods** Sperrgut.
bull Haussier, Haussespekulant;
~ *(v.)* auf Hausse spekulieren;
~ **the market** Preise hochtreiben, Kurse steigern; ~ **account** *(US)* Hausseengagement.
bulldog clip Büroklammer.
bulletin Nachrichtenblatt, -sendung, Bulletin.
bullion [Gold-, Silber]barren;
~ **point** Goldpunkt; ~ **reserve** Goldreserve.
bullish steigend, haussetendenziös, haussierend;
~ **tendency (tone)** Haussestimmung, -tendenz. •
bumping *(US)* Beibehaltung langjähriger Angestellter bei Entlassungen.
bunch of orders Auftragsbündel.
bunched *(US, stock exchange)* fortlaufend notiert;
~ **costs** pauschalierte Kosten; ~ **income** für längeren Zeitraum in einem Steuerjahr anfallendes Einkommen.
bundle sale Koppelungsverkauf.
buoy [Anker]boje, Bake, Seezeichen;
~ *(v.)* **the economic index** dem Konjunkturindex Auftrieb geben.
buoyancy *(market)* Elastizität, Erholungsfähigkeit, *(taxes)* inflationsbedingter Anstieg.
buoyant *(market)* sehr fest, steigend.
burden Gemein-, Handlungskosten;
~ *(v.)* **with a mortgage** mit einer Hypothek belasten; ~ **with taxes** besteuern;
~ **absorption rate** Gemeinkostenverrechnung; ~ **adjustment** Unkostenaufteilung; ~ **center** Kostenstelle.
bureau Amts-, Geschäftszimmer, Büro.
Bureau | of the Census *(US)* Statistisches Bundesamt; ~ **of Employment Security** *(US)* Sozialversicherungsbehörde; ~ **of Old-Age and Survivors Insurance** *(US)* Versicherungsaufsichtsamt.
bursary Stipendium, *(Br.)* Schatzmeisteramt.
business *(bargain)* Abschluß, Geschäft, *(total box-office receipts)* Gesamteinnahme, *(calling)* Beruf, Geschäft, Beschäftigung, Gewerbe, Geschäftszweig, *(commercial house)* Geschäfts-, Handelsbetrieb, Firma, Geschäft, *(customers)* Kundschaft, *(shop)* [Laden]geschäft, Geschäftslokal, *(turnover)* Umsatz;
away on ~ geschäftlich verreist; **strictly for** ~ nur zu Geschäftszwecken;
~ **done** *(stock exchange)* getätigte Börsenabschlüsse;
big ~ *(US)* Großunternehmen, -industrie; **capital-oriented** ~ kapitalintensives Unternehmen; **over-the counter** ~ Tafelgeschäft; **family-owned** ~ Familienbetrieb; **fancy-goods** ~ Modewarengeschäft; **investment** ~ Anlagegeschäft; **losing** ~ verlustbringendes Geschäft; **mail-order** ~ Versandhausgeschäft; **private** ~ Privatwirtschaft; **retail** ~ Einzelhandelsgeschäft; **slower** ~ Umsatzrückgang; **small**

~ *(US)* Mittel- und Kleinbetriebe, gewerblicher Mittelstand;

~ **on joint account** Konsortialgeschäft; ~ **in used cars** Gebrauchtwagengeschäft; ~ **done for the monthly clearance** Ultimogeschäft; ~ **of same nature** gleichartiger Geschäftsbetrieb; **to be about one's master's** ~ für seinen Dienstherrn tätig sein; **to be in** ~ **for o. s.** auf eigene Rechnung arbeiten; **to be well versed in** ~ geschickter Geschäftsmann sein; **to carry on the** ~ **under one's name** Geschäft unter seinem eigenen Namen führen; **to do** ~ **as a banker** Bankier sein; **to double** ~ Umsatz verdoppeln; **to go into** ~ **for o. s.** sich selbständig machen; **to go out on** ~ *(sales agent)* auf [Vertreter]tour gehen; **to have a share in the** ~ Geschäftsanteil haben; **to plough back in** ~ wieder im Geschäft anlegen; **to quit** ~ sich aus dem Geschäft[sleben] zurückziehen; **to transact** ~ geschäftlich tätig sein; **to wind up a** ~ Geschäft liquidieren;

~ **acumen** Geschäftssinn; ~ **address** Büroadresse; ~ **administration** *(US)* Betriebswirtschaft[slehre]; ~ **advertising** Wirtschaftswerbung; ~ **analyst** Konjunkturanalytiker; **to be a long-term** ~ **asset** zu den langfristigen Aktivposten eines Unternehmens zählen; ~ **auditing service** Buch- und Betriebsprüfung; ~ **briefs** Kurznachrichten aus der Wirtschaft; ~ **car** Firmenwagen; ~ **card** Visiten-, Geschäftskarte; ~ **climate** Konjunkturklima; ~ **college** *(US)* Handelsakademie, -schule; **to graduate from a** ~ **college** *(US)* [etwa] Kaufmannsprüfung bestehen; ~ **connection** Geschäftsverbindung, befreundete Firma; ~ **correspondent** Geschäftsfreund; ~ **cycle** Konjunkturzyklus, -ablauf; ~ **directory** Handelsadreßbuch; ~ **downturn** Konjunkturrückgang; ~ **economics** *(Br.)* Geschäftspolitik, *(economic theory, Br.)* Betriebswirtschaftslehre; ~ **enterprise** gewerbliches Unternehmen, Gewerbebetrieb; ~ **errand** Geschäftsbesorgung; ~ **failure** Zahlungseinstellung; ~ **forecaster** Konjunkturprognostiker; ~ **getting** Akquisition; ~ **hand** kaufmännische Handschrift; ~ **hazard** Unternehmerwagnis; **after** ~ **hours** nach Geschäftsschluß; ~ **indicator** Konjunkturbarometer; ~ **insurance** Betriebsversicherung; ~ **interest** Geschäftsanteil; ~ **letter** Geschäftsbrief; ~ **licence** Gewerbebilanz; ~ **loan** Betriebs-, Geschäftskredit; ~ **location** geschäftliche Niederlassung; ~ **lunch[eon]** Arbeitsessen; ~ **name** Firmen-, Geschäftsname;

~ **office** Geschäftslokal; ~ **page** Wirtschaftsteil einer Zeitung; **unethical** ~ **practices** standeswidriges Geschäftsgebaren; ~ **premises** Geschäftslokal; ~ **profit tax** Gewerbesteuer; ~ **reply card (envelope,** *US)* [bezahlte] Rückantwort, Freiumschlag; ~ **research** Konjunkturforschung; ~ **secret** Geschäftsgeheimnis; ~ **seminar** Wirtschaftsseminar; ~ **slump** konjunkturelle Baissezeit; ~ **stagnation** Geschäftsstockung; ~ **tax** Gewerbesteuer; ~ **trainee** kaufmännischer Lehrling; **upward** ~ **trend** konjunkturelle Aufwärtsbewegung; ~ **user** gewerblicher Verbraucher; ~ **year** Geschäftsjahr.

businessman Kauf-, Geschäftsmann;
to be ~ **all the time** sich nur für das Geschäft interessieren.

bust *(bankruptcy)* Pleite, Bankrott.

busy beschäftigt, betriebsam, *(tel., US)* besetzt;
~ **hours** *(traffic)* Hauptverkehrszeiten.

buy Kauf, Kaufmöglichkeit, Geschäft;
~ *(v.)* [an-, ab]kaufen, käuflich erwerben, *(auction, Br.)* ersteigern, erstehen;
~ **bulk or packed goods** Ware lose oder verpackt kaufen; ~ **[at] first hand** direkt beziehen; ~ **on impulse** auf Grund plötzlicher Eingebung kaufen; ~ **ready-made** von der Stange kaufen; ~ **for a rise** auf Hausse spekulieren; ~ **on a scale** zu festen Preisen kaufen; ~ **on the instal(l)ment (deferred payment,** *US)* **system** auf Raten (Stottern, Abzahlung) kaufen.

buy *(v.)* **out a partner** seinen Partner auszahlen.

buyer [An]käufer, Abnehmer, Erwerber, Einkäufer, Kaufinteressent;
no ~s Brief; ~s **over** mehr Brief als Geld;
seriously disposed ~ ernsthafter Reflektant.

buyer's | market Käufermarkt; ~ **resistance** Käuferwiderstand.

buying An-, Einkauf, Kauf, Kaufen;
direct ~ Direkteinkauf, -bezug; **space** ~ Buchen von Anzeigenraum; ~ **outright** *(stocks)* Kassakauf;
~ **on margin** *(stock exchange)* Effektendifferenzgeschäft;
~ **area** Einzugsgebiet; ~ **association** Einkaufsgenossenschaft; ~ **choice** Sortimentsbreite; **go-slow** ~ **pattern** zurückhaltendes Einkaufsverhalten; ~ **quota** Einkaufskontingent; ~ **wave** Käuferansturm.

by | -bidder Scheinbieter; ~-**business** Nebengeschäft; ~-**product** Abfall-, Nebenprodukt.

C

cab [Miet]wagen, Auto, Taxe, Taxi
~**company** Taxiverleih; ~ **rank** Taxistand.
cabin *(airplane)* Flugzeugkabine, Pilotensitz;
~ **baggage** Hand-, Bordgepäck; ~ **class** *(ocean ship)* Luxusklasse; ~ **passenger** Kajütsfahrgast.
cable Kabel[depesche];
~ *(v.)* kabeln, depeschieren, drahten;
~ **address** Kabel-, Telegrammadresse; ~ **order** Kabelauftrag; ~ **rate** telegrafische Auszahlung.
ca'canny absichtliche Arbeitsverzögerung, *(factory)* künstliche Produktionseinschränkung.
calculate *(v)* berechnen, kalkulieren, Berechnungen anstellen, *(price)* kalkulieren;
~ **closely** knapp kalkulieren; ~ **the selling price** Verkaufspreis berechnen.
calculated risk wohlabgewogenes Risiko.
calculating machine Rechenmaschine.
calculation Be-, Er-, Ausrechnung, Voranschlag;
ät the lowest ~ bei niedrigster Berechnung; **on a strictly commercial rate-of-return** ~ bei reinem Rentabilitätsdenken;
unit ~ Einzelkalkulation;
~ **of cost** Selbstkostenrechnung; ~ **of earning power (productiveness, yield)** Rentabilitätsberechnung;
~ **item** Kalkulationsfaktor.
call Ruf, Ernennung, *(bonds)* Aufruf [zur Einziehung], *(broker's note)* Schlußnote, *(demand)* Nachfrage, *(for founds)* Zahlungsaufforderung, *(option)* Bezugsoption, *(stock exchange, Br.)* Differenz-, Zeitgeschäft;   .
collect ~ *(US)* R-Gespräch; **first** ~ *(stock exchange)* Notierung; **long-distance telephone** ~ *(US)* Ferngespräch; **transferred charge** ~ *(Br.)* R-Gespräch;
~ **for bids** öffentliche Ausschreibung; ~ **for margin** Nachzahlungsaufforderung für Aktionäre; ~ **of more** *(Br.)* Nochgeschäft; ~ **of a salesman** Vertreterbesuch;
~ *(v.) (issue bonds)* Schuldverschreibungen kündigen;
~ **a meeting of the creditors** Gläubigerversammlung einberufen; ~ **an option** Prämiengeschäft eingehen.
call *(v.)* **in** *(debts)* [Forderung] einziehen, *(loan, mortgage)* [Kredit, Hypothek] kündigen;
call *(v.)* **off** | **a boycott** Boykott aufheben; ~ **workers** Arbeitskräfte abziehen.
call, to make a ~ **on shares** Einzahlung auf Aktien verlangen;
~**back** *(salesman)* nachfassender *(zweiter)* Vertreterbesuch; ~**back pay** Überstundenbezahlung
~ **box** *(Br.)* Telefon-, Fernsprechzelle, Münzfernsprecher; ~ **car** Funktaxi; ~ **deposits** Sichteinlagen; ~ **market** Markt für tägliches Geld; ~ **money** *(Br.)* Tagesgeld; ~ **prefix** *(tel.)* Vorwählnumer; ~ **slip** Vertreterbericht.

called *(bonds)* zur Rückzahlung rufen;
to be ~ **for** postlagernd.
calling on customers Kundenbesuch.
calling | **card** Visitenkarte; ~ **round** Besuchstour.
calm *(stock exchange)* still, lustlos.
campaign Werbekampagne, -feldzug;
advertising ~ Einführungsfeldzug; ~ **cream** ~ erfolgversprechendster Werbefeldzug;
~ **to raise funds** Sammelaktion.
can Kanister *(tin, US)* [Konserven]dose;
~ **industry** *(US)* Konservenindustrie.
cancel Rückgängigmachung, Annullierung;
~ *(v.)* one's **booking** Platzbestellung rückgängig machen; ~ **a check** *(US)* (cheque, *Br.)* Scheck stornieren; ~ **a trademark registration** Warenzeichen im Register löschen.
cancellation Annullierung, Ungültigkeitserklärung *(countermanding)* Storno, Abbestellung;
~ **of a firm in the register of business names** Löschung einer Firma im Handelsregister; ~ **of a licence** Lizenzrücknahme; ~ **of an order** Auftragsstreichung; ~ **of a premium** Prämienstornierung; ~ **of securities** Kraftloserklärung verlorengegangener Wertpapiere; ~ **of unissued shares** Kaduzierung von Aktien;
~ **mark** Entwertungsmarke.
cancelling price Abstandssumme.
canned goods *(US)* Konserven.
canons of taxation gesunde Steuergrundsätze.
canteen Kantine, *(buffet)* Erfrischungsstand;
industrial (works) ~ Betriebskantine;
~ **keeper** Kantinenwirt.
canvas Packleinwand.
canvass Auftrags-, Kundenwerbung;
~ *(v.) (advertisements)* Inserate sammeln, *(customers)* [Kunden] besuchen, akquirieren;
~ **from door to door** hausieren gehen.
canvasser *(advertisements)* Annoncenwerber, *(salesman)* Handlungsreisender;
book ~ Subskribentensammler; **freight** ~ Frachtenmakler; **insurance** ~ Versicherungsvertreter.
canvassing *(advertisements)* Annoncenakquisition, *(orders)* Akquirieren;
door-to-door ~ Hausierertum;
~ **department** Kundenwerbeabteilung.
capacity *(factory machine)* Leistungsfähigkeit, *(ship)* Ladungs-, Tragfähigkeit;
in managerial ~ in leitender Stellung;
earning ~ Rentabilität; **operating** ~ Leistungsfähigkeit bei voller Kapazitätsausnützung; **taxable** ~ Steuerkraft;
~ **to earn a rental return** Ertragswertseignung; ~ **to pay** Zahlungsfähigkeit;
to be working to ~ voll ausgelastet (beschäftigt) sein; **to operate close to (at near)** ~ Betriebskapazität beinahe (fast) voll ausnützen;
~ **costs** Kosten bei voller Betriebsnutzung.

capital Kapital[ien], Stammvermögen, *(funds)* [Geld]mittel, *(proprietorship)* Eigenkapital; **active** ~ Betriebs-, Umlaufkapital; **advanced** ~ eingebrachtes Kapital; **authorized** ~ genehmigtes Kapital; **borrowed** ~ Fremdmittel; **circulating** ~ Umlaufvermögen; **fixed** ~ Anlagevermögen; **invested** ~ Einschuß, Einlage; **nominal** ~ *(Br.)* Grund-, Gründungs-, Stammkapital, *(US)* nominelles Kapital; **share** ~ *(Br.)* Grund-, Aktienkapital;
to convert into ~ kapitalisieren; **to infuse fresh** ~ neues Kapital zuführen; **to live on the** ~ von der Substanz leben; **to make holes in (inroads on) one's** ~ sein Kapital angreifen; **to write down** ~ Kapital herabsetzen; **to write off** ~ Kapitalzusammenlegung vornehmen;
~ **account** Kapitalkonto; ~ **adjustment** Kapitalberichtigung; ~ **allowance** *(Br.)* steuerlich zulässige Abschreibungen auf das Anlagevermögen; ~ **appreciation** *(Br.)* Kapitalaufstockung; ~ **appropriations** bereitgestellte Subventionsmittel; ~ **demand** Kapitalbedarf; ~ **depreciation account** Kapitalentwertungskonto; ~ **expenditure cutback** Investitionsdrosselung; ~ **flight** Kapitalflucht; **misappropriated** ~ **funds** Kapitalfehlleitung.
capital-gains | account Kapitalgewinnkonto; ~ **tax** Kapitalzuwachssteuer.
capital goods Investitionsgüter, Anlagewerte.
capital | grant Kapitalzuschuß; ~**-intensive** kapitalintensiv; ~ **investment** Investitionskapital; ~ **to service its** ~ **investment** Kapitaldienst sicherstellen; ~ **issue restrictions** Emissionssperre; ~ **loss** Kapitalverlust; ~ **market** Geld-, Kapitalmarkt; ~ **reconciliation statement** *(Br.)* Ausweis über die Verwendung von Kapitalmitteln; ~ **resources (bank)** Eigenkapital; ~**-short** kapitalknapp; ~ **spending boom** Investitionsgüterkonjunktur.
capital stock *(US)* Aktien-, Grund-, Stammkapital, *(amount to be paid in)* Kapitaleinlage;
~ **exchange offer** Aktienumtauschangebot.
capital yields tax *(Br.)* Kapitalertragssteuer.
capitalism Kapitalismus.
capitalization Kapitalisierung, Aktivierung, *(capital stock)* Grund-, Gesellschaftskapital;
~ **of interest** Hinzuschlagen der Zinsen zum Kapital.
capitalize *(v.)* aktivieren, kapitalisieren, auf Kapitalkonto übernehmen.
capitalized expenses kapitalisierte (auf Kapitalkonto übernommene) Ausgaben.
captain | of industry Wirtschaftsführer; ~'s **manifest** Ladungsverzeichnis, -manifest; ~'s **protest** Havarieattest, Seeprotest.
captive shop *(US)* Betriebsladen, dem Betrieb gehöriges Geschäft.
car *(US, railroad carriage)* [Eisenbahn]waggon, *(car)* Wagen, Kraftfahrzeug;
dining ~ *(US)* Speisewagen; **freight** ~ *(US)* geschlossener Güterwagen; **low-milage** ~ wenig ge-

fahrener Wagen; **sleeping** ~ *(US)* Schlafwagen; **to pick up a** ~ Auto abschleppen;
~ **allowance** Auto-Zuschuß; ~ **demurrage charges** *(US)* [Waggon]liegegelder; ~ **hire service** *(Br.)* Automietverleih; ~ **insurance** Kraftfahrzeugversicherung; ~ **licence** Kraftfahrzeugpapiere; ~**-mile revenue** Unterhaltungsaufwand für ein Auto; ~ **park** *(Br.)* Parkplatz; ~ **park attendant** *(Br.)* Parkwächter; ~ **rental** Wagenmiete; ~ **rental agency** Mietwagenvertretung, -verleih; ~**-sleeper express** Ferienreisezug.
caravan *(Br.)* Wohnwagen[anhänger].
card Karte, Billet, *(business)* Visiten-, Geschäftsanzeige, *(notice)* Mitteilung, Ankündigung;
index ~ Kartothek-, Karteikarte; **insurance** ~ Versicherungskarte; **rate** ~ Anzeigenpreisliste;
to ask for one's ~s um seine Entlassungspapiere bitten.
card-index Kartei, Kartothek;
~ *(v.)* katalogisieren, Kartei anlegen.
card | rate Anzeigentarif; **punch** ~ **system** Lochkartensystem.
cardboard Pappe, Kartonpapier.
care | of public money Verwaltung öffentlicher Gelder; ~ **of securities** Effektenverwaltung.
career Laufbahn, Karriere, Werde-, Entwicklungsgang, Beruf;
to carve out a ~ **for s. o.** j. lancieren; **to spend one's entire** ~ **on the financial side** sich beruflich lediglich mit finanzwirtschaftlichen Fragen beschäftigen;
~ **advancement** berufliche Förderung; ~**-building bureau** Berufsberatungsstelle; ~ **prospects** Laufbahnaussichten.
cargo [Schiffs]fracht, [Schiffs]ladung, Frachtgut;
general ~ Stückgüterladung; **homeward** ~ Retourfracht; **short-landed** ~ bei Schiffsankunft festgestellte Fehlmenge;
to discharge a ~ Ladung löschen;
~ **agent** Frachtspediteur; ~ **aircraft** Transportflugzeug; **hot** ~ **ban** Belieferungsverbot [für bestreikten Betrieb]; ~ **[-carring] capacity** Ladefähigkeit; ~ **insurance** Güterfrachtversicherung; ~ **manifest** Ladungsverzeichnis; ~ **revenue** Frachteinnahmen; ~ **steamer** Frachtdampfer; ~ **to divert a** ~ **vessel** Frachter umleiten.
carhop *(US)* Bedienung im Autorestaurant.
carload *(US)* Waggon-, Wagenladung;
~ **freight** *(US)* Waggonfracht; **less-than-** ~ **freight** *(US)* Stückgut; **mixed** ~ **freight** *(US)* Sammel-, Stückgutladung, Stückgüter; **less-than-**~ **order** *(US)* Stückgüterauftrag; **less-than-**~**rate** *(US)* Stückgütertarif.
carlot *(US)* Waggon-, Güterwagenladung;
~ **rate** Waggontarif; **mixed** ~ **rate** Sammelladungstarif; ~ **shipment** Waggonladung.
carriage Fuhr-, Transportgeschäft, *(cost of transport, Br.)* Transportkosten, *(railway, Br.)* Eisenbahnwaggon;
~ **forward** Spesennachnahme; ~**-free (paid)** frachtfrei, franko, frei Haus;

express ~ *(Br.)* Eilzugwagen; through ~ *(Br.)* Kurswagen;
~ **by air** Lufttransport; ~ **on hire** Beförderung gegen Entgelt; ~ **by land** Landtransport; ~ **by sea** Seetransport;
~ **account** Frachtkonto; ~ **rate** Frachtsatz, -rate; ~ **receipt** Ladeschein; ~ **trade** Luxusindustrie.

carrier Fuhr-, Rollfuhr-, Transportunternehmer, Frachtführer, Spediteur, *(aircraft)* Lufttransportgesellschaft;
common ~ [bahnamtlicher] Spediteur; **connecting** ~ Korrespondenzspediteur; **contract** ~ bahnamtlicher Rollfuhrunternehmer; **inland** ~ Binnenfrachtführer; **private** ~ Gelegenheitsspediteur;
common ~ **by air** Luftfrachtspediteur; ~ **by sea** Seefrachtführer; ~ **and forwarding agent** Spediteur;
~**s' manifest** Frachtladungsverzeichnis.

carry *(v.)* **as asset[s]** aktivieren, auf der Aktivseite [einer Bilanz] aufführen; ~ **in the books** in den Büchern führen (ausweisen); ~ **a customer** Kunden anschreiben lassen; ~ **a financial page** *(journal)* Wirtschaftsteil enthalten; ~ **an insurance** versichert sein; ~ **an interest of 5 %** mit 5 % verzinslich sein; ~ **as liability (liabilities)** passivieren, als Passiva behandeln; ~ **an amount to reserve** Betrag der Reserve zuweisen; ~ **securities** *(US)* Wertpapiere durchhalten; ~ **goods in stock** Waren auf Lager halten.

carry forward *(v.)* vortragen, übertragen, *(stock exchange)* prolongieren.

carry on *(v.)* **a business under one's name** Geschäft unter seinem Namen fortführen.

carry out *(v.)* | **a commission** sich eines Auftrags entledigen; ~ **a product** Posten umbuchen.

carryback *(US)* Verlustausgleich.

carryforward *(balance sheet)* Vortrag;
tax-loss ~ Steuerverlustvortrag.

carrying Beförderung, Transport;
~ **over** *(stock exchange, Br.)* glatte Prolongation; ~ **agent** Spediteur; ~ **business** Speditionsgeschäft; ~ **capacity** Lade-, Tragfähigkeit; ~ **charges** Betriebs-, Lagerkosten; **high** ~ **costs** *(inventory)* hohe Unterhaltungskosten; ~ **day** *(Br.)* Report-, Prämien-Erklärungstag; ~**-over business** *(Br.)* Prolongations-, Report-, Kostgeschäft; ~ **value** Buchwert; ~ **van** Speditionswagen.

carryover *(Br.)* Report, Prolongation, *(taxation)* Verlustvortrag.

cartage Fuhrlohn, Frachtgebühr;
regular ~ **company** Bahnspediteur.

carted goods Rollgut.

cartel Kartell[konvention];
marketing ~ Absatz-, Vertriebskartell;
~ **agreement** Kartellvertrag, -vereinbarung; ~ **price** gebundener Preis, Kartellpreis.

cartelize *(v.)* kartellisieren, zu einem Kartell zwingen.

carter Fuhrmann, [Roll]fuhrunternehmer.

case Kiste, Behälter, Kasten;
~**s and casks** Rollgut.

cash Bargeld, -zahlung, bares Geld, Barmittel, *(balance sheet)* Kassenbestand, *(stock exchange, US)* per Kasse;
in [ready] ~ [in] bar, in klingender Münze; **short of** ~ knapp bei Kasse; **for 3 %** ~ 3 % Skonto für Barzahlung;
loose ~ Klein-, Münzgeld; **net** ~ bar ohne Abzug; **petty** ~ Portokasse;
~ **in advance** netto Kasse im Voraus; ~ **in bank (at bankers)** *(balance sheet)* Bankguthaben; ~ **on delivery** Empfänger bezahlt, Vorauskasse; ~ **against documents** Kasse gegen Dokumente; ~ **in (on) hand** Bargeld, Barbestand, -vorrat, Kassenbestand; ~ **in vaults** *(US)* Barbestand einer Bank;
~ *(v.)* zu Geld machen, realisieren;
~ **a bill** Wechsel einlösen;
to balance the ~ Kassensturz machen; **to be rolling in** ~ im Geld schwimmen; **to free up bogged-down** ~ Bargeldreserven freisetzen; **to lock up one's** ~ **in one's trade** sein Geld ins Geschäft stecken; **to send** ~ **on delivery** per Nachnahme schicken;
~ **account** Kassa-, Kassenkonto; ~ **adjustment** Barregulierung; ~ **advance** Bar-, Kassenvorschuß; ~ **balance** Geldbestand, Barguthaben; **adverse** ~ **balance** Kassendefizit; ~ **business** Kassa-, Bar-, Lokogeschäft.

cash-and-carry *(US)* Verkauf gegen Barzahlung und ohne Kundendienst;
~ **wholesaler** Abholgroßhändler.

cash | **cheque** *(Br.)* Barscheck; ~ **clerk** Kassierer; ~ **credit** Bar-, Kontokorrentkredit; ~ **diary** Kassenkladde; ~ **disbursement[s]** Kassenausgang, -auszahlungen; ~ **discount** Bar[zahlungs]rabatt, Kassaskonto; ~ **distribution** Barausschüttung; ~ **drain** Kassenanspannung; ~ **drawing** Barabhebung; ~ **funds** Barmittel, ~**-heavy** äußerst liquide, sehr flüssig; ~ **indemnity** Mankogeld; ~ **journal** Kassenjournal; ~ **line** Kreditlinie; ~ **market** Kassamarkt; ~ **note** Kassenanweisung; ~ **order** *(stock exchange)* Kassaorder; ~ **position** Flüssigkeit, Liquiditätslage; ~ **price** Bar-, Effektivpreis, *(stock exchange)* Kassakurs; ~ **rate** *(cheque, Br.)* Scheckkurs; ~ **receipt** Kassenquittung; ~ **record** Kassenbeleg; ~ **refund** Barvergütung; ~ **reserve** *(investment fund)* Barmittel; **minimum** ~ **reserve** *(bank)* Mindestreserve; **operating** ~ **reserve** Betriebsmittelrücklage; ~ **short** *(US)* Kassendefizit; ~ **store** *(US)* Barzahlungsgeschäft; ~ **surrender value** *(life insurance)* Rückkaufwert; ~ **transaction** Kassa-, Bargeschäft; ~ **voucher** Kassenbeleg.

cashbook Kassa-, Verkaufsbuch; Kassenstrasse.

cashflow Dividendenausschüttung zuzüglich Abschreibung, Bruttoertragsziffer;
~ **position** Bruttoertragslage.

cashier Kassierer, Kassenführer, -wart.

cashier's | **check** *(US)* Kassen-, ~ **desk** Zahlstelle; ~ **receipt** Kassenquittung, Bankscheck.

cashless payment *(US)* bargeldlose Zahlung.

cast *(v.)* **interest** Zinsen ausrechnen;
~ **goods** Ramschwaren.

casual Aushilfsarbeiter, -kraft;
~ **customer** Lauf-, Gelegenheitskunde; ~ **emolument** Nebeneinnahme; ~ **worker** Gelegenheitsarbeiter.
casualty insurance *(US)* Unfallversicherung.
cats and dogs *(US)* billige Spekulationspapiere.
catalog(ue) Katalog, Verzeichnis, Liste, *(price list)* Preisverzeichnis, *(prospectus)* Prospekt;
trade ~ Versandhauskatalog;
~ **business** Versandhausgeschäft; ~ **price** Katalog-, Listenpreis; ~ **store** Versandhausgeschäft.
catastrophe reserve Katastrophenrücklage.
catch *(v.)* **on** *(article)* populär werden, einschlagen.
catchpenny article Schleuderartikel, Schundware.
category of risks Gefahrenklasse.
cater *(v.)* verpflegen, liefern, *(for airliner)* fertige Menüs anliefern;
~ **for the needs of customers** Kundenbedürfnisse befriedigen.
caterer Menülieferant, Gaststättenbetrieb.
catering | **contractor** Vertragslieferant für Betriebskantinen; ~ **costs** Verpflegungskosten; ~ **department** Werksküche, Betriebskantine; ~ **establishment** Gaststättenbetrieb; ~ **industry** Gaststättengewerbe.
caution money *(Br.)*[hinterlegte] Kautionssumme.
caveat emptor Gewährleistungsausschluß.
cease *(v.)* *(firm)* erlöschen, *(payment)* fortfallen;
~ **to do business** Geschäftsbetrieb einstellen; ~ **payment** *(bank)* Zahlungen einstellen;
~ **and desist order** *(US)* Wettbewerbsverbot.
ceiling Höchstbetrag, -preis;
retail ~ **price** Verbraucherhöchstpreis; ~ **wages** festgesetzte Höchstlöhne.
census Volkszählung, Totalerhebung;
industrial ~ Betriebszählung;
~ **data** Erhebungsangaben; ~ **paper** Haushaltsfragebogen.
central Zentrale, Zentralstelle, *(telephone, US)* Fernsprechamt, -vermittlung;
~ **administration** Hauptverwaltung; ~ **area shop** Geschäft im Stadtzentrum; ~ **bank policy** Politik der Bundesnotenbank; ~ **business district** Hauptgeschäftsgegend; ~ **market** Hauptabsatzgebiet; ~ **valuation committee** Steuerveranlagungsausschuß.
centre *(Br.)*, **center** *(US)* Zentralstelle, Zentrum, wichtiger Platz, Mittelpunkt;
business (commercial) ~ Geschäftszentrum; **shopping** ~ Einkaufszentrum;
~ **spread** doppelseitige Anzeige.
certificate [amtliche] Bescheinigung, Bestätigung, *(customs)* Geleitzettel, *(policy)* Transportpolice, *(record)* Beleg, Urkunde, *(stock)* Zertifikat, Anteilschein;
audit ~ Prüfungsbescheinigung; **benefit** ~ Lebensversicherungspolice; **clearance** ~ Zollerlaubnisschein; **customhouse** ~ Bescheinigung für zollfreie Wiederausfuhr; **gold** ~ *(US)* Goldzertifikat; **insurance** ~ Versicherungsschein; **motor-vehicle registration** ~ Kraftfahrzeugbrief; **organization** ~

(US, bank) Konzessionsurkunde; **tax-reserve** ~ Steuergutschein;
~ **[payable] to bearer** Inhaberpapier; ~ **of clearance inward** Einfuhrbescheinigung; ~ **of clearance outward** Ausfuhrbescheinigung; ~ **of the customhouse** Zollquittung; ~ **of employment** Beschäftigungsnachweis; ~ **of inventory** Bestandsprüfungsbescheinigung; ~ **of origin** Ursprungszeugnis, Herkunftsbescheinigung; ~ **of posting** Postquittung; ~ **of priority** Dringlichkeitsbescheinigung; ~ **of renewal** Erneuerungsschein; ~ **of stock** (US) Aktienzertifikat; ~ **of tonnage** Meßbrief; ~ **of transfer** *(Br.)* [Effekten]lieferungsbescheinigung; ~ **of warranty** Garantieschein;
~ *(v.)* Bescheinigung ausstellen;
to buy in ~s on a no-load basis Investmentanteile ohne Provisionsaufschlag erwerben.
certificated amtlich zugelassen, *(Br.)* diplomiert;
~ **bankrupt** *(Br.)* Gemein-, Konkursschuldner.
certification *(of a check, US)* Bestätigungs-, Gültigkeitsvermerk;
~ **mark** Gütezeichen.
certified *(attested)* bescheinigt, *(licensed)* amtlich zugelassen;
~ **carrier** Spediteur im Güterfernverkehr; ~ **financial statement** mit Prüfungsvermerk versehene Bilanz.
certify *(v.)* bescheinigen;
~ **a check (cheque,** *Br.)* Scheck [als gedeckt] bestätigen.
cessation | **of imports** Einfuhrstopp; ~ **from work** Arbeitseinstellung, -niederlegung.
cestui que trust Treuhandnehmer.
chain *(advertising agency)* zusammenarbeitende Gruppe, *(branch)* Kettenunternehmen, Filialbetrieb;
~ **banking** *(US)* Filialbankbetrieb; ~ **discount** Stufenrabatt; ~ **retailing organization** Einzelhandelskette; ~ **store** Kettenladen, Einheitspreisgeschäft.
chair *(chairman)* Präsident, Vorsitzender;
~ **car** *(railroad, US)* Salonwagen.
chairman Obmann, Vorsitzender, Präsident;
~ **of the board** Verwaltungsratsvorsitzender; ~ **of the executive board** Vorstandsvorsitzender.
chalk *(v.)* **it up** Rechnung auflaufen lassen.
chamber *(Exchequer, Br.)* Schatzamt;
~s *(business use, Br.)* Geschäftsräume;
~ **of Commerce** Handelskammer;
to live in ~s *(Br.)* möbliert wohnen;
chance bargain Gelegenheitskauf.
Chancellor of the Exchequer *(Br.)* Schatzkanzler.
Chandler Act *(US)* Konkursordnung.
change *(balance returned)* Wechselgeld, *(exchange)* Tausch, *(stock exchange, Br.)* Börse;
small ~ Wechsel-, Kleingeld;
~ **in the economic activities** konjunktureller Wandel; ~**s in the direction of a firm** Veränderungen im Vorstand; ~**s in prices** Preisveränderungen; ~ **in rates** Anzeigenpreisänderung; ~ **of trade name** Firmenänderung;

~ *(v.)* **about** *(prices)* schwanken; ~ **hands at** . . . *(stock exchange)* umgesetzt werden mit; ~ **one's profession** umsatteln.

change-over | **costs** Umstellungskosten; ~ **employment** Übergangsbeschäftigung.

channel | **of distribution (trade)** Absatzweg; **~s and outlets** Vertriebskanäle;
~ **freight** Kanalfracht.

channelling of scarce materials Steuerung von Engpaßwaren.

character *(reputation)* Ruf, Leumund;
~ **of business** Geschäftstyp;
~ **reference** persönliche Referenzen.

charge *(bookkeeping)* Belastung, *(care)* Aufsicht, Gewahrsam, Obhut, Sorge, *(financial burden)* Belastung, finanzielle Last, *(fee)* Gebühr, Taxe, *(load)* Last, Belastung, Fracht, *(price)* geforderter Preis, Forderung, Kosten, *(on property)* [Vermögens]belastung;
at his own ~ auf seine Kosten; **free of** ~ unentgeltlich, gratis, kostenfrei, spesenfrei, *(delivery)* frei Haus; **no** ~ **is made for packing** Verpackung wird nicht berechnet;
account-carrying ~ Kontospesen; **consular** ~ Konsulargebühr; **deferred** ~ passiver Rechnungsabgrenzungsposten; **maintenance** ~ *(banking)* monatliche Bankspesen; **reserve** ~ *(postage)* Gebühr bezahlt Empfänger; **service** ~ Dienstleistungsgebühr;
~ **for depreciation** Abschreibungskosten; ~ **for overdraft** Überziehungsprovision;
~ *(v.)* *(costs)* erheben, *(debit)* anlasten, belasten, in Rechnung setzen, debitieren, *(fix price)* berechnen;
~ **forward** nachnehmen; ~ **s. th. on the bill** etw. auf die Rechnung setzen; ~ **commission** Provision berechnen; ~ **the old price** früheren Preis berechnen;
to make an additional ~ nachberechnen;
~ **account** *(US)* Kunden-, Anschreibungskonto; ~ **customer** Kredit-, Teilzahlungskunde; ~ **card** Kundenkreditkarte.

charges *(accessory expenses)* Spesen, Gebühren;
adding ~ einschließlich der Spesen; **liable to** ~ gebührenpflichtig;
advertising ~ Insertionsgebühren; **auction** ~ Versicherungsgebühren; **bank** ~ Bankspesen; **business** ~ Geschäftsspesen; **capital** ~ [aktivierungspflichtiger] Kapitalaufwand; **carrying** ~ Verwaltungsgebühren; **collect-on-delivery** ~ Nachnahmespesen; **dead** ~ Betriebsunkosten; **deferred** ~ **[to expense]** *(balance sheet)* transitorische Posten; **demurrage** ~ Liegegebühren; **forwarding** ~ Versandspesen; **landing** ~ Löschungsgebühren; **overhead** ~ Generalunkosten; **packing** ~ Verpackungskosten; **postal** ~ Portokosten; **underabsorbed** ~ zu niedrig angesetzte Gemeinkosten;
~ **paid in advance** Kostenvorschuß; ~ **to be collected** Nachnahmegebühren.

chargeable der Besteuerung unterliegend;
~ **income** steuerpflichtiges Einkommen; ~ **weight** frachtpflichtiges Gewicht.

charitable mildtätig, karitativ, gemeinnützig;
~ **contribution** *(income tax return)* Beiträge für wohltätige Zwecke; ~ **foundation** milde Stiftung.

charity Wohltätigkeit;
~ **collection** Sammlung zu wohltätigen Zwecken.

charm price optischer Preis, Blickfangpreis.

chart Karte, *(US)* graphische Darstellung, *(in tabular form)* Tabelle, Schaubild;
organizational ~ Organisationsplan;
~ **of accounts** Kontenplan.

charter Chartern, Mieten, Befrachten, *(US, of corporation)* Satzung;
bank ~ Bankenprivileg; **time** ~ Zeitcharter;
~ *(v.)* chartern, *(bank)* privilegieren;
to go on ~s Charterflugzeug benutzen;
~ **airline** Chartergesellschaft; ~ **plane** Charterflugzeug; ~ **rates** Befrachtungstarif.

chartered befrachtet, gechartert;
~ **bank** *(Br.)* priviligierte Bank; ~ **exemption** *(Br.)* zugestandene Steuerfreiheit.

chartering business Charter-, Frachtgeschäft.

charterparty Befrachtungs-, Frachtvertrag.

cheap *(price)* billig, niedrig, preiswert, wohlfeil;
to sell dirt-~ zu Schleuderpreisen verkaufen;
~ **fare** ermäßigter Fahrpreis; ~ **money** billige Geldsätze; ~ **money policy** Niedrigzinspolitik.

cheapen *(v.)* billiger werden, im Preis sinken.

cheapening of money Geldverbilligung.

check [Gepäck]aufbewahrungsschein, *(cheque, US)* Scheck, Zahlungsanweisung *(control)* Aufsicht, Kontrolle, *(cloakroom, US)* Garderobenmarke, *(voucher)* Bon, Gutschein; **cashier's** ~ Kassenscheck; **rubber** ~ ungedeckter Scheck; **storage** ~ *(railroad)* Lagerschein;
~ *(v.)* kollationieren, Abschriften vergleichen;
~ **the books** Bücher revidieren; ~ **in with a hotel** *(US)* sich [bei einem Hotel] anmelden; ~ **investments** Subventionen bremsen; ~ **off goods** Bestandsaufnahme machen; ~ **[off] names on a list** Namen auf einer Liste abhaken; ~ **out** *(US)* Hotel nach Rechnungsbegleichung verlassen;
~ **out luggage** *(Br.)* Gepäck abholen; ~ **production** Produktion drosseln;
to bounce a ~ Scheck platzen lassen;
~ **account** *(US)* Gegenrechnung; ~ **alteration and forgery insurance** *(US)* Scheckversicherung; ~ **-in** *(airport)* Abfertigung; **no** ~ **-in time** *(airport)* kein Meldeschluß.

checkbook Scheckbuch, Kontrollbuch;
~ **money** *(US)* Giralgeld.

checking Kontrolle, *(advertising)* Steuerprüfung, *(inventory)* Jnventurkontrolle;
~ **of accounts** Bücherrevision; ~ **of baggage** *(US)* Gepäckaufgabe; ~ **of quality** Qualitätsprüfung; ~ **account** *(US)* Scheckkonto, Girokonto.

checkoff *(US)* Lohnabzug von Gewerkschaftsbeiträgen durch den Betrieb;
~ **system** *(US)* Lohnabzugsverfahren.

checkout | **clerk** Kontrollangestellter; ~ **counter** Abfertigungsschalter.

checkroom *(US)* Gepäckaufbewahrung.
checkup of the cash Kassenrevision.
cheerful *(market)* freundlich, lebhaft, etw. fester.
cheque *(Br.)* (check, *US*) Scheck;
 advised ~ advisierter Scheck; bearer ~ Inhaberscheck; blank ~ Blankoscheck; crossed ~ *(Br.)* Verrechnungsscheck; ~ dated ahead vordatierter Scheck; dishono(u)red ~ nicht eingelöster Scheck; kite ~ ungedeckter Scheck; postal ~ Postscheck; stopped ~ gesperrter Scheck;
 ~s in hand Scheckbestand;
 to cash a ~ Scheck zur Einlösung vorlegen; to cross a ~ Verrechnungsscheck ausstellen; to present a ~ for payment Scheck zur Zahlung vorlegen; to raise a ~ Scheck höher beziffern;
 ~ account Giro-, Scheckrechnung, Girokonto; ~ alteration Scheckfälschung; ~ clearing system Scheckverrechnungssystem; ~ collection Scheckinkasso.
chief | accountant Hauptbuchhalter; ~ agent Generalvertreter; ~ executive [officier] Vorstandsmitglied; ~ market Hauptabsatzmarkt.
choice article[s] (goods) Qualitätsware.
choicest quality erlesene Qualität.
chop *(brand)* Marke, Sorte;
 ~ *(v.)* prices Preise stark herabsetzen.
cipher *(v.)* chiffrieren, verschlüsseln;
 ~ code Telegrammcode; ~ text verschlüsselter Text.
circle Wirkungsgebiet, -kreis, Einflußsphäre;
 specialist ~s Fachwelt.
circular Zirkular, Rundschreiben, *(advertisement)* Prospekt;
 ~ cheque *(Br.)* Reisescheck; ~ letter Laufzettel, Rundschreiben; ~ offer Prospektangebot; ~ ticket Fahrscheinheft; ~ tour (trip) Rundreise, -fahrt.
circulate *(v.)* | bills Wechsel girieren; ~ freely (slowly) *(money)* hohe (niedrige) Umlaufgeschwindigkeit haben.
circulating | assets Umlaufvermögen; ~ notes Notenumlauf.
circulation umlaufende Zahlungsmittel;
 out of ~ außer Kurs [gesetzt];
 active ~ Notenumlauf;
 to recall (withdraw) from ~ außer Kurs setzen, aus dem Verkehr ziehen;
 ~ privilege Banknotenprivileg.
circumstances Vermögensverhältnisse;
 in easy ~ gut situiert;
 to live in narrow ~ in ärmlichen Verhältnissen leben.
circumstanced, well in guten Verhältnissen.
city [Groß]stadt, *(center)* Stadtmitte, Innenstadt, Geschäftsgegend;
 to be in the ~ Geschäftsmann sein;
 ~ article Börsenbericht; ~ collections Stadtinkassi; at ~ expenses auf Kosten der Stadt; ~ levy städtische Umlage; ~ man *(Br.)* Finanz-, Geschäftsmann, *(bank)* Bankangestellter; ~ news Börsennachrichten; ~ price Großhandelspreis, *(stock exchange)* Börsennotierung.

civic enterprise Kommunalbetrieb.
civil | bonds *(US)* Schuldverschreibungen der öffentlichen Hand; ~ commotion insurance Aufruhrversicherung; ~ employment bürgerlicher Beruf; ~ loan *(US)* öffentliche Anleihe; ~ year Kalenderjahr.
claim Klageanspruch, *(advertising)* Werbeanspruch, *(insurance)* Versicherungsanspruch, *(mining)* Mutung;
 assigned ~ abgetretene Forderung; book ~ Buchforderung; outlawed ~ *(US)* verjährte Forderung; preference (preferential, priority) ~ *(bankruptcy)* abgesonderte Befriedigung; provable ~ *(bankruptcy)* anmeldefähige Forderung; proved ~ *(bankruptcy)* anerkannte Konkursforderung; statutebarred ~ verjährte Forderung; unsecured ~ *(bankruptcy)* Masseanspruch;
 ~ for benefit Unterstützungsanspruch; ~ against the estate Masseanspruch; ~ of exemption *(US)* Aussonderungsanspruch; ~ for maintenance Unterhaltungsanspruch;
 ~ *(v.)* benefits Unterstützungsansprüche stellen;
 to adjust a ~ Versicherungsanspruch regulieren; to buy up a ~ for cash Anspruch in bar abfinden; to make a ~ in respect of a defect Mängelrüge vorbringen; to prove a ~ [Konkurs]forderung nachweisen; to write off a doubtful ~ *(Br.)* zweifelhafte Forderung abschreiben;
 ~ adjuster (insurance) Schadensregulierer; ~ costs *(insurance)* Regulierungskosten; ~ form Schadensformular; ~ settlement *(insurance)* Anspruchsregulierung.
claimant Antragsteller, Forderungsberechtigter, *(bill of exchange)* Regreßnehmer.
clamp | *(v.)* ceilings on prices Höchstpreise festsetzen; ~ down on liquidity Liquiditätsbestimmungen verschärfen.
clampdown on credit Kreditbeschränkung.
class Art, [Wert]klasse, *(quality)* ausgezeichnete Qualität, Grad, Güteklasse, Sorte;
 trading ~ Geschäftsleute; the working ~es Arbeiterstand, -schaft;
 my ~ of business meine Kundschaft; ~ of consumers Verbraucherschicht; ~ of risk *(insurance)* Gefahrenklasse;
 ~ *(v.)* einstufen, gruppieren, klassifizieren, ordnen, eingruppieren;
 ~ bonds in Serien ausgegebene Schuldverschreibungen; high-~ goods erstklassige Erzeugnisse; first-~ matter Briefpost; second-~ matter Drucksachen; ~ price Preis für gehobene Schichten; ~ rate Grundgehalt, -tarif, *(insurance)* Tarifprämie.
classification Rangordnung, Eingruppierung, Klassifizierung, *(salaries)* Einstufung;
 freight ~ Frachttarif; job (occupational) ~ Berufszugehörigkeit;
 ~ of accounts Kontengliederung; ~ of properties Vermögensschichtung;
 ingrade ~ change niedrigere Einstufung ohne Lohnkürzung; ~ plan Stellenplan; ~ rating Tarifeinstufung.

classified | **advertisements** kleine Anzeige; ~ **directory** Branchenadreßbuch; ~ **service** *(US)* gehobener Dienst.

classify *(v.)* einstufen, klassifizieren, nach Klassen einteilen, *(customs)* tarifieren.

clause Klausel, Absatz, Paragraph;
acceleration ~ Fälligkeitsklausel; **escalator** ~ Notgleitklausel; **memorandum** ~ *(insurance)* Freizeichnungsklausel; **most-favo(u)red-nation** ~ Meistbegünstigungsklausel; **saving** ~ Vorbehaltsklausel; **sue-and-labo(u)r** ~ *(insurance)* Selbstbehaltsklausel.

clean | **acceptace** bedingungsloses (vorbehaltloses) Akzept; ~ **of lading** echtes Konnossement; ~ **credit** nicht dokumentarisch gesicherter Trassierungskredit.

clear *(cargo)* unbefrachtet, leer, ohne Ladung, *(claim)* unanfechtbar, *(net)* netto, ohne Abzug;
~ **of charges** spesenfrei; ~ **of income tax** nach Abzug der Einkommensteuer;
~ *(v.) (check)* im Clearingwege abrechnen, *(debt)* bezahlen, begleichen, glattstellen, *(gain)* netto verdienen, *(pay dues)* ausklarieren;
~ **the balance** Saldo ausgleichen; **not to** ~ **one's expenses** nicht einmal seine Unkosten decken; ~ **by instal(l)ments** in Raten abzahlen; ~ **one's luggage through the customs** *(Br.)* sein Gepäck zollamtlich abfertigen lassen; ~ **a shop** ausverkaufen; ~ **a thousand £ a year** netto 1000,— Pfund jährlich verdienen.
~ **amount** Nettobetrag; ~ **annuity** steuerfreie Rente; ~ **business day** Bankschalertag; ~ **loss** Nettoverlust; ~ **market value** echter Verkehrswert.

clearance *(airplane)* Abfertigung, *(cheque)* Ver-, Abrechnung, *(certificate of clearing)* Zollschein, *(customs)* Zollabfertigung;
~ **inwards** Ein[gangsde]klarierung;
to effect customs ~ Zollabfertigung vornehmen;
~ **certificate** Unbedenklichkeitsbescheinigung, *(ship)* Zollbescheinigung; ~ **charges** Zollabfertigungsgebühren; ~ **sale** Räumungsverkauf.

clearing Abrechnungsverfahren, -verkehr;
~ **of an account** Kontoglattstellung; ~ **of goods** *(liquidation)* [Total]ausverkauf;
~ **balance** Verrechnungssaldo, -spitze; ~ **item** Abrechnungsposten; ~ **office** Konversionskasse; ~ **rate** Verrechnungskurs; ~ **unit** Verrechnungseinheit.

clearinghouse *(Br.)* Abrechnungs-, Girozentrale;
~ **business** Abrechnungsverkehr; ~ **system** Girosystem.

clerical | **assistant** Bürogehilfe; ~ **position** Bürotätigkeit.

clerk *(employee)* kaufmännischer Angestellter, Kontorist, *(US, shop assistant)* Handelsgehilfe, Verkäufer;
bookkeeping ~ Buchhalter; **copying** ~ Expedient; **head** ~ Bürovorsteher, -vorstand; **shipping** ~ Expedient, *(US)* Spediteur; **signing** ~ *(Br.)* Handlungsbevollmächtigter.

client *(customer)* Kunde, Auftraggeber.

clientele Kundschaft *(of professional men)* Praxis; **upper-income** ~ gutverdienende Kundschaft.

climate *(company)* Betriebsklima;
business ~ Konjunkturklima.

clipper Schnelldampfer, Verkehrsflugzeug.

clipping *(of coupons)* Abtrennung;
~ **service** *(US)* Zeitungsausschnittdienst.

cloakroom Gepäck[aufbewahrungs]raum;
~ **fee** Aufbewahrungsgebühr.

clock | **card** Stechkarte; ~ **hours** *(time study)* Ist-Zeit.

close Abschluß, Anzeigenschluß;
~ **of navigation** Schiffahrtssperre;
~-**down** Betriebsstillegung;
~ *(v.)* **at 185¹/₂ against 185** *(stock exchange)* mit 185¹/₂ gegen 185 schließen; ~ **an account** Konto abschließen; ~ **a bankruptcy** Konkursverfahren einstellen; ~ **down** *(factory)* Betrieb schließen (stillegen), *(stop work)* Schicht machen; ~ **down for holidays** Betriebsferien machen; ~ **a submission list** Subskriptionsliste schließen; ~ **a year in the red** Jahr mit Verlust abschließen;
~ *(a.) (capital)* knapp, *(stock exchange)* Schluß fest;
~ **money** teures Geld; ~ **price** scharf kalkulierter Preis.

closed | **today** heute Betriebsruhe;
~ **account** abgeschlossenes Konto; ~ **door** *(tariff policy)* Tarifbegünstigung.

closed-end fund *(US)* Investmentfonds mit begrenzter Emissionshöhe.

closed | **professions** gesperrte Berufszweige; ~ **shop** gewerkschaftspflichtiger Betrieb.

closeout *(US, clearance sale)* Teilausverkauf.

closing *(advertising)* Anzeigenschluß, *(shutting)* Schließung, Stillegung;
earlier ~ früherer Ladenschluß; **fiscal** ~ Rechnungsabschluß; **half-day** ~ *(Br.)* früher Ladenschluß; **steady** ~ *(stock exchange)* fester Schluß;
~ **of an account** Rechnungsabschluß;
~ **agent** Abschlußagent; ~ **bid** Höchstgebot; ~ **date** *(advertising)* Anzeigenschluß; ~-**down (out) sale** Räumungsschlußverkauf; ~ **quotation** Schlußnotierung; ~ **time** Ladenschluß; ~ **trial balance** bereinigte Probebilanz.

Coal and Steel Community Montanunion.

coastal shipping Küstenschiffahrt.

coasting trade Küstenhandel.

cocket *(Br.)* Zollpassierschein, *(seal)* Zollsiegel.

code Code, Geheimschrift, Chiffrierschlüssel;
to write a dispatch in ~ Code benützen;
~ **address** Chiffreanschrift; ~ **clerk** Chiffrierbeamter; ~ **key** Chiffrierschlüssel; ~ **telegram** Chiffretelegramm.

codetermination parietätische Mitbestimmung.

coffee | **break** *(US)* Kaffeepause; ~ **room (shop,** *US) (hotel)* Frühstückszimmer, -raum.

coin Münze, Geldstück, *(hard money)* Hartgeld;
~ *(v.)* **money** Geld prägen (scheffeln);
~-**box telephone** *(US)* Münzfernsprecher.

coinage, debased Münzverschlechterung.
coinsurance clause Selbstbehaltsklausel.
coinsure *(c.)* mit-, rückversichern.
coinsurer Selbstversicherer.
cold training *(US)* vorsorgliche Ausbildung leitender Angestellter.
collapse | of a bank Bankkrach; ~ of prices Preiszusammenbruch, -sturz.
collateral Sicherheitsgegenstand, Pfand *(security)* Deckung, Sicherheit;
  to borrow on the ~ of securities Darlehn gegen Lombardierung von Wertpapieren aufnehmen;
  ~ acceptance Interventions-, Notakzept; ~ advance Lombardvorschuß; ~ credit gedeckter Kredit, *(securities)* Lombardkredit; ~ endorsement Gefälligkeitsgiro; ~ holdings Lombardbestände; ~ loan Lombardkredit; ~ value Lombard[ierungs]wert.
collaterate *(v.) (US)* Verpfändung von Wertpapieren vornehmen.
collect [an]sammeln, *(cheques)* einziehen, einlösen, *(taxes)* erheben;
  ~ a claim Forderung eintreiben;
  ~ call *(tel.)* R-Gespräch; ~ shipment Frachtnachnahme.
collect on delivery *(C. O. D.) (US)* Zahlung gegen Nachnahme, zahlbar bei Lieferung;
  ~ fee Nachnahmegebühr.
collecting | agency Inkassostelle, -büro; ~ box Sammelbüchse; ~ business Inkasso[geschäft]; ~ clerk Kassenbote.
collection Inkasso, *(bill, debts)* Einziehung, Einzug, *(taxes)* Einziehung;
  house-to-house ~ Haussammlung; slow ~s schleppend eingehende Inkassobeträge;
  ~ of charges Spesennachnahme; ~ by the customer Selbstabholung; ~ on delivery *(US)* Zahlung gegen Nachnahme; ~ of freight charges Frachteninkasso; ~ of patterns Musterkollektion; ~ at the source Quellenbesteuerung;
  to effect ~s Inkassi besorgen;
  ~ agency (agent) Inkassobüro, -stelle; ~ business Inkassogeschäft; ~ item Inkassoabschnitt; ~ letter *(US)* Mahnschreiben; ~ order form Postauftragsformular.
collective | account Sammelkonto; ~ agreement *(bargaining)* Tarifvertrag, -vereinbarung; ~ bargaining Tarifverhandlungen; ~ bill of lading Sammelkonnossement; ~ call *(tel.)* Konferenzgespräch; ~ consignment Sammelladung; ~ insurance Gruppenversicherung; ~ mark Verbandszeichen; ~ number *(tel.)* Sammelanschluß, -nummer; ~ ticket Sammelfahrschein; ~ wage agreement Lohntarifvertrag.
collector Sammler, *(customs)* Zolleinnehmer, *(debts)* Inkassobeamter;
  rent ~ Mieteinnehmer;
  ~of internal revenues *(US)* Finanzamtsleiter; ~ of taxes *(Br.)* Steuereinnehmer.
collision Kollision, *(car)* Karambolage;
  ~ of interests Interessenkonflikt;
  ~ insurance *(US)* Kaskoversicherung.
colo(u)r | ad *(US)* mehrfarbige Anzeige; ~ block *(Br.)* Farbklischee.
colo(u)rable | claim *(bankruptcy)* aussonderungsberechtigte Forderung; ~ transaction Scheingeschäft.
column Zahlenkolonne, Spalte, Kolumne;
  advertisement ~s Anzeigenteil; financial ~s Handels-, Wirtschaftsteil.
columnar | [system of] bookkeeping amerikanische Buchführung; ~ sheet Kolonnenbogen.
combination Konzern, Interessengemeinschaft;
  price ~ Preiskartell;
  ~ in restraint of trade Wettbewerbskartell; ~ milage and rate prorate *(US)* kombinierter Frachttarif; ~ offer Kopplungsangebot; ~ rate kombinierter Anzeigenpreis, *(railway)* Durchfrachtsatz, -tarif.
combine Trust, Konzern, Pool;
  buying (purchasing) ~ Einkaufsverband;
  ~ *(v.)* fusionieren, zusammenschließen;
  ~ price Verbandspreis.
combined | certificate of value and origin *(Br.)* kombiniertes Wert- und Ursprungszeugnis; ~ annual fee pauschale Jahresgebühr; ~ income *(married couple)* gemeinsames Einkommen; ~ wholelife insurance gemischte Lebensversicherung auf den Erlebens- und Todesfall.
come *(v.)* into | a business in ein Geschäft eintreten; ~ property Vermögen erben (erwerben).
comfortable independence finanzielle Unabhängigkeit.
commencing salary Anfangsgehalt.
commendatory letter Empfehlungsbrief.
commerce [Handels]verkehr, Handel;
  active ~ Außenhandel mit eigenen Schiffen; maritime ~ Handelsschiffahrt.
Commerce Department *(US)* Handels-, Wirtschaftsministerium.
commercial *(broadcasting, television)* Patronats-, Werbesendung, *(traveller, Br. coll.)* Handelsreisender, Vertreter;
  ~ *(a.)* geschäftlich, kaufmännisch, gewerblich, kommerziell;
  ~ acceptance credit Warenrembourskredit; ~ advertising Wirtschaftswerbung; ~ agency *(US)* [Kredit]-auskunftei; ~ appointment kaufmännische Beschäftigung; ~ association Wirtschaftsvereinigung; ~ books Geschäftsbücher; ~ broker Produktenmakler; ~ car Nutzfahrzeug, Geschäfts-, Lieferwagen; ~ correspondence course Handelskorrespondenzkurs; ~ directory Branchenadreßbuch; ~ domicile Sitz der gewerblichen Niederlassung; ~ medium-sized ~ establisment des gewerblichen Mittelstandes; ~ hotel Durchgangshotel; ~ letter Geschäftsbrief; ~ newspaper Wirtschaftszeitung, Börsenblatt; ~ paper Schuldschein; ~ prospects Geschäftsaussichten; ~ risk Geschäftsrisiko, Unternehmerwagnis;
  ~ room *(hotel, Br.)* Besprechungs-, Konferenz-

zimmer; ~ **shipping** Handelsschiffahrt; ~ **size** marktfähige (gängige) Größe; ~ **terms** Lieferklauseln; ~ **treaty** Handelsvertrag, Wirtschaftsabkommen; ~ **use** gewerbliche Nutzung.

commission Kommission[sgebühr], [Makler]provision, *(brokerage)* Courtage;

free of ~ provisionsfrei;

accrued ~ Provisionsforderung; **counterbalance** ~ Stornogebühr; **overdraft** ~ Überziehungsprovision; **overriding** ~ Abschlußprovision des Generalvertreters; **underwriting** ~ Abschlußprovision, Bonifikation;

~ **for domicil[at]ing** Domizilprovision; ~ **of the stock exchange** Börsenzulassungsausschuß;

~ *(v.)* beauftragen, bevollmächtigen, ermächtigen, *(ship)* in Dienst stellen;

to buy and sell on ~ Provisionsgeschäfte machen; ~ **account** Provisionskonto, -rechnung; ~ **agent** Kommissionär; **to be paid (operate) on a** ~ **basis** als Provisionsvertreter (auf Provisionsgrundlage) arbeiten; ~ **charge** Provision, *(broker)* Courtage[satz]; ~ **selling** Verkauf auf Provisionsbasis.

commissioner Beauftragter, Bevollmächtigter, *(committee member)* Ausschußmitglied;

⚲ **of Audit** Oberster Rechnungshof; ~ **of banking** *(US)* Bankenkommissar.

commit *(v.)* | **an act of bankruptcy** Konkursvergehen begehen; ~ **o. s. on easing money** sich für Geldmarkterleichterungen einsetzen.

commitment Verbindlichkeit, [finanzielle] Verpflichtung, *(stock exchange, US)* [Börsen]engagement;

advance ~ Kreditzusage; **fortnightly** ~s Mediofälligkeiten;

to meet one's ~s seinen Verpflichtungen nachkommen; **to shorten** ~s Aufträge zurückziehen; ~ **commission** Bereitstellungsprovision.

committee Ausschuß, Kommission, Komitee;

appraisement ~ Bewertungsausschuß; **assessment** ~ Veranlagungsausschuß; **Economic and Finance** ⚲ *(UNO)* Wirtschafts- und Finanzausschuß; **shop** ~ *(Br.)* Betriebsrat;

~ **of creditors** Gläubigerbeirat; ~ **of inspection** *(Br. bankruptcy)* Gläubigerausschuß; ⚲ **of Supply** *(Br.)* Haushaltsausschuß.

commodities Waren, Artikel, Gebrauchsgüter;

agricultural ~ landwirtschaftliche Erzeugnisse; **bulk** ~ Massengüter; **price-maintained** ~ preisstabile Waren; **rationed (scarce)** ~ Mangelware; ~ **[not] under control** [nicht] bewirtschaftete Waren.

commodity [Handels]ware, [Gebrauchs]artikel;

~ **advance** Warenbevorschussung; ~ **aid** projektgebundene Hilfe; ~ **classification** Warenverzeichnis; ~ **futures** Warentermingeschäft; ~ **money** *(US)* Indexwährung; ~ **rate** *(airline)* Vorzugstarif.

common *(a.)* [allgemein] üblich, *(inferior)* geringwertig, *(public)* öffentlich;

⚲ **Agriculture Policy** Agrarpolitik der Europäischen Gemeinschaften; ~ **capital stock** *(US)* Stammkapital.

common carrier *(US)* Spediteur, gewerbsmäßiger Frachtführer.

common | **enterprise** Gemeinschaftsbetrieb; ~ **hazard** *(fire insurance)* allgemeine Feuersgefahr; ~ **labo(u)rer** ungelernter Arbeiter.

Common Market Gemeinsamer Markt; ~ **Community** Europäische Wirtschaftsgemeinschaft.

common | **purse** gemeinsame Kasse; ~ **seal** *(Br.)* Firmensiegel; ~ **share** *(Br.)* Stammaktie, -anteil.

communal trading (untertaking) Kommunal-, Gemeindebetrieb.

communication Verkehrsverbindung, -weg;

commercial ~s geschäftliche Mitteilungen; **postal** ~ Postverbindung;

~ **satellite** Nachrichtensatellit.

community Gemeinwesen, Gemeinde, Öffentlichkeit;

conventional ~ vertraglich vereinbarte Gütergemeinschaft;

~ **of [rights and] interests** [Rechts- und] Interessengemeinschaft;

~ **property** *(married couple, US)* Errungenschaftsgemeinschaft.

commutation Ablösung, Ablösungssumme, *(US, travel(l)ing on a commutation ticket)* Benutzung einer Dauerkarte;

~ **of an annuity** Rentenablösung;

~ **fare** *(US)* Abonnementsfahrpreis; ~ **rates** *(US)* Zeitkartentarif; ~ **ticket** *(US)* Zeit-, Dauerkarte.

commute *(v.)* [Lasten]ablösen, *(commutation ticket)* pendeln, Dauerfahrkarte benutzen, *(pay in gross)* durch Kapitalzahlung abfinden.

commuter *(US, railroad ticket)* Zeitkarteninhaber, Pendler;

~ **train** Vorort-, Pendler-, Nah-, Berufsverkehrszug.

commuting *(US)* Nah-, Berufsverkehr, Pendeln; ~ **business** *(US)* Pendlerverkehr.

company [Handels]gesellschaft, Firma, Unternehmen, Betrieb;

accepting ~ *(insurance)* Rückversicherer; **affiliated** ~ Tochter-, Konzerngesellschaft; **ceding** ~ *(insurance law)* Erstversicherer; **debtor** ~ Schuldnerin; **family-held** ~ Familienunternehmen; **guarantee** ~ Kautionsversicherungsgesellschaft; **joint-stock** ~ *(Br.)* Aktiengesellschaft, *(US)* [etwa] Kommanditgesellschaft auf Aktien; **limited [liability]** ~ *(Br.)* [etwa] Gesellschaft mit beschränkter Haftung; **nonprofit [-making]** ~ gemeinnützige Gesellschaft; **one-man** ~ *(US)* Einmanngesellschaft; **operating** ~ Betriebsgesellschaft; **public-utility** ~ öffentlicher Versorgungsbetrieb; **shipping** ~ Reederei; **subsidiary** ~ Organ-, Schachtelgesellschaft; **direct-writing** ~ Rückversicherungsgesellschaft;

to administer a ~ **from red to black** Betrieb aus den roten Zahlen herausführen; **to float (found) a** ~ Gesellschaft gründen; **to register a** ~ Firma handelsgerichtlich eintragen lassen; **to wind up a** ~ Gesellschaft auflösen (liquidieren);

~ **address** Firmenanschrift; ~ **benefit** betriebliche Sozialbeihilfe; ~ **cafeteria** Betriebskasino; ~ **car**

firmeneigener Wagen; ~ **dwelling (flat)** Werkswohnung; ~ **meeting** Gesellschafterversammlung; ~'s **name** Firmenname; ~ **policy** Unternehmenspolitik; ~ **property** Firmen-, Betriebsvermögen; ~ **town** *(US)* Werkssiedlung.
comparative income statement vergleichende Gewinn- und Verlustrechnung.
compensable death schadenersatzpflichtiger Unfalltod.
compensate *(v.)* ausgleichen, kompensieren; ~ **s. o. for a loss** j. für einen Verlust entschädigen.
compensation [Schaden]ersatz, *(counterbalance)* Ausgleich[ung], Kompensation, *(US, customs)* Ausgleichszoll, *(indemnification)* Entgelt, Abstandsgeld, Entschädigung, *(salary, US)* Lohn, Gehalt, Vergütung; **dismissal** ~ Abfindung; **sickness** ~ Krankengeld; **year-end** ~ Jahresabschlußvergütung; ~ **in cash** Barabfindung; ~ **for pain and suffering** *(US)* Schmerzensgeld; **to accept** ~ sich abfinden lassen; **Workmen's** ≙ **Act** Arbeiterunfallversicherungsgesetz; ~ **business** Kompensationsgeschäft.
compensatory | **damages** *(US)* Ersatz des tatsächlichen Schadens; ~ **duty** Ausgleichszoll; ~ **fiscal policy** antizyklische Konjunkturpolitik; ~ **interest** Zinseszinsen; ~ **time off** Ausgleichsurlaub für Überstunden.
compete *(v.)* im Wettbewerb stehen; ~ **for a job** sich um einen Posten bewerben.
competing | **brands** Konkurrenzmarken; ~ **business** Konkurrenzgeschäft.
competition Konkurrenz[kampf], Wettbewerb; **cutthroat** ~ Schmutzkonkurrenz; **fair** ~ lauterer Wettbewerb; **knocking** ~ herabsetzende Werbung; **to throw open a job to** ~ Position ausschreiben; ~ **clause** Wettbewerbsklausel.
competitive konkurrenzfähig, wettbewerbsfähig; ~ **advertising** *(US)* aggressive Werbung; ~ **article** Konkurrenzerzeugnis; ~ **bidding** Submissionsverfahren; ~**distorting** wettbewerbsverzerrend; ~ **exhibition** Leistungsschau; ~ **firm** Konkurrenzfirma; ~ **tendering** Ausschreibung.
competitor Bewerber, *(firm)* Konkurrenzfirma.
complaint Beanstandung, Reklamation, Mängelrüge, *(insurance)* Schadenanzeige; ~**s department** Reklamationsabteilung.
complementary | **goods** komplementäre Güter; ~ **line** verwandtes Sortiment.
complete | **audit** Jahresrevision; **to have** ~ **charge of a business** Geschäft vollständig allein leiten; ~ **voucher copy** vollständiges Belegexemplar.
completed transaction abgeschlossenes Geschäft.
complimentary | **account** Werbungskonto; ~ **copy** Freiexemplar; ~ **ticket** Freikarte.
composite | **advertisement** Kollektivanzeige; ~ **index number** Generalindex.
composition Übereinkunft, *(sum paid to compound)* Vergleichs-, Abfindungssumme; ~ **in bankruptcy** Konkurs-, Zwangsvergleich; **to**

make a ~ **with one's creditors** sich mit seinen Gläubigern akkordieren; ~ **tax** pauschalierte Steuer.
compound [Schuld] ablösen, *(settle in bulk)* pauschalieren; ~ **with one's creditors** Arrangement mit seinen Gläubigern treffen; ~ **one's interest quarterly** Zinsen vierteljährlich bezahlen; ~ **amount** Zinseszinsbetrag; ~ **duty** gemischter Wertzoll; ~ **interest** Zinseszinsen.
comprehensive | **coverage** *(insurance, US)* Teilkasko; ~ **liability and property damage insurance** *(US)* Haft- und Diebstahlautoversicherung.
comptroller Rechnungsprüfer, Revisor; ≙ **General** *(US)* Präsident des Bundesrechnungshofs.
compulsory | **arbitration** Zwangsschlichtung; ~ **insurance against third party risks** Unfallhaftpflichtversicherung; ~ **syndicate** Pflichtkartell.
computation Schätzung, Überschlag; **income-tax** ~ Einkommensteuerberechnung; ~ **table** Berechnungstafel.
compute *(v.)* er-, be-, ausrechnen, *(estimate)* Überschlag machen, kalkulieren, überschlagen; ~ **a bill** Verfall[stag] eines Wechsels ausrechnen.
computed tare Durchschnittstara.
conceal *(v.) (balance sheet)* verschleiern.
concealed loss unbemerkt gebliebener Verlust.
concealment Verschleierung, *(insurance law)* Anzeigenpflichtverletzung.
concentration Konzentration, Konzentrierung; **market** ~ Absatzkonzentration.
concern Betrieb, Handelsgeschäft, [industrielles] Unternehmen, Firma, Geschäft; **big** ~ Großbetrieb; **commercial** ~ [Handels]firma, Geschäftsbetrieb; **paying** ~ rentables Geschäft; **to have a** ~ **in a business** Geschäftsanteil besitzen.
concession Vergünstigung, Zugeständnis, *(customs)* Zollzugeständnis, *(US)* Gewerbeerlaubnis, Lizenz; **international** ~internationale Niederlassung; **price** ~ Preiszugeständnis; ~**s on depreciation** Abschreibungsvergünstigungen; **to let out on a** ~ **basis** im Konzessionswege vergeben; ~ **fee** Konzessionsgebühr.
conciliation, industrial Schlichtungswesen in der Wirtschaft.
conclusion of a bargain Geschäftsabschluß.
condemn *(v.) (building)* für gebrauchsunfähig erklären, *(goods)* beschlagnahmen, konfiszieren; ~ **as a lawful prize** für gute Prise erklären.
condemnation Beschlagnahme, Einziehung, Konfiskation, *(ship)* Seeuntauglichkeitserklärung; ~ **money** *(US)* Entschädigungsbetrag.
condemned property enteignetes Grundstück.
condensed balance sheet Bilanzauszug.
condition Bedingung, Auflage, Klausel; **deliverable** ~ lieferfähiger Zustand; **distressed** ~ Notlage; **market** ~**s** Absatzverhältnisse; ~**s of labo(u)r** Arbeitsbedingungen.

conditional | **acceptance** bedingte Annahme; ~ **indorsement** beschränktes Giro; ~ **sales contract** Kauf[vertrag] unter Eigentumsvorbehalt.

condominium [apartment] *(US)* Eigentumswohnung.

conduct | **of business** ordnungsmäßige Geschäftsleitung;
~ *(v.)* **a business** Geschäft betreiben; ~ **correspondence** Korrespondenz führen;
~ **money** *(travel(l)ing expenses)* Reisegeld.

conference Beratung, Besprechung;
news ~ Pressekonferenz; **world economic** ~ Weltwirtschaftskonferenz;
~ **call hookup** Sammelgesprächsschaltung; ~ **room** Konferenz-, Besprechungszimmer; ~ **selling** Verkaufsaktion im Vorführungsraum.

conferring of a contract Auftragserteilung.

confidential | **clerk** Privatsekretär; ~ **communication** vertrauliche Mitteilung.

confirm *(v.)* **by letter** brieflich bestätigen.

confirmation Bestätigung[sschreiben];
~ **of balance** Kontokorrentbestätigung; ~ **of an order** Auftragsbestätigung.

confirmatory note *(carrier, US)* Übernahmebescheinigung.

confiscate *(v.)* **contraband goods** Schmuggelwaren mit Beschlag belegen.

confiscation Beschlagnahme, Konfiszierung;
~ **order** Beschlagnahmeverfügung.

confiscatory | **rates** kostenmäßig nicht gedeckte Tarifsätze; ~ **taxes** ruinöse Steuern.

conformity, to enter in gleichlautend buchen.

confusion | **of debts** Untergang von Forderungen; ~ **of goods** Warenvermischung; ~ **of trademarks** Verwechslung von Warenzeichen.

congest *(v.)* **the market** Markt überschwemmen.

congestion charge *(shipping)* Frachtzuschlag.

conglomerate Zusammenballung, *(industrial concern, US)* Konzern[gruppe], Großkonzern.

congress Tagung, Kongreß;
~ **center** Kongreßzentrum.

connected | **expenses** notwendige Aufgaben; ~ **load** Gesamtbelastung.

connecting carrier Anschlußreederei.

connection (connexion, *Br.)* Anschluß, *(customers)* Kundschaft, Klientele;
business ~ Geschäftsverbindung; **financial** ~ kapitalmäßige Bindung; **first-rate** ~**s** erstklassiger Kundenkreis;
to dispose over wide ~**s** über gute Beziehungen verfügen.

conscience money *(Br.)* anonyme Steuernachzahlung, Reugeld.

conscript *(v.)* *(labo(u)r)* dienstverpflichten;
~ **capital** Kapital der staatlichen Zwangswirtschaft unterwerfen.

conscription of labo(u)r Dienstverpflichtung.

consecutive quotation laufende Notierung.

consequential damages mittelbarer Schaden.

conservation of assets Erhaltung von Vermögenswerten.

consideration *(bill of exchange)* Valuta, *(compensation)* Entschädigung, Vergütung;
~ **bargained for** vereinbarte Gegenleistung; **valuable** ~ Gegenwert, Vertragsinteresse;
~ **money** Gegenwert in Geld.

consign übergeben, *(deposit in bank)* [in die Bank] einzahlen, hinterlegen, *(transmit)* [Waren] übersenden, ausliefern.

consignation Hinterlegung, Zusendung.

consigned | **goods** Kommissionsware; ~ **money** anvertrautes Geld.

consignee [Waren]empfänger, Kommissionär.

consignment Übertragung, *(commission)* Kommission, Kommissionsauftrag, *(depositing)* Hinterlegung, *(goods consigned)* [Waren]sendung;
on ~ kommissionsweise; **shipping on** ~ auf eigene Rechnung versandt;
mixed ~ Sammelladung; **small** ~**s** Stückgut;
~ **on approval** Auswahl-, Ansichtssendung; ~ **in specie** Barsendung;
to make out a ~ Frachtbrief ausstellen; **to take goods on** ~ Waren in Kommission nehmen;
~ **goods** Konsignationswaren; ~ **invoice** Kommissionsrechnung; ~ **note** Warenbegleit-, Ladeschein.

consolidate *(v.)* vereinigen, zusammenziehen, *(shares)* [Aktien] zusammenlegen;
~ **companies** Firmen zusammenschließen.

consolidated vereinigt, fundiert, konsolidiert;
~ **balance sheet** Konzernbilanz; ~ **delivery system** gemeinsames Auslieferungssystem; ~ **group** Konzerngruppe; ~ **loan** fundierte Anleihe; ~ **shipment** *(Br.)* Sammelladung.

consolidation Konsolidierung, *(market)* [Be]festigung, *(merger)* Fusion;
~ **of mortages** Zusammenschreibung von Hypotheken; ~ **of shares** Zusammenlegung des Aktienkapitals;
~ **balance sheet** Fusionsbilanz.

consols *(Br.)* fundierte Staatsanleihe.

consortium Konsortium, Syndikat, Gruppe;
~ **of banks** Finanz-, Bankenkonsortium;
~ **aid** Konsortialhilfe.

constant costs konstante Kosten.

constituent | **company** Gründergesellschaft; ~ **territory of a customs unit** Collunionsteilnehmerland.

construction | **company** Baufirma; ~ **cost index** Baukostenindex; ~ **industry** Bauwirtschaft; **public** ~ **project** öffentliches Bauvorhaben.

constructive baulich, *(law)* angenommen, fingiert;
to claim ~ **damages** Ersatz des mittelbaren Schadens verlangen; ~ **[total] loss** *(marine insurance)* fingierter Totalverlust.

consular | **agency** konsularische Vertretung; ~ **certificate** Konsulatsbescheinigung; ~ **fees** Konsulatsgebühren; **to prepare a** ~ **invoice** Konsulatsfaktura ausstellen.

consultancy agreement Beratungsvertrag.

consultant [ständiger] Gutachter, Berater;
~ **on business policy** Berater der Geschäftsleitung;
~ **service** Beratungsdienst.

consulting | **agreement** Beratungsvertrag; ~ **engineering firm** Industrieberatung.

consumer Verbraucher, Konsument, Abnehmer;
bulk ~ Großverbraucher;
~ **acceptance** Kaufbereitschaft; ~ **advertisement** Endverbraucherwerbung; ~ **behavio(u)r** Verbraucherverhalten; ~ **buying** Verbrauchsnachfrage;
~ **credit** Verbraucher-, Kundenkredit ~ **durables** langlebige Konsum-, Gebrauchsgüter ~ **goods** Konsum-, Verbrauchsgüter; ~ **industry** Konsumgüterindustrie; ~ **instal(l)ment credit** Abzahlungskredit; ~ **loan company** *(US)* Finanzierungsgesellschaft für Kleinkredite; ~ **mail panel** postalische Verbraucherbefragung; ~ **market** Konsum-, Verbrauchsgütermarkt; ~**orientated** konsumbewußt; ~ **panel** repräsentative Verbrauchergruppe; ~ **price index** Verbraucherpreis-, Lebenshaltungsindex; ~ **purchasing power** Konsumentenkaufkraft; ~ **research** Konsumgütermarkt; ~ **spending spree** Ausgabenfreudigkeit der Verbraucherschaft.

consuming area Verbrauchsgebiet.

consumption Verbrauch, Verzehr, Konsum;
domestic ~ Inlandsverbrauch; **low oil** ~ *(car)* geringer Ölverbrauch;
~ **of costs** Kostenverzehr;
to enter goods for ~ Waren zum freien Verkauf einführen;
~ **capacity** Kaufkraft einer Verbraucherschicht; ~ **credit** Konsumentenkredit; ~ **economy** Verbrauchswirtschaft; ~ **goods** Verbrauchsgüter; ~ **goods industry** Verbrauchsgüterindustrie; ~ **line** Verbrauchskurve; ~ **market** Verbrauchermarkt; ~ **voucher** Bedarfsdeckungsschein.

contact man Verbindungsmann, Behördenvermittler.

container [Versand]behälter, Kanister;
~ **car** Behälterwagen.

contango *(Br., stock trade)* Reportprämie, Prolongationsgebühr, Kursaufschlag;
~ **business** *(Br.)* Report-, Kost-, Prolongationsgeschäft; ~ **rate** *(Br.)* Prolongationsgebühr.

contest [Verbraucher]wettbewerb.

continental | **bills** *(Br.)* Wechsel auf Plätze des europäischen Kontinents; ~ **tour** *(Br.)* Europareise.

contingencies unvorhergesehene Ausgaben, *(balance sheet)* Eventualverbindlichkeiten;
~ **reserve** Reservefonds, Notrücklage.

contigency ungewisses (zufälliges) Ereignis;
~ **fund** außerordentliche Reservefonds; ~ **reserve** Delkredererückstellung.

contingent [Pflicht]anteil, [Beteiligungs]quote, Kontingent;
~ **account** *(Br.)* Delkrederekonto; ~ **annuity** Rente; mit unbestimmter Laufzeit; ~ **beneficiary** *(insurance)* bedingt Begünstigter; ~ **liability** Eventualverpflichtung; ~ **order** gekoppelter Auftrag; ~ **reserve** Rückstellung für unvorhergesehene Ausgaben.

continuance of a firm Fortbestand einer Firma.

continuation Weiterführung, *(Br., stock exchange)* Prolongation, Kostgeschäft;

fortnightly ~ *(Br.)* Medioprolongation;
~ **bill** *(Br.)* Prolongationswechsel; ~ **business** *(Br.)* Prolongations-, Report-, Kostgeschäft; ~ **day** *(Br.)* Reporttag.

continue *(v.)* | **a business** Geschäft fortführen; ~ **in demand** fortlaufend gefragt sein.

continued | **account** Übertrag; ~ **bonds** *(US)* prolongierte Obligationen.

continuing | **account** Kontokorrentkonto; ~ **appropriation** nicht verbrauchte Etatsanteile; ~ **guaranty** *(US)* Kreditbürgschaft.

continuity | **in advertising** fortlaufender Werbeeinsatz; ~ **of employment** Beschäftigungskontinuität; ~ **premium** Zugabenwerbung in Sammelform.

continuous | **audit** laufende Revisionsarbeiten; ~ **inventory** permanente Bestandsaufnahme.

contra | **account** Gegen-, Wertberichtigungskonto; ~ **entry** *(Br.)* Gegenbuchung, Storno.

contraband Konter-, Schmuggel-, Bannware;
~ **trade** Schmuggel.

contract Vertrag, Auftrag, Verdingung;
costplus-a fixed-fee ~ Vertrag mit Preisfestsetzung nach den Kosten zuzüglich Verrechnung fester Zuschläge; **exclusive-dealing** ~ Ausschließlichkeitsvertrag; **fixed-price** ~ Festpreisvertrag; **fixed price-incentive fee** ~ Festpreisvertrag mit Leistungszuschlägen; **fixed-price** ~ **with provision for redetermination of price** *(US)* Festpreisauftrag mit Neufestsetzung des Preises; **hire-purchase** *(Br.)* **(instal(l)ment)** ~ Abzahlungsvertrag; **loan** ~ Darlehnsvertrag; **underwriting** ~ Konsortialvertrag; ~ **of apprenticeship** Lehr[lings]vertrag; ~ **of employment** Arbeits-, Dienstvertrag; ~ **in restraint of trade** Kartellvereinbarung; ~ **by tender** Submission, Ausschreibung; ~ **of warranty** Garantieversprechen; ~ **for work and labo(u)r (service)** Werkvertrag; ~ **for work and materials** Werklieferungsvertrag;
(v.) ~ **liabilities** Verpflichtungen eingehen;
to be awarded a juicy government ~ fetten Regierungsauftrag erhalten; **to break a** ~ vertragsbrüchig werden; **to buy on** ~ fest kaufen; **to confer the** ~ Zuschlag erteilen;
~ **award** Auftragserteilung, Vergabe öffentlicher Aufträge; ~ **bond** Unternehmerkaution; ~ **hours** vertragliche Arbeitszeit; ~ **price** Submissions-, Lieferpreis; ~ **shop** *(US)* Akkordbetrieb; ~ **trade (trading)** *(stock exchange)* Termingeschäft; ~ **work** *(US)* Akkordarbeit.

contracting **[for work]** Gedinge-, Akkordwesen;
~ **price** Lieferungspreis; ~ **state** Vertragsstaat.

contraction | **of debts** Schuldenaufnahme; ~ **in production** Produktionseinschränkung.

contractive tendencies Abschwächungstendenzen.

contractor *(employer)* Unternehmer, *(supplier)* Auftragnehmer, [Submissions]lieferant;
carting ~ Rollfuhrunternehmer.

contribute *(v.)* zuwenden, beitragen;
~ **capital** Kapital einbringen; ~ **equally towards the losses sustained by a firm** Geschäftsverluste zu gleichen Teilen tragen.

contributed capital eingezahltes Grundkapital.
contribution Masseverteilung, *(capital)* Einlagekapital, *(membership due)* Beitrag, *(share)* Prämienanteil;
  liable to ~ beitragspflichtig;
  capital ~ Kapitalaufbringung; employee's ~ *(social insurance)* Arbeitnehmeranteil; employer's ~ *(social insurance)* Arbeitgeberanteil; national *(Br.)* insurance (social security, *US*) ~ Sozialversicherungsbeiträge;
  ~ in cash Bareinlage; ~ in kind Sacheinlage; ~ to a pension trust *(balance sheet)* Beiträge zur Altersversorgung;
  ~ clause *(fire insurance)* Umlegungsbestimmung;
  ~ margin Deckungsbeitrag; ~ rate Beitragssatz.
contributor Spender, Leistungspflichtiger.
contributory beitragspflichtiges Mitglied, *(shareholder, Br.)* solidarisch haftender Aktionär;
  ~ *(a.)* beitragspflichtig;
  ~ basis Beitragsgrundlage; ~ scheme of insurance Umlageverfahren einer Versicherung.
control *(economic planning)* Bewirtschaftung, *(supervision)* Aufsicht, Kontrolle, Steuerung;
  commodity ~ Warenbewirtschaftung; economic ~ Zwangsbewirtschaftung; foreign exchange ~ Devisenbewirtschaftung; price ~ Preisüberwachung; production ~ Produktionslenkung; quality ~ statistische Güteüberwachung; rent ~ Mieterschutz;
  ~ in ownership interests ausschlaggebender Kapitalanteil; ~ of profits Gewinnbeschränkung;
  ~ *(v.)* bewirtschaften, überwachen;
  ~ the economic life of a region Wirtschaftsleben einer Gegend entscheidend beeinflussen; ~ housing Wohnungsmarkt bewirtschaften;
  to have ~ of an undertaking an der Spitze eines Unternehmens stehen;
  ~ account Hauptbuchsammel-, Kontrollkonto; ~ zone *(traffic)* Nahverkehrsbezirk.
controlled gelenkt, bewirtschaftet, *(price)* preisgestoppt;
  government- ~ unter Staatsaufsicht;
  ~ company beherrschtes Unternehmen; ~ economy Planwirtschaft; ~ house der Mieterschutzgesetzgebung unterliegendes Haus; ~ price gebundener Preis.
controller Rechnungsprüfer, Revisor;
  ~ of the currency *(US)* Bankenkommissar.
controlling | body Aufsichtsbehörde; ~ company Holding-, Dachgesellschaft; ~ interest Kapitalmehrheit; ~ stockholder Aktienmajoritätsbesitzer.
convenience | goods *(US)* Bedarfsdeckungs-, Verbrauchsgüter; ~ store Bedarfsartikelgeschäft.
convention | money gemeinsame Währung; ~ tariff Vertragstarif.
conventional | community vertragliche Gütergemeinschaft; ~ design gängige Sorte; ~ interest vereinbarter Zinssatz; ~ necessities Güter des gehobenen Bedarfs.
conversion Umwandlung, *(enterprise),* Umstellung, *(of debentures)* Umtausch, Konversion, Konver-

tierung, *(reduction of foreign exchange)* Umrechnung, Umwechslung;
loan ~ Anleiheumwandlung;
  ~ into a company Vergesellschaftung; ~ into flats Umbau in Appartmentwohnungen; ~ into nontaxable form steuerfreie Anlage; ~ of rooms to office use Zweckentfremdung einer Wohnung;
  ~ account Umstellungskonto; ~ balance Konversionsguthaben; ~ key Umrechnungsschlüssel; ~ table Umrechnungstabelle.
convert *(v.)* realisieren, versilbern, *(change money)* um-, einwechseln, konvertieren;
  ~ funds to one's own use fremdes Geld für sich verwenden; ~ into finished products zu Fertigwaren verarbeiten; ~ shares Aktien zusammenlegen.
convertibility Konvertierbarkeit;
  ~ agreement Konversionsabkommen.
convertible *(a.)* umwandelbar, konvertierbar, *(reducible)* umrechenbar;
readily ~ into cash sofort realisierbar;
  ~ bonds Wandelschuldverschreibungen.
converting permit Verarbeitungsgenehmigung.
convey *(v.)* befördern, transportieren.
conveyance Auflassung, Umschreibung, Liegenschaftsübertragung, *(transfer)* Abtretung, Zession, *(transporting)* Spedition, Über-, Versendung, Transport, *(vehicle)* Fahrzeug;
  ~ by aircraft Lufttransport; ~ by sea Beförderung auf dem Wasserweg.
conveyer, conveyor Frachtführer;
  ~ assembly line Fließbandmontage; ~ band (belt) Fließ-, Förderband.
cook *(v.)* a balance sheet Bilanz frisieren.
cooling-off period *(strike law)* Abkühlungszeit.
cooperation Zusammenarbeit, *(economic association)* genossenschaftlicher Zusammenschluß.
cooperative Genossenschaft, Gemeinschaft;
  marketing ~ Absatzgenossenschaft;
  ~ advertising *(Br.)* Gemeinschaftswerbung; ~ buying gemeinsamer Warenbezug; ~ credit association Kreditgenossenschaft; ~ movement Genossenschaftsbewegung; ~ shop *(Br.)* Konsum[geschäft], Konsumladen.
copartnership Teilhaberschaft, Sozietät;
  labo(u)r ~ Arbeitergewinnbeteiligung.
copy Durchschlag, Abschrift, *(advertisement)* Werbung, Reklame-, Anzeigentext;
  attested ~ beglaubigte Abschrift; carbon ~ Durchschlag; complimentary ~ Werbenummer; disparaging ~ herabsetzende Werbung; reason-why ~ *(advertising)* Überzeugungsreklame;
  ~ of invoice Rechnungsdurchschlag;
  ~ appeal Attraktivität der Anzeigenaussage; ~ approach Textaufhänger; ~ date Anzeigenschluß, *(broadcasting)* Werbefunkschluß.
copying | apparatus Verfielfältigungsapparat; ~ cost Kopierunkosten; ~ paper Durchschlagpapier.
copywriter [Werbe]texter.
core, hard Restbestand [der Arbeitslosigkeit].
corner Aufkäufergruppe;

~ *(v.)* **the market** Waren zu Spekulationszwecken aufkaufen;

~ **influence** *(land)* wertsteigernder Faktor.

corporate vereinigt, verbunden, *(company)* inkorporiert, körperschaftlich, gesellschaftlich;

~ **action** zustimmungspflichtige Gesellschaftertätigkeit; ~ **assets** Gesellschaftsvermögen; ~ **bonding** *(insurance)* Sammeldepot; ~ **books** *(US)* Geschäftsbücher einer Aktiengesellschaft; ~ **creditor** Firmen-, Gesellschaftsgläubiger; ~ **customer** Firmenkunde; ~ **election** *(US)* Vorstandswahl; ~ **headquarters** Zentrale; ~ **image** Vorstellungsbild eines Unternehmens in der Öffentlichkeit; ~ **income tax** *(US)* Körperschaftsteuer; ~ **net worth** Eigenkapital; ~ **policy** Unternehmenspolitik; ~ **profit** Gesellschaftsgewinn; ~ **proprietorship** Gesellschaftskapital; ~ **seal** *(US)* Firmensiegel; ~ **tax** Körperschaftssteuer.

corporation *(US)* Kapital-, Aktiengesellschaft, *(municipal enterprise, US)* Kommunalbetrieb;

affiliated ~ *(US)* Organ-, Konzern-, Zweiggesellschaft; **banking** ~ *(US)* Aktienbank; **consolidated** ~ Schachtelgesellschaft; **membership** ~ *(US)* eingetragener Verein; **parent** ~ Mutter-, Dachgesellschaft; **public** ~ *(Br.)* Wirtschaftsunternehmen der öffentlichen Hand; **subsidiary** ~ Organgesellschaft;

~ **capital** *(US)* Gesellschaftskapital; ~ **charter** *(US)* Gründungsurkunde.

correct *(v.)* **an amount** Rechnungsbetrag berichtigen.

correcting entry Berichtigungsbuchung.

correction of an account Kontoberichtigung.

correspond *(v.)* in Geschäftsbeziehungen (im Briefwechsel) stehen;

~ **to sample** dem Muster entsprechen.

correspondence Briefverkehr, Schriftwechsel, Korrespondenz, Geschäftsverbindung;

~ **classes** Fernunterricht; ~ **clerk** Korrespondent; ~ **ticket** Umsteigefahrschein.

correspondent Briefpartner, *(US, banking)* Korrespondenzbank, *(business friend)* Geschäftsfreund, *(employee)* Korrespondent;

banking ~ Bankverbindung.

corresponding entry gleichlautende Buchung.

cost [Un]kosten, Geschäftskosten, Spesen, Auslagen, Aufwand, Kostenbetrag, *(loss)* Verlust;

all ~**s included** unter Einschluß sämtlicher Kosten; **at** ~ zum Selbstkostenpreis, *(investment fund)* auf Anschaffungsbasis, *(stock exchange)* zu Ankaufskursen; **at less than** ~ unter Einkaufspreis;

actual ~ Selbst-, Gestehungskosten; **agreed** ~**s** vereinbarte Spesen; **billed** ~ Kosten vor Abzug des Bardiskonts; **depreciation** ~**s** Abnutzungsaufwand; **factory overhead** ~**s** allgemeine Betriebsunkosten; **first** ~ Selbstkostenpreis; **invoice** ~ Einkaufspreis; **landed** ~ *(customs)* Anlieferungspreis; **overhead** ~**s** Fertigungsgemeinkosten; **prime** ~ Selbst-, Gestehungskosten, Anschaffungswert; **production** ~ Produktionsaufwand; **running** ~**s** laufende Unkosten; **sal-**

vage ~ *(insurance)* Bergungskosten; **social** ~ Soziallasten; **standard** ~ vorkalkulierte Kosten; **lower-unit** ~**s** niedrige Stückkosten; ~, **insurance and freight** (cif) Kosten, Versicherung und Fracht; ~ **of collection** Einzugsspesen; ~ **of delivery** Liefer-, Versandkosten; ~**s of goods and services** Preis für Güter und Dienstleistungen; ~ **of labo(u)r** Löhne und Gehälter.

cost of living Lebenshaltungskosten;

~ **allowance** Teuerungszuschlag; ~ **escalator** Lohngleitklausel; ~ **index** Lebens[haltungs]kostenindex.

cost | of maintenance Instandhaltungskosten; ~ **of money** Geldbeschaffungskosten;

~ *(v.)* kosten, zu stehen kommen, *(calculate)* Preis kalkulieren;

~ **the earth** kleines Vermögen kosten;

to carry ~**s** Kostenfolgen haben; **to cut** ~**s throughout a company** ganzen Betrieb kostenmäßig durchforsten; **to sell at** ~ zum Einkaufspreis verkaufen.

cost | absorption Kostenwertberichtigung; ~ **accountant** [Betriebs]kalkulator; ~ **accounting** betriebliches Rechnungswesen, [Selbst]kostenberechnung; ~ **averaging** *(stock exchange)* Kostenausgleich; ~ **book** *(mining)* Kuxbuch; ~ **cutter** Sparkommissar; ~ **estimate** Kostenvoranschlag; ~ **or market whichever is lower method** *(balance sheet, US)* Niederstwertprinzip; ~ **pass-alongs** Kostenabwälzung.

cost-plus *(US)* Lohnaufwand plus Material und Unternehmergewinn;

~ **contract** Werklieferungsvertrag.

cost | price Kosten-, Wareneinstandspreis; ~**-push inflation** kostentreibende Inflation; ~ **records** Spesenzettel; ~ **Rentabilitätsberechnung**.

costermonger *(Br.)* Straßenhändler, Höker.

costing Preisberechnung, Rentabilitätsberechnung, Kostenkalkulation;

direct (marginal, *Br.)* ~ Grenzplankostenrechnung.

cottage *(Br.)* Werks-, Arbeiterwohnung;

~ **industry** Heimarbeit, -industrie.

council | of economic advisers wirtschaftlicher Beirat; ~ **flat** *(Br.)* Sozialwohnung.

count *(v.)* **the daily receipts** Kassensturz machen.

counter Schalter, *(luggage)* Gepäckannahme, -ausgabe, *(shop)* Ladentisch, Kasse;

over the ~ *(US, securities)* im Freiverkehr;

~ **account** Gegenkonto, Kontrollregister; ~ **advertising** Abwehrwerbung; ~ **assurance** Rückversicherung; **over-the-** ~ **business** Schaltergeschäft; ~ **check** *(US)* Blankobank-, Kassenscheck; ~ **display** Ladentischauslage; **over-the-** ~ **market** *(US)* Freiverkehrsmarkt; **under-the-** ~ **sales** ungesetzlicher Ladenverkauf; ~ **trading** Schalterverkehr, freihändiger Effektenverkauf.

counterbill Gegenwechsel.

counterbond Rückbürgschaft.

countercyclical compensatory goernment policy antizyklische Konjunkturpolitik.

counterfeit Fälschung, *(spurious note)* falsche Banknote;
~ *(v.)* **coins** falschmünzen.
counterfeiter of banknotes Banknotenfälscher.
counterfoil Kontrollabschnitt, -blatt, *(coupon)* Kupon, *(luggage)* Gepäckzettel, *(talon)* Abschnitt, Talon;
~ **waybill** Frachtbriefdoppel.
counterinsurance Rückversicherung.
countermand Widerruf, Annullierung, Storno;
~ *(v.)* **payment** Zahlungsauftrag stornieren.
counteroffer Gegengebot, -offerte.
counterorder Abbestellung, Stornierung.
counterpart Kopie, Duplikat;
~ **fund** Gegenwertmittel, -fonds.
countersecurity Gegen-, Rückbürgschaft.
countervailing | **charge** Ausgleichsabgabe; ~ **credit** Gegenakkreditiv; ~ **duty** Ausgleichs-, Kompensationszoll, Umsatzausgleichssteuer.
country, underdeveloped Entwicklungsland;
~ **with a high (low) monetary standard** valutastarkes (valutaschwaches) Land;
~ **bank** *(Br.)* Provinzbank; ~ **store** *(US)* Dorfladen; ~ **trade** Binnenhandel.
coupon *(advertising)* Einsendeabschnitt, *(dividend warrant)* Gewinnanteilschein, *(interest warrant)* Zinsschein, Kupon, *(ration ticket, Br.)* [Lebensmittel]kartenabschnitt, *(ticket)* Gutschein, Kassenzettel, Bon;
free gift ~ Gutschein;
to detach ~**s** Kupons abtrennen;
~ **bond** *(US)* Inhaberschuldverschreibung; ~ **holder** Kuponinhaber; ~ **scheme** Werbeaktion mit beigefügten Kupons; ~ **sheet** Zinsscheinbogen;
~ **tax** Kuponsteuer.
course *(journey)* Fahrt, Reise, *(stock exchange)* Wechselkurs, [Kurs]notierung;
in-company ~ innerbetrieblicher Ausbildungskursus;
[ordinary] ~ **of business** normaler Geschäftsgang, -ablauf; ~ **of exchange** *(Br.)* Wechselkurs[zettel];
to act in the ordinary ~ **of one's business** im Rahmen der üblichen Geschäftsbedingungen handeln.
courtesy card Gutschein.
cover Hülle, Emballage, *(backing of notes)* Geld-, Notendeckung, *(envelope)* Kuvert, [Brief]umschlag, *(security)* Sicherheit, Deckung, Bürgschaft;
under ~ unter Kreuzband; **without** ~ ungedeckt;
additional ~ Deckungszuschuß; **provisional** ~ vorläufige Deckungszusage;
~ *(v.) (by insurance)* decken, *(reimburse)* ausgleichen;
~ **a bill** Deckung für einen Wechsel anschaffen; ~ **liabilities** Verpflichtungen nachkommen; ~ **over a loan** Anleihe überzeichnen; ~ **short sales** Fixgeschäfte abdecken; ~ **a territory** *(salesman)* Bezirk bearbeiten;
to lodge stock as ~ Aktien als Deckung hinterlegen; **to run off one's** ~ Kautionssumme einbüßen;

~ **address** Deckadresse; ~ **afloat (in transit)** Deckung angeschafft; ~ **folder** eingelegter Prospekt; ~ **note** *(Br.)* vorläufige Deckungszusage.
coverage *(advertising)* Streubreite, -dichte, *(agreement)* Geltungsbereich, *(insurance)* Versicherungsschutz, -umfang, *(market reached)* Reichweite, *(statistics)* erfaßter Bereich;
extended ~ *(fire insurance)* zusätzlicher Versicherungsschutz; **term-life** ~ Risikolebensversicherungsschutz.
covered | **by the amount insured** voll durch die Versicherung gedeckt;
~ **job** *(US)* pflichtversicherte Tätigkeit; ~ **waggon** *(Br.)* geschlossener Güterwagen.
covering *(stock exchange)* Deckungskauf;
~ **agreement** Mantelvertrag; ~ **entry** falsche Buchung; ~ **purchase** Deckungskauf.
craft Beruf, Gewerbe, *(aircraft)* Flugzeug;
customs ~ Zollboot;
~ **union** *(US)* Fachgewerkschaft; ~ **worker** Facharbeiter.
craftsmanship Handwerkerstand.
crank *(v.)* **up production** Produktion ankurbeln.
crash Karambolage, *(banking)* Bankkrach, *(stock exchange)* Zusammenbruch;
~ *(v.) (business)* pleite gehen, *(car)* karambolieren;
~ **job** Sofortauftrag.
cream campaign Werbefeldzug im erfolgversprechendsten Gebiet.
create *(v.)* | **capital goods** Kapitalgüter schaffen; ~ **a demand** Bedarf hervorrufen; ~ **money** Geld schöpfen; ~ **a trust** Treuhandverhältnis begründen.
creation | **of currency (money)** Geldschöpfung; ~ **of work** Arbeitsbeschaffung.
creative copy außergewöhnlicher Werbetext.
credentials Empfehlungsschreiben.
credit Kredit, *(credit side of account)* Haben, *(income tax, US)* abzugsfähiger Betrag, Freibetrag, *(letter of credit)* Akkreditiv, Kreditbrief, *(reputation for solvency)* Kreditwürdigkeit, Bonität, *(sum placed at disposal)* Guthaben, Gutschrift;
at three months' ~ Ziel gegen drei Monate;
acceptance ~ Akzeptkredit; **blank** ~ Blankokredit;
confirmed ~ *(Br.)* bestätigter Kredit; **consumer** ~ Abzahlungskredit; **countervailing** ~ Gegenakkreditiv; **documentary** ~ Dokumentenkredit; **earned-income** ~ *(US)* Steuerabzug für Arbeitseinkommen; **global** ~ Rahmenkredit; **hire-purchase (instal(l)ment)** ~ Abzahlungskredit; **joint** ~ Konsortialkredit; **open** ~ Kontokorrentkredit; **overdrawn** ~ überzogener Kredit; **reserve bank** ~ *(US)* [etwa:] Kassenkredit bei der Landeszentralbank; **revocable** ~ widerrufliches Akkreditiv; **stand-by** ~ Kreditzusage; **tied** ~ projektgebundener Kredit;
~ **on joint account** Metakredit; ~ **against securities** Lombardkredit; ~ **granted by supplies** Lieferantenkredit;
~ *(v.)* im Haben buchen, gutschreiben, *(grant credit)* kreditieren, [auf] Kredit geben;

to buy on ~ auf Kredit (Borg, Rechnung) kaufen; **to confirm a** ~ Akkreditiv bestätigen; **to exceed a** ~ Kreditlinie überschreiten; **to pledge one's husband's** ~ im Rahmen der Schlüsselgewalt kaufen; ~ **accommodation** Kreditfazilität; ~ **account** kreditorisch geführtes Konto; ~ **advice** Gutschriftsanzeige; ~ **allocation** Kreditkontingentierung; ~ **approval** Kreditzusage; ~ **balance** Guthaben, Aktivsaldo; **retail** ~ **bureau** (US) Einzelhandelskreditauskunftei; ~ **card** Kreditkarte; ~ **coupon plan** bargeldloses Verkaufssystem; ~ **currency** Buch-, Giralgeld; ~ **folder** Kreditakte; ~ **form** (US) Kreditvordruck; ~ **interest** Habenzinsen; **to run over the** ~ **limit** (Br.) eingeräumten Kredit überziehen; ~ **memorandum** (US) Gutschrift[anzeige], ~ **money** Buch-, Giralgeld; ~ **note** Gutschrift[anzeige]; ~ **restraint** (restriction) Kreditrestriktion, -drosselung; ~ **service charge** Kreditgebühr; ~ **slip** (Br.) Einzahlungsbeleg, Bon; ~ **solvency** (standing status) Bonität; **to buy on** ~ **terms** Im Kreditwege erwerben; ~ **transfer** bargeldlose Überweisung; **to pass a** ~ **vote** Kreditgesuch bewilligen; ~ **voucher** Einzahlungsbeleg.
creditor Gläubiger, Kreditor;
catholic ~ erstklassig gesicherter Gläubiger; **general** ~ Massegläubiger; **preferential** (Br.), **preferred** (US) ~ (bevorrechtigter) [Konkurs]gläubiger; **secured** ~ (US) absonderungsberechtigter Gläubiger;
~ **with a colo(u)rable claim** aussonderungsberechtigter Gläubiger; ~ **at large** einfacher Konkursgläubiger;
to compound (compose) with ~**s** mit Gläubigern einen Vergleich schließen;
~ **country** Gläubigerland; ~**debtor relation** Gläubiger-Schuldner-Verhältnis; ~**s' ledger** Kreditorenbuch.
crop [Getreide]ernte;
~ **insurance** Ernteversicherung.
cross (v.) (bill of exchange) querschreiben;
~ **acceptance (accommodation,** Br.) Wechselreiterei; ~ **account** (Br.) Rikambiorechnung; ~ **bill** (bill of exchange, Br.) Rück-, Gegenwechsel; **to make** ~ **entries** Gegenbuchungen vornehmen; ~ **order** (stock exchange) Kompensationsorder; ~ **trade** (US) Börsenkompensationsgeschäft.
crossing (cheque, Br.) Verrechnungsvermerk.
crowd | **of eager shoppers** kauflustige Menge;
~ (v.) **a debtor** Schuldner bedrängen;
to pull in the ~**s** Massenpublikum anziehen.
crowded hours Hauptverkehrszeit.
crown property (Br.) fiskalisches Eigentum.
cruise ship Vergnügungsdampfer.
crumble (v.) abbröckeln, Kursrückgang erleiden;
~ **up an estate** Gut parzellieren.
cultivate (v.) **the market** Marktpflege betreiben.
cultivated area Anbaugebiet.
cum | **dividend** mit (einschließlich) Dividende; ~ **drawing** inklusive Ziehung; ~ **new** mit Bezugsrecht auf junge Aktien.

cumulative | **dividend** Dividende auf kumulative Vorzugsaktien; ~ **fund** (Br.) thesaurierender Fonds; ~ **preference stocks** (US) kumulative Vorzugsaktien.
curb (US) Nach-, Freibörse, -verkehr;
on the ~ (US) nach-, außerbörslich, im Freiverkehr;
~ **on dividend rises** Dividendenstopp; ~ **of exports** Ausfuhrbeschränkung;
~ (v.) (business cycle) dämpfen, zügeln;
~ **the production** Produktion drosseln;
~ **broker** (US) Freiverkehrsmakler; ~ **exchange** (US) Freiverkehrsbörse.
curio | **dealer** Antiquitätenhändler; ~ **shop** Antiquitätengeschäft.
currency (circulation of money) [Geld]umlauf, [Geld]zirkulation, umlaufendes Geld, (legal tender) Zahlungsmittel, (standard) Währung, Valuta, (validity of money) Gültigkeit;
automatic ~ elastische Währung; **credit** ~ Buch-, Giralgeld; **deposit** ~ (US) bargeldloses Zahlungsmittel; **foreign** ~ Devisen-, Fremdwährung; **fractional** ~ (US) Kleingeld; **managed** ~ manipulierte Währung;
~ **of a bill** Laufzeit eines Wechsels;
~ **account** Valuta-, Währungskonto; ~ **appreciation** Wechselkursaufwertung; ~ **area** Währungsgebiet; ~ **assets** Devisenguthaben; ~ **bonds** Valutaobligationen; **[free]** ~ **country** [nicht] devisenbewirtschaftetes Land; **soft** ~ **country** land mit unstabiler Währung; **holiday** ~ **demands** Anforderungen für Ferien- und Reisegelder; ~ **dumping** Valutadumping; ~ **principle** Golddeckungsprinzip; ~ **snake** Währungsschlange; ~ **supply** Zahlungsmittelversorgung; ~ **unit** Zahlungsmitteleinheit.
current (a.) (circulating) zirkulierend, umlaufend, kursierend, (negotiable) kurs-, verkehrsfähig, (salable) [markt]gängig, leicht verkäuflich;
~ **account** laufendes (offenes, tägliches) Konto, Kontokorrentkonto; ~ **assets** (balance sheet, Br.) kurzfristiges Umlaufvermögen; ~ **capital** Betriebskapital; ~ **catalog(ue)** derzeit gültiger Verkaufskatalog; ~ **deposits** Kontokorrenteinlagen; ~ **exchange** Tageskurs; ~ **goods** Verbrauchsgüter; ~ **liabilities** kurzfristiges Fremdkapital; ~ **maintenance** Unterhaltungsaufwand; ~ **market value** Zeit-, Tageswert; ~ **money** Landeswährung; ~ **operating expenses** laufende Betriebsunkosten; ~ **position** (banking) Liquiditätsstatus; ~ **price** Tages-, Marktpreis; ~ **quality** gängige Qualität; ~ **yield** Effektivverzinsung.
curtail (v.) **production** Produktion drosseln.
cushion of stock Aktienvorrat, -polster.
Custodian | **of Enemy Property** (Br.) Treuhänder für Feindvermögen;
♀ **account** Depotkonto; ♀ **bank** Depotbank.
custodianship (US) Effektenverwaltung, Depotgeschäft;
~ **receipt** (US) Depotschein.

custody | **of property** Vermögensverwaltung; ~ **of se-curities** *(Br.)* Aufbewahrung von Wertpapieren; **to place securities in safe** ~ Wertpapiere ins Depot legen.

custom *(customers)* Kundschaft, Klientel, *(duty)* Abgabe, Gebühr, Zoll;
~ **of the port** Hafenusancen, -brauch;
~ *(a.) (US)* auf Bestellung angefertigt, bestellt.

customs *(duty)* Steuer, Zoll;
to clear through the ~ zollamtlich abfertigen;
~ **administration** Zollverwaltung; ~ **barrier** Zollschranke; ~ **bill of entry** Zolleingangsdeklaration;
~ **clearing house** Zollabfertigungsstelle; ~ **debenture** Zollrückschein; **to evade** ~ **duty** Zollhinterziehung begehen; ~ **invoice** Zollfaktura; ~ **letter** Zollbenachrichtigung; ~ **official** Zollbeamter; ~ **territory** Zollanwendungsgebiet; **to enter into a** ~ **union** einer Zollunion beitreten.

customer [Geschäfts]kunde, Debitor, Mandant, Klient, *(purchaser)* Abnehmer, Käufer;
against the interests of ~s kundenfeindlich; **accidental (casual)** ~ Laufkunde; **price-finicky** ~ preisempfindlicher Käufer; **regular (standing, steady)** ~ Stammkunde;
~ **agent** Exportgroßhändler; ~ **allowance** Kundenrabatt; ~ **complaint** Reklamation, Mängelrüge; ~ **country** Abnehmerland; ~ **register** Kundenliste; ~**s' room** Kundenberatungszimmer.

customhouse Zollamt, -haus, -abfertigungsstelle;
to clear the ~ Zoll entrichten;
~ **agent (broker)** Zollmakler, -agent; ~ **bond** Zoll-Steuerschein; ~ **clearance (entry)** Zolldeklaration.

cut *(capital)* [Kapital]herabsetzung, *(interest)* Zinskupon, *(reduction)* [Preis]ermäßigung;
salary ~ Gehaltskürzung;
~ **in consumption** Verbrauchsrückgang; ~ **in rates** Gebührensenkung;
~ *(v.)* kürzen, Abstriche vornehmen, *(bookkeeping)* [Verlust] abbuchen, abschreiben;
~ **business** Geschäft aufgeben; ~ **the discount rate** Diskont[satz] herabsetzen; ~ **an inventory** Lager abbauen; ~ **a melon** *(US)* außerordentliche Dividende verteilen.

cut | **down** s. one's allowances jds. Spesen herabsetzen; ~ **up for sale** ausschlachten;
~ **price shop** Diskontgeschäft; ~**-rate** *(US)* herabgesetzter (äußerster) Preis.

.**cutback** *(workers)* Arbeitskräfteabbau, *(US)* Reduzierung, Kürzung, Abbau, Abstrich;
~ **in capital spending** Kürzung von Investitionsvorhaben.

cutoff date Inventurtermin.

cutthroat | **competition** existenzgefährdender Wettbewerb; ~ **price** mörderischer (ruinöser) Preis.

cutting Preisdrückerei, Konkurrenzunterbietung;
~ **of inventory** Lagerabbau; ~ **the melon** *(US)* Ausschüttung einer außerordentlichen Dividende.

cycle, business Konjunkturzyklus, -rhythmus.

cyclical zyklisch, konjunkturrhythmisch;
~ **boom** Hochkonjunktur; ~ **downswing (downturn)** Konjunkturabschwung; ~ **industry** konjunkturabhängige Industrie; ~ **policy** Konjunkturpolitik; ~ **swing** Konjunkturumschwung; ~ **upsurge** konjunktureller Auftrieb.

D

dabble *(v.)* **on the stock exchange** ein bißchen an der Börse spekulieren.

daily | **allowance** Tagesspesen; ~ **breader** *(Br.)* Pendler, Zeitkarteninhaber; ~ **earnings** Tagesverdienst; ~ **quotation** Tagesnotierung; ~ **routine** Alltagsbeschäftigung.

damage Schaden, Beschädigung, Nachteil, Beeinträchtigung, *(loss)* Verlust, Einbuße; ~**s** Schadensersatz[anspruch], Schadensbetrag, Schadloshaltung; **liquidated** ~**s** vertraglich festgesetzte Schadenssumme; ~**s at law** gesetzlicher Schadenersatzanspruch; ~**s for pain and suffering** *(Br.)* Schmerzensgeld; **to be answerable for** ~**s** schadenersatzpflichtig sein; ~**s claim** Schadenersatzanspruch; ~ **survey** *(average)* Havariegutachten.

damaged goods Ausschuß[ware].

dampen *(v.)* **inflation** Inflation zügeln.

dandy note *(Br.)* Zollfreigabeschein.

danger money Gefahrenzulage, -geld.

dangerous premises gefährliche Betriebe.

data Angaben, Unterlagen, Zahlenmaterial; **personal** ~ **and testimonial** Bewerbungsunterlagen.

date Datum und Ortsangabe, *(of bill of exchange)* Ausstellungstag, *(fixed day)* Termin; **[average] due** ~ [durchschnittlicher] Verfalltag [eines Wechsels], Fälligkeitstermin; **earliest** ~ **available** frühester Antrittstermin; **mailing** ~ Versandtermin; **value** ~ *(bookkeeping)* Wertstellungstermin; ~ **of delivery** [Ab]liefer[ungs]termin; ~ **of invoice** Rechnungsdatum; ~ **of maturity** Fälligkeits-, Verfalltag; ~ **of payment** Zahlungstermin; ~ **of shipment** Versandtermin; ~ *(v.)* **ahead** *(cheque)* vordatieren; ~ **stamp** Datum-, Poststempel.

day, business Geschäftstag; **lay** ~**s** Liegetage; **trading** ~ Börsentag; ~ **of entry** Einklarungs-, Einschiffungstag; ~**s of grace** Verzugs-, Respekttage; **to put aside for a rainy** ~ Notgroschen zurücklegen. ~**-to**-~ **money** täglich fälliges Geld, Tagesgeld; ~ **letter** *(US)* Brieftelegramm; ~ **off** freier Tag, Ruhe-, Ausgehtag; ~**'s receipts** Tageseinnahme; ~ **ticket** Rückfahrkarte mit eintägiger Gültigkeit.

daybook Journal, Memorial, Tagebuch, Kladde.

daylight-saving time Sommerzeit.

daywork Zeitlohn-, Schichtarbeit.

dead *(a.)* flau, still, umsatz-, geschäftslos; ~ *(v.)* **a letter** Brief als unzustellbar erklären; ~ **account** *(Br.)* umsatzloses Konto; ~ **article** Ladenhüter; ~ **assets** unproduktive [Kapital]anlagen; ~ **capital** brachliegendes Kapital; ~ **file** abgelegte Akte; ~ **freight** Leer-, Faulfracht; ~ **hours** umsatzschwache Geschäftszeit; ~ **load** Ei-

gengewicht; ~ **loss** Totalverlust; ~ **season** Sauregurkenzeit; ~ **security** *(Br.)* wertlose Sicherheit; ~ **stock** *(farming)* totes Inventar, *(unsalable goods)* unverkäufliche Bestände; ~ **time** Verlustzeit, *(wages)* Lohnausfall.

deadline *(US)* Fristablauf, letzter [Ablieferungs]termin; ~ **for tenders** Ausschreibungsfrist.

deadwood *(unsalable stock)* Ladenhüter.

deal *(advertising)* Gratisangebot, *(bargain)* Handel, Geschäft, Abschluß, Transaktion; **forward** ~ Zeitgeschäft; ~ **on joint account** Metageschäft; ~ **on the stock exchange** Börsencoup; ~ *(v.)* **in an article** Artikel führen; ~ **in a line** in einer Branche tätig sein. **to make a little** ~ **in stocks as a feeler** Markt mit kleinen Börsenumsätzen abtasten.

dealer Händler, Kaufmann, *(retailer)* [Wieder]verkäufer, Fachgeschäft; **franchised** ~ zugelassener Händler; **local** ~ Platzvertreter; **money** ~ Devisenhändler; **secondhand** ~ Altwarenhändler; ~ **in used cars** Gebrauchtwagenhändler; ~ **in fancy goods** Modewarengeschäft; ~ **in stocks** *(US)* [Effekten]händler; ~**'s abatement** Händlerrabatt; ~ **aid** *(advertising)* werbliche Unterstützung des Händlers; **to sell below** ~ **costs** unter dem normalen Handelspreis verkaufen; ~ **markup** kaufmännische Verdienstspanne; ~ **survey** Einzelhandelserhebung.

dealing Geschäft, Handel, Abschluß; **exclusive** ~**s** Ausschließlichkeitsverbindungen; **foreign-exchange** ~**s** Devisenhandel; **inter-office** ~**s** *(securities)* Telefonverkehr; ~ **for the account** *(Br.)* Termin-, Zeitgeschäft; ~ **for cash** Kassageschäft; ~ **in stocks** *(Br.)* Effektenhandel, -geschäft.

death | **benefit** Hinterbliebenenversorgung, Sterbegeld; ~ **duty** *(Br.)* Nachlaß-, Erbschaftssteuer.

debase *(v.)* entwerten, verfälschen.

debenture *(acknowledgement of debt)* Schuldanerkenntnis, *(bond)* Obligation, *(Br.)* Pfandbrief, *(drawback)* Rückzollschein; **mortgage** ~ *(Br.)* Hypothekenpfandbrief; ~ **bond** *(US)* festverzinsliche Schuldverschreibung, *(Br.)* Pfandbrief, *(customs)* Rückzollschein; ~ **stock** *(US)* Vorzugsaktie, Anleiheschuld, *(Br.)* Schuldverschreibung.

debentured goods Rückzollgüter.

debit Debet[posten], Soll, *(entry on debit side)* Kontobelastung, Lastschrift; ~ *(v.)* | **an account** Konto belasten; ~ **account** Debet-, Debitorenkonto; ~ **advice** Lastschrift; ~ **balance** Soll-, Debetsaldo; ~ **interest** Sollzinsen; ~ **side** Debet-, Sollseite.

deblock *(v.)* **frozen accounts** eingefrorene Guthaben freigeben.

debt Schuld, Verschuldung, Forderung;
deep[ly involved] in ~ überschuldet;
active ~s Außenstände; **bad** ~s *(US)* Dubiosen, *(Br.)* uneinbringliche Außenstände; **book** ~ Buchschuld; **doubtful** ~s *(Br.)* Dubiosen; **frozen** ~s Stillhalteschulden; **funded** ~ Anleiheschuld; **judgment** ~ vollstreckbare Forderung; **preferential (preferred)** ~ *(bankruptcy)* bevorrechtigte Forderung; **not provable** ~ unbegründete Konkursforderung;
~s **in arrears** Schuldenrückstand;
to appropriate ~s Zweckbestimmung von Zahlungen festlegen; **to be head over ears (up to the eyes) in** ~ *(fam.)* bis an die Ohren in Schulden stecken; **to expand the floating** ~ kurzfristige Verschuldung vergrößern; **to prove** ~s *(bankruptcy)* Konkursforderungen nachweisen; **to settle one's** ~s sich mit seinen Gläubigern arrangieren;
~-**collecting agency (business)** Inkassobüro; ~ **equity ratio** Verbindlichkeiten zu Eigenkapitalverhältnis; ~ **financing** Finanzierung mittels Forderungsabtretung; ~ **instrument** Schuldtitel; ~ ~ **refunding** Umschuldung; **National** ⌾ Register Staatsschuldbuch; **to meet** ~ **service charges** Belastung des Schuldentilgungsdienstes erfüllen.
debtor Schuldner, Debitor, *(debit side)* Soll-, Passivseite;
bill ~ Wechselschuldner; **judgment** ~ Vollstreckungsschuldner;
~ **in account current** Kontokorrentschuldner;
poor ~'s **oath** Offenbarungseid; ~ **warrant** Besserungsschein.
decartelization Entflechtung.
deceptive mark irreführendes Warenzeichen.
decimal currency Dezimalwährung.
deck | **cargo** Deckgüter; ~ **class** Touristenklasse.
declaration *(bankruptcy)* Anmeldung, *(customs)* Zolldeklaration, *(insurance)* Angabe des Versicherungswertes;
income-tax ~ *(Br.)* Einkommensteuererklärung; ~ **outwards** *(Br.)* Zollausfuhrerklärung;
~ **of dividends** Dividendenausschüttung; ~ **of property** Vermögensanmeldung; ~ **of value** Wertanzeige;
~ **form** Begleitadresse.
declare *(v.)* Erklärung abgeben, anmelden, *(customs)* [zollamtlich] deklarieren;
~ **o. s. a. bankrupt** sich für zahlungsunfähig erklären, seinen Konkurs anmelden; ~ **a dividend** Dividende ausschütten; ~ **one's income** seine Einkommensteuererklärung abgeben; ~ **for public sale** zum Verkauf anbieten; ~ **the value** Wert [bei der Verzollung] angeben.
declared *(customs)* zollamtlich erklärt, deklariert;
~ **capital** festgesetztes Kapital; ~ **dividend** ausgeschüttete Dividende.
decline *(business cycle)* Abschwächung, Abschwung, Abnahme, *(deterioration)* Verfall, Verschlechterung, *(prices)* Fallen, Sinken, Sturz, Rückgang, *(stock exchange)* Kursrückgang, -abschlag, Baisse;
business ~ Rezession;

~ **in demand** Nachfragerückgang; ~ **in earnings** Ertragsminderung; ~ **in sales** Umsatzrückgang; ~ **in value** Wertminderung.
~ *(v.)* *(decrease)* abnehmen, geringer werden, *(price)* fallen, weichen, sinken, *(stock exchange)* nachgeben;
~ **in economic usefulness** sich verschleißen; ~ **the responsibility** *(insurance)* Haftpflicht ablehnen;
to sell at a ~ mit einem Abschlag verkaufen.
declining | **balance depreciation** degressive Abschreibung; ~ **market** nachgebende Kurse.
decode *(v.)* [Funkspruch] entziffern, dechiffrieren.
decontrol Abbau der Zwangswirtschaft;
~ **of imports** Einfuhrliberalisierung;
~ *(v.)* Zwangswirtschaft abbauen.
decontrolled frei, liberalisiert.
decrease Verringerung, Kürzung;
~ **in consumption** Verbrauchsrückgang; ~ **in value** Wertverringerung;
~ *(v.)* abnehmen, geringer werden, *(quotations)* zurückgehen, schwächer liegen.
decreasing costs abnehmende Unkosten.
decree in bankruptcy Konkurseröffnungsbeschluß.
decurrent rent nachschüssige Rente.
deduct *(v.)* | **cost** Kosten absetzen; ~ **the discount** Skonto abziehen; ~ **5 % from the wage** 5 % vom Lohn einbehalten.
deductible | **from income tax** einkommensteuerabzugsfähig;
~ **clause** *(insurance)* Selbstbehaltsklausel.
deduction Abrechnung, Absetzung, Abzug, Kürzung, *(rebate)* Abschlag, Rabatt, *(reserve)* Rückstellung, abzugsfähiger Betrag;
admitted as ~ steuerabzugsfähig;
fixed ~s feststehende Lohnabzüge; **income** ~s *(balance sheet)* Erlösschmälerungen; **marital** ~ *(gift and estate)* Freibetrag für die Ehefrau; **standard** ~ *(US)* abzugsfähiger Pausch[al]betrag;
~ **from gross income** Abzug von Betriebsausgaben; ~ **of tax at source** quellensteuerabzug; ~ **of input tax** Vorsteuerabzug;
~ **card** Lohnsteuerkarte; ~ **limit** Freibetragsgrenze.
deed Urkunde, Dokument, Schriftstück;
composition ~ *(Br.)* Gläubigervergleich; **purchase** ~ Kaufvertrag;
~ **of arrangement** *(Br.)* Vertrag; ~ **of partnership** Gesellschaftervertrag.
deface *(v.)* **the coinage** Währung verschlechtern.
defaced stamp entwertete Briefmarke.
defalcation Unterschlagung, Veruntreuung.
default *(contract)* Vertragsverletzung, *(failure to perform)* [Zahlungs]verzug;
on (upon) ~ **of payment** mangels Zahlung;
~ **in delivery** Lieferverzug;
~ *(v.)* in Verzug geraten, [Raten]zahlungen nicht einhalten, *(become insolvent)* zahlungsunfähig werden;
to make ~ seinen Verbindlichkeiten nicht nachkommen;
~ **fee** Säumnisgebühr; ~ **fine** Verspätungszuschlag; ~ **interest** Verzugszinsen.

defaulted bonds *(US)* notleidende Obligationen.

defaulter säumiger Zahler (Schuldner), *(insolvent debtor, Br.)* zahlungsunfähiger Schuldner.

defeating of creditors Gläubigerbenachteiligung.

defect Mangel, Manko, Fehler, Defekt;
latent (hidden) ~ versteckter (verborgener) Mangel [beim Kauf]; **redhibitory** ~ Gewährleistungs-, Wandlungsfehler;
to be liable for ~s der Mängelhaftung unterliegen.

defective article Fehlfabrikat.

defence | *(Br.)* **defense** *(US)* **award** Rüstungsauftragsvergabe; ~ **contractor** Rüstungsbetrieb.

defer *(v.)* *(balance sheet)* als Rechnungsabgrenzung behandeln.

deferral Vertagung, Verschiebung, *(accounting method)* Rechnungsabgrenzung;
~ **of investment program(me)s** zurückgestellte Investitionsvorhaben.

deferred | **accounts receivable** noch nicht fällige Forderungen; ~ **asset** *(balance sheet)* transistorischer Posten; ~ **charge [to expense]** *(US)* Posten der Rechnungsabgrenzung; ~ **credits to income** *(balance sheet)* passive Rechnungsabgrenzungen; ~ **demand** Konsumverzicht; ~ **payment sale** *(US)* Abzahlungsgeschäft; ~ **revenue** antiziparorische Passiva, ~ **shares** *(Br.)* Nachzugsaktien; ~ **taxes** *(balance sheet)* Steuervorauszahlungen.

deficiency *(short balance)* Unterbilanz, *(defect)* Fehler, Mangel, *(deficit)* Manko, Fehlbetrag;
~ **in stock** [Lager]fehlbestand; ~ **in weight** Gewichtsmanko;
~ **advances** *(Br.)* Vorschüsse der Bank von England; ~ **appropriations** *(US)* Nachtragsbewilligung; ~ **pagments** Agrarpreissubventionen; ~ **statement** *(US)* Verlustbilanz, -abschluß.

deficient | **amount** Fehlbetrag; ~ **delivery** Mankolieferung.

deficit Defizit, Ausfall, Verlust, Manko, *(short balance)* Unterbilanz;
balance-of-payments ~ Zahlungsbilanzdefizit; **operating** ~ Betriebsverlust;
~ **in taxes** Steuerausfall, Minderaufkommen;
to make good a ~ Verlust ausgleichen; **to slip into** ~ in rote Zahlen geraten;
~ **account** Verlustkonto; ~ **area** wirtschaftliches Verlustgebiet; ~ **spending** öffentliche Verschuldung durch Anleiheaufnahme.

deflate *(v.)* **a currency** Zahlungsmittelumlauf einschränken.

deflation Deflation;
~ **of credit** Kreditrestriktion.

deflationary policy Deflationspolitik.

defraud | *(v.)* **a creditor** Gläubiger betrügen; ~ **the customs** Zoll hinterziehen.

defraudation of the revenue Steuerhinterziehung.

defray |s. **one's expenses** jds. Spesen bestreiten.

defunct company im Handelsregister gelöschte Gesellschaft.

degree Grad, Rang, Klasse, *(university)* Diplom;
high ~ **of liquidity** starke Liquiditätsposition; ~ **of risk** Gefahrenumfang.

degression *(taxation)* Degression.

degressive tax degressive Steuer.

del credere *(Br.)* Delkredere, Bürgschaft;
~ **account** Delkrederekonto; ~ **commission** Delkredereprovision.

delay Verzögerung, Verzug, *(respite)* Stundung, Aufschub, Verschiebung, Frist;
~ **of creditors** Gläubigerbenachteiligung; ~ **in delivery** Lieferverzug; **~s in execution of order** Auftragsverzögerung;
~ *(v.)* **creditors** Gläubiger hinhalten;
~ **time** betrieblich bedingte Verlustzeit.

deliberalization Entliberalisierung.

delinquent rückständig;
~ **list** Liste der Steuerschuldner; ~ **tax** *(US)* Steuerrückstand.

deliver *(v.)* *(goods)* [ab]liefern, ausliefern, *(hand over)* einliefern, abgeben, aushändigen;
~ **luggage** Gepäck zustellen; ~ **the mail** Post bestellen; ~ **within the specified time** fristgerecht liefern.

deliverable condition (state) lieferfähiger Zustand.

delivered | **free** frei Haus;
to be ~ **free railway station** frei Bahnstation geliefert werden.

delivering charges Lieferspesen.

delivery Anfuhr, Ein-, Ab-, Auslieferung, *(handing over)* Überbringung, Aushändigung;
at the time of ~ im Zeitpunkt der Lieferung; **by special** ~ *(US)* durch Eilboten; **cash** *(Br.)* **(collect, US) on** ~ **(C. O. D.)** Zahlung gegen Nachnahme, *(stocks)* gegen Kasse;
bad ~ *(stock exchange)* nicht lieferbar; **door** ~ *(US)* Hauszustellung; **express** ~ *(Br.)* Eilzustellung; **less-than-carload** ~ Stückgutlieferung; **mail** ~ Postzustellung; **special** ~ *(US)* durch Eilboten;
~ **in arrears** rückständige Lieferung; ~ **of a telegram** Telegrammzustellung;
to be late in ~ im Lieferverzug sein; **to sell for** ~ auf Lieferung verkaufen; **to take orders for future** ~ Warenbestellungen entgegennehmen;
~ **bonus** Auslieferungsprämie; ~ **boy** Laufbursche; ~ **charge** Zustellgebühr; **[scheduled]** ~ **date** [festgesetzter] Liefertermin; ~ **delay** Lieferverzögerung; ~ **note** Bordereau, Lieferschein; **lengthening** ~ **periods** länger werdende Lieferfristen; ~ **slip** Auslieferungszettel.

demand Nachfrage, Bedarf;
in [great] ~ **[sehr]** gefragt; **payable on** ~ zahlbar auf Verlangen;
backlog ~ Bedarfsreserve; **market** ~**s** Marktbedürfnisse; **pent-up** ~ *(US)* Nachholbedarf; **wage** ~**s** Lohnforderungen;
~ **for every description** Nachfrage nach allen Qualitäten; ~ **for payments** Zahlungsaufforderung;
to be in brisk ~ lebhaft begehrt werden; **to pay on** ~ bei Vorzeigung zahlen;
~ **analysis** Bedarfsanalyse; ~ **deposit** fällige Sorteinlage; ~ **draft** *(US)* Sichtwechsel; ~ **management** Nachfragesteuerung; ~ **price** *(stock exchange)* Geldkurs; ~ **quotation** *(stock exchange)* Geldnotiz;

demolition contractor Abbruchunternehmer.
demonetization Außerkurssetzung, Entwertung.
demonstration *(stock exchange)* Börsenmanöver;
bearish ~ *(Br.)* Baissebewegung; **bullish** ~ *(Br.)* Haussebewegung;
~ **farm** Musterfarm.
demurrage *(railway)* Wagenstandsgeld, *(ship)* Überliegegeld, Verzugskosten;
~ **charges** Liegegebühren, [Wagen]standgeld.
denationalization Reprivatisierung.
denomination *(money)* Sorte, Nennwert, *(shares)* Stückelung, *(weight)* Gewichtseinheit;
of low ~ kleingestückelt.
dent | **in earnings** Ertragseinbuße;
to put a big ~ **in the economy** Konjunkturkurve einbeulen.
department *(US)* Dienst-, Regierungsstelle, Ministerium, *(branch of business)* Branche, Geschäftszweig, *(field)* Fachgebiet;
accounting ~ Buchhaltung; **appointments** ~ Personalabteilung;
~**of Commerce** *(US)* Wirtschaftsministerium; ~ **of Labor** *(US)* Arbeitsministerium; ~ **of the Treasury** *(US)* Finanzministerium, Schatzamt;
~ **head** Abteilungsvorstand, -leiter, Dezernent;
~ **store** *(US)* Warenhaus.
departmental accounting dezentralisiertes Rechnungswesen.
departure | **lounge** Abflughalle; ~ **station** Versandbahnhof.
depend *(v.)* **on foreign supplies** auf ausländische Lieferungen angewiesen sein.
dependant | **benefit** *(Br.)* Invalidenrente; ~ **relative allowance** *(Br.)* Steuerfreibetrag für Familienangehörige.
dependency | **benefit** *(Br.)* Leistung an Unterhaltsberechtigte; ~ **bonus** Kinderzulage.
deplete *(v.)* *(store)* erschöpfen, *(taxation)* abschreiben.
depletion Substanzverringerung, -verlust, *(US, taxation)* Abschreibung;
~ **of capital** Kapitalentblößung;
~ **allowance** *(charges, expenses)* Abschreibung für Substanzverringerung.
deposit *(in bank)* eingezahltes Geld, [Geld]einlage, Einzahlung, *(first instalment)* Anzahlung, *(giving in trust)* Aufbewahrung, Verwahrung;
for ~ **only** nur zur Sicherheit;
~ **bank** Depositenguthaben; **blocked** ~ gesperrtes Depot; **fixed** ~ Kündigungsgeld; **irregular** ~ Sammeldepot; **safe** ~ Tresor, Stahlkammer; **savings** ~ Spareinlage; **time** ~ *(US)* Festgeld;
~ **at call** *(Br.)* Sichteinlage; ~**s by customers** *(balance sheet)* Fremdgelder; ~**s and drawings** Einzahlungen und Abhebungen; ~**s at short notice** kurzfristige Einlagen; ~**s at post office** Postscheckguthaben; ~**s with suppliers** geleistete Anzahlungen;
~ *(v.)* *(goods)* deponieren, hinterlegen, in Verwahrung (ins Depot) geben;

~ **the duty** [**repayable**] Zollgarantie leisten; ~ **securities** Wertpapiere hinterlegen;
to make a ~ Pfand hinterlegen, *(banking)* Einzahlung leisten;
~ **account** *(US)* Guthaben[konto]; **to have a** ~ **account with the Federal Reserve Bank** *(US)* Konto bei der Landeszentralbank unterhalten; ~ **banking** Depositengeschäft; ~ **business** *(loan bank)* Lombardgeschäft, Depotgeschäft; ~ **certificate** Hinterlegungsschein, Festgeldbescheinigung; ~ **company** *(Br.)* Hinterlegungsstelle; ~ **currency** *(US)* Giral-, Buchgeld; ~ **ledger** *(Br.)* Depotbuch; ~ **liabilities** Kontokorrentverpflichtungen; ~ **rate** Habenzinssatz; ~ **receipt** Einzahlungsbeleg; ~ **warrant** Hinterlegungsschein.
depositary bank *(US)* Depotbank.
depositing business Depotgeschäft.
deposition Hinterlegung, Aufbewahrung.
depositor Hinterleger, Einzahler, Einleger;
checking-account ~ Kontokorrentkunde.
depository Verwahrungsort, Hinterlegungsstelle, *(goods)* Lagerhaus, Stapelplatz, Magazin;
night ~ Nachttresor.
depot Aufbewahrungsort, -raum, *(stores)* Lager[haus], -platz, Magazin, Depot;
freight ~ *(US)* Güterbahnhof; **storage** ~ Lagerhaus;
~ **for spares** Ersatzteillager.
depreciable abschreibungsfähig, abschreibbar;
~ **amount** Abschreibungsbetrag; ~ **value** Abschreibungsgrundwert.
depreciate *(v.)* *(currency)* ab-, entwerten, *(decline)* im Wert (Preis) sinken (fallen), *(write off)* abschreiben;
~ **the pound** Pfund abwerten.
depreciated | **cost** Restbuchwert; ~ **currency** notleidende Währung.
depreciation Wertminderung, Entwertung, *(provision for ~ in balance sheet)* Abschreibung[srückstellung], *(writing off)* Abschreibung;
liable to ~ abschreibungsfähig;
accrued ~ Wertberichtigung für Abbuchung; **faster capital goods** ~ schnellere Abschreibungsmöglichkeit für Anlagegüter; **straight-line** ~ lineare Abschreibung;
to allow for ~ für Abschreibungen zurückstellen;
to spread one's ~ **over several years** seine Abschreibungen steuerlich über mehrere Jahre verteilen;
~ **allowance** Abschreibungsmöglichkeit, -betrag; ~ **date** Abschreibungsstichtag; ~ **rate** Abschreibungsquote; ~ **reserve** Rückstellung für Abschreibungen, Wertminderungsrücklagen.
depressed flau, gedrückt, matt, mißgestimmt, *(price)* herabgesetzt, gesenkt;
~ **area** *(Br.)* Notstandsgebiet.
depression *(prices)* Fallen, Sinken, [Preis]senkung, *(stock exchange)* Baisse, *(trade)* Depression, Tiefstand, Konjunkturtief;
~ **of the market** Baissestimmung; ~ **of prices** Kurs-, Preiseinbruch;

to show a ~ Konjunkturrückgang erfahren;
~ **low** Konjunkturmulde.
derating of local taxes ·Befreiung von Gemeindesteuern.
derationed goods freigegebene Waren.
derelict ship aufgegebenes Schiff, Wrack.
derivative deposit Lombarddepot.
derived income abgeleitetes Einkommen.
description *(sort)* Qualität, Sorte, Art, Gattung;
~s *(Br., stock exchange)* Wertpapiere;
leading ~s *(Br.)* führende Werte;
~ **of securities** Effektengattung.
descriptive labelling übliche Etikettierung.
design *(pattern)* Muster, Modell;
industrial ~ gewerbliches Muster;
⊆ **Act** *(Br.)* Geschmacksmustergesetz; ~ **patent**
(US) geschütztes Geschmacksmuster.
desire to buy Kaufinteresse.
desk Pult, Schreibtisch, *(clerical performance)* Büro-,
Kanzleiarbeit, *(counter)* Ladentisch;
pay ~ Kassenschalter;
~ **audit** Buchprüfung auf Grund mitgenommener
Belege; ~ **jobber** Grossist ohne eigenes Lager; ~
tray Briefkorb.
destination station Bestimmungsbahnhof.
detach *(v.)* **coupons due** verfallene Zinsscheine ablösen.
detached parcels of goods gesonderte Warenpartien.
detailed account spezifizierte Rechnung.
deteriorate *(v.)* an Wert verlieren, Wertminderung erfahren, *(goods)* verderben, *(trade)* zurückgehen.
deterioration Wertminderung, *(wear and tear)* Verschleiß;
~ **of purchasing value of money** Verschlechterung
der Kaufkraft.
determination of quotas Kontingentfestsetzung.
detour ticket Umsteigefahrschein.
devalorization Abwertung.
devaluate *(v.)* abwerten, devaluieren.
devaluation [Währungs]abwertung, Entwertung.
develop *(v.)* | **building lots** Bauland erschließen; ~
weakness *(market)* schwach werden.
developable position ausbaufähige Stellung.
developed entwickelt, *(building ground)* baureif;
highly ~ **countries** hoch industrialisierte Länder;
less ~ **countries** Entwicklungsländer.
developing countries Entwicklungsländer.
development Ausbau, Förderung, *(land)* Erschließung;
ripe for ~ baureif;
housing ~ Wohnsiedlung;
~ **of building ground** Baulanderschließung; ~ **of**
foreign trade Außenhandelsentwicklung;
~ **agency** Grundstückserschließungsgesellschaft;
~ **man** Entwicklungshelfer; ~ **area** *(Br.)* Fördergebiet; **industrial** ~ **company** Industrieförde-
rungsgesellschaft; ~ **expenses** *(land)* Erschlie-
ßungskosten; ~ **loan** Entwicklungsanleihe; ~ **pro-**
ject Entwicklungsvorhaben.
deviation *(insurance)* Risikoveränderung;
~ **of actual cost** Istkosten-Abweichung;

~ **clause** *(international goods traffic)* Toleranz-,
Abweichungsklausel.
diary Tagebuch, *(journal)* Journal, *(tickler)*Verfallbuch, Vormerk-, Terminkalender.
dictating machine, dictaphone *(Br.)* Diktiergerät.
dictation Diktat [schreiben];
to take ~ Diktat aufnehmen; **to transcribe** ~ Diktat auf die Schreibmaschine übertragen.
difference | **in prices** Preisunterschied, -differenz; ~ **in**
rates Kursunterschied;
to split the ~ strittigen Preisunterschied teilen.
differential *(in prices)* Kursgefälle, *(difference in*
rates) Frachtdifferenz, *(difference in wages)* Lohngefälle;
inter-industry ~ industrielles Lohngefälle;
~ **duty** Vorzugs-, Differentialzoll; ~ **piece-rate**
system Stücklohnverfahren; ~ **rate** Ausnahme-
frachtsatz.
dilute *(v.) (stocks)* verwässern;
~ **labo(u)r** ungelernte Arbeiter einstellen.
dilution | **of labo(u)r** Einstellung ungelernter Ar-
beiter; ~ **of stocks** Aktienverwässerung.
dime store *(US)* Einheitspreisgeschäft.
diminished proceeds Mindererlös.
diminishing | **productivity** Produktivitätsrückgang;
~ **utility** Grenznutzen.
diminution | **of profits** Gewinnschrumpfung; ~ **of**
taxes Steuerherabsetzung;
to show a considerable ~ beträchtlichen Ertragsrückgang aufweisen.
dining car Speisewagen.
dip *(business cycle)* zurückgehen, *(stock exchange)*
[ab]sinken;
change) [ab]sinken.
direct | *(v.)* **a parcel correctly** Paket ordnungsgemäß
beschriften;
~ **advertising** Konsumentenwerbung; ~ **buying**
Direkteinkauf; ~ **costs** Selbstkosten; ~ **costing**
Grenz[plan]kostenrechnung; ~ **endorsement** *(US)*
Vollgiro; ~ **exchange** fester Umrechnungskurs; ~
insurer Erstversicherer; ~ **labo(u)r cost** Fertigungs-
löhne; ~ **loss** versicherter Schaden; ~~**mail ad-**
vertising *(shot)* Postversandwerbung, -wurfsen-
dung; ~~**material costs** unmittelbarer Materialaufwand; ~ **purchase** Beziehungskauf; ~ **sale** **(selling)**
Direktverkauf; ~ **shipment** Direktversand; ~ **train**
durchgehender Zug; ~~**writing company** *(carrier)*
Rückversicherungsgesellschaft.
directed economy gelenkte Wirtschaft, Planwirtschaft.
direction *(address)* Adresse, Aufschrift, Anschrift,
(board) Vorstand, Direktion, Direktorium, *(capi-*
tal control) Bewirtschaftung, *(managing)* Leitung,
Geschäftsführung;
~ **of consumption** Verbrauchslenkung; ~s **for use**
Gebrauchsanweisung, -vorschrift;
~ **card** *(luggage)* Gepäckzettel.
director Direktor, Vorsteher, Leiter, Geschäftsführer, *(on the board)* Aufsichtsratsmitglied;
acting ~ *(Br.)* geschäftsführendes Vorstandsmit-

glied; **ordinary** ~ einfaches Vorstandsmitglied;
~ **of labo(u)r affairs (relations)** Arbeitsdirektor;
~ **of sales** Verkaufsleiter, -chef;
~ **meeting** Aufsichtsratssitzung; ~ **percentage of
profit** Vorstandstantieme; ~ **report** Vorstandsbericht.

directorate Direktorium, Direktion, Geschäftsleitung, *(office of director)* Aufsichtsratsposten;
interlocking ~s Schachtelaufsichtsrat.

directory Adreßbuch;
classified trade ~ Branchenadreßbuch;
~ **of suppliers** Bezugsquellennachweis.

dirt-cheap zu einem Spottpreis, spottbillig.

disability Erwerbsunfähigkeit;
general ~ *(law)* Geschäftsunfähigkeit;
~ **benefit** Invalidenrente; ~ **rate** Invaliditätsgrad.

disable | *(v.)* **an estate** Gut verwirtschaften; ~ **a ship**
Schiff außer Dienst stellen.

disabled *(a.)* invalide, berufs-, dienstuntauglich, erwerbsunfähig, *(legally incompetent)* geschäftsunfähig;
~ **person** Erwerbsunfähiger.

disablement Arbeits-, Berufs-, Erwerbsunfähigkeit,
Invalidität, *(incapacity)* Geschäftsunfähigkeit,
partial ~ Teilinvalidität;
~ **annuity** Invaliditäts-, Invalidenrente; ~ **insurance** Invaliden-, Invaliditätsversicherung.

disagio Abschlag, Disagio.

disaster area Katastrophengebiet.

disburse *(v.)* [Geld] auszahlen, auslegen;
~ **s. one's full and entire part** jem. seinen Anteil
voll auszahlen.

disbursement Ausgabe, Auslage;
capital ~s Kapitalaufwendungen; **dividend** ~s Dividendenausschüttungen;
~ **account** Auslagenaufstellung.

disc parking Parkscheibe.

discardment *(asset)* Außerbetriebssetzung.

discharge *(crew)* Abmusterung, *(dismissal)* Verab-
schiedung, Entlassung, *(payment of debt)* Tilgung,
Abgeltung, *(unloading)* Entladen;
in full ~ zum vollen Ausgleich;
unjust ~ unberechtigte Entlassung;
~ **of a bankrupt** Konkursaufhebung; ~ **of business**
Geschäftsbesorgung; ~ **for cause** begründete Entlassung;
~ *(v.) (dismiss)* entlassen, *(pay)* entrichten, tilgen,
abgelten, *(seaman)* abmustern;
~ **an account** Konto ausgleichen; ~ **a bill** Wechsel
einlösen; ~ **cargo** entladen, Ladung löschen; ~ **the
directors from responsibilities** Vorstand entlasten;
~ **from liabilities** von der Haftpflicht befreien.

discharged bankrupt entlasteter Konkursschuldner.

discharging expenses Löschungskosten.

disclaim *(v.)* **liability** *(insurance)* Deckung ablehnen.

disclose *(v.)* Versicherungsfall anzeigen;
~ **a material inadequacy in the reserve** Unange-
messenheit der Reserven herausstellen.

disclosure Enthüllung, *(balance sheet)* Offenlegung
in Fußnoten im Revisionsbericht.

discontinuance | **of business** Geschäftseinstellung; ~
of subscription Abbestellung eines Abonnements.

discount *(bill of exchange)* Diskont, Zinsabzug, *(deduction)* Abzug, Abstrich, *(disagio)* Disagio, *(discounting)* Diskontierung, *(insurance)* Prämien-
nachlaß, *(rebate)* Rabatt, Preisnachlaß, *(shop, US)*
Einzelhandelsladen mit Rabattsystem;
adjusted ~ Staffelkonto; **bond** ~ Pfandbriefagio;
~**dealer's** ~ Händlerrabatt; ~ **earned** Diskonterlös; **frequency** ~ *(advertising)* Serienrabatt; **patronage** ~ Treuerabatt; **trade** ~ Rabatt für Wiederverkäufer;
~ **of a bill** Wechseldiskont; ~ **for quantities**
Mengenrabatt;
~ *(v.)* abziehen, Rabatt gewähren;
~ **the market** Marktentwicklungen im voraus berücksichtigen;
to allow ~ Ermäßigung (Rabatt) gewähren, Skonto einräumen; **to be at a** ~ unter Pari stehen; **to buy
at a** ~ mit Disagio kaufen; **to open at a slight** ~
(stock exchange) leicht abgeschwächt eröffnen; **to
sell at a** ~ mit Verlust verkaufen, (v. i.) unter
Pari stehen;
~ **bills** Diskonten; ~ **bookseller** Sortimentsbuch-
händler; ~ **charges** Diskontspesen; ~ **holdings**
(US) Wechselbestand; ~ **house** *(Br.)* Diskont-,
Wechselbank, *(retailing)* Diskontgeschäft, Billig-
laden; ~ **market** *(Br.)* Wechsel-, Diskontmarkt;
Markt für kurzfristige Wertpapiere; ~ **piracy**
Skontoschinderei; ~ **quotation** Disagionotierung;
to lower the ~ **rate** Diskontsatz herabsetzen; ~
shop *(US)* Diskontladen; ~ **terms** Diskont-,
Rabattbedingungen.

discountable diskontierbar, diskontfähig.

discounting of bills (notes) Wechseldiskontierung.

discovery *(insurance)* Versicherungsanzeige;
~ **of one's assets** *(bankrupt)* Darlegung (Offen-
barung) seiner Vermögensverhältnisse;
~ **period** Anzeigespielraum für Verluste.

discretionary beliebig, willkürlich, dem Gutdünken
überlassen, dem Ermessen anheimgeben;
~ **buying power** frei verfügbare Kaufkraft; ~ **order**
(stock exchange) Vertrauensorder; ~ **trust** Investmentgesellschaft mit breitgestreutem Aktienportefeuille.

discriminating | **duty** Differentialzoll; ~ **treatment**
diskriminierende Behandlung.

discrimination | **against** Schlechterstellung; ~ **in
customs duties** Zolldiskriminierung; ~ **in prices**
Preisdifferenzierung, -spaltung.

discriminatory | **duty** Prohibitivzoll; ~ **taxation**
steuerliche Vorzugsbehandlung.

disease, industrial (vocational) Berufskrankheit.

disequilibrium in the balance of payments unausgeglichene Zahlungsbilanz.

dishono(u)r Akzeptverweigerung, Nichthonorierung;
~ *(v.)* **a bill** Wechsel Not leiden lassen.

dishono(u)red check *(US)* **(cheque,** *Br.)* nicht eingelöster Scheck.

disincentive *(fiscal policy)* Abschreckungsmittel.
~ **to business** negative Konjunktureinwirkung.
disinclination to buy Kaufunlust.
disinflation Inflationsabbau durch gezielte Maßnahmen.
disinvestment *(US)* Zurückziehung von Anlagekapital, *(reductions of inventories)* Lagerabbau.
dislocation | **of the currency** Währungsverfall; ~ **of workers** Umsetzung von Arbeitskräften.
dismantlement Aus-, Abbau, Demontage.
dismantling list Demontageliste.
dismemberment | **benefit** Versehrtenunterstützung bei Gliederverlust; ~ **compensation** Gliedertaxe.
dismiss *(v.)* [aus dem Dienst] entlassen;
~ **the crew** Schiffsvolk abdanken; ~ **without notice** fristlos entlassen.
dismissal [Dienst]entlassung;
~ **without notice** fristlose Entlassung;
~ **compensation (wage)** Abstandgeld, Entlassungsentschädigung, -ausgleich, -gehalt.
disparagement of goods Verunglimpfung von Konkurrenzerzeugnissen.
disparaging competition herabsetzende Werbung.
dispatch Spedition, Versandunternehmen, *(sending)* Absendung, Beförderung, Versand;
ready for ~ versandfähig;
~ **of fast goods** Eilgutabfertigung; ~ **by rail** Bahnversand;
~ *(v.)* abschicken, expedieren, befördern;
~ **a business** Geschäft erledigen; ~ **goods to their destination** Waren an ihren Bestimmungsort dirigieren;
~ **agency** Telegrafenbüro; ~ **goods** Eilfracht, -gut;
~ **money** *(Br.)* Vergütung für schnelles Entladen;
~ **note** *(Br.)* Versandanzeige; ~ **service** Expedition, ~ **station** Versandstation.
dispatcher Expedient, Absender;
train ~ Fahrdienstleiter.
dispatching | **clerk** Expedient, Abfertiger; ~ **office** Abfertigungsstelle, Expedition.
dispersal | **of assets** Anlagenstreuung; ~ **of industrial facilities** aufgelockerte Ansiedlung industrieller Fertigungsbetriebe.
dispersion | **of industry** industrielle Auflockerung; **wide** ~ **of ownership** breite Eigentumsstreuung.
displaced shares nicht notierte Aktien.
displacement *(factory)* Verlagerung, *(ship)* Tonnengehalt, Tonnage, Wasserverdrängung;
load ~ Ladetonnage;
~ **of funds** anderweitige Kapitalverwendung; ~ **of labo(u)r** Freisetzungen.
display *(goods)* [Schaufenster]auslage;
counter ~ Ladentischauslage; **window** ~ Dekorationsfenster;
~ *(v.)* *(goods)* zeigen, zur Ansicht vorlegen;
~ **advertising** Schlagzeilenwerbung; ~ **cabinet** Vitrine; ~ **contractor** Ausstellungsunternehmen; ~ **figure** Schaufensterpuppe; ~ **kiosks** Werbebauten; **window-** ~ **material** Dekorationsmaterial; ~ **window** Dekorations-, Auslagefenster.

disposable | **goods** disponible (sofort verfügbare) Ware, Wegwerfgüter; ~ **income** *(Br.)* *(social accounting)* frei verfügbares Einkommen nach Steuern.
disposal (sale) Absatz, Verkauf;
~ **of a piece of business** Erledigung einer geschäftlichen Angelegenheit; ~ **of property** Vermögensverfügung;
to have large capital at one's ~ große Kapitalbeträge zur Verfügung haben;
~ **instruction** Verkaufsanweisung.
dispose *(v.)* Verfügung treffen, verfügen über, disponieren;
~ **of one' business** sein Geschäft verkaufen; ~ **of large capital** mit großem Kapital arbeiten.
disposition Einteilung, Verteilung, Anordnung, *(control)* freie Verfügung[smacht], *(sale)* Verkauf;
~ **of net income (profit)** Verwendung des Reinerlöses.
dispossess *(v.)* Räumungsverfahren durchführen.
disproportion of supply and demand Mißverhältnis zwischen Angebot und Nachfrage.
disputed | **claims office** *(insurance)* Rechtsabteilung;
~ **title** bestrittenes Eigentumsrecht.
dissection of accounts Kontenaufgliederung.
dissentient shareholder Minderheitsaktionär.
dissolution Auflösung, Löschung, Liquidation;
~ **sale** Liquidationsverkauf.
dissolve *(v.)* auflösen, liquidieren, *(antitrust law, US)* entflechten.
distinctive name Markenname.
distrain *(v.)* **upon a debtor** gegen einen Schuldner zwangsvollstrecken.
distrained goods gepfändete Waren.
distress Beschlagnahme, Pfändung, Zwangsvollstreckung, *(taxation)* Steuerpfändung, *(want)* Notlage, Notstand;
to levy (put in) a ~ **on s. th.** etw. mit Beschlag belegen, Zwangsvollstreckung betreiben;
~ **call** Hilferuf, *(ship)* Notsignal; ~ **merchandise** notleidende Waren; ~ **warrant** Pfändungsbeschluß; ~ **work** Notstandsarbeiten.
distressed notleidend, *(seized)* gepfändet;
~ **area** Elends-, Notstandsgebiet.
distribute *(v.)* auf-, verteilen, zur Verteilung bringen, *(advertising)* streuen;
~ **the assets** *(partners)* sich auseinandersetzen;
~ **equally** *(stock)* repartieren; ~ **in a fixed ratio** aufschlüsseln.
distributing | **agency** Vertriebsgesellschaft; ~ **agent** Großhandelsvertreter; ~ **trade** Verteilergewerbe, Absatzwirtschaft.
distribution *(advertising)* Streuung, *(apportionment)* Auf-, Ein-, Zu-, Verteilung, *(marketing)* Absatz und Vertrieb;
charitable ~ milde Gabe, Spende;
~ **of assets of a bankrupt's estate** Schluß-, Masseverteilung; ~ **of dividends** Dividendenausschüttung; ~ **of the net gain** Verteilung des Reingewinns; ~ **of losses** Verlustaufteilung; ~ **of prof-**

its Reingewinnverwendung; ~ of risk Risikoverteilung; ~ of trading profits Ausschüttung von Börsengewinnen; ~ of wealth Vermögen-, Güterverteilung;
~ agreement Vertriebsvereinbarung; ~ area Absatzgebiet; ~ cartel Absatz-, Vertriebskartell; ~ costs (expense) Vertriebsunkosten.

distributive | cost accounting Zuschlagskalkulation; ~ trades Verteilergewerbe.

distributor Verteiler, Wiederverkäufer, (agent) Bezirksvertreter;
~ audit Warenbestandsprüfung; ~ discount Wiederverkäuferrabatt.

district [Verwaltungs]bezirk, (fig.) Arbeitsgebiet; central shopping (business) ~ Hauptgeschäftsgegend; high-rent (low-rent) residential ~ teure (billige) Wohngegend;
~ devoted to industry rein industrielle Gegend; to work a ~ Bezirk bearbeiten;
~ agent Bezirksvertreter; ~ agreement Ortstarif; ~ auditor Bezirksrevisor.

disturbed market lebhafte, bewegte Börse.

diversification Diversifikation, Anlagenstreuung;
~ in manufacturing weitgestreutes Produktionsprogramm; ~ of product lines Auffächerung des Warensortiments; ~ of risk Risikoverteilung;
to owe one's performance to ~ seinen Erfolg einem breitgefächerten Produktionsprogramm verdanken;
~ program(me) weitgestreutes Produktionsprogramm.

diversified (capital) verteilt angelegt, risikomäßig gestreut, (production program(me)) aufgefächert.

diversify (v.) (capital) Risikostreuung betreiben, gestreut anlegen, (corporation) Produktionsprogramm auffächern;
~ into outside banking seine Tätigkeit auf bankfremde Geschäfte ausdehnen; ~ away from a business Geschäftssparte aufgeben; ~ into commercial markets sich dem kommerziellen Sektor intensiver zuwenden.

diversion Unterhaltung, Zeitvertreib, (change of route, Br.) Umleitung;
favo(u)rite ~s bevorzugte Freizeitbeschäftigung; ~ of manpower Arbeitskräfteverteilung.

divert (v.) to one's personal use für sich persönlich (für eigene Zwecke) verwenden (abzweigen).

divide (v.) a bankrupt's estate Konkursmasse ausschütten.

dividend Dividende, Gewinnanteil, (bankruptcy) [Konkurs]quote, Rate;
cum ~ (Br.) mit (einschließlich) Dividende, samt Kupon; ex ~ ohne (exklusive) Dividende; ~ off (US) ohne Dividende; ~ on (US) einschließlich Dividende;
cash ~ Bardividende; declared ~ ausgeschüttete Dividende; life insurance ~ Prämie; liquidation ~ Liquidationsquote; optional ~ Gratisaktie mit Wahlrecht der Barabfindung; passed ~ ausgefallene Dividende; preferred ~ Vorzugsdividende; stock ~ (US) Gratisaktie;

~s in arrear Dividendenrückstände; ~ of a bankrupt's estate Konkursquote;
to declare a stock ~ Gratisaktien ausgeben; to rank for the ~ dividendenberechtigt sein;
~ accumulation Dividendenansammlung; ~ announcement Dividendenerklärung; ~ cutting Dividendenkürzung; ~ payers (US) Dividendenpapiere; ~ reinvestment wiederangelegte Dividendenausschüttungen; ~ warrant Dividenden-, Gewinnanteilschein.

division (industry) Fachgruppe;
payroll ~ Lohnabteilung;
~ of a bankrupt's estate Ausschüttung der Konkursmasse; ~ of markets Abgrenzung der Verkaufsgebiete; ~ into shares Stückelung.

divulge (v.) information preisgeben.

do (buy up, Br.) Wechsel aufkaufen;
~ badly schlechte Geschäfte machen; ~ odd jobs Gelegenheitsarbeiten verrichten.

dock Dock, Kai, Schiffswerft, (landing pier) Landungs-, Anlageplatz, Pier, (railroad, US) Laderampe, (wage cut) Lohnkürzung, (warehouse) Lager-, Packhof;
~ (v.) (go into dock) ins Dock gehen, docken;
~ a workman's wages Arbeitslohn kürzen;
~ charges (dues) Dockgebühren, Hafengeld; ~ facilities Dockanlagen; ~ receipt (Br.) Lagerschein, (US) Kaiannahme-, Ablieferungsschein; ~ warrant (Br.) Docklagerschein.

docker (Br.) Schauermann, Hafen-, Dockarbeiter, Ablader.

docket (agenda, US) Tagesordnung, (customhouse warrant, Br.) Zollquittung, Passierzettel, (delivery order, Br.) Lieferschein, (label) Etikett, (purchasing permit, Br.) Einkaufsgenehmigung;
~ (v.) mit Etikett versehen, etikettieren.

docking of pay (US) Lohnabzug.

dockmaster Hafenmeister, -kommissar.

document Beweis-, Beleg-, Schriftstück, Urkunde; accompanying ~ Begleitpapier; shipping ~s Verschiffungs-, Frachtpapiere, Verladedokumente; ~s against acceptance Dokumente gegen Akzept; ~s against payment Kasse gegen Dokumente; ~s of shipment Verladepapiere;
~ (v.) mit den notwendigen Papieren versehen, (prove by documents) urkundlich belegen;
~ bill Dokumententratte; ~ credit Dokumentenkredit; ~ tax Urkundensteuer.

documentary | bill (draft) Dokumententratte; ~ credit Dokumentenakkreditiv; ~ proof Urkundenbeweis.

dodge (v.) a tax Steuer umgehen.

dole (Br.) Arbeitslosenunterstützung, -geld;
to be on (draw) the ~ (Br.) stempeln gehen;
~ drawer (Br.) Stempelbruder.

dollar | acceptance Dollarakzept; ~ country zum Dollarblock gehöriges Land.

domestic (a.) (inland) inländisch, innerstaatlich, einheimisch;
~ activity Binnenkonjunktur; ~ agency Stellen-

vermittlung; ~ **bill** Inlandswechsel; ~ **consumption** Inlandverbrauch; ~ **currency** Landeswährung; ~ **industry** Heim-, Hausindustrie; ~ **market** Binnenmarkt; ~ **workshop** Heimarbeitsbetrieb.

domicile *(bill of exchange)* Zahlstelle, *(dwelling)* Wohnung;
commercial ~ Wohnsitz der gewerblichen Niederlassung;
~ **of origin** *(contract)* Erfüllungsort;
~ *(v.)* domizilieren, zahlbar stellen.

domiciled bill Domizilwechsel.

domiciliation Zahlbarstellung, Domizilangabe.

donated surplus Portefeuille eigener Aktien.

donee country Empfängerland.

door Tür, *(mar.)* Luke;
to close the ~s *(banking)* Schalter schließen; **to pay for articles at the** ~ Waren bei [der] Lieferung bezahlen.

door-to-door | **market** Hausverkauf; ~ **service** bahnamtlicher Rollfuhrdienst.

dope *(advertising)* Waschzettel.

dormant | **account** umsatzloses Konto; ~ **capital** totes Kapital; ~ **partner** stiller Teilhaber; ~ **stock** Ladenhüter; ~ **warrant** Blankovollmacht.

double | **accident benefit** *(Br.)* doppelte Leistung bei Unfalltod; ~–**bill** *(v.)* doppelte Spesen in Rechnung stellen; ~–**billing technique** System der doppelten Rechnungsausstellung; ~ **bottom** *(US, stock exchange)* äußerster Tiefstand; ~–**entry bookkeeping** doppelte Buchführung; ~ **option** Stellagegeschäft, ~–**page spread** doppelseitige (zweiseitige) Anzeige; ~–**taxation agreement** Doppelbesteuerungsabkommen; ~ **time** Lohnzuschlag für Nachtarbeit.

doubtful debts, notes and accounts *(US)* dubiose Forderungen.

down Abwärtsbewegung;
~ *(a.)* *(goods)* wenig gefragt, *(prices)* heruntergegangen, gefallen;
cash ~ gegen bar;
~ *(v.)* **tools** *(Br.)* Arbeit niederlegen, streiken;
to be ~ **5 degrees** um fünf Punkte gefallen sein; **to mark goods** ~ Waren billiger setzen;
~ **cycle** rückläufiger Konjunkturzyklus; ~ **payment** *(Br.)* Bar-, Sofortzahlung, *(US instalment)* Anzahlung[sbetrag]; ~ **time** *(factory, US)* betrieblich bedingte Verlustzeit.

downgrade, to be on the *(business)* schlecht gehen, *(price)* fallen, sinken.

downgrading of property niedrigere Vermögenseinstufung.

downpay *(US)* Anzahlung.

downshift in rates Tarifsenkung.

downstairs merger Fusion der Mutter- mit der Tochtergesellschaft.

downswing, cyclical Konjunkturabschwung.

downtown *(US)* **district** Geschäftsgegend.

downtrend Konjunkturrückgang;
~ **in new orders** Auftragsrückgang.

downturn *(business activity)* Abwärtsbewegung, Flaute, Konjunkturabschwächung;
~ **in the market** rückläufige Marktbewegung.

downward | **movement** Abwärtsbewegung; ~ **swing** Konjunkturabschwung; ~ **tendency** Baisse; ~ **[business] trend** Konjunkturabschwächung.

dowry insurance Aussteuerversicherung.

drab | **earnings** geringfügige Erträgnisse; ~ **to be on the** ~ **side** schlecht verdienen.

draft *(allowance)* Gutgewicht, *(on bank)* [Zahlungs]-anweisung, *(bill of exchange)* Tratte, Handelswechsel, *(drawing of money)* Geldabhebung;
arrival ~ Tratte mit beigefügten Verschiffungsdokumenten; **bank[er's]** ~ Banktratte, **documentary** ~ Dokumententratte; ~s **receivable** *(balance sheet)* Debitoren aus Wechselforderungen;
~ **[payable] at sight** Sichttratte, -wechsel;
~ *(v.)* **in a new management** neue Geschäftsleitung einsetzen;
to advise a ~ Tratte ankündigen (avisieren); **to have a quick** ~ reißend abgehen; **to make a** ~ **on one's account** Kontoabhebung vornehmen; **to negotiate a** ~ Tratte begeben;
~ **book** *(Br.)* Wechsel[kopier]buch; ~ **collection** Wechselinkasso; ~ **credit** Remboursedkredit; ~ **economy** gelenkte Wirtschaft, Planwirtschaft.

drag | **on recovery** konjunkturelle Bremse;
~ *(v.)* schlecht (flau) gehen;
~ **clause** *(tariff law)* Sammelklausel.

drain *(money)* Abzüge, [Geld]abfluß;
foreign ~ Kapitalabwanderung;
~ **of bullion** *(Br., gold)* Goldabfluß; ~ **on liquidity** Liquiditätsanspannung;
~ *(v.)* **a country** Land völlig ausplündern;
to be a ~ **on s. one's purse** jds. Geldbeutel in Anspruch nehmen; **to throw money down the** ~ Geld zum Fenster hinauswerfen.

draw *(attraction)* Zug-, Anziehungskraft, Schlager, Zugartikel, *(lottery)* Ver-, Auslosung, Ziehung;
box-office ~ Kassenschlager; **Christmas** ~ Weihnachtslotterie;
~ **on reserves** Anspannung der Reserven;
~ *(v.)* | **away customers** Kunden abspenstig machen; ~ **back** Rückvergütung erhalten, *(bill)* zurücktrassieren, *(duty)* als Rückzoll bekommen; ~ **by lot** *(bonds)* ver-, auslosen; ~ **in one's expenditure** sich in seinen Ausgaben einschränken; ~ **on one's capital** sein Kapital angreifen.

draw up | **a balance sheet** Bilanz aufstellen; ~ **an estimate** Kostenvoranschlag machen.

draw upon one's savings seine Ersparnisse angreifen.

draw | **a bill of exchange** Wechsel ziehen (trassieren);
~ **a check** *(US)* **(cheque,** *Br.)* **upon an account** Scheck auf ein Konto ziehen; ~ **a commission on a transaction** Provision aus einem Geschäft beziehen; ~ **heavily on the credit market** Kreditmärkte stark in Anspruch nehmen; ~ **a regular income** regelmäßige Einkünfte beziehen; ~ **on s. o. on sight** Sichtwechsel auf j. ziehen;
to be a big ~ starke Anziehungskraft ausüben.

drawback *(money remitted)* Rückvergütung, -erstattung, *(refund of duty)* Export-, Zollrückvergütung, Rückzoll;
~ **slip** Verrechnungsbeleg.

drawee *(bill)* [Wechsel]bezogener, Trassat.

drawer Aussteller, Trassant, Ordergeber.

drawing *(bill of exchange)* Ziehen, Ausstellen, Trassieren, *(of bonds)* Auslosen, *(cashing)* Ab-, Erhebung;
personal ~s Privatentnahmen;
~s on account current Kontokorrentabhebungen;
~ account Girokonto, *(agent)* Spesen-, Vorschußkonto; ~ credit Trassierungskredit; ~ rate *(bills)* Briefkurs; ~ right Auslosungsrecht.

drawn bonds ausgeloste Obligationen (Schuldverschreibungen).

drift *(v.) down (prices)* abbröckeln.

drive *(advertising campaign)* Werbefeldzug, *(money collection, US)* Geldsammlung, *(US, sale under price)* Schleuderverkauf, *(US, stock exchange)* Baisseangriff;
export ~ Exportförderung;
~ a good bargain Geschäft zu einem guten Abschluß bringen; ~ up the prices Preise in die Höhe treiben; ~ one's workmen too hard seine Arbeitskräfte übermäßig ausnützen.

droop *(v.) (prices)* fallen, abflauen, abbröckeln.

drop *(prices)* Fallen, Sinken, Rückgang, *(stock exchange)* Einbruch, Baisse;
~ in earnings Ertragsrückgang; ~ in investments Investitionsschwund; ~ in sales Umsatzrückgang; ~ *(v.) (correspondence)* einschlafen, *(prices)* fallen, sinken;
~ out of the management arrangement on 60 days' notice sich mit einer zweimonatigen Kündigung aus einer Vereinbarung über die Vorstandsbesetzung zurückziehen;
~ a lot of money on a deal bei einem Geschäft viel Geld einbüßen; ~ in quality Qualitätsrückgang erfahren;
~ shipment Direktverkauf durch Grossisten ohne eigenes Lager.

drop off in profits Gewinnrückgang.

drove of tourists Touristenstrom.

drug on the market unverkäufliche (schlecht verkäufliche) Ware, Ladenhüter.

drum *(v.) (US)* [Kunden] werben;
~ up business Geschäft ankurbeln.

drummer *(US)* Handlungsreisender, Vertreter.

dry | *(v.) up (labo(u)r reserves)* versiegen;
~ capital unverwässertes Gesellschaftskapital;
~ goods *(US)* Textilwaren, Textilien.

dual | **pricing** Doppelpreissystem; **~-use package** wiederverwendbare [Ver]packung, Mehrwegpackung.

dubious undertaking unsicheres Unternehmen.

duck *(v.)* a payment Zahlungsverpflichtung nicht einhalten.

dud *(banknote, sl.)* falsche Banknote;
~ check *(US)* (cheque, *Br.*) ungedeckter Scheck; ~ stock unverkäufliche Waren.

due *(charge)* Gebühr, *(membership)* Beitrag;
~ *(a.)* gebührend, *(mature)* fällig, [sofort] zahlbar, *(owing)* schuldig, zustehend, geschuldet;
until ~ bis zur Verfallzeit;

~ at call täglich fällig;
amount debts ~ and owing Aktiva und Passiva; rent ~ fällige Miete; tax ~ Steuersoll;
~ from banks *(balance sheet)* Nostroguthaben; ~ to banks *(balance sheet)* Nostroverpflichtungen;
to be ~ to retire Altersgrenze erreicht haben; to become (fall) ~ zahlbar [fällig] werden;
~ and reasonable care im Verkehr erforderliche Sorgfalt; ~ and proper notice fristgerechte Kündigung.

dues *(club)* [Vereins]beitrag, Abgaben, Gebühren;
union ~ Gewerkschaftsbeiträge;
~ checkoff automatische Beitragseinbehaltung.

dull geschäftslos, flau;
~ performer *(stock exchange)* schlechtgehendes Papier; ~ sale schleppender Absatz.

dullness Börsenflaute, Lustlosigkeit;
~ in the stock market flaue Stimmung auf dem Aktienmarkt.

dummy Attrappe, Strohmann, *(model)* [Ausstellungs]muster, *(sham package)* Leer-, ʾSchaupakkung;
~ advertisement fingierte Annonce; ~ concern Scheinunternehmen; ~ transaction Scheingeschäft.

dump *(v.) (stock exchange)* Effektenpakete billig abstoßen; *(trade)* Ware in großer Menge billig auf den Markt bringen, *(export trade)* Dumping betreiben.

dumping Deponie, *(export trade)* Warenausfuhr zu Schleuderpreisen, *(price)* Preisunterbietung;
foreign exchange ~ Valutadumping.

dun Zahlungsaufforderung.

dunning letter Mahnbrief.

duplicate gleichlautende Abschrift, *(second of exchange)* Sekundawechsel;
~ of invoice Rechnungsdoppel;
~ receipted bills quittierte Rechnungen in doppelter Ausfertigung; ~ receipt Quittungsduplikat.

duplicating machine Vervielfältigungsapparat.

durable goods, durables langlebige Gebrauchsgüter, dauerhafte Konsum-, Kapitalgüter.

duration | **of benefits** Unterstützungszeitraum; ~ of offer Gültigkeit einer Offerte.

Dutch treat getrennte Kasse.

dutiable goods zollpflichtige Waren.

duty *(customs)* Zoll[gebühren], Eingangsabgabe, *(fee)* Gebühr, Taxe, Auflage, *(impost)* [Verbrauchs]abgabe, *(obligation)* Verbindlichkeit, Verpflichtung;
exempt from (free of) ~ *(customs)* zollfrei, *(fees)* gebühren-, spesenfrei, *(tax)* steuer-, abgabenfrei;
liable to ~ *(customs)* zollpflichtig; off ~ dienstfrei, außerdienstlich; ~ off unversteuert, unverzollt;
additional ~ Zollaufschlag, Steuerzuschlag; commercial *(Br.)* (compensation, compensative, countervailing, *US)* ~ Ausgleichszoll; compound ~ Mischzoll; prohibitive ~ Schutzzoll; retaliatory ~ Vergeltungs-, Kampfzoll; ad valorem ~ Wertzoll; ~ to account Rechnungs[legungs]pflicht; ~ charged by weight Gewichtszoll; ~ on increment value Wertzuwachssteuer;

to go through free of ~ zollfrei passieren; **to pay ~ on** versteuern, *(customs)* verzollen, Zoll entrichten;
~ **change** Tarifänderung; ~ **drawback** Zollrückvergütung; **~-free return** zollfreie Wiedereinfuhr; **~-free shop** zollfreier Laden.

dwelling, furnished möblierte Wohnung; **industrial ~** Werkwohnung; **uncontrolled (unrestricted) ~** freier (nicht bewirtschafteter) Wohnraum; **lower-price (low-rental) ~ unit** billiges Mietshaus.

dwindling | of stocks Lagerschrumpfung;
~ **assets** Vermögensverfall.

E

early | -bird price Werbe-, Einführungspreis; ~ **closing** früher Geschäfts-, Ladenschluß.

earmark Identitäts-, Kennzeichen;
~ *(v.) (finance)* zweckbestimmen, vorsehen;
~ **a check** Scheck sperren; ~ **for a key position** für eine Schlüsselstellung ausersehen.

earmarked | account zweckgebundenes Konto; ~ **gold** Goldreserve bei ausländischen Bankinstituten.

earn *(v.)* erwerben, gewinnen, *(wages)* verdienen;
~ **one's bread and butter** sich seinen Lebensunterhalt selbst verdienen; ~ **interest** Zinsen bringen.

earned | freight verdiente Transportkosten; ~ **income** Arbeits-, Erwerbseinkommen; ~ **income relief** *(Br.)* Steuervergünstigung für Berufstätige; ~ **surplus** Betriebsgewinn; ~ **unappropriated surplus** *(US)* Gewinnvortrag.

earner Verdiener, Erwerbstätiger;
wage ~ Lohnempfänger.

earnest money Draufgabe, -geld.

earning | advancement Einkommensanstieg; ~ **asset** *(Federal Reserve Bank, US)* gewinnbringende [Kapital]anlage; ~ **capacity** Rentabilität; **~ -capacity value** Ertragswert.

earnings *(income)* Einkommen, Einkünfte, Bezüge, *(profit)* Gewinn, Ertrag, Erlös, *(salary)* Gehalt, *(wages)* Verdienst, Arbeitslohn;
accumulated ~ *(balance sheet)* Gewinnvortrag; **after-tax ~** Gewinn nach Steuern; **daily ~** Tagesverdienst; **gross ~** Bruttoeinnahmen; **hourly ~** Stundenlohn; **pretax ~** Gewinn vor Steuern; **retained ~** *(US)* Gewinnvortrag;
~ **of management** Unternehmerlohn;
to plough back ~ Gewinn nicht entnehmen;
~ **base** Ertragsposition; ~ **dip** Ertragsrückgang;
~ **increase** Ertragssteigerung; ~ **statement** Gewinn- und Verlustrechnung.

ease, a fractional Kursabschwächung um einen Bruchteil;

~ **of money** Geldflüssigkeit;
~ *(v.)* **off** abschwächen, *(prices)* nachlassen, fallen;
~ **a fraction** *(prices)* etw. abbröckeln; ~ **the economic situation** Konjunktur entspannen.

easier *(stock exchange)* leichter, niedriger;
to become ~ abflauen;
~ **money** leichteres (billigeres) Geld.

easiness on the money market Geldmarktflüssigkeit.

easing | [up] in credit kreditpolitische Erleichterungen; ~ **of cyclical conditions** Konjunkturentspannung; ~ **of monetary policy** Liquiditätsverbesserungen für den Bankenapparat.

easy *(commodity)* wenig gefragt, *(market)* ruhig, weichend, flau, lustlos *(money)* flüssig, billig;
to be an ~ finish *(money market)* am Schluß leicht sein; ~ **market** *(stock exchange)*, freundliche Börse; ~ **money market** *(US)* Bankenliquidität, Geldmarktflüssigkeit; ~ **terms** günstige Geschäftsbedingungen.

eat *(v.)* **up savings** Ersparnisse aufbrauchen.

economic [volks]wirtschaftlich, nationalökonomisch;
~ **activity** konjunkturelle Aktivität; ~ **adviser** Wirtschaftsberater; ~ **aid** Wirtschaftshilfe; ~ **assets** Wirtschaftsgüter; ~ **atmosphere** Konjunkturatmosphäre; ~ **boom** Konjunkturaufschwung; ~ **climate** Konjunkturklima; ~ **commentary** Wirtschaftskommentar; ⁰ **Commission for Europe** *(ECE)* Europäische Wirtschaftskommission; ~ **cooperation** wirtschaftliche Zusammenarbeit; ⁰ **and Social Council** Wirtschafts- und Sozialrat; ~ **dip** Konjunkturrückschlag; ~ **efficiency** Wirtschaftlichkeit; ~ **espionage** Wirtschaftsspionage; ~ **fluctuations** Konjunkturschwankungen; ~ **forecast** Konjunkturvorschau; ~ **forecaster** Konjunkturbeobachter; ~ **growth** Steigerung des Sozialprodukts; ~ **indicator** Konjunkturanzeichen, -in-

dikator, -barometer; ~ **independence** Autarkie; ~ **interest** Kapitalanteil; ~ **life** *(asset)* wirtschaftliche Nutzungsdauer; ~ **-lot size** rationelle Stückzahl; ~ **news** Nachrichten aus dem Wirtschaftsleben; ~ **order quantity** wirtschaftliche Auftragsgröße; ~ **picture** Konjunkturbild; ~ **policy** Konjunktur-, Wirtschaftspolitik; ~ **policymaker** Konjunkturpolitiker; ~ **profit** Grenzkostenergebnis; ~ **program(me)** Konjunkturprogramm; ~ **prospects** Konjunkturaussichten; ~ **recovery** konjunkturelle Belebung; ~ **rent** *(Ricardo)* Grundrente; ~ **reprisals** wirtschaftliche Repressalien; ~ **research** Konjunkturforschung; ~ **sanctions** wirtschaftliche Sanktionen; ~ **self-sufficiency** wirtschaftliche Autarkie; ~ **slowdown** Konjunkturabschwächung; ~ **supremacy** wirtschaftliche Übermacht; ~ **survey** Wirtschaftsbericht; ~ **trend** konjunktureller Entwicklungsverlauf; ~ **trough** Konjunkturtief; ~ **upswing** Konjunkturanstieg; ~ **use** Nutzungsdauer.

economical [volks]wirtschaftlich, *(thrifty)* sparsam; ~ **operation** rentabler Betrieb; **to be of low ~ strength** nicht krisenfest sein.

economics [Volks]wirtschaft, *(savings)* Ersparnisse, *(science Br.)* Volkswirtschaftslehre, Nationalökonomie.

economies of scale Kostenersparnisse durch optimale Betriebsvergrößerung, Kostendegression.

economize *(v.)* sparsam wirtschaften, überflüssige Ausgaben vermeiden, sich einschrränken.

economy *(economics)* [Volks]wirtschaft, Nationalökonomie, *(thrift)* Sparsamkeit, Ökonomie, Ersparnis;

competitive ~ Wettbewerbs-, Konkurrenzwirtschaft; **flat** ~ Konjunkturflaute; **free-enterprise** ~ freie Marktwirtschaft; **industrial** ~ gewerbliche Wirtschaft; **labo(u)r-tight** ~ angespannte Arbeitslage; **planned** ~ [staatliche] Plan-, Zwangswirtschaft, staatlicher Dirigismus; **slowing** ~ Konjunkturabschwächung;

~ **in fuel consumption** *(car)* geringer Benzinverbrauch;

to cool the ~ Konjunkturabkühlung herbeiführen; **to get the** ~ **back on the tracks** Konjunktur wieder zum Anlauf bringen; **to give the** ~ **a shot in the arm** *(US)* der Wirtschaft eine Konjunkturspritze geben; **to keep the** ~ **in high gear** Wirtschaft auf Hochtouren laufen lassen; **to put the** ~ **on a richer monetary diet** für wirtschaftliche Liquidität sorgen; **to stabilize the** ~ stabile Konjunkturpolitik betreiben;

~ **car** Kraftfahrzeug der Mittelklasse; ~ **class** *(airplane)* Touristenklasse; ~ **market** Absatzgebiet für billige Artikel; ~**-priced** vergleichsweise preisgünstig.

edge *(v.)* **down** *(prices)* schwächer tendieren.

editor, city *(Br.)* Redakteur des Wirtschaftsteils, *(US)* Lokalredakteur; **financial** ~ *(US)* Wirtschaftsredakteur.

editorial advertisement redaktionell aufgemachte Anzeige.

education, business Handelsschulbildung.

educational | **advertising** Aufklärungsreklame; ~ **tariff** Schutzzoll.

effect | *(v.)* **a corresponding entry** gleichlautende Buchung vornehmen; ~ **customs clearance** sich zollamtlich abfertigen lassen; ~ **an insurance** Versicherung abschließen; ~ **payment** Zahlung bewirken; ~ **foreign exchange transactions** Abschlüsse in Devisen tätigen.

effective | **in advertising** werbewirksam; ~ **capital** Betriebskapital; ~ **demand** wirksame Gesamtnachfrage; ~ **interest yield** Effektivverzinsung; ~ **output** Nutzleistung; ~ **value** Effektivwert.

effects *(cash)* Barbestand, -vorräte, *(property)* Vermögenswerte, Habseligkeiten;

~ **not cleared** *(Br.)* noch nicht verrechnete Abschnitte; **personal** ~ persönliche Gebrauchsgegenstände.

efficiency Leistungsfähigkeit, Wirtschaftlichkeit; **marginal** ~ Grenznutzen; **operating** ~ Betriebsleistung;

~ **apartment** Zimmer mit Dusche und Kochnische; ~ **audit** Wirtschaftlichkeitsprüfung; ~ **bonus plan** Leistungslohnsystem; ~ **engineer** *(US)* Rationalisierungsfachmann; ~ **wages** Leistungslohn.

eight-hour [working] day Achtstunden[arbeits]tag.

elasticity | **of demand** Nachfrage-, Bedarfselastizität; ~ **of supply** Angebotselastizität.

electricity | **consumption** Stromverbrauch; ~ **cut** Stromsperre.

eligibility for [re]discount [Re]diskontfähigkeit; ~ **to serve as collateral** *(US)* Deckungsfähigkeit; ~ **for vacation** Urlaubsanspruch.

eligible *(banking)* bank-, diskontfähig;

~ **for pension** pensionsberechtigt; ~ **for relief** fürsorge-, unterstützungsberechtigt; ~ **to serve as collateral** *(US)* lombardfähig;

to be ~ **for the dividend received exclusion provided by the Internal Revenue Code** das von der Steuergesetzgebung vorgesehene Schachtelprinzip genießen;

~ **investment** *(US)* mündelsichere Anlage; ~ **paper** *(US)* rediskontfähiges und lombardfähiges Papier.

eliminate *(v.)* **an account** Konto auflösen.

elimination | **of competition** Ausschaltung der Konkurrenz; ~ **of wholesalers** Umgehung des Großhandels.

embargo Hafensperre, Blockade;

outright economic ~ vollständige Sperre des Wirtschaftsverkehrs; **gold** ~ Goldausfuhrverbot; **hostile** ~ völkerrechtswidriges Embargo;

~ *(v.)* Blockade (Embargo) verhängen, Handelsverkehr sperren;

to lift the ~ Beschlagnahme aufheben.

embark *(v.)* sich einschiffen, an Bord gehen;

~ **on a business** Geschäft eröffnen; ~ **capital in trade** sein Geld unternehmerisch arbeiten lassen.

embarkation card *(airport)* Abflugkarte.

embarrassed in Geldverlegenheit;

~ **business** zerrüttete Verhältnisse; ~ **estate** überschuldeter Besitz.

embarrassment finanzielle Bedrängnis, Zahlungsschwierigkeit, Geldverlegenheit.

embezzle *(v.)* **the funds of a ward** sich an Mündelgeldern vergreifen.

embezzlement of trust money Depotunterschlagung.

emerge | *(v.)* **with small advances** *(stock exchange)* mit kleinen Kursaufbesserungen schließen.

emergency | address Notadressat; ~ aid program(me) Notstands-, Soforthilfeprogramm; ~ amortization beschleunigte Abschreibung; ~ job Aushilfsstellung; ~ loss Elementarschaden; ~ sale Notverkauf; ~ tax Krisensteuer; ~ train Hilfszug; ~ [relief] work Notstandsarbeit.

emission Ausgabe, Emission;
above par ~ Überpari-Emission.

emit *(v.)* a bill of credit Kreditbrief ausstellen.

emolument Nutzen, Gewinn, Vergütung;
~s Aufwandsentschädigung, Nebeneinkünfte.

employ Beschäftigung[sverhältnis], Stellung;
out of ~ stellungs-, erwerbs-, arbeitslos;
~ *(v.)* anstellen, einstellen, *(use)* gebrauchen;
~ an expert accountant Buchsachverständigen zuziehen;
to be in s. one's ~ bei jem. beschäftigt (angestellt) sein, in jds. Diensten stehen.

employed beschäftigt, angestellt, berufstätig;
gainfully ~ gegen Entgelt beschäftigt, erwerbstätig; permanently ~ festangestellt;
~ capital produktives Kapital; self- ~ person selbständiger Erwerbstätiger.

employee *(Br.),* employe *(US)* Angestellter, Arbeitnehmer, Gehaltsempfänger;
black-coated ~ *(Br.)* höherer Büroangestellter; covered ~ versicherter Angestellter; full-time ~ ganztägig beschäftigter Angestellter; substandard ~ untertariflich bezahlter Arbeiter;
~ appraisal Angestelltenbeurteilung; ~ benefits Sozialleistungen; ~ benefit paid by company *(national insurance)* vom Arbeitnehmer bezahlter Sozialversicherungsanteil, Arbeitgeberanteil; ~ discount Rabatt für Werksangestellte; ~ election Betriebswahl; ~ home Werkswohnung; ~ layoff Belegschaftsabbau; ~ profit sharing Gewinnbeteiligung der Arbeitnehmer; ~ roster Stellenbesetzungsplan; ~ stock Belegschaftsaktie; ~ suggestion system betriebliches Vorschlagwesen; ~'s withholding exemption certificate Lohnsteuerfreibetragsformular.

employer *(business)* Unternehmer, Arbeitgeber, Dienstherr;
most recent ~ letzter Arbeitgeber;
~ and his agent Auftraggeber und Auftragnehmer; ~s' association Arbeitgeberverband; ~ contribution *(national insurance)* Arbeitgeberanteil; ~'s liability insurance Betriebshaftpflichtversicherung.

employment Beschäftigung, Tätigkeit, Geschäft, Beruf, *(situation)* unselbständige Arbeit, Stelle, [An]stellung, Beschäftigungs-, Angestellten-, Dienst-, Arbeitsverhältnis, *(use)* Gebrauch, An-, Verwendung;

in public ~ im öffentlichen Dienst; out of ~ stellen-, arbeits-, beschäftigungslos;
fluctuating ~ stetiger Arbeitsplatzwechsel; full ~ Vollbeschäftigung; full-time ~ Ganztagsbeschäftigung; gainful ~ Erwerbstätigkeit; guaranteed ~ garantierter Jahreslohn; part-time ~ Halbtagsbeschäftigung, Kurzarbeit; probationary ~ Probeanstellung; self-~ selbständige Tätigkeit;
~ of capital Kapitalanlage;
to find ~ for s. o. j. unterbringen;
~ agency Stellenvermittlungsbüro; ~ agreement Dienstvertrag; ~ application blank Bewerbungsformular; ~ bureau Arbeits-, Stellennachweis; to terminate an ~ contract without notice *(US)* Dienstverhältnis fristlos kündigen; ~ exchange *(Br.)* Arbeits-, Stellennachweis; ~ history beruflicher Werdegang; ~ interview persönliche Vorstellung; ~ public ~ office *(US)* staatlicher Arbeitsnachweis; ~ papers Arbeitspapiere; ~ period Beschäftigungszeit; selection ~ tax *(Br.)* Lohnsummensteuer.

empties leere Fässer, Leergut.

empty Leergut, -material, *(car)* Leerwagen;
~ taxi freies Taxi; ~ weight *(airplane)* Eigen-, Leergewicht.

encashment | of debts Schuldeneinziehung;
~ charges Einzugsspesen; ~ order Inkassomandat; -auftrag.

encumber *(v.)* dinglich belasten.

encumbered estate [hypothekarisch] belasteter Grundbesitz.

encumbering goods Sperrgüter.

encumbrance [Grundstücks]belastung;
free from ~s schulden-, lastenfrei, entschuldet;
to free an estate of ~s Grundstück entschulden.

end | of the month Ultimo;
to be at the ~ of one's resources seine Mittel aufgebraucht haben;
~-of-month-figures Monatsendstände; ~-processing plant Weiterverarbeitungsbetrieb; ~-year pressure Jahresultimobeanspruchung.

endorsable girierbar, indossierbar;
~ instrument Orderpapier.

endorse *(v.)* indossieren, girieren, begeben;
~ generally blanko girieren.

endorsee Girat, Indossat[ar].

endorsement Giro, Indossament, *(insurance)* [Versicherungs]nachtrag, Zusatz[klausel];
accommodation ~ Gefälligkeitsindossament; blank ~ Blankoindossament; general ~ Vollindossament; restrictive ~ Rektagiro, -indossament;
~ made out to bearer Inhaberindossament; ~ without recourse Giro ohne Verbindlichkeit.

endorser Girant, Indossant, *(guarantor of bill)* Aval, Wechselbürger;
preceding (previous, prior) ~ Vor[der]mann.

endowed ausgestattet, dotiert.

endowment assurance *(Br.)* Versicherung auf den Erlebensfall, Aussteuer-, Erlebensversicherung; ~ period Erlebenszeit.

enfacement Wechselvermerk auf der Vorderseite.

enforce *(v.)* **payment by legal proceedings** Zahlung gerichtlich beitreiben.

enforceable einklagbar, vollstreckbar.

enforced liquidation Zwangsvergleich.

enforcement Geltendmachung, Vollstreckung; ~ **of a lien** Pfandverwertung; ~ **proceedings** Vollstreckungsverfahren.

engage *(book)* [Platz] bestellen, belegen, *(employ)* einstellen, anstellen, in Dienst nehmen; ~ **in business** Geschäftsmann werden; ~ **in a line of business** in einer Branche tätig sein; ~ **rooms at a hotel** Zimmer in einem Hotel bestellen; ~ **seamen** Seeleute anmustern.

engaged belegt, besetzt, beschäftigt; ~ **signal (tone)** Besetztzeichen.

engagement Stellung, Stelle, Ein-, Anstellung, Beschäftigung, Engagement; **without** ~ freibleibend, ohne Gewähr; **bear** ~**s** *(stock exchange)* Engagements der Baissepartei; **bull** ~**s** Engagements der Haussepartei; **fresh** ~ Neueinstellung; ~ **of seamen** Anmusterung von Seeleuten; **to have found a lucrative** ~ gut bezahlten Posten gefunden haben; **to have numerous** ~**s for next week** vollbesetzten Terminkalender haben; **to meet one's** ~**s** seinen Verbindlichkeiten nachkommen; ~ **book** Terminkalender, Merkbuch.

engross *(v.) (monopolize)* Markt monopolisieren.

enhance *(v.)* | **in price** im Preis steigen; ~ **the value of land** Grundstückswerte steigen lassen.

enlarge | *(v.)* **one's business** sein Geschäft ausdehnen; ~ **the payment of a bill** Wechsel prolongieren; ~ **one's premises** anbauen.

enlargement | **of business** Geschäftsausdehnung; ~ **of capacity** Kapazitätserweiterung.

enlist *(v. i.)* anstellen, einstellen, engagieren; ~ **the aid of the court** Hilfe des Gerichts in Anspruch nehmen.

enlistment Anwerbung, Einstellung; ~ **allowance** *(US)* Treueprämie.

enliven *(v.)* **business** Konjunktur ankurbeln.

enrol(l) *(v.)* Namen in einer Liste eintragen; ~ **workers** Arbeitskräfte einstellen.

enrol(l)ment | **fee** Einschreibgebühr; ~ **office** Registratur.

entangle *(v.)* **o. s. with moneylenders** sich mit Geldleihern einlassen.

enter *(v.) (become a party)* eingehen, kontrahieren, unterzeichnen, *(book)* eintragen, [ver]buchen; ~ **into a binding agreement** bindende Verpflichtung eingehen; ~ **a bill short** Wechsel Eingang vorbehalten gutschreiben; ~ **into business relations** neue Geschäftsverbindungen anknüpfen; ~ **upon a career** Laufbahn einschlagen; ~ **into the channels of distribution** *(customs)* in den freien Verkehr überführen; ~ **on the credit side** im Haben buchen; ~ **at the customhouse** zollamtlich deklarieren; ~ **goods** Waren zur Verzollung deklarieren; ~ **an item in the ledger** Posten im Hauptbuch eintragen; ~ **into partnership** sich assoziieren; ~ **into the rights of a creditor** Gläubigerstellung erhalten; ~ **a seaman on the ship's books** Seemann anheuern; ~ **short** zu wenig deklarieren; ~ **up** Buchungen vervollständigen.

entering Einschreibung, Eintragung; ~ **short** Gutschrift, Eingang vorbehalten.

enterprise Unternehmen, -nehmung, Geschäft, [Gewerbe]betrieb *(venture)* Spekulation; **business (commercial)** ~ geschäftliches (gewerbliches) Unternehmen, Gewerbebetrieb; **family-owned** ~ Familienbetrieb; **free** ~ freies Unternehmertum; **industrial** ~ Gewerbebetrieb; **manufacturing** ~ Fabrikationsbetrieb; **municipal** ~ Gemeindebetrieb; **nationalized** ~ verstaatlichtes Unternehmen; **nonprofit** ~ gemeinnütziger Betrieb; **publicity-owned** ~ Unternehmen der öffentlichen Hand; **semi-public** ~ gemischtwirtschaftliches Unternehmen; **wildcat** ~ Schwindelunternehmen; **free-** ~ **economy** freie Unternehmerwirtschaft; **free-** ~ **system** freie Marktwirtschaft.

entertain *(v.)* Gäste haben, bewirten; ~ **business connections** Geschäftsbeziehungen unterhalten.

entertainment Unterhaltung, Gastfreundschaft, Bewirtung, Repräsentation; ~ **allowance** Aufwandentschädigung; ~ **duty** *(Br.)* Vergnügungssteuer.

enthusiasm for work Arbeitslust, -freude.

entice *(v.)* **away customers** Kunden von jem abziehen.

entire | **income** Gesamteinkommen; **to be** ~ **master of one's property** völlig frei über sein Vermögen verfügen können.

entitled | **to alimony** *(wife)* unterhaltsberechtigt; ~ **to damages** zum Schadenersatz berechtigt.

entity accounting Konzernbuchführung.

entrance Eintrittsgebühr, *(right of admission)* Zulassung, Zutritt, Zugang; ~ **except on business** Unbefugten ist der Eintritt verboten; ~ **to the harbo(u)r** Hafeneinfahrt; ~ **certificate** Aufnahmebescheinigung; ~ **duty** Einfuhr-, Eingangszoll; ~ **rate** Anfangslohn.

entrepôt Zollniederlage, Lager-, Stapelplatz.

entrepreneur Unternehmer.

entrepreneurial | **activity** Unternehmertätigkeit; ~ **business venture** unternehmerisches Risiko; ~ **profit** Unternehmergewinn.

entrust *(v.)* **an employee with executive functions** Angestellten mit Führungsaufgaben betrauen; ~ **s. o. with the sale** jem. den Verkauf übertragen.

entry Besitzergreifung; *(customs)* [Zoll]deklaration, Einklarierung, *(item in accounts)* [Buchungs]posten, gebuchter Posten; **adjusting (adjustment) [journal]** ~ Berichtigungsbuchung; **debit** ~ Lastschrift; **fraudulent** ~ Falschbuchung; ~ **inwards** Einfuhrdeklaration; ~ **outwards** Ausfuhrdeklaration; **prime** ~ *(customs)* vorläufige Zolldeklaration; **reversing** ~ Stornobuchung; ~ **under bond** Einfuhr unter Zollvormerkschein;

~ **into the Common Market** Beitritt zum Gemein-samen Markt; ~ **and departure of a vessel** Ein- und Auslaufen eines Schiffes; ~ **for duty-free goods** De-klaration für zollfreie Waren; ~ **closed to traffic** gesperrt für Fahrzeuge aller Art; ~ **for ware-housing** Transiterklärung;
   to adjust an ~ Buchung berichtigen; **to cancel an** ~ Posten streichen; **to make a false (wrong)** ~ irrtümlich buchen; **to pass an** ~ **in conformity** gleichlautend buchen; **to reverse an** ~ Buchung stornieren;
   ~ **age** Eintrittsalter; ~ **form** Anmeldeformular; ~ **money** Eintrittsgeld; ~ **visa** Einreisevisum.

envelope Briefumschlag, -hülle, -kuvert;
   commercial ~ Geschäftsumschlag; **penalty** *(US)* Briefumschlag frei durch Ablösung; **self-addressed** ~ Freiumschlag;
   ~ **addresser** Adressiermaschine; ~ **sealer** Briefver-schlußmaschine; ~ **stuffer** Postwurfsendung.

equal | **to cash** so gut wie bares Geld;
   ~ **distribution of taxes** Steuergleichheit; ~ **pay** gleiche Entlohnung.

equality of freight rates Frachtenausgleich.

equalization | **of supplies** Bedarfsausgleich;
   ~ **account** *(Exchequer, Br.)* Subventionsfond; ~ **fee** Ausgleichsumlage; ~ **office** Ausgleichskasse; ~ **pay** Teuerungszulage; ~ **reserve** Ausgleichsrück-lage.

equalize *(v.)* **accounts** Konten ausgleichen.

equated abstract of account Staffelauszug.

equation | **of currency** Währungsausgleich; ~ **of supply and demand** Gesetz von Angebot und Nach-frage; ~ **of interest** Zinsstaffel; ~ **of payments** Fest-stellung des mittleren Zahlungstermins.

equilibrium | **of the balance of payments** Zahlungs-bilanzgleichgewicht;
   ~ **price** Wettbewerbspreis.

equip *(v.)* **a shop with tools** Betrieb installieren.

equipment Betriebs-, Geschäftseinrichtung, Gerät, Maschinenanlage, *(rolling stock)* Wagenpark;
   capital ~ Kapitalausrüstung, -ausstattung; **factory** ~ Betriebseinrichtung, -ausstattung; **idle** ~ nicht ausgenutzte Betriebsanlagen; **optional** ~ *(car)* Zu-satzausstattung;
   to replace worn-out ~ abgenutzte Anlagen er-setzen;
   ~ **lease** Maschinenmiete.

equitable | **assignment** [etwa] stille Abtretung; ~ **gar-nishment** Forderungspfändung; ~ **lien** Sicherungs-, Treuhandgut.

equities Dividendenpapiere, *(Br.)* Stammaktien;
   selected ~ ausgesuchte Anlagenwerte.

equity *(business interest)* Nettoanteil, *(capital)* Wert des Grundkapitals, Eigenkapital;
   ~ **of redemption** Hypothekenablösungsrecht;
   to build ~ *(contract system)* Eigenkapital an-sparen;
   to participate on an ~ **basis** sich kapitalmäßig be-teiligen; ~ **capital** Eigenkapital; ~ **dilution** Ver-wässerung des Eigenkapitals; ~ **financing** Kapital-

beschaffung durch Aktienausgabe; ~ **issue** Aktien-emission; ~ **market** Aktienmarkt; ~ **ratio** Eigen-kapitalkoeffizient.

equivalence of exchange Kurs-, Währungsparität.

erection cost Errichtungs-, Montagekosten.

erosion from inflation Inflationserosion.

error in addition Additionsfehler.

escalation price gleitender Preis.

escalator *(clause)* automatischer Ausgleich;
   ~ **clause** Wertsicherungs-, Gleit-, Indexklausel, *(prices)* gleitende Preisskala, Preisgleitklausel, *(wages)* Lohngleitklausel.

escape Unterhaltung, Entspannung;
   ~ **clause** Rücktrittsklausel; ~ **period** Rücktritts-frist.

escrow | **account** Treuhandkonto; ~ **department** Hinterlegungsabteilung einer Bank.

essential | **goods** lebenswichtige Güter; ~ **industry** kriegswichtiger Betrieb.

essentials lebenswichtige Güter.

establish *(v.)* gründen, etablieren, ansiedeln;
   ~ **o. s.** sich niederlassen (selbständig) machen;
   ~ **standard cost at a high level** Kosten hoch vor-kalkulieren; ~ **a domicile** Wohnsitz begründen.

established feststehend, *(employed)* fest angestellt;
   well- ~ **business** gut eingeführtes Geschäft; ~ **civil servant** *(Br.)* Planstelleninhaber; ~ **merchant** selb-ständiger Kaufmann; ~ **post** Planstelle; ~ **products** im Markt gut eingeführte Produkte.

establishment *(abode)* Niederlassung, fester Wohn-sitz, *(house of business)* [Geschäfts]unternehmen, Firma, Geschäft, Betrieb, Anlage, Etablissement, *(personnel)* Personalbestand, Planstelle, *(place in life)* Lebensstellung, Versorgung, Einkommen, Gehalt;
   on the ~ fest angestellt, in einer Planstelle;
   branch ~ Zweigbetrieb, -geschäft; **commercial** ~ gewerbliche Niederlassung; **industrial** ~ Industrie-unternehmen; **manufacturing** ~ Fabrikationsbe-trieb; **one-man** ~ Einmannbetrieb;;
   ~ **of a company** Gesellschaftsgründung; ~ **of a common customs tariff** Aufstellung eines gemein-samen Zolltarifs; ~ **of a partnership** Begründung eines Gesellschaftsverhältnisses;
   ~ **fund** Sozialversicherungsfonds.

estate *(assets)* Eigentum, [Gesamt]besitz, *(of bank-rupt)* Konkursmasse, *(landed property)* Grund-stück, Grund-, Landbesitz, Grundeigentum, Be-sitzung;
   ~ **brought in** eingebrachtes Gut; **industrial** ~ Kom-paktsiedlung; **personal** ~ Mobiliarvermögen; **real** ~ Immobilien, Liegenschaften; **separate** ~ Vorbe-haltsgut der Ehefrau, *(partner)* Sonder-, Privat-vermögen;
   ~ **from year to year** von Jahr zu Jahr verlängerte Pacht;
   to administer an ~ Nachlaß verwalten;
   ~ **agency** *(Br.)* Immobilienbüro; ~ **car** *(Br.)* Kom-biwagen; ~ **duty** *(Br.)* Erbschafts-, Nachlaßsteuer; ~ **tax** *(US)* Erbschafts-, Nachlaßsteuer.

Estimates, the Etat, Haushaltsplan.

estimate Vor-, Kosten[vor]anschlag, *(estimation)* Bewertung, [Ab]schätzung, Taxe;
building ~ Baukostenanschlag; **plant** ~s Betriebsbudget; **supplementary** ~s Haushaltsnachtrag;
~ **of income** Einkommenschätzung; ~ **of productiveness** Rentabilitätsberechnung;
~ *(v.)* [ab]schätzen, veranschlagen, bewerten;
~ **the productive capacity of land** Grundstück bonitieren; ~ **roughly** überschlagen;
to employ a more conservative ~ vorsichtige Kalkulation zugrunde legen.

estimated | **amount** Schätzungsbetrag; ~ **charges** Kostenvoranschlag; ~ **cost** Sollkosten.

estimating | **clerk** Kalkulator; ~ **cost system** Standardkostenrechnung.

European | **Free Trade Association** kleine Freihandelszone; ~ **Monetary Agreement** Europäisches Währungsabkommen; ~ **plan** *(US)* Zimmervermietung ohne Frühstück.

evacuation Evakuierung, [Betriebs]verlagerung.

evade | *(v.)* **one's creditors** sich seinen Gläubigern entziehen; ~ **customs duty** Zollhinterziehung begehen; ~ **paying taxes** sich von der Steuerzahlung drücken.

evaded income tax hinterzogene Einkommensteuer.

evaluate *(v.)* bewerten, abschätzen;
~ **on a hurry-up basis** Bewertung im Blitzverfahren vornehmen.

evasion, fiscal (tax) Steuerverkürzung, -umgehung.

even *(account)* schuldenfrei, ausgeglichen, *(stock exchange, Br.)* glatt;
~ *(v.)* **out** *(prices)* sich einpendeln; ~ **out fluctuations in earning power** Ertragsschwankungen ausgleichen; ~ **up** *(stock exchange)* glattstellen.;
to break ~ ohne Verlust arbeiten, Gewinnschwelle erreichen.

evening up *(odd lots)* Spitzenausgleich, *(US, stock exchange)* Glattstellung.

evict *(v.)* *(tenant)* Zwangsräumung betreiben.

eviction | **notice** Räumungsbefehl; ~ **proceedings** Räumungsverfahren.

ex | **all** ausschließlich aller [Dividenden]rechte; ~ **factory** ab Fabrik (Werk); ~ **interest** ohne Zinsen; ~ **quay** ab Kai; ~ **rights** ohne Bezugsrecht.

exact *(v.)* *(fees)* erheben, *(payments)* eintreiben;
to be ~ **in one's payments** pünktlich zahlen, pünktlicher Zahler sein;
to tender the ~ **amount** Nachschußsumme aufbringen; ~ **interest** Zinsen auf Basis von 365 Tagen.

exaction of taxes Steuereintreibung.

exaggerated | **demand** Übernachfrage; ~ **price** übersetzter Preis.

examination *(of accounts)* Revision, Nachrechnung, *(real-estate purchase)* Grundbucheinsicht;
competitive ~ Wettbewerb; **qualifying** ~ Fach-, Eignungsprüfung;
~ **of financial conditions** Prüfung der wirtschaftlichen Verhältnisse; ~ **of luggage** *(Br.)* Gepäckrevision.

examine *(v.)* | **the books** Bücher prüfen (revidieren); ~ **item by item** Punkt für Punkt durchgehen.

exceed *(v.)* **a prescribed amount** Limit überschreiten; ~ **in value** wertmäßig übertreffen.

exception *(document)* Vorbehaltsklausel, *(insurance contract)* Risikoausschluß;
~ **to classification** Tarifänderung;
to take ~ **to an audit report** Revisionsbericht beanstanden.

exceptional | **offer** Ausnahmeangebot; ~ **position** Vorzugsstellung; ~ **price** Sonderpreis; ~ **tariff** Ausnahmetarif.

excess | **of expenditure over revenues** Ausgaben-, Unkostenüberhang; ~ **of exports** Ausfuhrüberschuß; ~ **of purchasing power** Kaufkraftüberhang; ~ **of weight** Mehrgewicht;
to be in ~ **of the demand** Bedarf übersteigen;
~ **amount** überzahlter Betrag, Mehrbetrag; ~ **baggage** *(US)* Mehrgepäck; ~ **capacity** Überkapazität; ~ **deductions** Sonderfreibetrag; ~ **expenditure** Mehrausgaben; ~ **freight** Frachtzuschlag; ~ **hour** Überstunde; ~ **insurance** Selbstbehalt; ~ **loss insurance** Exzedentenrückversicherung; ~ **payment of income tax** Einkommensteuerüberzahlung; ~ **postage** Nachgebühr, Strafporto; ~ **profit** Wucher-, Über-, Kriegs-, Mehrgewinn; ~ **reserve** *(US)* außerordentliche Reserve; **to mop** ~ **spending power** überschüssige Kaufkraft abschöpfen; ~ **value** Mehrwert.

excessive | **in amount** zu hoch angesetzt;
~ **bail** überhöhte Kaution; ~ **boom** überhitzte Konjunktur; ~ **demand** Nachfrageüberhang; ~ **interest** Wucherzins[en].

exchange *(barter transaction)* Tauschgeschäft, -handel, *(currency)* Währung, Valuta, *(market)* Börse, *(of money)* Ein-, Umwechslung, *(rate of exchange)* [Wechsel]kurs, *(tel.)* Fernsprechamt;
at the ~ **of** zum Kurs von; **with** ~ *(US)* zuzüglich Einzugsspesen;
commercial ~ Warenbörse; **direct** ~ fester Umrechnungskurs; **domestic** ~ Inlandwechsel; **labour** ~ *(Br.)* Arbeitsamt; **nontaxable** ~ steuerfreier Majoritätskauf; **pegged** ~ gestützter Wechselkurs; **shipping** ~ Frachtenbörse; **stock** ~ Wertpapierbörse;
~ **of the day** Tageskurs; ~ **for forward (future) delivery** Devisentermingeschäft; ~ **without variation** keine Kursveränderungen;
~ *(v.)* [um]tauschen, ver-, austauschen, auswechseln, *(money)* [um]wechseln;
to be hammered on the ~ *(Br.)* für zahlungsunfähig erklärt werden;
~ **account** *(US)* Wechsel-, Valutakonto; ~ **accrual** Devisenzugänge; ~ **advice** Börsenbericht; ~ **allowance** Devisenzuteilung; ~ **bank** Devisenbank; ~ **board** Kursanzeigetafel; ~ **broker** Wechsel-, Börsen-, Kurs-, Devisenmakler; ~ **calculation** Kursberechnung; ~ **commission** Wechselprovision; ~ **commitments** Devisenengagements; ~ **dealer** *(Br.)* Devisenhändler; ~ **dealings** *(Br.)* Devisenhandel,

-geschäft; ~ **differene** Kursdifferenz, -spanne; ~ **embargo** Devisensperre; ~ **Equalization Account** *(Br.)* Währungsausgleichskonto; ~ **fee** Devisengebühr; ~ **fluctuations** Kursschwankungen; ~ **list** Kurszettel; ~ **market** Devisenmarkt; ~ **office** Wechselstube; ~ **premium** Agio; ~ **profit** Kursgewinn; ~ **floating** ~ **rates** bewegliche Wechselkurse; ~ **reserve** Devisenpolster; ~ **restrictions on payments and transfers** devisenrechtliche Beschränkungen; **foreign** ~ **risk** Kurs-, Währungsrisiko; ~ **telegram** Kursdepesche.

exchangeable goods Tauschprodukte.

Exchequer *(Br.)* Staatskasse, Fiskus, *(Ministry of Finance, Br.)* Schatzamt, Finanzministerium; ~ **aid** *(Br.)* staatliche Mittel; ~ **bonds** *(Br.)* langfristige Schatzanweisungen.

excisable [verbrauchs]steuerpflichtig, steuerbar.

excise indirekte Steuer, *(monopoly duty)* Monopolsteuer-, gebühr, *(tax on consumption)* Waren-, Verbrauchssteuer, Akzise; ~ **bond** Zolldurchlaßschein; ~ **licence** *(US)* Schankkonzession; ~ **office** *(Br.)* Regieverwaltung; ~ **tax** *(US)* Verbrauchsabgabe.

exclusion | **of benefits** *(social insurance)* Leistungsausschluß; ~**s from gross income** steuerfreie Einkünfte.

exclusive | **of costs** ausschließlich der Kosten; ~ **of packaging** Verpackung ausgenommen; ~ **agency** Alleinvertretung; ~ **agreement** Exklusivvertrag; ~ **dealing** Markenbindung; ~ **employment** einzige Beschäftigung; ~ **hotel** Hotel der Spitzenklasse; ~ **right** Exklusivrecht.

exclusivity stipulation *(Br.)* Konkurrenzverbot.

excursion Ausflug, Vergnügungsreise; ~ **ticket** Touristenkarte, Ferienbillet; ~ **train** Sonder-, Vergnügungs-, Ferienzug.

execute *(v.) (judgment)* vollstrecken, vollziehen; ~ **an order at best** Auftrag bestens ausführen; ~ **orders in listed securities on a commission basis** Effektengeschäfte auf Provisionsbasis durchführen.

executed sale Kauf mit Eigentumsübertragung.

executing creditor Vollstreckungsgläubiger.

execution Durch-, Ausführung, *(seizure)* Pfändung, [Zwangs]vollstreckung; **unsatisfied** ~ fruchtlose Pfändung; ~ **of an order** Auftragserledigung; ~ **of policy** Ausstellung eines Versicherungsscheines; **to be exempt from** ~ nicht der Zwangsvollstreckung unterliegen; ~ **creditor** Vollstreckungsgläubiger; ~ **debtor** Vollstreckungsschuldner.

executive *(US)* leitender Angestellter, Führungskraft; **fringe** ~ tantiemenberechtigte Führungskraft; **junior** ~ Nachwuchskraft; **top** ~ **appointment** Spitzenposition; ~~**class car** Auto für gehobene Ansprüche; ~ **compensation package** massierte Sondervergünstigungen für leitende Angestellte; ~ **department** Vorstandsressort;

top ~ **management** Unternehmensleitung *(US)* Vorstand einer AG; ~ **personnel** Führungskräfte; ~ **recruiter** Unternehmensberater; ~ **rotation** turnusmäßige Versetzung leitender Angestellter; ~ **shuffle** Umbesetzungen im Vorstand; ~ **trainee** Nachwuchskraft; ~ **work** leitende Tätigkeit.

exemplary damages Buße, Bußgeld.

exempt | **from charges** spesenfrei; ~ **from execution** pfändungsfrei, unpfändbar; ~ *(v.) o. s.* **from liability** sich freizeichnen; ~ **commodities** nicht unter den Tarif fallende Waren; ~ **property** pfändungsfreies Vermögen.

exempted amount Pfändungsfreibetrag.

exemption Befreiung, Ausnahme[stellung], Ausnahmeregelung, *(execution)* pfändungsfreier Betrag, Pfändungsfreibetrag *(income tax, US)* [Steuer-]freibetrag; **dependency** ~ *(US)* Steuerfreibetrag für Kinder; **flat** ~ *(US)* Pauschbetrag; **old-age** ~ *(US)* Altersfreibetrag; **withholding** ~ *(employee) (US)* Lohnsteuerfreibetrag; ~ **from [customs] duty** Abgaben-, Zollfreiheit; ~ **from liability** Haftungsausschluß; ~ **clause** *(Br.)* Freistellungsklausel; ~ **credit** *(US)* Steuerfreibetrag.

exercise | **of options** Ausübung des Prämienrechts, Optionsausübung; ~ *(v.)* **the right to subscribe to new stock** Bezugsrecht ausüben.

exhaust *(v.)* | **the land** Raubbau treiben; ~ **a quota** Kontingent erschöpfen.

exhausted *(policy)* abgelaufen, *(reserves)* erschöpft.

exhibit *(auditing)* Status, Vermögensverhältnisse, *(document)* Beweisstück, Beweismittel, Beleg, *(enclosure)* Anlage, Beilage, *(exhibited article)* Ausstellungsgegenstand; ~ *(v.)* **goods at a fair** Waren auf einer Messe ausstellen; ~ **large profits** große Gewinne ausweisen.

exhibited articles Ausstellungsgut, Messegüter.

exhibiting firm Aussteller.

exhibition Ausstellung, Schau, Messe, *(exhibit)* Ausstellungsobjekt; **export** ~ Exportausstellung, -messe; **industrial** ~ Industrie-, Gewerbeausstellung; ~ **of documents** Urkundenvorlage; **to stage an** ~ Ausstellung veranstalten; ~ **board** Messe-, Ausstellungsleitung; ~ **grounds** Messe-, Ausstellungsgelände; ~ **site** Messe-, Ausstellungsgelände; ~ **stand** Messe-, Ausstellungsstand.

exhibitor Aussteller, Messeteilnehmer.

exit permit Ausreiseerlaubnis.

exodus of capital Kapitalflucht.

exorbitant | **demand** (übertriebene) Forderung; ~ **price** Wucherpreis; ~ **rates** wucherische Zinssätze.

expansion Ausdehnung, Ausbreitung; **currency** ~ Vermehrung des Zahlungsmittelumlaufs; ~ **of assortment** Sortimentsausweitung; ~ **of credit** [übermäßige] Kreditausweitung; ~ **of machinery**

Vervollkommnung des Maschinenparks; ~ **in the money supply** Geldausweitung, -schöpfung; ~ **of sales** Umsatzausweitung;

~ **site** Expansionsgelände).

expectancy of life *(insurance)* Lebenserwartung, mutmaßliche Lebensdauer.

expectation of loss Verlustkalkulation.

expedited freight Expreßgut.

expend *(v.)* verwenden, auslegen, ausgeben.

expendable verbrauchbar, kurzlebig;

~ **package** verlorene Packung, Einwegpackung.

expenditure Ausgaben, [Kosten]aufwand, [Un]kosten, Spesen, *(laying out of money)* Ausgabe, Aufwendungen;

actual ~ Istausgabe; ~ **not budgeted for** außerplanmäßige Ausgaben; **capital** ~ Kapitalaufwand; **extraordinary and outside** ~ außerordentliche und betriebsfremde Aufwendungen; **nonrecurring** ~ einmalige Ausgaben; **professional** ~ Werbungskosten;

~ **to be charged to income** aus dem Erfolg zu deckende Aufwendungen; ~ **for repair** Instandsetzungskosten; ~ **for wages** Lohnaufwand;

tu cut ~ Ausgaben senken; **to plan one's** ~ sein Geld einteilen;

~ **ceiling** Ausgabenhöhe; ~ **rate** [höchstzulässiger Unkostensatz.

expense Ausgabe, Auslage, Aufwendungen, Spesen, **after (deducting)** ~s nach Abrechnung der Spesen; **at public** ~ auf Staatskosten; **free of** ~ kostenfrei; **involving** ~ mit Kosten verknüpft; **with out-of-pocket** ~ gegen Erstattung der baren Unkosten; **actual** ~s Barauslagen; **advanced** ~ Spesen-, Kostenvorschuß; **collection** ~ Inkassokosten; **delivery** ~s Zustellungs-, Versandkosten; **direct** ~ unmittelbarer Kostenaufwand; **factory overhead** ~ Fertigungsgemeinkosten; ~s **charged forward** gegen Nachnahme der Kosten; **overhead** ~s Geschäfts-, Handlungsunkosten; **prepaid** ~s*(balance sheet)* active Rechnungsabgrenzungsposten; **running** ~s *(car)* Unterhaltungskosten;

~ **in carrying on business** laufende Geschäftsunkosten; ~ **for management and administration** Betriebs- und Verwaltungskosten;

to allocate general ~s Gemeinkosten umlegen; **to allow s. o. his** ~s jem. seine Spesen ersetzen; **to break down** ~s [Un]kosten (Spesen) aufschlüsseln; **to cut down** ~s Unkostenetat (Spesenetat) kürzen; **to recover** ~s sich für den Betrag seiner Spesen erholen; **to run on** ~s *(car)* auf Geschäftskosten laufen;

~ **account** Spesen-, Aufwandkonto; ~ **allowance** Aufwandsentschädigung; ~ **budget** Spesenetat; ~ **prepayment** Spesenvorschuß; ~ **report** Spesenabrechnung.

experience, bad-debt Erfahrung mit faulen Schuldnern; **business** ~ Geschäftserfahrung, Routine;

~ *(v.)* **an advance** Kurssteigerung erfahren;

~ **rating** Leistungsbeurteilung; ~ **tables** Sterblichkeitstafeln.

expert Fachmann, Spezialist, Autorität; **among** ~s in Fachkreisen, in der Fachwelt;

~ **in contracting** Vergabeexperte; ~ **in handwriting** Schriftsachverständiger;

according to ~ **advice** nach dem Urteil des Sachverständigen; ~**'s report** fachmännisches Gutachten, Sachverständigenurteil; ~ **workman** Facharbeiter.

expiration Erlöschen, Verfall, Fälligwerden;

~ **of the period of notice** Ablauf der Kündigungsfrist; ~ **of free time** befristete Entladezeit;

~ **date** Verfalltermin; ~ **list** *(insurance)* Fälligkeitsliste.

expire Gültigkeit verlieren, verfallen.

expired *(ticket)* abgeknipst, ungültig;

~ **bill** fälliger Wechsel; ~ **cost** unnützer Kostenaufwand; ~ **licence** erloschene Konzession; ~ **policy** abgelaufene Police.

expiring date Verfalltstag.

expiry of period *(time)* Fristablauf.

exploit *(v.)* | **a mine** Bergwerk betreiben; ~ **a patent** Patent verwerten; ~ **the national resources of a country** Bodenschätze eines Landes ausbeuten.

exploitation, industrial industrielle Verwertung;

~ **of a country** Erschließung eines Landes; ~ **of a coal mine** Betrieb eines Bergwerks; ~ **of workers** Ausbeutung von Arbeitern;

~ **rights** Ausbeutungsrechte.

export Export, [Waren]ausfuhr, Exportgut;

capital ~ Kapitalausfuhr; **invisible** ~ unsichtbare Ausfuhr;

to produce for ~ für das Exportgeschäft herstellen; ~ **advertising** Exportwerbung; ~ **agent** Exportvertreter; ~ **authorization** Exportgenehmigung; ~ **bounty** Ausfuhrprämie; ~ **clearance** Ausfuhrabfertigung; ~ **clerk** Exportsachbearbeiter; ~ **credit guarantee** *(Br.)* Hermesbürgschaft; ~ **dealer** Exporthändler; ~ **duty** Ausfuhrabgabe; ~ **finance concern** Exportfinanzierungsgesellschaft; ~ **gold point** Goldausfuhrpunkt; ~ **incentives** Exportvergünstigungen; ~ **licence** Exportbewilligung; ~ **merchant** Exportkaufmann, -firma; ~ **order** Exportauftrag; ~ **promotion** Exportförderung; ~ **specification** *(Br.)* Ausfuhrerklärung; ~ **surplus** Export-, Ausfuhrüberschuß; ~ **trade** Aktivhandel; ~ **Trade Act** *(US)* Außenhandelsgesetz.

exported article Exportartikel.

exporting country Ausfuhr-, Exportland.

exposition *(US)* [Verkaufs]ausstellung.

exposure of goods for sale Freihalten von Waren.

express Eilbeförderung, Eilbrief, *(Br., messenger)* Eilbote, *(train)* Schnell-, Expreßzug; **limited** ~ *(US)* FD-(Fernschnell-)Zug;

~ *(v.)* **a letter** Brief per Eilboten schicken;

to travel ~ D-Zug benutzen;

railway ~ **agency** bahnamtlicher Rollfuhrdienst; ~ **bill of lading** *(Br.)* Eilgutladeschein; ~ **business** *(US)* Speditionsgewerbe, -geschäft; ~ **company** *(US)* Paketbeförderungsgesellschaft; ~ **delivery** *(Br.)* Eil-, Expreßzustellung; ~**delivery fee**

(Br.) Eilzustellgebühr; ~ **freight** *(US)* goods *(Br.)* Eilfracht, Eilgut; ~ **highway** *(US)* Schnellverkehrsstraße; ~ **letter** *(Br.)* Eilbrief; ~ **liner** *(US)* Schnelldampfer; **by** ~ **messenger** *(Br.)* durch Eilboten, expreß; ~ **money order** *(US)* telegrafische Geldüberweisung; ~ **train** D-(Expreß-) Zug.

expression of par values Paritätenfestsetzung.

expressway *(US)* Schnell[verkehrs]straße.

extend *(v.)* ausdehnen, ausbauen, *(shorthand)* [Kurzschrift] in Kurrentschrift übertragen; ~ **a balance** Saldo vortragen (übertragen); ~ **a bill of exchange** Wechsel prolongieren; ~ **an invoice** Rechnung spezifizieren; ~ **a passport** Paß verlängern; ~ **the protest** *(ship)* Verklarung ablegen; ~ **the statute of limitations** Verjährungsfrist verlängern.

extended | coverage *(fire insurance)* zusätzlicher Versicherungsschutz; ~**term policy** prolongierte Kurzversicherungspolice.

extension Erweiterung, Vergrößerung, *(to building)* An-, Erweiterungsbau, *(prolongation)* Verlängerung, Prolongation, *(tel.)* Nebenanschluß; ~ **of business** Geschäftsausweitung; ~ **of capacity** Kapazitätsausweitung; ~ **of working hours** Arbeitszeitverlängerung; ~ **of payment** Zahlungsaufschub; ~ **of time** Nachfrist; ~ **agreement** Prolongationsabkommen; ~ **night** verlängerte Polizeistunde.

extent *(of loan)* Höhe, *(valuation, Br.)* Abschätzung [von Land], Bewertung; ~ **of credit** Kredithöhe; ~ **of liability** Haftungsumfang; ~ **of taxation relief** Umfang der Steuervergünstigung; **to be liable to the** ~ **of one's property** mit seinem ganzen Vermögen haften.

external auswärtig, außenwirtschaftlich; ~ **account** Ausländerguthaben; ~ **aid** Auslandshilfe; ~ **assets** Auslandsvermögen; ~ **audit** außerbetriebliche Revision; ~ **commerce** Außenhandel; ~ **deficit** Passivsaldo der Zahlungsbilanz; ~ **economy** Außenwirtschaft; ~ **sales** *(balance sheet)* Fremdumsatz.

extinguishment of debts Schuldentilgung.

extort *(v.)* **fees** unstatthafte Gebühren erheben.

extortion Erpressung, *(extortionate charge)* Geldschneiderei, Wucher; ~ **in office** Amtsunterschlagung.

extra *(s. th. in addition)* Zugabe, *(charge added)* Zuschlag; ~**s** Nebengebühren, Neben-, Sonderausgaben; ~ **charge** [Sonder]zuschlag; ~ **charges** Nebenspesen, Nachforderung; ~ **discount** Sonder-, Extrarabatt; ~ **dividend** Zusatzdividende, Bonus; ~ **expense insurance** Betriebsstillstandsversicherung; ~ **fare** Zuschlag[skarte]; ~ **-hazardous employment** *(insurance)* besonders gefährliche Beschäftigung; ~ **hour** Überstunden; ~ **laydays** [Über]liegetage; ~ **luggage** *(Br.)* zuschlagspflichtiges Gepäck; ~ **postage** Nachporto, Portozuschlag; ~ **premium** Zusatzprämie; ~ **work** Überstundenarbeit.

extract of account Exzerpt, Konto-, Rechnungsauszug.

extraneous | expenses Fremdaufwendungen; ~ **income** Fremderträge.

extraordinary | general meeting *(Br.)* außerordentliche Hauptversammlung; ~ **income** außerordentliche Erträge, Fremderträge; ~ **reserve** Sonderrückstellung.

extravagant expenses übermäßiger Aufwand.

exurban shopping center *(US)* (centre, *Br.)* außerhalb der Stadt gelegenes Einkaufszentrum.

eye appeal (catcher) *(advertisement)* Blickfang.

F

fabricant Hersteller, Fabrikant.
fabricate *(v.) (build)* bauen, errichten, *(forge)* fälschen, *(manufacture)* verfertigen, fabrizieren, erzeugen, herstellen, anfertigen.
fabricated account gefälschte Rechnung.
fabricating parts Zulieferungsteile.
fabrication Fabrikation, Anfertigung, Herstellung; ~ **tax** Fabrikations-, Produktionssteuer.
fabulous wealth sagenhafter Reichtum.
face *(coin)* Bild-, Vorderseite, *(document)* Wortlaut, *(exact amount)* genauer Betrag, *(nominal amount)* Nennwert, -betrag, Nominalwert;
~ **of invoice** Rechnungsbetrag; ~ **of policy** Versicherungswert;
to be regular on its ~ *(check)* äußerlich in Ordnung sein;
~ **amount** *(instrument)* Nominal-, Nennbetrag; ~ **rate** *(loan)* Nettosatz; ~ **value** Nominal-, Nennwert.
facilitation of payments Zahlungserleichterungen.
facilities Erleichterungen, Fazilitäten;
credit ~ Kreditfazilitäten; **owned** ~ betriebseigene Fertigungsstätten; **productive** ~ Produktionseinrichtungen;
~ **of payment** Zahlungserleichterungen.
facing | matter *(advertising)* textanschließend; ~ **slip** *(US)* Aufklebezettel, Paketadresse.
facsimile | document Faksimileabschrift; ~ **signature** faksimilierte Unterschrift.
facts about turnover Umsatzangaben.
factor *(agent)* [Verkaufs]kommissionär, [Abschluß]agent, Handelsvertreter, *(manager)* Geschäftsführer, Disponent;
cost ~ Kostenfaktor;
~ **of merit** Gütefaktor;
~ *(v.)* als Verwalter tätig sein, *(consignment)* auf Kommissionsbasis verkaufen;
~ **one's accounts** sich Betriebsmittelkredit durch Debitorenabtretung beschaffen;
~'s **lien** [etwa] Sicherungsübereignung.
factorage Kommissions-, Provisionsgebühr.
factoring *(US)* Warenbevorschussung, Debitorenverkauf;
notification (old-line) ~ Forderungsankauf mit Anzeige an den Drittschuldner;
~ **system** *(US)* Absatzfinanzierungssystem.
factory Fabrikationsstätte, Fabrik[anlage], Werk-, Fertigungsanlage, *(trading station)* Faktorei, Handelsniederlassung;
[direct] from ~ *(US)* ab Fabrik (Werk);
nonoperating ~ stillgelegter Betrieb;
~ **at work** betriebsfertige Anlage;
~ **overhead account** Fertigungsgemeinkostenkonto; ~ **accounting** Betriebsbuchhaltung; ~ **Act** *(Br.)* Gewerbeordnung; ~ **canteen** [Betriebs]kantine; ~ **cost** Herstellungs-, Fertigungsgemeinkosten; ~ **council** *(Br.)* Betriebsrat; ~ **extension** Betriebser

weiterung; ~ **fleet** Fahrabteilung; ~ **inspection** Gewerbepolizei; ~ **inventory** Betriebsinventar; ~ **management** Betriebsleitung; ~ **manager** Betriebs-, Fabrikleiter; ~ **overheads** Fertigungsgemeinkosten; ~ **owner** Fabrikbesitzer; ~ **payroll** Betriebslohnliste; ~ **price** Preis ab Werk; ~ **production** Industrieproduktion; ~ **property** Betriebsgrundstück; ~ **regulations** gewerbepolizeiliche Anordnungen; ~ **rejects** Ausschußware; ~ **snackshop** *(US)* Werks-, Betriebskantine; ~ **worker** Fabrikarbeiter.
fail *(v.) (go bankrupt)* Zahlungen einstellen, Konkurs machen, *(harvest)* mißraten;
~ **in one's undertakings** mit seinen Unternehmungen Schiffbruch erleiden.
failing *(a.)* **circumstances** *(bank)* insolvent, zahlungsunfähig.
failure Fehlen, Mangel, *(bankruptcy)* Konkurs, Bankrott, *(insolvency)* Zahlungseinstellung;
~ **to meet the deadline** Fristüberschreitung; ~ **to meet one's engagements** schuldhafte Nichterfüllung; ~ **to pay a bill** Nichthonorierung eines Wechsels;
~ **rate** Ausfallrate.
fair Messe, Ausstellung, Jahrmarkt;
industries ~ Industrieausstellung; **outdoor** ~ Messe im Freigelände;
to attend a ~ Ausstellung (Messe) besuchen; **to exhibit goods at a** ~ Waren auf einer Messe ausstellen;
~ **attendance** Messebesuch; ~ **catalog(ue)** Messekatalog; ~ **dealer** Messebesucher; ~ **directory** Ausstellerverzeichnis; ~ **site** Ausstellungs-, Messegelände.
~ *(a.) (equitable)* reel, billig, gerecht, kulant, angemessen, *(favo(u)rable)* günstig, aussichtsreich;
~ **to middling** ziemlich gut bis mittelmäßig;
~ **average quality** Durchschnittsqualität; ~ **and reasonable compensation** angemessene Entschädigung; ~ **market value** üblicher Marktpreis; ~ **price** angemessener, (marktgerechter) Preis; ~ **trade** *(US)* Lauterkeit des Wettbewerbs; ~-**trade** preisbindungsmäßig; ~-**trade agreement** *(US)* Preisbindungsabkommen; ~ **cash market value** gemeiner Wert, üblicher Marktpreis.
fairgoer Messebesucher.
fake *(v.)* **a balance sheet** Bilanz fälschen (verschleiern, frisieren);
~ **check customer** *(US)* Scheckfälscher.
faked balance sheet gefälschte Bilanz.
fall Fallen, Sinken, Sturz, Rückgang *(stock exchange)* Kurssturz, -einbruch;
heavy ~ *(prices)* scharfer Rückgang;
~ **in the bank rate** Diskontsenkung; ~ **of the currency** Geldentwertung; ~ **in stocks** Weichen der Kurse; ~ **in the value of money** Geldwertverlust;

~ *(v.)* sich vermindern, abnehmen, fallen, sinken, *(prices)* stürzen;
~ **behind with one's payments** mit seinen Zahlungen in Rückstand geraten; ~ **within the budget** haushaltsrechtlich genehmigt sein; ~ **off in quality** in der Qualität nachlassen; ~ **short** knapp werden; **to be likely to** ~ *(prices)* zur Schwäche neigen; **to buy on a** ~ fixen;
~-**back pay** *(pieceworker)* garantierter Mindestlohn; ~-**off in the economy** Konjunkturabfall.

falling | **in sales** Absatz-, Umsatzrückgang;
~ **market** Baissemarkt; ~ **prices** weichende Kurse.
falling-off of orders Auftragsrückgang.

false falsch, *(sham)* nachgemacht, unecht;
~ **balance sheet** gefälschte (frisierte) Bilanz; ~ **coin** Falschgeld; ~ **papers** falsche Schiffspapiere; ~ **return** unrichtige Einkommensteuererklärung; ~ **weight** Fehlgewicht.

falsification | **of accounts** Bücherfälschung; ~ **of competition** Wettbewerbsverzerrung.

falsify *(v.)* **the accounts** Bücher fälschen.

family | **allowance** *(Br.)* Familienzuschlag, -beihilfe;
~ **brand** Dachmarke; ~ **business** Familienbetrieb;
to be ~ -**employed** als mithelfendes Familienmitglied tätig sein; ~ **industry** Hauswirtschaft; ~ **run concern** Familienunternehmen; ~ **settlement** *(Br.)* Erbauseinandersetzung; ~ **size** Groß-, Haushaltspackung.

fancy | **article** Mode-, Luxusartikel; ~ **goods** Galanterie-, Luxuswaren; ~ **price** Liebhaberpreis; ~ **stocks** *(US)* unsichere Spekulationspapiere.

fare Fahrgeld, -preis, Überfahrtsgeld;
airline ~ Flugpreis; **return** ~ Rückfahrschein; -fahrkarte; **round-trip excursion** ~**s** Ausflugstarif; ~ **hike** Fahrpreiserhöhung; ~ **stage** *(Br.)* Fahrpreiszone, Tarifgrenze, Teilstrecke.

farm landwirtschaftlicher Betrieb, Bauerngut.

faulty goods nicht einwandfreie Ware.

favo(u)r Gefälligkeit, Privileg, Vergünstigung;
~ *(v.)* **a creditor** Gläubiger begünstigen;
to balance in ~ **of s. o.** jem. gutschreiben; **to be out of** ~ aus der Mode gekommen sein.

favo(u)rable | **balance of trade** aktive Handelsbilanz;
~ **exchange rate** günstiger Umrechnungskurs; **specially** ~ **rate** Sondertarif.

favo(u)rite | **s** *(market)* Spitzenwerte;
~ **brand** bevorzugte Marke.

feasibility study Projekt-, Vorstudie.

featherbedding *(US, unionism)* Anstellung nicht benötigter Arbeitskräfte.

feature *(advertising)* Aufhänger, *(newspaper)* besonders aufgemachter Artikel;
~ *(v.)* **high-priced items** sich auf teure Qualitätserzeugnisse spezialisieren.

featured articles Sonderangebot.

federal | **bank account** *(US)* [etwa] Girokonto bei der Landeszentralbank; ~ **currency** *(US)* Landeswährung; ~ **funds** *(banking, US)* Zentralbankgeld; ~ **rediscount rate** *(US)* [etwa] Diskontsatz der Landeszentralbank; ~ **Reserve Bank** *(US)* [etwa] Lan-

deszentralbank; ~ **transfer tax** *(US)* Effektenumsatzsteuer.

Federation of British Industries [etwa] Arbeitgeberverband.

fee *(advertising)* Agenturvergütung; *(entrance money)* Eintrittsgeld, *(honorarium)* Honorar, Vergütung, Entgelt, *(sum payable to public officer)* [amtliche] Gebühr, Taxe;
liable to a ~ gebührenpflichtig;
attendance ~**s** Präsenzgeld; **author's** ~ Tantieme;
booking ~ Vormerkgebühr; **collection** ~ Inkassogebühr; **director's** ~ Aufsichtsratstantieme; **filing** ~**s** [Konkurs]anmeldegebühr; **flat** ~ Pauschalgebühr; **insurance** ~ Versicherungskosten; **late-letter** ~ Nachtzustellungsgebühr; **safe-custody** ~ Aufbewahrungsgebühr; **underwriting** ~ Übernahmespesen;
to draw one's ~**s** seine Tantiemen kassieren; **to pocket large** ~**s** große Honorare einstreichen;
~ **note** Gebührenberechnung; ~ **scale** Gebührenstaffel.

feeder *(railway)* Zubringerzug, *(road)* Zubringer;
~ **airport** Hilfsflugplatz; ~ **line** Zubringerlinie; ~ **plant** Zulieferungsbetrieb.

fellow | **board member** Vorstandskollege; ~ **drawer** Mitaussteller eines Wechsels; ~ **worker** Mitarbeiter, Berufskamerad, Kollege.

ferry Fähre, Fährschiff;
~ *(v.)* Fährdienst versehen;
~ **fare** Fährgeld; ~ **service** Fährbetrieb.

fetch *(v.)* **and carry** lediglich Handlanger sein.

fiat money *(US)* Papiergeld ohne Deckung.

fictitious fingiert, fiktiv, frei erfunden, *(assumed)* angenommen, *(counterfeit)* nachgemacht, unecht;
~ **assets** fiktive Vermögenswerte; ~ **bargain** Scheingeschäft; ~ **bill** *(Br.)* Kellerwechsel; ~ **profit** Scheingewinn; ~ **sale** Proformaverkauf; ~ **value** fiktiver Wert.

fidelity | **bond** Kaution gegen Veruntreuung; ~ **guarantee insurance** *(Br.)* Kautionsversicherung; ~ **insurance** *(US)* Kautions-, Garantieversicherung.

fiduciary *(a.)* treuhänderisch, anvertraut, *(notes)* fiduziär, ungedeckt;
~ **account** Treuhandkonto; ~ **agent** Treuhänder; ~ **bond** Kautionsverpflichtung; ~ **circulation** *(Br.)* ungedeckter Notenumlauf; ~ **debtor** Treunehmer; ~ **issue** *(Br.)* ungedeckte Notenausgabe; ~ **loan** ungedeckter Personalkredit; ~ **money** Giralgeld.

field [Fach]gebiet, Bereich, Arbeitsgebiet, *(market)* Absatzgebiet, Markt;
in the ~ im Außendienst;
coal ~ Kohlenrevier; **oil** ~ Ölvorkommen;
~ **of application** Anwendungsbereich; ~ **of business activity** geschäftlicher Tätigkeitsbereich;
to work in the ~ im Außendienst tätig sein;
~ **auditor** Außenbeamter der Revision; ~ **costs** Plazierungskosten eines Produkts; ~ **investigation** Umfrage, Marktforschung; ~ **investigator** Marktforscher, -befrager; ~ **manager** Gebietsverkaufs-

leiter; ~ **office** Außenstelle; ~ **sales manager**
Außenstellenleiter; ~ **survey** Absatz-, Marktforschung; ~ **warehouse** Außenlager; ~ **warehousing**
(US) Lagerung sicherungsübereigneter Waren.
fieldwork Außenarbeit, -dienst, -einsatz.
fieldworker Marktbefrager.
fighting brand Kampfmarke.
figure *(amount)* Betrag, Wert, *(number)* Zahl, Ziffer,
(pattern) Muster, *(price)* Preis;
  at the best ~ bestens;
  hard ~**s** zuverlässiges Zahlenmaterial; **released
  Board of Trade** ~**s** vom Handelsministerium veröffentlichte Ziffern; **revised** ~**s** bereinigte Zahlen;
  standard ~**s of distribution** Absatzkennzahlen;
  ~ *(v.)* **up the costs** Kosten veranschlagen (berechnen);
  to assess on ~**s** auf Zahlen basieren; **to buy at a low**
  ~ billig erwerben; **to run into three** ~**s** *(costs)* in die
  Hunderte gehen; **to run into five** ~**s** *(income)*
  fünfstellig sein;
  ~ **code** Zahlenkode, Telegraphenschlüssel.
figurehead Gal(l)ions-, Repräsentationsfigur.
file Aktenstück, -ordner, Sammelmappe, Ordner;
  for our ~**s** zu den Akten;
  card-index ~ Kartothek, Kartei; **credit** ~ Kredit-
  registratur; **dead** ~**s** abgelegte Akten; **tickler** ~
  Terminkalender;
  ~ *(v.)* zu den Akten nehmen, *(hand in)* einreichen,
  vorlegen;
  ~ **an application** Antrag einreichen; ~ **a bankruptcy
  petition** Konkursantrag stellen; ~ **letters in alphabetical order** Briefe alphabetisch ablegen; ~ **ih
  order of date** chronologisch ablegen; ~ **a plan**
  (bankruptcy) Vergleichsvorschlag machen; ~ **an
  incometax return** Einkommensteuererklärung abgeben; ~ **by subject matter** nach Sachgebieten ablegen;
  to place a report on one's ~ Bericht zu seinen Akten
  nehmen;
  ~ **cabinet** Aktenschrank; ~ **card** Kartei-, Karto-
  thekkarte, Ablage; ~ **cover** Aktendeckel; ~ **folder**
  Aktenhefter, -ordner; ~ **mark** Eingangsvermerk;
  ~ **number** Akten-, Geschäftszeichen; ~ **signal** Kartenreiter.
filing *(registration)* Anmeldung, Einreichen, Einreichung, Registrierung, [Akten]ablage;
  chronological ~ chronologische Ablage; **subject** ~
  Ablage nach Sachgebieten;
  ~ **of an application** Antragstellung; ~ **of bankruptcy
  petition** Einreichung des Konkursantrages; ~ **of
  claim** Forderungsanmeldung; ~ **of records** Akten-
  ablage;
  ~ **box** Karteikasten; ~ **cabinet** Kartothek, Kartei,
  Aktenschrank; ~ **jacket** Aktenhefter; **central** ~
  system Zentralregistratur.
fill | *(v.)* **an order** *(US)* Auftrag ausführen; ~ **a vacancy**
  Stelle besetzen.
fill in *(Br.)* | **a form carelessly** Formular flüchtig aus-
  füllen; ~ **a job** Stellung besetzen.
fill out a bill *(US)* Wechselformular ausfüllen.

fill-in reorder Lagerbestellung.
filled, orders ausgeführte Aufträge.
filler paper Ersatzeinlagen für Ringbuch.
filling | **of a contract** Auftragsabwicklung; ~ **of va-
  cancies** Neubesetzung erledigter Stellen;
  ~ **station** *(US)* Tankstelle.
film advertisement Filmwerbung, Kinoreklame.
final | **account** Abschlußrechnung; ~ **consumer** End-
  verbraucher; ~ **date for payment** äußerster Zahlungstermin; ~ **dividend** Schlußdividende, *(liquidation)* Schlußquote; ~ **instal(l)ment** letzte Rate; ~
  product Endprodukt; ~ **quotation** Schlußkurs; ~
  utility theory Grenznutzenlehre.
finance Finanzwirtschaft, Finanzen, Geldwesen;
  ~**s** Staatseinkünfte, -finanzen;
  disordered ~**s** zerrüttete Finanzverhältnisse; **sound**
  ~**s** gesunde Finanzgebarung;
  ~ *(v.)* Geldgeschäfte machen, finanzieren, Kapital
  beschaffen;
  ~ **away** *(US)* [Geld] verschieben; ~ **the costs of an
  undertaking** Geldmittel für ein Unternehmen zur
  Verfügung stellen; ~ **with short-term money** mit
  kurzfristigen Geldmitteln finanzieren;
  to jeopardize one's ~**s** seine Finanzlage gefährden;
  to put s. one's ~**s on a healthy basis** j. finanziell
  sanieren;
  ~ **bill** *(US, banking)* Finanzierungs-, Mobilisie-
  rungswechsel; ~ **charges** Finanzierungskosten;
  sales ~ **company** Absatzfinanzierungsgesellschaft;
  ~ **demand** Finanzbedarf; ~ **house** Finanzierungsinstitut; ^º **Ministry** Finanzministerium; ~ **office**
  (company) Finanzressort; ~ **stamp** Effektenstempel.
financial finanziell, fiskalisch, geldlich;
  ~ **accounting** Finanzbuchhaltung; ~ **agent** Fi-
  nanz-, Darlehensmakler; ~ **aid** finanzielle Hilfe; ~
  arrangement Finanzierungsplan; ~ **assets** Geld-
  vermögen; ~ **basis** Kapitalbasis; ~ **bond** Kaution;
  ~ **circumstances** Vermögensverhältnisse; ~ **column**
  (newspaper) Handels-, Wirtschaftsteil; ~ **controller** Leiter der Finanzabteilung; **to get (fall, run)
  into** ~ **difficulties** in Zahlungsschwierigkeiten geraten; ~ **drag** finanzielle Belastung; ~ **editor** *(US)*
  Wirtschaftsredakteur; ~ **embarrassment** Geldverlegenheit; ~ **forecasting** Beurteilung der finanziellen Entwicklung; ~ **gap** Finanzierungslücke; ~
  hardship finanzielle Misere; ~ **health** gesunde Finanzgebarung; ~ **investment** Geldmarktanlage; ~
  lease Maschinenpachtvertrag [ohne Wartung]; ~
  management Finanzplanung; ~ **market** Markt für
  Investitionspapiere; ~ **news** Börsenbericht; ~ **organization** Finanzierungsinstitut; ~ **page** *(newspaper)* Wirtschaftsteil; ~ **paper** Börsenblatt, *(US)*
  Gefälligkeitswechsel; ~ **performance** Finanzgebarung; **sound** ~ **position** Kapitalkraft; ~ **report**
  Bericht über die Vermögenslage; ~ **resources** Fi-
  nanzierungsquelle, Geldmittel; ^º **Secretary to the
  Treasury** *(Br.)* Staatssekretär für Finanzen; **to be
  in a poor (weak)** ~ **situation** finanziell schlecht gestellt sein; ~ **soundness** Solidität; ~ **specialist**
  Finanzfachmann; ~ **standing** Kapitalkraft, Boni-

tät; ~ **statement (status)** Status, Vermögensaufstellung; ~ **transaction** Finanztransaktion; **to slide into deep** ~ **troubles** in ernsthafte finanzielle Schwierigkeiten geraten; ~ **year** *(Br., private)* Geschäfts-, Bilanz-, Betriebs-, Wirtschaftsjahr, *(state, Br.)* Finanz-, Rechnungs-, Etatsjahr.

financially sound (strong) finanz-, kapitalkräftig; ~ **weak** finanz-, kapitalschwach.

financier Finanzmann, Geldgeber.

financing Finanzierung, Kapitalbeschaffenheit; **accounts receivable** ~ *(US)* Finanzierung durch Abhebung von Warenforderungen; **foreign-trade** ~ Außenhandelsfinanzierung; **long-term** ~ langfristige Finanzierung; **medium-range** ~ mittelfristige Finanzierung; **preliminary** ~ Vorfinanzierung;

to find favo(u)rable ~ günstige Finanzierungsmöglichkeiten beschaffen; **to switch** ~ sich anderweitig Finanzierungsrückhalt verschaffen;

~ **agency** Finanzierungsgesellschaft; **long-term** ~ **funds** langfristige Finanzierungsmittel; ~ **package** gebündeltes Finanzierungsangebot.

find *(v.)* | **for o. s.** sich selbst versorgen; ~ **the money** Geld beschaffen; ~ **a situation abroad** Stellung im Ausland finden.

finder Finder *(customs)* Zolldurchsucher; ~'s **fee** *(banking)* Maklerprovision; ~'s **reward** Finderlohn.

finding *(of lost property)* Fund; ~ **of capital** Kapitalbeschaffung.

fine Geldbuße, Reugeld, Strafsumme; ~ *(a.) (gold, silver)* fein, rein; **to be cut very** ~ *(price)* scharf kalkuliert sein; **to cut one's profit too** ~ zu niedrige Gewinnspanne haben; ~ **bank bill** erstklassiger Bankwechsel; ~ **papers** *(Br.)* prima Diskonten; ~ **work** Qualitätsarbeit.

finish Nach-, Fertigbearbeitung; ~ *(v.) (el., gas, water)* installieren, *(perfect)* fertig bearbeiten.

finished goods Fertigwaren, -erzeugnisse.

finishing *(manufacture)* Veredelung, Über-, Neu-, Verarbeitung, *(el., gas, water)* Installation, Installierung; ~ **industry** Veredelungsindustrie; ~ **mill** Fertigstraße; ~ **process** Veredelungsverfahren; ~ **product** Fertigerzeugnis.

fire, unfriendly *(insurance)* Schadenfeuer; ~ *(v.) (from service) (US sl.)* [feuern], herauswerfen, -schmeißen;

~ **company** *(Br.)* Feuerversicherungsanstalt, *(US)* Feuerwehr; ~ **insurance** Feuerversicherung, -assekuranz; ~ **insurance risk** Feuerversicherungsrisiko; ~ **office** *(Br.)* Feuerversicherungsanstalt, Brandkasse; ~-**resisting steel cabinet** feuerfester Stahlschrank.

firm Firma, Betrieb, Geschäft, Unternehmen, [Handels]haus, *(firm name)* Firmenname; **affiliated** ~ Zweigniederlassung; **dissolved (defunct)** ~ erloschene Firma; **import** ~ Importhaus;

old-established ~ alteingesessene Firma; **solid** ~ solides Geschäft; **spot** ~ Barzahlungsgeschäft; **world-renowned (universally known)** ~ Firma mit Weltruf;

~ **of builders and contractors** Bauunternehmen; ~ **of good repute** renommierte Firma; ~ **of stockbrokers** Maklerfirma, Börsenkommissionsgeschäft;

to enter a ~ **as partner** in einer Firma als Teilhaber eintreten;

~'s **assets** Geschäftsaktiva, Firmenvermögen; ~'s **capital** Geschäfts-, Firmenkapital; ~'s **debts** Gesellschaftsverbindlichkeiten; ~'s **name** Firmenname, -bezeichnung;

~ *(v.)* **up** *(stock exchange)* festliegen, anziehen; **to buy** ~ fest (auf feste Rechnung) kaufen; ~ **bargain** fester Abschluß; ~ **bid** *(dealer in securities)* festes Kaufgebot, Abnahmeverpflichtung; ~ **limit** feste Preisgrenze; ~ **market** feste Börse; ~ **order** Fixauftrag; ~ **quotation** *(stock exchange)* verbindliche Kursnotierung.

firmness in calls *(stock exchange)* Festigkeit der Sätze für tägliches Geld.

first | **of exchange** Primawechsel; ~ **board** *(stock exchange)* erste Kursnotierung; ~-**chop** *(Br.)* prima, erstklassig.

first-class erstklassig, ausgesucht; ~ **mail** *(US)* Briefpost; ~ **quality** Produkt erster Wahl; ~ **references** prima Referenzen.

first | **cost** An-, Einkaufs-, Selbstkostenpreis; ~-**hand** direktbezogen; ~-**in,** ~-**out** Zuerstentnahme der älteren Vorräte und Bilanzierung zum jeweiligen Buchwert; ~-**mortgage** erstrangig, -stellig; ~ **purchaser** Ersterwerber; ~ **quality** prima Qualität; ~-**rate firm** erstklassiges Unternehmen; ~ | **refusal** erstes Anrecht; ~ **right of purchase** Vorkaufsrecht; ~ **teller** Kassierer für Auszahlungen.

fiscal *(a.)* steuerlich, fiskalisch; ~ **agent** *(banking)* Zahlstelle; **to close its** ~ **books** Steuerabschluß machen; ~ **deficiencies** steuerpolitische Nachteile; ~ **earnings** zu versteuernde Einnahmen; ~ **evasion** *(Br.)* Steuerverkürzung, -umgehung; ~ **period** Geschäfts-, Rechnungsperiode, Steuerabschnitt; ~ **policy** steuerpolitische Maßnahmen, Steuer- und Geldpolitik; ~ **provisions** steuerrechtliche Vorschriften; ~ **year** *(US)* Geschäfts-, Rechnungs-, Finanz-, Haushalts-, Etatsjahr, *(Br.)* Steuerjahr.

fit *(a.)* **for acceptance** lieferfähig; ~ *(v.)* **o. s. for a post** sich die für eine Stellung notwendigen Kenntnisse verschaffen.

fitness for employment Arbeitsfähigkeit.

five | **and-dime store** *(US)* Einheitspreisgeschäft; ~-**figure income** fünfstelliges Einkommen; ~-**star hotel** Fünfsternehotel.

fix Klemme *(ship)* Besteckaufnahme; ~ *(v.)* **the budget** Etat aufstellen; ~ **damages** Entschädigung festsetzen; ~ **a deposit for two months** Guthaben für zwei Monate festlegen; ~ **the income**

tax Einkommensteuerrichtlinien erlassen; ~ **a price** Preis bestimmen; ~ **quotas for import** Einfuhrkontingente verteilen; ~ **the value of an entry (item)** Buchungsposten valutieren.

fixed unveränderlich, fest, festgelegt, *(bill of exchange, Br.)* ohne Respekttage;
to be well ~ *(US)* finanziell gut dran sein;
~ **allowance** Fixum; ~ **assets** Anlagevermögen; ~ **charges** Generalkosten, ~ **costs** feste Kosten; ~ **deposit** Festgeld; ~ **draft** Tratte ohne Respekttage; ~ **exchange** Mengennotierung; ~ **exchange rate** fester Wechselkurs; ~ **fund** *(US)* Investmentfonds mit feststehendem Portefeuille; ~-**interest bearing** festverzinslich; ~ **mortgage** Festgeldhypothek; ~ **parity** feste Parität; ~ **price** Festpreis; ~ **property** Liegenschaften; ~-**resale price** in der zweiten Hand gebundener Preis; ~ **shift** gleichbleibende Arbeitsschicht.

fixture feste Anlagen, Inventarstück, *(person)* Planstelleninhaber, *(time loan)* kurzfristiger Kredit.

flag, house Reedereiflagge;
~ **discrimination** unterschiedliche Anwendung des Zolltarifs.

flaring advertisement marktschreierische Werbung, sensationell aufgemachte Anzeige.

flash check *(US)* (cheque, *Br.)* ungedeckter Scheck.

flat *(Br.)* Etagen-, Mietwohnung, Appartement;
self-contained ~ abgeschlossene Mietwohnung;
~ **in the attic** Mansardenwohnung; ~ **in a quiet neighbo(u)rhood** ruhig gelegene Wohnung;
~ *(a.)* *(standard)* einheitlich, gleichmäßig, pauschal, *(stock exchange)* lustlos, flau, *(US, without interest)* franko;
to go ~ **with losing operations** Verlustgeschäft erleiden; **to loan stocks** ~ Wertpapiere zinslos lombardieren;
~ **broke** *(US sl.)* völlig pleite; ~ **catcher** Lockartikel; ~ **cost** Selbstkosten-, Gestehungspreis; ~ **exemption** *(US)* steuerlicher Pauschalfreibetrag; ~-**letting business** Vermietungsgeschäft; ~ **rate** Einheits-, Pauschalsatz, Kleinverbrauchertarif, *(el., US)* Grundgebühr, *(advertising)* Pauschal-, Anzeigenfestpreis; ~-**rate reduction** genereller Lohnsteuerfreibetrag.

flatness in advertising business Anzeigenflaute.

flattening of economic growth Abflachung der Wachstumskurve.

fleet, mercantile Handelsflotte;
~ **of trucks** [Last]kraftwagenpark;
~ **car** Geschäfts-, Betriebs-, Firmenwagen; ~ **insurance** *(automobiles)* Gruppenversicherung.

flexible | **currency** elastische Währung; ~ **exchange rate system** System flexibler Wechselkurse; ~ **fund** *(US)* Investmentfonds mit auswechselbarem Portefeuille; ~ **schedule** bewegliches Arbeitszeitprogramm; ~ **working hours scheme** gleitende Arbeitszeit.

flier *(leaflet, US)* Flugblatt, *(train)* Expresszug, *(US sl.)* Spekulationskauf eines Außenseiters.

flight *(distance covered)* Flugentfernung, -strecke, Fliegen, [Flug]reise;

commercial ~ Linienflug; **scheduled** ~ fahrplanmäßiger Flug;
~ **from taxation** Steuerflucht;
~ **cancellation** Flugstornierung; ~ **reservation** Flugplatzreservierung; ~ **seat number** reservierte Flugplatznummer.

flimsy Durchschlag[papier], Kopie.

flip-flop Umlegemappe.

float *(checks, coll.)* im Einzug befindliche Schecks;
~ *(v.)* umlaufen, *(give currency to)* in Umlauf bringen, *(put on the market)* auf den Markt bringen;
~ **a bond issue** Schuldverschreibungen ausgeben;
~ **a new business company** neue Gesellschaft gründen.

floater *(of company)* Gründer, *(insurance)* Pauschalversicherung;
commercial ~ *(US)* Reisegepäckversicherung;
~ **policy** Pauschalversicherung.

floating Finanzierung, *(exchange rate)* Wechselkursfreigabe, Freigabe der Wechselkurse;
bloc ~ Blockfloaten;
~ **of a company** Gesellschaftsgründung;
~ *(v.)* umlaufend, zirkulierend, *(debt)* schwebend, unfundiert;
~ **assets** Umlaufkapital, Betriebsmittel; ~ **cargo** schwimmende Fracht; ~ **debt** unfundierte Schuld; ~ **exchange rates** flexible Wechselkurse; ~ **policy** *(Br.)* *(fire insurance)* gleitende Neuwertversicherung; ~ **rates** freie Wechselkurse, *(ocean freight)* Seefrachsätze; ~ **trade** Seefrachthandel.

flood | **of demands** Konsumwelle;
~ *(v.)* **the market** Markt überschwemmen.

floor *(minimum of prices, US)* Mindestpreishöhe, *(stock exchange)* Börsensaal;
on the ~ in der Fabrikhalle, am Arbeitsplatz;
~ **broker** Börsenmakler; ~ **plan service** Autoabzahlungsgeschäft; ~ **price** Mindestpreis; ~ **trader** *(US)* auf eigene Rechnung spekulierendes Börsenmitglied.

floorwalker *(US)* Ladenaufsicht, Empfangschef.

flop *(sl.)* wirtschaftlicher Mißerfolg, Fiasko.

flotation Kapitalbesorgung, Inumlaufbringen, Begebung, *(of a loan)* Auflegung, Lancieren;
new capital ~s Neuemissionen.

flotsam and jetsam Strandgut.

flourish *(v.)* **goods** Ware im Schaufenster auslegen.

flow *(output)* Produktionsmenge, *(production)* Arbeitsablauf;
~ **of capital** Kapitalwanderung; ~ **of commodities** Warenverkehr; ~ **of tourists** Touristenstrom; ~ **of work** Arbeitsablauf;
~ *(v.)* **in (orders)** eingehen, hereinströmen;
~ **chart** Schaubild, Flugdiagramm; ~ **process chart** Arbeitsablaufbogen; ~ **system** Fließbandfertigung, Bandmontage.

fluctuating | **market** Marktschwankungen; ~ **market value** veränderlicher Markt-, Kurswert; ~ **quotations** schwankende Kurse.

fluctuation Schwanken, fluktuieren, Fluktuation;
~ **on bank accounts** Kontenumsätze; ~s **of currency**

Währungsschwankungen; ~s **of the discount rate** Diskontbewegungen; ~s **in the money market** Geldmarktschwankungen.

fluid | **assets** *(US)* Umlaufvermögen; ~ **savings** noch nicht wieder angelegte Ersparnisse.

flurry *(stock exchange)* kurzer Börsenauftrieb.

flush of money mit Geld wohl versehen.

fly *(v.)* **befor you buy** Produktionsaufträge erst nach positiv verlaufenen Modellversuchen erteilen; ~ **a kite** auf Gefälligkeitswechsel borgen; ~**-by-night corporation** *(US)* Unternehmen von zweifelhaftem Wert; ~ **sheet** Flugblatt.

flying | **exhibiton** Wanderausstellung; ~ **squadron** fliegende Arbeitskolonne.

foist *(v.)* **one's wares upon the public** seine schlechte Ware unter die Leute bringen.

fold *(v.)* *(Br.)* fallieren, bankrott werden, *(production)* einstellen; ~ **up** aus einem Geschäft aussteigen.

folder Aktendeckel, *(folded circular)* Broschüre.

follow *(v.)* **a trade** Gewerbe ausüben.

follow-on contract Anschlußauftrag.

follow-up *(advertising)* nachfassende Befragung, *(salesman)* nachfassende Tätigkeit; ~ **of orders** Terminüberwachung; ~ **advertising** Erinnerungswerbung; ~ **file** Wiedervorlagenmappe; ~ **letter** nachfassender Werbebrief; ~ **order** Anschlußauftrag.

food, frozen Tiefkühlkost; **to ration** ~ Lebensmittel rationieren, ~ **allowance** Verpflegungszulage; ~ **deficit area** Nahrungsmittelzuschußgebiet; ~ **industry** Nahrungsmittelindustrie; ~**-processing company** Lebensmittelverarbeitungsbetrieb, ~ **shortage** Nahrungsmittelknappheit.

foot | *(v.)* **a bill** *(US)* Rechnung bezahlen; **to have found its** ~ **again** *(market)* sich stabilisiert haben.

footing Kolonnadenaddition, *(entry money)* Einstandsgeld, *(sum total)* Gesamtsumme.

footloose industry standortungebundene Industrie.

forbearance Stundung, Nachsicht, Zahlungsaufschub; ~ **money** Verzugszinsen.

force *(employees)* Belegschaft; **main** ~ **of demand** Schwergewicht der Nachfrageentwicklung; ~ **of production** Produktivkräfte; ~ *(v.)* **down prices** Preise drücken; ~ **up** *(prices)* in die Höhe treiben.

forced | **agreement** Zwangsvergleich; ~ **currency** Zwangswährung; ~ **loan** Zwangsanleihe; ~ **quotations** fiktive Kurse; ~ **sale** Zwangsverkauf; ~ **savings** Zwangssparen.

forecast Vorhersage, Prognose; ~ *(v.)* **the course of a business** Konjunkturprognose vornehmen.

forecaster Konjunkturberater, -politiker.

forecasting Konjunkturprognose; **long-range** ~ Langfristprognose; ~ **sales** Absatzvorschau.

foreclose *(v.)* **on a mortgage** *(US)* aus einer Hypothek die Zwangsvollstreckung betreiben.

foreclosure Zwangsvollstreckung in das unbewegliche Vermögen; ~ **sale** *(US)* Zwangsversteigerung.

foredate *(v.)* voraus-, vordatieren.

foreign | **acceptance** Außengeltung; **for** ~ **account** für fremde Rechnung; ~ **affiliate** ausländische Tochtergesellschaft; ~ **aid** Auslandshilfe; ~**-aid program** *(US)* Auslandshilfsprogramm; ~ **assets** Devisen-, Fremdwerte; ~ **bill** [**of exchange**] Fremdwährungswechsel; ~ **coins and notes** [ausländische] Sorten; ~ **commerce** *(US)* Außenhandel; ~**-controlled** überfremdet; ~**-correspondence clerk** Auslandskorrespondent; ~ **credit balance** aktive Zahlungsbilanz; ~ **Credit Insurance Association** *(US)* [etwa] Hermesversicherungs AG; ~ **currency** Devisen, Fremdwährung; ~ **currency account** Devisen-, Währungskonto; ~ **debit balance** passive Zahlungsbilanz; ~ **debt** Auslandsverschuldung; ~ **deposits** Auslandsguthaben.

foreign exchange ausländischer Wechselkurs, Devisenkurs, *(money)* Devisen, Auslandsvaluten; **to apply for** ~ Devisen beantragen; ~ **allotments** Devisenzuteilung; ~ **allowance** Devisenfreibetrag; ~ **bank** Devisenbank; ~ **bill** Fremdwährungswechsel; ~ **broker** Devisenmakler; ~ **control** *(US)* Devisenbewirtschaftung; ~ **equalization fund** Devisenausgleichsfonds ~ **guaranty** Kurssicherung; ~ **list** *(US)* Devisenkurszettel; ~ **rates** Devisenkurse; ~ **regulations** Devisenbewirtschaftungsvorschriften; ~ **reserves** Devisenreserven; ~ **shortage** Devisenknappheit; ~ **transaction** Devisengeschäft.

foreign | **-going ship (vessel)** Schiff auf großer Fahrt; ~ **interests** ausländische Beteiligungen; ~ **labo(u)r** Fremdarbeiter; ~ **loan** Auslandsanleihe; ~ **make** Auslandsfabrikat; ~ **market** Markt der Auslandswerte; ~ **money department** Sortenabteilung; ~ **money order** internationale Postanweisung; ~ **notes** Sorten; ~ **postal money order** Auslandspostanweisung; ~ **quota** Devisenkontingent; ~ **sector** Außenwirtschaftsbereich.

foreign trade Außen-, Auslandshandel; Außenwirtschaft; ~ **agency** Außenhandelsstelle; ~ **zone** *(US)* Zollausschlußgebiet, Freihandelszone.

foreigners *(stock exchange)* Auslandswerte.

foreman Vorarbeiter, Werkmeister, -führer.

forestall *(v.)* **the market** durch Ankauf den Markt beherrschen.

forestalling produktionsorientierte Wirtschaftspolitik; ~ **the market** Aufkaufen.

forfeit Reugeld, Vertragsstrafe; ~ *(v.)* *(confiscate)* einziehen, konfiszieren; ~ **a bond** Kaution verfallen lassen; ~ **the right to a pension** Ruhegehaltsanspruch verlieren; ~ **shares** Aktienanteile kaduzieren; ~ **money** Reugeld, Abstandssumme.

forfeiture Konfiskation, Vermögenseinziehung, *(fine)* Buße, Einbüßung, Geldstrafe;
~ **of bond** Pfandverwirkung; ~ **of one's property** Vermögenseinziehung, -konfiskation; ~ **of shares for the failure of paying a call** Kaduzierung von Aktien.

forge *(v.)* falschmünzen;
~ **ahead** *(stock exchange)* Führung übernehmen;
~ **ahead 13 points to 567** um 13 Punkte auf 567 steigen.

forged | **money** Falschgeld; **to put** ~ **notes into circulation** Falschgeld in Umlauf setzen.

forger of bank notes Banknotenfälscher.

forgery | **of bills** Wechselfälschung;
~ **insurance** Versicherung gegen Scheckfälschung.

form *(bidding)* Angebotsblankett, -formular, *(document with blanks)* Formular, Formblatt, Vordruck;
application ~ Bewerbungsformular; **blank** ~ Formvordruck; **income-tax** ~ Einkommensteuerformular; **listing** ~ *(banking)* Sammelaufgabeformular; ~ **of payment** Zahlungsmodus; ~ **of statement** Bewertungsformular; ~ **of tender** Submissionsbogen; ~*(v.)* **a company** *(Br.)* Gesellschaft gründen; ~**s close** *(Br., advertising)* Anzeigenschluß; ~ **letter** Muster-, Standard-, Formularbrief.

formal requirements Formvorschriften.

formalities, customs Zollformalitäten.

formation Gründung, Errichtung;
~ **of cartels** Kartellbildung; ~ **of a company (corporation)** Gesellschaftsgründung; ~ **of prices** Preisbildung.

formula, price Preisformel.

fortnightly | *(Br.)* **bill** Mediowechsel; ~ **loans** Mediogeld; ~ **settlement** Medioabrechnung.

fortune *(property)* Vermögen, Mittel;
to come into (inherit) a ~ reiche Erbschaft machen; **to spend a** ~ **over one's business** enorm viel Geld in sein Geschäft stecken;
~ **sheet** Aufstiegsmöglichkeitstabelle.

forward *(stock exchange)* auf Ziel (Zeit);
balance carried ~ Saldovortrag; **please** ~ bitte nachsenden;
~ *(v.)* absenden, befördern, versenden, nachsenden;
~ **by express train** als Eilgut befördern; ~ **goods to a customer** Kunden beliefern;
to buy ~ auf Lieferung (Zeit) kaufen; **to date a check** *(US)* **(cheque,** *Br.)* ~ Scheck vordatieren;
~ **business** *(stock exchange)* Termingeschäft; ~ **cover** Kurssicherung; ~ **deal** *(Br.)* Zeit-, Termingeschäft; ~ **dollar** Termindollar; ~ **exchange** Devisenterminhandel; ~ **exchange rate** Devisenterminkurs; ~ **quotation** Terminnotierung; ~ **securities** Terminwerte, -papiere; ~ **transaction** Zeit-, Termingeschäft.

forwarded telegram nachgesandtes Telegramm.

forwarder [Ab]sender, Spediteur;
freight ~ Güterexpedition.

forwarding Versendung, Verschickung, Absendung, Übersendung, Versand, Expedition, Spedition;
~ **advice** Versandanzeige; ~ **agency** *(US)* Speditions-, Versandgeschäft; ~ **agent** Spediteur; ~ **charges** Versandspesen, Speditionsgebühren; ~ **clerk** Expedient; ~ **department** Expeditionsabteilung; ~ **expenses** Versandspesen, Speditionsgebühren; ~ **firm** Speditionsgeschäft; ~ **instructions** Versandvorschriften; ~ **note** Frachtbrief; ~ **office** Speditionsbüro, Abfertigungsstelle.

foul bill of lading einschränkendes Konnossement.

found *(US)* incl. Unterkunft und Verpflegung;
~ *(v.)* **a fortune** Grundlage für ein Vermögen legen.

foundation Gründung, [Firmen]errichtung, *(endowed institution)* Anstalt, Stiftung;
charitable ~ milde Stiftung;
to lay the ~**s of a business** Geschäftsvoraussetzungen schaffen.

founder member Gründungsmitglied.

founder's shares (stocks) Gründeraktien, -anteile.

fourth | **[bill] of exchange** Quartalswechsel; ~**-class matter** *(US)* Warensendungen, Paketpost.

fractional | **amount** Bruchteil; ~ **bond** Teilschuldverschreibung; ~ **changes** *(stock exchange)* geringfügige Veränderungen; ~ **coin** Scheidemünze; ~ **lot** *(US fam.)* nicht offiziell an der Börse gehandelte Abschnitte; ~ **reserves** *(banking)* vorgeschriebene Mindestreserven; ~ **share** kleingestückelte Aktie.

franchise *(sole agency, US)* Alleinverkaufsrecht, *(Br., insurance)* Mindestgrenze, Selbstbehalt, *(licensing, US)* Lizenz[vergabe], *(privilege)* Vorrecht, Sonderstellung, Konzession;
~ **agent** *(US)* Lizenzvertreter; ~ **broker** *(US)* Lizenzmakler; ~ **dealer** *(US)* Lizenznehmer; ~ **operation** *(US)* Lizenzvertretung; **to supply** ~ **service** *(US)* Dienste einer Generalvertretung zur Verfügung stellen; ~ **tax** *(US)* Konzessionssteuer.

franchisee *(US)* Konzessions-, Lizenznehmer.

franchiser *(US)* Lizenz-, Konzessionsvergeber.

franchising *(US)* Lizenz-, Konzessionserteilung.

frank *(v.)* freimachen, portofrei machen.

franking | **machine** Freimachungs-, Frankiermaschine; ~ **privilege** *(US)* frei durch Ablösung.

fraternal insurance *(US)* Sterbekasse.

fraudulent | **alienation** Vollstreckungsvereitelung; ~ **balance sheet** gefälschte Bilanz; ~ **bankruptcy** betrügerischer Bankrott; ~ **conveyance** Gläubigerbenachteiligung; ~ **entry** Falschbuchung.

free frei, selbständig, unabhängig, *(without cost)* frei, kostenlos;
carriage ~ Fracht bezahlt; **duty-** ~ zollfrei; ~ **from breakage** bruchfrei; ~ **of debt** schuldenfrei; ~ **of all average** nicht gegen große und besondere Havarie versichert; ~ **of capture and seizure** Beschlagnahmerisiko ausgeschlossen; ~ **of charge and postage paid** gratis und franko; ~ **of commission** provisionsfrei; ~ **to the door** frei Haus; ~ **in and out stowed** frei ein und aus und gestaut; ~ **on board (fob)** fob, franko Bord, frei Schiff, *(US)* **on truck** *(Br.)* frei Eisenbahn; ~ **station** bahnfrei; ~ **on truck** *(Br.)* frei LKW ab Lager;

~ *(v.)* **rationed goods** bewirtschaftete Ware freigeben;
to be ~ **with one's money** nicht so genau rechnen, großzügig wirtschaften;
~ **accommodation** freie Wohnung; ~ **allowance** Freigepäck; ~ **balance** unverzinstes Guthaben; ~-**of-capture-and-seizure clause** Aufbringungs- und Beschlagnahmeklausel; ~ **currency** frei konvertierbare Währung; ~-**currency country** nicht devisenbewirtschaftetes Land; ~-**enterprise system** freie marktwirtschaft; ~-**for-all** offener Wettbewerb; ~ **gift** Werbegeschenk, Zugabe; ~ **goods** zollfreie Waren; ~ **items** *(US)* spesenfreie Inkassi; ~-**lance** *(a.)* freiberuflich; ~ **list** Freiliste [zollfreier Gegenstände], Zollfrei-, Liberalisierungsliste; ~ -**market economy** freie Marktwirtschaft; ~-**market price** Freiverkehrskurs; ~ **movement** Freizügigkeit; ~-**port area** Freihafengebiet; ~ **puff** *(Br.)* kostenlose redaktionelle Werbung; ~ **share** Gratisaktie; ~ **ticket** Freifahr-, Freikarte; ~ **trade** Freihandel, zollfreier Verkehr, ~-**trade area** Freihandelszone; ~ **trial** kostenlose Warenprobe.
freedom | of association Koalitionsfreiheit; ~ **of competition** Wettbewerbsfreiheit; ~ **of exchange operations** freier Devisenverkehr; ~ **of price formation** freie Preisbildung; ~ **of trade** Gewerbefreiheit.
freehold | flat Eigentumswohnung; ~-**land society** *(Br.)* Parzellierungsgesellschaft.
freeway *(US)* plankreuzungsfreie Fernverkehrsstraße, Autobahn.
freeze | on pay and prices Lohn- und Preisstopp; ~ **on wages** Lohnstopp;
~ *(v.)* *(accounts)* einfrieren, blockieren, sperren, *(vurtail civilian use)* rationieren, *(prices)* auf bestimmter Höhe halten, *(wages)* gesetzlich festlegen;
~ **action on a merger** Fusionsbeschluß inhibieren; **to put a** ~ **on hirings** Einstellungsstopp verfügen.
freezing | of payments Stornierung von Zahlungen; ~ **of prices** *(US)* Preisstopp; ~ **of foreign property** Einfrierung ausländischer Guthaben.
freight *(cargo)* Schiffsladung, (~ *line)* Frachtlinie, *(load)* Fracht, Ladung, *(tonnage)* Frachtraum, Laderaum, *(transport charges)* Frachtkosten, Fuhrlohn;
by ~ *(US)* per Frachtgut (Eisenbahn); **free of** ~ **and duty** frachtfrei verzollt;
additional ~ Frachtaufschlag; **advance[d]** Frachtvorschuß; **carload** ~ *(US)* Sammelfracht; **dead** ~ Fehl-, Fautfracht; **less-than-carload** ~ *(US)* Stückgut[sendungen]; **ocean** ~ Transatlantikfracht; **original** ~ Vorfracht; ~ **outward and home** Hin- und Herfracht; **perishable** ~ leicht verderbliches Frachtgut; **phantom** ~ Transportkosten;
~ **and carriage** *(Br.)* See- und Landfracht; ~ **and charges prepaid** fracht- und spesenfrei; ~ **pro rata** Distanzfracht;
~ *(v.)* befrachten, in Fracht nehmen, beladen, *(transport, US)* verfrachten, als Frachtgut befördern;

~ **by parcels** Stückgüter laden; ~ **out a ship** Schiff verchartern; ~ **through** durchfrachten;
to book ~ Frachtraum belegen;
~ **absorption** Frachtnachlaß; ~ **agency** *(US)* Güterabfertigungsstelle; ~ **agent** *(US)* Frachtspediteur; ~ **bill** *(US)* Frachtbrief; ~ **broking** Frachtmaklergeschäft; ~-**car shortage** *(US)* Waggonknappheit; ~ **clerk** Speditionsangestellter; ~ **container** Transportbehälter; ~ **density** Verkehrsdichte im Güterfernverkehr; ~ **depot** *(US)* Güterbahnhof; ~ **equalization** *(US)* Frachtausgleich; ~ **list** *(US)* Kontenzettel, Ladungsverzeichnis, Frachtbrief; ~ **mileage** nach Kilometern berechneter Frachttarif; ~ **note** *(Br.)* Frachtrechnung, -brief; ~ **office** *(US)* Güterausgabe, -abfertigung; ~ **rate** Fracht-, Gütertarif; **[long-distance]** ~ **traffic** *(US)* Güter[fern]verkehr; **by fast** ~ **train** *(US)* Schnellgüterzug; ~ **wagon** *(US)* Güterwagen, Waggon; ~ **warrant** *(US)* Frachtbrief; ~ **yard** *(US)* Güterbahnhof.
freighter Verlader, Verfrachter, *(aeroplane)* Frachtflugzeug, *(cargo steamer)* Frachtschiff.
freighting Befrachtung;
~ **by the case** Stückgutbefrachtung; ~ **on measurement** Maßfracht.
frequency *(trains)* Verkehrshäufigkeit, Dichte;
~ **of loss** Schadenshäufigkeit;
~ **discount** Mengenrabatt.
frequent *(v.)* **fairs** Messen besuchen, Märkte beziehen;
~ **customer** Dauerkunde.
fresh | apprentice unerfahrener Lehrling; ~ **demand** erneute Kauflust.
frictional unemployment Fluktuationsarbeitslosigkeit.
friendly society *(Br.)* Versicherungsverein auf Gegenseitigkeit, Hilfskasse.
frills Extras, *(US, insurance)* neuartige Versicherungsleistungen.
fringe[s *(employees)* zusätzliche Sozialaufwendungen, Nebenleistungen;
~ **benefits** lohnunabhängige Einkommensteile, *(US, director)* Aufwandsentschädigungen, Gewinnbeteiligung, *(pension provision)* Pensionsleistung, *(wage earner, US)* Lohnneben-, Sozialleistungen.
front *(individual representing company)* Aushängeschild, Strohmann, nomineller Vertreter;
to show a bold ~ *(stock exchange)* feste Haltung zeigen;
~-**end load** hohe Anfangsbelastung.
frozen *(account)* eingefroren, blockiert, gesperrt, *(not liquid)* nicht flüssig, *(price)* preisgebunden;
~ **capital** festliegendes Kapital; ~ **cargo** Gefrierladung; ~ **debts** Stillhalteschulden; ~ **inventory** unabsetzbares Lager; ~ **price** eingefrorener Preis, Stoppreis.
fuel Brennstoff, Betriebs-, Kraft-, Treibstoff;
~ *(v.)* tanken, *(ship)* bunkern;
~ **allocation** Benzinzuteilung; ~ **consumption** Brennstoffverbrauch; ~ **supply** Treibstoffversorgung.

fulfil, fulfill *(US)* *(v.)* a contract Vertrag erfüllen.
fulfilment of a contract Vertragserfüllung.
full voll, ganz, völlig, vollständig, *(hotel)* besetzt;
  payment in ~ zum Ausgleich aller Forderungen;
  to receipt in ~ per Saldo quittieren;
  ~ **age** Mündigkeit, Volljährigkeit; ~ **board** *(Br.)*
  Vollpension; **~-cost principle** Vollkostenrech-
  nung; ~ **economic price** nicht subventionierter
  Preis; ~ **employment** Vollbeschäftigung; ~ **indorsement** Vollgiro; **~-line department** reichlich sorti-
  mentiertes Warenhaus; ~ **lot** *(US)* [Börsen]ab-
  schlußeinheit; **~-page advertisement** ganzseitige
  Anzeige; **to be retired on** ~ **pay** mit vollen Bezügen
  pensioniert werden; ~ **position** *(advertising)* bevorzugte Placierung; ~ **rates of custom duties** allgemeiner Zolltarif; ~ **set** *(bill of lading)* vollständiger Formularsatz.
full-time hauptamtlich, -beruflich, ganztätig;
  to run ~ im Schichtbetrieb laufen;
  to employ on a ~ **basis** ganztägig beschäftigen; ~
  job ganztägige Beschäftigung.
full timer ganztägig Beschäftigter.
fully paid shares voll eingezahlte Aktien.
functional amtlich, *(statistics)* repräsentativ;
  ~ **building** Zweckbau; ~ **classification** Gliederung
  nach Sachgebieten; ~ **depreciation** Abschreibung
  auf Rationalisierungsinvestitionen; ~ **discount**
  Funktions-, Händlerrabatt; ~ **wholesaler** Engros-
  vertreter.
fund [flüssiges] Kapital, Geldsumme, *(capital stock)*
  Grund-, Stamm-, Betriebskapital einer Bank, *(investment company)* Anlagefonds, *(money set apart)*
  Fonds, zweckgebundene Vermögensmasse, [Son-
  der]vermögen;
  ~ **aid** ~**s** Hilfsgelder; **cash-heavy** ~ liquider Fonds;
  closed-end ~ Investmentfonds mit begrenzter
  Emissionshöhe; **consolidated** ~ konsolidierte
  Staatsschuld; **cumulative** ~ thesaurierender
  Fonds; **depreciation** ~ Abschreibungsreserve;
  employees' pension ~ Pensionsfonds für Angestellte; **fixed** ~ Investmentfonds mit feststehendem
  Portefeuille; **flexible** ~ Investmentfonds mit wech-
  selbarem Portefeuille; **general revenue** ~ Kom-
  munalvermögen; **managed** ~ Investmentfonds mit
  veränderlichem Portefeuille; **old-age pension** ~
  Pensionskasse; **open-end** ~ Investmentfonds mit
  beliebiger Investitionshöhe; **operating** ~ Betriebsmittel; **provident** ~ Unterstützungsfonds; **sick-
  benefit** ~ Betriebskrankenkasse; **sinking** ~ Amortisationsfonds; **unemployment** ~ [etwa]Sonderver-
  mögen der Bundesanstalt für Arbeitslosenversicherung;
  ~ *(v.)* *(convent floating debt, Br.)* [schwebende
  Schuld] fundieren, konsolidieren, kapitalisieren;
  (invest in funds, Br.) Geld in Staatspapieren anlegen;
  ~ **interest arrears** Zinsrückstände kapitalisieren;
  to run a hot ~ Topf heißen Geldes verwalten;
  ~ **administration** *(investment fund)* Vermögensverwaltung; ~ **decision** *(investment trust)* Anlageent-

scheidung; ~ **manager** Vermögensverwalter; ~
  money *(investment fund)* Anlagekapital; ~ **raiser**
  Mittelaufbringer; **to launch a** ~**-raising drive** große
  Sammelaktion starten; **sinking-~ tax** Anleihe-
  steuer.
funds *(Br.)* Staatspapiere, *(pecuniary resources)*
  [Geld]mittel, Gelder, Finanzmittel, Kapital[ien].
  for lack of ~ mangels Barmittel; **without** ~ **in hand**
  ohne Deckung;
  consolidated ~ *(Br.)* fundierte Staatsschuld, Konsols; **earmarked** ~ zweckbestimmte Mittel; **employed** ~ Betriebsvermögen; **insufficient** ~ *(banking)* ungenügende Deckung; **original** ~ Stammkapital; **trust** ~ Treuhandvermögen; **unapplied** ~
  [unappropriated] ~ nicht verwendete (verteilte)
  Mittel;
  ~ **at disposal** verfügbare Mittel;
  to be in ~ flüssig (bei Kasse) sein, *(bank)* zahlungsfähig sein, *(firm)* kapitalkräftig sein; **to buy** ~
  Renten[werte] kaufen; **to deposit** ~ **with a trustee**
  Beträge für die Pensionskasse zurückstellen; **to
  funnel** ~ **to one's own use** Vermögen für seine pri-
  vaten Zwecke mißbrauchen; **to have DM 10 000 in**
  ~ 10 000,— DM in Staatspapieren angelegt haben;
  to make a call for ~ Kapitalerhöhung vornehmen;
  to provide with ~ für Deckung sorgen; **to vote the**
  ~ Haushaltsmittel bewilligen;
  sufficient-~ clause *(banking)* Guthabenklausel;
  ~ **statement** Vermögensnachweis, Bewegungsbilanz, Finanzflußrechnung.
funded verzinslich angelegt, *(capitalized)* kapitali-
  siert, *(converted into permanent debt)* fundiert;
  long-term ~ **capital** langfristig angelegte Gelder;
  ~ **debt (indebtedness)** *(Br.)* langfristige Anleiheschuld.
fundholder Fondsbesitzer, Rentier.
funding Schuldenkonsolidierung, *(investing)* Anlage
  in Staatspapieren;
  ~ **loan** Konsolidierungsanleihe.
funeral allowance Sterbegeld.
furnish *(v.)* einrichten, versehen mit, *(provide)* versorgen, [be]liefern, ver-, beschaffen;
  ~ **s. o. with cover (funds)** jem. Deckung zur Verfügung stellen; ~ **a bill with stamps** Wechsel verstempeln.
furnished apartment möbliertes Zimmer.
furnishings and fixtures Inventar, Mobiliar und Zubehör.
furniture and office equipment Büroeinrichtung.
further | **to our letter of yesterday** im Nachgang zu
  unserem gestrigen Schreiben; ~ **signature required**
  (bill, check) zweite Unterschrift fehlt.
future |s *(US)* Termingeschäfte, -handel, Liefe-
  rungskäufe;
  commodity ~s *(US)* Warentermingeschäfte;
  ~s contract *(US)* Termingeschäft, Lieferungsvertrag; **to soll for** ~ **delivery** auf Termin verkaufen;
  ~s exchange *(US)* Devisenterminhandel; **~s market** *(US)* Terminmarkt; **~s purchase** *(US)* Terminkauf; **~s rate** *(US)* Kurs für Devisenterminge-
  schäfte, Terminsatz.

G

gain Gewinn, Ertrag, Überschuß, Vorteil;
for purpose of ~ zu Gewinnzwecken; **with the object of** ~ in gewinnsüchtiger Absicht;
~s *(emoluments, US)* Einkommen, Verdienst, Einkünfte, *(stock exchange)* [Kurs]gewinn;
ceasing ~ entgangener Gewinn; **clear** ~ Netto-, Reingewinn; **taxable** ~ besteuerungsfähiger Gewinn;
~ **in assets** Anlagenzugang;
~ *(v.)* verdienen, erwerben, *(improve)* an Wert gewinnen, *(prices)* sich bessern;
~ **an advantage over one's competitors** seine Konkurrenten überflügeln; ~ **three points** *(stock exchange)* sich um drei Punkte verbessern;
to register small ~s kleine Gewinne verzeichnen;
~ **sharing** *(bonus system)* Gewinnbeteiligung.
gainful einträglich, gewinnbringend, vorteilhaft;
~ **occupation** Erwerbstätigkeit.
gainings Verdienst, Ertrag, Gewinn, Einkommen.
gamble *(v.)* **on a fall** auf Baisse spekulieren; ~ **away one's fortune** sein Vermögen verspielen.
gambling | **in futures** Differenzgeschäft; ~ **on the stock exchange** Börsenspekulation.
gang Arbeiterkolonne;
breakdown ~ *(Br.)* Unfallhilfstrupp.
gap Lücke, *(insurance)* Wartezeit;
~ **in interest rates** Zinsgefälle; ~ **in the market** Marktlücke; ~ **in supplies** Angebots-, Versorgungslücke.
garage Garage, Autohalle;
lockup ~ Einzelgarage; **open** ~ Sammelgarage; ~ **fee** Standgeld.
garnish *(v.)* Pfändungsbescheid zukommen lassen, Zahlungsverbot erlassen;
~ **the wages** Lohnpfändung vornehmen.
garnishee | **account** Sperrkonto [des Drittschuldners]; ~ **order** Pfändungs- und Überweisungsbeschluß.
gasoline *(US)* Benzin, Brenn-, Betriebsstoff;
~ **allowance** Kraftstoffzuteilung, ~ **attendant** Tankwart; ~ **container** Benzinkanister; ~ **price** Benzinpreis; ~ **station** Tankstelle; ~ **tax** Benzin-, Treibstoffsteuer.
gate Eingang, *(aerodrome)* Flugsteig, *(entrance money)* Eintrittsgeld.
gather *(v.)* | **in debts** Schulden einkassieren; ~ **rents** Mieten einziehen.
gazette *(Br.)* Staatsanzeiger, Gesetz-, Amtsblatt;
~ *(v.)* **a case of bankruptcy** Konkursfall bekanntgeben.
gear *(v.)* **to consumer needs** sich dem Verbraucherbedürfnis anpassen; ~ **production to the capacity of a plant** betriebliche Produktionskapazität voll ausfahren.
geared to export exportorientiert.
gearing *(capital)* festverzinslicher Anteil am Gesamtkapital;
high ~ Kapitalintensität.

general | **advertising** überregionale Werbung; ~ **agent** Generalvertreter, -bevollmächtigter; $\simeq$ **Agreement on Tariffs and Trade (GATT)** Allgemeines Zoll- und Handelsabkommen; ~ **assignment** *(banking)* Mantelzession; ~ **audit** Jahresabschlußprüfung; ~ **bill of lading** Sammelkonossement; ~ **bookkeeper** Hauptbuchhalter; ~ **burden** Handlungsunkosten; ~ **cargo** Stückgut, Sammelladung; ~ **cash** Betriebsmittel; ~ **consumption** Massenkonsum; ~ **contingency reserve** allgemeine Delkredererückstellung; ~ **contractor** Generalunternehmer; ~ **creditor** nicht bevorrechtigter Gläubiger; ~ **dealer** *(Br.)* Gemischtwarenhändler, Krämer; ~ **endorsement** Blankogiro; ~ **freight** Stückgutfracht; ~ **ledger** Hauptbuch; ~ **line jobber** Großhändler mit breitem Sortiment; ~ **management trust** Kapitalanlagegesellschaft mit veränderlichem Anlagefonds; ~ **manager** Generaldirektor; ~ **meeting** Generalversammlung; ~ **partner** Komplementär; ~ **partnership** Offene Handelsgesellschaft; ~ **post** ortsübliche Postzustellung; ~ **records** Buchungsunterlagen; ~ **shop** Gemischtwarenhandlung; ~ **tariff** *(customs)* Einheitstarif.
genuine echt, rein, unverfälscht, authentisch, *(business)* solid, reell;
~ **article** Markenartikel; ~ **purchaser** ernsthafter Reflektant.
get *(Br. mining)* Ertrag, Fördermenge, Ausbeute;
~ *(v.)* **(earn)** verdienen, *(purchase goods)* besorgen, auftreiben, [Waren] beziehen;
~ **commodities from abroad** seine Ware außerhalb beziehen; ~ **in debts** Schulden hereinbekommen; ~ **into a line of business** in eine Branche einsteigen; ~ **one's living** sein Auskommen haben; ~ **off false coin** falsches Geld loswerden; ~ **off one's merchandise** seine Ware losschlagen; ~ **off without a loss** seine Unkosten gerade decken; ~ **only a small profit** nur geringen Nutzen erzielen; ~ **the sack** *(sl.)* gefeuert werden; ~ **through one's fortune** sein Vermögen durchbringen; ~ **up an article for sale** Ware zum Verkauf ausstellen.
gift Schenkung, Geschenk, *(in shop)* Zugabe;
tax-free ~ steuerfreie Schenkung;
~ **advertising** Zugabewerbung; ~ **coupon** Wertgutschein; ~**loan** *(v.)* als zinsloses Darlehen geben; ~ **package (parcel)** Geschenkpackung, Liebesgabensendung; ~ **selection catalog(ue)** Geschenkartikelkatalog; ~**tax exemption** *(US)* Schenkungssteuerfreibetrag; ~ **wrapping** Geschenkpackung.
gilt-edged investment mündelsichere Kapitalanlage.
gimmick *(US)* Sensationswerbung.
giro *(Br.)* Postscheck;
~ **account** *(Br.)* Postscheckkonto.
give *(v.)* | **away the prizes** Preisverteilung vornehmen;
~ **bail** Bürgschaft leisten, Kaution stellen; ~ **bonds** Sicherheiten bestellen; ~ **a buying order** Kaufauftrag erteilen; ~ **for the call** *(stock exchange)* Vor-

prämie kaufen; ~ **for the put** *(stock exchange)* Rückprämie verkaufen; ~ **on** *(Br., stock)* in Prolongation geben, hineingeben.

give out | **by contract** [in Submission] vergeben; ~ **handbills** Prospekte verteilen.

give | **a receipt** Quittung ausstellen; ~ **and take** Gewinn und Verlust durchschnittlich ausgleichen.

give up *(stock exchange)* Auftraggeber benennen; ~ **business** sich vom Geschäft zurückziehen; ~ **effects to one's creditors** sich für zahlungsunfähig erklären.

give the value date [Schecks] einbuchen.

giveaway *(leaflet)* Handzettel, *(seller, US)* Prämie, Zugabe, Gutschein.

giver Schenker, Spender, *(of option money)* Prämienkäufer;
~ **of a bill** Wechselaussteller; ~ **of a guaranty** Wechselbürge; ~ **of an option** *(Br.)* Prämienkäufer, Optionsgeber.

giving up [of a business] Geschäftsaufgabe.

global | **charges** Pauschalspesen; ~ **insurance** Pauschalversicherung; ~ **value adjustment** Sammelwertberichtigung.

glut *(market)* Überangebot, -fluß, -sättigung;
~ **in the market** Marktfülle; ~ **of money** Geldschwemme.

go *(v.)* | **ahead sturdily** *(prices)* scharf anziehen; ~ **back to the drawer** Regreß nehmen; ~ **bust** Pleite machen; ~ **down** *(orders)* zurückgehen, *(price)* fallen, sinken, *(sales)* zurückgehen; ~ **equal shares** gleichen Anteil haben; ~ **heavily into the red** *(US)* schwere finanzielle Verluste erleiden; ~ **in for a competition** sich an einem Wettbewerb beteiligen; ~ **into business** Kaufmann werden; ~ **partnership with s. o.** sich mit jem. assoziieren; ~ **off quickly** reißenden Absatz finden; ~ **on a relief fund** von einem Unterstützungsfonds leben; ~ **out of business** Geschäft aufgeben; ~ **out of fashion** unmodern werden; ~ **over an account** Rechnung durchsehen; ~ **slow** *(workers)* Bummelstreik durchführen; ~ **through one's apprenticeship** seine Lehrzeit durchmachen; ~ **through one's bills** seine Rechnung durchgehen; ~ **up sharply** *(prices)* scharf anziehen; ~ **upon tick** *(fam.)* auf Pump kaufen;
to be all the ~ *(fashion)* höchst modern sein (der letzte Schrei, die große Mode) sein.

go-slow *(Br.)* planmäßiges Langsamarbeiten, Arbeiten nach Vorschrift, Bummelstreik.

going, ~, **gone!** *(auction)* zum ersten, zum zweiten, zum dritten!;
~ **concern** im Betrieb befindliches Unternehmen; ~ **price** Tagespreis; ~**-out-of-business sale** Totalausverkauf; ~ **short** *(US)* Baissespekulation; ~ **[-concern] value** Betriebswert.

gold Gold, *(coin)* Goldmünze;
on ~ auf Goldbasis;
twenty-four carat ~ 24karätiges Gold;
~ **in ingots** Stangengold;
~ **bar** Goldbarren; ~ **backing** Golddeckung; ~ **bloc** Goldwährungsblock; ~**-bullion standard** Gold-

kern-, Goldbarrenwährung; ~ **clearance fund** *(US)* Goldausgleichsfonds; ~**-exchange standard** Golddevisenwährung; ~ **export point** oberer Goldpunkt; ~ **stock** Goldbestand, -vorrat.

golden handshake Abfindung für vorzeitiges Ausscheiden.

gone *(auction)* zugeschlagen, *(trade)* ruiniert;
~ **away, no address** unbekannt verzogen.

good [öffentliches] Wohl, *(balance sheet)* Habenseite;
~ *(a.)* gültig, unverfälscht, *(financially sound)* zahlungs-, kreditfähig, gut, solid, solvent, reell;
as ~ **as ready money** so gut wie Bargeld;
~ **address** gute Wohngegend; ~ **cause** Entlassungsgrund; **to constitute [a]** ~ **delivery** *(stock exchange)* lieferbar sein; ~**-faith taker** gutgläubiger Erwerber; **to be earning** ~ **money** hoch bezahlt werden; ~ **trade paper** diskontfähiger Warenwechsel.

goods Waren, Handelsware, -güter, *(railway)* Güter[ladung], Fracht[gut], Ladung;
ascertained ~ *(law)* Speziessachen; **bale** ~ Ballengüter; **bonded** ~ Waren unter Zollverschluß; **branded** ~ Markenartikel, -ware, -erzeugnisse; **bulk[y]** ~ Sperrgut; **carted** ~ Rollgut; **consumer (consumption)** ~ Konsum-, Verbrauchsgüter; **convenience** ~ *(US)* persönliche Gebrauchsgegenstände; **durable** ~ langlebige Güter; **duty-free** ~ zollfreie Waren; **fast-moving (-selling)** ~ Ware mit hoher Umsatzgeschwindigkeit; **fungible** ~ Gattungssachen; **high-volume and highly acceptable branded consumer** ~ hochwertige Massenkonsumgüter; **homeproduced (homemade)** ~ heimische Fabrikate; **industrial** ~ Produktionsgüter; **invoiced** ~ fakturierte Ware; **job** ~ Ausschußware; **low-class (-quality)** ~ minderwertige Ware; **manufactured** ~ Fertigerzeugnisse; **measurement** ~ Maßgüter; **packaged** ~ abgepackte Ware; **quota (rationed)** ~ bewirtschaftete Waren; ~ **selling like hot dogs (wildfire)** schnell vergriffene Waren; **trashy** ~ Schundware; **unascertained** ~ Gattungssachen; **uncleared** ~ zollhängige Waren; **valuable** ~ Wertgegenstände;
~ **billed to customer** dem Kunden in Rechnung gestellte Ware; ~ **in the process of clearing** zollhängige Waren; ~ **dangerous in themselves** von Natur aus gefährliche Sachen; ~ **to declare** anmeldepflichtige Waren; ~ **exhibited for sale** Ausstellungsartikel; **heavy** ~ **laden in bulk** Sturzgüter; ~ **in parcels** Stückgut; ~ **lying in pledge** verpfändete Waren; ~ **in process** Halbfabrikate; ~ **shipped in bulk** Sperrgut; ~ **in short supply** Mangelware; ~ **in transit** unterwegs befindliche Güter;
to buy ~ **wholesale** engros einkaufen; **to lay in** ~ Waren auf Lager nehmen; **to stop** ~ **in transit** kaufmännisches Zurückbehaltungsrecht ausüben; **to take** ~ **on consignment** Waren in Kommission nehmen;
~ **account** Warenkonto, -rechnung; ~ **agent** *(Br.)* Bahnspediteur; ~ **agreement** Warenabkommen; ~ **delivery and collection** *(Br.)* Rollfuhrdienst; ~ **depot** *(Br.)* Güterschuppen; ~ **exchange** Produk-

tenbörse; ~ **loft** *(Br.)* Güterspeicher; ~ **office** *(Br.)* Güterabfertigung; ~ **rates** *(Br.)* Gütertarif; ~ **service** *(Br.)* Güter-, Frachtverkehr; ~ **station** *(Br.)* Güterbahnhof; **long-distance** ~ **traffic** *(Br.)* Güterfernverkehr; ~ **train** *(Br.)* Güterzug; **to send by** ~ **train** *(Br.)* als Frachtgut senden; ~ **transport** *(Br.)* Güterverkehr; ~ **waggon** *(Br.)* Güterwaggon; ~ **yard** *(Br.)* Güterbahnhof.

goodwill Firmenwert, geschäftliches Ansehen, *(customers)* [Stamm]kundschaft, Kundenkreis, Klientele;
~ **advertising** institutionelle Werbung, Image-, Prestigewerbung.

governing market trends marktbestimmende Entwicklungen.

government | **annuities** Staatsrenten; ~ **bank** Staatsbank; ~ **bidding process** staatliches Ausschreibungsverfahren; ~ **borrowing** staatliche Schuldenaufnahme, Staatsverschuldung; ~ **business** Staatsaufträge, *(~ corporation)* Wirtschaftsunternehmung der öffentlichen Hand, Staatsunternehmen; ~ **contract** öffentlicher Auftrag; ~ **depository** *(US)* staatliche Kapitalsammelstelle; ~ **enterprise** Wirtschaftsbetrieb der öffentlichen Hand; ~ **export credit insurance** staatliche Ausfuhrversicherung; ~ **funds** fundierte Staatspapiere; **~-owned enterprise** Regie-, Staatsbetrieb; **to stay free of** ~ **ownership** der Verstaatlichung entgehen; ~ **securities** *(Br.)* Staatsanleihe; ~ **spending** *(Br.)* Ausgaben der öffentlichen Hand.

governmental enterprise Staats-, Regiebetrieb, Wirtschaftsunternehmen der öffentlichen Hand.

grace [Zahlungs]frist;
to give a creditor a week's ~ seinem Gläubiger eine Frist von einer Woche gewähren;
~ **period** *(credit)* tilgungsfreie Zeit.

grade Grad, Klasse, *(job evaluation)* Lohnklasse, *(of quality)* Güteklasse, -grad, Qualität;
of finest ~ erste Qualität;
similar ~ **of bond** gleichartige Obligation; **like** ~ **and quality** gleiche Beschaffenheit und Güte;
~ *(v.)* sortieren, *(quality)* in Güteklassen einteilen;
~ **label(l)ing** Güteklassebezeichnung.

grading | **of commodities** Wareneinteilung nach Güteklassen; ~ **of premiums** Beitragsstaffelung.

graduated | **interest** gestaffelte Zinsen; ~ **tariff** Staffeltarif; ~ **tax** gestaffelte Steuer.

graduation | **of prices** Preiseinstufung; ~ **of wages** Lohnstaffelung.

graft *(US)* Korruption, Schmiergeld.

grain | **exchange** Getreidebörse; ~ **futures** Getreidetermingeschäfte.

grant Bewilligung, Gewährung *(of right)* Verleihung, Konzession, *(sum granted)* Zuschuß, finanzielle Hilfe;
capital ~ Kapitalzuschuß; **maintenance** ~ Unterhaltszuschuß; **supplementary** ~ Nachbewilligung; **~-s-in-aid** *(US)* Staats-, öffentliche Zuschüsse, Subvention; ~ **of credit** Kreditbewilligung;
~ *(v.)* gewähren, bewilligen, zugestehen;

~ **an advance** Vorschuß bewilligen; ~ **an exemption** Steuerfreibetrag gewähren; ~ **a loan against securities** Wertpapiere lombardieren; ~ **a respite** stunden;
~-aided subventioniert.

granting of a loan Darlehnsgewährung.

graphic design Werbestil.

gratification Honorar, Zuwendung, Lohn.

gratuitous unentgeltlich, umsonst, gratis, *(without consideration)* ohne Gegenleistung.
~ **advice** kostenloser Rat; ~ **allowance** Pension, Ruhegeld; ~ **bailee** unentgeltlicher Verwahrer.

graving dock Trockendock.

gravy *(bribe, sl.)* Bestechung, Schiebung.

gray market grauer Markt.

grease Schmiergelder.

green | **stamp** *(US)* Rabattmarke; **in the** ~ **tree** in guten Verhältnissen.

grind *(v.)* **down with taxes** übermäßig besteuern.

grocer Lebensmittel-, Gemischt-, Kolonialwarenhändler.

grocery *(US)* Kolonialwarengeschäft.

groceteria *(US)* Selbstbedienungsladen.

gross *(advertising)* Bruttotarifpreis;
by the ~ in Bausch und Bogen, *(at wholesale)* im Großhandel;
~ **adventure** Bodmereidarlehen; ~ **amount** Roh-, Bruttobetrag; ~ **average** Großhavarie; ~ **average hourly earnings** Bruttodurchschnittsverdienst; ~ **deposits** Einlagenbestand; ~ **dividend** Bruttodividende; ~ **domestic product** Bruttosozialprodukt zu Marktpreisen; ~ **investment in fixed assets** Bruttoanlageninvestition; ~ **margin** Bruttohandelsspanne; ~ **national debt** National-, Staatsschuld; ~ **national product** Bruttosozialprodukt; ~ **national product gap** Vollbeschäftigungslücke; ~ **profit** Roh-, Bruttogewinn; ~ **receipts** Bruttoertrag, Brutto-, Roheinnahmen; ~ **rental** Bruttomiete; ~ **revenue** Roheinkünfte; ~ **salary** Bruttogehalt; ~ **sales** Bruttoumsatz; ~ **value** Bruttowert; ~ **wage** Bruttolohn; ~ **yield** *(stocks)* Bruttorendite.

ground Grund und Boden, *(building site)* Baustelle, *(person's property in land)* Grundbesitz;
~s Ländereien, (Grundbesitz), *(city)* städtische Anlagen, Garten-, Parkanlagen;
~s **for giving notice** Kündigungsgrund;
~ *(v.)* gründen, bauen, errichten, *(airplane)* Startverbot erteilen, *(ship)* auf Grund laufen;
to break the ~ Absatzmarkt öffnen; **to hold one's (their)** ~ *(prices)* sich behaupten; **to move into new high** ~ neue Höchstkurse erreichen.

ground floor Erd-, Untergeschoß, Parterre, *(US, price of shares)* Aktienvorzugspreise eines neugegründeten Unternehmens;
to get (be let) in on the ~ sich zu den Gründerbedingungen beteiligen;
~ **rent** Grundabgabe, Reallast.

group Gruppe, Klasse, *(business concern)* Konzern;
advisory ~ Beratergruppe; **multiproduct** ~ Konzern mit breitgestreutem Produktionsprogramm;
~ **of banks** Bankenkonsortium;

~ *(v.)* [sich] gruppieren, in Gruppen einteilen; ~ **account** Konzernabschluß; ~ **annuity insurance** kollektive Rentenversicherung; ~ **banking** *(US)* Filialbankwesen; ~ **buying** Sammeleinkauf; ~ **charter rate** Reisegesellschaftstarif; ~ **discount** *(advertising)* Mengenrabatt bei Belegen mehrerer Zeitungen; ~ **incentive** Gruppenakkord; ~ **insurance** Kollektiv-, Betriebsversicherung; ~ **piece rate** Gruppenakkord; ~'s **sales** Konzernumsatz.

grow *(v.)* wachsen, zunehmen, *(make progress)* beruflich vorankommen, vorwärtskommen; ~ **flat** *(business)* stocken.

growth Wachstum; **of foreign** ~ fremden Ursprungs, ausländisch; **slow economic** ~ geringe Wachstumsperiode; ~ **in consumption** Konsumsteigerung; ~ **of savings deposits** Spareinlagenzuwachs; ~ **area** Wachstumsgebiet; ~ **industry** Wachstumsindustrie; **to come to the end of the** ~ **line** Wachstumsgrenze erreicht haben; ~ **prospects** Wachstumsaussichten; ~ **rate** Zuwachs-, Wachstumsrate; **zero** ~ **rate** zum Stillstand führende Wachstumsrate; ~ **recession** Wachstumsrückgang; ~ **target** Wachstumsziel.

guarantee *(Br.)* Bürgschaft, Garantie, Gewähr[leistung], *(guarantor)* Garant, Gewährsmann, Bürge, *(security)* Sicherheit, Kaution; **without** ~ ohne Gewähr; **bank** ~ Bankgarantie; **conditional** ~ Ausfallbürgschaft; **deficit** ~ Ausfallbürgschaft; ~ **of delivery** Liefergarantie; ~ **of bill of exchange** Wechselbürgschaft, Aval; ~ *(v.)* sicherstellen, gewährleisten, *(stand bail)* bürgen, Bürgschaft leisten; ~ **[due payment of]** a **bill** Wechselbürgschaft leisten; ~ **that the debts will be paid** Schuldenbezahlung garantieren; ~ **s. th. as genuine** für die Echtheit eines Artikels garantieren; **to call upon a** ~ Sicherheit in Anspruch nehmen; **to cancel a** ~ Garantie annullieren; **to make a** ~ **stick** Garantieansprüche durchsetzen; **to raise claims**

under a ~ Garantie in Anspruch nehmen; ~ **commission** Dekredereprovision; ~ **contract** Bürgschafts-, Garantievertrag; ~ **deposit** Sicherheitshinterlegung, *(insurance)* Kautionsdepot; ~ **fund** *(Br.)* Garantie-, Reservefonds; ~ **pay** garantierte Mindestzahlung; ~ **registration card** Garantieschein; ~ **stock** Deckungsstock.

guaranteed | **bill of exchange** avalierter Wechsel; ~ **bond** Garantieschein; ~ **employment** garantierte Mindestbeschäftigung; ~ **position** *(advertising)* garantierte Placierung; ~ **stocks** *(US)* Aktien mit Dividendengarantie; ~ **wage plan** Lohnabkommen mit garantierter Mindestbeschäftigungszeit.

guarantor Bürge, Gewährsmann, Garant, Avalist; ~ **of a bill (note)** Wechselbürge.

guaranty *(US)* Garantie, Bürgschaft[sversprechen, -vertrag], Kaution, Gewähr[leistung], *(security)* Pfand, Sicherheit, Sicherheitssumme; **absolute** ~ Bürgschaft ohne Einrede der Vorausklage, selbstschuldnerische Bürgschaft; **conditional** ~ Ausfallbürgschaft; ~ **of collection** *(US)* Ausfallbürgschaft; ~ **of payment** *(US)* selbstschuldnerische Bürgschaft; **to ask for a** ~ Garantie (Kaution) verlangen; **to stand back of a** ~ Gewährleistungsansprüche erfüllen; ~ **account** Sicherstellungskonto; ~ **agreement (contract)** *(US)* Bürgschaftsvertrag.

guard *(v.)* **by clauses** durch vertragliche Bestimmungen absichern.

guardian Vormund, *(curator)* Kurator, Verwahrer; ~ **of property** Vermögensverwalter.

guest [Hotel]gast, *(motorcar)* Mitfahrer; ~ **room** *(hotel)* Fremdenzimmer.

guidance, vocational Berufsberatung; ~ **of production** Produktionslenkung.

guide Ratgeber, Berater, *(guidebook)* Reiseführer; **railway** ~ Kursbuch, Fahrplan.

guidebook Reisehandbuch, -führer.

guiding price Richtpreis.

gutter bleed *(advertising)* Innenausschnitt.

H

haberdasher Kurzwarenhändler.

habit survey Untersuchung von Verbrauchergewohnheiten.

habitation tax Gebäudesteuer.

hack Tagelöhner, Gelegenheitsarbeiter.

haggle *(v.)* about the price um den Preis feilschen.

half | **commission** *(stock exchange)* halbe Provision; ~-**day job** Halbtagsbeschäftigung; ~ **holiday** freier Nachmittag; ~ **pay** Ruhegehalt, -geld; **to be on** ~-**time** nur halbtags arbeiten; ~-**time job** Halbtagsbeschäftigung; ~-**timer** Halbtagsarbeiter, *(student, Br.)* Werkschüler, -student.

hallmark Feingehaltsstempel.

hammer | *(v.)* *(Br.)* für zahlungsunfähig erklären; ~ **the market** *(US)* Baisseangriff machen; **to bring to the** ~ versteigern, verauktionieren.

hand *(worker)* [Hand]arbeiter; **for one's own** ~ im eigenen Interesse; **in** ~ *(cash)* bar, in klingender Münze, *(stocked)* vorrätig. **small** ~ gewöhnliche Korrespondenzschrift; **to be in the ~s of moneylenders** von Wucherern ausgebeutet werden; **to change ~s** Besitzer wechseln; **to have still some money on** ~ Reserven haben; **to sign in one's own** ~ eigenhändig unterschreiben; ~ **baggage** *(US)* **luggage,** *(Br.)* Handgepäck; ~-**medown** *(fam., US)* Konfektionsanzug, *(a.)* von der Stange (fertig) gekauft; ~-**to-mouth buying** unmittelbare Bedarfsdeckung; ~-**to-mouth existence** unsichere Existenz.

handbill Flugblatt, Reklame-, Werbeprospekt.

handicraft handwerklicher Beruf, Handwerk; **local** ~ ortsansässiges Gewerbe.

handle *(v.)* *(item)* manipulieren, *(manage)* behandeln, handhaben, *(transport)* befördern, weiterleiten; ~ **a lot of money** größere Geldsumme verwalten; ~ **any sort of business** Geschäfte aller Art erledigen.

handling Abwicklung, Handhabung, *(transportation)* Beförderung, Weiterleitung; ~ **of cargo** Umstauen der Ladung; ~ **of the economy** Konjunktursteuerung; ~ **of flights** Flugabfertigung; ~ **capacity** Umschlagkapazität; ~ **charge** *(stock exchange)* Manipulationsgebühr; **special** ~ **parcel** *(US)* Schnellpaket.

handout [Werbe]prospekt, Broschüre, Waschzettel; ~ **material** Informationsmaterial.

handyman Aushilfsarbeiter, -kraft, Faktotum.

harbo(u)r, **commercial** Handelshafen; **landlocked** ~ Binnenhafen; **short-term** ~ **for one's cash** kurzfristige Barmittelanlage; ~ **of transshipment** Umschlaghafen; **to call at a** ~ Hafen anlaufen; ~ **authority** Hafenamt; ~ **dues** Hafengebühren.

hard *(prices)* hoch, starr; **to be** ~ **hit** große Verluste erlitten haben; **to be** ~

up for money sich in Geldverlegenheit befinden; ~ **cash** *(cash on hand)* Barbestand, *(coin)* Hartgeld; ~ **core** *(unemployment)* Arbeitslosengrundsatz; ~ **currency** harte Währung; ~-**currency country** währungsstarkes Land; ~ **goods** *(US)* Gebrauchsgüter; ~ **sell** aggressive Verkaufspolitik; **to be a** ~ **spot** *(stock exchange, US)* festliegen.

hardening of the market Versteifung am [Geld]markt.

hardship allowance Härtezulage.

harmonization *(tariff, taxes)* Abstimmung.

harvest [Getreide]ernte, *(fig.)* Ertrag, Gewinn; ~ **prospects** Ernteaussichten.

haul Transportweg, -strecke; **long** ~**s** Fernverkehr; **short** ~**s** Nahverkehr. *(v.)* **freight** Frachtgut befördern.

haulage *(cartage)* Rollfuhr, *(charges)* Beförderungs-, Transportkosten; ~-**contracting business** Fuhr-, Rollfuhrunternehmen; **road** ~ **industry** Speditionsgewerbe.

hauling | **costs** Zubringer-, Zustellungskosten; ~ **rates** Transporttarif.

haven, tax Steuerparadies.

hawker Wandergewerbetreibender.

hawking Wander-, Hausierergewerbe.

hazard *(insurance law)* versicherbares Risiko; ~**s not covered** ausgeschlossene Risiken; **moral** ~ subjektives [Versicherungs]risiko; ~ **bonus** Gefahrenzulage, Risikoprämie; ~ **classification** *(insurance)* Risikoklassifizierung.

hazardous | **goods** gefährliche Güter; ~ **insurance** Risikoversicherung; ~ **speculation** gewagte Spekulation; ~ **work bonus** Risikoprämie.

head *(category)* Kategorie, Abschnitt, Rubrik, Kapitel, *(chief)* Chef, Leiter, Vorsteher, *(item)* [Rechnungs]posten; **department** ~ Abteilungsleiter; **real** ~ **of the business** eigentlicher Kopf des Unternehmens; ~ **of a letter** Briefkopf; ~ **and front of an undertaking** Seele eines Unternehmens; ~ *(v.)* rubrizieren, *(direct)* richten, leiten; ~ **a list** Liste eröffnen (anführen); **to be** ~ **over heels in debt** total verschuldet sein; **to have a good** ~ **for business** guter Geschäftsmann (kaufmännisch gewandt) sein; ~ **agency** Generalagentur; ~ **agent** Generalvertreter; ~ **clerk** Geschäftsführer, Bürovorsteher; ~ **firm** Stammhaus; ~-**hunt** *(fig.)* Jagd auf Nachwuchskräfte; ~ **office** Hauptgeschäftsstelle; ~-**office expense** Unkosten der Zentrale; ~-**on location** bevorzugte Placierung von Außenwerbung; ~ **organization** Spitzenverband; ~ **tax** *(US)* Einwanderungssteuer.

heading on the customs tariff Zollposition.

headquarters Hauptgeschäftsstelle, -sitz.

health | **of earnings** gesunde Ertragslage; ~ **benefit** Kassenleistung; ~ **insurance** Krankenversicherung; **National** ~ **Insurance** *(Br.)* Staatliche

Krankenversicherung; ~ **welfare benefit** Kranken-
zulage.
heavy *(a.) (order)* umfangreich, *(stock exchange)* flau,
schlecht;
~ **baggage** *(US)* großes Gepäck; ~ **buyer** Großabnehmer; **~-duty** hochbesteuert; ~ **fall in stocks**
heftiger Kursrückgang; ~ **firm (house)** bedeutende
Firma; ~ **lift** *(mar.)* Schwergut; ~ **orders** umfangreiche Aufträge; ~ **sale** guter Absatz.
hedge *(stock exchange)* Sicherungsgeschäft;
~ *(v.)* Sicherungsgeschäft abschließen.
to put ~s **in a contract** Vertrag verklausulieren;
~ **buying** Vorratseinkäufe; ~ **clause** *(US)* Vorbehalt[sklausel]; ~ **selling** Deckungs-, Sicherungs-
kauf.
hedging Abschluß von Deckungsgeschäften.
helicopter terminal Hubschrauberlandeplatz.
help Hilfek[leistung], Unterstützung;
~-wanted ads Stellenanzeigen.
hiatus in demand Nachfragelücke.
hidden | defect versteckter (verborgener) Mangel; ~
reserves stille Rücklagen; ~ **tax** indirekte Steuer.
high Höchststand, *(business)* Aufschwungjahr;
to be at an all-time ~ *(prices, US)* höher denn je
stehen; **to be** ~ **in office** hohe Stellung bekleiden;
to continue ~ Höchstkurs beibehalten;
~-bracket people Einkommensteuerzahler in den
oberen Steuerstufen; **~-class goods** Produkte erstklassiger Qualität; **~-class hotel** erstklassiges (Ia)
Hotel; **~-cost enterprise** kapitalintensives Unternehmen; **to buy at a** ~ **figure** teuer einkaufen; ~
finance Hochfinanz; **~-geared** *(capital)* überkapitalisiert; **~-grade fuel** Qualitätsbenzin; ~ **money**
(US) teures Geld; **to ~-pressure customers** Kunden
bearbeiten; **~-pressure salesmanship** rasante Verkaufstechnik; **~-price work** überproportionale
Akkordarbeit; ~ **rate of interest** hoher Zinssatz;
~ **sea[s]** hohe (offene) See; ~ **society** obere Zehn-
tausend; **~-ticket instalment sales** hochwertige Ab-
zahlungsverkäufe.
highjacking Flugzeugentführung, Luftpiraterie.
highway öffentlicher Verkehrsweg, Fernverkehrs-,
Landstraße erster Ordnung;
express ~ Schnellverkehrsstraße;
~ **transportation** *(US)* Güterfernverkehr.
hire Miete, *(payment for ~)* Mietpreis, Miete, *(act of
hiring, US)* An-, Einstellung;
for ~ zu vermieten, *(taxi)* frei;
~ **for work and labo(u)r** Werklieferungsvertrag;
~ *(v.)* mieten, pachten, *(engage, US)* ein-, anstellen;
~ **a crew** Mannschaft anmustern; ~ **by the day** in
Tagelohn nehmen;
to borrow through ~ Abzahlungskredit aufnehmen.
hire-purchase *(Br.)* Raten-, Abzahlungskauf, -ge-
schäft, Abstottern;
~ **agreement** Teil-, Ab-, Ratenzahlungsvertrag;
~ **company** Abzahlungsfinanzierungsgesellschaft;
~ **price** Preis bei Ratenzahlung; **to sell on the** ~
system auf Abzahlung verkaufen.

hired aircraft Charterflugzeug.
hiring Mieten, *(worker)* An-, Einstellung;
maximum ~ **age** höchstzulässiges Einstellungs-
alter; ~ **quota** Einstellungsquote; ~ **scheme** Anwer-
bungsplan.
historical cost ursprüngliche Anschaffungskosten;
(public-utility accounting) nachträglich errechnete
Selbstkosten.
history sheet Personalbogen.
hive *(v.)* **off profitable activities to the private sector** er-
tragreiche Teilgebiete reprivatisieren.
hoard *(v.)* **up treasure** Vermögen ansammeln.
hoarding Hortung, Hamstern, *(billboard, Br.)* Re-
klamefläche, Anschlagbrett.
hold Einfluß, *(ship)* Schiffs-, Stau-, Laderaum;
~ **on the resources** Rückgriff auf die Hilfsquellen;
~ *(v.)* **(prices)** sich halten, *(retain)* rückbehalten;
~ **a job down** *(coll.)* Beruf weiter ausüben; ~ **on to**
one's oil shares seine Ölaktien durchhalten; ~ **out**
for a higher price besseres Angebot abwarten; ~ **up**
well *(securities)* sich gut behaupten.
~ **s. o. liable** j. haftpflichtig machen; ~ **the market**
Stützungsaktion unternehmen; ~ **the purse** Kas-
senwart sein; ~ **in safe custody** verwahren; ~ **shares**
in a business Geschäftsanteile besitzen; ~ **stocks for**
a rise Aktien in Erwartung von Kurssteigerungen
zurückhalten.
holdback pay *(US)* einbehaltene Lohngelder.
holder *(property, stocks)* Inhaber, Besitzer;
bona-fide ~ gutgläubiger Besitzer; **season-ticket** ~
Dauerkarteninhaber; **small-fund** ~ Kleinrentner;
~ **of an annuity** Rentenempfänger; ~ **in due course**
rechtmäßiger Wechsel-, Scheckinhaber; ~ **of a lien**
Pfandgläubiger;
to be made out in the name of the ~ auf den Inhaber
lauten.
holding *(interest)* Beteiligung, Anteil, *(stocks held)*
Aktienbesitz, *(store)* Vorrat, Lager;
collateral ~s Lombardbestand; **diversified** ~s weit-
gestreute Anlagebeteiligungen; **gold and foreign-**
exchange ~s Gold- und Devisenbestände;
~ **the market** *(US)* Marktstützung; ~s **of securities**
Wertpapierportefeuille;
to divide land into small ~s Land parzellieren;
~ **area** *(airplane)* Warteraum; ~ **company** Hol-
ding-, Dachgesellschaft; ~ **period** *(income tax)* Be-
sitzdauer.
holdover *(advertising)* nicht gebrachte Anzeige.
holdup *(railway)* Betriebsstockung;
personal ~ **insurance** *(US)* Überfallversicherung.
hole | in the wall *(sl.)* Kleinstbetrieb;
to make a large ~ **in one's savings** Loch in seine Ersparnisse reißen;
~-and-corner business anrüchiges Geschäft.
holiday *(US)* [arbeits]freier Tag, Ruhetag, *(vacation,*
Br.) Ferien, Urlaub, Erholungsaufenthalt;
bank ~ Bankfeiertag; **paid** ~ *(Br.)* bezahlter Urlaub;
to take a ~ sich einen Tag frei nehmen;
~ **booking** Urlaubsreservierung; ~ **home** Ferien-

haus; ~ **layoffs** Entlassungen während der Urlaubszeit; ~ **pay** Urlaubsgeld, Feiertagszuschlag; ~ **shutdown** ferienbedingte Schließung; ~ **travel** Urlaubs-, Ferienreise.

home Wohnung, Haus, Heim;
without permanent ~ ohne festen Wohnsitz; **council** ~ *(Br.)* Sozialwohnung;
~ **address** Privatanschrift; ~ **building industry** *(US)* Wohnungsbauwirtschaft; ~ **commodities** Landesprodukte; ~ **currency** Binnenwährung; ~ **delivery** Lieferung frei Haus; ~ **descriptions** *(Br.)* heimische Wertpapiere; ~ **financing** Eigenheimfinanzierung; ~ **freight** Her-, Rückfracht; ~ **industry** einheimische Industrie, *(carried on at home)* Haus-, Heimindustrie; ~**-foreign insurance** *(Br.)* Korrespondenzversicherung; **paid** ~ **leave** bezahlter Heimaturlaub; ~ **mail** *(Br.)* Inlandpost; ~**-owning member** Eigenheimbesitzer; ~ **port** Heimathafen; ~**-produced goods** Inlandserzeugnisse; ~ **site** Wohngrundstück; ~ **trade** *(Br.)* Binnen-, Inlandshandel; ~**-trade navigation** Küstenverkehr; ~**-use entry** *(Br.)* Einfuhrdeklaration für Inlandsverbrauch; ~ **value** Inlandswert.

homecroft *(Br.)* landwirtschaftliche Nebenerwerbssiedlung.

homeowner *(US)* Haus-, Eigenheimbesitzer.

homestead *(US)* Eigenheim;
business ~ *(US)* gewerblich genutztes Eigenheim; ~ **exemption** *(US)* Zwangsvollstreckungsfreigrenze.

hono(u)r *(v.) (accept bill)* akzeptieren, annehmen, *(pay bill)* einlösen, bezahlen, honorieren;
~ **a bill at maturity** Wechsel bei Verfall einlösen.

hono(u)rable understanding formlose Wettbewerbsabrede.

hoops, to go through the Konkurs anmelden.

horizontal files Flachregistratur.

hospital benefits Krankenhauszuschuß.

hospitalization insurance *(US)* Zusatzversicherung für Krankenhausaufenthalt.

host [Quartier]wirt, Gastgeber;
~ **country** Gastland.

hot *(note)* neu, *(stolen goods)* heiß, geschmuggelt;
to sell like ~ **cakes** wie warme Würstchen (Semmeln) weggehen; ~ **money** heißes Geld.

hotel Hotel, Gasthof, -haus;
private ~ *(Br.)* Pension; **upper-bracket** ~ Hotel der gehobenen Mittelklasse;
to book a ~ *(Br.)* Hotelzimmer bestellen; **to register with a** ~ Anmeldezettel im Hotel ausfüllen; ~ **accommodation** Hotelunterbringung; ~ **bill** Hotelrechnung; ~ **bookings** Hotelreservierungen; ~ **guide** Hotelverzeichnis; ~ **industry** Hotelgewerbe; ~ **register** Fremdenbuch; ~ **regulations** Haus-, Gästeordnung; ~ **reservation** Zimmerreservierung.

hotelkeeper Gastwirt, Wirt, Hotelbesitzer.

hour Stunde, *(television)* feststehende Sendung;
after ~**s** nach der Geschäftszeit, nach Dienstschluß (Feierabend);

actual ~**s** effektive Arbeitszeit; **business** ~**s** Geschäftsstunden, -zeit; **official** ~**s** *(stock exchange)* Börsenzeit; **rush** ~**s** Hauptgeschäftszeit; **final** ~ **of trading** Börsenschluß; **scheduled** ~**s of work** festgesetzte Arbeitszeit;
to be dealt with after ~**s** *(stock market)* im Telefonverkehr gehandelt werden; **to pay s. o. by the** ~ j. stundenweise bezahlen;
~**s convention** Arbeitszeitabkommen.

house Haus, Heim, Wohnung, *(firm)* Handelsfirma, -haus, *(Br., stock exchange)* Börse;
apartment ~ Mietshaus; **boarding** ~ Fremdenpension; **commission** ~ Maklerfirma; **company** ~ Werkswohnung; **executive-level** ~ Haus für gehobenere Ansprüche; **first** ~ *(cinema)* Frühvorstellung; **originating** ~ Konsortialführerin; **solvent** ~ zahlungsfähige Firma;
~ **for sale with immediate possession** sofort bezugsfertiges Haus;
~ **agency** Häusermakler; ~ **bill** Filialwechsel; ~ **brand** Eigenmarke; ~ **delivery** Lieferung frei Haus; **inhabited** ~ **duty** Hauszinssteuer; ~ **hunter** Wohnungssuchender; ~ **item** *(Br.)* eigener Scheck; ~ **journal** Werkzeitung; **external** ~ **organ** Aktionärszeitschrift; ~ **price** *(Br.)* Börsenpreis; ~ **Ways and Means Committee** *(US)* Haushaltsausschuß.

house-to-house | **canvassing** Akquirieren; ~ **selling** Direktverkauf an der Haustür.

household | **consumption** Haushaltsverbrauch; ~ **delivery** Direktlieferung an die Haushaltungen.

housekeeper allowance (relief, Br.) Steuerfreibetrag für Hausangestellte.

housekeeping allowance Haushaltungsgeld.

housing (charges) Lagergeld, *(house building)* Wohnungsbau, *(lodging)* Wohnung, Herberge;
additional ~ zusätzlicher Wohnraum; **factory-built** ~ vorfabrizierte Wohnungseinheit; **federally financed low-cost** *(US)* **(low-income)** ~ sozialer Wohnungsbau; **upper-level** ~ Wohnung für gehobenere Ansprüche;
~ **aid** Wohnungsbeihilfe; ~ **allowance** Wohnungszuschuß; ~ **finance** Wohnungsfinanzierung; ~ **industry** Wohnungswirtschaft; ~ **mortgage** Eigenheimhypothek; **low-cost** ~ **program(me)** Programm für die Beschaffung billiger Mietwohnungen; **privately financed** ~ **unit** freifinanzierte Wohnung.

huckster Hausierer, Straßenverkäufer.

hull insurance [Schiffs]kaskoversicherung.

husbanding of capital vorsichtige Kapitalverwendung.

hush money Schweigegeld.

hypothecary | **claim** Hypothekenforderung; ~ **value** Beleihungs-, Lombardwert.

hypothecate *(v.)* verpfänden, hypothekisieren.

hypothecation Verpfändung, Beleihung, *(securities)* Lombardierung, *(ship)* Verbodmung;
~ **bond** Bodmereischein; ~ **certificate** *(US)* Lombardschein; ~ **value** Beleihungs-, Lombardwert.

I

ice-free harbo(u)r eisfreier Hafen.

ideas man *(advertising, Br.)* Ideenspezialist.

ideal | **capacity** Betriebsoptimum; ~ **standard** optimale Standardkosten.

identifiable property feststellbare Vermögenswerte.

identification | **card** Personalausweis; ~ **papers** Legitimationspapiere.

identy card [Personal]ausweis, Kennkarte.

idle *(capital)* unproduktiv, tot, brachliegend, *(not operating)* außer Betrieb, stillstehend, *(unoccupied)* unbeschäftigt, erwerbslos;
to be ~ *(machine)* brachliegen; **to run** ~ *(factory)* stilliegen;
~**-plant expenses** Stillstandskosten; ~ **tenement** leerstehende Wohnung; ~ **time** Leerlaufzeit.

illegal | **interest** ~ Wucherzinsen; ~ **strike** wilder Streik; ~ **trade** Schmuggel, Schleichhandel.

illicit | **dealer** Schwarzhändler; ~ **profits** unerlaubte Gewinne; ~ **work** Schwarzarbeit.

illiquid nicht flüssig, *(bank)* illiquide;
~ **position** angeschlagene Liquiditätsposition.

image *(advertising)* Vorstellungs-, Leitbild; **corporate** ~ Leitbild eines Unternehmens.

imbalance in payments unausgeglichene Zahlungsbilanz.

imitation of trademarks Warenzeichenverfälschung.

immediate unverzüglich, sofort, *(first hand)* unmittelbar, aus erster Hand;
~ **annuity** sofort fällige Rente; ~ **benefit** sofortiger Versicherungsschutz; **for** ~ **delivery** sofort lieferfähig; ~ **demand** Nachfragestoß; **with** ~ **possession** *(house)* sofort bezugsfähig.

immobilization | **of capital** Kapitalfestlegung; ~ **of liquid funds** Liquiditätsbindung.

immobilize *(v.)* Kapital festlegen.

immovable estate Liegenschaften.

impact *(advertisement)* Stoßkraft, Intensität;
~ **of a tax** *(Br.)* Steuerbelastung.

impairment of capital Kapitalverminderung.

impediment to trade Handelsschranken.

imperfect competition *(US)* unvollständige Konkurrenz, ungleiche Wettbewerbsbedingungen.

Imperial preference *(Br.)* Zollbegünstigung.

impersonal account Sachkonto.

implements and machinery *(factory)* Inventar.

implied guarantee gesetzliche Gewährleistung.

import Einfuhr, Import, Auslandszufuhr;
capital ~ Kapitalimport; **invisible** ~**s** unsichtbare Einfuhr, passive Dienstleistungen; **nonquota** ~**s** nicht kontingentierte Einfuhrartikel;
~ **of foreign capital** ausländische Kapitaleinfuhr;
~**s in excess of exports** Einfuhrüberschuß;
~ *(v.)* **duty-free** zollfrei einführen;
~ **allocation** Einfuhrzuteilung; ~ **authorization** Einfuhrbewilligung; ~ **business** Importgeschäft; ~ **commerce** Passivhandel; ~ **credit** Importkredit; ~ **deposit** *(Br.)* Importdepot; ~ **firm** Importhaus; ~

Importfirma; ~ **limitation** Einfuhrbegrenzung; ~ **list** Einfuhrliste; ~ **monopoly** Einfuhrmonopol; ~ **specie point** unterer Goldpunkt; ~ **trade** Passiv-, Importhandel, -geschäft.

importation | **in bond** Einfuhr unter Zollverschluß; **temporary** ~ **papers** Zollpapiere für vorübergehende Einfuhr.

imported commodities (goods) Einfuhrwaren.

importer Importeur, Importkaufmann.

impose *(v.)* **an embargo** Embargo verhängen; ~ **inferior goods upon s. o.** jem. minderwertige Ware aufdrängen.

imposition of taxes Steuerausschreibung.

impost Abgabe, Steuer, *(import duty)* Einfuhrzoll; ~**s** Gefälle.

impressed stamp eingedrucktes Postwertzeichen.

imprest Spesenvorschuß;
~ **account** Spesen-, Vorschußkonto; ~ **fund** *(petty cash)* Portokasse; ~ **system** bargeldloser Zahlungsverkehr.

improve *(v.)* verbessern, *(land)* kultivieren, meliorieren, *(market)* erholen, sich kräftigen, *(refine)* veredeln, verfeinern;
~ **the conditions of the poor** bessere Lebensbedingungen für die Armen herbeiführen; ~ **a property** Werterhöhungen an einem Grundstück vornehmen.

improved | **goods** veredeltes Erzeugnis; ~ **site** erschlossenes Gelände.

improvement *(advance)* Steigen, Anziehen, Steigerung, *(agriculture)* Bodenverbesserung, Melioration, *(betterment of building)* Werterhöhung, *(refining)* Veredelung, *(stock market)* Kursanstieg; **beneficial** ~**s** wertsteigernde Meliorationen; **necessary** ~**s** werterhaltende Gebäudeverbesserungen; **widely spread** ~ *(stock exchange)* Kursanstieg auf breiter Front; **voluntary** ~ Verschönerungsarbeiten;
~ **in pay** Gehaltsaufbesserung; ~ **in rates** Tarifverbesserung; ~ **in stocks** Erholung der Aktienkurse;
~ **course** Fortbildungskursus; ~ **grants** Wohngebäude-, Meliorationszuschüsse; ~ **industry** Veredelungswirtschaft; ~ **trade** Veredelungsverkehr.

impulse buying Spontan-, Stimmungskäufe.

imputed | **cost** kalkulatorische Kosten; ~ **notice** zurechenbare Kenntnis; ~ **price** Schattenpreis.

in *(additional)* als Zugabe, *(fashion)* in Mode, modern, *(train)* angekommen;
~**-between** Zwischenhändler; ~**-grade salary decrease** tarifliche Niederstufung; ~**-house fund** versicherungseigener Infestmentfonds; ~**-plant shop** Werksladen; ~**-plant training** *(US)* Werkstattausbildung.

inability | **to pay** Zahlungsunfähigkeit; ~ **to supply goods** Lieferunfähigkeit.

inactive *(business)* still, *(stock exchange)* flau, reserviert, lustlos;

~ **capital** brachliegendes Kapital; ~ **money** gehortetes Geld; ~ **securities** Effekten mit geringen Umsätzen.

inanimate *(market)* flau, unbelebt, lustlos.

inaugurate | *(v.)* **an air service** Fluglinienverkehr aufnehmen; ~ **a life insurance** Lebensversicherung abschließen.

incapable of managing one's own affairs in some jurisdictions beschränkt geschäftsfähig.

incapacitated arbeitsunfähig, geschäftsunfähig; ~ **worker** Invalide, Erwerbsunfähiger.

incapacity to act in law Geschäftsunfähigkeit.

incentive [Leistungs]anreiz, *(salesman)* Leistungsprämie;
to lack ~ *(market)* lustlos sein;
~ **bonus** Leistungszulage; ~ **pay** Leistungslohn; ~ **plan** Prämienwesen; ~ **premium** Gratiskupon; ~ **taxation** zyklisches Steuersystem; ~ **wage plan (system)** Leistungslohnsystem.

inchoate | **cheque** *(Br.)* nicht fertig ausgefüllter Scheck; ~ **instrument** *(Br.)* Blankoakzept.

incidence | **of loss** Schadenshäufigkeit; ~ **of a tax** Steuerbelastung, -anfall, -wirkung.

incidental earnings Nebenverdienst.

inclination to buy Kaufneigung, -lust, -interesse.

incline *(v.)* **to rise** *(market)* zur Festigkeit neigen.

inclusive | **charge** Gesamtgebühr; ~ **terms** *(at a hotel)* alles inbegriffen.

income Einkommen, Einnahmen, Einkünfte;
adjusted gross ~ *(US)* steuerpflichtiges Bruttoeinkommen; **deferred** ~ *(accounting)* antizipatorische Passiva; **accrued expense and deferred** ~ *(balance sheet)* Rechnungsabgrenzung; **earned** ~ Erwerbseinkommen, Einkünfte aus gewerblicher Tätigkeit; **national** ~ Volkseinkommen; **nonrecurring** ~ einmalige Erträgnisse; **occupational** ~ Einkünfte aus selbständiger Arbeit (freiberuflicher Tätigkeit); **operating** ~ Betriebseinnahmen; **pretax** ~ Einkommen vor [Abzug der] Steuern; **professional** ~ Einkünfte aus freiberuflicher Tätigkeit; **retained** ~ *(US)* unverteilter Reingewinn; **retirement** ~ Ruhegehalt; **tax-exempt** ~ steuerfreie Einkünfte; **taxable** ~ steuerpflichtiges Einkommen; **trading** ~ Einkünfte aus Gewerbebetrieb; **unearned** ~ *(investment)* arbeitsloses (fundiertes) Einkommen, Kapitalertrag; **wage** ~ Einkünfte aus nicht selbständiger Arbeit;
~ **in the $ 15 000—20 000 bracket** Einkommen zwischen 15 000 und 20 000 Dollar; ~ **from capital** Einkünfte aus Kapitalvermögen; ~ **not charged under any other heading** *(income-tax form, Br.)* sonstige Einkünfte; ~ **received from social insurance** Bezüge aus der Sozialversicherung; ~ **from sales** Umsatzerlöse, Veräußerungsgewinne; ~ **for the year** Jahresgewinn;
to average one' ~ seine Einkünfte über mehrere Jahre verteilen; **to exceed one's** ~ über seine Verhältnisse leben; **to report as taxable** ~ [als Einkommen] versteuern;
~ **account** Ertragsrechnung; **national** ~ **accounting** Volksvermögensrechnung; ~ **averaging** Durchschnittsbesteuerung; ~ **basis** Rendite [eines Wertpapiers]; ~ **bracket** Einkommensteuergruppe; ~ **deductions** Erlösschmälerungen; ~ **earner** *(US)* Einkommensbezieher; ~ **engineering** *(US)* Haushaltsaufstellung; **upper** ~ **family** gut verdienende Familie; ~ **increment** Einkommenssteigerung; ~ **limit** [Einkommensteuer]freigrenze; ~ **policy** Rentenversicherung zugunsten eines überlebenden Dritten; ~**yielding property** Einkünfte aus Kapitalvermögen; ~ **realization** Gewinnrealisierung; ~ **receiver** Einkommensempfänger; ~ **redistribution** Einkommensumverteilung; ~ **relief** *(Br.)* Einkommensteuererleichterung; ~ **return** *(US)* Rendite, ~ **splitting** Splitting; ~ **statement** *(US)* Gewinn- und Verlustrechnung; ~ **surtax** Einkommensteuerzuschlag.

income tax Einkommensteuer.
normal ~ *(US)* Einkommensteuer; **withholding** ~ Lohnsteuerabzug;
~ **on corporations** *(US)* Körperschaftssteuer; ~ **on individuals** *(US)* Einkommensteuer für natürliche Personen;
~ **age exemption** altersbedingte Einkommensteuerfreigrenze; ~ **credit** *(US)* Einkommensteuervergünstigung; ~ **deductions** Abzüge vom steuerpflichtigen Einkommen; ~ **form** Einkommensteuerformular; ~ **relief** *(Br.)* Einkommensteuervergünstigung; **to file one's** ~ **return** Einkommensteuererklärung abgeben.

incoming *(accruing)* erwachsend, *(order)* einlaufend; ~ **partner** neu eintretender Gesellschafter; ~**stocks** Warenzugänge.

inconvertibility *(banknotes)* Nichteinlösbarkeit.

inconvertible *(banknotes)* nicht einlösbar, *(debentures)* nicht konvertierbar, unkonvertierbar.

incorporate *(v.)* als Aktiengesellschaft eintragen;
~ *(a.)* inkorporiert, *(registered)* amtlich eingetragen;
~ **body** Körperschaft.

incorporated inkorporiert, registriert, als juristische Person eingetragen;
~ **in the United Kingdom** mit Sitz in England;
to be ~ Rechtspersönlichkeit erlangen;
~ **accountant** *(Br.)* staatlich geprüfter Bücherrevisor; ~ **bank** *(US)* Aktienbank; ~ **company** rechtsfähige Handelsgesellschaft, *(US)* Aktiengesellschaft.

incorporation Körperschaft, *(forming of corporation)* Inkorporierung, Körperschaftsbildung, *(registration)* [amtliche] Eintragung, Registrierung; ~ **fee** Eintragungsgebühr.

incoterms Regeln für die Auslegung handelsüblicher Vertragsformen.

, **increase** *(advance)* Ansteigen, Erhöhung, Steigerung, *(augmentation)* Vergrößerung, Wachstum, Erweiterung, Zunahme;
17 % ~ 17 %ige Zuwachsrate; **interest** ~ Zinserhöhung; **price** ~ Preis-, Kurserhöhung;
~ **in the bank rate** Diskonterhöhung; ~ **in (of)**

capital Kapitalerhöhung; ~ of capital stock *(US)* Kapitalaufstockung; ~ in cost Kostensteigerung; ~ of the currency Geldvermehrung; ~ in demand wachsende Nachfrage; ~ of [their] special deposits with the Bank of England [etwa] Mindestreservenerhöhung bei der Bundesnotenbank; ~ in efficiency Leistungssteigerung; ~ of liquidity Liquiditätsverbesserung; ~ in productivity Produktivitätssteigerung; ~ in range of goods Sortimentserweiterung; ~ in the rediscount rate *(US)* Diskontsatzerhöhung; ~ of salary Gehaltszulage; ~ in unemployment Zunahme der Arbeitslosigkeit; ~ in wages Lohnanstieg;
~ *(v.)* erhöhen, steigern, vermehren, *(v. i.)* anwachsen, [an]steigen, zunehmen;
~ the borrowings at the bank Bankkredit in erhöhtem Maße in Anspruch nehmen; ~ the original capital by ... Grundkapital um ... erhöhen; ~ paper circulation Notenumlauf steigern; ~ in value im Wert steigen.
increased demand Bedarfszunahme, Mehrbedarf.
increment Zunahme, [Wert]zuwachs;
annual ~ *(salary)* jährliche Gehaltssteigerung; marginal ~ Mindestwerterhöhung; pension ~ Pensionsaufstockung; unearned ~ Wertzuwachs;
~ income tax Gewinnzuwachssteuer; ~ value duty Wertzuwachssteuer.
incumbered verschuldet, belastet.
incumbrance *(mortgage)* Hypothekenbelastung.
incur *(v.)* | debts Schulden machen; ~ losses Verlust erleiden.
indebted verschuldet, schuldenbelastet;
to be contingently ~ aus Giroverbindlichkeiten schulden.
indebtedness Verschuldung, Schulden[last],
excessive ~ Überschuldung; long-term ~ langfristige Verschuldung.
indemnification Entschädigung, Vergütung, Schadloshaltung, Ersatzleistung, Schadenersatz;
special ~ Sondervergütung.
indemnify entschädigen, schadlos halten, Schadenersatz leisten;
~ s. o. for expenses incurred jem. seine Spesen ersetzen; ~ s. o. for a loss j. für einen Verlust entschädigen.
indemnity Entschädigungsbetrag, -summe, Schadenersatz, *(compensation)* Entschädigung, Abfindung;
cash ~ Mankogeld; lump-sum ~ Pauschalabfindung;
~ against liability Haftungsfreistellung;
to waive a claim to ~ auf Schadenersatzansprüche verzichten;
~ bond *(US)* Ausfallbürgschaft; ~ contract Schuldübernahmevertrag; ~ letter *(Br.)* Garantieverpflichtung, Ausfallbürgschaft.
indent *(export order)* Auslandsauftrag;
ration ~ *(Br.)* Bezugsschein;
~ *(v.)* [Auslands]auftrag erteilen.
indented im Lehrlingsverhältnis.

indenture Lehrvertrag;
trust ~ *(US)* Treuhandvertrag;
~ *(v.)* in die Lehre geben.
indentured im Lehrlingsverhältnis.
independent | accountant *(US)* Wirtschaftsprüfer; in an ~ capacity selbständig; ~ contractor selbständiger Unternehmer; to have an ~ income privatisieren; ~ means eigenes Vermögen.
indeterminate obligation Gattungsschuld.
index Inhalts-, Namenverzeichnis, Index, [Sach]register, Tabelle, Kennziffer;
tied to the ~ indexgebunden;
card ~ Kartei, Kartothek; cost-of-living ~ Lebenshaltungsindex; national-production ~ Index der industriellen Nettoproduktion; share-price ~ *(Br.)* Aktienindex; stock-exchange ~ Börsenindex;
~ of general business activity Konjunkturindex; ~ of retail prices Einzelhandelsindex; ~ of stocks *(US)* Aktienindex;
~ card Karteikarte; ~ clause Indexklausel.
index number *(statistics)* Index[zahl], Indexziffer;
~ of cost of living Lebenskosten-, Lebenshaltungsindex; ~ of wholesale prices Großhandelsindex.
indication | of origin Ursprungsbezeichnung; ~ of price Preisangabe.
indicator Indikator, Meßgröße;
~ of business Konjunkturbarometer.
indirect | action *(advertising)* Prestigewerbung; ~ bill Domizilwechsel; ~ cost Fertigungsgemeinkosten; ~ exchange indirekte Devisenarbitrage; ~ labo(u)r Gemeinkostenlöhne; ~ liability Eventualverbindlichkeit; ~ rates *(Br.)* per Pfund notierte Devisenkurse; ~ relief *(double taxation)* Anrechnungsverfahren; ~ tax indirekte Steuer.
individual | assets Privatvermögen [eines Gesellschafters]; ~ bargaining Einzeltarifverhandlung; ~ credit Personalkredit; ~ earnings pro-Kopf-Einkommen; ~ income tax *(US)* Einkommensteuer; ~ location *(advertising)* Sonderplacierung; ~ proprietor alleiniger Geschäftsinhaber.
indoor | relief Anstaltspflege; ~ work Haus-, Heimarbeit.
indorsable girierbar, indossabel, indossierbar.
indorse *(v.)* indossieren, girieren, begeben;
~ in full voll girieren.
indorsed in blank in Blanko giriert.
indorsee Girat, Indossat, Indossatar.
indorsement Giro, Indossament, Indossierung;
without ~ ungiriert;
absolute ~ *(US)* unbeschränktes Giro; accommodation ~ Gefälligkeitsindossament; blank ~ Blankoindossament; direct ~ *(US)* Vollgiro; partial ~ Teilindossament; qualified ~ Giro ohne Verbindlichkeit; ~ required Giro fehlt; restrictive ~ Rektaindossament;
~ without recourse Giro ohne Verbindlichkeit.
indorser Girant, Indossant, Begebender;
accommodation ~ Gefälligkeitsgirant; preceding (previous, prior) ~ Vordermann.
inducement to buy Kaufanreiz.

indulgence Zahlungs-, [Wechsel]stundung.
industrial Gewerbetreibender, Industrieller;
~s *(stock exchange)* Industriewerte;
~ *(a.)* industriell, gewerblich, industrialisiert;
~ **accession** Bearbeitungszuschlag; ~ **accident** Fabrik-, Betriebsunfall; ~ **accounting** Betriebsbuchhaltung; ~ **adviser** *(US)* Betriebsberater; ~ **agreement** Tarifabkommen; ~ **arbitration** gewerbliche Schiedsgerichtsbarkeit; ~ **bill** Industrieakzept; ~ **building** gewerblich genutztes Gebäude; ~ **canteen** Betriebskantine; ~ **capital** Gewerbekapital; ~ **census** Betriebszählung; ~ **city** Fabrikstadt; ~ **complex** Industriekomplex; ~ **concern** Industrieunternehmen, -betrieb; ~ **conflict** Arbeitskonflikt; ~ **conscription** *(US)* Arbeitsdienstpflicht; ~ **consumer** gewerblicher Verbraucher; ~ **death benefit for widows and other dependants** *(Br.)* Invalidenrente für Familienangehörige; ~ **development company** Erschließungsgesellschaft; ~ **disease** Berufskrankheit; ~ **division** Fachgruppe; ~ **economy** gewerbliche Wirtschaft; ~ **engineering** Fertigungssteuerung; ~ **enterprise** gewerblicher Betrieb; ~ **estate** *(Br.)* Industrieerwartungsland; ~ **exhibition** Gewerbeausstellung; ~ **features** *(stock exchange)* Industriewerte; ~ **hazard** Betriebsrisiko; ~ **investment** Vermögensanlage in Industriewerten; ~ **labo(u)rer** Fabrikarbeiter; ~ **leader** Wirtschaftsführer; ~ **line** Betriebseisenbahn; ~ **loan** Industriekredit; ~ **loan company** gewerbliche Kreditgenossenschaft; ~ **management** Betriebsführung; ~ **market** Investitionsgütermarkt; ~ **mobility** Freizügigkeit der Arbeitskräfte; ~ **partnership** *(US)* Arbeitergewinnbeteiligung; ~ **pension plan** betriebliche Altersversorgung; ~ **and provident society** *(Br.)* Erwerbsgenossenschaft; ~ **regulations** gewerbepolizeiliche Bestimmungen; ~ **retail store** werkseigener Verkaufsladen; ~ **savings** Werksparen; ~ **sickness insurance fund** Betriebskrankenkasse; ~ **site** Fabrikgrundstück; ~ **track** Fabrikgleis; ~ **use** Gewerbezweck; ~ **user** gewerblicher Verbraucher; ~ **worker** Industrie-, Fabrikarbeiter.
industries, hard-goods devisenstarke Industriezweige; **secondary** ~ weiterverarbeitende Industrie; **to shut down whole** ~ ganze Industriezweige stillegen.
industry Industrie *(branch of ~)* Branche, Gewerbe-, Wirtschafts-, Industriezweig;
automobile (automotive, *US)* ~ Kraftfahrzeugindustrie; **basic** ~ Grund[stoff]industrie; **capital-goods** ~ Investitionsgüterindustrie; **coal, iron and steel** ~ Montanindustrie; **consumer (consumption [goods])** ~ Verbrauchsgüterindustrie; **continuous** ~ Industriebetrieb mit durchgehender Arbeitszeit; **infant** ~ schutzzollbedürftige Industrie; **medium-sized** ~ Mittelbetriebe; **octopied** ~ dezentralisierter Großbetrieb; **producer-goods** ~ Produktionsgüterindustrie; **retail** ~ Einzelhandelsgewerbe; **sophisticated** ~ Industrie für Güter des gehobenen Bedarfs; **sweated** ~ unterentlohntes Gewerbe;
to create ~ **from the ground up** Industriebetrieb auf der grünen Wiese beginnen;

~ **competition** industrieller Wettbewerb; ~ **executives** industrielle Führungskräfte; ~ **label** gewerbliche Schutzmarke; ~ **slump** industrielle Rezession; ~**wide bargaining** Tarifverhandlungen für einen gesamten Industriebereich.
ineligible paper *(US)* nicht diskontfähiges Papier.
inexperienced worker ungelernter Arbeiter.
inferior *(a.)* minderwertig, mittelmäßig, ziemlich schlecht, zweitklassig, [im Wert] geringer; ~ **goods** minderwertige Ware; ~ **position** unbedeutende (untergeordnete) Stellung.
inflate *(v.)* **the currency** Geldumlauf künstlich steigern, Inflation herbeiführen.
inflated | currency Inflationswährung; ~ **prices** künstlich überhöhte Preise; ~ **stocks** überhöhte Lagerhaltung.
inflation Inflation, [Geld]entwertung;
cost-push ~ kostentreibende Inflation; **creeping** ~ schleichende Inflation; **wage-push** ~ durch Lohnsteigerung bedingte Inflation;
to bring ~ **under control** Inflation in den Griff bekommen; **to prime** ~ Inflation anheizen; **to slow down** ~ Inflationsrate verlangsamen.
~ **boom** inflationistische Konjunktur; ~**induced** inflationsbedingt; ~**prone goods** inflationsempfindliche Waren; ~ **rate** Inflationsrate.
inflationary | adjustment Inflationsausgleich; ~ **gain** Inflationsgewinn; ~ **gap** inflatorische Lücke; ~ **pressure** Inflationsdruck; ~ **spiral** Inflations-, Preisspirale.
inflow of capital Kapitalzufluß.
influence | of rationalization Rationalisierungseffekt; ~ **peddler** Regierungskontakter.
influx | of foreign exchange *(US)* Devisenzuflüsse; ~ **of wealth** Wohlstandszunahme.
informal record *(bookkeeping)* inoffizielle Buchungsunterlage.
information, inside vertrauliche Mitteilung;
~ **agency** Informationsbüro, -stelle; ~ **bureau** *(US)* Auskunftei; ~ **manager** Leiter der Marktforschung; ~ **stand** *(fair)* Auskunftsstand; ~ **window** Auskunftsschalter.
informative labeling Herkunftsbezeichnung.
infringement | of contract Vertragsbruch; ~ **of a trademark** Warenzeichenverletzung, Markenfälschung.
ingot of gold Goldbarren.
inhabited-house duty Hauszinssteuer.
inherent defect (vice) *(law of contract)* innewohnender (versteckter) Mangel.
inheritance tax *(US)* Nachlaß-, Erbschaftssteuer.
initial | allocation Erstausstattung; ~ **allowance** *(Br.)* Sonderabschreibung für Neuanschaffungen; ~ **capital** Anfangs-, Gründungs-, Einlegekapital; ~ **capitalization** Erstausstattung; ~ **carrier** Aufgabespediteur; ~ **cost** Anschaffungspreis; ~ **dividend** *(Br.)* Abschlagsdividende; ~ **payment** Anzahlung; ~ **placing of securities** Erstabsatz von Wertpapieren; ~ **salary** Anfangsgehalt.
initial(l)ed | check *(US)* **(cheque,** *Br.)* Scheck mit geprüfter Unterschrift.

initiation fee Aufnahme-, Eintrittsgebühr.

injection of capital Kapitalspritze.

injunction Vorschrift, richterliche Verfügung.

injure *(v.) (damage)* beschädigen, Schaden zufügen, *(impair)* schädigen, beeinträchtigen;
~ **s. one's interests** jds. Interessen (Rechte) beeinträchtigen.

injury [Be]schädigung, Schaden;
disabling ~ Dienstbeschädigung; **occupational** ~ Betriebs-, Arbeitsunfall;
~ **suffered by goods** Warenbeschädigung; ~ **to one's reputation** Kreditgefährdung, -schädigung;
~ **benefit** *(Br.)* Unfallrente.

inland | **carrier** Binnenfrachtführer; ~ **commodities** Landesprodukte; ~ **duty** Binnenzoll; ~ **mail** *(Br.)* Inlandpost; ~ **marine insurance** Binnentransportversicherung; ~ **market** Binnenmarkt; ~ **money order** Inlandspostanweisung; ~ **product** einheimisches Fabrikat; ~ **revenue** *(Br.)* Steuereinnahmen;
♀ **Revenue Office** *(Br.)* Einkommensteuerverwaltung; ♀ **Revenue stamp** *(Br.)* Stempel-, Steuermarke; ~ **transportation insurance** Binnentransportversicherung.

· **inner reserves** *(finance)* stille Reserven.

innkeeper's liability Gastwirtshaftung.

innocent | **goods** nicht geschmuggelte Waren; ~ **holder for value** gutgläubiger Besitzer.

inofficial | **dealings** *(stock exchange)* Freiverkehr; ~ **market** Freiverkehrsmarkt.

inoperative account *(Br.)* umsatzloses Konto.

input | **price** Kostengüterpreis; ~ **tax** Vorsteuer.

inquire *(v.)* **the price** nach dem Preis fragen, Preis erfragen.

inquiry Nachforschung, -frage, Anfrage;
without ~ *(stock exchange)* nicht gesucht;
~ **agency** Auskunftei; ~ **office** Auskunftsbüro, -stelle, Auskunftei, *(railway)* Auskunftschalter.

inroad Überfall, *(fig.)* Ein-, Übergriff;
to make ~s **upon s. one's savings** Loch in jds. Ersparnisse reißen.

inscribe *(v.)* **across the face of a bill** auf der Rückseite eines Wechsels girieren.

inscribed stock börsenmäßig gehandelte Buchwerte, Schuldbuchgiroforderungen.

inscription Registrierung von Namenspapieren;
~ **form** Anmeldeformular.

insecure | **investment** unsichere Kapitalanlage; ~ **load** unbefestigte Ladung.

insert *(advertising)* Inserat, Anzeige, *(extra leaf, US)* Beilage, Beilagenprospekt, Beihefter, Beileger, *(postal service)* Drucksache;
~ *(v.) (in newspaper)* [Anzeige] einrücken lassen, inserieren;
~ **in a catalog(ue)** in einen Katalog aufnehmen; ~ **a coin in a slot machine** Münze in einen Automaten einwerfen.

insertion | **of an advertisement** Anzeigenaufgabe;
~ **schedule** Erscheinungsplan.

inset Einlage, Beilage, *(advertising)* Einschaltseite.

inside | **address** Innenadresse; ~ **board** *(US)* Füh-

rungsgremium aus leitenden Angestellten; ~ **broker** *(Br.)* amtlich zugelassener Makler.

insiders eingeweihte Kreise, *(Br.)* Börsenmakler.

insolvency Insolvenz, Unvermögen, Überschuldung, Zahlungsunfähigkeit, -einstellung, Fallisement, Konkurs;
commercial ~ Geschäftsinsolvenz; **national** ~ Staatsbankrott; **voluntary** ~ vom Gemeinschuldner beantragtes Vergleichsverfahren;
~ **of an estate** Nachlaßüberschuldung;
to declare one's ~ sich für zahlungsunfähig erklären, seine Zahlungen einstellen;
~ **fund** Insolvenzenfonds; ~ **laws** *(Br.)* Vergleichsordnung; ~ **proceedings** Vergleichsverfahren; ~ **statute** *(US)* Vergleichsordnung.

insolvent *(a.)* überschuldet, zahlungsunfähig, illiquide, insolvent, bankrott;
to be adjudged ~ für bankrott erklärt werden;
~ **debtor** Gemein-, Konkursschuldner.

inspect *(v.)* | **the books** Bücher revidieren (einsehen);
~ **a car** [Auto]inspektion durchführen; ~ **the extent of the damage** Schaden besichtigen.

inspecting order Prüfungsauftrag.

inspection Prüfung, Kontrolle, Revision, *(car)* Inspektion;
subject to ~ prüfungspflichtig;
factory ~ gewerbepolizeiliche Überprüfung, Gewerbeaufsicht; **shipping-point** ~ Prüfung am Versandort;
~ **of documents** Akteneinsicht; ~ **of goods** Besichtigung der Ware;
~ **certificate** Prüfungsbescheinigung; ~ **cost** Abnahmekosten; ~ **stamp** Kontrollmarke; ~ **tour** Besichtigungsreise.

inspector Aufseher, Aufsichtsbeamter, Prüfer, *(customs)* Zollaufseher, -beamter;
factory ~ Gewerbeaufseher;
♀ **of Taxes** *(Br.)* Finanzamtleiter.

installation Betriebseinrichtung, Werk, Fabrikanlage, *(setting up)* Installierung, Einbau, Montage;
~s **under construction** *(balance sheet)* Anlagen im Bau.

instal[l]ment *(installation)* Aufstellung, Installierung, Einbau, Montage, *(part payment)* Raten-, Ab-, Teilzahlung, Rate;
by ~s ratenweise, in Raten;
first ~ Anzahlung; **sinking-fund** ~ Ablösungsrate;
~ **of purchase price** Kaufpreisrate;
to be behindhand with an ~ mit einer Rate im Rückstand sein; **to be published in** ~s in Fortsetzungen veröffentlicht werden; **to issue a loan in** ~s Anleihe in Stücken ausgeben; **to vote credits in** ~s Kredit nur ratenweise bewilligen;
~ **account** Abzahlungskonto; ~ **business** Raten-, Abzahlungsgeschäft; ~ **buying** Abzahlungskauf, Teilzahlungsgeschäft; ~ **credit business** Teil-, Abzahlungsgeschäft; ~ **house** *(US)* Kundenkreditbank; ~ **method of accounting** Buchungsmethode mit Realisierung der Rohgewinne bei Ratenein-

gang; ~ **mortgage** Amortisationshypothek; ~ **obligations** Teilzahlungsverpflichtungen; ~ **payment** Teil-, Abschlags-, Ratenzahlung; **on the ~ plan** auf Abzahlung[sbasis]; **to buy on the ~ plan** auf Raten kaufen; ~ **receivables** *(balance sheet)* Abzahlungsverträge; ~ **system** Abzahlungs-, Raten-, Teilzahlungssystem.
instant dismissal fristlose Entlassung.
institute | **for business-cycle research** Konjunkturinstitut;
~ *(v.)* **[bankruptcy] proceedings against** [Konkurs]verfahren eröffnen;
~**cargo clause** *(Br.)* zusätzliche Frachtdeckungsklausel.
institution Anstalt, Institut, *(EG)* Organ, *(society)* Stiftung, Gesellschaft;
banking ~ Bankinstitut; **charitable** ~ wohltätige (milde) Stiftung; **nonprofit-making** ~ gemeinnützige Einrichtung.
institutional | **advertising** *(US)* Eigen-, Vertrauens-, Goodwill-, Repräsentations-, Firmenwerbung; **to prosper on** ~ **business** im Kapitalanlagegeschäft erfolgreich sein; ~ **campaign** Goodwillwerbung; ~ **clients** Anlagepublikum; ~ **investor (lender)** Kapitalsammelstelle.
instruct *(v.)* **a clerk in bookkeeping** Angestellten in die Buchführung einweisen.
instruction Anordnung, [An]weisung, Auftrag, Vorschrift;
shipping ~**s** *(US)* Versandanweisung;
~**s for use** Gebrauchsanweisung;
~ **booklet** Gebrauchsanweisung; ~ **manual** Betriebsanweisung.
instrument Dokument, Urkunde, Papier;
bearer ~ Inhaberpapier; **negotiable** ~ begebbares Papier; **nonnegotiable** ~ Rektapapier;
~ **payable to order** Orderpapier.
insufficiency of assets ungenügende Deckung.
insufficient | **assets** unzureichende Aktiva; ~ **funds** *(bill of exchange)* ungenügende Deckung; ~ **packing** mangelhafte Verpackung.
insurable | **interest** Versicherungsinteresse; ~ **value** Versicherungswert.
insurance Versicherung, Versicherungsprämie, -summe;
accident benefit ~ Unfallversicherung; **accounts receivable** ~ Debitorenversicherung; **air passengers'** ~ Fluggastversicherung; **[compulsory] automobile** ~ *(US)* Kraftfahrzeug[haftpflicht]versicherung; **automobile personal liability and property damage** ~ *(US)* Kaskoversicherung; **baggage** ~ *(US)* Reisegepäckversicherung; **business** ~ Versicherung leitender Angestellter; **business interruption** ~ Betriebsstillstandversicherung; **check (cheque,** *Br.)* **alteration and forgery** ~ Versicherung gegen Scheckfälschungen; **commercial accident** ~ Betriebsunfallversicherung; **compensation** ~ *(US)* Arbeiterunfallversicherung; **comprehensive motorcar** ~ *(Br.)* Vollkaskoversicherung; **voluntarily continued** ~ freiwillige Weiterversiche-

rung; **contractors' public liability and property damage liability** ~ Unternehmerhaftpflicht- und Schadenversicherung; **contributory** ~ Versicherung mit Selbstbehalt; **convertible term** ~ Risikoumtauschversicherung; **disability (disablement)** ~ Invaliditätsversicherung; **employers' liability** ~ Betriebshaftpflichtversicherung; **endowment** ~ Versicherung auf den Erlebensfall, Aussteuerversicherung; **fidelity** ~ *(US)* Kautionsversicherung; **free** ~ kostenloser Versicherungsschutz; **furniture-in-transit** ~ Umzugsversicherung; **group** ~ Kollektivversicherung; **hazardous** ~ Elementarschadensversicherung; **hospital benefit** ~ Krankenhauszuschußversicherung; **hull** ~ *(airplane, ship)* Kaskoversicherung; **industrial [life]** ~ *(US)* Volks-, Kleinlebensversicherung; **joint life** ~ Überlebensversicherung; **public liability** ~ öffentliche Haftpflichtversicherung; **limited payment** ~ Lebensversicherung mit abgekürzter Prämienlaufzeit; **luggage** ~ *(Br.)* Reisegepäckversicherung; **marine (maritime)** ~ Seeschadenversicherung; **National** ⚬ *(Br.)* Sozialversicherung; **paid-up** ~ beitragsfreie Versicherung; **partnership** ~ Teilhaberversicherung; **property damage liability** ~ Sachschadenversicherung; **registered-mail** ~ Versicherung für eingeschriebene Postsendungen; **rent** ~ Mietverlustversicherung; **residence burglary** ~ Einbruchsversicherung; **safe-deposit box** ~ Depotversicherung; **shipping** ~ *(US)* Transportversicherung; **sickness** ~ *(US)* Krankenversicherung; **single-premium** ~ Lebensversicherung gegen Zahlung einer einmaligen Prämie; **supplementary** ~ Zusatzversicherung; **survivorship** ~ Hinterbliebenen-, Überlebensversicherung; **tenant's liability** ~ Mieterhaftpflichtversicherung; **term** ~ Kurzversicherung; **tourist weather** ~ Reisewetterversicherung; **unemployment** ~ Arbeitslosenversicherung; **whole-life** ~ Lebensversicherung auf den Todesfall, reine Todesfallversicherung; **workmens' compensation** ~ *(US)* Berufsunfallversicherung;
~ **against damage to property** Sachschadenversicherung; ~ **on hull and appurtenances** *(ship)* Kaskoversicherung; ~ **against loss by redemption (redemption at par)** Kursverlustversicherung; ~ **against all risks** Versicherung gegen alle Gefahren; ~ **in transit** Transitversicherung; ~ **of value** Valoren-, Wertversicherung;
to arrange an ~ Versicherung abschließen; **to carry** ~ **against legal liability** gesetzliche Haftpflichtversicherung unterhalten; **to receive** £ **10 000** ~ Versicherungssumme in Höhe von 10 000 £ ausgezahlt bekommen; **to surrender an** ~ Versicherungspolice zurückkaufen; **to write** ~ als Versicherer tätig sein;
National ⚬ **Act** *(Br.)* Sozialversicherungsgesetz; ~ **adjuster** Schadensregulierer; ~ **agency** Versicherungsagentur; ~ **agent** Versicherungsvertreter; ~ **benefit** Versicherungsleistung; **to be engaged in the** ~ **business** im Versicherungsgewerbe tätig sein; ~ **certificate** Versicherungsbescheinigung; **to settle**

~ **claims** Versicherungsansprüche regulieren; ⁀ **Commissioner** *(US)* Landesaufsichtsamt für das Versicherungswesen; **mutual life** ~ **company** Lebensversicherungsverein auf Gegenseitigkeit; ~ **consumer** Versicherungsnehmer; ~ **contract** Versicherungsvertrag; **national** ~ **contributions** *(Br.)* Sozialversicherungsbeiträge; **social** ~ **contributions** *(US)* Sozialversicherungsbeiträge; ~ **coverage** Versicherungsschutz; ~ **fraud** Versicherungsbetrug; **National** ⁀ **Fund** *(Br.)* Sozialversicherungsstock; ~ **money** Versicherungssumme; ~ **note** vorläufiger Deckungsschein; ~ **office** Versicherungsanstalt; **extended-term** ~ **option** Wahlrecht der beitragsfreien Lebensversicherung; ~ **period** Versicherungszeit; ~ **policy** Versicherungspolice; ~ **premium** Versicherungsprämie; ~ **regulation** Regulierung eines Versicherungsfalles; ~ **salesman** Versicherungsvertreter; **contributory** ~ **scheme** beitragspflichtiges Versicherungssystem; ~ **technician** Versicherungsmathematiker; ~ **trade** Versicherungsgewerbe; ~ **umbrella** Versicherungsschutz.

insure *(v.)* versichern, sich versichern lassen, Versicherung abschließen, *(guarantee)* garantieren, verbürgen, sicherstellen;
~ **for a larger amount** nachversichern; ~ **one's house against fire** sein Haus feuerversichern; ~ **against illness** Krankenversicherung abschließen; ~ **a number in a lottery** auf eine besondere Lotterienummer setzen; ~ **s. th. against all risks** für etw. eine Generalpolice nehmen.

insured Versicherter, Versicherungsnehmer;
amount ~ Versicherungssumme, Deckungsbetrag; ~ **letter** *(Br.)* Wertbrief; ~ **person** Versicherungsnehmer.

insurer Versicherer, Versicherungsträger.

intangible assets immaterielle Werte.

integrated | **commercial** eingeblendete Werbesendung; ~ **economy** Verbundwirtschaft; ~ **store** *(US)* Kettenladen; ~ **trust** vertikaler Konzern.

integration | **of markets** Marktverflechtung;
‚ ~ **process** Integrationsprozeß.

intelligence, shipping Schiffahrtsnachrichten;
~ **bureau (department)** Auskunftsabteilung.

intending buyer (purchaser) Kaufinteressent, -reflektant.

intensive intensiv, ertragssteigernd.

intent | **on business** geschäftlich interessiert;
~ **application** ernstliche Bewerbung.

interagent Vermittler, Mittelsmann.

interbank clearings Lokalumschreibungen.

intercept | *(v.)* **the trade** Handel behindern.

intercity | **check (cheque,** *Br.)* **-clearing service** Scheckaustausch innerhalb einer Stadt; ~ **differential** Ortsklassen[lohn]ausgleich; ~ **train** Nahverkehrszug.

intercompany | **debt** Konzernschulden; ~ **elimination** *(consolidated balance sheet)* Konzernausgleich; ~ **operations** Geschäftsverkehr zwischen Konzerngesellschaften; ~ **profit** Konzernbuchgewinn.

interconnecting flight Anschlußflug.

intercorporate | **privilege** *(US)* Schachtelprivileg; ~ **stockholding** *(US)* Schachtel[besitz].

intercourse [Geschäfts]verkehr, Handelsverbindung.

interdiction of commerce Handelsverbot.

interest *(advantage)* Vorteil, Interesse, Belange, Nutzen, *(on loan)* Zinsen, Zinsfuß, Verzinsung, *(right)* [An]recht, Anspruch, *(share)* Beteiligung, Anteil; **and** ~ zuzüglich Stückzinsen; **at legal** ~ zum gesetzlichen Zinsfuß; **in the public** ~ im öffentlichen Interesse; **paying [no]** ~ [un]verzinslich; **without** ~ franko Zinsen;
accrued ~ aufgelaufene [aber noch nicht fällige] Zinsen, *(bonds)* Stückzinsen; **anticipatory** ~ Zinsvorauszahlungen; **business** ~ Geschäftsanteil; **collected in advance** ~ Zinsvorauszahlungen; **compound** ~ Zinseszinsen; **controlling** ~ Mehrheitsbeteiligung, ausschlaggebender Kapitalanteil; **debit** ~ Sollzinsen; ~ **due** Schuld-, Passivzinsen, fällige Zinsen; ~ **earned** Sollzinsen; **equated** ~ Staffelzinsen; **excessive** ~ Wucherzinsen; **government** ~s staatliche Beteiligungen; **graduated** ~ Staffelzinsen; **gross** ~ Bruttozinsen; **insurable** ~ Versicherungsinteresse; ~ **due** Schuld-, Passivzinsen, fällige Zinsen; **majority controlling** ~ ausschlaggebende Mehrheitsbeteiligung; **moneyed** ~ Finanzwelt; **mortgage** ~ Hypothekenzinsen; **one-third** ~ Drittelbeteiligung; **ordinary** ~ *(US)* auf Basis von 360 Tagen berechnete Zinsen; **partnership** ~ Gesellschaftsanteil; ~ **payable** fällige Zinsen; **pecuniary** ~ finanzielle Interesse; **pure** ~ Nettozinsen; ~ **receivable** *(US)* ausstehende Zinsen; **shipping** ~ Reedereibetrieb; **short** ~ *(stock exchange)* Baisse-engagement; **statutory** ~ gesetzlicher Zinssatz; **vital** ~s lebenswichtige Interessen;
~ **on arrears** Verzugszinsen; ~ **on capital** Kapitalverzinsung; ~ **on credit balances** Habenzinsen; ~ **on debit balances** Debit-, Sollzinsen; ~ **for default** Verzugszinsen; ~ **of legatee** Vermächtnisanspruch; ~ **in the nature of investments** *(balance sheet)* beteiligungsähnliche Ansprüche; ~ **pro and contra** Soll- und Habenzinsen; ~ **on shares** Stückzinsen;
to act in s. one's ~ für fremde Rechnung tätig werden; **to add the** ~ **to the capital** Zinsen zum Kapital schlagen; **to bear** ~ Zinsen tragen, sich verzinsen, verzinslich sein; **to buy an** ~ **in a firm** Geschäftsanteil übernehmen; **to carry a low rate of** ~ niedrig verzinslich sein; **to compute** ~ Zinsen berechnen; **to give s. o. financial** ~ **in a business** j. an einem Geschäft beteiligen; **to have an** ~ **in a business** Geschäftsanteil besitzen; **to have an** ~ **in an estate** erbberechtigt sein; **to hold a 10 %** ~ zehnprozentige Beteiligung besitzen; **to invest money at** ~ Geld verzinslich anlegen; **to lend at short** ~ kurzfristiges Darlehen gewähren; **to live on the** ~ **received from one's capital** von den Zinsen seines Vermögens leben; **to pay 8 per cent** ~ **on a loan** Kredit mit 8 % verzinsen; **to put out at** ~ verzinslich anlegen; **to raise the** ~ Zinssatz erhöhen; **to travel abroad in the**

~s of a business firm Geschäftsinteressen einer Firma im Ausland wahrnehmen; **to work out the** ~ Zinsen ausrechnen; **to yield high** ~ hohe Rendite erzielen;

~ **account** Zinsenkonto; **compound** ~ **basis** Zinseszinsbasis; ~**bearing investment** verzinsliche Kapitalanlage; ~ **charges** *(balance sheet)* Zinsen-[dienst]; ~ **cost** Habenzinsen; ~ **coupon** Zinsschein, -abschnitt, -kupon; ~ **expense** Zinslast; ~**free loan** unverzinsliches Darlehen; ~ **lottery** Prämienlotterie; ~ **numbers** Zinszahlen; ~ **payment date** Zinstermin; ~ **rate adjustment** Zinsanpassung; ~ **rate ceiling** Zinshöchstsätze; ~ **rebate (reduction)** Zinsnachlaß; **fixed-** ~ **securities** festverzinsliche Papiere; ~ **sheet** Zinsbogen; ~ **statement** Zinsenaufstellung; ~ **warrant** Zinsabschnitt, -kupon; ~ **yield** Zinsertrag, Rendite.

interested [mit]beteiligt, *(bias(s)ed)* parteiisch; **to be** ~ reflektieren; **to be financially** ~ **in a business** an einem Unternehmen finanziell beteiligt sein.

interfere | *(v.)* **with private business** in die Privatwirtschaft eingreifen; ~ **with s. one's interests** jds. Interessen beeinträchtigen.

interference Störung, Beeinträchtigung, Einmischung, *(clashing of interests)* Interessenkonflikt.

interfirm comparative studies Betriebsvergleich.

interim | **account** Zwischenkonto; ~ **agreement** vorläufige Vereinbarung; ~ **aid** Überbrückungshilfe; ~ **balance [sheet]** Zwischenabschluß; ~ **bill** Interimswechsel; ~ **credit** Zwischenkredit; ~ **dividend** Abschlagsdividende; ~ **factor** vorläufiger Konkursverwalter; ~ **financing** Zwischenfinanzierung; ~ **injunction** einstweilige Verfügung; ~ **order** vorläufige Anordnung; ~ **receipt** Zwischenquittung; ~ **stock certificate** *(US)* Interimsaktie.

interior *(a.) (domestic)* in-, binnenländisch; ~ **bank** *(US)* Provinzbank; ~ **display** Innenauslage; ~ **economy** Materialverwaltung; ~ **trade** Binnenhandel.

interline fare Teilstreckenfahrpreis.

interlocked enterprises verflochtene Unternehmen.

interlocking | **of several undertakings** Verschachtelung verschiedener Unternehmungen.

~ **combine** Konzernverflechtung; ~ **directorate** *(US)* Schachtelaufsichtsrat; ~ **right** *(US)* Schachtelprivileg.

interloper wilder (unkonzessionierter) Händler.

intermediary Mittelsmann, -person, *(trader)* Zwischenhändler,

~ **bank** eingeschaltete Bank.

intermediate | **account** Zwischenabrechnung; ~ **goods** Halbfabrikate; ~ **lag** Anlaufverzögerung; ~ **reply** Zwischenbescheid; ~**term** mittelfristig; ~ **trade** Zwischenhandel.

intermittent unemployment vorübergehende Arbeitslosigkeit.

internal innerstaatlich, binnen-, inländisch; ~ **account** Inlandskonto; ~ **audit** innerbetriebliche Revision; ~ **commerce** *(US)* Binnenhandel; ~ **consumption** Inlandsverbrauch; ~ **currency** Binnenwährung; ~ **monopoly** Binnenmonopol; ~ **national debt** innere Staatsschuld; ~ **navigation** Binnenschiffahrt; ~ **price** Versicherungspreis; ~ **revenue** *(US)* Staatseinkünfte aus inländischen Steuern; ~ **service** *(airline)* Inlandsflugverkehr; ~ **tariff** Binnenzoll; ~ **transaction** Buchhaltungsvorgang.

international *(a.)* zwischenstaatlich;

⌀ **Air Transport Association (IATA)** Internationaler Luftverkehrsverband; ⌀ **Bank for Reconstruction and Development** Internationale Wiederaufbaubank; ⌀ **Chamber of Commerce** Internationale Handelskammer; ⌀ **Development Agency** Internationale Entwicklungsstelle; ~ **economics** Außenwirtschaftstheorie, -politik; ⌀ **Labo(u)r Office** Internationales Arbeitsamt; ~ **market** *(stock exchange)* Markt für international gehandelte Wertpapiere; ⌀ **Monetary Fund** Weltwährungsfonds; ~ **money order** Auslandspostanweisung; ~ **payments** zwischenstaatlicher Zahlungsverkehr; ~ **price** Weltmarktpreis; ~ **reply coupon** internationaler [Rück]antwortschein; ~ **stocks** *(US)* international gehandelte Wertpapiere; **Standard** ⌀ **Trade Classification** Internationales Warenverzeichnis für den Außenhandel; ~ **transit** Transitverkehr.

interoffice | **memo** innerbetrieblicher Aktenvermerk; ~ **slip** Laufzettel.

interpretation | **of a contract** Vertragsauslegung; ~ **of statistics** Auswertung von Statistiken.

interruption | **of business** Unterbrechung des Geschäftsbetriebs; ~ **of traffic** Verkehrsstörung.

interstate commerce *(US)* zwischenstaatlicher Handel.

interurban traffic Überlandverkehr.

intervene *(v.)* **in case of need** als Notadressat intervenieren.

intervention Einmischung, Einschaltung, Dazwischentreten, Vermittlung;

direct ~ **in the economy** staatliche Intervention in die Wirtschaft.

~ **buying** *(International Monetary Fund)* Interventionskäufe.

intra-enterprise conspiracy Absprache zwischen Konzernunternehmen.

intrastate | **rate** *(US)* zwischenstaatlicher Tarif; ~ **shipment** binnenstaatlicher Versand.

introduce | *(v.)* **a new fashion** neue Mode aufbringen; ~ **new ideas into a business** Neuerungen in einem Geschäft einführen; ~ **an insurance** Versicherung vermitteln.

introduction | **of business** Anbahnung eines Geschäfts; ~ **of convertibility** Übergang zur Konvertierbarkeit; **progressive** ~ **of a common customs tariff** schrittweise Einführung eines gemeinsamen Zolltarifs.

introductory campaign *(advertising)* Einführungswerbung.

invade *(v.)* **a city** *(tourists)* Stadt überschwemmen; ~ **the principal** Kapital angreifen.

invalid Kranker, Gebrechlicher, Dienst-, Arbeitsunfähiger;

~ **check** *(US)* **(cheque**, *Br.)* unvollständiger Scheck; ~ **a letter of credit** ungültiger Kreditbrief.
invalidation of securities Kraftloserklärung von Wertpapieren.
invalidity *(US)* Arbeits-, Dienstunfähigkeit.
invention | **made by employees** Angestelltenerfindung; **to put an** ~ **to commercial use** Erfindung gewerblich verwerten.
inventories Lager-, Warenbestände, *(balance sheet)* Vorräte;
~ **at the lower of cost or market** Warenbestände zum Anschaffungs- oder niedrigeren Marktpreis angesetzt.
inventory Inventar[verzeichnis], Bestandsnachweis, -verzeichnis, *(inventory taking, US)* Bestandsaufnahme, Inventur, *(list of securities)* Stückeverzeichnis;
beginning ~ Anfangsinventar; **book** ~ *(US)* Buchinventar; **finished-goods** ~ Fertigwarenlager; -bestand; **low** ~ geringe Lagervorräte; **merchandise** ~ Warenbestand, -lager; **opening (original)** ~ Anfangs-, Eröffnungsinventar; **perpetual** ~ *(US)* buchmäßig geführtes Inventar; **physical** ~ Inventur; **raw-material[s]** ~ Rohstoffbestände; **top-heavy** ~ übervolles Lager; **unsold** ~ Lagerbestand; **work-in-process** ~ Halbfabrikate-Anfangsbestand;
~ **at cost** Inventar zum Anschaffungspreis; ~ **of property** Vermögensverzeichnis, *(bankruptcy proceedings)* Masseverzeichnis;
~ *(v.)* Verzeichnis anlegen, Inventar aufnehmen, inventarisieren, Inventur machen;
to draw up an ~ Inventar aufnehmen; **to keep down an** ~ Lagervorräte knapp bemessen; **to liquidate an** ~ *(US)* Lager (Vorräte) abbauen;
~ **account** Inventar-, Sachkonto; ~ **accumulation** Inventaranreicherung; ~ **audit** Bestandsprüfung; ~ **book** Inventarbuch; **perpetual** ~ **card** Lagerkarte; ~ **control** Vorratsbewirtschaftung; -bestand ~ **cut-off date** Inventurtag; ~ **growth** Lagerzunahme; ~ **increase** Lagerauffüllung; ~ **loan** Lagerfinanzierung durch mittel- oder langfristigen Kredit; ~ **markup** Rohgewinnaufschlag auf den Inventarwert; ~ **price decline** *(balance sheet, US)* Wertminderung der Vorräte; ~ **profit** Buchgewinn; ~ **reduction** Lagerabbau; ~ **reserve** Wertberichtigung der Vorratsvermögens; ~ **schedule** Bestandsverzeichnis; ~ **shrinkage** Bestandsverlust, Schwund; ~ **taking** Bestandsaufnahme; ~ **turnover** Umschlagsfähigkeit des Lagerbestands; ~ **writedown** Inventarabschreibung.
invest *(v.)* investieren, [Geld] anlegen, unterbringen, [Kapital] einschießen, placieren;
~ **advantageously** zinstragend anlegen; ~ **one's fortune in life annuities** sich in eine lebenslängliche Rente einkaufen; ~ **capital** Kapital anlegen investieren; ~ **in house property** Wohngrundstück erwerben; ~ **one's money to good account** sein Geld vorteilhaft anlegen; ~ **one's money in stocks and shares** sein [ganzes] Geld in Aktien anlegen.

invested capital Anlagekapital.
investigate *(v.)* **statistically** statistische Erhebungen anstellen.
investigation of a company's affairs Revision der Geschäfte einer Gesellschaft;
~ **service** Zollfahndungsdienst.
investigative | **agency** Fahndungsbehörde; ~ **unit** Zollfahndungsstelle.
investing | **institution** Kapitalsammelstelle; ~ **member** *(loan society Br.)* noch nicht zugeteilter Bausparer; ~ **public** Kapitalmarktpublikum.
investment [Kapital]anlage, Vermögensanlage, *(investing)* Investierung, Placierung, *(money put in)* [Kapital]einlage, Einschuß, Beteiligung, Anlage[kapital];
~s **abroad** Auslandsanlagen, auswärtige Investitionsvorhaben; **domestic** ~s Inlandsinvestitionen; **financial** ~ Geldmarktanlage; **fixed-income** ~ festverzinsliche Werte; **fixed-property** ~ Anlagevermögen; **gilt-edged (high-grade)** ~ mündelsichere Kapitalanlage; **intangible** ~[s] immaterielle Anlagewerte; **legal** ~ *(US)* mündelsichere [Kapital]anlage; **long-term** ~s *(balance sheet, US)* Wertpapiere des Anlagevermögens; **nonoperating fixed** ~ außerbetriebliche Anlagen; **other** ~s *(balance sheet)* diverse Anlagewerte; **public** ~[s] [Kapital]-investitionen der öffentlichen Hand; **trust[ee]** ~ *(Br.)* mündelsichere Kapitalanlage;
~ **in capital goods** Kapitalanlagegüterinvestition; ~ **in men** Ausbildungskosten; ~ **in plant and equipment** Betriebsausstattung; ~ **of net profit** Verwendung des Reingewinns; ~s **undertaken for rationalization purposes** Rationalisierungsinvestitionen; ~ **in securities** Wertpapieranlage, *(balance sheet)* Wertpapierbestand;
to court ~s Investitionstätigkeit hofieren; **to cut back on** ~ Investitionstätigkeit verringern; **to hold down** ~ **in new facilities** Neuanlagegeschäft drosseln; **to make a good** ~ vorteilhaft anlegen; **to plow** *(US)* **(plough,** *Br.)* **in foreign** ~s Auslandsinvestitionen vornehmen; **to single out for** ~ zur Anlage empfehlen; **to slow down** ~ Investitionstempo drosseln;
~ **account** Einlage-, Beteiligungskonto, Konto, Beteiligungen, *(building society)* Bausparvertrag; ~ **accounting** Anlagenbuchführung; ~ **advice** *(Br.)* Kapitalanlagenberatung; ~ **adviser** Anlage-, Effektenberater; ~ **aid** Investitionshilfe; ~ **allowance** Investitionsfreibetrag; ~ **backlogs** Investitionsüberhang; ~ **bank[er]** Effektenbank, Emissionshaus; ~ **banking** Emissionsgeschäft; ~ **bonds** festverzinsliche Anlagepapiere; ~ **boom** Investitionskonjunktur; ~ **business** Anlagegeschäft; ~ **buying** Anlagekäufe; ~ **capital** Anlage-, Investitionskapital; ~ **community** Anlagepublikum; ~ **company** Kapitalanlage-, Investmentgesellschaft; **open-end** ~ **company** Investmentgesellschaft mit beliebiger Emissionshöhe; ~ **consultant** Anlageberater; ~ **costs** Investitionsaufwand; ~ **counsel[or]** *(US)* Anlageberater; ~ **credit** Investitions-, langfristiger

Anlagekredit; ~ **decision** Investitionsentschluß; ~ **earnings** Beteiligungserträge; ~ **experience** Erfahrungen im Investitionsgeschäft; **failure** Fehlinvestition; ~ **financing** Anlagenfinanzierung; ~ **fund** Investmentfonds; ~ **grant** Investitionszuschuß; ~ **house** Anlageberatungsfirma; ~ **income** *(US)* Einkünfte aus Kapitalvermögen; ~ **industry** Investitionsgüterindustrie; ~ **inflow** *(building society)* Zugänge an Bausparverträgen; ~ **loan** Investitionskredit; ~ **management** Effektenverwaltung *(investment trust)* Anlagenberatung; ~ **paper** Anlagepapier; **monthly** ~ **plan** Sparvertrag mit monatlichen Raten; ~ **policy** Investitionspolitik, *(investment fund)* Anlagebestimmungen; ~s **portfolio** Effektenportefeuille; ~ **program(me)** Investitionsprogramm; ~ **project** Investitionsprojekt; ~ **rating** *(US)* Anlagenbewertung; ~ **ratio** Investitionsquote; ~ **restrictions** Investitionsbeschränkungen; ~ **return (revenue)** Kapitalverzinsung, *(shares)* Kapital-, Anlagenrendite; ~ **risk** Investitions-, Anlagerisiko; ~ **securities** erstklassige Anlagepapiere; ~ **tax credit** Steuervergünstigungen für Investitionen, Investitionsprämie.

investment trust Investmenttrust, -gesellschaft, Effektenfinanzierungsgesellschaft; ~ **buying** Anlagekäufe der Investmentgesellschaften; ~ **certificate** an der Börse gehandeltes Investmentzertifikat; ~ **securities** Fondswerte einer Kapitalgesellschaft.

investor Kapitalanleger, -geber, Geldanleger; ~s Anlagepublikum; **high-bracket** ~ Kapitalgeber mit hoher Einkommensteuerprogression; **institutional** ~ Kapitalsammelstelle.

invigoration of business Ankurbelung der Wirtschaft.

invisible | **balance** Dienstleistungsbilanz; ~ **exports** unsichtbare Ausfuhr, aktive Dienstleistungen; ~ **imports** unsichtbare Einfuhren, passive Dienstleistungen.

invitation | **to bid** *(US)* Stellenausschreibung, -anzeige; ~ **to the public to subscribe to a loan** Subskriptionsaufforderung; ~s **for tenders with discretionary award of contracts** freihändige Ausschreibung.

invite | *(v.)* **applications for a position** Stelle ausschreiben; ~ **public competition** öffentlichen Wettbewerb ausschreiben; ~ **shareholders to subscribe capital** Aktionäre zur Zeichnung auffordern.

invoice [Waren]rechnung, Faktura, Nota; **as per** ~ **on the other side** laut umstehender Rechnung; **on transmitting the** ~ bei Übersendung der Faktura; **consular** ~ Konsulatsfaktura; **customs** ~ Zollfaktura; **legalized** ~ beglaubigte Faktura; **pro-forma** ~ fingierte Rechnung; **sales** ~ Verkaufsrechnung; **shipping** ~ Versandrechnung; ~ *(v.)* Faktura erteilen, fakturieren; **to enter in the** ~ auf die Rechnung setzen; **to get the consular** ~s **legalized** Konsulatsfakturen beglaubigen lassen; **to sell at a loss on the** ~ unter dem fakturierten Wert verkaufen;

~ **amount** Rechnungsbetrag; ~ **clerk** Fakturist; ~ **cost** Bruttoeinkaufspreis; **combination sales-order-shipper** ~ **form** kombiniertes Auftrags- und Versandrechnungsformular; ~ **number** Rechnungsnummer; ~ **price** Rechnungs-, Fakturapreis; ~ **weight** Rechnungsgewicht.

invoiced | **goods** fakturierte Waren; ~ **price** fakturierter Preis, Rechnungsbetrag.

invoicing Rechnungsausstellung, Fakturieren.

involuntary | **bankrupt** Zwangsgemeinschuldner; ~ **bankruptcy** durch Gläubigerantrag herbeigeführter Konkurs; ~ **conversion** Zwangskurs; ~ **transfer** Forderungsübergang kraft Gesetzes.

involve | *(v.)* **additional charges** mit weiteren Kosten verbunden sein; ~ **o. s. in debt** sich verschulden.

inward | **bill of lading** Importkonnossement; ~ **duty** *(Br.)* Eingangs-, Binnenzoll; ~ **manifest** Zolleinfuhrerklärung.

iron note *(fam.)* erstklassig abgesicherter Schuldschein.

irredeemable *(annuities, bonds)* unkündbar, untilgbar, unablösbar, *(paper currency)* nicht einlösbar; ~ **annuity** unablösbare Rente; ~ **foreign exchange standard** Golddevisenwährung.

irregular *(a.) (stock exchange)* uneinheitlich, schwankend; ~ **customer** Laufkunde; ~ **payments** unregelmäßige Zahlungen.

irresponsible debtor unzuverlässiger Schuldner.

irretrievable loss unersetzlicher Verlust.

irrevocable [letter of] credit *(US)* unwiderruflich bestätigtes Akkreditiv.

island position *(advertising)* Inselplacierung.

isometric standard Preisindexwährung.

issuance *(US)* Ausgabe, Aus-, Verteilung; ~ **of checks** Scheckausstellung; ~ **of licence** *(US)* Lizenzerteilung; ~ **of stocks** *(US)* Aktienemission.

issue *(bill of exchange)* Ausstellung, *(newspaper)* Nummer, Ausgabe, *(securities)* Emission, Reihe, Ausgabe; **first** ~ erste Serie; **high-risk** ~s risikoreiche Werte; **industrial** ~s Industriewerte; **junior** ~s *(shares)* junge Aktien; **national bond** ~ Staatsanleihe; **security** ~ Wertpapieremission; **[new]** ~ **of bank notes** Banknotenausgabe; ~ **of a bill of exchange** Wechselausstellung; ~ **of a check** *(US)* **(cheque,** *Br.)* Scheckausstellung; ~ **of an order** Erlaß einer Verfügung; ~ **above par** Überpariemission; ~ **below par** Unterpariemission; ~ **of a prospectus** *(Br.)* Auflegung zur Zeichnung durch Prospekte; ~ **of securities** Wertpapieremission; ~ **of shares** *(Br.)* Aktienausgabe; ~ **of stocks** *(US)* Aktienemission;

~ *(v.) (bill of exchange)* ausstellen, *(loan)* begeben, *(notes)* in Umlauf setzen, ausgeben, emittieren, *(policy)* ausfertigen;

~ **to the bearer** auf den Inhaber ausstellen; ~ **a check** *(US)* **against an account** Guthabenscheck ausschreiben; ~ **bad checks** *(US)* ungedeckte Schecks ausstellen; ~ **a prospectus** Prospekt lancieren;

to bring a campaign to a successful ~ Werbefeldzug erfolgreich abschließen; **to make ~s to the army** Lieferungen für die Armee durchführen; **to make a new ~ of capital** Kapitalerhöhung vornehmen;

~ **bank** Noten-, Emissionsbank; ~ **department** *(Bank of England)* Notenausgabestelle; **property** ~ **form** Materialausgabeschein; ~ **house** Emissionshaus; ~ **par** *(Br.)* Parikurs; ~ **price** Ausgabe-, Emissionskurs; **capital** ~ **restrictions** Emissionssperre.

issued capital *(Br.)* **(capital stock,** *(US)* effektiv ausgegebenes Kapital.

issuing | **bad checks** *(US)* Scheckbetrug;
~ **agency** Emissionsstelle; ~**house** *(Br.)* Emissionshaus, Finanzierungsbank; ~ **syndicate** Begebungskonsortium.

item Gegenstand, *(bill)* Geld-, Rechnungsposten, *(bookkeeping)* Position, Posten, Buchung, Abschnitt, *(GATT)* Tarifnummer;
availability ~s *(US)* langfristige Einlagen; **balance-sheet** ~s Bilanzposten; **bookkeeping** ~ Buchungsposten; **combined** ~s Sammelsendungen; **debit** ~ Lastschriftposten; **deferred** ~ Rechnungsabgren-

zungsposten; **hard-to-sell** ~s schwer verkäufliche Waren; **house** ~ *(Br.)* eigener Scheck; **monitory (pro-memoria)** ~ *(balance sheet)* Merkposten; **rationed** ~ bewirtschafteter (rationierter) Artikel; **registered** ~s eingeschriebene Sendungen; **suspense (transitory)** ~ (transistorischer Posten; **valuation** ~ Wertberichtigungsposten;

~s **on the agenda** Punkte auf der Tagesordnung; ~ **included in the budget** Titel des Haushaltsplans; ~ **not in stock** nicht auf Lager befindliche Ware; ~ **of value** Wertgegenstand;
to cancel an ~ Posten stornieren; **to number the** ~s **in a catalog(ue)** Katalogposten numerieren.

itemize *(v.)* *(US)* einzeln aufführen, spezifizieren, detaillieren, nach Posten aufgliedern;
~ **accounts** einzelne Rechnungsposten angeben; ~ **a bill** Rechnung spezifizieren.

itemized | **account** spezifizierte Rechnung; ~ **appropriation** detaillierte Mittelzuweisung.

itinerant | **exhibiton** Wanderausstellung; ~ **merchant** Wandergewerbetreibender; ~ **showman** Schaubudenbesitzer; ~ **trade** Wandergewerbe.

itineration Geschäftsreise.

J

jack Gelegenheitsarbeiter, Handlanger;
pilot's ~ Lotsenflagge;
~-**of-all-trades** Faktotum, Universalgenie;
~-**pot winner** Kassenschlager.

jam *(traffic)* Verstopfung, Stockung, Stauung.

Jason clause *(ship)* Versicherungsklausel gegen verborgene Mängel.

jeopardize | *(v.)* **one's business** geschäftliche Verluste riskieren; ~ **one's finances** sich in finanzielle Ungelegenheiten bringen.

jeopardizing a creditor's interests Gläubigergefährdung.

jeopardy assessment *(income tax)* sofortige Steuerveranlagung wegen befürchteten Steuerausfalls.

jerque *(v.)* *(Br.)* zollamtlich untersuchen;
~ **note** *(Br.)* Eingangszollscheine.

jet | **aircraft** Düsenflugzeug; ~ **freight** Düsenfrachtgut.

jetsam, flotsam and treibendes Wrack- und Strandgut, Schiffbruchsgüter.

jettison of cargo Ladungswurf.

job [An]stellung, Stelle, Position, Posten, Arbeitsplatz, -stelle, Beruf, Berufstätigkeit, *(piece of business)* Geschäft, Auftrag,
by the ~ im (auf) Akkord, im Stücklohn, *(for a lump sum)* zu einem Pauschlapreis; **out of a** ~ arbeitslos;

blind alley ~ Beruf ohne Aufstiegsmöglichkeit; **full-time** ~ ganztägige Beschäftigung; **higher-level** ~ *(US)* gehobenere Stellung; **odd** ~ Gelegenheitsarbeit; **skilled factory** ~ Facharbeiterberuf; **white-collar** ~ Stehkragenberuf;
~ *(v.)* *(deal corruptly)* Schiebungen begehen, in die eigene Tasche wirtschaften, *(deal in stocks, Br.)* mit Aktien handeln, Maklergeschäfte betreiben, *(do odd jobs)* Gelegenheitsarbeiten machen, *(sublet)* Arbeit auf feste Rechnung geben, im Akkord vergeben, *(undertake work at agreed price)* Arbeit auf feste Rechnung übernehmen, *(wholesale business, US)* Großhandel betreiben *(work by the job)* im Akkord (gegen Stücklohn) arbeiten;
~ **in bills** Wechselmakler sein; ~ **a contract** Auftrag an seine Lieferanten weitervergeben; ~ **shares** Kursmakler sein;
to apply for a ~ sich um eine Stelle bewerben; **to be at a dead end in one's** ~ beruflich in einer Sackgasse sein; **to find s. o. a.** ~ jem. eine Beschäftigung verschaffen; **to have a regular** ~ einer regelmäßigen Beschäftigung nachgehen; **to learn on the** ~ seine Berufsausbildung am Arbeitsplatz bekommen; **to put out a** ~ **on commission** Arbeit in Regie vergeben; **to reeducate on the** ~ am Arbeitsplatz umschulen; **to switch a** ~ Berufswechsel vornehmen; **to throw up one's** ~ seine Stellung aufgeben;

~ **analysis** *(US)* Arbeitsstudie; ~ **applicant** Stellenbewerber; ~ **attendance** Einhaltung der Arbeitsstunden; ~ **breakdown** berufliche Aufschlüsselung; ~ **card** Auftragsabrechnungskarte; ~ **classification index** *(US)* Berufsgruppenindex; ~ **cost ledger** Auftragskostenbuch; ~ **cost sheet** Auftragskostensammelblatt; ~ **costing** Kostenrechnungssystem; ~ **counsellor** *(US)* Berufsberater; ~ **creation** Arbeitsbeschaffung; ~ **description** *(US)* Stellenbeschreibung; ~ **difficulty allowance** Zuschlag für schwierige Arbeiten; ~ **discrimination** *(US)* berufliche Diskriminierung; ~ **efficiency** berufliche Leistungsfähigkeit; ~ **evaluation** Arbeitsplatzbewertung; ~ **factor** Bewertungsmerkmal; ~ **goods** Ramsch-, Partie-, Schleuderware; ~ **hazard** Berufsrisiko; ~**hop** *(v.)* Arbeitsplatz (Beruf) häufig wechseln; ~ **hunting** Arbeitssuche; ~ **jockey** Postenjäger; ~ **joy** Arbeitslust; ~ **leasing** Zeitarbeit; ~ **line** Ramsch-, Partieware; ~ **loss** Arbeitsplatzverlust; ~ **lot** Ramschwaren; **to buy as a ~ lot** partieweise kaufen; ~**lot production** Kleinserienfertigung; **odd~ man** Gelegenheitsarbeiter; ~**market** Stellen-, Arbeitsmarkt; ~ **number** Arbeitsauftragsnummer; ~ **openings** offene Stellen; ~ **order** *(US)* Fabrikationsauftrag; ~**order cost accounting** *(US)* Arbeitsauftragskosten-, Stückerfolgsrechnung, Zuschlags-, Serienkalkulation; ~**order cost sheet** *(US)* Kostenrechnungsblatt; ~**order number** *(US)* Fabrikationsauftragsnummer; ~ **pattern** Stellenbesetzungsplan; ~ **pricing** Lohnkostenkalkulation; ~ **processing** Lohnveredelung; ~ **production** *(US)* Einzelfertigung; ~**questionnaire** beruflicher Fragebogen; ~ **rate** Akkordrichtsatz; ~ **record** berufliche Vergangenheit; ~ **rotation** *(US)* Arbeitsplatzwechsel [innerhalb eines Betriebes]; ~ **security** Sicherheit des Arbeitsplatzes; ~ **seniority** *(US)* Dienstalter; ~ **shop** Spezialteilebetrieb; ~ **ticket** *(US)* Akkord-, Arbeitslaufzettel; ~ **time** Arbeits-, Stückzeit; **[on the]** ~ **training** *(US)* Ausbildung am Arbeitsplatz; ~ **vacancy** unbesetzter Arbeitsplatz; **to do** ~ **work** im Akkord arbeiten; ~ **worker** Akkordarbeiter.

jobber *(casual labo(u)rer)* Gelegenheitsarbeiter, *(day labo(u)rer)* Tagelöhner, Dienstmann, *(middleman, US)* Zwischen-, Großhändler, *(piece worker)* Stücklohnarbeiter, *(speculator)* Schieber, Börsenspekulant, *(stock exchange, Br.)* Effekten-, Fondshändler;

desk ~ Grossist ohne eigenes Lager (mit Streckengeschäft); **local** ~ Platzmakler; **wagon** ~ *(US)* Grossist mit eigenem Lager;
~ **in bills** *(Br.)* Wechselreiter.

jobbing Zwischen-, Großhandel, *(job work)* Akkord-, Stücklohnarbeit, *(speculation)* Spekulation[sgeschäft], *(stock exchange dealings, Br.)* Börsen-, Effektenhandel, *(wholesale business, US)* Großhandel;
~ **in bills** Wechselarbitrage;
~ **house** *(US)* Großhandelshaus; ~ **production** Auftragsfertigung.

jobholder Festangestellter, Stelleninhaber.

jobless *(US)* erwerbs-, arbeitslos;
~ **army** Arbeitslosenarmee.

join *(v.)* sich zusammentun, bei-, eintreten;
~ **documents to a report** einem Bericht Unterlagen beifügen; ~ **one's father's firm** in das väterliche Geschäft eintreten; ~ **stock with s. o.** sein Kapital zusammenschießen.

joint | **account** gemeinsame Rechnung, Konsortial-, Metakonto; ~ **and survivor annuity** Überlebensrente; ~ **cargo** Sammelladung; ~ **costs** Schlüssel-, Umlagekosten; ~ **credit** Konsortialkredit; ~ **creditor** Gesamtgläubiger; ~ **debtor** Solidarschuldner; ~ **guaranty** solidarische Haftung; ~ **liability** gesamtschuldnerische Verpflichtung; ~ **lives** *(life insurance)* verbundene Leben; ~ **owner** Miteigentümer, *(ship)* Mit-, Partenreeder; ~ **product** Kuppelprodukt; **on** ~ **profit and loss** auf gemeinschaftlichen Gewinn und Verlust; ~ **promissory note** solidarischer trockener Wechsel; ~ **purse** gemeinsame Kasse; ~ **rate** *(railway)* Sammeltarif; ~ **return** *(income tax, US)* gemeinsame Veranlagung von Ehegatten.

joint stock Gesellschafts-, *(Br.)* Aktienkapital;
~ **company** *(Br.)* Aktiengesellschaft, AG, *(US)* Offene Handelsgesellschaft auf Aktien.

joint | **undertaking** Gemeinschaftsunternehmen, Partizipationsgeschäft; ~ **use** Mitbenutzung; ~ **venture** Gemeinschaftsunternehmen, *(contracting)* Arbeitsgemeinschaft, *(banking)* Metageschäft, *(ownership)* Beteiligungsverhältnis.

joint and several gesamtschuldnerisch;
~ **liability** gesamtschuldnerische Haftung; ~ **note** *(US)* gesamtschuldnerisches Zahlungsversprechen.

jointly and severally liable gesamtschuldnerisch haftbar.

journal *(bookkeeping)* Journal, Memorial, *(periodical)* Zeitschrift, *(ship)* Logbuch;
bills-payable ~ Wechselverfallbuch; **bills-receivable** ~ Wechseldebitorenbuch; **cash receipts** ~ Kasseneingangsjournal; **multi-column** ~ Mehrspaltenjournal; **trade** ~ Handelsblatt;
to bring the cash through the ~ Kasse journalisieren; **to post into the** ~ ins Journal übertragen; ~ **entry** Journaleintragung; ~ **number** Geschäftszeichen; ~ **voucher** Buchungsbeleg.

journey Reise, Weg, Route;
~ **abroad** Auslandsreise; **official** ~ Dienstreise.

journeyman Lohnarbeiter, Geselle, Gehilfe;
approved ~'s **rate** Gesellenlohn.

judgment, enforceable vollstreckbares Urteil;
~ **for costs** Kostenurteil, -entscheidung; ~ **by default** Versäumnisurteil;
to enforce (execute) a ~ Urteil vollstrecken;
~ **creditor** Vollstreckungsgläubiger; ~ **debt** vollstreckbare Forderung; ~ **debtor** Vollstreckungsschuldner; ~ **note** Schuldschein mit Unterwerfungsklausel; ~ **rate** *(fire insurance)* Selbsteinschätzung.

jump in exports plötzlicher Ausfuhranstieg;
~ *(v.) (prices)* emporschnellen, sprunghaft ansteigen, *(in promotion)* überspringen;
~ **one's bail** *(US)* Bürgschaft schießen (Kaution verfallen) lassen; ~ **into new high ground** *(prices)* sprunghaft steigen und einen neuen Höchstkurs erzielen; ~ **into new purchase** sich auf Neuerwerbungen stürzen;
to get the ~ **on one's competitors** seine Konkurrenz überflügeln; **to go up with a** ~ *(stock exchange)* plötzlich in die Höhe gehen.

junior | **accountant** Hilfsprüfer; ~ **bondholder** Neubesitzer; ~ **execution** Anschlußpfändung; ~ **mortgage** nachstellige Hypothek; ~ **partner** Juniorpartner; ~ **security** zweitrangige Sicherheit.
junk Trödel, Kram, Altmaterial;
~ **auto** Schrottwagen; ~ **dealer** Trödler; ~ **goods** Ramsch[waren].
justify | *(v.)* **a lunch as business expense** Mittagessen über Spesen abrechnen; ~ **a trip with good business reasons** Geschäftsreise mit zwingenden Gründen belegen.

K

keen | **demand** hektische Nachfrage; **to have a** ~ **eye for a bargain** Nase für gute Geschäfte haben.
keep *(livelihood)* Unterhalt, Kost;
~ *(v.)* **an account** Konto unterhalten; ~ **back s. th. from s. one's wages** etw. von jds. Lohn einbehalten;
~ **boarders** Pensionäre haben; ~ **the cash** Kassierer sein; ~ **[back] one's payments** seine Zahlungen einhalten; ~ **in safe custody** sicher aufbewahren;
~ **for sale** feilhalten; ~ **steady** *(prices)* sich behaupten; ~ **in stock** auf Lager halten, [Artikel] führen.
keep up | **up a correspondence** Schriftwechsel unterhalten; ~ **with the Joneses** *(Br.)* hohen Lebensstandard halten; ~ **one's payments** seinen Zahlungsverpflichtungen nachkommen;
keep, to work for one's gegen freie Station arbeiten.
kerb *(stock exchange, Br.)* Freiverkehrsbörse;
~**[-stone] broker** *(Br.)* Freiverkehrsmakler; ~ **exchange** *(Br.)* Freiverkehrsbörse; ~ **market** *(Br.)* Freiverkehrsmarkt; ~ **prices** *(Br.)* Freiverkehrskurse.
key *(advertising)* Kennziffer, -wort, Chiffre, Kontrollziffer, *(leading position)* Schlüsselposition;
golden (silver) ~ Bestechungsgeld;
~ **of distribution** Verteilungsschlüssel;
~ **appointments** [Besetzung von] Schlüsselpositionen; ~ **businessmen** führende Geschäftsleute; ~ **currency** Leitwährung; ~ **customer** wichtigster Kunde; ~ **date** Stichtag; ~ **financial nation** finanzstarkes Land; ~ **industrial emporium** wirtschaftliche Schlüsselstellung; ~ **industry** Schlüsselindustrie; **[turn]-**~ **job** Schlüsselstellung; ~ **money** Handgeld, Anzahlung, *(tenant)* Mietvorauszahlung, verlorener Baukostenzuschuß; ~**-money rates** Geldleitsätze; ~ **number** Kennziffer, Chiffre;

~ **rate** *(banking)* Leitzinssatz, *(insurance)* nach Gefahrenklassen eingeteilte Grundprämie.
keyed | **address** Kennzifferanschrift; ~ **advertising** Kennziffer-, Chiffrewerbung.
keying of advertisements Chiffrewerbung.
keynote idea *(advertising)* Hauptgedanke.
kick *(fashion)* neuester Modefimmel, letzter Schrei;
~ *(v.)* **up earnings** Gewinn hochschrauben;
to get the ~ *(sl.)* rausfliegen, gefeuert werden.
kill *(v.)* **a wire** Telegramm widerrufen.
kind Qualität, Art, Klasse, Gattung, Sorte;
in cash or in ~ in bar oder in Sachleistungen;
~ **of securities** Effektengattung;
to pay in ~ in Naturalien zahlen.
kite Keller-, Reit-, Gefälligkeitswechsel;
~ *(v.) (bill)* Reitwechsel ausstellen, *(check, US)* Scheckbetrag fälschen;
to fly a ~ Gefälligkeitswechsel ziehen;
~ **mark** *(Br.)* Qualitätszeichen, Standardnormstempel.
kiting stocks *(US)* Hinauftreiben von Aktienkursen.
knock | *(v.)* **down** *(auction)* zuschlagen, *(lower in price)* stark drücken; ~ **off** vom Preis abziehen, Preisabstrich vornehmen, *(work, sl.)* Feierabend machen;
~**-for** ~ **agreement** *(insurance)* Regreßverzichtsvereinbarung.
knockdown price Werbe-, Spottpreis, *(auction)* äußerster Preis, Mindestpreis.
knocking down copy *(Br.)* herabsetzende (aggressive Werbung, herabsetzender Werbetext.
knockout *(Br.)* Scheinauktion.
know-how praktisches Wissen, Fachkenntnisse;
industrial ~ industrielle Produktionserfahrungen.
knowledge of business Geschäftskenntnisse, -erfahrung.

L

label *(branded goods)* Schutzmarke, *(short name)* Bezeichnung *(parcel)* Paketzettel, -adresse, Aufkleber, *(adhesive stamp)* Aufklebemarke, *(ticket)* Etikett, Anhänge-, Bezeichnungsschild, Aufklebe-, Warenadreßzettel;
gummed ~ Aufklebeadresse; **baggage** *(US)* **(luggage,** *Br.)* ~ Gepäckadresse, -anhänger;
~ *(v.)* mit Etikett versehen, etikettieren, [Waren] [aus]zeichnen, beschildern;
~ **an article for sale** Gegenstand mit Preiszettel versehen;
to sell under a secondary ~ als zweitklassige Ware verkaufen.
labelling Etikettierung, Auszeichnung;
informative ~ Herkunftsbezeichnung.
labo(u)r Arbeit[skraft], *(operatives)* Arbeitskräfte;
casual ~ Gelegenheitsarbeit; **direct** ~ Fertigungslohn; **drafted** ~ dienstverpflichtete Arbeitskräfte; **indirect** ~ Gemeinkostenlöhne; **organized** ~ *(US)* gewerkschaftlich organisierte Arbeit; **semi-skilled** ~ angelernte Arbeitskräfte; **unskilled** ~ ungelernte Arbeitskräfte; **work-in-process** ~ Halbfabrikatelöhne;
~ **agreement** *(US)* Kollektivvertrag; ~ **allocation** Arbeitseinsatz; ~ **budget** Lohn- und Gehaltsetat; ~ **charge** Lohnkostenanteil; ~ **colony** Arbeitersiedlung; ~ **conscription** Arbeitsdienstpflicht; ~ **cost** Lohnkosten; ~ **court** *(US)* Arbeitsgericht; ~ **Department** *(US)* Arbeitsministerium; ~ **exchange** *(Br.)* Arbeitsnachweis; **total possible** ~ **force** Arbeitskräftereserven; **~-force dropouts** Belegschaftsabgänge; ~ **management contract** betriebliche Lohnvereinbarung; ~ **pass** Arbeitsgenehmigung; ~ **piracy** *(US)* Abwerbung von Arbeitskräften; ~ **recruitment** Anwerbung von Arbeitskräften; ~ **representative** Arbeitnehmervertreter; ~ **turnover** Arbeitsplatzwechsel.
labo(u)rer [ungelernter] Arbeiter;
day ~ Tagelöhner; **factory** ~ Fabrikarbeiter; **permanent** ~ Stammarbeiter.
lack | **of capital** Kapitalmangel; ~ **of sales** ungenügender Umsatz.
laden | **in bulk** mit Massengut beladen; ~ **with parcels** mit Stückgütern befrachtet.
lading port Verlade-, Versandhafen.
lag | **in collection** Inkassorückstand; ~ **in investments** stagnierende Investitionstätigkeit.
land *(balance sheet)* Grundstücke, *(landed property)* Grundbesitz, Grund und Boden;
developed ~ Bauland; **third-party** ~ *(balance sheet)* fremde Liegenschaften; **undeveloped** ~ unerschlossenes Gelände;
~**, buildings, plant and machinery** *(balance sheet, Br.)* Sachanlagen;
~ *(v.) (discharge)* [Waren] ausladen, löschen, *(go ashore)* landen, anlegen, an Land gehen;
to acquire ~ **in advance of development** Vorratsgelände erwerben;

~ **acquisition** Grundstückserwerb; ~ **agency** *(US)* Immobilien-, Maklerbüro; ~ **agent** Grundstücks-, Gütermakler, *(steward, Br.)* Gutsverwalter; ~ **boom** Baulandkonjunktur; ~ **broker** *(Br.)* Grundstücksmakler; ~ **carrier** Fernspediteur; ~ **developer** Grundstückserschließungsgesellschaft;
undeveloped ~ **duty** *(Br.)* Bauland-, Bauplatzsteuer; **~-office business** *(fam., US)* Bombengeschäft; ~ **purchase** Grundstückskauf; ~ **register** *(Br.)* Grundbuch; ~ **surveyor** Landmesser; ~ **tax** *(US)* Grundsteuer; ~ **value** Grundstücks-, Bodenwert; ~ **value tax** Wertzuwachssteuer für Grundstücke.
landed | **price** Preis frei Bestimmungshafen; ~ **terms** franko Löschung.
landing Landung, Landen, *(discharge)* Löschung [einer Ladung];
~ **bill** *(ship)* Landungsrolle; ~ **certificate** Löschungsschein; ~ **fee** Landegebühr; ~ **field** Landeplatz, Rollfeld; ~ **order** *(Br.)* Zollpassierschein; ~ **permit** Löscherlaubnis; ~ **surveyor** *(Br.)* Oberzollaufseher; ~ **waiter** Zollbeamter.
landlord *(innkeeper)* Gastwirt, *(landowner)* Gutsherr, *(lessor)* Mietherr, Vermieter, Hauswirt;
~**'s warrant** Vermieterpfandrecht.
languid *(market)* flau, matt, schleppend, lustlos.
lapsed policy ungültige (verfallene) Versicherungspolice.
large | **customer** Großabnehmer; ~ **establishment** Großbetrieb; ~ **income** hohes Einkommen; **~-lot production** Massenerzeugung; **~-lot trader** *(stock exchange)* Pakethändler.
large-scale | **business (enterprise)** Großbetrieb, -unternehmen; ~ **consumer** Großverbraucher; ~ **consumer advertising** breitgestreute Verbraucherwerbung; ~ **manufacture** Massenherstellung; ~ **production** Serienproduktion.
large share in the management, to take a an der Geschäftsführung entscheidend beteiligt sein.
last | **column** Schlußspalte; **~-day business** Ultimogeschäft; **~-in, first-out** *(inventory taking)* Zuerstentnahme der neueren Vorräte und Bilanzierung zum jeweiligen Buchwert; ~ **quotation** Schlußnotierung.
late | **bag** *(Br.)* Briefkasten mit Spätleerung; ~ **delivery** Spätzustellung.
latent | **defects** verborgene Mängel; ~ **reserve** Stille Reserve.
launch *(v.)* | **an advertising campaign** Werbefeldzug starten; ~ **an appeal** Sammelaktion starten; ~ **a new enterprise** neues Geschäft (Unternehmen) gründen; ~ **a loan** Anleihe auflegen;
~ **advertising** *(US)* Einführungsanzeige.
launching cost Anlaufkosten.
lavish expenditure zügellose Ausgabenwirtschaft.
law Recht, Gesetz, Statut;
antitrust ~ Kartellgesetzgebung; ~ **bankrupt (bank-**

ruptcy) ~ Konkursrecht; **business** ~ Gewerberecht; commercial ~ Handelsrecht; **trademark** ~ Warenzeichenrecht;
~ **of diminishing returns** Gesetz vom abnehmenden Bodenertrag; ~ **of property** Sachenrecht; ~ **of supply and demand** Gesetz von Angebot und Nachfrage;
~ **business** Rechtsangelegenheit.
lawful | day Werktag; ~ **goods** *(US)* zum Export freigegebene Waren.
lay *(sl., job)* Betätigungsfeld, Beschäftigung, Branche, *(terms of sale, US)* Verkaufsbedingungen;
~ *(v.)* **aside money for one's old age** für sein Alter sparen; ~ **down** *(ship)* auf Stapel legen; ~ **in goods** Waren einlagern; ~ **provisions** Vorräte anlegen; ~ **stocks pretty heavily** sich kräftig eindecken, erhebliche Lagerankäufe tätigen.
lay off | **at short notice** kurzfristig entlassen; ~ **a risk** Rückversicherung abschließen.
lay on duties on import Einfuhrzoll erheben.
lay out one's money carefully sein Geld sorgfältig anlegen.
lay | **-away** *(US)* zurückgelegte Ware; ~ **days** Liegezeit, Liegetage, Löschzeit.
layoff [vorübergehender] Personalabbau, *(strike)* Arbeitseinstellung;
~ **benefit** Entlassungsentschädigung.
layout *(advertisement)* Aufriß, Layout, Ideenskizze, *(display of goods)* Ausgestaltung des Verkaufsraums, Aufmachung;
workplace ~ Arbeitsplatzgestaltung.
lead führende Rolle, Führung, Leitung;
~s **and lags in trade** Schwankungen im Handelsverkehr;
~ *(v.)* leiten, leitende Stellung einnehmen; ~ **all competitors** gesamte Konkurrenz übertreffen; ~ **the fashion** Mode machen;
~ **-in** *(advertising)* (suggestiver Beginn) einer Anzeige; ~ **seal** Plombe.
leader *(advertisement)* Blickführungslinie, *(article of trade)* Zug-, Anreiz-, Lockartikel;
industrial ~ Wirtschaftsführer; **loss** ~ Lockartikel; ~ **of a cartel** Kartellvorsteher; **traditional** ~s **on prices** seit je führende Werte;
to become the ~ **in establishing pricing policies** Preisführerschaft übernehmen.
leading | **agent of a firm** Hauptrepräsentant einer Firma; ~ **bank** Konsortialführerin; ~ **fashion house** führender Modesalon; ~ **figures in finance, industry and trade** führende Persönlichkeiten des Finanz- und Wirtschaftslebens; ~ **share** Spitzenwert; ~ **shareholder** Hauptaktionär; ~ **underwriter** Erstversicherer.
leaflet Zettel, Flug-, Werbeblatt, Broschüre.
leakage Leckwerden, Verlust, Schwund, *(of capital)* Kapitalverlust.
lease Verpachtung, Pacht, Miete, *(contract)* Pacht-, Mietvertrag, -verhältnis;
on expiration of the ~ nach Ablauf des Mietvertrages;

building ~ Erbpacht, -baurecht; **commercial** ~ Mietvertrag für gewerblich genutzte Räume; **equipment** ~ Maschinenpachtmiete; **service** ~ *(US)* Maschinenpacht- und wartungsvertrag;
~ *(v.)* **[out]** [ver]pachten, [ver]mieten; ~ **business property** Geschäftsgrundstück vermieten;
~ **arrangement** Pachtvereinbarung; ~ **back** Rückkaufgarantie; ~**-lend** *(US)* Pacht- und Leihvertrag; ~ **period** Miet-, Pachtzeit, -dauer.
leased | **car** *(US)* Mietauto, -wagen, Leihwagen; ~ **property** Pachtgrundstück, Mietgegenstand.
leasehold Pachtgrundstück, Pachtung;
~ **building** Mietshaus, Zinshaus; ~ **improvements** Werterhöhungen während der Pachzeit.
leasemonger Pachtmakler, Vermietungsbüro.
leave *(of absence, US)* Urlaub, Ferien;
full-pay ~ vollbezahlter Urlaub; **sick** ~ Krankheits-, Genesungsurlaub;
~ *(v.)* **a balance of $ 1 000 to your debit** Saldo von $ 1 000 zu Ihren Lasten aufweisen; ~ **one's bag in the cloakroom** seinen Koffer zur Gepäckaufbewahrung geben; ~ **in bond** unter Zollverschluß lassen; ~ **harbo(u)r** auslaufen; ~ **nothing but debts** nichts als Schulden hinterlassen; ~ **at one's own volition** von sich aus kündigen; ~ **off flat** *(stock exchange)* flau schließen.
ledger Hauptbuch, *(register)* Register;
accounts-payable ~ Kontokorrentbuch für Kreditoren; **accounts-receivable** ~ Kontokorrentbuch für Debitoren; **daily mail** ~ Brieftagebuch; **factory** ~ Betriebshauptbuch; **goods-bought** ~ Wareneinkaufsbuch; **goods-sold** ~ Warenverkaufsbuch; **payroll** ~ Lohn-, Gehaltsliste;
to balance the ~ Hauptbuch saldieren; **to enter into the** ~ in das Hauptbuch eintragen; **to post up the** ~ Hauptbuch vollständig nachtragen;
~ **abstract** Hauptbuchauszug; ~ **account** Hauptbuchkonto; ~ **clerk** Buchhalter; ~ **keeper** Hauptbuchführer; ~**-type journal** amerikanisches Journal.
left | **luggage** *(Br.)* zur Aufbewahrung gegebenes Gepäck; ~**-luggage office** *(Br.)* Handgepäckaufbewahrung.
legacy Vermächtnis, Legat;
preferential ~ Vorausvermächtnis;
~ **duty** *(Br.)* Vermächtnissteuer.
legal | **capacity** Geschäftsfähigkeit; ~ **coin** gesetzliche Zahlungsmittel; ~ **custodian** amtliche Hinterlegungsstelle; ~ **debt margin** *(municipal accounting)* zugelassene Überschuldung; ~ **disability** Geschäftsunfähigkeit; ~ **investments** *(US)* mündelsichere Anlagepapiere; ~ **obligation to support** Unterhaltspflicht; ~ **quay** *(Br.)* Zollkai; ~ **reserve** *(banking)* gesetzliche Rücklage.
leisure frei verfügbare Zeit, Freizeit;
~ **business** Freizeitindustrie; ~**-time market** Freizeitmarkt.
leisured classes wohlhabender Bevölkerungsteil.
lend *(v.)* [ver]leihen, ausleihen, Darlehen geben;

~ **on bottomry** auf Bodmerei geben; ~ **on collateral** Lombardkredit gewähren; ~ **an employee to s. o.** Angestellten zu jem. abstellen; ~ **money on contango** Reportgeschäfte machen; ~ **money at interest** Geld auf Zinsen ausleihen; ~ **money on mortgage** Hypothekendarlehn geben.

lender Anleihe-, Kredit-, Darlehnsgeber; ~ **on bottomry** Bodmereigeber.

lending Ver-, Ausleihen, Darlehnsgewährung; **international** ~ internationaler Kreditverkehr; ~ **fee** Leihgebühr; ~ **institute** Geldinstitut; ~ **policy** Darlehens-, Kreditpolitik; ~ **rate** *(US)* Lombard-, Leihsatz.

less-than-carload *(railroad, US)* Stückgut[sendung].

let *(Br.)* Vermeiten, Vermietung, Verpachtung; ~ *(v.)* *(lease)* vermieten, verpachten; ~ **a farm to a tenant** Hof verpachten; ~ **a firm down** Firma herunterwirtschaften; ~ **a house furnished** Haus möbliert vermieten; ~ **works and supplies** Arbeiten und Lieferungen vergeben; ~**alone principle** Grundsatz des freien Wettbewerbs (der freien Wirtschaft).

letdown in sales Absatz-, Umsatzrückgang.

letter Buchstabe, *(one who lets)* Vermieter; **business** ~ Geschäftsbrief; **cable** ~ Brieftelegramm; **caller's** ~ postlagernder Brief; **collection** ~ Inkassoschreiben; **commercial** ~ Geschäftsbrief; **follow-up** ~ *(advertising)* nachfassender Werbebrief; **night** ~ *(US)* Brieftelegramm; **recommendatory** ~ Empfehlungsschreiben; **registered** ~ Einschreiben; **short-paid** ~ ungenügend frankierter Brief; ~ **of allotment** *(Br.)* Bezugsrechtsmitteilung; ~ **of application** Bewerbungsschreiben, *(for shares, Br.)* Zuteilungsantrag; ~ **of authority** Akkreditivermächtigung; ~**s of business** *(Br.)* Gewerbelizenz; ~ **of consignment** Frachtbrief.

letter of credit Akkreditiv, Kreditbrief; **commercial** ~ *(US)* Rembourskredit; **confirmed** ~ bestätigtes Akkreditiv; **documentary** ~ Dokumentarakkreditiv; **mutual** ~ Gegenakkreditiv; **revolving** ~ sich automatisch erneuerndes Akkreditiv; **traveller's** ~ Reisekreditbrief.

letter | **of delegation** Inkassovollmacht; ~ **of engagement** Anstellungsschreiben; ~ **of indemnity** *(Br.)* Ausfallbürgschaft, *(US)* Konnossementsgarantie; ~ **of intent** Absichtserklärung; ~ **of licence** *(bankruptcy proceedings)* Stillhalteerklärung; ~ **of recommendation** Befürwortungsschreiben; ~ **of regret** *(stock exchange, Br.)* Mitteilung über die Ablehnung einer Aktienzuteilung; ~ **of withdrawal** Kündigungsschreiben; ~ **book** Kopierbuch; ~**s-despatched book** *(Br.)* Briefausgangsbuch; ~ **file** Briefordner, Schnellhefter; ~**s-received book** *(Br.)* Briefeingangsbuch.

letterhead Briefkopf, *(business use)* Geschäftsbogen.

letting of works and supplies Auftragsvergabe.

level Höhe, Niveau, *(rank)* Rang, Stand, Stellung; **on middle-management** ~ auf dem Gebiet der mittleren Führungskräfte; **bargain** ~ niedrigster Preis (Kurs); **year-ago** ~ Vorjahrsniveau;

~ **of earnings** Ertragsniveau; ~ **of prices** Preisstand, -niveau; ~ **of commodity prices at wholesale** Großhandelsindex; **to carry to higher price** ~**s** zu Kurssteigerungen führen; ~ **annuity** gleichbleibende Rente; ~**premium system** Kapitaldeckungsverfahren.

levelling | **out of business fluctuations** Konjunkturausgleich; ~ **of premiums** *(insurance)* Bildung von Durchschnittsprämien.

leverage *(capital)* festverzinslicher Anteil des Gesamtkapitals, *(fig.)* Einfluß, Macht, Druckmittel, *(profit)* zum Umsatz disproportionale Tendenz; ~ **fund** Investmentfonds mit Leihkapital.

leveraged position disproportionale Gewinnsituation.

levy Eintreibung, *(collecting of tax)* [Steuer]erhebung, -abgabe, *(distraint)* Pfändung, Beschlagnahme, *(tax)* Umlage, Abgabe, Steuer; **capital** ~ Vermögensabgabe; **yearly pension** ~ Jahresbeitrag zum Pensionsfonds; **excess-profits** ~ *(Br.)* Sondergewinnsteuer; ~ **on real estate** Abgabe auf das Grundvermögen; ~ *(v.)* beschlagnahmen, pfänden, *(tax, contribution)* erheben, eintreiben; ~ **a distress on** Pfändung vornehmen; ~ **customs duties** Zölle erheben; ~ **a tax on dividend distribution** Kapitalertragssteuer erheben.

liabilities *(balance sheet)* Passiva, Passivmasse, *(in bankruptcy)* Schulden, Konkursmasse; **assets and** ~ Aktiva und Passiva; **capital** ~ Kapitalverschuldung; **contingent** ~ *(balance sheet, Br.)* Rückstellung für zweifelhafte Schulden, Eventualverpflichtungen; **current** ~ *(balance sheet)* kurzfristige Verbindlichkeiten; **fictitious** ~ fiktive Kreditoren; **foreign** ~ Auslandsverpflichtungen; **intercompany** ~ Konzernverbindlichkeiten; **long-term** ~ langfristige Verbindlichkeiten; **net** ~ Nettoverbindlichkeiten nach Abzug der liquiden Aktiven; **reserve-carrying foreign** ~ mindestreservepflichtige Auslandsverbindlichkeiten; **sight** ~ sofort fällige Verbindlichkeiten; ~ **on account of acceptances** Akzeptverbindlichkeiten; ~ **upon bills** Wechselverpflichtungen; ~ **in foreign exchange** Devisenverpflichtungen; ~ **due on presentation** Sichtverbindlichkeiten; ~ **subject to reserve requirements** rücklagepflichtige Verbindlichkeiten;

to discharge one's ~ seinen Verbindlichkeiten nachkommen;

~ **adjustment** *(Br.)* Schuldnervergleich.

liability *(bankrupt)* Schuldenmasse, *(debt)* Schuld, Obligo, Verbindlichkeit, *(title of credit side)* Passivseite; **absolute** ~ Gefährdungshaftung; **civil** ~ zivilrechtliche Schadenersatzverpflichtung; **employers'** ~ Unfallhaftpflicht der Arbeitgeber; **endorser's** ~ Wechselhaftung; **income-tax** ~ Einkommensteuerschuld; **individual** ~ persönliche Haftung; **joint and several** ~ gesamtschuldnerische Haftung; **limited**

~ Haftungsbeschränkung; ~ over *(US)* Regreß-
pflicht; **primary** ~ selbstschuldnerische Haftung;
reserve ~ *(life insurance)* Nachschußpflicht; **secondary** ~ Ausfallhaftung; **vicarious** ~ Haftung für
den Erfüllungsgehilfen;
~ **to render account** Rechnungslegungspflicht; ~
for animals Tierhalterhaftung; ~ **to discover** Aus-
kunftspflicht; ~ **of innkeeper** Gastwirtshaftung; ~
for maintenance Unterhaltspflicht; ~ **to pay** Zahlungsverpflichtung; ~ **to recourse** Regreßhaftung;
to be exonerated from ~ von der Haftung befreit
werden; **to carry limited** ~ **in a partnership** kom-
manditistisch beteiligt sein;
Employers' ≗ **Act** Unfallhaftpflichtgesetz; **limited**
~ **company** Gesellschaft mit beschränkter Haftung (GmbH); ~ **item** *(balance sheet)* Passiv-,
Schuldposten; ~ **loss** Haftungsschaden; ~ **side**
Passivseite; ~ **verification** Bewertung von Verbindlichkeiten.
liable *(answerable)* haftbar, haftpflichtig, *(obliged)*
verpflichtet, verbunden, verantwortlich;
primarily ~ unmittelbar (selbstschuldnerisch)
haftbar; **secondarily** ~ subsidiär haftbar;
~ **to account** rechenschaftspflichtig; ~ **for (to pay)
damages** schadenersatzpflichtig; ~ **to pay taxes**
steuer-, abgabenpflichtig; ~ **to recourse** regreßpflichtig;
to be ~ **jointly and severally** gesamtschuldnerisch
haften; **to be** ~ **for one's wife's debts** für die Schulden der Ehefrau aufkommen müssen; **to be** ~ **for
the debt of the principal** für den Hauptschuldner
haften; **to be** ~ **to the extent of one's property** mit
seinem ganzen Vermögen haften; **to be vicariously**
~ für den Erfüllungsgehilfen haften.
liaison | **committee** Verbindunsausschluß; ~ **consult-
ant** Kontaktmann.
liberal | **professions** freie Berufe; ~ **settlement** kulante
Bedingungen.
liberalized capital account liberalisiertes Kapitalkonto.
liberty | **to come and go** Niederlassungsfreiheit; ~ **of
the globe** *(marine insurance)* geographisch unbeschränkter Versicherungsschutz; ~ **of trade** Ge-
werbefreiheit.
licence, license *(patent law)* Patentausnützung, *(motorcar)* Führerschein, *(permit)* Erlaubnis[schein],
Genehmigung, Berechtigungsnachweis, *(trade)* Lizenz, Konzession, Gewerbeschein;
subject to a ~ lizenzpflichtig;
building ~ Baugenehmigung; **business** ~ Gewerbekonzession; **driving** *(Br.)* **(driver's,** *US)* ~ Führerschein; **excise** ~ *(Br.)* Schankkonzession; **hawker's**
~ Wandergewerbeschein; **local taxation** ~ gebührenpflichtige Genehmigung; **professional** ~ Genehmigung zur Ausübung eines Berufes; **motor-
vehicle** ~ Kraftfahrzeugzulassung;
~ **to manufacture** Herstellerlizenz; ~ **to use** Be-
nutzungsschein;
license *(Br. and US) (v.) (business)* konzessionieren,
Konzession (Lizenz) erteilen;

~ **s. o. to keep an inn** Gastwirtskonzession erteilen;
to apply for a ~ Konzession beantragen; **to build
under** ~ lizenzmäßig herstellen; **to disqualify a** ~
Führerschein einziehen;
~ **arrangement** Lizenzabkommen; ~ **fee[s]** Lizenzgebühr[en]; ~ **number** *(US)* polizeiliches Kennzeichen.
licenced, licensed amtlich zugelassen, befugt, konzessioniert, privilegiert;
~ **construction** Lizenzbau; ~ **dealer** konzessionierter Händler; ~ **firm** Lizenznehmer.
licencee, licensee *(US)* Lizenz-, Konzessionsinhaber,
Lizenznehmer, -träger, *(patent law)* Patentberech-
tigter.
licencing, licensing *(US)* Lizenz-, Konzessionserteilung;
~ **of process** Lizenzierung von Herstellungsverfahren;
~ **agreement** Lizenzabkommen; ~ **income** Lizenz-
einkünfte; ~ **requirements** gewerbepolizeiliche
Voraussetzungen.
lie | *(v.)* **over** *(remain unpaid)* nicht zur Verfallszeit be-
zahlt werden;
~ **up** *(ship)* außer Dienst (Fahrt) sein, aufliegen.
lien Zurückhaltungs-, Pfandrecht;
carrier's ~ Frachtführerpfandrecht; **common-law**
~ gesetzliches Zurückbehaltungsrecht; **warehouseman's** ~ Lagerhalterpfandrecht;
to enforce a ~ Pfandrecht verwerten.
life *(agreement)* Geltungsdauer, Laufzeit;
good ~ *(life insurance business)* gesunder Versicherungsnehmer; **useful** ~ Nutzungsdauer;
working ~ Arbeitsjahre;
~ **of a letter of credit** Laufzeit eines Akkreditivs;
~ **and soul of a company** Seele eines Unternehmens;
to hold an office (a post) for ~ auf Lebenszeit
(lebenslänglich) angestellt sein; **to insure one's** ~
Lebensversicherung abschließen; **to retire from
active** ~ in den Ruhestand treten;
~ **annuitant** Leibrentenempfänger; ~ **annuity** Le-
bens-, Leibrente.
life assurance *(Br.)* Lebensversicherung;
industrial ~ Volks-, Kleinlebensversicherung;
straight ~ Versicherung auf den Todesfall.
life | **beneficiary** lebenslänglicher Nutznießer; ~
company Lebensversicherungsgesellschaft; ~ **expectancy** Lebenserwartung.
life insurance Lebensversicherung;
business ~ Teilhaberversicherung; **industrial** ~
(US) Volks-, Kleinlebensversicherung; **limited-
pay** ~ *(US)* Lebensversicherung mit abgekürzter
Prämienzahlung; **ordinary** ~ *(US)* Lebensversicherung auf den Todesfall;
~ **in force** Lebensversicherung mit laufender Beitragszahlung; ~ **with (without) profits** *(Br.)* Lebensversicherung mit (ohne) Gewinnbeteiligung;
~ **agent** Lebensversicherungsvertreter; ~ **fund** Prämienreserve; ~ **policy** Lebensversicherungspolice;
~ **premium** Lebensversicherungsprämie.

life | **interest** Leibrente; ~ **office** Lebensversicherungsbüro; ~ **pensioner** Leibrentner; ~ **table** Sterblichkeitstabelle, Sterbetafel; ~ **underwriter** Lebensversicherer.
lifeless *(stock exchange)* lustlos, matt, flau.
lift *(Br.)* Aufzug, *(advancement)* Beförderung;
~ *(v.)* **a control** *(trade)* Bewirtschaftungsmaßnahmen aufheben; ~ **restrictions on instal(l)ment buying** Beschränkungen auf dem Abzahlungsgebiet aufheben; ~ **the top** *(stock exchange, US)* Höchstkurs heraufsetzen.
light | **cargo** Leichtgut; ~ **displacement** Leertonnage; ~ **freight** Leichtgüter; ~ **taxation** geringe Besteuerung; ~ **trading** schwacher [Börsen]umsatz.
lighterage Löschungs-, Leichtergebühren.
limit Grenze, *(duration of validity)* Gültigkeitsdauer, *(price)* Preisgrenze, Limit;
age ~ Altersgrenze; **cartage** ~ Zustellbezirk; **credit** ~ *(Br.)* Kreditlinie; **fiduciary** ~ Höchstgrenze für ungedeckte Notenausgabe; **firm** ~ Festorder; **increased** ~ *(liability insurance)* erhöhte Versicherungssumme; **standard** ~ *(liability insurance)* normale Versicherungssumme;
basic ~ **for property damage** versicherter Sachschadensgrundbetrag;
~ *(v.)* *(price)* limitieren, Limit vorschreiben, *(restrict)* beschränken;
to exceed the ~ *(broker)* Limit ([Preis]grenze) überschreiten; **to reach the** ~**s of one's resources** an der Grenze seiner Mittel ankommen;
~ **order** *(broker)* limitierter [Börsen]auftrag.
limitation Be-, Einschränkung, Begrenzung, *(prescription)* Verjährung[sfrist];
statutory ~ gesetzliche Verjährungsfrist;
~ **of a claim** Anspruchsverjährung; ~ **of (on) dividends** Dividendenbeschränkung; ~ **of hours** Arbeitszeitbeschränkung; ~**s upon production** Produktionsbeschränkungen.
limited begrenzt, limitiert, *(company)* mit beschränkter Haftung;
~ **audit** abgekürzte Prüfung; ~ **capacity** beschränktes Fassungsvermögen, *(legal capacity)* **(**beschränkte Geschäftsfähigkeit; ~ **[liability] company** *(Br.)* *(corporation, US)* Gesellschaft mit beschränkter Haftung (GmbH); ~ **life assets** Kapitalanlagegüter mit beschränkter Lebensdauer; ~ **mail** Bahnpost; ~ **market** beschränkte Absatzmöglichkeiten; ~ **order** Limit, limitierte [Börsen]order; ~ **partnership** Kommanditgesellschaft; ~ **price** Kurslimit; ~**-price store** *(US)* Kleinpreisgeschäft, Billigwarenhaus.
linear increase of taxation lineare Steuererhöhung.
line *(branch of business)* Branche, Geschäfts-, Gewerbezweig, *(class of goods)* Warengattung, -sortiment, Posten, Partie, *(production)* Fertigungsserie, *(sphere of business)* Fach, Arbeits-, Fachgebiet, Tätigkeitsfeld, *(telecommunication)* Fernverbindung, *(tel.)* Leitung, Anschluß, *(traffic)* Verkehrs-, Omnibus-, Eisenbahnlinie.
above the ~ *(Br.)* zum ordentlichen Etat gehörig;
below the ~ *(balance sheet)* unter dem Strich;

agate ~ *(advertising)* Anzeigenmaß, Zeile; **assembly** ~ Fließband; **busy** ~ *(US)* besetzte [Telefon]leitung; **cheap** ~ preiswerte Ware; **competitive** ~ Konkurrenzerzeugnis; **feeder** ~ Zubringer; **gross** ~ *(insurance)* Höchstgrenze; **industrial** ~ Fabrikgleis; **leading** ~ Spezialität, Reklameartikel; **net** ~ *(insurance)* Höchstgrenze des Selbstbehalts; **run-of-the-mile** ~ einfaches Durchschnittserzeugnis; **trunk** ~ *(tel., Br.)* Fernverbindung;
~ **of credit** *(US)* Kreditlinie; ~ **of manufacture** Fabrikationszweig; ~ **of travel** Reiseroute;
to change one's ~ **of business** Geschäftszweck ändern; **to deal in a** ~ Artikel führen; **to hold the** ~ **on costs** Kostenniveau halten; **to hold the** ~ **on prices** Preise stabil halten; **to sell its losing** ~ mit Verlust arbeitenden Fertigungsbetrieb verkaufen; **to trace a flat** ~ *(stocks)* keinen Kursanstieg aufweisen; **to write a** ~ *(underwriter)* Teilrisiko übernehmen;
~ **advertising** Produktionswerbung; **one-~** **business** Spezial-, Fachgeschäft; **full** ~ **forcing** *(US)* Abnahmezwang für alle Produkte; ~ **shutup** Fertigungsaufgabe.
liner Linienschiff, Passagierdampfer, Linienflugzeug;
~ **freighting** Stückgutbefrachtung; ~ **service** Linienverkehr.
liquid flüssig, liquid, sofort realisierbar;
~ **assets** *(balance sheet, US)* Umlaufvermögen; ~ **current assets** kurzfristige Forderungen; **to hold savings in** ~ **form** Ersparnisse liquide angelegt haben; ~ **loan** Liquiditätskredit; ~ **position** *(banking)* Liquiditätsstatus; ~ **reserve** *(banking business)* Mindest-, Liquiditätsreserven; ~ **securities** leicht absetzbare Papiere; ~ **strength** hoher Liquiditätsgrad.
liquidate *(v.)* abrechnen, abwickeln, glattstellen, saldieren, *(firm)* liquidieren, auflösen, *(v. i.)* in Liquidation gehen;
~ **the assets of a bankrupt** Konkursmasse liquidieren; ~ **an inventory** *(US)* Lager abbauen; ~ **one's stock of goods** sein Lager abstoßen.
liquidated | **account** der Höhe nach feststehender Saldo; ~ **damages** festgesetzte Schadenssumme, Konventionalstrafe.
liquidating | **balance sheet** Liquidationsbilanz; ~ **distribution** Masseverteilung; ~ **dividend** Liquidationsanteil; ~ **value** Liquidationswert.
liquidation Abrechnung, Abwicklung, *(company)* Liquidation, Liquidierung, *(evening up)* Glattstellung;
adjudicated ~ Zwangsliquidation; **inventory** ~ *(US)* Lagerabbau;
~ **of an annuity** Rentenablösung; ~ **of assets** Anlagenverwertung; ~ **of debts** Schuldentilgung; ~ **of long positions** *(stock exchange)* Glattstellung von Hausse-Engagements;
to come in for heavy ~**s** *(stock market)* umfangreichen Gewinnrealisationen unterworfen sein;
~ **account** Liquidationskonto; ~ **dividend** Schlußdividende; ~ **fund** Tilgungsfonds; ~ **value** Liquidationswert.

liquidator Liquidator, Abwickler, Masseverwalter.
liquidity [Geld]flüssigkeit, Liquidität;
newly created ~ Liquiditätsausweitung; **surplus** ~ Liquiditätsüberhang;
to be based on ~ liquiditätsmäßig sichtbar werden; **to build** ~ liquiditätspolitische Maßnahme treffen; **to have no effect on** ~ liquiditätspolitisch neutral sein; **to strain** ~ angespannte Liquiditätspolitik betreiben;
~ **arrangement** Liquiditätsabsprache; ~-**creating effect** Liquiditätsauswirkung; **to establish itself firmly on the international** ~ **map** sich auf internationalen Märkten eines ausgezeichneten Liquiditätsrufes erfreuen; ~ **margin** Liquiditätsspielraum; ~ **measures** Liquiditätsmaßnahmen; ~ **pinch** Liquiditätsbeengung; ~ **position** Liquiditätsstatus; ~ **pressure** Liquiditätsdruck; ~ **requirements** Liquiditätsvorschriften.
list Liste, Register, Adressenverzeichnis, Aufstellung, *(docket)* Terminliste;
black ~ Boykottliste; **cargo** ~ Ladeverzeichnis; **credit** ~ Liste der kreditfähigen Kunden; **free** ~ Freiliste [zollfreier Gegenstände]; **official** ~ *(stock exchange, Br.)* amtliche Börsennotierung; **price** ~ Preisverzeichnis, -liste; **shopping** ~ Einkaufszettel; **specie** ~ Geldsortenzettel; **stock-exchange** ~ *(Br.)* Kursblatt; **subscription** ~ Subskriptionsliste; **trade** ~ Preisliste, Geschäftskatalog;
~ **of assets** Vermögensverzeichnis, *(bankruptcy)* Masseverzeichnis, *(estate)* Nachlaßverzeichnis; ~ **of charges** Gebührenordnung; ~ **of creditors of a bankrupt** Konkurstabelle; ~ **of customers** Kundenkartei; ~ **of foreign exchanges** *(Br.)* Devisenkurszettel; ~ **of exhibitors** Ausstellerverzeichnis; ~ **of [market] quotations** *(Br.)* Börsen-, Kurszettel; **stockbroker's** ~ **of recommendation** Liste empfohlener Börsenwerte; ~ **of shareholders** *(Br.)* Aktionärsverzeichnis; ~ **of subscribers** Subskriptions-, Abonnentenliste; ~ **of suppliers** Lieferantenliste; ~ *(v.)* in einer Liste eintragen, [listenmäßig] erfassen, registrieren, aufzeichnen, *(stock exchange, US)* [Effekten] an der Börse einführen; ~ **in a catalog(ue)** in einen Katalog aufnehmen; ~ **property with a broker** *(US)* einem Makler Grundstückseigentum an die Hand geben; **to be struck from the** ~ *(insolvency)* für zahlungsunfähig erklärt werden; **to rent** ~**s** *(list broker)* Adressenverzeichnisse leihweise zur Verfügung stellen;
~ **broker** Adressenbüro; ~ **price** Katalogpreis.
listed registriert, *(of stocks, US)* börsenfähig, amtlich notiert.
listing Katalogisierung, Inventarisierung, *(real estate)* Maklerbeauftragung;
exclusive ~ ausschließlicher Maklerauftrag; ~ **of property for taxation** *(US)* Vermögensteuererklärung; **official** ~ **note** *(stock exchange US)* Zulassungsbescheid.
listless trading *(US)* Freiverkehr.

live *(v.)* **on one's capital** von seinem Kapital leben; ~ **economically** sparsam wirtschaften; ~ **at s. one's expense** jem. auf der Tasche liegen; ~ **off government checks** *(US)* **(cheques,** *Br.)* von staatlicher Unterstützung leben; ~ **up to the letter of a contract** Vertrag bis zum letzten I-Tüpfelchen erfüllen; ~ *(a.)* **assets** wohlfundierte Anlagewerte; ~ **letter book** Tageskopiebuch; ~ **load** Nutzlast.
livelihood [Lebens]unterhalt, Existenz[grundlage];
to earn one's ~ seinen Lebensunterhalt verdienen.
lively *(stock exchange)* flott, lebhaft.
livery *(allowance of food)* Deputat.
living Wohnen, Aufenthalt, *(livelihood)* Nahrung, [Lebens]unterhalt, Auskommen, Existenz;
substandard ~ asoziale Wohnweise;
to scrape one's ~ sein Leben fristen;
~ **separate and apart** *(income-tax statement)* getrennt lebend;
~ **allowance** Unterhaltszuschuß; ~ **cost** Lebenshaltungskosten; ~ **standard** Lebensstandard; ~ **wage** Existenzminimum.
load Fuhre, Last, Ladung, Fracht, *(insurance)* Verwaltungskostenzuschlag, *(loading capacity)* Tragfähigkeit, *(work)* Arbeitspensum;
gross ~ Bruttobelastung; **no** ~ Nullast; **peak** ~ Spitzenbelastung;
~ *(v.)* [auf]laden, *(add to the selling price)* Aufschlag vornehmen, *(insurance)* Prämienzuschlag für Verwaltungskosten erheben, *(take aboard)* Ladung übernehmen;
~ **in bulk** *(ship)* Sturzgüter laden; ~ **in parcels** Stückgüter laden;
~ **capacity** Trag-, Ladefähigkeit; ~ **displacement** Wasserverdrängung, Ladetonnage.
loaded with securities mit Effekten stark eingedeckt.
loading [Be]laden, Aufladen, *(freight)* Ladung, Fracht, *(instalment system, Br.)* Aufschlag, *(insurance)* Prämienaufschlag zu den Verwaltungskosten, *(investment trust)* Ausgabekostenzuschlag zuzüglich Erwerbskosten der Wertpapiere, *(ship)* Schiffsladung, *(statistics)* Zuschlag zur Erzielung eines gewogenen Indexes;
daily ~**s** Tagesversand;
~ **area** Ladefläche; ~ **berth** Ladestelle; ~ **capacity** *(vehicle)* Fassungsvermögen; ~ **dock** Ladedock; ~ **platform** Ladebühne, -rampe; ~ **point** Verladeort; ~ **profit** *(insurance)* Aufschlagsgewinn.
loan Anleihe, Darlehn, Kredit, *(advance)* Vorschuß;
thrown out of ~**s** *(stocks)* nicht lombardfähig;
accommodation ~ Überbrückungskredit; **amortized (amortizing)** ~ Tilgungsdarlehn; **bank** ~ Bankkredit; **bottomry** ~ Bodmereigeld; **call** ~ sofort rückzahlbares Darlehn; **collateral** ~ *(US)* Lombardkredit; **commercial** ~ Warenkredit; **crop** ~ Ernte[finanzierungs]kredit; **day** ~ Tagesgeld; **demand** ~ Tagesgeld; **fiduciary** ~ ungesicherter Personalkredit; **fixed-value** ~ wertbeständige Anleihe; **forced** ~ Krediterhöhung infolge Kontoüberziehung; **foreign-currency** ~ Währungskredit; **gap** ~ Überbrückungskredit; **gilt-edged** ~ mündel-

sichere Anleihe; **government[al]** ~ Staatsanleihe, öffentliche Anleihe; **line-of-credit** ~ Kredit in festgesetzter Höhe; **local-authority** ~ *(Br.)* Kommunalanleihe; **medium-term** ~ längerfristiger Kredit; **municipal** ~ Stadt-, Kommunalanleihe; **nonliquid** ~ eingefrorener Kredit; **oversubscribed** ~ überzeichnete Anleihe; **public** ~ öffentliche Anleihe; **redemption** ~ Tilgungsanleihe; **relief** ~ Notstandskredit; **secured** ~ gesicherter (gedeckter) Kredit; **security** ~ Lombardkredit; **sight** ~ gegen Sichtwechsel gewährtes Darlehn; **tied** ~ zweckgebundene Anleihe; **trade** ~ *(US)* Warenkredit; ~ **against borrower's note** Schuldscheindarlehn; ~ **on bottomry** Bodmereigeld; ~ **without interest** zinsloses Darlehn; ~ **at notice** kündbares Darlehn; ~ **for use** Gebrauchsüberlassung, Leihe; ~ *(v.)* **[out]** [aus]leihen, gegen Zinsen ausleihen, Darlehn gewähren; ~ **on collateral** gegen Sicherheit Kredit gewähren; ~ **on interest** auf Zinsen ausleihen; **to draw a** ~ **in tranches** Anleihe in Abschnitten in Anspruch nehmen; **to float a** ~ Anleihe lancieren; **to meet a** ~ **when due** fälligen Kredit zurückzahlen; **to offer a** ~ **for subscription** Anleihe zur Zeichnung auflegen; **to oversubscribe a** ~ Anleihe überzeichnen; **to place a** ~ Anleihe unterbringen; **to replenish a** ~ zusätzliche Sicherheiten stellen; **to service a** ~ Zinsendienst einer Anleihe durchführen; **to subscribe for (to, *Br.*) a** ~ Anleihe zeichnen; **to sweeten a** ~ *(sl.)* erstklassige Sicherheiten stellen; **to turn thumbs down on a** ~ Kreditanfrage ablehnen; ~ **account** Darlehns-, Kreditkonto; ~ **agreement** Darlehnsvertrag; ~ **business** *(securities)* Lombardgeschäft; ~ **commitments** Anleiheverpflichtungen; ~ **committee** Kreditausschuß; ~ **embargo** Kreditsperre; ~ **envelope** Sicherheitenmappe; ~ **shark** *(US)* wucherischer Geldverleiher, Kredithai; **mutual** ~ **society** *(Br.)* Darlehnskassenverein auf Gegenseitigkeit; ~ **talks** Kreditverhandlungen; ~ **terms** Anleihebedingungen; ~ **value** Beleihungs-, Lombardwert; **to be waiting at the** ~ **window** am Darlehnsschalter Schlange stehen.

loaned employee abgestellter Angestellter.

loanmonger Darlehns-, Finanzmakler.

lobby Halle, Vestibül, *(pressure group)* Interessen-, Machtgruppe, Lobby;
~ *(v.)* **a bill** Gesetz [als Interessent] beeinflussen.

lobbying office Kontaktbüro.

local │ acceptance Platzakzept; ~ **agent** Bezirksvertreter; ~ **agreement** Ortstarif; ~ **bill** Platzwechsel; ~ **bond** *(Br.)* Kommunalschuldverschreibung; ~ **bonus** Ortszuschlag, -zulage; ~ **branch** Zweigstelle, Filiale; ~ **business** Platz-, Lokogeschäft; ~ **charges** *(banking)* Platzspesen; ~ **currency** Landeswährung; ~ **customer** Stammkunde; ~ **freight** Fracht im Nahverkehr; ~ **letter** Ortsbrief; ~ **rate** Ortstarif; ~**rates** *(Br.)* Kommunalabgaben; ~ **traffic** Vorortverkehr; ~ **transaction** Platzgeschäft.

locate *(v.)* **a factory** Fabrik, Fabrikgelände (Standort für eine Fabrik) auswählen; ~ **one's office** sein Büro unterbringen.

located in A mit dem Sitz in A.

location *(advertising)* Raum für Außenwerbung, *(place of settlement)* Niederlassung, *(position)* Lage, Standort, Belegenheit, Stellung, Platz, Stelle; **in a desirable** ~ verkehrsgünstig gelegen; **high-rent** ~ Geschäftsgegend mit hohen Mieten; **individual** ~ *(advertising)* Sonderplacierung; **suitable** ~ **for new factories** gute Standortlage für neue Fabriken; ~ **factor** *(US)* Immobilienmakler.

lock *(v.)* │ **out** *(labo(u)rers)* aussperren; ~ **up capital** Kapital blockieren.

locked warehouse Zollager.

lockup *(car)* Autobox, Einzelgarage, *(invested capital)* festgelegtes Kapital.

lodge *(v.)* *(deposit)* hinterlegen, in Verwahrung geben, *(quarter)* aufnehmen, unterbringen, einquartieren, *(reside as a lodger)* als Mieter wohnen, logieren; ~ **a claim** Forderung anmelden; ~ **documents** Urkunden hinterlegen; ~ **a proof of debt with the official receiver** Forderung beim Konkursverwalter anmelden; ~ **as security** als Sicherheit hinterlegen; ~ **one's valuables in the bank** seine Wertsachen ins Bankdepot geben.

lodger [Unter]mieter, Pensionär, Kostgänger.

lodging Logis, [Miet]wohnung, Unterkunft, Behausung, möbliertes Zimmer;
board and ~ Unterkunft und Verpflegung; **unfurnished** ~**s** Leerzimmer;
~ **of security** Sicherheitsleistung;
to let ~**s** *(Br.)* Zimmer vermieten;
~ **allowance** Wohnungsgeldzuschuß; ~ **house** [billige] Pension, Hotel garni; **common** ~ **house** *(Br.)* Obdachlosenasyl.

lodgment *(deposit of customer)* Bankdepot, *(depositing)* Hinterlegung, Deponierung.

loft building *(US)* Speichergebäude.

log Tagebuch, Schiffsjournal.

logbook *(car, US)* Fahrtnachweis, *(ship)* Schiffsjournal, Bord-, Logbuch.

long *(stock exchange, US)* Haussier;
~**s and shorts** Hausse- und Baissegeschäft;
to be ~ **on cash** flüssig sein; **to be** ~ **of the market** *(US)* mit Effekten hinreichend versehen sein;
~ **account** *(US)* Engagements der Haussepartei;
~**, heavy or bulky articles** Sperrgut; ~**-dated** langfristig; ~ **day** Arbeitszeit mit Überstunden; ~ **-distance** Fernamt, Fernvermittlung;

lond-distance │ cable Fernkabel; ~ **call** Ferngespräch, *(Europe)* Auslandsgespräch; ~ **freight traffic** Güterfernverkehr; ~ **goods traffic** *(Br.)* Güterfernverkehr.

long │ exchange *(Br.)* langfristiger Devisenwechsel; ~ **firm** *(Br.)* Schwindelfirma; ~ **-form report** *(auditing)* detaillierter Revisionsbericht; ~ **hauls [on the railway]** Güterfernverkehr; ~ **-haul freight traffic** Güterfernverkehr; ~ **interest** *(US)* Engagements der Haussepartei; ~ -lived **assets** langlebige Wirtschaftsgüter; ~ **market** *(US)* nicht mehr aufnahmefähiger Markt; ~ **pull** *(US)* Effektenspekulation auf lange Sicht; ~ **side** *(stock exchange, US)* Haussepartei.

long-term | **appointment** Dauerstellung; ~ **compensation** *(income tax)* Einkünfte für in mehreren Jahren geleistete Arbeit.

longevity pay *(US)* Prämie für langjährige Betriebszugehörigkeit.

longshoreman *(US)* Schauermann, Kaiarbeiter.

look | *(v.)* **down a list** Liste durchsehen; ~ **for a job** sich nach einer Stellung umsehen.

loose *(unpacked)* unverpackt, lose; ~ **capital** brachliegendes Kapital; ~ **combinations** *(cartel, US)* lockere Vereinbarungen (Zusammenschlüsse).

loose-leaf | **binder** Loseblatt-, Ringbuch, Sammelmappe, Schnellhefter; ~ **ledger** Loseblattbuchführung.

loosen *(v.)* **the lid on tight money** Geldmarktverknappung beseitigen.

lorry *(Br.)* Lastkraftwagen, -auto, *(railway)* offener Güterwagen, Rungenwagen; ~ **driver** *(Br.)* Fernlastfahrer.

lose *(v.)* verlieren, einbüßen, *(prices)* zurückgehen; ~ **a business** Kundschaft verlieren; ~ **ground** *(prices)* zurückgehen; ~ **money by a bad investment** sich verspekulieren; ~ **in value** Wertminderung erleiden.

losing | **bargain** schlechtes Geschäft; ~ **business** Verlustgeschäft; ~ **price** Verlustpreis.

loss Verlust, *(damage)* Schaden, Einbuße, Einbüßung, *(disadvantage)* Nachteil, Ausfall, *(insurance)* Versicherungsschaden; **after charging of all** ~es nach Abschreibung aller Verluste; **upon the occurrence of a** ~ beim Schadenseintritt; **actual** ~ *(insurance)* Verlust in Höhe des Zeitwerts [des versicherten Gegenstandes]; **average** ~ Havarieschaden; **book** ~ buchmäßiger Verlust; ~ **carried forward** *(balance sheet, Br.)* Verlustvortrag; **clear** ~ Nettoverlust; **constructive total** ~ *(insurance)* fingierter Totalschaden; ~ **deductible** *(income tax)* steuerlich abzugsfähiger Verlust, Verlustabzug; **fire** ~ Brandschaden; **marine** ~ Verlust auf See; **normal** ~ natürlicher Schwund; **partial** ~ Partialschaden; **property** ~ Vermögensschaden; **salvage** ~ *(marine insurance)* Bergungsschaden; **shock** ~ *(insurance)* Katastrophenschaden; **trading** ~ Betriebs-, Geschäftsverlust; **use and occupancy** ~ Betriebsunterbrechungsschaden; **wage** ~ Lohnausfall; ~ **in assets** Anlagenabgang; ~ **from bad debts** Verlust aus zweifelhaften Forderungen; ~ **on exchange** Kursverlust; ~ **incurred by breach of contract** Vertrauensschaden; ~ **fully covered by insurance** durch die Versicherung voll gedeckter Schaden; ~ **not compensated by insurance** von der Versicherung nicht gedeckter Schaden; ~ **of overseas markets**

Verlust überseeischer Absatzgebiete; ~ **occasioned by breach of contract** Vertrauensschaden; **national** ~ **in potential output** nicht genutzte volkswirtschaftliche Wachstumsmöglichkeit; ~ **of profits** Gewinnrückgang; ~ **of prospective profits** entgangener Gewinn; **recession-induced** ~ **of revenue** rezessionsbedingter Steuerausfall; ~ **of a ship with all hands** Schiffsuntergang mit der gesamten Besatzung; ~ **of trade** Handelsrückgang; ~ **in transit** Transportschaden; ~ **of useful value** *(depreciation, Br.)* unvorhergesehene Entwertung; **to assess a** ~ Schaden abschätzen; **to be at a** ~ **for money** in Geldverlegenheit sein; **to be responsible for a** ~ für einen Schaden haften; **to claim damages for** ~ **of expectation of life** Schadenersatz für geringer gewordene Lebenserwartung verlangen; **to close with a** ~ mit Verlust abschließen; **to charge off (deduct)** ~es Verluste abschreiben; **to cut one's** ~es rechtzeitig zu spekulieren aufhören; **to get off without a** ~ sich salvieren; **to hold s. o. harmless from a** ~ j. von einer Schadenersatzverpflichtung freistellen; **to incur heavy** ~es große Verluste erleiden; **to retrieve a** ~ Verlust wieder einbringen; **to run at a** ~ mit Verlust arbeiten; **to settle a** ~ Schadensfall regeln; **to work at a** ~ mit Unterbilanz arbeiten;

profit and ~ **account** Gewinn- und Verlustkonto; ~ **adjustment** Schadensregulierung; ~ **advice** Schadensanzeige; ~ **assessment** Schadensfeststellung; ~ **and damage claim** *(transportation)* Transportschadensforderung; **to plunge into the** ~ **column** in die Verlustzone (rote Ziffern) geraten; ~ **deduction** Verlustabzug; ~ **leader** *(shop)* Reklamepreis, Lockartikel, Köder; ~ **prevention** Schadenverhütung; ~-**producing factor** Verlustfaktor; ~ **ratio** *(insurance)* Schadensquote; ~ **relief** *(income-tax statement)* Verlustanrechnung; ~ **reserve** *(insurance)* Rücklage für laufende Risiken.

lost verloren, abhanden gekommen, in Verlust geraten, *(broken down)* ruiniert; ~ **or not** ~ *(marine insurance)* rückwirkende Versicherungsschutzklausel; ~ **property** Fundsachen; ~-**property office** Fundbüro; ~ **time** Verlustzeit.

lot Teil, Anteil, *(duty, Br.)* Abgabe, Steuer, *(goods)* Waren-, Lieferposten, Partie, Sendung, *(item)* Posten, Artikel, *(lottery)* Los, *(plot of land)* Bauplatz, [Grundstücks]parzelle; **in** ~s in Partien, posten-, partienweise; **broken** ~ Partieware, Restposten, *(stock exchange)* Bruchschluß; **even (full)** ~ voller Börsenschluß; **job** ~ Ramschwaren; ~ *(v.)* **out** in Partien aufteilen, *(land)* parzellieren; **to be redeemed by** ~ zur Rückzahlung ausgelost werden; **to dispose of a** ~ **at reduced prices** Partie zu zurückgesetzten Preisen abgeben; ~ **money** *(auction sale)* Aktuionsgebühr; **economic** ~ **size** wirtschaftliche Losgröße.

lottery Verlosung, Ausspielung, Lotterie; **charity** ~ Tombola; **class (Dutch)** ~ Klassenlotte-

rie; **interest** ~ Prämienanleihe; **number** ~ [Zahlen]-lotto; **serial** ~ Serienlotterie;
~ **agent** Lotterieeinnehmer; ~ **bond** Prämienanleihe; ~ **list** Ziehungsliste; ~ **ticket** [Lotterie]los.
lotto Zahlenlotto.

low *(a.)* niedrig, *(prices)* billig, gedrückt;
~ **in cash** knapp bei Kasse;
~-**cost production facilities** günstige Produktionsverhältnisse; ~-**duty goods** niedrig verzollte Waren; ~-**geared** *(capital)* unterkapitalisiert; ~ **gearing** Herabsetzung des Fremdkapitalanteils; ~ **level** Tiefstand [der Kurse]; ~-**price countries** Billigpreisländer; ~ **price group** niedrige Preisgruppe; ~ **station in life** bescheidene Berufsposition; **to be in** ~ **water** schlecht bei Kasse sein.

lower *(v.)* | **the bank rate** Diskontsenkung vornehmen; ~ **the currency** Währung verschlechtern; ~ **the price of goods** Warenpreise heruntersetzen; ~-**bracket** zur unteren Steuergruppe gehörend; ~ **of cost or market principle** *(balancing)* Niederstwertprinzip; **valued at the** ~-**of-cost-or-market price** *(balance sheet)* bewertet zum Einstands- oder Marktwert.

lowering | **of the bank rate** Diskontsenkung; ~ **of prices** Preisherabsetzung, *(stock exchange)* Kursabschwächung.

lowest | **bid** Mindestgebot; ~ **bidder** Mindestbietender; ~ **quotation** niedrigster Kurs.

luggage *(Br.)* [Reise]gepäck, Passagiergut;
free ~ Freigepäck; **left** ~ Aufbewahrungsgepäck; **personal** ~ Handgepäck; **registered** ~ aufgegebenes Gepäck;
to examine the ~ Gepäck zollamtlich revidieren; **to send one's** ~ **in advance** sein Gepäck aufgeben; ~ **chit** Gepäckschein; ~ **counter** Gepäckschalter; ~ **examination** zollamtliche Gepäckrevision; ~ **registration window** Gepäckschalter.

lull *(stock exchange)* Geschäftsstille, Flaute.

lump, in the im ganzen, in Bausch und Bogen, pauschal;
~ *(v.)* **the expenses** Unkosten aufteilen; ~ **items together** *(balance sheet)* Posten zusammenwerfen; ~ **fee** Pauschalgebühr; ~ **price** Pauschalpreis; ~ **sum** einmalige Summe, Pauschalbetrag; ~ -**sum allowance** Pauschalvergütung.

luncheon voucher Essenmarke;
to buy ~s im Abonnement essen.

lure *(v.)* labo(u)r **into other jobs** Arbeitskräfte zum Berufswechsel verführen.

luxuries tax Luxussteuer.

luxury | **apartment** Luxuswohnung; ~ **article** Luxusartikel; ~ **hotel** Hotel der Spitzenklasse; ~ **industry** Luxuswarenindustrie; ~ **tax** Luxussteuer.

M

mace-proof pfändungsfrei.

machine Maschine, Apparat, Vorrichtung;
copying ~ Kopierpresse;
~ **accountant** Maschinenbuchhalter; ~ **burden unit** Maschinen-, Platzkostensatz; ~ **downtime** *(US)* Maschinenbrachezeit.

machinery | **and plant** Maschinen und maschinelle Anlagen;
~ **replacement** Erneuerung des Maschinenparks.

machining | **allowance** Zuschlag für maschinelle Bearbeitung; ~ **operation** Bearbeitungsvorgang.

made | **to order** auf Bestellung gemacht (angefertigt);
~ **out to order** an Order ausgestellt; ~ **bill** *(Br.)* indossierter Wechsel; ~-**up clothes** Konfektionsware, -kleidung.

magazine Warenlager, Speicher, Vorratsraum;
~ **advertisement** Zeitschriftenreklame.

mail Post[sendung], Postsachen, Brief-, Paketpost;
by return of ~ *(US)* postwendend, umgehend;
bulk ~ Postwurfsendung; **closed** ~ versiegelte Postsäcke im zwischenstaatlichen Durchgangsverkehr; **first-class** ~ *(US)* Briefpost; ~ *(railway)* Bahnpost; **second-class** ~ *(US)* Zeitungen; **special-delivery** ~ Eilbotensendung; **third-class** ~ *(US)* Drucksachen;

~ *(v.)* *(US)* mit der Post senden, zum Versand bringen, zur Post geben, auf der Post ausliefern;
to dispatch the ~ Post abfertigen; **to sell by** ~ im Postversandwege verkaufen;
direct ~ **advertising** Einzelwerbung durch die Post; ~ **advertising reply** *(US)* Werbeantwort; ~ **carrier** *(US)* Postbote; ~ **classification** Postversandarten; ~ **delivery** *(US)* Postzustellung; ~ **department** Expedition[sabteilung]; ~-**in premium** Zugabe gegen eingesandten Kupon; ~ **matter** Postsendungen, -sachen, Briefpost; ~ **order** Postauftrag, -versand.

mail-order | **advertising** Versandhauswerbung; ~ **business** Versandgeschäft, -handel; ~ **catalog(ue)** Versandhauskatalog; ~ **firm (house)** Versandhaus, -geschäft, -unternehmen; ~ **selling** Verkauf durch Versandgeschäft; ~ **store** Auslieferungsstelle einer Versandfirma; ~ **wholesaler** Versandgroßhändler.

mail | **payment (remittance)** briefliche Überweisung; **in-the-**~ **price** Preis frei Haus; ~ **service** *(US)* Postdienst, -verkehr, -zustellung; **two-tiered** ~ **system** zweistufiges Posttarifsystem; **by** ~ **train** als Frachtgut; ~ **transfer** Postüberweisung, briefliche Auszahlung.

mailed application schriftlicher Antrag.
mailing | **address** Postanschrift; ~ **cartoon** Versandkarton; ~ **clasp** *(US)* Musterklammer; ~ **charges** *(US)* Postgebühren; ~ **department** Expedition-[sabteilung]; ~ **list** Postversandliste, Adressenkartei; ~ **machine** Adressiermaschine; ~ **piece** Postwurfsendung; ~ **shot** Postwerbeexemplar; ~ **tube** Papp-, Versandrolle.

main | **artery** Hauptverkehrsweg; ~ **business** Hauptgeschäft; ~ **catalog(ue)** Hauptkatalog; ~ **establishment** Hauptniederlassung; ~ **supplier** Hauptlieferant.

maintain *(v.)* | **an action in one's own name** im eigenen Namen klagen; ~ **a correspondence** Briefwechsel führen; ~ **an office** Geschäftsstelle unterhalten; ~ **fixed resale prices** Preisbindung der zweiten Hand beibehalten; ~ **reserves** Reserven halten.

maintained *(stock exchange)* behauptet;
~ **price** gebundener Preis.

maintenance *(keeping in repair)* [laufend] Unter-, Instandhaltung, Wartung, *(subsistence)* [Lebens]-unterhalt, Unterhaltsmittel;
entitled to ~ unterhaltsberechtigt;
resale price ~ Preisbindung der zweiten Hand;
separate ~ *(US)* Unterhalt bei Getrenntleben;
~ **of the poor** Fürsorge [für die Armen]; ~ **of prices** Preisstützung, -bindung; ~ **of resale prices by local dealers** Preisbindung der zweiten Hand;
~ **arrears** rückständige Unterhaltszahlungen; ~ **allowance** Unterhaltszuschuß; ~ **cost** Instandhaltungs-, Betriebs-, Wartungs-, Unterhaltungskosten; ~ **grant** Unterhaltszuschuß; ~ **order** *(Br.)* Unterhaltsurteil; ~ **service** Wartung; ~ **wages** das Existenzminimum deckender Lohn.

major | *(v.) (US)* **in business administration** sich auf Betriebswirtschaft spezialisieren;
~ **consumer goods** hochwertige Gebrauchsgüter;
~ **swing** *(US)* Marktentwicklung über einen größeren Zeitraum.

majority Mehrheit, Majorität, *(full age)* Mündigkeit, Volljährigkeit;
~ **in amount** *(company)* kapitalmäßige Mehrheit;
~ **of creditors** Gläubigermehrheit; ~ **of shares** (stock, *US*) Aktienmehrheit;
to control a ~ **of votes** über die Stimmenmehrheit (Majorität) verfügen;
~ **interest** Mehrheitsbeteiligung; ~**-owned** im Mehrheitsbesitz; ~ **shareholder** Mehrheitsaktionär.

make Erzeugnis, Fabrikat, Marke, Warenzeichen, *(brand)* [Marken]produkt, *(machine)* Bauart, Typ;
of first-class ~ in hervorragender Verarbeitung; ~ **on the** ~ *(sl.)* profitgierig;
our own ~ unser eigenes Fabrikat; **standard** ~ Normalausführung;
~ *(v.)* machen, *(gain)* verdienen, *(manufacture)* fabrizieren, [ver]fertigen, herstellen;
~ **an allowance** Rabatt geben; ~ **an assignment** sein Eigentum auf den Konkursverwalter übertragen; ~ **a bargain** Geschäft abschließen; ~ **default** seinen Verpflichtungen nicht nachkommen;

~ **good arrears** Rückstände begleichen; ~ **good a deficiency (loss)** Schaden decken; ~ **a living** seinen Lebensunterhalt verdienen; ~ **one's mark** unterschreiben; ~ **one's market** sein Warenlager absetzen; ~ **money by economies** einsparen; ~ **an offer** Offerte abgeben; ~ **to order** auf Bestellung anfertigen; ~ **an additional payment** Nachzahlung leisten; ~ **a return** Steuererklärung abgeben.

make away with one's fortune sein Vermögen durchbringen.

make out ausstellen, ausfertigen;
~ **an account** Rechnung ausstellen.

make over abtreten, übertragen;
~ **one's estate** sein Vermögen hinterlassen.

make up *(accounts)* ausgleichen, *(compensate)* wiedergutmachen, ersetzen, entschädigen;
~ **the average** Dispache machen; ~ **an inventory** Inventur machen.

make-up | **pay** *US)* Akkordzuschlag; ~ **work** nachgeholte Arbeitszeit.

maker *(of bill)* Wechselgeber, -aussteller, *(manufacturer)* Hersteller, Produzent, Erzeuger, Fabrikant;
accommodation ~ Gefälligkeitsaussteller.

making up | **the accounts (books)** Kontenabschluß; ~ **a balance sheet** Bilanzaufstellung; ~ **for losses** Verlustausgleich;
~ **day** *(Br.)* Prämienerklärungs-, tag, zweiter Liquidationstag; ~ **price** *(Br.)* Liquidationspreis, -kurs.

maladjustment | **in the balance of payments** Störungen der Zahlungsbilanz; ~ **of prices** Preisschere.

malproduction Überproduktion.

malversation of public money Amtsunterschlagung.

man | **of business** Geschäfts-, Kaufmann; ~ **of means (property)** begüterter Mann; ~ **on the spot** örtlicher Vertreter; ~ **of straw** vorgeschobene Person, Strohmann;
~**-days lost** verlorene Arbeitstage; ~**-hour** Arbeitsstunde; ~ **rating** Leistungseinstufung.

manage *(v.)* verwalten, [Betrieb] leiten, *(contrive)* fertigbringen, bewerkstelligen;
~ **with $ 100** mit 100 Dollar auskommen können.

managed | **currency** manipulierte Währung; ~ **economy** Planwirtschaft.

management Verwaltung, Betrieb, *(company)* Geschäftsleitung, Verwaltungsspitze, Direktion, [Geschäfts]vorstand, *(executives)* leitende Angestellte, Führungskräfte;
under new ~ unter neuer Leitung;
advanced ~ mittlere Führungsschicht; **bad** ~ schlechte Betriebsführung; **brand** ~ Markenbetreuung; **debt** ~ *(US)* Bundesschuldenverwaltung; **factory** ~ Fabrikleitung; **middle** ~ *(US)* mittlere Führungsschicht;
central ~ **of a combine** Konzernleitung; ~ **of a corporation** Verwaltungsspitze einer Gesellschaft; ~ **by decision rules** Betriebsführung anhand eines Verhaltenskatalogs; **poor** ~ **of expenditure** schlechte Ausgabenwirtschaft; ~ **by innovation** Betriebs-

führung durch ständiges Streben nach Systemerneuerung; ~ **and labo(u)r** Tarifpartner; ~ **by objectives** Betriebsführung durch Zielvorgabe; **to dismantle central** ~ zentralgesteuerte Verwaltungsspitze auflösen; **to have a voice in the** ~ in der Verwaltung (Leitung) mitzureden haben; **to supply the** ~ **with advice** dem Vorstand beratend zur Verfügung stehen;

~ **accounting** Rechnungswesen für bestimmte Betriebsführungsbedürfnisse; ~ **board** Vorstandsgremium; ~ **cash-incentive scheme** Tantiemenregelung für leitende Angestellte; ~ **committee** Geschäftsführungsausschuß; ≙ **Committee** *(EG)* Direktorium; ~ **consultant** Unternehmens-, Industrieberater; ~ **consulting firm** Beratungsfirma; **top-level** ~ **decision** Entscheidung auf höchster Ebene; ~ **engineering** *(US)* Betriebstechnik; ~ **expense** Verwaltungskosten, ~ **fee** Vorstandsvergütung, *(investment trust)* Verwaltungskosten, -gebühr; ~ **fund** Investmentfonds mit veränderlichem Portefeuille; ~ **game** Betriebsplanspiel; ~ **hierarchy** Betriebshierarchie; ~ **investment company** Kapitalanlagegesellschaft mit Freizügigkeit in der Anlagepolitik; ~ **partition** betriebliche Mitbestimmung; ~ **policy** Unternehmenspolitik; **top-level** ~ **position** Spitzenposition; ~ **report** Vorstandsbericht; **to come into the** ~ **scene** in den Vorstand gelangen, ~ **seminar** Nachwuchsseminar; ~ **switch** Austausch von Vorstandsmitgliedern; **top** ~ **team** Spitzengremium; **to update its** ~ **techniques** Führungsapparat modernisieren; ~ **trainee** Nachwuchskraft, Führungsnachwuchs; ~ **trust** Kapitalanlagegesellschaft mit freizügiger Anlagenverwaltung; **general** ~ **trust** Investmentgesellschaft mit breitgestreutem Aktienportefeuille.

manager Verwalter, Leiter, Vortsteher, *(conducter of business)* Betriebsleiter, -führer, Geschäftsführer, Unternehmensleiter, Direktor, Vorsteher; ~**s** Direktion, Vorstand;

acting ~ Betriebsleiter, geschäftsführender Direktor; **bank** ~ Bankdirektor; **branch** ~ Filialleiter; **departmental** ~ Abteilungsleiter; **hotel** ~ [Hotel]- geschäftsführer; **marketing** ~ Vertriebsleiter; **personnel** ~ Personaldirektor; **produktion** ~ Produktionsleiter; **sales** ~ Leiter der Verkaufsabteilung; **technical** ~ technischer Direktor; ~ **of credit** Kreditfachmann;

to be a bad ~ nicht einteilen können; **to be an excellent** ~ sehr gut wirtschaften können; ~ **underwriter** Konsortialführer.

managerial führend, unternehmerisch, direktorial; ~ **authority** Führungsbefugnisse; **in a** ~ **capacity** in leitender Stellung; ~ **decisions** Maßnahmen der Betriebsleitung; ~ **economics** *(US)* allgemeine Betriebswirtschaftslehre; **at** ~ **level** auf Vorstandsebene; **high-income** ~ **people** Führungskräfte mit hohem Einkommensniveau; ~ **position (post)** führender Posten, leitende Stellung; ~ **qualities** Unternehmereigenschaften; ~ **staff** Geschäfts-, Betriebsleitung.

managing Geschäftsführung, Betriebsleitung; ~**board** Verwaltungsrat, Direktorium; ~ **clerk** Geschäftsleiter, -führer, Bevollmächtigter, Prokurist, Bürovorsteher, leitender Angestellter; ~ **commitee** Verwaltungsausschuß; ~ **company** *(Br.)* Verwaltungsgesellschaft; ~ **director** *(Br.)* geschäftsführendes Vorsltandsmitglied; ~ **owner of a ship** Korrespondenzreeder.

mandate Mandat, Vollmacht, Geschäftsbesorgungsvertrag.

mandatory | **removal** zwangsweise Entlassung; ~ **retirement age** vorgeschriebenes Pensionsalter.

manifest *(customs)* Zolldeklaration, *(invoice)* Lade-, Warenverzeichnis, Frachtliste, -brief; **bonded** ~ Freigut; **cargo** ~ Ladeverzeichnis.

manifold | **book** Durchschreibebuch; ~ **paper** Vervielfältigungspapier, Saugpost.

manipulate *(v.)* | **accounts** Bücher frisieren; ~ **the currency** Währung manipulieren; ~ **the market** *(stock exchange)* Markt beeinflussen.

manipulation *(stock exchange)* Kursbeeinflussung, -manipulierung; ~ **of accounts** Kontenfälschung; ~ **of the currency** Währungsmanipulation.

manner | **of conveyance** Beförderungsart; ~ **of delivery** Versandform.

manpower menschliche Arbeitskraft, *(labo(u)r force)* verfügbare Arbeitskräfte, Personalbestand; **to recruit** ~ *(US)* Arbeitskräfte einstellen; ~ **budget** Personaletat; ~ **inventory** Personalkartei; ~ **policy** personalpolitische Grundsätze eines Unternehmens; ~ **program(me)** Arbeitsbeschaffungsprogramm; ~ **situation** Arbeitsmarktlage.

manual Vorschriften-, Instruktions-, Handbuch.

manufacture Herstellung, Verarbeitung, Fabrikation, Verfertigung, Anfertigung, Produktion, *(line of industry)* Industrie-, Fabrikationszweig; **direct-marketing** ~ Fabrikhandel; **domestic** ~ einheimisches Fabrikat; **durable** ~**s** Dauergüter; **nondurable** ~**s** Verbrauchsgüter; **serial** ~ Serienfabrikation; **wholesale** ~ Massenherstellung; ~ *(v.)* fabrikmäßig (maschinell) herstellen, fabrizieren, Produktionsstätten unterhalten, produzieren, ausstoßen.

manufactured fabrikmäßig hergestellt; ~ **article** Fabrikware.

manufacturer Fabrikant, Hersteller[firma]; **direct-marketing (-selling)** ~ Fabrikhändler; **lowercost** ~ billigerer Herstellungsbetrieb.

manufacturer's | **agent** *(US)* Werksvertreter; ~ **brand** Fabrikmarke; ~ **catalog(ue)** Preisliste; ~ **cost** Herstellungskosten; ~ **mark** Fabrikmarke; ~ **number** Fabrikationsnummer; ~ **sales price** Verkaufspreis ab Fabrik; ~ **own shop** betriebseigene Verkaufsfiliale.

manufacturing [fabrikmäßige] Herstellung, Verarbeitung, Fabrikation; **quantity** ~ Massenherstellung, erzeugung; ~ *(a.)* gewerbetreibend, fabrikatorisch; ~ **account** Fabrikationskonto; ~ **acquisition** betriebliche Neuerwerbung; ~ **business** Gewerbebetrieb; ~ **company** *(Br.)* Produktionsgesellschaft, Fabrikationsbetrieb; ~ **consumer** gewerblicher Verbraucher; ~ **cost** Anfertigungs-, Fabrikationskosten; ~ **cost sheet** Fabrikationskostenaufstellung; ~ **economics** Produktionskostensenkung; ~ **engineer** Betriebsingenieur; ~ **enterprise (establishment)** gewerblicher Betrieb, Fertigungs-, Produktions-, Fabrikationsbetrieb; ~ **expenses** Fertigungsgemeinkosten; ~ **facilities** Produktionsanlagen; ~ **group** Herstellergruppe; ~ **industry** Fertigungsindustrie; ~ **knowhow** industrielle Produktionserfahrungen; ~ **labo(u)r** Fabrikationslöhne; ~ **method** Produktionsverfahren; ~ **output** Fabrikausstoß; ~ **population** Arbeiterbevölkerung; ~ **price** Fabrik-, Herstellungspreis, ~ **process** Herstellungsmethode, Fertigungsverfahren; ~ **requirements** betriebstechnische Anforderungen; ~ **schedule** Fertigungsplan; ~ **secret** Fabrikationsgeheimnis; ~ **subsidiary** Zulieferungsbetrieb; ~ **tag** Laufzettel; ~ **trade** gewerbliche Wirtschaft.

margin *(cover)* Deckung, Anschaffung, *(difference)* Marge, Differenz, Spielraum, [Handels]spanne, Bruttogewinn, *(insurance)* Verwaltungskostenzuschlag, *(net earnings)* Überschuß, Reingewinn, *(stock exchange)* Sicherheitssumme, Einschuß; dealer's ~ Großhandelsspanne; gross ~ Bruttogewinnspanne; **liquidity** ~ Liquiditätsspielraum; **narrow** ~ geringe Verdienstspanne; **post-tax** ~ Gewinnspanne nach Abzug der Steuern; **profit** ~ Verdienstspanne, Bruttogewinn;
~ **of consumption** Sättigungsgrad; ~ **for unforeseen expenses** Reserve für unvorhergesehene Ausgaben; ~ **of production** Rentabilitätsgrenze; ~ **quality** Qualitätszeichen;
~ *(v.) (stock exchange)* Einschuß leisten;
~ **up** *(broker)* Deckung für Kursverluste stellen;
to buy on ~ *(US)* gegen Sicherheitsleistung kaufen; **to cut** ~s Verdienstspannen herabsetzen; **to put up more** ~ Nachschußzahlung leisten;
~ **account** *(US)* Einschußkonto; ~ **business (buying)** *(US)* Effektendifferenzgeschäft; **narrow** ~ **line** enge Gewinnspanne; ~ **rate** *(securities)* Lombardsatz; ~ **requirements** *(stock exchange, US)* Mindesteinzahlungsbetrag; ~ **trading** *(US)* Effektendifferenzgeschäft.

marginal gerade noch rentabel, zum Selbstkostenpreis;
~ **analysis** Grenzplankostenrechnung; ~ **balance** Bruttogewinn; ~ **company** Grenzbetrieb; ~ **costing** *(Br.)* Grenzplankostenrechnung; ~ **costs** nahe der Rentabilitätsgrenze stehende Kosten; ~ **disutility** *(US)* Arbeitsunlustigkeit; ~ **income** Deckungsbeitrag, Bruttogewinn; ~ **income statement** Ergebnisrechnung auf der Basis variabler Kosten; ~ **labo(u)r** unrentable Arbeitskräfte; ~ **producer** Betrieb an der Grenze der Rentabilität; ~ **productivity of labo(u)r** Grenzproduktivität der Arbeit; ~ **propensity to save** an der Grenze liegende Sparfreudigkeit; ~ **rate** Höchststeuersatz; ~ **relief** *(Br.)*

ermäßigter Steuersatz für die untersten Einkommensgruppen; ~ **supply** Spitzenangebot; ~ **trading** Effektendifferenzgeschäft; ~ **utility** Grenznutzen.

marine, mercantile (merchant) Handelsmarine;
~ **insurance** See[schadenstransport]-versicherung; ~ **interest** Bodmereizinsen; ~ **loan** Bodmereidarlehn; ~ **perils** See[transport]gefahr; ~ **registry** *(Br.)* Eintragung ins Schiffsregister; ~ **store** *(Br.)* Trödelgeschäft; ~ **stores** Schiffsbedarf; ~ **underwriter** Seeschadensversicherer.

marital deduction *(estate tax, US)* Freibetrag der Ehefrau.

maritime | **affairs** Schiffahrtsangelegenheiten; ~ **blockade** Seeblockade; ~ **insurance** Seeversicherung.

mark *(quality)* Marke, Nummer, Qualität, Sorte, *(sign)* [Kenn]zeichen, Eigentumszeichen, *(stock exchange, Br.)* Kursfestsetzung, Notierung, *(ticketing label)* Preiszettel, -angabe, Warenzettel, *(trademark)* Handels-, Fabrik-, Schutzmarke; **below the** ~ unterdurchschnittlich;
blocked ~ *(Germany)* Sperrmark; **certification** ~ *(US)* Güte-, Verbandszeichen; **price** ~ Preiszettel, -auszeichnung;
~ **of origin** Ursprungsbezeichnung; ~ **of quality** Güte-, Qualitätszeichen;
~ *(v.)* markieren, bezeichnen, kennzeichnen;
~ **a cheque** *(Br.)* Scheck bestätigen; ~ **down** *(goods)* niedriger auszeichnen, *(stock exchange)* niedriger notieren; ~ **down the discount rate** Diskontsenkung vornehmen; ~ **out** *(price tag)* mit Preisangaben versehen; ~ **stock** *(stock exchange, Br.)* Kurswerte notieren;
to lodge an objection to the ~ *(stock exchange)* *Br.)* gegen eine Kursfestsetzung protestieren.

markdown *(US)* niedrigere Auszeichnung, Preisherabsetzung;
~ **of securities** Neubewertung von Effekten;
~ **price** herabgesetzter Kleinhandelspreis.

marked *(price)* mit Preisen versehen, ausgezeichnet;
to be ~ **down** *(stock exchange)* niedriger notiert werden;
~ **check** *(US)* gekennzeichneter Scheck; ~ **cheque** *(Br.)* bestätigter Scheck; ~ **improvement** *(stock exchange)* deutliche Besserung.

market Markt, *(business situation)* Handelsverkehr, Wirtschaftslage, *(fair)* Messe, Jahrmarkt, *(marketing)* Absatz, Abnehmer, *(market price)* Marktpreis, Kurs, *(profit)* Umsatz, Gewinn, Vorteil, *(stock exchange)* Börse, Verkehr, *(trading area)* Absatzmarkt, -gebiet, -bereich;
at the ~ *(US)* zum Börsenkurs, bestens; **in the free** ~ außerbörslich; **in a rising** ~ bei steigenden Kursen; **with a brisk** ~ bei guten Umsätzen;
advancing ~ steigende Marktpreise; **bear** ~ Baisse; **black** ~ Schwarzmarkt; **bond** ~ Pfandbriefmarkt; **broad** ~ aufnahmefähiger Markt; **bull** ~ Hausse; **buyers'** ~ Käufermarkt; **capital** ~ Kapitalmarkt; **cheerful** ~ lebhafte Börse; **commodity** ~ Waren-, Rohstoffmarkt, Warenbörse; **Common** ℓ Ge-

meinsamer Markt; **over-the-counter** ~ *(US)* Freiverkehr[sbörse]; **curb** ~ *(US)* Freiverkehrsmarkt; **domestic** ~ inländischer Absatzmarkt; **down** ~ rückläufige Kurse; **employment** ~ Stellenmarkt; **equity** ~ Aktienmarkt; **featureless** ~ lustlose Börse; **fluctuating** ~ schwankende Nachfrage; **freight** ~ Frachtenbörse; **gilt-edged** ~ *(Br.)* Markt für mündelsichere Wertpapiere; **glutted** ~ übersättigter Markt; **heavy** ~ schleppender Absatz; **limited** ~ beschränkt aufnahmefähiger Markt; **narrow** ~ lustloser Markt, geringe Umsätze; **off-board** ~ *(US)* Markt für nicht notierte Wertpapiere; **open** ~ Freiverkehr; **outside** ~ außerbörslicher Kurs; **out-of-town** ~ *(US)* Regionalbörse; **principal** ~ Hauptabsatzgebiet; **property** ~ *(Br.)* Immobilienmarkt; **resistant** ~ widerstandsfähiger Markt; **securities** ~ Effektenbörse; **sellers'** ~ Verkäufermarkt; **spot** ~ Kassamarkt, Barverkehr; **street** ~ *(Br.)* Nachbörse, Freiverkehr; **strong** ~ feste Börse; **thin** ~ geringe Umsätze; **unofficial** ~ Freiverkehr; **untapped** ~ unerschlossene Absatzgebiete; **weekly** ~ Wochenmarkt; ~ **for bonds** Pfandbriefmarkt; ~ **for futures [delivery]** Terminmarkt; ~ **for mortgages** Hyptheken markt;

~ *(v.)* *(deal)* handeln, Handel treiben, Märkte besuchen;

~ **one' block of shares** sein Aktienpaket auf dem Markt unterbringen;

to apportion the ~ Markt aufspalten; **to be in the** ~ sich interessieren für, als Käufer auftreten; **to be on the** ~ *(stock exchange)* angeboten werden; **to boom the** ~ Kurse in die Höhe treiben; **to bring one's eggs (hogs) to the wrong (bad)** ~ schlechtes Geschäft machen; **to bull the** ~ auf Hausse kaufen; **to come out of the** ~ angeboten werden; **to depress the** ~ Kurse drücken; **to find a ready** ~ guten Absatz haben; **to force out of the** ~ vom Markt vertreiben; **to give a fillip to the** ~ der Börse Auftrieb geben; **to glut the** ~ Markt überschwemmen; **to hold the** ~ Stützungsaktion unternehmen; **to jump into the** ~ plötzlich Kaufaufträge erteilen; **to meet with a ready** ~ aufnahmefähigen Markt finden; **to open up new** ~**s** neue Märkte erschließen; **to play the stock** ~ an der Börse spekulieren; **to rescue the** ~ Stützungsaktion unternehmen; **to rig the** ~ *(Br.)* Kurse in die Höhe treiben;

~ **analysis** Marktuntersuchung, Konjunkturdiagnose; ~ **analyst** Konjunkturdiagnostiker; ~ **average** durchschnittliche Kursentwicklung; ~ **capacity** Aufnahmefähigkeit des Marktes; ~ **comment** Börsenbericht; ~ **data** Absatzzahlen, -ziffern; ~ **discount** *(Br.)* Privatdiskont; ~ **distortion** Marktverzerrung; ~ **flexibility** Nachfrageflexibilität; ~ **fluctuations** Konjunkturschwankungen, *(stock exchange)* Kursschwankungen; ~ **forecast** Konjunkturprognose; ~ **growth** Wachstumsmarkt; ~ **hole** Marktlücke; ~ **investigation** Marktbeobachtung; ~ **leaders** Spitzenreiter; ~ **letter** *(US)* Börsenbrief; ~ **level** Preisniveau; ~ **monopoly** Absatzmonopol;

~ **news** Börsenbericht; **open** ~ **operatiopn** Offenmarktgeschäft; ~ **order** *(US)* *(stock exchange, US)* Billigstens-, Bestauftrag, Bestensorder; ~ **outlook** Konjunkturaussichten; ~ **pattern** Probemuster; ~ **penetration** Marktdurchdringung; ~ **performers** führende Börsenwerte; **to turn the world into a global** ~ **place** seine Erzeugnisse auf dem ganzen Erdball verkaufen; ~ **price** Marktpreis, *(US)* Wiederbeschaffungswert, *(cost of market, whichever is lower)* Wert nach dem Niederstwertprinzip, *(stock exchange)* Effekten-, [Börsen]kurs, Kurswert; ~ **profit** Kursgewinn; ~ **quota** Absatzkontingent; ~ **quotation** [Börsen]notierung; ~ **rate** *(discount rate, Br.)* Diskontsatz [der Londoner Banken und Wechselmakler], *(stock exchange, US)* Tages-, [Börsen]kurs, Kurswert; **short-term** ~ **rate** kurzfristiger Geldsatz; ~ **recession** Konjunkturrückgang; ~ **report** *(stock exchange)* Kurs-, Börsenbericht; ~ **research** Marktforschung; ~**research specialist** Konjunkturforscher; ~ **resistance** Widerstandsfähigkeit des Marktes; ~ **rigger** Kurstreiber; ~ **sentiment** Börsenstimmung; ~ **share** Marktanteil; ~ **spots** *(US)* Effekten mit Sonderbewegungen; ~ **study** Marktuntersuchung; ~ **survey** Marktuntersuchung; ~ **swing** *(US)* Konjunkturperiode; ~ **tip** Börsentip; ~ **trends** Konjunkturentwicklung; ~ **trend analysis** Konjunkturdiagnose; ~ **value** Gemein-, Kauf-, Marktwert, *(stock exchange)* Kurswert; **fair and reasonable** ~ **value** Verkehrswert; **open** ~ **value** *(inheritance tax, Br.)* Verkehrswert.

marketable *(salable)* marktfähig, lieferbar, *(stock exchange)* börsenfähig, -gängig, notiert; ~ **equities** börsengängige Dividendenwerte; ~ **prices** herrschende Marktpreise; ~ **securities (stocks)** *(balance sheet, US)* Wertpapiere des Umlaufvermögens.

marketeer *(US)* Verkäufer, Händler, *(stock exchange)* Abgeber, Verkäufer.

marketing Absatzwirtschaft, -planung, Absatz[wesen], -bemühungen, -politik, Marktversorgung, Vertrieb[slehre]; **associative (cooperative)** ~ genossenschaftliches Absatzwesen; **commodity** ~ Warenabsatz, -vertrieb; **orderly** ~ *(US)* Selbstbeschränkungsabkommen;

to do one's ~ seine Einkäufe machen;

~ **adviser** Absatzberater; ~ **agreement** Vertriebsvereinbarung; ~ **area** Absatzbereich, -gebiet; ~ **behavio(u)r** marktorientiertes Verhalten; ~ **campaign** Absatzfeldzug; ~ **channels** Absatzwege; ~ **conception** Absatzkonzeption; ~ **consultant** freiberuflicher Vertriebsberater; ~ **corporation** *(US)* Vertriebsgesellschaft; ~ **director** Leiter der Vertriebsabteilung; ~ **drive** Absatzfeldzug; ~ **expense(s)** Vertriebsunkosten; ~ **expert** Marktsachverständiger; ~ **financing** Absatzfinanzierung; ~ **knowhow** Absatz-, Vertriebserfahrungen; ~ **man** Vertriebsfachmann; ~ **mix** *(US)* Absatzplanung; ~**oriented** absatzbewußt; ~ **outlet** Einzelhandelsgeschäft; ~ **outlook** Absatzkonjunktur; ~ **planning**

Absatzplanung; ~ **policy** Vertriebs-, Absatzpoli-
tik; ~ **quota** Sollvorgabe für den Absatz; ~ **regulation** *(EC)* Marktordnung; ~ **research** Markt-,
Absatzforschung; ~ **territory** Absatzbezirk.
marking Kennzeichnung, Markierung, *(check, US)*
Bestätigungsvermerk, *(stock exchange, Br.)* Kursnotierung;
~ **clerk** *(stock exchange, Br.)* Kursmakler; ~ **requirements** Kennzeichnungsvorschriften.
markon *(US)* Kalkulationsaufschlag.
markup Handelsspanne, Kalkulationsaufschlag,
*(difference between cost and retail price of mer-
chandise)* Rohgewinnaufschlag [auf den Einkaufs-
preis];
individual ~ Einzelkalkulationsaufschlag;
~ **on cost** Kalkulationsaufschlag auf den Einstandspreis; ~ **on selling prices** Handelsspanne;
~ **percentage** Bruttogewinnsatz.
marshal *(v.)* ordnen, aufstellen, arrangieren;
~ **the assets** Aktiva [im Konkurs] (Verteilungsplan) feststellen; ~ **creditors** Rangordnung der
Gläubiger festlegen; ~ **securities** Sicherheiten aufteilen.
marshal(l)ing | **of assets** *(bankruptcy)* Feststellung der
Aktiva, Aufstellung eines Verteilungsplanes; ~ **of
securities** Aufteilung der Sicherheiten.
masked advertising Schleichwerbung.
mass | **advertising** Massenwerbung; ~ **appeal** Mas-
senanreiz; ~ **discount** Mengenrabatt; ~ **dismissals**
Massenentlassungen; ~ **picketing** massiertes
Streikpostenaufgebot; ~**produce** *(v.)* fabrikmäßig
herstellen.
mass production Massenproduktion, -fabrikation,
Serienproduktion;
standardized ~ Fließbandarbeit;
~ **car** Serienwagen; ~ **industry** Massengüterin-
dustrie.
mass | **purchasing power** Massenkaufkraft; ~ **un-
employment** Massenarbeitslosigkeit.
master Kapitän, Schiffer, *(craft)* Handwerksmeister,
(employer) Prinzipal, Arbeitgeber, Lehrherr;
little ~ *(journeyman, Br.)* Geselle;
~ **agreement** Manteltarifabkommen; ~ **budget** Ge-
samtetat; ~ **freight agreement** Rahmenfrachtab-
kommen; ~ **hand** Fachmann, Spezialist; ~ **mariner**
Handelskapitän; ~ **summary sheet** Betriebsbe-
rechnungsbogen; ~ **workman** Werkmeister, Vorarbeiter.
match Artikel gleicher Qualität;
~ *(v.)* **new cars on the market** neue Autotypen auf
dem Markt einführen; ~ **the sample** mit dem Muster übereinstimmen.
matching *(balance sheet)* periodische Abgrenzung
von Aufwand und Ertrag.
mate's receipt Steuermannsquittung.
material Werkstoff, Material;
~**s consumed** *(balance sheet)* Materialverbrauch;
direct ~**s** Fertigungsmaterial;
labo(u)r and ~**s** Arbeitslohn und Materialkosten;
indirect ~**s and supplies** Materialgemeinkosten;
to buy a house for its ~ Haus auf Abbruch kaufen;

~ **accounting** Materialabrechnung; ~ **change of
user** *(building, Br.)* wesentliche Gebrauchsände-
rung; ~ **consumption** Materialverbrauch; ~ **control**
Materialprüfung; ~ **cost burden rate** Materialge-
meinkostenzuschlag; ~ **damage** Sachschaden; ~ **-
flow** Werkstoffdurchlauf; ~**received report** *(US)*
Materialempfangsbescheinigung; ~ **requisiton slip**
Materialentnahmeschein; ~ **supplies** Materialvor-
rat.
matter Angelegenheit, Sache, *(business)* Geschäft;
first-class ~ *(US)* Brief- und Paketsendungen;
second-class ~ *(US)* Zeitungen und Zeitschriften;
third-class ~ *(US)* Drucksachen; **fourth-class** ~
(US) Paketpost, Mustersendungen; **inquired** ~
(stock exchange) Geld gesucht; ~ **insured** versicherter Gegenstand;
~ **of public concern[ment]** öffentliche Angelegenheit.
matured | **claim** fällige Forderung; ~ **coupon** noch
nicht zur Zahlung eingereichter Kupon.
maturity Fälligkeit, Verfall[zeit];
to have a ~ **of twenty years** zwanzigjährige Laufzeit haben; **to pay before** ~ vor Fälligkeit bezahlen;
~ **age** *(insurance)* Endalter; ~ **date** Fälligkeitstag,
-termin; ~ **index (tickler,** *US)* Terminkalender,
Verfallbuch.
maximum Höchstbetrag, *(bid)* Höchstgebot, *(price)*
Höchstsatz, -preis;
~ **amount** Höchstbetrag; ~ **capacity** *(production)*
Produktionsoptimum; ~ **hiring age limit** *(US)*
Höchsteinstellungsalter; ~ **price** Höchstpreis,
(stock exchange) Höchstkurs; ~ **and minimum tariff** Doppeltarif; ~ **tax rate** Steuerhöchstsatz; ~
wage[s] Höchst-, Spitzen-, Maximallohn.
meal ticket Beköstigungs-, Essensbon;
to buy ~**s** im Abonnement essen.
mean *(value)* Durchschnitts-, Mittelwert;
~ *(a.) (average)* Durchschnitts-, Mittelwert;
~ *(a.) (average)* mittel, durchschnittlich;
to be rather ~ **over money matters** in finanziellen
Dingen äußerst kleinlich sein;
~ **average** gewogener Mittelwert; ~ **competition**
unlauterer Wettbewerb; ~ **due date** mittlerer Verfalltag; ~ **rate of exchange** Durchschnittskurs.
means [Geld]mittel, Einkommen, *(property)* Vermögen;
of small ~ minderbemittelt;
current ~ Umlaufvermögen; **private** ~ Privatver-
mögen;
~ **of communication** Verkehrsmittel; **major** ~ **of
income** Haupteinnahmequelle; ~ **of payment** Zahlungsmittel;
to be of independent ~ finanziell unabhängig sein;
to have ample ~ **at one's disposal** reichliche Mittel
zur Verfügung haben;
~ **test** *(Br.)* Bedürftigkeitsnachweis.
measure Maß, Ausmaß, Umfang, Grad;
made to ~ nach Maß angefertigt;
~ **of damages** Umfang der Schadenersatzberech-
nung; ~**s of economy** Sparmaßnahmen;
~ **cargo (goods)** Sperrgut.

measured | **goods** sperrige Güter; ~ **ton** Raumtonne.
measurement | **goods** Maßgüter; ~ **ton** Raumtonne.
mechanical bookkeeping Durchschreibebuchhaltung.
media Media, Medien, Werbeträger;
commissionable ~ provisionspflichtige Medien;
mass ~ Massenmedien;
~ **allocation** Streuung; ~ **clerk** Mediasachbear-
beiter; ~ **concept** Werbekonzeption; ~ **cost** Werbe-
kosten; ~ **man** Steuerplaner; ~ **research** Werbe-
trägerforschung; ~ **schedule** Streuplan.
medium Mittel, Medium, Organ, *(advertisement)*
Werbeträger, -mittel;
through the ~ **of a goods agent** mit Hilfe (unter
Inanspruchnahme) eines Spediteurs;
advertising ~ Werbeträger; **circulating** ~ Um-
laufs-, Tauschmittel;
~ **of exchange** *(currency)* Valuta, *(exchangeable
article)* Tauschmittel, ~ **of payment** Zahlungsmittel;
~ *(a.)* mittelmäßig, gewöhnlich;
~ **and small-scale enterprises** Mittel- und Kleinbetriebe; ~ **price** Mittelpreis; ~ **price range** mittlere Preislage; ~**quality goods** Produkte mittlerer
Qualität; ~**sized business** Mittelbetrieb, mittleres
Unternehmen.
meet | *(v.) (company)* tagen, *(pay)* begleichen;
~ **a bill** Wechsel einlösen; ~ **the claims of one's
creditors** seine Gläubiger befriedigen; ~ **the deadline** Frist einhalten; ~ **the demand** Bedarf decken;
~ **the demands for payment** Zahlungsansprüche
befriedigen; ~ **with a loss** Verlust erleiden; ~ **with
due protection** *(bill)* honoriert werden.
meeting Besprechung, Sitzung, Tagung;
annual general ~ *(Br.)* ordentliche Jahreshaupt-,
Generalversammlung; **company** ~ *(Br.)* Gesellschafterversammlung; **company-wide** ~ Konzern-
tagung; **extraordinary** ~ *(Br.)* außerordentliche
Hauptversammlung; **overflow** ~ Parallelversamm-
lung; **sales** ~ Vertretertagung;
~ **of the [executive]board** Vorstandssitzung; ~
of creditors Gläubigerversammlung; ~ **of directors**
Direktionssitzung; ~ **of shareholders** *(Br.)* **(stockholders,** US) Aktionärs-, Generalversammlung;
to call a ~ **of the shareholders** *(Br.)* Hauptversammlung einberufen.
melon *(US)* außerordentliche Dividende, Gratisaktie, größerer Bonus.
member, advanced *(building society, Br.)* zugeteilter
Bausparer; **paying** ~ förderndes Mitglied; **unad-
vanced** ~ *(building society, Br.)* noch nicht zugeteilter Bausparer;
~ **of the executive board** *(US)* Vorstandsmitglied;
~ **of the board of directors** Aufsichtsratsmitglied;
~ **banks** *(US)* Mitgliederbanken [des Federal-
Reserve-Systems].
memorandum Vereinbarung, Vertragsurkunde, *(record of events)* Exposé, Memorandum, *(short note)*
Notiz, Vermerk, *(statement of goods sent)* Bordereau, Lieferschein [im Kommissionsverkauf];
to be shipped on ~ kommissionsweise versandt;

common ~ *(Lloyd's, Br.)* Deckungsausschluß für
Bruchschäden; **urgent** ~ Dringlichkeitsvermerk;
~ **of association** *(Br.)* Gründungsurkunde, Gesellschaftsvertrag, -statuten; ~ **of insurance** vorläufiger Deckungsschein;
~ **articles** *(insurance mortgage)*, vom Versicherungsschutz ausgeschlossene Gegenstände; ~ **bill**
Lieferschein; ~ **buying** Kauf mit Rückgaberecht; ~
check *(US)* befristeter Scheck; ~ **clause** *(insurance)*
Ausschluß-, Freizeichnungsklausel; ~ **goods
(package,** US) Kommissionswaren; ~ **sale** Kommissionsverkauf.
mercantile | **academy** Handelshochschule; ~ **agency**
(US) Kreditauskunftei; ~ **agent** *(Br.)* Kommissionär, Handelsvertreter; ~ **bank** Handelsbank; ~
bill Warenwechsel; ~ **career** kaufmännische Laufbahn; ~ **credit** Warenkredit; ~ **creditor** Waren-
gläubiger; ~ **directory** Branchenverzeichnis; ~
establishment Handelsniederlassung; ~ **law** See-,
Verkaufs-, und Handelsrecht; ~ **marine** Handelsmarine; ~ **paper** Warenwechsel; ~ **practice** Handelsbrauch; ~ **report** Bericht einer Kreditauskunftei; ~ **store** *(US)* Ladengeschäft; ~ **system** Merkan-
tilsystem; ~ **vessel** Handelsschiff.
merchandise, merchandize *(US)* Ware[n], Artikel,
Erzeugnis;
as-in ~ zurückgesetzte (reduzierte) Ware; **branded**
~ Markenartikel; **high-cost** ~ Waren in hoher
Preislage; **higher-margin** ~ Waren mit hoher Gewinnspanne; **marked-down** ~ im Preis herabgesetzte Ware; **price-fixed** ~ preisgebundene Waren;
quality ~ Qualitätsware; **staple** ~ Haupterzeug-
nisse; **trademarked** ~ Markenartikel;
~ **shipped by air** auf dem Luftwege beförderte
Güter; ~ **at the beginning of the month** Bestand am
Monatsanfang; ~ **on consignment** Kommissionsware; ~ **on memorandum** Kommissionswaren; ~
in transit Transitware;
~ *(v.) (US)* Handel treiben, handeln, Geschäfte
machen, Absatz steigern;
~ **account** Warenkonto; ~ **allowance** Warenra-
batt; ~ **assortment** Warensortiment; ~ **broker** Produktenmakler; ~ **car** Güterwagen; ~ **control** Wa-
renkontrolle; ~ **cost** Einkaufskosten abzüglich
Warenskonto; ~ **inventory** *(balance sheet)* Warenbestand; ~ **lines** Warensortiment; ~ **manager** Leiter der Ein- und Verkaufsabteilung; **gross** ~ **margin** Bruttoverdienstspanne; ~ **mark** *(Br.)* Warenzeichen; ~ **mix** Zusammensetzung des Sortiments;
~ **procurement cost** Warenbeschaffungskosten; ~
receivables *(balance sheet)* Warenforderungen; ~
shipment Warenversand; ~ **stock** Warenlager; ~
trade surplus Warenhandelsüberschuß; ~ **turnover**
Lagerumschlag; ~ **valuation** Lagerbewertung.
merchandising, merchandizing *(US)* Absatzvorberei-
tung durch Vertriebsplanung, Absatzförderung,
Verkaufspolitik;
~ **department** Vertriebsabteilung; ~ **director** Leiter
der Verkaufsförderungsabteilung; ~ **establishment** Handelsfirma; **gross** ~ **margin** Bruttoge-

winnspanne; ~ **plan** Verkaufsförderungsplan; ~
show Warenmesse; ~ **support** Verkaufsunter-
stützung bei Einzelhändlern.
merchant [Groß]kaufmann, *(agent)* Vertreter, Handlungsreisender, *(shopkeeper, US)* Ladenbesitzer,
Einzelhändler, Krämer;
  commission ~ Kommissionär; **established** ~ selbständiger Kaufmann; **export** ~ Exportkaufmann;
  ~ **s' accounts** kaufmännische Buchführung; ~ **appraiser** Schätzer im Zollbescheidverfahren; ~
  banker *(Br.)* Handels-, Remboursbank; **~'s basket**
  (statistics) Warenkorb; ~ **flag** Handels-, Reedereiflagge; **war-riddled** ~ **fleet** durch den Krieg stark
  mitgenommene Handelsflotte; ~ **middleman** Kommissionär; ~ **prices** Engrospreise; ~ **service** Handelsschiffahrt, -marine, Seehandel; ~ **ship** Handelsschiff; ~ **shipper** [Import]zwischenhändler,
  (Br.) Exporthändler; ~ **shipping** Handelsschiff-
  fahrt.
merchantable lieferbar, *(salable7* verkäuflich, gangbar, gängig, marktgängig;
  in a ~ **condition** in handelsfähigem Zustand; ~
  quality Ware mittlerer Art und Güte, marktgängige Ware.
merchantman Handelsschiff, Kauffahrer.
merge *(v.)* verschmelzen, fusionieren.
merger Verschmelzung, Fusion[ierung], [Firmen]-
zusammenschluß;
  bank ~ Bankenfusion; **conglomerate** ~ *(US)* Fusion branchenfremder Unternehmen;
  ~ **of funds** Kapitalzusammenlegung;
  to rule òn ~s für Fusionsgenehmigungen zuständig
  sein;
  ~ **agreement** Fusionsvereinbarung; ~ **application**
  Fusionsantrag; ~ **bid** Fusionsangebot; ~ **clearance**
  (US) Fusions-, Konzentrationsgenehmigung; ~
  company fusionierende Gesellschaft; ~ **decision**
  Fusionsbeschluß.
merit Verdienst, Vorzug, Wert;
  on the ~s or in terms of amount dem Grunde oder
  der Höhe nach;
  to admit a claim on the ~s Anspruch dem Grunde
  nach anerkennen;
  ~ **bonus** Leistungsprämie; **~-pricing system** *(motorcar insurance)* Kraftfahrzeugversicherungs-
  system mit Prämien für unfallfreies Fahren; ~
  rating *(US)* Leistungseinstufung; ~ **salary increase**
  (US) Leistungszulage.
message Nachricht, Bestellung, Mitteilung, *(advertising)* Werbeaussage;
  ~ **in code** verschlüsselte Nachricht;
  to run ~s Botendienste tun;
  ~ **form** Depeschen-, Telegrammformular.
messenger Bote, Läufer, *(bank)* Kassenbote;
  express ~ *(Br.)* Eilbote; **special** ~ *(US)* Eilbote.
metal │ **industry** Metallindustrie; **~-processing industry** metallverarbeitende Industrie.
method Verfahren, Verfahrensweise, Methode;
  working ~ Fabrikationsverfahren;
  unfair ~s of competition unlauterer Wettbewerb;

of depreciation Abschreibungsart; ~ **of financing**
Finanzierungsweise; ~ **of payment** Zahlungsweise;
~ **of production** Produktionsverfahren.
metropolitan │ **area** Großstadtgebiet; ~ **plan** *(advertising)* Ortsverbreitungsplan.
mid-month account Medioabrechnung.
middle │ **-bracket income** mittleres Einkommen; ~
-class zum Mittelstand gehörig; **the upper** ~ **classes**
gehobener Mittelstand; ~ **[market, *Br*]** price Mit-
telkurs.
middleman Zwischenhändler, Makler, *(gobetween)*
Mittelsmann, -person, Vermittler;
  functional ~ Zwischenmakler; **produce** ~ Produktenmakler.
middling mittelfein, von mittlerer Art und Güte;
  good ~ **quality** gute Mittelsorte.
midyear │ **demands** Anforderungen zum Halbjah-
resultimo; ~ **dividend** Halbjahresdividende.
migrant worker Wanderarbeiter.
migration of capital Kapitalabwanderung.
mil(e)age *(allowance for travel(l)ing expense)* Fahrt-
entschädigung, Kilometergeld;
  ~ **per gallon** Kraftstoffverbrauch auf 100 km;
  low-~ car wenig gefahrenes Auto; ~ **rate** Kilo-
  metersatz.
mill *(factory)* Fabrik, Werk;
  ~ **out of work** stillgelegter Betrieb;
  ~ **hand** Fabrikarbeiter; ~ **shutdown** Fabrikschlie-
  ßung.
mine Zeche, Bergwerk, Grube;
  ~s *(shares)* Mo'ntanwerte, Kuxe;
  abandoned ~ verlassener Bau;
  to shut down a ~ Grube auflassen.
mineral │ **deposit** Mineralvorkommen; **~-oil tax** Mi-
neralölsteuer; ~ **royalty** Bergregal.
minimum │ **of capital** Mindestkapital; ~ **of existence**
Existenzminimum;
  to stand at a ~ *(stock exchange)* sehr niedrig stehen;
  ~ **benefit** Mindestunterstützungssatz; ~ **bill of lading charge** Minimalfracht; ~ **cash reserve** Pflicht-
  reserve; ~ **deposit** Mindesteinlage, -anzahlung; ~
  lending rate *(Br.)* Mindestausleihungsrediskont-
  satz; ~ **maintenance** notwendiger Lebensunterhalt; ~ **paid-in capital** *(US)* Mindestkapital; ~
  period of employment Mindestbeschäftigungszeit;
  ~ **rate** Mindestsatz, -kurs, *(wages)* Mindestlohn-
  satz; ~ **resale price** gebundener Preis auf der Stufe
  des Endverbrauchs; ~ **guaranteed wage** garantierter Mindestlohn.
mining Grubenbetrieb, Bergbau;
  open-cast ~ Tagebau;
  ~ **claim** Mutung; ~ **company** Zechen-, Bergwerks-
  gesellschaft; ~ **franchise** Abbaukonzession; ~ **securities** Montanwerte.
Minister │ **of Agriculture, Fisheries and Food** *(Br.)*
Ernährungs-, Landwirtschaftsminister; ~ **of Economics (Economic Affairs)** *(Br.)* Wirtschaftsmi-
nister; ~ **of Housing and Local Government** *(Br.)*
Wohnungsbauminister; ~ **of Labour** *(Br.)* Arbeits-
minister; ~ **of Power** *(Br.)* Minister für Energie-

minister; ~ of **Social Security** *(Br.)* Sozialminister; ~ of **Transport** *(Br.)* Verkehrsminister.

ministry *(Br.)* Ministerium, Regierung.

Ministry, Air *(Br.)* Luftfahrtministerium;
~ of **Housing and Local Government** *(Br.)* Wohnungsbauministerium; ~ of **Labour** *(Br.)* Arbeitsministerium; ~ of **Power** *(Br.)* Energieministerium; ~ of **Supply** *(Br.)* Versorgungsministerium.

minor | **coin** *(US)* Scheidemünze; ~ **loss** *(insurance)* Bagatell-, Kleinschaden.

minority Minorität, Minderheit, -zahl, *(state of being a minor)* Minderjährigkeit;
blocking ~ Sperrminorität;
~ **holder** Minoritätsaktionär.

mint Münze, Münzplatz, -amt, -anstalt;
in ~ **condition** *(of coins)* funkelnagelneu; ~ **par of exchange** festes Wechselpari.

minute *(Br., notes)* Notiz, Memorandum, Exposé;
up to the ~ hypermodern;
~ **account** spezifizierte Rechnung.

minutes Niederschrift, Sitzungsbericht;
board ~ Vorstandsprotokoll.

misapplication of funds Veruntreuung von Geldern.

misapply *(v.)* **public money** öffentliche Gelder veruntreuen.

misappropriate *(v.)* widerrechtlich verwenden, veruntreuen.

misappropriated capital [Kapital]fehlinvestition.

misappropriation unrechtmäßige Verwendung, Entwendung, Veruntreuung, *(wrong appropriation)* [Kapital]fehlleitung, Mißwirtschaft.

misbranding of commodities Falschbezeichnung von Waren als Markenartikel.

miscarriage of goods Verlustsendung.

miscarry *(v.)* *(letter)* verlorengehen.

miscellaneous | **assets** *(balance sheet)* verschiedene Anlagegüter; ~ **collections of goods** gemischte Warensendungen; ~ **investments** *(balance sheet)* verschiedene Beteiligungen.

misconduct, professional standeswidriges Verhalten; ~ of **the tenant** unzumutbares Verhalten des Mieters.

misdirect *(v.)* **capital** Kapitalfehlleitung vornehmen.

misdoings of advertising Reklameauswüchse.

misemployment *(money)* Fehlinvestition.

misentry falscher Eintrag, Falschbuchung.

misinvestment Fehlinvestition.

mismanagement Mißwirtschaft, schlechte Verwaltung (Geschäfts-, Betriebsführung).

misrepresent *(v.)* falsche Tatsachen vorspiegeln.

misrepresentation, material *(insurance)* absichtliches Verschweigen von für die Versicherungsgesellschaft bedeutsamen Tatsachen.

misrouted freight fehlgeleitete Sendung.

missed profit entgangener Gewinn.

missing items verlorene Postsendungen.

mistake Fehler, Mißgriff, *(law)* Geschäftsirrtum;
~ **in calculation** Rechen-, Kalkulationsfehler; ~ **as to the existence of the subject matter** Irrtum über die Geschäftsgrundlage; ~ **in labelling** Auszeich-

nungsfehler; ~ **as to the nature of the subject matter** Motivirrtum.

mistaken | **identity** Identitätsverwechslung; ~ **investment** Fehlinvestition.

misuse of public funds Unterschlagung öffentlicher Gelder.

mixed | **account** gemischtes Konto; ~ **assortment** gemischtes Sortiment; ~ **cargo** Stückgutladung; ~ **cargo rate** *(Br.)* Stückgütertarif; ~ **carload rate** *(US)* Stückgütertarif; ~ **economy** gemischte Wirtschaftsform, -ordnung; ~ **enterprise** gemischtwirtschaftliches Unternehmen; ~ **income** Einkünfte aus selbständiger und nichtselbständiger Arbeit; ~ **price** Mischpreis; ~ **tariff** kombinierter Zolltarif.

mobile shop fahrbare Verkaufsstelle, Verkaufswagen.

mobilization of funds Flüssigmachen von Kapital.

mock auction Scheinauktion.

mode | of **employment** Beschäftigungsart; ~ of **payment** Zahlungsweise; ~ of **process** Herstellungsprozeß, -verfahren.

model *(car)* Bauart, *(design)* Entwurf, *(exemplary piece)* Muster[stück], *(exhibition)* Ausstellungsstück, Verkaufsmodell;
previous year's ~ Vorjahrsmodell;
~ **agreement** Manteltarifabkommen; ~ **enterprise** Musterbetrieb; ~ **stock** Spezialsortiment.

moderate | **income** bescheidenes Einkommen; ~ **priced** billig, preiswert.

modular housing vorfabrizierte Wohnungseinheiten.

monetary geldlich, finanziell, monetär;
~ **Agreement** Währungsabkommen; ~ **area** Währungsgebiet; ~ **claim** Geldforderung; ~ **cooperation** Zusammenarbeit auf dem Währungsgebiet; ~ **correction** Geldwertkorrektur; ~ **ease** Geldmarkterleichterungen; ~ **economics** Geldwirtschaft; **International** ~ **Fund** Welt-, Internationaler Währungsfonds; **to provide fully to the increasing** ~ **needs** zunehmenden Geldbedarf hunderprozentig decken; **to hold to restrictive** ~ **policies** harte Geldmarktpolitik treiben; **to relax** ~ **policy** geldmarktpolitische Erleichterungen zulassen; ~ **policy devices** geldpolitische Maßnahmen; **to handle the** ~ **side** sich um die geldpolitische Aufgabe kümmern; **in the** ~ **sphere** in geldwirtschaftlicher Hinsicht; ~ **standard** Währungseinheit; ~ **and fiscal techniques** Geldmarktinstrumentarium.

money Geld[sorte], Münze, *(amount of money)* Geldbetrag, -summe, *(legal tender)* Zahlungsmittel, *(wealth)* Geld, Reichtum, Vermögen;
at a heavy cost of ~ unter schweren Geldopfern; **for** ~ *(stock exchange)* netto Kasse; **for ready** ~ gegen bar; **ready** ~ **only** nur gegen Barzahlung; **active** ~ lebhafter Geldmarkt; ~ **advanced** Vorschuß; **barren** ~ totes Kapital; **base** *(Br.)* **(bogus)** ~ Falschgeld; **borrowed** ~ Fremdmittel; **call** ~ *(US)* tägliches Geld, Tagesgeld; **caution** ~ Kaution; **condemnation** ~ Entschädigungsbeitrag; **counterfeit** ~ Falschgeld; **credit** ~ Giralgeld; **dear** ~

knappes (teures) Geld; **demand** ~ tägliches Geld, Tagesgeld; **deposit** ~ *(Br.)* Buch-, Giralgeld; **earnest** ~ An-, Handgeld; **easy** ~ flüssiger Geldmarkt; **entrance** ~ Eintrittsgeld; **foreign** ~ ausländische Zahlungsmittel; **fractional** ~ Wechsel-, Kleingeld; **fugitive** ~ Fluchtgeld; **happy** ~ für Vergnügungszwecke vorgesehener Geldbetrag; **hot** ~ heißes Geld; **hush** ~ Schweigegeld; **immobilized** ~ festgelegtes Geld; **key** ~ *(Br.)* Mietvorauszahlung; **lawful** ~ *(US)* gesetzliches Zahlungsmittel; .**longterm** ~ langfristiges Geld; **near** ~ *(US)* geldähnliche Forderungen, leicht liquidierbare Einlagen; ~ **owing to us** *(balance sheet)* Guthaben; ~ **paying no interest** brachliegendes Kapital; **pin** ~ Nadelgeld; **pocket** ~ Taschengeld; ~ **received** Geldeingänge; **rent** ~ Pachtzins; **scrip** ~ *(US)* Schwundgeld; **smart** ~ Schmerzensgeld, Reu-, Abstandsgeld; **soft** ~ *(US sl.)* Papiergeld; **substitute** ~ Zahlungssurrogat; **surplus** ~ *(foreclosure proceedings)* im Zwangsversteigerungsverfahren erzielter Überschuß; **till** ~ *(banking)* Kassenbestand;

~ **of account** Landeswährung; ~ **on account** Guthaben; ~ **in circulation** Zahlungsmittelumlauf; ~ **withdrawn from circulation** aus dem Verkehr gezogenes Geld; ~ **for the monthly clearance** Ultimogeld; ~ **lying idle** brachliegendes Geld; ~ **on short notice** kurzfristige Gelder; ~ **no object** Geld spielt keine Rolle; ~ **put by for a rainy day** Sparpfennig; **to advance** ~ Geld vorschießen (vorstrecken); **to advance** ~ **on securities** Wertpapiere lombardieren; **to be coining** ~ Dukatenesel sein, im Geld schwimmen; **to call in** ~ Kapital kündigen; **to come into one's own** ~ Verfügungsgewalt über sein Geld bekommen; **to convert into** ~ versilbern; **to create** ~ Geldschöpfung vornehmen; **to deposit** ~ **with a bank** Geld bei einer Bank einzahlen; **to embark** ~ Geld hineinstecken; **to favo(u)r easier** ~ sich für Erleichterungen des Geldmarktverkehrs einsetzen; **to handle large sums of** ~ große Geldbeträge verwalten; **to have** ~ **in a business** an einem Unternehmen beteiligt sein; **to husband one's** ~ sparsam mit seinem Geld umgehen (wirtschaften); **to leave all one's** ~ **to charity** sein gesamtes Vermögen für wohltätige Zwecke hinterlassen; **to live with little** ~ mit wenig Geld auskommen; **to look after one's** ~ seine paar Groschen zusammenhalten; **to pay** ~ **down (in ready ~)** bar [auf den Tisch des Hauses] bezahlen; **to put** ~ **into circulation** Geld unter die Leute bringen; **to put out** ~ **at interest** Geld verzinslich anlegen; **to remit** ~ Geld überweisen; **to take up** ~ **at the bank** Bankkredit aufnehmen; **to throw one's** ~ **away** unnützen Aufwand treiben;

~ **agent** Geldwechsler; ~ **allowance** Barvergütung; ~ **bargain** Effektivgeschäft; ~ **box** Sparbüchse; **ready-**~ **business** Kassageschäft; ~ **dealer** Geldwechsler; ~ **demand** Geldbedarf; ~ **gap** Finanzierungslücke; ~ **gift** Geldspende, -geschenk; ~ **grant** Geldbewilligung; ~ **jobber** *(Br.)* Geldhändler, -makler; ~ **letter** *(US)* Geld-, Wertbrief; ~ **loser** Verlustbetrieb.

money market Geldmarkt; ~ **indebtedness** Geldmarktverschuldung; ~ **instrument** Geldmarktpapier; ~ **rates** Geldmarktsätze.

money order *(M.O.)* Zahlungs-, Geld-, Postanweisung; **domestic postal** ~ Inlandspostanweisung; **postal** ~ *(US)* Postanweisung; ~ **telegram** telegrafische Geldüberweisung.

money | **payment** Geldrente; ~ **pinch** [zeitweilige] Geldknappheit; ~**-proof** unbestechlich; ~ **rate** Geldmarktsatz; **easy** ~ **rates** leichte Geldmarktsätze; ~ **relief** Geldentschädigung, -unterstützung; ~ **request** Geldanforderung; ~ **reserve** Barreserve; ~ **saver** wirtschaftlicher Artikel; ~ **squeeze** [zeitweilige] Geldklemme; ~ **stringency** Geldknappheit; ~ **substitute** Zahlungssurrogat; ~ **supply** Geldbedarf, -versorgung; ~**-supply** economist Geldtheoretiker; ~ **teller** Kassierer; ~ **transaction** Geld-, Effektivgeschäft; ~ **transactions** Geldverkehr; ~ **transfer** Geldüberweisung; ~ **transfers** Zahlungsverkehr; ~ **troubles** Geldsorgen; ~ **value** Gestehungs-, Kurswert; **to get one's** ~**'s worth** etw. für sein Geld bekommen.

moneyed pekunär, finanziell, *(wealthy)* mit Geld versehen, reich, vermögend; ~ **aristocracy** Geldadel; ~ **capital** liquide Vermögenswerte; ~ **interests** finanzielle Belange, Hochfinanz.

moneylender Geldgeber, -verleiher.

moneylending gewerbsmäßiger Geldverleih.

monitory | **item** *(balance sheet)* Merkposten; ~ **letter** Mahnschreiben.

monopolistic | **agreement** Monopolabkommen; ~ **control** Monopolkontrolle; ~ **position (situation)** Monopolstellung; **to split a** ~ **structure** Monopolstellung beseitigen.

monopolize *(v.)* monopolisieren, Monopol besitzen; ~ **a business** Monopolstellung haben.

monopoly Monopol[stellung], Alleinherstellungsrecht; **artificial** ~ gesetzliches Monopol; **buyer's** ~ Nachfragemonopol; **government** ~ Staatsmonopol; **market** ~ Marktbeherrschung; **state-buying** ~ staatliches Einkaufsmonopol; **trade** ~ Handelsmonopol; ~ **in the issue of bank notes** Banknotenmonopol; ~ **of foreign trade** Außenhandelsmonopol; **to break up a** ~ Monopol auflösen; ~ **capitalism** Monopolkapitalismus; ~ **charge** Kartellklage; ~ **committee** Kartellaufsichtsbehörde; ~ **price** Monopolpreis; ~ **system of foreign trade** Außenhandelsmonopol.

monopsony Nachfragemonopol.

month | **under report** Berichtsmonat; **three** ~**s' draft** Dreimonatspapier; **three** ~**s money** Vierteljahresgeld.

monthly | **accruals** Ultimofälligkeiten; ~ **instal(l)ment** Monatsrate; ~ **rental** Monatsmiete; ~ **report of the labo(u)r force** monatliche Meldung über den Beschäftigungsstand; ~ **requirements** Ultimobedarf;

~ **return** *(Br.)* Monatsausweis; ~ **season ticket** Monatskarte.

moonlighter *(US)* Doppelverdiener.

moral | hazard *(insurance)* Risiko falscher Angaben; ~ **suasion** Maßhalteappell, Seelenmassage.

moratorium Moratorium, Zahlungsaufschub, Stillhalteabkommen.

mortality Steblichkeit[sziffer], Sterbehäufigkeit; ~ **table** Sterbetafel, Sterblichkeitstabelle.

mortgage hypothekarische Belastung, Hypothek, Hypothekenbrief;
bulk ~ *(US)* Verpfändung ganzer Bestände; **construction** ~ Bauhypothek; **instal(l)ment** ~ Tilgungs-, Amortisationshypothek; **option** ~ Landesdarlehn mit Grundbuchsicherung; **ordinary** ~ Verkehrshypothek; ~**s payable** *(general ledger, US)* hypothekarische Verpflichtungen; **purchase-money** ~ Restkaufgeldhypothek;
to assume a ~ Hypothek [unter Anrechnung auf den Kaufpreis] übernehmen; **to execute a** ~ aus einer Hypothek zwangsvollstrecken; **to raise a** ~ **on a house** Haus beleihen;
~ **amortization** Hypothekentilgung; ~ **bond** Hypothekenpfandbrief; ~ **business** Hypothekengeschäft; ~ **buying** Hypothekenanlagenkäufe; ~ **certificate** *(US)* Hypothekenbrief; ~ **creditor** Hypothekengläubiger; ~ **debenture** *(Br.)* hypothekarisch gesicherte Schuldverschreibung, Hypothekenpfandbrief; ~ **finance (financing)** Hypothekenfinanzierung; ~ **foreclosure** Zwangsvollstreckung aus einer Hypothek; ~ **interest** Hypothekenzinsen; ~ **lending** Hypothekenausleihungen; ~ **loan** Hypothekarkredit; ~ **market** Hypothekenmarkt; ~ **payment delinquency** nicht eingehaltene Hypothekenrate; ~ **sales** Hypothekenabschlüsse; ~ **term** *(Br.)* Laufzeit einer Hypothek.

mortgaged property belastetes Grundeigentum.

mortgagee Pfand-, Hypothekengläubiger;
~ **clause** *(fire insurance)* Hypothekenklausel.

mortmain tote Hand.

mortuary table *(insurance, US)* Sterblichkeitstabelle.

most-favo(u)red nation | clause Meistbegünstigungsklausel; ~ **policy** Präferenzpolitik; ~ **principle** Meistbegünstigungsprinzip; ~ **rate** Meistbegünstigungssatz; ~ **treatment** Meistbegünstigung.

motion picture business Filmgeschäft, -branche.

motor [Verbrennungs]motor, *(motorcar)* Kraftwagen, Motorfahrzeug, Automobil;
~ **cavalcade** Autokolonne; ~ **company** Autofirma; ~ **industry** *(Br.)* Kraftfahrzeug-, Automobilindustrie; **to carry a public liability** ~ **insurance** *(Br.)* Autohaftpflichtversicherung unterhalten; ~ **lorry** *(Br.)* Lastkraftwagen; ~ **traffic** Kraftfahrzeug-, Autoverkehr; ~ **transport** Lastwagentransport; ~ **transportation insurance** Kraftfahrzeugversicherung; ~ **truck** *(US)* Lastkraftwagen; ~ **van** *(Br.)* Liefer-, Lastwagen.

motor vehicle Kraftfahrzeug;
~**s passenger insurance** *(Br.)* Insassenversicherung; ~ **production** Automobilproduktion; ~ **registra**-

tion Kraftfahrzeuganmeldung; ~ **registration certificate** *(US)* Kraftfahrzeugbrief; ~ **tax** *(US)* Kraftfahrzeugsteuer.

motorcar *(Br.)* Auto, Automobil, Kraftfahrzeug; ~ **industry** *(Br.)* Kraftfahrzeug-, Automobilindustrie.

motorway *(Br.)* Autobahn.

mount *(v.)* montieren, zusammenbauen.

movable goods bewegliches Vermögen, Mobilien.

movables Mobilien, bewegliches Vermögen.

move *(v.)* *(change residence)* weg-, ver-, umziehen;
~ **briskly ahead** *(prices)* rasch steigen (anziehen); ~ **backward** *(economy)* zurückgehen, nachlassen; ~ **down** *(prices)* zurückgehen; ~ **into a new high** *(prices)* neuen Höchststand erreichen; ~ **one's lodgings** seine Wohnung wechseln; ~ **up sharply** scharf anziehen; ~ **violently** *(stock exchange)* heftig reagieren.

movement *(market activity)* Umsatz, *(stock exchange sl.)* Kursbewegung;
downward ~ Abwärtsbewegung; **free** ~ Freizügigkeit; **no** ~ *(stock exchange)* ohne Umsatz; ~ **in demand** Nachfrageverlagerung; ~ **of freight (goods)** Waren-, Güterverkehr; ~ **of prices** Preisentwicklung.

movie | admission price Kinoeintrittspreis; ~ **advertisement** Kinoreklame.

moving Umzug, *(transfer of official)* Versetzung;
~ **into a new flat** Einzug in eine neue Wohnung; **to be** ~ **up** *(prices)* aufwärts gehen, anziehen; ~ **allowance** *(US)* Umzugsgeld; ~ **company** *(US)* Möbelspediteur.

muddle *(v.)* **| account books** Buchführung durcheinanderbringen; ~ **away a fortune** Vermögen durchbringen.

multicorporate enterprise *(US)* Konzern.

multifamily dwelling Mehrfamilienhaus.

multilateral | clearing system multilateraler Verrechnungsverkehr; ~ **system of payments** multilaterales Zahlungssystem.

multipart freight bill Frachtrechnung in mehrfacher Ausfertigung.

multiple, price-earnings Kurs-Ertragsmultiplikator; ~ **chain** Filialunternehmen im Einzelhandel; ~ **basing point system** *(US)* Preissortsystem; ~ **currency system** Devisenverrechnungssystem; ~ **delivery contract** Sukzessivlieferungsvertrag; ~ **exchange rates** multiple Wechselkurse; ~ **listing** Anhandgeben von Grundstücken an mehrere Makler; ~ **piecework system** Stücklohnverfahren; ~ **price** Mengenrabattpreis; ~ **production** Serienherstellung; ~ **rate system** System multipler Wechselkurse; ~ **share** Mehrstimmrechtsaktie; ~ **shift operation** Schichtbetrieb; ~ **shop** *(Br.)* Kettenladen; ~ **taxation** Mehrfachbesteuerung.

multistor(e)y car park (garage) Parkhochhaus.

municipal | accounting kommunales Rechnungswesen; ~ **bonds** *(US)* Kommunalschuldverschreibungen; ~ **compensation** *(US)* Konzessionsabgabe; ~ **credit** Kommunalkredit; ~ **enterprise** Kommunalbetrieb; ~ **rates** *(Br.)* Kommunalabgaben; ~ **stock** *(Br.)* Kommunalobligation; ~ **trading** gemeindliche Gewerbetätigkeit.

mushroom *(v.)* **into a production order** lawinenartigen Produktionsauftrag auslösen.

mutual | **assurance company** Versicherungsverein auf Gegenseitigkeit; ~ **fund** *(US)* Kapitalanlage-,

Investmentgesellschaft; ~ **fund insurance package** mit einer Lebensversicherung gekoppeltes Investmentzertifikat; ~ **insurance** Versicherung auf Gegenseitigkeit; ~ **loan association** *(US)* Bausparkasse; ~ **savings bank** *(US)* genossenschaftsähnliche Sparkasse.

N

nail, on the auf der Stelle, sofort; **to pay on the** ~ bar (pünktlich) bezahlen.

naked | **debenture** *(Br.)* ungesicherte Schuldverschreibung; ~ **deposit** unentgeltliche Verwahrung.

name Name, Bezeichnung, Benennung, *(reputation)* Ruf, Renommee; **in the** ~ **and behalf of** im Namen und im Auftrag von; **in one's own** ~ **and on one's own account** in eigenem Namen und für eigene Rechnung; **brand** ~ Markenname; **business** ~ [Handels]firma, Firmenname; **corporate** ~ *(US)* Firmenname; **first-class** ~ *(bill of exchange)* erstklassige Adresse; **trade[mark]** ~ Markenname; **to be in s. one's** ~ *(share)* auf jds. Namen eingetragen sein; **to be made out in the** ~ **of the holder** auf den Inhaber lauten; **to have one's** ~ **in the Gazette** für bankrott erklärt werden; **to supply** ~**s of prospects** Anschriften potentieller Kunden liefern; ~ **brand** Markenartikel.

narrow | **circumstances** *(coll.)* beschränkte Verhältnisse; ~ **fortune** kleines Vermögen; ~ **market** *(stock exchange)* flauer Markt; ~ **profit margin** schmale Verdienstspanne; **in** ~ **straits** in Geldverlegenheit.

national | **assistance** *(Br.)* staatliche Fürsorge, Sozialhilfe; ~ **bank** *(US)* National-, Staats-, Landesbank; ~ **bank tax** *(US)* Notenbanksteuer; ~ **bankruptcy** Staatsbankrott; ~ **Bankruptcy Act** *(US)* Konkursordnung; ⌂ **Board for Prices and Incomes** *(US)* Preisüberwachungsstelle; ~ **currency** Landeswährung; ~ **Debt Commissioner** *(Br.)* [etwa] Bundesschuldenverwaltung; ~ **economic accounting** volkswirtschaftliche Gesamtrechnung; ~ **economy** Volkswirtschaft, Nationalökonomie; ~ **enterprise** Staatsbetrieb; ~ **finance** Staatsfinanzen; ~ **Giro Service** *(Br.)* Postscheckdienst; ⌂ **Health Insurance** *(Br.)* Krankenversicherung; ⌂ **Institute of Economic and Social Research** *(Br.)* Konjunkturinstitut; ⌂ **Insurance Act** *(Br.)* Sozialversicherungsgesetz; ~ **insurance benefits** *(Br.)* Sozialversicherungsleistungen; ~ **insurance card** *(Br.)* Sozialversicherungskarte; ~ **insurance contribution**

(Br.) Sozialversicherungsbeitrag; ~ **insurance fund** *(Br.)* Sozialversicherungsstock; ~ **monetary commission** Währungsausschuß; ~ **product** *(Br.)* Sozialprodukt; ~ **savings certificate** *(Br.)* Sparkassengutschein; ⌂ **Tax Association** *(US)* Verband der Steuerzahler.

nationalization indemnity *(Br.)* Sozialisierungsentschädigung.

native | **labo(u)r** einheimische Arbeitskräfte; ~ **product** Landeserzeugnis.

natural | **business year** normales Geschäftsjahr; ~ **loss** natürlicher Schwund; ~ **price** durchschnittlicher Marktpreis; ~ **product** Rohprodukt.

navigable | **road** Wasserstraße; ~ **waters** schiffbare Gewässer.

near money *(US)* geldähnliche Forderungen, leicht liquidierbare Einlagen.

nearness to market Marktnähe.

necessaries Bedarfsartikel, -gegenstände; **travel** ~ Reisebedürfnisse; **to pledge the husband's credit for** ~ *(Br.)* [etwa] Schlüsselgewalt ausüben; **to procure the bare** ~ Existenzminimum sicherstellen.

necessary article Bedarfsartikel.

need *(destitution)* Not[stand], -lage, Bedürftigkeit, *(requirement)* Bedarf, Nachfrage; **in** ~ **of assistance** hilfsbedürftig, *(Br.)* fürsorgebedürftig; **monetary** ~**s** Geldbedarf; ~ **for foreign exchange** Devisenbedarf; ~ **for liquidity** Liquiditätsbedürfnis; **to aim at the** ~**s of a customer** auf die Wünsche eines Kunden abstellen; **to examine the** ~ **for granting a licence** Bedarfsfrage bei einer Erteilung einer Konzession prüfen.

needy family unterstützungsbedürftige Familie.

negative investment Desinvestition.

neglect | **of business** Geschäftsvernachlässigung; ~ *(v.)* **to pay one's debts** seine Schulden nicht bezahlen.

negligence Nachlässigkeit, *(law)* Fahrlässigkeit; **collateral** ~ positive Vertragsverletzung; **contribu-**

tory ~ mitwirkendes (konkurierrendes) Verschulden; **ordinary** ~ *(US)* Mangel der im Verkehr erforderlichen Sorgfalt.

negotiability Börsenfähigkeit, Indossierbarkeit, Begebbarkeit.

negotiable verhandlungsfähig, aushandelbar, *(bankable)* börsen-, bankfähig, *(endorsable)* begebbar, durch Indossament übertragbar, *(realizable)* verwertbar;

~ **without endorsement** einfach übertragbar; ~ **on the stock exchange** börsenfähig;

~ **bill** durch Indossament übertragbarer Wechsel; ~ **bill of lading** Orderfrachtbrief; ~ **document** Order-, Inhaberpapier jeder Art; ~ **instrument** begebbares Wertpapier, auf Zahlung von Geld gerichtetes Order- und Inhaberpapier; **quasi-~ instrument** unrechtes Orderpapier; **Uniform ≈ Instruments Act** *(US)* Wertpapiergesetz; ~ **securities** durch Indossament übertragbare Wertpapiere.

negotiate *(v.) (bill)* begeben, unterbringen, *(confer with)* ver-, unterhandeln;

~ **a contract in exhausting detail** Vertrag bis zu den kleinsten Kleinigkeiten aushandeln; ~ **by delivery only** formlos übertragen; ~ **a draft** Tratte ankaufen; ~ **a loan** Anleihe begeben; ~ **for new premises** in Mietverhandlungen stehen; ~ **on better terms** günstigere Verhandlungsposition haben.

negotiating group Verhandlungsgruppe.

negotiation Vertragsabschluß, *(issue)* Begebung, Übertragung, Unterbringung;

commercial ~s Handelsbesprechungen; **detailed** ~s Einzelbesprechungen; **tariff** ~s Zollverhandlungen;

~ **of a bill of exchange** Begebung eines Wechsels; ~ **of a draft** Trattenankauf; ~ **of a loan** Übernahme einer Anleihe;

~ **credit** Trattenankaufskredit; ~ **package** Verhandlungspaket; ~ **price** Übernahmekurs, -preis.

negotiator Verhandlungsführer, Unterhändler, *(broker)* Makler, *(mediator)* Vermittler.

neighbo(u)rhood, low-income niedrige Einkommensgegend;

~ **bank branch** *(US)* Depositenkasse; ~ **improvements** Anliegerbeiträge.

nest egg Sparpfennig, -groschen.

net Netz *(advertising)* Agenturnetto, *(net income)* Reingewinn, -ertrag, Nettoeinkommen;

~ **in advance** Nettokasse im Voraus;

~ *(v.)* Reingewinn erzielen, netto verdienen;

~ **amount** Rein-, Nettobetrag; ~ **avails** *(discounted note)* Diskonterlös, *(US)* Nettoerlös, Gegenwart; ~ **bonded debt** *(municipal accounting, US)* Schuldscheinverpflichtungen; ~ **book amount** wertberichtigtes Anlagevermögen; ~ **cash** netto Kasse, bar ohne Abzug; ~ **change in business inventories** *(national income accounting)* Nettobestandsveränderung; ~ **cost** Selbstkostenpreis; ~ **current assets** Betriebskapital; ~ **earnings** Nettoverdienst, Effektivlohn; ~ **income** Reinertrag; ~ **liabilities** reine Schulden nach Abzug der flüssigen Aktiva; ~

load Nutzlast; ~ **loss** Netto-, Reinverlust; ~ **national product** Nettosozialprodukt; ~ **proceeds** Reinertrag; ~ **profit[s]** Reinerlös, -gewinn, Nettogewinn; ~ **profit from operation (operating profit)** Betriebsreingewinn; ~ **profit on sales** Nettoverkaufserlös; ~ **rate of interest** Nettozinsfuß; ~ **rental** *(Br.)* Nettomiete; ~ **rest** reiner Überschuß; ~ **retention** *(reinsurance)* Selbstbehalt; ~ **return** Nettoumsatz, *(banking)* Nettoausweis, *(of a bond)* Nettoertrag; ~ **savings** Nettoersparnisse; ~ **surplus** *(US)* Reingewinn [nach Ausschüttung der Dividende]; ~ **ton** Nettoregistertonne; ~ **tonnage** Nettoregistertonnage; ~ **value** Nettowert; ~ **realizable value** *(Br.)* realisierbarer Verkaufserlös; ~ **value added** Wertschöpfung; ~ **worth** reiner Wert, *(stockholder)* Nettoanteil, (US) Eigenkapital; ~ **yield** effektive Rendite.

network *(advertising)* Stellennetz, *(broadcasting)* Sendernetz;

basic ~ Sendergruppe; **highway** ~ Straßennetz;

to sell through a ~ of 550 dealers über ein Netz von 550 Vertragshändlern verkaufen.

never-never *(sl., Br.)* Stottern, Abzahlen.

new | for old *(insurance)* neu für alt; ~ **and useful** *(patent law)* Neuheit;

~ **acquisition** Neuerwerbung; ~ **book department** Sortimentsabteilung; ~ **business commission** Abschlußprovision; ~ **car sales** Neuwagengeschäft; ~ **financing** Erstfinanzierung; ~ **hiring** Neueinstellungen; ~ **home starts** Neubauten.

news, commercial Handelsteil, Börsenteil;

~ **advertisement** Zeitungsannonce; ~ **agency** Pressedienst; ~ **blackout** Nachrichtensperre; ~ **bulletin** Nachrichtensendung; ~ **dealer** *(US)* Zeitungshändler.

newscast Nachrichtensendung.

newspaper Zeitung, Journal, Blatt;

commercial ~ Börsenblatt, Wirtschaftszeitung;

to subscribe to a ~ *(US)*, **to take in a ~** *(Br.)* Zeitung halten (beziehen, abonnieren);

~ **advertisement** Zeitungsannonce, -inserat; ~ **clipper** *(US)* Ausschnittbüro; ~ **real-estate pages** Immobilienteil einer Zeitung; ~ **space** *(advertising)* Anzeigenraum; ~ **wrapper** Kreuz-, Streifband.

newsreel Wochenschau.

newsroom Nachrichtenzentrale.

newsstand distribution *(US)* Kioskabsatz.

next to reading matter anschließende Anzeige.

night | employment Nachtarbeit; ~ **letter[gram]** *(US)* Brieftelegramm; ~ **school** Fortbildungsschule, [etwa] Volkshochschule; ~ **-shift bonus** Nachtschichtvergütung.

no | a/c *(account)* kein Konto;

~ **agents** *(house sale, Br.)* Makler verboten; ~ **change given** Geld abgezählt bereithalten; ~ **-claim bonus** *(Br.)* Schadensfreiheitsrabatt; ~ **funds** keine Deckung; ~ **par** ohne Nennwert; ~ **-par value stock** *(US)* nennwertlose Aktie; ~ **-purpose loan** nicht zweckgebundener Kredit; ~ **reduction** feste Preise.

nominal | account Erfolgskonto, *(Br.)* Sachkonto; ~ **amount** Nominal-, Nennbetrag; ~ **assets** *(US)* Buchwerte; ~ **capital** Grund-, Gründungs-, Stammkapital *(corporation)* autorisiertes Aktienkapital, Grundkapital, *(US)* geringfügiges Kapital, Nominalkapital; ~ **hours** nach dem Tarif vorgesehene Arbeitszeit; ~ **interest** Normalverzinsung; ~ **market** fast umsatzlose Börse; ~ **par** Nenn-, Nominalwert; ~ **partner** *(Br.)* Scheingesellschafter; ~ **rent** sehr geringe Miete; ~ **wage** Nominallohn; ~ **yield** Nominalverzinsung.

nomination of beneficiary *(life insurance)* Einsetzung eines Begünstigten.

nominee Kandidat, vorgeschlagener Bewerber, *(man of straw)* vorgeschobene Person, Strohmann, *(recipient of annuity, grant)* Leibrenten-, Zuschußempfänger.

nonacceptance *(of a bill)* Akzeptverweigerung, *(of goods)* Annahmeverweigerung.

nonadmitted assets *(insurance accounting)* ungeeignete Deckungsmittel.

nonassessable stock *(US)* voll eingezahlte Aktie.

nonbanking business bankfremdes Geschäft.

nonbusiness days Sonn- und Feiertage.

nonclearing countries Länder ohne Verrechnungsabkommen.

noncommercial | enterprise gemeinnütziges Unternehmen; ~ **quantities** nicht zum Handel geeignete Mengen.

nonconsolidated *(balance sheet)* nicht konsolidiert.

noncontingent preference stock *(Br.)* kumulative Vorzugsaktie.

noncontributory pension plan beitragsfreies Pensionssystem.

nondeductible *(income tax)* nicht abzugsfähig.

nondescript arbeitsunfähig, Invalide.

nondisclosure *(insurance law)* Verletzung der vorvertraglichen Anzeigepflicht.

nondiscretionary trust *(Br.)* Investmentfonds mit festgelegten Anlagewerten.

nondurable consumer goods kurzlebige Verbrauchsgüter.

nonforfeiture value *(insurance)* Rückkaufswert.

nongraded products unsortierte Ware.

noninterest-bearing securities unverzinsliche Werte.

nonliability Haftungsausschluß.

nonnegotiability notice Sperrvermerk.

nonnegotiable bill Rektawechsel.

nonnotification basis Forderungsabtretung in stiller Form.

nonoperating | expense Erlösschmälerungen; ~ **factory** stillgelegte Fabrik.

nonparticipating | countries *(ECU)* Nichtmitgliedsstaaten; ~ **insurance** nicht gewinnbeteiligte Versicherung.

nonpayment Zahlungsverweigerung.

nonpiecework bonus plan Gruppenprämiensystem.

nonproduction bonus Prämie für Produktionsstilllegung.

nonproductive labo(u)r Gemeinkostenlohn.

nonprofit | agreement Gewinnausschließungsvereinbarung; ~-**making corporation (enterprise)** gemeinnütziges Unternehmen.

nonquota goods nicht kontingentierte Waren.

nonresidence *(foreign exchange)* Ausländereigenschaft.

nonresident *(USA)* Devisenausländer.

nonreturnable package Einwegpackung.

nonscheduled *(US)* nicht fahrplanmäßig.

nonsked business *(US)* Charterfluggeschäft.

nontariff barrier Zollfreigrenze.

nontrader Nichtkaufmann.

nonwage demands lohnfremde Forderungen.

nonwarranty clause Freizeichnungsklausel.

normal | loss natürlicher Schwund; ~ **return** Normalverzinsung; ~ **tax** *(US)* Basissteuer.

nostro accounts Nostrokonten.

not | to be had *(market report)* fehlt; ~ **paying** unrentabel; ~ **provided for** keine Deckung.

notarial charges Notariatsgebühren.

note Notiz, Vermerk, *(account)* Rechnung, *(bank note)* Banknote, *(bond)* Schuldschein, *(promissory note)* Schuldschein, Solawechsel; **accommodation** ~ Gefälligkeitswechsel; **bought and sold (broker's)** ~ Schlußschein; **country** ~ Provinzwechsel; **covering** ~ *(insurance)* vorläufige Deckungszusage; **credit** ~ Gutschriftsanzeige; **customs** ~ Zollvormerkschein; **debit** ~ Lastschriftanzeige; **delivery** ~ Lieferschein; **demand** ~ *(Br.)* Steuerbescheid; **dispatch** ~ Versandanzeige; **foreign coins and** ~**s** Sorten; **jerque** ~ Zolleinfuhrbescheinigung; **joint and several** ~ *(US)* gesamtschuldnerisches Zahlungsversprechen; **joint promissory** ~ solidarischer trockener Wechsel; ~**s payable** *(balance sheet, US)* Wechselverbindlichkeiten; **promissory** ~ Schuldschein, Solawechsel; ~**s receivable** *(balance sheet, US)* Wechselforderungen; **shipping** ~ Warenbegleitschein; **treasury** ~ *(US)* Kassenschein; ~ **of blocking** Sperrvermerk; ~**s and small change** Banknoten und Kleingeld; ~ **of charges** *(Br.)* Gebührenrechnung; ~ **of exchange** Kursblatt; ~ **of expenses** *(Br.)* Spesenrechnung; ~ **of hand** *(Br.)* eigener (trockener) Wechsel; ~ **of prepayment** Frankovermerk; ~ **of protest** Protestnote; ~ **of specie** Sortenverzeichnis; ~ **(v.) a bill (draft)** Wechselprotest erheben; ~ **an order** Auftrag vormerken; **to issue [bank]** ~**s** Banknoten ausgeben; **to make good on a** ~ Wechsel einlösen; ~ **broker** *(US)* Disskont-, Wechselmakler; ~ **collection** Wechselinkasso; ~ **cover** Notendeckung; ~-**issuing privilege** Banknotenprivileg; ~ **paper** Schreibpapier; ~ **tickler** *(US)* Wechselverfallbuch.

noted before the official hours vorbörslich.

notice *(instruction)* Anordnung, Unterweisung, *(public advertisement)* [öffentliche] Bekanntmachung, *(warning)* Warnung, Kündigung; **at a moment's** ~ jederzeit kündbar; **at short** ~ kurzfristig; **subject to change without** ~ freibleibend;

due ~ rechtzeitige Kündigung; **immediate ~ Scha-densanzeige**; **written ~** schriftliche Kündigung; **~ in advance** Voranzeige; **~ of arrival** Eingangs-bestätigung; **~ of assessment** Steuerbescheid; **~ of assignment** Abtretungsbenachrichtigung; **~ of defect** Mängelrüge; **~ of deposit** *(Br.)* Hinterlegungs-bescheid; **~ of discharge** Kündigungsmitteilung; **~ of dismissal** Entlassungsbescheid; **~ of exemption** *(taxation)* Freistellungsbescheid; **~ to leave** Kündigung; **~ of meeting** Einberufung der Haupt-versammlung; **~ of opposition** *(patent law)* Ein-spruchseinlegung; **~ of protest** *(US)* Protestbe-nachrichtigung; **~ to quit** Mietkündigung; **~ of receipt** Empfangsbescheinigung, Rückschein; **~ of redemption** Bekanntmachung über die Einlösung und Tilgung von Wertpapieren; **~ of removal** An-zeige über die erfolgte Geschäftsverlegung; **~ of suspension of payments** Benachrichtigung über die Zahlungseinstellung; **~ of termination of treaty** Vertragsaufkündigung; **~ of withdrawal** *(securi-ties)* Kündigung von Wertpapieren; **~ in writing** schriftliche Mitteilung (Kündigung); **to be under six months'** ~ halbjährlich kündbar sein; **to be under** ~ **to leave (quit)** gekündigt sein; **to dismiss s. o. without ~** j. sofort (fristlos) ent-lassen; **to give ~ of cancellation of the insurance policy** Versicherung kündigen; **to put a ~ in the papers** Annonce in die Zeitung setzen; **to stick up a** ~ Bekanntmachung anschlagen; **to waive ~** auf Einhaltung der Kündigungsfrist verzichten; **~ board** *(Br.)* Schwarzes Brett, Aushang, An-schlagtafel; **~ period** Kündigungsfrist.

notification *(advertisement)* [Werbe]anzeige, *(giving)* public notice) Bekanntmachung, Mitteilung; **official ~** amtliche Bekanntgabe; **~ of an accident** Unfallanzeige; **to operate on a ~ basis** Forderungsabtretung offenlegen; **~ type of a loan** Kreditgewährung mit offengelegter Forderungsabtretung.

notify *(v.)* bekanntgeben, amtlich mitteilen; **~ a claim** Anspruch anmelden; **~ the police of a loss** Verlustanzeige bei der Polizei abgeben.

notifying bank avisierende Bank.

novelties neueingeführte Artikel, Modeartikel.

novelty *(patent law)* Neuheit, *(trade)* Werbegeschenk-[artikel]; **to constitute a bar as to ~** neuheitsschädlich sein; **~ advertising** Warenprobenverteilung.

nuisance Ärgernis, Mißstand, Belästigung, *(damage to neighbo(u)ring property)* Immissionen; **~ industries** Emissionsbetriebe; **~ tax** unwirt-schaftliche Steuer.

nulla bona Unpfändbarkeitsbescheinigung.

nullify *(v.)* **all rate and position protections** *(adver-tising)* alle Rabattvorteile und Vorzugsplacierun-gen aufheben.

number [An]zahl, Ziffer, Haus-, Zimmer-, Telefon-nummer, *(copy)* Exemplar, Heft, Nummer; **back** ~ Ladenhüter, *(newspaper)* altes [Zeitungs]-exemplar; **collective ~** *(tel.)* Sammelnummer; **con-secutive ~s** fortlaufende Zahlen; **ex-directory ~** *(tel.)* Geheimnummer; **file ~** Aktenzeichen; **index** ~ Indexzahl; **invoice ~** Rechnungsnummer; **red ~s** *(interest)* Zinszahlen; **reference ~** Aktenzeichen; **serial ~** Serien-, Fabriknummer; **supply ~** Bestell-nummer; **toll-free ~** gebührenfreier Telefonanruf; **~ of a car** polizeiliches Kennzeichen; **~ of entry** Buchungsnummer; **~ of persons employed** Be-schäftigtenzahl; **~ of units** Stückzahl; **~ *(v.)* (add)** zusammenzählen, aufrechnen, *(assign a number)* numerieren; **to appear in ~s** lieferungsweise erscheinen; **to dial a** ~ [Telefon]nummer wählen; **to take a car's ~** Auto polizeilich anmelden; **box ~ ad** *(US)* Schließfachnummerinserat; **~ plate** *(car)* Nummernschild; **~s pool** Zahlenlotto.

numbered account Nummernkonto.

numbering, consecutive fortlaufende Numerierung.

nurse | *(v.)* **an account** *(Br.)* faules Konto versuchs-weise sanieren; **~ an infant industry** neugegründe-ten Industriezweig fördern; **to have a lot of unsalable stocks to ~** unverkäuf-liches Lager auf dem Halse haben.

O

oath of manifestation *(US)* Offenbarungseid.
obituary notice Todesanzeige, Nachruf.
object Gegenstand, Sache, Zweck, *(tax)* [Steuer]-objekt;
money no ~ Geld spielt keine Rolle; **salary no** ~ *(advertisement)* Gehalt Nebensache;
with the ~ **of gain** in gewinnsüchtiger Absicht;
~ **of a company** Gesellschaftszweck.
objection Einspruch, Beanstandung, Reklamation.
obligation *(bond)* Verpflichtungsschein, Schuldschein, -verschreibung, Obligation, *(liability)* Verbindlichkeit, Leistung;
of ~ unumgänglich, obligatorisch; **no** ~ unverbindlich;
business ~ Geschäftsverbindlichkeit; **determinate** ~ Speziesschuld; **financial** ~ Zahlungsverpflichtung; **indeterminate** ~ Gattungsschuld; **long-term** ~ langfristige Verbindlichkeit; **secondary** ~ Nebenleistung; **solidary** ~ Solidarverpflichtung; **tax-free** ~s steuerfreie Obligationen;
~ **to accept the goods** Abnahmeverpflichtung; ~ **to buy** Kaufzwang; **legal** ~ **of convertibility** gesetzliche Einlösungspflicht; ~ **to disclose** Anzeigenpflicht bei Versicherungsabschluß; ~s **of a landlord** Vermieterpflichten; ~ **in respect of maintenance** Unterhaltspflicht; ~ **to pay** Obligo;
to assume ~s Verbindlichkeiten übernehmen; **to fulfil(l) one's** ~s **under a contract of sale** seinen Verpflichtungen vertragsgemäß nachkommen; **to repudiate financial** ~s sich finanziellen Verpflichtungen entziehen.
obligatory | **agreement** bindende Abmachung; ~ **disposition** Mußvorschrift; ~ **insurance** Pflichtversicherung.
obliging entgegenkommend, gefällig, kulant.
obligor Schuldner, *(bonds)* Obligationsschuldner.
obliterating stamp Entwertungsstempel.
observation | **form** *(time study)* Beobachtungsposten; ~ **train** *(US)* gläserner Zug.
obsolescence Unbrauchbarkeit, Überalterung;
~ **of stock** Lagerveralterung.
obsolete securities *(US)* aufgerufene und ungültig gemachte Wertpapiere.
obstruct | *(v.)* **navigation** Schiffahrt behindern; ~ **process** Zwangsvollstreckung vereiteln.
obstructing highways Verkehrsbehinderung auf öffentlichen Straßen.
obstruction | **of bankruptcy** Konkursverschleppung; ~ **to navigation** Behinderung der Schiffahrt.
obtain *(v.)* | *(v.)* **an advance of money** Vorschuß erhalten; ~ **goods** Waren beziehen; ~ **a loan of money by application** beantragtes Darlehn erhalten; ~ **nothing** *(creditor)* leer ausgehen.
obtainable, freely frei erhältlich;
~ **on the market** an der Börse gehandelt; ~ **from all stockists** in allen einschlägigen Geschäften zu haben.

obvious risk klar erkennbares Risiko.
occasional | **labo(u)r** Gelegenheits-, Aushilfsarbeit;
~ **licence** *(Br.)* beschränkte Schankkonzession; ~ **purchase** Gelegenheitskauf.
occupancy expenses Hausinstandhaltungskosten.
occupation *(business)* Geschäft, Gewerbe, *(calling)* Beruf, *(employment)* Beschäftigung, Berufsarbeit, -tätigkeit, -leben, Tätigkeit;
as a regular (permanent) ~ hauptberuflich; **without a permanent** ~ ohne feste Beschäftigung;
business ~ berufliche Beschäftigung; **clerical** ~ Bürotätigkeit; **entry** ~ Anfangsberuf; **light** ~ leichte Beschäftigung; **minor** ~ Nebenberuf; -beschäftigung; **no** ~ ohne Beruf; **paramount** ~ *(taxation)* überwiegende Beschäftigung;
~ **for o. s.** Eigennutzung;
to be in a reserved ~ kriegswichtigen Beruf ausüben; **to choose an** ~ Berufswahl treffen; **to look for an** ~ **suited to one's abilities** sich nach einer geeigneten Beschäftigung umsehen;
~ **census** Berufszählung; ~ **road** *(Br.)* Zufahrts-, Privatstraße; ~ **tax** Gewerbesteuer.
occupational | **accident** Berufsunfall; ~ **category (class)** Berufsgruppe; ~ **classification** Berufszugehörigkeit; ~ **description** Berufsbezeichnung; ~ **disease** *(Br.)* Gewerbe-, Berufskrankheit; ~ **hazard** Berufsrisiko; ~ **immobility** *(labo(u)rer)* nicht vorhandene Umsetzfähigkeit; ~ **index** Berufsgruppenindex; ~ **injury** Berufsunfall; ~ **mobility** *(labo(u)rer)* Umsetzfähigkeit; ~ **risk** Berufsrisiko; ~ **shift** Berufswechsel; ~ **training** berufliche Ausbildung, Berufs-, Fachausbildung; ~ **wage** Branchentariflohn.
occupied beschäftigt, ausgelastet, *(hospital)* belegt, *(seat)* besetzt, belegt;
fully ~ *(enterprise)* vollbeschäftigt;
~ **population** werktätige Bevölkerung.
occupier Besitzer, Inhaber, Grundstückseigentümer;
~ **of a shop** Ladeninhaber.
occupy *(v.)* | *(o. s.)* sich beschäftigen, *(s. o.)* j. beschäftigen, *(be in)* innehaben, *(lodge)* bewohnen;
~ **a dual capacity** mit sich selbst kontrahieren.
occurence of loss Versicherungsfall.
ocean | **bill of lading** Seekonnossement; ~ **carrier** Seehafenspediteur; ~ **-carrying trade** Hochseeschiffahrt; ~ **lane** Schiffahrtsroute; ~ **manifest** *(US)* Ladungsverzeichnis; **packed for** ~ **shipment** seeverpackt; ~ **shipping** Atlantikfrachtverkehr.
odd *(left over)* überzählig, *(numbers)* ungerade;
~ **-come shorts** Überreste, Abfälle; ~ **jobs** Gelegenheitsaufträge.
odd lot ungerade Menge, Restpartie, *(auction sale)* Auktionsposten, *(stock exchange)* gebrochener Börsenschluß;
~ **broker (dealer,** *US)* Makler in kleinen Effektenabschnitten.
odd | **man** Gelegenheitsarbeiter; **to make up the** ~

money Summe vollmachen; ~ **size** nicht gängige Größe.

oddments Reste, Abfälle, Ramschwaren.

off *(market)* in einer Flaute, flau, lostlos, *(quality)* minderwertig, von schlechter Qualität, *(sold out)* ausgegangen;

better ~ bessergestellt; **dividend** ~ ausschließlich Dividende;

to allow 2 per cent ~ for ready money 2 % Diskont bei Barzahlung gewähren; **to be ~ three points** *(stock exchange)* drei Punkte tieferliegen; **to give the staff a day** ~ der Belegschaft einen Tag frei geben;

~**beat advertising** ausgefallene Reklame; ~**board market** *(US)* Markt für nicht notierte Werte; ~**brand** nicht markengebunden; **for** ~**consumption** *(alcoholics, Br.)* zum Mitnehmen; ~**the-job accident** Unfall außerhalb der Arbeitszeit; ~ **limits** *(US)* beschlagnahmefrei; ~**peak hours** verkehrsschwache Stunden; ~ **the record** nicht zur Veröffentlichung bestimmt, inoffiziell; ~**season** stille (tote) Saison, Vor- und Nachsaison; ~**schedule** *(US)* außer[fahr]planmäßig.

offer Offerte, Angebot, *(stock exchange)* Angebot, Brief;

at the best possible ~ bestens; **on** ~ *(stock exchange)* Brief, angeboten;

best ~ Meist-, Höchstgebot; **not binding** ~ freibleibendes Angebot; **firm** ~ verbindliche Offerte; **free** ~ freibleibendes Angebot; **special** ~ Vorzugsangebot; **subscription** ~ Zeichnungsaufforderung; ~ **in blank** Blankoofferte; ~ **to buy** Kaufgesuch; ~ **without engagement** freibleibende (unverbindliche) Offerte; ~ **of service** Geschäftsempfehlung; ~ **subject to prior sale (subject unsold)** freibleibendes Angebot, Zwischenverkauf vorbehalten;

~ *(v.)* Angebot machen, offerieren;

~ **bills for discount** Wechsel zum Diskont einreichen; ~ **without engagement** unverbindlich offerieren; ~ **firm** fest anbieten; ~ **goods at 15 per cent off the regular price** Waren 15 % unter Preis anbieten; ~ **guarantee** *(Br.)* Delkredere stehen; ~ **a loan** Kreditofferte machen; ~ **o. s. for a post** sich für eine Stellung in Vorschlag bringen; ~ **a price** Preisangebot machen; ~ **a reward** Belohnung aussetzen; ~ **for sale** offerieren, feilbieten;

to avail o. s. of an ~ von einem Angebot Gebrauch machen; **to close with an** ~ Angebot annehmen; **to hold an** ~ **open** Angebot aufrechterhalten; **to make a firm** ~ fest an die Hand geben; **to vary the terms of an** ~ Angebotsbedingungen abändern; **to withdraw an** ~ Angebot zurückziehen;

~ **price** *(stock exchange)* Briefkurs.

offered, freely stark angeboten; **nothing** ~ *(market report)* fehlt;

~ **down** *(US)* unter der letzten Notierung angeboten; ~ **firm** fest angeboten.

offering ~**s** *stock exchange, US)* Material;

~ **date** Verkaufstermin; ~ **price** *(investment trust)* Ausgabe-, Verkaufspreis.

office *(branch)* Zweigniederlassung, *(bureau)* Geschäftszimmer, Kanzlei, Geschäftsstelle, Kontor *(governmental agency)* Amt, Dienststelle, Behörde, *(governmental office)* Amtszimmer, *(life insurance company, Br.)* Versicherungsgesellschaft, *(profession)* Geschäft, Beruf, *(ministry)* Ministerium;

through the good ~**s of a friend** durch die gütige Vermittlung eines Freundes;

booking ~ Fahrkartenschalter; **box** ~ Schalter; **branch** ~ Filialbüro; **complaints** ~ Beschwerdestelle; **dispatching** ~ Abfertigungsstelle; **Excise** ⌾ Regieverwaltung; **fire [insurance]** ~ *(Br.)* Feuerversicherungsgesellschaft; **forwarding** ~ Versand-, Expeditionsabteilung; **head** ~ Hauptgeschäft; **lost-property** ~ Fundbüro; **lucrative** ~ einträgliche Pfründe; **luggage** ~ *(Br.)* Gepäckannahme; **notary's** ~ Notariatsbüro; **paying** ~ Zahlstelle; **permanent** ~ ständiges Büro; **receiving** ~ [Paket]annahmestelle; **reception** ~ Empfangsbüro; **main regional** ~ Kopffiliale; **registered** ~ *(of a company)* eingetragener Geschäftssitz; **registry** ~ Stellenvermittlungsbüro; **shipping** ~ *(US)* Versand-, Speditionsbüro; **vacant** ~ freie Stelle;

⌾ **of Business Economics** *(US)* Statistisches Bundesamt; ~ **of a chairman** Präsidentenamt; ~ **of destination** *(Br.)* Bestimmungspostamt; ~ **of dispatch** Abfertigungsstelle, *(post office)* Abgangs-, Aufgabeamt; ⌾ **of Emergency Preparedness** *(US)* Technische Nothilfe; ~ **of posting** *(Br.)* Aufgabepostamt; ⌾ **of Price Administration** *(US)* Preisprüfungsamt; ~ **for reservation of seats** Platzkartenschalter;

to act in virtue of one's ~ in amtlicher Eigenschaft handeln; **to be called to** ~ ins Ministerium berufen werden; **to be in** ~ amtieren; **to be working in an** ~ Büroarbeit verrichten; **to enter upon** ~ (Stellung) antreten; **to maintain an** ~ Büro unterhalten; **to oust a rival from** ~ Konkurrenten aus einer Stellung verdrängen; **to resign one's** ~ sein Amt niederlegen; **to stand for an** ~ kandidieren; **to work in an** ~ Büroangestellter sein;

~ **accommodation** Büroräume, -unterbringung; ~ **appliances** Bürobedarfsartikel, -ausstattung; ~ **books** Geschäftsbücher; ~ **boy** Laufbursche; ~ **building** Bürogebäude; ~ **clerk** Kontorist, Handlungsgehilfe; ~ **copy** *(Br.)* amtlich erteilte Abschrift; ~ **fixtures** Büroinventar; ~ **gossip** Büroklatsch; ~ **hands** *(US)* Büropersonal; ~ **hours** Dienst-, Geschäfts-, Bürostunden, Geschäftszeit; ~ **hunter** Stellenjäger; ~ **keeper** Bürovorsteher; ~ **machine** Büromaschine; ~**operating costs** Geschäfts-, Bürounkosten; ~ **paper** *(US)* Finanzierungswechsel; ~ **premises** Geschäftsgrundstück, räume; ~ **rent** Büromiete; **to furnish a room** Büroraum zur Verfügung stellen; ~ **routine** Geschäftsbetrieb, -praxis; ~ **staff** Büropersonal; ~ **stamp book** Portokasse; ~ **stationery (supplies)** Bürobedarf, -material; ~ **use** Benutzung als Geschäftsraum; ~ **worker** Büroangestellter, -kraft.

officeholder *(US)* Amts-, Stelleninhaber.

officer Beamter, Angestellter, *(company)* leitender Angestellter, Direktor;
while an ~ in dienstlicher Eigenschaft;
corporate ~ leitender Angestellter; **customhouse** ~ Zollbeamter; **established** ~ planmäßiger Beamter; **local government** ~ *(Br.)* Kommunalbeamter; **preventive** ~ Zollfahndungsbeamter; **relieving** ~ *(Br.)* Sozialfürsorger;
~ **of the board** Vorstandsmitglied; ~ **in charge** Sachbearbeiter; ~**s and staff** leitende Angestellte und sonstiges Personal.

official Beamter, Angestellter;
higher-echelon ~ Beamter des gehobenen Dienstes; **top[-ranking]** ~ Spitzenkraft;
~ *(a.)* behördlich, amtlich, offiziell, dienstlich, *(authorized)* bevollmächtigt;
~ **authorization** amtliche Genehmigung; ~ **business** dienstliche Angelegenheit, Dienstsache; ≙ **Business** *(mail, US)* Dienstpost; ~ **channels** Instanzenweg; ~ **hours** Geschäfts-, Dienst-, Bürozeit, Amts-, Dienststunden; ~ **list** *(stock exchange)* Liste der zum Börsenhandel zugelassenen Werte; ~ **paid** *(Br.)* portofrei; ~ **quotation** offizielle [Kurs]notierung; ~ **receiver** *(Br.)* Zwangsverwalter; ~ **register** *(US)* Amtsblatt; ~ **tour** Dienstreise; ~ **use** only nur für den Dienstgebrauch; ~ **year** Geschäftsjahr.

offset *(set-off, US)* Gegenposten, -rechnung, -forderung[en], Ausgleich, Ver-, Aufrechnung;
~*(v.)* *(US)* kompensieren, ver-, aufrechnen, ausgleichen;
~ **earlier losses** frühere Verluste ausgleichen;
~ **account** Verrechnungskonto; ~ **agreement** Verrechnungsabkommen; ~ **payments** Devisenausgleich.

offsetting entry Storno-, Gegenbuchung.

offshore *(US)* im Ausland getätigt;
~ **order** *(US)* Auslands[hilfs]auftrag.

oil Öl;
~ **company** Ölgesellschaft; ~ **concession** Erdölkonzession; ~ **industry** Erdölindustrie; ~ **occurrence** Erdölvorkommen.

old-age | **annuity** Alters-, Invalidenrente; ~ **benefit** *(US)* Altersversorgung; ~ **benefit taxes** *(US)* Sozialabgaben; ~ **exemption** *(US)* Altersfreibetrag; ~ **insurance** Altersversicherung; ~ **pension** *(Br.)* Alters-, Invalidenrente; ~ **and survivor's insurance** *(US)* Sozial-, Alters- und Hinterbliebenenversorgung.

old | **-established firm** alteingesessene Firma; ~ **stock** Ladenhüter.

omnibus | **account** *(Br.)* Sammelkonto; ~ **credit** *(Br.)* Warenkredit; ~ **deposit** Girosammeldepot; ~ **train** *(Br.)* Personen-, Bummelzug.

on | **-carrier** übernehmender Spediteur; ~**-the-job accident** Betriebs-, Arbeitsunfall; ~**-sale date** Verkaufstermin.

oncost *(Br.)* Gemein-, Regiekosten.

one | **-armed bandit** *(US)* Spielautomat; ~**-day loan**

(US) Vierundzwanzigstundenkredit; ~**-family house** Einfamilienhaus; ~**-line business** Spezial-, Fachgeschäft; ~**-man business (firm.,** *US)* Einmannbetrieb; ~**-price** Festpreis; ~**-price article** Einheitspreisware, -artikel; ~**-price store** Einheitspreisgeschäft; ~**-third down** $^1/_3$ Anzahlung; ~**-time purchaser** Laufkunde; ~**-time rate** Einmaltarif; ~**-trip container** *(US)* Einwegbehälter; ~**-way only** *(Br.)* Einbahnstraße; ~**-way package** Wegwerfpackung; ~**-way traffic** Einbahnverkehr.

onerous goods unwirtschaftliche Artikel.

onionskin Luftpostpapier; *(typewriter)* Durchschlagpapier.

open | **all night** ganze Nacht geöffnet; ~ **to the public** für den öffentlichen Verkehr freigegeben; ~ **to residents only** frei für Anlieger; ~ **for subscription** zur Zeichnung aufgelegt;
~ *(v.) (shop)* Betrieb aufnehmen;
~ **active** *(stocks)* von Anfang an gefragt sein; ~ **a the budget** Haushaltsvoranschlag vorlegen; ~ **a business** Geschäft eröffnen; ~ **up a country to trade** Land für den Handel erschließen; ~ **a credit** Kredit gewähren; ~ **at a slight discount** *(stock exchange)* leicht abgeschwächt eröffnen; ~ **a highway** Verkehrsweg zur öffentlichen Benutzung freigeben; ~ **a letter of credit** Akkreditiv eröffnen; ~ **negotiations** Verhandlungen einleiten; ~ **steady** *(stock exchange)* fest eröffnen; ~ **a trade** Gewerbe beginnen; ~ **up business relations** in Geschäftsverbindung treten; ~ **up to the tourist trade** für den Fremdenverkehr erschließen;
~ **account** laufendes Konto, Kontokorrentkonto; ~ **book account** *(US)* laufende Rechnung; ~ **cheque** *(Br.)* Barscheck; ~ **claim** *(insurance)* noch nicht entschiedener Versicherungsanspruch; ~ **competition** freier Wettbewerb; ~ **credit** *(US)* Kontokorrentkredit.

open-end | **commercial** Werbefilm mit eingeblendeten Händleradressen; ~ **fund** *(US)* Investmentfonds mit beliebiger Emissionshöhe; ~ **transcription** Standardwerbeprogramm; ~ **wage contract** Tarifvertrag mit Lohngleitklausel.

open market Freiverkehr, Offenmarkt;
~ **credit** Schuldscheindarlehn; ~ **policy** Offenmarktpolitik der Notenbank; ~ **purchases** Käufe am offenen Markt.

open | **order** *(US)* bis zum Widerruf gültiger Auftrag; ~**-plan office** Großraumbüro; ~ **policy** *(insurance, Br.)* Pauschalversicherung; ~ **port** Freihafen; ~**-price system** *(US)* Preisinformationssystem; ~ **rate** *(advertising)* Anzeigengrundpreis; ~ **rates** *(US)* Geldsätze am offenen Markt; ~ **shop** *(US)* nicht gewerkschaftspflichtiger Betrieb.

opencast production Übertageförderung.

opening *(off account)* Errichtung, Eröffnung, *(letter)* Briefanfang, *(opportunity)* Gelegenheit, Chance, *(stock exchange)* Eröffnung;
active ~ *(stock exchange)* lebhafte Eröffnung; **unfilled jobs** ~ Angebot offener Stellen;
~ **in a bank** freie Stelle bei einer Bank; **attractive**

~s on managerial levels Aufstiegschancen in der Betriebshierarchie; ~ for subscription Auflegung zur Zeichnung;
~ balance Eröffnungsbilanz; ~ bid Eröffnungsangebot; ~ capital Grund-, Stamm-, Anfangskapital; ~ hours Eröffnungszeit; ~ price (quotation, rate) Anfangskurs; ~ stock Anfangsinventar.

openjaw *(air travel)* Rundflugkarte mit variablem Endflugplatz.

operate *(v.)* funktionieren, laufen, in Betrieb sein, *(handle)* handhaben, betätigen, *(machine)* bedienen, betreiben, *(stock exchange)* operieren;
~ an account Konto unterhalten; ~ for one's own account auf eigene Rechnung betreiben; ~ above capacity überlasten; ~ at below two thirds of capacity nur zwei Drittel der Betriebskapazität ausnützen; ~ against one's client gegen die Interessen seines Kunden handeln; ~ economically sparsam wirtschaften; ~ for a fall auf Baisse spekulieren; ~ at a profit mit Gewinn betreiben; ~ for a rise auf Hausse spekulieren; ~ in global spread weltweite Unternehmungen betreiben; ~ a state-wide system of branches Filialen im ganzen Land unterhalten.

operating | of a motor vehicle *(US)* Führen eines Kraftfahrzeugs;
to be ~ at a high level voll beschäftigt sein; to be ~ at a loss mit Verlust arbeiten;
~ account Betriebskonto; ~ cash reserve Betriebsmittelrücklage; ~ cost Betriebsunkosten; ~ dummy Scheinunternehmen; ~ efficiency Betriebsleistung, Wirtschaftlichkeit; ~ income Betriebseinkommen; ~ loss Betriebsverlust; ~ performance income statement Betriebsergebnisrechnung; ~ rate Beschäftigungsgrad, *(US)* Grad der Kapazitätsauslastung; ~ statement *(US)* Gewinn- und Verlust-, Betriebsabrechnung; ~ surplus Betriebsüberschuß, -gewinn; ~ unit Betriebseinheit.

operation *(efficacy)* Wirksamkeit, Wirkung, Geltung, *(enterprise)* Unternehmen, Betrieb, *(management)* Leitung, *(machine)* Bedienung, Handhabung;
in full ~ vollbeschäftigt, *(machine)* in vollem Betrieb; ready for ~ betriebsfertig; reliable in ~s betriebssicher;
authorized ~ Betriebsgenehmigung; automatic ~ *(tel.)* Selbstwählverkehr; banking ~s Bankgeschäfte; bearish ~ Blankoabgabe; continuous ~ Tag- und Nachtbetrieb; economic[al] ~ wirtschaftliche Betriebsführung, Wirtschaftlichkeit; financial ~ Finanztransaktion; inter-company ~s Verrechnungs-, Konzerngeschäfte; scheduled ~ *(US)* fahrplanmäßiger Betrieb; thriving ~ florierendes Unternehmen;
~ for own account Nostrotransaktion; ~ in futures *(stock exchange)* Termingeschäft;
to be in ~ in Betrieb sein, funktionieren; to commence ~s in Betrieb nehmen; to slim down ~s Geschäftsvolumen verringern; to suspend ~s Geschäftstätigkeit einstellen;
~ analysis chart Bewertungsformblatt; ~ card Arbeitskarte; ~ costs Betriebskosten; ~ manager Betriebsleiter; ~ sheets Betriebsabrechnungsbogen.

operational betrieblich, betriebsbedingt, *(airliner)* einsatz-, betriebsbereit;
~ accounting Betriebsabrechnung; ~ blindness Betriebsblindheit; ~ deficit Betriebsdefizit; ~ expenditure Betriebsaufwand; ~ loss Betriebsverlust; ~ setup Betriebsschema.

operative *(artisan)* Handwerker, *(machinist)* Mechaniker, Maschinist;
~ building ~ Bauarbeiter; ~ skilled ~ Facharbeiter; ~ *(a.)* wirksam, gültig, *(in operation)* tätig, in Betrieb, betriebsfähig.

operator Bedienungsperson, *(manager, US)* Unternehmer, Betriebsführer, -leiter;
black-market ~ Schwarzhändler; gasoline-station ~ Tankstellenbesitzer; market ~ [berufsmäßiger] Spekulant;
~ of a motor vehicle *(US)* Kraftfahrzeugführer.

opinion Ansicht, Stellungnahme, *(auditor)* Testat, *(legal expert, Br.)* Rechtsgutachten;
expert ~ Sachverständigengutachten;
~ leader meinungsbildende Persönlichkeit; ~ list *(Br.)* Kundenauskunftsbuch; ~ poll (survey, test) Meinungsbefragung; public ~ research Meinungsforschung.

opportunity [günstige] Gelegenheit, Chance; employment ~ Beschäftigungsmöglichkeit;
~ to buy Einkaufsmöglichkeit; ~ for work Arbeitsgelegenheit;
~ chart Beförderungstabelle; ~ costs alternative Kosten, Wartekosten.

opposition *(bankruptcy proceedings)* verweigerte Entlastung, *(patent law)* Pateneinspruch, *(trademark)* Widerspruch.

optimal size optimale Betriebsgröße.

optimum capacity Höchstleistungsfähigkeit.

option *(choice)* freie Wahl, Alternative, *(put and call)* Börsentermingeschäft, Terminhandel;
at one's ~ nach Wahl; on the exercise of an ~ aufgrund der Ausübung eines Bezugsrechtes; buyer's ~ Vorprämie; call ~ Bezugsoption, Vorprämie[n-geschäft]; first ~ Vorhand [beim Kauf]; put ~ Rückprämie[ngeschäft]; unexercised ~ nicht ausgeübtes Optionsrecht;
~ to put Käufers Wahl, Option; ~ of redemption Rückkaufsrecht; ~ to subscribe to new shares (on new stock, US) Bezugsrecht auf junge Aktien; to abandon an ~ Optionsrecht nicht ausüben; to buy an ~ on stock Bezugsrecht kaufen; to buy a call ~ Vorprämie kaufen; to call an ~ *(Br.)* Prämiengeschäft eingehen; to deal in ~s *(Br.)* Prämiengeschäfte machen; to have an ~ on a piece of land Grundstücksvorkaufsrecht haben; to rent a building with the ~ of purchase Haus mit Vorkaufsrecht mieten; to take up an ~ Kaufoption ausüben;
~ agreement Bezugsrechtsvereinbarung; ~ bond Optionsanleihe; ~ business Terminhandel; ~ buyer Prämienkäufer; ~ certificate to bearer Inhaberzertifikat; ~ deal *(Br.)* Prämiengeschäft; ~

exercise Optionsausübung; ~ **market** *(Br.)* Termin-, Prämienmarkt; ~ **money** *(Br.)* Prämiengeld; ~ **rates** *(Br.)* Prämiensätze; ~ **stock** *(Br.)* Prämienwerte.

optional *(a.)* freigestellt, fakultativ, beliebig; ~ **at extra cost** auf Wunsch gegen besondere Berechnung; ~ **with the buyer** nach Käufers Wahl; ~ **bonds** *(US)* jederzeit kündbare Obligationen; ~ **clause** Fakultativklausel; ~ **equipment** *(car)* Extra-, Sonderausstattung; ~ **price** Prämienkurs; ~ **retirement** Pensionierung auf eigenen Wunsch.

order Auftrag, Bestellung, Order, Kommission, *(direction)* Anordnung, [An]weisung, *(decree, Br.)* Verfügung, Erlaß, *(entry permit, Br.)* Freikarte, *(social status)* Stand, Gesellschaftsschicht; **by ~ and for account of** im Auftrag und auf Rechnung von; **in good ~ and well conditioned** gut und wohlerhalten; **in running ~** betriebsfertig; **made to ~** auf Bestellung angefertigt; **out of ~** nicht betriebsfähig; **payable to ~** zahlbar an Order; **to ~** *(check)* an Order; **additional ~** Nachbestellung; **big-ticket ~** *(stock exchange)* Großauftrag; **~s booked** Auftragsbestand; **good until cancelled ~** auf Widerruf gültiger Auftrag; **delivery ~** Lieferanweisung; **disbursing ~** Auszahlungsverfügung; **filled ~s** erledigte Aufträge; **foreign (international) money ~** Auslandspostanweisung; **garnishee ~** Pfändungs- und Überweisungsbeschluß; **landing ~** *(Br.)* Zollpassierschein; **market ~** *(US)* Bestens-Order; **matched ~s** *(US)* gekoppelte Börsenaufträge; **money-losing ~** Verlustauftrag; **purchasing ~** Bestellung; **receiving ~** *(Br.)* Konkursbeschluß; **repeat ~** Nachbestellung; **stop payment ~** Auszahlungssperre; **working ~** betriebsfähiger Zustand; **~ for the account** *(stock exchange)* Terminauftrag; **~ on a bank** Überweisungsauftrag; **~s on the book** *(US)* gebuchte Aufträge; **~ of discharge** *(Br.)* (for discharge, *US)* Konkursaufhebungsbeschluß; **~ for goods** Warenauftrag; **~s on hand** Auftragsbestand; **~ to pay (for payment)** Zahlungsanweisung; **~ to quit** *(Br.)* Räumungsbefehl; **~ for the settlement** *(stock exchange, Br.)* Terminauftrag; ~ *(v.)* bestellen, Auftrag aufgeben, in Auftrag geben; **~ an account to be blocked** Konto sperren lassen; **~ in advance** vor[aus]bestellen; **~ goods from the sample** laut Muster bestellen; **to be in good working ~** voll betriebsfähig sein, **to be made out to ~** an Order lauten; **to cancel an ~** abbestellen; **to canvass ~s** Aufträge hereinholen; **to execute all ~s in strict rotation** Aufträge in der Reihenfolge des Eingangs erledigen; **to personally handle an ~** sich persönlich um eine Auftragserledigung kümmern; **to make a bill payable to ~** Wechsel an Order ausstellen; **to place an ~** Auftrag erteilen; **to revoke an ~** Auftrag stornieren; **~ bill** Orderpapier; **~ bill of lading** Orderfrachtbrief, -konnossement; **~ blank** *(US)* Bestellzettel, Auftragsformular; **~ book** Auftragsbuch; **length-**

ening ~ books wachsender Auftragsbestand; **~ cheque** *(Br.)* Orderscheck; **~ filling** Auftragserledigung; **~ form** Bestellschein; **~ instrument** Orderpapier; **~ placing** Auftragsvergabe.

ordinaries *(Br.)* Stammaktien.

ordinary *(employment)* ständiges Dienst- und Anstellungsverhältnis, *(tavern)* fester Mittagstisch; **~ annuity** nachschüssige Rente; **~ bill of exchange** Handelswechsel; **~ capital** Stammkapital; **~ care** im Verkehr übliche Sorgfalt; **~ creditor** Massegläubiger; **~ dealings** gewöhnliche Zahlungsbedingungen; **~ debts** Masseschulden; **~ depreciation** normale Abschreibung; **~ dividend** Stammdividende; **~ endowment insurance** abgekürzte Lebensversicherung; **~ life insurance** *(US)* (assurance, *Br.)* Lebensversicherung auf den Todesfall; **~ interest** Zinsen auf Basis von 360 Tagen; **~ negligence** *(US)* leichte Fahrlässigkeit; **~ prudent person** normaler Durchschnittsmensch; **~ seaman** Leichtmatrose; **~ share** Stammaktie; **~ stockholder** *(US)* Stammaktionär; **~ train** fahrplanmäßiger Zug.

organ company *(US)* Organgesellschaft.

organization Organisation, Vereinigung, Verband, *(organizing)* Gestaltung, Einrichtung, Bildung; **administrative ~** Verwaltungsapparat; **business ~** Geschäftsgründung; **marketing ~** Absatzorganisation; **nonprofit ~** gemeinnützige Einrichtung; **professional ~** berufsständische Vertretung; **top-heavy ~** kopflastige Verwaltung; **♀ for European Economic Cooperation (OEEC)** Europäischer Wirtschaftsrat; **♀ for the Maintenance of Supplies** *(Br.)* Technische Nothilfe; **~ for standardization** Normenausschuß; **~ arrangement** Organisationsplan; **~ certificate** Gründungsurkunde; **~ chart** Organisationsschema; **~ cost** *(US)* Gründungskosten.

organizational | chart Organisationsschema; **~ picketing** organisierte Streikposten.

organize *(v.)* organisieren, gründen, veranstalten; **~ a corporation** *(US)* Aktiengesellschaft gründen; **~ a fair** Messe aufziehen.

organized market Interessenzusammenschluß zwecks einheitlicher Verkaufspolitik.

original Original, Erstanfertigung; **~ advertisement (advertising)** Einführungsreklame; **~ assets** Anfangskapital; **~ bill** *(US)* Primawechsel; **~ capital** *(US)* Gründungs-, Stamm-, Grundkapital; **~ contractor** Hauptlieferant; **~ cost** Anschaffungs-, Erwerbskosten; **~ invoice** Originalrechnung; **~ price** Anschaffungs-, Einkaufspreis; **~ share** *(Br.)* Stammaktie; **~ subscriber** Ersterwerber; **~ syndicate** *(US)* Übernahmekonsortium; **~ value** Anschaffungswert.

ostensible agency Vertretung ohne Vertretungsmacht.

other | income *(balance sheet)* sonstige Erträge; **~ investment** *(balance sheet)* diverse Analgewerte.

oust *(v.)* **from the market** vom Markt verdrängen.

out *(let)* vermietet, verpachtet, *(of office)* außer Dienst, *(used up)* verbraucht;

~ **of bond** vom unverzolten Lager; ~ **of cash** nicht bei Kasse; **~-of-date** unmodern, veraltet *(Br., cheque)* Einlösungsfrist abgelaufen; **~-of-line rate** übertariflicher Lohn; ~ **of order** außer Betrieb; **~-of-pocket** in bar bezahlt; ~ **of a situation** ohne Stellung; **~-of-stock** nicht am Lager (vorrätig); ~ **of time** *(ship)* überfällig; **~-of-town collections** *(US)* auswärtige Inkassi; ~ **of trim** *(cargo)* schlecht gestaut;

to be ~ **on account of illness** wegen Krankheit der Arbeit fernbleiben; **to be** ~ **of all** keinen Pfennig mehr besitzen; **to be** ~ **on business** geschäftlich unterwegs sein; **to be** ~ **at interest** verzinslich angelegt sein; **to go** ~ in den Streik treten, streiken; ~ **benefit (pay)** Arbeitslosenunterstützung; ~ **and home voyage** Hin- und Rückreise.

outbidding höheres Gebot, Mehrgebot.
outbound *(ship)* nach dem Ausland bestimmt.
outdoor | **advertising** Außenwerbung; ~ **relief** *(Br.)* Sozialhilfe, Fürsorgeunterstützung; ~ **work** Außenarbeit.
outflow | **of cash** Kassenabgänge; ~ **of funds** Guthabenabgang; ~ **of gold** Goldabfluß.
outgoing | **long-distance call** abgehendes Ferngespräch; ~ **train** abfahrender Zug.
outing, factory Betriebsausflug.
outlawed claim *(US)* verjährter Anspruch.
outlay Ausgaben, -lagen, [Kosten]aufwand;
cash ~ Barauslagen; **first (initial)** ~ Anschaffungskosten; **professional** ~ Werbungskosten.
outlet *(bulk buyer)* Großabnehmer, *(fig.)* Betätigungsfeld, *(market)* Absatzfeld, -gebiet; **cash** ~ Kassamarkt.
outlook, business Konjunkturaussichten.
output *(machine)* Leistung[sfähigkeit], *(mine)* Ausbeute, *(quantity produced)* Produktion, Ausstoß, Ertrag;
annual ~ Jahresproduktion; **domestic** ~ Inlandserzeugung; **industrial** ~ Industrieproduktion; **peak** ~ Höchstleistung;
~ **of a colliery** Förderung eines Kohlenbergwerks; ~ **per man-shift** *(mining)* Schichtleistung; ~ **in volume** mengenmäßige Erzeugung;
to cut back ~ Ausstoß verringern; **to match** ~ **to the absorption capacities** Förderung den Absatzmöglichkeiten anpassen;
~ **bonus** Produktionsprämie; ~ **capacity** Produktionskapazität; ~ **figures** Produktionszahlen; ~ **quota** Förderungskontingent; ~ **rate** Ausstoßziffer; ~ **target** Produktionsziel.
outright völlig, gänzlich, total, *(on the spot)* sofort; **to buy** ~ *(US)* gegen sofortige Lieferung (per Kasse) kaufen; **to pay s. o.** ~ j. voll auszahlen; ~ **acceptance** vorbehaltlose Annahme; ~ **owner** Volleigentümer; ~ **purchase** fester Kaufabschluß; ~ **sale** Abschluß zu einem festen Verkaufspreis.
outrun *(v.)* **one's credit** seinen Kredit überschreiten; ~ **increases in productivity** Produktivitätszunahme wettmachen; ~ **one's income** über seine Verhältnisse leben.

outside | **one's official functions** außerdienstlich; ~ **activities** außerberufliche Beschäftigung; ~ **agent** Außenvertreter; ~ **artist** *(advertising)* freier Mitarbeiter; ~ **broking** freie Maklertätigkeit; ~ **capital** Fremdkapital; ~ **director** *(US)* freier Berater des Vorstandes; ~ **financing** Fremdfinanzierung; ~ **funds** Fremdmittel; ~ **loan** amtlich nicht notierte Anleihe; ~ **market** Freiverkehr[smarkt]; ~ **securities** Freiverkehrswerte.
outsider Außenseiter, Nichtfachmann, *(price maintenance)* an Preisabsprachen nicht gebundener Betrieb, *(stock exchange)* Freiverkehrsmakler.
outsize Übergröße.
outstanding offenstehend, rückständig; ~ **capital stock** *(US)* ausgegebenes Aktienkapital; ~ **coupons** notleidende Zinsscheine; ~ **debts** [Aktiv]außenstände; ~ **interest** Zinsrückstände; ~ **notes** Wechselumlauf.
outtrade *(v.)* umsatzmäßig überflügeln.
outward | **appearance** *(goods)* äußere Aufmachung; ~ **bill of lading** Exportkonnossement; ~ **journey** *(Br.)* Aus-, Hinreise; ~ **mail department** Postversandabteilung, Expedition.
over Überschuß, Mehrbetrag;
cash shorts and ~s *(US)* Kassenüberschüsse und Fehlbeträge;
to recover ~ *(US)* Regreß nehmen; ~ **the counter** *(US)* freihändig, im Freihandel verkauft; **~-the-counter business (trade)** *(US)* Schalterverkehr, außerbörslicher Effektenhandel.
overage of cash *(US)* Kassenüberschuß.
overall | **budget** Gesamtetat; ~ **demand** gesamtwirtschaftliche Nachfrage; ~ **elasticity of supply** volkswirtschaftliche Angebotselastizität; ~ **increase of prices** generelle Preiserhöhung; ~ **limitation** *(income tax, US)* Anrechnung im Ausland insgesamt gezahlter Steuern; ~ **quota** Globalkontingent; ~ **rate** Pauschalsatz.
overassessment zu hohe Steuerveranlagung.
overcapitalize *(v.)* überkapitalisieren.
overcertification Ausstellung eines Überziehungsschecks, *(US)* Bestätigung eines ungedeckten Schecks.
overcertify *(v.)* *(US)* ungedeckten Scheck bestätigen.
overcharge Mehrbelastung, zuviel berechneter Betrag, *(public utility)* überhöhter Tarif; ~ **of freight** zuviel berechnete Fracht; ~ *(v.)* zuviel fordern, anrechnen.
overcharged prices übersetzte Preise.
overcheck *(US)* Überziehungsscheck.
overcrowded | **labo(u)r market** Überangebot an Arbeitskräften; ~ **profession** übersetzter Berufszweig; ~ **region** Ballungsgebiet.
overdiscount *(v.)* **the market** *(US)* erwartete Hausse am Markte überschätzen.
overdraft, overdraught *(Br.)* Kontoüberziehung, Kreditüberschreitung;
to have an ~ sein Konto überzogen haben; ~ **commission** Überziehungsprovision; **to grant a firm** ~ **facilities** einer Firma Kreditfazilitäten zur Verfügung stellen.

overdrawing Kontȯüberziehung.
overdrawn | **account** überzogenes Konto, Kontoüberzug;
to be ~ at the bank bei der Bank im Debet sein.
overdue rückständig, *(bill)* notleidend, *(train)* überfällig;
~ **amount** rückständiger Betrag; ~ **interest** Verzugszinsen.
overemployment Überbeschäftigung.
overenter *(v.)* zu hoch deklarieren.
overestimate *(v.) (balance sheet)* überbewerten.
overextension Überschuldung eines Betriebes.
overhaul Überprüfung, gründliche Untersuchung, *(car)* Generalüberholung;
~ *(v.)* überholen, reparieren, *(accounts)* erneut prüfen, genau überprüfen, *(stock)* abschreiben.
overhauling of stock Lagerabschreibung.
overhead(s) fortlaufende (fixe) Kosten, Betriebs-, Gemeinkosten, Generalunkosten;
factory ~ Fertigungsgemeinkosten; **overabsorbed ~** Gemeinkostenüberdeckung;
factory ~ account Betriebs-, Fertigungsgemeinkostenkonto; ~ **allocation** Aufteilung der Generalunkosten; ~ **charges (costs, expenses)** Handlungs-, General-, allgemeine Unkosten, Regiekosten; ~ **company** Dachgesellschaft; ~ **distribution** Gemeinkostenumlage; ~ **organization** Dachorganisation; ~ **price** Pauschal-, Gesamtpreis.
overinsurance Überversicherung.
overinvestment in inventories übermäßige Kapitalinvestitionen in Warenbeständen.
overissue Überemission, Papiergeldinflation.
overlying mortgage *(US)* nachstellige Hypothek.
overnight | **charge** Nachtzuschlag; ~ **loan** *(US)* Tagesgeld; ~ **stay** Übernachtung.
overpayment Überzahlung.
overrate *(v.)* zu hoch schätzen (veranlagen).
overriding | **clause** Aufhebungsklausel; ~ **commission** *(insurance business, Br.)* dem Generalvertreter verbleibender Provisionsanteil.
overrun *(v.)* **the constable** *(fam.)* über seine Verhältnisse leben.
oversea(s) | **advertising** Auslandswerbung; ~ **bank** Überseebank; ~ **business** Überseehandel mit Nie- Auslandskunde; ~ **company** *(Br.)* Gesellschaft mit Niederlassung in England; ~ **countries** Überseeländer; ~ **investment** Auslandsinvestitionen; ~ **postage rates** *(Br.)* Auslandsporto; ~ **sales** Umsätze im Überseegeschäft; ~ **trade service** Außenhandelsorganisation.
overseer Vorarbeiter, Werkmeister, Aufseher;
~ **of the customs** Zollinspektor; ~ **of the poor** *(Br.)* Sozialamt.
overselling übertriebene Verkaufspolitik.
overside delivery Überbordauslieferung.
oversold market *(US)* infolge von Baisseverkäufen überlasteter Markt.
overstay *(v.)* **one's market** *(US)* richtigen Zeitpunkt zum Verkauf verpassen.
overstock Überfluß, -vorrat, zu großes Lager;

~ *(v.)* **with goods** übermäßig (über den Bedarf) mit Waren eindecken.
oversubscribe *(v.)* [Anleihe] überzeichnen.
overtake *(v.)* **the boom** Konjunktur überhitzen.
overtaxation Übersteuerung.
overtime Überstunden, -schicht;
to be paid extra for ~ Überstundengelder erhalten;
to employ ~ Überstunden machen lassen;
~ **allowance** Überstundenvergütung; ~ **ban** Überstundenverbot; ~ **bonus (compensation, premium)** Mehrarbeitszuschlag, Überstundengelder; ~ **rate of time and a half** anderthalbfacher Tarifsatz für Überstunden.
overtrade *(v.) (stock exchange)* ohne kapitalmäßige Deckung spekulieren.
overwrite *(v.)* Superprovision zahlen.
owe *(v.)* schulden, schuldig sein;
~ **for one's house** noch Schulden auf seinem Haus haben.
owing, amount ausstehender Betrag; **rent ~** Mietrückstand;
to have money ~ Geld ausstehen haben.
own *(v.)* besitzen, Eigentümer sein;
~ **beneficially** nießbrauchberechtigt sein; ~ **subsidiaries outright** Tochtergesellschaften hundertprozentig besitzen;
to be [working] on one's ~ selbständig sein; **to have no resources of one's ~** über kein Vermögen verfügen; **to hold one's ~ in competitive markets** sich wettbewerbsmäßig (auf dem Markt) durchsetzen; **for one's ~ account** auf eigene Rechnung; ~ **brand** Eigen-, Hausmarke; ~ **consumption** Eigenverbrauch; ~ **financing** Eigenfinanzierung; ~ **insurer** Selbstversicherer; ~ **retail store** betriebseigener [Verkaufs]laden.
owner Besitzer, Eigentümer, Eigner, Inhaber *(entrepreneur)* Unternehmer, *(shipowner)* Reeder;
at ~'s risk auf eigene Gefahr;
beneficial ~ Nießbrauchberechtigter, Nutznießer; **builder ~** Bauherr; **equitable ~** wirtschaftlicher Eigentümer; **managing ~** Korrespondenzreeder; **part ~** Bruchteilseigentümer; **person not the ~** Nichteigentümer; **policy ~** Versicherungsnehmer; **previous ~** Vorbesitzer; **riparian ~** Flußanlieger; **trademark ~** Warenzeicheninhaber;
~ **and charterer** Reeder und Verfrachter;
~ **of a banking account** Bankkontoinhaber; ~ **of an automobile** Kraftfahrzeughalter; ~ **of a business** Geschäftsinhaber; ~ **of a patent** Patentinhaber; ~ **of a ship** Schiffsreeder;
~**-driver** Selbst-, Herrenfahrer; ~**-occupied dwelling** Eigentumswohnung.
ownership Eigentum, Eigentumsrecht, Besitz;
under new ~ unter neuer Leitung;
equitable ~ wirtschaftliches Eigentum; **industrial ~** Besitz der Produktionsmittel; **stock ~** Aktienbesitz;
to be under foreign ~ von ausländischem Kapital kontrolliert werden; **to retain ~ in one's policy** Begünstigter bleiben;

~ **distribution** Eigentumsverteilung; ~ **interest** Gesellschaftsanteil; **to exercise** ~ **powers** Eigentumsrechte ausüben; ~ **purchase** Eigentumserwerb; ~ **representation** Vertretung der Anteilseignerseite; ~ **representative** Vertreter der Anteilseigner; ~ **securities** Dividendenpapiere.

P

pace *(stock exchange, Br.)* Stellagegeschäft.

pace | *(v.)* **the general increase of living cost** preistreibend für die Lebenshaltungskosten sein; ~ **the market** Schrittmacher abgeben.

pack *(bale)* Ballen, *(bundle)* Bündel, *(parcel)* Paket, Pack[en], Verpackungseinheit;
loose or in ~**s** lose oder verpackt;
~ *(v.)* **out** auspacken, *(ship)* abladen;
~ **up one's wares** seine Waren in Ballen verpacken.

package *(advertising issue)* Werbematerial für Händler, *(bale)* Waren, Ballen, Kollo, Gebinde, *(bargaining)* Tarifabschluß, *(charge for packing)* Pakkerlohn, *(packing)* Verpacken, Verpackung, *(packing material)* Verpackung, Emballage, *(parcel, US)* Paket;
collect-on-delivery ~ *(US)* Nachnahmepaket; ~ **export** ~ *(US)* Ausfuhrkolli; **express** ~ *(US)* Eilpaket;
~ **of monetary relief** ganzes Bündel geldmarkterleichternder Maßnahmen;
~ *(v.)* verpacken, in Pakete packen;
to send a ~ **collect** *(US)* **(cash,** *Br.)* **on delivery** Paket als Nachnahme schicken;
~ **advertising** Versandwerbung; ~ **car** Waggon für Stückgutladungen; ~ **conveyor** [Versand]behälter; ~ **deal** Kopplungsgeschäft; ~ **freight** *(US)* Stückgutsendungen; ~ **offer** Kopplungsangebot; ~ **settlement** gebündeltes Übereinkommen; ~ **size** Paketgröße; ~ **tour** Pauschalreise.

packaged | **goods** abgepackte Ware; ~ **tour** *(US)* Pauschalreise.

packaging [Ver]packen, Verpackung;
fancy ~ Luxuspackung;
~ **costs** Verpackungskosten; ~ **material** *(US)* Verpackungsmaterial; ~ **slip** Packzettel.

packed | **for exportation by sea** seemäßig verpackt;
~ **parcels** Stückgutsendung.

packet Pack[en], *(Br.)* kleines Paket, Päckchen;
postal ~ *(Br.)* Postpaket; **registered** ~ *(Br.)* Einschreibepaket;
to earn a ~ Haufen Geld verdienen;
~ **boat** Postdampfer, Paketboot.

packing [Ver]packen, Einpacken, Verpackung;
~ **extra** Verpackung wird besonders berechnet;
without ~ netto;
defective ~ mangelhafte Verpackung; **nonreturnable** ~ Verpackung zum Wegwerfen; ~ **ordered** vorschriftsmäßige Verpackung; **seaproof (seaworthy)** ~ seetüchtige (seefeste) Verpackung, Seeverpackung;

~ **at cost** Verpackung zum Selbstkostenpreis;
~ **agent** Verpacker; ~ **case** Pappkarton, -kiste; ~ **company (house, plant)** *(US)* Konservenfabrik; ~ **credit** Versandbereitstellungskredit; ~ **industry** *(US)* Konservenindustry; ~ **list** Pack-, Versandliste; ~ **material** Verpackungsmaterial; ~ **plant** Verpackungsbetrieb; ~ **sheet** Packleinwand; ~ **slip** Packzettel.

page Seite, Blatt, *(print)* Kolumne;
advertising ~ Anzeigenseite;
~**s of advertising** Anzeigen-, Reklameteil;
one-time black-and-white ~ **rate** Anzeigenpreis für eine Schwarzweißseite.

paid bezahlt, *(on receipted bill)* Zahlung erhalten;
carriage ~ frachtfrei; **postage** ~ frei[gemacht];
to be ~ **out in cash by the postman** Geld durch Zahlkarte überwiesen erhalten; **to be** ~ **out of the town funds** auf der städtischen Lohnliste stehen;
~ **check** *(US)* **(cheque,** *Br.)* eingelöster Scheck; ~ **badly** ~ **situation** schlecht bezahlte Stellung; ~ **work** Lohnarbeit.

paid-in | **capital** eingezahltes Kapital, Einlagekapital;
~ **surplus** *(profit, US)* nicht entnommener Gewinn.

paid-up | **addition** *(life insurance)* Summenzuwachs [durch stehengelassene Prämie]; ~ **capital** voll eingezahltes Kapital, *(corporation)* eingezahltes Grundkapital; ~ **value** *(life insurance)* Umwandlungswert.

palm | *(v.)* **off old stock on a client** einem Stammkunden Lagerreste (Ladenhüter) aufschwatzen;
~ **grease** *(sl.)* Bestechungsgeld.

paltry debts Bagatellschulden.

pamphlet Flugblatt, -schrift, Streitschrift, Broschüre, Prospekt.

panel Forum, Gremium, *(health service, Br.)* Kassenarztliste;
on the ~ *(Br.)* als Kassenarzt zugelassen;
~ **of consumers** Verbraucherausschuß;
to be on the ~ auf der Liste stehen, *(health service, Br.)* als Kassenarzt zugelassen sein;
~ **envelope** Fensterbriefumschlag; ~ **patient** *(Br.)* Kassenpatient.

panic *(stock exchange)* Börsenpanik, Kurssturz;
~ **buying (purchases)** Angst-, Hortungskäufe.

paper Papier, Pappe, *(bill)* Wechsel, *(document)* Dokument, *(negotiable instrument)* Wertpapier;
accommodation ~ Gefälligkeitswechsel; **bank[able]** ~ Bankakzept; **brown** ~ Packpapier; **commodity** ~ Warenwechsel; **eligible** ~ *(US)* [zentral]bankfähiger Wechsel; **foreign** ~ Luftpostpapier; **photo-**

copying ~ Lichtpauspapier; **shipping** ~s Versand-
papiere; **trade** ~ Fachzeitschrift, Verbandsorgan,
(bill of exchange), Kunden-, Warenwechsel;
~s **of a business concern** Geschäftsunterlagen;
to have one's ~s **viséd** Visum erhalten;
~ **book** Formularbuch; ~ **clip** Büro-, Briefklam-
mer; ~ **credit** offener Wechselkredit; ~ **currency**
(circulation) Papiergeld-, Banknotenumlauf,
(money) Papiergeld, Banknoten, *(standard)* Pa-
pierwährung; ~ **fastener** Musterklammer; ~
money Papiergeld, Banknoten, Scheine; ~ **profits**
Papiergewinne, unrealisierte Gewinne; ~ **work**
Schreibarbeit.

par *(face value)* Pari, Nennwert;
above (below) ~ über (unter) Pari; **at** ~ **al pari,**
zum Nennwert; **on a** ~ *(Br.)* durchschnittlich;
issue ~ Emissionskurs; **nominal** ~ Nominalwert;
~ **of exchange** Wechselpari[tät], Parikurs;
~ **collection** Inkasso zum Pariwe:t; ~ **exchange**
rate *(International Monetary Fund)* Wechselkurs-
satz; ~ **line** *(of stock)* Aktienmittelwert; ~ **list** *(US)*
Pariliste, Paritätstabelle; ~ **value** Pari-, Nennwert,
Parität; **no** ~ **value stock** *(US)* nennwertlose Aktie,
Quotenaktie.

parcel *(bundle)* Bündel, Ballen, *(of goods)* Posten,
Partie, Menge, Ware, *(luggage)* Gepäck-
stück, *(package)*[Post]paket, Versandstück, *(piece
of land)* [Grundstücks]parzelle, Stück Land,
(packet, US) Päckchen;
express ~ Eilpaket; **insured** ~ *(Br.)* Wertpaket;
numbered ~ Wertpaket; **special-handling** ~ *(US)*
Schnellpaket;
~ **of goods** Warenpartie; ~ **of shares** Aktienpaket;
~ *(v.)* *(cut up into lots)* parzellieren;
~ **goods** Waren in Partien aufteilen;
~ **bill** Paketeingangszettel; ~ **cartage** *(Br.)* Paket-
zustellung; ~ **delivery company** Paketfahrtgesell-
schaft; ~ **delivery service** Paketzustellungsdienst.
~ **post** Paketpost.
parcel-post | **insurance** Paketversicherung; ~ **window**
Paketschalter.
parcel | **shipment** Muster-ohne-Wert-Sendung; ~
sticker Paketaufklebeadresse.
pare | *(v.)* **[down]** **expenditures** Kosteneinsparung
vornehmen; ~ **the work force** Belegschaft verringern, Belegschaftsabbau herbeiführen.
parent | **company (concern, corporation, establish-
ment)** Mutter-, Dach-, Holding-, Gründergesell-
schaft, Stammhaus; ~ **plant** Stammwerk.
pari passu *(creditors)* gleichberechtigt.
paring of employment Beschäftigungsrückgang.
parish *(Br.)* Gemeindebezirk;
poor-law ~ *(Br.)* Fürsorgebehörde, -verband, Sozialamt;
to be (go) on the ~ Sozialhilfe beziehen.
parity Parität, Parikurs, Pariwert;
at the ~ **of** zum Umrechnungskurs;
commercial ~ *(US)* Handelsparität; **gold** ~ Gold-
parität; **purchasing power** ~ Kaufkraftparität;
to be at a ~ pari stehen; **to crawl one's** ~ seine
Währungsparität langsam ändern;

~ **clause** Paritätsklausel; ~ **payments** Auszahlungen zum Parikurs; ~ **table** Paritätstabelle.
parking Parken;
low-cost night-time ~ billige Parkmöglichkeiten
während der Nachtzeit;
no-~ **area** Parkverbotsgebiet; ~ **bay** reservierter
Parkplatz; ~ **garage** *(US)* Hochhausgarage; **guaranteed** ~ **lot** *(US)* bewachter Parkplatz; ~ **meter**
Parkuhr; **[public]** ~ **place** [öffentlicher] Parkplatz;
~ **ticket** Parkzettel, *(US)* gebührenpflichtige Verwarnung wegen falschen Parkens.
part Teil, Stück, *(of a loan)* Tranche, Teilbetrag,
(share) Anteil, Bestandteil, Partie;
spare ~ Ersatzteil;
~ **of a business** Teilbetrieb;
~ *(v.)* **with one's money** mit dem Geld heraus-
rücken, sein Scheckbuch zücken;
to contribute in ~ **to the expense of production** Produktionskosten teilweise übernehmen; **to keep
back** ~ **of the price** Teil des Preises zurückhalten;
~ **delivery** Teillieferung; ~s **depot** Ersatzteillager;
~ **loads** Stückgüter; ~ **payment** Teil-, Raten-, Abschlagszahlung; ~ **payment on account** Akontozahlung eines Teilbetrages; ~ **time** verkürzte Arbeitszeit.
part-time nebenberuflich;
~ **employment** Kurzarbeit, Halbtags-, Teilzeitbeschäftigung; ~ **job** Halbtagsstelle; ~ **school** Fort-
bildungsschule; ~ **worker** Kurzarbeiter, Halbtagskraft.
part-timer Aushilfs-, Kurzarbeiter, Halbtagskraft.
partial | **amount** Teilbetrag; ~ **average** besondere
(einfache) Havarie; ~ **delivery** Teillieferung; ~
payment plan Abzahlungsplan; ~ **shipment** Teil-
sendung, -lieferung.
participate *(v.)* teilnehmen, gewinnbeteiligt sein;
~ **in a loss** am Verlust beteiligt sein.
participating | **bonds** *(US)* Vorzugsobligationen; ~
capital stock *(US)* mit zusätzlichen Dividendenberechtigung ausgestattetes Aktienkapital; ~ **certificate** Genußschein; ~ **contract** *(insurance law)*
Gewinnbeteiligungsvertrag; ~ **dividend** Vorzugsdividende.
participation Mitwirkung, Teilnahme, *(banking)*
Konsortialbeteiligung;
financial ~ Kapitalbeteiligung;
~ **in dividends** Dividendenberechtigung;
to take up a financial ~ sich kapitalmäßig beteiligen;
~ **account** Beteiligungs-, Konsortialkonto; ~ **share**
Anteilschein.
particular|s **of an account** einzelne Abrechnungs-
posten; ~s **of sale** *(auction sale)* detaillierte Ob-
jektbeschreibung;
~ **costs** direkte Kosten; ~ **custom** Ortsgebrauch; ~
partnership Gelegenheitsgesellschaft.
parties, contracting vertragschließende Parteien; ~
primarily liable *(on commercial papers)* unmittelbar Wechselverpflichtete.
partner Beteiligter, Teilnehmer, *(in partnership)* Teil-

haber, Gesellschafter, Kompagnon, Partner, Sozius;

active (acting) ~ geschäftsführender Teilhaber, Komplementär; **apparent** ~ Scheingesellschafter; **dormant** ~ stiller Teilhaber; **junior** ~ Juniorchef; **limited** ~ Kommanditist; **managing** ~ geschäftsführender Gesellschafter; **ordinary** ~ *(Br.)* unbeschränkt haftender Teilhaber; **outgoing** ~ ausscheidender Gesellschafter; **secret** ~ stiller Teilhaber; **senior** ~ Seniorchef; **silent (sleeping, Br.)** ~ stiller Gesellschafter; **trade** ~ Handelsvertragspartner; **unlimited** ~ haftender Gesellschafter; Komplimentär; persönlich;

to admit as ~ als Teilhaber aufnehmen; **to be personally liable as a** ~ als Gesellschafter persönlich haften; **to join a firm as** ~ Gesellschafter werden, als Teilhaber eintreten;

~**like stake** teilhaberähnliches Interesse.

partnership *(articles)* Gesellschaftsvertrag, *(business association)* [offene] Handels-, Personalgesellschaft;

with a view to ~ mit der Aussicht späterer Beteiligung;

commercial ~ Handelsgesellschaft; **dormant** ~ stille Teilhaberschaft; **general** ~ offene Handelsgesellschaft; **industrial** ~ *(US)* Gewinnbeteiligung der Arbeitnehmer; **limited** ~ Kommanditgesellschaft; **ordinary** ~ *(US)* offene Handelsgesellschaft; **secret** *(US)* **(silent, sleeping, Br.)** ~ stille Beteiligung; ~ **wanted** *(advertisement)* Teilhaber gesucht;

~ **in syndicate** Konsortialbeteiligung;

to be in ~ **with** s. o. mit jem. assoziiert sein; **to bring one's skill into a** ~ seine Arbeitskraft in eine Gesellschaft einbringen; **to dissolve a** ~ Gesellschaft auflösen; **to give** s. o. **a** ~ **in the business** jem. einen Geschäftsanteil überlassen; **to retire from a** ~ als Teilhaber ausscheiden;

~ **agreement** Gesellschafter-, Teilhabervertrag; ~ **articles** Gesellschaftssatzung; ~ **assets** Gesellschaftsvermögen; **within the scope of the** ~ **business** im Rahmen der Gesellschaftertätigkeit; ~ **creditor** Gesellschaftsgläubiger; ~ **debt** Gesellschaftsschuld; ~ **income** Firmeneinkommen; **limited** ~ **interest** Kommanditanteil; ~ **property** Firmenvermögen; ~ **purpose** Gesellschaftszweck.

party [Vertrags]partei, -partner, Kontrahent;
for account of a third ~ zugunsten eines Dritten; **accommodated** ~ Begünstigter; **innocent** ~ gutgläubiger Dritter; **working** ~ Arbeitsgruppe;
~ **entitled to a claim** Anspruchsberechtigter; ~ **liable for cost** Kostenschuldner;
third-~ **insurance** Haftpflichtversicherung; **third**-~ **risk** Regreßrisiko.

pass Personalausweis, Paß, Passierschein;
customhouse ~ Zollbegleitschein; **free** ~ *(railway)* Freifahrtschein; **international travelling** ~ Carnet;
~ *(v.)* **an account** Rechnung genehmigen; ~ **an item to the current account** *(Br.)* Posten verbuchen; ~ **along** *(price)* abwälzen; ~ **forged coins** Falschgeld

in Umlauf bringen; ~ **in conformity** gleichlautend buchen; ~ **the customs** zollamtlich abgefertigt werden; ~ **a customs entry** zur Verzollung deklarieren; ~ **to** s. **one's debit** j. belasten (debitieren); ~ **a dividend** *(US)* Dividende ausfallen lassen; ~ **off one's goods as those of another make** *(US)* seine Waren unter falschem Warenzeichen vertreiben; ~ **on rising cost without becoming incompetitive** gestiegene Kosten ohne Verschlechterung der Wettbewerbssituation weitergeben; ~ **by sale** *(title of goods)* beim Verkauf übergehen.

~ **check** *(US)* Passierschein; ~ **duty** Durchgangszoll.

passage *(Br.)* Durchgang, [Haus]flur, Korridor, *(channel)* Fahrwasser, Kanal, *(crossing)* Überfahrt, *(money)* Fahrgeld, -preis;
on his ~ **home** auf seiner Heimreise;
assisted ~ Reise-, Fahrgeldzuschuß;
to book one's ~ seine Schiffskarte (Flugkarte) lösen;
~ **broker** *(Br.)* Auswanderungsagent.

passbook *(Br.)* Konto-, Einzahlungsbuch.

passenger Passagier, Reisender, Fahrgast, *(airplane)* Fluggast;
cabin ~ Kajütenpassagier; **individual** ~ Einzelreisender; **public transit** ~ Benutzer öffentlicher Verkehrsmittel; **steerage** ~ Passagier dritter Klasse; **through** ~ Durchreisender; **tourist** ~ Passagier der Touristenklasse;
~ **agent** *(US)* Schalterbeamter; ~ **baggage** *(US)* Reisegepäck; ~ **car** *(US)* **(carriage, Br.)** Personen- [kraft]wagen; ~ **density** Verkehrsdichte; ~ **fare** Personenfahrpreis; ~ **goods** Passagiergut; ~ **list** Passagierliste; ~ **luggage** *(Br.)* Reisegepäck; ~ **rates** Personentarif; ~ **reservation** Flugreservierung; ~ **service charge** Fluggastgebühr; ~ **tariff** Personen-, Beförderungstarif; ~ **ticket** Fahrkarte, -schein, *(airplane)* Flugkarte, -schein, *(ship)* Schiffskarte; **commutator** ~ **traffic** *(US)* Zeitkartenverkehr; **by** ~ **train** als Eilgut.

passing | **counterfeit money** Inumlaufsetzen von Falschgeld; ~ **of property** Eigentumsübergang; ~ **of risk** *(conveyance)* Gefahrenübergang;
~ **off** Kennzeichenmißbrauch.

passive | **bond** unverzinsliche Schuldverschreibung; ~ **trade balance** *(US)* passive Handelsbilanz.

passport Reisepaß;
official ~ Amtspaß; **ship's** ~ Seepaß;
~ **inspection** Paßkontrolle.

paste-on label Aufklebeadresse.

patent Patent[urkunde], *(licence)* Konzession;
improvement ~ Vervollkommnungspatent; **interfering** ~ Kollisionspatent; **pioneer** ~ Stammpatent;
~ **for invention** Erfindungspatent;
to defeat the right to a ~ Patentanspruch zu Fall bringen; **to file an application for a** ~ **abroad** Auslandspatent anmelden; **to infringe a** ~ Patent verletzen; **to lodge an opposition to a** ~ Patentwiderspruch anmelden; **to work a** ~ Patent ausüben (verwerten);

~ *(a.)* gesetzlich geschützt, patentiert;
~ **article** Markenartikel; ~ **defect** offener Mangel;
~ **filing** Patentschrift; ~ **goods** Markenartikel; ~
infringement Patentverletzung; ~ **specification** Patentbeschreibung.

patented article Markenartikel.

patron Gönner, Mäzen, *(restaurant)* Stammgast, *(shop)* Stammkunde, Klient.

patronage Protektion, Gönnerschaft, Schirmherrschaft, *(shop)* Kundschaft, Besucherkreis, Klientele;
~ **discount** Treuerabatt; ~ **dividend** *(US)* Rabattmarke, Rückvergütung; ~ **system** Vetternwirtschaft.

patronize *(v.)* [als Kunde (häufig)] besuchen, *(favo(u)r)* begünstigen, protektionieren.

patronizer Gönner, Förderer, Wohltäter, *(client)* regelmäßiger Kunde, *(restaurant)* Stammgast.

pattern Muster[exemplar], Modell, Schema, *(sample)* Warenprobe;
according to ~ mustergetreu; **as per** ~ **enclosed** laut beiliegender Qualitätsprobe;
reference ~ Ausfallmuster;
~ **of consumption** Verbrauchsstruktur; ~ **of investment** Investitionsschema; ~ **of trade** Handelsstrom; ~ **of working** Arbeitsrezept;
to work from a ~ nacharbeiten;
~ **agreement** Modellabkommen, -tarif; ~ **card** Musterkarte; **by** ~ **post** als Muster ohne Wert; ~ **shop** Modellwerkstätte.

pauper relief Armenunterstützung.

pavilion *(exhibition)* Ausstellungszelt, -pavillon.

pawn Pfandgegenstand;
to lend on ~**s** Darlehen gegen Pfandbestellung gewähren; **to put in** ~ ins Leihhaus tragen, versetzen;
~ **money** Pfandgebühr; ~ **ticket** Pfandschein.

pawnbroker's business *(shop)* Pfandleihe, Leihhaus.

pawned stock *(Br.)* lombardierte Wertpapiere.

pawnshop Pfand-, Leihhaus, Pfandleihanstalt.

pay Entgelt, Entschädigung, *(reward)* Belohnung, *(salary)* Gehalt, Dotierung;
in the ~ **of** beschäftigt (angestellt) bei; **more to** ~ nicht genügend frankiert;
additional ~ Gehaltsaufbesserung; **back** ~ Lohnrückstand; **basic** ~ Grundgehalt, -lohn; **extra** ~ Zulage; **gross** ~ Bruttogehalt; **half** ~ Wartegeld; **leave** ~ Urlaubsgeld; **minimum call** ~ *(US)* Mindestlohn für nur stundenweise Tätigkeit; **overtime** ~ Überstundenzuschlag; **takehome** ~ Nettogehalt; ~ **in advance** Vorausschußzahlung; ~ **after stoppage** *(Br.)* Nettogehalt; ~ **before stoppage** *(Br.)* Bruttogehalt;
~ *(v.)* zahlen, Zahlung leisten, bezahlen *(reward)* belohnen, *(yield)* sich rentieren, Gewinn abwerfen;
~ **into an account** auf ein Konto einzahlen; ~ **on account** Anzahlung leisten; ~ **in advance (by anticipation)** pränumerando (vor Fälligkeit) zahlen; ~ **back** Schulden abdecken; ~ **the balance** Unterschiedsbetrag begleichen; ~ **beforehand** pränume-

rando zahlen; ~ **a bill** Zeche bezahlen; ~ **a [further] call on shares** Teilzahlung auf Aktien leisten; ~ **cash [down]** bar bezahlen; ~ **one's creditors in full** seine Gläubiger voll befriedigen; ~ **one's debt to the last penny** seine Schulden auf Heller und Pfennig bezahlen; ~ **a dividend out of capital** Dividende vom Kapital zahlen; ~ **on the dot** ganz pünktlich bezahlen; ~ **extra duty** Steuerzuschlag bezahlen; ~ **the full fare** vollen Fahrpreis zahlen; ~ **half the cost** Kosten hälftig tragen; ~ **due hono(u)r to a draft** Wechsel honorieren; ~ **a check** *(US)* **(cheque,** *Br.)* Scheck einlösen; ~ **in monthly instal(l)ments** monatliche Teilzahlung leisten.

pay into | an account auf ein Konto einzahlen; ~ **court** Geld bei Gericht hinterlegen.

pay off ausbezahlen, *(pay in full)* tilgen, [vollständig] ab[be]zahlen;
~ **bonds** Obligationen einlösen; ~ **one's creditors** seine Gläubiger voll befriedigen; ~ **the crew** Mannschaft abmustern; ~ **a loan** Darlehen zurückzahlen; ~ **a mortgage** Hypothek amortisieren.

pay | out s. o. j. abfinden; ~ **one's passage** seine Überfahrt bezahlen; ~ **the piper** Unkosten tragen; ~ **s. o. from (out of) one's own pocket** j. aus der eigenen Tasche bezahlen; ~ **promptly** pünktlich bezahlen; ~ **according to the quality of the work** Lohn nach der Leistung bemessen; ~ **on receipt** postnumerando zahlen; ~ **the rent annually in advance** Jahresmiete im voraus bezahlen; ~ **one's own shot** seinen Anteil an der Rechnung bezahlen; ~ **on the spot** [in] bar bezahlen; ~ **through the nose** sich neppen lassen; ~ **one's way** seinen Verbindlichkeiten nachkommen, genug zum Lebensunterhalt verdienen; **to be in s. one's** ~ bei jem. angestellt sein; **to be a good** ~ *(US)* gute Zahlungsmoral haben; **to keep s. o. in one's** ~ jem. Lohn und Brot geben;
~ **agreement** Lohnabkommen; ~ **bill** Gehalts-, Lohnliste, *(Br.)* Kassen-, Zahlungsanweisung; ~ **boost** Gehaltsanstieg; **upper** ~ **brackets** höhere Besoldungsgruppen; ~ **check** *(US)* Gehaltsscheck; ~ **clerk** Lohnbuchhalter; ~ **cut** Gehaltskürzung; ~ **desk** Kasse[nschalter]; ~ **differential** Lohnunterschied, -gefälle; ~ **envelope** Lohntüte; ~ **guest** Pensionär; ~ **hospital** Privatkrankenhaus; ~ **jump** starker Gehaltsanstieg; ~ **list** Lohnliste; ~ **negotiations** Lohnverhandlungen; ~ **off stage** Gewinnschwelle; ~ **package** gebündeltes Lohnangebot; ~ **packet** Lohntüte; ~ **phone** *(tel., US)* Münzfernsprecher; ~ **rise** *(Br.)* Gehaltserhöhung; ~ **scale** *(US)* Lohntabelle, Gehaltsskala; ~ **schedule** Lohntabelle; ~ **sheet** Gehälterliste; ~ **slip** Lohnzettel; **incentive** ~ **system** Akkordlohnsystem; ~ **voucher** *(Br.)* Zahlungs-, Kassenanweisung.

pay-as-you-earn (PAYE) *(Br.)* Lohnsteuereinbehaltung, -abzug.

payable zahlbar, *(due)* fällig, schuldig, *(profitable)* rentabel ertragreich;
~**s** *(US)* Verbindlichkeiten; Kreditoren;
accounts ~ *(balance sheet)* Passiva, Buchschulden;
bills ~ *(balance sheet)* Wechselverbindlichkeiten;

~ **at address of payee** am Wohnsitz des Empfängers zahlbar; ~ **to bearer** auf den Inhaber (überbringer) lautend; ~ **on demand** zahlbar bei Anforderung, *(bill)* bei Verlangen (bei Sicht) zahlbar; ~ **in monthly instal(l)ments** monatlich abzahlbar; ~ **to order** an Order (auf den Namen) lautend; ~ **on presentation** bei Vorlage (Sicht) zahlbar; ~ **upon submission of proof of identity** zahlbar gegen Vorlage des Personalausweises; ~ **against surrender of shipping documents** zahlbar gegen Aushändigung der Begleitpapiere;

to be ~ **on the 15th prox.** am 15. des nächsten Monats fällig sein; **to make a bill** ~ **to s. o.** Wechsel an jds. Order ausstellen; **to make an expense** ~ **out of public funds** Summe zur Zahlung aus der Staatskasse anweisen.

paybox *(Br.)* Kasse, Schalter.

payday *(stock exchange, Br.)* Lieferungs-, Zahltag.

payee Zahlungsempfänger;
~ **of a bill of exchange** Wechselnehmer, Remittent; ~ **of a check** *(US)* **(cheque,** *Br.)* Scheckempfänger.

payer, dilatory (slow, tardy) säumiger Zahler.

paying | **off** Abtragung, Tilgung, *(mortgage)* Amortisation; ~ **off the creditors** Gläubigerbefriedigung; ~ **out** Auszahlung, *(partner)* Abfindung; ~ *(a.)* einträglich, rentabel, gewinnabwerfend; **not** ~ unrentabel;
~ **agent** [Kupon]zahlstelle; **to put its relationship on a** ~ **basis** seine Beziehungen finanziell untermauern; ~ **boarder** Kostgänger; ~ **concern** rentables Unternehmen; ~ **cashier** Auszahlungsbeamter; ~ **counter** Auszahlungsschalter; ~ **guest** Feriengast, Pensionär.

paying-in | **book** *(Br.)* Einzahlungsbuch; ~ **form** Einzahlungsformular; ~ **slip** *(Br.)* Einzahlungsbeleg, -schein.

payload Lohnkostenanteil, *(plane, ship)* Nutzlast.

paymaster Kassierer für Auszahlungen.

payment *(bill)* Einlösung, *(creditor)* Befriedigung, *(of debt)* Begleichung, Abtragung, *(paying)* [Be]zahlung, Ein-, Auszahlung, Entrichtung;
in ~ **of our account** zum Ausgleich unserer Rechnung; **as** ~ **for your services** als Vergütung für Ihre Dienste; **in lieu of** ~ an Zahlungs Statt; **in default of** ~ mangels Zahlung; **on** ~ **of costs** unter Auferlegung der Kosten;
additional ~ Nachschuß, Zuzahlung; **advance** ~ **(anticipated,** *US)* Vorauszahlung; **benefit** ~ Unterstützungszahlung; **cash [down]** ~ Barzahlung; ~ **countermanded** Zahlung gesperrt; **deferred** ~ *(US)* Ratenzahlung; **ex gratia** ~ *(third-party insurance)* freiwillige Entschädigungsleistung; **final** ~ Rest-, Abschlußzahlung; **general** ~**s** allgemeiner Zahlungsverkehr; **loss** ~ Auszahlung der Schadenssumme; **lump-sum** ~ Pauschalzahlung; **overtime** ~**s** Überstundengelder; **parity** ~**s** [Aus]zahlungen zum Parikurs; **part** ~ Teil-, Raten-, Abschlagszahlung; **prompt** ~ sofortige Bezahlung; **revolving** ~**s** wiederkehrende Zahlungen; **stopped** ~ Zahlungseinstellung; **supplementary** ~ *(relief)* Zusatzunterstützung;

~ **on account** An-, Abschlags-, Akontozahlung, Anzahlungssumme; ~ **in advance (by anticipation)** Voraus-, Vorschuß-, Pränumerandozahlung; ~ **in arrears** Nachtrags-, Rückstandszahlung; ~**s due and from foreign countries** internationaler Zahlungsverkehr; ~ **into court** Hinterlegung bei Gericht; ~ **must be made upon delivery of the goods** Zahlung bei Eingang der Waren; ~ **of dividends** Dividendenzahlung, *(out of a bankrupt's estate)* Abschlagsverteilung; ~ **for hono(u)r** Ehreneintritt; ~ **during illness** Gehaltsfortzahlung im Krankheitsfall; ~ **by instal(l)ments** Ratenzahlung; ~ **of interest** Verzinsung; ~ **in kind** Sach-, Naturalleistung, -entlohnung, Sachbezüge; ~ **during leave** Urlaubsgeld; ~ **supra protest** Ehren-, Interventionszahlung; ~ **in ready money** Barzahlung; ~ **by result** Leistungs-, Stück-, Erfolgslohn; ~ **to suppliers** Lieferantenzahlungen; ~ **as you feel inclined** Zahlung nach Belieben;

to accept in ~ in Zahlung nehmen; **to anticipate** ~ Zahlung vor Fälligkeit leisten; **to be admitted in** ~ gesetzliches Zahlungsmittel sein; **to be behind with one's** ~**s** mit seinen Zahlungen im Rückstand sein; **to be slow in** ~ schlechte Zahlungsmoral haben; **to default on** ~ mit den Zahlungen in Verzug kommen; **to demand prompt** ~ auf sofortiger Bezahlung bestehen; **to evade** ~ sich einer Zahlungsverpflichtung entziehen; **to extend the time of** ~ Zahlungsfrist verlängern; **to keep international** ~**s in balance** Zahlungsbilanz im Gleichgewicht halten; **to make a subsequent** ~ nachbezahlen; **to meet the** ~**s** Ratenzahlungen einhalten; **to miss a** ~ **on one's home** mit einer Hypothekenrate in Verzug kommen; **to pass an account for** ~ Etattitel zur Zahlung anweisen; **to postpone** ~ Zahlung aufschieben; **to present a check** *(US)* **(cheque,** *Br.)* **for** ~ Scheck zur Einlösung vorlegen; **to require** ~ **on delivery** Zahlung Zug um Zug verlangen; **to stand surety for the** ~ **of a sum** für den Eingang eines Betrages bürgen; **to take in (as)** ~ an Zahlungs Statt annehmen;

~ **agreement** Zahlungsabkommen; ~ **balance** Zahlungsbilanz; ~**s deficit** Zahlungsbilanzdefizit; ~ **imbalance** Zahlungsgleichgewichtigkeit; ~ **order** Auszahlungsanweisung; ~ **period** Zahlungsfrist; ~ **sheet** *(Br.)* Lohn-, Gehälterliste.

payola *(sl.)* Bestechungs-, Schmiergelder.

payroll *(US)* Lohnliste, Gehälterliste;
on the ~ angestellt; **accrued** ~**s** *(balance sheet)* fällige Löhne; **to be off the** ~ *(US)* arbeitslos (entlassen) sein; **to be on the** ~ *(US)* auf der Lohnliste stehen; **to cut the** ~ **by 10 %** *(US)* zehnprozentige Lohnkürzung durchführen;
~ **account** *(US)* Lohnkonto; ~ **clearing account** *(US)* Lohnverrechnungskonto; ~ **clerk** *(US)* Lohnbuchhalter; ~ **deductions** *(US)* Lohnsteuerabzüge; ~ **employment** *(US)* lohnsteuerpflichtiger Beruf; ~ **period** *(US)* Gehaltsperiode; ~ **records** *(US)* Lohnsteuerunterlagen; ~ **sheet** *(US)* Lohn- und

Gehaltsliste; ~ **tax** *(US)* Lohnsummensteuer; ~ **voucher** *(US)* Lohnzettel.

peacetime economy Friedenswirtschaft.

peak Gipfel, Höhepunkt, *(el., traffic)* Hauptbelastung, Stoßzeit;
~ **of the demand** Spitzenbedarf; ~ **capitalism** Hochkapitalismus; ~ **demand** Spitzenbedarf; **off-~ flights** gering belegte Flugzeiten; ~ **hours** Stoßzeit, Hauptgeschäftszeit; **to reach** ~ **levels** *(stock exchange)* Höchstkurse erzielen; ~ **output** Produktionsmaximum; ~ **price** Höchstpreis, -kurs; **to handle the seasonal ~ problems** mit dem Problem der saisonalen Spitzenbelastung fertig werden; ~ **sales period** Hauptgeschäftszeit; ~ **season** Hochsaison; ~ **time** konjunktureller Wellenberg; ~ **value** Spitzen-, Höchstwert; ~ **wage** Spitzenlohn.

peculation [Amts]unterschlagung.

pecuniary geldlich, finanziell, pekuniär;
~ **aid** finanzielle Unterstützung; ~ **benefit** geldlicher Vorteil, Vermögensvorteil; ~ **compensation** Geldentschädigung; ~ **difficulty (embarrassment)** Geldverlegenheit, -sorgen; **for** ~ **gain** in gewinnsüchtiger Absicht; ~ **legacy** Geldvermächtnis; ~ **loss** Vermögensverlust; ~ **prejudice** Vermögensnachteil; ~ **present** Geldgeschenk; ~ **requirements** Geldbedarf; **for** ~ **reward** gegen Entgelt.

peddle *(v.)* hausieren, Wandergewerbe betreiben;
~ **through its branch offices** durch das eigene Filialnetz vertreiben; ~ **without a licence** ohne Gewerbeschein tätig sein.

peddler's licence Wandergewerbe-, Hausierschein.

peg *(stock exchange)* Kurs-, Marktunterstützung;
off the ~ von der Stange [gekauft];
~ *(v.) (price)* [Kurs] stützen, stabilisieren;
~ **the market** Kursstützungen durchführen; ~ **a price** Preis stützen; ~ **the value of the pound to the dollar** Kurs des Pfundes an den Dollar anhängen; ~ **the wages at** Löhne stoppen bei.

pegged price subventionierter Preis, *(stock exchange)* Stützkurs.

pegging *(market, price)* Kurs-, Preisstützung;
wage-~ efforts Lohnstabilisierungsbemühungen.

penalty *(for nonfulfilment of contract)* Vertrags-, Konventionalstrafe;
~ **envelope** *(US)* Briefumschlag frei durch Ablösung; ~ **postage** Strafporto.

pence rates *(Br.)* in Pennys notierte Devisenkurse.

pending risks laufende Versicherungsrisiken.

penny *(Br.)* Penny, *(fig.)* Heller, Kleinigkeit;
to the last ~ bis zum letzten Heller;
to cost a pretty ~ schönes Stück Geld kosten; **to look at every** ~ jeden Pfennig zweimal umdrehen; ~ **bank** *(Br.)* Sparkasse.

pennyworth wohlfeiler Kauf, gutes Geschäft.

pension Pension, Rente, Ruhegehalt, -geld, *(board and lodging)* Pension, Fremdenheim;
entitled (eligible) to a ~ pensionsberechtigt, -fähig, versorgungsberechtigt;
contributory ~ beitragspflichtige Pension; **life** ~

lebenslängliche Rente; **old-age** ~ *(Br.)* Alters-, Invalidenrente; **portable** ~ übertragbarer Pensionsanspruch; **retiring (retirement)** ~ Ruhegehalt; **survivor's** ~ Hinterbliebenenrente; **widow's** ~ Witwenrente;
~ *(v.)* pensionieren, in den Ruhestand versetzen, Ruhegehalt gewähren, *(v/i)* in Pension sein;
to apply for retirement (to be retired) on a ~ um seine Pensionierung einkommen; **to be awarded a** ~ Pension erhalten (beziehen); **to be entitled to a** ~ pensionsberechtigt sein; **to go on a** ~ in den Ruhestand treten; **to qualify for a** ~ Pensionsvoraussetzungen erfüllen; **to retire on a** ~ pensioniert werden, sich pensionieren lassen, in den Ruhestand treten; **to supplement one's** ~ zu seiner Pension hinzuverdienen;
~ **account** Pensionskasse; **Old-Age ~s Act** *(Br.)* Altersversorgungsgesetz; ~ **benefit** Pensionszahlung; ~ **costs** Pensionslasten; **Old-Age ~ Fund** Altersversorgungskasse; ~ **improvements** Verbesserung der Pensionsleistungen; **old-age** ~ **insurance** Altersversicherung; ~ **payment** Pensionszahlung, Versorgungsleistung; ~ **plan** Pensions-, Altersversorgungsplan, Pensionskasse;
company-financed ~ **plan** planbeitragsfreies Pensionssystem; **noncontributory** ~ **plan** planbeitragsfreie Pensionskasse; ~ **reserve** Rückstellung für Ruhegeldverpflichtungen; ~ **rights** Ruhegehaltsanspruch; **occupational** ~ **scheme** betriebliche Altersversorgung, Ruhegeldordnung; **to be a participant in a** ~ **scheme** pensionsberechtigt sein; ~ **scheme arrangment** Pensionsvereinbarung; **to make contributions to the** ~ **trust** Beiträge zur Pensionskasse leisten.

pensionable ruhegehalts-, pensionsfähig, -berechtigt;
~ **age** Pensionsalter; ~ **post** pensionsberechtigte Stellung.

pensionary *(Br.)* Pensionär, Ruhegehaltsempfänger;
~ **provisions** Pensionsbestimmungen.

pensioner Rentner, Ruhegehaltsempfänger;
old-age ~ Bezieher einer Altersversorgung.

pensioning warrant Pensionszusicherungsschein.

per | advance im voraus; ~ **advice** laut Abzeige; ~ **bearer** durch Überbringer; ~ **capita sales** *(turnover)* Pro-Kopf-Umsatz; ~ **rail** per Achse.

percents festverzinsliche Wertpapiere.

perceivable risk übersehbares Risiko.

percentage Prozent[satz], *(allowance)* Tantieme, *(commission)* Provision, *(of earned income)* Gewinnbeteiligung;
expressed as a ~ prozentual ausgedrückt;
contract ~ vertraglich ausgehandelter Provisionssatz; **director's** ~ Vorstandstantieme;
~ **of the incentive rate** Leistungslohnanteil; ~ **on profit** Gewinnanteil; ~ **of recovery** *(US)* Konkursquote; ~ **of sales** Umsatzprovision;
to allow a ~ **on all transactions** Umsatzprovision gewähren; **to get a good** ~ **in one's outlay** fast alle Spesen ersetzt bekommen;
~ **depletion** *(income tax)* für Substanzvermögen

zugelassener Abschreibungssatz; ~ **distribution** Tantiemeverteilung; **fixed ~ fee** fester Provisionssatz; **fixed ~ method** gleichmäßige Abschreibung vom Buchwert; ~ **premium** Anteilsprämie; ~ **tare** Bruttotara.

perfect | competition *(US)* uneingeschränkter Wettbewerb; ~ **usufruct** uneingeschränkter Nießbrauch.

performance | of contract Vertragserfüllung; ~ **of earnings** Gewinnentwicklung; ~ **in kind** Naturalleistung;
to give an uneven ~ *(stock exchange)* unruhiges Bild abgeben; **to turn in another strong** ~ *(stock exchange)* erneuten Auftrieb erhalten;
~ **appraisal** Leistungsbeurteilung; ~ **bond** *(US)* Submissions-, Bietungsgarantie; ~ **bonus** Leistungsprämie; ~ **budget** Istetat; ~ **chart** Leistungsdiagramm; ~ **rating** Leistungsbeurteilung.

performer *(stock exchange)* Erfolgsaktie.

peril Risiko, Gefahr;
at one's (your) ~ auf eigene (Ihre) Gefahr; **excepted ~s** Freizeichnung für Schäden; **marine** ~ Seetransportgefahr;
excepted ~ clause Freizeichnungsklausel.

period *(break)* Pause, Absatz, *(portion of time)* Laufzeit, Zeit[abschnitt], Zeitraum, Periode;
accounting ~ Rechnungsabschnitt; **busy** ~ Hauptgeschäftsstunden; **credit** ~ Laufzeit eines Kredits; **fiscal** ~ Steuerabschnitt; **limitation** ~ Verjährungsfrist; **operating** ~ Betriebsdauer; **subscription** ~ Zeichnungsfrist; **waiting** ~ *(insurance)* Karenzzeit; ~ **of vocational (professional) adjustment** Einarbeitungszeit; ~ **of apprenticeship** Lehr-, Lehrlingszeit; ~ **of assessment** Veranlagungszeitraum; ~ **for claims** Mängelrügefrist; ~ **of depression** Depressionsphase; **minimum** ~ **of employment** [Mindest]- beschäftigungszeit; ~ **of exchange** Umtauschfrist; ~ **of guarantee** Garantiezeit; ~ **of notice** Kündigungsfrist; ~ **to run** Laufzeit; ~ **of proposed stay** beabsichtigte Aufenthaltsdauer; ~ **of warranty** Gewährleistungsfrist.

periodic | audit laufend durchgeführte Revision; ~ **charges (cost, expense)** wiederkehrende Aufwendungen.

periodical Magazin, [periodische] Zeitschrift;
~ **advertising** Zeitschriftenwerbung; ~ **payments** wiederkehrende Zahlungen.

perishable | cargo verderbliche Ladung; ~ **commodities** Verbrauchsgüter; ~ **goods** leicht verderbliche Waren;.

permanent | abode ständiger Aufenthaltsort; ~ **appointment (assignment)** feste Anstellung, Dauerstellung; ~ **assets** *(accounting)* Anlagevermögen; ~ **disability** Vollinvalidität; ~ **employee** Festangestellter; ~ **life insurance** jährlich kündbare Lebensversicherungspolice; ~ **portfolio** *(securities)* Daueranlage.

permission Erlaubnis, Genehmigung;
without ~ unbefugt;
owner's ~ Erlaubnis des Eigentümers;

~ **by the authorities** behördliche Genehmigung; ~ **to reside** Aufenthaltsgenehmigung; ~ **to transact business** Gewerbegenehmigung.

permissive | provision Kannvorschrift; ~ **wage-adjustment clause** genehmigte Lebenshaltungskostenklausel; ~ **waste** Vernachlässigung notwendiger Gebäudereparaturen.

permit Erlaubnis[schein], Genehmigung, *(customs)* Zollgeleit-, Zollfreischein, *(licence, Br.)* Lizenz, Zulassung, Konzession;
building ~ *(US)* Baubewilligung; **exit** ~ Ausreisegenehmigung; **export** ~ Ausfuhrgenehmigung; **labo(u)r** ~ Arbeitsgenehmigung; **special** ~ Sondergenehmigung;
~ **for home consumption** Zollfreischein für im Lande verbleibende Waren; ~ **of transit** Transitschein.

perpetual | annuity ewige Rente; ~ **inventory** *(US)* buchmäßig laufend geführtes Inventar, Buchinventur.

perquisite Verdienst, Einkommen, *(gratuity)* Sondervergütung.

person | domiciled here Wohnsitzberechtigter; ~ **insured** Versicherter; ~ **s interested** Interessenten;
~ **of full age and capacity** Volljähriger und Geschäftsfähiger; ~ **of private (independent) means** Rentner, finanziell Unabhängiger; ~ **of ordinary prudence** normaler Durchschnittsmensch.

personal *(a.)* *(private)* privat, vertraulich, *(claim)* obligatorisch, *(property)* persönlich, beweglich;
~ **accident insurance** Unfallversicherung; ~ **account** Kundenkonto, *(private account)* Privatkonto; ~ **allowance** *(income tax, Br.)* persönlicher Steuerfreibetrag; ~ **articles** persönliche Gebrauchsartikel; ~ **baggage** *(US)* Handgepäck; ~ **consumption** privater Verbrauch; ~ **contribution to social insurance** *(US)* Arbeitnehmerbeitrag zur Sozialversicherung; ~ **credit** Personalkredit; ~ **data and testimonials** Bewerbungsunterlagen; ~ **earnings** ~ Einkünfte aus freiberuflicher Tätigkeit; ~ **exemption** *(taxation, US)* persönlicher Freibetrag; ~ **files** Handakten; ~ **finance company** Kundenkreditgesellschaft; ~ **income tax** *(US)* Einkommensteuer; ~ **liability insurance** Privathaftpflichtversicherung; ~ **relief** *(Br.)* persönlicher Freibetrag; ~ **service business** *(US)* Dienstleistungsgewerbe; ~ **use** Eigenbedarf.

personnel Personal, Belegschaft, *(ship)* Besatzung, Mannschaft;
sales ~ Verkaufspersonal; **skilled** ~ Fachkräfte.
~ **budget** Personalausgaben; ~ **chart** Stellenbesetzungsplan; ~ **data** Personalangaben; ~ **files (folders)** Personalakten; ~ **management** Personalführung; ~ **mobility** Belegschaftsfluktuation; ~ **performance** betriebliche Leistungen; ~ **records** Personalunterlagen, -akten; ~ **shakeup** personelle Umbesetzungen; ~ **transfer** innerbetriebliche Umsetzungen.

persuasive advertising stark überzogene Werbung.

petition [schriftliches] Gesuch, Antrag, Eingabe;
creditor's ~ Konkurseröffnungsantrag eines Gläubigers;

~ **for arrangement** Vergleichsantrag; ~ **for discharge** [of a bankrupt] *(US)* Antrag auf Aufhebung des Konkursverfahrens;
to file an involuntary ~ Zwangskonkurs beantragen.
petitioning creditor Konkursgläubiger.
petrol *(Br.)* Benzin, Sprit, Treibstoff;
~ **allowance** Benzinzuteilung; ~ **consumption** Benzinverbrauch; ~ **station** Tankstelle.
petty | **amounts** geringfügige Beträge; ~ **average** Vergütung für kleinere Reiseunkosten eines Schiffes; ~ **cash** Portokasse; ~ **debts** Läpper-, Bagatellschulden; ~ **journal** Kladde; ~ **patent** *(US)* Gebrauchsmuster; ~ **wares** Kurzwaren.
phase Stadium, Phase, Etappe;
~ *(v.)* **out low-margin products** Erzeugnisse mit niedriger Gewinnspanne produktionsmäßig auslaufen lassen.
photostatic copy *(US)* Fotokopie.
physical | **assets** Sachanlagevermögen; ~ **depreciation** Gebrauchsabschreibung; ~ **inventory** tatsächlich aufgenommenes Inventar; ~ **turnover** mengenmäßiger Umsatz.
pick *(v.)* **up** *(market)* sich erholen;
~ **a bargain** gutes Geschäft machen; ~ **bargains** *(stock exchange)* Gewinne mitnehmen; ~ **for a song** *(sl.)* spottbillig kaufen.
picket Streikposten, -wache;
~ *(v.)* Streikposten stehen;
to cross the ~ **line** sich als Streikbrecher betätigen.
picketing Aufstellen von Streikposten;
secondary ~ *(US)* betriebsfremde Streikposten.
pickup *(bargain)* Gelegenheitskauf, *(small commercial body)* Liefer-, Kleinlastwagen;
~ **in employment** Beschäftigungsanstieg; ~ **in orders** Auftragszunahme;
~ **and delivery service** Abhol- und Zustelldienst; ~ **truck** *(US)* schneller Lkw, Abholfahrzeug.
piece | **of business** Geschäftsangelegenheit; ~ **of land** Stück Land, Parzelle; ~ **of luggage** *(Br.)* Gepäckstück;
to be paid by the ~ Stücklohn erhalten;
~ **broker** Restehändler; ~ **cost** Stückkosten; ~ **goods** Meter-, Schnittware; ~ **labo(u)r** Stück-, Akkordarbeit; ~ **price** Stückpreis; ~**-price system** Akkordsystem, Stücklohnverfahren.
piece rate Stücklohn-, Akkordlohnsatz;
~ **earnings** Akkordverdienst; ~ **system** Prämienlohnsystem; ~ **work** Akkordarbeit.
piecemeal stückweise, Stück für Stück;
to buy only ~ nur stückweise einkaufen;
~ **contracts** Einzelaufträge.
piecework Akkord-, Gedingearbeit;
high ~ progressiver Leistungslohn;
to put s. o. on ~ j. im Akkord beschäftigen;
~ **bonus** Akkordzuschlag; ~ **pay** Akkord-, Stücklohn; ~ **rate** Akkordrichtsatz; ~ **system** Akkordlohnsystem.
pieceworker Akkord-, Stückarbeiter.
pier Hafendamm, Landungsplatz, Mole, Kai.

pigeonhole [Brief]fach, Ablagefach, Zettelkasten.
piggyback [rail]service Huckepackverkehr.
piggly-wiggly-store *(US)* Lebensmittelautomat.
pilot Flugzeugführer, Pilot, Flieger, *(ship)* Lotse;
compulsory ~ Zwangslotse;
~ **boat** Lotsenboot; ~ **flag** Lotsenflagge; ~ **lot** Null-, Versuchsserie; ~ **production** Versuchsproduktion.
pin money *(daughter)* Nadelgeld, *(outworker)* Heimarbeiterlohn.
pinch *(stock exchange)* plötzliche Kurssteigerung;
money ~ zeitweilige Geldknappheit;
~ **on profits** Erlösdruck.
pinched im Druck, in Bedrängnis;
to be ~ darben, *(stock exchange)* plötzlich zu Deckungskäufen gezwugen sein;
~ **circumstances** beschränkte Verhältnisse.
pioneer patent Stammpatent.
pirate *(v.)* **designs** Gebrauchsmuster kopieren.
pithead price Zechen-, Grubenpreis.
pitch *(street trade, Br.)* Verkaufsstelle, Stand.
privotal industry Schlüsselindustrie.
place Ort, Ortschaft, Platz, Stelle, *(employment)* [An]stellung, Amt;
out of a ~ stellenlos;
confidential ~ Vertrauensstellung; **permanent** ~ Dauerstellung; **shipping** ~ Versandort;
~ **of abode** Wohnsitz; ~ **of business** Geschäftssitz, gewerbliche Niederlassung; ~ **of delivery** Lieferungs-, Erfüllungsort; ~ **of destination** Bestimmungsort; ~ **of entry** Zollhafen; ~ **of issue** Ausstellungsort; ~ **of origin** Ursprungsort; ~ **of shipment** [Ver]ladestelle; ~ **of transshipment** Umschlagplatz; ~ **of work** Arbeitsplatz;
~ *(v.)* *(invest)* investieren, Investition vornehmen, *(loan)* placieren, unterbringen;
~ **to s. one's account** jem. in Rechnung stellen; **to new account** auf neue Rechnung vortragen; ~ **a contract** Auftrag vergeben; ~ **on file** zu den Akten nehmen; ~ **goods** Ware absetzen; ~ **an issue** Emission unterbringen; ~ **pressure on the money market** Druck auf dem Geldmarkt verursachen; ~ **a sum at the disposal of s. o.** jem. einen Geldbetrag zur Verfügung stellen; ~ **surplus stock** überschüssige Waren loswerden;
to book a ~ sich einen Platz reservieren lassen;
to go ~**s and see things** Touristenreise machen;
~ **hunter** Stellenjäger.
placemanship *(Br.)* Futterkrippenwirtschaft.
placement Unterbringung *(employees, US)* Arbeitseinsatz, *(investment)* Investition, Anlage, *(securities, US)* Placierung;
~ **of funds** Kapitalverwendung;
~ **agency** *(US)* Stellenvermittlung; ~ **bureau** *(US)* Arbeitseinsatzbüro, Berufsberatungsstelle; ~ **consulter** *(US)* Berufsberater; ~ **service** *(US)* Berufsberatungsdienst.
placing | **of an advertisement (advertising)** Anzeigenaufgabe, -placierung; ~ **of a loan** Anleiheplacierung; ~ **of an order** Auftragserteilung.

plain dealing lauteres (reelles) Geschäftsgebaren.

plan *(arrangement)* Anordnung, System, Plan;
financing ~ Finanzierungsplan; **investment** ~ Investitionsvorhaben;
~ **of arrangement** Vergleichsvorschlag; ~ **or readjustment** Sanierungsprogramm; ~ **of redemption** Amortisationsplan; ~ **to encourage thrift** Sparanreizsystem; ~ **for zoning** Flächennutzungsplan.

plane, chartered Charterflugzeug;
to allow a ~ **into revenue service** Flugzeug für Linienverkehr freigeben;
~ **reservation** Flugplatzreservierung.

planned dirigistisch;
~ **economy** Planwirtschaft; ~ **obsolescence** geplante Veralterung.

planning Planung, Bewirtschaftung;
private ~ industrielle Zukunftsplanung;
~ **agency** Planungsbehörde; ~ **measures** dirigistische Maßnahmen; ~ **Minister** *(Br.)* Planungsminister; **to pass the** ~ **stage** über das Entwurfsstadium hinausgelangen.

plant [Werk-, Betriebs-, Fabrik]anlage, Fabrik;
fully automated ~ vollautomatisiertes Werk; **competing** ~ Konkurrenzbetrieb; **newly established** ~ neu in Betrieb genommene Anlage; **government-operated** ~ Staatsbetrieb; **limited-capacity** ~ Betrieb mit begrenzter Kapazität; **manufacturing** ~ Fabrikationsbetrieb; **model** ~ Musterbetrieb;
~ **and equipment** *(balance sheet)* Maschinen und Einrichtungen; ~ **in process of conversion** Umstellungsbetrieb; ~ **working with a deficit** Verlustbetrieb;
to move a ~ **to another locality** Betriebsverlagerung durchführen; **to run a** ~ Betrieb leiten;
~ **account** Anlagekonto; ~ **addition** Betriebserweiterung; ~ **assets** Betriebsanlagewerte; ~ **blindness** Betriebsblindheit; **idle** ~ **capacity** betriebliche Reservekapazität; ~ **costs** Betriebsunkosten; ~ **efficiency** betriebliche Leistungsfähigkeit; ~ **gate** Fabriktor; ~ **improvements** Betriebsverbesserungen; ~ **inventory** Betriebsinventar; ~ **layout** betriebliche Anlagenplanung, Betriebsanlage; ~ **ledger** Betriebshauptbuch; ~ **location** Fabriklage, Betriebsbelegenheit; ~ **management** *(US)* Betriebsführung, Werksleitung; ~ **manager** *(US)* Werk-, Betriebsleiter; ~ **premises** Fabrikgebäude; ~ **processing** Werksveredelung; ~ **program(me)** Produktionsprogramm; ~ **rationalization** Betriebsrationalisierung; ~ **shutdown** Betriebsschießung, -einstellung; ~ **site** Betriebsgrundstück, Fabrikgelände; ~ **tour** Betriebsbesichtigung; ~ **utilization** Ausnutzung der Betriebskapazität; ~ **value** Betriebswert; ~-**wide burden rate** Gemeinkostenzuschlag.

platform Bahnsteig;
unloading ~ Abladeplatz;
~ **car** *(US)* **(carriage,** *Br.*) offener Güterwagen; ~ **ticket** Bahnsteigkarte.

play *(v.)* **away a fortune** Vermögen verspielen.

pleasure Vergnügen, *(discretion)* Gutdünken;

to serve at the ~ **of the board** an Vorstansweisungen gebunden sein;
~ **trip (travel)** Vergnügungsreise, Ausflug.

pledge Pfand[gegenstand], Faustpfand;
~ **of personal property** Verpfändung beweglichen Eigentums; ~ **of stocks** Aktienverpfändung;
~ *(v.)* versetzen, verpfänden, Pfand bestellen;
~ **securities with a bank for payment of a loan** Effekten bei einer Bank lombardieren lassen;
to take out of ~ Pfand auslösen;

pledged | as security sicherheitsübereignet;
~ **article** Pfandobjekt; ~ **assets** Pfandsicherheit; ~ **merchandise** sicherungsübereignete Waren; **to levy against the** ~ **property** Vollstreckung in den Pfandgegenstand betreiben; ~ **securities** lombardierte Effekten.

pledging of securities Wertpapierlombardierung.

plot Grundstück, Parzelle, Bauplatz;
~ **of unbuilt ground** unbebautes Grundstück.

plough, *(v.)* **plow** *(US)* **back the profits of a business** Geschäftsgewinn sofort wieder anlegen.

plum *(melon, US sl.)* Gratisaktie.

plunged into debt völlig verschuldet.

plus Gewinnfaktor;
to be in the $ 3 000 ~ **range** in der Preislage von 3 000 Dollars aufwärts liegen; ~ **value** Mehrbetrag, Wertzuwachs.

poach *(v.)* **employees** Angestellte abwerben.

pocket Tasche, *(for money)* Geldbeutel, -sack;
out of one's own ~ aus der eigenen Tasche;
~ *(v.)* sich unrechtmäßig aneignen, einheimsen;
to be in ~ gut bei Kasse sein; **to be out of** ~ Verluste haben; **to line one's** ~s sich bereichern;
~ **agreement** Nebenabrede; **out-of-**~ **expenses** bare Auslagen, Spesen.

point Punkt, Stelle, Ort, *(agenda)* Punkt, Einzel-, Teilfrage, *(ration coupon)* Punkt;
bullion ~ Goldpunkt; **gold** ~ Goldausfuhrpunkt; **unloading** ~ Entladestelle;
turning ~ **in s. o.'s career** Wendepunkt in jds. Laufbahn; ~ **of destination** Bestimmungsort; ~ **of entry** Zoll-, Eingangshafen; ~**s from letters** Auszüge aus Leserbriefen; ~ **of loading** Verladeort; ~ **of origin** *(US)* Herkunfts-, Ursprungsort;
to be on ~**s** bewirtschaftet sein; **to decline 5** ~**s um 5** Punkte nachgeben;
~-**of-purchase display** Verkaufsförderungsmittel;
~ **system** *(job evaluation)* Punktbewertungssystem.

policy Methode, Verfahren, Taktik, Politik, *(investment fund)* Geschäftspolitik, *(lotto, US)* Zahlenlotto, *(insurance)* Versicherungsschein, [-]police;
additional ~ Nachtrags-, Zusatzpolice; **all-risks** ~ *(car)* Universalversicherungspolice; **blank** ~ Policenformular; **blanket** ~ *(US)* Pauschalpolice; **buy-American** ~ Kaufbindungspolitik; **convertible term** ~ umwandelbare Lebensversicherungspolice; **depreciation** ~ Abschreibungspolitik; **economic** ~ Wirtschaftspolitik; **endowment assurance** ~ *(Br.)* abgekürzte Lebensversicherungspolice; **expired** ~ abgelaufene Versicherungspolice; **freight**

~ Frachtpolice; **inflationary** ~ Inflationspolitik; **insurance** ~ Versicherungspolice; **labo(u)r** ~ Arbeitsmarktpolitik; **lasped** ~ verfallene Police; **liability** ~ Haftpflichtversicherungspolice; **life** ~ Lebensversicherungspolice; **marine insurance** ~ Seeversicherungspolice; **mixed** ~ *(Br.)* Zeit- und Reiseversicherung; **monetary** ~ Währungspolitik; **ordinary life** ~ Lebensversicherungspolice mit gleichbleibenden Prämien; **straight (whole) life** ~ Versicherungspolice auf den Todesfall; **nonassessable** ~ *(US)* nachschußfreie Versicherungspolice; **nonparticipating** ~ nicht gewinnberechtigte Police; **open** ~ *(Br.)* Police ohne Wertangabe; **fully paid-up** ~ prämienfreie Versicherung; **limited-payment** ~ Versicherung mit begrenzter Prämienzahlung; **rental value** ~ Mietausfallversicherung; **single** ~ Einzelpolice; **stock [-rate]** ~ Lebensversicherungspolice ohne Gewinnbeteiligung; **supplementary** ~ Zusatzpolice; **survivorship annuity** ~ Rentenversicherungspolice zugunsten eines überlebenden Dritten; **time** ~ Zeitpolice; **tourist floater** ~ Reisegepäckversicherungspolice; **valued** ~ Police mit Wertangabe; **wage-freezing price-lowering** ~ Lohnstopp- und Preissenkungspolitik; **whole life** ~ Lebensversicherungspolice auf den Todesfall; ~ **of active ease** Liquiditätspolitik; ~ **of marine insurance** Seeversicherungspolice; **to cancel a** ~ Versicherung aufheben; **to lend money on a** ~ Police beleihen; **to take out a** ~ sich versichern lassen; ~ **book** Policenregister; ~ **broker** Versicherungsmakler; ~ **drafting** Policenausfertigung; ~ **duty** Versicherungssteuer; ~ **form** Policenformular; ~ **meeting** geschäftspolitische Tagung; ~ **number** Policennummer; ~ **owner** Versicherungsnehmer; ~ **playing** *(US)* Lottospielen; ~ **proof of interest** *(marine insurance)* als Nachweis des Anspruchs genügt die Police; ~ **shop** *(US)* Lottoannahmestelle; ~ **slip** *(US)* Wettkarte, Lottoschein; ~ **year** Versicherungsjahr.

policyholder Versicherungsnehmer.

pollution | **of the air** Luftverschmutzung; **to meet** ~ **standards** den Anforderungen des Umweltschutzes entsprechen.

pool Interessengemeinschaft, -verband, *(arrangement between companies)* Kartell, Ring, Pool, Gewinngemeinschaft; ~s Lotto, *(shipping business)* Gewinnabrechnungsgemeinschaften; **money** ~ *(US)* in Krisenzeiten operierende Bankengruppe; **gross-money** ~ Gewinnbeteiligungskartell; ~ **purchasing** ~ Einkaufsgemeinschaft; **typing** ~ Gemeinschaftssekretariat; ~ **of liquidity** Liquiditätsfonds; ~ *(v.)* zusammenwerfen, *(coordinate)* zusammenfassen, koordinieren, *(join a pool)* einer Interessengemeinschaft unterwerfen, Kartell bilden, kartellieren, *(share profits)* [Gewinne] teilen, poolen;

~ **expenses** sich an den Kosten schlüsselmäßig beteiligen, Unkosten aufschlüsseln; ~ **orders** Aufträge kartellisieren; ~ **patents** Patente zusammenwerfen; **to win a fortune from the** ~s beim Toto ein Vermögen machen; ℒ **Betting Act** Lottogesetz; ~ **filler** Lottospieler.

pooling | **of accounts** Kontenzusammenlegung; ~ **of freights** *(US)* Frachtenverrechnungsabkommen; ~ **of interests** Interessenvereinigung; ~ **of risks** Risikoverteilung [innerhalb eines Unternehmens]; ~ **agreement (contract)** Poolvertrag, Kartellabkommen.

poor ärmlich, besitzlos, *(debtor)* arm, mittellos, *(profit)* dürftig, schlecht; ~ **debtor** pfändungsfreier Schuldner; ~ **debtor's oath** *(US)* Offenbarungseid; ~ **-law relief** öffentliche Fürsorge; ~ **market** schleppender Warenabsatz; ~ **quality** schlechte Qualität.

pop, in *(Br. sl.)* versetzt, auf der Pfandleihe; ~**-and-mom shop** Tante Emma Laden.

popular | **article** zugkräftiger Artikel; ~ **price** volkstümlicher Preis.

popularity poll *(US)* Beliebtheitsumfrage.

population Bevölkerung, Einwohnerzahl; **working-class** ~ werktätige Bevölkerung; ~ **redistribution** Umverteilung der Bevölkerung; ~ **shift** Bevölkerungsverschiebung.

port [See]hafen, Flughafen, *(opening in a ship)* Ladeluke, -pforte; **bonded** ~ Hafen mit Zollager; **discharging** ~ Entladehafen; **free** ~ Freihafen; **loading** ~ Verladehafen; **maritime** ~ Seehafen; ~ **of call** Anlauf-, Anlegehafen, *(airplane)* Anflughafen; ~ **of clearance** Abgangshafen; ~ **of departure** Abgangs-, Abfahrtshafen, *(airplane)* Abflughafen; ~ **of destination** Bestimmungshafen; ~ **of distress** Nothafen; ~ **of embarkation** Ausgangshafen; ~ **of entry** Zollabfertigungshafen; ~ **of sailing** Abgangshafen; ~ **of transit** Transithafen; ~ **of transshipment** Umschlaghafen; **to call at a** ~ Hafen anlaufen, *(airplane)* Flughafen anfliegen; **to clear a** ~ aus einem Hafen auslaufen; **to close a** ~ Hafen sperren; ~ **administration** Hafenverwaltung; ~ **bill of lading** Hafenkonnossement; ~ **charges (dues)** Hafengebühren; ~ **equalization** Frachtbasis; ~ **facilities** Hafenanlagen; ~ **regulations** Hafenordnung; ~ **warden** *(US)* Hafenaufseher, -meister.

portable pension übertragbarer Pensionsanspruch.

portfolio Bestand, Portefeuille, *(minister)* Geschäftsbereich, Portefeuille, Ressort; **insurance** ~ Versicherungsbestand; **investment** ~ Wertpapierportefeuille; ~ **of bills** Wechselportefeuille, -bestand; **to resign one's** ~ sein Ministerium abgeben; ~ **bill** Portefeuillewechsel; ~ **description** *(investment fund)* Wertpapieraufstellung; ~ **manager** Vermögens-, Effektenverwalter; ~ **switch** Effektenaustausch.

portion Teil, Stück, *(dowry)* Mitgift, Heiratsgut, Aussteuer, *(inheritance)* Erb[an]teil, *(share)* Anteil, Quote;

aggressive ~ *(investment trust, US)* risikoreichere Effektenbestand; **defensive** ~ *(investment trust, US)* risikoärmere Effektenanlage; **legal** ~ Pflichtteil;

unused ~ **of credit** offener Kreditbetrag; **unsold** ~ **of an issue** unverkaufte Emissionsspitze; ~ **policy** Aussteuerpolice.

position *(advertising)* Placierung, *(airplane)* Standort, *(financial condition)* finanzielle Verfassung, *(employment)* Anstellung, Stelle, Stellung, Platz, *(ship)* Besteck, Position, Schiffsort, *(tariff)* Tarifnummer;

advanced ~ gehobene [Dienst]stellung; **balance-of-payments** ~ Zahlungsbilanzposition; **bear** ~ Baisseposition; **bull** ~ Hausseposition; **cash** ~ Kassenstand; ~ **closed** *(post office)* hier keine Abfertigung; **current** ~ *(bank)* Liquiditätslage; **fiduciary** ~ Vertrauensstellung; **financial** ~ Vermögenslage; **high-paying** ~ hochbezahlte Stellung; **managerial** ~ leitende Stellung; ~ **offered** Stellenangebot; **preferred** ~ *(advertising)* Sonderplacierung; **quick** ~ Liquidität eines Unternehmens; **senior** ~ leitende Stellung; **short** ~ Baisseposition; **well-paid** ~ gut dotierte Stellung; ~ **of an authority** verantwortungsvolle stellung; **customer's** ~ **at the bank** Kundenbeurteilung durch die Bank; ~ **of influence** einflußreiche Position; ~ **with good prospects** ausbaufähige Stellung; **to apply for a** ~ sich um eine Stellung bewerben; **to be in an established** ~ in Amt und Würden sein; **to build up a sizable** ~ **in stocks** *(US)* beträchtliches Aktienpaket zusammenkaufen; **to change one's** ~ seine Stellung wechseln; **to find the** ~ *(ship)* orten; **to fix a ship's** ~ Position eines Schiffes bestimmen; **to hold a high-level** ~ führende Stellung einnehmen; **to maintain a** ~ **in sound stocks** auf guten Werten sitzen bleiben; **to work o. s. into a good** ~ sich hocharbeiten;

~ **bookkeeping** *(securities market)* Liste der eingegangenen Verpflichtungen; ~ **charge** Placierungsaufschlag.

possession Sachherrschaft, Besitz[tum];

constructive ~ mittelbarer Besitz; **physical** ~ unmittelbarer Besitz; **vacant** ~ bezugsfertiges Haus; **to be let with immediate** ~ bezugsfertig zu vermieten; **to take** ~ **of an estate** Erbschaft antreten; ~ **proceedings** *(Br.)* Räumungsverfahren.

post Amt, Stelle, [An]stellung, Posten, *(item)* Rechnungsposten, *(letter box, Br.)* Post-, Briefkasten, *(postal matters, Br.)* Postsendungen, *(stock exchange, US)* Börsenstand;

by return (earliest) ~ *(Br.)* mit umgehender Post; **book** ~ *(Br.)* Drucksachenpost; **confidential** ~ Vertrauensposten; **established** ~ Planstelle; **general** ~ *(Br.)* Früh-, Morgenpost; **halfpenny packet** ~ *(Br.)* Päckchenpost; **holiday** ~ Ferienbeschäftigung; **newspaper** ~ *(Br.)* Drucksachenpost; **parcel** ~ *(Br.)* Paketpost;

~ **of authority** einflußreiche Stellung; ~ *(v.)* *(appoint to post)* ernennen, *(letter, Br.)* aufgeben, zur Post geben, mit der Post befördern, *(transfer to ledger)* [ins Hauptbuch] übertragen; ~ **no bills!** Zettelankleben verboten; ~ **an announcement on the notice board** Hinweis am Schwarzen Brett anbringen; ~ **at the counter** *(Br.)* am Schalter aufgeben; ~ **an entry** Buchung vornehmen; ~ **gains** Gewinne verzeichnen; ~ **up an account** Konto abschließen;

to advertise a ~ Stelle ausschreiben; **to be given a** ~ **as general manager** zum Generaldirektor ernannt werden; **to dispatch (forward, send) by** ~ *(Br.)* mit der Post senden (schicken); **to take up one's** ~ seine Stellung antreten;

~ **bag** *(Br.)* Postbeutel; ~ **-dated check** vordatierter Scheck; ~ **directory** *(Br.)* Postadreßbuch; ~ **hours** *(Br.)* Schalterstunden.

post office Post[amt];

general ~ *(GPO)* Hauptpostamt; **railway** ~ Bahnpostamt;

~ **address** *(US)* Postanschrift; ~ **clerk** Postbeamter; ~ **order** *(Br.)* Zahlungs-, Postanweisung; ~ **savings bank** *(US)* Postsparkasse.

postage Porto[gebühr], Briefporto, Portospesen;

~ **free, free of** ~ freigemacht, portofrei, franko; ~ **unpaid** unfrankiert;

additional ~ Portozuschlag, Nachgebühr; ~ **due** Strafporto; **ordinary** ~ einfaches Porto; **overseas** ~ *(Br.)* Auslandsporto; **underpaid** ~ ungenügende Freimachung;

~ **to be collected** unter Portonachnahme;

to charge the ~ **to the consumer** dem Kunden Portogebühren in Rechnung stellen; **to pay the** ~ Brief freimachen (frankieren);

~ **book** Portokassenbuch; **special handling** ~ **charge** *(US)* Eilzustellgebühr; ~ **envelope** *(US)* Freiumschlag; ~ **meter [machine]** *(US)* Frankiermaschine, Freistempler; ~ **rates** Postgebühren, -tarif; ~ **stamp** Briefmarke, Postwertzeichen.

postal | address Postanschrift; ~ **building** Postamt, -gebäude; ~ **card** *(US)* Postkarte; ~ **cash order** Postnachnahme; ~ **collection order** *(US)* Postauftrag; ~ **delivery** Postzustellung; ~ **directory** [Post]adreßbuch; ~ **district** Zustellbezirk; ~ **lot** Postgewicht; ~ **money order** *(US)* Postanweisung; ~ **order** *(Br.)* Postanweisung [für kleinere Beträge]; ~ **principle** *(US)* Postprivileg; ~ **receipt** Posteinlieferungsschein; ~ **regulations** postalische Bestimmungen.

postal savings | account *(US)* Postsparkassenkonto; ~ **bank** *(US)* Postsparkasse; ~ **certificate** *(US)* Postsparkarte; ~ **deposit** *(US)* Postsparguthaben.

postal | service Postverkehr; ~ **cancellation stamp** Postentwertungsstempel; ~ **subscription rate** Postbezugspreis; ~ **survey** postalische Umfrage; ~ **trade** Postversandwesen; ~ **tube** Rohrpost; ~ **weight** Postgewicht; ~ **wrapper** Streif-, Kreuzband; ~ **zone number** *(Br.)* Postleitzahl.

postcard *(Br.)* Postkarte;

picture ~ Ansichts[post]karte; **replay-paid** ~ *(Br.)* Postkarte mit Rückantwort.

postclosing balance sheet berichtigte Bilanz.

postdate *(v.)* später datieren, nachdatieren.

posted gebucht, *(well-informed)* unterrichtet;
to keep s. o. ~ **[on]** j. auf dem laufenden halten; ~ **rate** *(US)* Briefkurs für ausländische Valuta.

postentry nachträgliche [Ver]buchung;
to pass a ~ Nachverzollung durchführen.

poster [Laden]plakat, Anschlagzettel;
bill ~ Zettelankleber; **time** ~ Aushängefahrplan; ~ **design** Plakatentwurf; ~ **display** Plakatwerbung; ~ **pillar** Anschlag-, Litfaßsäule.

posting *(advertisement)* Anschlag[werbung], Plakatierung, *(bookkeeping)* Übertragung in das Hauptbuch, *(letter, Br.)* Aufgabe bei der Post, Posteinlieferung;
fly ~ wilder Anschlag;
~ **bill** Anschlagzettel, Plakat; ~ **operation** Buchungsverfahren.

postmann of the walk Revierbriefträger.

postmark Datum-, Tages-, Entwertungs-, Poststempel.

postpaid portofrei, Porto bezahlt, frankiert.

postwar economic recovery wirtschaftliche Wiederbelebung der Nachkriegszeit.

potential, economic Wirtschaftspotential; **working** ~ Arbeitskräftepotential, -reserven;
~ **buyer** Kaufinteressent; ~ **earnings** geschätzte Verdienstmöglichkeiten; ~ **market** Absatzmöglichkeiten, -chancen; ~ **resources** latente Hilfsquellen.

poverty Bedürftigkeit, Mittellosigkeit;
to be below the ~ **line** Mindesteinkommensgrenze unterschreiten.

power *(authority)* Vollmacht, Berechtigung, Befugnis, Ermächtigung, *(competency)* Zurechnungsfähigkeit, *(state)* Land, Staat, Regierung, Macht;
by virtue of ~ of attorney laut Vollmacht; outside the ~s *(corporation)* außerhalb des ordnungsgemäßen Geschäftsbereichs;
bargaining ~ *(trade union)* Tarifabschlußvollmacht; **buying** ~ Kaufkraft; **discretionary** ~ Ermessensbefugnis; **earning** ~ Ertragsfähigkeit; **economic** ~ Wirtschaftspotential; **financial** ~ finanzielle Leistungsfähigkeit; **full** ~s [General]vollmacht; **lending** ~ Ausleihungsbefugnis;
~ **to operate on an account** Verfügungsberechtigung über ein Konto; ~ **of an agent** Vertretungsmacht; ~ **of attorney** Handlungs-, Vertretungsvollmacht, notarielle Vollmacht; ~ **to collect** Inkassovollmacht; ~ **to contract** Abschlußvollmacht; ~ **coupled with an interest** [etwa] Vollmacht unter Ausschluß des Selbstkontrahierens; ~ **of the purse** *(US, Congress)* Zweckbestimmungsbefugnis;
to act in excess of one's ~ seine Befugnisse überschreiten; to invest (furnish) s. o. with full ~s jem. Generalvollmacht erteilen;
~ **blackout** Stromausfall; ~ **consumption** Stromverbrauch; ~ **shutdown** Stromsperre.

practice Brauch, Gewohnheit, Praktik, *(working method)* Arbeitsweise;
business ~s *(cartel law)* Geschäftspraktiken; **deceptive business** ~s *(US)* unlautere Machenschaften; **commercial** ~ Handelsbrauch; **sharp** ~ Schiebung.

precarious living unsichere Erwerbsquelle.

precept Steuerzahlungsauftrag.

precinct, shopping Geschäftsgegend.

precious wertvoll, kostbar;
to have ~ **little money** left kaum mehr Geld übrig haben; ~ **metal** Edelmetall.

preclosing trial balance Probebilanz.

precut house Fertighaus.

predatory | **practices** rücksichtslose Wettbewerbsmethoden; ~ **price differential** *(US)* gezielte Kampfpreise.

predecessor company Geschäftsvorgänger[in].

predetermined cost vorkalkulierte Kosten.

predicted cost Standard-, Normalkosten.

preempt *(v.)* Vorkaufsrecht erwerben.

preemption Vorkauf[srecht];
~ **claimant** Vorkaufsberechtigter; ~ **entry** Vormerkung; ~ **price** Vorkaufspreis.

preemptive right Vorkaufsrecht, *(stockholder, US)* Bezugsrecht.

prefabricate *(v.)* genormte Hausteile vorfertigen.

prefabricated house Fertighaus.

prefabricator Fertighausbetrieb.

prefer *(v.)* vorziehen, Vorzug geben, *(creditors)* bevorzugt befriedigen;
~ **one creditor over others** Gläubiger bevorzugen; ~ **to a higher post** befördern.

preference Bevorzugung, Vorzug, *(in bankruptcy)* Vorrang, vorzugsweise Befriedigung, *(customs, Br.)* Meistbegünstigung[skauf], Präferenz;
~s *(stock exchange)* Vorzugsaktien;
fraudulant ~ *(in bankruptcy)* Gläubigerbegünstigung; **recoverable** ~ Aussonderungsrecht;
~ **as to assets** *(dissolution of company)* Vorzugsbehandlung im Falle einer Liquidation; ~ **of creditors** Gläubigerbegünstigung; ~ **as to dividends** Dividendenbevorrechtigung;
to give a ~ einem [Gläubiger] vorzugsweise Befriedigung gewähren;
~ **area** Präferenzgebiet; ~ **bonds** *(Br.)* Prioritätsobligationen, Prioritäten; ~ **claim** privilegierte Forderung; ~ **dividend** *(Br.)* Vorzugsdividende; ~ **freight** *(US)* zu Vorzugsbedingungen beförderte Fracht; ~ **income** steuerlich begünstigte Einkünfte; ~ **items** *(taxation)* steuerlich begünstigte Posten; ~ **loan** Prioritätsanleihe; ~ **margin** Präferenzspanne; ~ **offer** Sonderangebot; ~ **shares** *(Br.)* Prioritäts-, Vorzugsaktien; **participating** ~ **shares** *(Br.)* Vorzugsaktien mit zusätzlicher Dividendenberechtigung; ~ **stockholder** *(US)* Vorzugsaktionär.

preferential bevorzugt, bevorrechtigt;
to treat a creditor's claim as ~ Gläubigerforderung absondern;

~ **arrangement** *(GATT)* Präferenzabmachung; ~ **assignment** Vermögensübertragung auf die Konkursgläubiger; ~ **claim** bevorrechtigte Forderung, Vorzugsrecht, Absonderungsanspruch; ~ **creditor** *(Br.)* absonderungsberechtigter Gläubiger; ~ **debt** bevorrechtigte [Konkurs]forderung; ~ **dividend** *(Br.)* Vorzugsdividende; ~ **loan** *(Br.)* Prioritätsanleihe; ~ **payments** *(bankruptcy proceedings, Br.)* bevorrechtigte Gläubigerbefriedigung; ~ **price** Vorzugspreis; ~ **rate** *(customs)* Präferenzzollsatz; ~ **share** *(Br.)* Prioritätsaktie; ~ **tariff** *(Br.)* Meistbegünstigungstarif; ~ **tariff area** Zollvorzugsgebiet; ~ **treatment** Vorzugsbehandlung, *(bankruptcy)* Absonderung; **to enjoy a** ~ **treatment** *(customs)* Präferenz genießen.

preferred mit einem Vorrecht ausgestattet, bevorzugt, bevorrechtigt;
~ **bond** Prioritätsobligation; ~ **claim** bevorrechtigte Konkursforderung; ~ **creditor** bevorrechtigter [Konkurs]gläubiger; ~ **debt** bevorrechtigte [Konkurs]forderung; ~ **dividend** *(US)* Vorzugsdividende; ~ **position** *(advertising)* bevorzugte Placierung; ~ **risk plan** *(US)* Schadensfreiheitsrabatt; ~ **stocks** *(US)* Vorzugsaktien.

prefinance *(v.)* vorfinanzieren.

prejudice Vorurteil, Befangenheit, *(detriment)* Beeinträchtigung, Nachteil, Schaden;
without ~ ohne Obligo (Verbindlichkeit);
~ *(v.)* s. one's interests jds. Interessen beeinträchtigen.

preliminary | **advice** Voravis, -anzeige; ~ **balance sheet** Vorbilanz; ~ **calculation** Vorkalkulation; ~ **estimate** Kostenvoranschlag; ~ **expenses** *(company, Br.)* Gründungskosten; ~ **financing** Vorfinanzierung; ~ **proof** *(insurance)* erster Schadensnachweis.

premerger notification *(US)* vorausgehende Fusionsmitteilung.

premises dazugehöriger Grund und Boden, Grundstück, Haus und Nebengebäude, Geschäftsräume, -lokal;
on the ~ im Betrieb;
bank ~ Bankgebäude; **decontrolled** ~ im weißen Kreis gelegene Wohnung; **exhibition** ~ Ausstellungsräume; **factory** ~ Fabrikgrundstück; **licensed** ~ *(Br.)* Schanklokal; **residential** ~ Wohngebäude, -grundstück;
~ **account** Grundstücks-, Liegenschaftskonto.

premium *(agio)* [Wechsel]agio, Aufgeld, Zuschlag, *(bonus)* Bonus, Prämie, *(insurance)* Versicherungsprämie, *(special offer)* Gratis-, Sonder-, Vorzugsangebot, *(shop)* Rabattmarke, *(stock exchange)* Prämie, Reugeld;
at a ~ über Pari, *(fig.)* hoch im Kurs;
additional ~ Prämienzuschlag; **bleed** ~ *(advertising)* Anschnittszuschlag; **current** ~ Folgeprämie; **earned** ~ Prämieneinkommen; **fluctuating** ~ veränderliches Agio; **insurance** ~ Versicherungsprämie; **natural** ~ Mindestprämie zur Fortsetzung der Versicherung; **outstanding** ~s Prämienrückstände;

risk ~ Nettoprämie; **stock** ~ *(life insurance)* Gewinnbeteiligung; **unearned** ~ *(life insurance)* Prämienreserve;
~ **of apprenticeship** Lehrgeld; ~ **for the call** Vorprämie[ngeschäft]; ~ **on capital stock** Emissionsagio; ~ **on exchange** Wechselagio; ~ **for [single] option to put** Rückprämie[ngeschäft];
to be at a ~ über Pari stehen; **to command a** ~ Agio genießen; **to pay a** ~ **to an agent** Provision an einen Vertreter zahlen; **to sell at a** ~ über Pari stehen, *(v. t.)* mit Gewinn verkaufen;
~ **bond** Prämienschein; ~ **bonds** *(Br.)* Prämienanleihe; ~ **brand** Markenerzeugnis; ~ **drawing** Prämienziehung; ~ **hunting** Börsenspiel, Agiotage; **single** ~ **insurance** Lebensversicherung gegen Zahlung einer Einmalprämie; ~ **loan** Prämienanleihe; ~ **offers** *(US)* Zugabenangebot; ~ **overtime** Überstundenzuschlag; ~ **rebate** Prämienrabatt; ~ **reminder** *(insurance company)* Mahnschreiben; **unearned** ~ **reserve** *(insurance)* Prämienreserve, Deckungskapital; ~ **reserve fund** Deckungsstock; ~ **savings bond** Prämienbon; ~ **statement** Beitragsabrechnung; ~ **token** Prämien-, Gutschein.

prepaid vorausbezahlt, *(post)* frankiert, freigemacht, portofrei;
carriage ~ frachtfrei;
~ **assets** *(balance sheet)* transitorische Posten; ~ **expenses** aktive Rechnungsabgrenzungsposten; ~ **reply** Freiantwort, [Rück]antwort bezahlt; ~ **telegram** Rückantworttelegramm.

preparation | **of a budget** Etatsvorbereitung; ~ **of a form** Ausfüllung eines Formulars.

preparatory work *(plant)* Fertigungsvorbereitung.

prepare | *(v.)* **a balance sheet** Bilanz aufstellen; ~ **the way for negotiations** Weg für Verhandlungen ebnen.

prepays *(balance sheet)* Anzahlungen an Lieferanten.

prepayment Anzahlung, Voraus-, Pränumerandozahlung, *(post)* Freimachung, Frankierung;
without ~ unfrankiert, unfrei;
compulsory ~ Freimachungszwang;
~**s for capital additions** *(balance sheet, US)* Anzahlungen für Neuanlagen; ~ **of interest** Zinsvorauszahlung;
~ **clause** Vorfälligkeitsklausel; ~ **fee** Freimachungsgebühr.

preproduction model Herstellungsmuster.

prerecorded | **broadcast** Bandaufnahme; ~ **tape** Konserve.

prescribed | **industrial disease** *(Br.)* Berufskrankheit; ~ **form** vorgeschriebenes Formblatt; ~ **position** *(advertisement)* vorgeschriebene Placierung.

prescription Vorschrift, Ersitzung.

preselection *(tel.)* Vorwahl.

preselling Vorverkauf eines Produkts.

present *(v.)* *(bill)* vorlegen, präsentieren, *(show)* zeigen, darbieten;
~ **again** *(cheque)* wieder vorlegen; ~ **a balance of $ 100 to your credit** Saldo von 100 Dollar zu Ihren Gunsten aufweisen;

~ **capital** tatsächlich eingezahltes Kapital; ~ **estate** gegenwärtiges Vermögen; ~ **money** bares Geld; ~ **price** Tagespreis; ~ **value** Bar-, Tages-, Zeitwert.

presentation *(advertising)* Aufmachung, Markenausstattung, *(advertising agency)* Werbeplanvorlage, *(bill of exchange)* Präsentierung, Vorlegung, Vorlage;

personal ~ persönliche Vorstellung;

~ **of the annual balance sheet** Vorlage des Jahresabschlusses;

to be payable on ~ bei Vorlage zahlbar werden; ~ **draft** *(US)* Sichtwechsel.

presentment of a bill Wechselvorlage.

preside *(v.)* **over a business** Geschäft führen.

president *(of corporation, US)* Generaldirektor, Vorsitzender des Vorstandes;

~ **of the Board of Trade** *(Br.)* Handelsminister.

press Zeitungswesen, Journalismus;

before going to ~ vor Redaktionsschluß; **ready for** ~ druckfertig, -reif;

~ **of business** Drang der Geschäfte;

~ *(v.)* **a claim** auf einer Forderung bestehen; ~ **down heavily** *(tax)* sich drückend bemerkbar machen; ~ **for payment** auf Zahlung drängen;

~ **advertisement** Zeitungsanzeige; ~ **agency** Pressebüro; ~ **clipping** *(US)* Zeitungsausschnitt; ~ **date (day)** Redaktionsschluß; ~ **money** Handgeld.

pressed | **by one's creditors** von seinen Gläubigern bedrängt; ~ **for funds (money)** geldknapp, in Geldverlegenheit.

pressure, economic wirtschaftlicher Druck; **monetary** ~ Geldknappheit;

~ **of demand** Nachfragedruck, -sog; ~ **on liquidity** Liquiditätsanspannung; ~ **on the money market** Versteifung des Geldmarktes; ~ **of the prices** *(stock exchange)* Kursdruck; ~ **of taxation** Steuerbelastung;

to be under ~ *(stock exchange)* gedrückt liegen; **to put** ~ **on the management** Vorstand unter Druck setzen;

~ **bargaining** unter Streikdruck stehende Tarifverhandlungen; ~ **group** Interessenverband, -gruppe.

prestige | **advertising** Repräsentationswerbung; ~ **merchandise** Prestigeartikel.

pretax profit Gewinn vor Steuern.

prevailing | **price** gegenwärtiger Preis; ~ **tone** *(stock exchange)* Grundtendenz.

prevention | **of accidents** Unfallverhütung; ~ **of loss** Schadensverhütung.

preventive | **officer** *(Br.)* Beamter des Zollfahndungsdienstes; ~ **service** *(Br.)* Küstenschutz-, Zollfahndungsdienst.

previous | **application** *(patent law)* Voranmeldung; ~ **career** bisherige Tätigkeit; **our** ~ **communications** unsere Vorkorrespondenz; ~ **day** *(stock exchange)* letzter Notierungstag; ~ **endorser** Vor[der]mann; ~ **quotation** letzte Notierung.

prewar | **holdings** Vorkriegsbeteiligungen; ~ **price** Friedens-, Vorkriegspreis; ~ **rent** Friedensmiete.

price Preis, Kauf-, Marktpreis, *(cost)* Kosten, *(re-*

ward) Lohn, Belohnung, *(stock exchange)* Kurs[wert];

at all ~s in jeder Preislage; **at the lowest** ~ bei billigster Berechnung; **at current market** ~s *(stock exchange)* zum Tageskurs; **at a low** ~ billig; **at one** ~ zu festem Preis; **at a reduced** ~ mit Preisnachlaß; **within the limits of this** ~ in derselben Preislage;

~ **is no object** der Preis spielt keine Rolle;

adjustable ~ Staffelpreis; **administered** ~ amtlich festgesetzter Preis; **advertised** ~ *(newspaper)* Bezugspreis; **asked** ~ *(stock exchange)* Briefkurs; **asking** ~ Preiserwartung; **average cost** ~ Durchschnittsgestehungspreis; **bargain** ~ Ausverkaufspreis; **bid** ~ gebotener Preis, *(stock exchange)* Geldkurs; **bottom** ~ *(stock exchange)* niedrigster Kurs; **cash** ~ Bar-, Kassapreis, *(stock exchange)* Kassakurs; **catalog(ue)** ~ Listenpreis; **ceiling** ~ [amtlicher] Höchstpreis; **city** ~ *(stock exchange)* Börsenkurs; **class** ~ überhöhter, vom Kunden akzeptierter Preis; **close** ~ scharf kalkulierter Preis; **closing** ~ *(stock exchange)* Schlußnotierung; **competitive (competitor's)** ~ Wettbewerbspreis; **contract** ~ Lieferpreis; **controlled** ~ gebundener Preis; **cost** ~ Selbstkosten-, Einstandspreis; ~ **cut very fine** scharf kalkulierter Preis; **cut-rate** ~ Schleuderpreis; **cutthroat** ~ Schleuderpreis der Konkurrenz; **declining** ~s fallende Kurse; **discount** ~ Wiederverkaufspreis; **early-bird** ~ Reklamepreis; **equity** ~s Kurse von Dividendenwerten; **exorbitant** ~ Wucherpreis; **factory** ~ Preis ab Fabrik; **fair market** ~ marktgerechter Preis; **fancy** ~ Liebhaberpreis; **firm** ~s *(stock exchange)* feste Kurse; **first** ~ Anschaffungspreis; **fixed** ~ Festpreis; **floor** ~ Mindestpreis; **forward** ~ *(Br.)* Terminkurs; **frozen** ~ Stoppreis; **futures** ~ *(Br.)* Terminkurs; **give-away** ~ Schleuderpreis; **going-market** ~ gängiger Marktpreis; **gross** ~ Bruttopreis; **guiding** ~ Richtpreis; **highest** ~ Höchstkurs; **home-market** ~ Inlandspreis; **industrial share** ~s Notierungen für Industriewerte; **issue** ~ Emissionskurs; **kerb** [-**stone**] ~ *(Br.)* Freiverkehrskurs; **knockdown** ~ Reklamepreis; **limited** ~ Kurslimit; **in-the-mail** ~ Preis frei Haus; **making-up** ~ *(Br.)* Verrechnungs-, Liquidationskurs; **managed (manipulated)** ~ manipulierter (gesteuerter) Preis; **market** ~ Tages-, Marktpreis, *(stock exchange)* Tages-, Börsenkurs; **minimum resale** ~ in der zweiten Hand gebundener Preis; **natural** ~ durchschnittlicher Marktpreis; **offer[ed]** ~ *(stock exchange)* Briefkurs; **opening** ~ *(stock exchange)* fester Kurs, Eröffnungskurs; **parity** ~ Parikurs; **peak** ~ *(stock exchange)* Höchstkurs; **pegged** ~ gestützter Kurs; **pithead** ~ Preis ab Schacht; **prewar** ~ Vorkriegs-, Friedenspreis; **prohibitive** ~ unerschwinglicher Preis; **put-up** *(auction)* Mindestgebot; **put and call** ~ Stellagekurs; **quantity** ~ Mengenpreis; **~s quoted** Kursnotierung; **replacement** ~ Wiederbeschaffungskosten; **resale** ~ Wiederverkaufspreis; **fixed resale** ~ gebundener Preis; **retail** ~ Einzelhandelspreis;

selling ~ Laden-, Verkaufspreis; **share ~** Aktienkurs; **sidewalk ~** Freiverkehrskurs; **skyrocketing ~** Phantasiepreis; **standardized ~** genormter Preis; **at-station ~** Preis ab Versandbahnhof; **stiff ~s** Apothekerpreise; **stop ~** stoppter Preis, Stoppreis; **subscription ~** Bezugspreis; **suggested ~** empfohlener Richtpreis; **supported ~** subventionierter Preis; **time ~** Preis bei Ratenzahlung; **today's ~** Tageskurs; **trade ~** Engrospreis; **wholesale ~** Großhandels-, Engrospreis; **wide ~s** stark divergierende Preise, *(stock exchange)* starke Kursunterschiede; **~ for the account** *(Br.)* Terminkurs; **~ for cash** *(stock exchange)* Kassakurs; **~ subject to change without notice** Preis freibleibend; **~ covering the costs of production** kostendeckender Preis; **~ of the dinner exclusive of wine** Preis des trockenen Gedecks; **~ fixed by the government** Festpreis; **~ after hours** nachbörslicher Kurs; **~s laid down by the manufacturer** vom Hersteller festgesetzte Verkaufspreise; **~ of money** Kapitalmarktzins; **~ inclusive of postage and packing** Preis einschließlich Porto und Verpackung; **~s shaded for quantities** Mengentarifpreise; **~ at station** Preis frei Station; **~ ex store** Preis bei sofortiger Lieferung; **~ per unit** Stückpreis; **~ at works** Fabrikpreis; **~** *(v.) (appraise)* abschätzen, bewerten, *(fix price)* Preis festsetzen; **~ goods** Waren auszeichnen; **~ o. s. out of the market** sich durch überhöhte Preise den Markt entfremden; **to abate a ~** Preis nachlassen; **to administer a ~** Richtpreis festsetzen; **to advance the ~** Kurs erhöhen; **to be marked by a decline of ~s** im Zeichen der Baisse stehen; **to beat down a ~** Preis herunterhandeln; **to calculate a ~** Preis kalkulieren; **to cut ~s to the minimum** Preise schärfstens kalkulieren; **to depress the ~** Kurse drücken; **to establish a ~** Preis amtlich festsetzen; **to fall in ~** im Kurs fallen; **to flatten ~s** *(stock exchange)* Kurse abschwächen; **to freeze ~s** *(US)* Preisstopp durchführen; **to jump ~s** Preise sprunghaft erhöhen; **to keep ~s on an even level** Preise stabil halten; **to make an allowance upon the ~** Preisabschlag gewähren; **to pay a heavy ~** mit Geld aufwiegen; **to pay top ~s** Höchstpreise zahlen; **to peg ~s** Preise stützen, *(stock exchange)* Kurse stützen; **to prescribe minimum ~s** Mindestverkaufspreise für den Einzelhandel vorschreiben; **to quote a ~** Kurs notieren; **to remain stationary at yesterday's ~** sich auf dem gestrigen Kursniveau halten (behaupten); **to sell goods subject to a condition as to the ~** Ware mit Preisbindungsklausel verkaufen; **to sell under cost ~** unter dem Selbstkostenpreis abgeben; **to slash ~s** Preise stark ermäßigen; **to stick to the fixed ~** Limit einhalten; **~s are advancing** Kurse ziehen an; **~s are easing off** Kurse bröckeln ab; **~s become firmer** Kurse werden fest; **~s have eased [off]** Kurse sind abgeschwächt; **~s have hardened** Kurse zogen an; **~s have improved** Kurse liegen gebessert; **~s rise sharply** Preise (Kurse) ziehen heftig an;

~ abatement Preisnachlaß; **~ action** Preismaßnahme; **~ adjustment** Preisausgleich *(stock exchange)* Kurskorrektur; **♀ Administrator** *(US)* Preiskommissar; **~ advance** Kurssteigerung; **~ agreement** Preiskonvention, -absprache; **~ arrangement scheme** Preisbindungsvereinbarung, Preisbindung der zweiten Hand; **♀s and Income Board** *(Br.)* Preis- und Lohnbehörde; **~-bound** preisgebunden; **~ calculation** Preiskalkulation; **~ cartel** Preiskartell; **~ catalog(ue)** Preisliste; **~ change slip** Preisänderungsmitteilung; **♀ Commission** *(Br.)* Preisüberwachungsstelle; **~ concession** Preiszugeständnis; **administration ~ control** staatliche Preisüberwachung; **~-controlled** preisgebunden; **~ current** Preisliste, -verzeichnis; **~-cutting move** Preissenkungsaktion; **to lead the ~-cutting wave** Preisbrechergruppe anführen; **~ decontrol** Aufhebung der Preisüberwachungsvorschriften; **~ deduction** Preisnachlaß; **~ determination** *(stock exchange)* Kursbildung; **~ dip** Preisrückgang; **~ discrimination** *(US)* Preisdiskriminierung; **~ earnings ratio** Kurs-Ertrags-Verhältnis; **~ estimate** Preiskalkulation; **~ fixing** Preisfestsetzung, *(cartel law)* Preisabsprache; **~ resale** *(Canada)* Preisbindung der zweiten Hand; **~-fixing conspiracy** Preisverabredung; **~ fluctuations** *(stock exchange)* Kursschwankungen; **~ formula** Preisformel; **~ freeze** Preisstopp; **~ guidelines** Preisrichtlinien; **~ increase (increment)** Preisanhebung, -erhöhung; **~ increase rate** Preissteigerungsrate; **~ index** Preisindex; **consumer ~ index** Preisindex für die Lebenshaltung, Verbraucherindex; **retail ~ index** Preishandelspreisindex; **~ index number** Preisindexzahl; **~ intervention** *(stock exchange)* Kursintervention; **~ leader** *(US)* Preisführer; **~ line** *(US)* Einheitspreis; **~ list** Preisverzeichnis, *(stock exchange)* Kurszettel.

price maintenance Preisbindung [für Markenartikel]; **resale ~** Preisbindung der zweiten Hand; **~ agreement** Preisbindungsabsprache.

price|-maintained articles Produkte mit stabilen Preisen; **~ mark** Preiszettel; **~ merry-go-round** Preiskarussell; **to be in a downward ~ movement** abwärts gerichtete Kursbewegung haben; **~ oscillations** Preis-, Kursschwankungen; **~ pattern** Preisschema; **~ pause** Preispause; **~ range** Preisskala, -lage, -spanne; **to carry the full ~ range** Erzeugnisse aller Preisklassen führen; **~ recommendations** Preisempfehlungen; **~ reduction** Preisherabsetzung; **~ relief** Preisstützung; **~ ring** Verkaufskartell, *(stock exchange)* Börsenkonsortium; **~ risk** Kursrisiko; **~ rollback** staatliche Preissenkungsaktion; **~ schedule** Preisliste; **~ shading** Preisnachlaß aus Konkurrenzgründen; **~ spiral** Preisspirale; **~ spread** *(US)* Preisspanne; **~ stabilization pact** Preisstabilisierungsabkommen; **one-~ store** Einheitspreisgeschäft; **~ subsidy** Preissubvention; **~ support** Kurs-, Preisstützung; **~ swing** Kursumschwung; **delivered ~ system** *(US)* Preisbindungssystem; **~ tag** Preiszettel; **~ variation**

clause Preisgleitklausel; ~ **weakness** *(stock exchange)* Kursabschwächung.

priced | **at** mit Preisen (Preisangabe) versehen, ausgezeichnet;
budget-~ *(US)* preisgünstig; **high-~** hochbewertet, teuer; **thrift-~** *(US)* preisgünstig;
to be clearly ~ *(goods)* sorgfältig ausgezeichnet sein; **to be ~ right** preislich richtig liegen.

pricing Preiskalkulation, -festlegung, -bestimmung; **cost-based ~** kostenorientierte Preisbildung; **zone ~** *(freightage, US)* Preisfestsetzung nach Zonengebieten;
~ in code verdeckte Preisauszeichnung;
~ formula Preisberechnungsmethode; **~ policy** Preispolitik; **~ schedule** Kalkulationstabelle.

pricking note Ausfuhrversandliste.

primary | **beneficiary** Hauptnutznießer; **~ benefit** *(social insurance)* Grundrente; **~ bill** Primawechsel; **~ boycott** unmittelbarer Boykott; **~ deposits** *(US)* effektive Einlagen; **~ industry** Grundstoffindustrie; **~ liability** selbstschuldnerische Haftung; **~ obligator** *(US)* selbstschuldnerischer Bürge; **~ reserve** *(banking)* Kassenreserve.

prime Primasorte, auserlesene Qualität;
~ banker's acceptance *(US)* Primadiskonten; **~ bill** *(US)* prima (erstklassiger) Wechsel; **~ contractor** Hauptlieferant; **~ cost** *(cost price)* Selbstkosten-, Gestehungspreis, Gestehungskosten; **~ cost burden rate** Gemeinkostenzuschlagssatz auf Basis der Einzelkosten; **~ entry** vorläufige Zolldeklaration; **~ quality** vorzügliche Qualität; **~ [lending] rate** *(US)* Bankzinssatz für erstklassige Firmen, Eckkredit-, Leitzinssatz; **~ trade bill** *(US)* erstklassiger Handelswechsel.

principal *(capital)* Grundkapital, Kapital[summe], *(chief)* Chef, Leiter, *(debtor)* Hauptschuldner, *(employer of agent)* Auftrag-, Vollmachtgeber, *(proprietor)* Unternehmer, Geschäftsinhaber;
only ~s will be dealt with *(newspaper)* Vermittler verbeten;
~ and agent Auftraggeber und Auftragnehmer; **~ and charges** Kapital und Spesen; **~ with interest accrued** Kapital samt abgelaufene Zinsen;
to be liable as a ~ selbstschuldnerisch haften; **to make incursions into the ~** Kapital angreifen;
~ agent Generalvertreter; **~ amount** Kapitalbetrag; **~ establishment** Zentrale, Stammhaus; **~ market** Hauptabsatzgebiet; **~ place of business** Hauptniederlassung; **~ shareholder** Großaktionär.

principle|s of accounting Buchführungsmethoden; **~ of settlement** Vergleichsgrundlage.

print Druck, [Druck]auflage;
in ~ *(at hand)* vorrätig, auf Lager; **in small ~** kleingedruckt;
blue ~ Lichtpause.

printed | **application form** gedrucktes Antragsformular; **~ and mixed consignment** Postwurfsendung; **~ matter (paper,** *Br.)* Drucksache, -schrift; **~ paper rate** *(Br.)* Drucksachentarif, -porto.

printing | **charges (costs, expenses)** Druckkosten;.
~ establishment Druckerei, graphischer Betrieb; **~ machine** *(Br.)* Schnellpresse; **~ trade** Druckergewerbe.

prior | **to deduction of taxes** vor [Abzug der] Steuern, brutto; **~ to maturity** vor Fälligkeit;
~ art *(patent law)* Stand der Technik; **~ endorser** Vordermann; **~ lien** Pfandrecht; **~ mortgage** vorrangige Hypothek; **~ redemption** vorzeitige Tilgung.

priority *(bankruptcy)* Rangfolge, *(order that takes priority)* Dringlichkeitsauftrag, *(preference)* Dringlichkeit, Priorität, Vorzug[srecht];
convention ~ Verbandspriorität;
~ of creditors Gläubigervorrang; **~ of invention** Erfindungspriorität; **~ of liens** Rangordnung von Pfandrechten; **to be given ~** bevorzugt abgefertigt werden; **to come under ~** zur ersten Dringlichkeitsstufe gehören; **to give top ~ in the allocation** hinsichtlich der Zuteilung höchste Dringlichkeitsstufe zuerkennen; **to have ~ over s. o. in one's claim on mortgaged property** jem. im Grundbuch vorgehen;
~ bonds Prioritätsobligationen, Prioritäten; **to receive ~ consideration** bevorzugt behandelt (abgefertigt) werden; **~ delivery** Vorzugslieferung; **~ holder** Vorzugsberechtigter; **~ job** Schlüsselberuf; **~ list** Dringlichkeitsliste; **~ notice** *(real estate law,* *Br.)* Vormerkung; **~ redemption** vorzeitige Tilgung; **~ telegram** dringendes Telegramm; **~ treatment** Vorrangsbehandlung.

privacy Vertraulichkeit, Intimsphäre;
~ scrambler *(tel.)* Verschlüsselungsmaschine.

private *(a.)* privat, persönlich, *(not known)* vertraulich, nicht öffentlich, *(unofficial)* nicht amtlich, außerdienstlich, -geschäftlich;
to go ~ *(company)* in ein Privatunternehmen umgewandelt werden;
~ account Privatguthaben; **~ accountant** *(US)* betriebseigener Revisor; **~ arrangement** gütlicher Vergleich; **~ bank** Privatbank[haus]; **to sell by ~ bargain** unter der Hand verkaufen; **~ bill of exchange** Kundenwechsel; **~ boarding house** Privatpension; **~ box** Abhol-, Schließfach; **~ brand** Hausmarke; **to enter ~ business** in die Wirtschaft gehen; **~ company** *(Br.)* Personengesellschaft; **~ consumption** privater Konsum, Selbst-, Eigenverbrauch; **~ debts** persönliche Schulden; **~ enterprise** privatwirtschaftliche Aktivität, Privatwirtschaft; **to pass into ~ hands** in Privathand übergehen; **~ hotel** Fremdenheim; **~ liability** persönliche Haftung; **~ limited company** *(Br.)* Gesellschaft mit beschränkter Haftung; **to live on ~ means** von seinem Vermögen leben; **~ rate of discount** *(Br.)* Diskontsatz der Geschäftsbanken; **~ room** *(hotel)* reserviertes Besprechungszimmer; **~ sale** freihändiger Verkauf; **~ secretary** Privatsekretär[in]; **~ siding** Werksanschluß; **~ trader** selbständiger Unternehmer; **~ trust** Familienstiftung.

privilege [Vor]zugs-], Sonderrecht, Vergünstigung,

(marine insurance) Frachtzuschlag, *(stock exchange, US)* Spekulations-, Prämien-, Stell-, Zeitgeschäft;
circulation ~ Notenbankprivileg; **commercial** ~ Gewerbeberechtigung; **financial** ~ Finanzhoheit;
~ **in bankruptcy** Konkursvorrecht; ~ **of operating a business** Gewerbeberechtigung;
~ **broker** *(US)* Prämienmakler; ~ **tax** *(US)* Konzessionssteuer.

privileged bevorrechtigt, privilegiert;
~ **from distress** nicht pfändbar, unpfändbar;
~ **communication** Berufsgeheimnis; ~ **debt** bevorrechtigte Konkursforderung; ~ **share** Vorzugsaktie; ~ **shareholder** Vorzugsaktionär; ~ **stockholder** *(US)* Vorzugsaktionär.

privity Eingeweihtsein, *(participation in interest)* Interessengemeinschaft;
~ **of contract** vertragliche Bindung.

prize Preis, Prämie, *(lottery)* Treffer, [Lotterie]gewinn, *(ship)* Prise;
first (grand, great, highest) ~ großes Los, Hauptgewinn; **lottery** ~ Lotteriegewinn;
to award a ~ Preis zuerkennen; **to draw a** ~ **in a lottery** Lotteriegewinn machen;
~ **bounty** Prisengeld; ~ **competition (contest)** Preisausschreiben; ~ **scholarship** Freiplatz, -stelle; **to draw a** ~**winning ticket** Gewinnlos ziehen.

probability | of survival Erlebenswahrscheinlichkeit;
~ **sample** zufallsgesteuerte Stichprobenauswahl.

probable life mutmaßliche Lebensdauer.

probation Probe, Eignungsprüfung;
on ~ auf Probe, widerruflich;
~ **appointment** Probeanstellung.

probationer auf Probe Angestellter, Probekandidat.

probusiness *(US)* wirtschaftsfreundlich eingestellt.

procedure of reorganization Sanierungsverfahren.

proceed | *(v.)* with an application Antrag bearbeiten;
~ **with one's journey** seine Reise fortsetzen.

proceedings, bankruptcy Konkursverfahren; **composition** ~ Vergleichsverfahren, -verhandlungen;
to file Chapter TEN ~ *(US)* Vergleichsverfahren beantragen; **to take [legal]** ~ **for the recovery of a debt** Forderung einklagen.

proceeds Erlös, Ertrag, Einnahmen, Einkünfte *(of bills)* Diskonterlös, *(of cheque)* Gegenwert;
business ~ Geschäftseinnahmen; **foreign-exchange** ~ Devisenerlös; **gross** ~ Brutto-, Rohertrag; **net** ~ Netto-, Reinertrag, Nettoerlös; **quantity** ~ Mengenertrag;
~ **of an auction** Versteigerungserlös; ~ **to go to local charities** für örtliche Wohltätigkeitseinrichtungen bestimmte Erträge; ~ **of a liquidation** Liquidationserlös;
to credit the ~ **to an account** Konto mit dem Gegenwert erkennen.

process Rechtsstreit, Prozeß, *(course of action)* Vorgang, Verfahren, *(method of production)* [Arbeits]prozeß, -stufe;
during the ~ **of removal** während des Umzugs;

executory ~ Vollstreckungsverfahren; **finishing** ~ Veredelungsverfahren; **industrial** ~ industrielles Herstellungsverfahren; **secret** ~ Geheimverfahren;
~ **of industrialization** Industrialisierungsprozeß;
~ **of manfacture** Herstellungsverfahren, Produktionsprozeß;
~ *(v.) (finish)* veredeln, weiterverarbeiten;
to be in ~ **of manufacture** in Arbeit sein;
~ **account** Fabrikationskonto; ~ **chart** Arbeitsablaufdiagramm; ~ **costing** Kostenrechnung für Serienfertigung; ~ **costs** Verarbeitungskosten.

processed products Veredelungserzeugnisse.

processing Be-, Verarbeitung, Veredelung;
contract ~ Lohnveredelung;
~ **in bond** Zollveredelung; ~ **under a job contract** Lohnveredelung;
~ **company** Weiterverarbeitungsbetrieb; ~ **cost** Fabrikations-, Herstellungskosten; ~ **country** Veredelungsland; ~ **enterprise** Verarbeitungs-, Veredelungsbetrieb; ~ **industry** verarbeitende Industrie; ~ **permit** Verarbeitungsgenehmigung; ~ **restriction** Verarbeitungsbeschränkung; ~ **stage** Veredelungsstufe; ~ **tax** *(US)* Veredelungs-, Verarbeitungssteuer.

procuration *(brokerage fee)* Maklergebühr, *(instrument)* [etwa:] Prokura, Vollmacht, Bevollmächtigung, Vertretungsmacht;
branch ~ [etwa:] Filialprokura; **single (sole)** ~ Einzelvollmacht;
~ **of a loan** Anleihebeschaffung.

procure | *(v.)* acceptance Akzept einholen; ~ **capital** Kapital beschaffen.

procurement Beschaffung, Besorgung;
~ **of funds** Mittelaufbringung; ~ **of a loan** Anleihevermittlung;
~ **agency** *(US)* Beschaffungsstelle; **normal** ~ **channels** normaler Beschaffungsweg.

procuring agency Beschaffungsbehörde.

produce Erzeugnis, Produkt;
agricultural ~ landwirtschaftliche Erzeugnisse; **gross** ~ Rohertrag; **home (inland)** ~ inländische Bodenerzeugnisse; **raw** ~ Rohmaterial;
~ *(v.) (farming)* Ertrag bringen (liefern), erzeugen, *(manufacture)* [Güter] erzeugen, herstellen, ausstoßen, produzieren, fabrizieren;
~ **accounts for inspection** Bücher zur Revision vorlegen; ~ **a certificate** Bescheinigung vorlegen; ~ **heavy crops** reiche Ernten erbringen; ~ **mainly for export** in der Hauptsache für den Export anfertigen; ~ **at an economic figure** rentabel produzieren; ~ **an invention** Erfindungsgegenstand herstellen; ~ **one's passport** seinen Paß vorzeigen; ~ **a power of attorney** Vollmacht vorlegen;
~ **advance** Produktivkredit; ~ **broker** Produkten-, Warenmakler; ~ **dealer** Produktenhändler; ~ **exchange** Produktenbörse; ~ **market** Produkten-, Warenmarkt.

producer Hersteller, Erzeuger, Produzent;
domestic ~ inländischer Erzeuger; **high-cost** ~

teurer Herstellungsbetrieb; **inland** ~ Inlandser-
zeuger; **marginal** ~ Betrieb an der Grenze der
Rentabilität;
~ **advertising** Herstellerwerbung; ~ **association**
Produzentenverband; ~'s **brand** Herstellermarke;
~ **cooperative** landwirtschaftliche Absatzgenossenschaft; ~ **costs** Gestehungskosten; ~ **goods industry** Produktionsgüterindustrie; ~'s **liability insurance** *(US)* Gewährleistungsversicherung des
Produzenten; ~ **price** Produzenten-, Erzeuger-
preis.
producing | **for stock** Lageranfertigung;
raw material ~ **area** Rohstoffgebiet; ~ **center
(centre,** *Br.)* Produktionszentrum; ~ **country**
Produktionsland; ~ **facilities** Fabrikationsanla-
gen; ~ **unit** Produkt[ions]einheit.
product Erzeugnis, Produkt, Fabrikat, Artikel;
~**s** *(Br., interest)* Zinszahlen, -nummern;
advertised ~**s** Reklameartikel; **agricultural** ~**s** landwirtschaftliche Erzeugnisse; **black** ~**s** *(interest,
Br.* schwarze [Zins]nummern; **credit** ~**s** *(Br.)* Ha-
benzinsnummern; **debit** ~**s** *(Br.)* Sollzinsnum-
mern; **established** ~ gut eingeführter Artikel; **factory** ~ gewerbliches Erzeugnis; **finished** ~**s** Fertigerzeugnisse; **half-finished** ~**s** Halbfabrikate; **high-
quality** ~**s** Qualitätserzeugnisse; **inferior** ~ minderwertige Ware; **inland** ~ einheimisches Fabrikat; [**total**] **gross national** ~ Bruttosozialprodukt;
nongraded ~**s** nicht sortierte Artikel; **price-maintained** ~**s** preisstabile Erzeugnisse; **rival** ~ Konkurrenzerzeugnis; **spinoff** ~**s** anfallende Nebenprodukte; **waste** ~ Abfallprodukt;
~**s of one' labo(u)r** Früchte seiner Arbeit;
to showcase new ~**s** neue Produkte vorführen;
~ **control** Fertigungsüberwachung; ~ **cost** Produktionsaufwand; ~ **differentiation** Produktdifferen-
zierung; ~ **diversification** reichhaltiges Produktionsprogramm; ~ **engineer** Fertigfabrikatsinge-
nieur; **diversified** ~ **lines** breit gestreutes Warensortiment; ~ **manager** Markenbetreuer; ~ **mix** ge-
mischtes Produktionsprogramm, Fertigungssor-
timent; ~ **quality** Produktionsqualität; ~ **research**
Marktforschung für ein neues Erzeugnis; ~ **sales
breakdown** Umsatzaufschlüsselung; ~ **sharing** Deputatentlohnung; **finished** ~ **stage** Fabrikations-
reife; ~ **warranty** Mängelgewähr.
production Hervorbringen, Herstellung, Ausstoß,
Fertigung, Fabrikation, Produktion;
ready to go into ~ fertigungs-, produktionsreif;
annual ~ Jahresproduktion; **contracting** ~
schrumpfende Produktion; **copyrighted** ~**s** *(US)*
urheberrechtlich geschützte Veröffentlichungen;
economic (factory) ~ gewerbliche Produktion, industrielle Erzeugung; **flow** ~ Fließarbeit, -band-
fertigung; **high-cost** ~ mit hohen Selbstkosten arbeitende Industrie; **increased** ~ Produktionssteigerung; **individual** ~ Einzelanfertigung; **large-scale**
~ Massenfertigung; Großserienproduktion; **moving-band** ~ Produktion am laufenden Band;
quantity ~ Massenproduktion; **secondary** ~ ver-

arbeitende Industrie; **serial (series)** Serienherstellung; **soft goods** ~ Produktion schnell verbrauch-
barer Güter; **standardized** ~ genormte Produktion;
~ **in bulk** Massenherstellung; ~ **of goods** Güter-
erzeugung; ~ **of manufactured goods** Herstellung
von Massengütern; ~ **for stock** Vorrats-, Lager-
anfertigung;
to curb (curtail) the ~ Produktion drosseln; **to form the bulk of** ~ wesentlichen Teil
der Produktion ausmachen; **to go into** ~ *(new factory)* Produktion aufnehmen; **to hive off** ~ Produktionsaufträge in einem fremden Werk herstellen lassen; **to increase** ~ Produktionssteigerung
herbeiführen; **to operate at full** ~ mit voller Kapazität arbeiten; **to round off one's** ~ sein Produktionsprogramm abrunden; **to start full** ~ mit der
Serienproduktion beginnen; **to tailor** ~ **to demand**
Produktion der Nachfrage anpassen;
~ **account** Fabrikations-, Produktionskonto; ~
allocation program(me) *(US)* kriegsbedingte Produktionslenkung; ~ **bonus** *(US)* Leistungsprämie;
~ **capacity** Leistungsfähigkeit, Produktionskapazität; ~ **capital** Produktivkapital; ~ **car** Serienwagen; ~ **control** Produktionslenkung, Fertigungssteuerung; ~ **costs** Gestehungskosten, Produktionsaufwand; ~ **credit association** *(US)* landwirtschaftliche Kreditgenossenschaft; ~ **cut** Dros-
selung der Produktion; ~ **diversions** Produktions-
bereich; ~ **engineer** Fertigungs-, Betriebsingenieur; ~ **engineering** Fertigungstechnik; ~ **enterprise** Produktionsbetrieb; ~ **facilities** Produktionseinrichtungen; ~ **force** Belegschaft; ~ **goods**
Produktionsgüter; ~ **goods industry** Produktionsgüterindustrie; ~ **grant** *(Br.)* Produktionsprämie;
~ **line** Förder-, Transport-, Fließband, Ferti-
gungsstraße; **empty** ~ **line** auftragsloser Ferti-
gungszweig; **to halt** ~ **lines** einzelne Produktions-
zweige stillegen; ~ **machinery** Produktionsanlage;
~ **management** Produktionssteuerung; ~ **order**
Fabrikationsauftrag; ~ **overhead charges** Fertigungsgemeinkosten; ~ **plan** Produktionsprogramm; ~ **price** Fabrikations-, Herstellungspreis;
~ **rationalization** rationalisiertes Produktionsverfahren; ~ **statement** Produktionsbilanz; ~ **target**
Produktionsziel; ~ **time** Fertigungszeit; **individual**
~ **time** Stückzeit.
productive leistungsfähig, produzierend, produktiv,
(yielding in abundance) ertragreich, ertragsfähig;
~ **apparatus** Produktionsapparat; **national** ~
capacity Sozialproduktvolumen; ~ **capital** Produktivkapital; ~ **burden center** *(US)* (centre, *Br.)*
Fertigungskostenstelle; ~ **enterprise** ertragbrin-
gendes Unternehmen; ~ **establishment** Produktionsstätte; ~**-motivated basic premium** vermö-
genspolitisch motivierte Sockelprämie; ~ **property**
Produktionsvermögen; ~ **unit** Produktionsstätte.
productivity, productiveness Ertragsfähigkeit, wirtschaftliche Leistungsfähigkeit, Produktivität;
marginal ~ Grenzproduktivität;

~ **agreement** Produktivitätsvereinbarung; ~ **bargaining** am Produktivitätszuwachs orientierte Tarifvereinbarung; **to settle for rises based on a ~ rate** Tariferhöhungen auf Produktivitätszunahmesätze abstellen; **~-related pay hike** produktivitätsgekoppelter Lohnanstieg.

profession Berufsschicht, -stand, freier Beruf, freiberufliche Tätigkeit;
commercial ~ Kaufmannsstand, -beruf; **crowded ~** überfüllter (übersetzter) Beruf;
~ or vocation *(income tax, Br.)* freie oder sonstige selbständige Berufe;

professional Berufsangehöriger, *(expert)* Fachmann, *(stock exchange)* Berufsspekulant, *(university man)* Geisteswissenschaftler, Akademiker;
~ *(a.)* beruflich, fachlich, berufsmäßig; *(expert)* fachmännisch;
~ activity [frei]berufliche Tätigkeit; **~ association** Berufsverband; **to be of ~ caliber** sich für einen Beruf besonders eignen; **~ classification** Berufszugehörigkeit; **~ confidence** Berufsgeheimnis; **~ discretion** Schweigepflicht; **~ earnings** Einkünfte aus freiberuflicher Tätigkeit; **~ employment** Berufstätigkeit; **~ ethics** Standespflichten; **~ examination** Fachprüfung; **~ expenditure** *(income tax statement)* Werbungskosten; **~ government** Berufsbeamtentum; **~ journal** Fachzeitschrift; **~ liability** Unternehmerhaftpflicht; **in a ~ manner** fachmännisch; **~ privilege** anwaltliches Vorrecht; **~ qualifications** fachliche Eignung; **~ school** Berufs-, Fachschule; **~ standards** berufsethische Grundsätze; **~ training** Berufs-, Fachausbildung; **~ worker** freiberufliche Arbeitskraft.

profit *(advantage)* Nutzen, Vorteil, *(gain)* Gewinn, [Rein]ertrag, Erlös, Verdienst, Profit;
with a view to ~ in gewinnsüchtiger Absicht;
actual ~ Effektivgewinn; **anticipated ~** Gewinnerwartung; **book ~** Buchgewinn; **clear (clean) ~** Netto-, Reingewinn, ertrag; **distributed ~** ausgeschütteter Gewinn; **exchange ~** Kursgewinn; **gross ~** Bruttoertrag; **intercompany ~s** Konzernerlöse; **~ left** stehengelassener Gewinn; **net ~** Nettoertrag; **net trading ~** Geschäftsreinertrag; **paper ~** unrealisierter (rechnerischer) Gewinn; **pure ~** Unternehmerreingewinn; **taxable ~** steuerpflichtiger Gewinn; **undistributed net ~** *(Br.)* unverteilter Reingewinn;
~s of (from) capital Kapitalerträge; **~s on exchange** Kursgewinne; **~ from operations** *(US)* Unternehmergewinn; **~s of profession or vocation** Einkünfte aus freiberuflicher Tätigkeit; **~s before taxation** Ertrag vor Abzug der Steuern; **~ per unit** Erlös pro Verkaufseinheit;
~ *(v.)* nützen, von Vorteil, profitieren;
~ by the tendency Kurstendenz ausnützen;
to ascertain the ~ Gewinn feststellen; **to clear a ~** Reingewinn erzielen; **to hold down ~s** Gewinne niedrig halten; **to lock in the ~** Gewinn kassieren; **to make illicit ~s** unerlaubte Gewinne einstreichen; **to operate at a ~** mit Gewinn arbeiten; **to**

plow (plough, *Br.)* **back ~s into research** Gewinnrücklagen für Forschungszwecke einsetzen; **to put down to ~ and loss** in die Erfolgsrechnung einsetzen; **to shove up ~s** Gewinnchancen verbessern; **to siphon off ~s** Gewinnabschöpfung vornehmen; **to turn a healthy ~** angemessene Gewinne erzielen;
~ account Gewinnkonto, Erfolgsrechnung; **to pass to the ~ and loss account** auf Gewinn- und Verlustkonto buchen; **~ contribution** Deckungsbeitrag, Bruttogewinn; **to turn the ~ corner** Gewinnschwelle überschreiten; **~-earning capacity** Ertragsfähigkeit, Rentabilität; **~ dip** Gewinnrückgang; **excess ~s duty** *(Br.)* Mehrgewinnsteuer; **~ erosion** Gewinnerosion; **~ and loss expenses** Handlungsunkosten; **~ forecast** Ertragsvorschau; **~ margin** Verdienst-, Gewinnspanne; **~ picture** Ertragsbild; **~ share** Erlösanteil; **~ sharing** *(employees)* Gewinnbeteiligung; **~ situation** Ertragslage; **~ squeeze** Gewinnverdeckung; **~ taking** *(stock exchange)* Gewinnsicherung, -realisierung; **~-taking sales** Realisierungsverkäufe; **~s tax** *(Br.)* Ertragssteuer; **excess-~s tax** *(US)* Mehrgewinnsteuer.

profitability | **graph** Rentabilitätsdiagramm; **~ level** Gewinnschwelle.

profitable gewinnbringend, ertragreich, einträglich, wirtschaftlich, rentabel;
to be ~ for all sich für alle auszahlen; **to stay ~** Gewinnposition beibehalten;
~ basis Gewinnschwelle; **~ enterprise** rentabler Betrieb; **~ investment** lohnende Kapitalanlage; **to put on a ~ track** Rendite erwirtschaften.

profiteer Geschäftemacher, Schieber, Schwarzhändler, Wucherer, Kriegsgewinnler.

profiteering Geschäftemacherei, Wuchergeschäfte.

profitmonger Wucherer.

proforma | **account** Proformarechnung, fingierte Verkaufsrechnung; **~ bill** Keller-, Gefälligkeitswechsel; **~ receipt** Scheinquittung; **~ transaction** Scheingeschäft.

program(me) Programm, Plan;
aid ~ Hilfsprogramm; **crash ~** Sofortprogramm; **housing ~** Wohnungsbauprogramm; **working ~** Arbeitsplan;
~ budget Istetat.

progress Fortgang, Verbesserung, Fortschritt;
economic ~ wirtschaftlicher Aufschwung; **technological** technologischer Fortschritt;
to bring about a better ~ of representation seine Repräsentationspflichten verstärkt wahrnehmen; **~ chart** Entwicklungsdiagramm; **~ report** Tätigkeitsbericht; **~ sharing** Erfolgsbeteiligung am Produktivitätszuwachs.

progression wages gestaffelte Löhne.

progressive | **assembly** Fließbandmontage; **~ removal of restrictions** stufenweiser Abbau von Beschränkungen; **~ tax** progressive Steuer; **~ wage rate** Progressivlohn.

prohibited | **articles** Schmuggelware, Konterbande; **~ risk** *(insurance)* nicht versicherungsfähiges Interesse.

prohibition | of **exports** Exportverbot; ~ of **issue** Emissionssperre.
prohibitionism Schutzzollsystem.
prohibitive | **cost** untragbare Kosten; ~ **duty** Schutz-, Sperrzoll; ~ **tax** prohibitive Steuer.
project Projekt, Plan, Entwurf, Vorhaben;
   development ~ Entwicklungsvorhaben; **hush** ~ Geheimprojekt; **investment** ~ Investitionsvorhaben;
   ~ **supported by taxes** aus Steuern finanziertes Projekt;
   ~ **funds** Projektmittel; ~ **team** Projektgruppe.
projected financial statement zukünftiger Finanzstatus.
prolong (v.) (bill of exchange) prolongieren.
prolongation [Frist]verlängerung, (bill of exchange) Prolongation, Prolongierung;
   ~ **of time** Nachfrist.
   ~ **business** Prolongationsgeschäft.
promise | **to pay** [the debt of another] Zahlungsversprechen; ~ **of reward** Auslobung.
promising market erfolgversprechender Absatzmarkt.
promissory note Schuldschein, (bill of exchange) eigener (trockener) Wechsel, Eigen-, Solawechsel;
   ~ **made out to bearer** Inhaberwechsel; ~ **made out to order** Ordertratte.
promote befördern, (advertise, US) Reklame machen, (float) gründen;
   ~ **a bill in Parliament** Gesetzentwurf initiieren;
   ~ **a new business company** (Br.) neue Gesellschaft gründen.
promoter Förderer, (of joint stock company) Gründer;
   ~'s **shares** (stocks, US) Gründeraktien.
promoting syndicate (Br.) Gründerkonsortium.
promotion (advertising, US) Reklame, Werbung, (furtherance) Unterstützung, Begünstigung, Förderung;
   direct-mail ~ (US) Werbung durch Postversand; **sales** ~ Verkaufswerbung, -förderung; **volume incentive** ~ mengenmäßige Leistungsförderung;
   ~ **of employment** Arbeitsbeschaffung; ~ **of industries** Förderung der Wirtschaft; ~ **by seniority** Beförderung nach dem Dienstalter; ~ **of tourism** Fremdenverkehrsförderung;
   to be on one's ~ zur Beförderung anstehen;
   ~ **allowance** (US) Reklamenachlaß; ~ **and advertising costs** (US) Werbungskosten; ~ **department** (US) Werbeabteilung; ~ **expense** Gründungsaufwand; ~ **roster** Beförderungsliste; ~ **shares** (stock, US) Gründeraktien.
promotional | **arrangements** Beförderungsbestimmungen; ~ **chart** Beförderungstabelle; ~ **material** (US) Werbematerial; ~ **raise** (US) (rise, Br.) Gehaltsaufbesserung bei einer Beförderung; ~ **value** (US) Werbewert.
prompt Ziel, Zahlungsfrist;
   ~**s** (Br.) sofort lieferbare Ware;
   to pay ~**ly** pünktlicher Zahler sein;

~ **attention to an order** sofortige Auftragserledigung; **for** ~ **cash** gegen Barzahlung; ~ **delivery** Lieferung innerhalb kürzester Frist; ~ **service**. prompte Bedienung; ~ **shipment** sofortiger Versand.
prone to crisis krisenanfällig..
proof (print.) Korrekturfahne;
   brush ~ (print.) Bürstenabzug; **clean** ~ (print) Revisionsbogen;
   ~ **of claim** (bankruptcy) Forderungsanmeldung;
   ~ **of one's identity** Legitimation; ~ **of loss** (fire insurance) Schadensanzeige;
   to lodge a ~ **in bankruptcy** zur Konkurstabelle anmelden; **to pay s. o. a sum upon submission of** ~ **of identity** jem. gegen Vorlage seines Personalausweises einen Betrag auszahlen;
   ~ **sheet** (slip) Korrekturbogen, Druckfahne.
propaganda (publicity) Reklame, Werbetätigkeit, Werbung;
   ~ **barrage** Werbehindernis; ~ **efforts** Werbeanstrengungen; ~ **leaflet** Werbeprospekt; ~ **writings** Reklameschriften, Werbematerial.
propensity | **to buy** Kauflust; ~ **to consume** Konsumfreudigkeit; ~ **to spend** Ausgabebereitschaft.
proper | **authority** zuständige Behörde; **through the** ~ **channels** auf dem Dienstwege; **due and** ~ **notice** ordnungsgemäß zugestellte Kündigung; **at the** ~ **rate** zum Tarifsatz; ~ **receipt** rechtsgültige Quittung.
propertied classes begüterte Kreise.
properties Liegenschaften, Immobilien.
property Vermögen[sgegenstand], (ownership) Eigentum[srecht], (piece of ~) Grundstück, Stück Land;
   on one's own ~ auf eigenem Grund und Boden; **alien** ~ Ausländervermögen; **built-on** ~ bebautes Grundstück; **charged** ~ belastetes Grundstück; **community** ~ (US) Güter-, Errungenschaftsgemeinschaft; **confiscated** ~ beschlagnahmtes Vermögen; **dotal** ~ eingebrachtes Gut der Ehefrau; **exempt** ~ (bankruptcy) konkursfreies Eigentum; **foreign-owned** ~ Ausländervermögen; **government** ~ fiskalisches Eigentum; **incorporeal** ~ immaterielle Vermögenswerte; **intangible** ~ immaterielle Vermögenswerte; **landed** ~ Grundbesitz; **leased** ~ Pachtgrundstück; **lost** ~ Fundgegenstände; **mixed** ~ bewegliches und unbewegliches Vermögen; **personal** ~ Mobiliarvermögen, (inheritance) beweglicher Nachlaß; ~ **reserved** (Br.) Rückstellung für Abschreibungen; **residential** ~ Wohngrundstück; **restituted** ~ rückerstatteter Vermögensgegenstand; **tangible** ~ greifbare Vermögenswerte; **aggregate taxable** ~ steuerpflichtiges Gesamtvermögen; **waterfront** ~ Ufergrundstück;
   ~ **of a capital nature** Kapitalvermögen; ~ **acquired during marriage** Errungenschaft; ~ **to be reported** anmeldepflichtiges Vermögen;
   to alienate ~ Vermögen veräußern; **to be free with other people's** ~ mit fremdem Geld leichtsinnig umgehen; **to be liable to the extent of one's** ~ mit

seinem ganzen Vermögen haften; **to get a** ~ **free from all encumbrances** Grundstück lastenfrei erwerben; **to have a small** ~ **in the country** etw. Grundbesitz haben; **to price a** ~ Verkaufspreis für ein Grundstück festsetzen; **to realize one's** ~ sein Vermögen flüssigmachen; **to remove** ~ *(bankrupt)* Vermögensstücke beiseite schaffen; **to seize** ~ Vermögen beschlagnahmen; **to take private** ~ for public use Privatgrundstücke für öffentliche Zwecke enteignen;
~ **account** Sach-, Immobilien-, Anlagenkonto; ~ **assets** Vermögenswerte; ~ **capital** in Wertpapieren angelegtes Kapital; ~ **company** Immobiliengesellschaft; ~ **damage [liability] insurance** Sachschadenversicherung; ~ **development costs** [Grundstücks]erschließungskosten; ~ **dividend** Sachwertdividende; ~ **finance consultant** Vermögensberater; ~ **income** Einkünfte aus Land- und Forstbesitz; ~ **increment tax** Wertzuwachssteuer; ~ **issue form** Materialausgabeschein; ~ **loss** Vermögensverlust, -schaden; ~ **market** *(Br.)* Immobilienmarkt; **lost-** ~ **office** Fundbüro; ~, **plant and equipment** *(balance sheet, US)* Grundstücke und Gebäude, Maschinen und maschinelle Anlagen; ~ **settlement** Vermögensregelung; ~ **statement** Vermögensaufstellung; ~ **tax** *(Br.)* Grund- und Gebäudesteuer, *(US)* Vermögenssteuer; ~ **value** Vermögenswert.

proportion *(ratio)* Verhältnisziffer;
in ~ **to** anteils-, verhältnismäßig, proratarisch; **relative** ~**s** Größenverhältnis, Proportionen;
~ **of reserves to liabilities** Verhältnis der Reserven zu den Verbindlichkeiten;
to be out of ~ **to one's income** zum Einkommen in keinem Verhältnis stehen; **to divide expenses in equal** ~**s** Unkosten umlegen.

proportional | **assessment** anteilsmäßige Veranlagung; ~ **rate** Proportionalsatz, *(railroad)* Distanztarif; ~ **share** Quote, ~ **taxation** Proportionalbesteuerung.

proposal Vorschlag, Antrag, *(insurance)* Versicherungsantrag, *(trade)* Lieferungsangebot;
sealed ~ verschlossenes Angebot;
~ **for a subscription** Subskriptionsangebot;
~ **bond** Bietungsgarantie.

propose *(v.)* **to an insurance company** Versicherungsantrag stellen.

proprietary Grundstückseigentum, *(ownership)* Eigentumsrecht;
landed ~ Grundbesitzer;
~ **account** Kapitalkonto; ~ **articles** Monopolartikel, *(branded goods, US)* Markenartikel; ~ **capital** Eigenkapital; ~ **company** *(US)* Holdinggesellschaft; ~ **goods** *(US)* Markenartikel; ~ **insurance** *(Br.)* Prämienversicherung; ~ **name** gesetzlich geschützter Name.

proprietor Inhaber, Eigentümer, Besitzer;
landed ~ Grundeigentümer; **registered** ~ eingetragener Gebrauchsmusterinhaber;
~ **of a business** Geschäfts-, Firmeninhaber; ~ **of a**

hotel ~ Hotelbesitzer; ~**s in a joint stock company** *(Br.)* Aktionäre;
~**s' capital** Eigenkapital; ~**s' capital account** Kapitalkonto; ~ **income** Vermögenseinkünfte.

proprietorial attitude Unternehmereinstellung.

proprietorship Eigentumsrecht, Eigenbesitz, Eigentum, *(balance sheet, US)* Eigenkapital;
corporate ~ *(US)* Gesellschaftskapital; **single** ~ *(US)* Einzelfirma;
~ **account** Kapitalkonto.

prorata | **freight** Distanzfracht; ~ **premium** verdiente Prämienanteil; ~ **rate** anteilige Prämie.

prorate *(v.) (assess, US)* anteilmäßig veranlagen.

prorated expenses *(US)* Schlüsselgemeinkosten.

prosecute *(v.)* **a trade** einem Gewerbe nachgehen.

prospect Aussicht, *(consumer, US)* potentieller Verbraucher, (Käufer), Reflektant;
cyclical ~**s** Konjunkturaussichten;
future ~**s of an undertaking** Zukunftsaussichten eines Unternehmens;
~ *(v.)* **for gold** nach Gold schürfen; ~ **for oil** nach Öl bohren;
to have good ~**s** Erbschaftsaussichten haben; **to have nothing in** ~ keine Stellung in Aussicht haben; **to injure one's** ~**s** seiner Karriere schaden.

prospecting licence Schürfrecht.

prospective | **buyer** potentieller Käufer, Kaufinteressent, -reflektant; ~ **consumer** potentieller Verbraucher; ~ **damage** mittelbarer Schaden, entgangener Gewinn; ~ **investors** anlagesuchendes Publikum.

prospectus Prospekt, Werbeschrift, *(of a new company)* Zeichnungsangebot, Subskriptionsanzeige, *(price list)* Preisliste;
to send out a ~ Propsekt versenden;
~ **company** *(Br.)* Gründungsgesellschaft.

prospertiy Wohlstand, Gedeihen, Blütezeit;
national ~ Volkswohlstand; **peak** ~ Hochkonjunktur; **specious** ~ Scheinblüte, -konjunktur; ~ **era** wirtschaftliche Blütezeit; ~ **index** Wohlstandsindex; ~ **phase** Konjunkturperiode.

protect | *(v.)* **a bill at maturity** Wechsel bei Verfall einlösen; ~ **s. one's interests** jds. Interessen wahrnehmen.

protected | **industries** *(US)* durch Zollschranken geschützte Industriezweige; ~ **profit stop** *(US)* limitierte Verkaufsorder.

protection Schutz, Protektion, *(economy)* Schutzzollpolitik, *(insurance)* Versicherungsschutz;
~ **of registered design** Geschmacksmusterschutz; ~ **of interests** Wahrnehmung von Interessen; ~ **of tenants** Mieterschutz; ~ **of trademarks** Warenzeichenschutz;
to find due ~ *(bill)* akzeptiert (honoriert) werden; ~ **and indemnity insurance** Schiffshaftpflichtversicherung; ~ **money** *(US)* Bestechungsgelder; **trade** ~ **society** Gläubigerschutzverband.

protectionism Schutzzollsystem.

protectionist Schutzzollpolitiker;
~ **sentiment** wachsender Protektionismus.

protective | **clause** Freizeichnungsklausel; ~ **duty** Schutzzoll; ~ **measures** Abwerhmaßnahmen; ~ **system** Schutzzollsystem; ~ **[customs] tariff** Abwehrzoll, Schutzzoll[tarif].

protest Verwahrung, Einspruch, Protest, *(bill of exchange)* Wechselprotest;
  no ~ *(bill)* ohne Kosten; **under** ~ unter Vorbehalt; **extended** ~ *(navigation)* Seeprotest, Verklarung; ~ **waived** ohne Protest (Kosten);
  ~ **for nonpayment** Wechselprotest mangels Zahlung;
  ~ *(v.)* **a bill** Wechselprotest einlegen; ~ **a bill for nonpayment** Wechsel mangels Zahlung protestieren;
  to accept under ~ unter Vorbehalt annehmen; **to enter a** ~ Protest erheben (einlegen); **to enter a** ~ **in case of damage** Verklarung über die Beschädigung eines Schiffes einlegen; **to lodge a** ~ Verwahrung einlegen; **to make a written** ~ schriftlich Einspruch einlegen; **to pay a bill under** ~ Wechsel unter Protesterhebung einlösen;
  ~ **certificate** Protesturkunde; ~ **charges (expenses, fees)** Protestkosten, -spesen.

protested | **for nonacceptace** mangels Annahme protestiert; ~ **for nonpayment** mangels Zahlung protestiert;
  to return a bill ~ Wechsel unter Protest zurückgehen lassen.

protocol Verhandlungs-, Sitzungsbericht, Protokoll.

prototype Muster, Modell, Prototyp, Ausgangsbaumuster, Erstausführung;
  ~ **production** Musterproduktion.

provable claim anmeldungsfähige Konkursforderung.

prove *(v.) (bankruptcy)* [Forderung im Konkursverfahren] geltend machen, *(print.)* Probeabzug machen;
  ~ **to be a forgery** sich als Fälschung herausstellen; ~ **one's identity** sich legitimieren.

proved | **damages** festgestellter Schadenersatzanspruch; ~ **debt** festgestellte [Konkurs]forderung.

provide for | **s. o.** für jeds. Lebensunterhalt sorgen; ~ **a bill** Deckung für einen Wechsel anschaffen; ~ **payment** Deckung anschaffen, für Zahlung (Deckung) sorgen.

provide | **a bill with acceptance** Wechsel mit Akzept versehen; ~ **s. o. with cover** jem. Deckung anschaffen.

provided vorgesehen, vorgeschrieben;
  not ~ **for** keine Deckung;
  ~ **by the articles of the association** in den Satzungen der Gesellschaft vorgesehen; ~ **in the budget** in den Etat eingestellt; **to be well** ~ **with capital** kapitalkräftig sein.

provident | **bank** Sparkasse; ~ **benefit** Fürsorgeunterstützung; ~ **company** Wirtschaftsgenossenschaft; ~ **fund** Hilfskasse, Pensionsfonds; **miners'** ~ **fund** Knappschaftskasse; ~ **reserve** Sonderrücklage; ~ **society** *(Br.)* Wirtschaftsgenossenschaft.

provider Ernährer, Versorger, Lieferant;
  universal ~s Waren-, Kaufhaus.

province [Wissens]gebiet, Fach, *(region)* Gebiet, Landstrich, Gegend, *(sphere of action)* Geschäftskreis, Bereich, Wirkungskreis.

provincial market *(Br.)* Regionalbörse.

provision Vorkehrung, Maßnahme, *(balance sheet)* Rückstellung, Rücklage, *(clause)* Klausel, Vorschrift, *(remittance)* Übermachung, Deckung, *(stipulation)* Bestimmung, Vorschrift;
  after ~ **for contingencies** nach Rückstellungen für unvorhergesehene Ausgaben;
  ~s Lebensmittel, Proviant, *(reserve, Br.)* Rückstellungen und Wertberichtigungen;
  fiscal ~s steuerrechtliche Bestimmungen; ~s **running out** ausgehende Vorräte; **standard** ~s *(insurance)* allgemeine Versicherungsbedingungen; **tax-law** ~s steuerrechtliche Bestimmungen;
  ~ **of capital** Kapitalbeschaffung, -bereitstellung; ~ **for deferred repairs and renewals** Rückstellungen für Reparaturen und Erneuerungen; ~ **for depreciation** Entwertungsrücklage; ~ **for the future** Vorsorge für die Zukunft; ~ **for outstanding losses** *(insurance)* Schadensreserve; ~ **for obsolescence** Rückstellung für Überalterung; ~ **for replacement of inventories** *(US)* Rückstellung für Auffüllung des Lagerbestandes;
  to break into ~s Vorräte anbrechen; **to lay in a store of** ~s Vorratslager anlegen; **to make** ~s *(balance sheet)* Rückstellungen bilden; **to make** ~s **for one's old age** Vorkehrungen für sein Alter (Altervorsorgebestimmungen) treffen;
  wholesale ~ **business** Lebensmittelgroßhandel; ~ **dealer** Lebensmittelhändler.

provisional *(a.)* vorläufig, provisorisch, zeit-, einstweilig, kommissarisch, interimistisch;
  ~ **arrangement** Provisorium; ~ **bond** Zwischen-, Interimsschein; ~ **booking** provisorischer Abschluß; ~ **invoice** vorläufige Rechnung; ~ **receipt** Zwischenquittung.

proviso Bedingung, Klausel, Vorbehalt;
  ~ **in case of war** Kriegsklausel.

proximity to transportation Verkehrsnähe, nahe Verkehrsbelegenheit.

proxy [Handlungs]vollmacht, Stellvertretung, *(for meeting of shareholders)* Stimmrechtsermächtigung, *(representative)* Rechts-, Stellvertreter, Bevollmächtigter;
  irrevocable ~ *(shareholders' meeting, Br.)* unwiderruflich erteilte Vollmacht;
  to send in ~ **against (in favo(u)r)** *(shareholders' meeting)* sein Stimmrecht durch einen Bevollmächtigten dagegen (dafür) ausüben lassen;
  ~ **form** Vollmachtsformular; ~ **power** Depotstimmrechtsermächtigung.

prudent buisness man umsichtiger Kaufmann.

prudential | **committee** *(US)* Beratungs-, Verwaltungsausschuß, Beirat; ~ **insurance** Volksversicherung.

public Öffentlichkeit, Allgemeinheit;
  general investing ~ analgsuchende Publikum;
  ~ *(a.)* öffentlich [bekannt], staatsbürgerlich, staatlich;

to go ~ *(company)* in eine öffentlich-rechtliche Gesellschaftsform umwandeln;
[certified] ~ **accountant** *(US)* Bücherrevisor, Wirtschaftsprüfer; ~ **administration** Regie; ~ **appointment** Staats[an]stellung; ~ **assistance** *(US)* Sozialhilfe, Fürsorgeunterstützung; ~ **auction** öffentliche Versteigerung; ~ **bonds** Staatsanleihe, -schuldverschreibungen; ~ **business** Staatsbetrieb; ~ **call box** *(Br.)* öffentliche Fernsprechzelle; ~ **company** *(Br.)* gemeinwirtschaftliche Unternehmung; ~ **credit** Staatskredit; ~ **debt** *(US)* Staatsschuld; ~ **deposits** *(Br.)* Zentralbankguthaben der öffentlichen Hand; ~ **economist** Nationalökonom; ~ **economy** Volkswirtschaftslehre; ~ **expenditures** Ausgaben der öffentlichen Hände; **at the** ~ **expense** auf Kosten des Steuerzahlers; ~ **finances** Finanzwirtschaft; ~ **house** *(Br.)* Schankwirtschaft, Kneipe; ~ **institution** gemeinnütziges Unternehmen; ~ **liability insurance** Haftpflichtversicherung; ~ **ownership** Staatseigentum, *(municipal accounting)* Kommunalbesitz; ~ **pension** Staatspension; ~ **relations** öffentliche Meinungspflege, Kontaktpflege, Öffentlichkeitsarbeit; ~ **relief** *(US)* öffentliche Fürsorge; ~ **revenue** Staatseinkünfte; ~ **sale** Auktion; ~ **service company (corporation, enterprise,** *US)* öffentlicher Versorgungsbetrieb; ~ **store** Zollniederlage; ~ **telephone** Münzfernsprecher; ~ **tender** Ausschreibung; ~ **transport** öffentliche Verkehrsmittel.

public utility [öffentlicher] Versorgungsbetrieb; ~ **bonds** Versorgungswerte; ~ **company (corporation, establishment, undertaking)** öffentlicher Versorgungsbetrieb, Versorgungsunternehmen.

public | warehouse [öffentlicher] Speicher; ~ **way** Landstraße; ~ **works project** *(US)* Arbeitsbeschaffungsprojekt.

publication Veröffentlichung, öffentliche Bekanntmachung;
business ~ Wirtschaftswerbung.

publicity Öffentlichkeit, *(advertising)* Propaganda, Werbung;
to create favo(u)rable ~ positive Reaktionen in der Öffentlichkeit auslösen;
~ **agency** Werbeagentur; ~ **bureau** Anzeigenannahmestelle; ~ **campaign** Werbefeldzug, -aktion; ~ **manager** Werbeleiter.

publish *(v.)* verlegen, publizieren, veröffentlichen;
~ **counterfeit money** Falschgeld in Umlauf setzen.

publishing business Verlagsbuchhandel.

puff *(v.) up goods* Warenpreis in die Höhe treiben.

puffing *(Br.)* übertriebene Anpreisung;
harmless ~ *(US)* überzogene Werbung.

pull *(influence, sl.)* politischer Einfluß, Protektion, gute Beziehungen;
~ **of demand** Nachfragesog;
~ *(v.)* seine Beziehungen spielen lassen;
~ **in the cash** Außenstände eintreiben; ~ **down the prices of stocks** Aktienkurse herunterdrücken;
to be a heavy ~ **upon s. one's purse** jem. teuer zu stehen kommen;
~~**out supplement** herausnehmbare Beilage.

pump priming *(US)* konjunkturelle Initialzündung, Ankurbelung der Wirtschaft.

purchase Kauf, Einkauf, Erwerbung, Anschaffung, *(annual return from land)* Jahresertrag;
at thirty years' ~ zum Dreißigfachen des Jahresertrages;
advance ~ Vorratseinkauf; **bulk** ~ Mengen-, Großeinkauf; **compulsory** ~ *(Br.)* Enteignung; **firm** ~ Festkauf; ~ **forward** Terminkauf, Kauf auf Zeit (Lieferung); **futures** ~ *(US)* Terminkauf; **hire** ~ *(Br.)* Abzahlungskauf, -geschäft; **open-market** ~ Käufe am offenen Markt; **outright** ~ *(bank)* Übernahme auf den Konsortialwege, *(US)* Kauf gegen sofortige Lieferung; **speculation (speculative)** ~s Meinungs-, Spekulationskäufe;
~ **on account** Kauf auf Kredit ([feste] Rechnung);
~ **on approval** Kauf auf Probe; ~ **for cash** Kauf gegen bar; ~ **on commission** Kommissionskauf; ~ **for future delivery** *(US)* Lieferungs-, Terminkauf; ~ **by description** Gattungskauf; ~ **of a home** Eigenheimerwerb; ~ **according to (by) sample (pattern)** Kauf nach Probe; ~ **of securities** Effektenerwerb; ~ **on the deferred payment system** *(US)* Abzahlungskauf;
~ *(v.) (acquire)* erstehen, [käuflich] erwerben, *(buy)* kaufen, ab-, an-, einkaufen, anschaffen;
~ **on account (credit)** auf Rechnung kaufen; ~ **at auction** ersteigern; ~ **for future delivery** *(US)* auf Lieferung kaufen; ~ **a portion of a new issue** Konsortialanteil einer Anleihe übernehmen;
to acquire by ~ käuflich erwerben; **to cancel a** ~ Kauf rückgängig machen; **to have some ~s to make** einige Besorgungen zu erledigen haben; **to live on one's** ~ einträgliche Beschäftigung haben;
~ **account** Wareneingangskonto; ~ **agreement form** Kaufvertragsvordruck; ~ **allowance** Preisnachlässe; ~ **book** Wareneingangsbuch; ~ **commitments (balance sheet)** Konsortialverpflichtungen; ~ **contract** *(stock exchange)* Schlußnote; ~ **diary** Einkaufszettel; ~ **invoice** Eingangsrechnung; ~ **money** Kaufpreis, -summe; ~ **observation** Beobachtung der Kaufgewohnheiten; ~ **order** Kunden-, Kaufauftrag, Bestellung; ~ **pattern** Käuferverhalten; ~ **price** Anschaffungs-, Erwerbs-, [Ein]kaufpreis, Kaufsumme; ~ **record** Einkaufsbeleg; ~ **requisition** Bedarfsmeldung; ~ **requisition number** Bestellnummer; ~ **returns account** Retourenkonto.

purchaser Käufer, Erwerber, Abnehmer *(auction)* Ersteigerer;
bona-fide ~ gutgläubiger Erwerber; **intending (prospective)** ~ [Kauf]reflektant, Kaufinteressent; **onetime** ~ Laufkunde;
~ **in bad faith** bösgläubiger Erwerber;
to find (meet with) ~s Abnehmer finden.

purchasing Kauf[en], Einkauf, Ankauf, Erwerb;
~ **agent** Einkaufssachbearbeiter; ~ **association** Einkaufsgenossenschaft; ~ **cartel** Abnehmerkartell; ~ **combine** Einkaufsgemeinschaft; ~ **costs** Warenbeschaffungskosten; ~ **country** Käuferland; ~ **order** Kaufauftrag, Bestellung.

purchasing power Kaufkraft;
    excessive ~ Kaufkraftüberhang;
    ~ of the population Massenkaufkraft;
    ~ parity Kaufkraftparität; **to skim off ~ surplus**
    überschüssige Kaufkraft abschöpfen.
pure unverfälscht, rein, *(gold)* massiv;
    ~ competition *(US)* freier Wettbewerb; **~ endow-**
    ment insurance Kapitalversicherung auf den
    Erlebensfall.
purge *(v.)* **the finances of a country** Finanzen eines
    Landes in Ordnung bringen.
purse Börse, [Geld]beutel, Portemonnaie, *(sum col-*
    lected) Geldsammlung, -geschenk;
    heavy (long, well-lined) ~ wohlgespickte (volle)
    Börse; **ill-lined ~** leeres Portemonnaie; **public ~**
    Staatsschatz;
    to be beyond one's ~ etw. nicht erschwingen kön-
    nen; **to live within one's ~** seinen Verhältnissen ent-
    sprechend leben;
    ~ bearer Kassenwart.
pursue *(v.)* **one's business** seinen Geschäften (seinem
    Beruf) nachgehen; **~ a trade** Gewerbe betreiben.
pursuit of a trade Gewerbeausübung.
push *(pep)* Unternehmungsgeist, Energie, Schwung,
    upward ~ on costs Kostenauftrieb;
    ~ *(v.)* **ahead about six points** etwa sechs Punkte
    gewinnen; **~ goods** Waren aufdrängen; **~ shares**
    (stock exchange) Schwindelaktien an der Börse
    unterbringen; **~ one's wares** seine Waren absetzen;
    to get a job by ~ seine Position reiner Protektion
    verdanken.
put *(stock exchange)* Rückprämie;
    ~ and call Stellagegeschäft, Geschäft auf Geben
    und Nehmen; **~ of more** Nach[lieferungs]geschäft,
    Nochgeschäft auf Geben (in Verkäufers Wahl);
    ~ *(v.)* **a business deal across** Geschäft erfolgreich
    abschließen; **~ a good deal of money aside** schönes
    Stück Geld zurücklegen; **~ away for one's old age**
    Geld für seine alten Tage zurücklegen; **~ down to**
    s. one's account jem. in Rechnung stellen; **~ down**
    one's expenditure seine Ausgabenwirtschaft ein-
    schränken.

put in *(in bank)* einlegen, *(employ)* einstellen, *(file)*
    vorlegen, einreichen, *(ship)* einlaufen;
    ~ an advertisement Annonce in die Zeitung ein-
    rücken lassen; **~ a distress** Zwangsvollstreckung
    betreiben; **~ an extra hour's work** Überstunde
    machen; **~ operation** in Betrieb setzen; **~ store** ein-
    lagern; **~ a trade** in die Lehre geben.
put | capital into a business Geld in ein Geschäft
    stecken; **~ money into an undertaking** Geld in ein
    Geschäft stecken.
put off auf die lange Bank schieben *(forged money)*
    in Umlauf setzen;
    ~ one's creditors seine Gläubiger hinhalten.
put | on an (a new) article on the market Ware auf dem
    Markt anbieten, neue Artikel lancieren; **~ it on**
    during the holiday season während der Ferienzeit
    höhere Preise verlangen; **~ a price on each article**
    jeden Artikel einzeln auszeichnen.
put out to apprentice in die Lehre geben.
put through a business deal Geschäft zu einem er-
    folgreichen Abschluß bringen;
put to | great expense große Unkosten verursachen; **~**
    the money to a good use Geld vernünftig anlegen; **~**
    large sums to reserve große Rückstellungen ma-
    chen.
put up *(increase)* erhöhen, heraufsetzen, (Aktien)
    übernehmen, *(at a hotel)* übernachten [in];
    · in barrels in Fässern verpacken; **~ funds** Geld
    aufbringen; **~ a notice** Bekanntmachung anschla-
    gen; **~ the rate of a tax** Steuersatz anheben; **~ a**
    vessel for freight Schiff zur Verladung vormerken.
put and call Geschäft auf Geben und Nehmen,
    Stellagegeschäft.
put-up | job abgekartete Sache; **~ price** *(auction)*
    Taxpreis.
pyramid *(stock exchange)* ständig zunehmender Bör-
    sengewinn;
    ~ *(v.)* *(stock exchange)* *(US)* [Aufträge] zu Speku-
    lationszwecken sich häufen lassen.
pyramiding Verschachtelung, *(monopoly position)*
    finanzielle Monopolstellung;
    ~ business Schachteltransaktion.

Q

qualification [erforderliche] Befähigung, persönliche Begabung, [berufliche] Eignung, Qualifikation, *(of corporate director)* Aktienkapital eines Pflichtvorstandsmitgliedes;
subject to ~ Änderung vorbehalten;
professional ~s fachliche Qualifikationen; **property** ~ Eigentumsnachweis;
~ **for benefit** Unterstützungsvoraussetzung; ~ **for dividend** Dividendenberechtigung; ~s **for a public office** Beamteneigenschaften; ~ **for pension** Pensionsberechtigung;
to accept without ~ vorbehaltlos annehmen; **to hold the** ~s [berufliche] Voraussetzungen erfüllen; ~ **card** Personalbogen; ~ **form** Bewerbungsformular; ~ **shares** Pflicht-, Qualifikationsaktien [eines Vorstandsmitgliedes].

qualified *(authorized)* autorisiert, befugt, berechtigt, *(eligible)* berechtigt, qualifiziert, geeignet, befähigt;
~ **to list** *(shares)* börsenfähig;
~ **acceptance** Annahme unter Vorbehalt; ~ **certificate** *(auditing)* eingeschränkter Prüfungsbericht; ~ **indorsement** Giro ohne Verbindlichkeit; ~ **plan** (trust, *US*) steuerlich begünstigter Gewinnbeteiligungs- oder Pensionsplan; ~ **sale** Kauf unter Eigentumsvorbehalt; ~ **seaman** Maat; ~ **worker** Facharbeiter.

qualify *(v.)* qualifizieren, berechtigen, sich eignen, Befähigung besitzen, *(modify)* einschränken, modifizieren;
~ **a security for sale to the public** Wertpapier zur Börsenzulassung anmelden; ~ **for dividend** dividendenberechtigt sein; ~ **for a pension** zur Pensionierung anstehen.

qualifying | **agreement** *(Br.)* Lombardschein; ~ **certificate** Befähigungsnachweis; ~ **period** Anwartschaftszeit [in der ˙Sozialversicherung], Warte-, Karenzzeit; ~ **shares** *(US)* [nach Statuten] vorgeschriebener Aktienbesitz.

quality Güte, Qualität, Wert, *(faculty)* Eigenschaft, Fähigkeit, *(grade)* Gütegrad, Sorte, Marke;
of first (prime) ~ feinster Sorte, von bester Qualität; **varying in** ~ von ungleicher Güte; **bottom** ~ schlechte Qualität; **choicest** ~ feinste Sorte; **fair average** ~ Durchschnittsqualität; **inferior** ~ abfallende Qualität; **medium (middling)** ~ Mittelsorte, Sekundaqualität; **good merchantable** ~ gute Qualität und Beschaffenheit; **standard** ~ Durchschnittsqualität; **sterling** ~ allererste Qualität; **warranted** ~ zugesicherte Eigenschaft;
~ **of commodities** Handelswert einer Ware;
to act in the ~ **of an agent** als Vertreter handeln; **to check the** ~ Qualitätsprüfung vornehmen; **to stock only one** ~ nur eine Sorte führen;
~ **area** Güteklasse; ~ **complaint** Qualitätsrüge; ~ **control** Qualitätskontrolle, statistische Güteüberwachung; **medium-**~ **goods** Waren mittlerer Qualität und Güte; ~ **grade** Qualitätssorte, -stufe; ~ **inspection** *(Br.)* Abnahmeprüfung; ~ **label** Gütezeichen; ~ **product** Qualitätserzeugnis; ~ **specification** *(Br.)* Güte-, Abnahmevorschriften; ~ **workmanship** Qualitätsarbeit.

quantitative | **index** Mengenindex; ~ **sales** Mengenkonjunktur.

quantity Quantität, Quantum, Menge;
minimum commercial ~ handelsübliche Mindestmenge;
~ **buyer** Großabnehmer, Grossist; ~ **contract** Gattungskauf; ~ **description** Mengenbezeichnung; ~ **discount** Großhandels-, Mengenrabatt; ~ **production** Massenproduktion; ~ **rate** Mengen-, Grossistentarif; ~ **surveyor** *(Br.)* Preiskalkulator, Bausachverständiger; ~ **turnover** mengenmäßiger Umsatz.

quarantine Quarantäne[station];
to be out of ~ Quarantäne hinter sich haben;
~ **flag** Quarantäneflagge.

quarter *(mar.)* Posten, *(of town)* Stadtviertel, (of year) Vierteljahr, Quartal;
from authoritative ~ von maßgebender Seite; **business** ~ Geschäftsgegend, -viertel; **financial** ~s Finanzkreise; **manufacturing** ~ Fabrikviertel;
to apply to the proper ~ sich an die zuständige Stelle wenden; **to have free** ~s umsonst wohnen; **to owe several** ~s **rent** mehrere Mietraten schuldig sein; **to shift one's** ~s umziehen;
~s **allowance** Beköstigungsgeld; ~ **bill** Quartalsabrechnung; ~ **stock** *(US)* Viertelsaktie.

quarterly | **account** Quartalsrechnung; ~ **dividend** Vierteljahresdividende.

quasi | **agreement** *(antitrust law, US)* aufeinander abgestimmtes Verhalten; ~**-governmental corporation** halbstaatliche Einrichtung; ~ **prosperity** Scheinkonjunktur.

quay Schiffslandeplatz, Anlegestelle, Kai;
to discharge at the ~ am Kai löschen;
~ **dues** Kaigebühren; ~ **receipt** Kai-Empfangsschein.

queer | **bill** fauler Wechsel; ~ **transaction** verdächtiges Geschäft.

question |s **of currency** Währungsfragen;
~ *(v.)* **the computation of an account** Kontoabrechnung nicht anerkennen;
~ **form** Fragebogen.

questionnaire, questionary Fragebogen.

queue | **of cars** Fahrzeug-, Autoschlange;
~ *(v.)* **up** *(Br.)* Schlange stehen.

queuing line Warteschlange.

quick schnell, sofort, prompt, *(in business)* geschäftsgewandt;
~ **assets** *(balance sheet, US)* flüssige (liquide) Anlagen, Umlaufvermögen; ~**-assets ratio** *(US)* Liquiditätsgrad; ~ **liabilities** kurzfristig rückzahl-

bare Schulden; ~-lunch bar Imbißstube, Schnell-restaurant.

quickie strike von den Gewerkschaften nicht genehmigter (wilder) Streik.

quit | of charges spesenfrei;
~ (v.) business sich vom Geschäft zurückziehen; ~ scores Konto ausgleichen;
to give notice to ~ Mieter kündigen.

quitclaim deed Grundstücksübertragungsurkunde.

quitter (US) Arbeitsunlustiger, Drückeberger.

quitting clause (US) Dienstschlußklausel.

quorum Beschlußfähigkeit;
to lack a ~ beschlußunfähig sein.

quota Kontingent, Quote, (bankruptcy) [Konkurs]-quote, (share) [Verhältnis]anteil, Rechnungs-, verhältnismäßiger Anteil, prozentuale Beteiligung;
subject to a ~ kontingentiert;
exhausted ~ erschöpftes Kontingent; export ~ Ausfuhrquote; foreign-exchange Devisenkontingent; marketing ~ Absatzkontingent; sales ~ Verkaufskontingent; tariff-rate ~ Zollkontingent;
~ of profits Gewinnanteil;
to allow unfilled ~s to carry into next year unausgenutzte Quoten ins nächste Jahr übertragen lassen; to contribute one's ~ seinen Anteil bezahlen; to exceed a ~ Kontingent überziehen; to use up a ~ Kontingent erschöpfen;
~ accountancy Quotenabrechnung; ~ agent Kontingentträger; ~ bargaining Quotenaushandlung; ~ goods kontingentierte (bewirtschaftete) Waren; ~ increase Quotenerhöhung; ~ restriction Kontingentierung; ~ share Kontingentsanteil, (reinsurance) Quote.

quotation zitierte Stelle, Belegstelle, Zitat, (stock exchange) [Kurs]notierung, Börsennotierung, Effektenkurs, -notiz;
at the present ~ zum gegenwärtigen Kurs; without official ~ ohne Kurs;
bid ~s Geldkurs; closing ~ Schlußnotierung; daily ~s Kursblatt; fluctuating ~ schwankender Kurs; latest ~s from the stock exchange letzte Kursnotierungen; nominal ~ Notiz ohne Umsätze; official ~ amtliche Notierung; opening ~ Eröffnungskurs; price ~ (stock exchange) Kursnotierung; today's ~ heutige Notierung;
~s for forward delivery Terminnotierungen; ~ of [foreign] exchange [rates] Devisen-, Valutanotierung; ~ of a price Preisangabe; ~ of specie Geldkurszettel; ~ on the stock market Börsenkurs; to admit for ~ on the stock exchange zur Notierung zulassen; to give a ~ for building a house Kostenvoranschlag für einen Hausbau vornehmen;
~ board Kurstafel; ~ ticker (US) Börsenfernschreiber.

quote (v.) zitieren, (state price) Preise angeben, (stock exchange) Kurse börsenmäßig feststellen;
~ a price Preisangebot machen, (stock exchange) Kurs notieren; ~ references Referenzen angeben.

quoted | on exchange börsengängig;
to be ~ consecutively fortlaufend notiert werden; ~ investments at costs (balance sheet, Br.) börsengängige Wertpapiere zum Anschaffungskurs; ~ list (Br.) amtlicher Kurszettel; ~ price Preisangebot, (stock exchange) Kursnotierung; ~ value Kurswert.

R

rack Gestell, Verkaufsständer;
   baggage *(US) (luggage, Br.)* ~ Gepäcknetz, -ablage; **unloading** ~ Abladeplatz;
   ~ **jobber** *(US)* Großlieferant eines Kaufhofs.
racket *(sharp practices, US)* Schiebung.
racketeer *(US)* Schieber, Erpresser.
rackrent *(Br.)* jahresübliche Miete.
radio Rundfunk, Radio;
   ~ **address** Rundfunkansprache; ~ **advertising** Hörfunkwerbung; ~ **newsreel** *(Br.)* Nachrichtensendung; **to sponsor a** ~ **program(me)** Finanzierung eines Rundfunkprogramms übernehmen; ~ **spot** kurze Werbedurchsage; ~ **taxi** Funktaxi.
raffle *(lottery)* Ausspielung, Verlosung, Tombola.
rag | **and bone dealer** *(Br.)* Lumpensammler; ~ **fair** Trödelmarkt; ~ **money** *(US)* entwertetes Papiergeld.
raid *(prices)* Druck, *(stock exchange)* Kursdruck;
   ~ **on a bank** Banküberfall; ~ **on the reserves** Angreifen der Reserven;
   ~ *(v.)* **the market** Kurse durch Verkäufe dfücken;
   ~ **the labo(u)r market** Arbeitsmarkt leerpumpen; ~ **the reserves** Reserven angreifen.
rail *(railway)* Schiene, *(ship)* Reling;
   by ~ per [Eisen]bahn; **ex** ~ **ab Bahnhof**;
   to forward by ~ mit der Bahn befördern;
   ~ **freight** [Eisen]bahnfracht; ~ **freight revenue** Frachteinnahmen; ~ **piggyback** Huckepackverkehr; ~ **and water terminal** Güterumschlagstelle.
railroad *(US)* Eisenbahn, Schienenweg;
   ~ **bill of lading** Eisenbahnfrachtbrief; ~ **carloading** Bahnfrachtsendung; ~ **carrier** bahnamtlicher Spediteur; ~ **fare** Fahrkarte; ~ **freight car** Güterwagen; ~ **passenger car** Personenwaggon; ~ **stocks** Eisenbahnwerte.
railway *(Br.)* Eisenbahn, Schienenweg;
   factory ~ Werksbahn;
   ~ **advertising** Eisenbahnwerbung; ~ **advice** Eisenbahnavis; ~ **carriage** Bahnfracht; ~ **consignment note** Bahnfrachtbrief; ~ **delivery** Bahnzustellung; ~ **express agency** bahnamtlicher Spediteur; ~ **express business** Eilgutverkehr; ~ **goods traffic** Güterverkehr; ~ **parcels** Bahnfrachtgut; ~ **passenger duty** Beförderungssteuer; ~ **terminal** Kopfbahnhof; ~ **ticket** [Eisenbahn]fahrkarte.
rain | **check** *(US)* Einlaßkarte für Ersatzveranstaltung; ~ **insurance** Regenversicherung.
raise | **in (of) wages** *(Br. coll.)* Gehalts-, Lohnerhöhung;
   ~ *(v.)* **the bank rate** *(Br.)* Diskontsatz erhöhen; ~ **a blockade** Blockade aufheben; ~ **capital** Kapital aufnehmen; ~ **cash** Geld auftreiben; ~ **a check** *(US)* Scheckziffern in betrügerischer Absicht erhöhen; ~ **the discount** Diskont[satz] erhöhen; ~ **exports** Ausfuhr steigern; ~ **funds by subscription** Geld durch Zeichnung aufbringen; ~ **the level of prices** Preisniveau anheben; ~ **a loan** Anleihe auf-

nehmen; ~ **money on an estate** Geld (Hypothek) auf ein Grundstück aufnehmen; ~ **production to a maximum** Produktion auf den Höchststand bringen; ~ **a tariff** Tariferhöhung vornehmen.
raising | **of the bank rate** *(Br.)*Diskonterhöhung; ~ **of capital** Kapitalaufbringung; ~ **of a claim** Geltendmachung eines Anspruchs; ~ **of postal** *(Br.)* **(postage,** *US)* **rates** Portoerhöhung; ~ **of rents** Mietsteigerung.
rake-off *(US sl.)* Gewinnanteil, Provision.
rally *(meeting, US)* Tagung, Treffen, *(stock exchange)* [schnelle] Erholung, [Preis]aufschwung.
random | **distribution** Zufallsverteilung; ~ **sample** Stichprobe; ~ **sampling** Stichprobenerhebung.
range *(area)* Gebiet, Spannweite, Bereich, Fächer, *(stock exchange)* Schwanken der Kurse;
   comprehensive ~ gute Auswahl; **price** ~ *(stock exchange)* Kursbewegung, -bildung; **salary** ~ Gehaltsklasse;
   ~ **of activities** Betätigungsfeld; ~ **for cable transfers** Satz für Kabelauszahlungen; ~ **of customers** Kundenkreis; ~ **of earnings to be effected** betroffene Einkommensgruppen; ~ **of goods** Produktangebot; **wide** ~ **of items** großes Warenangebot; ~ **of patterns** Musterkollektion; ~ **of validity** Gültigkeitsbereich;
   ~ *(v.)* einordnen, -reihen, klassifizieren; ~ **between 2 and 8** zwischen 2 und 8 schwanken; **to have a wide** ~ **of goods** über ein großes Sortiment verfügen; **to move in a narrow** ~ geringe Kursschwankungen aufweisen.
rank *(order of precedence)* Rang[ordnung], *(position in life)* Rang, Klasse, Stand, [soziale] Stellung;
   of prior ~ im Range vorgehend, vorrangig;
   cab ~ *(Br.)* Taxistand;
   ~**s of middle management** Schicht der gehobenen Angestellten;
   ~ *(v.)* bevorrechtigt sein, Vortritt haben, *(range in a class)* einordnen, klassifizieren;
   ~ **a creditor** Rangordnung eines Gläubigers bestimmen; ~ **for the July dividend** *(Br.)* schon im Juli an der Dividendenausschüttung teilnehmen; ~ **high in public favo(u)r** großes Ansehen in der Öffentlichkeit genießen;
   ~**-and-file union member** einfaches Gewerkschaftsmitglied.
ranking | **of assets** Rangfolge von Konkursgegenständen; ~ **of a creditor** Gläubigerrang; ~ **of mortgage** Hypothekenrang;
   ~ *(a.)* **for dividend** dividendenberechtigt.
ransom | **demand** Lösegeldforderung; ~ **money** Lösegeld; ~ **price** Wucherpreis.
rapid | **mass transport** Schnelltransport von Massengütern; ~ **transit** *(US)* Nahschnellverkehr.
rata, pro verhältnismäßig, anteilig.
ratable verhältnis-, anteilsmäßig, *(municipal tax, Br.)* umlage-, kommunalsteuerpflichtig;
   ~ **freight** Distanzfracht; ~ **value** Steuermeßwert.

rate *(advertising)* Anzeigenpreis, *(broadcasting)* Minutenpreis, *(electricity, gas)* Abgabenpreis, *(estimate)* Preis, Veranschlagung, Anschlag, Berechnung, Taxe, *(public charge)* Gebühr, Leistungsentgelt, *(insurance)* Prämiensatz, *(marine insurance)* Risikoklasse;

all the same ~ zum gleichen Preis; **at the best possible** ~ bestens, bestmöglich; **at a cheap (low)** ~ wohlfeil, billig; **at the current** ~ zum Tageskurs; **at the highest** ~ **of exchange** zum höchsten Kurse; **at a** ~ **of 4 percent** zu einem [Zins]satz von 4 %; **~s** *(municipal taxes, Br.)* Gemeindeabgaben; Kommunalsteuern,

first-~ erstklassig; **third-~** von minderwertiger Qualität;

advanced ~ erhöhter Frachtsatz; **advertising** ~ Anzeigentarif; **asked** ~ Briefkurs; **bank** ~ *(US)* Diskont[satz]; **base (basic)** ~ *(wages)* Ecklohntarif; **blanket** ~ Pauschaltarif; **buying** ~ Ankaufskurs; **call** ~ Satz für täglich fälliges Geld; **carload** ~ *(US)* Waggonfrachtrate; **class** ~ *(insurance)* Tarifprämie; **clock card** ~ garantierter Stundenlohn; **closing** ~ Schlußkurs; **combination through** ~ kombinierter Durchgangsfrachtsatz; **commission** ~ Provisionssatz; **commodity** ~ *(airliner, US)* Vorzugstarif; **continental** ~**s** Sorten und Devisenkurse auf europäischen Plätzen; **cost-per-thousand** · ~ *(advertising)* Tausenderpreis; **customs** ~ Zollsatz; **death** ~ Sterblichkeitsziffer; **deposit** ~ Habenzinssatz; **discount** ~ Diskont[satz]; **distance** ~ Distanzfrachttarif; **drooping** ~**s** rückläufige Kurse; **effective** ~ Effektivzins; **entrance** ~ *(US)* Anfangsgehalt, -lohn; **exceptional** ~ Ausnahmetarif; **exchange** ~ Wechsel-, Umrechnungskurs; **factory overhead** ~ Fertigungsgemeinkostensatz; **first** ~ erste Qualität; **flat** ~ *(advertising)* Anzeigenfestpreis; **flat mil(e)age** ~ Kilometerpauschale; **freight** ~**s** *(US)* Gütertarif; **graduated** ~ Staffeltarif; **half** ~ halber Fahrpreis; **income tax** ~ Einkommensteuersatz; **insurance** ~ Versicherungsprämie; **interest** ~ Zinssatz; **job** ~ Akkordrichtsatz; **less-than-carload (LCL)** ~ *(US)* Stückguttarif; **line** ~ Mindesttarifsatz; **loan** ~ Darlehnszinssatz; **local** ~**s** *(shipping)* Ortstarif; **lowest [possible]** ~ Mindestpreis, -satz; **market** ~ Marktpreis, *(Br., discount rate)* Diskontsatz, *(stock exchange)* amtlicher Kurs, Börsenkurs; **minimum plant** ~ betrieblicher Mindestlohn; **mixed carload** ~ *(US)* Stückguttarif; **mortality** ~ Sterblichkeit[sziffer]; **mortgage** ~ Hypothekenzinssatz; **municipal** ~**s** *(Br.)* Kommunalumlage; **net U. K.** ~ *(Br.)* Steuersatz nach Anrechnung der Doppelsteuer; **occupational** ~ üblicher Stundenlohn; **official** ~ *(stock exchange)* amtlicher Kurs; **one-time** ~ *(advertising)* Seitenpreis, Einmaltarif; **open-market** ~**s** *(US)* Geldsätze am offenen Markt; **part-time** ~ Lohn für nicht ganztägig beschäftigte Arbeitskräfte; **preferential** ~**s** Vorzugssatz, -tarif; **prime** ~ *(US)* Leitzinssatz; **private** ~ *(Br.)* Privatdiskontsatz; **public utility** ~**s** Gebührnisse öffentlicher Betrie-

be; **quantitiy** ~ Mengentarif; **regular** ~ *(wages)* Normallohn; **renewal** ~ Prolongationssatz; **scale** ~ *(Br.)* Staffeltarif; **special** ~ Zweckabgabe, Vorzugssatz; **specific** ~ *(insurance)* Sondertarif; **spot** ~ Platzkurs; **standard** ~ Einheitstarif; **straight piece** ~ reiner Stücklohn; **subminimum** ~ untertariflicher Lohn; **tapering** ~**s** Staffeltarif; **telegram** ~ Wortgebühr; **through** ~ *(Br.)* Frachtsatz für Ladungen unter 50 kg; **time** ~ Zeitlohn; **transient** ~ Anzeigentarif für Einzelinsertion ohne Rabatt; **uniform** ~ Einheitsgebühr, -tarif; **water** ~**s** *(Br.)* Wassergeld;

~s and taxes Gebühren und Abgaben, *(Br.)* Kommunalabgaben und Steuern; ~ **of absenteeism** Abwesenheitsquote; **~-in-aid** *(Br.)* kommunale Ausgleichsumlage; ~ **of assessment** Steuersatz; ~ **of benefits** Leistungshöhe; ~ **of contango** Prolongationsgebühr; ~ **of corporation tax** Körperschaftssteuersatz; **letter postage** ~ **for foreign countries** *(Br.)* Auslandsbriefporto; ~ **for delivery** Löschquantum; ~ **of depreciation** Abschreibungssatz; **preferential** ~ **of duty** *(Br.)* Präferenzzoll; ~ **of change** Kursstand, -verhältnis *(bills of exchange)* Wechsel-, Devisen, Umrechnungskurs; ~ **of exchange** Zwangskurs; ~ **of expansion** Expansions-, Zuwachsrate; ~ **of economic growth** Wachstumsrate des Sozialprodukts; ~ **of income tax** Einkommensteuersatz; ~ **of insurance** Versicherungsprämie; ~ **of interest** Zinsfuß; ~ **of issue** Emissionskurs; ~ **for loans on collateral** Lombardsatz; **hourly** ~ **of pay** Stundenlohnsatz; ~ **of productivity** Produktivitätsrate; ~ **of redemption** Rückzahlungskurs; ~ **of return[s]** *(US)* Kapitalverzinsung; **low** ~ **of return** geringe Rendite; ~ **of shipping** Frachttarif; ~ **of subscription** Bezugspreis, *(stock exchange)* Zeichnungskurs; ~ **of turnover** Umschlagsgeschwindigkeit; ~ **of unemployment** Arbeitslosenprozentsatz;

~ *(v.) (appraise)* [ab]schätzen, [be]werten, taxieren, *(assess)* einschätzen, besteuern, *(employees)* beurteilen;

~ **s. o. up** *(insurance)* j. höher (in eine höhere Prämiengruppe) einstufen;

~ **a building for insurance purposes** Gebäude für die Versicherung schätzen lassen; ~ **heavily** kräftig beisteuern; ~ **s. one's property at $ 100 per annum** 100 $ Vermögenssteuer für j. festsetzen; ~ **the tare** Tara berechnen;

to accord s. o. favo(u)rable ~**s** einen günstigen Tarif zugestehen; **to advance the** ~ Kurs heraufsetzen; **to be quoted at the** ~ **of ...** zum Kurs von ... notiert werden; **to cut the** ~ **of discount** Diskont herabsetzen; **to fix** ~**s** *(stock exchange)* Kurse festsetzen, *(tariff policy)* tarifieren; **to lay a** ~ **on a building** Hauszinssteuer erheben; **to sell s. th. at a reasonable** ~ etw. zu einem vernünftigen Preis verkaufen; **to trim slightly the current** ~ **of spending** Umfang der vorgesehenen Investitionen leicht verringern;

~ **adjustment** Prämienregulierung; **~-aided person**

(Br.) Unterstützungsempfänger; ~ **announcement** *(advertising)* Mitteilung über die Anzeigentarife; ~ **base** Richtsatz; ~ **card** *(advertising)* Preistafel, Anzeigentarif, -preisliste; ~ **change** Prämienänderung; ~ **collection** Umlagenerhebung; ~ **collector's office** Stadtsteueramt; ~ **cutting** Tarifermäßigung; ~ **deficiency grant** *(Br.)* Ausgleichszahlungen an finanzschwache Gemeinden; ~ **fixing** Kursfestsetzung, *(piece wage)* Akkordberechnung; ~ **holder,** *(advertising)* Komplettierungsanzeige, Rabattkunde, -schinder, *(US)* Dauerinserat; ~ **making** *(insurance)* Prämienfestsetzung; ~ **-making association** Tarifverband; ~ **notification** *(tel.)* Gebührenansage; ~ **receipt** *(Br.)* Kommunalabgabenquittung; ~ **scale** *(US)* Staffel-, Zonentarif; **joint** ~ **setting** Lohnfestsetzung durch Betriebsführung und Betriebsrat.

rateable verhältnismäßig, anteilmäßig, *(customs)* zollpflichtig, *(municipal tax)* abgaben-, kommunalsteuerpflichtig; ~ **value** *(Br.)* Einheitswert.

rated value of property Mietertragswert eines Grundstückes.

ratepayer *(Br.)* Kommunalsteuerpflichtiger.

ratification of directors' acts Entlastung des Vorstands, Vorstandsentlastung.

rating *(amount fixed, Br.)* Gemeindesteuerbetrag, Umlage[betrag], *(appraisal)* Bemessung, Bewertung, Einschätzung, Taxierung, *(assessment, Br.)* [Steuer]einschätzung, Heranziehung zu einer Umlage, *(banking)* Bonitätsprüfung, *(financial standing)* finanzielle Stellung, *(position)* finanzielle Stellung [eines Unternehmers]; ~s *(stock exchange, US)* Effektenbewertung; **credit** ~ *(US)* Bonitätsprüfung; **efficiency** ~ *(US)* Leistungsbeurteilung; **employee** ~ *(US)* Angestellteneinstufung; ~ **merit** ~ *(US)* Leistungsbeurteilung; **qualification** ~ *(US)* Eigenschaftsbeurteilung; **service** ~ *(US)* Leistungsanalyse; **special** ~ *(US)* Kreditauskunft; ~ **of the entire mortgage pattern** Abschätzung zwecks hypothekarischer Beleihung; ~ **agreement** Tarifvereinbarung; ~ **area** *(Br.)* Umlagenbezirk; ~ **authority** *(Br.)* kommunale Steuerbehörde; ~ **bureau** Prämien-, Tarifbüro, *(insurance business)* Zweckverband; ~ **flop** vom Publikum abgewertetes Fernsehprogramm; ~ **office** Prämienberechnungsstelle; ~ **scale** Schätz-, Beurteilungsskala; ~ **table** *(securities, US)* Bewertungssystem; ~ **valuation** *(Br.)* Grundsteuereinschätzung.

ratio Verhältnis[zahl], Verteilungsschlüssel, Koeffizient, *(balance sheet)* Wertverhältnis; **bond-stock** ~ Renditeverhältnis; **cash position** ~ Kassenstandskoeffizient; **clearing** ~ Verrechnungsschlüssel; **current position** ~ Flüssigkeitsverhältnis (Liquiditätsstatus) eines Unternehmens; **equity** ~ Verhältnis der Aktiva zu den Passiva; **inventory turnover** ~ Umschlagshäufigkeit der Vorräte; **loss** ~ *(insurance)* Schadens-

quote; **price-earnings** ~ Kurs-Gewinnverhältnis; ~ **of allotment** Zuteilungsquote; ~ **of current assets to total liabilities** Verhältnis der flüssigen Aktiven zu den gesamten Verbindlichkeiten; ~ **of distribution** Verteilungsschlüssel; ~ **of exchange** Wechselparität; ~ **of indebtedness to net capital** Verschuldungskoeffizient; ~ **of sales to receivables** Kontoumsatz.

ration Ration *(rationing)* Zuteilung; **off the** ~ nicht bewirtschaftet, punktfrei; **basic petrol** ~ Benzinnormalzuteilung; ~ *(v.) (conrol)* rationieren, in Rationen zuteilen, der Zwangsbewirtschaftung unterwerfen, *(currency)* kontingentieren; ~ **coupon** Lebensmittelkartenabschnitt; ~ **period** Zuteilungsperiode.

rationalization Rationalisierung, Wirtschaftlichkeit, wirtschaftliche Vereinfachung; ~ **boom** Rationalisierungskonjunktur; ~ **efforts** Rationalisierungsanstrengungen.

rationed rationiert, [zwangs]bewirtschaftet; ~ **goods** bewirtschaftete Güter.

rationing | **of consumption** Verbrauchsregelung; ~ **of credit** Kreditkontingentierung; ~ **of foreign exchange** Devisenbewirtschaftung; ~ **card** Zuteilungskarte; ~ **system** Rationierungssystem.

rattener *(Br.)* Saboteur.

rattling trade florierendes Geschäft.

raw *(land, US)* unkultiviert, unbebaut, *(not manufactured)* roh, unbe-, unverarbeitet.

raw material Rohmaterial, -stoff; ~**s used** Rohstoffverbrauch; ~ **s and supplies** *(balance sheet)* Roh-, Hilfs- und Betriebsstoffe; ~ **inventory** Rohstofflager; ~ **shortage** Rohstoffknappheit.

reach-me-down|s Konfektionskleidung, -ware; ~ *(a.)* zum Gebrauch fertig, billig, *(clothes)* konfektioniert.

reacquired capital stock Portefeuille eigener Aktien.

react *(v.)* **markedly lower** *(stock exchange)* mit erheblich niedrigeren Notierungen einsetzen.

reaction, sharp *(stock exchange)* scharfer Rückschlag; **to suffer a slight** ~ leichten [Kurs]rückgang erleiden.

reader | **advertisement** Textanzeige, redaktionelle Anzeige; ~ **traffic** Leserprozentsatz.

readership analysis Leseranalyse, -umfrage.

readiness | for delivery (to deliver) Lieferbereitschaft; ~ **to invest** Anlageneignung.

reading | of the balance sheet Bilanzlesen; ~ **matter** Lesestoff, *(newspaper)* redaktioneller Teil; ~ **notice** redaktionell aufgemachte Anzeige.

readjustment Wiederanpassung, -herstellung, *(of business enterprise)* [wirtschaftliche] Sanierung; **debt** ~ Schuldenregelung; ~ **of capital stock** Berichtigung des Aktienkapitals.

ready [gebrauchs]fertig, verfügbar, einsatzbereit,

(market) aufnahmefähig, geneigt, *(money)* flüssig, bar;

~ **for collection** abhol-, abrufbereit; ~ **for dispatch** versandbereit; ~ **for occupancy** bezugsfertig; ~ **for sea** seeklar; ~ **for shipment** versandfertig; ~ **to take off** *(airplane)* flugklar; ~ **for working** betriebsfertig;

~ **assets** verfügbare Vermögenswerte; ~ **cable** Platzkurs; ~ **capital** Umlaufkapital; ~ **cash** Barzahlung.

ready-made | **-clothes** Konfektionsartikel, -ware; ~ **shop** Konfektionsgeschäft.

ready | **market** aufnahmefähiger Markt; ~ **money** Bargeld; **to find a** ~ **sale** gut gehen, schnell Absatz finden; ~**-to-wear** konfektioniert.

real | **account** Bestands-, Sachkonto; ~ **amount** Istbestand.

real estate unbewegliches Vermögen, Immobiliarvermögen, Liegenschaften, Grundbesitz, *(balance sheet)* unbebaute und bebaute Grundstücke;

developed ~ bebautes Grundstück; **industrial** ~ gewerblich genutztes Grundstück; **mortgaged** ~ [hypothekarisch] belastetes Grundstück.

real-estate | **account** Liegenschaftskonto; ~ **bank** Bodenkreditbank; ~ **broker** Immobilienmakler; ~ **columns** *(newspaper)* Immobilien, Grundstücksmarkt; ~ **dealing** Grundstücksgeschäft; ~ **development project** Landerschließungsvorhaben; ~ **exchange** Grundstückstausch; ~ **firm** Terraingesellschaft; ~ **investment** Anlage in Grundstücken; ~ **investment trust** Immobilieninvestmentfonds; ~ **levy** Grundbesitzabgabe; ~ **loan** hypothekarisch gesicherter Kredit; ~ **manager** Grundstücksverwalter; ~ **map** Grundbuchblatt; ~ **mortgage note** Hypothekenpfandbrief; ~ **offering** Grundstücksangebot; ~ **picture** Grundstücksbeschreibung; ~ **recording** *(US)* Grundbucheintragung; ~ **recording office** *(US)* Grundbuchamt; ~ **register** *(US)* Grundbuch; ~ **syndicate** Terraingesellschaft; ~ **tax** *(US)* Grundsteuer; ~ **value** Grundstückswert; ~ **venture** Bodenspekulation.

real | **income** Realeinkommen; ~ **investment** Sachanlage; ~ **price** effektiver Preis; ~ **purchasing power** effektive Kaufkraft; ~ **tare** Nettotara; ~ **wages** Reallohn.

realizable *(convertible into capital)* kapitalisierbar, *(salable)* verkäuflich, umsetzbar;

~ **assets** effektiver Bestand; ~ **stock** börsengängige Papiere.

realization Kapitalisierung, *(converting into money)* Flüssigmachung, Liquidation, Versilberung, *(evening up)* Glattstellung;

compulsory ~ Zwangsglattstellung;

~ **of a pledge** Pfandverwertung; ~ **of profit** Gewinnrealisierung;

~ **[and liquidation] account** Glattstellungs-, Liquidationskonto; ~ **clause** Verwertungsklausel; ~ **price** Liquidations-, Verkaufspreis; ~ **value** Liquidations-, Realisationswert.

realize *(v.) (convert into capital)* kapitalisieren, *(con-*

vert into money) flüssig-, zu Geld machen, in Geld umsetzen, realisieren, verwerten, versilbern, erlösen, *(even up)* glattstellen, aktivieren;

~ **assets** Vermögenswerte flüssigmachen; ~ **a [high] price** [hohen] Preis erzielen.

realized | **income** tatsächlich verbrauchtes Einkommen; ~ **profit (revenue)** realisierter Gewinn.

realizing order Glattstellungsauftrag.

reallot *(v.)* repartieren.

realty Grundbesitz, -eigentum, Immobilien;

to convert ~ **into personalty** unbewegliches in bewegliches Vermögen umwandeln;

~ **company** *(US)* Grundstücksgesellschaft; ~ **transfer tax** *(US)* Grunderwerbsteuer.

reappraisal Neubewertung.

rearrangement | **of debts** Schuldenregelung; ~ **of a time-table** Fahrplanänderung.

reason-why advertising Aufklärungswerbung.

reasonable *(current)* gangbar, *(fair)* angemessen, solide, reell, *(moderate)* mäßig, billig;

~ **care and diligence** im Verkehr erforderliche Sorgfalt; ~ **cause to believe a debtor insolvent** ausreichender Verdacht für das Vorliegen der Zahlungsunfähigkeit eines Schuldners; ~ **man** normaler Durchschnittsmensch; ~ **notice** angemessene Kündigungsfrist; ~ **price** mäßiger Preis; ~ **wear and tear** übliche Abnutzung.

reassessment Neuveranlagung, *(revalorization)* Aufwertung, *(securities)* Bereinigung;

~ **of taxes** Berichtigungsveranlagung.

reassignment Rückübertragung, Wiederabtretung.

reattachment wiederholte Pfändung.

rebate [Preis]nachlaß, Rabatt, Abzug, Abstrich, *(banking)* Bonifikation, *(drawback)* Rückzoll;

less ~ abzüglich Rabatt;

dealer's ~ Händlernachlaß, -rabatt; **freight** ~ Frachtnachlaß; **quantity** ~ Mengenrabatt;

~ **on bill not due** Wechseldiskontabzug; ~ **of interest** Zinsermäßigung, -vergütung;

~ *(v.)* Nachlaß gewähren, Rabatt zugestehen; **to allow a** ~ **on an account** Rechnungsnachlaß gewähren.

rebook *(v.)* umbuchen.

rebuilding of liquidity Liquiditätsverbesserung.

recall | **for redemption** Aufforderung zur Rückzahlung;

~ *(v.)* **from circulation** aus dem Verkehr ziehen; ~ **a wire** Telegramm widerrufen.

recapitalization of business [Geschäfts]sanierung.

recapitalize *(v.)* kapitalisieren, neufinanzieren, sanieren.

recapture *(confiscation, US)* Enteignung.

recede *(v.)* [im Wert] zurückgehen, *(prices)* weichen, nachgeben;

~ **fractionally** *(stock exchange)* abbröckeln.

receding prices weichende (nachgebende) Kurse.

receipt *(bill)* Rechnung, Quittung, Kassenbon, *(of letter)* Empfang, Inempfangnahme, *(luggage)* Aufgabeschein;

as per ~ **enclosed** laut beiliegender Quittung; **on** ~ **of the draft** bei Eingang des Wechsels;

~s *(goods)* eingehende Waren, *(money received)* eingehende Gelder, Einkünfte;
accountable ~ Buchungsbeleg; **actual** ~s Effektiveinnahme; **application** ~ *(shares, Br.)* Zeichnungsbescheinigung; **bank** ~ Depotschein; **box-office** ~s Kasseneinnahmen; **current** ~s *(US)* Umlaufvermögen; **customhouse** ~ Zollquittung; **daily** ~s Tageseinnahme; **delivery** ~ Lieferschein; **dock** ~ Kaiempfangsschein; **gross** ~s Bruttoeinnahme[n]; **interim** ~ Zwischenquittung; **net** ~s Nettoeinkommen, Betriebsüberschüsse; **nonnegotiable warehouse** ~ Rektalagerschein; **postal** ~ Posteinlieferungsschein; **renewal** ~ Erneuerungsschein; **tax** ~s Steueraufkommen;
~ **in blank** unausgefüllte Quittung; ~s **of the day** Tageskasse; ~ **of deposit** Einzahlungsbescheinigung; ~ **in full** Schlußquittung; ~ **in duplicate** doppelt ausgefertigter Empfangsschein; ~ **of an order** Auftragseingang; ~ **that is not in order** unvollständige Quittung;
~ *(v.)* Quittung ausstellen, quittieren;
~ **a hotel bill** Quittungsstempel auf eine Hotelrechnung setzen;
to acknowledge [the] ~ Empfang bestätigen; **to be in [the]** ~ **of a good income** gutes Einkommen haben; **to count the** ~s Kasse schließen; **to enter as** ~ als Einnahme buchen; **to get a** ~ **for money spent** Spesenzettel erhalten; **to give** ~ **in full** per Saldo quittieren;
~ **book** Quittungsbuch; ~ **form** Quittungsformular; ~ **stamp** Quittungsstempel.
receipted bill of exchange quittierter Wechsel.
receivable ausstehend, noch als Eingang zu erwarten, auf Zahlung wartend, zu zahlen;
~s *(US)* Forderungen, Außenstände, Debitoren [aus Buch-, Wechselforderungen];
accounts ~ *(US)* Buchforderungen; **bills** ~ *(US)* Wechselforderungen, Rimessen; **currents** ~ *(balance sheet, US)* Umlaufvermögen; **long-term** ~s *(US)* langfristige Debitoren;
~s **from customers** *(balance sheet, US)* Kundenforderungen;
~ **assets** ausstehende Guthaben; ~s **turnover** Forderungsumschlag.
receive *(v.)* | **in advance** vorausempfangen; ~ **for collection** zum Inkasso übernehmen; ~ **stolen goods** als Hehler fungieren; ~ **an order** Auftrag entgegennehmen.
received [Zahlung] erhalten, empfangen, *(generally accepted)* authentisch, echt;
cash ~ Betrag bar erhalten;
~ **on account** als Akontozahlung erhalten;
~ **stamp** Eingangsstempel.
receiver Empfänger, Adressat, Übernehmer, *(bankruptcy, US)* Konkurs-, Masseverwalter, *(money)* Einnehmer, *(official liquidator, Br.)* Zwangsverwalter, *(shipping business)* Ladungsempfänger, *(teller)* Kassierer;
~ **general of the public revenue** *(Br.)* Obersteuereinnehmer;

~ **of customs** Zolleinnehmer; ~ **of goods** Warenempfänger; ~ **of wreck** *(Br.)* Strandvogt;
to petition for the appointment of a ~ *(US)* Antrag auf Geschäftsaufsicht stellen;
~ **'s certificate** Beschlagnahmeverfügung.
receivership Vermögensverwaltung, *(bankruptcy, Br.)* Zwangs-, Konkursverwaltung, Geschäftsaufsicht;
under ~ in Konkurs;
to go into ~ bankrott werden; **to make application for** ~ Antrag auf Geschäftsaufsicht stellen.
receiving An-, Abnahme, Empfangnahme;
~ **of goods** Warenannahme;
~ **cashier** Kassierer am Einzahlungsschalter; ~ **counter** Briefannahmestelle; ~ **house** *(goods, Br.)* Auslieferungslager; ~ **note** Lade-, Versandschein; ~ **order** *(Br.)* Veräußerungsverbot, Konkurseröffnungsbeschluß; ~ **room** Empfangsraum, *(goods)* Wareneingangsstelle; ~ **slip** Wareneingangsschein; ~ **teller** Einzahlungskassierer.
reception *(acceptance)* Inempfangnahme, *(admission)* Zulassung, Aufnahme;
~ **of deposits** Annahme von Einlagen;
~ **desk** Empfang[sbüro]; ~ **office** *(hotel)* Empfang[sbüro].
receptionist Empfang, Empfangschef, -dame.
recess *(break)* [Arbeits]pause.
recession [Preis-, Kurs]rückgang, Rückschlag, *(cyclical movement)* Rezession, Konjunkturrückgang, -rückschlag, -flaute; .
initial violent ~ anfängliches starkes Nachgeben [der Kurse]; **trade** ~ wirtschaftlicher Rückschlag; ~ **in business** Konjunkturrückgang; ~ **in profits** Gewinnrezession;
to come out of a ~ Rezession gerade hinter sich gebracht haben; ~ **borne** rezessionsgesteuert; ~ **money** Abstandsgeld; **anti-**~ **policy** Politik der Konjunkturbelebung; ~ **-proof** rezessionsunempfindlich; ~ **year** Jahr wirtschaftlichen Rückgangs.
recharter Weiterbefrachtung.
recipient Empfänger, Empfangsberechtigter, *(benefited party)* Bedachter;
~ **of an allowance** Zuschußempfänger; ~ **of a pension** Ruhegehaltsempfänger.
reciprocal | **insurance** *(US)* Versicherung auf Gegenseitigkeit; ~ **trade agreement** Gegenseitigkeitsabkommen.
reciprocity | **dealings** Gegenseitigkeitsgeschäfte; ~ **principle** Gegenseitigkeitsprinzip.
reckon *(v.)* *(compute)* berechnen, kalkulieren, *(count)* rechnen;
~ **a business generally as prosperous** Geschäftsbranche generell für gewinnträchtig halten; ~ **the cost of a holiday** Kostenaufwand eines Urlaubs ausrechnen; ~ **one's total indebtedness** sich über den Umfang seiner Schulden klarwerden; ~ **rent in the cost of living** Mietanteil in die Lebenshaltungskosten mit einbeziehen; ~ **up one's losses** Verlustbilanz aufstellen.

reckoning *(computing)* [Be]rechnung, *(counting)* Rechnung, Rechnen, Zählen, Zählung;
  without ~ the travel(l)ing expenses Reisespesen ungerechnet;
  to be out of one's ~ sich verrechnet haben; **to work out the ship's ~** Besteck berechnen (nehmen).
reclamation *(banking)* Differenzbetrag [in der Scheckverrechnung], *(protest)* Reklamation, Beschwerde;
  ~ proceedings *(US)* Aussonderungsverfahren.
reclassify *(v.)* neu einstufen, umgruppieren.
recognition test Wiedererkennungstest.
recognizance Kaution, Sicherheitsleistung.
recognized | **agent** Vertreter; **~ merchant** Gewerbesteuerpflichtiger.
recognizee Schuldscheinnehmer.
recognizor Schuldscheinaussteller.
recommend *(v.)* **a price** als [Richt]preis empfehlen.
recommendation Befürwortung, Empfehlung;
  with a favo(u)rable ~ befürwortend.
recommendatory, letters Einführungsschreiben.
recommended price unverbindliche Preisempfehlung.
recompense *(amends)* Entgelt, Ersatz, Entschädigung, *(reward)* Belohnung, Vergeltung;
  as ~ for your trouble für Ihre Mühewaltung;
  to work without ~ unentgeltlich tätig sein.
reconcile *(v.)* *(accounts)* abstimmen, postenweise vergleichen, kollationieren;
reconcilement of bank statement *(Br.)* Anerkenntnis des Rechnungsabschlusses, Saldenbestätigung.
reconciliation | **of [bank] accounts** Kontenabstimmung; **~ of surplus** Gewinnberichtigung;
  ~ account Berichtigungskonto; **~ date** *(banking)* Abstimmungstermin.
reconditioning charge Instandsetzungskosten.
reconfirm *(v.)* **a reservation** Buchung bestätigen.
reconfirmation notice *(airplane)* Buchungsbestätigung.
reconsign umleiten, umadressieren.
reconstruct *(v.)* **a company** *(Br.)* Gesellschaft sanieren.
reconstruction *(house)* Um-, Wiederaufbau, *(reorganization, Br.)* Wiederaufbau, Reorganisation, Sanierung;
  ~ credit Ankurbelungskredit; **≗ Finance Corporation** *(US)* Kreditanstalt für Wiederaufbau; **~ loan** Wiederaufbaukredit.
reconversion *(industry)* Wiederumstellung;
  ~ of stock Aktienumwandlung.
reconvert *(v.)* **industry** Wirtschaft wieder auf Friedensproduktion umstellen.
record *(document)* Urkunde, Dokument, *(minutes)* Aufzeichnungen, Niederschrift *(peak performance)* Höchst-, Spitzenleistung, Rekord, *(register)* Tabelle, Register, Liste, Verzeichnis;
  off the ~ *(US)* inoffiziell, nicht zur Veröffentlichung bestimmt;
  accounting ~s Buchungsbelege, -unterlagen; **old ~s** Registratur; **payroll ~** Gehälterliste; **progressive ~s** laufend geführte Aufzeichnungen; **supporting ~s** Buchungsbelege;

~ of attendance Anwesenheitsliste; **~s of a bank** Bankbelege;
~ *(v.)* buchen, eintragen, *(in minutes)* protokollieren, Protokoll führen, *(put down in writing)* aufzeichnen, verzeichnen, registrieren;
  ~ gains Gewinne verzeichnen; **~ a payment on the reverse side of a letter of credit** Zahlung auf der Rückseite eines Kreditbriefes notieren;
  to appear on the ~ aktenmäßig feststehen; **to be shown only as a ~** nur als Merkposten bestehen; **to cancel a ~ in the real-estate register** *(US)* Eintragung im Grundbuch löschen; **to keep a ~ of one's expenses** Spesenbelege sammeln; **to speak off the ~** nicht für die Öffentlichkeit bestimmte Bemerkungen machen;
  ~ card *(US)* Karteikarte; **~ keeping** Unterlagenführung; **~ low** Rekordtiefstand; **to enter at close to ~ rates** nahezu Höchstsätze erreichen.
recordable eintragungs-, registrierfähig.
recorded | **tape** besprochenes Band; **~ time value** *(rating)* festgelegter Zeitfaktor.
recorder of deeds *(US)* Urkundbeamter der Geschäftsstelle, Geschäftsstellenleiter.
recording Registrierung, Eintragung, Protokollierung, Aufzeichnung;
  ~ of a mortgage Hypothekeneintragung;
  ~ consent Eintragungsbewilligung; **~ medium** Buchungsbeleg; **~ officer** *(US)* Grundbuchbeamter; **~ system** *(filing)* Ablagesystem.
recoup *(v.)* *(cross action)* Schadenersatz im Wege der Gegenklage erhalten, *(recompense)* ersetzen, Ersatz leisten, entschädigen;
  ~ o. s. sich schadlos halten; **~ one's disbursements** seine Auslagen wieder hereinbekommen; **~ a loss** Verlust ausgleichen.
recourse Entschädigung, Schadloshaltung, Ersatzanspruch, [Regreß]recht, -anspruch;
  liable to ~ regreßpflichtig; **without ~** ohne Regreß (Obligo); **without ~ to public funds** ohne Inanspruchnahme öffentlicher Gelder;
  ~ to the capital market Inanspruchnahme des Kapitalmarktes; **~ to the endorser** Rückgriff auf den Indossaten; **~ to public money** Beanspruchung öffentlicher Mittel; **~ to a prior party** Sprungregreß;
  to be liable to ~ regreßpflichtig sein; **to have ~ to arbitration** Schiedsgericht anrufen; **to have ~ to the endorser of a note** sich beim Giranten erholen; **to preserve ~** Regreßrecht wahren; **to seek ~** Regreßansprüche stellen.
recover *(v.)* *(bankruptcy)* aussondern, *(collect)* einziehen, eintreiben, beitreiben, *(get back)* wiederbekommen, *(make up for)* wiedereinbringen, -gutmachen, *(market)* sich [wieder] erholen, ansteigen, anziehen, *(secure compensation)* sich schadlos halten, Regreß nehmen;
  ~ average Ersatz für Havarie erhalten; **~ the coupon** Kuponabschlag einbringen; **~ one's properly incurred expenses** gerechtfertigte Spesen erstattet bekommen; **~ its losses** *(stock market)* Verluste

wieder ausgleichen; ~ **the old level** alten Kursstand wieder erreichen; ~ **a pledged article** Pfand einlösen; ~ **shipwrecked goods** Güter aus einem verunglückten Schiff bergen.

recoverable | costs Kostenrückstand; ~ **debt** beitreibbare Schuld.

recovery Zurück-, Wiedererlangung, *(cyclical)* Aufschwung, Erholung *(debt)* Beitreibung, Einziehung, *(salvage)* Bergung, Rettung, *(stock exchange)* Erholung, Wiederbelebung, Festigung der Börse;
by way of ~ auf dem Regreßwege;
economic ~ Konjunkturanstieg; **financial** ~ finanzielle Gesundung; **industrial** ~ Wirtschaftsbelebung;
~ **of amounts outstanding** Eintreibung von Außenständen; ~ **of by-products** Gewinnung von Nebenprodukten; ~ **of damages** Erlangung von Schadensersatz; ~ **of the market** Kurserholung; ~ **of prices** Preisanstieg, *(stock exchange)* Kurserholung; ~ **of property** Wiedererlangung des Eigentums; ~ **of trade** Wiederbelebung des Handels; ~ **of waste** Abfallverwertung;
to experience a ~ *(market)* sich [wieder] erholen;
to seek ~ Regreß nehmen;
~ **charges** Einziehungskosten, -spesen; ~ **party** Abschleppkommando; **European** ≗ **Program(me) (ERP)** Europäisches Wiederaufbauprogramm; ~ **value** Ausschlachtungswert; ~ **vehicle** Abschleppwagen.

recreation Erholung, Arbeitsruhe, Freizeit;
~ **area** Erholungsgebiet; ~ **center (centre,** *Br.)* Erholungsstätte; ~ **guidance** Freizeitberatung; ~ **market** Freizeitindustrie.

recreational | activities Freizeitbeschäftigung; ~ **facilities** Erholungsmöglichkeiten; **company** ~ **program(me)** betriebliches Freizeitprogramm.

recruit *(v.) (crew)* anheuern, *(labor, US)* anwerben, anstellen, einstellen, *(recover)* sich erholen;
~ **supplies** Lager auffüllen.

recruiter *(plant, US)* Einstellungsleiter.

recruiting *(labor, US)* Einstellung [von Arbeitern]; **personnel** ~ Personalbeschaffung;
~ **firm** Rekrutierungsbüro.

recruitment *(labor, US)* Anstellung, Einstellung;
~ **of apprentices** *(US)* Lehrlingsanwerbung;
~ **sources** *(US)* Arbeitskräftereservoir; ~ **technique** *(US)* An-, Einstellungsverfahren.

rectification | of an account Ansatzberichtigung;
~ **of capital stock** Kapitalberichtigung.

rectify *(v.)* **entries** Eintragungen (berichtigen).

recuperate *(v.)* **a loss** sich für einen Verlust schadlos halten.

recuperation, economic wirtschaftliche Erholung, Konjunkturbelebung.

recurring cost *(US)* laufende Geschäftskosten.

recycle *(v.)* regenieren, *(finance)* Öldollar international wieder anlegen, *(refuse)* Müll aufbereiten.

recycling *(financing)* Rückführung von Öldollarkapital.

red *(balance sheet)* Schulden-, Debetseite, *(loss, US)* Verlust, Defizit, Schulden;
to be in the ~ *(US)* Verluste haben, im Debet sein; **to be wound up in the** ~ *(US)* mit Verlust liquidiert werden; **to climb (get, come) out of the** ~ *(US)* aus den roten Zahlen herauskommen; **to go into the** ~ *(US)* in die Verlustzone geraten; **to run in the** ~ *(US)* mit Verlust arbeiten;
~**carpet clause** *(letter of credit)* Vorschußklausel;
~**carpet treatment** großer Bahnhof; ~ **figures** *(balance sheet)* rote Zahlen, Verlustzahlen; **to cope with** ~ **ink** *(US)* mit dem Defizit fertig werden; ~**ink entry** *(US)* Verlusteintragung; ~ **interest** Sollzinsen; ~ **numbers** Zinszahlen; ~ **tapism** Bürkratismus.

redeem *(v.) (amortize)* amortisieren, *(buy off)* zurückzahlen, ablösen, *(pledge goods)* [wieder] einlösen;
~ **an annuity** Rente ablösen; ~ **a bill** Wechsel honorieren; ~ **a mortgage** Hypothek tilgen.

redeemable tilg-, amortisierbar, *(loan)* kündbar, *(recoverable)* ablöslich, auslösbar;
~ **in advance** vorzeitig tilgbar; ~ **in gold** in Gold rückzahlbar;
~ **annuity** Ablösungsrente; ~ **bonds** kündbare Obligationen; ~ **feature** Kündigungsrecht; ~ **loan** Tilgungsdarlehen; ~ **preferred stock** *(US)* rückkaufbare Vorzugsaktie.

redemption Amortisierung, Tilgung, *(coupon)* Gutscheineinlösung, *(investment trust)* Rückzahlung von Investmentanteilen, *(of pledge)* Aus-, Einlösung;
mandatory ~ Einlösung vor Verfall;
~ **of an annuity** Rentenablösung; ~ **of bank notes** Einlösung von Banknoten; ~ **of debts** Schuldentilgung; ~ **of land tax** Grundsteuerablösung; ~ **of shares (stocks,** *US)* Aktienrückkauf;
to call for ~ zur Einlösung aufrufen;
~ **account** Amortisationskonto; ~ **capital** Ablösungsbetrag; ~ **charge** *(investment fund)* Rücknahmespesen; ~ **clause** Einlösungsklausel; ~ **cost** *(investment trust)* Verkaufsspesen; ~ **fund** *(US)* Ablösungs-, [Schulden]tilgungsfonds; ~ **instal(l)ment** Tilgungsrate; ~**loan** Ablösungsanleihe; ~ **money** Tilgungsbetrag; ~ **mortgage** Amortisationshypothek; ~ **office** Amortisationskasse; ~ **plan** Schuldentilgungsplan; ~ **price** Rückzahlungspreis, *(investment fund)* Rücknahmepreis; ~ **rate** Tilgungsquote; ~ **reserve** Tilgungsrücklage; ~ **right** Auslosungsrecht; ~ **table** Amortisationsplan; ~ **value** Rückkaufswert.

redeploy | *(v.)* the assets of a company Vermögenswerte eines Unternehmens anderweitig einsetzen;
~ **the labo(u)r force** Arbeitskräfte umgruppieren.

redhibiton *(US) (sales contract)* Wandlung.

redhibitory defect (vice) *(US)* Gewährmangel.

redirect *(v.) (letter)* umadressieren, nachschicken.

rediscount Rediskont, *(US)* Diskont;
~ **credit** Rediskontkredit, *(US)* Diskontkredit; ~ **rate** Rediskontsatz, *(US)* Diskontsatz.

redistribution of income Einkommensumschichtung, -umverteilung.

redraft Rückwechsel, Rikambio[wechsel];
~ **charges** Rückwechselspesen.
redraw *(v.)* **upon** zurücktrassieren.
redress | *(v.)* **the balance of trade** Handelsbilanz ausgleichen;
to obtain ~ **from s. o.** gegen j. Regreß nehmen.
reduce *(v.)* ermäßigen, ab-, nachlassen, verbilligen, *(diminish in value)* herab-, heruntersetzen, reduzieren;
~ **the assessment on a building** Gebäude niedriger bewerten; ~ **the bank rate** Diskontsatz senken; ~ **the consumption** Verbrauch einschränken; ~ **debts** Schulden abbauen; ~ **the customs duties** Zollsätze herabsetzen; ~ **the establishment** Personalabbau durchführen; ~ **a fee** Gebühren ermäßigen; ~ **land to public use** Land für öffentliche Zwecke enteignen; ~ **money** Devisen umrechnen; ~ **the output** Produktion drosseln; ~ **pro rata** nach dem Verhältnis der Beträge kürzen; ~ **the share capital** Kapitalherabsetzung vornehmen.
reduced herabgesetzt, ermäßigt;
and ~ *(capital stock, Br.)* und herabgesetzt, mit herabgesetztem Kapital;
~ **annuity** verkürzte Rente; ~ **assessment** niedrigere Bewertung; ~ **capital** herabgesetztes Kapital; **at a** ~ **fee** für ein mäßiges Honorar; ~ **goods** Ausverkaufsware; ~ **liquidity** Liquiditätsbeengung; ~ **price** verbilligter Preis; **~-rate relief** *(Br.)* gestaffelte Steuerermäßigung.
reduction *(abatement)* Anschlag, Abzug, [Preis]-nachlaß, -ermäßigung, Rabatt, *(decreasing)* Herab-, Heruntersetzung; *(of foreign exchange)* [Devisen]umrechnung, *(waste)* Abgang, Schwund;
customs ~ Zollsenkung; **freight** ~ Frachtermäßigung; **no ~s** feste Preise; **tax** ~ Steuererleichterung; **wage** ~ Lohnsenkung;
~ **in the bank rate** Diskontsenkung; ~ **of capital** *(Br.)* Kapitalherabsetzung; ~ **for children** Kinderermäßigung; ~ **of debts** Schuldenabbau; ~ **of earning capacity** Erwerbsminderung; ~ **of expenses** Kosteneinsparung; ~ **in the freight rate** Frachtermäßigung; ~ **in hours of work (of working hours)** Arbeitszeitverkürzung; ~ **of an overdraft** Zurückführung einer Kontoüberziehung; ~ **in prices** Preisermäßigung, -abbau; ~ **of stock** Lagerabbau; ~ **in turnover** Minderumsatz; ~ **in value** Wertrückgang; ~ **of working hours** Arbeitszeitverkürzung;
to claim a ~ **of assessment** Neubewertung verlangen;
~ **formula** Umrechnungsformel.
redundancy payment *(Br.)* Abfindungszahlung bei Stillegung.
redundant labo(u)r überzählige Arbeitskräfte.
reemployment Wiedereinstellung, -beschäftigung.
reestablishment of currency Währungssanierung.
reexport[ation] | **prohibition** Wiederausfuhrverbot;
~ **trade** Wiederausfuhrhandel.
refer | *(v.)* **a check (cheque, Br.) to the drawer** Scheck an den Aussteller zurückgeben; ~ **to a**

former employer letzten Arbeitgeber als Referenz angeben.
referee in bankruptcy *(US)* Konkursrichter.
reference Bezugnahme, Hinweis, *(book)* Belegstelle, *(person giving information)* Referenz, Auskunftgeber, Gewährsmann;
for ~ zur Information **with further** ~ **to my letter** im Anschluß an mein Schreiben;
banker's ~ Bankauskunft; **first-class ~s** prima Referenzen;
~ **to be quoted in all communications** im Schriftwechsel anzugebendes Aktenzeichen;
~ **book** Nachschlagebuch; ~ **files** Handakten; ~ **initials** Diktatzeichen; ~ **number** Aktenzeichen.
refinancing plan Refinanzierungssystem.
refine *(v.* | *goods)* veredeln.
refining industry Veredelungsindustrie.
reflation Wirtschaftsbelegung durch Anhebung des Preisniveaus.
refloating of a company Reorganisation (Sanierung) einer Gesellschaft.
reflux of capital Kapitalrückfluß.
refreighter Unterbefrachter.
refresher course *(US)* Forbildungskurs.
refreshment | **car** Speisewagen; ~ **counter** Getränkeausschank; ~ **room** Büfett, Erfrischungsraum.
refund Rückvergütung, -erstattung;
tax ~ Steuererstattung.
~ **of the purchase price** Zurückerstattung des Kaufpreises;
~ *(v.) (fund anew)* [Anleihe] neu fundieren, *(pay back)* zurückzahlen, -erstatten;
~ **the cost of postage** Portospesen zurückvergüten; ~ **s. o. for all his expenses** jem. alle Unkosten ersetzen;
to obtain a ~ **of a deposit** *(customs)* Zollkaution zurückerstatten;
[tax] ~ **certificate** Steuerrückvergütungsschein; **tax** ~ **proceedings** Steuererstattungsverfahren.
refunding Rückvergütung, *(loan)* Neufundierung;
~ **of duties** Steuererstattung; ~ **at maturity** Anleihetausch vor Fälligkeit;
~ **bonds** Ablösungsschuldverschreibungen, Umtauschobligationen.
refusal ablehnende Antwort, Absage;
individual ~ *(antitrust law, US)* einzelne Abschlußverweigerung;
~ **of acceptance (to accept)** Annahmeverweigerung; ~ **to deal** *(antitrust law, US)* Liefersperre; ~ **of goods** Annahmeverweigerung; ~ **to supply** Auftragsverweigerung;
to buy the ~ Waren auf Termin kaufen; **to give the right of first** ~ Vorkaufsrecht einräumen;
refuse *(job goods)* Ausschuß[ware], Ramsch;
trade ~ gewerblicher Abfall;
~ *(v.)* **the acceptance** Abnahme (Annahme) verweigern; ~ **to back a bill** Giro verweigern.
regardless of expense(s) ohne Rücksicht auf die Kosten.
regimented industries unter staatlicher Aufsicht stehende Industrien.

region Bezirk, Distrikt, Bereich, Gegend;
overcrowded ~ Ballungsgebiet.

regional örtlich, lokal, regional;
~ association Regionalverband; ~ director Bezirksdirektor; ~ economic policy *(EC)* Standortpolitik; ~ exchange Provinzbörse.

register Register, *(ledger)* Journal, Kontobuch, *(official written record)* [amtliches] Register, Liste, Verzeichnis, *(registration)* Registrierung, Eintrag[ung];
cash ~ Registrierkasse; fixed-assets ~ Anlagenkartei; hotel ~ Fremdenbuch; public ~s öffentliche Bücher; share ~ *(Br.)* Aktionärsverzeichnis; ship's ~ Schiffsregister; trade ~ Handelsregister; voucher ~ Belegsammlung;
~ in bankruptcy Konkursrichter; ~ of births, deaths and marriages *(Br.)* Personenstandsregister; ~ of companies *(Br.)* Handelsregister; ~ of land charges *(Br.)* Hypothekenregister; ~ of members Mitgliederverzeichnis; ~ of membership of corporations *(US)* Vereinsregister; ~ of securities *(Br.)* lebendes Depot, Effektendepot; ~ of ships (shipping) Schiffsregister; ~ of taxes Hebeliste; ~ of trademarks Warenzeichenrolle;
~ *(v.) (enter in the minutes)* protokollieren, *(hotel register)* sich anmelden, *(letter)* einschreiben lassen, *(luggage)* aufgeben, *(record in list)* registrieren, [amtlich] eintragen, in eine Liste eintragen, amtlich erfassen;
~ bonds Obligationen auf den Namen eintragen; ~ a company Gesellschaft (Firma) handelsgerichtlich eintragen [lassen]; ~ small gains kleine Gewinne verzeichnen; ~ at a hotel Anmeldezettel im Hotel ausfüllen; ~ shares Aktien überschreiben lassen; ~ a stop *(check)* sperren lassen; ~ a trade Gewerbe anmelden; ~ a trademark Warenzeichen anmelden;
to remove a firm from the ~ Firma im Handelsregister löschen;
~ card Karteikarte; ~ office Registratur.

registered eingetragen, registriert, *(company)* handelsgerichtlich eingetragen, *(trademark)* gesetzlich geschützt;
to have one's luggage ~ *(Br.)* sein Gepäck aufgeben;
~ address feststehende Adresse; ~ bonds Namensschuldverschreibungen; ~ capital Grundkapital; ~ customer Stammkunde; ~ design eingetragenes Gebrauchsmuster; ~ items eingeschriebene Postsendungen; ~ letter Einschreibebrief, Wertbrief; ~ mail insurance *(US)* Postwertversicherung; ~ mail receipt *(US)* Posteinlieferungsschein; ~ pattern Gebrauchsmuster; ~ share *(Br.)* Namensaktie; ~ tonnage Registertonnage.

registrar *(Br.)* Registerführer, Urkundsbeamter;
⌀ of Companies Gesellschafts-, Handelsregister.

registration amtliche Eintragung, Registrierung, Erfassung, *(enrolment)* Anmeldung, *(securities)* Börsenanmeldung von Wertpapieren;
subject to ~ eintragungs-, anmeldepflichtig;

~ of business Gewerbeanmeldung; ~ of a company *(Br.)* handelsgerichtliche Eintragung einer Gesellschaft; ~ of land *(Br.)* Grundbucheintragung; ~ of a letter Briefaufgabe per Einschreiben; ~ of luggage *(Br.)* Gepäckaufgabe; ~ of trademarks Warenzeicheneintragung;
to require one's ~ registrierungspflichtig sein;
~ card Personalbogen; ~ certificate *(motor vehicle, US)* Kraftfahrzeugbrief; ~ fee Eintragungs-, Anmeldegebühr, *(post office)* Einschreibegebühr; ~ form Anmeldeformular; ~ number of a car Zulassungsnummer; ~ plate *(car, Br.)* polizeiliches Kennzeichen; ~ window Gepäckschalter.

registry *(employment office)* Arbeitsvermittlungsstelle, *(register)* Verzeichnis, *(registration)* Eintragung, Registrierung;
~ fee *(real estate)* Grundbuchkosten; *(post office)* Einschreibegebühr.

regrets only Antwort nur bei Absage erforderlich.

regular *(customer)* Stammkunde;
~ *(a.)* regelmäßig, satzungs-, ordnungs-, vorschriftsmäßig, *(train)* fahrplanmäßig;
~ agent ständiger Vertreter; ~ business laufende Geschäfte; ~ course of business normaler Geschäftsablauf; ~ employment feste Anstellung; ~ income festes Einkommen; ~ lot *(stock exchange)* handelbare Größe; ~ payments regelmäßig wiederkehrende Zahlungen; ~ place of business Betriebsstätte; to have no ~ profession keinen festen Beruf ausüben; ~ salary Fixum; ~ supplier regelmäßiger Lieferant; ~ traveller Dauerkarteninhaber; to have no ~ work keine bestimmte Tätigkeit ausüben.

regulate *(v.)* regulieren, *(business)* Geschäft abwickeln;
~ one's expenditure seine Ausgabenwirtschaft in Ordnung bringen.

regulation Regelung, Regulierung, Reglement;
building ~s Bauvorschriften; currency ~s Devisenbestimmungen; customs ~s Zollvorschriften; export ~s Ausfuhrbestimmungen; market ~s Marktordnung; postal ~s postalische Bestimmungen; safety ~s Sicherheitsbestimmungen; stock exchange ~s Börsenordnung; trade ~s *(US)* Wettbewerbsregeln;
~s of pay scale Tarifordnung; ~ of production Produktionslenkung;
~ charge Gewerbescheingebühr.

regulatory | agency *(US)* Durchführungsstelle, -behörde; ~ job Überwachungstätigkeit.

rehabilitate *(v.)* normalisieren, *(reorganize)* sanieren, *(workers)* umschulen.

rehabilitation *(buildings)* Restaurierung;
industrial ~ wirtschaftliche Wiedereingliederung; monetary ~ Währungssanierung;
~ center (centre, *Br.)* Umschulungszentrum; ~ loan Wiederaufbauanleihe; ~ plan Sanierungsplan.

rehypothecation Wieder-, Weiterverpfändung, *(securities)* zweite Lombardierung.

reimburse *(v.)* abgelten, entschädigen;

~ o. s. upon s. o. sich bei jem. bezahlt machen; ~ s. o. for his losses jds. Verluste übernehmen.

reimbursement Abgeltung, Ersatz[leistung], Entschädigung, Schadenersatz;
~ of charges Spesenvergütung; ~ for exports Ausfuhrrückvergütung;
~ card Nachnahmekarte; ~ charges Spesenvergütung; ~ credit Rembourskredit; ~ draft Rembourstratte; ~ fund Deckungskapital.

reimportation Wieder-, Rückeinfuhr.

reimposition erneute Besteuerung.

reinstate | *(v.)* the contents of a parcel Paketwert ersetzen; ~ an insurance Versicherung wiederaufleben lassen.

reinsurance Rück-, Gegenversicherung;
excess ~ Exzedentenrückversicherung; treaty ~ automatisch wirksame Rückversicherung;
~ by quota cession Quotenrückversicherung;
~ business Rückversicherungsgeschäft; ~ carrier Rückversicherer; ~ policy Rückversicherungspolice; ~ treaty Rückversicherungsvertrag.

reinsure *(v.)* nach-, rückversichern.

reinsured carrier rückversicherte Gesellschaft.

reinvestment of proceeds Wiederanlage des Erlöses.

reissue *(banknotes)* Wiederausgabe;
~ *(v.) (banknotes)* wieder begeben;
~ stamps Briefmarken nachdrucken.

reject *(job goods)* Ausschuß[ware];
~ *(v.)* an application Bewerbung ablehnen; ~ a check (cheque, *Br.)* Scheck zurückweisen; ~ goods delivered Warenlieferung beanstanden.

rejection Annahmeverweigerung;
~s *(job goods)* Ausschußware, -stücke;
~ of offer Angebotsablehnung;
~ slip Verwerfungsschein.

related | company Tochter-, Konzerngesellschaft;
~ cost notwendige Kosten.

relation Beziehung, Zusammenhang, Verhältnis;
business ~s geschäftliche Beziehungen; confidential ~(s) Vertrauensverhältnis; financial ~ kapitalmäßige Bindung;
to have business ~s with s. o. in Geschäftsbeziehungen mit jem. stehen.

relationship, agency Vertretungsverhältnis.

relative | cost relative Kosten; to live in ~ ease verhältnismäßig wohlhabend sein.

relax | *(v.)* a block ade Blockade lockern; ~ restrictions Beschränkungen abbauen.

relaxation | s in credit Krediterleichterungen; ~ of money rates Erleichterung des Geldmarktes.

release Entlastung, Entpflichtung, Entbindung, *(press)* Freigabe, Veröffentlichung, *(renunciation)* Verzicht[leistung], Aufgabe, Preisgabe;
general ~ *(of taxes)* allgemeine Steueramnestie;
~ of a blocked account Kontenfreigabe; ~ of a claim Forderungserlaß; ~ from debts Schuldenerlaß; ~ of liquid funds Liquiditätsfreisetzung; ~ from liability Haftungsfreistellung;
~ *(v.)* entlasten, entbinden, befreien, freistellen;
~ a blocked account Kontensperre aufheben; ~

capital Kapital flüssigmachen; ~ a mortgage Hypothek löschen; ~ to the press für die Presse freigeben; ~ a reserve Reserve auflösen;
to demand a ~ *(trustee)* Entlastung verlangen;
~ date Veröffentlichungstermin.

relevant | cost relevante Kosten; ~ document rechtserhebliche Urkunde.

reliability *(financial rating)* Kreditwürdigkeit, Solidität, Bonität;
~ in operation (service) Betriebssicherheit.

reliable *(solvent)* kreditwürdig, solide;
~ authority sicherer Gewährsmann; ~ security ordnungsgemäße Sicherheit.

relief *(assistance to the poor)* Wohlfahrts-, [Gemeinde]-unterstützung, Fürsorge, *(discharge)* Entlastung, *(reduction of taxes, Br.)* Ermäßigung, Steuerfreibetrag;
eligible for (entitled to) ~ *(Br.)* fürsorge-, unterstützungsberechtigt;
age ~ *(Br.)* Altersfreibetrag; double-taxation ~ *(Br.)* Anrechnung im Ausland gezahlter Steuern; earned-income ~ *(Br.)* Freibetrag für Arbeitseinkünfte; small-income ~ *(Br.)* gestaffelter Freibetrag für Einkommen von 250 bis 350 $; income-tax ~ *(Br.)* Steuervergünstigung, -abzug; out[door] ~ *(Br.)* Fürsorgeunterstützung, Sozialhilfe; public ~ *(US)* öffentliche Unterstützung, Sozialhilfe; reduced-rate ~ *(Br.)* gestaffelte Steuerermäßigung für kleine Einkommen;
~ against forfeiture *(tenant)* Vollstreckungsschutz;
~ to officers Vorstandsentlastung [durch den Betriebsprüfer];
to be on ~ *(US)* Sozialhilfe beziehen; to give ~ Entlastung erteilen;
~ agency Hilfsorganisation, -werk; ~ association Fürsorgeverband; ~ fund Hilfs-, Unterstützungsfonds; ~ office *(Br.)* Wohlfahrtsbehörde, Sozial-, Fürsorgeamt; ~ officer *(Br.)* Fürsorgebeamter; ~ program(me) Notstandsprogramm; ~ road Entlastungsstraße; ~ roll *(Br.)* Fürsorge-, Wohlfahrtsempfängerliste; to go on ~ rolls *(Br.)* Sozialunterstützung empfangen; ~ standards *(Br.)* normale Unterstützungssätze; ~ works Notstandsarbeiten.

reliever of the poor Sozialhelfer.

relieve *(v.) (exonerate)* entlasten, Entlastung erteilen, *(redress)* abhelfen, wiedergutmachen, *(subsist)* unterstützen, Unterstützung gewähren;
~ the common distress allgemeine Not lindern; ~ an emergency Notlage beheben; ~ hardships Härtefälle mildern; ~ s. o. from a liability j. von einer Haftung befreien; ~ the railway Eisenbahnverkehr entlasten.

relinquish *(v.) (abandon)* verlassen, aufgeben, abandonieren, *(renounce)* Verzicht leisten, verzichten;
~ a claim von einer Forderung Abstand nehmen;
~ a residence Wohnsitz aufgeben.

relinquishment Aufgabe, Überlassung, Abtretung;
~ of succession Erbschaftsausschlagung.

reloading Umladung, Umschlag;
~ charges Umschlagskosten, Umladegebühren.

relocate *(v.) (plant)* verlagern;
~ **an employee** Angestellten in die Zentrale zurückversetzen.
relocation Umsiedlung, *(plant)* Verlagerung;
~ **of industry** Industrieverlagerung;
~ **assistance** Umzugshilfe.
remain | *(v.)* **active in business** im Geschäft tätig bleiben; ~ **in existence** *(firm)* weiterbestehen; ~ **on hand (unsold)** unverkauft [liegen]bleiben; ~ **steady** *(prices)* sich behaupten; ~ **until called for** postlagernd aufbewahrt werden.
remainder [Rest]bestand, Restbetrag, *(arrears)* Rückstand, *(books)* Partieartikel;
~ **of order** Auftragsrest; ~ **of stocks** Restbestand; ~ **line** unverkaufter Restbestand.
remaining | **amount** Restbetrag; ~ **assets** *(bankruptcy)* Restmasse; ~ **credit balance** verbleibendes Guthaben; ~ **foreign exchange** nicht ausgenutzte Devisenbeträge.
remarking **of merchandise** Neufestsetzung von Warenpreisen.
remedy **allowance** *(Br.)* Toleranz, zulässige Abweichung.
reminder Mahnung, Hilfs-, Mahnzettel;
~ **of due date** Fälligkeitsavis;
~ **advertising** Erinnerungswerbung; ~ **letter** Mahnbrief; ~ **value** *(bookkeeping)* Erinnerungswert.
remiss **in paying one's bills** schludrig beim Bezahlen seiner Rechnungen.
remission Ermäßigung, Nachlaß;
conventional ~ ausdrücklicher Schuldenerlaß;
~ **of money** Geldüberweisung; ~ **of taxation** Steuerverkürzung.
remit *(v.) (cover)* Deckung anschaffen, *(make over)* überlassen, vermachen, abtreten, *(transmit)* überweisen;
~ **arrears of maintenance** Unterhaltsrückstände erlassen; ~ **a bill** Wechsel einlösen; ~ **by check (cheque,** *Br.)* mit Scheck bezahlen; ~ **home every month** monatlich Geld nach Hause schicken; ~ **by return of post** postwendend überweisen; ~ **the proceeds** Gegenwert anschaffen; ~ **samples** Muster vorlegen.
remittance Geldsendung, überweisung;
prepaid ~ portofreie Sendung;
capital ~s **abroad** Kapitalausfuhr; ~ **in cash** Barsendung; ~ **of cover** Regulierung eines überzogenen Kontos; ~ **of proceeds** Anschaffung des Gegenwertes; ~ **of profit** Gewinntransferierung;
to make (provide for) ~ Deckung (Gegenwert) anschaffen;
~ **account** Überweisungskonto; ~ **basis** *(income tax, Br.)* Versteuerung nur nach England überwiesener Beträge; ~ **form** Überweisungsformular; ~ **slip** Überweisungsträger.
remittee Überweisungsempfänger.
remnant [Über]rest, Überbleibsel, Rückstand;
~ **rate** Resteverkauf.
remote | **damage** nicht voraussehbarer, indirekter Schaden.

remoteness **of the market** Marktferne, -entlegenheit.
removal Entfernen, *(bankruptcy)* Beiseiteschaffen [von Vermögensgegenständen], *(changing of residence)* Umzug;
mandatory ~ zwangsweise Entlassung;
~ **to avoid taxes** Verlagerung aus Steuergründen; ~ **without proper cause** unberechtigte Entlassung; ~ **of directors** Abberufung des Vorstandes; ~ **from office** Amtsenthebung; ~ **of price ceilings** Beseitigung von Höchstpreisbestimmungen; ~ **from the stock-exchange list** Streichung der amtlichen Notierung;
~ **allowance** *(Br.)* Umzugskostenersatz; ~ **bond** Zollfreigabeschein; ~ **contractor** *(Br.)* Möbelspediteur; ~ **goods** *(Br.)* Umzugsgut; ~ **van** *(Br.)* Möbelwagen.
remove Wohnsitzveränderung, Umzug, *(discharge)* Absetzung;
~s **to convertibility** Übergang zur Konvertibilität;
~ *(v.) (bankruptcy)* [Vermögensgegenstände] beiseite bringen, *(business)* verlegen;
~ **from the agenda** von der Tagesordnung absetzen; ~ **a manager** Geschäftsführer abberufen; ~ **from the register** *(trademarks)* in der Warenzeichenrolle löschen; ~ **the seals** Plomben abnehmen.
removing **expenses** Umzugskosten.
remunerate *(v.) (pay)* honorieren, dotieren;
~ **s. o. for his trouble** j. für seine Bemühungen entschädigen.
remuneration *(fee)* Honorar, Dotierung, *(reimbursement)* Entgelt, Entschädigung, Vergütung;
without ~ unentgeltlich;
~ **of directors** Vorstandsvergütung; ~ **from a profession** Einkünfte aus freiberuflicher Tätigkeit; ~ **for salvage** Bergelohn;
to charge ~ Honorar liquidieren.
remunerative vorteilhaft, einträglich, lohnend, gewinnbringend, ergiebig, lukrativ;
~ **business** einträgliches Geschäft; ~ **employment** Erwerbstätigkeit; ~ **investment** lukrative Anlage.
render | *(v.)* **account** Rechnung [vor]legen; ~ **a profit** Gewinn abwerfen.
rendered, **to (per) account** laut erteilter (früherer) Rechnung.
renew *(v.)* wiederherstellen, restaurieren;
~ **a bill (draft)** Wechsel prolongieren; ~ **an order** nachbestellen; ~ **a stock of goods** Vorräte ergänzen.
renewable **term insurance** verlängerungsfähige Risikolebensversicherung.
renewal *(bill)* Prolongation;
~s *(balance sheet)* Neuanschaffungen;
~ **of a bill** Wechselprolongation; ~ **of a lease** Pachtverlängerung;
to grant a ~ **of a draft** Wechsel prolongieren; **to put through** ~s **at 2 per cent** Verlängerungen zum Satz von 2 % tätigen;
~ **bill** Prolongationswechsel; ~ **certificate** Talon;
~ **costs** Prolongationskosten; ~ **fund** Erneue-

rungsrücklage; ~ **premium** Folgeprämie; ~ **rate**
Prolongationssatz.

renounce | *(v.)* **a claim** auf eine Forderung verzichten;
~ **an inheritance** *(US)* Erbschaft ausschlagen.

renowned banking company bekanntes (angesehenes)
Bankhaus.

rent *(periodical payment)* [Wohnungs]miete, Mietzins, Pacht[zins], Pachtgeld, *(return of value)*
Einkommen[squelle];
for ~ zu vermieten;
~s Staatsanleihen, Rentenpapiere;
accrued ~ Mietrückstände; **advanced** ~ Mietvorauszahlung; **commercial** ~ wirtschaftlich berechtigter Mietzins; **current market** ~ übliche Miete;
dead ~ Bergregalabgabe; **economic** ~ Kostenvergleichsmiete; **imputed** ~ Mietwert der
eigengenutzten Wohnung im Einfamilienhaus;
office ~ Büromiete; **prewar** ~ Vorkriegs-, Friedensmiete; **residential** ~ Wohnungsmiete; **standard** ~ *(Br.)* normale Friedensrente [per 3. 8. 1914];
~ **issues and profits** Vermögenseinkünfte; ~s **and
profits of land** Einkünfte aus Grundbesitz; ~ **lying
in prender** *(Br.)* Mietbringschuld; ~ **lying in render**
(Br.) Mietholschuld;
~ *(v.)* mieten, [ab]pachten, *(borrow, US)* sich etw.
leihen, *(let for ~, US)* vermieten;
~ **a building with the option of purchase** Haus mit
Vorkaufsrecht mieten; ~ **a film** Film verleihen; ~
a flat and take over the furniture *(Br.)* Wohnung
mieten und die Möbel übernehmen; ~ **at $ 900 a
year** 900 Pfund an Miete im Jahr erbringen;
to be in arrears with one's ~ im Mietrückstand sein;
to command a high ~ hohe Miete erzielen; **to have
a house free of** ~ mietfrei wohnen; **to raise a lodger's** ~ j. in der Miete steigern;
~ **account** Mietkonto; ~**-a-car** Mietwagen; ~**-a-car
agency** **(firm, corporation)** Mietwagenverleih,
Autovermietungsfirma; ~ **allowance** Mietzuschuß; ~ **ceiling** Höchstmiete; ~ **charge** *(Br.)* Erbzins; ~ **control** *(Br.)* Mietschutz; **to occupy a
house** ~**free** Haus zur freien Miete bewohnen; ~
insurance Mietverlustversicherung; ~ **restrictions**
gesetzlicher Mieterschutz; ⁀ **Restriction Act** *(Br.)*
Mieterschutzgesetz; ~ **schedule** Mietertragstabelle; ~ **tax** Hauszinssteuer; ~ **tribunal** *(Br.)* Mieteinigungsamt.

rental Miet-, Pachteinnahme, [Brutto]mietertrag;
car ~ Automietgebühr; **subscriber's** ~ Fernsprechanschlußgebühr;
~ **agent** Häusermakler; ~ **allowance** Wohnungsgeld; ~ **car company** Mietwagenfirma; ~ **earnings**
(motion picture) Verleiheinnahmen; **to produce** ~
income Mieteinkünfte abwerfen; ~ **property** einträglicher Betrieb; ~ **right** *(Br.)* Erbpacht; ~
schedule Mietertragstabelle; **rent and** ~ **value insurance** Mietausfallversicherung.

rented car Leihwagen.

renter of a safe Safe-, Depotmieter.

renting | **of cars** Autovermietung; ~ **of safes** Schrankfachmiete.

renunciation | **of dower** Ausschlagung der Mitgift; ~
of guarantee Garantieverzicht;
~ **form** *(Br.)* Verzichtleistungsschreiben [für Bezugsrechte].

reopen | *(v.)* **a case of bankruptcy** Konkursverfahren
noch einmal aufrollen; ~ **a shop** Laden wiedereröffnen.

reorder Nach-, Neubestellung.

reorganization Neugestaltung, Um-, Reorganisation,
(company) Sanierung, Bereinigung, *(US)* Gläubigervergleich;
~ **under Chapter 10** *(US)* Vergleichsverfahren;
~ **of a corporation** *(US)* Vergleichs- und Sanierungsverfahren;
~ **account** *(US)* Vergleichskonto; ~ **bond** *(US)* Gewinnschuldverschreibung; ~ **measures** Sanierungsmaßnahmen; ~ **petition** *(US)* Vergleichsantrag; ~ **proceedings** *(US)* Vergleichsverfahren; ~
truste *(US)* Vergleichsverwalter.

reorganize reorganisieren, *(firm)* sanieren, *(economy)* wiederaufbauen;
~ **under Chapter 10** *(US)* Vergleichs- und Sanierungsverfahren durchführen.

repair Instandsetzung, Wiederherstellung, Reparatur, Ausbesserung, *(accounting)* Instandhaltungsaufwand;
in bad ~ *(house)* baufällig, in schlechtem Zustand;
in need of ~ instandsetzungsbedürftig;
road (street) ~s Straßeninstandsetzungsarbeiten;
tenant's ~s dem Mieter obliegende Reparaturen;
~ *(v.)* erneuern, ausbessern, instandsetzen, reparieren, *(machine)* überholen;
~ **damage** Schaden ersetzen; ~ **one's fortune** seine
Vermögensverhältnisse neu ordnen;
to be under ~ repariert werden;
[statutory] ~s **allowance (deduction)** [etwa] 7b-Abschreibung; ~ **costs** Reparatur-, Instandsetzungskosten.

reparation Instandsetzung, Wiederherstellung;
~ **payments** Reparationszahlungen.

repatriate | *(v.)* **capital** Kapital wieder ausführen; ~
earnings from foreign investments ausländische
Anlagenerlöse devisenmäßig vereinnahmen.

repatriation of dividend Dividendentransfer.

repay *(v.)* zurück[be]zahlen, rückerstatten;
~ **o. s.** sich erholen (schadlos halten);
~ **s. o. in full** j. voll befriedigen; ~ **a mortgage debt**
Hypothek tilgen.

repayable on demand auf Verlangen rückzahlbar.

repayment Rückzahlung, -vergütung, -erstattung;
~ **of a credit** Kredittilgung; ~ **of.principal** Kapitalrückzahlung;
~ **period** Rückzahlungszeitraum, *(hire purchase)*
Abzahlungsfrist, -periode.

repeat neue Bestellung, neuer Auftrag, Neubestellung, *(advertising)* Ersatz-, Erinnerungsanzeige;
~ *(v.)* **an article** nach-, neu bestellen; ~ **back a telegram** Telegramm kollationieren;
~ **order** Neu-, Nachbestellung, *(advertising)* Wiederholungsauftrag; ~ **sale** *(US)* Verkauf auf
Grund von Erinnerungswerbung.

repetition | **-paid telegram** kollationiertes Telegramm; ~ **work** Serienarbeit, -herstellung.

replace *(v.)* wieder-, rückerstatten, rückvergüten; ~ **fixed assets** Anlagen erneuern; ~ **stolen money** unterschlagenes Geld ersetzen.

replaced equipment Ersatzanschaffungen.

replacement *(accounting)* Anlagenerneuerung, *(destroyed building)* Wiedererrichtungskosten, *(substituting)* Ersatz-, Wiederbeschaffung; **holiday** ~ *(Br.)* Urlaubsvertretung; ~ **of inventories** Auffüllung des Lagerbestands; ~ **in kind** Naturalersatz; **to buy goods in** ~ Deckungskauf vornehmen; **to require goods in** ~ Ersatzlieferung verlangen; ~ **cost** Gestehungs-, Wiederbeschaffungskosten; ~ **cost new** Neuanschaffungswert; ~ **cost standard** *(balance sheet)* Wiederbeschaffungswert; ~ **fund** Erneuerungsrücklage; ~ **housing** Ersatzwohnung; ~ **method of depreciation** Abschreibung auf Basis der Wiederbeschaffungskosten; ~ **parts** Ersatz-teile; ~ **program(me)** Ausweichprogramm, *(investing)* Anlagenerneuerungsplan; ~ **rate** Wiederbeschaffungs-, Anlagenerneuerungssatz, *(employees)* Zu- und Abgangssatz; ~ **value** Ersatz-, Wiederbeschaffungswert.

replenish | *(v.)* one's **inventory** sein Lager auffüllen; ~ **a loan** zusätzliche Sicherheit leisten; ~ **a ship's stores** Schiffsvorräte ergänzen; ~ **one's stocks** sein Lager vervollständigen.

replenishment | **of a loan** Gestellung zusätzlicher Sicherheiten; ~ **of stocks** Lagerauffüllung; ~ **ship** Versorgungsschiff.

replevin *(bail)* Pfandauslösung, Selbsthilfeverkauf.

reply *(letter)* Antwortschreiben, Rückäußerung; **intermediate** ~ Zwischenbescheid; ~ **paid** [Rück]antwort bezahlt; **business** ~ **card** Werbeantwortkarte; ~ **coupon** *(advertising)* Bestellkupon; ~ **paid telegram (wire)** Telegramm mit bezahlter Rückantwort.

report Nachricht, Meldung, *(corporation)* Geschäfts-, Rechenschaftsbericht *(formal statement)* [Rechenschafts]bericht; **annual** ~ *(Br.)* Jahres-, Geschäftsbericht; **captain's** ~ Verklarung, Seeprotest; **credit** ~ Kreditauskunft; **damage** ~ *(insurance)* Schadensmeldung, -bericht; **expert's** ~ Sachverständigengutachten; **market** ~ Markt-, Preisbericht, *(stock exchange)* Börsen-, Kursbericht; **over-the-counter** ~s *(US)* Kursblatt für Freiverkehrswerte; **receiving** ~ Wareneingangsmeldung; ~ **on business [conditions]** Konjunkturbericht; ~ **of loss** Schadensmeldung; ~ **of survey** Havariegutachten; **false** ~ **of weight** falsche Gewichtsangabe. ~ *(v.)* *(customs)* deklarieren, *(state a fact)* melden, berichten, Bericht erstatten; ~ **an accident to the police** Unfallmeldung erstatten; ~ **directly to the President** dem Vorstandsvorsitzenden unmittelbar unterstehen; ~ **a marked improvement in business** Konjunkturaufschwung feststellen; ~ **progress** über den Stand einer Angelegenheit berichten;

to be **of good** ~ guten Leumund haben; **to cook a** ~ *(sl.)* Bericht frisieren; **to receive a** ~ **on a firm** Auskünfte über eine Firma erhalten;

reporting | **of property** Vermögensanmeldung; ~ **form** Berichtsformular, *(insurance)* Risikoformular; ~ **pay** Anwesenheitsgeld.

repository Verwahrungsort, *(shop)* Laden, *(warehouse)* Warenlager, Niederlage, Magazin; **furniture** ~ [Möbel]speicher.

repossess *(v.)* **goods** *(hire purchase)* auf Teilzahlung gekaufte Waren wieder in Besitz nehmen.

represent | *(v.)* **every facet of business** repräsentativen Querschnitt der gesamten Wirtschaft darstellen; ~ **the interests of the creditors** Gläubigerinteressen wahrnehmen.

representation *(accounting)* Vorstandserläuterung über die Geschäftspolitik für Revisionsbeamte, *(description)* Darstellung, -legung; ~s *(insurance)* Anzeige von Gefahrenumständen; ~ **abroad** Auslandsvertretung; **legal and general** ~ gerichtliche und außergerichtliche Vertretung; ~ **of interests** Interessenvertretung; ~ **in equal numbers** paritätische Vertretung; ~ **of ownership** Vertretung der Anteilseigner; **to have** ~ **at the bargaining table** am Verhandlungstisch vertreten sein; **to make** ~s **to the Inspector of Taxes about an excessive assessment** Einspruch beim Finanzamt gegen zu hohe Veranlagung einlegen; ~ **allowance** Aufwandsentschädigung.

representative [Stell]vertreter, Bevollmächtigter, Beauftragter, Agent, Repräsentant; ~ **abroad** Auslandsvertreter; **commercial** ~ Handelsvertreter; **lawful** ~ ordnungsgemäß bevollmächtigter Vertreter; **sales** ~ Vertreter; **sole** ~ *(firm)* General-, Alleinvertreter; ~ **capacity** Vertretereigenschaft; ~ **money** *(US)* Papiergeld; ~ **sample** Serienmuster; ~ **stock** *(US)* Standardwerte.

represented on the board im Aufsichtsrat vertreten.

repricing erneute Preisfestsetzung; ~ **clause** Preisänderungsklausel.

reprivatization Reprivatisierung.

reproduction Abdruck, Wiederherstellung, Reproduktion, Vervielfältigung; ~ **cost** Veredelungskosten, *(replacement)* Wiederbeschaffungskosten; ~ **standard** *(balance sheet)* Wiederbeschaffungswert.

reproductive service werbende Dienstleistungen.

repudiate *(v.)* **the national debt** *(US)* Staatsschuld nicht anerkennen.

repudiation *(of national debt)* Zahlungsverweigerung.

repurchase Wieder-, Wiederan-, Rückkauf; **with option of** ~ mit Rückkaufsrecht; ~ **of units** *(Br.)* Rücknahme von Investmentanteilen; ~ *(v.)* **short sales** Leerabgaben einer Position decken; ~ **cost** Wiederbeschaffungskosten; ~ **privilege** *(investment fund)* Rückgaberecht; ~ **value** Rückkaufswert.

reputation Leumund, guter Ruf, Ansehen, Renommée;
  business ~ geschäftliches Ansehen;
  to damage s. one's ~ Rufmord an jem. begehen;
  to live up to one's ~ standesgemäß leben.
reputed ownership vermutliches Eigentum.
request Bitte, [An]ersuchen, Aufforderung, *(demand)* Nachfrage, Anforderung;
  by (on) ~ bei Bedarf; **in** ~ gefragt, begehrt;
  vacation ~ *(US)* Urlaubsgesuch; **written** ~ Aufforderungsschreiben;
  ~ **for diminution of taxes** Steuerherabsetzungsantrag; ~ **for a holiday** *(Br.)* Urlaubsgesuch; ~ **for money (payment)** Zahlungsaufforderung, Mahnbrief; ~ **for respite** Stundungsgesuch;
  ~ *(v.)* **a brief delay** um eine kurze Fristverlängerung einkommen; ~ **s. o. to use his influence** jds. Beziehungen für sich einzusetzen suchen; ~ **a loan** Kredit beantragen;
  to deal with a ~ Antrag bearbeiten; **to send by** ~ auf Bestellung zuschicken;
  ~**s book** Beschwerdebuch; ~ **form** Bestellschein; ~ **program(me)** Wunschkonzert; ~ **stop** *(Br.)* Bedarfshaltestelle.
requested authority ersuchte Behörde.
require *(v.) (demand)* [an]fordern, verlangen, *(need)* benötigen, Bedarf haben an, brauchen;
  ~ **money** Geld kosten.
required idle time unvermeidliche Verlustzeit.
requirement [An]forderung, *(direction)* Vorschrift, *(need)* Bedarf, Erfordernis, Bedürfnis, *(qualification)* erforderliche Eigenschaft;
  additional ~ Mehrbedarf; **counter** ~**s** [Zahlungs]-anforderungen im Schalterverkehr; **financial monetary)** ~**s** Finanzbedarf; **monthly** ~**s** Ultimobedürfnisse; **personal** ~ Eigenbedarf; **statutory** ~**s** Satzungserfordernisse; **over-the-window** ~**s** Anforderungen im Schalterverkehr;
  ~**s for admission** Zulassungsvoraussetzungen; ~**s in goods** Warenbedarf;
  to be modest in one's ~**s** bescheidene Ansprüche stellen; **to meet s. one's** ~**s** jds. Bedarf decken; **to meet the** ~**s at a competitive price** preisgünstig liegen.
requisite Gebrauchsgegenstand, Bedarfsartikel;
  office ~**s** Büroartikel;
  ~ **capital** notwendiges Betriebskapital.
requisition Ersuchen, Auf-, Anforderung, *(formal application)* Anforderung[sschein];
  purchase ~ Ermächtigung der Einkaufsabteilung; **stores** ~ Lageranforderung;
  ~ **of material** Materialanforderung;
  ~ **blank** Anforderungsformular; ~ **form** *(Br.)* Bestell-, Auftragszettel; ~ **number** Bestellnummer.
requisitioning authority Erfassungsstelle.
reroute *(v.)* umleiten, *(air ticket)* umschreiben.
resale *(by default of payment)* Selbsthilfeverkauf, *(sale at secondhand)* Verkauf aus zweiter Hand, *(second sale)* Weiter-, Wiederverkauf;
  ~ **price** Wiederverkaufs-, Einzelhandelspreis; ⟲

Price Act *(Br.)* Preisbindungsgesetz; ~ **price agreement** Preisbindungsvereinbarung; ~ **price condition** Preisbindung; ~ **price fixing (maintenance)** Preisbindung der zweiten Hand, vertikale Preisbindung; ~ **value** Wiederverkaufswert.
rescind | *(v.)* **a bargain** von einem Geschäft zurücktreten.
rescinding a contract Vertragsannulierung.
rescission Rückgängigmachung, Rücktritt;
  ~ **for breach of warranty** *(US)* Wandlung wegen Gewährleistungsbruchs.
rescue Rettung, *(salvage)* Bergung;
  ~ **of goods restrained** Pfandbruch;
  ~ *(v.)* **the market** Stützungsaktionen unternehmen;
  ~ **party (squad)** Bergungsmannschaft, Hilfstrupp;
  ~ **ship** Rettungsschiff.
research *(advertising)* Marktforschung, Analyse, *(scientific)* Forschung[sarbeit];
  business ~ Konjunkturforschung; **listenership** ~ *(US)* Höreranalyse; **market** ~ Markt-, Absatzforschung; **opinion** ~ Meinungsbefragung;
  ~ **assignment** Forschungsauftrag; ~ **director** *(advertising)* Leiter der Marktforschung; ~ **material** Forschungsergebnisse; ~ **plant** Versuchsanlage; ~ **service** *(advertising)* Ausschnittdienst; ~ **study** Forschungstätigkeit.
resell *(v.)* weiter-, wiederverkaufen.
reservation *(clause)* Einschränkung, Vorbehalt[s-klausel], *(reserve)* Rückstellung, *(reserved room)* reserviertes Zimmer, *(of seats, US)* Vorbestellung, Buchung, Platzkarte;
  with the usual ~**s** unter üblichem Vorbehalt;
  continuing-plane ~ Anschlußbuchung; **flight** ~ Flugplatzreservierung;
  ~ **of earned surplus** Gewinnrückstellung; ~ **of title** Eigentumsvorbehalt;
  to accept s. th. without ~ etw. vorbehaltlos annehmen; **to cancel a** ~ Reservierung rückgängig machen; **to telegraph to a hotel for a** ~ Hotelzimmer telegrafisch vorbestellen;
  ~ **fee** Vormerk-, Reservierungsgebühr; ~ **form** Platzkartenformular.
reserve *(balance sheet)* Reserve, Rücklage, *(US)* Rückstellung, *(reservation)* Einschränkung, Vorbehalt, *(supply)* Vorrat, Reserve;
  under ~ vorbehaltlich; **without** ~ unbedingt, *(auction sale)* freier Verkauf;
  actual ~ Istreserve; **amortization** ~ Rücklagen zur Abschreibung langfristiger Anlagegüter; **available** ~frei verfügbare Reserven; **bad-debts** ~ Rücklagen für zweifelhafte Forderungen; **capital** ~ nicht steuerpflichtiger Kapitalgewinn; **operating cash** ~ Betriebsmittelrücklage; **company's** ~ nicht verteilter Gewinn, Betriebsrücklage; **contingency** ~ Delkredererückstellung; **declared** ~ ausgewiesene (offene) Rücklagen; **depreciation** ~ Entwertungsrücklage; **equalization** ~ Ausgleichsrücklage; **foreign-exchange** ~ Devisenpolster; **free** ~ *(banking, US)* [etwa] freie Guthaben bei der Landeszentralbank; **hidden** ~ stille Reserve; **lawful** *(US)*, **legal**

(Br.) ~ Mindestreserve; **liability** ~ Rückstellung für eingegangene Verbindlichkeiten; **loss** ~**s** *(insurance)* Rücklage für laufende Risiken; ~ **maintained** *(banking)* Ist-, Mindestreserve; **mental** ~ Mentalreservation; **official** ~ offene Reserven; **primary** ~ *(banking)* Kassenreserve; **provident** ~ Sonderrückstellung; **required** ~**s** Pflichtrücklagen; **revaluation** ~ Rückstellung für Neubewertungen; **secret** ~ stille Reserven; **statutory** ~ gesetzlich vorgeschriebene Reserve; **surplus contingency** ~ Rückstellung für mögliche Verluste am Reingewinn; **taxation** ~ Steuerrückstellung; **undisclosed** ~ stille Reserven; **valuation** ~ Wertberichtigung; ~ **for additions, betterments and improvements** Erneuerungsrücklage; ~ **to balance the budget** Ausgleichsrücklage; ~ **for bad debts** Rückstellung für Dubiose; ~ **for outstanding claims** *(insurance company)* Schadensreserve; ~ **for currency equalization** Rückstellung für Währungsausgleich; ~ **for debt redemption** Rückstellung für Schuldentilgung; ~ **for depletion** Wertberichtigungsposten auf Anlagen; ~ **for discounts** Rückstellung für Kontonachlässe; ~ **for dividends voted** Rückstellung für Dividendenausschüttungen; ~ **for possible inventory losses** Rückstellungen für mögliche Inventarverluste; ~ **for investment fluctuations** Rückstellungen für Anlageveränderungen; ~ **for loss on investment** Rücklagen für Anlagenverluste; ~ **for unearned premium** *(balance sheet)* Prämiumüberhang; ~ **for renewals and replacements** Erneuerungsrücklage; ~ **for sinking fund** Tilgungsrücklage; ~ **for wear, tear, obsolescence or inadequacy** Abschreibungsrücklage;
~ *(v.) (goods)* Waren zurückhalten; *(make reservation, US)* buchen, *(set aside)* reservieren, zurückstellen;
~ **one's decision** seine Entscheidung zurückstellen; ~ **money for unforeseen contingencies** Geld für unvorhergesehene Ereignisse zurücklegen; ~ **a seat for s. o.** Sitz (Platz) für j. reservieren;
to abolish a ~ Vorbehalt aufheben; **to accumulate** ~**s** Reseven ansammeln; **to be classifiable as** ~ den Rücklagen zugerechnet werden; **to be a draw on one's** ~**s** Reservenabbau verursachen; **to build up** ~**s** Rücklagen bilden; **to maintain** ~**s** Reserven unterhalten; **to overrun one's** ~**s** seine Rücklagen aufzehren; **to place (put) to** ~ dem Reservefonds zuführen; **to release a** ~ Rücklagen auflösen; **to shunt undisclosed sums into inner** ~**s** nicht offen gelegte Beträge in den stillen Rücklagen verstecken;
~ **account** Rückstellungs-, Delkredere-, Reservekonto; ~ **assets** Währungsguthaben; **Federal ♀ Bank** *(US)* [etwa] Landeszentralbank; ~**carrying** *(banking)* mindestreservepflichtig; ~**free base figure** [etwa] landeszentralbankfreie Einlagensumme; ~ **fund** Rücklage-, Reserve[fonds]; ~ **liability** *(life insurance, Br.)* Nachschußpflicht; ~ **position** Reservepolster; ~ **price** Mindestpreis; ~ **requirements** *(US)* Mindestreservevorschriften; ~ **value** *(insurance)* Prämienreserve.

reserved *(seat, US)* belegt, *(stock exchange)* zurückhaltend;
all seats ~ nur gegen Platzkarten; ~ **position** *(advertising)* reservierter Anzeigenplatz; ~ **prices** bescheidene Preise; ~**seat ticket** Platzkarte; ~ **share** Vorratsaktie; ~ **surplus** zweckgebundene Rücklage.
resettlement Umsiedlung, Wiedereingliederung; **occupational** ~ berufliche Umschulung.
reshape *(v.)* **a company** Firma umorganisieren.
reship *(v.)* wieder verladen, *(ship)* umladen.
reshipment Wiederversendung, -verladung.
reshipping cost Weiterversendungskosten.
reshuffling of top management Umbesetzung der Schlüsselpositionen in der Vorstandsspitze.
residence Aufenthalts-, Wohnort, [Wohn]sitz; ~ **abroad** Auslandsaufenthalt; **ordinary** ~ *(Br.)* steuerlicher Aufenthalt; **permanent** ~ [etwa] fester Wohnsitz;
~ **of a company (corporation)** Gesellschaftssitz; **to change one's** ~ seinen Wohnsitz verlegen;
~ **address** Privat-, Wohnsitzanschrift; ~ **certificate** Aufenthaltsgenehmigung; ~ **and outside theft insurance** Einbruchdiebstahlsversicherung.
resident Anwohner, Bewohner, Ortsansässiger, *(hotel)* Dauergast, *(Br.)* Deviseninländer; **national** ~ *(US)* Staatsangehöriger; ~ **agent** Empfangsbevollmächtigter; **U. K.** ~ **company** *(Br.)* Handelsgesellschaft mit Geschäftssitz in Großbritannien.
residential | **accommodation** Wohnmöglichkeit; ~ **allowance** Ortszulage; **low-(high-) rent** ~ **district** billige (teure) Wohnlage; ~ **hotel** Familienpension; ~ **taxpayer** unbeschränkt (inländischer) Steuerpflichtiger; ~ **trade** Lokalhandel.
residual | **amount** Restbetrag; ~ **cost** Restbuchwert; ~ **product** Abfall-, Nebenprodukt; ~ **value** *(balance sheet)* Restbuchwert.
residuary beneficiary Nachlaßbegünstigter.
residue Rest[betrag], *(balance)* Rechnungsrest.
resign | *(v.)* **an agency** Vertretung niederlegen; ~ **in a body** geschlossen zurücktreten; ~ **an inheritance** *(US)* Erbschaft ausschlagen; ~ **a managership** Vorstandsamt niederlegen.
resignation Verzichtleistung, *(membership)* Austritt[serklärung], *(office)* [Amts]niederlegung, Rücktritt;
involuntary ~ nahegelegte Kündigung; ~ **request** Rücktrittsersuchen.
resistance | **to wear** Verschleißfestigkeit; **to offer** ~ **in the public** von der Öffentlichkeit nicht positiv aufgenommen werden; **to show strong** ~ *(market)* sehr widerstandsfähig sein; ~ **level** *(stock market)* Widerstandsschwelle.
resistant *(stock exchange)* widerstandsfähig; ~ **to the slowdown** konjunkturunempfindlich.
resolution Resolution, Beschluß; **corporate** ~ *(US)* Hauptversammlungsbeschluß; **extraordinary** ~ *(bankruptcy)* qualifizierter Mehrheitsbeschluß, *(company, Br.)* mit 3/4 Mehrheit

gefaßter Hauptversammlungsbeschluß; **ordinary** ~ einfacher Mehrheitsbeschluß;

to put a ~ to the meeting Entschließung einbringen.

resort Aufenthaltsort, *(place of popular resort)* Urlaubsort;

health ~ Bade-, Kurort; **winter** ~ Winterkurort, -sportplatz;

~ **hotel** Ferien-, Kurhotel; ~ **project** Ferienprojekt.

resource Ausweg, Hilfsquelle, Behelf, *(reserve)* Vorrat, Reserve.

resources Hilfsmittel, -quellen; *(accounting, coll.)* Aktiva, Vermögenswerte;

without ~ mittellos;

a company's ~ Gesellschaftskapital; **inexhaustible** ~ unerschöpfliche Bodenschätze;

natural ~ **of a country** natürliche Bodenschätze eines Landes; ~ **in men** Menschenreserve;

to be thrown upon one's own ~ auf sich selbst angewiesen sein; **to have exhausted all** ~ alle Reserven aufgebraucht haben; **to make the most of one's** ~ sein Kapital schwerpunktartig einsetzen; **to open up new** ~ neue Hilfsquellen erschließen.

respect Ansehen, Achtung, Ruf;

world-wide ~ Weltgeltung;

~ *(v.)* **one's own interests** eigene Interessen berücksichtigen.

respectable| **amount** bedeutende Summe; **to belong to the** ~ **middle class** zum gehobeneren Mittelstand gehören; ~ **firm** angesehenes Haus; **to have a** ~ **income** schönes Einkommen haben.

respite Aufschub, *(Br.)* Frist, Termin, Nachsicht;

additional (after) ~ Nachfrist;

~ **for payment** Zahlungsaufschub, Stundung;

to accord a ~ Frist zugestehen; **to accord a** ~ **for payment of a draft** Wechsel prolongieren;

~ **money** Prolongationsgebühr.

respited freight gestundete Fracht.

respond *(v.)* **in damages** *(US)* schadensersatzpflichtig sein.

respondentia Bodmerei auf die Schiffsladung.

responsibility Verantwortlichkeit, *(solvency, US)* Zahlungsfähigkeit, Solidität;

without ~ ohne Verbindlichkeit (Obligo);

~ **of one seeking a loan** Kreditfähigkeit eines Darlehnsnehmers;

to assume [the] ~ **for another's debts** Haftung für j. übernehmen; **to pass** ~ **down the line** Verantwortungsbereich dezentralisieren;

~ **costing** verantwortlich aufgeteilte Kostenkalkulation.

responsible *(accountable)* rechnungspflichtig, *(legally accountable)* zurechnungs-, geschäftsfähig, *(liable)* haftpflichtig, *(solvent)* zahlungsfähig, solvent, solid;

jointly and severally ~ solidarisch [gesamtschuldnerisch] haftbar; **primarily** ~ unmittelbar haftpflichtig;

to be ~ **for a loss** für einen Verlust aufkommen müssen; **to be** ~ **for maintenance** unterhaltspflichtig sein; **to be** ~ **for the petty cash** Portokasse

verwalten; **to hold the carrier** ~ **for the full value** vollen Schadenersatz vom Spediteur verlangen;

~ **age** geschäftsfähiges Alter, Mündigkeit; ~ **business** zahlungsfähige (solvente) Firma; ~ **job** Vertrauensstellung; ~ **partner** persönlich haftender Gesellschafter (Teilhaber).

rest *(abode)* Wohnstätte, *(balance)* Rest, [Rechnungs]saldo, *(balance sheet, Br.)* Bücherabschluß, Bilanzierung, *(remainder)* [Über]rest;

net ~ Nettoüberschuß;

~ **capital** *(Br.)* Reservefonds, -kapital; ~ **center (centre, Br.)** Erholungsstätte, -zentrum; ~ **fund** *(banking)* Mindestreserve; ~ **room** Aufenthalts-, Tagesraum, *(US)* Waschraum, Toilette.

restaurant Gastwirtschaft, -stätte, Lokal, Restaurant;

~ **business** Gaststättengewerbe; ~ **car** *(US)* Speisewagen; ~ **tax** Schanksteuer.

restitution Wiedererstattung, *(return)* Restitution, Wiedergutmachung;

~ **in kind** Naturalrestitution; ~ **of the purchase money** Rückerstattung des Kaufpreises;

to be liable to make ~ rückerstattungspflichtig sein; ~ **treaty** Wiedergutmachungsabkommen.

restitutory right Rückerstattungsanspruch.

restock *(v.)* *(US)* Vorrat ergänzen.

restoration *(currency)* Sanierung, *(reparation)* Instandsetzung, *(return)* Wiedergabe;

~ **of a building** Gebäudeinstandsetzung; ~ **of goods in distraint** Pfandfreigabe.

restore *(v.)* zurückgeben, -erstatten, *(repair)* instandsetzen, reparieren;

~ **a ruin[ed building]** verfallenes Gebäude instandsetzen; ~ **money to the owner** Geld dem Eigentümer zurückerstatten; ~ **confiscated property** beschlagnahmtes Vermögen freigeben.

restrain| *(v.)* **production** Produktion drosseln; ~ **trade** Wettbewerb beschränken.

restraining clause Konkurrenzklausel.

restraint [Verfügungs]beschränkung;

monetary ~ Geldverknappung; **unreasonable** ~ unlauterer Wettbewerb;

~ **on alienation** *(Br.)* Veräußerungsverbot; ~ **of princes and rulers** Verfügung von hoher Hand; ~ **of trade** Konkurrenzbeschränkung, -verbot; ~ **clause** Konkurrenz-, Wettbewerbsklausel.

restrict | *(v.)* **competition** Wettbewerb einschränken; ~ **to thirty miles an hour in built-up areas** Höchstgeschwindigkeit in geschlossenen Ortschaften auf 50 km beschränken; ~ **production** Produktion drosseln.

restricted | begrenzt, eingeschränkt, *(controlled)* bewirtschaftet, *(under reserve)* vorbehaltlich;

~ **area** *(US)* Zone mit Geschwindigkeitsbegrenzung; ~ **indorsement** beschränktes Giro; ~ **information** vertrauliche Information; ~ **receipts** zweckgebundene Einnahmen.

restriction Be-, Einschränkung, *(land register, Br.)* Veräußerungsbeschränkung, *(reservation)* Vorbehalt, *(zoning laws, US)* Baubeschränkung;

credit ~ Kreditrestriktion; **currency (foreign-ex-change)** ~s Devisenbeschränkungen; **rent** ~s *(Br.)* Mieterschutzbestimmungen;
~ **on benefit** *(insurance)* Karenz; ~ **of expenditure** Ausgabenbeschränkung; ~ **of output** Produktionsbegrenzung;
to abrogate ~s Beschränkungen aufheben; **to reimpose** ~s **on imports** Liberalisierung aufheben.

restrictive | **business practices** *(cartel law, Br.)* wettbewerbsbeschränkende Verhaltensweise; ~ **covenant** Konkurrenzvereinbarung; ~ **credit policy** Kreditdrosselungspolitik; ~ **indorsement** beschränktes Giro, Rektaindossament; ~ **injunction** Verbotsverfügung; ~ **policy** Restriktionspolitik; ~ **practices in industry** gewerbepolizeiliche Auflagen; ~ **trade agreement** *(Br.)* Kartellvereinbarung; ~ **Trade Practice Act** *(Br.)* Kartellgesetz.

result |s *(advertising)* Werbeerfolg, *(balance sheet, US)* Jahresergebnis;
profit ~ Gewinnergebnis;
~ *(v.)* **in a profit** Gewinn zeitigen;
~ **fee** *(Br.)* Erfolgshonorar.

resume | *(v.)* **business** Geschäft wiedereröffnen; ~ **negotiations** Verhandlungen wiederaufnehmen.

resumption of business Wiederaufnahme der Geschäftstätigkeit.

retail Klein-, Handverkauf, Detailgeschäft;
wholesale and ~ im Groß- und Einzelhandel;
~ *(v.)* Einzelhandelsgeschäft betreiben;
~ **advertising** Einzelhandelswerbung; ~ **book credit** Kundenkredit [des Kaufmanns]; ~ **charge account** Kundenkreditkonto; ~ **consignments** Stückgut; ~ **credit** *(US)* Kundenkredit; ~ **customer** Einzelhandelskunde; ~ **dealer** Einzel-, Kleinhändler, Wiederverkäufer; ~ **discount** Kleinhandelsrabatt; ~ **enterprise (establishment, firm)** Einzelhandelsunternehmen, -betrieb, -firma; ~ **house** Einzelhandelsgeschäft; ~ **margin** Kleinverkaufsspanne; ~ **markup** Handelsspanne; ~ **outlet** Einzelhandelsverkaufsstelle; ~ **[selling] price** Einzelhandels-, Detailpreis; ~ **ceiling price** Verbraucherhöchstpreis; ~ **price index** Einzelhandelspreisindex; ~ **price maintenance** Preisbildung der zweiten Hand; ~ **sales** Einzelhandelsumsatz; ~ **shop** *(Br.)* Klein-, Einzelhandelsgeschäft; ~ **spending boom** Einzelhandelskonjunktur; ~ **store** *(US)* Einzelhandelsgeschäft; ~ **trade** Einzelhändler; ~ **trading zone** zentrumnahes Geschäftsviertel; ~ **turnover** Einzelhandelsumsätze.

retailer Klein-, Wiederverkäufer;
limited-line ~ Inhaber eines Spezialgeschäftes;
~ **survey** Einzelhändlerbefragung.

retailing Detailverkauf, Einzelhandel;
large-scale ~ Massenfilialbetrieb.

retain *(v.)* *(book)* [Plätze] belegen;
~ **an agent** Vertreter beschäftigen; ~ **on a per-diem-plus-expense basis** auf Tages- und Unkostenbasis engagieren; ~ **title** sich das Eigentum vorbehalten.

retained | **earnings** thesaurierter Gewinn, Gewinnvortrag; ~s **income** Gewinnrücklage.

retainer Anhaltshonorar, *(formal retention)* Zurückbehaltung[srecht];
~ **of debts** Vorwegbefriedigungsrecht;

retaliate *(v.)* *(customs)* Kampfzölle (Retorsionszölle) erheben.

retaliation Repressalien, *(customs)* Retorsion.

retaliatory duty Kampfzoll.

retention Ein-, Bei-, Zurückbehaltung, *(reinsurance business)* Selbstbehalt;
title ~ Eigentumsvorbehalt;
~ **of goods** Warenhortung; ~ **of wages** Lohneinbehaltung;
~ **money** *(Br.)* Sicherheitssumme.

retire *(v.)* sich zurückziehen, *(board member)* abwählen, *(bookkeeping)* ausbuchen, *(give up office)* zurücktreten, ausscheiden, sich pensionieren lassen;
~ **under the age limit** sich aus Altersgründen pensionieren lassen; ~ **a bill** Wechsel einlösen; ~ **bonds** Obligationen aus dem Verkehr ziehen; ~ **coins from circulation** Münzen aus dem Verkehr ziehen; ~ **a loan** Anleihestücke zurückkaufen; ~ **by rotation** turnusgemäß ausscheiden; ~ **to consultant status** in Pension gehen, aber noch beratend tätig bleiben; ~ **a unit** Anlage außer Betrieb nehmen.

retired *(abandoned)* ausgebucht, *(bill)* zurückgezogen, eingezogen;
to live ~ im Ruhestand leben;
to be placed on the ~ **list at one's own request** auf eigenen Wunsch pensioniert werden; ~ **partner** ausgeschiedener Gesellschafter.

retirement *(bill)* Zurück-, Einziehung, *(board member)* Abwahl, *(bookkeeping)* Ausbuchung, *(from office)* Rück-, Austritt, Ausscheiden, Pensionierung, Ruhestand;
~s *(balance sheet)* Abgänge;
compulsory ~ Zwangspensionierung; **early** ~ frühzeitige Pensionierung;
~ **of a bill** Wechseleinlösung; ~ **from business** Aufgabe eines Geschäftes; ~ **of the public debt** *(US)* Tilgung der öffentlichen Schuld; ~ **of a partner** Ausscheiden eines Teilhabers; ~ **on full pension** Pensionierung mit vollem Ruhegehalt; ~ **of securities** Kraftloserklärung von Wertpapieren;
to choose early ~ **at sixty** sich mit sechzig vorzeitig pensionieren lassen; **to spend an active** ~ sich nach seiner Pensionierung noch betätigen;
~ **accounting method** Abschreibungsmethode; ~ **age** Altersgrenze; **to stay on past** ~ **age** über das pensionspflichtige Alter hinaus tätig bleiben; ~ **allowance** Altersrente; ~ **benefit** *(US)* Pensionszuwendung, -bezüge, Ruhegeld; ~ **eligibility** Pensionsberechtigung; ~ **income** Ruhegehaltsbezüge; ~ **pension** *(Br.)* Altersversorgung, Ruhegehalt; ~ **reserve fund** Tilgungsrücklage; ~ **unit** außer Betrieb genommene Anlage.

retiring | **of a bill** Wechseleinlösung; ~ **from business** Ausscheiden aus einem Geschäft;
~ **allowance** Ruhegehalt; ~ **director** ausscheidendes Vorstandsmitglied; ~ **president** bisheriger Präsident.

retool *(v.)* **industry** Industrie neu ausrüsten.

retraining scheme Umschulungsprogramm.

retrench *(v.)*Ausgaben einschränken, sparen; ~ **privileges** Vorrechte aufheben; ~ **this year** in diesem Jahr sehr sparsam leben.

retrenchment Einschränkung, Kürzung, Schmälerung, *(of employees)* [Beamten]abbau; ~ **of budgetary expenditure** Haushaltseinsparungen; ~ **of salary** Gehaltskürzung.

retrievable loss ersetzbarer Verlust.

retrieve | *(v.)* one's **fortune** sein Vermögen wiedererwerben; ~ **a loss** Verlust wieder einbringen.

retroactive pay rückwirkende Lohnerhöhung.

retrocession Rück-, Wiederabtretung, Rückübertragung, *(reinsurance)* Folgerückversicherung.

retrograde movement rückgängige [Kurs]bewegung.

return *(bailiff)* Vollzugsbericht, *(census)* Volkszählung, *(income tax)* [Einkommen]steuererklärung, *(journey)* Rückfahrt, -reise, *(repayment)* Rückzahlung, -erstattung, *(replacement)* Rückgabe, -lieferung, *(report)* statistischer Ausweis, *(yield)* Zinsertrag, [Anlage]verzinsung; **for collections and** ~s zwecks Einziehung und Überweisung; **in ~ for his services** als Entgelt für seine Tätigkeit; **on [sale | for]** ~ in Kommission; **without** ~ unentgeltlich, umsonst; ~s *(balance sheet)* Einkünfte aus Kapitalvermögen, *(goods returned)* Retour-, Rückwaren, Remittenden, *(redrafts, Br.)* retournierte Schecks; **amended** ~ Einkommensteuerberichtigung; **annual** ~ Jahresausweis, *(taxation, Br.)* jährliche [Einkommen]steuererklärung; **bank** ~ Bankausweis; **Board of Trade** ⌖s *(US)* Ausweis des Statistischen Bundesamtes, Handelsstatistik; **consolidated** ~ *(US)* Konzernbilanz; **corporate income-tax** ~ Körperschaftsteuerformular; **diminishing** ~s Ertragsrückgang; **duty-free** ~ zollfreie Wiedereinfuhr; **gross** ~s Bruttoeinnahmen; **income-tax** ~ Einkommensteuererklärung; **joint** ~ gemeinsame [Einkommen]steuererklärung; **normal** ~s landesübliche Kapitalverzinsung; **processed** ~ bearbeitetes Einkommensteuerformular; **recurring** ~s wiederkehrende Nutzungen; ~ **unsatisfied** *(bankruptcy)* mangels Masse unerledigt; ~ **of allotment** Aktienzuteilungsbericht; ~s **and allowances** *(balance sheet)* Retouren und Rabatte; ~ **on capital employed** Kapitalrendite; ~ **of contribution** Beitragsrückgewähr; ~ **of the day** Tagesumsatz; ~ **of empties** Rücksendung der Verpackung; **greater** ~ **on equity** höhere Kapitalrendite; ~ **of exchange** Rückwechselsrechnung; ~ **of expenses** Spesen-, Ausgabenaufstellung; ~ **of a gift** Widerruf einer Schenkung; ~ **of goods** Warenrückgabe; ~s **of payment** Rimessen, ~ **of premium** *(marine insurance)* Prämienrückgewähr; ~ **on sales** Gewinnspanne; ~ **to work** Wiederaufnahme der Arbeit; ~ *(v.)* zurück-, wiederkommen, *(send back)* zurückschicken, *(remit)* übermachen, retournieren, *(turnover)* umsetzen, *(yield)* einbringen, abwerfen;

~ **an overpaid amount** zuviel gezahltes Geld zurückgeben; ~ **a bill to drawer** Wechsel retournieren; ~ **the details of one's income** detaillierte Einkommensteuererklärung abgeben; ~ **five per cent** sich mit fünf Prozent verzinsen; ~ **to port** wieder in den Hafen einlaufen; ~ **a profit** Gewinn abwerfen; **to answer by** ~ **of mail** *(US)* postwendend antworten; **to bring a fair** ~ angemessenen Gewinn abwerfen; **to deliver goods on sale or** ~ Waren .in Kommission geben; **to file separate** ~s getrennte Einkommensteuererklärung abgeben, sich getrennt veranlagen lassen; **to get a good** ~ **on an investment** hohe Rendite abwerfen; **to make good** ~s gute Umsätze erzielen; **to process a** ~ Einkommensteuererklärung bearbeiten; **to take a first-class** ~ to X Rückfahrkarte erster Klasse nach X lösen; **to yield an easy (quick, short)** ~ rasch umgesetzt werden;

~s **account** Retourenkonto; ~ **air fare** Rückflugkarte; ~s **book** Retourenbuch; ~ **card** [Rück]antwortkarte, *(advertising)* Bestellkarte; ~ **cargo** Rückfracht; ~ **commission** Provisionsvergütung; ~ **coupon** Kupon in Form einer Bestellkarte; ~ **debit** Rückbelastung; ~ **draft** Rückwechsel; ~ **envelope** Freiumschlag; ~ **performance** Gegenleistung; ~ **premium** stornierte Prämie; ~ **reference** Wiedervorlage; ~ **tag** Rücksendeadresse; ~ **ticket** Rückfahrkarte.

returnable rückgabepflichtig, rückzahlbar.

returned | **empty** leer zurück; **to be** ~ **unfit for work** arbeitsunfähig geschrieben werden; ~ **articles** Remittenden; ~ **bill** Retourwechsel; ~ **goods** *(customs, US)* Rück-, Retourware; ~ **letter** unbestellbarer Brief; ~-**shipment rate** *(US)* verbilligter Frachtsatz für Leergut.

revalorize *(v.)* neu bewerten, aufwerten.

revaluation Neube-, Um-, Aufwertung; ~ **of fixed assets** Neubewertung des Anlagevermögens; ~ **of the currency** Neueinstufung der Währung; **quasi-**~ **measures** aufwertungsähnliche Maßnahmen; ~ **reserves** Rückstellung für Wertberichtigungen, Neubewertungsreserve.

revalue *(v.)* von neuem schätzen, aufwerten; ~ **assets** Anlagen reaktivieren.

revenue *(government board)* Finanzverwaltung, Fiskus, *(income)* Einkommen, Einnahme[n], Einkünfte, Ertrag, *(state's annual income)* Staatseinnahmen, Steueraufkommen, *(periodical yield from investment)* Nutzung, Ertrag, Rendite, Kapitalrente; **annual** ~ Jahreseinnahme; **customs** ~ Zolleinnahmen; **inland** *(Br.)* **(internal,** US**)** ~ Steuereinnahmen, -aufkommen; **land** ~ *(Br.)* Domänenerträge; **nonoperating** ~s betriebsfremde Einkünfte; **public** ~ Einkünfte der öffentlichen Hand; **recurring** ~s wiederkehrende Nutzungen; **taxable** ~ steuerbares Einkommen; **unearned** ~ Kapitalrente;

to defraud the ~ Steuern hinterziehen; **to produce less** ~ geringeres Steueraufkommen erzielen; ~ **account** Ertrags-, Gewinn- und Verlustkonto; ~ **agent** Finanzbeamter, *(customs)* Zollbeamter; ~ **assets** werbende Betriebsmittel; ~ **cutter** *(US)* Zollschiff, -kutter, -boot, -fahrzeug; ~ **cutter service** *(US)* Zolldienst; ~ **deduction** *(municipal accounting)* Erlösschmälerung; ~ **deficit** *(taxes)* Einkommen-, Steuerdefizit; ~ **drain** *(budgeting)* steuerlicher Verlustfaktor; ~ **estimates** Steuervorausschätzungen; ~ **expenditure** Kapitalaufwand; ~ **forecast** Steueraufkommensschätzung; ~ **frauds** Steuer-, Zollhinterziehungen; ~ **loss** Steuerverlust; ~ **office** Zollamt; ~ **officer** Steuer-, Zollbeamter; ~ **reserve** *(Br.)* *(balance sheet)* Ertragsrücklage; ~ **service** Zolldienst; ~ **shortage** unzureichendes Steueraufkommen; ~ **stamp** Banderole; **internal** ~ **taxes** inländische Steuern und Abgaben; ~ **tariff** Einkommensteuertarif.

reversal Stornierung, Gegenbuchung; ~ **in the money market** Liquiditätsumschwung.

reverse *(check)* Revers, *(coin)* Rückseite; ~ *(v.)* **the charge** *(tel., US)* R-Gespräch herstellen; ~ **an entry** Buchung stornieren; ~ **entry** Gegenbuchung, -eintrag; ~ **split-up** Aktiensplit, -zusammenlegung.

reversed call *(tel., US)* R-Gespräch.

reversing entry Stornierungsbuchung.

reversion *(deferred annuity)* Anwartschaftsrente, *(life insurance)* Versicherungssumme, *(right of succession)* Anwartschaft; ~ **claim** Anwartschaft[srecht].

reversionary | **additions** *(life insurance)* Summenzuwachs durch stehengelassene Prämien; ~ **annuity** einseitige Überlebensrente.

reversioner Anwartschaftsberechtigter.

review *(check)* [Nach]prüfung, *(periodical)* Zeitschrift; **market** ~ Marktbericht; ~ **of costs** Überprüfung einer Kostenrechnung; ~ *(v.)* **a price list** Preisliste berichtigen.

revise *(v.)* **one's estimates** Neukalkulation vornehmen.

revision Nachprüfung, Revision.

revitalization of the capital market Wiederbelebung des Kapitalmarktes.

revival *(market)* Wiederbelebung, -aufleben, Aufschwung, Erholung; ~ **in business** Geschäfts-, Konjunkturbelebung.

revive *(v.)* erneuern, *(stocks)* sich erholen, *(trade)* sich wiederbeleben, aufblühen; ~ **an industry** Industriezweig beleben.

revocable | **letter of credit** widerrufliches Akkreditiv; ~ **licence** widerrufliche Genehmigung.

revocation | **of agency** Widerruf des Auftragsverhältnisses; ~ **of a letter of credit** Akkreditivwiderruf.

revoke | *(v.)* **an agency** Vertretungsverhältnis aufheben; ~ **an authority** Vollmacht widerrufen; ~ **a letter of credit** Akkreditiv zurückziehen; ~ **a**

licence Lizenz zurücknehmen; ~ **an order** Auftrag stornieren;

revolving | **account** revolvierendes Konto; ~ **assets** Umlaufsvermögen; **secured** ~ **credit** Warenlombardkredit; ~ **fund** *(governmental accounting, US)* rückzahlbare Staatssubvention.

reward [Finder]lohn, [Geld]belohnung; **to offer a** ~ Belohnung aussetzen, Auslobung vornehmen, ausloben; ~ **system** Prämienlohnsystem.

rework expense Nacharbeitungskosten.

rid | *(v.)* **o. s. of an employee** Angestellten loswerden; ~ **one's estate of debt** seinen Grundbesitz schuldenfrei machen.

rider *(advertisement)* abschließender Kaufappell, *(of a bill)* Verlängerungszettel, Wechselallonge, *(insurance)* besondere Versicherungsvereinbarung.

rig Börsenmanöver.

rigger Preistreiber, *(stock exchange)* Kurstreiber.

rigging the market Kurstreiberei, Börsenmanöver.

right Recht, Anrecht, [Rechts]anspruch, *(application right)* Bezugsrecht auf Aktien; **cum ~s, ~s on** mit (inklusive) Bezugsrechten; **application** ~ *(Br.)* Bezugsrecht; **drawing** ~ Auslosungsrecht; **industrial** ~ gewerbliches Schutzrecht; **serial ~s** Veröffentlichungsrechte in Zeitungen und Zeitschriften; **shop ~s** Fabrikationsrechte; **stock** ~ *(US)* Bezugsrecht; **subscription** ~ *(Br.)* Bezugsrecht; ~ **to alimony** Unterhaltsanspruch [der Ehefrau]; ~ **of anticipation** Vorkaufsrecht; ~ **to draw benefits** *(social security)* Leistungsanspruch; ~ **of conversion** Umwandlungsrecht; ~ **to a dividend** Dividendenanspruch; ~ **of sole emption** Alleinverkaufsrecht; ~ **to issue bank notes** Banknotenprivileg; ~ **of maintenance** Unterhaltsanspruch; ~ **of preemption** Vorkaufsrecht; ~ **of priority** *(creditor)* Recht auf vorzugsweise Befriedigung im Konkursverfahren; ~ **of recourse** Rückgriffsrecht, Regreßrecht; **[sole]** ~ **to sell (of selling)** [alleiniges] Verkaufs-, Vertriebsrecht; ~ **of separation** Absonderungsanspruch; ~ **of stoppage in transit (to stoppage in transit)** Anhalte-, Rückrufrecht; **to forfeit the** ~ **of recourse** Regreßanspruch verlieren; **to have £ 400 in one's own** ~ über eine Jahresrente von 400 Pfund verfügen; **to reserve the** ~ **of property** Eigentum[srecht] vorbehalten; **~s dealings** *(US)* Handel in Bezugsrechten; **~s market** *(US)* Markt für Bezugsrechte.

rightful claimant Anspruchsberechtigter.

rigid economy sparsame Wirtschaftsführung.

ring Ring, Kartell, Syndikat, *(stock exchange)* Börsenkonsortium; **bull** ~ *(stock exchange)* Haussepartei; ~ **of dealers at an auction** Aufkäuferring bei einer Versteigerung; ~ **trading** *(Br.)* Händlerabsprachen.

rise Zuwachs, Zunahme, *(extra pay, US)* Zulage, Gehaltsaufbesserung, *(in prices)* Anziehen, Steigen, Preiserhöhung, *(stock exchange)* Aufschwung, Aufwärtsbewegung, Kursanstieg;

abrupt ~ scharfer Kursanstieg; **widely spread** ~ Kursanstieg auf breiter Basis;
~ **in the bank rate** *(Br.)* Diskonterhöhung; ~ **in costs** *(expenditure)* Kostensteigerung; ~ **in life** sozialer Aufstieg; ~ **in production** Produktionssteigerung; ~ **in profits** Gewinnanstieg; ~ **in sales** Absatzerhöhung; ~ **in the standard of living** Verbesserung des Lebensstandards; ~ **of stocks** *(US)* Aktienhausse;
~ *(v.)* *(adjourn)* auseinandergehen, Sitzung aufheben, sich vertagen, *(prices)* anziehen, [im Preise steigen], sich aufwärts bewegen, *(stock exchange)* sich bessern, anziehen, steigen;
~ **into new high ground** neuen Höchstkurs erzielen; ~ **by merit only** seinen Aufstieg allein sich selbst verdanken; ~ **from nothing** aus kleinsten Verhältnissen stammen; ~ **to order** zur Geschäftsordnung sprechen; ~ **from the ranks** von der Pike auf dienen;
to ask one's employer for a ~ *(US)* seinen Arbeitgeber auf Gehaltserhöhung ansprechen; **to buy for a** ~ auf Hausse spekulieren; **to have a sudden** ~ plötzlich im Kurs steigen; ~ **forecast** Kurssteigerungsprognose.
rising Steigen, Steigerung, Anziehen;
~ *(a.)* *(stock exchange)* kursanziehend; ~ **costs** steigende Kosten; ~ **market** Kursanstieg; ~ **tendency** Preiserhöhungstendenz, *(stock exchange)* Kursaufschwung.
risk Verlust, Risiko, *(insurance)* Wagnis, Verlustgefahr, *(object or person insured)* versicherte Person, versicherter Gegenstand;
at all ~**s** ohne Rücksicht auf Verluste; **at one's own** ~ auf eigene Gefahr;
abnormal ~ erhöhtes Risiko; **business** ~ Ausfall-, Geschäftsrisiko; **commercial** ~ Unternehmerwagnis; ~ **covered** gedecktes Risiko; **exchange** ~ Kursrisiko; **flat** ~ *(insurance)* Pauschalsatz; **marine (maritime)** ~ Seetransportgefahr; **tenant's** ~ Mieterhaftung; **uninsured** ~**s** ungedeckte Risiken; ~ **of breakage** Bruchgefahr; ~ **incident to employment** Berufsrisiko, Haftpflicht; ~ **of investment** Anlagen-, Investitionsrisiko; ~**s and perils of the sea** Seegefahr; ~**s of an undertaking** unternehmerisches Risiko; ~ **of war** Kriegsrisiko;
~ *(v.)* **one's fortune** sein Vermögen einsetzen;
to assume all ~**s** Risiko übernehmen; **to class as high** ~ zum besonders hohen Risiko erklären; **to cover a** ~ für ein Risiko die Versicherung übernehmen; **to spread the** ~ Risiko verteilen, *(reinsurance)* Rückversicherungsrisiko atomisieren; **to take a** ~ **on a cargo** Ladung versichern; **to underwrite a** ~ Versicherung unter Risikoteilung übernehmen;
~ **bearer** Risikoträger; ~ **[-bearing] capital** Spekulations-, Risikokapital; ~ **money** Kaution, *(cashier)* Manko-, Fehlgeld; ~ **taking** Risikoübernahme, Gefahrtragung.
rival | **s in business** Konkurrenten;

~ *(v.)* konkurrieren, in Wettbewerb treten;
~ **business concern** Konkurrenzunternehmen; ~ **supply** Konkurrenzangebot.
river, navigable schiffbarer Fluß;
~ **bill of lading** Flußladeschein.
road [Land]straße, Verkehrs-, Fahrweg, *(mining)* Förderstrecke, *(waterway)* Wasserweg;
by ~ mit dem Lastauto, im Straßentransport; **at the** ~ geschäftlich unterwegs;
access ~ Zufahrtsstraße, Zubringer; **adopted** ~ *(US)* vom Kommunalverband unterhaltene Straße; **arterial** ~ Hauptverkehrsstraße; ~ **closed ahead** gesperrt für den Durchgangsverkehr; ~ **open to traffic** für den öffentlichen Verkehr freigegebene Straße; **no through** ~ Sackgasse; ~ **versus rail** Wettbewerb zwischen Schiene und Straße;
to be off the ~ *(car)* aus dem Verkehr gezogen sein; **to be on the** ~ *(bus)* im Betrieb sein, *(traveller)* auf Reisen (Tour) sein;
~ **accident** Auto-, Verkehrsunfall; ~ **behavio(u)r** Verkehrsdiziplin; ~ **check** Straßen-, Verkehrskontrolle; ~ **conditions** Straßenzustand; **long-distance** ~ **haulage** Güterkraftverkehr; ~ **tax** *(Br.)* Straßenbenutzungsgebühr; ~ **traffic control** Verkehrsregelung; ~ **transport** *(Br.)* Straßen-, Güterkraftverkehr.
roadbook Straßenatlas, Autoreiseführer.
roaring business Bombengeschäft.
rock-bottom price äußerst kalkulierter Preis.
roll Verzeichnis, Liste, Rolle;
assessment ~ Steuer-, Hebeliste; **bank** ~ Banknotenbündel; **rent** ~ Pachtaufkommen;
~ *(v.)* **back** *(US)* Preise durch Subventionsmaßnahmen senken; ~ **in money** im Geld schwimmen; ~ **over bank loans on a continuing basis** Bankkredite revolvierend einsetzen;
~**-on, ~-off service** Huckepackverkehr.
rolling | **adjustment** *(US)* Konjunkturdämpfung auf einzelnen Gebieten; ~ **capital** Betriebskapital; ~ **charges** Rollgeld; ~ **stock** Eisenbahnbetriebsmittel, Wagenpark.
room Zimmer, Raum, *(mining)* Abbaustrecke;
auction ~ Auktionslokal; **furnished** ~ möbliertes Zimmer; **strong** ~ Tresor, Stahlkammer; ~ **and board** Kost und Logis;
to book a hotel ~ Hotelzimmer bestellen; **to live in furnished** ~**s** möbliert wohnen;
~ **fee** Zimmerpreis; ~ **trader** *(US)* auf eigene Rechnung spekulierendes Börsenmitglied.
rotate *(v.)* **in office** sich turnusmäßig abwechseln.
rotation geregelter Stellenwechsel, Turnus, *(advertising)* ständig wiederholte Werbeserie;
job ~ *(US)* Arbeitsplatzwechsel;
~ **training** Praktikantenausbildung.
rough | **balance** Probe-, Rohbilanz; ~ **book** Kladde; ~ **calculation** flüchtige Berechnung, Voranschlag.
round *(tour)* Rundreise, Tour, Rundgang;
visiting ~ Inspektionsfahrt;
~**-of-wage increase** globale Anhebung des Lohn-

niveaus; ~ **of negotiations** Verhandlungsrunde; ~ of visits Besuchstour;

~ *(v.)* **off one's property** sein Gelände arrondieren; **to show s. o. ~ the factory** j. die Fabrik besichtigen lassen;

in ~ figures in runden Zahlen; **~-table conference** Konferenz am runden Tisch; ~ **tour** Rundreise; ~ **transaction (turn)** abgeschlossenes Börsengeschäft; ~ **trip** Rundreise, -fahrt.

round-trip air fare Rundreiseflugkarte; ~ **excursion fare** Rundreise-, Ausflugsfahrkarte.

roundabout *(detour, US)* Umleitung, *(road junction, Br.)* Kreisel-, Rundverkehr.

roundsman *(Br.)* Laufbursche, Lieferbote.

route *(airplane)* Fluglinie, -route, -strecke, *(insurance)* Transportweg, *(road)* [Reise]route, Weg, [Bundes]straße, *(salesman)* Verkaufstournee, *(ship)* Schiffahrtsweg, Kurs;

en ~ unterwegs;

bus ~ Omnibusstrecke; **trade ~** Handelsstraße;

low-cost ~ to raise capital to finance expansion billiger Finanzierungsweg für Betriebsausweitungen; ~ **of travel** Beförderungsweg;

~ *(v.)* befördern, leiten, dirigieren, *(post)* mit Postleitvermerk versehen;

to build regular ~s feste Verkaufstournee festlegen; **to pick up ~ 10** *(US)* der Bundesstraße 10 folgen;

~ **card** Arbeitsablaufkarte; ~ **forecast** Streckenvorhersage, Flugwetterdienst; ~ **instructions** Leitvermerk; ~ **items** *(US)* Boteninkassi.

routine gewohnheitsmäßiger Verlauf, Trott, Routinesache, *(matter of form)* Brauch, Formsache, Dienstweg;

business (office) ~ üblicher Arbeitsgang;

to be only ~ reine Formsache sein;

~ **board** Dienstplan; ~ **business** Routinearbeit; ~ **business letter** üblicher Geschäftsbrief; ~ **expenditure** tägliche Ausgaben; ~ **visit** Routinebesuch.

routing | **of salesmen** Festlegung der Verkaufsrouten von Vertretern;

~ **clerk** *(US)* Abfertigungsbeamter; ~ **sheet** Arbeitsfolgenplan; ~ **slip** Laufzettel.

royalty *(copyright)* Autorenanteil, Tantieme, Honorar, *(licence)* Lizenzgebühr, *(patent)* Patentgebühr, *(share in profit)* Gewinn-, Ertragsanteil;

accrued ~ Tantiemenforderung; **director's ~** Aufsichtsratstantieme;

~ **of 10 % on the published price** zehn Prozent vom Ladenverkaufspreis;

on a ~ basis gegen Zahlung einer Lizenzgebühr; **~-free licence** gebührenfreie Lizenz; ~ **statement** Lizenzabrechnung.

rubber | **check** *(coll., US)* ungedeckter (geplatzter) Scheck; ~ **stamp** Gummistempel; **~-stamp** *(v.)* sich genau nach den Vorschriften richten; **~-stamp commitments** *(US sl.)* Zahlungsverpflichtungen routinemäßig erledigen.

rude produce Rohprodukt.

ruin Ruin, finanzieller Zusammenbruch;

~ *(v.)* **s. one's good reputation** Rufmord an jem. begehen.

ruinous | **expenditure** ruinöser Aufwand; ~ **price** Schleuder-, Verlustpreis.

rule Rechtsverordnung, Vorschrift, Verfügung;

under the ~s *(stock exchange)* börsenmäßig;

formal ~s Formvorschriften; **shop ~s** Betriebssatzung; **standing ~** Geschäftsordnung;

~s for admission Zulassungsbedingungen; **~s of a cartel** Kartellvorschriften; **~s for a credit** Kreditrichtlinien; **liberalized ~s on depreciation** günstige Abschreibungsmodalitäten; **~s on expense-account spending** Spesenrichtlinien; **~s of the stock exchange** Börsenordnung; **~s of taxation** Steuerrichtlinien;

~ *(v.)* **around** 7¹/₂ % zu etwa 7¹/₂ % umgehen; ~ **high** *(prices)* hoch liegen, hohes Kursniveau haben; ~ **off an account** Konto abschließen;

to break the ~ of a cartel gegen eine Kartellvereinbarung verstoßen; **to loosen ~s on depreciation** Abschreibungsmodalitäten lockern; **to work to ~** streng nach Vorschrift arbeiten;

ruling | **classes** privilegierte Klassen; ~ **price** gegenwärtiger (geltender) Preis, Tages-, Durchschnittspreis.

rummage Ausschuß, Ramsch, *(search by customs officials)* zollamtliche Durchsuchung;

~ **goods** Ausschußware; ~ **sale** Fundsachenversteigerung, Ramschverkauf.

run *(class of goods)* Sorte, Qualität, *(course)* Lauf, Gang, Fortgang, *(great demand)* Absatz, starker Zulauf, starke Nachfrage, Ansturm, *(output)* Betriebsleistung, Ausstoß, *(tenure of office)* Amtszeit, *(validity)* Gültigkeitsdauer, Laufzeit;

inaugural ~ Jungfernfahrt;

~ **on a bank** Ansturm auf eine Bank, ~ **of business** Geschäftsgang; **ordinary ~ of buyers** übliche Käuferschicht; ~ **of the market** Marktverlauf; ~ **of mill** Durchschnittserzeugnis; **trial ~ of a plant** Probelauf einer Fabrik; ~ **on oil stocks** ungeheure Nachfrage nach (Sturm auf) Erdölaktien;

~ *(v.)* *(circulate)* [um]laufen, in Umlauf sein, *(customers)* Run veranstalten, *(become due)* laufen, fällig werden, *(function)* funktionieren, arbeiten, im Betrieb sein, *(price)* sich stellen [auf], *(railway)* in Betrieb sein, verkehren, *(time)* verstreichen, vergehen;

~ **aground** *(ship)* auflaufen, stranden; ~ **at pari** *(shares)* Pari stehen; ~ **down the goods of a competitor** Konkurrenzware anschwärzen; ~ **for profit** auf Renditebasis betreiben.

run into | **debt** sich in Schulden stürzen; ~ **five figures** fünfstelligen Betrag ausmachen; ~ **heavy selling** schwer verkaufen lassen; ~ **money** *(coll.)* ins Geld gehen.

run off *(clear)* (Lager) räumen, *(bill of exchange)* ablaufen, fällig werden, *(stock exchange)* rückläufig sein;

~ **with the cash** mit der Kasse durchbrennen; **run out** *(loan)* erschöpft werden, *(passport)* ablaufen, *(stock)* zu Ende gehen, ausgehen.

run over one's account seine Konten durchgehen.

run through | **an account** Rechnung überfliegen; ~ **one's property** sein Vermögen durchbringen.

run up sich summieren, *(force up prices)* hinauftreiben, in die Höhe schrauben, *(rise in price)* im Preise steigen, anziehen; ~ **an account** auf Rechnung kaufen, *(bill)* anschreiben; ~ **a big bill in a hotel** große Hotelrechnung machen; ~ **a score** anschreiben lassen.

run | **an account with a shop** bei einem Laden auf Rechnung einkaufen; ~ **a bus company** *(US)* Omnibusunternehmen betreiben; ~ **day and night** *(trains)* Tag und Nacht verkehren; ~ **a factory at a loss** in einer Fabrik mit Verlust arbeiten; ~ **flat** *(business)* auf niedrigen Touren laufen, auf Sparflamme kochen; ~ **letters into a file** Briefe abheften; ~ **a cheap line** billige Artikel verkaufen; ~ **at par** auf Pari stehen; ~ **on schedule** *(US)* fahrplanmäßig verkehren; ~ **short** knapp werden, zur Neige gehen; ~ **a stand** Kiosk besitzen; **to be** ~ **at small cost** *(car)* billig im Betrieb sein; **to come down with a** ~ *(prices)* ruckartig fallen; **to give s. o. a.** ~ **for his money** jem. für sein Geld etw. bieten; **to pay in the long** ~ sich auf die Dauer bezahlt machen (auszahlen).

run-up *(airplane)* Anflug, *(motor car)* Probelauf; **high-cost** ~ hoher Kostenaufwand; ~ **in the money supply** Geldbedarfzunahme; ~ **of prices** *(US)* Kurssteigerung, -anstieg.

runabout | **ticket** *(railway, Br.)* Netzkarte; ~ **utility vehicle** Kombiwagen.

runaway | **cost** schnell steigende Kosten; ~ **inflation** zügellose (hemmungslose) Inflation.

running *(currency)* Laufzeit, Gültigkeitsdauer, *(functioning)* Laufen, Betrieb; ~ **in** *(car)* Einfahren; ~ **of trains** Zugverkehr; ~ *(a.)* *(circulating)* umlaufend, *(current)* laufend, offen, *(working)* in Betrieb; **to be** ~ **again** *(hotel)* wieder in Betrieb sein; **to have ceased** ~ *(factory)* Betrieb eingestellt haben, *(hotel)* geschlossen haben; ~ **account** Kontokorrent[konto], Verrechnungskonto; ~ **costs** Betriebs[un]kosten; ~ **days** Ladetage; ~ **engagements** laufende Verpflichtungen; ~ **form** *(insurance)* Risikoformular; ~ **idle** *(machine)* Leerlauf; ~ **interest** laufende Zinsen; **in** ~ **order** betriebsfertig; ~ **yield** *(Br.)* laufende Verzinsung.

rural cooperative *(US)* landwirtschaftliche Genossenschaft.

rush Andrang, Ansturm, Geschäftsandrang, *(demand)* äußerst lebhafte Nachfrage, *(traffic)* [Verkehrs]andrang; ~ **of orders** Auftragsstrom; ~ **on mining stocks** Nachfrage nach Montanaktien; ~ *(v.)* **s. o. for an article** *(sl.)* jem. einen überhöhten Preis für einen Artikel abjagen; ~ **through an order for goods in three days** Warenauftrag in drei Tagen ausliefern; ~ **hour** verkehrsstarke Zeit, Verkehrsandrang, Stoßgeschäftszeit; ~**-hour traffic** Spitzenverkehr; ~ **job** *(order)* Eilauftrag; ~ **work** schludrige Arbeit.

S

sabotage, economic Wirtschaftssabotage.
sack *(v.)* *(dismiss, sl)* feuern, an die Luft setzen, Laufpaß geben, fristlos kündigen;
to **hold the ~ for the whole of the balance unpaid** *(fam., US)* Haftung für den unbezahlten Rechnungssaldo übernehmen.
sacrifice Gewinnverlust;
general average ~s Aufopferungen der großen Havarie;
to sell at a ~ zu jedem Preis losschlagen;
~ price Verlustpreis; **~ sale** Verlustverkauf.
sacrificed goods spottbillige Waren, *(marine insurance)* aufgeopferte Güter.
safe *(bank)* Schließ-, Bank-, Stahlkammerfach, Depot, *(strong box)* Tresor, Geldschrank, Safe;
fireproof ~ feuerfester Geldschrank;
~ *(a.)* wohlbehalten, gefahrlos, sicher;
~ to operate betriebssicher;
to consider s. o. ~ for a credit of $ 4 000 j. für einen Kredit von 4 000 Dollar gut halten;
iron ~ clause *(insurance business)* Safeklausel; **~ custodies** *(Br.)* Depotgeschäft.
safe custody sicherer Gewahrsam, *(banking, Br.)* Verwahrung, [Wertpapier]depot;
~ of securities *(Br.)* Effektenverwaltung;
~ account *(Br.)* Depotkonto, Effektendepot; **~ business** *(Br.)* Depotgeschäft; **~ charges** *(Br.)* Depot[verwaltungs]gebühr; **~ receipt** *(Br.)* Depotquitttung.
safe deposit Geldschrank, Tresor, Stahlkammer, *(US)* [Bank]depot, Depotverwahrung;
safe-deposit feuer-, einbruchsicher;
~ balance Depotguthaben; **~ box** Schließ-, Tresor-, Stahl-, Bankfach, Safe; **~ box insurance** Depotversicherung; **~ facilities** Schließfachmiete; **~ keeping** *(US)* Aufbewahrung in Stahlkammern; **~ vault** *(US)* Stahl-, Schließfach.
safe | estimate vorsichtige Schätzung; **~ investment** [mündel]sichere Anlage; **from a ~ quarter** aus zuverlässiger Quelle.
safeblower Geldschrankknacker.
safeguard Sicherung, Schutz, *(protection)* Schutzvorrichtung;
~ *(v.)* **an industry** Schutzzölle für einen Industriezweig festsetzen.
safeguarding | of credits Kreditbesicherung; **~ of the currency** Währungssicherung;
♀ of Industry Act *(Br.)* Gewerbeschutzgesetz; **~ duty** *(Br.)* Schutzzoll.
safekeeping sichere Aufbewahrung, *(bank)* Depot-[aufbewahrung];
to have jewels in ~ Schmuck im Tresor haben.
safety Sicherheit, Schutz, Gefahrlosigkeit;
~ belt Rettungsgürtel, *(car)* Anschnallgürtel; **~ box** Panzerschrank; **~ fund** *(banking)* Mindestreserven; **~ inspection of factories** gewerbepolizeiliche Überprüfung der Betriebssicherheit; **~**

load zulässige Belastung; **~ vault** Panzergewölbe, Stahlschrank.
sag *(stock market)* Baisse;
~ *(prices)* nachgeben, gedrückt sein, sinken, abflauen, sich abschwächen.
sagging | of the market Kursabschwächung;
~ market abgeschwächter Markt, nachgebende Kurse.
sail *(v.)* **to schedule** *(US)* fahrplanmäßig auslaufen.
sailing Abfahrt, Auslaufen;
~ card Verladeanweisung; **~ date** *(ship)* Abfahrtszeit.
salable verkäuflich, *(marketable)* absatz-, marktfähig, absetz-, gang-, umsetzbar, einschlagend;
~ stock börsengängige Papiere.
salaried fest angestellt, besoldet;
~ clerk Büroangestellter; **high-~ officials** hochbezahlte Angestellte.
salary Gehalt, Besoldung, Dienstbezüge, Lohn;
accrued ~ Gehaltsrückstände; **advance ~** Gehaltsvorschuß; **commencing ~** Anfangsgehalt; **~ expected** *(advertisement)* Gehaltsansprüche; **stating ~** *(advertisement)* Gehaltsangabe; **top[level] ~** Spitzengehalt; **weekly ~** Wochenlohn;
~ by arrangement Gehalt nach Vereinbarung; **~ of a member of Parliament** Aufwandsentschädigung eines Abgeordneten, Diäten; **~ no object** *(newspaper)* Gehalt ist Nebensache;
to apply for a boost (increase, rise) in ~ um Gehaltserhöhung einkommen; **to carry an attractive ~** mit gehobeneren Gehaltsansprüchen verbunden sein; **to draw a fixed ~** fest angestellt sein; **to pay a ~** besolden, Gehalt zahlen;
~ account Gehaltskonto; **~ advance** Gehaltsvorschuß; **~ bracket** Gehaltsklasse, Besoldungsgruppe; **~ classification** Gehaltseinstufung; **demotional ~ decrease** Gehaltskürzung infolge anderer Einstufung; **~ differential** Sonderzulage für erschwerte Arbeitsbedingungen; **~ group** Gehalts-, Besoldungsgruppe; **present ~ level** augenblickliche Bezüge; **~ open** *(advertising)* Gehalt ist Verhandlungssache; **~ rise** Gehaltssteigerung; **~ roll** Gehälterliste; **~ a secondary consideration** *(advertisement)* Gehalt ist Nebensache.
sale Verkauf, Veräußerung, Kaufvertrag, *(clearance sale)* Inventur-, Saisonaus-, Saisonschlußverkauf;
at the time of ~ beim [Ver]kauf[s]abschluß; **for (on) ~** zu verkaufen; **no ~s** ohne Umsatz; **slow of ~** schlecht verkäuflich; **subject to prior ~** Zwischenverkauf vorbehalten;
advance ~ Vorverkauf; **annual ~** Jahresumsatz; **bearish ~** Leerabgabe; **bulk ~** Verkauf in Bausch und Bogen; **catalog(ue) ~** Versandgeschäft; **clearance (cheap) ~** Ausverkauf; **close-out ~** Schluß-, Ausverkauf; **consolidated outside ~** *(balance sheet)* Umsatz an die Kundschaft; **direct ~** Verkauf ohne Zwischenhändler; **distress ~** Notverkauf; **execu-**

tion *(US)* ~ Zwangsversteigerung; **executory** ~ [Ver]kauf unter Eigentumsvorbehalt; **going-out-of business** ~ Totalausverkauf; **gross** ~s Bruttoumsatz; **hedging** ~ Deckungsverkauf; **instal(l)ment** ~ Abzahlungsgeschäft; **intercompany** ~s Umsätze innerhalb eines Konzerns; **mail-order** ~ *(US)* Verkauf auf Grund übersandten Katalogs; **matched** ~s *(stock exchange)* gekoppelte Börsengeschäfte; **memorandum** ~ Kommissionsverkauf; **offhand** ~ freihändiger Verkauf; **open-market** ~s Verkäufe am offenen Markt; **public** ~ öffentliche Versteigerung; **repeat** ~ Kauf auf Grund von Erinnerungswerbung; **rummage** ~ Ramschverkauf; **seasonal** ~ Saisonschlußausverkauf; **shore** ~s *(stock exchange, US)* Leerverkauf, Verkauf ohne Deckung; **summer** ~s Sommerschlußverkauf; **under-the-counter** ~ Verkauf unter dem Ladentisch; **wash** ~ Börsenscheingeschäft; **white** ~ weiße Woche; **winter** ~ Winterschlußverkauf;
~ **on account** Verkauf auf Rechnung; ~ **on approval** Kauf auf Probe; ~ **by sealed bids** Submissionsverkauf; ~ **to the highest bidder** Zuschlag an den Meistbietenden; ~ **ex bond** Verkauf ab Zollager; ~ **on consignment** Verkauf auf Kommissionsbasis; ~ **below cost** Abgabe unter Selbstkostenpreis; ~ **for prompt delivery** Verkauf zur sofortigen Lieferung; ~ **by description** Gattungskauf; ~ **with all faults** Verkauf wie es steht und liegt; ~ **of ascertained goods** Spezieskauf; ~ **of unascertained goods** Gattungskauf; ~ **in gross** Partieverkauf; ~ **on inspection** Kauf nach Besichtigung; ~ **in lots** Verkäufe in Partien; ~ **with option of repurchase** Verkauf mit Rückkaufsrecht; ~ **by order of the court** gerichtliche Versteigerung; ~ **to pattern** Verkauf nach Muster; ~ **of real property** Grundstücks[ver]kauf; ~ **and return** Verkauf mit Rückgaberecht; ~ **by sample** Kauf nach Probe (Muster); ~ **of services** auf Dienstleistungsgeschäft; ~s **on speculation** Meinungsverkäufe; ~ **on the spot** Verkauf an Ort und Stelle; ~ **on the deferred payment system** *(US)* Abzahlungsgeschäft; ~ **on trial** Verkauf zur Probe; **to achieve world-wide** ~ weltweiten Absatz haben; **to be dull of** ~ sich schwer verkaufen lassen; **to be of quick** ~ reißend Absatz finden; **to find no** ~ nicht untergebracht werden können; **to make** ~s **on credit to retail customers** seinen Einzelhandelskunden Warenkredit einräumen; **to push** ~s Absatz vorantreiben; **to put up for** ~ feilbieten; **to rack up big** ~s dick verdienen; **to ring up the** ~ Betrag registrieren; **to roll up the** ~s Umsatzsteigerung erzielen;
on ~, **owner retiring from business** wegen Geschäftsaufgabe zu verkaufen;
~ **catalog(ue)** Verkaufskatalog; ~ **goods** Ramschwaren; ~ **note** *(broker, US)* Schlußnote; ~ **ring** *(auction)* Aufkäufergruppe.

sales | **account** Warenausgangskonto, *(advertising agency)* Kundenetat; ~ **agency** Verkaufsorganisation; ~ **agent** *(US)* Handels-, [General]vertreter; **conditional** ~ **agreement** Kaufvertrag mit Eigen-

tumsvorbehalt; ~ **approach** Verkaufsgesichtspunkt; ~ **association** Vertriebsgesellschaft; ~ **booth** Verkaufsbude; ~ **call** Vertreter-, Kundenbesuch; ~ **cartel** Absatz-, Rayonierungskartell; ~ **channel** Vertriebsweg; ~ **check** *(US)* Kassenzettel, -beleg; ~ **commission** Abschlußprovision; ~ **company** Vertriebsgesellschaft; ~ **crisis** Absatzkrise, Umsatztief; ~ **demonstration** Verkaufsvorführung; ~ **discount** Kundenrabatt; ~ **drive** verstärkter Werbeeinsatz; ~ **efforts** verstärkte Absatzbemühung; ~ **executive** Verkaufsleiter; ~ **figures** Absatzziffern, Umsatzwerte; ~ **finance company** *(US)* Absatzfinanzierungsgesellschaft; ~ **force** *(US)* Verkaufspersonal, Absatzstab; ~ **and service force** Verkaufs- und Kundendienstnetz; ~ **gimmicks** *(US sl.)* Verkaufstrick; ~ **inducement** Kaufanreiz; ~ **jump** sprungartiger Umsatzanstieg; ~ **ledger** Debitorenbuch; ~ **letter** Werbebrief; ~ **load** *(investment trust)* Verkaufsspesen; ~ **manager** Verkaufsleiter; ~ **manual** Handbuch für Verkäufer; ~ **marketing conference** Absatzgremium; ~ **mix** *(US)* Sortiment; ~ **monopoly** Vertriebsmonopol; ~ **office** Verkaufsbüro; ~ **order** Verkaufsauftrag; ~ **organization** Vertriebsorganisation; ~ **outlet** *(US)* Vertriebsstelle; **to hire extra** ~ **people** zusätzliches Verkaufspersonal einstellen; ~ **premium** Umsatz-, Abschlußprämie; **to speed up the** ~ **process** für beschleunigten Umsatz Sorge tragen; ~ **prohibition** Veräußerungsverbot; ~ **promotion** Vertriebs-, Absatzförderung; ~ **proportion** Absatzquote; ~ **prospects** Vertriebsaussichten; ~ **quota** Sollvorgaben im Verkauf; ~ **record** Kassenbeleg; ~ **representation** Verkaufsaktion; **to tailor one's** ~ **representation** sein Verkaufsprogramm darauf abstellen; ~ **resistance** Kaufunlust; ~ **situation** Marktlage; ~ **slip** Kassenschein, -beleg; ~ **staff** Verkaufspersonal; ~ **supervisor** Außenrevisor; ~ **syndicate** Absatzgemeinschaft; ~ **tax** *(US)* Umsatzsteuer; ~ **terms** *(US)* Absatz-, Vertriebsbedingungen; ~ **territory** Absatzgebiet; ~ **ticket** *(US)* Kassenschein, -beleg; ~ **training** Verkäuferschulung; ~ **trend** Umsatzentwicklung; ~ **trip** Vertretertour; ~ **volume** Umsatzvolumen.

salesfolder illustrierter Klappprospekt.
salesman Kaufmann, *(US)* [Laden]verkäufer; **carpet-bagging** ~ unseriöser Vertreter; **travelling** ~ Geschäfts-, Provisionsreisender.
salesmanship Kunst des Verkaufens; **high-pressure** ~ zielbewußte Verkaufsmethode; **unfair** ~ unlautere Verkaufspraktiken.
saloon Saal, Halle, *(bar, Br.)* Bar[raum]; **dining** ~ *(ship)* Speisesaal; ~ **car** *(Br.)* Luxuswagen, Limousine.
saloonkeeper *(US)* Gastwirt, Kneiper.
salt *(v.)* **an account** gepfefferte Rechnung ausstellen; ~ **the books** Geschäftsbücher frisieren.
salvage Bergelohn, *(property saved)* gerettetes Gut, Bergungsgut, *(recovery of waste)* [Abfall]verwertung;
civil ~ Bergeleistung, Schiffsrettung;

to assets the amount payable as ~ Höhe des Berge-
lohnes festsetzen; to make ~ of a shipwrecked
cargo Bruchlandung;
~ agreement Bergungsvertrag; ~ boat Bergungs-
fahrzeug; ~ corps *(US)* Technische Nothilfe [für
Brandkatastrophen usw.]; ~ crane Abschlepp-
kran; ~ money Bergegeld, Rettungslohn; ~ service
Seenotdienst; ~ ship Bergungsdampfer; ~ value
(marine insurance) Bergungs-, Schrottwert.

sample [Waren]probe, Qualitätsprobe, [Stück]mu-
ster, *(opinion poll)* Befragte, *(statistics)* Stichprobe, Querschnitt;
annexed ~s anhängende Muster; biased ~ ver-
zerrte Stichprobe; ~ displayed vorgelegte Probe;
~s only Muster ohne Wert; pattern ~ Muster-,
Probestück; quota ~ Quotenstichprobe; random
~ Zufallsstichprobe; sealed ~ verschlossenes Muster; ~ taken offhand Stichprobe;
~ of goods Warenprobe; ~ for inspection An-
sichtsmuster; ~ of no commercial value Muster
ohne Wert;
~ *(v.)* bemustern;
to assort ~s Muster zusammenstellen; to be up to
~ mustergetreu sein; to keep a stock of ~s Musterlager unterhalten; to order goods from the ~ nach
dem Muster bestellen; to take ~s at random Stichproben entnehmen;
~ assortment Musterkollektion; ~ bag Musterkof-
fer; ~ balance sheet Bilanzmuster; ~ card Musterkarte; ~ collection Mustersendung, [Muster]kol-
lektion; ~ fair Mustermesse; ~ offer Probeauftrag; ~ packet Mustersendung; by ~ post als
Muster ohne Wert; ~ statistic Teilerhebung; ~
stock Musterlager, -kollektion.

sampling Musterstück, Mustersammlung, *(marketing)* Marktforschung durch genaues Studium
einer repräsentativen Käuferschicht, *(representative investigation)* Auswahl eines repräsentativen
Querschnitts;
acceptance ~ Stichprobenentnahme bei der Abnahme; bulk ~ planlose Stichprobenauswahl; quota ~ Quotenauswahlverfahren; random ~ Entnahme von Stichproben;
~ distribution Stichprobenverteilung; ~ error Aus-
wahlfehler; ~ unit *(statistics)* Auswahleinheit.

sanctions, economic wirtschaftliche Sanktionen.

sanitary | installations sanitäre Einrichtungen; ~ serv-
ice Gesundheitsdienst.

satellite | airfield Ausweich-, Feldflughafen; ~
surburb Satellitenstadt.

satiate *(v.)* the market Markt sättigen.

satisfaction Begleichung, Bezahlung, Tilgung;
job ~ *(US)* Arbeitsfreude;
~ of a creditor Gläubigerbefriedigung; ~ of record *(US)* Hypothekenlöschung;
to enter ~ Hypothek im Grundbuch löschen;

satisfactory pension auskömmliche Pension.

satisfy *(v.)* [Schaden]ersatz leisten, Schulden bezahlen;
~ an accord Vergleich durchführen; ~ one's creditors seine Gläubiger befriedigen.

saturate *(v.)* *(market)* sättigen.

saturation of conumser demands Marktsättigung.

save *(v.)* retten, bewahren, *(abstain from expending)*
[ein]sparen, Ersparnisse machen;
~ for one's old age für sein Alter sparen; ~ 30 %
on costs versus competitors 30 % kostengünstiger
als die Konkurrenz arbeiten; ~ labo(u)r Arbeitskräfte einsparen; ~ middlemen's profit Provision
sparen.

saving Sparvorgang, Sparen;
~s Ersparnis[se], Spartätigkeit, erspartes Geld;
collective ~ Werksparen; compulsory ~ Zwangs-
sparen; personal ~s private Spartätigkeit; tax ~s
Steuerersparnisse;
~s for education Ausbildungsrücklage; ~ of expense Kostenersparnis;
to be careful of one's small ~s äußerst sparsam
wirtschaften; to dig into ~s to pay current debts
seine Ersparnisse zur Schuldenbezahlung angreifen; to encourage ~ Sparförderungsmaßnahmen
ergreifen; to keep one's ~s in the post office Post-
sparguthaben besitzen; to live on one's ~s von
seinen Ersparnissen leben;
~ bond Sparbon; ~s certificate Rabattmarke; ~
investment *(US)* erstklassiges Anlagepapier; ~ ratio Sparquote.

savings account Spar[kassen]guthaben.

savings bank Sparkasse;
post-office *(Br.)* *(postal)* ~ Postsparkasse.

savings-bank | account Sparkonto, -guthaben; ~ [de-
posit] book Sparkassenbuch; ~ investment *(US)*
mündelsicheres Anlagepapier; ~ investment rates
Sparzinssätze.

savings | bonds *(US)* kleingestückelte Obligationen; ~
box Sparbüchse; ~ deposits Spargelder, -einlagen;
~ plan Prämienplan; ~ rate Sparrate; ~ stamp *(US)*
Rabattmarke; ~ withdrawals Spareinlagenabgän-
ge.

scab *(US)* Nichtgewerkschaftler, Streikbrecher;
~ work *(US)* Schwarz-, Streikarbeit.

scale Waagschale, *(gradation)* Gradeinteilung, Ab-
stufung, *(measure)* Maßstab, Skala, *(tariff)* Tabelle, Staffel, Tarif;
on a ~ *(stock exchange)* zu verschiedenen Kursen
limitiert; on a descending ~ *(tax)* degressiv;
cost-of-living sliding ~ Gleitlohntarif; salary ~
Gehaltstabelle; wage ~ Lohnskala, -staffel, -tabel-
le;
~ of benefits Unterstützungsumfang; ~ of charges
Gebührenordnung, -tabelle; ~ of discount Rabatt-
staffel; high ~ of financing hoher Finanzierungs-
umfang; ~ of prices Preisskala, -staffel; ~ of salaries Gehaltsordnung; ~ of taxation Steuersatz,
-klasse;
~ *(v.)* a debt Schuld reduzieren; ~ down an
allotment Zuteilung repartieren; ~ down wages
Lohnsenkung vornehmen; ~ up income tax 10 per
cent Einkommensteuersätze 10 % heraufsetzen;
to be at the top of the ~ Tabelle anführen; to buy on
a ~ *(stock exchange, US)* seine Zukäufe über eine
Baisseperiode verteilen;

~ **buying** *(US)* Wertpapierkauf zu verschiedenen Zeiten; ~ **graduation** Tarifstaffelung.

scalp *(US)* kleiner Weiterverkaufsgewinn.

scant | **allowance** knappe Zuteilung; ~ **supply** geringer Vorrat.

scanty | **income** kümmerliches Einkommen; ~ **means** unzureichende Geldmittel.

scarce articles (commodities, goods, materials) knappe Waren, Mangelwaren.

scarcity Verknappung, Mangel, Teuerung; ~ **of currency** Devisenmangel; ~ **of housing** Wohnungsnot; ~ **of labo(u)r** Mangel an Arbeitskräften; ~ **of tonnage** Mangel an Schiffsraum.

scare | **on the stock exchange** Börsenpanik; ~ **buying** Angstkäufe.

scatter diagram *(statistics)* Streubild.

schedule *(additional clause)* Zusatzartikel, *(annex to income tax)* Einkommensteuererläuterung, *(bankruptcy, US)* Konkursbilanz, *(covering note)* Begleitschreiben, *(income-tax bracket, Br.)* Einkommensteuerklasse, *(income-tax form)* Einkommensteuerformular, *(list annexed)* Anlage, Anhang, *(railway guide, US)* Fahrplan, *(rider)* Zusatzurkunde, *(statistics)* Fragebogen, *(timetable)* Ablauf-, Zeit-, Stundenplan, *(written statement)* Tabelle, Liste;

according to (on) ~ *(US)* [fahr]planmäßig; **aging** ~ Fälligkeitstabelle; **cost** ~ Kostenaufstellung; **demand** ~ Bedarfsliste; **itemized** ~ Einzelaufstellung; **production** ~ Produktionsprogramm; ~ **of accounts payable** *(US)* Kreditorenverzeichnis; ~ **of accounts receivable** *(US)* Debitorenverzeichnis; ~ **to a balance sheet** Bilanzanlage; ~ **of commissions** Provisionstabelle; ~ **of concessions** *(GATT)* Zollzugeständnisliste; ~ **of encumbrances** Verzeichnis der hypothekarischen Belastungen; ~ **of insertions** Datenplan der Anzeigen; ~ **of planes** Flugplan; ~ **of prices** Preisverzeichnis; ~ **of property** Vermögensaufstellung;

~ *(v.)* Liste (tabellarisch) zusammenstellen; ~ **production** Produktion programmieren; **to be finished on** ~ termingemäß fertig werden; **to catch up with** ~ Terminplan wieder einhalten; **to fall behind** ~ Planziel nicht erreichen; **to file one's** ~ *(US)* Konkursanmeldung vornehmen; ~ **change** *(US)* Fahrplanänderung.

scheduled | **airline service** *(US)* Linienverkehr; ~ **cost** vorkalkulierte Kosten; ~ **price** Listenpreis; ~ **taxes** *(Br.)* veranlagte Steuern; ~ **territories** *(Br.)* Länder des Sterlingblocks.

scheduling *(US)* Fertigungsplanung.

scheme *(deceased's estate, Br.)* Verteilungsplan, *(plan)* Plan, Entwurf, Projekt, Vorhaben, *(statement)* [tabellarische] Aufstellung, Liste, Schema; **allocation** ~ Zuteilungsplan, **bubble** ~ Schwindelunternehmen;

~ **of arrangement** *(Br.)* Vergleichsvorschlag; ~ **of a lottery** Lotterie-, Ziehungsplan; ~ **of redemption** Amortisationsplan.

school, commercial *(Br.)* Handelsschule; ~ **continua-** tion ~ Fortbildungsunterricht; **industrial** ~ Fach-, Berufs-, Gewerbeschule; **language** ~ Sprachenschule; **technical** ~ Gewerbe-, Fach-, Berufsschule; **trade** ~ *(US)* Handels-, Berufsschule.

science | **of industrial administration** Betriebswirtschaftslehre; ~ **of future** Futurologie.

scientific management wissenschaftliche Betriebsführung.

scoop *(v.)* **in a large profit** Sondergewinn einstreichen; **to earn a lot of money in one** ~ auf einen Schlag viel Geld verdienen.

scope *(law)* Gültigkeitsbereich, Geltungsgebiet, *(sphere of action)* Aufgaben-, Wirkungskreis, Reichweite, Betätigungsfeld; ~ **of audit** Prüfungsumfang; ~ **of [agent's] authority** Vollmachtsumfang; **to act within the** ~ **of one's authority** im Rahmen seiner Vertretungsmacht handeln.

score | *(v.)* auf Rechnung setzen, anschreiben; ~ **an advance** Kursgewinn verzeichnen; ~ **up debts** Schulden machen; **to run up a** ~ *(Br.)* Schuldkonto anwachsen lassen.

scot Beitrag, Abgabe; **to pay** ~ **and lot** auf Heller und Pfennig bezahlen.

scrabble *(v.)* **the pennies together** Pfennige zusammenkratzen.

scrap Schrott, Abfall, Ausschuß, Altmaterial; ~ *(v.)* verschrotten, ausrangieren; ~ **company** Schrottfirma; ~ **material** Abfallmaterial; ~ **price** Schrottpreis.

scrape *(v.)* **a living** sich kümmerlich durchbringen.

scrapping facilities Schrottverwertungsanlage.

scratch | *(v.)* **along** sich mühsam durchschlagen; ~ **around for funds** auf der Kapitalsuche sein; **to start from** ~ ganz unten anfangen; ~ **collection** Zufallskollektion.

screen *(car)* Windschutzscheibe, *(television)* Bild-, Fernsehschirm; ~ *(v.)* **candidates** *(US)* Bewerber sieben; ~ **advertising** Filmwerbung.

screw | *(v.)* **down prices** Preise herunterdrücken; ~ **up the rents** Mieten unmäßig erhöhen.

scrip Interims-, Zwischen-, Bezugs-, Berechtigungsschein; **stock** ~ *(US)* Berechtigungsschein für den Bezug von Aktien; ~ **bonus** *(Br.)* Gratisaktie; ~ **certificate** *(US)* Zertifikat, *(Br.)* Interims-, Zwischenschein; ~ **company** *(US)* Kommanditgesellschaft auf Aktien; ~ **issue** *(Br.)* Ausgabe von [Gratis]berichtigungsaktien; ~ **money** *(US)* Schwundgeld.

scrupulous in money matters in Geldsachen äußerst pingelig.

sea See, Seegang, Ozean, Meer; **in the open** ~ auf hoher See; **ready for** ~ seefertig; ~**-borne commerce** Überseehandel; ~ **damage** Seeschaden; ~**-damaged** havariert; ~ **letter** Schiffspaß; ~**-proof packing** Überseeverpackung.

seagoing vessel Hochseeschiff.
seal Siegel[abdruck], Dienstsiegel, *(customs)* Plombe, Verschluß;
~ **broken** ~ erbrochenes Siegel; **common** *(Br.)* **(corporate,** *US)* ~ Firmensiegel; **customhouse** ~ Zollverschluß, -plombe;
to affix a ~ *(customs)* plombieren; **to break the** ~ **of a letter** Briefgeheimnis verletzen; **to remove the** ~**s from a package** Ware aus dem Zoll freigeben.
sealed versiegelt, *(with lead)* plombiert;
~ **bid** *(US)* Submissionsangebot im versiegelten Umschlag.
sealing | **label** Verschlußmarke; ~ **wax** Siegelwachs.
seaman, able-bodied Vollmatrose; **merchant** ~ Handelsschiffer.
search Durchsuchung, Überprüfung;
house ~ Haus[durch]suchung;
~ **of luggage** *(Br.)* Gepäckrevision;
~ *(v.)* **a register** Grundbuch einsehen;
~ **party** *(Br.)* Suchtrupp, Rettungskolonne; ~ **warrant** Haus-, Durchsuchungsbefehl.
season Jahreszeit, Saison *(increased business activity)* Hauptverkaufs-, geschäftszeit;
in ~ *(market)* günstig auf dem Markt zu haben;
busy ~ Hauptsaison; **dead (dull, off)** ~ tote Jahreszeit;
~ **business** Saisongeschäft; ~ **ticket** *(Br.)* Eisenbahnabonnement, Dauer-, Zeit-, Abonnements-, Monatsfahrkarte;
seasonal saisonbedingt, -üblich, jahreszeitlich bedingt;
~ **adjustment** Konjunkturausgleich; ~ **allowance** Frühbezugsrabatt; ~ **articles** Saisonartikel; ~ **business** Saisongeschäft; ~ **clearance** *(US)* **(closing-out,** *Br.)* **sale** Saisonschlußverkauf; ~ **demand** saisonbedingte Nachfrage; ~ **fluctuations** saisonale Schwankungen; ~ **industries** saisonbedingte Industrien; ~ **sickness** sommerliche Flaute; ~ **slump** saisonbedingter Geschäftsrückgang; ~ **trade** Saisongewerbe; ~ **trend** saisonbedingter Konjunkturaufschwung; ~ **unemployment** konjunkturelle Arbeitslosigkeit; ~ **worker** Saisonarbeiter.
seasonally adjusted saisonbereinigt.
seat Sitz, *(establishment)* [Gesellschafts]sitz, Hauptniederlassung;
reserved ~ reservierter (numerierter) Platz;
~ **on a board** Vorstands-, Aufsichtsratssitz;
to book ~**s** Plätze [vor]bestellen (reservieren lassen);
~ **belt** *(aircraft)* Rettungs-, Sicherheitsgurt; ~ **reservation** Platzbelegung.
seaworthy packing seegemäße Verpackung.
second *(of exchange)* Sekunda[wechsel];
~**s** *(goods)* Mittelsorte, Waren mittlerer Art und Güte *(zweite Qualität);*
~ **car** Zweitwagen.
second-class zweitklassig, -rangig;
to go (travel) ~ zweiter Klasse reisen;
~ **mail** *(US)* Zeitungspost.

second | **distress** Anschlußpfändung; ~ **floor** *(Br.)* zweite Etage, *(US)* erste Etage, erster Stock; ~ **lien** nachrangiges Pfandrecht; ~**rate** zweitrangig, -klassig, minderwertig; ~ **teller** Kassierer für Einzahlungen.
secondarily liable *(US)* mittelbar haftpflichtig.
secondary | **boycott** mittelbarer Boykott; ~ **calling** Nebenberuf; ~ **credit** *(US)* Gegenakkreditiv; ~ **creditor** nachstehender Gläubiger; ~ **distribution of securities** nachbörslicher Wertpapierhandel; ~ **liability** *(US)* Eventualverpflichtung; ~ **reserve** *(banking)* Sekundärliquidität; ~**use package** weiterverwendungsfähige Packung.
secondhand aus zweiter Hand, gebraucht, antiquarisch;
~ **bookshop** Antiquariat; ~ **car** Gebrauchtwagen; ~ **hirer** Untermieter; ~ **market** Trödlermarkt.
secrecy of correspondence Post-, Briefgeheimnis.
secret, business Geschäftsgeheimnis; **manufacturing** ~ Fabrikationsgeheimnis;
~ **account** Geheimkonto; ~ **commission** *(agent)* verbotene Sonderprovision; ~ **[manufacturing] process** geheimes Herstellungsverfahren; ~ **partner** stiller Teilhaber; ~ **reserves** stille Reserven.
secretarial | **clerk** Büroangestellter; ~ **facilities** Büromitbenutzung; ~ **pool** Gemeinschaftssekretariat; ~ **work** Büro-, Sekretariatsarbeit.
secretary Sekretär[in], *(of society)* Schriftführer;
German-language ~ deutschsprachige Sekretärin; ⌾ **of Commerce** *(US)* Handelsminister; ⌾ **of the Treasury [Department]** *(US)* Finanzminister, Schatzkanzler.
section Dezernat, *(sleeping compartment)* Schlafwagenabteil;
busy ~ belebter Stadtteil; **commercial** ~ Geschäftsviertel; **shopping** ~ Einkaufsgegend;
to contract in several ~**s** *(stock exchange)* in verschiedenen Effektengruppen Abschlüsse tätigen;
~ **chief (manager)** Abteilungsleiter.
sectional | **interests** lokale Interessen; ~ **price list** Einzelprospekt; ~ **strike** Teilstreik.
sector | **of economy** Wirtschaftsgebiet, -zweig; **private** ~ **of industry** im Privatbesitz befindliches Industrievermögen.
secure *(v.)* sich verschaffen, erwerben, erlangen;
~ **an application** [Versicherungs]antrag entgegennehmen; ~ **a business** Abschluß erzielen; ~ **a creditor** Gläubiger sicherstellen; ~ **an interest** Beteiligung erwerben; ~ **higher prices** bessere Preise erzielen; ~ **a room in a hotel** Hotelzimmer bestellen; ~ **a better share of the market** sich einen größeren Marktanteil sichern;
~ **investment** sichere Kapitalanlage.
secured | **by mortgage** hypothekarisch gesichert;
~ **account** abgesichertes Konto; ~ **advance** Lombardkredit; ~ **creditor** absonderungsberechtigter (dinglich gesicherter) Gläubiger; ~ **note** lombardgesicherter Schuldschein.
securities Sicherheiten, *(bonds)* [Wert]papiere, Effekten[bestände], Stücke;

bearer ~ Inhaberpapiere; **collateral** ~ lombardierte Wertpapiere; ~ **deposited** hinterlegte Effekten; **dividend-paying** ~ börsengängige Dividendenwerte[**drawn** ~ ausgeloste Wertpapiere; **fixed-interest-bearing** ~ festverzinsliche Werte; **gilt-edged** ~ *(Br.)* mündelsichere Wertpapiere; **good-delivery** ~ lieferbare Effekten; **government** ~ *(Br.)* Staatsobligationen; **high-grade** ~ hochwertige Effekten; **higher-yield** ~ Wertpapiere mit höherer Rendite; **industrial** ~ Industrieobligationen; **fixed-interest-bearing** ~ festverzinsliche Werte; **listed** ~ *(US)* amtlich notierte Werte; **marketable** ~ börsengängige (fungible) Effekten; **marketable** ~ **at cost** *(balance sheet)* börsenfähige Wertpapiere zu Ankaufskursen; **nontaxable** ~ *(US)* Wertpapiere mit steuerfreien Zinserträgen; **nonvoting** ~ stimmrechtlose Wertpapiere; **quoted** ~ notierte Werte; **registered** ~ *(Br.)* Namenspapiere; **suffering** ~ notleidende Werte; **tax-exempt** ~ ertragssteuerfreie Wertpapiere; **trustee** ~ *(Br.)* mündelsichere Wertpapiere; **undigested** ~ *(US)* vom Markt noch nicht aufgenommene Wertpapiere; **unlisted** ~ *(US)* nicht notierte Werte;
~ **dealt in for the account** Terminpapiere;
~ **on hand** Effektenbestand; ~ **quoted on the spot market** Kassapapiere, werte;
to advance money on ~ Effekten lombardieren; **to be loaded up with** ~ mit Effekten sehr stark eingedeckt sein; **to call in** ~ Papiere einziehen; **to commute** ~ in Kost gegebene Effekten auswechseln; **to deposit** ~ **in safe custody** *(Br.)* Wertpapiere ins Depot einliefern; **to introduce (list,** *US,* **market)** ~ einführen; **to marshal** ~ Sicherheiten aufteilen; **to take** ~ **on a commission basis** Wertpapiere in Kommission nehmen;
~ **account** Stückekonto; ~ **assistant** Sicherheitenbearbeiter; ~ **blotter** *(US)* Effektenstrazze; ~ **book** *(Br.)* Lebendes Depot[konto]; ~ **broker** Effektenmakler; ~ **business** Effekten-, Wertpapiergeschäft; ~ **company** *(US)* Effektenverwertungsgesellschaft; ~ **custody** Depotverwahrung; ~ **holdings** Effektenportefeuille; ~ **issue** Effektenemission; ~ **journal** *(Br.)* Effektenstrazze; ~ **ledger** *(Br.)* Effektenkonto, totes Depot; ~ **prices** Effektenkurse; ~ **quotation** Wertpapiernotierung; ~ **tax** Wertpapiersteuer; **stolen** ~ **traffic** Handel mit gestohlenen Wertpapieren.

security Sicherheit, Schutz, *(cover)* Sicherheit, Sicherheitsleistung, *(guarantee)* Bürgschaft, Bürge; **able to put up** ~ kautionsfähig; **pledged as** ~ sicherungsübereignet; **without** ~ ungedeckt;
collateral ~ zusätzliche Deckung, Lombarddeckung; **floating** ~ auswechselbare Kreditsicherung; ~ **owned** vorhandene Sicherheit; **shifting** ~ auswechselbare Kreditsicherung; **trust** ~ *(US)* mündelsichere Anlage; **underlying** ~ dingliche Sicherheit;
~ **for costs** Kostenvorschuß; ~ **by mortgage** hypothekarische Sicherstellung; ~ **of tenure** Mieterschutz;

to afford ~ Sicherheit stellen; **to furnish (give)** ~ Bürgschaft, (Kaution, Garantie) leisten; **to furnish a bill with** ~ Wechsel decken; **to lend money on** ~ Geld gegen Sicherheiten ausleihen; **to lend money without** ~ Blankokredit gewähren; **to lodge stock as additional** ~ Aktien als Lombardsicherheit hinterlegen; **to pledge as** ~ zu Sicherheitszwecken übereignen; **to stand** ~ **for a signature** Unterschrift avalieren;
~ **account** Effektenkonto; ~ **analyser** Effektenberater; ~ **bill** Kautions-, Garantiewechsel; ~ **bond** Bürgschaftsschein; ~ **exchange** Wertpapierbörse; ~ **holdings** Effektenbestand; ~ **market** Effekten-, Wertpapiermarkt, Effektenbörse; ~ **prices** Effektenkurse; ~ **sales** Wertpapierverkäufe.

segregated | **account** *(US)* Sonderkonto; ~ **appropriation** *(fund, US)* gesonderte Zweckbestimmung.

seize *(v.)* **property on an execution** Zwangsvollstreckung durchführen.

seizure Beschlagnahme, Einziehung, Konfiskation, *(distraint)* Pfändung, Arrest, *(ship)* Aufbringung; ~ **under a prior claim** Vorpfändung; ~ **of property** Vermögensbeschlagnahme;
to be subject to ~ der Beschlagnahme unterliegen; **to lift the** ~ Pfändung aufheben;

select table Sterblichkeitstabelle.

selected | **applicant** erfolgreicher Bewerber; ~ **investments** ausgesuchte Anlagewerte.

selection Auslese, Auswahl, Kollektion;
in a wide ~ **of fields** auf verschiedensten Sparten; **adverse** ~ *(life insurance)* Ausscheiden der besseren Risiken; **portfolio** ~ optimale Planung einer Wertpapieranlage;
~ **of media** *(advertising)* Auswahl der Werbeträger;
~ **committee** Bewerbungsausschuß.

selective | **advertising** gezielte Werbung; ~ **demand** spezifischer Bedarf; ~ **driver plan** *(US)* Versicherungsnachlaß für unfallfreies Fahren, Schadensfreiheitssystem; ~ **employment tax** *(Br.)* Lohnsummensteuer; ~ **strength** *(stock exchange)* auf Spezialwerte beschränkte feste Haltung.

self | **-addressed card** Rückantwortkarte; ~**-addressed envelope** Freiumschlag; ~**-appraisal** *(taxation)* Selbsteinschätzung; ~**-assessment** [steuerliche] Selbsteinschätzung; ~**-consumption** Eigenverbrauch; ~**-contained flat** *(Br.)* abgeschlossene Wohnung; ~**-contained house** *(Br.)* Einfamilienhaus; ~**-contained industries** autarke Industriezweige; ~**-cost** Gestehungs-, Selbstkostenpreis; ~**-drive cars for hire** *(Br.)* Autovermietung für Selbstfahrer; ~**-employed person** selbständiger Erwerbstätiger; ~**-employment income** Einkünfte aus selbständiger Erwerbstätigkeit; ~**-financing** Selbstfinanzierung; ~**-liquidating** sich automatisch abdeckend; ~**-liquidating premium** Warenprobe zum Selbstkostenpreis; ~**-mailer** Werbesache mit Rückantwort; ~**-retention** *(insurance business)* Selbstbehalt; ~**-service restaurant** Restaurant mit Selbstbedienung, Automatenrestaurant; ~-service shop (store, *Br.*) Selbstbedienungsladen;

sell, hard *(US)* energische Verkaufstechnik;

~ *(v.)* verkaufen, käuflich überlassen, losschlagen, anbringen, veräußern, *(turn over)* umsetzen; ~ **abroad** exportieren; ~ **for the account** *(Br.)* auf Termin verkaufen; ~ **by [public]** (at, *US*) **auction** öffentlich versteigern; ~ **badly** schwer abgehen; ~ **a bear** auf Baisse spekulieren; ~ **at best** *(stock exchange)* zum Höchstkurs verkaufen; ~ **by bulk** in Bausch und Bogen verkaufen; ~ **like hot cakes** reißenden Absatz finden; ~ **on commission** auf Kommissionsbasis verkaufen; ~ **below cost price (less than cost)** unter Selbstkostenpreis verkaufen; ~ **over the counter** *(stock exchange, US)* im Freiverkehr handeln; ~ **dirt-cheap** verschleudern; ~ **at a discount** *(stock exchange)* unter Pari stehen; ~ **divisions to raise cash** einzelne Fertigungszweige zum zweck der Liquiditätsverbesserung aufgeben; ~ **in dribs and drabs** in kleinen Partien verkaufen; ~ **forward (for future delivery)** auf Termin verkaufen; ~ **hard (heavily)** schlechten Absatz finden; ~ **insurance** Versicherungsvertreter sein; ~ **an interest** ([Kapital]beteiligung) verkaufen; ~ **an issue** en bloc Emission en bloc begeben; ~ **machinery as junk** Maschinen auf Abbruch verkaufen; ~ **off** ausverkaufen, Lager räumen; ~ **by order of the court** gerichtlich versteigern; ~ **out** ausverkaufen, Lager räumen; ~ **out against a client** *(stock exchange)* Börsenorder gegen die Interessen des Auftraggebers ausführen; ~ **by the piece** stückweise verkaufen; ~ **at a premium** *(stock exchange)* über Pari stehen; ~ **readily** guten Absatz finden; ~ **at a sacrifice** Verlustverkauf tätigen; ~ **at public sale** *(US)* verauktionieren, versteigern; ~ **by sample** nach Muster verkaufen; ~ **on a scale** *(stock exchange, US)* seine Verkäufe über eine Hausseperiode verteilen; ~ **for settlement** *(Br.)* auf Termin verkaufen; ~ **short** *(stock exchange)* ohne Deckung verkaufen, fixen; ~ **to the trade** an Wiederverkäufer verkaufen; ~ **for value** entgeltlich überlassen; ~ **a wide variety of goods** großes Warensortiment haben; ~ **by the weight** dem Gewicht nach verkaufen; ~ **wholesale** *(Br.)* (at wholesale, *US*) en gros verkaufen;

~-**off** *(stock exchange)* Glattstellenverkauf; ~-**out** Ausverkauf.

seller Verkäufer, Veräußerer, *(stock exchange, Br.)* Abgeber;

bear ~ Baissespekulant; **best** ~ Verkaufsschlager; **forward** ~ Terminverkäufer.

seller's | commission Absatzprovision; ~ **option** Terminverkauf; **to hold subject to the** ~ **order** zur Verfügung des Käufers halten.

sellers *(stock exchange)* Brief;

more buyers than ~ *(Br.)* mehr Geld als Brief.

selling Verkauf[en], Absatz, Vertrieb, *(stock exchange)* Verkäufe, Umsätze;

direct ~ Direktverkauf; **direct-to-customer** ~ Beziehungskauf; ~ **forward** Terminkäufe; **heavy** ~ größere Abgaben; **house-to-house** ~ Hausierhandel; **low-pressure** ~ unaufdringliche Verkaufsmethodik; **mail-order** ~ *(US)* Versandhausgeschäft; ~ **off (out)** *(stock exchange)* Exekutionsverkauf; ~ **stocks short** Blankoverkäufe, Fixgeschäfte; ~ **a bear** *(Br.)* Baissespekulation; ~ **below cost price** Verkauf unter Selbstkosten; ~ **by direct mail** Versandhausgeschäft; ~ **with premium** Zugabewesen; ~ **on a scale** *(US)* Aufgabe von Kauf- und Verkaufsorders zu verschiedenen Zeiten; ~ **by wholesale** Großhandelsverkäufe;

to be ~ **fast** schnell weggehen; **to turn into heavy** ~ sich schwer verkaufen lassen;

~ **account** Betriebskonto; ~ **accounts receivable outright** *(US)* Debitorenverkauf; ~ **agent** Absatzvertreter; ~ **area** Absatzgebiet; ~ **brokerage** Verkaufskommission; ~ **commission** Verkaufsprovision; ~ **costs** Vertriebskosten; ~ **efforts** Absatzanstrengungen; ~ **and administrative expense** *(income statement)* Verwaltungskosten; ~ **group** Absatzgremium, *(banking)* Verkaufskonsortium; ~ **office** Verkaufsbüro; ~ **order** Verkaufsorder; ~ **power** Werbekraft; ~ **pressure** Verkaufsdruck, *(stock exchange)* drängendes Angebot; **to be under** ~ **pressure** *(market)* durch Verkäufe gedrückt liegen; ~ **price** Laden[verkaufs]preis, *(stock exchange)* Briefkurs; ~ **space** Verkaufsfläche; ~ **staff** Verkaufspersonal; ~ **stop order** *(US)* limitierte Verkaufsorder; ~ **syndicate** [Emissions]konsortium.

semiannual interest halbjährliche Zinsen.

semifinished products Halbfertigwaren, -fabrikate.

semifixed fund Investmentfonds mit begrenzt auswechselbarem Portefeuille.

semiskilled worker angelernter Arbeiter.

send *(v.)* schicken, senden, zum Versand bringen, *(remit)* überweisen;

~ **in an application** Antrag einreichen; ~ **on approval** zur Ansicht schicken; ~ **in one's bill** seine Rechnung schicken; ~ **out circulars** Rundschreiben verschicken; ~ **goods to a fair** Messe beschicken; ~ **goods to the market** Markt beliefern; ~ **on one's luggage** *(Br.)* sein Gepäck aufgeben; ~ **in (up) one's name** sich anmelden [lassen]; ~ **off by post** zur Post geben; ~ **in one's papers** um seine Entlassung einkommen; ~ **prices up** Preise hinaufschrauben, *(stock exchange)* Kurse in die Höhe treiben; ~ **a telegram** Telegramm aufgeben.

sending | away of an employee Entlassung eines Angestellten;

~ **station** Versandstation, Aufgabestelle.

senior Dienstälterer, -ältester, Rangältester;

~ *(a.)* älter, bevorrechtigt, vorrangberechtigt, *(service)* rang-, dienstälter;

~ **accountant** leitender Buchhalter, *(auditing)* selbständiger Revisionsbeamter; ~ **bonds** Vorzugsobligationen; ~ **capital** *(Br.)* Stammkapital; ~ **clerk** Bürovorsteher; ~ **officer** *(enterprise, US)* leitender Angestellter; ~ **shares** *(Br.)* Stamm-, Vorzugsaktien.

seniority höheres Dienstalter;
~ **allowance** *(US)* Dienstalterzulage; ~ **pay** *(US)* Dienstalters-, Beförderungszulage.

sensitive | **to business movements** konjunkturempfindlich;
to be ~ **to a downturn** auf konjunkturelle Verschlechterungen empfindlich reagieren.

sentimental | **damage** *(insurance)* Wertminderung;
~ **value** Liebhaberwert.

separable costs Produktionskosten.

separate *(v.)* [ab]trennen, *(bankruptcy)* aus-, absondern, ausscheiden, *(corporation)* auflösen;
~ **into small fields** in kleine Parzellen aufteilen;
~ **account** Sonderkonto; **under** ~ **cover** im besonderen Umschlag; ~ **estate** Sondervermögen, *(married woman)* eingebrachtes Gut, Vorbehaltsgut; ~ **property** *(US)* Sondervermögen, *(married woman)* Vorbehaltsgut; ~ **return** getrennte Steuererklärung; ~ **satisfaction** *(bankruptcy)* abgesonderte Befriedigung; ~ **trade** Proprehandlung.

separation Trennung, Teilung, *(bankruptcy proceedings)* Absonderung, Aussonderung;
~ **of estate** Gütertrennung.

sequester [Zwangs]verwalter, Treuhänder;
~ *(v.)* zwangsverwalten, sequestrieren;
~ **alien property** Feindvermögen beschlagnahmen.

sequestration Beschlagnahme, *(bankruptcy)* Zwangsverwaltung;
to award ~ **of estate** Vermögensbeschlagnahme anordnen.

serial *(broadcasting)* Sendereihe, *(publication)* Serie, Veröffentlichungsreihe, Lieferungswerk;
~ **advertisements** Anzeigenserie; ~ **bond** Serienobligation; ~ **construction** Serienherstellung, Massenfabriktion; ~ **number** Fabrikationsnummer; ~ **production** Fließarbeit, Serienfertigung, Massenproduktion.

serialization serienmäßige Herstellung.

serialize *(v.)* serienmäßig herstellen.

series | **discount** *(advertising)* Wiederholungsrabatt;
~ **production** Serienherstellung, Massenproduktion.

servant Dienstbote, Diener, Bediensteter, *(law)* [Erfüllungs]gehilfe, *(official)* Angestellter;
civil ~ *(Br.)* Verwaltungs-, Staatsbeamter; **hired** ~ Lohndiener.

serve *(v.)* dienen, im Dienst stehen, Dienst leisten, *(office)* verwalten, amtieren, fungieren, *(public utility)* versorgen;
~ **one's articles** in der Lehre sein; ~ **with a bankruptcy notice** Konkurseröffnungsbeschluß zustellen; ~ **a customer** Kunden bedienen; ~ **one's own interests** den eigenen Interessen dienen; ~ **the town with gas** Stadt mit Gas versorgen.

service Dienst[leistung], Arbeitsleistung, Bedienung, *(delivery of a writ)* Zustellung, *(machine)* Betrieb, *(for purchasers)* Kundendienst, Service;
15 per cent for ~ 15 % für die Bedienung;

on Her Majesty's ~ *(Br.)* portofrei, [etwa] frei durch Ablösung; **out of** ~ außer Betrieb; **retired from** ~ in Pension;
~ **abroad** Auslandsdienst; **administrative** ~ Verwaltungstätigkeit; **after-sales** ~ Kundendienst **bus** ~ Omnibusverkehr, -verbindung; **career** ~ Berufsbeamtentum; **cartage** ~ Rollfuhrdienst; **civil** ~ *(Br.)* Staats-, Verwaltungs-, öffentlicher Dienst; **collection** ~ Inkassodienst; **contributing** ~ [auf die Pension] anrechnungsfähige Dienstzeit; **door-to-door airport limousine** ~ Flugplatzabholdienst; **essential** ~s lebenswichtige Betriebe; **express delivery** ~ Express-, Eilgutverkehr; **freight** ~ Frachtverkehr; **honorary** ~ ehrenamtliche Tätigkeit; **loan** ~ Anleihedienst; **mail** ~ Postzustellung; **outdoor** ~ Außendienst; **passenger** ~ Personenverkehr; **phone-and-delivery** ~ telefonischer Bestell- und Lieferbetrieb; **good postal** ~ gute Postverbindungen; **press** ~ Pressedienst; **prompt** ~ schnelle Bedienung; **public** ~ *(US)* Staatsdienst; **regular twenty-fourhour** ~ durchgehender Betrieb; **secretarial** ~ Bürotätigkeit; **shuttle** ~ Pendelverkehr; **store-door** ~ Hauszustellung; **take-out** ~ Lieferung frei Haus; **telephone** ~ Telefonverkehr; **train** ~ Zugverkehr; **water** ~ Wasserversorgung; ~ **of capital** Kapitaldienst; ~ **of custodianship** *(US)* Depotverwaltung; ~ **of debts** Schuldendienst; ~ **to stockowners** *(US)* Aktionärspflege;
~ *(v.)* instandhalten, Pflegedienst übernehmen;
to have one's car ~**d regularly** sein Auto laufend zum Kundendienst bringen;
to add 10 per cent to the bill for ~ 10 % Bedienungszuschlag auf die Rechnung setzen; **to be in the civil** ~ *(Br.)* Staatsbeamter sein, im Beamtenverhältnis stehen; **to be introduced into regular** ~ in den Fahrplan aufgenommen werden; **to buy a television with** ~ **for six months** Fernsehgerät mit halbjähriger Garantie kaufen; **to cut back** ~ Dienstbetrieb einschränken; **to extend tailor-made** ~s auf den einzelnen Kunden zugeschnittene Dienstleistungen ausweiten; **to make use of s. one's** ~s von jds. Angebot Gebrauch machen; **to provide with intelligent** ~ guten Kundendienst haben; **to retire from** ~ in den Ruhestand treten; **to run joint** ~s gemeinsam betreiben; **to sell one's** ~ **country-wide** seine Tätigkeit über das ganze Land ausdehnen; **to take out of** ~ aus dem Verkehr ziehen;
~ **agreement** Dienstvertrag, -vereinbarung; ~ **allowance** Aufwandsentschädigung; ~ **area** *(broadcasting)* Sendebereich, *(town gas)* Versorgungs-, Liefergebiet; **personal** ~ **business** *(US)* Dienstleistungsgeschäft; ~ **call** *(tel.)* Dienstgespräch; ~ **center** *(US)* (centre, *Br.)* Reparaturwerkstätte; ~ **charge** Dienstleistungsgebühr, *(banking)* Vermittlungs-, Bearbeitungsgebühr, *(investment trust)* Verwaltungsgebühr, *(restaurant)* Bedienungszuschlag, Trinkgeld; ~ **control** Dienstaufsicht; ~ **cost** abschreibungsfähige Kosten; **to transfer one's** ~ **credits** seine zusätzlichen Sozialansprüche abtreten; ~ **department** Hilfsbe-

trieb, *(shop)* Kundendienstabteilung; ~ **economy** Dienstleistungsindustrie; ~ **engineer** Wartungsingenieur; ~ **fee** Zustellungsgebühr; ~ **field** Dienstleistungsbereich; ~ **flat** *(Br.)* Etagenwohnung mit Bedienung; ~ **instructions** Betriebsvorschriften; ~ **life** *(asset, Br.)* Lebensdauer; ~ **pension** Beamtenpension; ~ **rating (review)** Leistungsbeurteilung; ~ **report** Eignungsbericht; ~ **sector** Dienstleistungsbereich; ~ **staff** Beamtenkörper; ~**station** Kundendienstwerkstatt; ~ **store** Dienstleistungsbetrieb; ~ **transactions** Dienstleistungsverkehr; ~ **undertaking** Dienstleistungsbetrieb; ~ **unit** *(balance sheet)* Gebrauchseinheit; ~ **wholesaler** Effektivgroßhändler; ~**-yield basis [of depreciation]** Abschreibungsberechnungsgrundlage.

servicing *(US)* Kundendienst; ~ **of government debt** Staatsschuldendienst.

session Sitzung, Tagung, Versammlung; **budget** ~ Haushaltsberatungen; **full** ~ Plenarsitzung, Plenum.

set *(broadcasting receiver)* Rundfunk-, Fernsehempfänger, *(of goods)* Serie, Satz, Sortiment, Garnitur, Kollektion; ~ **of bills** Satz Wechsel; **complete** ~ **of bills of lading** vollständiger Satz Konnossemente; ~ **of patterns** Musterkollektion; ~ *(v.)* **one's hand to a document** Urkunde unterzeichnen; ~ **the price of a house** Verkaufspreis für ein Haus festsetzen.

set apart beisetelegen, reservieren, bestimmen für, *(bankruptcy)* aussondern; ~ **funds for a purpose** Sonderfonds einrichten.

set aside *(annul)* außer Kraft setzen, annullieren, *(money)* beiseite legen; ~ **an agreement** Vertrag für ungültig erklären.

set down schriftlich niederlegen, niederschreiben; ~ **to s. one's account** auf jds. Rechnung setzen; ~ **o. s. down in a hotel register** Berufsangabe bei der Hotelanmeldung vornehmen.

set in action (operation, into operation) in Gang setzen, in Betrieb nehmen.

set off *(Br.)* an-, aufrechnen, in Gegenrechnung bringen, gegen einen Posten validieren.

set up errichten, *(auction)* zur Auktion bringen, *(in business)* sich etablieren, sich selbständig machen; ~ **one's abode** seinen Wohnsitz begründen; ~ **an account** Konto eröffnen; ~ **s. o. up in business** j. [geschäftlich] etablieren; ~ **s. o. up in funds** j. mit Geldmitteln versehen; ~ **a manufactory** Fabrikationsbetrieb errichten; ~ **reserves** Rückstellung bilden (vornehmen); ~ **one's son in a trade** seinem Sohn ein Geschäft einrichten.

set | aside *(US)* [Lebensmittel]reservefonds; ~ **prices** feste Preise; ~ **work** Serienfabrikat.

setback *(stock exchange)* Rückschlag, Verschlechterung; ~ **in production** Produktionsrückgang.

setting | aside Absonderung, *(claims)* Zurückweisung; ~ **up** Etablierung, Errichtung, Gründung.

settle *(v.)* *(agree)* ab-, ausmachen, übereinkommen,

vereinbaren, *(buy plot of land)* sich ankaufen, *(establish o. s. in business)* Geschäft gründen, sich geschäftlich niederlassen, sich etablieren, *(liquidate)* abwickeln, liquidieren, *(pay bill)* Rechnung bezahlen, begleichen, glattstellen; ~ **an account** Rechnung begleichen; ~ **an affair out of court** sich außergerichtlich vergleichen; ~ **an annuity** Rente aussetzen; ~ **the average** Havariekosten aufmachen; ~ **one's son in business** seinen Sohn in der Wirtschaft unterbringen; ~ **with one's creditors** sich mit seinen Gläubigern vergleichen; ~ **down** *(market)* sich beruhigen, *(price)* sich einpendeln; ~ **down to a new job** sich in einer neuen Stellung einarbeiten; ~ **an estate** Nachlaß verteilen (regulieren); ~ **one's liabilities** seinen Verpflichtungen nachkommen; ~ **a pension** Ruhegehalt aussetzen; ~ **property** Nacherbschaft festlegen; ~ **the terms of freight** Fracht bedingen.

settled *(balanced)* abgerechnet, abgeschlossen, ausgeglichen, *(daughter)* versorgt, verheiratet, *(done)* erledigt, *(paid)* beglichen, bezahlt; **as good as** ~ so gut wie abgemacht; ~ **abode** fester Wohnsitz; ~ **account** beglichene Rechnung, *(banking)* schriftlich anerkanntes Kontokorent; ~ **income** festes Einkommen; ~ **production** stetige Produktion.

settlement *(adjustment)* Beilegung, Erledigung, *(agreement)* Übereinkommen, Vereinbarung, Abkommen, Abmachung, *(of annuity)* Aussetzung einer Rente, *(colony)* [An]siedlung, Kolonie, abgesonderte [Fremden]niederlassung, landwirtschaftliches Siedlungsgebiet, *(establishment)* Niederlassung, *(establishment in life)* Unterbringung, Einstellung, Versorgung, *(estate)* Auseinandersetzung, *(liquidation)* Liquidation, *(of a pauper)* Unterstützungswohnsitz, *(payment)* Begleichung, Bezahlung, *(legal residence)* gesetzlicher Aufenthaltsort, *(settling of accounts)* Abrechnung, Saldierung, Abschluß; **for monthly** ~ per Ultimo; **claim** ~ Schadensregulierung; **extra-judicial** ~ außergerichtlicher Vergleich; **fortnightly** ~Medioabrechnung; **mid-month** ~ Medioliquidation; **out-of-court** ~ außergerichtlicher Vergleich; **pro-rata** ~ proratarische Befriedigung; **special** ~ *(stock exchange)* Sonderabrechnung; **wage** ~ Lohnabkommen; **yearly** ~ Jahresabschluß; ~ **of account** Rechnungsbegleichung; ~ **by arbitration** schiedsrichterliche Entscheidung; ~ **of average** Havarieaufmachung, Dispache; ~ **with one's creditors** Gläubigervergleich; ~ **of interbank debits and credits** interne Abrechnung der Banken; ~ **of hardship cases** Härteregelung; ~ **of a loss** Schadensregulierung; ~ **of transactions** Ausgleich des Zahlungsverkehrs; ~ **in trust** Güterrechtsvertrag; **to arrange a** ~ **with s. o.** Vergleich mit jem. abschließen; **to buy for** ~ auf Lieferung kaufen; **to have reached a** ~ sich vergleichsweise geeinigt haben;

~ **account** Liquidations-, Regulierungskonto; ~

bargain *(stock exchange)* Termingeschäft; ~ **day** *(London stock exchange)* Skontierungs-, Liquidationstag; ~ **offer** Vergleichsangebot; ~ **office** Liquidationskasse; ~ **price** Terminkurs; ~ **project** Besiedlungsplan; ~ **right** Auseinandersetzungsanspruch; ~ **sheet** *(banking)* Abschlußbogen; ~ **terms** *(bankruptcy)* Liquidationsbedingungen.

settling | **of accounts** Rechnungsbegleichung; ~ **day** *(clearing day)* Abrechnungs-, Skontierungstag, Abrechnungstermin, *(pay day)* Zahl-, Erfüllungstag; ~ **period** Abrechnungsperiode; ~ **price** Liquidationspreis.

setup Arbeitsstab, Organisation; **economic** ~ Wirtschaftssystem; ~ **costs** Gründungskosten; ~ **time** Einrichte-, Umstellungszeit.

several | **debt** Einzelschuld, -verpflichtung; ~ **estate** Sondervermögen; ~ **note** Zahlungsversprechen.

several, joint and solidarisch, gesamtschuldnerisch; ~ **bond** Solidarverpflichtung; ~ **guarantee** gesamtschuldnerische Bürgschaft; ~ **mortgage** Gesamthypothek; ~ **obligation** Gesamtschuldverhältnis.

severalty Sondervermögen, Bruchteileigentum; ~ **owner** Bruchteilseigentümer.

severance | **allowance** Trennungsentschädigung; ~ **benefit** *(US)* Entlassungsabfindung, *(pension plan)* Übergangsentschädigung; ~ **pay** *(US)* Entlassungsabfindung, Härteausgleich.

severe | **competition** scharfe Konkurrenz, scharfer Wettbewerb; ~ **illness** *(life policy)* schwere Krankheit.

shade *(small degree)* geringer Grad, Kleinigkeit, Nuance, Spur, Idee, *(stock exchange)* Schattierung, Nuance; ~ *(v.) (prices)* allmählich sinken.

shading *(stock exchange)* geringfügiger Kursrückgang.

shadow factory *(mil.)* Schatten-, Tarn-, Ausweichbetrieb.

shady | **business** dunkles Geschäft; ~ **financier** zweifelhafter Finanzier.

shaken credit geschwächter Kredit.

shakeout Produktionsaufgabe, *(economic situation)* Nachlassen der wirtschaftlichen Aktivität.

shakeup Umbesetzung, -organisation.

shaking out *(US)* Börsenmanöver.

shaky firm unzuverlässige Firma.

sham Betrug, Schein, fauler Zauber, Schwindel; ~ **bid** Scheingebot, fingiertes Angebot; ~ **boom** Scheinkonjunktur; ~ **package** Schaupackung; ~ **payment** fingierte Zahlung; ~ **purchase** Scheinkauf; ~ **transaction** fingiertes Geschäft.

share *(bankrupt's estate)* [Konkurs]quote, *(of capital)* Kapitalanteil, Gesellschaftsanteil, *(contribution)* Beitrag [bei Geldsammlungen], *(mining ~)* Kux, *(of profits)* Beteiligung, [Gewinn]anteil, *(quota)* Kontingent, Quote, *(royalty)* Tantieme; ~ **and** ~ **alike** zu gleichen Teilen; **baby** ~ Kleinaktie; **bearer** ~ Inhaberaktie; **bonus** ~ Genuß-, Gratisaktie; **business** ~ Geschäftsanteil; **common**

~ *(US)* Stammaktie; **deposited** ~ hinterlegte Aktie; **dividend** ~ Gratisaktie; **forfeited** ~s kaduzierte Aktien; **guaranteed** ~ Aktie mit garantierter Mindestdividende; **initial** ~ Gründeranteil; **inscribed** ~ Namensaktie; **legal** ~ Pflichtteil; **limited partner's** ~ Kommanditanteil; **listed** ~ notierte Aktie; **loaned** ~ lombardierte Aktie; **mining** ~ Kux; **nonvoting** ~ nicht stimmberechtigte Aktie; **no-par value** ~ *(US)* nennwertlose Aktie; **ordinary** ~ *(Br.)* Stammaktie; **paid-up** ~ Vollaktie; **participating** ~ dividendenberechtigte Aktie; **partnership** ~ Geschäftsanteil; **participating preference** ~ *(Br.)* mit zusätzlicher Gewinnbeteiligung ausgestattete Vorzugsaktie; **preferred** ~ *(US)* Prioritäts-, Vorzugsaktie; **qualification** ~s für eine Vorstandsstellung erforderlichen Aktienbesitz; **redeemable preference** ~ *(Br.)* rückkaufbare Vorzugsaktie; **stock** ~ Stammaktie; **narrowly traded** ~s nur im kleinsten Kreis gehandelte Aktien; **unclaimed** ~ herrenlose Aktie; **underwriting** ~ Konsortialbeteiligung; **utility** ~s Versorgungswerte; **voting** ~ Stimmrechtsaktie;

~s **and securities** *(balance sheet)* Kapitalvermögen; ~ **of benefit** Nutzanteil; ~s **in capital** Geschäftseinlage; ~s **at a discount** Aktien unter dem Nennwert; **[allocated]** ~ **of exports** Ausfuhrkontingent; ~ **in an inheritance** *(US)* Erbanteil; ~ **of the market** Marktanteil; ~ **payable to bearer** Inhaberaktie; ~ **of proceeds** Gewinnanteil, Tantieme; ~ **cum rights** Aktie mit Dividendenschein; ~ **of stock** Aktie, Kapitalanteil; ~ **in a syndicate** Konsortialanteil; ~s **that yield high interest** Aktien mit hoher Rendite;

~ *(v.)* **and** ~ **alike** Gewinne und Verluste zu gleichen Teilen tragen; ~ **with s. o. in the costs** sich mit jem. die Unkosten teilen; ~ **one's estate between one's heirs** sein Vermögen unter die Erben aufteilen; ~ **losses** Verluste aufteilen; ~ **in the expanding market** sich an der Marktausweitung beteiligen; ~ **an office with s. o.** Büro mit jem. teilen, Bürogemeinschaft mit jem. haben; ~ **in profits** gewinnbeteiligt sein;

to allot ~s Aktien zuteilen; **to apply for** ~s *(Br.)* Aktien zeichnen; **to claim one's proportionate** ~ seinen [vollen] Anteil beanspruchen; **to deposit** ~s **for the general meeting** Aktien zur Generalversammlung anmelden; **to go** ~ **and** ~ zu gleichen Teilen beteiligt sein; **to go half** ~s **with s. o.** Metageschäfte mit jem. machen; **to have a** ~ **in a bank** an einer Bank beteiligt sein; **to hold** ~s **in a company** Aktionär einer Gesellschaft sein; **to own control of** ~ Aktienmajorität besitzen; **to pay off** ~s Aktien einziehen; **to place** ~s **with the public** Aktien beim Publikum plazieren; **to subscribe to (for,** *Br.)* ~s Aktien zeichnen; **to take a personal** ~ **in a work** an einer Sache persönlich Anteil nehmen; ~ **account** Aktien-, Kapitalkonto; ~~**acquisition scheme** *(Br.)* Gewinnbeteiligungssystem für Arbeitnehmer; ~ **applicant** Aktienzeichner; ~ **bonus** Gewinnprämie, Aktienbonus, *(Br., split up)* Split;

~ **broker** Aktienmakler; ~ **capital** Geschäfts-, Aktienkapital; **to reduce** ~ **capital** Zusammenlegung des Aktienkapitals vornehmen; ~ **certificate** *(Br.)* Aktienzertifikat, -promesse, Mantel; ~ **deposit account** Stückkonto; ~-**for**-~ **exchange** *(stock exchange)* Umtauschverhältnis eins zu eins; ~ **index** *(Br.)* Aktienindex; ~ **ledger** *(Br.)* Aktionärsverzeichnis; ~ **market** Aktienmarkt; ~-**the-work plan** *(US)* Kurzarbeitvereinbarung; ~ **price** Aktienkurs; ~ **quotation** Aktiennotierung; ~ **register** *(Br.)* Aktienregister; ~ **warrant [to bearer]** *(Br.)* Inhaberaktie.
sharecropper *(US)* Deputant, Pächter.
shareholder Aktieninhaber, Aktionär;
chief (principal) ~ Hauptaktionär; **dissenting** ~ opponierender Aktionär; **preferential** ~ Vorzugsaktionär;
to tap ~**s with rights offering** Aktionären mit Bezugsrechten Geld aus der Tasche locken.
shareholders' ǀ **approval** Genehmigung durch die Anteilseigner; ~ **committee** Aktionärsausschuß; ~ **meeting** Aktionärsversammlung; ~ **newsletter** Aktionärsbrief; ~ **register** *(Br.)* Aktionärsverzeichnis.
shareholding interest Aktienbeteiligung.
shareholdings Beteiligungen, Aktienbesitz.
sharepusher *(Br.)* Aktienschwindler.
sharing, cost Kostenbeteiligung;
fair ~ **of burden** gerechte Lastenverteilung; ~ **the market** Marktaufteilung;
~ **plan** *(US)* Gewinnbeteiligungssystem.
shark ǀ Schwindler, Betrüger, Gauner.
sharp ǀ **business** Schwindel, Gaunerei; ~ **practices** Beutelschneiderei, Schmutzkonkurrenz; ~ **swings** *(stock exchange)* starke Kursschwankungen.
shave *(US sl.)* übermäßiger Diskont, Wucherzins;
~ *(v.)* **the budget estimates** Haushaltsvoranschlag kürzen.
sheet *(advertising)* großformatige Anzeige;
attendance ~ Anwesenheitsliste; **cost** ~ Kostenaufstellung; **loose** ~ loses Blatt; **order** ~ Bestellschein; **tear** ~ *(US)* Belegstück; **time** ~ *(employee)* Arbeitsblatt, -zettel, *(railway)* Aushängefahrplan; ~ **of coupons** Kuponbogen; ~ **of wrapping paper** Bogen Packpapier.
shelf Gestellbrett, Sims, [Waren]fach, Regal;
on the ~ *(fig.)* auf dem Abstellgleis;
to have on the ~ auf Lager haben;
~ **space** Stellfläche; ~ **warmer** Ladenhüter.
shell *(company)* Firmenmantel, *(ship)* Rumpf.
sheltered industries (trades) durch Einfuhrzölle geschützte Industriezweige.
sheriff's sale *(Br.)* Zwangsversteigerung.
shift Verlagerung, *(makeshift)* Notbehelf, Ausweg, Hilfsmittel, *(working hours)* [Arbeits]schicht;
day ~ Tagesschicht; **dropped** ~ Fehl-, Feierschicht; **extra** ~ Sonderschicht;
~ **in monetary policy** geldmarktpolitische Änderungen; ~ **of prices** Kursverschiebung;
~ *(v.)* verschieben, *(capital)* umschichten, *(cargo)* verrutschen, *(goods)* über-, umladen;

~ **for a living** sich durchschlagen; ~ **orders** Aufträge verlagern; ~ **slightly** *(prices)* sich leicht verändern; ~ **from full-time schedules to part-time** vom Status der Vollbeschäftigung zur Kurzarbeit übergehen;
to drop ~**s** Feierschichten einlegen; **to work in** ~**s** Schichtarbeit verrichten;
~ **allowance (differential)** Schichtzuschlag, -ausgleich; ~ **operation** Schichtbetrieb; ~ **wage** Schichtlohn.
shifting ǀ **of cargo** Verschiebung der Ladung; ~ **of income** Einkommensverlagerung; ~ **of risk** Risikoabwälzung;
~ **ballast** *(marine)* übergehender Ballast.
ship Schiff, *(airplane)* Flugzeug;
convoy ~ Begleitschiff; **merchant** ~ Kauffahrtei-, Handelsschiff;
~ **under average** havariertes Schiff;
~ *(v.)* *(on board)* verschiffen, laden, [Ware], einnehmen, einladen, *(forward, US)* verfrachten, verladen, versenden, abschicken, *(transport)* durch Schiffe befördern;
~ **in bulk** lose verladen; ~ **in carlots** in Waggonladungen versenden; ~ **goods by instal(l)ments** Ware in Teilladungen versenden; ~ **goods by express train** als Eilgut schicken;
to break up a ~ Schiff ausschlachten; **to launch a** ~ Schiff vom Stapel [laufen] lassen; **to put a** ~ **in commission** Schiff in Dienst stellen; **to unload a** ~ Schiff entladen;
~'**s agent** Schiffsmakler, -agent; ~'**s articles** Heuervertrag; ~'**s bill** Bordkonnossement; ~ **broker** Schiffs-, Frachtenmakler; ~ **chandler** Schiffslieferant; ~'**s days** Entladetage; ~'**s distress signal** Schiffsnotsignal; ~'**s hold** Schiffs-, Verladeraum; ~'**s husband** Korrespondenz-, Mitreeder; ~'**s newspaper** Bordzeitung; ~ **order** Schiffsbauauftrag; ~'**s papers** Schiffspapiere; ~'**s protest** Havarieerklärung, Verklarung; ~'**s register** Schiffsregister; ~ **stores** Schiffsbedarfsmagazin.
shipboard container Schiffsbehälter.
shipbuilder's yard Schiffswerft.
shipbuilding ǀ **industry** Schiffsbau[industrie]; ~ **order** Schiffsbauauftrag.
shipload Schiffsladung, -last.
shipment Verschiffung, *(consignment)* [Waren]sendung, Ladung, Frachtgut *(US, forwarding)* Spedition, Expedition;
ready for ~ versandbereit;
drop ~ Auftragssendung; **general-commodity** ~ Sammelgutladung; **high-cost peak** ~ teure Frachtsendungen in Spitzenverkehrszeiten; **less-than-carload** ~ *(US)* Stückgutsendung; **prompt** ~ prompte Verladung; **short** ~ Minderlieferung; **through** ~ Durchgangsfracht;
~ **on deck** Verladung auf Deck; ~ **of gold** Goldversand; ~ **at less-than-carload lot** *(US)* Stückgutversand; ~ **by sea** Seetransport.
~ **account** Versandkonto; ~ **operation** Frachtbetrieb.

shipowner Reeder, Schiffseigentümer, -eigner;
~'s **office** Reederei.
shipped an Bord gebracht, verschifft, verladen;
~ **by express** per Expreß [versandt];
~ **bill of lading** Bordkonossement.
shipper Verschiffer, Ab-, Verlader, *(US, land transport)* Versender, Spediteur, Verfrachter;
all-purpose ~ Universalspediteur;
~'s **manifest** *(US)* Ausfuhrdeklaration; ~'s **memorandum** Konnossement; ~'s **papers** Schiffs-, Verladepapiere; ~'s **representative** Speditionsagent.
shipping Verladung, Verladen, *(dispatch, US)* Versand, Versendung, Spedition;
coastal ~ Küstenschiffahrt; **idle** ~ aufgelegte Tonnage; **maritime** ~ Seeschiffahrt;
~ **of goods** Güterversendung, Warenversand;
~ **advice** Versandbenachrichtigung; ~ **agency** Speditionsgeschäft; ~ **agent** Schiffsmakler, Reedereivertreter; ~ **agreement** Schiffahrtsabkommen; ~ **announcement** *(US)* Versandanzeige; ~ **company** Reedereigesellschaft; ~ **container** *(US)* Versandbehälter; ~ **contract** *(US)* Frachtvertrag; ~ **costs** *(US)* Versandkosten; ~ **date** *(US)* Versandtermin; ~ **documents** Schiffspapiere, *(US, land transport)* Versand-, Verladepapiere; ~ **dues** Schiffsabgaben; ~ **exchange** Frachtenbörse; ~ **expenses** Verladungskosten, Schiffsspesen, *(US)* Versand-, Fracht-, Transportkosten; ~ **facilities** *(US)* günstige Versand-, Frachtmöglichkeiten; ~ **industry** Schiffsbau; ~ **instruction** *(US)* Versandanweisung; ~ **insurance** *(US)* Transportversicherung; ~ **intelligence** Schiffahrtsnachrichten; ~ **master** *(Br.)* Heuerbaas; ~ **note** *(Br.)* Waren-, Lade-, Frachtannahme-, Warenbegleitschein; ~ **office** *(US)* Speditionsbüro, *(Br.)* Heuerbüro; ~ **papers** Schiffspapiere; ~ **point** *(US)* Versandort; ~ **port** Versand-, Ausfuhr-, Ladehafen; ~ **room** *(US)* Versand-, Verpackungsraum; ~ **route** Schiffahrtsweg; ~ **service** *(US)* Frachtdienst; ~ **stretch-outs** *(US)* Überstunden im Speditionsgewerbe; ~ **trade** Reedereibetrieb, *(US)* Speditionsgeschäft; **average** ~ **weight** Durchschnittsverladegewicht.
shipwreck Schiffbruch, Wrack.
shipwright Schiffbauer, Werftbesitzer.
shoestring *(US sl.)* völlig unzureichendes Kapital;
~ **margin** *(US)* völlig ungenügende Deckung.
shoot Schuttabladestelle;
~ *(v.)* **into new high ground** *(prices)* in rascher Steigerung neue Höchstkurse erzielen; ~ **the moon** *(Br. sl.)* mit der Kasse durchbrennen.
shop [Kauf]laden, [Laden]geschäft, *(occupation)* Geschäft, Gewerbe, Beruf, *(plant)* Betrieb, Fabrik, *(premises)* Geschäftslokal;
antique ~ Antiquitätenladen; **closed** ~ *(US)* gewerkschaftspflichtiger Betrieb; **erecting** ~ Montagehalle; **junk** ~ Ramschladen; **mobile** ~ [Lebensmittel]laden; **the other** ~ die Konkurrenz; **repair** ~ Reparaturwerkstatt; **stationer's** ~ Schreibwarenhandlung; **struck** ~ bestreikter Betrieb; **union** ~ *(US)*

gewerkschaftspflichtiger Betrieb; **well-stocked** ~ wohlassortierter Laden;
~**-by-phone** telefonische Einkaufserledigung;
~ *(v.)* kaufen, einkaufen [gehen], Besorgungen [Einkäufe] machen;
~ **regularly at A's** regelmäßig bei A kaufen;
to buy a ~ **with all fixtures** Laden mit der gesamten Ausstattung erwerben; **to clear a** ~ ausverkaufen; **to close up a** ~ Geschäft schließen; **to go through the** ~s *(apprentice)* Lehre durchmachen; **to keep** **[a]** ~ Ladenbesitzer sein; **to manage a** ~ Geschäft führen; **to open a** ~ Laden eröffnen; **to patronize a** ~ regelmäßig in einem Laden einkaufen; **to round the** ~s **looking for s. th.** Läden nach etw. abklappern; **to shut up** ~ Laden zuschließen (dichtmachen), *(give up)* Geschäft aufgeben, sich vom Geschäftsleben zurückziehen, Bude zumachen, *(stock working)* Feierabend machen; **to smell of the** ~ sich nur für seinen Beruf interessieren; **to work in the** ~s in der Fabrik arbeiten;
~ **advertising** Ladenwerbung; ~ **agreement** Betriebstarifvertrag; ~ **assistant** *(Br.)* Handlungsgehilfe, Ladenangestellter, Verkäufer; ~ **audit** Händlerbefragung; ~ **buying** *(stock exchange)* Berufskäufe; ~ **case** Vitrine; ~ **clerk** Verkäufer, Ladenangestellter; ~ **closing** Ladenschluß; ~ **committee** *(US)* Betriebsrat; ~ **cost** Fabrikkosten; ~ **discipline** Betriebsdisziplin; ~ **fittings** *(Br.)* Ladeneinrichtung; ~ **foreman** Werkmeister; ~ **front** Ladenfront, Schaufenster, Auslage; ~ **hours** Verkaufszeiten; **closed** ~ **provisions** *(trade union, US)* Mitgliedschaftszwang; ~ **rent** Lokal-, Geschäfts-, Ladenmiete; ~ **right** *(patent law, US)* Herstellungs-, Fabrikatiosnrecht; ~ **rules** Betriebsanordnungen; ~**-soiled** angeschmutzt; ~ **steward** Betriebsobmann.
shopboard Ladentisch.
shopbreaking Ladeneinbruch, -diebstahl.
shopkeeper *(Br.)* Geschäfts-, Ladeninhaber, Ladenbesitzer, *(shelf warmer)* Ladenhüter.
shopmark Markenzeichen.
shopper Ladenbesucher, Käufer.
shopping Einkauf, Einkäufe, Besorgungen;
to do some ~ einige Einkäufe (Besorgungen) erledigen;
~ **area** Geschäftsgegend, -viertel; ~ **bag** Einkaufstasche; ~ **basket** Einkaufskorb, *(statistics)* Warenkorb; ~ **goods** *(US sl.)* erst nach Preisvergleich gekaufte Waren; ~ **hours** [Laden] Verkaufszeit; ~ **list** Einkaufsliste, Besorgungszettel; ~ **parade** Ausstellungsraum; ~ **street** Ladenstraße.
shoppy | **street** Laden-, Geschäftsstraße; ~ **talk** Fachsimpelei.
shopwalker [Geschäfts]aufsicht im Laden, Empfangschef.
shopwindow Schaufenster;
to dress a ~ Auslage herrichten;
~ **advertising** Schaufensterwerbung, -reklame.
shopworn angestaubt, beschädigt.
short *(bear)* Baissespekulant, Baissier, Fixer;

~s and overts Überschüsse und Fehlbeträge;
~ in [the] cash Kassendefizit, -manko;
~ *(a.)* knapp *(securities)* blanko, deckungslos, *(at short sight)* plötzlich, kurzfristig, mit kurzer Laufzeit;
~ of liquid assets (funds) liquiditätsbeengt; ~ of cash knapp bei Kasse; ~ of hands knapp an Arbeitskräften; ~ of stock kapitalarm;
to be $ 10 ~ zehn Dollar zu wenig [in der Kasse] haben; to be ~ of an article Ware im Augenblick nicht vorrätig haben; to be ~ in one's payments säumiger Zahler sein; to be ~ of petrol kein Benzin mehr haben; to be ~ of staff an Personalmangel leiden; to be in ~ supply beschränkt lieferbar sein; to be ~ of trading capital nicht über ausreichendes Betriebskapital verfügen; to run ~ of provision(s) knapp an Vorräten werden; to sell ~ ohne Deckung verkaufen, auf Baisse spekulieren;
~ account *(Br.)* Baisseposition; ~ amount Minderbetrag; ~ bill Wechsel auf kurze Sicht; to be on ~ commons nicht genug zum Essen haben; ~ covering *(US)* Deckungskauf; ~-dated kurz[fristig]; ~ delivery Teil-, Minderlieferung; ~-distance goods traffic *(Br.)* Güternahverkehr; ~ engagements Baisseengagements; ~ exchange *(Br.)* kurzfristiger Devisenwechsel; ~ haul freight traffic Güternahverkehr; ~ holiday Kurzurlaub; ~ hours Kurzarbeit; ~ interest *(insurance)* Überversicherung, *(of the market, US)* Baisseengagements; ~-landed zu knapp geliefert; ~-lived assets kurzlebige Wirtschaftsgüter; ~ loan fund *(Br.)* Tagesgeldmarkt; ~ market Baissemarkt; at ~ notice kurzfristig kündbar; to invest [money, capital] at ~ notice [Geld, Kapital] kurzfristig anlegen; ~ notice charge Kleinanzeigenzuschlag; ~ offer Baisseangebot; ~ order *(restaurant)* Schnellgericht; ~ position *(investment fund)* Baisseengagement, Leerverkaufsposition; ~ rate Devisenkurs für kurzfristige Wechsel, *(advertising, US)* ermäßigter Tarif; ~ return of interest *(insurance)* Rückvergütung; ~ sale schneller Absatz, *(stock exchange, US)* Verkauf ohne Deckung, Leerverkauf, Blankoabgabe, Fixgeschäft; ~ seller Leerverkäufer, Fixer; ~ shipment Minderlieferung; ~ stock *(US)* Baisseengagements; ~ subject Kurzfilm, Beiprogramm; ~-term borrowings kurzfristige Geldaufnahmen; ~-time *(v.)* s. o. j. als Kurzarbeiter beschäftigen; to be on ~ time *(factory)* kurzarbeiten; ~-time treasury bills unverzinsliche Schatzanweisungen; U-Schätze; ~-time work Kurzarbeit; ~ weight Fehlgewicht, Manko; to give ~ weight knapp abwiegen;
~ of liquid assets Liquiditätsbeengung; ~ in the cash Kassendefizit; ~ of foreign currency Devisen-

knappheit; ~ in money accounts mangelnde Flüssigkeit; ~ of mortgage money knappes Hypothekenangebot; ~ of rolling stock unzureichendes Betriebsmaterial; ~ in weight Untergewicht; ~ of work Auftragsmangel.

shortcoming Unzulänglichkeit, Mängel, Defizit; ~ goods Mangelwaren.

shorten *(v.)* commitments Aufträge zurückziehen.

shortening of policy Abkürzung der Versicherungsdauer.

shortfall in revenue Einnahmerückgang.

shorthand Stenografie, Kurzschrift;
to take notes in ~ sich stenografische Aufzeichnungen machen; to transcribe ~ Stenogramm übertragen;
~ clerk Stenokontoristin.

shorthaul *(US)* Güternahverkehr.

shot | in the arm *(business cycle)* Konjunkturspritze; ~ in the locker *(fig.)* Rückhalt, letzte Reserve.

show Vorführun, Vorstellung, Schau *(exhibition)* Ausstellung, *(window display)* Auslage;
on ~ on our premises bei uns zu besichtigen; automobile ~ *(US)* Autoausstellung; one-man ~ Alleinunterhaltung; trade ~ *(Br.)* Gewerbeausstellung;
~ *(v.)* an advance *(industrials)* Kurssteigerung aufweisen; ~ a balance in s. one's favo(u)r Saldo zu jds. Gunsten auf-, ausweisen; ~ small gains *(stock exchange)* kleine Gewinne verzeichnen; ~ a cheap line of goods billige Waren feilbieten; ~ a loss mit Verlust abschließen; ~ a good tone *(stock exchange)* fest liegen (sein);
~ bill Verzeichnis der ausgelegten Waren; ~ boat Vergnügungsdampfer; ~ business Vergnügungs-, Unterhaltungsindustrie, Schaugeschäft; ~ card Reklameplakat, *(business card)* Muster-, Geschäftskarte.

showboard Anschlagtafel, Schwarzes Brett.

showcase Auslagekasten, Schaukasten, Vitrine.

showing *(film)* Vorführung, *(outdoor advertising)* Anschlageinheit;
to have a poor financial ~ in einer schlechten Finanzlage sein; to make a ~ on cost sich kostenmäßig auswirken, kostenmäßig durchschlagen.

showpiece Ausstellungsgegenstand, -stück.

shrink *(v.)* *(income)* zusammenschrumpfen.

shrinkage Schwund, Verlust, *(allowance)* Refaktie, Nachlaß, *(trade)* schrumpfen, Schrumpfung;
profit ~ Gewinnschrumpfung;
~ of the export trade Exportrückgang; ~ of stocks Lagerverlust.

shuffle of holdings Beteiligungsumstellungen.

shut *(v.)* *(business)* stillegen, schließen, [Betrieb] einstellen;
~ the door upon further negotiations Tür zur weiteren Verhandlungen zuschlagen; ~ out of foreign markets vom Auslandsmärkten ausschließen; ~ up shop Laden schließen (dichtmachen), Bude zumachen.

shutdown *(closing of plant, US)* Stillegung, Schließung, vorübergehende Betriebsstillegung;

shortage *(bootleneck)* Engpaß, *(deficiency)* Fehl-, Minderbetrag, -menge, Defizit, *(weight)* Gewichtsverlust, -abgang, Manko;
owing to ~ of staff mangels Arbeitskräften;
housing ~ Wohnungsnot; manpower ~ fehlende Arbeitskräfte; wartime ~ kriegsbedingte Verknappung;

plant-wide ~s umfassende Betriebsstillegungen; ~ **costs** Kosten der Betriebseinstellung.

shuttle Pendelverkehr; ~ **bus** im Pendelverkehr eingesetzter Bus; ~ **car** Triebwagen; ~ **service** Pendelverkehr; ~ **train** Zubringer-, Vorort-, Pendelzug.

shyster *(US)* Hamsterer, Schieber, *(legal business)* Winkelkonsulent, -advokat, Rechtsverdreher.

sick | **allowance** Krankengeld; ~ **benefit** *(Br.)* Krankenhilfe; ~ **certificate** Krankenschein; ~ **insurance** Krankenversicherung; ~ **market** *(US)* flaue Börse.

sickness | **allowance** *(US)* Krankengeld; ~ **benefit** *(Br.)* Leistungen im Krankheitsfall; ~ **fund** Krankenkasse; ~ **insurance** Krankenversicherung.

side Gegend, Bezirk, Nachbarschaft; **credit** ~ Kreditseite; **debit** ~ Soll-, Debetseite; **to be on the high** ~ *(prices)* hoch sein.

sideline Seitenlinie, *(goods, US)* zusätzliche Waren, *(profession)* Nebenberuf, -beschäftigung.

sidetrack *(US)* totes Gleis, Anschluß-, Fabrik-, Neben-, Abstellgleis;

sight *(bill of exchange)* Sicht, Vorzeigung; **at** ~ bei Sicht (Vorkommen); **in** ~ *(on the market)* vorhanden; **on sale** ~ **unseen** *(US)* ohne Besichtigung zu verkaufen; **commercial** ~ Handelsakzept; ~ *(v.)* **a bill** Wechsel mit Sicht versehen; **to give s. o.** ~ **into the business** jem. geschäftlichen Einblick gewähren; ~ **bill** Sichtwechsel, -tratte; ~ **deposits** täglich fällige Gelder, Sichteinlagen; ~ **draft** Sichttratte; ~ **rate** Kurs für Sichtpapiere.

sighting a bill *(US)* Präsentieren eines Wechsels.

sightseeing | **bus** Aussichts-, Rundfahrtautobus; ~ **tour** Stadtrund-, Besichtigungsfahrt.

sign [An]zeichen, *(advertising)* Werbeschild, *(shop)* Laden-, Aushängeschild; **road** ~ Wegweiser, **traffic** ~ Verkehrszeichen; ~s **of slowdown** konjunkturelle Abschwächungshinweise; ~ **o. s.** sich anmelden; ~ **as attorney-in-fact** in Vollmacht unterschreiben; ~ **away one's interest in an estate** auf Grundstücksansprüche verzichten; ~ **a check** *(US)* **(cheque, Br.)** Scheck unterschreiben; ~ **up for evening classes** sich zu Kursen für die Erwachsenenbildung anmelden; ~ **for the goods** Warenempfang bestätigen; ~ **off** *(radio, US)* Funkstille ansagen, *(relinquish one's claims)* verzichten, *(stop work)* Arbeitsschluß registrieren; ~ **on** *(broadcasting)* Sendebetrieb eröffnen, *(factory)* anwerben, einstellen; ~ **the ship's articles** sich anheuern lassen; **to show** ~s **of improvement** Besserungstendenzen erkennen lassen.

signal for inflation Inflationszeichen.

signature Unterschriftsleistung, Unterzeichnung; **blank** ~ Blankounterschrift; **counter** ~ Gegenzeichnung; **facsimile** ~ Faksimileunterschrift; **fictitious (forged)** ~ Unterschriftsfälschung; ~ **missing** Unterschrift fehlt;

to have one's ~ **legalized** seine Unterschrift beglaubigen lassen; ~ **book** *(bank)* Unterschriftenverzeichnis.

signboard Aushänge-, Firmenschild.

signing | **clerk** *(Br.)* Prokurist; ~ **fee** Zeichnungsgebühr; ~ **power** Unterschriftsvollmacht.

silent partner *(Br.)* stiller Teilhaber.

silver, fine Feinsilber; **standard** ~ Münzsilber; ~ **bar** Silberbarren.

simple | **average** einfache Havarie; ~ **contract** formloser Vertrag; ~ **contract debt** nicht bevorrechtigte [Konkurs]forderung; ~ **interest** Kapitalzinsen; ~ **majority** einfache Mehrheit.

simulated | **account** fingierte Rechnung; ~ **sale** Scheinkauf.

simulcast *(television)* Direktübertragung.

single *(railway, Br.)* Einzelfahrkarte; ~ **allowance** *(income tax, Br.)* persönlicher Freibetrag; ~ **bill** Solawechsel; ~-**employer bargaining** Einzeltarifverhandlung; ~-**entry bookkeeping** einfache Buchführung; ~-**family dwelling (home)** Einfamilienhaus; ~-**line store** Spezialwarengeschäft; ~-**name paper** *(US)* Solawechsel; ~-**part production** Einzelanfertigung; ~-**plant bargaining** Einzeltarifverhandlung; ~-**rate letter** einfacher Brief; ~-**step income statement** *(US)* Gewinn- und Verlustrechnung in Kontoform; ~ **tariff** autonomer Tarif; ~ **track** eingleisige Strecke; ~ **trader** *(Br.)* Einzelkaufmann.

sink *(v.)* *(amortize)* tilgen, amortisieren, *(prices)* sinken, fallen, niedriger werden, *(ship)* sinken; ~ **half of one's fortune in a new business undertaking** Hälfte seines Vermögens in einem neuen Geschäft anlegen; ~ **the level of prices** Kursniveau vertiefen.

sinking of debts Schuldentilgung.

sinking fund Schuldentilgungs-, Ablösungsfonds, Amortisationsfonds, -kasse; **to raid the** ~ Tilgungsfonds zweckentfremden; ~ **income** Erträgnisse des Amortisationsfonds; ~ **method of calculating depreciation** Abschreibungsmethode mit steigenden Quoten; ~ **reserve** Tilgungsrücklage.

siphon *(v.)* **off funds** Mittel abschöpfen.

sit *(v.)* **on (upon) a committee** Ausschußmitglied sein; ~ **at a high interest** hohe Zinsen zahlen müssen; ~-**down strike** Sitzstreik.

site Lage eines Grundstückes, *(plot of land)* Bauplatz, -grund, -gelände, Gelände; **delivered [on]** ~ Lieferung frei Baustelle; **erection** ~ Aufstellungsort; **fair** ~ Ausstellungs-, Messegelände; **home** ~ Eigenheimgrundstück; ~ **of an industry** Sitz einer Industrie; ~ *(v.)* **a new factory** neues Fabrikgelände festlegen; ~ **development** Baulanderschließung; ~ **land** Baugelände; ~ **value** [steuerlicher] Einheitswert.

sitting Sitzung, TAgung; **all-night** ~ Nachtsitzung; ~ **fee** *(Br.)* Sitzungsgeld.

situated, badly finanziell schlecht gestellt sein.

situation Lage, Zustand, Situation, *(building)* Geschäftslage, *(employment)* [An]stellung, Stelle, Posten;
financial ~ Status; **hazardous** ~ gefährlicher Arbeitsplatz; **labo(u)r** ~ Arbeitsmarktlage; **~s required** *(newspaper)* Stellengesuche; **~s vacant** Stellenangebot;
to apply for a ~ sich um eine Stelle umtun (bewerben); **to throw up a** (Beschäftigung) aufgeben.
situs Belegenheit, Lageort, *(plant)* Geschäftssitz; **business** ~ steuerlicher Geschäftssitz.
size Größe, Nummer, Maß, Umfang, Format;
of all ~s in allen Größen;
odd ~ nicht gängige Größe; **stock** ~ Lagergröße; ~ **of income** Höhe des Einkommens; ~ **of order** Auftragsvolumen;
to seek ~ **rather than quality** mehr auf Quantität als auf Qualität gehen.
sized nach Größen geordnet;
large-~ in Großformat.
skeleton Gerüst, Gestell, *(building)* Rohbau, *(plant)* Stammpersonal;
~ **agreement** Rahmenabkommen; ~ **bill** Wechselblankett; ~ **contract** Manteltarif; ~ **letter** Blankoformular.
sketch Übersicht, überschlägige Berechnung; **first (rough)** ~ Rohentwurf.
skid in profits Gewinnabfall.
skilled gelernt, geschickt, bewandert;
to be ~ **in a business** fachlich ausgebildet sein; ~ **labo(u)r** Fachkräfte, -arbeiter; ~ **trades** Spezialberufe; ~ **worker** Facharbeiter.
skim *(v.)* **surplus purchasing power** überschüssige Kaufkraft abschöpfen.
skimming off excess profits Gewinnabschöpfung.
skip *(debtor, US)* unbekannt verzogener Schuldner; ~ *(v.)* **bail** Kaution verfallen lassen;
~ **tracing** *(US)* Ausfindigmachung eines säumigen Schuldners.
sky | **advertising** Luftwerbung; ~ **sign** Leucht-, Lichtreklame; ~ **tourist** Touristenfluggast; ~ **train** *(US)* Airbus.
skyrocket *(v.)* *(prices, US)* in die Höhe schnellen.
skyscraper Wolkenkratzer, Hochhaus.
slack Nachlassen, Flaute, *(coll.)* Ruhepause;
~ **in the economy** Konjunkturflaute;
to be ~ *(stock market)* lustlos sein, *(trade)* stocken;
~ *(a.)* *(stock exchange)* unbelebt, geschäftslos, flau, lustlos, still;
~ **business** ruhiges Geschäft; ~ **demand** spärliche Nachfrage; ~ **period (season)** stille (tote) Saison.
slacken *(v.)* *(stock exchange)* nachlassen.
slackening tendency Abschwächungstendenz.
slackness | **of business** Geschäftsstockung; ~ **of the market** Flaute.
slash [Preis]nachlaß, Abstrich;
~ *(v.)* **a budget** Etat zusammenstreichen; ~ **costs** Unkosten drastisch reduzieren; ~ **production** Produktion einschränken; ~ **taxes** Steuern kräftig ermäßigen.

slaughtered price Schleuderpreis.
slave | **labo(u)r** Zwangsarbeit; ~ **labo(u)rer** Zwangsarbeiter.
sleeper Schlafplatz, *(US)* Ladenhüter;
~ **train** Schlafwagen.
sleeperette Schlafkoje.
sleeping | **accommodation** Schlafgelegenheit;
~ **account** totes Konto; **to book a** ~ **car** Schlafwagenplatz bestellen; **~-car ticket** Schlafwagenkarte; ~ **partner** *(Br.)* stiller Teilhaber; ~ **partnership** *(Br.)* Kommanditgesellschaft.
slice | **of budget** Etatsanteil; ~ **of a commission** Provisionsanteil.
slick | **business deal** aalglattes Geschäft; ~ **salesman** gerissener Geschäftsmann.
slide Dia[positiv], *(film)* Filmband;
~ **in the interest rate** nachlassende Zinssätze; ~ **in values** Absinken der Kurse;
~ *(v.)* **down** *(prices)* abgleiten;
~ **advertising** Diapositivwerbung; ~ **lecture** Lichtbildervortrag.
sliding | **rate of interest** Staffelzins; ~ **scale** *(advertising)* Nachlaß-, Rabattstaffel, *(prices)* bewegliche Preisskala, *(wages)* bewegliche Lohnskala, gleitender Lohntarif; **~-scale price** Staffelpreis.
slight decline *(stock exchange)* geringe Abschwächung.
slip *(advertising)* Aufkleber, *(banking)* Formularstreifen, *(bill of exchange)* Anhang, *(of paper)* Zettel, Blatt Papier;
bank ~ Girozettel; **betting** ~ Wettschein; **binding** ~ *(insurance law)* vorläufige Deckungszusage; **sales** ~ Kassenzettel; **wage** ~ Lohn[abrechnungs]zettel; ~ **book** Quittungs-, Belegbuch; ~ **system** Belegbuchhaltung.
slogan *(advertising)* Werbetext, -spruch, Slogan.
slopshop billiger Konfektionsladen.
slopwork Serienarbeit, *(clothes)* Konfektionskleidung.
slot machine [Verkaufs]automat.
slow *(business)* zurückgeblieben, schleppend, flau, *(debtor)* säumig, saumselig;
~ *(v.)* **down economy** Konjunktur verlangsamen;
to go ~ *(workers)* Bummelstreik durchführen, streng nach Vorschrift arbeiten;
~ **assets** feste (fixe) Anlagen; ~ **goods traffic** Frachtgutverkehr; ~ **train** Bummelzug.
slowdown Arbeitsverlangsamung, Bummelstreik;
~ **in business** verlangsamte Konjunktur; ~ **in investment** Investitionsverlangsamung; ~ **in price increase** nachlassender Preisanstieg;
~ **strike** *(US)* Bummelstreik.
slowing down | **of the economy** Konjunkturverlangsamung; ~ **in prices** verlangsamter Preisanstieg.
slum Elendsgasse, -quartier;
~ **area** Elendsgebiet; ~ **clearance** Städtesanierung.
slumberette Schlafsitz [im Flugzeug].
slump *(of prices)* Fall, [plötzliches] Fallen der Preise, Preissturz, *(stock exchange)* Einbruch, Baisse, *(trade cycle)* Konjunkturrückgang;

~ **in the franc** Sturz des Frankenkurses; **heavy** ~ **in cotton prices** scharfer Einbruch der Baumwollpreise; ~ **in sales** Absatzkrise, rapider Umsatzrückgang; ~ **in stocks** Aktiensturz; ~ **clause** Baisseklausel; ~**-proof** krisenfest.

slush fund *(US)* Reptilien-, Bestechungsfonds.

smalls *(advertising)* Kleinanzeigen.

small | **ad** Kleinanzeige; ~ **bonds** *(US)* Obligationen in kleinen Stückelungen; ~ **business** *(US)* gewerblicher Mittelstand, Klein- und Mittelbetriebe; ~ **change** Wechselgeld; ~ **consignments** Stückgut; ~ **denominations** kleine Stücke; ~ **hand** gewöhnliche Korrespondenzschrift; ~**-income allowance** *(Br.)* Freibeträge für niedrige Einkommen; ~**-loan company** *(US)* genossenschaftliche Darlehnskasse; ~ **resources** unbedeutende Mittel; ~ **tradesman** Minderkaufmann.

smallholder *(Br.)* Kleinlandbesitzer, *(savings)* Kleinsparer, *(stock ownership)* Kleinaktionär.

smalltime organization Schmalspurorganisation.

smallwares Kurzwaren.

smart | **bargainer** pfiffiger Geschäftsmann; ~ **money** Reu-, Abstandsgeld, *(indemnification, US)* Schmerzensgeld.

smash *(banking)* Bankkrach, *(collision)* Zusammenstoß, *(commercial failure)* Zusammenbruch, Bankrott; ~ *(v.) (bankrott)* gehen, zusammenbrechen.

smuggle *(v.)* **through the customs** durch den Zoll schmuggeln.

smuggled goods Schmuggelware.

smuggling, currency Devisenschmuggel.

snap *(easy job, US sl.)* Druckposten; ~ *(v.)* **at an offer** sich auf ein Angebot stürzen; ~ **check** stichprobenartige Überprüfung.

social | **accounting** Sozialstatistik; ~ **cost** Soziallasten; ~**-economic balance sheet** Sozialbilanz.

social insurance *(US)* Sozialversicherung; ~ **benefits** *(US)* Sozialversicherungsleistungen; ~ **contributions** *(US)* Sozialversicherungsbeiträge.

social | **relief** Sozialfürsorge; ~ **saving** kollektives Sparen.

social security soziale Sicherheit *(US)* Sozialversicherung, *(Br.)* Sozialhilfe; ~ **adjustment** *(US)* Anpassung der Sozialversicherungsleistungen; ~ **card** *(US)* Sozialversicherungskarte; ~ **check** *(US)* Auszahlung der Sozialrente; ~ **contribution** *(US)* Sozialversicherungsbeitrag; ~ **payments** *(US)* Sozialabgaben, -leistungen; ~ **service** *(US)* Sozialversorgung; ~ **tax** *(US)* Sozialversicherungsbeitrag, Zwangsbeiträge zur Sozialversicherung.

social | **service** Wohlfahrt, Fürsorge; ~ **services** Sozialleistungen, Sozial-, Fürsorgeeinrichtungen; ~ **welfare** *(US)* soziale Wohlfahrt, Sozialhilfe; ~ **worker** Fürsorgebeamter, Sozialfürsorger.

socialize *(v.)* sozialisieren, verstaatlichen, vergesellschaften.

society *(association)* Verein[igung], Verband, *(partnership)* Gesellschaft, *(trade partnership)* Berufsgenossenschaft;

benevolent ~ *(Br.)* Versicherungsverein auf Gegenseitigkeit; **building** ~ *(Br.)* Bausparkasse; **co-operative** ~ *(Br.)* Konsumverein; **cooperative productive** ~ Produktionsgenossenschaft; **incorporated** ~ *(US)* eingetragener (rechtsfähiger) Verein; **mutual** ~ Unterstützungsverein auf Gegenseitigkeit; **registered** ~ *(Br.)* eingetragener Verein.

sociologist, industrial Betriebssoziologe.

soft *(stock exchange)* nachgiebig, unstabil; ~ **currency** weiche Währung; ~**-currency country** währungsschwaches Land; ~**-drink industry** alkoholfreie Getränkeindustrie; ~ **money** Papiergeld; ~**-pedal** *(v.)* **one's claims** seine Forderung abschwächen.

softening in business conditions Konjunkturabschwächung.

softness in demand Nachfrageschwäche.

sold | **by auction** in der Auktion verkauft; ~ **out** ausverkauft, nicht mehr vorrätig; **not to be** ~ unverkäuflich sein; ~ **ledger** Verkaufsbuch, -journal; ~ **note** *(broker, Br.)* Schlußschein, -note.

sole | **account** alleinige Rechnung; ~ **agency** Alleinvertretung; ~ **bill** Solawechsel; ~ **corporation** Einmanngesellschaft; ~ **heir** Universalerbe; ~ **occupation** ausschließliche Beschäftigung; ~ **proprietor** Einzelkaufmann; ~ **right of negotiation** Ausschließlichkeitsrecht; ~ **trade** Monopol; **feme-**~ **trader** Kauffrau.

solicit | *(v.)* **for custom** um Kundschaft werben; ~ **orders** sich um Aufträge bemühen; ~ **subscriptions** Abonnenten werben.

solicitation | **of business** Geschäftsanfrage; ~ **of customers** Kundenwerbung.

solicitor *(law court, Br.)* [nicht plädierender Rechts]anwalt, Rechtsbeistand.

to retain a ~ *(Br.)* Anwalt betrauen.

solid *(credit rating)* kreditfähig, *(honest)* gediegen, solide; ~ **business firm** solides Unternehmen; ~ **gold** gediegenes Gold.

solution of financial troubles Behebung finanzieller Schwierigkeiten.

solvency Zahlungsfähigkeit, Liquidität, Solvenz; ~ **rules** Liquiditätsbestimmungen.

solvent *(able to pay)* zahlungsfähig, solvent, liquid, *(credit rating)* kreditfähig, -würdig, *(financially sound)* leistungsfähig, *(solid)* solide; ~ **estate** liquider Nachlaß.

song, for a mere um ein Spottgeld.

sophistication geistige Differenziertheit, *(technics)* hochentwickelter Stand der Technik.

sordid gains unerlaubte Gewinne.

sort Sorte, Klasse, *(brand)* Marke, *(kind)* Gattung, Art, *(quality)* Güte, Qualität; **of** ~**s** unsortiert, gemischt; ~ *(v.)* **out** *(law of bankruptcy)* aussondern.

sorting | **out** *(law of bankruptcy)* Aussonderung; ~ **machine** Sortiermaschine.

soul of an enterprise Seele eines Geschäfts.

sound *(v.)* | **a capitalist with regard to a proposed investment** Kapitalgeber wegen der Finanzierung eines Unternehmens ansprechen; ~ **in damages** Schadenersatzansprüche begründen;
~ *(a.)* gesund, unversehrt, *(credit rating)* kreditfähig, -würdig, *(firm)* solide, reell;
~ **bank** seriöse Bank; ~ **commercial credit** geschäftliches Ansehen; ~ **currency** gesunde Währung; ~ **financial postion** gesunde Finanzverhältnisse; ~ **ship** seetüchtiges Schiff.

source Ursprung, *(authority)* Gewährsmann;
at the ~ *(taxation* an der Quelle;
~**s close to the bank** der Bank nahestehende Kreise;
~ **of earnings** Einkommensquelle;
to open up new ~**s** neue Quellen erschließen; **to pay a tax at the** ~ Quellensteuer entrichten.

souvenir shop Geschenkartikelgeschäft.

space *(advertising, US sl.)* Anzeigenraum, -teil;
blank ~ freie Stelle; **cargo** ~ Laderaum; ~ **required** Platzbedarf;
to apply for ~ sich zu einer Messe anmelden; **to contract for** ~ Anzeigenraum sicherstellen;
~ **advertisement** seitenteilige Anzeige; ~ **buyer** Werbungsmittler; ~ **buying** Anzeigenbelegung; ~ **rates** Anzeigentarif; ~ **schedule** Datenschema, Streuplan.

spare Reserve-, Ersatzteil, Extrastück;
~*(v.)* **no expenses** keine Kosten scheuen;
~ **capacity** *(Br.)* ungenützte Kapazität; ~ **capital** flüssiges Kapital; ~ **money** Notgroschen; ~ **part** Ersatzteil; ~ **room** Besuchs-, Fremdenzimmer;
~**time activities** Freizeitgestaltung; ~ **tyres** *(Br.)* (tires, *US)* Ersatzbereifung.

speaking clock *(tel.)* Gesprächsuhr.

special *(correnspondent)* Sonderberichterstatter, *(newspaper)* Extrablatt, *(railway)* Sonderzug;
~ **acceptance** eingeschränktes Akzept; ~ **account** Sonder-, Separatkonto; ~ **allowance** Sondervergütung; ~ **area** *(Br.)* Notstandsgebiet; ~ **audit** außerplanmäßige Revision; ~ **bonus** Sonderzulage; ~ **branch** *(trade)* Spezialität, Fachgebiet; ~ **capital** Kommanditkapital; ~ **contingency reserve** Sonderrücklage; ~ **delivery** *(US)* Eilzustellung; ~ **deposits** *(Bank of England, Br.)* Mindestreserven; ~ **dictionary** Fachwörterbuch; ~ **dividend** Superdividende; ~ **drawing rights** *(International Monetary Fund)* Sonderziehungsrechte; ~ **guarantee** *(US)* Kreditbürgschaft; ~ **handling** *(US, postal service)* Einschreiben; ~ **knowledge required** erforderliche Spezialkenntnisse; ~ **lien** Zurückhaltungsrecht; ~ **messenger** *(US)* Eilbote; ~ **order** Fabrikationsauftrag; ~ **partner** Kommanditist; ~ **permit** Ausnahmegenehmigung; ~ **position** *(advertising)* Vorzugsplacierung; ~ **rate** Vorzugstarif; ~ **restraint of trade** auf bestimmte Gebiete beschränktes Konkurrenzverbot; ~ **stocks** *(US)* Spezialwerte, Favoriten; ~ **subject** Wahlfach; ~ **supplement** Sonderbeilage; ~ **train** Sonderzug.

specialist Fachmann, -arbeiter, Spezialist, Sachverständiger;

accounting ~ Buchprüfungsspezialist; **radio and television** ~ Fachgeschäft für Radio und Fernsehen;
~ **circles** Fachkreise; ~ **staff** Fachkräfte.

specialize *(v.)* **in (on)** [sich] spezialisieren auf, als Spezialfach betreiben.

specialized | **fair** Fachmesse; ~ **worker** Facharbeiter.

specialty *(goods)* Neuheit, Spezialität, Spezialartikel, *(special pursuit)* Spezial-, Fachgebiet;
~ **contract** formbedürftiger Vertrag; ~ **gift** Werbegeschenk; ~ **goods** Marken-, Spezialartikel; ~ **shop** (store, *US)* Spezial[artikel]geschäft; **departmental** ~ **store** Gemischtwarengeschäft.

specie Hart-, Metallgeld, Bargeld, gemünztes Geld;
to pay in ~ in klingender Münze zahlen.
~ **account** Sortenkonto; ~ **consignment** Barsendung.

specific | **deposit** Sonderdepot; ~ **duty** *(customs)* Mengenzoll; ~**order cost system** Kostenrechnungssystem für auftragsweise Fertigung; ~ **performance** effektive Vertragserfüllung; ~ **tariff** Mengentarif.

specification genaue Angabe, Spezifikation, *(patent)* Patentbeschreibung, -schrift, *(securities)* namentliches Stückeverzeichnis;
building ~**s** Ausschreibungsbedingungen, Baukostenvoranschlag; **export** ~ *(Br.)* Ausfuhrerklärung; **job** ~ *(US)* Arbeitsplatzbeschreibung;
~**s of a car** technische Daten eines Autos; ~ **of disbursements** Spesenaufstellung; ~ **of numbers** Nummernverzeichnis; ~ **of weight** Gewichtsnota.

specified | **account** detaillierte Rechnung; ~ **goods** Speziessachen; **in** ~ **instalments** in festgesetzten Raten.

specify | *(v.)* **a place of payment** Zahlungsort angeben.

specimen Muster, Muster-, Probestück;
~ **of signature** Unterschriftsprobe;
~ **book** Musterbuch; ~ **rate** Vorzugssatz.

spectacular *(advertising)* Werbegroßanlage, *(newspaper advertisement)* großformatige Anzeige.

speculate | *(v.)* **in atomic shares** mit Atomaktien spekulieren; ~ **for differences** *(Br.)* Differenzgeschäfte machen.

speculating | **in contangos** Reportgeschäft;
~ **manoeuvre** Spekulationsmanöver; ~ **transactions** Spekulationsgeschäfte.

speculation Spekulation, gewagtes Unternehmen;
bad ~ Fehlspekulation; **bull** ~ Haussespekulation;
~ **for a fall** Baissespekulation; ~ **in stocks** *(US)* Aktienspekulation.

speculative | **buying** Spekulations-, Meinungskäufe;
~ **damage** vorausberechneter Schaden; ~ **gain** Spekulationsgewinn; ~ **purchases** Meinungskäufe; ~ **stock** *(US)* Spekulationspapier.

speculator | **for a fall** Baissespekulant; ~ **in property** Grundstücksspekulant.

speech, maiden Jungfernrede; **opening** ~ Eröffnungsrede.

speed, cruising *(car)* Reisegeschwindigkeit;
~ **of turnover** Umschlagshäufigkeit;

~ (v.) up production Produktionsausstoß erhöhen; ~ goods (Br.) Eilgut; ~ recorder Fahrtenschreiber.

speedup of production beschleunigter Produktionsausstoß.

spell Arbeitszeit, Beschäftigung; sinking ~ (export) rückläufige Periode.

spend (v.) (employ) aufwenden, (money) verausgaben, ausgeben, (use up) verbrauchen; ~ on advertising für Werbungszwecke ausgeben; ~ an estate in gaming Vermögen verspielen; ~ one's leisure time seine Freizeit verbringen; ~ money with a free hand flott Geld ausgeben.

spendable earnings Nettoeinkommen.

spending Ausgabe, Ausgabenwirtschaft; capital ~ Kapitalaufwand; deficit ~ öffentliche Verschuldung durch Anleiheaufnahme; to hold ~ down Ausgabenwirtschaft einschränken; to increase its ~ on plant Betriebsinvestitionen erhöhen; ~ decision Ausgabenentscheidung; to show ~ forbearance sich in den Ausgaben Beschränkungen auferlegen; ~ income verfügbares Einkommen; ~ priorities vordringliche Ausgabeposten; to be off on a ~ spree Geld mit vollen Händen ausschütten; ~ unit Verbrauchereinheit.

sphere | of activity (action) Tätigkeits-, Arbeits-, Geschäfts-, Wirkungskreis; ~ of business Geschäftsrahmen.

spinoff (income tax, US) Aktientausch; ~ products Abfallerzeugnisse.

spiral, wage-price Lohn-Preis-Spirale.

spiral(l)ing of costs Kostenspirale.

spirit, business (commercial) Geschäftssinn.

splinter operation Kleinbetrieb.

split Teilung (shares, US) Aktiensplit, (taxation) Einkommensaufteilung; ~ (v.) the income (US) Steuereinkommen aufspalten; ~ commission geteilte Provision; ~ off (US) Aktientausch; ~ opening (US) Eröffnungsnotierung mit stark abweichenden Kursen; ~ quotation (US) Notierung in Bruchteilen; ~ shift unterbrochene Arbeitsschicht; ~-ups (US) Bonus in Form aufgeteilter Aktien.

splitting Spaltung, (income tax, US) getrennte Veranlagung, (shares) Aktiensplit.

spoiled, spoilt schadhaft, beschädigt; ~ goods verdorbene Ware; ~ stamps ungültige Briefmarken; ~ work Ausschuß.

spoils system (US) Futterkrippenwirtschaft.

sponsor (advertising) Auftraggeber, (furtherer, US) Gönner, Förderer, Schirmherr; ~ (v.) fördern, unterstützen, (braodcasting) Sendeprogramm fördern;

sponsored, government staatlich unterstützt.

sponsorship (broadcasting) Patentstelle.

spot Ort, Platz, Fleck, Stelle, (film, US) Kurzszene, (local goods) Lokoware; in a ~ (sl.) in schwieriger Lage (der Klemme); hot ~ Touristenattraktion;

to be without a ~ on one's reputation blütenweiße Weste haben; to deal with a supplier on the ~ Platzgeschäfte machen; to do a ~ of work ein bißchen arbeiten; ~ (a.) sofort lieferbar, zahlbar; ~ announcement (US) Werbedurchsage, -einblendung, -spot; to buy on a ~ basis gegen bare Kasse kaufen; ~ broker Kassa-, Platzmakler; ~ business Platz-, Lokogeschäft; ~ cash (US) bares Geld, Barzahlung; ~ check Prüfung an Ort und Stelle; ~-credit approval sofort erteilte Kreditgenehmigung; ~ delivery Kassalieferung; ~ goods Lokoware; ~ market Loko-, Kassamarkt; ~ parcels sofort lieferbare Stücke; ~ quotations Kassakurs; ~ transaction Effektivgeschäft.

sqout, up the (coll.) versetzt, verpfändet.

spread Verbreitung, (advertising) Streuung, (underwriters' commission) Konsortialprovision, (margin, US) Spanne, Differenz; double-page ~ doppelseitige Anzeige; price ~ Kursdifferenz; ~ of risk Risikoverteilung; ~ (v.) out goods for sale Waren zum Verkauf ausbreiten; ~ out income Einkommen [steuerlich] verteilen; ~ the cost of an asset over its useful life Anschaffungskosten eines Wirtschaftsguts auf seine Nutzungsdauer verteilen; ~ instal(l)ments over several months Abzahlungsraten auf mehrere Monate verteilen; ~ over the entire taxable year steuerlich über das ganze Jahr verteilen; ~-work system Arbeitsstreckenverfahren.

spreading of work Arbeitsstreckung.

spreadover (advertising) Streuplan, (industry) Arbeitsstundenanpassung.

spring | resort Kurort; ~ sales (shopping) Frühjahrseinkäufe, -besorgungen.

spurious bank bill Falschgeldschein.

spurt plötzliches Anziehen der Preise; upward ~s Kurssprünge.

squaring of accounts Kontenabstimmung.

squeeze Klemme, Geldverlegenheit, (scarcity) Knappheit, wirtschaftlicher Engpaß; credit ~ Kreditrestriktion; money ~ Liquiditätsbeendung; ~ (v.) the bears (stock exchange) zu Deckungskäufen zwingen; ~ down prices Preise (Kurse) herunterdrücken.

stability | of prices Kurs-, Preisstabilität; ~ of value Wertbeständigkeit.

stabilization Stabilisierung, Festigung; wage ~ board (US) Lohnausgleichsstelle; ~ fund Währungsausgleichsfonds; ~ loan Aufwertungsanleihe.

stabilizing factors of the market Kursstützungsfaktoren.

stable (a.) beständig, fest, stabil, (goods) haltbar, dauerhaft, (in value) wertbeständig, unveränderlich; ~ in price preisstabil; ~ currency stabile Währung; ~ job Dauerbeschäftigung.

staff [Geschäfts], Betriebspersonal, Angestellte, Belegschaft, Personalbestand, Mitarbeiterstab;
on the regular ~ fest angestellt;
editorial ~ Redaktion[sstab]; efficient ~ gut geschultes Personal; field ~ Außenkräfte; temporary ~ Aushilfspersonal;
to be on the ~ zur Belegschaft gehören; to be on the regular ~ im festen Angestellenverhältnis stehen; ~ auditor Betriebsrevisor; ~ department Personalabteilung; ~ magazine Werkzeitschrift; ~ pension fund (Br.) [Angestellten]pensionskasse; ~ shares (Br.) Belegschaftsaktien; ~ vacations Betriebsferien.
staffing schedule (US) Stellenbesetzungsplan.
stag nicht an der Börse zugelassener Makler, (stock exchange, Br.) Konzertzeichner;
~ party Herrenabend, -gesellschaft.
stage Abschnitt, Stadium, [Entwicklungs]phase, Etappe, (traffic) Abschnitt, Teilstrecke;
landing ~ Landungsbrücke; manufactured ~ abgeschlossenes Produktionsstadium;
~ of negotiations Stand der Verhandlungen; ~s of production Produktionsstufen.
stagflation mit langsamem Wachstum des Sozialprodukts gekoppelte Inflation.
stagger (prices) Schwanken;
~ (v.) the annual holidays Zeit der großen Ferien aufteilen.
staggering | of hours Staffelung der Arbeitszeit;
~ of shifts Kurzarbeit.
stagging the market (Br.) Beeinflussung der Börsenkurse durch Konzertzeichnungen.
stagnancy Mattheit, Lustlosigkeit, Stockung, Flaute.
stagnant market stagnierender Markt, matte Börse.
stagnation of business Geschäftsstille, -stockung.
stake (capital) Einschuß, Einlage, (share) Anteil;
~ in ownership Eigentumsanteil;
~ (v.) out a claim Grundstück abstecken;
to have a ~ in the lottery in der Lotterie spielen;
~ money Einsatz, Wettgebühr.
stale flau, (impaired in legal force) verjährt;
~ articles unmoderne Waren; ~ bear (bull) geschlagener Baissier (Haussier); ~ demand verjährter Anspruch; ~ news abgestandene Neuigkeiten.
stall Verkaufsstand, -bude, Marktbude;
~ (v.) a debt Schuld in Raten abtragen;
~ rent Standgeld, -gebühr.
stalwarts of the market führende Marktwerte.
stamp (brand) Firmenzeichen, Etikette, (mark) Stempel, (postage) Frei-, Briefmarke, Postwertzeichen;
free of ~ (stock exchange) börsenumsatzsteuerfrei;
affixed ~ Aufklebemarke; bill ~ Wechselstempel; cancelling ~ Entwertungsstempel; finance ~ Stempelmarke; inland-revenue ~ (Br.) Steuer-, Gebührenmarke; receipt ~ Quittungsmarke; savings ~ (Br.) Sparmarke;
~ on securities (US) Effektenstempel;
~ (v.) ver-, abstempeln, (coin) prägen, (mail) freimachen, frankieren;
~ a document Urkunde verstempeln;

to affix a ~ Stempel aufdrücken;
~ book Portobuch; ~ booklet Briefmarkenheft; ~ dealer Briefmarkenhändler; exempt from ~ duty stempelsteuerfrei; ~ pad Stempelkissen; ~ tax (US) Stempelsteuer.
stamped | envelope Freiumschlag, -kuvert; ~ shares abgestempelte Aktie; ~ weight geeichtes Gewicht.
stamping Verstempeln, (mail) Frankierung;
~ machine Frankiermachine.
stand Stand, Verkaufsbude, -stand, (business situation, US) Geschäftslage;
fair ~ Messestand; market ~ Marktbude;
~ in a trade exhibition Ausstellungsstand;
~ (v.) by an agreement sich an eine Vereinbarung halten; ~ bail for s. o. für j. Kaution stellen; ~ at cost at . . . (balance sheet) mit einem Herstellungspreis von . . . zu Buch stehen; ~ idle (factory) stilliegen; ~ first on the list Liste anführen; ~ shot to s. o. j. freihalten; ~ for more wages Lohnerhöhung fordern;
~ space Ausstellungsfläche.
standard Standard, [Güte]grad, (average) Durchschnitt, (coinage) gesetzlicher Feingehalt, Münzfuß, (currency) Währung[sstandard], (norm) Norm, Normentyp, Richtwert, (quality) Standardqualität, (sample) Muster, (value) Wertmesser, -einheit (weight) Normalgewicht;
by European ~s nach europäischen Maßstäben;
bimetallic ~ Doppelwährung; credit ~s Kreditrichtlinien; gold- ~ Goldstandard; gold-bullion ~ Goldkernwährung; gold-exchange ~ Golddevisenwährung; multiple ~ Indexwährung; professional ~ berufsethische Grundsätze; tabular ~ Indexwährung;
~s of business forms einheitliche Geschäftsmethoden; normal ~ of interest üblicher Zinsfuß; ~ of living (life) durchschnittliche Lebenshaltung, Lebensstandard; ~ of prices Preisniveau, -spiegel; ~ of wages Lohnniveau; ~ of weight Gewichtseinheit;
to promote high ~s hohe Qualitätsansprüche stellen; to reach a high ~ of efficiency hohen Leistungsgrad erreichen; to set a high ~ of business morality hohe Anforderungen an die Geschäftsmoral stellen;
~ (a.) normal, vorschriftsmäßig, (stable) stabil, wertbeständig;
~ account form Einheitskontoblatt; ~ automobile public liability policy (US) allgemeine Kraftfahrzeughaftpflichtpolice; ~ broadcast Mittelwellenfunk; ~ capacity Durchschnittsleistung; ~ car Standardausführung; ~ claim Valutaschuld; ~ clause (currency) Währungsklausel; ~ cost Richtkosten, vorkalkulierte Kosten; ~ -cost system Normalkostenrechnung; silver-~ country Silberwährungsland; ~ deduction (income tax) Pauschalabzug für Geschäftsunkosten, Sonderausgabenpauschale; ~ design Regelausführung; ~ family (statistics) Normalfamilie; ~ form Einheitsformular; ~ gauge (railway) Normalspurweite; ~ gold

Münzgold; ⌀ **and Poor's Indices** *(US)* Indexziffern der Börsenkurse; ~ **labo(u)r rate** Grundlohn einschließlich der Normalzuschläge; ~ **make** Normalausführung; ~ **mark** Feingehaltsstempel; ~ **mortgage clause** *(fire policy)* Auszahlungsklausel bei der Hypothekengewährung; ~ **output** Sollleistung; ~ **performance** Vorgabeleistung; ~ **piece wage** Einheitsstücklohn; ~ **price** Richt-, Einheitspreis; ~ **profit** Bruttoverdienst; ~ **quality** durchschnittliche Güte (Qualität); ~ **rate** Grundpreis *(taxation, Br.)* [Steuer]normalsatz; ~**-run quantity** wirtschaftliche Losgröße; ~ **stocks** Standardwerte, Favoriten; ~ **tax** *(US)* Basissteuer; ~ **unit** Standardformat; ~ **wage rates** Tariflohnsätze; ~ **working day** Normalarbeitstag.

standardization Normung, Standardisierung, Eichung, Typisierung, Vereinheitlichung;
monetary ~ Währungsangleichung;
~ **of factories** Betriebsvereinheitlichung;
~ **committee** Normenausschuß.

standardized | **product** Einheitserzeugnis; ~ **sheet size** Standardformat.

standby *(technics)* Not-, Zusatz-, Reservegerät;
~ **agreement** *(banking)* Garantie des Direktabsatzes; ~ **arrangement** Stillhaltevereinbarung; ~ **cost** fixe Kosten; ~ **credit** Kreditzusage.

standing Rang[dienstalter], Stand, *(repute)* Stellung, Bonität;
credit ~ Kreditwürdigkeit;
~ **of a commercial house** bewährter Ruf einer Firma; ~ **idle** *(factory)* Stilliegen;
~ **charges** konstante Kosten; ~ **custom** Usance; ~ **customer** Dauerkunde; ~ **offer** gleichbleibendes Angebot; ~ **order** Dauerauftrag; ~ **room only** nur Stehplätze; ~ **wages** festes Gehalt.

standstill Stillstand, Stockung;
to be at a ~ stocken, *(factory)* nicht in Betrieb sein;
~ **agreement** Stillhalteabkommen.

staple *(chief product)* Haupterzeugnis, *(emporium)* Handelszentrum;
foreign ~ Ausfuhrmonopol;
~ **articles (commodities, goods)** Massen-, Hauptartikel, Hauptprodukte, Stapelwaren; ~ **place** Hauptniederlage.

start Start, *(airplane)* Abflug, *(departure)* Abfahrt, Abreise, *(machine)* Inbetriebsetzung;
~*(v.) (airplane)* abfliegen, *(depart)* abreisen, *(production)* anlaufen;
~ **in business** in ein Geschäft einsteigen; ~ **s. o. in business** j. etablieren; ~ **a fund** Geldversammlung veranstalten; ~ **the price** erstes Gebot abgeben; ~ **from scratch again** wieder von vorn anfangen;
to muddle at the ~ *(business)* schlechten Start haben.

starting | **of an enterprise** Geschäftsbeginn; ~ **of production** Anlauf der Erzeugung;
~ **credit** Anlaufkredit; ~ **platform** Abfahrtsbahnsteig; ~ **price** Anfangskurs; ~ **salary** Anfangsgehalt.

startup cost Start-, Anlaufkosten.
starvation wage Hungerlohn.
state [Zu]stand, Lage, *(financial situation, Br.)* Status, *(government)* Staat[swesen], Land;
in the native ~ *(product)* unbearbeitet;
daily ~ tägliche Geschäftsübersicht; **financial** ~ Vermögenslage; ~ **member** ~ Mitgliedsland;
~ **of an account** Kontostand; ~ **of business** Geschäftslage; ~ **of a commercial house** Vermögensverhältnisse einer Firma; ~ **of destination** Bestimmungsland; ~ **of the market** Konjunktur-, Marktlage;
~ *(v.)* **an account** Rechnung spezifizieren; ~ **the average** aufnehmen;
to be in a ~ **of distress** in bedrängter Lage sein; **to live in** ~ großen Aufwand treiben;
~ **aid** staatliche Unterstützung (Hilfe); ~**-aided** subventioniert; ~ **bank** *(US)* staatlich konzessionierte Bank; ~ **bank examiner** *(US)* Bankenkommissar; ~ **banking department** *(US)* Bankenaufsicht; ~**-buying organization** staatliche Einkaufsgesellschaft; ~ **cabin** Luxuskabine; ~**-controlled** unter Staatsaufsicht; ~ **debt** Staatsschuld; ~ **enterprise** Regiebetrieb; ~ **grant** Staatszuschuß; ~ **liability** Staatshaftung; ~ **monopoly** Staatsmonopol; **to transfer to** ~ **ownership** *(US)* verstaatlichen; ~ **planning agency** staatliche Planungsbehörde; ~ **property** *(US)* fiskalisches Vermögen; ~ **supervision** Staatsaufsicht; ~**-taxed** besteuert; ~ **trading** Regiebetrieb; ~ **unemployment insurance tax** Arbeitslosenversicherungsbeitrag.

stated | **account** spezifizierte Rechnung; ~ **capital** *(balance sheet, US)* ausgewiesenes Gesellschaftskapital; ~ **salary** festes Gehalt; ~ **value** festgestellter Wert.

statement *(abstract of account)* [Konto]auszug, *(account rendered)* [Rechenschafts]bericht, *(balance sheet, US)* Bilanz, *(bank)* Bankausweis, *(estimate)* Vor-, Kostenanschlag, *(of property)* Vermögensstand;
as per enclosed ~ laut anliegendem Verzeichnis;
accounting ~ Revisionsbericht; **application of funds** ~ Ausweis über die Verwendung des Grundkapitals; **average** ~ Havarieaufmachung; **closing** ~ [Ab]schlußbericht; **detailed** ~ Spezifikation; **earnings** ~ Gewinn- und Verlustrechnung; **financial** ~**s** Gewinn- und Verlustrechnung; **income** ~ *(US)* Gewinn- und Verlustrechnung; **official** ~ Kommuniqué; **operating** ~ Erfolgsbilanz; ~ **rendered** Rechnungsaufstellung; **weekly** ~ Wochenausweis; **working** ~ Geschäftsbericht;
~ **of account** Konto[korrent]auszug; **statutory** ~ **of affairs** Vermögensaufstellung, Status; ~ **of application of funds** Verwendungsnachweis, Bewegungsbilanz; ~ **of assets and liabilities** Bilanzaufstellung; ~ **of average** Havarieaufmachung; ~ **of charges** Kostenrechnung; ~ **of exchanges** Kursbericht; ~ **of fees** Gebührentarif; ~ **of goods** Lagerbestand; ~ **of income and accumulated earnings** *(US)* Gesamtergebnisrechnung; ~ **of income**

and expenses Gewinn- und Verlustrechnung; ~ of income and surplus *(corporation, US)* Jahresbericht nebst Bilanz sowie Gewinn- und Verlustrechnung; ~ of particulars Spezifikation; ~ of prices Preisliste, -verzeichnis; ~ of net proceeds Reinertragsübersicht; ~ of profit and loss *(US)* Gewinn- und Verlustrechnung; ~ of operating results *(US)* Ergebnisrechnung; ~ of sales done Umsatzbilanz; ~ of size Größenangabe; ~ of stockholder's equity Ausweis über die Verwendung des Grundkapitals; ~ of earned surplus Kapitalzuwachsbilanz;

to certify its financial ~ Bestätigungsvermerk erteilen; to publish a ~ Erklärung veröffentlichen; to send s. o. a. ~ of the amount owing to him jem. ein Schuldanerkenntnis schicken;

~ analysis *(US)* Bilanzanalyse, -kritik; ~ date *(US)* Bilanzierungstag; ~ form Gewinn- und Verlustrechnung in Staffelform; ~ wages Akkordlohn.

station Station, Stelle, *(broadcasting)* Funkstation, Sender, *(office)* Amt, Stellung, Posten, *(railway)* Haltestelle, Bahnhof;

[delivered] free of ~ bahnfrei; left at ~ till called for bahnlagernd;

ambulance ~ Unfallstation; filling ~ Tankstelle; forwarding ~ Versandbahnhof; goods ~ *(Br.)* Güterbahnhof; [omni]bus ~ Omnibusbahnhof; petrol ~ *(US)* Tankstelle; police ~ Polizeiwache; shunting ~ Verschiebebahnhof; telegraph ~ Telegraphenamt; terminal ~ Kopf-, End-, Sackbahnhof; trading ~ Handelsniederlassung;

~ of destination Bestimmungsbahnhof;

~ announcement (break) *(radio)* Pausen-, Sendezeichen; ~ hall Bahnhofshalle; ~ hotel Bahnhofshotel; at-~ price Preis ab Versandbahnhof; ~ wagon *(US)* Kombiwagen.

stationary | prices stabile Preise; ~ sum Fixum.

stationer Schreibwarenhändler.

stationery Bürobedarf; Papierwaren, Schreibmaterialien, *(letter paper)* Briefpapier;

office ~ Büromaterial; ~ department Materialverwaltung; ~ shop (store, *US*) Schreibwarenhandlung.

statistical | code number Nummer des statistischen Warenverzeichnisses; ~ expert Statistiker; ~ number *(export trade)* Ausfuhrnummer des statistischen Warenverzeichnisses.

statistics Statistik, statistische Unterlagen;

commercial ~ Handelsstatistik; distribution ~ Absatzkenzahlen;

~ of employment Beschäftigungszahlen;

status [geschäftliche] Lage, Geschäftslage, Status, *(position of affairs)* Finanz-, Vermögenslage;

without any official ~ ohne offiziellen Auftrag;

financial ~ Finanzlage, -status; marital ~ Familienstand;

~ of aliens Ausländereigenschaft; ~ of ownership Eigentumsverhältnisse;

~-plus Statusgewinn; ~ symbol Statussymbol.

statute Satzung, Statut, Gesellschaftsvertrag;

according to ~ satzungsgemäß; not subject to the ~ of limitations unverjährbar;

local ~ Ortsstatut; regulatory ~ Ausführungsbestimmung;

♀ at Large *(US)* Bundesgesetzblatt; ~ of limitations gesetzliche Verjährungsvorschriften;

to apply the ~ of limitations Verjährungsvorschriften anwenden; to plead the ~ of limitations Verjährung einwenden; to toll the ~ of limitations Verjährungsvorschriften unterbrechen;

~-barred *(Br.)* erlöschen, verjährt; ~ roll Gesetzblatt.

statutory statuten-, satzungsgemäß;

~ agent gesetzlicher Vertreter; ~ company (corporation) Körperschaft des öffentlichen Rechts; ~ factor's lien Sicherungseigentum an einem Warenlager mit wechselndem Bestand; ~ holiday gesetzlicher Feiertag; ~ interest gesetzliche Zinsen; ~ lien gesetzliches Zurückbehaltungsrecht; ~ limitation Verjährungsfrist; ~ meeting *(Br.)* gesetzlich vorgeschriebene Generalversammlung; ~ office *(corporation, US)* Büroadresse; ~ regime *(US)* gesetzlicher Güterstand; ~ report *(Br.)* gesetzlich vorgeschriebener Gründungsbericht; ~ reserve gesetzlich vorgeschriebene Reserve; ~ tenant *(Br.)* Mieter mit Kündigungsschutz.

stay Halt *(ship)* Aufenthalt, *(suspension of judical proceedings)* Aussetzung, Einstellung;

main ~ of a business Rückgrat eines Geschäfts; ~ at a health resort Kuraufenthalt;

~ *(v.)* execution Zwangsvollstreckung aussetzen; ~ at a hotel in einem Hotel wohnen;

~-in strike *(Br.)* mehrtägiger Sitzstreik.

steady ständig, *(price)* fest[stehend];

~ *(v.)* *(stock exchange)* sich festigen;

to grow ~ *(market)* stabil werden;

~ customer Stammkunde; ~ demand gleichbleibende Nachfrage.

steal *(v.)* s. one's thunder *(advertising)* jem. mit einer Überraschungsreklame zuvorkommen.

steamship company Schiffahrtsgesellschaft.

steel | cartel Stahlkartell; ~ consumption Stahlverbrauch; ~ industry Stahlindustrie; ~ price Stahlpreis; ~ stocks *(US)* Montan, Stahlaktien.

steep price unverschämter Preis.

steer *(v.)* near receivership auf den Konkurs zusteuern.

steerage passenger Zwischendeckpassagier.

steering committee Lenkungsausschuß.

step | *(v.)* into a fortune spielend zu einem Vermögen gelangen; ~ up production Produktion steigern;

~ bonus Leistungsprämie, Stufenakkord.

step-up | in inventory growth lagerzyklischer Aufschwung; ~ in output Ausstoßsteigerung.

sterling | account Pfundkonto; ~ bloc Sterlingblock; ~ invoice in Pfund zahlbare Rechnung.

stevedore Ab-, Belader, Stauer, Schauermann.

steward Inspektor, *(property)* [Vermögens]verwalter, *(ship)* Steward, Kellner;

land ~ *(Br.)* Güterverwalter.

stick | *(v.)* **bills** Zettel ankleben, plakatieren; ~ **it on during the busy season** während der Saison enorm hohe Preise verlangen; ~ **out for higher pay** auf höherem Lohn bestehen; **~on label** Aufklebezettel.

sticker *(US)* Aufklebezettel, *(drug)* Ladenhüter.

stiff | **bill** überhöhte Rechnung; ~ **card** *(sl.)* formelle Einladung; ~ **market** stabile Marktlage.

stiffening of prices Anziehen der Preise, *(capital market)* Versteifung am Geldmarkt.

stimulation of business activity Konjunkturanregung, -förderung, -stimulus.

stint *(mining)* Schicht, Tageswerk, *(task prescribed)* bestimmtes Arbeitspensum; **to do one's daily ~** seiner täglichen Beschäftigung nachgehen; **to work by ~s** auf Schicht arbeiten.

stipulate | *(v.)* **for the best material to be used** erstklassige Materialverwendung vereinbaren; ~ **payments in gold** Zahlungen auf Goldbasis vereinbaren; ~ **the terms of a contract** Vertragsbedingungen festsetzen.

stipulated | **damages** Konventionalstrafe; ~ **premium** Vertragsprämie.

stipulation Abmachung, Vereinbarung, *(condition)* Bedingung, Klausel; **exclusivity ~** Wettbewerbsausschluß; **reciprocity ~** Gegenseitigkeitsklausel; ~ **of payment** Zahlungsvereinbarung; ~ **in restraint of trade** Konkurrenzklausel.

stock *(Br., capital ~)* Grundstock, Geschäfts-, Stamm-, Grundkapital *(loan capital, Br.)* Anleihekapital, *(share capital, US)* Anfangskapital, Aktienkapital, *(provisions)* Vorrat, *(ready money)* Barschaft, *(share)* Aktie, *(share paid in)* Einlage, [Gesellschafts]anteil, *(store)* Lagervorrat, Warenbestand;

carried in ~ lagervorrätig; **ex ~** ab Lager; **out of ~** nicht ausverkauft, nicht mehr auf Lager; **active ~** *(US)* lebhaft gehandelte Aktien; **actual ~** Istbestand; **assented ~** *(US)* im Sammeldepot hinterlegte Aktien; **authorized ~** *(US)* genehmigtes Kapital; **barometer ~s** *(US)* Standardwerte; **bonus ~** Gratisaktie; **unissued capital ~** nicht ausgegebenes Aktienkapital; **consignment ~** Konsignationsware; **convertible ~** umtauschfähige Aktie; **corporation ~s** *(Br.)* Kommunalobligationen; **cumulative preferred ~** *(US)* Vorzugsaktie mit Dividendennachzahlungsverpflichtung; **dead ~** totes Inventar, **debenture ~** Vorzugsaktie; **deposited ~** Garantieaktie; **distributing ~** Auslieferungslager; **dormant ~** Ladenhüter; **fancy ~** *(US)* unsichere Spekulationspapiere; **ficititious ~** verwässerte Aktie; **floating ~** flüssiges Kapital; **food ~s** Lebensmittelvorräte; **foreign ~s** *(Br.)* Valutapapier, Auslandswerte; **gilt-edged ~** *(Br.)* mündelsichere Wertpapiere; **gold ~** Goldbestand; **growth ~s** Wachstumswerte; **high-quality ~** Spitzenwert; **incoming ~** Wareneingänge; **inscribed ~s** *(Br.)* Schuldbuchgiroforderungen, börsenmäßig gehandelte Buchwerte; **issued ~** *(US)* effektiv ausgegebenes Aktien-

kapital; **joint ~** Aktien-, Stammkapital; **listed ~** *(US)* an der Börse notierte Aktie; **~s loaned** lombardierte Effekten; **majority ~** *(US)* Aktienmehrheit; **merchandise ~** Warenlager; **municipal ~s** *(Br.)* Kommunalobligationen, -schuldverschreibungen; **~s negotiable on the ~ exchange** börsenfähige Aktien; **noncumulative preferred ~** *(US)* Vorzugsaktie ohne Dividendenbezugsrecht; **nonvoting ~** nicht stimmberechtigtes Aktienkapital; **~ offered** *(stock exchange)* Abgabematerial; **opening ~** Anfangsbestand; **option ~** *(Br.)* Prämienwerte; **original ~** Grund-, Stammkapital; **par-value ~** *(US)* Nennwertaktie; **phantom ~s** nur buchmäßig gutgeschriebe Aktien; **preference ~** *(Br.)* Prioritäts-, Vorzugsaktie; **preferred ~** *(US)* Vorzugs-, Prioritätsaktie; **public ~s** Staatsobligationen; **registered ~** *(Br.)* Namensaktie; **reserve ~** Reservelager; **rolling ~** [Eisenbahn]-betriebsmaterial; **surplus ~** Inventarüberschuß; **treasury ~** *(US)* Portefeuille eigener Aktien; **trustee ~s** mündelsichere Anlagepapiere; **unissued capital ~** *(US)* genehmigtes noch nicht ausgegebenes Kapital; **voting ~** *(US)* Stimmrechtsaktie; **watered ~** verwässertes Aktienkapital; **well-assorted (-selected) ~** wohlassortiertes Lager;

~ **of bills of exchange** Wechselbestand; ~ **on commission** Kommissionslager; ~ **of gold** Goldvorrat; ~ **of goods** Warenlager; ~ **in (on) hand** Lagerbestand, Warenvorrat; ~ **of merchandise** Warenvorrat; ~ **in process** in der Verarbeitung befindliches Material; ~ **of raw materials** Rohstofflager; ~ **of spare parts** Ersatzteillager; ~ **in trade** Betriebsmaterial, -mittel, -kapital, *(goods)* Warenbestand;

~ *(v.)* auf Lager nehmen, *(have in stock)* Waren auf Lager halten (führen), *(store)* aufspeichern, sammeln; ~ **varied goods** (verschiedenste Warengattungen) führen; ~ **a shop with goods** Ladengeschäft assortieren; ~ **up** sich eindecken, Lager auffüllen, bevorraten;

to be in ~ vorrätig (auf Lager) sein, *(cash)* bei Kasse sein, Geld haben; **to be long of ~** *(US)* mit Aktien eingedeckt sein; **to be out of ~** vergriffen sein; **to be short of ~** *(US)* Aktien gefixt haben; **to buy the whole ~ of a business** Geschäft in Bausch und Bogen kaufen; **to carry heavy ~** umfangreiche Lagervorräte haben; **to exercise the right to subscribe to [acquire] new ~** *(US)* Bezugsrecht auf junge Aktien ausüben; **to give on ~** *(Br.)* in Prolongation geben, hineingeben; **to have all one's fortune in ~s** sein ganzes Vermögen in Aktien angelegt haben; **to invest one's money in a safe ~** sein Geld in mündelsicheren Papieren anlegen; **to keep in ~** auf Lager haben; **to lay in fresh ~s** Neuanschaffungen vornehmen; **to lay a ship on the ~s** Schiff auf Kiel legen; **to make for ~** lagermäßig herstellen; **to pay a call on ~** Einzahlung auf Aktienleisten; **to refill the ~** Lagerbestand ergänzen; **to run down ~s** Lager abbauen; **to set a low**

value on a ~ *(US)* Aktienwert niedrig ansetzen, **to slaughter** ~s Bestände verschleudern; **to take** ~ Inventar (Lagerbestand) aufnehmen, Inventur machen, **to take in** ~ **for a borrower** *(US)* Aktien hereinnehmen; **to take in** ~ **without charging** Effekten glatt hereinnehmen; **to work on** ~ lagermäßig herstellen;
~ **account** *(capital, Br.)* Kapitalkonto, *(goods)* Waren[bestands]konto; ~ **accounting** Lagerbuchhaltung; ~ **adventurer** *(Br.)* Aktien-, Fondsspekulant; ~ **allotment warrant** *(US)* Aktienbezugsschein; ~ **analyst** Effektenberater; ~ **appreciation** Kapitalerhöhung; ~ **arbitration** *(Br.)* Effektenarbitrage, ~ **articles** Serienware, Lagerartikel; ~ **book** *(shares, US)* Hauptbuch der Aktionäre, *(Br.)* Effektenbuch; ~ **boom** Effektenhausse; ~ **bubbling** *(US)* Aktienschwindel; ~ **building** Lageraufstockung; ~ **capital** Grund-, Stammkapital; ~ **card** Inventarkarte; ~ **certificate** *(US)* Kapitalanteilschein, *(Br.)* Aktienzertifikat; ~ **check** Bestandsaufnahme; ~ **control** Lagerkontrolle; ~ **dealer** Viehhändler; ~ **deposit** *(Br.)* Wertpapierdepot; ~ **dividend** *(US)* Gratisaktie.
stock exchange [Wertpapier]börse, Effekten-, Aktien-, Fondsbörse, Fondsmarkt;
to admit for quotations (list, *US***) on the** ~ zur Börsennotierung zulassen; **to be dealt in on the** ~ an der Börse gehandelt werden.
stock-exchange | **agent** Börsenvertreter; ~ **bank** *(US)* Effektenbank; ~ **broker** Börsen-, Effekten-, Fondsmakler; ~ **business** Effektenhandel; ~ **commission** Effektenprovision; ~ **customer** Börsenbesucher; ~ **holiday** *(Br.)* Börsenfeiertag; ~ **list***(Br.)* Börsen-, Kurszettel, Kursblatt; **to remove shares from the** ~ **list** Aktien von der Notierung absetzen; ~ **operations** Börsengeschäfte; ~ **order** Börsenorder, -auftrag; ~ **price** Börsenkurs; ~ **securities** börsengängige Wertpapiere; ~ **tax** Börsenumsatzsteuer.
stock | **girl** Lagerarbeiterin; ~ **indicator** Börsentelegraph; ~ **issue** *(US)* Aktienausgabe; ~ **ledger** *(inventory)* Inventarbuch, *(shares, US)* Aktionärsverzeichnis.
stock market Effekten-, Wertpapierbörse, Aktien-, Börsen-, Effektenmarkt;
dull ~ Börsenflaute, Börsenkurse;
to play the ~ *(coll.)* auf dem Aktienmarkt spekulieren;
~ **boom** *(US)* Aktienhausse; ~ **credit** Lombardkredit; ~ **favo(u)rite** Kursfavorit; ~ **gain** Börsengewinn; ~ **loss** Börsenverlust; ~ **report** *(US)* Kursblatt; ~ **rise** Anstieg der Aktienkurse; ~ **sentiment** Börsenstimmung; ~ **setback** Kursrückschlag; ~ **trading** Effektenverkehr; ~ **trend** Börsenentwicklung.
stock | **model** *(car)* Serienmodell; ~ **option** *(US)* Aktienbezugsrecht [für Betriebsangehörige]; ~ **order** Lagerauftrag; ~ **position** Vorratslage; ~ **power** *(US)* Börsenvollmacht; ~ **premium** *(US)* Aktienagio; ~ **price** *(US)* Aktienkurs, -preis; ~

printer Börsentelegraph; ~ **purse** Gemeinschaftskasse; ~ **quotation** *(US)* Aktiennotierung; ~ **receipt** *(Br.)* Effektenquittung; ~ **reduction** Lagerabbau; ~ **register** *(US)* Aktienverzeichnis; ~ **requisition** Entnahmeschein; ~ **right** *(US)* [Aktien]bezugsrecht; ~ **scrip** *(US)* Interimsaktie; ~ **shortage** Warenknappheit; ~ **size** lagergängige (stets vorrätige) Größe; ~ **subscription** *(US)* Aktienzeichnung; ~**subscription right** Aktienbezugsrecht; ~ **ticker** Börsentelegraf; ~ **trading without transfer** stückeloser Effektenverkehr; ~ **transaction** Börsengeschäft; ~ **transfer** *(Br.)* Wertpapier-, Aktienübertragung; ~ **transfer tax** *(US)* Börsenumsatzsteuer; ~ **trend** *(US)* Börsentendenz; ~-**trial order** Lagerprobeauftrag; ~ **turnover** Lagerumschlag; ~ **voucher** Bestandsbeleg; ~ **warehouse** Warenlager; ~ **warrant** *(US)* Aktienbezugsschein, *(Br.)* Aktienzertifikat; ~ **watering** Kapitalverwässerung;
stockbroker Aktien-, Effekten-, Börsen-, Fonds-, Kurs-, Geldmakler, Effektenhändler.
stockbroking *(Br.)* Effektengeschäft, -transaktion.
stocked geführt, auf Lager, vorrätig;
~ **by all retailers** durch den Einzelhandel zu beziehen.
stockholder *(US)* Aktionär, Effekten-, Aktieninhaber, *(Br.)* Effekten-, Fondsbesitzer, Anteilseigner, *(capitalist)* Kapitalist;
controlling ~ Aktienmajoritätsbesitzer; **ordinary** ~ *(US)* Stammaktionär;
~ **action** *(US)* Aktionärsklage; ~ **relations** *(US)* Aktionärspflege. ,
stockholders' | **equity** *(US)* Eigen-, Gesellschaftskapital; ~ **meeting** *(US)* Hauptversammlung.
stockholding *(US)* Aktien-, Effektenbesitz;
~ **interests in foreign banks at cost** *(balance sheet)* Aktien auswärtiger Banken zum Anschaffungspreis.
stockist *(Br.)* Fachgeschäft, -händler.
stockjobber *(Br.)* Börsenmann, -jobber, -spekulant, *(US)* Fondsmakler, Effektenhändler.
stockjobbery *(Br.)* Aktien-, Effektenspekulation, *(US)* Kurstreiberei, -beeinflussung.
stockkeeper Lagerhalter.
stockowner *(US)* Aktien-, Effektenbesitzer.
stockpile Vorrat, Reserve, [Vorrats]lager;
to cut back drastically on the ~s drastischen Lagerabbau durchführen;
~ **dispositions** Lagerdispositionen.
stockpiling Lager-, Vorratswirtschaft, -bildung;
to step up one's ~ **pace** Tempo der Lageranreicherung beschleunigen.
stocktaking Aufnehmen der Bestände, Lager-, Bestands-, Inventur[aufnahme];
physical ~ tatsächliche Inventaraufnahme;
~ **sale** Inventurausverkauf.
stop Sperrung, Sperre, *(for check)* Sperrauftrag, *(ship)* Anlegestelle, *(stop order)* limitierter Börsenauftrag;
bus ~ [Omni]bushaltestelle; **conditional** ~ Bedarfshaltestelle; **price** ~ Preisstopp;

~ *(v.) (check)* sperren, *(close down)* stillegen, *(stock exchange)* limitierten Börsenauftrag geben; ~ **an account** Konto sperren; ~ **bankruptcy proceedings** Konkursverfahren einstellen; ~ **business** Betrieb einstellen; ~ **at an inn** in einem Gasthaus einkehren; ~ **a neighbo(u)r's light** dem Nachbarn die Aussicht verbauen; ~ **payments** Zahlung sistieren, Auszahlung sperren; ~ **supplies** Lieferung einstellen; ~ **work** in Streik treten;
to come to a dead ~ im Verkehr steckenbleiben; to put a ~ to expenses Spesenaufwand begrenzen; to run without a ~ *(train)* durchfahren;
~ **card** *(checks)* Sperrliste; ~ **list** *(trade association)* schwarze Liste, Boykottliste; ~**-loss order** limitierter [Börsen]auftrag; ~ **order** Verkaufsstopp, *(check)* Schecksperre, *(stock exchange, US)* limitierter Börsenauftrag; ~**-payment** Zahlungssperre; ~**-and-go policy** antizyklische Steuerung der Konjunktur durch Staat und Notenbank; ~**-press news** *(Br.)* letzte (neueste) Nachrichten; ~ **price** Stopppreis.
stopgap Notbehelf, Lückenbüßer, Aushilfe; ~ **advertisement (advertising)** Füllanzeige, Füller.
stopover *(US)* Fahrtunterbrechung, *(plane)* Zwischenlandung, Flugunterbrechung; ~ **ticket** Rundreisefahrkarte.
stoppage Anhalten, Unterbrechung, *(closing down)* [Betriebs]stillegung, *(deduction of salary)* Gehaltsabzug, *(stopping payment)* Zahlungseinstellung, *(stopping work)* Arbeitseinstellung; ~ **of business** Betriebseinstellung; ~ **of pay** Lohneinbehaltung; ~ **at source** *(taxation)* Quellenbesteuerung; ~ **in transit[u]** Ausübung des Zurückhaltungsrechts an unterwegs befindlichen Waren.
stopping | time Arbeitsschluß; ~ **train** Bummelzug.
storage *(cost)* Lagergeld, -miete, -spesen, -zins, *(space)* Lagerraum, *(storing)* [Ein]lagerung, Einlagern;
~ **in transit** Zwischenlagerung;
to put into cold ~ [Plan] auf Eis legen; to take goods out of ~ Waren sortieren;
~ '**accommodation** Lagerungsmöglichkeit; ~ **area** Lagerräume; ~ **business** Lagerungsgeschäft; ~ **charges** *(costs)* Lagerungsgebühren; ~ **operation** Lagerbetrieb; ~ **track** Abstellgleis; **cold-~ vessel** Gefrierschiff; ~ **yard** Lagerhof.
store *(abundance)* Überfluß, Fülle, *(Br.)* Aufbewahrungsort, Lager[haus], Magazin, [Waren]speicher, Depot, Niederlage, *(department store)* Kauf-, Warenhaus, *(shop, US)* Geschäft, Laden[geschäft];
ex ~ ab Lager; **in** ~ vorrätig, auf Lager; **the** ~**s** *(Br.)* Konsumverein;
appraiser's ~ *(US)* Zollspeicher; **basement** ~ Laden im Parterre; **bonded** ~ Entrepot, Zollniederlage; **contractor's** ~ Materiallager; **cooperative** ~ *(US)* Konsumgenossenschaft, -verein, Konsum; **general** ~ Gemischtwarenhandlung, *(US)* Kauf-, Warenhaus; **high-class service** ~ *(US)* Geschäft mit erstklassiger Bedienung; **independent** ~ *(US)*

selbständiges Einzelhandelsgeschäft; **integrated** ~ *(US)* Kettenladen; **marine** ~**s** Schiffsbedarf; **multiple** ~ Kettenladenunternehmen; **one-price** ~ *(US)* Einheitspreisgeschäft; **public** ~ *(US)* öffentlicher Speicher; **single-line retail** ~ Einzelhandelsfachgeschäft; **specialty** ~ *(US)* Spezial[artikel]geschäft; **utility-operated** ~ *(US)* betriebseigener Laden; **limited-price variety** ~ billiges Warenhaus;
~ **of money** Geldreserve; ~ **for rent** vermieteter Laden;
~ *(v.)* aufbewahren, [ein]lagern, auf Lager haben, aufs Lager bringen;
~ **furniture** Möbel auf den Speicher geben; ~ **goods** Waren einlegen; ~ **a ship with provisions** Schiff verproviantieren; ~ **up** auf Lager nehmen, *(money)* thesaurieren;
to create a ~ Depot errichten; to have a good ~ of provisions in the house ausreichende Vorräte im Haus haben; to lay in ~ Vorrat anlegen; to take out of ~ auslagern;
~ **account** Lagerkonto; ~ **book** Lager-, Bestandsbuch; ~**-brand items** *(US)* ladeneigene Erzeugnisse; ~ **card** *(US)* Reklamekärtchen [zur Beschreibung der Ware]; ~ **detective** *(US)* Ladendetektiv; ~ **display** *(US)* Ladenauslage; ~**-door delivery, ~-door service** *(US)* Zustellung frei Haus; ~ **furniture** *(US)* Speichermöbel; ~**s ledger** Lagerhauptbuch; ~ **ledger card** Lagerkarte; ~ **manager** *(US)* Geschäftsführer, -leiter; ~ **owner** *(US)* Ladenbesitzer; ~ **paper** Werkzeitung; ~ **rental** *(US)* Ladenmiete; ~ **shed** Materialschuppen; ~ **supplies** Lageranlieferung; ~ **window** *(US)* Schaufenster.
storefront *(US)* Ladenfront.
storekeeper *(Br.)* Lagerhalter, -verwalter, *(shop, US)* Ladenbesitzer, Händler.
storeroom Abstell-, Proviant-, Lagerraum.
storing [Ein]lagern, Lagerhaltung;
~ **business** Lagergeschäft; ~ **charges** Lagergebühren; ~ **number** Lagernummer.
story *(account)* Darstellung, Bericht, *(US)* Stockwerk, Etage;
attic ~ Mansarde; **first** ~ erste Etage, *(US)* zweite Etage;
~ **rights** Drehbuchrechte.
stow | *(v.)* **a wag(g)on** Waggon beladen.
stowage *(charges)* Stauerlohn, *(store room)* Laderaum, -tonnage, Nutzraum, *(stowing)* Verstauung;
to shift the ~ umstauen;
~ **certificate** Stauattest; ~ **plan** Stauplan.
stowaway blinder Passagier.
straddle *(US)* Gegentransaktion, Stellagegeschäft.
straight *(account)* geordnet, in Ordnung, *(without discount, US)* ohne Mengenrabatt;
to find the accounts ~ Bücher in Ordnung befinden;
~ **accounts** sorgfältig geführte Konten; ~ **bill of lading** *(US)* auf den Namen ausgestelltes Konnossement; ~ **commercial** eingeblendete Werbedurchsage; ~ **dealings** korrektes Geschäftsgeba-

ren; ~ **income** Normaleinkommen; ~ **life insurance** *(US)* Versicherung auf den Todesfall; ~-**line method of calculating depreciation** *(US)* Abschreibungsmethode nach Quoten, lineare Abschreibung; ~ **note** *(US)* Namenspapier; ~ **piece-rate plan** Stücklohnsystem; ~ **salary** festes Gehalt.

strain Anstrengung, -spannung, Bemühung;
~ **on credit** Kreditanspannung;
~ *(v.)* **one's powers** seine Befugnisse überschreiten; **to be a ~ on s. one's resources** j. finanziell sehr in Anspruch nehmen; **to place great ~s on the economy** Wirtschaft großen Belastungen aussetzen.

straits Meerenge, *(fig.)* Verlegenheit, Klemme.

stranglehold, to loosen its ~ on the money supply Geldhahn wieder aufdrehen.

straw | bail wertlose Bürgschaft; ~ **bid** *(US)* Scheingebot.

stray customer gelegentlicher Kunde.

stream | of cars Autokette; ~ **of dividends** Dividendenstrom.

streamer Wimpel, *(advertising)* Streifenanzeige.

streamline *(v.)* modernen Verhältnissen anpassen, rationalisieren, modernisieren;
~ **a tax-collection system** Steuereintreibungsverfahren modernisieren.

street Straße, *(stock exchange, Br.)* Nachbörse, *(curb market)* Freiverkehr;
[done] in the ~ nachbörslich; **on easy ~** *(US)* in guten Verhältnissen;
adopted ~ Kommunalstraße; **one-way ~** Einbahnstraße; **no-waiting ~** Parkverbotsstraße;
to put workers on the ~ Arbeiter auf die Straße setzen; **to sell on the ~** *(Br.)* an der Nachbörse verkaufen, *(curb market)* im Freiverkehr verkaufen;
~ **certificate** *(US)* formlos übertragene Aktie; ~ **collection** Straßensammlung; ~ **industry** Hausierergewerbe; ~ **market** *(Br.)* Freiverkehrsmarkt; ~ **prices** *(Br.)* *(curb market)* Freiverkehrskurse; ~ **sale** Straßenhandel.

strength *(market)* feste Haltung, *(stock exchange)* Festigkeit;
competitive ~ Wettbewerbsfähigkeit; **selective ~** *(stock exchange)* auf Spezialwerte beschränkte feste Haltung;
~ **of the staff** Personalbestand;
to negotiate on the ~ of samples auf Grund der Vorlage von Mustern verhandeln.

stress | of competition Wettbewerbsdruck; ~ **of money** Geldanspannung;
~ **disease** Managerkrankheit.

stretch Grundriß, Abriß, *(land)* Strich, Land;
~ **of authority** Vollmachtmißbrauch;
~ *(v.)* **one's credit** seinen Kredit überschreiten;
~-**out** *(US)* Arbeitsintensivierung (Überstundenzeit) ohne Lohnerhöhung.

stricken ship angeschlagenes Schiff.

strict | censorship strenge Zensur; **in ~ confidence** streng vertraulich; ~ **cost price** scharf kalkulierter Herstellerpreis; ~ **liability** Gefährdungshaftung.

strike Streik, [Arbeits]ausstand, Arbeitseinstellung, -niederlegung;

buyer's ~ Käuferstreik; **flash ~** wilder Streik; **general ~** Generalstreik; **go-slow ~** Dienst nach Vorschrift; **industry-wide ~** Streik innerhalb eines ganzen Industriezweiges; **lightning ~** Streik ohne vorherige Ankündigung; **outlaw ~** wilder Streik; **quickie ~** *(US)* wilder Streik, Kurzstreik; **selective ~** schwerpunktartig durchgeführter Streik; **sitdown ~** Sitzstreik; **slowdown ~** Streik durch Verlangsamung der Arbeit; **stay-in ~** *(Br.)* mehrtägiger Sitzstreik; **warning ~** Warnstreik;
~ **against bad working conditions** Streik wegen schlechter Arbeitsbedingungen; ~ **for higher pay** Streik für höhere Löhne;
~ *(v.)* in einen Streik eintreten, streiken, *(cease working)* Feierabend machen, *(find oil)* auf ein Öllager stoßen;
~ **a balance** bilanzieren; ~ **a bargain** Geschäft [ab]schließen; ~ **a dividend** Dividende ausschütten; ~ **a docket** *(bankruptcy proceeding, Br.)* Antrag auf Konkurseröffnung stellen; ~ **on the job** durch Arbeitsverlangsamung streiken; ~ **off 2 %** 2 Prozent abziehen; ~ **off the register** im Register löschen; ~ **out a new plan of finance** neuen Finanzierungsplan ersinnen; ~ **it rich** *(US)* reiche Geldquelle entdecken; ~ **a ship off the list** Schiff abwracken;
to bar a ~ Streik verbieten; **to be on ~** streiken;
~ **aid** Streikbeihilfe; ~ **benefit** Streikunterstützung; ~-**bound** vom Streik betroffen; **no-~ clause** Streikverbotsklausel; ~ **director** Streikleiter; ~-**free labo(u)r** am Streik unbeteiligte Arbeitskräfte; ~ **fund** Streikkasse; ~ **notice** Streikankündigung; ~ **replacement** Ersatz für Streikausfälle; ~ **vote** Urabstimmung.

strikebreaker Streikbrecher.

strikemonger Streikhetzer.

striking a balance Saldierung, Bilanzziehung.

string Bindfaden, Schnur, *(clause, US)* Geheimklausel;
no ~s attached nicht verklausuliert;
~ **development** Stadtrandsiedlung.

stringency Knappheit, *(money market)* Gedrücktheit;
credit ~ Kreditverknappung; **foreign-exchange ~** Devisenknappheit.

stringent stock market angespannte Börse.

strip Streifen, *(advertising)* Streifenanzeige;
flight ~ Notlandestreifen;
~ *(v.)* **a factory** Fabrik demontieren.

strong *(stock exchange)* fest, widerstandsfähig;
~ **demand** lebhafte Nachfrage.

strongbox Geldschrank, Stahlkassette, -fach.

strongroom Panzergewölbe, Stahlkammer.

structural unemployment strukturelle Arbeitslosigkeit.

structure, cost ~ Kostengefüge; **financial ~** Kapitalstruktur; **market ~** Marktgefüge;
~ **of an organization** Aufbau einer Organisation.

stub *(check book, US)* Kontrollabschnitt, Talon, *(railroad, US)* kurze Nebenstrecke.

study Studie, sorgsame Untersuchung, *(room)* Arbeits-, Herren-, Studierzimmer;
market ~ Marktanalyse;
~ **of productivity** Produktivitätsstudie;
~ *(v.)* only one's own interests nur sein eigenes Interesse im Auge haben;
~ **commission** Arbeitsausschuß; ~ **group** Studiengruppe.

stuff *(article)* Ware, *(cash, soll.)* Bargeld;
household ~ Einrichtungsgegenstände.

stumer *(cheque, Br. sl.)* ungedeckter Scheck.

stunt *(advertising)* Reklameschlager;
publicity ~ Werbefeldzug.

style Art, Stil, Typ, *(firm)* Firma, Firmenname;
under the ~ **of** unter der Firma (dem Namen);
fast-selling ~ schnell verkäuflicher Modeartikel;
~ *(v.)* anreden, *(US, boost)* Reklame machen, *(fashion)* Mode kreieren;
~ **name** Fabrikations-, Geschäfts-, name; ~ **show** Modeschau; ~ **trend** Modewechsel.

styling industrielle Formgebung.

subagency Untervertretung, Spezialagentur.

subcontract *(v.)* als Zulieferant übernehmen;
~ **work** Unterlieferantentätigkeit.

subcontractor Zulieferant, Unterlieferant.

subject [Gesprächs]thema, Gesprächsgegenstand, *(constitutional law)* Staatsangehöriger;
~ **of our negotiations** Gegenstand unserer Verhandlungen; ~ **of a tax** Steuerträger;
~ **to alterations** Änderungen vorbehalten; ~ **to change without notice** freibleibend; ~ **to the deposit of collateral security consisting of first stocks** *(US)* gegen Hinterlegung erstklassiger Aktien; ~ **to duty** zollpflichtig; ~ **to reservation** unter Vorbehalt; ~ **to stamp duty** stempelsteuerpflichtig; ~ **to the terms of the contract** vorbehaltlich der Vertragsbestimmungen;
to be ~ **to 4 % discount** 4 % Rabatt genießen;
~ **catalog(ue)** systematischer Katalog, Schlagwörterkatalog; ~ **filing** Ablage nach Sachgebieten; ~ **index** Sachregister, -index; ~ **matter** Stoff, [Verhandlungs]gegenstand; ~ **matter insured** Versicherungsgegenstand; ~ **matter of patent** patentfähiger Gegenstand.

sublease Unterpacht, -miete, -vermietung;
~ *(v.)* part of its production Produktionsaufträge teilweise bei Fremdbetrieben unterbringen.

sublettee Untermieter.

subletter Untervermieter.

subliminal advertising unterschwellige Werbung.

subminimum rate untertariflicher Lohn.

submission Schiedsgerichtsvereinbarung, *(bidding)* Submission;
~ **of account** Rechnungsvorlage; ~ **of proof of identity** Identitätsnachweis.

submit | *(v.)* an application Gesuch einreichen; ~ **goods to a careful examination** Waren einer genauen Untersuchung unterwerfen; ~ **proof of identity** Identitätsnachweis führen; ~ **a statement of one's affairs** Liquidationsbilanz aufstellen; ~ **a tender** Offerte unterbreiten.

subordinate | **interests** untergeordnete Interessen; ~ **partner** *(Br.)* nicht persönlich haftender Gesellschafter.

subordinated | **debt** im Range nachgehender Forderung; ~ **offer** verstecktes Angebot.

subrogation assignment Abtretungserklärung.

subscribe *(v.)* beitragen, -steuern, *(loan, shares)* zeichnen, *(newspaper)* abonnieren, vorbestellen, subskribieren, *(sign)* unterschreiben, unterzeichnen;
~ **an amount** Geldsumme aussetzen; ~ **to a relief fund** für einen Unterstützungsfonds Geld stiften.

subscribed gezeichnet;
to be ~ **several times** mehrfach überzeichnet sein; ~ **capital stock** Nominalkapital; ~ **risk** *(insurance)* übernommene Gefahr.

subscriber Abonnent, Bezieher, Subskribent, *(loan)* Zeichner, *(signer)* Unterzeichner, *(tel.)* Fernsprechteilnehmer;
original ~ Stammaktionär;
~ **to charity** Spender; ~ **to a periodical** Zeitschriftenabonnent;
~ **analysis** Abonnentenanalyse; ~**s' insurance** Abonnentenversicherung; ~**'s line** Anschlußleitung, Telefon-, Fernsprechanschluß; ~**'s number** Teilnehmernummer; ~ **trunk dialling** *(Br.)* Selbstwählfernverkehr.

subscription *(amount subscribed)* Subskriptionssumme, Beitrag, Gebühr, *(for shares)* [Anteils]zeichnung, *(member, Br.)* Mitgliedsbeitrag, *(newspaper)* Bezug, Abonnement, Subskription;
by ~ im Abonnement; **by public** ~ im Wege einer öffentlichen Sammlung;
annual ~ Jahresabonnement; **charitable** ~ Spende für wohltätige Zwecke; **deductible** ~ steuerabzugsfähiger Beitrag;
~ **to stock** *(US)* Aktienzeichnung; ~ **to charity** wohltätige Spende; ~ **by conversion of securities** Bezugsrecht bei Anleiheumwandlung; ~ **for new shares** *(Br.)* Bezug junger Aktien;
to be offered for ~ zur Zeichnung aufliegen; **to drop one's** ~ Abonnement aufgeben; **to get up a** ~ Sammlung ins Leben rufen; **to raise the** ~ Beitragserhöhung vornehmen; **to take out a year's** ~ Jahresabonnement nehmen;
~ **agent** *(US)* Abonnentenwerber; ~ **blank** *(US)* Subskriptionsvordruck, Zeichnungsformular; ~ **charge** Subskriptionsgebühr; ~ **costs** Bezugsgebühren; ~ **fee** Abonnenten-, Subskriptionspreis; ~ **form** *(order form)* Bestellschein; ~ **list** *(newspaper)* Zeichnungsliste, *(shares)* Subskriptionsliste; ~ **offer** Zeichnungsangebot; ~ **period** Bezugsdauer; ~ **price** Subskriptions-, Bezugspreis; ~ **privilege** *(US)* Zeichnungsberechtigung; ~ **right** Bezugs-, Optionsrecht; ~ **sale** Abonnementsverkauf; ~ **warrant** *(US)* Bezugsrecht, Subskriptionsschein.

subsequent | **additions** *(balance sheet)* Zugänge; ~ **assessment** Nachveranlagung; ~ **endorser** Hintermann; ~ **insurance** Nachversicherung; ~ **mortgage** nachrangige Hypothek.

subsidiary Tochtergesellschaft, Ableger, Filiale;
major ~ Hauptniederlassung;

~ **account** Hilfskonto; ~ **activity** Nebentätigkeit; ~ **bodies** nachgeordnete Stellen; ~ **company (corporation)** Tochter-, Organgesellschaft; ~ **journal** Hilfskontobuch; ~ **payments** Hilfsleistungen auf finanziellem Gebiet; ~ **retail business** Zweiggeschäft; ~ **source of income** zusätzliche Einkommensquelle; ~ **treaty** Subsidienvertrag; ~ **worker** Hilfskraft, -arbeiter.

subsidies *(state)* Subsidien, Hilfsgelder.

subsidize *(v.)* durch Staatsgelder unterstützen, subventionieren, aus öffentlichen Geldern fördern, Zuschuß gewähren.

subsidized | **export** subventionierter Export; ~ **housing** Wohnungsbauhilfe; ~ **lunch** Verpflegungszuschuß.

subsidy *(allowance)* Zuschuß, *(subvention)* [Staats]-subvention, Subsidien, Beihilfe aus öffentlichen Geldern, öffentlicher Zuschuß; **governmental** ~ Staatszuschuß; **nonasset-creating** ~ nichtvermögenswirksame Zuschüsse; ~ **fund** Unterstützungsfonds; ~ **requirements** Zuschußbedarf.

subsistence Existenz, [Lebens]unterhalt, *(provisioning)* Versorgung, Verpflegung; **reasonable** ~ angemessener Unterhalt; ~ **allowance** Unterhaltszuschuß; ~ **level** Existenzminimum; **bare** ~ **wage** Lohnminimum.

substandard unter der gesetzlich vorgeschriebenen Norm, unterdurchschnittlich; ~ **business** *(life insurance)* Risikogeschäft; ~ **goods** Ausschußware; ~ **housing** Elendsquartier; ~ **risk** anomales Risiko.

substantial | **business firm** solide (kapitalkräftige) Firma; ~ **damages** Schadenersatz für tatsächlich eingetretenen Schaden; ~ **landlord** Großgrundbesitzer.

substitute *(imitation)* Nachahmung, *(material)* Ersatz[mittel], Surrogat, Austauschwerkstoff; ~ **for travel** Reiseersatz, -spesen; ~ **performance** Ersatzvornahme.

subtenant Untermieter, -pächter.

suburb Vorstadt, Außenbezirk; **high-income** ~ wohlhabendes Viertel.

suburban | **apartment** Vorstadtwohnung; ~ **traffic** Vorortverkehr; ~ **train** Vorortzug.

subway Straßenunterführung, *(Br.)* Fußgängertunnel; ~ **system** *(US)* Untergrundbahnnetz.

success, box-office Kassenschlager.

succession *(estate of deceased person)* Nachlaß, Erbfall, *(office)* Nachfolge im Amt; ~ **of crops** Fruchtwechsel; ~ **duty** *(US)* Erbschafts-, Erbanfallsteuer, *(Br.)* Erbschaftssteuer für unbewegliches Vermögen.

successor company Nachfolgegesellschaft.

sudden chance *(stock exchange)* Umschwung.

sue *(v.)* gerichtlich belangen, Klage anstrengen; ~ **for claims on bills of exchange** Wechselforderungen einklagen; ~ **for damages** Schadenersatzklage anstrengen;

~ **and labo(u)r clause** *(marine insurance)* Selbstbehaltsklausel.

suffer | *(v.)* **a slight decline** *(stock exchange)* leichten Rückgang erfahren; ~ **a depreciation** Wertminderung erfahren.

sufferance *(customs, Br.)* Zollvergünstigung; **to leave in** ~ [Wechsel] nicht honorieren; ~ **wharf** *(Br.)* Freihafenniederlage.

sufficiency hinlängliches Auskommen, Unterhalt; ~ **of fuel** genügend Betriebsstoff.

sufficient genügend, hinlänglich, ausreichend; **not** ~ *(bill, check)* ungenügende Deckung; ~ **in numbers** *(quorum)* beschlußfähig.

suggestion, credit Kreditvorschlag; ~**s for improvement** Verbesserungsvorschläge; ~ **box** Beschwerdebriefkasten; ~ **scheme** *(US)* betriebliches Vorschlagswesen.

suit Rechtsstreitigkeit, Prozeß, Klage; ~ **on dumping** Dumpingverfahren.

sum Summe, [Geld]betrag, Posten; ~ **assured** Versicherungssumme; **lump** ~ Pauschalsumme; ~ **reserved** Rückstellungsbetrag; ~**s due from banks** *(balance sheet)* Bankguthaben; ~ **of the digits** digitale Abschreibung; ~ **chargeable to reserve** aus der Rücklage zu deckender Betrag; **to lend small** ~**s** kleine Beträge ausleihen; **to pay over a** ~ Summe abführen.

summarized balance sheet Bilanzauszug.

summarizing | **account** Sammelkonto; ~ **sheet** [tabellarische] Zusammenstellung.

summary kurze Inhaltsangabe, Abriß, *(abstract)* Auszug; **periodic** ~ periodischer Bilanzauszug; ~ **of balance sheet changes** Ausweis über die Verwendung des Grundkapitals; ~ **account** Übersichts-, Sammelkonto.

summarily, to dismiss fristlos entlassen.

summit organization Spitzenverband.

summon *(v.)* vorladen, vor Gericht zitieren; ~ **s. o. for debt** j. auf Bezahlung einer Schuld verklagen.

summons to pay Zahlungsbefehl.

Sunday opening Offenhalten am Sonntag.

sundries | **account** Spesenkonto, Konto für Diverse; ~ **debit form** Spesenbelastungsformular.

sundry | **debtors** diverse Debitoren; ~ **money owing** verschiedene Schuldbeträge; ~ **samples** Musterauswahl; ~ **securities** *(market report)* Nebenwerte.

sundryman Krämer, Gemischtwarenhändler.

superannuate *(v.)* Pensionierungsalter erreichen, *(send into retirement)* in den Ruhestand versetzen.

superannuated management pensionsreifer Vorstand.

superannuation Ruhegehalt, Pension, Alterszulage; ~ **allowance** Pension, Ruhegehalt; ~ **fund** Pensionskasse.

supercommission Superprovision.

superfluity of money Geldüberhang.

superintendence Oberaufsicht, Überwachung.

superintendent of agents *(insurance)* Bezirksdirektor.

superior *(a.)* vorzüglich, überlegen, *(in rank)* rangälter, vorgesetzt;
~ **articles** erstklassige Ware; ~ **quality** vorzügliche Beschaffenheit.
supermarket großes Lebensmittelgeschäft mit Selbstbedienung, Selbstbedienungsladen.
supernumerary überzählig, außeretatsmäßig.
supertax *(Br.)* Zusatz-, Über-, Mehrgewinnsteuer, *(income tax)* Einkommensteuerzuschlag.
supervision Überwachung, Aufsichtsführung;
disciplinary ~ Dienstaufsicht;
~ **of cartels** Kartellaufsicht; ~ **of manufacture** Fertigungskontrolle; ~ **of the stock exchange** Börsenaufsicht.
supervisor in a factory Betriebsaufseher, Werksleiter.
supervisory body Kontrollorgan.
supplement Zusatz, Ergänzung, Nachtrag, *(extra charge)* Preisaufschlag;
commercial ~ Handelsbeilage; **Exchequer** ~**s** *(Br.)* Staatszuschüsse zur Sozialversicherung.
supplemental | **appropriation** Nachtragsbewilligung;
~ **cost** Preisaufschlag; ~ **wages** Lohnzulage.
supplementary | **advertising** Ergänzungswerbung; ~ **allowance** Zusatzrente; ~ **banking functions** irreguläre Bankgeschäfte; ~ **benefit** *(Br.)* Sozialhilfe, staatliche Fürsorge; ~ **entry** Nachtragsbuchung; ~ **fee** *(post)* Nachgebühr; ~ **income** Nebenverdienst; ~ **load** Beiladung; ~ **order** Nachbestellung; ~ **policy** Nachtragspolice; ~ **sickness insurance** Krankenzusatzversicherung.
supplied | **daily** täglich beliefert; ~ **to trade only** Lieferung nur an Wiederverkäufer.
supplier Auslieferer, Lieferant;
~**s** *(balance sheet)* Lieferantenschulden;
regular ~ Stammlieferant;
~ **of addresses** Adressenverlag; ~ **of services** Erbringer von Dienstleistungen;
~ **company** Zulieferungsbetrieb; ~'**s financing** Lieferantenfinanzierung.
supplies *(allowance)* Unterhaltungszuschuß, *(balance sheet)* [Hilfs]material, Hilfs- und Betriebsstoffe, *(goods furnished)* Lieferungen, Belieferung, *(grant of money, Br.)* bewilligter Etat;
adequate ~ ausreichende Vorräte; **money** ~ Geldangebot;
~ **in a factory** Materiallager; ~ **on a deferred payment basis** *(US)* Warenlieferungen auf Abzahlungsbasis;
to cut off s. one's ~ jem. (den Zuschuß sperren); **to withhold** ~ **from a dealer** Händler nicht mehr beliefern;
~ **industry** Zulieferungsindustrie.
supply *(allowance)* Zuschuß, Beitrag, *(demand)* Angebot, *(provision)* [Be]lieferung, Eindeckung, Beschaffung, *(store)* Vorrat, Lager;
aggregate ~ Gesamtangebot; **essential** ~ lebenswichtiger Bedarf; **fresh** ~ Nachschub; **fuel** ~ Benzinversorgung; **a month's** ~ Monatsbedarf; **rival** ~ Konkurrenzangebot; **visible** ~ dem Markt zur Verfügung stehende Warenmenge;
~ **and demand** Angebot und Nachfrage;

~ **of capital** Kapitalbereitstellung; ~ **of energy** Energieversorgung; ~ **of goods** Güterversorgung; ~ **on hand** vorhandene Vorräte; ~ **of raw material** Rohstoffversorgung; ~ **of power** Stromversorgung;
~ *(v.)* *(fill as substitute)* als Ersatzmann einspringen, *(pay additionally)* nachzahlen, nachschießen, *(procure)* be-, verschaffen, liefern, Lieferant sein, besorgen;
~ **an article from abroad** Ware von außerhalb beziehen; ~ **the deficiency** Defizit decken; ~ **the public demand** einem öffentlichen Bedürfnis genügen; ~ **electricity to a town** Stromversorgung einer Stadt übernehmen; ~ **a family** Familie unterhalten; ~ **an interpreter** Dolmetscher stellen; ~ **the needs** Bedarf decken; ~ **a ship with provisions** Schiff verproviantieren; ~ **only to wholesalers** nur den Großhandel beliefern;
to cut off ~ Zufuhr abschneiden; **to hold a post on** ~ Stellung vorübergehend innehaben; **to stay well ahead of** ~ Nachfrage nicht befriedigen können;
~ **agreement** Lieferabkommen; ~ **area** Versorgungsgebiet; ~ **business** Zulieferungsindustrie; ~ **center** *(US)* (centre, *Br.)* Versorgungsstelle; **to defer fulfilment of** ~ **contracts** Erfüllung von Lieferungsverträgen aussetzen; ~ **curve** Angebotskurve; ~ **line** Nachschubweg; ~ **office** Beschaffungsamt; ~ **position** Versorgungslage; ~ **price** Angebotspreis; **electric** ~ **service** Stromversorgung; **tight** ~ **situation** angespannte Versorgungslage; ~ **store** Auslieferungslager; ~ **undertaking** Zuschußbetrieb.
support Unterstützung, Hilfe[stellung], *(stock exchange)* Stützungsaktion;
without government ~ ohne Staatszuschuß;
banking ~ Stützungsaktion durch die Banken;
price ~ Preisstützung;
~ *(v.)* unterstützen, unterhalten;
~ **o. s.** seinen Lebensunterhalt selbst verdienen; ~ **by taxes** aus Steuern finanzieren;
to be one's family's sole ~ alleiniger Versorger seiner Familie sein; **to offer a salary and** ~ **for the year** Gehalt und Lebensunterhalt für ein Jahr anbieten;
~ **buying** *(stock exchange)* Interessenkäufe; ~ **costs** Unterhaltungskosten.
supported price Stützungspreis.
supporting | **order** Interventionsauftrag, Stützungskäufe; ~ **schedule** erläuternde Aufstellung [für die Steuererklärung].
suppression of a newspaper Beschlagnahme einer Zeitung.
surcharge *(advertising)* Preisaufschlag für Placierungswünsche, *(exessive charge)* Überforderung, -teuerung, *(extra charge)* Zuschlag[sgebühr], Gebührenzuschlag, Abgabe, *(postage)* Straf-, Zuschlags-, Nachporto;
~ **of electricity** Mehrverbrauch an Strom; ~ **on imports** Einfuhrabgabe;
~ *(v.)* überfordern, -teuern, *(postage)* Nachporto erheben.

surety Bürgschaft[sleistung], Garantie-, Bürgschaftsschein, *(guaranty)* Sicherheit, Pfand, Kaution;

joint ~ Solidarbürgschaft, -bürge;

~ **for the payment of a bill** Wechselbürgschaft; **to become (go)** ~ bürgen, Bürgschaft übernehmen; ~ **acceptance** Avalakzept; ~ **bond** Garantieverpflichtung; ~ **commission** Garantieprovision; ~ **company** *(US)* Kautionsversicherungsgesellschaft; ~ **credit** Avalkredit; ~ **losses** *(balance sheet)* Verluste aus Bürgschaftsverpflichtungen.

surface | **mail** *(Br.)* Gesamtpost außer Luftpost; ~ **traffic** Land- und Binnenwasserverkehr; ~ **working** Tagebau.

surge | **of capacity** Kapazitätszunahme; ~ **in orders** Auftragsflut; ~ **in sales** Verkaufswelle; ~ *(v.)* **ahead** *(prices)* plötzlich steigen.

surplus Überfluß, *(balance sheet, US)* Rücklagen, *(exceeding amount)* Überschuß, Mehrertrag, Plus, *(excess profit)* Gewinnüberschuß, *(excess value)* Mehrwert, *(undivided profit)* unverteilter Reingewinn;

accumulated ~ Kapitalreserve; ~ **agriculture** ~ Überschüsse der Landwirtschaft; **appropriated** ~ *(US)* zweckgebundene Rücklage; **balance-of-payments** ~ Zahlungsbilanzüberschuß; ~ **brought forward** Gewinnvortrag; **divisible** ~ *(life insurance)* Dividendenguthaben; **donated** ~ stehengelassener Gewinn; **earned** ~ *(US)* thesaurierter Gewinn, freie Rücklage; **dated unearned** ~ Geschäftsgewinn ab Sanierung; **unappropriated earned** ~ unverteilter Reingewinn, *(balance sheet, US)* Gewinnvortrag, -rücklage; **free** ~ *(insurance)* freie Rücklage; **gross** ~ Bruttoüberschuß; **life-insurance** ~ Prämien-, Dividendenguthaben; **reappraisal** ~ Wertänderungsgewinn;

~ **of appreciation** Gewinn aus einer Buchwerterhöhung; ~ **of assets over liabilities** Bilanzüberschuß; ~ **from consolidation** Konsolidierungsgewinn; ~ **of exports** Exportüberschuß; ~ **of spending power** überschüssige Kaufkraft;

~ **account** Gewinnüberschußkonto; ~ **accumulation** Gewinnansammlung; ~ **area** [wirtschaftliches] Überschußgebiet; ~ **assets** *(Br.)* Liquidationswert einer Gesellschaft; ~ **capacity** freie Kapazität; ~ **contingency reserve** Verlustreserve; ~ **dividend** *(US)* außerordentliche Dividende; ~ **earnings** *(US)* unverteilter Reingewinn; ~ **fund** *(US)* außerordentlicher Reservefonds; ~ **manpower** Überschuß an Arbeitskräften; ~ **profit** *(US)* unverteilter Reingewinn; ~ **receipts** Einnahmeüberschuß; ~ **reinsurance** Exzedentenrückversicherung; ~ **reserve** *(US)* zweckgebundene Rücklage; ~ **statement** Gewinnverwendungsrechnung; ~ **value** Mehr-, Überwert, *(taxation)* freies Einkommen über dem Existenzminimum.

surrender Aufgabe, Preisabgabe, Verzicht;

~ **of a bankrupt's property** Übertragung der Konkursmasse auf die Gläubiger; ~ **of a charter** Konzessionsverzicht; ~ **of profits** Gewinnabführung;

~ *(v.)* übergeben, aushändigen, *(real-estate law)* [Grundstück] auflassen;

~ **an insurance [policy]** Lebensversicherungspolice zurückkaufen; ~ **a ship** Schiff aufgeben; —**of-profit agreement** Gewinnabführungsvertrag; ~ **value** *(life insurance)* Rückkaufswert.

surrounding risk gefahrerhöhende Nachbarschaft.

surtax Zusatz-, Zuschlagsteuer, Steuerzuschlag, -aufschlag, Ergänzungsabgabe;

~ *(v.)* Zuschlagsteuer erheben;

~ **brackets** Mehreinkommensteuerstufe; ~ **net income** *(US)* Nettoeinkommen nach Abzug der Steuerfreibeträge.

survey Sachverständigengutachten, *(inspection)* Besichtigung, *(market research)* Marktuntersuchung, -analyse;

cadastral ~ Katasterplan; **consumer** ~ Verbraucherumfrage; **dealer** ~ Händlerbefragung; **fresh** ~ Nachvermessung;

~ **of productiveness** Rentabilitätsbild;

~ *(v.)* **a building** Gebäude amtlich abnehmen; ~ **and value a parish** Einheitswerte in einer Gemeinde festlegen;

~ **certificate** Besichtigungsschein; ~ **charges** Vermessungsgebühren; ~ **report** *(of ship)* Havarie-, Schadenszertifikat.

surveying officer Vermessungsbeamter.

surveyor *(architect, Br.)* [ausführender] Architekt, Baumeister, *(clerk of works)* Bauleiter, *(customs, US)* Zollaufseher, -inspektor, *(of ships)* Havariekommissar;

quantitiy ~ *(Br.)* Preiskalkulator;

~ **of the mines** Bergwerksinspektor; **land** ~ **and valuer** Katasterbeamter; ~ **of weights and measures** *(Br.)* Eichmeister;

~**'s fees** Bauabnahmegebühren.

survival | **tables** Sterbetafeln; ~ **value** Erhaltungswert.

surviving company übernehmende Gesellschaft.

survivor | **s' benefit** *(US)* Leistungen an Hinterbliebene; ~**s' insurance** *(US)* Hinterbliebenenversicherung.

survivorship annuity Überlebensrente.

suspend *(v.)* | **a cashier pending investigation** Kassierer während der Untersuchung beurlauben; ~ **payment of one's debt** seine Zahlungen einstellen.

suspended | **account** transitorisches Konto; ~ **pocket filing** Hängeregistratur.

suspense Unentschiedenheit, Schwebe;

to keep a bill in ~ Wechsel Not leiden lassen;

~ **account** transitorisches Konto, Interimskonto; ~ **entries** transitorische Buchungen; ~ **item** offenstehender Posten, *(balance sheet)* Rechnungsabgrenzungsposten.

suspension Aufschub, einstweilige Aufhebung, vorläufige Einstellung;

~ **of air service** Einstellung des Flugverkehrs; ~ **of an automobile** Abmeldung eines Kraftfahrzeugs; ~ **of a bank** Liquidation einer Bank; ~ **of business** Einstellung des Geschäftsbetriebes; ~ **of** the gold standard Aufhebung des Goldstandards; ~ of payments Zahlungseinstellung; ~ of the statute of limitations Unterbrechung der Verjährung; ~ of work Arbeitseinstellung.

sustain | (v.) competition es mit der Konkurrenz aufnehmen; ~ a loss Verlust erleiden.

sutaining program (US) rundfunkeigene Sendung.

sustentation fund Unterstützungsfonds.

swamped | with orders mit Aufträgen überschüttet; to be ~ with debts bis über die Ohren in Schulden stecken.

swap [Devisen]swap, Tausch-, Swapgeschäft; ~ arrangement Swapabkommen; ~ rate Swapsatz.

swear (v.) an estate at $ 100 000 Nachlaßwert mit 100 000 Dollar angeben.

sweat (v.) (labo(u)rers) ausbeuten, schinden, schlecht bezahlen; ~ a practitioner Praktikanten ausnutzen.

sweated | industries unterbezahlte Industriezweige; ~ money Hungerlohn.

sweating Lohndrückerei, Ausbeutung.

sweatshop (US sl.), Ausbeutungsbetrieb.

sweep (v.) the board ganzen Gewinn einstreichen; to make a clean ~ of one's staff sein gesamtes Personal auswechseln.

sweeten (v.) a loan (US) hochwertige Aktien lombardieren.

swindling, insurance Versicherungsbetrug.

swing (trade agreement) Swing, Kreditmarge; in full ~ in vollem Betrieb (Gang); market ~ Konjunkturumschwung; to be given full ~ in the conduct of business voll in die Geschäftsführung eingeschaltet werden; to

live in the full ~ of prosperity Hochkonjunktur erleben; ~ credit kurzfristiger Auslandskredit.

switch (economy) Umstellung, (exchange trade) Switchgeschäft; ~ (v.) (export trade) Switchgeschäfte machen; ~ into growth stock in Wachstumswerte umsteigen; ~ out of stocks into high-yielding bonds aus Aktien in hochverzinsliche Obligationen umsteigen.

sworn appraiser vereidigter Sachverständiger.

sympathetic strike Solidaritäts-, Sympathiestreik.

syndicate Konsortium, Syndikat, Verband; banking ~ Bankenkonsortium; market ~ Börsensyndikat; original ~ (US) Übernahmekonsortium; underwriting ~ Emissionskonsortium; ~ account Beteiligungs-, Konsortialkonto; ~ agreement Konsortialvertrag; ~ business Konsortialgeschäft; ~ company Immobilienbeteiligungsgesellschaft; ~ credit (loan) Konsortialkredit; ~ manager Konsortialführer; ~ transaction Konsortialgeschäft.

system, accounting Buchführungswesen; clearing ~ Verrechnungssystem; currency ~ Währungssystem; dial ~ Selbstwählverkehr; domestic ~ Heimindustrie; inland-transport ~ Binnentransportwesen; manifold ~ Vervielfältigungsmethode; quota ~ Kontingentierungswesen; ~ of arbitration Schlichtungswesen; ~ of payment by results Akkordlohnsystem.

systematic | advertising zielbewußte Werbung; ~ sampling systematische Marktuntersuchung.

tab 192

T

tab Etikett, Schildchen, Anhänger, Kartenreiter, *(US, account)* Konto, Rechnung;
to foot the ~ Rechnung bezahlen; **to keep ~s on the expenses** Spesenwirtschaft im Auge behalten; **to keep ~s on the state of the economy** Konjunkturpolitik im Griff behalten.

table Verzeichnis, Liste, Tabelle;
conversion ~ Umrechnungstabelle; **mortality** ~ Sterblichkeitstabelle; **redemption** ~ Tilgungsplan; **wage-tax** ~ Tabelle zur Berechnung der Lohnsteuer;
~ **of charges** Gebührenverzeichnis; ~ **of depreciation** Abschreibungstabelle; ~ **of fares** Eisenbahntarif; ~ **of insurance** Versicherungstarif; ~ **of interest** Zinstabelle; ~ **of parities** Paritätentafel; ~ **of wages** Lohntabelle;
~ *(v.)* Tabelle anlegen, in eine Liste eintragen, in ein Verzeichnis aufnehmen;
~ **board** *(US)* Verpflegung, Kost.

tabloid paper Boulevardblatt.

tabular | **bookkeeping** *(US)* amerikanische Buchführung; ~ **composition** Tabellensatz; ~ **standard** Preisindexwährung; ~ **value** Tabellenwert.

tabularize *(v.)* tabellieren, tabellarisch anordnen.

tack *(lease)* Pachtvertrag;
~ *(v.)* **securities** *(Br.)* Sicherheiten zusammenfassen.

tacking *(mortgage, Br.)* Hypothekenvereinigung, *(securities)* Zusammenfassung.

tag Etikette, [Bezeichnungs]schild, *(label indicating price)* Preisauszeichnung, -zettel, *(luggage)* Gepäckanhänger, -zettel, *(luggage)* Gepäckanhänger, Gepäckadresse.

licence ~ Steuermarke;
~ *(v.)* auszeichnen, etikettieren, mit Preiszetteln versehen;
~ **addresser** Gepäckanhänger.

take *(Br., leasing)* Pachtland, *(theater)* Kasse, Einnahme;
~ *(v.)* **in advance** im Vorverkauf erwerben; ~ **legal advice** sich anwaltlich beraten lassen; ~ **a broadcast on tape** Rundfunksendung auf Band aufnehmen; ~ **for the call** Vorprämie verkaufen; ~ **the chair** Präsidium übernehmen; ~ **on credit** anschreiben lassen; ~ **a day off** sich einen Tag frei nehmen; ~ **discount** Diskont in Anspruch nehmen; ~ **on discount** diskontieren, in Diskont nehmen; ~ **the public fancy** beim Publikum sehr gut aufgenommen werden; ~ **firm** fest übernehmen; ~ **an interest in an enterprise** sich an einem Unternehmen finanziell beteiligen; ~ **lodgings** sich einmieten; ~ **a loss** Verlust erleiden; ~ **a newspaper** Zeitung halten; ~ **office** Büroräume mieten; ~ **s. o. into partnership** j. als Teilhaber aufnehmen; ~ **for the put** Rückprämie kaufen; ~ **a ship** sich einschiffen; ~ **stock** Lagerbestand aufnehmen; ~ **$ 400 a week** wöchentlich 400 Dollar verdienen.

take away customers Kunden abfangen.

take in Aufnahme gewähren, *(goods)* hereinnehmen, *(stock exchange)* *(Br.)* in (Prolongation) nehmen;
~ **cargo** Ladung einnehmen; ~ **part payment** sich mit Teilzahlungen einverstanden erklären.

take into account einberechnen, -kalkulieren.

take off *(airplane)* abfliegen, starten, *(bus)* aus dem Verkehr ziehen, *(deduct)* [Preis]senken;
~ **a trial balance** Rohbilanz erstellen; ~ **a ship off the active list** Schiff außer Dienst stellen.

take on | **charter** chartern; ~ **credit** anschreiben lassen; ~ **extra work** zusätzliche Arbeiten übernehmen.

take out | **of bond** aus dem Zollverschluß nehmen;
~ **a licence** sich eine Lizenz geben lassen; ~ **summons** Zahlungsbefehl erwirken.

take over | **the assets and liabilities** mit Aktien und Passiven übernehmen; ~ **the railways** Eisenbahn verstaatlichen.

take up | **an agency** Vertretung übernehmen; ~ **a bill** Wechsel honorieren; ~ **money** Geld aufnehmen; ~ **an option** Bezugsrecht ausüben; ~ **under rebate** *(Br.)* Wechsel diskontieren; ~ **shares** Aktien beziehen.

take-home pay Lohntüte, Netto-, Effektivlohn.

take-over, takeover *(management)* Übernahme der Geschäftsführung;
~ **agreement** Übernahmevertrag; ~ **price** Übernahmepreis.

taker Abnehmer, Käufer, Kunde;
~ **of a bill** Wechselnehmer; ~ **for a call** Verkäufer einer Vorprämie; ~ **of an option** Optionsnehmer; ~**in** Heimarbeiter, *(factory)* Faktor, *(stock exchange, Br.)* Hereinnehmer, Kostnehmer.

taking Entnehmen, Entnahme, *(receipts)* [Geld]einnahme, *(ship)* Aufbringung;
inventory ~ Bestandsaufnahme, Inventur; ~ **an order** Auftragsannahme; ~ **a risk** Risikoübernahme; ~ **samples** Musterziehung;
~ **over of a business** Geschäftsübernahme; ~ **up bills under rebate** *(Br.)* Wechseldiskontierung.

takings Einnahmen, Eingänge, Einkünfte;
to check the day's ~ Kassensturz machen.

talk, confidential vertrauliches Gespräch;
~**s about entry** Beitrittsverhandlungen; ~**s about** ~**s** *(US)* Sondierungsgespräche;
~ **s. o. into buying s. th.** jem. etw. aufschwatzen; **to squelch** ~ **of a liquidity pinch** um das Liquiditätsgerede zu beenden.

tally *(account)* Rechnung, [monatliche] Abrechnung, *(coupon)* Kupon, *(label)* Etikett, Schild, Anhänger, Kennzeichen, *(list of goods)* Warenliste, *(pass book)* Gegenbuch [des Kunden];
by the ~ nach dem Stück;
~ *(v.)* kontrollieren, abhaken, *(count by the piece)* [Ladung] stückweise nachzählen, *(label)* Waren bezeichnen, etikettieren;
to buy by the 100 ~ hundertstückweise kaufen;

~ **business** *(Br.)* [einzelnes] Abzahlungsgeschäft; ~ **clerk** Frachtkontrolleur, ~ **out** *(US)* Lieferschein; ~ **sheet** *(US)* Kontrolliste; ~ **shop** *(Br.)* Abzahlungsgeschäft.

talon *(Br.)* Erneuerungsschein, Talon, Zinskupon; ~ **tax** *(Br.)* Talonsteuer.

tamper *(v.)* **with the cash** sich an der Kasse vergreifen.

tampering of a balance sheet Bilanzfrisur.

tangible | **assets** körperliche Wirtschaftsgüter, greifbare Vermögenswerte, Sachanlagevermögen; ~ **value** *(going concern)* Betriebswert.

tanker fleet Tankerflotte.

tap *(brand, fam.)* Sorte, Marke, *(pub)* Schankwirtschaft, Schenke;
on ~ auf Lager, verfügbar;
~ *(v.)* **capital** Kapital angreifen; ~ **the money market heavily** Geldmarkt stark in Anspruch nehmen; ~ **issue** *(treasury bills, Br.)* Placierung außerhalb des Publikumsverkehrs; ~ **rate** *(Br.)* Diskontsatz für kurzfristige Schatzwechsel.

tape Papierband [des Börsentelegrafs], *(recording)* Ton-, Magnetofonband;
red ~ Bürokratismus, Amtsschimmel;
~ **abbreviations** Börsenabkürzungen; ~ **machine** *(Br.)* [Börsen]fernschreiber; ~ **price** notierter Kurs; ~ **quotations** Kabelnotierungen.

tare tote Last, Tara;
average ~ Durchschnittstara; **customs** ~ Zollgewicht; **real** ~ Nettotara;
~ **and tret** Tara und Gutgewicht;
~ *(v.)* Tara in Abzug bringen (vergüten);
~ **account (note)** Abgangs-, Tararechnung; ~ **weight** Taragewicht.

target wirtschaftliches Planziel, Soll, Vorgabe;
output ~ Produktionsziel;
~ **audience** Zielgruppe; ~ **cost** vorkalkulierte Kosten; ~ **date** Abschlußtermin, Stichtag; ~ **price** *(EC)* Übernahme-, Vertragspreis.

tariff Zoll[tarif], Zollverzeichnis, *(list of charges)* Taxe, Tarif, *(Br., prices in restaurant)* Preisliste;
agricultural ~ Agrarzoll; **bargaining** ~ Verhandlungstarif; **compound** ~ gemischter Zolltarif; **contractual** ~ Vertragszoll; **countervailing** ~ Ausgleichszoll; **electricity** ~ Stromtarif; **exceptional** ~ *(Br.)* Ausnahmetarif; **flexible** ~ Staffel-, Stufentarif; **hotel** ~ *(Br.)* Zimmerpreise; **local** ~ Binnentarif; **most-favo(u)red-nation** ~ Meistbegünstigungstarif; **preferential** ~ Vorzugszoll; **protective** ~ Schutzzoll; **railway (railroad,** *US)* Frachttarif; **retaliatory** ~ Vergeltungszoll; **revenue** ~ Finanz-, Einfuhrzoll; **sliding-scale** ~ Gleitzoll; **time-of-the-day** ~ *(Br.)* Nachtstromtarif; **valuation** ~ Wertberechnungsskala;
~ **of fares** Fahrpreisverzeichnis;
~ *(v.)* Tarifwert festsetzen, taxieren, *(customs)* mit Zoll belegen, *(fix a price)* Preis festsetzen;
to increase the ~ Zölle erhöhen; **to subject to** ~ den Zollbestimmungen unterwerfen;
~ **adjustment** Zollangleichung; ~ **agreement** Zollabkommen; ~ **barriers** Zollschranken; ~**-bound**

zollpflichtig; ~ **concession** Tarifzugeständnis; ~**-cutting agreement** Zollsenkungsabkommen; ~ **discrimination** benachteiligende Zollbehandlung; ~ **duty** Zolltarif, Tarifzoll; ~ **heading** Position des Zolltarifs, ~ **item** Tarifposition; ~ **negotiations** Zollverhandlungen; ~ **plank** Tarifgrundsätze; ~ **platform** zollpolitische Forderungen; ~ **protection** Schutzzollsystem; ~ **quota** Zollkontingent; ~ **rate** Gebühren-, Zollsatz, Tarifsatz; ~ **revenue** Zolleinnahmen; ~ **rollback** Tarif-, Zollsenkung; **autonomous** ~ **system** Zollautonomie; **to schedule the** ~ **value** *(Br.)* Tarifwert festsetzen; ~ **wall** Zollmauer.

task Aufgabe, *(piece rate)* Mindestleistung;
~ **bonus system** Prämienakkordsystem; ~ **force** *(US)* Arbeitsstab; ~ **master** Vorarbeiter, Aufseher; ~ **wage** Akkord-, Stücklohn.

taskmaster Vorarbeiter, Aufseher.

taskwork Stück-, Akkordarbeit.

tax [Staats]steuer, Abgabe, *(contribution)* Beitrag, *(fee)* Gebühr;
after [**deduction for**] ~**es** nach Abzug der Steuern;
liable to ~ steuerpflichtig;
accumulated-earnings ~ *(US)* Sondersteuer für nicht ausgeschüttete Gewinne; **accrued** ~**es** *(balance sheet)* Steuerschulden; **assessed** ~ veranlagte Steuer; **betterment** ~ *(Br.)* Wertzuwachssteuer; **beverage** ~ Getränkesteuer; **business** ~ Gewerbesteuer; **capital-gains** ~ Kapitalzuwachssteuer; **capital-stock** ~ Vermögenssteuer; **capital-yields** *(Br.)* Kapitalertragssteuer; **corporation [income]** ~ *(US)* Körperschaftssteuer; **death** ~ *(US)* Erbschaftssteuer; **deferred** ~**es** *(balance sheet)* Steuervorauszahlungen; ~ **due** Steuerschuld; **estate** ~ *(US)* Nachlaßsteuer; **excise** ~ *(US)* Sonderumsatz-, Gewerbesteuer; **export** ~ Ausfuhrabgabe; **Federal income** ~ *(US)* Einkommensteuer; **gift** ~ *(US)* Schenkungssteuer; **increment value** ~ Wertzuwachssteuer; **individual income** ~ *(US)* Einkommensteuer; **inheritance** ~ *(US)* Nachlaß-, Erbschaftssteuer; **landed-property** ~ Grundsteuer; **licence** ~ Lizenzgebühr; **local** ~**es** *(US)* Kommunalabgaben; **municipal** ~**es** *(US)* Kommunalabgaben; **nonresident** ~ Kurtaxe; **normal** ~ *(US, income tax)* Basissteuer; **profits** ~ *(Br.)* Körperschaftssteuer; **purchase** ~ *(US)* [Einphasenwaren]umsatzsteuer; **real-estate** ~ *(US)* Grundsteuer; **road-using** ~ Straßennutzungsgebühr; **sales** ~ *(US)* [Waren]umsatzsteuer; **social security** ~ *(US)* Zwangsbeitrag zur Sozialversicherung; **stamp** ~ *(US)* Stempelsteuer; **stock-transfer** ~ *(US)* Börsenumsatzsteuer; **turnover** ~ *(Br.)* Umsatzsteuer; **ad-valorem** ~ *(US)* Wertsteuer; **value-added** ~ Mehrwertsteuer; **wealth** ~ Vermögenssteuer; **withheld** ~**es** einbehaltene Steuern; **withholding** ~ *(US)* Quellen-, Kapitalertragssteuer *(wage earner)* einbehaltene Lohnsteuer;
~ **on consumption** Verbrauchs-, Aufwandsteuer;
~ **on freight transportation** *(US)* Verkehrssteuer;
~ **on income or profits from trades, profession or**

vocation Steuern auf Einkünfte aus selbständiger Arbeit; ~ **on real estate** *(US)* Grund[stücks]-steuer; ~ **on stock-exchange dealings** *(Br.)* **(on stock sales,** *US)* Börsenumsatzsteuer;

~ *(v.) (assess)* veranlagen, festsetzen, taxieren, abschätzen, ansetzen, *(impose a tax)* mit Abgaben (Steuern) belegen, besteuern;

~ **away** wegsteuern; ~ **with a higher rate** mit einem höheren Satz versteuern;

to assess ~**es upon** Steuern festsetzen; **to be liable for income** ~ einkommensteuerpflichtig sein; **to charge back** ~**es** nachträglichen Steuerbescheid erlassen; **to collect** ~**es** Steuern eintreiben; **to defraud a** ~ Steuer hinterziehen; **to drop a** ~ Steuer niederschlagen; **to impose a** ~ **on s. th.** etw. mit Steuer belegen; **to levy a** ~ **on dividend distribution** Kapitalertragssteuer erheben; **to pass on a** ~ Steuer abwälzen; **to pay** ~**es** versteuern; **to relieve from** ~**es** Steuerfreiheit gewähren;

~ **abatement** Steuernachlaß; ~ **accruals** *(US)* Steuerforderungen; ~ **advantage** Steuervorteil; ~ **allowance** *(Br.)* Steuervergünstigung, -freibetrag; ~ **anticipation certificate** *(US)* Steuergutschein; ~ **anticipation notes** *(US)* kleingestückelte Steuergutscheine; ~ **appeal** Steuereinspruch; ~ **assessment** *(Br.)* Steuerveranlagung; ~ **assessor** Veranlagungsstelle; ~ **auditor** *(US)* Steuerprüfer; ~ **avoidance** Steuerumgehung, -vermeidung; ~ **balance sheet** *(US)* Steuerbilanz; ~ **base** Besteuerungsgrundlage, Steuerobjekt; ~ **benefit** steuerliche Vergünstigung; **to put the** ~ **bite on** Steuerschraube anziehen; ~ **bracket** Steuergruppe, -stufe; ~ **break** *(US)* Steuervergünstigung; ~ **burden** Steuerlast; ~ **charge** Steuerbelastung; ~ **class** Steuerklasse; ~ **classification** steuerliche Einstufung; ~ **code** Abgabenordnung; ~ **collection procedure** Steuereinziehungsverfahren; ~ **collector** Steuereinnehmer; ~ **collector's district** Steuerbezirk; ~ **commissioner** *(Br.)* [Steuer]veranlagungsbehörde; ~ **concession** steuerliches Zugeständnis; ~ **consultant** Steuerberater; ~ **counsel[lor]** Helfer in Steuersachen; ~ **credit** *(US)* Steuergutschrift; -freibetrag; ~ **deadline** Steuertermin; ~**deductible** steuerabzugsfähig; ~ **deferral** *(US)* Steuerstundung; ~ **deficit** Steuerausfall; ~ **demand** Steuerbescheid; ~ **dodger** Steuerhinterzieher; ~ **evader** *(US)* Steuerhinterzieher; ~ **evasion** *(US)* Steuerhinterziehung; ~**exempt** *(US)* steuerfrei, -abgabenfrei; ~**exempt amount** *(US)* Steuerfreibetrag; ~ **expert** Steuersachverständiger; ~ **ferrets** Steuerfahndung; ~ **file** Steuerakte; ~**free allowance** *(Br.)* Steuerfreibetrag; ~**free transaction** steuerfreies Wertpapiergeschäft; ~ **haven** Steuerparadies, -oase; ~ **impact** *(Br.)* Steuerbelastung; ~ **lawyer** *(US)* Anwalt in Steuersachen; ~ **liability** Steuerschuld; ~ **list** Hebeliste, *(real-estate tax)* Liste säumiger Steuerzahler; ~ **loophole** steuerliches Hintertürchen; **to declare a** ~ **loss against future earnings** Steuerverlust vortragen; ~ **morale** Steuermoral; ~ **office** *(US)* Finanzamt; ~ **payments**

Steuerzahlungen; ~ **penalty** Steuersäumniszuschlag; **[local]** ~ **power** [kommunales] Besteuerungsrecht; ~ **practitioner** *(Br.)* Steuerberater; ~ **preference income** steuerlich begünstigte Einkünfte; ~**preparation service** Steuerberatungsdienst; ~ **privilege** steuerliche Vergünstigung; ~ **progression** Steuerprogression; **income** ~ **rate** Einkommensteuersatz; ~**rate schedule** Steuertabelle; ~ **rebate for exporters** Ausfuhrsteuerrückvergütung; **flat-rate** ~ **reduction** lineare Steuersenkung; **on-the-spot** ~ **refund** sofortige Steuerrückvergütung; ~ **regulations** steuerrechtliche Bestimmungen; ~ **relief** Steuervergünstigung, *(Br.)* Steuerfreibetrag; ~ **remission bill (certificate)** Steuergutschein; ~ **reserve** Steuerrückstellung; **to prepare an income**- ~ **return** Einkommensteuerformular ausfüllen; ~ **revenue gains** erhöhte Steuereinnahmen; ~ **roll** *(US)* Hebeliste; ~ **savings** Steuerersparnisse; **to offer** ~ **service** seine Dienste als Steuerberater anbieten; ~ **sharing** *(US)* Finanzausgleich; ~ **sheet** Steuerkarte; **to create a** ~ **shelter** einer steuerlichen Belastung ausweichen; ~**shelter deal** steuerbegünstigtes Geschäft; ~ **statement (status)** Steuerbilanz, -status; ~**supported** steuerlich begünstigt; ~ **surcharge** Einkommensteuerzuschlag; ~ **table** [Lohn]steuertabelle; **to benefit** ~**wise** steuerlich profitieren; ~ **withholding** Steuerabzug; ~ **writeoffs** steuerlich zulässige Abschreibungen *(US)*; ~ **yield** Steueranfall.

taxable Steuerpflichtiger;

~ *(a.)* [be]steuerbar, steuer-, abgaben-, veranlagungspflichtig;

to be ~ **as ordinary income** als normales Einkommen zu versteuern sein; ~ **class of goods** steuerpflichtige Waren; ~ **income** steuerpflichtiges Einkommen; ~ **period** Veranlagungszeitraum; ~ **profit** steuerpflichtiger Gewinn; ~ **year** *(US)* Veranlagungs-, Steuerjahr.

taxation Besteuerung, Steuerwesen, *(appraisal)* Abschätzung, [Steuer]veranlagung;

adjusted for ~ steuerbereinigt; **exempt from** ~ steuer-, abgabenfrei;

double ~ Doppelbesteuerung; **future** ~ *(balance sheet, Br.)* Steuerrückstellung; **minimum** ~ Steuermindestsatz; **multiple** ~ *(different states)* Mehrfachbesteuerung; **municipal** ~ Kommunalabgaben; **subsequent** ~ Nachversteuerung;

to allow (make provisions) for ~ Steuerrückstellung vornehmen, für Steuern zurückstellen;

anti-double ~ **agreement** Doppelbesteuerungsabkommen; ~ **cut** Steuersenkung; ~ **equalization reserve** *(balance sheet, Br.)* Steuerausgleichsrücklage; ~ **reserve** Steuerrücklage.

taxeater Wohlfahrts-, Unterstützungsempfänger, *(plant)* staatlich subventionierter Betrieb.

taxed, heavily hochbesteuert;

to be ~ **at lower income rates** zu niedrigen Einkommensteuersätzen veranlagt werden.

taxi [Auto]taxe, Taxi, Kraftdroschke;

~ **aircraft** Flugtaxi; ~ **driver** Taxichauffeur; ~ **stand (rank,** *Br.)* Taxistand, -haltestelle.

taxing | area Steuerdistrikt; ~ **unit** Steuerobjekt, -subjekt.

taxpayer Steuerzahler, -pflichtiger;
~ **in arrears** rückständiger Steuerpflichtiger.

tea | break *(Br.)* Frühstückspause; ~ **shop** *(Br.)* Imbißstube.

team Arbeitsgemeinschaft, -gruppe;
~ **of workmen** Schicht.

tear-off calendar Block-, Abreißkalender.

teaser advertisement *(US)* Rätselreklame.

technical handwerksmäßig, technisch, fachlich, *(stock exchange, US)* manipuliert;
~ **instructor** Gewerbelehrer; ~ **library** Fachbücherei; ~ **manager** technischer Direktor; ~ **sales representative** technischer Verkäufer; ~ **training** Fachschul-, Berufsausbildung.

technological | gap technischer Rückstand, technologische Lücke; ~ **unemployment** entwicklungsmäßig bedingte Arbeitslosigkeit.

telecommunication | satellite Nachrichtensatellit; ~ **traffic** Fernmeldeverkehr.

telegram Telegramm, Drahtnachricht, Depesche;
cipher ~ Schlüsseltelegramm; **decorative** ~ Schmuckblatt-Telegramm; **money-order** ~ telegraphische Geldüberweisung;
~ **delivered by mail** *(Br.)* Brieftelegramm;
to deliver a ~ Telegramm aufgeben; **to inquire by** ~ telegrafisch anfragen;
~ **address** Telegrammadresse; ~ **rate** Wort-, Telegrammgebühr.

telegraph | code Telegrammschlüssel; ~ **form** Depeschen-, Telegrammformular.

telegraphic | acceptance Drahtakzept; ~ **answer** Drahtantwort; ~ **money order** telegrafische Geldanweisung.

telephone Fernsprecher, Telefon;
automatic ~ Selbstanschluß; **inter-office** ~ Hausanlage;
~ *(v.)* telefonieren, Ferngespräch führen;
to be on the ~ telefonisch erreichbar sein;
~ **alphabet** Fernsprechalphabet; **automatic** ~ **answering service** Fernsprechauftragsdienst; ~ **booth** Telefonzelle; ~ **charges** Fernsprechgebühren; ~ **directory** Fernsprech-, Teilnehmerverzeichnis; ~ **exchange** Fernsprechamt, Vermittlung; ~ **information service** Fernsprechauskunftsdienst; ~ **line** Telefonleitung, Anschluß; ~ **number** Fernsprechnummer; ~ **order** telefonisch aufgegebene Bestellung; ~ **reservation** Festzeitgespräch; ~ **trade** *(stock exchange)* Telefonverkehr, -handel; ~ **subscriber** Fernsprechteilnehmer.

teleprinter Fernschreiber;
~ **connection** Fernschreibanschluß; ~ **line** Fernschreibleitung; ~ **user** Fernschreibteilnehmer.

teletype Fernschreiber, *(network)* Fernschreibnetz;
~ **communication** Fernschreibverkehr; ~ **operator** Fernschreiber.

television Fernsehen;
cable ~ Kabelfernsehen; **closed-circuit** ~ innerbetriebliches Fernsehnetz; **commercial** ~ Werbefernsehen;

to broadcast on ~ im Fernsehen übertragen; **to speak on** ~ Fernsehansprache halten;
~ **ad revenues** Fernsehwerbeeinnahmen; ~ **advertising** Werbefernsehen; ~ **announcer** Fernsehkommentator; ~ **broadcast** Fernsehsendung; ~ **channel** Fernsehkanal; ~ **commercial** Fernsehwerbesendung; ~ **course** Unterrichtskurs im Fernsehen; **canned** ~ **item** Fernsehkonserve; ~ **news show** Tagesschau; ~ **pickup van** Fernsehaufnahmewagen; ~ **program(me)** Fernsehprogramm; ~ **ratings** Beliebtheitstest; ~ **rights** Fernsehrechte; ~ **screen** Bild-, Fernsehschirm; ~ **spot commercials** kurze Fernsehwerbesendungen; ~ **station** Fernsehstation, -sender; ~ **transmission** Fernsehübertragung; ~ **viewer** Fernsehzuschauer.

telex *(US)* Fernschreiber;
~ **call charge** Fernschreibgebühr; ~ **connection** Fernschreibanschluß; ~ **line** Fernschreibleitung; ~ **unit** Fernschreibstelle; ~ **user** Fernschreibteilnehmer.

teller *(bank, US)* Kassierer, Schalterbeamter;
paying ~ Kassierer für Auszahlungen.

temporary *(a.)* vorläufig, kommissarisch, einst-, zeitweilig, vorübergehend, provisorisch;
~ **admission** zeitweilig zollfreie Einfuhr; ~ **appointment** Ernennung auf Widerruf; ~ **employment** vorübergehende Erwerbstätigkeit; ~ **investment** Zwischenanlage.

tenancy Pacht[verhältnis], Mietverhältnis, Miete;
business ~ gewerbliches Mietverhältnis;
to hold a life ~ **of a house** lebenslängliches Wohnrecht haben.

tenant Besitzer, Inhaber, Mieter, Pächter;
outgoing ~ ausziehender Mieter;
~ **for life** Nießbrauchbesitzer; ~ **from month to month** monatlich kündbarer Mieter;
to let out to ~s vermieten, verpachten;
~**'s fixtures** Pachtzubehör; ~**'s risk** Mieterhaftung.

tenantable repair *(house)* bewohnbarer Zustand.

tend | *(v.)* **to rise** leichte Aufwärtsbewegung erkennen lassen; ~ **a store** Ladenaufsicht haben.

tendency Vorliebe, Hang, Zug, *(stock exchange)* Richtung, Neigung, Tendenz, Strömung;
bearish (downward) ~ Baissetendenz; **bullish** ~ Haussetendenz; **general** ~ Grundrichtung; **price-raising** ~ kurstreibende Tendenz; **reserved** ~ zurückhaltende Stimmung; **sagging** ~ abschwächende Tendenz; **strong upward** ~ Haussetendenz;
~ **of the money market** Geldmarktentwicklung; **stronger** ~ **in prices** Kursbefestigung; ~ **toward protectionism** protektionistische Strömung;
to show a declining ~ sich abschwächen; **to show a rising** ~ sich festigen.

tender *(estimate of costs)* Kostenanschlag, *(legal ~)* Zahlungsmittel, *(offer)* [Lieferungs]angebot, Offerte, Anerbieten, Submission, *(ship)* Begleitschiff;
by ~ auf dem Submissionswege;
government ~ staatliche Ausschreibung; **lawful (legal, Br.)** ~ gesetzliches Zahlungsmittel; **sealed** ~ versiegeltes Submissionsangebot;

~ **of rent due** Andienung der fälligen Miete;
~ *(v.)* [Lieferungs]angebot machen;
~ **the amount of rent** Miete andienen; ~ **a bill for discount** Wechsel zur Zahlung einreichen; ~ **and contract for a supply** Lieferungsvertrag abschließen; ~ **for work on contract** sich an einer Ausschreibung beteiligen;
to accept the ~ Zuschlag erteilen; **to invite ~s [for a piece of work]** Ausschreibung veranstalten, Auftrag ausschreiben;
~ **allotment price** Zuteilungskurs; ~ **period** Bewerbungsfrist.

tenement Wohnhaus, Mietwohnung, *(apartment house, US)* Mietskaserne.

tenor *(bill of exchange)* Laufzeit.

tentative | balance sheet vorläufige Bilanz; **in a ~ stage** im Versuchsstadium.

tenure Grundbesitz, *(lease)* Pacht, Mietkontrakt;
communal ~ Gütergemeinschaft;
~ **in office** Amtsdauer;
~ **provision** Kündigungsbestimmung.

term Fachausdruck, *(appointed day)* Termin, *(condition)* [Vertrags]bedingung, *(currency)* Laufzeit;
in ~s of money dem Geldwerte nach; **in ~s of service** an Dienstjahren; **on deferred ~s** *(US)* auf Raten (Abzahlung); **on most moderate ~s** bei billigster Berechnung;
business ~ Geschäftsausdruck; **cash ~s** gegen bar; **conventional ~s** übliche Zahlungsfristen; **easy ~s** bequeme Raten, Zahlungserleichterungen; **reasonable ~s** *(price)* annehmbarer Preis;
~ **of a bill of exchange** Laufzeit eines Wechsels; **~s of business** Geschäftsbedingungen; **~s of conveyance** Beförderungsbedingungen; ~ **of a credit** Laufzeit eines Kredits; **~s of delivery** Liefer-, Bezugsbedingungen; ~ **of discount** Diskonttage; ~ **of guarantee** Garantiefrist; ~ **of an insurance** Versicherungsdauer; **~s of an issue** Emissionsbedingungen; ~ **of notice** Kündigungsfrist; **~s of partnership** Gesellschaftsvertrag; **~s of payment** Zahlungsbedingungen; **~s inclusive of service** Preise einschließlich Bedienung; ~ **of subscription** Bezugsfrist; **~s of tender** Ausschreibungsbestimmungen, Submissionsbedingungen; **~s of trade** Austauschrelationen, -verhältnis; **~s to the trade** Wiederverkaufspreis;
to be for a ~ of 15 years *(loan)* fünfzehnjährige Laufzeit haben; **to come to ~s** sich vergleichen; **to extend the ~** Zahlungsfrist verlängern; **to give s. o. special ~s** jem. einen Sonderpreis machen; **to keep to the ~s of the agreement** der Abrede gemäß handeln;
short-~ **borrowing** kurzfristige Geldaufnahme; ~ **file** Lieferkartei; ~ **insurance** Kurz-, Risikolebensversicherung; ~ **policy** Zeitpolice; **long-~** **transaction** langfristige Finanztransaktion.

terminable kündbar, auflösbar, rückzahlbar;
~ **annuity** *(Br.)* Zeitrente, abgekürzte Rente; ~ **mortgage** Amortisationshypothek.

terminal Flughafenabfertigungsgebäude, *(railroad,*

US) Endbahnhof, End-, Kopfstation;
rail and water ~ Umschlagplatz;
~ **area** Flugplatzgelände; ~ **building** Abfertigungs-Flughafengebäude; ~ **job** Beruf ohne Aufstiegsmöglichkeiten; ~ **leave pay** Entlassungsgeld; ~ **market** *(products, Br.)* Terminmarkt; ~ **payment** *(US)* letzte Ratenzahlung; ~ **reserve** *(life insurance)* Prämienreserve zum Jahresschluß; ~ **value** Endwert.

terminate *(v.)* **a contract** Vertragsverhältnis beenden;
~ **employment without notice** fristlos kündigen

termination | of a contract Vertragsbeendigung; ~ **of offer** Angebotsbegrenzung.

terminus *(railway, Br.)* Kopfbahnhof, -station, Sack-, Endbahnhof.

territorial | allocation Marktaufteilung; ~ **application** Geltungsbereich; ~ **waters** Hoheitsgewässer.

territory Gebiet, Territorium, Geltungsbereich, *(salesman)* Reisegebiet, Vertreterbezirk;
to work one's ~ intensively seinen Vertreterbezirk gründlich bearbeiten.

test Testverfahren, Prüfungsmittel, -verfahren;
acceptance ~ Abnahmeprüfung; **aptitude** ~ Eignungsprüfung; **job** ~ berufliche Eignungsprüfung; **means** ~ Bedürftigkeitsnachweis;
~ *(v.)* **a coin for weight** Münze auf das vorschriftsmäßige Gewicht prüfen;
~ **audit** stichprobenweise Prüfung; ~ **car** Versuchswagen, -modell; ~ **flight** Versuchsflug; ~ **number** Kontrollnummer, Stichzahl [im Telegrammverkehr]; ~ **series** Versuchsserie; ~ **shipment** Probeverzollung; ~ **site** Versuchsgelände.

testament Testament, letztwillige Verfügung.

testimonial Dienstleistungszeugnis, -bescheinigung.

testing *(advertising)* Erfolgskontrolle;
~ **engineer** Prüfingenieur; ~ **load** Probebelastung.

theory | of chances Wahrscheinlichkeitsrechnung; **quantity ~ of money** Quantitätstheorie; ~ **of probabilities** Wahrscheinlichkeitsrechnung.

thin | attendance spärlicher Besuch; **not worth a ~ dime** *(US)* keinen roten Heller wert; ~ **margin** *(US)* sehr knappe Deckung.

things | corporeal körperliche Gegenstände;
~ **in action** immaterielle Güterrechte; ~ **of value** Wertgegenstände.

third Drittel, *(law)* Dritter, dritte Person;
~s Waren minderwertiger Qualität;
~ **of exchange** Wechseldrittausfertigung;
to travel ~ [class] dritter Klasse reisen;
for ~ account für fremde Rechnung; ~ **class** *(US, postal service)* Drucksache; ~ **party** dritte Person, Dritter, *(proceedings)* Nebenintervenient, Streitgenosse.

third-party | accident insurance *(Br.)* Unfallhaftpflichtversicherung; ~ **funds** Fremdgelder; ~ **order** *(US)* Zahlungsverbot an Drittschuldner; ~ **risk policy** *(Br.)* Haftpflichtpolice.

thoroughfare Durchfahrt, Verkehrsader, Hauptverkehrsstraße;

thread mark *(bank note)* Faserzeichen.

three | **-fourth majority** Dreiviertelmehrheit; ~ **months' draft** Dreimonatswechsel; ~**-per-cents** *(Br.)* dreiprozentige Papiere.

threshold | **agreement** Tarifvertrag mit Indexklausel; ~ **price** Eingangs-, Schwellenpreis.

thrift Wirtschaftlichkeit, Sparsamkeit, Ökonomie; ~ **box** Sparbüchse; ~ **deposit** Spargelder.

through | **bill of lading** Transit-, Durchkonnossement; ~ **bookings** Pauschalreisen; ~ **car** *(US)* **(carriage, coach** *Br.)* Kurs-, Durchgangswagen; ~ **freight [business]** Durchgangsfracht[geschäft]; ~ **rate** *(US)* Durchgangssatz, Tarif, Durchfracht; ~ **shipment** durchgehende Ladung; ~ **traffic** Transit-, Durchgangsverkehr; ~ **waybill** durchgehender Frachtbrief.

throw | *(v.)* **into the bargain** drauf-, dazugeben; ~ **goods on the market** Waren auf den Markt werfen; ~ **open to the public** zur öffentlichen Benutzung freigeben; ~ **up one's job** seine Stellung aufgeben.

throwaway Wurf-, Streusendung, Reklamezettel.

tick *(account, fam.)* Rechnung, *(fam., credit)* Kredit, Pump, *(sign of control)* Vermerk, Kontrollzeichen, Haken, Häkchen; **on** ~ *(coll.)* auf Pump; ~ *(v.)* **off items in an account** Rechnungsposten abhaken; **to open a** ~ **account for s. o.** *(Br.)* Kreditkonto für j. eröffnen.

ticker Börsentelegraf, -fernschreiber; ~ **firm** Börsenmakler; ~ **service** *(US)* Tickerdienst;

ticket Einlaß-, Eintrittskarte, -schein, *(air travel)* Flugschein, *(label)* Etikett, Schildchen, Preiszettel, *(luggage)* Gepäckschein, *(pawn house)* Pfandschein, *(railway)* [Eisenbahn]fahrkarte, Fahrschein; **without a [valid]** ~ ohne gültigen Fahrausweis; **annual** ~ Jahresabonnement; **berth** ~ Schlafwagenkarte; **circular** ~ *(Br.)* Rundreisebillet; **cloakroom** ~ Garderobenschein, *(railway, Br.)* Gepäckaufbewahrungsschein; **collective** ~ Sammelfahrschein; **combined** ~ Fahrscheinheft für Bahn, Bus und Schiff; **commutation** ~ *(US)* Zeit-, Dauerfahr-, Abonnementsfahrkarte; **complimentary** ~ Freifahrschein; **coupon** ~ Fahrscheinheft; **delivery** ~ Lieferschein; **excursion** ~ [etwa] Sonntagsrückfahrkarte; **go-as-you-please** ~ Netzfahrkarte; **landing** ~ Landungskarte; **left-luggage** ~ *(Br.)* Gepäckaufbewahrungsschein; **lottery** ~ Lotterieschein, Los; **meal** ~ Essenbon; **parking** ~ *(US)* gebührenpflichtige Verwarnung; **point-to-point** ~ *(airline)* Rundreiseflugschein; **price** ~ Preiszettel; **reduced-rate** ~ *(Br.)* verbilligte Fahrkarte; **reserved-seat** ~ Platzkarte; **rover** ~ Netzkarte; **monthly season** ~ Monatskarte; **tourist** ~ Ferienfahrkarte; ~ *(v.)* etikettieren, numerieren, mit einem Etikett versehen, [Waren] auszeichnen; **to buy a** ~ Fahrkarte lösen; **to draw a prize-winning** ~ Lotteriegewinn ziehen; **to give s. o. a** ~ *(police)* gebührenpflichtige Verwarnung für j. ausstellen; **to turn in one's** ~ seine Fahrkarte bei der Sperre abgeben;

~ **advertising** Fahrscheinwerbung; ~ **agent** *(US)* Fahrkartenverkaufsstelle, *(theater)* Vorverkauf; ~ **counter** Fahrkartenausgabe; ~ **day** *(Br.)* Abrechnungs-, Liquidationstag; ~ **gate** Bahnsteigsperre; ~ **night** Benefizvorstellung; ~ **office** Fahrkartenbüro; ~ **seller** Fahrkartenverkäufer; ~ **slot machine** Fahrscheinautomat.

tickler *(US)* Vormerk-, Terminkalender; **maturity** ~ Wechselverfallbuch.

tie up | *(v.)* **capital** Kapital festlegen; ~ **a factory** Fabrik stillegen; ~ **production** Produktionsstopp vornehmen.

tie-in | **advertising** Anknüpfungswerbung; ~ **deal** Kopplungsgeschäft.

tie-on label Anhängeradresse, -zettel, Anhänger.

tie-up *(US)* Stillstand, Stockung, *(strike, US)* Ausstand, Streik, Arbeitseinstellung; ~ **advertising** kombinierte Werbeaktion.

tied | **to the index** indexgebunden; ~ **cottage** Deputatwohnung; ~**-up capital** festgelegtes Kapital.

tight in Geldverlegenheit, knauserig, knickerig, *(money)* knapp, angespannt; ~ **labo(u)r market** leerer Arbeitsmarkt; ~ **money market** angespannte Lage auf dem Geldmarkt.

tightening | **of a blockade** Blockadeverschärfung; ~ **of money conditions (the money market)** Versteifung des Geldmarktes, Liquiditätsanspannung.

till Geld-, Ladenkasse, Geldkassette, -lade; **to break into the** ~ Kasse angreifen; ~ **book** Kassenbuch, -strazze.

time Zeit, Zeitdauer, -abschnitt, *(broadcasting)* käufliche Werbezeit, *(wages)* Zeit-, Stundenlohn; **at the** ~ **of delivery** bei der Lieferung; **at the** ~ **of expiration** zur Verfallzeit; **in one's spare** ~ nach Feierabend; **additional** ~ Zusatzfrist; **appointed** ~ Termin; **broken** ~ Verdienstausfall; **chargeable** ~ *(tel.)* Gebührenminuten; **cooling** ~ *(strike law)* Abkühlungszeit; **dead** ~ *(factory?)* Verlustzeit; **dull** ~ stille Saison, Flaute; **free [allowance]** ~ standgeldfreie [Lade]zeit; **individual production** ~ Stückzeit; **part** ~ Kurzarbeit; **shipping** ~ Versandtermin; **short** ~ Arbeitszeitverkürzung; **spare** ~ Freizeit; ~ **worked** geleistete Arbeitsstunden; **working** ~ Betriebs-, Arbeitszeit; ~ **of accident** Unfallzeitpunkt; ~ **of admission** Aufnahmetermin; ~ **of arrival** Ankunftszeit; ~**s of delivery** *(postal service)* Zustellzeiten; ~ **of departure** Abflug-, Abfahrtszeit; ~ **for loading** Ladezeit; ~ **for payment** Zahlungsfrist; ~ **to run** *(bill of exchange)* effektive Laufzeit; ~ **when work begins** Arbeitsbeginn; ~ **when work ends** Arbeitsschluß; **to arrive on** ~ *(train)* fahrplanmäßig einlaufen; **to ask for** ~ um Fristverlängerung bitten; **to be always behind** ~ **with one's payments** seine Zahlungstermine nie einhalten; **to give** ~ **off** kurz beurlauben; **to keep** ~ Arbeitszeit registrieren; **to**

stipulate a ~ **for delivery** Lieferfrist festsetzen; **to work full** ~ ganztägig arbeiten;

~ **allowance** Zeitausgleich; ~ **bargain** Prämiengeschäft, *(stock exchange)* Lieferungs-, Fixgeschäft; ~ **bill** Nachsichtwechsel; ~ **buying** Belegen von Sendezeit; ~ **card** Stechkarte; ~ **clerk** *(works)* Zeitkontrolleur; ~ **clock** Stechuhr; ~ **deposit** *(US)* Einlage mit Kündigungsfrist; ~ **discount** *(advertising)* Mengenrabatt; ~ **freight** *(US)* Eilfracht; ~ **holder** *(advertising)* Komplettierungszeige; **spare**-~ **job** Freizeitbeschäftigung; ~ **limit for claims** Rügefrist; ~ **loan** längerfristiges Darlehn; ~ **method of calculating depreciation** *(US)* Abschreibungsmethode nach Quoten; ~ **and one half pay** Überstundenbezahlung; ~ **purchase** Fix-, Terminkauf; ~ **rate** *(US)* Zeitlohn; ~ **sheet** *(US)* Arbeitsblatt, Lohnliste; ~**-and-motion study** Rationalisierungsstudie; ~ **wage** Stundenlohn.

timetable Fahrplan, Kursbuch, Flugplan.

tip Trinkgeld, *(stock exchange)* Börsentip.

title [Rechts]anspruch, *(ownership)* Eigentum[stitel, -srecht];

without lawful ~ ohne Rechtsgrund;

~ **of an account** Kontobezeichnung; ~ **to a benefit** *(insurance)* Leistungsanspruch; ~ **of adverse possession** Eigentumserwerb durch Ersitzung; **to acquire the** ~ Eigentum erwerben; **to lower the** ~ **of the coinage** Währungsstandard senken; **to retain** ~ sich das Eigentum vorbehalten; ~ **deed** Eigentums-, Besitz-, Erwerbsurkunde, Grundstücksurkunde, Kaufvertrag; ~ **retention** Eigentumsvorbehalt; ~ **warranty** Rechtsmängelgewähr.

token *(premium)* Gutschein, Bon; ~ **imports** symbolische Einfuhr; ~ **money** Ersatzgeld; ~ **strike** Warnstreik.

tolerance *(US, customs)* Sperrgeld, Zollabgabe, *(in weight)* zugelassene [Gewichts]abweichung.

toll Abgabe, Gebühr, Zoll, *(market)* Standgeld, *(road)* Straßenbenutzungsgebühr, *(tel., US)* Ferngesprächsgebühr;

canal ~ Kanalgebühr; **town** ~ Gemeindeabgabe; ~ *(v.)* **the statute of limitations** Verjährungsfrist hemmen;

to pay the ~ Zoll entrichten; **to take heavy** ~**s of one's income** großen Einommensteil in Anspruch nehmen;

~ **call** *(tel.)* Ferngespräch; ~ **collector** Zolleinnehmer; ~ **exchange** *(tel.)* Schnell-, Nahverkehrsamt; **to call a** ~**-free number** kostenloses Ferngespräch führen; ~**-line dialing** *(US)* Selbstwählfernverkehr; ~ **road** *(US)* gebührenpflichtige Autobahn.

tommy shop (store, *US***)** Werkskantine.

ton Tonne[ngehalt], *(capacity)* Trag-, Ladefähigkeit; **freight** ~ Tonnenfracht; **gross register** ~ Bruttoregistertonne.

tone *(stock exchange)* Haltung, Stimmung;

bearish ~ flaue Stimmung; **prevailing** ~ Grundton, Grundhaltung der Börse; ~ **of restraint** zurückhaltende Tendenz.

tonnage Tonnage, Tonnengehalt, *(cubic capacity)* Lade-, Ladungsfähigkeit, *(merchant fleet)* Gesamttonnage;

deadweight ~ Lade-, Tragfähigkeit; **displacement** ~ Verdrängungstonnage; **gross** ~ Bruttoregistertonnage; **short** ~ Ladungsmanko; **waste** ~ ungenutzter Schiffsraum;

~ **car** *(US)* Güterwagen; ~ **certificate** Meßbrief; ~ **duty** *(Br.)* Tonnengeld; ~ **rate** *(US)* Lohnsatz por Tonne; ~ **rent** *(US)* Tonnengeld.

tool\|s of trade Rüstzeug zur Berufsausbildung; ~ *(v.)* **a factory** Fabrik mit den notwendigsten Maschinen ausstatten;

to lay down ~**s** Arbeit einstellen, streiken; ~**s rent** Werkzeugmiete.

toolings, furniture and fixtures *(balance sheet)* Werkzeuge, Betriebs- und Geschäftsausstattung.

top Spitze, Gipfel, *(position)* Spitzenstellung;

to buy at the ~ **of the market** zu Höchstkursen kaufen;

~ **adviser** Spitzenberater; ~ **appointment** Spitzenstellung; ~ **brackets** höchste Steuerstufen; ~ **gains** *(stock exchange)* Spitzengewinne; ~**-hat scheme** Bonussystem für leitende Angestellte; ~**-heavy** *(economics)* überkapitalisiert, *(nation)* finanziell überlastet, *(overorganized)* überorganisiert, *(securities)* überbewertet; **to be** ~**-heavy** *(administration)* Wasserkopf haben; ~**-level executive** Spitzenkraft; ~**-level negotiations** Verhandlungen auf höchster Ebene; ~ **management team** *(US)* Spitzengremium; ~ **price** Höchstkurs; ~ **priority** höchste Dringlichkeitsstufe; ~ **tax rate** steuerlicher Höchstsatz.

tort unerlaubte Handlung, Vergehen, Schaden; ~ **liability** Haftung aus unerlaubter Handlung.

total\|amount Gesamtbetrag; ~ **disability** Vollinvalidität; ~ **and permanent disability insurance** Versicherung gegen Vollinvalidität; ~ **loss** Totalverlust, *(fire insurance)* Totalschaden; ~ **proprietorship** Gesamteigenkapital; ~ **tonnage** Gesamttonnage.

touch Fühlungnahme, Verbindung, Kontakt, *(borrowing, sl.)* Anpumpen;

~ **and go** auf der Kippe; ~ *(v.)* **the bottom** niedrigsten Kursstand erreichen; ~ **shares of armament firms** in Rüstungswerten investieren; ~**-and-go business** riskantes Geschäft.

tour Reise, Tour, Rundfahrt, -reise, Ausflug;

all-expense ~ *(US)* kostenose Besichtigungsreise; **business** ~ Geschäftsreise; **conducted** ~ Gesellschaftsreise; **mystery** ~ Fahrt ins Blaue; **packaged** ~ *(US)* Gesellschaftsfahrt, -tour, Pauschalreise; ~ **of inspection** Besichtigungsreise; ~ *(v.)* **the fairs** Messen bereisen; ~ **operator** Touristikunternehmen.

touring exhibition Wanderausstellung.

tourism Fremdenverkehr, Tourismus;

to be mainly dependent for one's living on ~ hauptsächlich vom Fremdenverkehr leben; ~ **advertising** Fremdenverkehrswerbung.

tourist Vergnügungsreisender, Ausflügler, Tourist; ~ **advertising** Fremden[verkehrs]werbung; ~ **agency** Reisebüro; ~ **association** Fremdenverkehrsverband; ~ **bureau** *(US)* Reise-, Verkehrsbüro; ~ **class** Touristenklasse; ~ **deficit** Fremdenverkehrsdefizit; ~ **expenditure** Reisedevisen; ~ **guide** Fremdenführer; ~ **industry** Fremden[verkehrs]industrie; ~ **office** *(Br.)* Reisebüro; ~ **promotion** Fremdenverkehrsförderung; ~ **season** Reisezeit; ~ **trade** Fremdenverkehr[sgewerbe]; ~ **voucher** Touristengutschein.

tout Schlepper, Kundenwerber; ~ *(v.)* Kunden akquirieren (werben).

tow *(v.)* a **broken car** kaputtes Auto abschleppen; ~ **car** Abschleppwagen.

tower *(aviation)* Kontrollturm; ~ **block** *(Br.)* Wohnhochhaus.

town Stadt, Ort, *(business center)* Stadtzentrum, *(municipal administration)* Stadt-, Gemeindeverwaltung; **on the** ~ *(US)* auf städtische Unterstützung (Fürsorge) angewiesen; **company** ~ *(US)* Firmen-, Werkssiedlung; **manufacturing** ~ Industriestadt; ~ **agent** Stadtvertreter; ~ **cheque** *(Br.)* Clearing im Finanzzentrum von London; ~ **council** Stadtrat, Magistrat; ~ **councillor** *(Br.)* Stadtrat[smitglied]; ~ **dues** städtische Abgaben; ~ **rates** Kommunalabgaben; ~ **travel(l)er** *(Br.)* Platzreisender.

trace *(v.)* **lost goods** verlorene Warenpartie wiederfinden.

tracer *(railroad, US)* Laufzettel, Umlauf[schreiben], *(US, collecting business)* Inkassobericht; ~ **information** *(US)* Inkassoauskunft.

track *(mar.)* Fahrrinne, -wasser, *(railway)* Bahnstrecke, Schienenweg; **North Atlantic** ~ Nordatlantikroute; **occupied** ~ belegtes Gleis; **to keep on the** ~ auf dem laufenden halten.

trade Handel, *(business)* [Gewerbe]betrieb, ˙Geschäft, *(business situation)* Geschäftslage, *(business world)* Fach-, Geschäftswelt, Kaufmannschaft, *(customer)* Kundschaft, *(line)* Branche, Fach, Geschäftszweig, *(occupation)* Gewerbe, Erwerbszweig; **in the same** ~ im gleichen Metier; ~ **supplied to** ~ **only** Lieferung nur an Wiederverkäufer; **without a** ~ ohne Beruf; **active** ~ Export; **barter** ~ Tauschhandel; **basic** ~ Schlüsselindustrie; **building** ~ Bauwirtschaft; **carrying** ~ Transportgewerbe; **catering** ~ Gaststättengewerbe; **clandestine**˙ ~ Schwarzhandel; **distributing (distributive)** ~ Absatzwirtschaft; **domestic** ~ Binnenhandel; **flourishing** ~ blühendes Geschäft; **foreign** ~ Außenhandel, Außenwirtschaft; **free** ~ Freihandel; **itinerant** ~ ambulantes Gewerbe, Wandergewerbe; **no lawful** ~ verbotenes Gewerbe; **licensed** ~ konzessioniertes Gewerbe; **little** ~ *(stock exchange)* geringe Umsätze; **manufacturing** ~ gewerbliche Wirtschaft; **roaring** ~

schwunghafter Handel; **retail** ~ Klein-, Einzelhandel; **small-scale** ~ Kleingewerbe; **telephone** ~ *(stock exchange)* Telefonverkehr; **world** ~ Weltwirtschaft; ~ **and industry** Handel und Wirtschaft; ~ **for own account** Eigengeschäft; ~ **for third account** Kommissionshandel; ~ **subject to licence** gewerbepolizeipflichtiger Betrieb; ~ **on cash terms** Bargeldverkehr; ~ **with transit goods** Durchgangs-, Transithandel; ~ *(v.)* handeln, Handel treiben, *(barter)* tauschen, Tauschhandel treiben; ~ **for own account** für eigene Rechnung abschließen.

trade in *(US)* eintauschen, in Zahlung geben; ~ **bills** Wechselreiterei treiben; ~ **one's 1978 Ford car for a new model** seinen 1978er Ford für das neueste Modell in Zahlung geben; ~ **futures** Termingeschäfte abschließen.

trade on | **the credulity of a client** Gutgläubigkeit eines Kunden ausnutzen; ~ **the equity** seine Geschäfte mit Fremdkapital finanzieren; ~ **freight** auf Fracht fahren.

trade | **under one's own name** Firma unter seinem eigenen Namen betreiben; ~ **upon one's past reputation** von seinem guten Namen leben; ~ **with** | **borrowed money** mit fremdem Kapital arbeiten; **to be in the** ~ Geschäftsmann sein; **to carry on a** ~ gewerblich tätig sein, Gewerbebetrieb ausüben; **to drive a good** ~ gutgehendes Geschäft haben; **to engage in foreign** ~ Exportgeschäfte machen; **to follow a** ~ Gewerbe (Handwerk) ausüben; **to foster** ~ Wirtschaft ankurbeln; **to leave off** ~ Geschäft aufgeben; **to open a** ~ Geschäft eröffnen; **to put s. o. to a** ~ j. in die Lehre geben, j. ein Handwerk (Beruf) erlernen lassen; **to restrain** ~ Wettbewerb einschränken; **to set up s. o. in** ~ j. geschäftlich etablieren;

~ **acceptance** Handels-, Kundenakzept, Warenwechsel; ~ **accounts payable** *(balance sheet, US)* Warenschulden; ~ **accounts receivable** *(balance sheet, US)* Forderungen aus Warenlieferungen und Leistungen, Warenforderungen; ~ **advertising** Händlerwerbung; ~ **agency** Handelsagentur; ~ **agent** Handelsvertreter; ~ **agreement** Handelsvertrag; ~ **allowance** Großhandelsrabatt, Rabatt für Wiederverkäufer; ~ **arbitrator** Wirtschaftsschlichter; ~ **association** Berufsgenossenschaft, Gewerbeverband; **[adverse]** ~ **balance** [passive] Handelsbilanz; ~ **barriers** Handelsschranken; ~ **bill** Kunden-, Waren-, Handelswechsel; ~ **catalog(ue)** Preisliste, -verzeichnis; ~ **center** *(US)* (**centre,** *Br.)* Wirtschaftszentrum; ~ **channels** Absatzwege, Vertriebskanäle; ~ **charge** *(Br.)* Nachnahmebetrag; ~ **colony** Handelskolonie; ~ **committee** Gewerbeausschuß; ~ **connections** Handels-, Wirtschaftsverbindungen; ~ **convention** Wirtschaftsabkommen; ~ **council** Ausschuß der gewerblichen Wirtschaft; ~ **credit** Lieferantenkredit; ~ **creditor** Lieferant; ~ **cycle** *(Br.)* Konjunkturzyklus; ~ **debts** Lieferantenschulden; ~ **deficit** Passivsaldo im Außenhandel; ~ **delegation** Wirtschaftsabordnung, Handelsdelegation; ~ **depression** Konjunkturkrise; ~ **description** Warenbezeichnung; ~ **directory** Branchenadreßbuch; ~ **discount** Rabatt [an Wiederverkäufer], Händlerrabatt; ~ **exhibition** Fach-, Gewerbeausstellung; ~ **expenses** Handelsunkosten; ~ **fair** *(Br.)* Gewerbeausstellung; ~ **fixtures** fest eingebaute Maschinenanlagen; ~ **folder** Wirtschaftsprospekt; ~ **group interchange** *(US)* Kundenkreditauskunftei; ~**-in** in Zahlung gegebene Ware; ~**-in value** Verrechnungswert; ~ **inspection** Gewerbeaufsicht; ~ **inspector** Gewerbeaufsichtsbeamter; ~ **journal** Handelsblatt, Fach-, Wirtschaftszeitschrift; ~ **kit** Berufskleidung; ~ **law** Gewerbeordnung; ~ **libel** *(US)* Anschwärzung der Konkurrenz; ~ **licence** Konzession; ~ **list** Preisliste [für Großhändler]; ~ **literature** Fachliteratur; ~ **margin** Handelsspanne; ~**-mark name** Markenname, Schutzmarke; ~ **monopoly** Handelsmonopol; ~ **name** Firmenname, *(trademark)* Warenzeichen; ~ **negotiations** Wirtschaftsverhandlungen; ~ **notes receivable** *(US)* Kundenwechsel; ~ **organization** Wirtschaftsverband; ~ **paper** Kunden-, Waren-, Handelswechsel; ~ **policy** Handelspolitik; ~**-policy initiative** handelspolitische Initiative; ~ **unfair ~ practices** unlauteres Geschäftsgebaren; ~ **premium** *(export business)* Ausfuhrprämie; ~ **price** Großhandels-, Wiederverkäuferpreis; ~ **promotion** Wirtschaftsförderung; ~ **publication** geschäftliche Bekanntmachung, *(newspaper)* Wirtschaftszeitschrift; ~ **receivables** *(US)* Forderungen aufgrund von Warenlieferungen; ~ **refuse** Industriemüll; ~ **representative** Handelsvertreter; ~ **returns** Handelsstatistik; ~ **revival** Wiederbelebung der Wirtschaft; ~ **road (route)** Handelsstraße; ~ **school** *(US)* Gewerbeschule; **to divulge ~ secrets** Betriebsgeheimnisse verraten; ~ **service** diplomate Handelsattaché; ~ **stamp** *(US)* Rabattmarke; ~ **surplus** Handelsüberschüsse; ~ **terms** Wiederverkaufspreisbestimmungen; ~ **union** *(Br.)* Gewerkschaft; ~ **unionist** Gewerkschaftsangehöriger; ~ **usage** Geschäfts-, Handelsbrauch, Usance; ~ **value** Verkehrs-, Handelswert; ~ **walls** Zollmauern; ~ **war** Wirtschaftskrieg.

traded-in-car in Zahlung genommener Wagen.

trademark Waren-, Handels-, Hersteller-, Schutz-, Fabrikzeichen, Handelsmarke;
associated ~s *(Br.)* verbundene Warenzeichen; **common-law ~** *(US)* nicht eingetragenes Warenzeichen; **registered ~** eingetragenes (geschütztes) Warenzeichen;
~ *(v.)* gesetzlich schützen lassen, als Warenzeichen eintragen;
to appropriate unlawfully s. **one's ~** jds. Warenzeichenrecht verletzen; **to expunge the registration of a ~** Eintragung eines Warenzeichens löschen; **to infringe a ~** Warenzeichen verletzen; **to register a ~** Warenzeichen eintragen lassen;

~ **law** Warenzeichenrecht; ~ **name** Schutzmarke; ~ **owner** Warenzeichen-, Schutzmarkeninhaber; ~**s register** Warenzeichenrolle.

trademarked commodities (goods) Markenartikel, -erzeugnisse.

trademaster Gewerbeschullehrer.

trader Händler, Handeltreibender, Handelsmann, Kaufmann, -herr, *(stock exchange, US)* freier (selbständiger) Makler;
big-block ~ Pakethändler; **clandestine (illicit) ~** Schwarzhändler; **door-to-door ~** fliegender Händler; **rgular ~** Handelsschiff; **retail ~** Einzelhändler; **small ~** Kleingewerbetreibender; **sole ~** Einzelkaufmann.

tradesman Gewerbetreibender, [Einzel]händler, Kaufmann mit offenem Ladengeschäft, *(craftsman, Br.)* Handwerker, Minderkaufmann;
cutting ~ Preisverderber;
to register with a ~ sich bei einem Geschäft (Laden) als Kunde eintragen lassen.

tradesmen | who supply us unsere Lieferanten; ~**'s entrance** Eingang für Lieferanten.

trading Handel treiben, Börsenhandel;
over-the-counter ~ *(US)* Handel mit nicht notierten Wertpapieren; **illicit ~** Schleich-, Schwarzhandel; **light ~** *(stock exchange)* schwache Umsätze; ~ **municipal ~** Kommunalbetrieb; **odd-lot ~** *(US)* Handel in kleineren Effektenstücken;
~ **in calls** *(Br.)* Vorprämiengeschäft; ~**-in In**-Zahlung-Geben; ~ **in futures** *(US)* Termingeschäft; ~ **in stocks** *(US)* Aktienhandel; ~ **on the equity** Fremdfinanzierung; ~ **on the short side** Baissetermingeschäft; ~ **under the name** Firmierung;
to be accepted for ~ on the stock exchange zum Handel an der Börse zugelassen sein; **to dominate ~** Marktgeschehen beherrschen;
~ *(a.)* gewerbe-, handeltreibend, kaufmännisch; ~ **account** Verkaufskonto; ~ **advantage** Geschäftsvorteil; ~ **area** *(US)* Wirtschaftsgebiet; ~ **association** Wirtschaftsvereinigung; ~ **capital** Betriebskapital; ~ **certificate** *(Br.)* Gewerbegenehmigung; ~ **company (corporation)** Handels-, Erwerbsgesellschaft, *(marketing)* Vertriebs-, Absatzgesellschaft; ~ **concern** Wirtschaftsunternehmen; ~ **estate** *(Br.)* Industriesiedlung; ~ **favo(u)rites** *(stock exchange)* führende Werte; ~ **firm** Handelshaus; ~ **handicap** Geschäftsnachteil; ~ **income** Einkünfte aus Gewerbebetrieb; ~ **licence** Gewerbekonzession; ~ **loss** Geschäfts-, Betriebsverlust; ~ **partner** Handelspartner; ~ **partnership** [Offene] Handelsgesellschaft; ~ **post** *(stock exchange, US)* Börsen-, Maklerstand; ~ **profit** *(Br.)* Geschäfts-, Betriebsgewinn; ~ **report** Geschäftsausweis; ~ **specialist** Börsenfachmann; ~ **stamp** Gutschein, Rabattmarke; ~ **unit** *(stock exchange)* Handelseinheit; ~ **year** Geschäfts-, Rechnungsjahr.

traffic *(exchange of goods)* Güteraustausch, *(movement of vessels)* Schiffsverkehr, *(total of passengers transported)* beförderte Personenzahl, *(trade)*

Handelsverkehr, *(transportation)* Verkehr, Transport-, Verkehrswesen;

air ~ Luftverkehr; **border** ~ Grenzverkehr; **business** ~ Berufsverkehr; **congested** ~ Verkehrsstauung; **goods** ~ *(Br.)* Güterverkehr; **grouped** ~ Sammelladungsverkehr; **less-than-carload** ~ *(US)* Stückgüterverkehr; **oncoming** ~ Gegenverkehr; **short-distance goods** ~ Nahgüterverkehr; **through (transit)** ~ Durchgangsverkehr;

~ **on a road** Verkehrsdichte, -stärke; **to be opened to** ~ in Betrieb genommen werden; **to divert the** ~ *(Br.)* Verkehr umleiten;

~ **accident** Verkehrsunfall; ~ **artery** Verkehrsweg; ~ **beacon** Verkehrsampel; ~ **circle** *(US)* Kreisverkehr; **Uniform** ≗ **Code** *(US)* Straßenverkehrsordnung; ~ **congestion** Verkehrsstauung; ~ **density** Verkehrsdichte; ~ **director** Verkehrsdezernent; ~ **diversion** *(Br.)* Verkehrsumleitung; ~ **island** Verkehrsinsel; ~ **jam** Verkehrsstockung; ~ **manager** Versandleiter, Vertriebsdirektor; **no-delay-~ office** *(tel.)* Schnellverkehrsamt; ~ **peak period** Verkehrsspitze; ~ **sheet** *(hotel)* Gesprächsbelegzettel; ~ **violation** *(US)* Verkehrsübertretung.

trailer *(advertising)* Werbedurchsage für ein Nebenprodukt, *(car)* Wohnwagen[anhänger].

train [Eisenbahn]zug;

connecting (corresponding) ~ Anschlußzug; **corridor** ~ D-Zug; **express** ~ Eil-, Schnellzug, Express; **fast goods** ~ *(Br.)* Eilgüterzug; **freight** ~ *(US)* Güterzug; **goods** ~ *(Br.)* Güterzug; **parliamentary** ~ *(Br.)* Bummelzug; **vestibule** ~ *(US)* D-Zug;

handy ~ **and bus** gute Eisenbahn- und Busverbindungen;

~ *(v.)* **s. o. to business** j. für das Geschäft anlernen; ~ **for free** umsonst ausbilden;

to forward by mail ~ als Eilgut befördern; **to send s. th. by goods** ~ *(Br.)* als Fracht versenden; ~ **connections** Zugverbindungen; ~ **crew** Fahrpersonal; ~ **dispatcher** Fahrdienstleiter; ~ **guard** *(US)* Zugschaffner; ~ **reservation** Platzkarte; ~ **schedule** *(US)* Fahrplan, Zugfolge; **to cut** ~ **service** Zugverkehr einschränken; ~ **warrant** [Fracht]begleitzettel.

trainee Volontär, Praktikant, Nachwuchskraft, Anlernling, *(course)* Kursusteilnehmer;

~ **course** Ausbildungslehrgang.

training Ausbildung, Anlernen;

apprenticeship ~ Lehrlingsausbildung; **blitz** ~ *(US)* Ausbildung in Schnellkursen; **cold-storage** ~ *(US)* Ausbildung von Nachwuchskräften; **employee** ~ innerbetriebliche Ausbildung; **in-plant** ~ Ausbildung am Arbeitsplatz; **[on-the-] job (job instruction)** ~ *(US)* Ausbildung am Arbeitsplatz; **technical** ~ Fachausbildung; **vocational** ~ Berufsausbildung;

~ **benefit** Ausbildungszuschuß; ~ **camp** Schulungslager; ~ **course** Lehrgang; ~ **program(me)** Ausbildungsprogramm; ~ **shop** Anlernwerkstatt; ~ **time on job** berufliche Ausbildungszeit.

tramway advertising *(Br.)* Straßenbahnwerbung.

transact *(v.)* **banking business of every description** sämtliche Bankgeschäfte ausführen.

transaction *(agreement by mutual concessions)* übereinkunft, Abmachung, Vergleich, Vertrag, *(negotiation)* Unter-, Verhandlung, *(piece of business)* Transaktion, Geschäftsabschluß, Geschäftsvorfall, Handel, Unternehmen, *(stock exchange)* Umsatz, Abschluß, Transaktion;

~**s amounting to several million pounds** Transaktionen in einer Höhe von mehreren Millionen Pfund; **bear** ~ Baissegeschäft; **budgeted** ~**s** im Haushaltsplan vorgesehene Geschäftsabschlüsse; **bull** ~ Haussespekulation; **cash** ~ Kassageschäft, Barverkauf; **dummy (fictions, pro-forma)** ~ Scheingeschäft; **foreign-exchange** ~ Devisengeschäft; **forward** ~ Sicht-, Termingeschäft; **market** ~ Börsengeschäft; **security** ~ *(stock exchange)* Effektentransaktion; **taxable** ~ steuerpflichtiges [Rechts]geschäft;

~ **for the account** *(Br.)* Börsentermingeschäft; ~ **for own account** Geschäft für eigene Rechnung; ~ **for third account** Kommissionshandel; ~ **contra bonus mores** sittenwidriges Rechtsgeschäft; ~**s of a firm** Firmenumsatz; ~ **in goods** Warenabschluß; ~ **in syndicate** Konsortialgeschäft;

to avoid a ~ Rechtsgeschäft anfechten; **to effect** ~**s** Abschlüsse tätigen; **to record** ~**s** Geschäftsvorfälle aufzeichnen;

~ **record** Geschäftsbeleg.

transatlantic │ rate Überseetarif; ~ **ship** Ozean-, Überseedampfer.

transcribe *(v.)* abschreiben, *(bookkeeping)* übertragen, *(shorthand notes)* aus dem Stenogramm in Kurrentschrift übertragen.

transfer Übertrag, Umbuchung, *(assignment)* Abtretung, Zession, *(changing the train)* Umsteigen, *(of employees)* Versetzung, *(railroad ticket, US)* Umsteiger, *(remittance)* Überweisung, Transferierung.

bank ~ Banküberweisung; **blank** ~ *(Br.)* Blankoindossament; **cable** ~ Kabelauszahlung;

~ **of balance** Saldoübertrag; ~ **of business** Geschäftsverlegung; ~ **for disciplinary reasons** Strafversetzung; ~ **of a factory** Fabrikverlegung; ~ **on London** Auszahlung London; ~ **of ownership** Eigentumsübertragung; ~ **to reserve** Rückstellung; ~ **of shares** *(Br.)* **(stocks, US)** Aktienumschreibung.

transferee Zessionar, Übernehmer; ~ **company** übernehmende Gesellschaft.

trans(s)hipment Umladung, Umschlag;

~ **bill of lading** Umladekonnossement; ~ **charge** Umladegebühr; ~ **harbo(u)r** Umschlaghafen.

trans(s)hipping traffic Umschlagverkehr.

transient │ arrangement befristetes Abkommen; ~ **guest** *(US)* Durchreisender1 ~ **hotel** *(US)* Durchgangshotel.

transire *(Br.)* Zollbegleitschein, -durchlaß.

transit Durchfahrt, Überfahrt, Durchgang, Transit; **lost in** ~ auf dem Transport verlorengegangen; **rapid** ~ *(US)* Schnellverkehr;

to enter goods as ~ Waren durchdeklarieren; ~ **account** Übergangskonto; ~ **agent** Zwischenspediteur; ~ **bond** Durchfuhrschein; ~ **ceritificate** Passierschein; ~ **department** *(US)* Abteilung für Inkasso auf auswärtigen Plätzen; ~ **duty** Transitabgabe; ~ **entry** *(customs)* Durchfuhr-, Transiterklärung; ~ **freight** Durch[gangs]fracht; ~ **goods** Transitgüter; **permit** Durchfuhrbescheinigung, Transiterlaubnis; ~ **rate** verbilligter Frachttarif für Durchgangsgüter; ~ **trade** Durchfuhrverkehr; ~ **visa** Durchreisevisum.

transition stage Übergangsstadium.

transitional arrangement Übergangsregelung.

transitory *(balance sheet)* transitorisch.

translate *(v.)* übersetzen, *(telegram)* dechiffrieren.

translating bureau *(US)* Übersetzungsbüro.

translation Übersetzung, *(cable)* Dechiffrierung.

translocation of industry Industrieverlagerung.

transmission Überbringung, -mittlung, Versand; ~ **on death** Übergang von Todes wegen; ~ **of goods** Warenversand, Spedition; ~ **of money** Geldüberweisung; ~ **business** Speditionsgeschäft, -handel.

transmit *(v.)* *(broadcast)* [durch Rundfunk] übertragen, *(forward)* [über]senden, befördern, *(transfer)* übertragen, überschreiben; ~ **onward** weiterleiten; ~ **property** Besitz übertragen.

transoceanic steamer Überseedampfer.

transport *(airplane)* Transportflugzeug, *(amount carried forward)* Übertrag, -schreibung, *(forwarding)* Beförderung, Verfrachtung, Verschiffung, Transport; **by public** ~ mit öffentlichen Verkehrsmitteln; **air** ~ Luftverkehr; **collective** ~ Sammeltransport; **door-to-door** ~ Beförderung von Haus zu Haus; **inland water** ~ *(US)* Binnenschiffahrtsverkehr; **interstate** ~ *(US)* zwischenstaatlicher Güterverkehr; **long-distance** ~ Fernverkehr; **marine (maritime)** ~ Beförderung auf dem Seewege; **passenger** ~ Personenbeförderung; **rail** ~ Güterverkehr; **road** ~ *(Br.)* Straßentransport; **short-distance** ~ Nahverkehr; **waterborne** ~ Beförderung auf dem Wasserweg; ~ **in bulk** Massenbeförderung; ~ *(v.)* transportieren, befördern, versenden; ~ **goods by truck** Güter verfrachten; ~ **advertising** *(Br.)* Verkehrsmittelwerbung; ~ **agency** Transportagentur; ~ **charges** Transportgebühren; ~ **company** *(Br.)* Spediteur; ~ **industries** Transportgewerbe; ~ **insurance** Transportversicherung; ~ **risk** Transportrisiko; **public** ~ **service** Verkehrsbetrieb; ~ **ship (vessel)** Frachter; ~ **trade** Transportgewerbe.

transportation Beförderung, *(charges)* Versand-, Transportkosten, *(forwarding)* Versendung, Versand, Transport, *(means of conveyance, US)* Transportmöglichkeiten, Beförderungsmittel; **common carrier** ~ Beförderung durch öffentliche Verkehrsmittel; **railroad freight** ~ *(US)* Bahnfrachtverkehr;

~ **by air** Beförderung auf dem Luftwege; ~ **of passengers** Passagierverkehr; ~ **accounting** Speditionsbuchführung; ~ **advertisement** *(US)* Verkehrsmittelwerbung; ~ **agency** Speditionsgesellschaft; ~ **carrier** Hauptspediteur; **public** ~ **company** öffentliches Verkehrsunternehmen; ~ **Department** *(US)* Verkehrsministerium; ~ **economy** Verkehrswirtschaft; ~ **expert** Verkehrssachverständiger; ~ **insurance** *(US)* Transportversicherung; ~ **means** Verkehrsmittel; ~ **rate** Verkehrstarif; ~ **schedule** Frachttabelle; ~ **space** *(US)* Transportraum; ~ **tax** *(US)* Beförderungs-, Transportsteuer.

transporter Verkehrsflugzeug.

travel Reise[n], Reiseverkehr; **pleasure** ~ Vergnügungsreise; ~ **on official business** Dienstreise; ~ **to clients** Kundenbesuch; ~ *(v.)* reisen, *(salesman)* Reisender sein; ~ **by air** per Flugzeug reisen; ~ **a good deal** oft verreisen; ~ **on expenses account** zu Lasten des Spesenkontos verreisen; ~ **by sea** Seeweg benutzen; **to use a car for personal** ~ Auto für Privatfahrten benutzen; ~ **advance** Reisekostenvorschuß; ~ **agent (agency)** Reisebüro; ~ **allowance** Reisespesen; ~ **bureau** *(Br.)* Reisebüro; ~ **and entertainment diary** Spesennachweisbuch; ~–**expense report** *(US)* Spesenabrechnung; ~ **folder** Reiseprospekt; ~ **insurance** Reiseversicherung; ~ **subsidy (subvention)** Reisekostenzuschuß;

traveller Reisender, Tourist, *(Br.)* Handlungsreisender; **expense-account** ~ Spesenritter; **town** ~ Platzvertreter; ~ **on commission** Provisionsvertreter.

traveller's | accident insurance Reiseunfallversicherung; ~ **book** Fremdenbuch; ~ **check** *(US)* (**cheque,** *Br.)* Reisescheck; ~ **guide** Reisehandbuch; ~ **hotel** Touristenhotel; ~ **sample** Gebrauchsmuster.

travelling | agent Provisionsreisender; ~ **auditor** Außenrevisor; ~–**expense account** Spesenkonto; ~ **post office** Bahnpost[amt]; ~ **salesman** *(US)* Handlungsreisender.

treasure-trove aufgefundener Schatz, Schatzfund.

treasurer *(club)* Schatzmeister, Kassenverwalter, -wart; **city** ~ *(Br.)* Stadtkämmerer.

treasury *(Br.)* Schatzamt, Finanzministerium, *(revenue office)* Staats-, Finanzkasse; ~ **bench** *(Br.)* Regierungs-, Ministerbank; ~ **bill** *(Br.)* Schatzanweisung, kurzfristiger Schatzwechsel; ~ **bond** *(Br.)* langfristige Schatzanweisung; ~ **Department** *(US)* Bundesfinanzministerium; ~ **securities** Eigenbestand an Wertpapieren; ~ **warrant** *(Br.)* Schatzanweisung.

treat Einladung, Bewirtung, *(Br.)* Staatsanleihe.

treatment, customs zollrechtliche Behandlung; **most-favo(u)red-nation** ~ Meistbegünstigung.

treaty [Staats]vertrag;
  arbitration ~ Schieds[gerichts]vertrag; **trade** ~
  Handelsabkommen;
  ~ **of navigation** Schiffahrtsabkommen;
  to enter into a ~ **of commerce** Handelsvertrag
  abschließen;
  ~ **duties** Vertragszölle; ~ **port** Vertragshafen; ~
  reinsurance automatisch wirksame Rückversicherung.

trend Entwicklung, Entwicklungstendenz, Trend;
  cost ~ Kostenentwicklung; **cyclical** ~ Konjunk-
  turverlauf; **downward** ~ Abwärtsbewegung; **upward** ~ Konjunkturanstieg;
  ~ **of business** Geschäftsgang; **decreasing** ~ **in costs**
  Kostendegression; **~s in the economy** konjunkturelle Entwicklungstendenzen; **expected** ~ **of the
  market** Konjunkturerwartungen;
  ~ **analysis** Konjunkturanalyse.

trespass *(property)* Beeinträchtigung, Eigentums-
  verletzung, -störung;
  ~ *(v.) (property)* widerrechtlich betreten;
  ~ **upon s. one's privacy** jds. Intimsphäre verletzen.

trial Prozeß[sache], *(test)* Probe, Versuch;
  to put a machine to further ~ Maschine weiter
  ausprobieren;
  ~ **balance** Probe-, Salden-, Vorbilanz; ~ **engagement** Probeanstellung; ~ **order** Probeauftrag; ~
  run Probelauf einer Fabrik, *(ship)* Versuchsfahrt.

triangular operation in exchange Devisenarbitrage in
  drei verschiedenen Währungen.

trim of the hold gute Verstauung der Ladung.

trip Fahrt, Reise, Tour, Abstecher, Spritzer;
  business ~ Geschäftsreise.

triptych Zollpassierschein, internationaler Autopaß.

truck Last[kraft]wagen, LKW, *(barter)* Tauschgeschäft, *(mining)* Lore, Hund, *(payment in goods)*
  Warenentlohnung, *(trade, Br.)* [offener] Güter-,
  Rungenwagen;
  baggage ~ Handgepäckwagen; **heavy** ~ schwerer
  Lastkraftwagen; **industrial** ~ Fernlaster; **motor**
  ~ Lastkraftwagen; **semi-trailer** ~ Sattelschlepper;
  ~ *(v.) (barter)* Tauschhandel treiben, *(be employed
  in driving)* Lastwagen fahren;
  ~ **for a living** sich als Lastwagenfahrer sein Geld
  verdienen;
  ~ **charges** Rollgeld; ~ **driver** LKWfahrer; ~ **production** Lastwagenproduktion; ~ **rates** Kilometergeld, Überlandfrachtsatz.

truckage Lastwagenbeförderung, Güterkraftverkehr.

trucking LKW-Transport, *(Br.)* Güterwagentrans-
  port;
  ~ **agency** Rollfuhrunternehmen, Güterspedition;
  ~ **firm** Rollfuhrunternehmen; ~ **fleet** Lastwagen-
  kolonne; ~ **industry** Lastwagenindustrie.

truckload *(Br.)* Waggon-, Sammelladung.

true | **to specimen** laut Muster;
  ~ **copy** gleichlautende Abschrift; ~ **discount** *(loan)*
  offenes Disagio; ~ **gold** reines Gold; ~ **reserve**
  (US) außerordentliche Reserve.

trunk *(box)* Reise-, Übersee-, Schrankkoffer, *(railway)* Hauptlinie, *(tel., Br.)* Fernleitung;
  ~ **call** *(Br.)* Ferngespräch; ~ **enquiries** *(Br.)* Fern-
  auskunft; ~ **line** *(US)* Hauptverkehrslinie, *(tel.,
  Br.)* Fernverbindung; ~ **zone** Fernverkehrsbe-
  reich.

trust Vertrauen, Treu und Glauben, *(US, corner)*
  Trust, Konzern, Ring, Kartell, *(credit)* Kredit,
  Borg, *(custody)* Treuverhältnis, *(depositing)* Aufbewahrung, Verwahrung, *(trust estate)* Treuhandvermögen, -gut;
  accumulation ~ Kapitalsammelstelle; **bare** ~ *(US)*
  Hinterlegungsstelle; **charitable** milde Stiftung;
  discretionary ~ *(Br.)* nach freiem Ermessen verwaltetes Treuhandvermögen; **fixed investment** ~
  (US) Kapitalanlagegesellschaft mit festgelegtem
  Effektenbestand; **pension** ~ Pensionsfonds; **protective** ~ *(US)* für einen Verschwender errichtete
  Stiftung; **simple** ~ *(US)* einfache Hinterlegungsstelle; **voluntary** ~ Unterstützungsfonds;
  ~ *(v.)* sein Vertrauen setzen, *(allow credit for)* kreditieren, borgen;
  ~ **one's affairs to a lawyer** mit seiner Vertretung
  einen Anwalt betrauen;
  to administer a ~ Treugut verwalten; **to deliver in**
  ~ in Verwahrung geben; **to hold on** ~ treuhänderisch verwalten; **to take goods on** ~ Waren
  auf Kredit beziehen;
  ~ **account** Treuhand-, Treuhänderkonto; ~ **administration** Treuhandverwaltung; ~ **agreement**
  (trustee) Sicherungsübereignunsvertrag; ~ **busting**
  (US sl.) Kartellentflechtung; ~ **company** Treuhandgesellschaft; ~ **corporation** *(Br.)* öffentliche
  Treuhandstelle; ~ **deed** Treuhandvertrag; ~ **deposit** Treuhänder-, Anderdepot; ~ **donor** Treugeber; ~ **estate** Treuhandvermögen, -gut; **to
  distribute a** ~ **estate** *(bankruptcy law)* Konkursmasse verteilen; ~ **fund** Treuhandgelder, treuhänderisch verwaltetes Vermögen, *(guardianship)*
  Mündelgeld, -vermögen; **~-and-agency fund** *(municipal accounting)* Zweckvermögen; ~ **[fund] investments** *(US)* mündelsichere Kapitalanlagen; ~
  money Stiftungsgelder, Mündelgeld; ~ **receipt**
  (banking) Sicherungsübereignungsurkunde; ~ **receipt transaction** Sicherungsübereignung; ~ **relation[ship]** Treuhandverhältnis; ~ **report** Treu-
  handbericht; ~ **security** mündelsichere Anlage; ~
  transaction fiduziarisches Rechtsgeschäft.

trustee Treuhänder, -nehmer, *(administrator)* Vermögensverwalter, -pfleger, Kurator;
  court-appointed ~ gerichtlich bestellter Vermögensverwalter; **judicial** ~ gerichtlich bestellter
  Pfleger; **public** ~ *(Br.)* amtliche Hinterlegungsstelle; **sole** ~ Einzeltreuhänder;
  ~ **for administration** Vermögensverwalter; ~ **of a
  bankrupt's estate** Konkursverwalter; ~ **in charitable uses** Kurator;
  ~ **and beneficiary** Treugeber und Treunehmer;
  ~ *(v.)* einem Treuhänder übergeben, *(serve as ~)*
  als Treuhänder fungieren;

to appoint a ~ Treuhänder ernennen; **to remove a** ~ Treuhänder abberufen;

~'**s account** Treuhänderkonto; ~ **committee** Treuhänderausschuß; ~ **instruments** *(Br.)* mündelsichere Kapitalanlagen; ~ **savings bank** *(Br.)* gemeinnützige Sparkasse; ~ **stock** *(US)* mündelsichere Wertpapiere.

trusteeship Treuhandverwaltung.

trustworthy guarantee einwandfreie Bürgschaft.

turn Vorteil, Nutzen, Profit, *(broker)* Courtage, *(job)* Beschäftigung, *(alternating order)* Reihenfolge, Turnus, *(stock exchange)* Umschwung, Wende, *(Br.)* Kursgewinn;

~ **of exchange** Kursaufbesserung;

~ *(v.)* **to acount** Vorteil ziehen, verwerten; ~ **bear** Baissier werden; ~ **around a company** Betrieb völlig umkrempeln; ~ **an honest penny** sein Brot ehrlich verdienen; ~ **one's job in** seine Stellung aufgeben; ~ **into cash (money)** flüssig-, zu Geld machen; ~ **a partnership into a limited company** Offene Handelsgesellschaft in eine Gesellschaft mit beschränkter Haftung umwandeln.

turn out *(crop)* ausfallen, *(produce)* [Fabrikat] ausstoßen;

~ **s. o. out of his lodgings** j. exmitieren.

turn over *(goods)* Umsatz haben.

turn-key contract *(US)* schlüsselfertiger Vertrag.

turndown in imports Einfuhrrückgang.

turned out to order auf Bestellung angefertigt.

turnout Erzeugnis, Produkt, *(strike, Br.)* Ausstand, Arbeitseinstellung, Streik.

turnover Umschlag, Geschäftsumsatz, *(reorganization)* Umbau-, Organisation;

annual ~ Jahresumsatz; **capital** ~ Kapitalumschlag; **finished-goods** ~ Umschlaghäufigkeit des Warenbestandes; **gross** ~ Bruttoumsatz; **inventory** ~ Lagerumschlag; **raw-material** ~ Umschlaghäufigkeit des Rohstofflagers; **last year's** ~ Vorjahresumsatz;

thorough ~ **of the operating force** komplette Betriebsumstellung; ~ **of the labo(u)r force** Fluktuation der Arbeitskräfte;

~ **account** Warenverkaufskonto; ~ **commission** Umsatzprovision; ~ **gain** Umsatzzuwachs; ~ **rate** Umsatzziffer, -quote; **capital** ~ **ratio** Umschlaghäufigkeit des Eigenkapitals; ~ **tax** *(Br.)* Umsatzsteuer; ~-**tax refund** *(Br.)* Umsatzsteuerrückvergütung.

turnpike Zollschranke, Schlagbaum;

~ **money** *(freeway)* Autobahngebühr; ~ **road** *(US)* gebührenpflichtige Autobahn.

two | -**decker** zweistöckiger Omnibus; ~-**family house** Zweifamilienhaus; ~-**job man** *(US)* Doppelverdiener; ~-**price system** System gespalteter Preise; ~-**tier gold market** gespalteter Goldmarkt.

tying agreement (contract) *(US)* Exklusiv-, Kopplungsvertrag.

type Art, Type, Muster, Gattung;

~ **of enterprise** Unternehmensform; ~ **of financing** Finanzierungsweise; ~**s of income** Einkunftsarten; ~ **of insurance** Versicherungsform; ~ **of wage plan** Lohnzahlungsmethode.

typing pool Gemeinschaftssekretariat.

typist Maschinenschreiber, Stenotypist;

shorthand ~ Stenotypistin.

U

ultimate | consumer End-, Letztverbraucher; ~ desti-
nation endgültiger Bestimmungsort.
umbrella organization Spitzen-, Zentralverband.
unable to pay zahlungsunfähig.
unaccounted for *(balance sheet)* nicht ausgewiesen.
unadmitted assets nicht bewertbare Aktiva.
unallotted shares nicht zugeteilte Aktien.
unapplied funds totes Kapital.
unappropriated *(money)* nicht ausgeschüttet, keiner
bestimmten Verwendung zugeführt;
~ budget surplus *(municipal accounting)* Haus-
haltsüberschuß; ~ earned surplus *(budgeting) (US)*
nicht verteilter Reingewinn.
unascertained | duties pauschalierte Steuerzahlun-
gen; ~ goods Gattungssachen.
unassessed *(property)* untaxiert, nicht veranlagt.
unauthorized agency Vertretung ohne Vertretungsmacht.
unavailed credit line nicht in Anspruch genommene
Kreditlinie.
unblock *(v.)* an account Konto freigeben.
uncalled capital noch nicht eingezahltes Kapital.
uncertain quotations *(Br.)* per Pfund notierte Devisenkurse.
uncertificated bankrupt *(Br.)* nicht rehabilitierter
Konkursschuldner.
unclaimed | dividends nicht abgehobene Dividenden;
~ wreck herrenloses Wrack.
uncommitted funds nicht zweckgebundene Mittel.
unconditional | offer vorbehaltloses Angebot; ~ order
unwiderruflich erteilter Zahlungsauftrag.
unconfirmed credit unbestätigtes Akkreditiv.
uncontrolled rent freie Miete.
uncovered ungedeckt, ohne Deckung, *(not insured)*
unversichert;
~ advance Blankovorschuß; ~ balance ungedeckter Saldo; ~ sales Leerverkäufe.
uncrossed cheque *(Br.)* offener Scheck, Barscheck.
undebased unverfälscht, nicht entwertet.
undelivered *(letter)* unbestellt, nicht zugestellt;
~ goods noch nicht gelieferte Waren.
undepressed market feste Börse.
underbill *(v.) (US)* Waren zu niedrig deklarieren.
undercapitalization Unterkapitalisierung.
undercharge *(v.)* zu wenig berechnen, zu niedrig in
Rechnung stellen.
undercut *(v.)* a competitor Konkurrenz unterbieten.
undercutter Preisunterbieter.
underdiscount *(v.)* the market *(US)* erwartete Baisse
im voraus berücksichtigen.
underground | bistro Kellerrestaurant; ~ working
Untertagebau.
underhand trade Schleich-, Schwarzhandel.
underinsurance Unterversicherung.
underlying | bonds *(US)* durch Vorranghypothek ge-
sicherte Obligation; ~ company *(US)* [vollständig
abhängige] Tochtergesellschaft; ~ lien *(US)* Vor-

rangpfandrecht; ~ syndicate *(US)* Übernahmekonsortium.
underprice *(US)* Schleuderpreis.
underprivileged area of a city Armenviertel einer
Stadt.
underrate *(v.)* unterbewerten, zu niedrig bewerten.
undersell *(v.)* unter dem Preis verkaufen, verschleudern, Konkurrenz unterbieten.
underselling price Schleuderpreis.
understanding, friendly gütliches Einvernehmen; re-
ciprocal ~ Gegenseitigkeitsvereinbarung.
undersubscribed loan nicht in voller Höhe gezeich-
nete Anleihe.
undertake | a business Geschäftsbesorgung überneh-
men; ~ the collection of a bill Wechsel zum Inkasso übernehmen; ~ a risk Risiko eingehen.
undertaker Unternehmer, *(speculator)* Spekulant,
(supplier) Lieferant.
undertaking Unternehmen, -nehmung, Betrieb, *(ob-*
ligation) eingegangene Verpflichtung, Engagement;
on the ~ auf die Zusicherung;
agricultural ~ landwirtschaftlicher Betrieb; business ~ Geschäftsunternehmen, Wirtschaftsbe-
trieb; contributory ~ Zuschußbetrieb; industrial ~
Gewerbebetrieb, gewerbliches Unternehmen; public-utility ~ öffentlicher Versorgungsbetrieb;
~ to pay Zahlungsversprechen.
undertenant Untermieter, -pächter.
undertone *(stock exchange)* Grundton, -stimmung,
Tendenz.
undervaluation Unterbewertung, *(customs)* Zoller-
klärung zu zu niedrigem Wert.
underweight Mindergewicht, Gewichtsabgang.
underwrite *(v.)* unterschreiben, *(guarantee)* Haftung
übernehmen, *(insurance business)* versichern, Ver-
sicherungsgeschäfte übernehmen, *(issue of securities)*
Effektenemission garantieren, *(marine insurance)*
Transportversicherungsgeschäft erledigen;
~ the cost of a project für die Finanzierung eines
Projekts geradestehen; ~ a risk Versicherung
unter Risikoverteilung übernehmen.
underwriter Unterzeichner, *(agent, US)* Versicherungsagent, *(banking)* Konsortialmitglied, *(insur-*
ance business) Assekuranzversicherung, Versiche-
rungsgeber, -träger, *(issue of securities)* Emissionsbank, Anleihegarant;
~s *(issue of securities)* Übernahmekonsortium,
Garantiesyndikat, -konsortium;
cargo ~ Frachtenversicherer; leading ~ *(banking)*
Konsortialführerin; life ~ *(US)* Lebensversicherungsvertreter;
~s group Emissions-, Garantiekonsortium.
underwriting *(insurance business)* Übernahme von
Versicherungen, *(issue of securities)* Emissions-
übernahmegeschäft;
firm ~ feste Übernahme;

~ **of a risk** Übernahme eines Versicherungsrisikos; ~ **agent** *(Br.)* Abschlußagent; ~ **agreement** Übernahmeabkommen, Konsortialvertrag; ~ **bank** Konsortialbank; ~ **business** Effektenemissionsgeschäft, *(insurance)* Versicherungsgeschäft; ~ **conditions** *(banking)* Zeichnungsbedingungen; ~ **contract** Konsortialvertrag; ~ **costs** Kapitalemissionskosten; ~ **deficit** Versicherungsverlust; ~ **fee** Übernahmespesen; ~ **group** [missions]konsortium; ~ **house** *(US)* Emissionsfirma; ~ **member** Konsortialmitglied; ~ **price** Übernahmekurs; ~ **profit** *(insurance)* Versicherungsgewinn; ~ **share** Konsortialanteil; ~ **syndicate** Emissions-, Garantiekonsortium.

undeveloped land *(Br.)* nicht erschlossenes Baugelände, *(balance sheet)* unbebaute Grundstücke.

undigested securities *(US)* nicht placierte Effekten.

undischarged bankrupt nicht rehabilitierte Konkursschuldner.

undisclosed | **agency** verdeckte Stellvertretung; ~ **buyer** ungenannter Käufer; ~ **reserves** stille Rücklagen.

undisposed unbegeben, unverkauft.

undistributed | **cost** Handlungs-, Generalunkosten; ~ **net income** unverteilter Reingewinn; ~ **profit** nicht ausgeschütteter Gewinn.

undivided | **profit** nicht ausgeschütteter Gewinn; ~ **share in land** Liegenschaftsanteil.

undo *(v.)* **a bargain** *(Br.)* Effektentransaktion glattstellen.

undrawn profit nicht entnommener Gewinn.

undue | **attachment** unberechtigte Pfändung; ~ **hardship** unbillige Härte; ~ **preference** Gläubigerbegünstigung.

unearned | **income** *(balance sheet)* transitorische Passiva, *(taxation)* Einkünfte aus Kapitalbesitz; ~ **increment** *(land)* unverdienter Wertzuwachs; ~ **premium reserve** *(life insurance)* Prämienreserve.

uneconomical unwirtschaftlich, unrentabel.

unemployed arbeits-, stellen-, erwerbslos; ~ **on relief** ausgesteuerter Arbeitsloser; ~ **capital** brachliegendes Kapital; ~ **person** Arbeitsloser.

unemployment Arbeits-, Erwerbslosigkeit; **chronic** ~ Dauerarbeitslosigkeit; **cyclical** ~ konjunkturbedingte Arbeitslosigkeit; **frictional** ~ fluktuierende Arbeitslosigkeit; **seasonal** ~ saisonbedingte Arbeitslosigkeit; ~ **benefit** *(Br.)* Arbeitslosenunterstützung; **to draw (receive)** ~ **benefit** Arbeitslosenunterstützung beziehen.

unemployment compensation *(US)* Arbeitslosenunterstützung; ~ **program(me)** Arbeitslosenunterstützungsprogramm; ~ **contributions** Arbeitslosenunterstützungsbeiträge.

unemployment insurance Erwerbslosen-, Arbeitslosenversicherung; **to qualify for** ~ Voraussetzungen für die Arbeitslosenunterstützung erfüllen; ~ **contribution** Arbeitslosenversicherungsbeitrag.

unemployment | **line** Arbeitslosenschlange; **to report to the** ~ **office** sich beim Arbeitsamt als beschäftigungslos melden; ~ **pay** Arbeitslosenunterstützung; ~ **rate** Arbeitslosenprozentsatz, -ziffer; ~ **roll** Arbeitslosenregister.

unencumbered schuldenfrei, *(real estate)* unbelastet, hypothekenfrei;

unengaged unbeschäftigt, stellenlos.

unentered nicht gebucht, *(customs)* unverzollt.

unexpended appropriation *(governmental accounting)* noch nicht ausgegebene, jedoch verplante Etatsmittel.

unexpired expense transitorische Aktiva.

unfair | **business practices** unlautere Geschäftsmethoden; ~ **competition** unlauterer Wettbewerb.

unfavo(u)rable | **balance of trade** passive Handelsbilanz; ~ **exchange** ungünstiger Kurs.

unfilled orders Auftragsbestand.

unfinished | **business** *(parliament)* unerledigte Punkte [der Tagesordnung]; ~ **goods** Halbfertigwaren.

unfit | **for business** geschäftsuntüchtig; **to be** ~ **for heavy traffic** nur wenig Verkehr aufnehmen können.

unfreeze *(v.)* **funds** Guthaben freigeben.

unfunded debt *(Br.)* schwebende (unfundierte) Schuld.

unfurnished room Leerzimmer.

unified | **bonds** Ablösungsschuldverschreibungen; ~ **stock** *(Br.)* konsolidierte Anleihe.

uniform | **accounting system** einheitliches Buchführungssystem; ~ **price** Einheitspreis; ~ **tariff** Einheitstarif; ~ **value** einheitlicher Wert.

uniformity in taxation gleichmäßige Besteuerung.

unilinear tariff Einheitstarif.

unincumbered schuldenfrei, unbelastet.

uninsured | **employment** versicherungsfreie Beschäftigung; ~ **parcel** nicht versichertes Paket; ~ **risk** ungedecktes Risiko.

union *(society)* Verein, Verband, Vereinigung, *(trade union)* Gewerkschaft; **amalgamated craft** ~ Fachgewerkschaft; **company** ~ *(US)* Betriebsgewerkschaft; **economic** ~ Wirtschaftsunion; **industrial** ~ Industriegewerkschaft; **local** ~ Ortsverein; **peaceful** ~ *(US)* wirtschaftsfriedliche Gewerkschaft; **to join a** ~ einer Gewerkschaft als Mitglied beitreten; ~ **agent** Gewerkschaftsvertreter; ~ **agreement** Tarifvertrag; ~ **assessments** Gewerkschaftsbeiträge, -umlage; ~ **bank** Gemeinwirtschaftsbank; ~ **card** Gewerkschaftsausweis; ~ **dues** Gewerkschaftsbeiträge; ~ **enterprise** gewerkschaftseigenes Unternehmen; **to apply to the** ~ **house** *(Br.)* sich an die Fürsorgebehörden wenden; ~ **member** Gewerkschaftsmitglied; ~ **scale** *(US)* gewerkschaftlich festgesetzter Lohntarif; ~ **steward** *(US)* Betriebsrat, -obmann.

unionize *(v.)* gewerkschaftlich organisieren.

unionized labo(u)r gewerkschaftlich organisierte Arbeitskräfte.

unissued capital *(Br.)* **(capital stock,** *US)* nicht ausgegebenes (emittiertes) Aktienkapital.

unit Stück, *(block of securities)* Effektenbündel, *(investment trust, Br.)* Investmentanteil;

bargaining ~ Tarifvertragspartei; **cost** ~ Kosteneinheit; **first-stage** ~ *(statistics)* Einheit der ersten Auswahlstufe; **low-rent** ~ *(US)* billiges Mietshaus; **monetary** ~ Währungseinheit;

~ **of account** [Ver]rechnungseinheit; ~ **of assessment (taxation)** Veranlagungsobjekt; ~ **of cost** Kostenträger;

~ **amount** Betrag pro Einheit; ~ **calculation** Einzelkalkulation; ~ **control** *(US)* buchmäßige Mengenkontrolle; ~ **costs** Stückkosten; ~ **evaluation** *(investment fund)* Anteilsbewertung; ~ **furniture** Anbaumöbel; ~ **holder** *(Br.)* Investment-, Anteilscheinbesitzer; ~ **price** Stück-, Einheitspreis; ~ **pricing store** Einheitspreisgeschäft; ~ **trust** *(Br.)* Kapitalanlagegesellschaft.

United Nations Economic and Social Council Wirtschafts- und Sozialrat der Vereinten Nationen.

unity, economic Wirtschaftseinheit.

universal | **agent** Generalbevollmächtigter; ~ **partnership** allgemeine Gütergemeinschaft; ~ **provider** *(Br.)* Gemischtwarenhändler.

unlawful picketing unerlaubtes Streikpostenstehen.

unlicensed nicht konzessioniert, ohne Lizenz;
~ **broker** freier Makler.

unlimited | **claim** ziffernmäßig nicht begrenzte Forderung; ~ **company** *(Br.)* Gesellschaft mit unbeschränkter Haftung; ~ **liability** unbeschränkte Haftpflicht; ~ **order** unlimitierter Börsenauftrag; **for an** ~ **time** unbefristet.

unliquidated damages vertraglich nicht festgesetzter Schadenersatzanspruch.

unlisted *(US, stock exchange)* unnotiert, nicht notiert.

unload *(v.) (securities)* abstoßen, verkaufen.

unloading | **berth** Lösch-, Ausladeplatz; ~ **charges** Abladegebühr; ~ **platform** Ausladebahnsteig; ~ **risk** *(insurance)* Löschrisiko.

unmarketable assets nicht realisierbare Aktien.

unmortgaged unverpfändet, unbelastet.

unoccupied unbeschäftigt, *(vacant)* unbewohnt.

unofficial | **broker** Freiverkehrs-, Kulissenmakler; ~ **market** *(Br.)* Nachbörse, *(curb market)* Freiverkehr.

unorganized labo(u)r gewerkschaftlich nicht organisierte Arbeitskräfte.

unpaid unbezahlt, nicht bezahlt *(not prepaid)* unfrankiert, nicht freigemacht;
~ **agent** ehrenamtlicher Vertreter; ~ **bill** nicht eingelöster Wechsel; ~ **capital** noch nicht eingezahltes Kapital; ~ **interest** rückständige Zinsen.

unpegged [von der Goldwährung] losgelöst.

unpicked samples nicht ausgewählte Proben.

unpriced nicht ausgezeichnet, ohne Preisangabe.

unprivileged creditor Massegläubiger.

unproductive wages Gemeinkostenlöhne.

unprofessional berufswidrig, keiner Berufsgruppe zugehörig;

~ **advertising** stümperhafte Reklame; ~ **conduct** standeswidriges Verhalten.

unprovided for unversorgt.

unqualified ungeeignet, untauglich, *(balance sheet approval)* uneingeschränkt, nicht qualifiziert.

unquoted | **list** *(Br.)* Freiverkehrsnotierung; ~ **securities** zur amtlichen Notierung nicht zugelassene Wertpapiere.

unrealized profit nicht realisierter Gewinn.

unreasonable *(price)* unbescheiden, unverschämt;
~ **restraint of trade** *(US)* unberechtigte Preisbindung.

unrecovered cost *(balance sheet)* nicht abschreibungsfähige Investitionskosten.

unredeemed pledge uneingelöstes Pfand.

unregistered | **company** nicht eingetragene Gesellschaft; ~ **letter** gewöhnlicher (einfacher) Brief.

unreliable unzuverlässig, *(business firm)* unsolide.

unremunerative work unbezahlte Arbeit.

unrest, labo(u)r Arbeiterunruhen.

unsafe paper *(stock exchange)* dubioses Papier.

unsalaried | **clerk** Volontär; ~ **employment** unbezahlte Beschäftigung.

unsal(e)able article Ladenhüter.

unsatisfied *(creditor)* nicht befriedigt;
~ **execution** erfolglose Zwangsvollstreckung.

unscramble *(v.)* entschlüsseln, dechiffrieren;
~ **a business concern** Konzern entflechten.

unsecured | **account** ungesichertes Kontokorrentkonto; ~ **claim** *(bankruptcy)* Masseanspruch; ~ **credit** Blankokredit; ~ **creditor** Massegläubiger.

unsettled *(account)* nicht ausgeglichen, (abgerechnet) *(market)* uneinheitlich, schwankend, *(not fixed in position)* in unsicherer Stellung, *(residence)* ohne festen Wohnsitz;
~ **bill** unbezahlte Rechnung; ~ **region** unbesiedelte Gegend.

unsheltered industry zollpolitisch nicht geschützte Industriezweige.

unskilled ungelernt, ungeschickt;
~ **labo(u)r** Handarbeit, mechanische Arbeit; ~ **manpower** ungelernte Arbeitskräfte.

unsold, subject to being Zwischenverkauf vorbehalten.

unsound | **finance** finanzielle Mißwirtschaft; ~ **investment** Fehlanlage.

unstamped nicht verstempelt, unfrankiert.

unsteady output schwankende Produktionsziffern.

unsuccessful applicant zurückgewiesener Bewerber.

untaxable nicht besteuerungsfähig.

untouched provisions unangetastete Vorräte.

unused | **capital** brachliegendes Kapital; ~ **room** unbenutztes Zimmer.

unvalued shares (stocks, *US)* Aktien ohne Nennwert, Quotenaktien.

unweighted index unbewerteter Index.

up Preisanstieg, Kursanstieg;
~**s and downs of employment** Schwankungen der Beschäftigungsziffer;
2 d ~ *(stock exchange)* 2 Pence höher;

to be ~ against bankruptcy vom völligen Bankrott bedroht sein; to go ~ *(prices)* steigen, in die Höhe gehen.

updating of inventory Lagerwirtschaft.

upgrade Aufsteigen, Aufstieg; ~ *(v.)* economically auf einen wirtschaftlichen Höchststand bringen.

upgrading of income Einkommensanstieg.

upkeep and improvements Unterhaltungsaufwendungen und Instandhaltungskosten.

uplift *(economics)* Konjunkturanstieg.

upper-bracket in der höheren Einkommensklasse.

upset price *(bankruptcy proceedings)* niedrigster Zuschlagswert.

upsurge | **in housing** Wohungsbaukonjunktur; ~ **in imports** rasanter Einfuhranstieg; ~ **in rates** kräftige Tariferhöhung.

upswing Aufschwung, konjunktureller Auftrieb; **seasonal** ~ Saisonaufschwung.

uptick in production Produktionsanstieg.

uptrend Aufschwung, konjunktureller Auftrieb.

upturn Aufschwung, Besserung, *(prices)* Aufwärtsbewegung, *(stock market)* Kursanstieg; ~ **in business (in the business cycle)** Konjunkturanstieg; -aufschwung; ~ **in wages** Lohnanstieg.

upvaluation Aufwertung.

upward steigend, anziehend; **to go** ~s *(prices)* in die Höhe gehen; ~ **business trend** Konjunkturaufschwung; ~ **movement** Aufwärtsbewegung, *(stock exchange)* Kursanstieg; ~ **tendency** steigende [Kurs]tendenz; ~ **tendency of prices** Preisauftrieb; ~ **tendency of wages** Lohnauftrieb.

urban | **area** Stadtgebiet; ~ **center** *(US)* (centre, *Br.)* Ballungsgebiet.

urge to buy Kaufwut; ~ **to merge** Fusionsneigung; ~ *(v.)* payment auf Zahlung drängen.

urgency dringende Notwendigkeit, Dringlichkeit.

urgent | **creditor** drängender Gläubiger; ~ **items** dringende Postsendung.

usage [Handels]brauch, Praxis, Usance, Sitte; **compulsory** ~ Benutzungszwang; **ordinary** ~ Verkehrssitte.

use Nutzen, Vorteil, *(custom)* Gewohnheit, Brauch, *(employment)* Gebrauch, Verwendung; **fit for** ~ betriebsfähig; **charitable** ~ Wohltätigkeitszweck; **industrial** ~ gewerbliche Verwertung; **personal** ~ *(tenant)* Eigenbedarf; **productive** ~ Gebrauchsüberlassung; ~ **of airfreight in delivery** Auslieferung auf dem Luftfrachtwege; ~ **of capacity** Kapazitätsausnutzung; ~ **of a fund** Inanspruchnahme eines Fonds; ~ *(v.)* [ge]brauchen, benutzen, verwenden; **to alter the** ~ **of premises** Wohnung zweckentfremden; **to make full** ~ **of** voll verwerten; ~ **charge** Benutzungsgebühr; **home** ~ **entry** *(customs)* Einfuhr zum eigenen Gebrauch; ~ **life** Nutzungswert; ~ **value** Gebrauchswert.

used gebraucht, ausgenutzt, *(clothes)* getragen; **hardly** ~ *(marine insurance)* fast neuwertig; ~ **car** Gebrauchtwagen.

useful | **life** Nutzungsdauer; ~ **load** Nutzlast.

user Benutzer, Verbraucher, *(buyer)* Abnehmer; **large** ~ Großabnehmer; ~ **fee** Benutzungsgebühr.

usual | **course of employer's trade** üblicher Geschäftsablauf; ~ **place of abode** gewöhnlicher Aufenthaltsort.

usurious | **contract** Wuchervertrag; ~ **interest** Wucherzinsen; ~ **price** Wucherpreis; ~ **transaction** Wuchergeschäft.

usury, to practise Wucher treiben.

utilities *(stock exchange, US)* Versorgungswerte.

utility Nutzen, Nützlichkeit, *(patent law)* Nutzungswert, *(corporation, US)* Versorgungsbetrieb; **of public** ~ gemeinnützig; **municipally owned** ~ kommunaler Versorgungsbetrieb; **public** ~ Versorgungsunternehmen; ~ **article** Gebrauchsgegenstand; ~ **equipment** Versorgungseinrichtungen; ~ **goods** Gebrauchsgüter, *(Br.)* Güter mit sozialem Preis; ~ **shares (stocks,** *(US)* Versorgungswerte; **public** ~ **undertaking** öffentlicher Versorgungsbetrieb; ~ **van (wag(g)on)** Mehrzweckfahrzeug.

utilization of plant capacities Kapazitätsausnutzung.

utilize *(v.)* **workers** Arbeitskräfte einsetzen.

uttering false notes Falschgeldverbreitung.

V

vacancies *(newspaper)* Stellenangebote.
vacancy Vakanz, offene (freie) Stelle, *(unbuilt area)* unbebautes (freies) Gelände;
~ **in the board of directors** nicht besetzter Direktorenposten;
to advertise a ~ freie Stelle ausschreiben.
vacant frei, unbesetzt, leer, herrenlos, *(house)* leerstehend, unbewohnt, frei;
to apply for a ~ **position** sich um eine freie Stelle bewerben; ~ **room** Leerzimmer.
vacate.*(v.)* für ungültig erklären, *(empty)* [Zimmer]-räumen, ausziehen;
~ **a charter** Satzung zurücknehmen; ~ **one's residence** seinen Wohnsitz aufgeben.
vacation *(US)* Urlaub, Ferien;
eligible for ~**s** *(US)* urlaubsberechtigt;
paid ~ *(US)* bezahlter Urlaub;
~ **of a house** Räumung eines Hauses; ~ **without pay** *(US)* unbezahlter Urlaub;
to have no ~ **from business** geschäftlich ununterbrochen in Anspruch genommen sein;
~ **allowance** *(US)* Urlaubsabgeltung; ~ **bonus** *(US)* Ferienzulage; ~ **eligibility** *(US)* Urlaubsberechtigung; ~ **home** *(US)* Ferienheim; ~ **paradise** *(US)* Ferienparadies; ~ **period** *(US)* Urlaubs-, Ferienzeit; ~ **privilege (right)** *(US)* Urlaubsanspruch; ~ **request** *(US)* Urlaubsgesuch; ~ **schedule** *(US)* Urlaubsplan; ~ **school** *(US)* Ferienkurs; ~ **shutdown** *(US)* Schließung, Werksferien.
vagabond wage Hungerlohn.
valid [rechts]gültig, rechtskräftig, *(enforceable)* durchsetzbar, *(ticket)* gültig.
validate *(v.)* **a claim** Anspruch anerkennen.
validation Gültigkeitserklärung, Validierung;
~ **of a fund** Errechnung des Fondwertes.
validity Rechtswirksamkeit, Gültigkeitsdauer.
valorization Aufwertung, *(US)* Preisstützung.
valorize *(v.)* aufwerten, valorisieren;
~ **prices** *(US)* Preise stützen (stabilisieren).
valuable Wertgegenstand, -sache;
~ **consideration** Vertragsinteresse, entgeltliche Gegenleistung; ~ **improvements** Wertsteigerungen.
value Wert, *(appraisal)* Einschätzung, *(assessed value)* Verkehrswert, *(bill of exchange)* [Wechsel]-summe, *(currency, Br.)* Währung, Valuta, *(market price)* Preis, Wert, *(quality goods)* preiswerte (reelle) Ware, Qualitätsware;
at ~ *(stock exchange)* zum Tageskurs; **for** ~ **received** Wert (Betrag) erhalten; **of inferior** ~ minderwertig;
accounting ~ Buch[ungs]wert; **actual** ~ Effektivwert, **added** ~ Mehrwert; **amenity** ~ Annehmlichkeitswert [eines Grundstücks]; **annual** ~ *(Br.)* Jahresertrag; **assessed** ~ Steuer-, Tax-, Einheitswert; **asset** ~ Substanzwert; **attached-business** ~ Verkehrswert; **book** ~ Buchwert; **cash** ~ *(insurance)* Rückkaufswert; **declared current** ~ Emis-

sionswert; **customs** ~ Zollwert; **earning-capacity** ~ kapitalisierter Wert; **face** ~ Nominal-, Nennwert; **full** ~ *(insurance business)* Ersatzwert; **going-concern** ~ Betriebswert; **insurance** ~ versicherbarer Wert; **invoice** ~ Fakturawert; **junk** ~ Schrottwert; **market** ~ Markt-, Tages-, Verkehrswert; **marketable** ~ Verkaufswert; **net annual** ~ *(income tax statement, Br.)* Nutzungswert des eigengenutzten Einfamilienhauses; **present** ~ Tageswert; **pre-war** ~ Vorkriegswert; **rental** ~ Mietertragswert; **replacement (reproduction cost)** ~ Wiederbeschaffungswert; **scrap** ~ Abschreibungswert; **sentimental** ~ Liebhaberwert; **starting** ~ Ausgangswert; **stock-exchange** ~ Börsenwert; **surrender** ~ *(insurance)* Rückkaufswert; **tax** ~ Steuerwert;
net ~ **added** *(national income accounting)* Wertabschöpfung; ~ **of capital stock** Anlagenwert; ~ **as new** Neuwert; ~ **of plant in successful operation** Betriebswert; ~ **at point of entry** Deklarationswert; ~ **in use** Nutzungs-, Gebrauchswert;
~ *(v.) (appraise)* [ab]schätzen, einschätzen, *(assets)* taxieren, *(banking)* valutieren, *(draw bill)* ziehen, trassieren, *(negotiate)* begeben, verkaufen;
~ **cheques on London** *(Br.)* Schecks auf London ausschreiben; ~ **the damage [done] at five pounds** Schaden auf fünf Pfund abschätzen; ~ **an estate** Einheitswert [eines Grundstücks] festsetzen;
to be liable to deteriorate in ~ einer Wertminderung ausgesetzt sein; **to get good** ~ **for one's money** sein Geld gut anlegen; **to go down in** ~ **all the time** fortgesetzten Wertverlusten ausgesetzt sein; **to offer good** ~ **for long-range investment purposes** für langfristige Anlagezwecke billig liegen; **to raise the face** ~ [Aktien] zum Nennwert berechnen; **to sell under the** ~ unter dem Preis ablassen; **to set a low** ~ **on a stock** *(US)* Aktie niedrig ansetzen;
~-**added tax** Mehrwertsteuer; ~ **appreciation** Wertsteigerung; **global** ~ **adjustment** Sammelwertberichtigung; ~-**given clause** Valutaklausel; ~ **date** *(bookkeeping)* Wertstellungstermin, *(check)* Eingangsdatum; **fixed percentage** ~ **increment** prozentual festgelegte Wertsteigerung; **no par** ~ **stock** *(US)* Aktie ohne Nennwert, Quotenaktie.
valued at the lower of cost or market *(balancing method)* zum Einstands- oder Marktwert bewertet.
valuer *(Br.)* Schätzer, Taxator.
van Last-, Transportwagen, *(Br.)* G-Wagen;
delivery ~ *(Br.)* Lieferwagen;
~ **driver** Lastwagenfahrer.
variable *(market)* veränderlich, wechselnd;
~ **annuity** *(pension scheme)* auf den Lebenshaltungsindex abgestellte Rente; ~ **cost** veränderliche (bewegliche) Kosten; ~ **deductions** variable Lohnabzüge; ~ **yield securities** Papiere mit schwankendem Ertrag.
variance *(in cost)* Kostenabweichung.
variation, seasonal saisonbedingte Schwankungen;
~**s in prices** Preisschwankungen.

variety *(collection)* Angebot, Sortimentsbreite;
  wide ~ of product lines weit gestreutes Warensortiment; ~ of patterns Mustersortiment;
  ~ chain store Kaufhaus, -hof; ~ shop Ge
  mischtwarenhandlung.
vary *(v.)* with the season *(prices)* saisonalen Schwankungen unterworfen sein.
vault *(safe)* Stahlkammer, Tresor;
  ~ deposit Verwahrstück.
vehicle Fahrzeug, Beförderungsmittel;
  commercial ~ Nutzfahrzeug; for-hire ~ Mietfahr-
  zeug;
  ~ business Fahrzeugindustrie.
vending machine Waren-, Verkaufsautomat.
vendor, vender Verkäufer, *(supplier, US)* Lieferer,
  Lieferant;
  ~ company einbringende Gesellschaft; ~'s lien
  Eigentumsvorbehalt.
venture *(goods)* schwimmendes Gut (Ware), *(object
  of speculation)* Spekulationsobjekt, *(risk)* Risiko,
  Wagnis, *(speculation)* [Handels]spekulation;
  joint ~ Beteiligungsgeschäft;
  ~ of exchange Valutarisiko;
  ~ *(v.) (risk)* unternehmen, wagen, riskieren;
  ~ capital Risikokapital.
verbal offer mündlich gemachtes Angebot.
verification *(auditing)* Bestätigung der Richtigkeit,
  (examination) Nachprüfung, Überprüfung;
  delivery ~ Wareneingangsbestätigung;
  ~ of the cash Kassenrevision;
  ~ statement Saldenbestätigung.
verify *(v.) (auditing)* Richtigkeit bestätigen, *(confirm)*
  bestätigen;
  ~ an account Richtigkeit eines Kontoauszuges bestätigen; ~ a calculation nachrechnen; ~ by invoices mit Rechnungen belegen.
versedness in trade Geschäftserfahrung.
vertical | amalgamation vertikaler Zusammenschluß;
  ~ price-fixing contract Preisbindung der zweiten
  Hand; ~ trust Verbundwirtschaft.
vessel Schiff, Seefahrzeug, *(aircraft)* Luftfahrzeug,
  -schiff;
  cargo ~ Frachtschiff; idle ~ stilliegendes Schiff;
  merchant ~ Handels-, Kauffahrteischiff.
vest *(v.)* in the trustee in bankruptcy *(Br.)* auf den
  Konkursverwalter übergehen.
vested interests wohlerworbene Rechte.
vestibule | train *(US)* Durchgangszug, D-Zug; ~
  training *(US)* Werkstattausbildung.
vetoing stock Sperrmajorität.
viability finanzielle Leistungsfähigkeit.
vicarious | agent Erfüllungsgehilfe; ~ liability Haf-
  tung für fremdes Verschulden (für den Erfüllungsgehilfen).
vice-president stellvertretender Vorsitzender.
victuals *(Br.)* Lebens-, Nahrungsmittel, Proviant.
victual[l]er Lebensmittelhändler;
  licensed ~ *(Br.)* Schankwirt.
video *(US)* Fernsehen;
  ~ bus Fernsehaufnahmewagen; ~ cartridge Fern-
  sehfilmkassette.

videotape recorder Fernsehbandaufnahme.
view *(inquiry)* Untersuchung, Prüfung, *(survey)*
  Übersicht, kurzes Gutachten.
  true and fair ~ *(balance sheet)* wahres und richtiges
  Bild;
  to give an order to ~ Besichtigungsgenehmigung
  erteilen.
visa, visé Sichtvermerk, Einreisegenehmigung, Visum;
  customs ~ Zollvermerk; entry ~ Einreisevisum;
  transit ~ Durchreisevisum;
  to mark a passport with ~ Paß mit Sichtvermerk
  versehen.
visible | envelope Fensterumschlag; ~ exports sicht-
  bare Ausfuhr; ~ reserves offene Reserven.
visit Besuch, *(search)* Durchsuchung, *(ship)* Flag-
  genkontrolle;
  domiciliary ~ *(Br.)* Haussuchung;
  ~ of a commercial traveller Vertreterbesuch.
visiting book Besucherliste.
visitor Besucher, [Kur]gast, Tourist, *(hotel)* Hotelgast, *(inspector of corporation)* Prüfer, Revisor,
  Inspekteur;
  anticipated ~s geschätzte Besucherzahlen;
  to attract foreign ~s Fremdenverkehr heben;
  ~s' book Fremdenbuch.
visual *(advertising)* Verkaufshilfe.
vital interests lebenswichtige Interessen.
vocation Eignung, *(occupation)* Beruf, Beschäftigung, Geschäft, Gewerbe;
  overcrowded ~s überfüllte (übersetzte) Berufe.
vocational | adviser Berufsberater; ~ adjustment Ein-
  arbeitung; ~ aptitude berufliche Eignung; ~ clinic
  Berufsberatungsinstitut; ~ counsel[ing] Berufsberatung; ~ disease Berufskrankheit; ~-guidance adviser Berufsberater; ~-guidance center *(US)*
  (centre, *Br.)* Berufsberatungsstelle; ~ reeducation
  [Berufs]umschulung.
vogue Mode *(popularity)* Popularität, Erfolg, Anklang, Beliebtheit.
voice, bigger größere Stimmrechte;
  to have a technical 50-50 ~ in the management
  ziffernmäßig zu 50 % an der Geschäftsführung
  beteiligt sein.
void *(a.) (unhabited)* unbewohnt, *(invalid)* nichtig,
  [rechts]unwirksam, rechtsungültig, kraftlos;
  ~ of seizable property unpfändbar;
  ~ money order verfallene Postanweisung.
voidable preference *(bankruptcy law)* Gläubigerbe-
  vorzugung.
volume Maß, Umfang, *(content)* Rauminhalt;
  ~ of business Geschäftsvolumen; ~ of investment
  Umfang der vorgenommenen Investitionen; ~ of
  traffic Streckenbelastung, Verkehrsleistung; ~ of
  work Arbeitsanfall;
  to deal in big ~s große Geschäftsabschlüsse (Umsätze) tätigen;
  ~ discount Mengenrabatt; ~-produce serienmäßig
  herstellen; ~ production Massenproduktion.
voluntary freiwillig, aus eigenem Antrieb, *(amicable)*
  gütlich, außergerichtlich;

~ **agency** freiwillige Hilfsorganisation; ~ **bankruptcy** selbst beantragte Konkurserklärung; ~ **contribution** Spende; ~ **conveyance** unentgeltliche Übereignung; ~ **reserves** freie Rücklagen; ~ **sale** Freiverkauf; ~ **staff** ehrenamtliche Mitarbeiter.

volunteer unentgeltlicher Erwerber, *(agent of necessity)* Geschäftsführer ohne Auftrag, *(in undeveloppend country, Br.)* Entwicklungshelfer.

vote Wahlergebnis, *(money granted)* bewilligte Summe, Geldbewilligung, Budget;
majority ~ Majoritätsbeschluß; **straw** ~ inoffizielle Probeabstimmung; **supplementary** ~ *(parl.)* Nachbewilligung;
~ *(v.)* **the appropriation** Haushaltsvoranschlag bewilligen; ~ **[on] the stock** Aktienstimmrecht ausüben; ~ **a sum for travel(l)ing expenses** Reisespesen in einer bestimmten Höhe bewilligen.

voting | **capital stock** stimmberechtigtes Aktienkapital; ~ **list of stockholders** *(US)* Liste der stimmberechtigten Aktionäre; ~ **power** Abstimmungsbefugnis; ~ **procedure by proxy** Stimmrechtsausübung durch Stellvertreter; **to transfer one's** ~ **shares** *(Br.)* seine Stimmrechte übertragen; ~ **trust certificate** *(US)* Stimmbindungszertifikat; ~ **trust certificate holder** *(US)* stimmgebundener Aktionär.

vouch *(v.)* *(confirm)* bestätigen, bezeugen, *(corroborate)* belegen, durch Urkunden erhärten.

voucher [Buchungs]beleg, Buchungsunterlage, *(evidence to disburse cash)* [Aus]zahlungsbeleg, *(receipt)* Gutschein, Rechnungsbeleg, Bon;
approved ~ anerkannter Beleg; **disbursement** ~ Zahlungsanweisung; **expense** ~ Spesenbeleg; **hotel** ~ Hotelgutschein; **meal** ~ Essensbon; **petty-cash** ~ Portokassenbeleg;
to file a ~ Beleg abheften; **to support by** ~**s** dokumentarisch belegen;
~ **audit** Prüfung der Auszahlungsbelege; ~ **check** *(US)* Verrechnungsscheck; ~ **clerk** Kreditorenbuchhalter; ~ **register** Belegverzeichnis.

voyage Seereise, *(journey)* Reise;
~ **insurance** Reiseversicherung.

vulnerable to inflation inflationsempfindlich.

W

wad of bank notes Bündel von Banknoten.

waddle *(v.)* **out of the alley** *(Br. sl.)* sich von der Börse zurückziehen, Zahlungen einstellen.

wage [Arbeits]lohn, Werklohn, *(production cost)* Lohnanteil, *(ship)* Heuer;
advance ~ Lohnvorschüsse; **back** ~**s** Lohnrückstände; **bootleg** ~**s** außertariflich gezahlte Löhne; **dismissal** ~ Entlassungsausgleich; **job** ~ Stück-, Akkordlohn; **journeyman** ~ Gesellenlohn; **living** ~ Existenzminimum; **occupational** ~ Facharbeiterlohn; **pegged** ~ künstlich gehaltener Lohn; **real** ~ Reallohn; **result** ~ Akkordlohn; **sliding** ~ gleitender Lohn; **standard** ~ Tariflohn; **superannuated** ~ untertariflicher Lohn; **time** ~ Zeit-, Stundenlohn; ~ **of management** *(superintendence)* Gehalt leitender Angestellter, *(owner-manager)* Unternehmergewinn;
to attach ~**s** *(Br.)* Lohn pfänden; **to cut** ~**s** Löhne kürzen; **to deduct from the** ~ vom Lohn abziehen; **to freeze** ~**s** Lohnstopp durchführen; **to retain** ~**s** Lohn einbehalten;
~ **accounting** Lohnabrechnung; ~ **adjustment** Lohnangleichung, -anpassung; ~ **agreement** Tarifvertrag; ~ **bargaining** Lohnverhandlungen; ~ **bill** Lohnliste; **National** ~ **Board** *(US)* staatliches Schlichtungsamt; **to tie** ~ **boosts to productive gains** Lohnanstieg mit Produktivitätszuwachs koppeln; ~ **bracket** Tarifklasse, Lohngruppe; ~ **check** *(US)* Lohnscheck; ~ **clause** Tarifklausel; ~ **clerk** Lohnbuchhalter; ~ **and salary control** Lohn- und Gehaltsüberwachung, -reglementierung; ~ **demands** Lohnforderungen; ~ **development** Entwicklung der Löhne; ~ **differentials** Tarifunterschiede; ~ **docket** Lohntüte; ~ **drift** Lohnauftrieb; ~ **earner** Lohn-, Gehaltsempfänger; ~ **earning employment** nicht selbständige Beschäftigung; ~ **escalation** gleitende Lohnregelung; ~ **factor in cost** Lohnkostenfaktor; ~ **formula** Lohn-, Tarifformel; ~ **freeze** Lohnstopp; ~ **garnishment** *(US)* Lohnpfändung; ~ **guidepost** Lohneckpfeiler; ~ **incentive payment plan** Leistungslohnsystem; ~ **income** Erwerbseinkommen; ~ **across-the-board** ~ **increase** umfassender Lohnanstieg, Lohnwelle; **national** ~ **index corrected to take out inflationary effects** inflationsbereinigter Lohnkostenindex; ~ **intensive** lohnintensiv; ~ **level** Lohnniveau; ~ **loss** Lohnausfall; ~ **packet** Lohntüte; ~ **pattern** Tarifordnung; **guaranteed** ~ **plan** Lohnabkommen mit garantierter Mindestbeschäftigungszeit; ~ **price guidelines** Richtwerte für die Lohn- und Preisentwicklung; ~ **price guideposts** Orientierungsdaten; ~ **qualification** [höherer] Lohnanspruch; ~ **raise** Lohnsteigerung; **hourly** ~ **rate** Stundenlohn; **to peg the** ~ **rates** Lohnniveau einfrieren; ~ **reopening** neue Lohnverhandlungen; ~ **scale** Lohnskala, Tarif; ~ **schedule** Lohntabelle; ~ **slip** Lohnabrechnungszettel; ~ **stop** Lohnstopp; ~ **supplement** Lohn-, Gehaltszulage; ~ **tax** Lohnsteuer.

waggon, wagon *(US)* Fuhrwerk, [Last]wagen, *(railway, Br.)* Gepäck-, Güterwagen, Waggon;
~s available Wagenbestand; box (covered) ~ *(Br.)* Güterwagen; **station** ~ *(US)* Kombiwagen;
~ **distributor (jobber)** *(US)* Großhändler ohne eigenes Lager; ~ **manifest** Ladeverzeichnis; ~ **train** *(US)* Güterzug.

wag(g)onload Wagenladung, Fuhre, *(railway, Br.)* Waggonladung.

wait | *(v.)* **out the market** *(sl.)* durch Zurückhaltung die Marktpreise beeinflussen; ~ **on with patterns** Muster vorführen;
~ **order** *(advertising)* Terminauftrag.

waiting Aufwartung, Bedienen;
in ~ dienstbereit;
no-~ area Halteverbotszone; ~ **list** Warteliste; ~ **period** *(insurance law)* Karenzzeit.

waive | *(v.)* **the age limit** über die Altersgrenze hinaus tätig bleiben; ~ **debts** Schulden erlassen.

waiver Aufgabe, Verzicht, *(declaration)* Verzichtleistung;
~ **of demand, notice and protest** Verzichtsleistung auf Wechselprotest; ~ **of the statute of limitations** Verzicht auf die Einrede der Verjährung.

walk Benehmen, Lebenswandel, *(line of business)* Distrikt, Route, *(postman)* Zustellbezirk, *(profession)* Fach, Laufbahn, Lebensweg;
~ *(v.)* **into one's stock of money** gehörigen Griff in seine Brieftasche tun;
~ **bill** *(Br.)* Platzwechsel; ~ **charges** *(Br.)* Inkassospesen; ~ **cheque** *(Br.)* Platzscheck.

walking | **charges** Einziehungskosten, -spesen; ~ **delegate** Gewerkschaftsvertreter, ~ **ticket (papers,** *US sl.)* Entlassungspapiere.

walkout *(coll.)* Arbeitsniederlegung.

wall *(bankruptcy)* Bankrott, Konkurs;
tariff ~ Zollmauer;
~ **advertisement** Maueranschlag; ₂ **-Street loan** Lombardkredit.

wangle *(v.)* **accounts** Konten frisieren.

want Mangel, *(need)* Erfordernis, Bedarf, Bedürfnis, Not, *(scarcity)* Knappheit;
for ~ **of acceptance** mangels Annahme; **for** ~ **of advice** mangels Bericht; **for** ~ **of payment** mangels Zahlung;
~ **of ordinary care** Mangel der erforderlichen Sorgfalt; ~ **of consideration** fehlende Gegenleistung; ~ **of money** Geldbedarf;
to be in ~ **of repair** reparaturbedürftig sein;
~ **ads** *(US)* kleine Anzeigen, Suchanzeigen, Stellengesuche; ~ **list** *(US)* Bestelliste.

wanted Kaufgesuch, *(stock exchange)* Geld gesucht; **help** ~ offene Stelle; ~ **immediately** für sofort gesucht.

wanton | **negligence** grobe Fahrlässigkeit; ~ **strike** wilder Streik.

war | **debt** Kriegsschuld; ~ **insurance** Versicherung gegen Kriegsgefahr; ~ **loan** *(Br.)* Kriegsanleihe; ~ **order** Rüstungsauftrag; ~**-risk clause** Kriegsklausel; ~**-risk insurance** Kriegsrisikoversicherung; ~ **profits tax** *(US)* Rüstungsgewinnsteuer.

ward Mündel, Pflegling, *(custody)* Obhut.

warden Vormund, *(institution)* Kustos, Kurator.

ware Ware, [Handels]artikel;
to puff one's ~s seine Ware anpreisen.

warehouse Lager[haus], Auslieferungslager, Magazin, Speicher;
bonded ~ Transitlager, Entrepot, Zollspeicher, -lager; **custodian** ~ *(US)* Konsignationslager; **customs** ~ Zollniederlage; **licensed** ~ *(US)* Lagerhaus für zollpflichtige Güter; **unbonded** ~ Zollfreilager;
~ *(v.)* *(customs)* unter Zollverschluß bringen, *(goods)* [Güter] [ein]lagern, auf Lager nehmen;
to deposit in a ~ auf den Speicher bringen;
~ **account** Lagerkonto; ~ **bond** *(customs)* Lagerschein, Zollverschlußschein; ~ **book** Bestandsbuch; ~ **business** Lagerungsgeschäft; ~ **certificate** *(US)* Lagerschein; ~**-to-~ clause** Transportversicherungsklausel; ~ **clerk** Lagerist; ~ **goods** Waren auf Lager; **bonded** ~ **goods** Güter unter Zollverschluß; ~ **keeper** Lageraufseher, -halter; ~ **keeper's certificate** *(Br.)* [nicht begebbarer] Lagerschein; ~ **loan** Warenbevorschussung; ~ **period** Zollagerfrist; ~ **receipt** *(US)* Lagerschein; ~ **rent** Lagermiete; **cooperative** ~ **society** Lagergenossenschaft; ~ **space** Speicherraum; ~ **warrant** Lagerschein.

warehouseman Lagerist, Lagerverwalter, -aufseher, *(trader)* gewerblicher Lagerhalter, *(worker)* Speicherarbeiter.

warehousing [Ein]lagerung, Lagern, Lagerhaltung;
field ~ *(US)* Lagerung sicherungsübereigneter Waren, Sicherungsübereignung;
~ **business** Lagerungsgeschäft; ~ **charges** Speichergebühren; ~ **company** Lagerhausgesellschaft; ~ **system** *(US)* Zollverschlußsystem.

warmup *(advertising)* Werbevorspann.

warn *(v.)* **a tenant out of the house** Räumungsurteil gegen einen Mieter erwirken.

warning [Vor]warnung, *(giving notice)* Kündigung;
at a minute's ~ fristlos, auf jederzeitige Kündigung;
to give the tenant ~ Mieter kündigen;
~ **and fee** *(Br.)* gebührenpflichtige Verwarnung.

warrant *(of attorney)* Prozeßvollmacht, *(authority)* Befugnis, Berechtigung, Ermächtigung, *(guarantor)* Bürge, Gewährsmann, *(order to pay)* Zahlungsanweisung, *(promissory note, US)* Schuldschein, *(to stock owner)* Options-, Bezugsberechtigungsschein, Bezugsrecht;
bond ~ *(Br.)* Zollbegleitschein; **deposit** ~ Depotschein; **dividend** ~ *(Br.)* Dividendenanteilschein; **dock** ~ *(Br.)* Waren-, Lagerschein; **interest** ~ Zinsschein; **municipal** ~ Kommunalschuldschein; **stock-allotment** *(US)* **(subscription,** *Br.)* ~ Berechtigungsschein zum Erwerb neuer Aktien; **tax-anticipation** ~ Steuergutschein;
~ **of distress** Pfändungsbeschluß; ~ **of merchantability** Gewährleistung, Garantieverpflichtung;
~ *(v.)* *(authorize)* befugen, bevollmächtigen, berechtigen, *(guarantee)* gewährleisten, garantieren, *(stand bail)* Bürgschaft leisten;

~ creditor *(municipal accounting)* Schuldschein-inhaber.
warranted garantiert, verbürgt, echt.
warranty Berechtigung, Ermächtigung, *(guaranty)* Gewähr[leistung], Garantie, *(insurance)* Versicherung der Richtigkeit der Angaben, *(voucher)* Bürgschaftsschein;
  express ~ *(US)* Sachmängelhaftung; **implied ~** gesetzliche Gewährleistung;
  ~ of fitness *(US)* Eignungsgarantie; **~ of quality** Mängelgewähr;
  ~ claim Garantieanspruch; **~ work** *(auto dealer)* Garantiereparaturen.
wartime | **boom** Rüstungshausse; **~ economy** Kriegswirtschaft.
wash *(stock exchange, US)* Börsenscheinverkauf;
  ~ *(v.)* **20 % out of costs in freight** Frachtkosten um 20 % kürzen.
wastage Verschwendung, Vergeudung, *(wear and tear)* Verschleiß, Abnutzung.
waste übermäßiger Verbrauch, *(cargo)* Verlust, Spillage, Schwund, *(extravagance)* Verschwendung, Wertverschleuderung, *(refuse)* Ausschuß, *(wear and tear)* Abnutzung, Verschleiß;
  equitable ~ normaler Verschleiß;
  ~ of money Geldverschwendung;
  ~ *(v.) (loss in value)* Wertminderung erleiden, *(squander)* verschwenden;
  ~ book Strazze, Kladde; **~ disposal** Abfallbeseitigung; **~ paper** Makulatur.
wasting assets kurzlebige Wirtschaftsgüter.
water | *(v.)* **the stock** Aktienkapital verwässern;
  to spend money like ~ Geld mit vollen Händen ausgeben;
  ~borne auf dem Wasserwege befördert; **~ carriage** Verschiffung; **~ charges** *(US)* Wassergeld; **~ line** Ladelinie.
watered capital (capital stock, *US)* verwässertes Aktienkapital.
wave | **of demand** Nachfragewelle; **~ of prosperity** Hochkonjunktur.
way [Verkehrs]weg, Straße *(method)* Verfahren, Methode, *(route)* Strecke;
  by ~ of negotiation(s) im Verhandlungswege;
  permanent ~ *(Br.)* Bahngleis-, Bahnkörper;
  ~ of business Geschäfts-, Berufszweig; **~s and means** Geldbeschaffung, Deckungsmittel;
  to be on the ~ *(stock exchange)* erhältlich sein; **to be on their ~** auf Achse (unterwegs) sein; **to be in the shipping ~** im Schiffshandel sein; **to live in a small ~** sehr bescheidenes Leben führen; **to make a penny go a long ~** sein Geld sehr genau einteilen, jeden Groschen dreimal umdrehen;
  ~s and means advance *(Br.)* offene Buchkredite der Bank von England an die Regierung; **~ rate** *(US)* Ortstarif; **~ station** Durchgangsbahnhof; **~ traffic** *(US)* Nah-, Ortsverkehr.
waybill Frachtbrief, -zettel, *(advice of dispatch)* Versandanzeige, *(freight car, US)* Frachtbrief, Warenbegleitschein;
  ~ number Frachtbriefnummer.

weak *(stock exchange)* schwach, flau;
  to hold ~ *(market)* flau liegen.
weaker tendency in prices Kursabschwächung.
weakness | **in the market** Abgleiten der Kurse; **~ in sterling** Pfundschwäche.
wealth Vermögen, Besitz, Reichtum;
  national ~ Volksvermögen;
  ~ flow Vermögensertrag; **~ tax** Vermögenssteuer.
wear Bekleidung;
  [natural] ~ and tear Verschleiß, Abnutzung durch Gebrauch.
weed | *(v.)* **a garden** *(fig.)* Betrieb durchforsten; **~ a stock of goods** Warenlager räumen.
weekend | **sale** Wochenendverkauf; **~ ticket** Sonntagsfahrkarte.
weekly | **allowance** wöchentliches Taschengeld; **~ instal(l)ment** wöchentliche Rate; **~ pay** Wochenlohn.
weigh *(v.)* in the gross Bruttogewicht feststellen.
weight Gewicht, *(market research)* Bewerten;
  additional ~ Gewichtszuschlag; **allowed free ~** Frei-, Reingewicht; **dead ~** Leer-, Eigengewicht; **gross ~** Bruttogewicht;
  ~ of packing Verpackungsgewicht;
  to be deficient in ~ kein volles Gewicht haben; **~ cargo** Schwergut; **~ note** Wiegeschein.
weighted index gewogener Index.
welfare Wohlergehen, Wohlfahrt, *(~ work, US)* soziale Einrichtungen, Fürsorgearbeit; Sozialhilfe;
  to be on ~ *(US)* Sozialhilfe beziehen;
  ~ agency *(US)* Sozialamt; **~ beneficiary** Sozialhilfempfänger; **~ benefits** Sozial-, Fürsorgeleistungen; **~ costs** Fürsorgelasten, Sozialaufwand; **~ facilities** Sozialeinrichtungen; **~ grant** Sozialzuschuß; **~ recipient** Sozialhilfempfänger; **~ work** fürsorgerische Tätigkeit, Sozialarbeit; **~ worker** Sozialfürsorger.
well | **-financed** mit reichlichen Mitteln ausgestattet; **~-landed** begütert; **~-positioned** in einer guten Stellung; **~-priced** preisgünstig; **~-stocked** reichhaltig; **~-versed firm** bekannte Firma.
wet-time pay Schlechtwetterzulage.
wharf Lande-, Lösch-, Ladeplatz, *(quay)* Kai, Dock, Pier, Anlegestelle;
  ~ dues Dockgebühren.
wharfage Umschlaggebühr, Kai-, Löschgeld.
wharfinger Kaiaufseher, -meister;
  ~'s certificate *(Br.)* Kaiablieferungsbescheinigung;
  ~'s warrant *(Br.)* Kailagerschein.
whispering campaign Flüsterpropaganda.
white-collar | **crime** *(US)* Wirtschaftsverbrechen; **~ job** *(US)* Bürotätigkeit; **~ man (worker)** *(US)* [Büro]angestellter.
white | **elephant** unrentables Geschäft; **~ paper** *(bill of exchange, Br.)* erstklassiger Wechsel; **~ sale** Weiße Woche, Ausverkauf.
whitewash *(Br.)* Rehabilitierung, Schuldnerentlastung.
whole | **life assurance** *(Br.)* Lebensversicherung auf den Todesfall, reine Todesfallversicherung; **~-time job** ganztägige Beschäftigung.

wholesale Großhandel, -verkauf, Engroshandel;
at ~ *(US)* en gros, *(fig.)* pauschal;
to be manufactured ~ serienmäßig hergestellt sein;
to buy goods ~ zu Großhandelspreisen einkaufen;
~ business Großhandels-, Engrosgeschäft; **~ cost**
Großhandels-, Grossisten-, Engrospreis; **~ dealer**
Grossist, Engroshändler; **~ discount** Großhandelsrabatt; **~ enterprise (establishment)** Großhandelsunternehmen; **~ group rate** pauschalierter
Gruppentarif; **~ manufacture** Serienfabrikation,
fabrikmäßige Herstellung; **~ margin** Großhandelsspanne; **~ merchant** Grossist; **~ peddler** Engroshändler mit Wagenverkauf; **~ price** Engros-,
Grossisten-, Großhandelspreis; **~ price index**
Großhandelspreis; **~ quotations** Großhandelspreise; **~ selling** Großhandelsverkauf; **~ trade**
Groß-, Engroshandel; **~ trader** Grossist.
wholesaler Engroshändler, Großhändler, Grossist.
drop-shipment **~** auftragsvermittelnder Großhändler; **mail-order ~** Versandgroßhändler.
wholesaling Großhandelsgewerbe.
wide | **-branched** weitverzweigt; **~ interests** vielseitige
Interessen; **~ opening** *(stock exchange)* stark voneinander abweichende Eröffnungskurse; **~ quotation** *(stock exchange)* große Kursspanne.
widow and orphan stock *(US)* mündelsichere Wertpapiere.
widow's | **allowance** *(Br.)* Witwengeld; **~ benefit** *(Br.)*
Hinterbliebenenbezüge.
wildcat *(business)* Schwindel-, unsolides Geschäftsunternehmen, *(coll.)* Spekulant;
~ (a.) unsicher, riskant, spekulativ;
~ bank *(US)* Schwindelbank; **~ brand** unerlaubtes
Markenzeichen; **~ credit market** Parallelmarkt;
~ finance unsolide Finanzverhältnisse; **~ securities**
hochspekulative Effekten; **~ strike (walkout)** wilder (unorganisierter) Streik, Spontanstreik.
will *(last will)* Testament, letztwillige Verfügung;
holographic ~ handschriftliches Testament; **mutual ~** gegenseitiges Testament;
~ (v.) one's money to a hospital sein Geld einem
Krankenhaus hinterlassen;
to be capable of making a ~ testierfähig sein;
to take out probate of a ~ sich einen Erbschein
auf Grund eines Testaments ausstellen lassen;
~call for lay-away vom Kunden anbezahlter und
zurückgelegter Gegenstand.
willingness to sell Abgabebereitschaft.
win *(v.)* | **a competition** Preisausschreiben gewinnen;
~ one's way up from poverty sich aus kleinsten
Verhältnissen emporarbeiten.
wind up *(v.)* abschließen, erledigen, *(bankruptcy, US)*
bankrott (Konkurs) machen, *(business)* Geschäft
aufgeben, auflösen, abwickeln, liquidieren;
~ the affairs of a partnership Gesellschaft liquidieren; **~ an estate** *(Br.)* Nachlaß regeln; **~ liabilities** Verbindlichkeiten ordnen; **~ in a top policy
position** höchstmögliche berufliche Position erreichen.
windfall profit unerwarteter Gewinn.

winding up Liquidation[sverfahren], Abwicklung
(Auflösung) eines Geschäftes, *(Br.)* Eröffnung des
Konkursverfahrens;
compulsory ~ Zwangsliquidierung, -auflösung;
voluntary ~ Selbstauflösung;
~ by arrangement Liquidationsvergleich; **~ subject
to the supervision of the court** Liquidation unter
Aufsicht des Gerichtes;
~ order Konkurs-, Liquidationsbeschluß; **~ sale**
Totalausverkauf.
window [Bank-, Post-]schalter, Schaufenster;
ticket ~ Fahrkartenschalter;
to display in the ~ im Schaufenster ausstellen;
~ advertising Schaufensterreklame; **~ clerk** *(US)*
Schalterbeamter; **~ display** Schaufensterdekoration; **~ display material** Dekorationsmaterial; **~
dresser** Schaufensterdekorateur; **~ dressing**
Schaufensterdekoration, *(balance sheet)* Bilanzverschleierung, *(bank statement)* kurzfristige Liquiditätsanhäufung, *(sham)* Aufmachung, Mache, Reklame; **~ envelope** Fensterumschlag; **~
shop** *(v.)* Schaufensterbummel machen; **~ streamer** *(advertising)* Fenster[auf]kleber.
winning number *(lottery)* Gewinnlos, -nummer.
winter | **catalog(ue)** Winterkatalog; **~ peak in demand**
winterlicher Spitzenbedarf.
wipe *(v.)* off | **the books** voll abschreiben; **~ a debit
balance** Debetsaldo abbuchen.
wire Telegramm, Depesche, Drahtnachricht;
~ (v.) back zurücktelegraphieren;
to pull the ~s for office sich durch Beziehungen eine
Stellung verschaffen; **to telephone a ~** Telegramm
telefonisch durchsagen;
~ acceptance Drahtannahme; **~ address** Telegrammanschrift; **~ collect** *(US)* Telegramm mit
bezahlter Rückantwort; **~ transfer** *(US)* telegrafische Geldüberweisung.
wireless | **licence** *(Br.)* Rundfunkgenehmigung; **~
licence fee** *(Br.)* Rundfunkgebühr; **~ station** Sender.
withdraw *(v.)* *(loan)* ablösen, *(money)* abheben, *(retire)* ausscheiden;
~ from circulation aus dem Verkehr ziehen; **~ from
a company** aus einer Firma ausscheiden; **~ an order** Auftrag widerrufen (stornieren); **~ securities
from a deposit** Effekten aus dem Depot nehmen;
~ from a warehouse Auslagerung vornehmen.
withdrawal Zurücknahme, -ziehung, *(from circulation)* Außerkurssetzung, *(money)* Abhebung, Entnahme, *(retirement)* Aus-, Rücktritt;
day-to-day ~s tägliche Abhebungen;
~ of an application Rücknahme einer Bewerbung;
~ of bank notes Einziehung von Banknoten; **~ of
capital** Kapitalentnahme; **~ of a deposit amount**
Aufhebung von Spareinlagen; **~ of a licence**
Lizenzentzug; **~ of an order** Auftragsstornierung;
~ of a partner Firmenaustritt; **~ of a sum of money**
Geldabhebung;
to give notice of ~ of bonds Rückzahlung von
Obligationen ankündigen;

~ **benefit** Abgangsregulierung; ~ **notice** *(banking)* Kreditkündigung; ~ **period** Kündigungsfrist; ~ **warrant** Auszahlungsermächtigung.

withhold | *(v.)* **so much out of s.** one's **pay** soundso viel von jds. Lohn einbehalten; ~ **supplies from a dealer** Lieferung verweigern; ~ **a tax from wage payment** Steuern bei der Lohnzahlung einbehalten.

withholding Zurückbehaltung, *(tax)* Steuereinbehaltung; ~ **means of support from dependants** Unterhaltsentzug; ~ **of wages** Lohneinbehaltung; ~ **agent** *(Br.)* lohnsteuerpflichtige Stelle; ~ **exemption** *(US)* Lohnsteuerfreibetrag; ~ **rate** *(employees)* Lohnsteuersatz, *(dividends)* Kapitalertragssteuersatz; ~ **regulations** *(US)* Lohnsteuerrichtlinien; ~ **table** *(US)* Lohnsteuertabelle; ~ **tax** *(US) (dividends)* Quellen-, Kapitalertragsteuer, *(employee)* Steuerabzug von Dienstbezügen; **personal** ~ **tax** *(US)* einbehaltene Lohnsteuer; ~ **tax table** *(US)* Lohnsteuertabelle.

without | **advice** ohne Bericht; ~ **extra charge** ohne Preisaufschlag; ~ **engagement** ohne Obligo, freibleibend; ~ **expenses** ohne Kosten; ~ **interest** franko Zinsen; ~ **resource** ohne Regreßmöglichkeit.

woman, career berufstätige Frau.

wording | **of a bill** Wechseltext; ~ **of a contract** Wortlaut eines Vertrages.

work Arbeit, Beschäftigung, *(act)* Tat, Tätigkeit, *(building plot)* Baustelle, Bauten, Anlagen, *(machine)* Betrieb, Arbeit, Leistung, *(occupation)* Beschäftigung, Beruf, *(performance)* Leistung; **at** ~ im Betrieb; **ex** ~**s** ab Fabrik; **capital** ~**s** öffentliche Bauten; **casual** ~ Gelegenheitsarbeit; **contract** ~ Akkordarbeit; **emergency** ~**s** Notstandsarbeiten; **holiday** ~ Ferienbeschäftigung; **illicit** ~ Schwarzarbeit; **part-time** Kurzarbeit; **sparetime** ~ Nebenbeschäftigung; **sub-contracted** ~ Zuliefertätigkeit; **unskilled** Hilfsarbeit; **white-collar** ~ *(US)* Bürotätigkeit; ~ **on the bonus system** Arbeiten auf Prämienbasis; ~ **according to the book** *(US)* Dienst nach Vorschrift; ~ **by the job** Akkordarbeit; ~ **in process** *(Br.)* **(progress,** *US) (balance sheet)* halbfertige Erzeugnisse; ~**-to-rule** *(Br.)* Dienst nach Vorschrift;

~ *(v.)* Arbeit haben, arbeiten, tätig sein, *(factory)* in Betrieb sein, *(operate)* [Bergwerk, Fabrik] betreiben, *(v. i.)* funktionieren, gehen, laufen; ~ **under a written six-month contract** mit halbjähriger Kündigungsfrist angestellt sein; ~ **a district** *(traveller)* Bezirk bearbeiten; ~ **in one's father's firm** im Betrieb seines Vaters mitarbeiten; ~ **full-time** ganztägig arbeiten; ~ **half-time** halbtags arbeiten; ~ **by the job** im Akkord arbeiten; ~ **on the assembly line** *(US)* am Fließband arbeiten; ~ **overtime** Überstunden machen; ~ **short-time** kurzarbeiten.

work off a stock of goods Warenposten losschlagen.

work out | **heavy deficits** mit schweren Verlusten ar-

beiten; ~ **interest** Zinsen berechnen; ~ **a coded message** verschlüsselten Funkspruch entziffern.

work up a connexion sich einen Kundenkreis schaffen.

work, to be in im Berufsleben stehen; **to be in regular** ~ fest angestellt sein; **to do one's** ~ **in an office** Büroangestellter sein; ~ **attitude** Einstellung zur Arbeit; ~ **camp** Arbeitslager; ~ **clothes** Arbeits-, Berufskleidung; ~ **creation** Arbeitsbeschaffung; ~ **dodger** Drückeberger; ~ **incentive** Arbeitsansporn; ~**-in-process inventory** *(US)* Bestand in Halbfabrikaten; ~**s manager** Betriebsleiter; ~ **order** Arbeitsanweisung; ~**s outing** Betriebsausflug; **relief** ~**s program(me)** Notstandsprogramm; ~ **rules** Arbeitsrichtlinien; ~ **sharing** Arbeitssenkung, Beschäftigung in Kurzarbeit; ~ **sheet** Bilanzvorbereitungsbogen; ~ **spreading** Arbeitsstreckung; ~**s steward** Betriebsobmann; ~ **week** Arbeitswoche.

workable competition *(US)* funktionsfähiger Wettbewerb.

workbook Arbeitsbuch.

workday of eight hours Achtstundentag.

worker Arbeiter, Arbeitnehmer, Arbeitskraft; **assembly-line** ~ *(US)* Fließbandarbeiter; **blackcoated** *(Br.)* Büroangestellter; **factory** ~ Fabrikarbeiter; **fellow** ~ Kollege; **foreign** ~ Gastarbeiter; **general** ~ ungelernter Arbeiter; **industrial** ~ Industriearbeiter; **job** ~ Akkord[lohn]arbeiter; **maritime** ~ *(US)* Transportarbeiter; **migrant** ~ Wanderarbeiter; **part-time** ~ Kurzarbeiter; **piece** ~ Akkordlohnarbeiter; **professional** ~ freiberufliche Arbeitskraft; **redundant** ~ überzähliger Arbeiter; **relief** ~ Notstandsarbeiter; **skilled** ~ Facharbeiter; **short-time** ~ Kurarbeiter; **two-job** ~ Doppelverdiener; **unskilled** ~ Hilfsarbeiter; **to recruit** ~**s** *(US)* Arbeiter anwerben (einstellen); ~**s' compensation** Unfallentschädigung; ~**'s dwelling** Arbeiterwohnung; ~**s' housing estate** Arbeitersiedlung; ~**'s season ticket** Arbeiterdauerfahrkarte.

workfellow Arbeitskamerad, Mitarbeiter, Kollege.

workforce Belegschaft.

working Arbeiten, Arbeitsweise *(of materials)* Bearbeitung, Verarbeitung, *(patent law)* Verwertung, *(setting into operation)* Inbetriebsetzung; **continuous** ~ Dauerbetrieb; **hard** ~ *(US)* Schwerarbeit; **intermittent** ~ Stoßbetrieb; ~ **of an account** Kontoführung; ~ **of business** Betrieb eines Unternehmens; ~ **out of interest** Zinsenberechnung; ~ **of mines** Bergbau; ~ **overtime** Überstunden; ~ **of a patent** Patentausnutzung; ~ *(a.)* arbeitend, werk-, berufstätig, *(operating)* betriebsfähig, funktionierend, im Gang; **to cease** ~ Betrieb einstellen; ~ **agreement** Interessengemeinschaft; ~ **assets** Betriebs-, Umlaufsvermögen; **reduced** ~ **capacity** Erwerbsminderung.

working capital Betriebs-, Umlaufkapital, Betriebsmittel, werbendes Kapital; **to beef up** ~ Betriebskapital verstärken;

~ **fund** Betriebsmittelfonds; ~ **ratio** *(US)* Verhältnis der flüssigen Aktiva zu laufenden Verbindlichkeiten, Liquiditätsgrad;

working | **card** *(US)* Gewerkschaftsmitgliedskarte; ~ **class** Arbeiterklasse; ~-**class family** Arbeiterfamilie; ~ **conditions** Arbeitsverhältnisse, *(machine)* Betriebszustand; ~ **cost** Betriebskosten; ~ **day** Werktag; ~ **dinner** Arbeitsessen; ~ **expenses** Betriebskosten; ~ **force** [Betriebs]belegschaft; ~ **hour** Arbeitsstunde; ~ **hours** Arbeitszeit; **to have a** ~ **knowledge of French** einige Kenntnisse im Französisch haben; ~ **life** Berufsleben; ~ **majority** arbeitsfähige Mehrheit; ~ **mean** *(statistics)* provisorischer Durchschnitt; ~ **men's cooperative society** *(Br.)* [Arbeiter]konsumverein; ~ **order** betriebsfähiger Zustand; ~ **overtime** Überstundenarbeit; ~ **papers** *(US)* Arbeitsunterlagen, -papiere; ~ **partner** aktiver Gesellschafter; ~ **people** Arbeiterschaft, Berufstätige; ~ **period** Produktionsperiode, Arbeitszeit; ~ **plant** Betriebsanlage; ~ **population** werktätige Bevölkerung; ~ **potential** Arbeitskräftepotential; ~ **power** *(machine)* Leistungsfähigkeit; ~ **result** Betriebsergebnis; ~ **scheme** Arbeitsplan, Fabrikationsprogramm; **to reduce** ~ **time** Arbeitszeit kürzen; ~ **woman** berufstätige Frau.

workman Arbeiter, *(artisan)* Handwerker; **good** ~ geschickter Arbeiter; **unskilled** ~ ungelernter Arbeiter.

workmanship Arbeitsausführung, Qualitätsarbeit, Wertarbeit; **excellent (honest)** ~ feinste Qualitätsarbeit; **faulty** ~ fehlerhafte Ausführung.

workmaster Werkmeister, Faktor.

workmen Arbeiter, Arbeitskräfte, Arbeitnehmer; ~'s **compensation** Unfallentschädigung; ~-**compensation insurance** *(US)* Betriebshaftpflichtversicherung.

workplace Arbeitsraum, -platz; ~ **layout** Arbeitsplatzgestaltung.

workroom costs Werkstattkosten.

workshop Betrieb, Werkstatt; ~ **training** Werkstattausbildung.

world *(sphere of business)* Berufssphäre; **business** ~ Geschäftswelt; **financial** ~ Finanzleute; ~ **of high finance** Hochfinanz; **to face** ~ **competition for export markets** auf dem Exportmarkt konkurrenzfähig bleiben; ~ **depression** Weltwirtschaftskrise; ~-**economic recovery** Erholung der Weltwirtschaft; ~ **fair** Weltausstellung; ~ **price** Weltmarktpreis; ~-**wide financial crisis** weltweite Finanzkrise.

worse, to be 1/2 *(stock exchange)* einen halben Punkt niedriger stehen.

worsening of the balance of payment Zahlungsbilanzverschlechterung.

worth *(equivalent)* Gegenwert, *(merit)* Verdienst, Ansehen; **net** ~ *(US)* Eigenkapital;

to be ~ *(cost)* kosten, wert sein, *(to be quoted)* notieren; **to be** ~ **a million** millionenschwer sein.

wrap of the news Kurzfassung der Nachrichten.

wrappage Verpackung, Packmaterial.

wrapper Kreuz-, Streifband.

wrapping, original Originalverpackung; ~ **material** Verpackungsmaterial.

wreck gestrandetes Schiff, Wrack; **total** ~ *(insurance)* Totalverlust; **worthless** ~ *(car)* Totalschaden; ~ *(v.)* Schiffbruch erleiden; ~ **a commercial house** Handelsfirma ruinieren; ~ **off a ship** Wrack abbrechen; ~ **commissioner** *(Br.)* Strandvogt, Bergungsleiter.

wrecked | **bank** ruinierte Bank; ~ **building** abgerissenes Gebäude; ~ **cargo** Wrackgut; ~ **freight** verlorene Fracht; ~ **goods** Strandgut; ~ **ship** schiffbrüchiges Schiff; ~ **train** entgleister Zug.

wrecker *(relief train)* Hilfszug, *(ship)* Bergungsdampfer, *(truck, US)* Abschleppwagen.

wrecking | **company** *(US)* Abbruchgesellschaft; ~ **service** *(US)* Abschleppdienst.

writ | **of assistance** Zolldurchsuchungsbefehl; ~ **of attachment** *(US)* Pfändungs- und Überweisungsbeschluß; ~ **of ejectment** *(US)* Räumungsurteil.

write | *(v.)* **an application** Bewerbungsschreiben verfassen; ~ **a call naked** Leerverkauf tätigen; ~ **a check** *(US)* (cheque, *Br.*) Scheck ausschreiben; ~ **shorthand** stenografieren.

write down aufschreiben, *(depreciate)* teilweise abschreiben, Buchwert herabsetzen, abbuchen; ~ **the capital** Kapitalherabsetzung vornehmen.

write off *(balance sheet)* vollständig abschreiben. ~ **so much for wear and tear** bestimmten Betrag für Abnutzung absetzen.

write up the value of an asset Wert einer Anlage (Anlagenwert) heraufsetzen.

write-up *(balance sheet, US)* Höherbewertung, *(property statement)* frisierte Vermögensaufstellung; ~ **of stock values** Lageraufwertung.

writedowns *(US)*, **write-downs** *(Br.)* Abschreibungen.

writeoff *(US)*, **write-off** *(Br.)* Abschreibung; **accelerated** ~ verkürzte (beschleunigte) Abschreibung; **complete** ~ *(airliner, car)* Totalverlust; ~**s for losses on foreign exchange** Abschreibungen für Devisenverluste.

writing back Storno-, Rückbuchung.

writing-down of capital Herabsetzung (Zusammenlegung) des Aktienkapitals.

writing off | **of a bad debt** Abschreibung einer zweifelhaften Forderung.

writing-up *(balance sheet)* Höherbewertung.

writing | **block** Schreibblock; ~ **limit** *(reinsurance)* Zeichnungsgrenze.

written | **agreement** schriftliche Vereinbarung; ~ **instrument** Urkunde.

wrongful dismissal unberechtigte Entlassung, Entlassung ohne Einhaltung einer Kündigungsfrist.

X, Y, Z

Xerox Fotokopie, Ablichtung.
yard Hof *(US)* Arbeitsplatz, Werkstätte;
   goods ~ Warenlager; **repair** ~ Ausbesserungswerft.
year, account Rechnungsjahr; **budgetary** ~ Haushaltsjahr; **business** ~ Geschäftsjahr; **economically depressing** ~ Jahr konjunkturellen Rückschlags; **financial** ~ Rechungs-, Steuerjahr, *(Br.)* Haushaltsjahr;
   ~ **of assessment** Veranlagungsjahr; ~ **of coverage** *(social insurance)* anrechnungsfähiges Jahr.
year-end adjustemnt *(US)* Ultimoausgleich.
yearly | **account** Jahres[ab]rechnung; ~ **income** Jahreseinkommen.
yellow journalism *(US)* Boulevardjournalismus.
yield *(crop)* Ernte, *(interest)* [Effektiv]verzinsung; *(stocks)* Rendite,
   net ~ Nettoerlös; **running** ~ *(Br.)* laufende Verzinsung; ~ **on shares (stocks,** *US)* Aktienrendite; ~ **of taxes** Steueraufkommen;
   ~ *(produce)* Zinsen tragen, *(produce)* [Ertrag] abwerfen;
   ~ **high interest** hochverzinslich sein, *(shares)* hohe Rendite bringen;
   to sell on a ~ **basis** unter Berücksichtigung der Ertragsaussichten Absatz finden; **fixed** ~ **investment** festverzinsliche Anlage.

zero Null *(scale)* Ausgangs-, Nullpunkt;
   ~-**growth rate** keine Zuwachsrate; ~-**rated** abgabenfrei.
zip *(post office, US)* Postleitzahl;
zone [Teil]gebiet, Zone, *(city planning, US) (parcel post, tel. US)* Tarifzone,, *(railway, tram)* Tarifzone -stufe, Teilstrecke;
   business ~ Geschäftsviertel; **free** ~ *(customs)* Zollausschuß-, Freihafengebiet; **limited-parking** ~ Kurzparkzone; **no-parking** ~ Parkverbotsgebiet;
   ~ *(v.)* nach (in) Zonen einteilen, *(railway tariff)* Tarif nach Teilstrecken festsetzen;
   ~ **for one-family residences** für die Errichtung von Einfamilienhäusern vorsehen;
   ~ **change** *(US)* Änderung der Bebauungsvorschriften; ~ **plan** *(advertising campaign)* Schwerpunktwerbung; ~ **rates** *(public utilities, US)* Zonentarif; ~ **ticket** Teilstreckenfahrkarte.
zoning *(city planning, US)* Aufstellung von Flächennutzungsplänen.
   spot ~ Bauausnahmegenehmigung für Errichtung von Geschäftshäusern;
   ~ **case** *(US)* Planfeststellungsverfahren; ~ **code** *(US)* Generalbebauungsplan; ~ **restrictions** *(US)* Bebauungsbeschränkungen; ~ **system** *(post)* Leitzahlsystem.
zoom *(v.) (prices)* senkrecht in die Höhe steigen.

Mini
Cambridge-Eichborn
German Dictionary

Mini
Cambridge-
Eichborn
German
Dictionary

Business
and Economics

**English–German
German–English**

Abbreviations

a   = adjective
Br.   = chiefly used in Great Britain
fam. = familiar
fig. = figurative
o.s. = oneself
s.o. = someone
sl.   = slang
US = chiefly used in the USA

Repetition sign

Entry words in bold type when repeated in
the paragraph are substituted by a
repetition mark (~).

Italics

A word printed in italics indicates the
particular field of meaning, within which
the head word is used.

Spelling

Where the American spelling differs from
the British, words have been printed as
follows:
catalog(ue), hono(u)r, instal(l)ment,
program(me), wag(g)on.

A

a| eine **Mark** at 1 Mark (each piece); ~ **jour** up to date; ~ **ab** *(wirksam)* effective, as of, *(Versandort)* ex; ~ **conto** on account; ~ **metà** on joint account.

abändern, Buchung to alter an entry.

Abänderung eines gekreuzten Schecks in einen Barscheck opening a crossing *(Br.).*

Abandonerklärung notice of abandonment.

Abbau *(einzelner Beamter)* dismissal, discharge, axe, *(Gebäude)* demolition;
~ **der Auftragspolster** working off the backlog of orders; ~ **der Handelsschranken** reduction of barriers of trade; ~ **der Preisüberwachungsvorschriften** price decontrol; ~ **der Zölle** tariff reduction.

abbauen *(Beamte)* to discharge, *(Betriebseinrichtungen)* to dismantle, to discard, *(Gehälter, Preise, Zölle)* to reduce, to cut;
Bewirtschaftungsvorschriften ~ to abolish state planning.

abbestellen to countermand, to cancel [an order], *(Zeitung)* to discontinue, to cancel a subscription.

Abbestellung *(Zeitung)* discontinuance.

abbezahlen to pay (clear) off, *(tilgen)* to repay.

abbrechen *(Arbeit)* to stop, to interrupt, to knock off *(US)*, *(Gebäude)* to pull (take) down, to demolish;
Streik ~ to call off a strike; **Verhandlungen** ~ to break off negotiations.

Abbröckeln der Kurse crumbling of prices.

abbröckeln *(Kurse)* to crumble [away], to ease off.

Abbruch *(Gebäude)* demolition, pulling down, *(Maschine)* dismantlement, *(Verhandlungen)* breaking off, interruption, rupture;
auf ~ **verkaufen** to sell as scrap (at demolition value); **Maschinen auf** ~ **verkaufen** to sell machinery as junk; .
~**arbeiten** demolition [work]; ~**preis** breakup price.

abbruchreif *(Gebäude)* due for demolition.

Abbruchunternehmer housebreaker, knacker, wrecking company (contractor) *(US).*

abbuchen *(abschreiben)* to write off (down), to cut, *(ausbuchen)* to abandon, to retire;
von einem Konto ~ to deduct from an account.

Abbuchung write-off, *(Ausbuchung)* abandonment, retirement.

abdecken *(Kredit)* to repay, *(Termingeschäft)* to cover; **fälligen Kredit** ~ to meet a loan when due.

Abdeckung | *(Schulden)* covering, settlement;
~ **eines Kredites** repayment of a loan; ~ **von Schulden** settlement of debts.

abdisponieren, Gelder to withdraw funds.

Abdruck print, copy, *(Nachdruck)* reproduction; **erster** ~ galley (first) proof.

abdrucken to print, to publish.

Abend| **ausgabe** late edition; ~**börse** evening market; ~**kasse** *(Theater)* box office; ~**zeitung** evening paper;

Aberkennung | **des Ruhegehalts** deprivation of pension; ~ **von Schadenersatz** disallowance of compensation.

abfahren *(Auto)* to drive off, *(Dampfer)* to sail, *(Zug)* to start, to move (steam) off, to pull out.

Abfahrt departure, start, setting.

Abfahrts|**bahnsteig** starting platform; ~**rampe** drive off; ~**signal** *(Schiff)* blue Peter; ~**zeit** time of departure, *(Dampfer)* sailing date.

Abfall waste, scrap, garbage *(US)*, refuse *(Br.).*

abfallen, gegenüber dem Muster to prove inferior to sample.

Abfall| **händler** junk dealer; ~**produkt** waste (by-, residual, spinoff) product; ~**verwertung** recovery (recuperation) of waste, salvage; ~**wirtschaft** utilization of waste products.

abfangen *(Briefe)* to intercept;
Kunden ~ to entice (steal) customers.

abfassen to word, *(in Kodesprache)* to code, *(Schriftstück)* to draw (get) up, to draft;
freundlich ~ to couch in polite words;

Abfassung | **einer Beschwerde** filing of a complaint; ~ **eines Reklametextes** copy writing.

abfertigen to forward, to dispatch, to send off, to expedite, *(zur Post geben)* to post *(Br.)*, to mail *(US)*, *(Zoll)* to clear;
j. bevorzugt ~ to give s. o. priority (preference); **Kunden** ~ to deal with (attend, serve) a customer.

Abfertigung dispatch[ing], expedition, expediting, forwarding, *(Flugplatz)* clearance, check-in;
zollamtliche ~ clearance of goods;
~ **zum freien Verzehr beantragen** to enter for consumption.

Abfertigungs|**dienst** dispatch service; ~**gebäude** *(Flugplatz)* terminal building; ~**schalter** checkout counter; ~**schein** forwarding note, *(Zoll)* permit, customs declaration; ~**stelle** office of dispatch, forwarding (dispatch[ing]) office, ~**zeit** handling time, *(Flugplatz)* check-in (ground-handling) time.

abfinden to pay off, to satisfy;
j. in bar ~ to pay s. o. a compensation in cash; **j. mit Geld** ~ to buy s. o. off.

Abfindung *(Angestellter)* layoff benefit, dismissal compensation, severance pay (benefit), *(Entschädigung)* compensation, satisfaction, indemnification, indemnity, *(Teilhaber)* buying out.

Abfindungs|**betrag** [amount of] compensation, indemnity; ~**zahlung** lump-sum payout, payoff, composition payment.

abflachen *(Konjunkturzyklus, Preisgefälle)* to flatten.

Abflauen der Kurse sagging of prices.

abflauen *(Börse)* to sag, to flatten out, to ease off, *(Konjunktur)* to recede, to slump.

Abflug flight, start, taking off, take-off, takeoff;
~**hafen** port of departure; ~**halle** departure lounge; ~**zeit** departure time.

Abfluß outflow, *(Gold, Kapital)* drain;
~ **heißen Geldes** hot-money outflow.

abführen *(Geldbetrag)* to pay over (off), to clear, to discharge.

Abfuhr|lohn cartage; ~**spediteur** cartage contractor.

Abgabe *(Aushändigung)* delivery, turning over, *(Kommunalsteuer)* rate *(Br.),* lot, *(Steuer)* duty, impost, imposition, tax, direct tax *(Br.), (Verbrauchssteuer)* excise, duty;
~ **von Anteilen** *(Rückversicherung)* ceding of quotas; ~ **einer Einkommensteuererklärung** filing of an income-tax return; ~ **einer Offerte** making an offer; ~ **unter Selbstkostenpreis** sale below cost.

Abgaben [public] dues;
frei von ~ duty-free, scot-free;
drückende ~ heavy burden; **öffentliche (staatliche)** ~ rates and taxes; **soziale** ~ social security contributions;
hohe ~ **bezahlen müssen** to be heavily taxed; ~ **erheben** to impose (collect) a duty (tax).

Abgabe|druck *(Börse)* sales pressure; ~**frist** filing term; ~**kurs** issue price; ~**material** *(Börse)* stock offered, offerings; ~**neigung** willingness to sell.

abgaben|frei exempt from taxation (taxes), tax-exempt (-free, *US)* nondutiable, *(Kommunalsteuer)* nonassessable, zero-rated; ~**pflichtig** dutiable, liable to duty (to pay taxes), assessable, taxable, customable, *(Kommunalsteuer)* rat(e)able.

Abgaben|pflichtiger taxpayer, ratepayer; ~ **wirtschaft** financial economy.

Abgabe|preis selling (sales) price, *(Gas, Elektrizität)* rate, *(Obligation)* issue price; ~**termin** *(Steuer)* date of payment.

Abgang *(Abfahrt)* departure, leaving, *(Abnahme)* decrease, reduction, *(Verlust)* waste, wastage, loss, decrease, *(beim Wiegen)* short weight, loss;
~ **vom Goldstandard** abandonment of the gold standard; **gleichmäßiger** ~ **von versicherten Leben** equal decrement of life.

Abgänge *(Bilanz)* losses, retirements.

Abgangs|bahnhof departure (starting) station, station of departure; ~**liste** shipping list; ~**postamt** dispatching office; **Zu- und** ~**satz** *(Belegschaft)* replacement rate; ~ **station** departure station, *(Fracht)* dispatching station; ~**zeit** time of departure, *(Fracht, Telegramm)* time of dispatch, *(Schiff)* time of sailing.

abgeben to deliver [up], *(Fahrkarte)* to give up, *(Gepäck)* to leave with, to deposit, *(verkaufen)* to sell, to dispose, to supply, to let have;
blanko ~ *(Börse)* to sell bear *(Br.)* (short, *US);* **Einkommensteuererklärung** ~ to file an income-tax return; **sein Gepäck** ~ to leave one's luggage at the luggage office *(Br.),* to check one's baggage in the baggage room *(US);* **Wechsel** ~ to draw value on s. o.

Abgeber *(Börse)* seller, giver, marketeer.

abgebrannt burned, *(pleite)* on the rocks (nut, *US sl.),* [stony]broke *(sl.),* cleaned out.

abgefertigt werden *(Zoll)* to pass the customs.

abgehen *(Absatz finden)* to sell, *(vom Betrag)* to be deducted, *(Flugzeug)* to start, *(Post)* to go, to leave,

(Schiff) to sail, to set out, to leave for, *(Zug)* to depart, to go (steam) off;
nur langsam ~ to go off heavily; **reißend** ~ to sell rapidly (like hot dogs, cakes).

abgehend|e Ladung outward cargo; ~**er Zug** departing train.

abgehoben withdrawn, *(Dividende)* cashed.

abgelaufen expired, exhausted, *(fällig)* due, mature, *(Steuerjahr)* ended;
~ **sein** *(Frist)* to have run.

abgelten to reimburse, to compensate;
Kapitalertragssteuer durch eine 30%ige Pauschalzahlung ~ to meet capital yield tax by a 30 per cent lump-sum payment; **Überstunden** ~ to pay for overtime.

Abgeltung discharge, payment.

abgemachter Preis price agreed upon.

abgerechneter Betrag amount deducted.

abgerundet|er Betrag round sum; ~**e Leistung** finished performance.

abgeschlossen|es Börsengeschäft round transaction; ~**e Wohnung** self-contained flat.

abgeschwächt *(Kurse)* easier, weaker, sagged;
etw. ~ eased off a fraction;
leicht ~ **eröffnen** to open at a slight discount; ~**e Börse** weaker prices.

abgesonderte Befriedigung *(Konkurs)* preferential treatment (payment).

abgestellter Angestellter loaned employee.

abgestuft *(Steuer)* gradual, gradational, graduated.

abgetragene Schuld liquidated debt.

Abgleiten der Kurse weakness in the market.

abgleiten *(Kurse)* to slide down, to weaken, *(Währung)* to slump, to go down;
sozial ~ to sink in the social scale.

abgrasen, Bezirk to work a distrikt; **Markt** ~ to exploit a selling area.

Abrenzungs|kosten deferrals and accruals; ~**posten** *(Bilanz)* deferred item.

abhandeln *(Preisnachlaß erwirken)* to beat down, to knock off the price.

abhanden gekommene Wertpapiere lost securities.

abhängen to depend upon, *(Konkurrenz)* to outdistance.

abhängig *(finanziell)* dependant;
von jem. ~ **sein** to eat s. one's salt; **in einem** ~**en Arbeitsverhältnis stehen** to belong to the wage-earning group.

Abhängigkeitsverhältnis *(Angestellter)* subordinate position.

abheben to draw, to withdraw, *(Dividenden)* to cash, to collect, *(Flugzeug)* to take off;
Geld von der Bank ~ to withdraw funds from the bank.

Abhebung| eines Geldbetrages withdrawal of a sum of money; ~ **vom Sparkonto** withdrawal of a deposit account.

Abhebungs|befugnis drawing right; ~**formular** withdrawal form.

abheften to file [away], to file in.

Abhol- und Zustelldienst pickup and delivery service.
abholen, j. vom Bahnhof ~ to meet s. o. at the station; **seine Briefe vom Schließfach** ~ to fetch (collect) one's letters from one's post-office box; **sein Gepäck bei der Gepäckaufbewahrung** ~ to claim one's luggage from the left-luggage office *(Br.)*.
Abholfach post-office (letter, private) box; **~gebühr** collection fee.
abkaufen, seinem Partner den Anteil to buy out a partner; **jem. den ganzen Vorrat** ~ to clear s. one's stock.
abklappern, Läden naeh etw. to round (trapes round) the shops looking for s. th..
abklingen *(Konjunktur)* to recede, to slacken.
Abkommen arrangement, agreement, understanding, *(Tarif)* bargain; **betriebsgewerkschaftliches** ~ shopcraft settlement; **multilaterales** ~ multilateral agreement; **~ über deutsche Auslandsschulden** London Agreement; **~ über wirtschaftliche Zusammenarbeit** Agreement on Economic Cooperation; **in den Bereich eines ~s fallen** to fall within the ambit of an agreement; **~ mit seinen Gläubigern treffen** to compound with one's creditors.
Abkommensland *(ECU)* elearing country.
abkühlen, sich *(Konjunktur)* to cool off.
Abkühlungszeit *(Streikrecht)* cooling-off period *(US)*.
Abkürzung der Versicherungsdauer shortening of policy.
Abladefrist free (unloading) time; ~ **gebühr** unloading charges; **~gewicht** shipping weight.
Abladen unloading, unlading, discharging.
abladen to unload, to unlade, to discharge, *(Lastwagen)* to detruck, *(Müll)* to dump, to shoot, *(Schiff)* to unship.
Abladeplatz unloading place (platform), *(Schiffsplatz)* port of discharge, unloading port.
Ablader unloader, *(Schiff)* shipper, dock labo(u)rer, docker *(Br.)*, stevedore.
Abladeschein weight certificate, certificate of discharge; **~vorrichtung** dumping service.
Ablage filing, *(abgelegte Akten)* filed material; **~ nach Sachgebieten** subject filing; **~korb** [filing] tray; **zentrales ~wesen** central filing system.
ablassen *(abgeben)* to let have, *(Preis reduzieren)* to abate, to reduce, to grant a reduction, to give a discount; **billig** ~ to sell cheap; **unter dem Selbstkostenpreis** ~ to sell below cost price; **Zug** ~ to dispatch (start) a train.
Ablauf *(First, Vertrag)* expiry, expiration; **bei ~ des Wechsels** when the bill matures; **~ der Kündigungsfrist** fulfil(l)ment of the notice period.
ablaufen *(fällig werden)* to fall due, to mature, to become payable, *(First)* to expire, to run down.
Ablauftermin expiration date, term, deadline *(US)*.
Ablegefach pigeon hole; **~korb** [letter] tray; **~mappe** filing jacket.

ablegen to [put on] file, to pigeonhole; **chronologisch** ~ to file in order of date.
ablehnen, Angebot to decline (refuse) an offer; **Gesuch** ~ to run down a request.
Ablehnungsbescheid notice of denial.
ablichten to blueprint, to photostat, to xerox.
Ablichtung blueprint, photostatic copy.
abliefern to deliver, to hand (turn) in; **Koupons** ~ to surrender coupons.
Ablieferung delivery, handing over, surrender; **zahlbar bei** ~ cash on delivery *(C. O. D.)*.
Ablieferungsfrist delivery date; **~prämie** [delivery] bonus, bounty; **~schein** bill of delivery, dock receipt; **~termin** day (date) of delivery, *(Londoner Börse)* settling day *(Br.)*.
ablösbar detachable, *(Anleihe)* callable, *(Rente)* redeemable.
ablösen *(Lasten)* to commute, *(Rente)* to redeem; **Hypothek** ~ to satisfy (pay off) a mortgage; **fällige Zinsscheine** ~ to detach coupons.
Ablösung discharge, settlement, liquidation, *(Anleihe, Renten)* redemption; **frei durch** ~ on Her (His) Majesty's service *(Br.);* **~ einer Hypothek** satisfaction of a mortgage.
Ablösungsanleihe redemption loan, consol bonds; **~bestimmungen** redemption provisions; **~fonds** sinking (redemption, *US*) fund; **~recht** redemption right; **~schuldverschreibungen** refunding (consolidated) bonds.
Abmachung transaction, bargain, engagement; **bindende** ~ binding arrangement; **wirtschaftliche ~en** trade agreement.
abmontieren to take down (to pieces), *(Werksanlagen)* to scrap, to dismantle.
abmustern *(Matrose)* to sign off, *(Schiffsbesatzung)* to discharge, to pay off.
Abnahme *(Absatz)* sale, *(Annahme)* acceptance, receiving, *(Gebäude)* final architect's certificate, *(Minderung)* decrease, decline, diminution, reduction, dwindling, abatement; **bei ~ von** on purchase of; **bei ~ größerer Mengen** if larger quantities are taken; **~ nach Stichproben** acceptance sampling; **~ der Vorräte** shrinkage of stocks; **gute ~ finden** to sell well, to find a ready sale (market); **~beamter** quality inspector *(Br.)* receiving clerk *(US)*; **~bereitschaft des Verbrauchermarktes** consumer acceptance; **~fahrt** *(Schiff)* acceptance on trial; **~garantie** *(Anleihekonsortium)* underwriting guarantee; **~kontrolle** quality control; **~kosten** inspection cost; **~verpflichtung** *(Effektenhändler)* firm bid; **im ~verzug sein** to be in default; **~vorschriften** quality specifications; **~zwang für alle Produkte** full line forcing *(US)*.
abnehmen to accept, to take delivery, *(geringer werden)* to decline, to decrease, to diminish, to abate, *(kaufen)* to buy, to purchase, *(Konjunktur)*, to slow down, to taper off, *(Nachfrage)* to fall off; **jem. sein ganzes Geld** ~ to fleece s. o.

of his last halfpenny; **den ganzen Posten** ~ to take the whole lot; **Waren** ~ to take delivery of goods.

Abnehmer taker, user, *(Käufer)* buyer, *(Kunde)* client; **alleiniger** ~ sole buyer; **keine** ~ *(Börse)* no buyers; **gewerblicher** ~ industrial customer; ~ **sein** to be in the market; ~**kartell** buying (purchasing) combine.

Abnutzung wear, waste, wastage, exhaustion; **maschinelle** ~ machine wear.

Abnutzungs|betrag depreciation amount; ~**gebühr** detriment *(Br.)*; ~**restwert** scrap value *(US)*.

Abonnement subscription, *(Bahn)* season *(Br.)* (commutation, *US)* ticket; **sein** ~ **abbestellen** to give up subscribing, to discontinue one's subscription; **im** ~ **essen** to buy luncheon vouchers (meal tickets, *US)*.

Abonnements|erneuerung renewal of subscription; ~**fahrkarte** season *(Br.)* (commutation, *US)* ticket; ~**karte** subscription (season, *Br.,* commutation, *US)* ticket, *(Theater)* coupon, *(Mittagessen)* luncheon voucher, meal ticket *(US)*; ~**preis** subscription [fee, price, rate]; ~**verkauf** subscription sale.

Abonnent subscriber; ~**en für eine Zeitung werben** to canvasss for a newspaper, to solicit subscriptions.

Abonnenten|preis subscription fee (rate, price); ~**schwund** downward trend in subscriptions; ~**versicherung** subscriber's (newspaper) insurance.

abonnieren to subscribe, to enter a subscription, *(Zeitung)* to take in *(Br.)* to keep *(US)*.

abrechnen to [give an] account, *(abziehen)* to deduct, *(einbehalten)* to recoup, *(Skonto gewähren)* to discount; **Effekten zum Kurs von . . .** ~ to credit (debit) with the proceeds of the securities at the price of . . .; **Spesen** ~ to account for expenses; **Tara** ~ to allow for the tare; **Wechsel** ~ to discount a bill of exchange.

Abrechnung *(Abzug)* deduction, discount, *(Scheckverkehr)* bank clearing; **nach** ~ **der Spesen** after deducting expenses (charges); **nach** ~ **der Steuern** after taxes; **innerbetriebliche** ~ intercompany squaring; **monatliche** ~ monthly tally; **wöchentliche** ~ weekly settlement; ~ **der Regionalbanken** country clearing *(Br.)*; ~ **über den Kauf (Verkauf) von Effekten** contract note *(Br.)*, bought note *(US)*; **im voraus bezahlte Beträge in** ~ **bringen** to allow for sums paid in advance.

Abrechnungs|bank clearinghouse agent; ~**blatt** *(Börsenmakler)* contract sheet, *(Konto)* summary sheet; ~**büro** clearinghouse; ~**kurs** making-up (settling) price; ~**posten** clearance item; ~**preis** settling price; ~**tag** settling (settlement, bargain, audit, cash) day, day of account, *(Devisenverkehr)* value date; ~**verfahren** clearinghouse system; ~**verkehr** clearing, clearinghouse business.

Abreißkalender tearoff block (calendar).

abrollen *(Spediteur)* to transport, to deliver.

Abrufauftrag make-and-take order *(US)*.

abrufen, Gelder to call in funds.

abrunden to round off.

Absatz *(Absatzmarkt)* market, outlet, *(Abschnitt)* paragraph, new line, article, *(Verkauf)* sale, disposal, selling, *(Vertrieb)* marketing, distribution; **flauer** ~ dead sale; **neuer** ~ fresh paragraph; **reißender** ~ rapid sales; ~ **von Industrieerzeugnissen** industrial marketing; ~ **an Private** private offering, *(Banken)* private placement of securities; **neuen** ~ **beginnen** to begin a new paragraph; **glänzenden** ~ **finden** to rub off in great style; **keinen** ~ **finden** to find no sale, *(Börse)* to find no buyers; **schlechten** ~ **finden** to sell hard (heavily); ~ **steigern** to increase the sale.

Absatz|analyse market analysis; ~**anstieg** spring sales sprint; ~**anstrengungen** sales drive; ~**bedingungen** market[ing] conditions, sales terms *(US)*; ~**bewußt** sales-minded (-oriented); ~**chance** opening; ~**chancen** sales prospects; ~**denken** marketing concept; ~**diagramm** sales curve; ~**fachmann** marketing (market-research) specialist; ~**feldzug** marketing (sales, selling) campaign, marketing drive; ~**finanzierung** marketing (sales) financing; ~**förderung** sales promotion, merchandizing; ~**forschung** marketing (market) research; ~**garantie** sales guarantee; ~**gebiet** market, trading (marketing, selling) area; **neue** ~**gebiete erschließen** to open up new markets; ~**genossenschaft** marketing cooperative, cooperative marketing association, *(landwirtschaftliche)* producer cooperative; ~ **honorar** royalty; ~**kalkulation** sales estimate; ~**kanäle** marketing channels; ~**kennzahlen** distribution indices; ~**konjunktur** seller's market; ~**konzeption** marketing conception; ~**kosten** distribution expenses (costs), marketing costs; ~**krise** sales crisis, slump in sales; ~**lenkung** sales control.

Absatzmarkt market, market (trading) area; **erfolgversprechender** ~ promising (seller's) market; ~ **eröffnen** to break the ground.

Absatz, neue ~**märkte erschließen** to open up new channels of trade; **mit sicheren** ~**möglichkeiten** certain to sell; ~**monopol** sales monopoly; ~**organisation** sales (selling) organization; **selektive** ~**politik** selective selling; ~**prognose** sales forecast; ~**provision** seller's commission; ~**stab** sales force (people, personnel); **planmäßige** ~**steigerung** sales drive; ~**stockung** stagnation in trade, stagnant market; ~**verhältnisse** market (marketing) conditions; ~**vorbereitung durch Vertriebsplanung** merchandizing *(US)*; ~**vorschau** forecasting sales; **ausschließlicher** ~**weg** exclusive distribution; ~**wesen** marketing [field (system)]; ~ **wirtschaft** [industrial] marketing, distributive trade; ~**zahlen** sales figures, market (marketing) data.

abschätzen *(bewerten)* to value, to valuate, to eval-

uate, to price, *(taxieren)* to appraise, to estimate, to tax;
Schaden auf fünf Pfund ~ to value the damage done at five pounds.

Abschätzung *(Bewertung)* valuation, evaluation, valuing, *(Schätzung)* estimate, appraisal, estimation, appraisement, taxation;
~ **zwecks hypothekarischer Beleihung** rating of the entire mortgage pattern; ~ **zur Festlegung der Erbschaftssteuer** appraisal for inheritance taxation purposes; ~**zu Steuerzwecken** appraisal for taxation purposes, assessed valuation *(US).*

Abschätzungsklausel agreed-value (appraisal) clause.

abschicken to send off, to dispatch, to forward, to ship *(US);*
Geld ~ to remit money.

Abschieds|besuch farewell call (visit); **sein** ~**gesuch einreichen** to tender one's resignation, to send in one's papers.

Abschlag *(Abzug)* deduction, reduction, *(im Kurs)* decline, discount, disagio, *(Preisminderung)* abatement, rebate, allowance, discount;
auf ~ in part payments, by instalments; **mit 12 %** ~ less 12 %;
mit einem ~ **verkaufen** to sell at a decline.

Abschlags|dividende interim (initial, *Br.)* dividend, dividend at interim *(on account); ~***verteilung** *(Konkurs)* distribution of dividend; ~**zahlung** partial payment, *(Teilzahlung)* part (initial) payment.

Abschleppdienst recovery (breakdown, wrecking, towing, wrecker, *US)* service.

abschleppen *(Auto)* to haul, to tow off (away).

Abschlepp|kommando recovery (breakdown) party; ~**wagen** recovery vehicle, wrecker *(US)*, breakdown van (lorry), tow car.

abschließen *(Brief)* to close, *(Geschäft)* to transact, *(Konto, Rechnung)* to settle;
aktiv ~ to show a balance in favo(u)r; **Anleihe** ~ to contract a loan; **Bilanz** ~ to strike (bring down) a balance; **Geschäftsjahr** ~ to close the business year; **mit Gewinn** ~ to show a profit; **für eigene Rechnung** ~ to trade for own account; **Versicherung** ~ to take out an insurance policy; **Vertrag** ~ to come (enter into) an agreement.

Abschluß conclusion, *(Bank)* bank return, *(Bilanz)* balance [sheet], *(an der Börse)* bargain, transaction, *(Effektenemission)* underwriting, *(Geschäft)* deal[ing], business, transaction, *(Werbebranche)* contract;
bei ~ **unserer Bücher** on (when) balancing (closing) our books;
jährlicher ~ annual balance; **provisorischer** ~ provisional booking;
~ **von Deckungsgeschäften** hedging; ~ **eines Kontos** closing an account; ~ **zu einem festen Verkaufspreis** outright sale;
Geschäft zum ~ **bringen** to make a bargain, to bring to a close; **mit einem guten** ~ **rechnen** to calculate on a good trade; **ohne** ~ **sein** *(Börse)* to be a blank.

Abschluß|anmeldung *(Umsatzsteuer)* final declaration; ~**bericht** closing statement; ~**bilanz** [annual] balance sheet; ~**buchung** closing entry *(US);* ~**einheit** *(Börse)* even (full, *US)* lot; ~**kosten** *(Versicherung)* initial expenses; ~**provision** [sales, new business, final] commission, *(Effektenemission)* underwriting commission, *(Generalvertreter)* overriding commission; ~**rabatt** *(Anzeigenplazierung)* time discount; ~**termin** target date, *(Anleihe)* closing date; ~**vollmacht** power to contract; ~**zahlung** complete payment, *(letzte Rate)* final instal(l)ment; ~**zeugnis** leaving certificate, diploma *(US).*

Abschlüsse business [done], *(Aufträge)* orders secured, *(Börse)* transactions, commitments;
kleine ~ odd lots; **vereinzelte** ~ spasmodic dealings; **wenig** ~ few sales;
größere ~ **tätigen** to make more sales; ~ **in Devisen tätigen** to effect exchange transactions.

Abschnitt *(Buch)* chapter, section, *(Kontrollblatt)* counterfoil, stub *(US)*, *(Lebensmittelkarte)* coupon, *(Scheck)* stub, counterfoil;
nicht offiziell an der Börse gehandelter ~ odd (fractional, *US)* lot; **noch nicht verrechnete** ~e effects not cleared;
~ **einer Anleihe** portion (slice) of a loan; ~e **auf auswärtigen Plätzen** out-of-town items *(US)*; ~e **auf uns** bills on us.

abschöpfen to skim off, *(Gewinne)* to tax away, to siphon off, *(Kaufkraft)* to absorb.

Abschöpfungs|beitrag auf Agrareinfuhren product of agricultural levies; ~**betrag** *(EG)* price adjustment levy.

abschreiben *(Bilanz)* to write (charge) off, to allow for depreciation;
Betriebsanlage ~ to write down an asset; **zweifelhafte Forderung** ~ to write off a doubtful *(Br.)* (bad, *US)* debt; **Kunden** ~ to regard a customer as lost; **Verluste** ~ to charge off (deduct, cut) losses; **voll (vollständig)** ~ to wipe off the books.

Abschreibung writeoff *(US)*, charge-off, writedown, *(für Substanzverringerung)* depletion, *(für Wertminderung)* [allowance for] depreciation, amortization;
nach ~ **aller Verluste** after charging off all losses;
7 b ~ allowance on premises, [statutory] repairs allowance (deduction); **beschleunigte** ~ accelerated depreciation, emergency amortization, rapid writeoff; **degressive** ~ declining-balance depreciation; **digitale** ~ sum of the year digits; **lineare** ~ straight-line [method of] depreciation; **verdiente** ~ amount of depreciation earned; **vollständige** ~ wholesale writing down; **steuerlich zulässige** ~**en** tax writeoffs *(US)*, capital allowance *(Br.);*
~ **auf das Anlagevermögen** depreciation on fixed assets ~**en für Devisenverluste** writeoffs for losses on foreign exchange; ~ **für Gebäudeabnutzung** reduction of premises account; ~ **auf den Maschinenpark** depreciation on machinery; ~**en auf Warenbestände** inventory writedowns; ~ **für Wertminderung** allowance for wear and tear;

~ **aussetzen** to interrupt depreciation; ~**[zeitlich] verteilen** to allocate depreciation; **seine ~en steuerlich über mehrere Jahre verteilen** to spread one's depreciation over several years.

Abschreibungs|aufwand depreciation expense (charges); ~**betrag** depreciable amount, amount written off; **⁻fähig** depreciable, liable to depreciaton; ~**formel** depreciation formula; ~**grundwert** depreciable value; ~**kosten** depreciation charges (expense).

Abschreibungsmethode depreciation (retirement, accounting) method;
direkte ~ direct method of depreciation; **gleichmäßige** ~ **vom Anschaffungswert** straight-line method of depreciation; **gleichmäßige** ~ **vom Buchwert** fixed-percentage (diminishing-value) method of depreciation; ~ **mit fallenden Quoten** reducing-fraction method of calculating depreciation.

Abschreibungs|modalitäten, günstigere liberalized rules on depreciation; **schnellere ~möglichkeit für Anlagegüter** faster capital-goods depreciation; **steuerliche ~politik** depreciation tax policy; ~**quote** depreciation rate; ~**restwert** scrap (depreciated) value; ~**richtlinien** depreciation guidelines (rules); ~**rücklage** reserve for wear, tear, obsolescence or inadequacy; ~**satz** depreciation rate (charge); **jährlichen ~ satz berechnen** to compute the annual depreciation rate; ~ **sätze variieren** to vary writeoffs; ~**stichtag** depreciation date; **systematisch durchgeführtes ~verfahren** depreciation accounting; ~**verlust** retirement loss.

Abschrift copy, transcript, transcription;
für gleichlautende ~ for copy conform;
notariell beglaubigte ~ notarized copy;
~ **beglaubigen** to attest a copy of record.

abschwächen, sich (*Konjunktur*) to soften, to depress, to level off, (*Kurse*) to weaken, to sag, to ease off;
seine Forderungen ~ to soft-pedal one's claims.

Abschwächung (*Konjunktur*) softness, decline, levelling off, (*Kurse*) ease, easing, sagging;
saisonbedingte ~ seasonal allowance;
~ **um einen Bruchteil** fractional ease; .~ **der Sätze für Festgeld** lowering of the time loan rates.

Abschwächungstendenz weaker (downward, slackening) tendency.

absenden to send off, to forward, to dispatch, to expedite, to consign, to ship (*US*), (*Brief*) to post (*Br.*), to mail (*US*), (*Geld*) to remit.

Absender (*Brief*) sender, dispatcher, forwarder;
im Fall der Nichtzustellung an ~ **zurück** in case of nondelivery return to the sender.

Absende|spediteur forwarding carrier; ~**stelle** station of dispatch, forwarding point, (*Post*) office of dispatch.

Absendung sending off, (*Brief*) posting (*Br.*), mailing (*US*), (*Güter*) forwarding, dispatch, consignment, shipping (*US*), shipment (*US*).

absetzbar (*abschreibungsfähig*) depreciable, liable to depreciation, (*börsengängig*) marketable, (*steuerlich*) deductible.

absetzen (*abziehen*) to deduct, (*vom Budget*) to take (strike) off, (*verkaufen*) to market, to sell;
Aktien von der Notierung ~ to remove shares from the stock exchange list; **mit Gewinn** ~ to sell at a premium; **mit Verlust** ~ to sell at a loss (discount); **seine Waren** ~ to clear one's stock;
sich nicht ~ **lassen** to find no sale (buyers); **sich schwer** ~ **lassen** to run into heavy selling.

Absetzung remove, removal, dismissal, (*Kosten*) deduction;
steuerfreie ~ **für Abnutzung** allowance for wear and tear; ~**en für Substanzverringerungen** depletion charges.

absichern, Kredit to cover a loan.

Absichtserklärung declaration (letter) of interest, letter of intent (*US*).

Absinken (*der Kurse*) decline, fall, drop;
~ **der Aktienkurse** stock-market slide.

absinken (*Kurse*) to decline, to recede, to fall.

absondern (*Konkurs*) to set apart (aside).

Absonderung preferential treatment, setting aside (apart).

Absonderungsanspruch preferential claim, claim of a secured creditor (of exemption, *US*).

absonderungsberechtigter Gläubiger preferential (secured) creditor.

abspenstig machen (*Kunden*) to entice (draw) away, to alienate.

Absprache understanding, arrangement;
registrierte ~ (*Kartellrecht*) registered agreement (*Br.*).

Abstands|geld recession money, compensation, (*Angestellter*) dismissal wage, (*Börse*) option money, (*Wohnungsmiete*) key money (*Br.*).

abstauben (*profitieren*) to snaffle, to sneak.

absteigen, in einem Hotel to put up at a hotel.

Abstellbahnhof sidings, railway (railroad, *US*) yard.

abstellen (*Auto, Flugzeug*) to park (*Br.*), (*Gas, Wasser*) to turn off, (*Personal*) to detach, (*Strom*) to cut off, (*Waggon*) to shunt, to sidetrack;
~ **auf** to gear, to tailor; **Angestellten** ~ to loan an employee; **Fähigkeiten** ~ to calculate maturity on a monthly basis.

Abstell|gleis storage track; ~ **raum** storage room, storeroom.

abstempeln to stamp, to postmark, to hallmark, (*entwerten*) to obliterate, to deface, to cancel.

abstimmen to [give one's] vote, to poll, (*ausgleichen*) to reconcile, to balance, to adjust.

Abstimmung vote, voting, poll, (*Bücher*) adjustment, balancing, squaring;
~ **der Interessen** agreement of interests; ~ **über einen Streik** strike vote;
sich bei der ~ **vertreten lassen** to vote by proxy.

Abstimmungstermin (*Konto*) reconciliation date.

abstoßen (*Effekten*) to unload, to sell off, (*Lagerbestände*) to clear, to get rid of.

Abstottern (*fam.*) nevernever.

abstreichen, etw. von der Rechnung to knock off the bill.

Abstrich|e beim Haushaltsvoranschlag budget economies;
~e machen (vornehmen) to retrench, to economize, to cut.
abtasten, Markt to sound the market.
Abteil, bestelltes reserved compartment.
Abteilung *(Abschnitt)* compartment, *(Betrieb, Verwaltung)* department, division;
federführende ~ initiating department;
~ **für Inkassi auswärtiger Plätze** transit department *(US);* ~ **zur Regulierung unbezahlter Rechnungen** *(Warenhaus)* adjustment bureau.
Abteilungs|chef department head; ~kosten departmental costs (expenses).
abtelegrafieren to countermand by wire.
abtragen *(Passivsaldo)* to work off, to acquit;
Hypothek ~ to sink (amortize) a mortgage.
abtrennen to separate, to sever, *(Kupon)* to clip.
abtretbar transferable, conveyable, assignabel.
abtreten to assign, to make over (an assignment), to sign over, *(zurücktreten)* to resign.
Abtretung assignment, cession, transfer;
~ **des Ersatzanspruches** subrogation assignment;
~ **des Versicherungsanspruches an den Hypothekengläubiger** mortgage endorsement.
Abtretungs|benachrichtigung notice of assignment;
~urkunde assignation, [deed of] assignment, quitclaim deed *(US).*
abwälzen *(Preiserhöhung)* to pass along, *(Steuer)* to shift, to pass on.
Abwanderung migration, *(Kapital)* exodus.
Abwärtsbewegung *(Konjunktur)* down, downtrend, downturn, *(Kurse)* bearish tendency;
sich in einer ~ **befinden** to be on a downslope.
abweisen to refuse, to reject, to turn down;
Forderung ~ to set a claim aside.
abwerben, Angestellte to entice servants, to poach employees.
Abwerbung | von Arbeitskräften labor piracy US, pirating; ~ **von Belegschaftsangehörigen** poaching of staff.
abwerfen, Gewinn to leave (yield) a profit, to be profitable, to pay; **netto** ~ to [yield] net.
abwerten to devalue, to devaluate, to depreciate.
Abwertung devalorization, devaluation.
Abwertungs|gewinn devalorization profit; ~politik devaluation policy.
Abwesenheit absence, nonattendance, *(vom Arbeitsplatz)* absenteeism.
Abwesenheits|liste absentees list; ~pfleger public administrator.
abwickeln to adjust, to settle, to transact, to effect, *(liquidieren)* to liquidate, to wind up;
Geschäft ~ to settle a business; **über ein Refinanzierungsinstitut** ~ to effect through a refinancing institution; **alte Verträge** ~ to work off old contracts; **zwangsweise** ~ to execute under the rules.
Abwicklung settlement, adjustment, handling, *(Liquidation)* liquidation, winding up, windup;
zwangsweise ~ execution under the rules;

außerkonkursrechtliche ~ **zugunsten der Gläubiger** assignment for the benefit of creditors.
Abwicklungs|bank liquidating bank; ~geschäft winding-up transaction; ~gesellschaft liquidating company; ~konto liquidation account; ~kosten handling costs.
abwracken, Schiff to break up a ship.
abzahlen to pay off, to acquit, to discharge debts;
Hypothek ~ to clear off a mortgage; **monatlich** ~ to pay in monthly instal(l)ments.
Abzahlung paying off, *(in Raten)* part (instalment) payment, payment by instalments (on the instalment, hire-purchase, *Br.* deferred-payment, *US,* plan);
~ **in bequemen Raten** easy payment;
auf ~ **kaufen** to buy on the instalment (hire-purchase, *Br.)* (deferred-payment *US)* system;
einem Kunden etw. auf ~ **verkaufen** to hire-purchase s. th. to a customer.
Abzahlungs|bank personal (small) loan company, hire-purchase finance house *(Br.);* **auf** ~ **basis** on the instalment plan (hire-pruchase, *Br.);* ~formular hire-purchase form; ~geschäft hire purchase *(Br.),* tally trade *(Br.),* instalment business (sale), sale on the deferred-payment system *(US);* ~kauf instalment buying (sale, selling), hire purchase *(Br.),* purchase on the deferred-payment system *(US);* ~kredit instalment (hire-purchase, *Br.,* deferred-payment, *US)* credit; ~kredit aufnehmen to borrow through hire purchase *(Br.);* ~preis instalment (time, hire-purchase, *Br.)* price; ~rate instalment, period payment; ~raten auf mehrere Monate verteilen to spread instalments over several months; **hochwertige** ~verkäufe high-ticket instalment sales; ~vertrag instalment contract, hirepurchase *(Br.)* (deferred-payment, *US)* agreement; **miteinander verbundene** ~verträge add-ons; **Auto im** ~wege bezahlen to buy a motor car and pay for it by monthly instalments;
abziehen to deduct, to recoup, *(drucktechn.)* to pull off, to strike (print) off, *(vom Lohn)* to withhold, to dock;
3 % ~ to allow 3 per cent; **vom Preis** ~ to knock off the price
Abzug deduction, reduction, *(Abdruck)* print, *(vom Lohn)* withholding, stoppage, docking *(Br.);*
nach ~ **der Einkommensteuer** clear of income tax;
nach (unter) ~ **der Zinsen** less interest accrued;
bar ohne ~ net (spot) cash, cash less discount; **unter** ~ **Ihrer Provision** deducting your commission;
3 % ~ **bei Barzahlung** 3 % discount for cash; ~ **für Geschäftsauslagen** deduction for expenses *(Br.);*
in ~ **bringen** to deduct, to allow a discount;
~ **machen** *(Druckerei)* to pull (work) off a proof, *(Foto)* to copy; ~ **von 4 % vornehmen** to strike off 4 per cent.
Abzüge, einkommensteuerfreie exemptions, deduction for taxes;
~ **von Gold** gold withdrawals; ~ **vor Verteilung des Reingewinns** surplus charges; ~ **für Werbungsko-**

sten *(Steuererklärung)* allowance for professional expenditure.

abzüglich | Diskont less discount; ~ **aller Kosten** clear of all expenses.

abzugsfähig deductible, allowable; **voll ~e Ausgaben darstellen** to be fully deductible current expenses.

abzweigen *(Geldbeträge)* to earmark, to set aside.

Achse, auf der on track (truck); **per ~** by car (carriage, land), *(Bahn)* per rail, by wag(g)on; **Drittel des Jahres auf der ~ sein** to be on the road about a third of the year.

Achtstundentag eight-hour day, 8hr day.

Ackerbau agriculture, farming.

Adressant addresser, *(Warensendung)* consignor; ~ **eines Wechsels** drawer of a bill.

Adressat addressee, *(Geldsendung)* payee.

Adresse address, direction, *(Geldmarkt)* borrower; **per ~** undercover, care of (c/o); **erste ~** *(Geldmarkt)* first-rate borrower, *(Wechsel)* first-class (prime, *US*) name.

Adressen|änderung change of address; **~büro** list broker (house); **~kartei** mailing list; **~nachweis** list broker; **~verlag** list broker; **~verzeichnis** list [of names].

adressieren to address, to direct, *(Güter)* to consign; **falsch ~** to misaddress, to misdirect.

Adressiermaschine addressing (mailing) machine, addressograph, envelope addresser.

Agentur [commission] agency business (office), factorship, representation; ~ **für Industriewerbung** industrial agency; ~ **für Öffentlichkeitsarbeit** public-relations firm; **~geschäft** agency business; **~tätigkeit** agency service; **~vergütung** agency [service] fee.

Agio agio, [exchange] premium, rate of (premium on) exchange, *(bei der Emission)* stock discount; ~ **genießen** to command (be at) a premium; **~erlös** paid-in surplus; **~geschäft** agiotage; **~konto** agio account.

Agiotage agiotage, premium hunting, stockjobbing.

Agrar |kredit agricultural credit; **~preisniveau** farm-price level.

Akkord *(Lohnform)* contract (job) work, piece-work, tut *(Br.)*, *(Vergleich)* agreement with one's creditors; **im ~ anstellen** to take in contract*(US)*; **im ~ arbeiten** to job, to do job work (piecework); **in ~ nehmen** to take in contract*(US)*; **mit seinen Gläubigern einen ~ zustandebringen** to compound with one's creditors.

Akkord|arbeit job (piece-rate contact, *US*) work, jobbing, tut (time) work *(Br.);* ~ **arbeiter** jobber, job worker, taskworker, pieceworker; **~bezahlung** piecework pay.

Akkordlohn piecework pay, piece wage (rate bonus); **niedrig bezahlte ~arbeit** tight job; **~arbeiter** pieceworker, job worker; **~satz** piece[work] rate formula; **~verdienst** piecework earnings.

Akkord|prämie piece-rate bonus; **~richtsatz** job

(piece, piecework) rate; **~zettel** job ticket; **~zuschlag** piecework bonus, make-up pay.

akkreditieren to accredit; **j.** ~ to open a credit in favo(u)r of s. o.

Akkreditiv [letter of] credit; **begebbares ~** negotiable credit; **bestätigtes ~** confirmed letter of credit; **teilbares ~** transferable credit *(US)*; **unbestätigtes ~** unconfirmed credit; ~ **mit Dokumentenaufnahme** documentary letter of credit; ~ **annullieren** to cancel a credit; ~ **bestätigen** to confirm a credit; ~ **eröffnen** to open a letter of credit; **~gestellung** opening of a credit in favo(u)r; **~vorschuß** packing credit *(Br.)*; **~widerruf** revocation of a letter of credit.

Akontozahlung payment on account, downpayment, instalment.

Akquisiteur canvasser, commercial travel(l)er, drummer *(US)*, *(Anzeigen)* space salesman *(US)*, *(Versicherung)* insurance agent.

Akquisitionsabteilung new-business department.

Akten files, records, rolls, documents, papers; **bei den ~** on file; **abgelegte ~** dead files, filed material; ~ **abteilungsweise ablegen** to file material departmentally; ~ **anfordern** to call in records; **zu den ~ legen** to lay on the shelves, to shelve, to pigeonhole; **~ablage** filing [of records]; **~ablage nach Sachgebieten** classified filing; **~auszug** note, abstract of records; **~einsicht haben** to have access to the files; **~koffer** attaché case, portfolio; **nach ~lage entscheiden** to decide on the record; **~mappe** brief (dispatch) case.

aktenmäßig feststehen to be on (a matter of, appear on the) record.

Akten |notiz memo[randum], note; **~ordner** file folder; **~schrank** filing (file) cabinet; **~schwanz** tab; **~spiegel** retention schedule; **~stoß** pile of documents; **~stück** file, record, document; **~verzeichnis** file index; **~wolf** shredding machine; **~zeichen** file (reference) number, *(im Brief)* ref; **~zeichen angeben** to quote a reference.

Aktie share [of stock], stock *(US);* **zu einem Agio abgegebene ~** premium stock *(US);* **im Clearingverkehr abgerechnete ~** clearinghouse stock *(US);* **ausgegebene ~n** issued shares (stocks, *US)*; **an Betriebsangehörige ausgegebene ~n** staff shares *(Br.)*, shares for the staff *(Br.)*, employee shares *(Br.);* **voll bezahlte ~** paid-up (full-paid) stock *(US);* **börsenfähige ~n** stocks negotiable on the stock exchange *(US)*; **dividendenberechtigte ~** participating share; **noch nicht eingezahlte ~** partly paid [up] share; **eingezogene ~** recalled share; **erstklassige ~n** high-grade shares *(Br.)*, blue chips *(US);* **gewinnberechtigte ~** participating share *(Br.)*, profit-sharing stock *(US);* **nur buchmäßig gutgeschriebene ~n** phantom stocks *(US); im* **Sammeldepot hinterlegte ~** assented stock *(US);*

kaduzierte ~n forfeited shares (stocks, *US*); kleingestückelte ~ fractional share; auf den Inhaber lautende ~ share warrant (stock certificate, *US*) to bearer; auf den Namen lautende ~ registered share; lombardierte ~ loaned share (stock, *US*); mündelsichere ~ trustee stock *(US)*; nachschußpflichtige ~ assessable stock *(US)*; neue ~ fresh (new, junior) share, fresh stock *(US)*; an der Börse nicht notierte ~n displaced shares, unlisted stocks *(US)*; an der Freiverkehrsbörse notierte ~n curb stocks *(US)*, nicht stimmberechtigte ~ nonvoting share (stock, *US*); im Einzeldepot verwahrte ~n nonassented stocks *(US)*; zur Börsennotierung zugelassene ~n quoted shares *(Br.)*, listed stocks *(US)*; ~n auswärtiger Banken zum Anschaffungspreis shareholding (stockholding, *US*) interest in foreign banks at cost; ~ ohne Besitzerschein inscribed stock *(US)*; ~n mit geringen Börsenumsätzen inactive stock *(US)*; ~ mit normaler Dividendenberechnung equity share; ~ mit Dividendenvorzugsberechtigung stock preferred as to dividends *(US)*; ~ mit garantierter Mindestdividende guaranteed share (stock, *US*); ~n mit hoher Rendite shares that yield high interest; ~n abstoßen to unload stocks *(US)*; 10 000 Pfund in ~n angelegt haben to have 10 000 in the stocks *(US)*; ~n zur Generalversammlung anmelden to deposit shares for the general meeting; Bezugsrecht auf junge Aktien ausüben to exercise the right to subscribe (acquire) new stock *(US)*; junge ~n beziehen to subscribe to (for) new shares (stocks, *US*); ~n an der Börse einführen to have shares admitted (stocks listed, *US*) at the stock exchange; ~n hereinnehmen to take in shares for a borrower, to borrow stock *(US)*; Einzahlung auf ~n leisten to pay a call on stocks *(US)*; ~n lombardieren to lend money on stock *(US)*; ~n in Prolongation nehmen to borrow (carry) stocks *(US)*; ~n an der Börse notieren to quote shares *(Br.)* (list stocks, *US*) on the stock exchange; in ~n spekulieren to play the stock market; ~ splitten to split a share (stock, *US*); aus ~n in hochverzinsliche Obligationen umsteigen to switch out of stocks into high-yielding bonds *(US)*; ~n als Kreditunterlage verwenden to apply shares as collateral security *(US)*; ~n zeichnen to apply (make application) for shares *(Br.)*, to subscribe to (for) shares; ~n voll zuteilen to allot shares to all applicants.

Aktien |abschnitt dividend warrant, coupon; ~ agio stock premium *(US)*; ~anteilschein share (stock, *US*) certificate; ~bank joint stock bank *(Br.)*, banking company (corporation, *(US)*); ~besitz shareholdings *(Br.)*, stockholdings *(US)*; ~besitzer shareholder *(Br.)*, holder of shares *(Br.)*, stockowner *(US)*, stockholder *(US)*; ~bestand portfolio; eigener ~bestand treasury stock *(US)*; ~bezugsrecht stock-option (subscription) right *(US)*; ~bezugsschein stock-subscription warrant *(Br.)*, stock (allotment) warrant *(US)*; ~bonus share bonus; ~emission shares (stock, equity) issue

issuance of stocks *(US)*; ~fachmann share (security, *US*) analyst; ~gattung class of stock *(US)*.

Aktiengesellschaft *(AG)* joint-stock company *(Br.)* (corporation, *US*), company limited by shares; an der Börse eingeführte ~ stock-exchange-listed company; ~ mit Dividendenbeschränkung limited-dividend corporation *(US)*; als ~ eintragen to incorporate *(US)*; ~ gründen to promote a joint stock company *(Br.)*, to organize a corporation *(US)*.

Aktien |handel dealing in shares *(Br.)*, stockjobbing, stockbrokerage; ~hausse share (stock, *US*) -market boom; ~index index of stocks, share price index *(Br.)*, ~inhaber shareholder *(Br.)*, stockholder *(US)*, holder of a stock *(US)*.

Aktienkapital share capital, stock, joint stock *(Br.)*, capital stock *(US)*; ausgegebenes ~ issued [capital] stock *(US)*, outstanding shares *(Br.)*; mit zusätzlicher Dividendenberechtigung ausgestattetes ~ participating capital stock *(US)*; autorisiertes ~ authorized share capital *(Br.)*, registered [capital] stock *(US)*; teilweise eingezahltes ~ part-paid stock *(US)*; genehmigtes ~ authorized capital, authorized capital stock *(US)*; stimmberechtigtes ~ voting capital stock *(US)*, voting stock of a company *(Br.)*; ~ erhöhen to increase the share *(Br.)* (stock, *US*) capital; ~ verwässern to water the stock *(US)*; ~ zusammenlegen to write down (off) capital.

Aktien |konto share *(stock, US)* account; ~kupon coupon.

Aktienkurs share (stock, *US*) price; ~e herunterbringen, -drücken to pull (hammer) down the prices of stock *(US)*; ~rückgang decline in stocks *(US)*; ~steigerung stock-market rise *(US)*; ~treiberei kiting stocks *(US)*.

Aktienmajorität controlling interest majoritiy, stock (stockholders') majority *(US)*; ~ besitzen to own control of shares.

Aktien |makler sharebroker *(Br.)*, stockbroker *(US)*, stockjobber *(US)*; ~mantel share (stock *US*) certificate; ~markt share *(Br.)* *(stocks, US, equity)* market; ~notierung share (stock, *US*) quotation.

Aktienpaket block (portion, parcel) of shares; mehrere hundert Aktien umfassende ~e round lot *(US)*; ~ abstoßen to unload a block of shares; beträchtliches ~ zusammenkaufen to build up a sizable position in stocks *(US)*.

Aktien |polster cushion of stocks; ~ portefeuille portfolio [of shares], stock portfolio *(US)*; ~rendite earnings per share, yield on shares (stocks, *US*); ~repartierung allotment of shares (stocks, *US*); ~schein share warrant *(Br.)*, stock certificate *(US)*; ~schwindel stock pushing *(Br.)*, stock bubbling *(US)*; ~spekulation agiotage, speculation in stocks *(US)*, stockjobbery *(Br.)*; ~split [reverse] split-up, splitting; ~streuung dispersal of stock ownership

(US); ~**tausch** exchange of shares (stock, *US* stock switch *(US)*, split off *(US);* ~**umtauschangebot** capital stock exchange offer *(US);* be**trügerischer** ~**verkäufer** sharepusher; ~**verpfändung** pledge of stocks *(US);* ~**verwässerung** dilution (watering) of stocks *(US);* ~**zeichner** applicant (subscriber) for shares, share applicant; ~**zeichnung** application (subscription) for shares *(Br.).*

Aktien |**zertifikat** share warrant (certificate) *(Br.),* stock warrant *(Br.)* (certificate, *US);* ~**zusammenlegung** split-back (-down), reverse split *(US);* ~**zuteilung** allotment (allocation) of shares.

Aktion *(Werbung)* drive, campaign; **konzertierte** ~ concerted action.

Aktionär shareholder *(Br.),* stockholder *(US);* **einfacher** ~ common stockholder *(US);* **opponierender** ~ dissenting shareholder (stockholder, *US);* **stimmgebundener** ~ voting-trust certificate holder *(US);* ~**e zur Zeichnung auffordern** to invite shareholders (stockholders, *US)* to subscribe the capital; ~**e zu einer Generalversammlung einberufen** to summon shareholders for a general meeting *(Br.).*

Aktionärs |**ausschuß** shareholders' committee; ~**brief** shareholder (stockholder, *US)* newsletter; ~**klage** shareholder suit (action), *(für die Gesellschaft)* stockholder's derivative action *(US);* ~**pflege** stockholder relations *(US),* service to shareholders *(Br.);* ~**register** subscribers' *(Br.)* (stockholders, *US)* ledger, stock book *(US);* ~**zeitschrift** external house organ.

Aktions | **ausschuß** executive committee; ~**radius** *(Flugzeug)* range of action, flying range, *(Schiff)* cruising range.

aktiv active, *(Bilanz)* on the asset side, favo(u)rable; **im Geldmarkt** ~ **sein** to appear as creditor in the money market; ~**e Handelsbilanz** favo(u)rable balance of trade; ~**e Konjunkturpolitik** anticyclical measures.

Aktiva, in der Substanz abnehmende wasting assets; **nicht bewertbare** ~ *(Versicherungswesen)* unadmitted assets; **flüssige** ~ circulating (current, quick, floating, fluid, *US)* assets; **immaterielle** ~ *(Patente usw.)* intangible assets; **nicht realisierbare** ~ sticky assets; **zur Verteilung für die Masse verfügbare** ~ *(Konkurs)* unpledged assets, assets at hand; ~ **einer Bank** bank's resources; **Verhältnis der flüssigen** ~ **zu den laufenden Verbindlichkeiten** working capital ratio *(US);* **als** ~ **behandeln** to carry as assets; ~ **im Konkurs feststellen** to marshal assets; ~ **und Passiva übernehmen** to take over accounts receivable and accounts payable *(US).*

Aktivforderungen accounts receivable.

aktivieren, in der Bilanz to carry as assets; **Gewinne** ~ to capitalize profits.

Aktivierung von Gewinnen capitalization of profits.

aktivierungspflichtiger Aufwand capital expenditure.

Aktiv |**masse** assets of a bankrupt's estate; ~**posten** asset, *(Bank)* credit item, *(Rechnungsabgrenzung)* deferred item; ~**saldo** active balance, *(Bank)* credit balance.

Aktivseite *(Bilanz)* active (assets) side; **auf der** ~ **[einer Bilanz] aufführen** to carry as assets; **sich auf der** ~ **Bilanz niederschlagen** to show up in black on the balance sheet.

aktuell topical, of current event, front-page; ~**er Kapitalbedarf** capital needed immediately.

Akzept [letter (bill) of] acceptance, *(akzeptierter Wechsel)* accepted bill (draft), acceptance bill; **mangels** ~ for want (in default) of acceptance; **mangels** ~ **zurück** returned for nonacceptance; **bedingtes** ~ qualified acceptance; **unbeschränktes** ~ clean (general) acceptance; ~ **per Intervention (ehrenhalber)** acceptance for (upon) hono(u)r (supra protest); **sein** ~ **einlösen** to meet one's draft, to hono(u)r (meet) an acceptance; **Wechsel mit** ~ **versehen** to provide a bill with acceptance.

Akzeptant im Konkurs acceptor bankrupt.

Akzept |**bank** acceptance (accepting) house, merchant banker *(Br.);* ~**bestand** bill holdings; ~**einlösung** bill discounting; ~**geschäft** bill brokerage.

akzeptieren to accept, *(Wechsel)* to hono(u)r; **blanko** ~ to accept in blank.

akzeptiert werden to go, *(Wechsel)* to find (meet) with due protection.

Akzept |**kredit** acceptance credit; ~**provision** accepting commission; ~**umlauf** bills in circulation; **mit** ~**vermerk versehen** to provide with acceptance; ~**verweigerung** nonacceptance, dishono(u)r.

Akzise excise, indirect tax, inland duty.

alimentieren, Konto to place an account in funds.

Allein |**berechtigung** exclusive (sole) right; ~**hersteller** sole manufacturer; ~**inhaber** sole owner (proprietor).

alleinstehend *(Anzeige)* island *(US)* (solid) position, solus position *(Br.) (Haus)* detached, *(unverheiratet)* unmarried.

Allein |**verkauf** exclusive sale, sales monopoly; ~**verkaufsrecht** exclusive privilege, *(Makler)* exclusive listing; ~**vertreter** sole (exclusive) agent; ~**vertretung** sole (exclusive) agency; ~**zeichnungsberechtigung** single signature.

alles inbegriffen terms inclusive, all-in *(Br.).*

Allgemeinunkosten overhead [charges], oncost *(Br.).*

Alltagsbeschäftigung daily routine.

alphabetischer Katalog dictionary catalog(ue).

alt gekauft bought secondhand.

Alt |**baumiete** pre-currency reform rent; ~**bestände** existing stock.

Alter age, *(Dienstalter)* seniority; **im arbeitsfähigen** ~ of working age; **anerkanntes** ~ *(Versicherung)* age admitted; **pensionsfähiges** ~ retiring age, age of retirement; **im pensionsfähigen** ~ **stehen** to be eligible of age to retire.

alternative Kosten opportunity costs.

Alternativwährung alternative (alternate) currency.

Alters|abschreibung depreciation for age; **~freibetrag** *(Einkommensteuer)* age allowance (relief, *Br.);* **~fürsorge** relief for old people; **~grenze** age limit (boundary), *(Beamter)* retirement age; **~rente** retirement allowance (pension, Br.), old-age pension; **~vergünstigungen gewähren** to make allowance for age; **~versicherung** old-age insurance; **~versorgung** old-age (retirement, Br.) pension scheme.

Altersversorgungs|kasse provident fund; **betrieblicher ~plan** industrial pension plan.

Alterszulage superannuation (seniority) allowance (pay).

Altmaterial salvage, scrap, junk; **~verwertung** recovery of waste, salvage.

Altwarenhändler secondhand dealer.

ambulanter Gewerbebetrieb street (door-to-door) trading, peddling, peddlery, peddlary *(Br.).*

Amortisations|anleihe amortization (amortized, redemption, *US);* **~darlehen** amortized loan; **~fonds** sinking (amortization, redemption, *US)* fund; **~fondsreserve** sinking-fund reserve; **~hypothek** instalment mortgage; **~kasse** sinking fund, redemption office; **~konto** redemption account; **~quote, ~rate** instalment, redemption rate.

amortisieren to amortize, to pay amortization, to redeem, *(bezahlen)* to liquidate.

Amt *(Anstellung)* appointment, *(Aufgabe)* business, charge, function, part, task, *(Behörde)* magistracy, board, agency, bureau, department, office, *(Telefonzentrale)* exchange, operator, central *(US);* **sich um ein ~ bewerben** to run for an office.

amtlich official, magisterial, officiary, ministerial; **nicht ~** nonofficial, unofficial, in an unofficial capacity, inofficial, private; **~ notiert** *(Börse)* officially quoted (listed, *US);* **~ beglaubigen** to legalize; **~ genehmigen** to license; **~e Notierung** *(Börse)* official quotation.

Amts|blatt official register *(US),* Gazette *(Br.);* **~einkünfte** emoluments.

anbahnen, neue Geschäftsverbindungen to open new business connections.

Anbahnung eines Geschäfts introduction of a business.

Anbau side building, lean-to, annex, enlargement.

anbauen to enlarge (extend) one's premises; **Hotelflügel ~** to build a new wing to a hotel.

Anbaufläche acreage, arable land.

anbieten, fest to offer firm; **zum Kauf ~** to offer for sale, to pitch.

Änderung|en vorbehalten subject to alteration; **~ der Abschreibungsrichtlinien** depreciation changes; **~ des Flächennutzungsplans** rezoning, zone change *(US).*

Andienung der fälligen Miete tender of rent due.

Andrang throng, run, congestion, rush, *(Verkehr)* rush hours, heavy traffic; **~ auf einer Bank** run on a bank.

anerkannt|e Forderung debt on record; **~er Gläubiger** judgment creditor.

anerkennen to acknowledge, to recognize, to warrant, *(Bilanzposten)* to allocate, *(genehmigen)* to ratify, *(zugeben)* to admit, or to allow, to avow; **Schulden nicht ~** *(Staat)* to repudiate debts; **seine Unterschrift nicht ~** to disown one's signature; **Wechsel ~** to hono(u)r (accept) a bill.

Anerkenntnis | des Bankauszugs verification form *(Br.),* reconcilement blank *(US)* (statement, *Br.);* **~ der Unterschrift** confession of signature; **~zahlung** acknowledgment, token payment.

Anfall *(Erbschaft)* reversion, accession, devolution, *(Ertrag)* yield, *(Steuern)* incidence; **~ von Zinsen** accrual of interest.

anfallen *(Arbeit)* to arise, to come to pass, *(Gewinn)* to yield, *(Waren)* to come on the market, *(Zinsen)* to accrue.

anfallend|e Nebenprodukte spinoff products; **~e Zinsen** accruing interest.

anfangen, ganz von unten (von vorn) to start from scratch.

Anfangs|abschreibung initial capital allowance; **hohe ~belastung** front-end load; **~gehalt** initial (starting) salary, (probationary) rate; **~guthaben** *(ECU)* initial credit balance; **~inventar** (opening, original) inventory, **~kapital** initial (original) capital, original assets; **~kurs** opening price (quotation); **~reserve** *(Lebensversicherung)* initial reserve; **~satz** initial rate; **~schuld** *(ECU)* initial debit balance; **~schwierigkeiten** breaking-in difficulties, teething troubles; **~stellung** initial assignment, entry (beginning) job; **~wartezeit** *(Versicherung)* initial waiting period.

anfechtbares Rechtsgeschäft voidable contract, *(Konkursschuldner)* voidable preference.

anfechten, Vertrag to rescind (avoid) a contract.

Anfechtung avoidance, rescission, contestation.

Anfechtungs|berechtigter rescinder; **~frist** time for repudiation.

anfertigen to make, to manufacture, to fabricate, to produce; **auf Bestellung ~** to make to order.

anfinanzieren to provide with initial credit facilities.

Anflug|hafen port of call; **~weg** route.

anfordern *(Material)* to require, to request.

Anforderungen | für Ferien- und Reisegelder holiday currency demands; **~ im Schalterverkehr** over-the-counter requirements; **hohe ~ an die Geschäftsmoral stellen** to set a high standard of business morality.

Anforderungsformular requisition blank.

Anfuhr zum Bauplatz transport to building site.

Anfuhr|kosten cartage; **~rechnung** cartage note.

Angabe indication *(Anweisung)* instruction, order, *(beim Zoll)* declaration; **ohne ~** *(Zoll)* undeclared; **~ von Einzelheiten** specification; **~ des Versicherungswertes** declaration of the value insured.

Angaben data, particulars; **nicht den ~ entsprechend** *(Versicherung)* not according to representations;

finanzielle ~ financial data; **sachdienliche** ~ pertinent information;
~ **zur Person** personalia, personal data.

angeben to state, to declare, to indicate, *(Preise)* to quote, *(Wert)* to declare;
seine Einkünfte zu niedrig ~ to understate one's income; **Paketwert** ~ to declare the value of a parcel; **Warenwert beim Zoll** ~ to enter goods at the customhouse.

Angebot offer, offering, overture, *(Auktion)* first (opening) bid *(Lieferungsvertrag)* tender, bid *(US)*, *(Warenangebot)* supply;
vorher abgesprochenes ~ collusive price; **bindendes** ~ firm offer; **einige** ~**e** *(Börse)* a few buyers; **freibleibendes** ~ free (not binding) offer; **gekoppeltes** ~ combination offer; **gleichbleibendes** ~ standing offer; **reichhaltiges** ~ abundant offers, sample offerings, variety; **verschlossenes** ~ sealed proposal; **verstecktes** ~ buried offer;
~ **an Arbeitskräften** supply of labo(u)r; ~ **und Nachfrage** supply and demand; ~ **offener Stellen** unfilled jobs offering;
~ **abgeben** to make an offer; ~ **ablehnen** to reject (decline, set aside, refuse) an offer; **zu** ~**en auffordern** to invite offers (tenders); **sein** ~ **erhöhen** to raise one's bid; **von einem** ~ **Gebrauch machen** to avail o. s. of an offer; **einem** ~ **näher treten** to entertain an offer; ~ **zurückziehen** to revoke (withdraw) an offer, to retract a bid.

angeboten *(Börse)* offered;
fest ~ offered firm;
billig ~ **sein** *(Effekten)* to be on the bargain counter; ~ **werden** *(Börse)* to be on (come into, come out of) the market;
~**e Ware** goods for sale.

Angebots|annahme offer acceptance; ~**elastizität** elasticity of supply; ~**formular** form; ~**kurve** supply curve; ~**liste** *(Effektenemission)* sheet offer *(US)*; ~**lücke** gap in supplies; ~**preis** supply price.

angefallene Kosten costs incurred.

angefertigt made to order;
einzeln ~ custom-built *(US)*.

angehen, Chef um Gehaltserhöhung to tackle the boss for a raise; **j. um Geld** ~ to tap s. o. for money.

Angeld earnest [money], bargain money, handsel.

Angelegenheit matter, affair, business, concern, line, *(Rechtsfall)* case;
dienstliche ~ official business; **kostspielige** ~ costly affair;
~ **freundschaftlich beilegen** to settle a matter amicably; **sich in jds.** ~**en einmischen** to meddle in s. one's concern; **in geschäftlichen** ~**en kommen** to come on business.

angelegt invested;
fest ~ locked (tied); **verteilt** ~ *(Kapital)* diversified.

angemeldet registered, incorporated *(US)*, *(Konkursforderung)* proved.

angemessen|e Belohnung adequate reward; ~**es Einkommen** fair income; **innerhalb** ~**er Frist** within reasonable time; ~**er Preis** reasonable price.

angenommen|er Wechsel accepted (hono(u)red) bill; ~**er Wert** fictitious value.

angeschlossene Bank member bank.

angesetzt *(Preis)* quoted, *(Termin)* fixed;
zu niedrig ~ short-posted, understated;

angespannt strained, tense;
stark ~ **sein** to be under pressure; ~**er Geldmarkt** tightness of money (in the money market).

angestellt employed, on the payroll;
im Büro ~ black-coated *(Br.)*, white-collar *(US)*; **fest** ~ salaried, in a permanent position.

Angestellte employee, lady clerk, *(pl.)* staff, salaried (black-coated, *Br.*, white-collar, *US*) men (people); **abgestellte** ~ loaned employees; **leitende** ~ senior staff, executive personnel;
~**e auf Zeit** temporary staff.

Angestellten|ausbildung employee training; ~**beurteilung** employee appraisal; ~**fluktuation** employee turnover; ~**gehalt** salary rate; ~**pension** employee pension *(Br.)*; ~**pensionsfonds** staff pension fund *(Br.)*; ~**rabatt** employee discount; ~**verhältnis** employee status; ~**versicherung** social security *(US)* (insurance); ~**zeitschrift** personnel periodical.

Angestellter employee, employe *(US)*, officer, offical, functionary, corporate;
ganztägig beschäftigter ~ full-time employee; **hoch bezahlter** ~ high-salaried employee; **hochgestellter** ~ high-ranking executive; **kaufmännischer** ~ clerk; **langjähriger** ~ longservice employee; **leitender** ~ senior executive, executive [employee], top (corporate, *US*) executive; **untergeordneter** ~ inferior clerk, nonpolicy-making functionary; **zeichnungsberechtigter** ~ confidential clerk; ~ **im öffentlichen Dienst** government employee, public (state) employee *(US)*; ~ **einer Bank** clerk; ~ **der Handelsmarine** merchant navy officer.

Angestellten | entlassen to discharge (dispose of) an employee; **zu den** ~ **gehören** to be on the establischment; ~ **zur disziplinarischen Bestrafung melden** to report an employee for misconduct; ~ **versetzen** to move an employee.

angleichen to adapt, to adjust, to assimilate, *(Handels- an Steuerbilanz)* to match;
Frachtsätze ~ to standardize (adjust) freight rates; **Währungen** ~ to align currencies.

Angleichung assimilation, adjustment, adaptation;
~**der Einheitswerte** equalization of assessments; ~ **der Frachtsätze** standardization of freight charges; ~ **der Gehälter** salary adjustment; ~ **der Preise** price adjustment; ~ **der Währungen** monetary alignment.

angliedern to affiliate, to annex, to assimilate.

Angreifen der Reserven raid on the reserves.

angreifen, seine Ersparnisse to make inroads on one's savings.

Angst|klausel *(Wechsel)* safety (without-recourse) clause; ~**verkauf** panic sale.

anhalten *(Auto)* to stop, to pull up;
bei Bedarf ~ to stop by request.

Anhandgeben von Grundstücken bei mehreren Maklern multiple listing *(US)*.
Anhang appendix, appendage, supplement, *(Testament)* codicil, *(Wechsel)* slip, allonge.
Anhängeadresse tag, tally, tie-on label.
anhängen to affix, to join, to annex;
einem Kunden alte Ladenhüter ~ to fob off old stock on a client.
anhängend *(Zinsschein)* attached;
~es Muster attached sample.
Anhänger adherent, supporter, *(Anhängeadresse)* tie-on label, tag, tally, tab;
~ des Freihandelssystems free trader.
anhäufen *(Reichtum)* to accumulate, to aggregate, *(Waren)* to hoard, to amass, to aggregate, to stockpile.
Anhäufung *(Kapital)* accumulation, *(Zinsen)* accrual.
Anhebung der Lebenshaltungskosten cost-of-living raise.
anheften, Preiszettel to label, to ticket *(US)*.
anheimfallen, der Fürsorge to fall upon the parish.
anheuern to engage, to enrol, to hire, to recruit *(US)*, *(Seeleute)* to sign on.
Ankauf buying, purchase, purchasing, acquisition;
~ von Industrieunternehmungen asset backing;
~ offener Warenforderungen factoring;
über den ~ eines Hauses verhandeln to negotiate for the purchase of a house.
ankaufen to purchase [land], to buy, to acquire;
sich ~ to settle; Wechsel ~ to discount a bill.
Ankaufs|entscheidung buying decision; ~ermächtigung authority to negotiate.
ankaufsfähig purchasable, *(Wechsel)* discountable.
Ankaufs|genehmigung purchase approval; ~kommission purchasing commission; ~kosten *(Kapitalanlagegesellschaft)* acquisition cost, sales charge; ~kurs buying rate; zu ~kursen at cost; ~preis purchase (cost) price; ~sätze *(Landeszentralbank)* buying (discount, rediscount, *US*) rates.
Anklang finden to go down, to find favo(u)r, *(Ware)* to meet with approval, to find a ready market.
anknüpfen, neue Geschäftsbeziehungen to enter new business relations.
Anknüpfungswerbung tie-in advertising.
ankommen *(Zug)* to come (pull) in, to be due;
bei einer Firma ~ to find employment with a firm;
beim Publikum ~ to get across with the audience;
pünktlich ~ to arrive on time (as scheduled, *US*).
Ankunfts|bahnhof station of arrival; ~bahnsteig arrival platform; ~tafel arrival board; ~zeit time of arrival.
ankurbeln to stimulate, *(Wirtschaft)* to boost;
Produktion ~ to step (pep, *US*) up production.
Ankurbelung der Wirtschaft stimulation (reorganization) of business, pump priming *(US)*.
Ankurbelungskredit reconstruction (pump-priming, *US*) credit.
Anlage *(angelegtes Geld)* invested capital, *(Anordnung)* disposition, arrangement, plan, *(Beilage)* enclosure, inclosure, exhibit, *(zu einem Bericht)*

annex, appendix, exhibit, *(Betrieb)* plant, works, *(Einbau)* installation, equipment, facility, *(Investition)* placement, placing, investment;
~n *(Bauten)* works, *(Bilanz)* assets, facilities, *(Stadt)* public garden (parks), pleasure ground;
abgeschriebene ~ retirement unit; ausgesuchte ~ choice investment; betriebsfertige ~ factory at work; später erworbene ~n after-acquired assets;
feste ~ fixture; neu in Betrieb genommene ~ newly established plant; gewinnbringende ~n earning assets; kurzfristige spekulative ~ speculation *(Br.)*, round transaction *(US)*; moderne ~n modern equipment; mündelsichere ~n gilt-edged (legal, *US*) security, legal (eligible, trustee) investment *(US)*; risikoärmere ~n *(Investmentfonds)* defensive portion *(US)*; risikoreiche ~n *(Investmentfonds)* aggressive portion *(US)*; städtische ~n public garden, pleasure ground, grounds, park; unproduktive ~n dead assets;
~n im Bau *(Bilanz)* installation under construction; ~ in Grundstücken real-estate investments; ~ einer Kartei card indexing; ~ in Staatspapieren funding;
~ abschreiben to write down an asset; zur ~ empfehlen to single out for investment; ~ zum Geschäftsmann haben to have a turn for business; Wert einer ~ heraufsetzen to write up the value of an asset; ~ außer Betrieb nehmen to retire a unit; in eine steuerfreie ~ umwandeln to convert an investment into a nontaxable form.
Anlage|aufwand investment expense; ~berater investment adviser (consultant, counsellor, *US*), security analyst *(US)*; ~beratung investment advisory service; ~beratungsfirma investment house (counselling firm, *US*); ~bestimmungen *(Kapitalanlagegesellschaft)* investment policy; ~bewertung *(Effekten)* investment rating; ausländische erlöse devisenmäßig vereinnahmen to repatriate earnings from foreign investments; ~geschäft investment banking (business); ~gesellschaft investment trust; ~gewinn investment gain, return, yield.
Anlagegüter assets, capital goods (equipment);
in der Bilanz nicht aufgeführte ~ nonledger assets; langfristige ~ permanent investments;
~ mit einer zehnjährigen Nutzungsdauer investment with a useful life of ten years.
Anlage|kapital invested (permanent) capital, capital (fixed) assets, fixed (stock) capital, *(Kapitalanlagegesellschaft)* investment fund; ~käufe investment buying, *(Investmentgesellschaft)* investment trust buying; ~kosten initial capital expenditure, first (prime) cost; [langfristiger] ~kredit investment credit; ~markt investment market.
Anlagen|ausschlachtung assets stripping; ~bewertung asset valuation; ~buchhaltung property accounting; ~neubewertung revaluation of assets; ~verzinsung yield, return; ~zugang accretion to fixed assets.
Anlagepapier investment paper (bill);
erstklassige ~e gilt-edged (trustee, *US*) securities,

savings investment *(US)*; **fest verzinsliche ~e** interest-bearing investments; **~publikum** buying (investing) public, stockholding elements, investors; **~rendite** investment return, yield; **~risiko** investment risk, **~streuung** diversification, dispersal of assets; **einzelne Betriebe zur ~streuung zwingen** to force some outfits into diversification; **~veränderung vornehmen** to switch investments; **~vermögen** capital (permanent, fixed) assets, investment estate, fixed capital (property) investment; **~verzinsung** investment return, yield; **langfristiges ~vorhaben** long-term capital project.

Anlagewerte invested capital, capital goods; **ausgesuchte ~** selected investments; **mündelsichere ~** gilt-edged stock *(Br.)*, trustee (legal) securities *(US)*; **~ mit begrenzter Lebensdauer** limited-life assets.

Anlage\williger would-be investor; **~zinsen** interest on capital outlay; **zu ~zwecken** for investment purpose.

anlasten, jem. die Spesen to charge the expenses to s. o.

Anlauf der Produktion starting of production.

Anlaufen eines Nothafens forced call.

anlaufen *(Betrieb)* to start; **~ lassen** *(Betrieb)* to put in operation, to start (set) working.

Anlauf\hafen port of call, call port; **~kapital** initial capital; **~kosten** launching (startup) costs; **~schwierigkeiten** initial difficulties, teething troubles.

anlegen *(bezahlen)* to spend, to pay, *(Fabrik)* to set up, to erect, to establish, *(Kapital)* to place, to invest; **auf drei Monate fest ~** to fix a deposit for ninety days notice; **gewinnbringend ~** to invest advantageously; **sein Geld in Hausgrundstücken ~** to invest one's money in house property; **sein Kapital fest ~** to tie (lock, *Br.*) up one's capital; **kurzfristig ~** to invest [money] at short notice; **langfristig ~** to make long-term investments; **mündelsicher ~** to acquire gilt-edged *(Br.)* (trustee, *US)* securities; **verzinslich ~** to put out at interest. ·

Anlegung von Kapital placing of funds, placement of capital, investment.

Anleihe loan, stock *(Br.)*, bond *(US)*; **abgelöste ~** retired (redeemed) loan; **aufgewertete ~** revalorized loan; **fundierte ~** consolidated (funded) loan; **hypothekarisch gesicherte ~** mortgage loan; **notierte ~** quoted loan; **amtlich nicht notierte ~** outside loan; **öffentliche ~** public (government, civil, *US)* loan; **steuerbegünstigte ~** privileged loan; **steuerfreie ~** tax-exempt loan; **überzeichnete ~** oversubscribed loan; **~n und verzinsliche Schatzanweisungen** loan issues and interest-bearing treasury bonds; **~ abschließen** to contract a loan; **~ auflegen** to float (launch) a loan; **~ zur Zeichnung auflegen** to offer a loan for subscription; **~ in Stücken ausgeben** to issue a loan in instalments; **bei jem. eine ~ machen**

to borrow money from s. o. **~ in Abschnitten in Anspruch nehmen** to draw a loan in tranches; **~ überzeichnen** to cover over (oversubscribe) a loan; **~ unterbringen** to negotiate (place) a loan.

Anleihe\abkommen loan agreement; **~abschnitt** slice of a loan; **~agio** loan premium; **~ausgabe** issue of a loan; **~dienst** redemption service; **~emission garantieren** to underwrite a loan; **~geschäft** loan business; **~kapital** loan fund (capital), bond capital, stock; **~kurszettel** stock list *(Br.)*, bond record *(US)*; **~placierung** placing of a loan; **noch nicht abgehobene ausgeloste ~stücke** allotted loans not yet collected; **~tilgung** redemption of a loan *(US)*; **~umwandlung** loan conversion; **~verzinsung** loan service; **Kapital auf dem ~wege aufbringen** to raise capital by the issue of a loan.

Anlern\ling learner, beginner, trainee, improver; **~lohn** learner's wage rate.

Anlieferung | auf dem See- oder Binnenwasserweg delivery by sea or inland waterway; **~ an Schiffsseite** delivery shipside; **~ auf der Straße** delivery by road.

Anlieferungs\preis *(Zoll)* landed costs.

Anlieger abutter, abutting (adjacent) owner, *(Verkehrsregelung)* local resident; **~beiträge** neighbo(u)rhood improvements, assessment bonds; **~straße** access road; **~verkehr** *(Straßenbild)* residents only.

anlocken *(Kunden)* to attract, to entice, to tout.

Anmelde\buch visitors' book.

anmeldefähige Forderung provable debt.

Anmeldeformular registration (application) form, *(Wettbewerb)* entry form; **~ ausfüllen** *(Hotel)* to sign a registration form.

Anmelde\frist *(Patent)* filing period; **~ gebühr** application (registration) fee.

anmelden to announce, to declare, to report, *(beim Zoll)* to enter; **Aktien zur Generalversammlung ~** to deposit shares for the general meeting; **Anspruch (Forderung) ~** to file (lodge) a claim; **Ferngespräch ~** to book a trunk call *(Br.)*, to put in (place) a long-distance call *(US)*; **Gewerbe ~** to register a trade; **Konkursforderung ~** to prove a debt; **sich zu einem Kursus ~** to enrol(l), to enlist; **Patent ~** to take out a patent; **Tratte ~** to advise a draft; **Waren zur Verzollung ~** to enter goods at the customhouse; **sich ~ lassen** to send in one's name.

anmeldepflichtig notifiable, reportable; **~e Absprache** *(Kartellrecht)* agreement subject to registration.

Anmelde\schein *(Polizei)* registration card; **~stelle** booking (filing, registration) office; **~zettel im Hotel ausfüllen** to register with a hotel.

Anmeldung notification, notice, report, announcement, filing, registration, application, *(im Hotel)* enquiries, reception, *(Verzollung)* declaration; **polizeiliche ~** report to (registration with) the police; **~ von den Akten zur Hauptversammlung** deposition

of shares for the general meeting; ~ **eines Ferngesprächs** booking of a telephone call; ~ **des Konkurses** petition in bankruptcy; ~ **einer Konkursforderung** proof of a debt; ~ **eines Warenzeichens** registration of a trademark;
~ **zurückziehen** to withdraw an application.

Anmeldungs|frist time of application; **~vordruck** application blank.

Annahme acceptance, accepting, *(Depositen)* reception;
mangels ~ *(Wechsel)* returned for want of [non]acceptance; **mangels ~ protestiert** protested for nonacceptance; ~ **verweigert** *(Brief)* refused, *(Wechsel)* acceptance declined;
~ **unter einer Bedingung** qualified acceptance; ~ **einer Erbschaft** entering upon an inheritance; **~verweigern** to decline (refuse) acceptance, to refuse [to take] delivery, *(Wechsel)* to dishono(u)r a bill for nonacceptance;
ausdrückliche **~erklärung** express acceptance; **~verweigerung** *(Waren)* rejection; **sich im ~verzug befinden** to have been put on notice to take delivery.

annehmen to accept, to receive, to take delivery, *(Wechsel)* to accept, to hono(u)r;
Angebot ~ to accept an offer; **einen anderen Namen** ~ to change one's name; **sich einer Sache** ~ to take care of s. th., to attend to a matter.

Annehmlichkeitswert *(Grundstück)* amenity value.

Annonce advertisement, insertion, ad;
fingierte ~ dummy advertisement;
~ **in die Zeitung einrücken lassen** to advertise.

Annoncen|akquisiteur advertising agent, canvasser; **~annahme** newspaper office; **~blatt** advertising paper; **~preisstaffel** advertising rates; **~werber** advertising (publicity) agent, canvasser.

annoncieren to advertise, to insert.

Annuität, hinausgeschobene deferred annuity; **lebenslängliche** ~ life annuity;
~ **mit begrenzter Laufzeit** terminable annuity.

annullieren *(Aufträge)* to cancel, to countermand, *(Vertrag)* to make void, to avoid, to annul, to rescind, to set aside.

Annullierung annulment, voidance, rescission, *(Aufträge)* cancellation, countermanding;
~ **eines Geschäfts** calling off a deal.

anordnen to order, *(anweisen)* to conduct;
Beschlagnahme ~ to levy an attachment order; **Freigabe** ~ to release an attachment; **Kontosperre** ~ to block an account.

Anordnung order, direction, instruction;
behördliche ~ government regulation;
~ **der Betriebsanlagen** departmental layout; ~ **der Nachlaßverwaltung** letters of administration; ~ **der Zwangsvollstreckung** attachment order.

anpassen *(Handels- und Steuerbilanz)* to match;
sich den Verhältnissen ~ to accommodate (adapt) o. s.

Anpassung, automatische *(Steuersystem)* built-in flexibility;

~ **der Sozialversicherungsleistungen** social security adjustment.

Anpassungs|klausel *(Löhne)* escalator clause, *(Steuer)* matsching clause; **~phase** settling-down phase.

anpreisen to recommend, to promote, to write up, to sell *(US)*.

Anpreisung, marktschreierische puff, patter.

anpumpen, j. to touch (tap, stick, *US)* s. o.

anrechnen to reckon *(abziehen)* to allow, to deduct, *(belasten)* to charge;
auf das Erbteil ~ to throw into hotchpot.

Anrechnung *(Abzug)* allowance, deduction, *(Belastung)* charge, charging, debit[ing];
~ **des Altwertes** *(Versicherung)* deduction (old) for new; ~ **im Ausland gezahlter Steuern** double taxation relief *(Br.)*, foreign tax credit *(US)*.

anrechnungsfähiges Jahr *(Sozialversicherung)* year of coverage.

Anrechnungsverfahren *(Doppelbesteuerung)* indirect relief.

Anreiz, preislicher price appeal;
steuerliche ~e für Investitionen investment tax incentives.

Anrufbeantworter, automatischer *(tel.)* automatic telephone answering machine.

ansammeln *(Kapital)* to accumulate, *(Vorräte)* to assemble, to pile (hoard) up, to stockpile;
sich ~ *(Zinsen)* to accrue; **Reserven** ~ to build up reserves.

ansässig resident, residing, domiciled, settled;
im Ausland ~ resident (living) abroad.

Ansatz amount set up, *(Abschätzung)* valuation, *(Haushaltungsvoranschlag)* appropriation, amount budgeted;
~berichtigung rectification of an account.

Ansätze | des Haushaltsplans budgetary appropriation; ~ **des Tarifs** tarif rates.

Ansatzstück *(Wechsel)* allonge.

anschaffen to provide, to procure, to make provision for, to furnish, *(kaufen)* to purchase;
Betrag bei einer Bank ~ to remit a sum to a bank; **Deckung** ~ to furnish with cover; **Vorräte** ~ to lay in stocks, to stockpile, to purvey.

Anschaffung provision, procurement;
~ **in bar** remittance in cash; ~ **des Gegenwertes** remittance of proceeds.

Anschaffungs|basis, auf *(Kapitalanlagegesellschaft)* at cost; **~kosten** costs of acquisition, acquisition (prime, original, first) cost, first (initial) outlay; **~kosten eines Wirtschaftsgutes auf die Nutzungsdauer verteilen** to spread the cost of an asset over its useful life; **~preis** purchase (original, cost, first) price; **~wert** cost, value, prime cost.

Anschlag notice, announcement, *(Plakat)* poster, posting, bill;
wilder ~ fly posting;
~ **an einer Mauer machen** to stick up a bill on a wall.

Anschlagbrett notice *(Br.)* (bulletin, *US)* board, billboard, hoarding, *(Bahn, Theater)* call board.

anschlagen *(bewerten)* to calculate, to value, *(Plakat)* to placard, to stick [up];
zu hoch ~ to overestimate.
Anschlags|preis *(Auktion)* upset price; ~wert estimated value.
Anschluß *(Bahn, Flugzeug, Strom)* connexion, connection *(US), (Telefon)* [telephone] line;
überall ~ haben to meet all trains;
~auftrag follow-up order; ~buchung *(Flug)* onto booking, booking onward; ~fahrkarte transfer ticket; ~nummer call number; ~zug connecting (corresponding) train, *(an Dampferlinie)* boat train.
Anschnittzuschlag bleed premium (charge).
Anschreibe|buch passbook; ~konto charge account.
anschreiben to charge, to debit, to book, to score, to chalk, to note down, to mark up;
~ lassen to take on credit (tick, *Br.,* the cuff, *US)* to run up a book (a score, bills).
Anschrift address, direction;
~en potentieller Kunden liefern to supply names of prospects.
Anschwärzung der Konkurrenz trade libel.
Ansehen, geschäftliches sound commercial credit, business reputation, goodwill.
ansehnlich|es Gehalt handsome salary; ~es Vermögen sizable fortune.
ansetzen *(abschätzen)* to rate, to assess, to value, *(Termin)* to appoint, to fix, to schedule;
zu hoch ~ to overestimate.
Ansicht, zur *(Kauf)* on approval (approbation), for inspection;
~sendung consignment (articles sent) on approval.
anspannen *(Kredit)* to strain, *(Reserven)* to tax.
Anspannung | des Geldmarktes monetary strain; ~ der Reserven draw on the reserves.
Ansprache der Zielgruppen *(Werbung)* cream plan.
ansprechende Werbung appealing advertising.
Anspruch claim, interest, right;
anerkannter ~ *(Konkurs)* proved claim (debt);
verjährter ~ stale demand, claim barred by the statute of limitations;
~ auf bevorrechtigte Befriedigung *(Konkursrecht)* privileged debt, preferential claim; ~ auf Schadenersatz claim for damages; ~ auf Unterstützung right of support; ~ auf betriebliche Zuschüsse zur Arbeitslosenunterstützung supplementary unemployment insurance credit;
~ in bar abfinden to buy up a claim for cash; ~ dem Grunde nach anerkennen to admit a claim on its merits; ~ als berechtigt nachweisen to prove a debt; j. beruflich in ~ nehmen to consult s. o. professionally; Hilfe eines Anwalts in ~ nehmen to retain a lawyer; Kredite bei der Bank in erhöhtem Maße in ~ nehmen to increase the borrowings at a bank.
Ansprüche, beteiligungsähnliche *(Bilanz)* interest in the nature of investments;
allen ~n genügen *(Hotel)* to satisfy all possible requirements.

Anspruchsbefriedigung satisfaction of a claim.
anspruchsberechtigt sein to become eligible.
Anspruchs|bewertung claims assessment; ~regulierung claim settlement; ~verzicht unterschreiben to sign a waiver.
Anstalt institute, [public] institution, home, establishment, asylum, *(Stiftung)* foundation;
öffentliche (öffentlich-rechtliche) ~ public institution, body corporate.
anstehen to queue (line) up, to stand in line *(US)*;
zur Pensionierung ~ to qualify for a pension.
Ansteigen *(Kurse, Preise)* rise, increase, advance;
raketenartiges ~ der Kurse skyrocketing *(US).*
ansteigen *(Kurse, Preise)* to rise, to increase, to advance, to climb, to improve, to head up;
steil ~ to rocket, to skyrocket *(US).*
anstellen to engage, to enlist, to employ, to hire *(US)*, to recruit;
j. fest ~ to put s. o. on the establishment; wieder ~ to reappoint, to reengage, to rehire *(US).*
Anstellung employment, situation, job, post, position, place, *(Einstellung)* engagement, enlistment, recruitment *(US),* hiring *(US)*;
feste ~ permanent appointment;
~ auf Lebenszeit appointment for life;
sich um eine staatliche ~ bewerben to solicit a government post; keine feste ~ haben to have no regular work.
Anstellungs|schreiben letter of appointment; ~vertrag employment contract.
Anstieg *(Preise, Kurse)* rise, rising, increase, advance, improvement, recovery, hike *(US);*
steiler ~ *(Börse)* upsurge;
~ der Aktienkurse stock-market rise; explosionsartiger ~ der Mieten rental explosion.
anstoßerregende Gewerbe offensive trade.
Anstrengungen | zur Absatzsteigerung sales promotional efforts; ~ zur Ausweitung des Produktionsprogramms diversification move.
Ansturm auf eine Bank run on a bank.
Anteil stake, [proportional] share, part, portion, *(Beteiligung)* interest, share, stock, holding, *(Quote)* quota, contingent, contribution pro rata;
~ am Ertrag portion of proceeds; ~ am Gewinn profit share; hoher ~ von Obligationen und Vorzugsaktien am Gesellschafskapital high leverage factor *(US);*
jem. seinen ~ auszahlen to pay s. o. out; seinen ~ an der Rechnung bezahlen to pay one's shot; ~ am Gewinn haben to participate in the profit.
Anteilsbewertung *(Investmentfonds)* unit evaluation.
Anteilschein share, participation certificate *(US)* (share), *(Aktie)* share (scrip, *US)* certificate, scrip, share of stock *(US), (Zinsschein)* coupon; ~ einer Kapitalanlagegesellschaft investment trust certificate, unit *(Br.);*
~besitzer shareholder *(Br.),* stockholder *(US), (Kapitalanlagegesellschaft)* unitholder *(Br.).*
anteilsmäßig ratable, pro rata, proportionate.
Anti|dumpingzoll antidumping duty; ~kapitalismus

anticapitalism; **~streikbewegung** back-to-work movement.

antizipative Aktiva accrued assets (receivables, *US*).

antizyklisch countercyclical, contracyclical, anticyclical;
~e **Konjunkturpolitik** countercyclical compensatory government (fiscal) policy.

Antrag offer, *(Börse)* marrying *(Br.)*, *(Gesuch)* application, petition, request, *(Offerte)* tender, *(Parl.)* motion, *(Vorschlag)* proposal;
schriftlicher ~ mailed *(US)* (written) application; ~ **auf Erteilung einer Gewerbelizenz (auf Geschäftseröffnung)** business application; ~ **auf Aufhebung des Konkursverfahrens** petition for discharge; ~ **ablehnen** to defeat (reject, dismiss, deny, vote down, throw out) a motion; ~ **auf die Tagesordnung setzen** to put a resolution on record; ~ **auf Konkurseröffnung (Erlaß eines Konkurseröffnungsbeschlusses) stellen** to file a petition [for a receiving order] in bankruptcy; ~ **auf Eröffnung des Vergleichsverfahrens stellen** to apply for permission to reorganize under the Bankruptcy Act.

Antragsformular application (entry, claim) form.

Antragsteller applicant, proponent, claimant.

Antragsvordruck application form (blank).

antreten, Dienst to report for work, to clock in.

Antritt einer Stellung taking up a job.

Antwort bezahlt reply paid, *(Telegramm)* answer prepaid *(A. P.)*;
umgehende ~ prompt answer, anser by return of post *(Br.)* (mail, *US*), reply on receipt;
~**karte** double postcard, reply (return) card;
~**telegramm** reply-paid telegram.

anvertrautes Geld trust fund.

Anwachsen von Zinsen accrual of interest.

anwachsen to grow, to increase, *(sich ansammeln)* to accumulate, *(Betrag)* to run up, *(Zinsen)* to accrue.

anwählen, direkt *(tel.)* to dial direct.

Anwalt lawyer, solicitor *(Br.)* attorney at law *(US)*, *(im Prozeß)* pleader, barrister-at-law, counsel, counsellor *(US)*;
~ **in Steuersachen** tax lawyer *(US)*;
~**beschäftigen** to retain a lawyer; **durch einen ~ vertreten sein** to be represented by counsel *(Br.)*.

Anwalts|besprechung conference with one's lawyer;
~**büro** lawyer's office, barrister's [writing] chamber, chambers; ~**firma** law firm, firm of solicitors *(Br.)*; ~**honorar** attorney's (lawyer's, solicitors') fee *(Br.)*.

Anwärter candidate, expectant, probationer.

Anwartschaft expectancy, expectation, remainder, *(Sozialversicherung)* qualifying period.

Anwartschaftsberechtigter reversioner.

Anwartschafts|recht beneficial estate, remainder (reversionary) interest; ~**rente** deferred annuity, reversion.

anweisen *(anordnen)* to direct, to order, *(überweisen)* to remit;
Betrag ~ to remit (send) an amount; **Geld telegrafisch** ~ to transfer money by cable.

Anweisung order, direction, *(Geldanweisung)* money order, *(Vorschrift)* regulation, specification;
kaufmännische ~ trade acceptance; **telegrafische** ~ cable order (transfer);
~**en auf auswärtige Plätze** orders payable at foreign banks;
~ **ausstellen** to draw a check *(US)* (cheque, *Br.*).

Anwendung application, appropriation, employment, use, utilization, exercise;
~ **besonders intensiver Verkaufsmethoden** high-pressure salesmanship; **unterschiedliche ~ des Zolltarifs** flag discrimination.

Anwendungsbereich range of application.

anwerben, Arbeitskräfte to enlist (recruit, *US*) labo(u)r.

Anwesenheits|gelder attendance (call) fee; ~**liste** roll, attendance sheet; ~**vergütung** attendance money.

anzahlen to pay on account, to make a first instalment (downpayment), to deposit *(US)*.

Anzahlung payment on account, downpayment, deposit *(US)*, part payment, *(Mietvorauszahlung)* key money *(Br.)*, *(Ratenzahlung)* first instalment;
erhaltene ~**en** *(Bilanz)* payments on account received; **geleistete** ~**en** deposits with suppliers *(US)*;
~**en bei Lieferanten** *(Bilanz)* prepayments *(US)*;
~ **leisten** to pay a deposit *(US)* (in a sum as a security).

Anzeichen konjunktureller Verschlechterungen signs of slowdown.

Anzeige [press] advertisement, ad *(US)*, insert, *(bei der Behörde)* declaration, report;
angeschnittene ~ *(Werbung)* bleed page; **redaktionell aufgemachte** ~ editorial style of (editorialized) advertisement; **einzeln stehende** ~ sole advertisement; **nicht gebrachte** ~ holdover; **kleine ~n** classified advertisements, small (want) ads *(US)*; **gegenüber dem Text placierte** ~ matter facing text; **umrandete** ~ boxed advertisement;
~ **von Gefahrenumständen** *(Versicherung)* material representations; ~ **über die erfolgte Geschäftsverlegung** notice of removal;
~ **aufgeben** to advertise.

anzeigen to announce, *(avisieren)* to advise, *(inserieren)* to advertise, to insert, to publish;
Protest ~ to give notice of dishono(u)r.

Anzeigen|abteilung advertisement *(Br.)* (advertising, *US*) department; ~**akquisiteur** [advertisement] canvasser, adman *(US)*; ~**beleg** voucher copy; ~**blatt der Wirtschaft** industrial advertiser; ~**erinnerungstest** blind product text; ~**erscheinungsplan** schedule of insertions; ~**expedition** advertising agency, space buyer; ~**friedhof** cocktail of ads *(US)*; ~**gebühren** advertising charges (fees), adrates *(US)*; ~**grundpreis** open (basic) rate, open time rate *(US)*; **auf der Auflage beruhende** ~**liste** circulation rate base; ~**plazierung** placing of advertising; **reservierter** ~**platz** reserved position; ~**preis** [advertising] rate; ~**preisliste** advertising rate card, rate announcement (card, *US*).

Anzeigenraum [advertising] space, lineage;
~ **belegen** to reserve (book) space;
~**belegung** space buying.

Anzeigenrichtsatz advertising rate base; ~**schluß** [copy] deadline *(US)*, close; ~**seite** advertising page (sheet), ~**tarif** advertisement *(Br.)* (space, *US*) rates, advertising charges, advertising rate base, rate card *(US)*; ~**teil** *(Zeitung)* advertisement columns, classified advertising; ~**text** copy; ~**texter** copywriter, ad writer *(US)*; ~**vertreter** newspaper (advertising, *Br.)* representative.

Anzeigepflichtverletzung *(Versicherung)* nondisclosure, concealment.

Anziehen *(Kurse, Preise)* advance, rise, rising, recovery, hardening, improvement;

anziehen *(Kunden)* to attract, to appeal, to draw, *(Kurse, Preise)* to rise, to go (move) up, to [be on the] advance, to harden, to recover, to rally;
Kapital ~ to attract capital; **raketenartig** ~ to skyrocket *(US)*.

Anziehungskraft auf Kunden appeal to customers.

Apparat apparatus, machine, machinery;
über den notwendigen ~ **verfügen** to be duly equipped.

Appartment flat *(Br.)*, apartment, *(Hotel)* suite (set) of rooms;
~**wohnung** flat dwelling *(Br.)*, apartment *(US)*.

Arbeit work, labo(u)r, *(Aufgabe)* task, assignment, *(Beschäftigung)* employment, achievement, job, occupation, *(Geschäft)* concern, business;
schlecht bezahlte ~ badly paid (journeyman) work; **tatsächlich geleistete** ~ hours worked; **vertraglich übernommene** ~ contract labo(u)r; **unselbständige** ~ employment;
~ **auf Prämienbasis** work on the bonus system; ~ **im Tagelohn** daywork; ~ **unter Tariflohn** scab work; ~**en und Lieferungen öffentlich ausschreiben** to invite tenders; ~ **einstellen** to stop working, to knock off, to lay down tools; **im Rahmen einer** ~ **liegen** to fall within the scope of a work; **bei jem. in Lohn und** ~ **stehen** to be in s. one's employ; ~**en und Lieferungen vergeben** to let out.

arbeiten to [be at] work, to labo(u)r, *(Kapital)* to yield, *(Mechanismus)* to work, to run, to operate;
im Akkord ~ to work by the job (piece), to do job work; **in einer Fabrik** ~ to work in the shops; **ganztägig** ~ to work full-time; **planmäßig langsam** ~ to work to rule *(Br.);* **bis spät in die Nacht** ~ to burn the midnight oil; **für eigene Rechnung** ~ to work for one's own account; **mit Verlust** ~ to operate at a loss; **ohne Verlust** ~ to break even; **Kapital** ~ **lassen** to put out money at interst.

arbeitende Bevölkerung working classes; ~**es Kapital** employed (invested) capital.

Arbeiter worker, workman, labo(u)rer, *(Handwerker)* artisan, tradesman;
angelernter ~ semi-skilled worker; **im Stundenlohn bezahlter** ~ hourly worker; **geistiger** ~ white-collar man (worker) *(US)*, blackcoated worker *(Br.);* **minderjähriger** ~ underage worker *(US)*;

gewerkschaftlich organisierte ~ unionized labo(u)r; **ungelernter** ~ manual (unskilled, inexperienced) worker;
~ **ausbeuten** to sweat labo(u)r; ~ **im Stücklohn bezahlen** to pay workmen by the piece; **ungelernte** ~ **einstellen** to dilute labo(u)r; ~ **auf die Straße setzen** to put workers on the street.

Arbeiterausschuß shop council, workers' committee; ~**aussperrung** lockout; ~**baracke** bunkhouse; ~**bedarf** manpower requirements; ~**dauerkarte** workmen's season ticket; ~**familie** working-class family; ~**gewinnbeteiligung** profit-sharing by the workmen, industrial partnership; ~**klasse** working (operative, labo(u)ring) class, Labo(u)r; ~**lebensversicherung** industrial insurance; ~**schaft** working people (classes); ~**schutzgesetz** Factory Act *(Br)*.

Arbeiterunfall industrial accident;
~**gesetz** Workmen's Compensation Act *(US)*; ~**versicherung** workmen's compensation *(US)* (employer's liability) insurance.

Arbeiterwochenkarte workmen's ticket; ~**wohnung** workman's dwelling, cottage.

Arbeitgeber employer [of labo(u)r], master;
letzter ~ most recent employer;
~**anteil** *(Sozialversicherung)* employer contribution; ~**haftpflichtversicherung** industrial accident insurance; ~**verband** association of employers, employers' association (organization), Federation of British Industries *(Br.)*.

Arbeitnehmer wage earner, working man, worker, employee, employed person, employe *(US)*;
gewinnbeteiligter ~ profit-sharing employee;
~**anteil** employee contribution, Federal unemployment tax *(US)*; ~**beitrag** *(Sozialversicherung)* federal unemployment tax *(US)*; ~**organisation** organized labo(u)r; **Arbeitgeber-** ~**verhältnis** industrial *(US)* (employee-employer) relations; ~**vertreter** shop steward, employees' representative, *(im Aufsichtsrat)* personnel (staff) representative.

Arbeitsablauf flow process.

Arbeitsamt labo(u)r exchange *(Br.)*, unemployment (labo(u)r) office;
sich beim ~ **melden** to report to the labo(u)r exchange (unemployment office).

Arbeitsandrang pressure of work; ~**antritt** taking up work; ~**aufgaben** job assignment; ~**auftragskostenrechnung** job-order cost accounting; ~**auftragsnummer** job number; **unmittelbarer** ~**aufwand** direct labo(u)r costs; ~**ausfall** loss of working hours; ~**ausschuß** study group (committee); ~**bedingungen** working (job) conditions, labo(u)r conditions; ~**beginn** time when work begins; ~**beginn registrieren** to clock in, to punch the clock *(US)*; ~**bereich** field of action (operation), sphere of activities; ~**bericht** job report; ~**beschaffung** job (work) creation; ~**beschaffungsbehörde** Public Works Administration *(US);* ~**beschaffungsprogramm** relief (public works) program(me); ~**beschaffungsstelle** job-creating agency.

Arbeits|bescheinigung certificate of employment, *(nach Entlassung)* discharge paper; **~bewertung** job evaluation *(US)* (rating); **~blatt** work (time) sheet; **~buch** workbook, time book; **~disziplin** shop discipline; **~durchlaufdiagramm** flow diagram; **~einsatz** employment of labo(u)r, placement, manpower management; **~einstellung** *(Anstellung)* employment, appointment, recruiting *(US)*, *(Betriebsschließung)* shutdown; **~einweisung** escort; **~einzugsgebiet** labo(u)r market area; **~erlaubnis** work permit, *(für Ausländer)* alien's labo(u)r permit; **~essen** working lunch, business luncheon.

arbeitsfähig employable, able-bodied, able to work; **~es Alter** working age.

Arbeits|fortschrittsbild *(Statistik)* Gantt progress chart; **~freude** job joy (satisfaction) *(US)*; **~gang** turn, period of work; **~gebiet** province, sphere, field of study (activity); **~gemeinschaft** team, *(mehrerer Industriebetriebe)* joint venture; **~genehmigung** authorization to start work, *(Einzelner)* labo(u)r (work) permit; **~gruppe** working party *(Br.)*, study

Arbeits|fortschrittsbild *(Statistik)* Gantt progress chart; **~freude** job joy (satisfaction) *(US)*; **~gang** turn, period of work; **~gebiet** province, sphere, field of study (activity); **~gemeinschaft** team, *(mehrerer Industriebetriebe)* joint venture; **~genehmigung** authorization to start work, *(Einzelner)* labo(u)r (work) permit; **~gruppe** working party *(Br.)*, study group, team, detail *(US)*; **²intensiv** (labo(u)r-intensive; **~jahre** working life; **~kapazität** working capacity; **~karte** operation card; **~kollege** mate, workfellow, fellow worker; **~kolonne** working party *(Br.)*, detail *(US)*; **~konflikt** industrial conflict.

Arbeitskraft working capacity (potential), *(Arbeiter)* worker, workman;

freiberufliche ~ professional worker;

seine ~ einbringen *(in Firma)* to contribute one's services; **menschliche ~ ersetzen** to displace human labo(u)r by machinery.

Arbeitskräfte workmen, labo(u)r [force], manpower, **knapp an ~n** short of hands, shorthanded; **angelernte ~** semi-skilled labo(u)r; **dienstverpflichtete ~** drafted labo(u)r; **knappe ~** shortage of labo(u)r, manpower shortage; **ungelernte ~** untrained (unskilled) labo(u)r; **zusätzliche ~** additional employees; **zwangsverpflichtete ~** conscript labo(u)r;

~ von einem Konkurrenzbetrieb abwerben to raid rival organizations; **ausländische ~ einsetzen** to immigrate foreign labo(u)r; **~ einstellen** to enrol(l) workers, to hire labo(u)r *(US)*; **~ umgruppieren** to redeploy the labo(u)r force;

~abbau cutback on manpower; **~bedarf** demand for labo(u)r, direct labo(u)r budget, manpower (labo(u)r) requirements; **~reserve** manpower reserve.

Arbeits|kreis study group (committee); **angespannte ~lage** labo(u)r-tight economy; **~laufzettel** job ticket; **~leistung** labo(u)r (worker) performance,

(Fabrik) output, *(Fähigkeit)* working capacity, *(Maschine)* load, payload; **~lohn** pay, earnings.

arbeitslos unemployed, out of (job), jobless;

Arbeitslosen|anstieg increase in unemployment; **~entwicklung positiv beurteilen** to be bullish about unemployment; **~fürsorge** unemployment relief; **~hilfe** unemployment benefit (pay); **~restsatz** hard core; **~rückgang** drop in unemployment; **~schlange** unemployment line.

Arbeitslosenunterstützung unemployment benefit *(Br.)* (pay, compensation, relief);

zusätzliche ~ extended benefit *(Br.)*;

~ beziehen to draw unemployment benefit *(Br.)* (compensation, *US*), to be on (draw) the dole *(Br.)*.

Arbeitslosenunterstützungs|anspruch unemployment claim; **~beiträge** unemployment contributions.

Arbeitslosenversicherung unemployment insurance.

Arbeitsloser unemployed person;

ausgesteuerter ~ unemployed person on relief.

Arbeitslosigkeit unemployment, joblessness;

entwicklungsmäßig (technisch) bedingte ~ technological unemployment; **flukturierende ~** frictional unemployment; **saisonbedingte ~** seasonal unemployment;

~ vergrößern to add to unemployment.

Arbeitsmarkt labo(u)r (wage, employment, job) market;

leerer ~ tight labo(u)r market;

~ leerpumpen to raid the labo(u)r market.

Arbeits|methode method of work (operation); **~minister** Minister of Labour *(Br.)*, Secretary of Labor *(US)*; **~ministerium** Ministry of Labour *(Br.)*, Department of Labor *(US)*, Labor Department *(US)*; **~moral** morale at work, employee morale; **~nachweis** employment agency (bureau, *Br.)*; **~niederlegung** cessation of work, work stoppage; **~ordnung** shop rules; **~papiere** employment (working) papers; **~paß** labo(u)r permit; **~pause** rest pause (period), break, recess *(US)*; **~pensum** load; **~pflicht** industrial conscription; **~plan** [working] program(me), *(Fabrikationsprogramm)* production plan;

Arbeitsplatz workplace, yard *(US)*, *(Stellung)* job [opening], situation;

am ~ on the floor;

gefährlicher ~ hazardous situation; **sicherer ~** safe place to work; **unbesetzter ~** job vacancy;

j. um seinen ~ bringen to jockey s. o. out of his job; **am ~ umschulen** to re-educate on the job; **~ausschreibung** bidding; **~beschreibung** job specification *(US)*; **~wechsel** labo(u)r flux (turnover); **häufiger ~wechsel** job-hopping.

Arbeits|potential potential labo(u)r force; **~produktivität** productivity of labo(u)r; **~prozeß** [working] process, *(Rechtsstreit)* labo(u)r suit; **neue Kräfte in den ~prozeß eingliedern** to absorb new workers in the labo(u)r force; **~qualität** quality of work; **~raum** workroom, workplace, *(Büro)* office, bureau; **~rückstände** work in arrear.

arbeitsscheu workshy, averse to (afraid of) labo(u)r.

Arbeits|schicht [work] shift, turn; ~schluß stopping time, time when work ends; ~schluß registrieren to clock out, to sign off; ~sitzung work session; ~stab setup, study group, task force; ~stelle place of work, workplace; ~streckung spreading of work; ~studie motion study, job analysis *(US)*; ~stufe stage, process; ~stunde man-hour, work-hour; auf ~suche gehen to apply for a job; ~suchender employment applicant; ~tag office (lawful, working) day, workday *(US)*; sein ~tempo verlangsamen to slack up one's pace of work; ~tisch desk, writing table, bench.

arbeitsunfähig unemployable, disabled, incapacitated, unable (unfit) to work;
teilweise ~ nondescript; vorübergehend ~ temporarily incapacitated; ~ geschrieben werden to be returned unfit for work.

Arbeitsunfähigkeit unemployability, incapacity (unfitness) to (for) work (from working).

Arbeits|unfähigkeitsbescheinigung certificate of disability; ~unfall industrial injury, on-the-job (industrial) accident; ~unlust worker dissatisfaction; ~unterbrechung stoppage of work, work stoppage; ~unterlagen working papers (sheet); ~verfahren working (operating) process; ~verhältnis employment, job, situation, place; ~vermittlung employment agency (bureau).

arbeitsverpflichtet werden to be liable to labo(u)r conscription.

Arbeits|vertrag employment contract *(US)*, labour contract ~verweigerung refusal to work, *(Sitzstreik)* sitdown (stay-in) strike; absichtliche ~verzögerung ca'canny, go-slow *(Br.)*; ~weise method of operation, working, *(Maschine)* function[ing].

Arbeitszeit working hours (period, time), job-time, hours of employment, spell, *(Maschine)* machining time, run, *(für einzelnes Stück)* time spent on a piece of work;
festgesetzte ~ scheduled hours of work; garantierte ~ guaranteed employment; gleitende ~ staggering of hours, flexible working hours *(Br.)*, flextime *(Br.)*; verkürzte ~ short (part) time; nach dem Tarif vorgesehene ~ nominal hours; ~ registrieren to clock;
~beschränkung limitation of hours; ~kontrolleur timekeeper, check clerk *(US)*; ~verkürzung shortening of one's working hours (time); ~verlust broken time.

Arbeits|zettel time sheet; ~zyklus operation cycle.

Arbitrage arbitrage, arbitration;
direkte ~ direct arbitration (arbitrage); indirekte ~ indirect (triangular, *US*) arbitrage;
~ über mehrere Zwischenplätze compound arbitrage.

Arbitrage|geschäft arbitrage dealings (transactions); ~klausel arbitration clause; ermittelter ~umrechnungskurs arbitrated rate; ~werte arbitrage stocks.

Archiv archives, [old] records, files;

~beamter archivist, recorder, keeper of the records; ~unterlagen permanent files.

Armen|fürsorge maintenance of the poor, poor relief *(Br.)*; ~küche soup kitchen.

arrangieren, sich mit seinen Gläubigern to compound (come to an arrangement) with one's creditors.

arrondieren, sein Gelände to round off one's property.

Art *(Ausführung)* mode, manner, *(Beschaffenheit)* kind, nature, shape, *(Sorte)* class, sort, order, species, category;
von mittlerer ~ und Güte middling;
eine ~ Börsenmakler a sort of stockbroker.

Artikel article, commodity, merchandise, product, line, item, match, lot, *(in der Zeitung)* article, [news] item, stuff;
groß aufgemachter ~ feature article; ausgegangener ~ out-of-stock item; glänzend gehender ~ runner; hochwertiger ~ article of high quality; schnell verkäuflicher ~ fast-selling item; stets vorrätige ~ stock articles; zugkräftiger ~ popular line;
~ mit stabilen Preisen price-maintained products; ~ mit hoher Umschlagsgeschwindigkeit article of quick sale;
~ vor Veröffentlichung durchsehen to sub-edit an article; ~ führen to deal in an article (a line); ~ nicht mehr führen to be out of an article; sich auf einen ~ spezialisieren to specialize in a line.

Assekuranz assurance *(Br.)*, insurance;
~versicherung insurance business, underwriting.

Asyl für Obdachlose casual ward, pauper asylum.

Atelier studio, designing deparment;
~leiter *(einer Werbeagentur)* art director.

Aufbau *(Wirtschaft)* rehabilitation, reorganization;
~ einer Gesellschaft finanzieren to rehabilitate a company financially;
~anleihe rehabilitation loan; ~kredit reconstruction credit.

aufbauen to build up, *(Maschine)* to assemble.

Aufbau|finanzierung financial rehabilitation; noch im ~stadium sein to be still in its infancy.

aufbessern *(Gehalt)* to raise, to increase.

Aufbesserung der Kurse improvement of prices.

Aufbewahren, zum for store;
einer Bank Geld zum ~ geben to deposit money in a bank.

aufbewahren to keep, to hive, *(Bank)* to deposit, *(Lager)* to store;
getrennt ~ to keep apart;
Urkunden bei der Bank ~ lassen to place documents on deposit with a bank.

Aufbewahrung *(Bank)* depositing, deposition, safe custody, safekeeping, *(Lagerung)* storage;
zur ~ übergeben to warehouse, to deposit, to leave in s. one's custody; sein Gepäck zur ~ übergeben to leave one's luggage at the cloakroom *(Br.)*, to check one's baggage *(US)*.

Aufbewahrungs|gebühr *(Bank)* safe-deposit fee, *(Lager)* storage charge, *(Gepäck)* cloakroom fee *(Br.)*, checkroom fee *(US)*; ~**ort** depository, repository, store, depot, place of deposit.

aufbieten *(Zinsscheine)* to summon;

aufbrechen to make a move, *(Safe)* to break up.

aufbringen to get up, *(beschaffen)* to procure, to provide;
Kosten ~ to afford (defray, meet) costs, to find the money; **Steuern** ~ to raise taxes.

Aufbringung *(Schiff)* capture at sea, seizure, *(bei Verlustanteil)* contribution;
~ **von Kapitalien** capital flo(a)tation.

Aufbringungs- und Beschlagnahmeklausel free of capture and seizure clause.

Aufdruck impression, imprint, lettering, enfacement, *(auf Postkarten)* surcharge.

Aufenthalt quarters, living, dwelling [place], *(Wohnsitz)* abode, residence, domicile;
ständiger ~ legal residence.

Aufenthalts|bestätigung residence certificate (permit); ~**dauer** duration (length) of stay; ~**erlaubnis** residence (stay) permit, *(für Ausländer)* registration certificate, alien's residence permit.

Aufenthaltsort whereabouts, domicile, habitation; **ohne festen** ~ of no fixed abode; **jetziger** ~ **unbekannt** present location unknown.

Aufenthaltsraum *(Betrieb)* rest (recreation) room, *(Hotel)* dayroom, lounge.

auferlegen, jem. die Kosten des Verfahrens to award the costs against s. o.

auffächern to diversify.

Auffächerung des Produktionsprogramms diversification into manufacturing.

auffangen, inflatorische Ausstrahlungen to cushion inflationary factors; **Kosten teilweise** ~ to pick up part of the costs.

auffordern, j. zur Zahlung to request payment from s. o.

Aufforderung | zur Beteiligung an einer Ausschreibung invitation to contract *(Br.)* (treat), bid invitation *(US)*; ~ **zur Zahlung** call for funds; ~ **zur Leistung einer Einschußzahlung im Effektendifferenzgeschäft** margin call *(US)*; **öffentliche** ~ **zur Zeichnung von Effekten** public offering (issue).

aufführen *(Posten)* to enter, to book, to record, to list.

Aufführung | eines einzelnen Buchungspostens itemization of an account; ~ **beruflich erforderlicher Eigenschaften** job specification.

auffüllen, Fonds to reestablish a fund; **Lager** ~ to restock, to replace; **Reserven** ~ to replenish reserves.

Auffüllung des Lagers replacement of inventories.

Aufgabe task, business, office, job, part, *(Absendung)* dispatch, *(Aufgeben)* abolition, *(Preisgabe)* relinquishment, release, waiver, *(Telegramm)* handing in;
erste ~ *(Kapitalmarkt)* first-rate borrower; **vordringlichste** ~ priority task, top priority job;
~ **von Ansprüchen** relinquishment of claims; ~ **einer Anzeige** placing of an advertisement; ~ **des Gepäcks** booking of luggage *(Br.)*, checking of baggage *(US)*; ~ **eines Geschäfts** giving up busi-

ness, *(Ruhestand)* retirement from business; ~ **von Kauf- und Verkaufsorders zu verschiedenen Zeiten** *(Börse)* selling on a scale *(US)*; ~ **einer guten Stellung** vacation of a good position;
~**bahnhof** dispatch point; ~**formular** telegram form.

Aufgabenbereich sphere of action (activities), duties, functions, competence, province, domain;
neuen ~ **übernehmen** to enter upon new duties.

Aufgaben|gebiet domain, purview, field of action, scope, assignment of duties, province, competence; ~**spezialisierung** functional specialization.

Aufgabe|ort place of origin; ~**postamt** office of dispatch; ~**stelle** sending station; ~**zeit** time of dispatch, code time.

aufgeben *(absenden)* to dispatch, *(anzeigen)* to advise to give notice, *(belasten)* to debit;
Annonce [in einer Zeitung] ~ to insert (run) an advertisement [in a newspaper]; **Anspruch** ~ to resign (waive) a claim; **Bestellung** ~ to [place an] order; **Gepäck** ~ to register (book) luggage *(Br.)*, to check baggage *(US)*; **Geschäft** ~ to give up one's (retire from) business; **Saldo** ~ to state the balance of an account; **seine Stellung** ~ to resign from one's post, to throw up (quit) one's job; **zum Verkauf** ~ to give a selling order.

Aufgeber sender, consignor, *(Fernspruch)* drafter, *(Postanweisung)* remitter.

Aufgebot *(Wertpapiere)* cancellation.

Aufgebotsverfahren *(Wertpapiere)* cancellation proceedings.

aufgegeben *(Schiff)* abandoned, derelict;
~**es Gepäck** registered luggage *(Br.)*, checked baggage *(US)*.

aufgelassen *(Grundstück)* conveyed, assured;
~**e Grube** shut-down mine.

aufgelaufen accrued, accumulated;
~**e Dividende** accumulated (accumulation) dividend; ~**e Kosten** accrued costs; ~**e Zinsen** interest accrued.

Aufgeld *(Börse)* premium, agio, price of exchange, *(Handgeld)* earnest (odd) money.

aufgelegt *(Anleihe)* issued, *(Schiff)* laid up;
zur Zeichnung ~ open for subscription.

aufgelockerte Bebauung low-density housing.

aufgenommene Gelder debts, accounts payable *(US)*.

aufgerufen called, *(Obligationen)* recalled;
~**e Banknoten** notes withdrawn from circulation.

aufgeschoben|er Bedarf deferred (pent-up) demand;
~**e Rente** deferred annuity.

aufgliedern to subdivide, to split up into, to analyse, to break down *(US)*;
Konten ~ to dissect accounts; **Konten nach ihrer Fälligkeit** ~ to age accounts; **Kosten** ~ to itemize costs.

Aufgliederung splitting up, analysis, breakdown *(US)*;
~ **einer Bilanz** analysis sheet; ~ **von Kosten** itemization (breakdown, *US*)of costs; ~ **nach Sachgebieten** functional classification.

aufheben *(aufbewahren)* to keep, to preserve, *(Waren)* to store, to lay up, to warehouse; **Baubeschränkungen** ~ to rezone; **Beschränkungen** ~ to lift restrictions; **Blockade** ~ to raise a blockade; **Embargo** ~ to take off an embargo; **Steuer** ~ to abolish a tax; **Zwangswirtschaft** ~ to decontrol.

Aufhebung *(Annullierung)* annulment, cancellation, nullification, abolishment, *(Gesetz)* abolition, abrogation, repeal, *(Sitzung)* adjournment; ~ **von Baubeschränkungen** rezoning; ~ **einer Beschlagnahme** release of an attachment; ~ **der Blockade** raising of a blockade; ~ **der Goldeinlösungspflicht** suspension of specie payment; ~ **des Goldstandards** suspension of the gold standard; ~ **einer Konkursanordnung** [order of] discharge; ~ **eines Pfändungsbeschlusses** cancellation of a garnishee order; ~ **der Preisbindung** abolition of resale price maintenance; ~ **eines Testamentes** revocation of will; ~ **der Wohnungszwangswirtschaft** derequisition; ~ **der Zwangsverwaltung** desequestration; ~ **der Zwangswirtschaft** decontrol, derationing.

Aufholkonjunktur backlog boom.

Aufkauf buying up, cornering; **spekulativer** ~ forestalling the market; ~ **von Industrieunternehmungen** asset backing.

aufkaufen to buy up, *(zur Verteuerung)* to corner.

Aufkäufer|gruppe corner, ring, pool, *(bei Auktionen)* sales ring; **Richtwerte setzender** ~**markt** primary market *(US)*.

Aufklärungswerbung educational advertisement *(Br.)*, reason-why advertising *(US)*.

Aufklebeadresse gummed (paste-on) label.

Aufkommen *(Steuer)* yield, accrual; ~ **der Verkehrswirtschaft** transportation money.

aufkommen *(bezahlen)* to answer (pay) for, to compensate, *(Mode)* to come into fashion; **für die Kosten** ~ to assume (defray) the costs; **für entstehende Schäden** ~ to be held liable for damages.

aufkündigen *(Anleihe, Kapital, Kredit)* to call in, to recall, *(Hypothek)* to foreclose.

Auflage *(Anweisung)* direction, condition, *(Belastung)* charge, *(Buch)* edition, impression, *(Steuer)* imposition, levy, duty, tax, custom; **mit einer hohen** ~ with a wide circulation.

Auflagen|anstieg circulation growth; **über Zeitungskioske abgesetzter** ~**teil** newsstand sales; ~**ziffer** circulation rate.

auflassen *(Grundstück)* to assure, to convey, to transfer, to surrender.

Auflaufen | von Kosten accruing costs, accumulation of charges; ~ **von Zinsen** accrual of interest.

auflaufen to amount to, to pile up, *(Kosten)* to accumulate, *(Schiff)* to strike ground, *(Schulden)* to run up, *(Zinsen)* to accrue.

Aufleben *(Handel)* revival, recovery, *(Versicherungsvertrag)* reinstatement.

aufleben *(Handel)* to revive, to recover.

auflegen *(Schiff)* to lay up, *(Steuern)* to impose; **Anleihe** ~ to float (raise, issue) a loan; **Subscribentenliste** ~ to open a subscription list; **Anleihe zur Zeichnung** ~ to invite subscriptions for (float) a loan.

aufliefern *(bei der Bahn)* to consign, to send, *(Briefe)* to post *(Br.)*, to mail *(US)*.

aufliegen to be open for inspection; **zur Zeichnung** ~ to be open for subscription.

Auflockerung des Kapitalmarktes easing of the capital market.

auflösen to dissolve, *(Firma)* to liquidate, to wind up, *(Konzern)* to split (break) up; **Geschäft** ~ to liquidate a business; **Konto** ~ to close (eliminate, *US*) an account; **Reserve** ~ to release a reserve.

Auflösung | eines Geschäfts liquidation (winding-up, wind-up, *US*) of a business; ~ **eines Kontos** closing (elimination, *US*) of an account; ~ **von Reserven** release of reserves.

Auflösungs|beschluß winding-up order; ~**bestimmungen** provisions for dissolution.

aufmachen, Artikel zum Verkauf to get up an article for sale; **Bilanz** ~ to make up (strike) a balance sheet; **Havarie** ~ to adjust an average; **Rechnung** ~ to make out an invoice.

Aufmachung make-up, rigout, set-out, window dressing, *(Anzeige)* presentation, layout, *(Schaupackung)* dummy, mannequin *(US)*, *(Seeschadensberechnung)* average adjustment; **äußere** ~ *(Ware)* outward appearance; **bloße** ~ mere show, eyewash; **große** ~ **eines Zeitungsartikels** featuring of an article.

Aufmerksamkeitserreger advertising approach, eye-catcher, eye stopper, attention getter.

Aufnahme reception, *(auf Band)* [tape] recording, *(Beherbergung)* accommodation, *(Kapital)* taking up, raising, *(Kredit)* borrowing, *(in Liste)* entry, listing; ~ **der Bestände** stocktaking, inventory taking; ~ **des Betriebs** going into operation; ~ **einer Tratte** hono(u)ring a bill of exchange; **günstige** ~ **finden** to have a favo(u)rable reception, *(Mode)* to come into fashion, to catch on, *(Waren)* to meet with a ready market (sale).

Aufnahme|bedingungen terms of admission, entrance requirements; ~**bescheinigung** entrance certificate.

aufnahmefähig *(Börse)* buoyant, *(kauflustig)* inclined to buy, *(Markt)* ready, active, receptive; **nicht mehr** ~ *(Markt)* saturated; **beschränkt** ~**er Markt** limited market.

Aufnahme|gebühr entrance (admission, registration, initiation, *US*) fee; ~**neigung** *(Börse)* willingness to absorb.

aufnehmen to receive, to take up, to take in, *(in die Bilanz)* to include into, *(Fahrgäste)* to pick up, *(Markt)* to absorb, *(Wertpapiere)* to assimilate; **Anleihe** ~ to raise (contract, float) a loan; **Betrieb** ~ to go into operation, to start working; **Diktat** ~

to take down in shorthand; **Geld gegen hypothekarische Sicherheit** ~ to borrow on mortgage; **Hypothek auf ein Haus** ~ to raise a mortgage on (mortgage) a house; **in eine Liste** ~ to [enter into a] list; **Protest** ~ **lassen** *(Wechselrecht)* to note a protest, to have a bill protested; **Schulden** ~ to contract debts; **Seeschadensberechnung** ~ to average; **herauskommende Ware glatt** ~ *(Börse)* to absorb all offerings.

aufräumen, sein Lager to sell off, to clear one's stock.

Aufräumungsarbeiten clearance, clearing away.

aufrechnen to balance, to settle, to square, *(in Gegenrechnung bringen)* to compensate, to set off *(Br.)*, to offset *(US)*.

Aufrechnung compensation setoff *(Br.)*, offset *(US)*.

aufrechterhalten, Angebot to hold open an offer; **Versicherung** ~ to carry an insurance.

Aufreißpackung tear-open wrapper.

aufrücken, in eine höhere Stelle to rise (be promoted) to a better position.

Aufruf *(zur Einziehung)* call, recall, *(Gläubiger)* summons; ~ **von Banknoten** (withdrawal) of bank notes; ~ **von Wertpapieren** retirement of securities.

aufrufen *(Banknoten)* to call in, to withdraw from circulation, *(Gläubiger)*, *(Obligationen)* to recall, to summon.

Aufruhrversicherung civil-commotion insurance.

aufsaugen *(Markt)* to absorb.

aufschieben, Termin to extend a time limit; **Zahlung** ~ to defer (postpone) payment.

Aufschlag *(Abzahlungssystem)* loading, *(Kurs)* rise, advance, improvement, *(Preis)* additional charge, markup, *(Steuer)* surtax, additional tax; ~ **auf den Einfuhrpreis** import markup.

aufschlagen to raise, to surcharge, *(im Kurs)* to look up, to advance; **auf den Preis** ~ to increase the price, to mark up.

aufschließen *(Grundstücke)* to develop, to improve, *(Märkte)* to open up, to develop.

Aufschließung *(Grundstücke)* development, improvement, *(Märkte)* opening, development.

aufschlüsseln to subdivide, to apportion, to classify, to analyse, analyze, to break down *(US)*; **Verkaufsgebiete** ~ to divide sales areas.

Aufschlüsselung apportionment, breakdown *(US)*; **berufliche** ~ job analysis (breakdown, *US)*; ~ **der Geschäftsunkosten** overhead allocation; ~ **von Verkaufsgebieten** division of sales areas.

Aufschub der Zwangsvollstreckung stay of execution.

Aufschwung *(Konjunktur)* upswing, uptrend, upturn *(US)*; ~ **des Handels** increase in trade; **plötzlicher** ~ **der Preise** sudden advance in prices; ~ **erleben (nehmen)** *(Kurse)* to go up, to advance; ~ **nehmen** *(Konjunktur)* to boom; **neuen** ~ **nehmen** to show renewed activity.

Aufschwungstendenz rising (upward) tendency.

Aufseher overseer, controller, surveyor, overlooker *(Br.)*, *(Laden)* shopwalker, floorwalker *(US)*.

aufsetzen, Bewerbung to write an application; **Rechnung** ~ to make out an invoice.

Aufsicht oversight, inspection, supervision; ~ **im Laden** shopwalker *(Br.)*, floorwalker *(US)*.

Aufsichtsamt | **für das Kreditwesen** Credit Control Board *(US)*; ~ **für das Versicherungswesen** State Insurance Commission (Commissioner, US).

Aufsichtsbeamter inspector, superintendent, supervisor, control officer, surveyor; ~**organ** controlling body; ~**rat** board of directors (governors), *(Einzelperson)* board member.

Aufsichtsratsmitglied board member; **nominelles** ~ guinea pig *(Br.)*.

Aufsichtsrats|**posten** directorship, directorate; ~**sitz** seat on the board; ~**sitzung** board meeting; ~ **tantieme** director's fee; ~**vorsitzender** chairman of the board of directors.

Aufstecker *(Werbemitteilung im Laden)* crowner.

aufstellen *(Bilanz)* to prepare, to strike, *(Kosten)* to specify, *(Maschine)* to instal(l), to mount, to assemble; **Inventar** ~ to [take an] inventory, to take stock; **Streikposten** ~ to picket; **Tagesordnung** ~ to fix the agenda.

Aufstellung statement, schedule, *(Maschine)* assembly, installation, mounting; **laut** ~ as per account [rendered]; **detaillierte** ~ detailed statement, specification, itemized schedule *(US)*; ~ **der Aktiven und Passiven** statement of assests and liabilities, schedule *(US)*; ~ **einer Bilanz** striking a balance, preparation of a balance sheet; ~ **von Investitionsplänen** capital budgeting; ~ **der Kosten** statement of accounts; **erläuternde** ~ **für die Steuererklärung** supporting schedule; ~ **eines Verteilungsplans** *(Konkurs)* marshalling of assets.

Aufstiegs|**bild** progress chart; ~**chancen in der Betriebshierarchie** attractive openings on managerial levels.

Aufstiegsmöglichkeit prospects, promotional opportunity, opportunity to advance (for growth); **keine** ~ blind-alley job.

aufstocken, Kapital to appreciate capital *(Br.)*.

Aufstockung *(Gebäude)* addition, *(Kapital)* increase of capital, capital appreciation *(Br.)*, *(Rohštoffvorräte)* stockpiling.

auftauen, Konto to unfreeze an account; **eingefrorenen Kredit** ~ to unblock a frozen credit.

aufteilen to divide, to distribute, to [re]partition, *(parzellieren)* to parcel, *(zuteilen)* to allot, to allocate; **Sicherheiten** ~ to marshal securities (assets).

Aufteilung distribution, partition, portionment; **anteilsmäßige** ~ prorata apportionment; ~ **des Absatzmarktes** market segmentation; ~ **der Generalunkosten** overhead allocation; ~ **der Provisionsgebühr** diversion of commission; ~ **der Sicherheiten** marshalling of securities.

Auftrag *(Anwalt)* mandate, brief, *(Anweisung)* direction, order, orders, instruction, indent, assignment, *(Bestellung)* sales order, *(Botengang)* errand, commission; `

im ~ [von] by order (attorney), in charge, on the authority; **im ~ und für Rechnung** by order and for account of;

eingehender ~ incoming order; **großer** ~ large (tall) order; **limitierter** ~ *(Börse)* limited order, stop-loss order *(US)*; **vordringlicher** ~ rush order;

~ **zum regulären Festpreis** straight-fixed price contract *(US)*; ~ **durch die Post** mail order *(US)*;

~ **annehmen** to book an order; ~ **annullieren** to cancel an order; ~ **ausführen** to deal with (execute, effect, *US*) an order; ~ **bearbeiten** to put a matter in hand; **sich um einen** ~ **bemühen** to be in the running for a contract; **jds.** ~ **buchen** to book (enter, secure) s. one's order; ~ **erteilen** to give (place, space) an order, to indent, *(Behörde)* to confer (award) a commission; **im ~ von jem. handeln** to act on behalf of s. o.; ~ **stornieren** to cancel (revoke, withdraw) an order; ~ **an seine Lieferanten weitergeben** to job a contract.

Aufträge, gebuchte orders on the book; **öffentliche** ~ public contracts; **unerledigte** ~ unfilled orders; **sich um** ~ **bemühen** to solicit orders; ~ **in der Reihenfolge des Eingangs erledigen** to execute all orders in strict rotation; ~ **verlagern** to shift orders; ~ **zurückziehen** to shorten commitments.

Auftraggeber contractor, *(Arbeitgeber)* employer, principal, *(Kunde)* client, customer, *(Werbung)* sponsor;

ungenannter (verdeckter) ~ undisclosed principal; ~ **und Auftragnehmer** employer and his agent.

auftragloser Geschäftsführer agent of necessity.

Auftrags|ablehnung denial (rejection) of an order; ~**abwicklung** filling a contract; ~**annahme** taking an order; ~**beschaffung** bidding for orders; ~**bestand** orders on hand, orders booked, unfilled orders *(US)*; ~**bestätigung** confirmation (acknowledgement) of an order; ~**buch** order (commission) book; ~**dienst** *(Telefon)* telephone-answering service; ~**eingänge** incoming orders; ~**erholung** pick-up in orders; ~**erledigung** prompt attention to an order; ~**erteilung** placing an order, *(Behörde)* allocation of contract, contract award; ~**formular** order form (sheet, slip, blank, *US*); **kombiniertes** ~ **und Versandrechnungsformular** combination sales-order-shipper invoice form.

auftragsgemäß handeln to act in compliance with one's orders.

Auftrags|geschäft commissional business; **wirtschaftliche** ~**größe** economic order quantity; ~**kürzung** cutback in orders; ~**liste** order book; ~**makler** drop shipper; ~**planung und -steuerung** production planning; **vorgedruckte** ~**postkarte** postcard order form; ~**rückgang** falling off of orders; **rückstand** back (unfilled) orders, backlog (coll.); ~**sendung** drop shipment; ~**stornierung** withdrawal of an order; ~**vergabe** placing an order, order placing, *(Behörde)* award of a contract, letting of works and supplies; ~ **volumen** size of orders.

auftragsweise Einziehung collection on a commission basis.

Auftrieb *(Börse)* buoyancy, *(Preise)* rising tendency (trend), upswing, upsurge;

~ **in der Wohnungswirtschaft** upsurge in housing; **erneuten** ~ **erhalten** *(Kurse)* to turn in another strong performance; ~ **haben** *(Konjunktur)* to boom.

Auftriebstendenz upward trend.

Aufwand expenditure, expense, outlay, cost, *(Luxus)* extravagance, luxury;

aktivierungspflichtiger ~ capital expenditure; **betriebsfremder** ~ nonoperating expenses; **an der Grenze der Wirtschaftlichkeit liegender** ~ marginal costs; **unnützer** ~ waste;

~ **der öffentlichen Hand** government spending; ~ **der gewerblichen Wirtschaft für Bauleistungen** nonresidential building outlay; **unnützer** ~ **an Zeit** waste of time;

großen ~ **treiben** to live in state (at rack and manager).

Aufwandsentschädigung expense allowance, *(leitender Angestellter)* fringe benefit.

Aufwands|posten expense item; ~**prinzip** *(Steuer)* sumptuary principle; ~**steuer** tax on consumption, use tax *(US)*.

Aufwärtsbewegung *(Börse)* advance, up, upward push, buoyant tone of the market; **konjunkturelle** ~ upward business trend; **der** ~ **nur langsam folgen** to lag behind the advance.

Aufwärts|entwicklung upward surge, upsurge, uptrend, upswing; ~**tendenz erkennen lassen** to show a tendency to improve.

aufweichen, Währung to soften the currency.

aufwenden, Kosten to defray expenses; **große Mühe** ~ to take great pains.

aufwendig expensive, costly, sumptuous, extravagant, *(Buch)* lavish, luxurious;

~**e Lebensführung** extravagant living.

Aufwendungen expenditure, expense;

außerordentliche und betriebsfremde ~ extraordinary and outside expenditure; **entstandene, aber noch nicht fällige** ~ accrued expense (payables account, *US*); **soziale** ~ social expenditure (disbursements); **werterhöhende** ~ improvements; **zusätzliche** ~ **für leitende Angestellte** executive fringes;

~ **für bezogene Waren** goods supplied; ~ **bestreiten** to defray the expenses.

Aufwendungs- und Instandhaltungskosten upkeep and improvements.

aufwerten to revalue, to [re]valorize, *(Anlagegüter)* to write up, to appreciate *(Br.)*.

Aufwertung [upward] revaluation, upvaluation; ~ **von Anlagen** appreciation *(Br.)* (writing up) of assets.

Aufwertungsanleihe stabilization loan.

aufzehren, sein Kapital to eat up one's capital.

Aufzeichnung memorandum, note, notation, *(Rundfunk)* transcript[ion], platter.

Aufzeichnungen notes, records;
~ **über den Kassenausgang** cash disbursement records.

Auktion auction [sales], public sale, outcry, vendue *(US)*;
zur ~ **bringen, in die** ~ **geben** to auction, to sell by (at, *US*) auction, to put up for sale, to set up; **auf einer** ~ **kaufen** to buy by (at, *US*) auction.

Auktionator auctioneer, appraiser *(US)*.

Auktions|bedingungen terms of auction; ~**gebühren** auction fees, lot money; ~**katalog**, ~**liste** auction bill, catalog(ue) of sale; ~**preis** auction price; ~**verkauf** auction sale, sale by (at, *US*) auction.

ausarbeiten to work out in detail, to plan.

Ausarbeitung eines Vertrages drafting of a contract.

Ausbau development, enlargement, extension;
~ **des Dachgeschosses** building of an attic; ~ **seiner Stellung** consolidation (strengthening) of one's position.

ausbauen to develop, to improve, *(Geschäft)* to extend, to expand;
Handelsbeziehungen ~ to strengthen trade relations; **Schuppen** ~ to convert a shed; **Strecke zweigleisig** ~ to double an existing track.

ausbaufähig *(Stellung)* promising, progressive.

Ausbesserungsarbeiten *(Straße)* road repairs.

Ausbeute yield, output, *(Kux)* dividend.

ausbeuten to turn to account, to make capital out of *(Arbeiter)* to sweat, to exploit, *(Bergwerk)* to work.

Ausbeutung exploitation, *(Bergwerk)* working;
~ **eines Unternehmens** milking an enterprise *(US)*.

Ausbeutungs|kosten cost of exploitation costs; ~**recht** right to exploit; ~**system** *(Arbeiter)* sweating system.

ausbezahlen to pay out (off);
bar ~ to pay cash down; **Teilhaber** ~ to buy out a partner.

Ausbildung, berufliche ~ professional training; **innerbetriebliche** ~ employee (in-plant, *US*) training;
~ **am Arbeitsplatz** training on the job *(US)*, on-the-job (in-plant) training *(US)*; ~ **leitender Angestellter** executive training *(US)*; ~ **in der Lehrlingswerkstatt** vestibule school training; ~ **in Schnellkursen** intensive courses, blitz training *(US)*;
akademische ~ **haben** to hve been through the university.

Ausbildungs|beihilfe educational (training) grant, training subsidy; ~**bestimmungen für Lehrlinge** apprenticeship regulations; ~**gang** educational background; **praxisbezogener** ~**gang** end-on course; ~**kosten** training costs, investment in men, *(Lehrlinge)* premium of apprenticeship; ~**kurs** training course, course of training; ~**kurs für Nachwuchskräfte** management trainee course; ~**leiter** chief instructor.

Ausbildungsprogramm apprentice (training) program(me), educational training scheme.

Ausbildungs|stätte training center *(US)* (centre, *Br.*, facilities); **berufliche** ~**zeit** training time on a job; ~**zuschuß** training benefit.

ausbleiben *(Zug)* to be overdue;
mit der Zahlung ~ to make default, to be in arrears with one's payment.

ausbooten, jem. to unship s. o., to chuck s. o. out.

ausbuchen to abandon, to retire.

Ausbuchung abandonment, retirement.

ausdehnen to extend, to expand, to step up;
seine Tätigkeit auf bankfremde Geschäfte ~ to diversify outside banking.

auseinandersetzen to explain, to set forth, to state; **sich** ~ to arrange, to settle, *(Erben)* to partition, *(Partner)* to distribute the assets; **sich mit seinen Gläubigern** ~ to come to terms (compound) with one's creditors.

Auseinandersetzung arrangement, settlement, *(Erbteilung)* distribution and partition, *(Partner)* distribution of assets.

Auseinandersetzungs|anspruch distribution share, settlement right; ~**bilanz** liquidating balance sheet.

auserlesene Ware choice goods.

ausfahren, Kapazität fast voll to operate at close to capacity.

Ausfahrt ride, *(aus einem Grundstück)* [point off] exit, way-out, *(Hafen)* mouth, *(Zug)* departure.

Ausfall *(Abfall)* refuse parts, waste, scrap, *(Maschine)* breakdown, failure, *(Stromausfall)* breakdown;
~**bürge** surety, bail absolute; ~**bürgschaft** indemnity letter (bond, *US*), guaranty of collection *(US)*.

ausfallen *(Einnahme)* not to be forthcoming, *(Ernte)* to turn out, *(Maschine)* to fail, to be out of action, to pack up *(sl.)*, *(Muster)* to be like the pattern, *(Sitzung)* not to take place, *(Stromversorgung)* to break down;
Dividende ~ **lassen** to omit a dividend.

Ausfall|muster reference (outturn) sample (pattern); ~**straße** arterial road (highway).

ausfertigen *(Abschrift)* to copy, to exemplify;
doppelt ~ to make out (deliver) in duplicate; **Kreditbrief** ~ to issue a letter of credit.

Ausfertigung make, copy, engrossment, exemplification, *(Urkunde)* execution;
für die Richtigkeit der ~ certified true copy; **vollstreckbare** ~ special execution;
in drei ~**en liefern** to make in three styles.

Ausflug outing, jaunt, [pleasure] trip, tour, [holiday] excursion, sally;
~ **zu verbilligten Preisen** cheap trip.

Ausflugs|autobus charabanc; ~**lokal** inn, roadhouse; ~**preise** excursion fares.

Ausfuhr export [trade], exportation;
für die ~ **bestimmt** earmarked for exportation; **unsichtbare** ~ invisible exports, indirect exporting; ~**abgabe** export duty (levy, tax), duty on export; **plötzlicher** ~**anstieg** jump in exports; ~**artikel** article of exportation, export article, *(pl.)* exports;

~auftrag export order; ~bescheinigung certificate of clearance outward; ~beschränkungen export restrictions; ~bewilligung export licence (permit).

ausführen *(Waren)* to export, to sell abroad; sämtliche Bankgeschäfte ~ to transact banking business of every discription; ~de Behörde enforcement agency, executive body.

Ausfuhr|entwicklung export trend; unerwartet hoher ~erfolg export bonanza; ~erklärung declaration (entry) outwards; ~finanzierung export financing; ~firma exporter; ~förderung export drive (promotion); ~garantie export guarantee; ~genehmigung export permit (licence), transire *(Br.);* ~geschäft export business; ~handel export (active, outward) trade; ~konnossement export bill of lading; ~kontingent export quota; ~kredit export credit; ~kreditversicherung export credit insurance; ~liste export list; ~monopol foreign staple, export monopoly; ~nummer des statistischen Warenverzeichnisses statistical number; ~prämie export premium, subsidy to exports; bounty on exportation, [king's] bounty *(Br.);* ~quote export quota; ~rückvergütung export rebate, tax rebate for exporters, reimbursement for exports; ~sperre embargo on exports; ~tonnage export tonnage.

Ausführung execution, carrying out, handling, *(Modell)* type, model, make, style; luxuriöse ~ more luxurious finish.

Ausführungsbestimmungen implementing (implemeal) provisions (regulations).

Ausfuhr|verbot prohibition of exports, export prohibition; ~verkaufsrechnung export sales note; ~versandliste pricking note; ~zoll export duty (tariff), customs outwards; exitus.

ausfuhrzoll|frei free of export duty; ~pflichtig liable to export duty.

Ausfuhrzuschuß subsidy on exports.

ausfüllen, Antragsformular to fill in an application blank; Einkommensteuererklärung ~ to prepare an income-tax return.

Ausfüllung eines Steuerformulars tax preparation.

Ausgabe expense, expenditure, outlay, *(Ausgabestelle)* booking office, *(Aushändigung)* giving (handing) out, *(Buch)* edition, set, *(Emission)* issue, issuance *(US)*, issuing; alte ~ *(Zeitung)* back number; billige ~ cheap edition; broschierte ~ pamphlet copy; amtlich genehmigte ~ sealed form; urheberrechtlich geschützte ~ copyrighted publication; ~ von Gratisaktien bonus issue; ~ eines Passes issue of a passport; ~ von Gratisaktien vornehmen to declare a stock dividend *(US)* (bonus share, Br.); ~bewilligung budgetary appropriation; ~kostenzuschlag zuzüglich Erwerbskosten der Wertpapiere *(Kapitalanlagegesellschaft)* loading; ~kurs issue price.

Ausgaben expenditure, expense, outgoings *(Br.);* abzugsfähige ~ deductible expenses; außerplanmäßige ~ expenditure not provided for in the budget; noch nicht fällige ~ accrued expenses; laufende ~ fixed (running) expenses, current (returning) expenditure; sachliche ~ material cost; sonstige ~ other payments, *(Bilanz)* nonoperating expenses; tatsächliche ~ out-of-pocket expenses; unproduktive ~ nonproductive expenses; unvorhergesehene ~ unforeseen expense (expenditure); verschiedene ~ *(Bilanz)* sundries; werbende ~ productive expenses; regelmäßig wiederkehrende ~ recurrent expenses; ~ pro Kopf der Bevölkerung per capita costs; ~ der öffentlichen Hand government spending; ~ für den Lebensunterhalt consumption expenditure; ~ im Reiseverkehr tourist spending; sich in den ~ Beschränkungen auferlegen to show spending forbearance; ~ beschneiden to cut expenditure; ~ bestreiten to defray the costs; große ~ machen to incur heavy expenses; überflüssige ~ vermeiden to economize; für unvorhergesehene ~ zurückstellen to allow (provide) for contingencies.

Ausgaben|abbau limitation of spending; rapider ~anstieg spending splurge; ~beleg voucher jacket, expense voucher; ~beschneidung cost cutting, expenditure cut; ~buch charge (housekeeping) book, book of charges; Einnahmen- ~-Buchführungssystem cost-book principle; ~formular voucher jacket; ~freudigkeit der Verbraucherschaft consumer spending; ~höchstgrenze festsetzen to set a limit to expenses, to put a ceiling on spending; ~stimmung spending mood; staatlicher ~stopp ceiling to government spending; ~wirtschaft spending.

Ausgabeposten expense (spending) item; ~ verschwinden lassen to draw the curtain on outlays.

Ausgabe|preis issue price, *(Kapitalanlagegesellschaft)* offering price; ~stelle issuing office, *(Fahrscheine)* ticket office, *(Gepäck)* counter; ~tag publication (issue) date; ~wert issue value.

Ausgangs|fakturenbuch sales book; ~fracht outbound transportation; ~körbchen out-tray (basket); günstige ~position haben *(bei Verhandlungen)* to get (be let) in on the ground floor; ~punkt *(Bahn)* point of departure, *(Preisbestimmung)* basing point; ~tarif *(Versicherung)* manual rate; ~werte *(Zeitstudie)* basic data; ~zoll export duty.

ausgeben *(Geld)* to spend, to expend, to disburse, to lay out, to outlay, *(Banknoten)* to issue; Anleihe ~ to float (issue, negotiate) a loan; 40 000 Dollar im Jahr ~ to live at the rate of $ 40,000 (spend $ 40,000) a year; Gratisaktien ~ to declare a stock dividend *(US)*; Paß ~ to issue a passport.

ausgebildet, beruflich professional; fachlich ~ specialized; voll ~ fully qualified.

ausgedrückt in terms of; prozentual ~ expressed as percentage.

ausgefallen *(Dividende)* passed.

ausgeführte Aufträge filled orders.

ausgeglichen even, square, liquidated, in balance; ~es Konto balanced account.

ausgehen *(Vorräte)* to run low, *(Waren)* to run short, to sell out.
ausgehend|e **Fracht** outward freight; ~e **Post** departing (outgoing) mail.
ausgelastet occupied, booked, *(Betrieb)* working to capacity;
   zu 85 % ~ sein *(Betrieb)* to operate at a rate of 85 % of capacity.
ausgelegter **Betrag** money disbursed.
ausgeloste **Pfandbriefe (Schuldverschreibungen)** bonds called for redemption.
ausgemachter **Preis** price agreed upon.
ausgeschriebene **Stelle** advertised post.
ausgeschütteter **Gewinn** distributed profit.
ausgesperrt *(Arbeiter)* locked out.
ausgestellt *(Kreditbrief)* issued, *(auf einer Messe)* on show, exhibited, *(Wechsel)* made out;
   an Order ~ und blanko giriert made out to order and indorsed in blank.
ausgesteuert **sein** *(Arbeitsloser)* to be out of benefit (unemployment relief).
ausgesuchte **Ware** choice quality (goods).
ausgezeichnet excellent, distinguished, A I, first-class (-rate), classic, boss *(US)*;
   nicht ~ *(im Schaufenster)* unpriced.
Ausgleich balancing, balancing, squaring, adjustment, *(Gegenkonto)* setoff *(Br.)*, offset *(US)*, *(Glattstellung)* evening up;
   zum ~ aller Forderungen in settlement of all claims;
   ~ von Angebot und Nachfrage equilibrium of supply and demand; **~ in bar** cash adjustment;
   ~ der Versicherungsrisiken spread of risk.
ausgleichen to equate, to make equal, to equalize, to adjust, to level, to balance, to square, *(glattstellen)* to even up, to settle;
   Haushaltsdefizit ~ to balance an adverse budget;
   Konto ~ to settle an account; **Verlust ~** to make up for a loss.
Ausgleichs|abgabe equalization levy, countervailing charge; ~**abkommen** clearing agreement; ~**ansprüche haben** to be entitled to a composition; ~**fonds** equalization (compensation) fund; ~**klausel** *(Lohnfestsetzung)* escalator clause *(US)*.
ausgleichspflichtig *(Erbe)* liable to put into hotchpot.
Ausgleichs|rücklage equalization reserve; ~**umlage** equalization fee, *(Montanunion)* levy, *(kommunale)* rate-in-aid *(Br.)*; ~**urlaub für Überstunden** compensatory time off; ~**zahlung** equalization payment, *(bei Entlassungen)* coordination allowance *(US)*, severance pay *(US)*; ~**zulage** cost-of-living allowance.
Ausgleichung *(Banken)* clearance, *(Erben untereinander)* [putting in] hotchpot;
   zur ~ unserer Rechnung in full discharge of our account.
ausgliedern to separate, *(Konzerngesellschaft)* to disembody, to disincorporate.
Ausgliederung **von Konzernkonten** intercompany elimination *(US)*.
ausgründen to disincorporate, to disembody.

aushandeln, **Preis** to negotiate a price.
Aushändigung delivery, handing over, disposition;
   zahlbar gegen ~ der Begleitpapiere payable against surrender of shipping documents.
Aushang notice, bulletin, *(Plakat)* poster, placard.
Aushängefahrplan time poster (table), schedule *(US)*.
aushelfen, **jem. mit Geld** to accommodate s. o. with money; **seinem Vater im Geschäft ~** to help one's father in the shop.
Aushilfe aid, assistance, *(Geld)* accommodation, *(Laden)* counter hand, *(Notbehelf)* makeshift;
   als ~ arbeiten to help out, to come as a stopgap.
Aushilfs|arbeit odd job; ~**arbeiter** handyman, part-timer, hired help (man, *US*), casual [labo(u)rer], temporary, stopgap; ~**personal** temporary staff; ~**sekretärin** relief secretary.
Auskämmungsprozess *(zur Freimachung von Arbeitskräften)* comb[ing] out *(Br. sl.)*.
ausklarieren *(Schiff)* to clear for sailing, *(Zollrecht)* to take out of bond.
Ausklarierung clearance outward.
Ausklarierungsschein *(Schiff)* clearance certificate.
Auskommen livelihood, living, support;
   genügendes ~ competence, competency;
   sein ~ haben to get (make) a living, to pay one's way; **sein gutes ~ haben** to be in easy circumstances.
auskommen, **mit etw.** to manage (do) with s. th.;
   mit seinem Geld ~ to make both ends meet; **mit wenig Geld ~** to live with little money.
auskömmliches **Gehalt haben** to earn enough to live on.
Auskunft information, intelligence, *(Schalter)* inquiry office, information desk *(US)*;
   ~ in Zollangelegenheiten tariff information;
   ~ über eine Firma erhalten to receive a report on a firm;
   sofortige ~ über Deckung erbeten *(für einen Scheck)* advise fate.
Auskunftei inquiry office (agency), *(Kreditauskunft)* credit agency, information bureau *(US)*.
Auskunfts|beamter inquiry clerk; ~**büro** inquiry office, information centre *(Br.)* (bureau, *US*); ~**pflicht** *(Versicherung)* liability to discover; ~**schalter** inquiry office, information desk (window, *US*); ~**stand** *(Messe)* information stand.
Auslade|bahnsteig unloading platform; ~**hafen** port of discharge; ~**kosten** unloading expenses.
ausladen to unload, to unlade, to discharge, to clear, *(Flugzeug)* to deplane, *(Lastwagen)* to detruck, *(Omnibus)* to debus *(US)*, (Schiff) to unship, to land, to lighten.
Ausladerampe unloading platform.
Auslage expense, outlay, laying out, disbursement, *(Schaufenster)* shop front (window);
   ~ innerhalb des Ladens interior display;
   ~ herrichten to dress a shop window.
Auslage|fenster display (show, *US*) window; ~**geld geben** to place in funds *(Br.)*; ~**material für Schaufenster** window material.

Auslagen expenses, outlay, cost[s], mise paid-on charges *(Br.)*;
bare ~ cash advances (disbursements); **erstattungsfähige** ~ reimbursable expenses; ~ **zu Lasten des Kunden** expenses charged to client's account;
seine ~ **aufschreiben** to keep a record of one's expenses; ~ **ersetzen (erstatten)** to reimburse (refund) the expenses.

Auslagen aufstellung specification of disbursements; ~**ersatz** reimbursement of expenses; ~**werbung** *(auf Ladentisch)* counter display.

auslagern to take out of store, to dislocate, to evacuate, to withdraw from a warehouse.

Auslagerung dislocation, evacuation.

Ausland foreign countries (parts);
im ~ **hergestellt** foreign-built (-made); **im** ~ **zahlbar** payable abroad;
vom ~ **kontrolliert werden** to be controlled by foreign interests.

Ausländer, ansässiger alien resident *(US)*.
~**guthaben**, ~**konto** external account; ~**konvertierbarkeit** convertibility for nonresidents.

ausländisch|e Absatzmärkte foreign markets; **in** ~**em Besitz** foreign-owned; ~**es Fabrikat** foreign [-made] product; ~**e Vermögensverwaltung** alien property custodian *(US)*; ~**e Zahlungsmittel** foreign money.

Auslands|absatz foreign market; ~**abteilung** foreign department; ~**anleihe** external (foreign) loan; ~**aufenthalt** residence (stay, time spent) abroad; ~**auftrag** indent, export order, *(Rüstungsauftrag)* offshore order; ~**bank** foreign (overseas) bank, foreign banking corporation *(US)*; ~**berichterstatter** foreign correspondent; ~**brief** foreign letter; ~**dienst** service abroad, foreign service *(US)*; ~**geschäft** export trade, *(einzelnes)* export business; ~**gespräch** *(Telefon)* external (foreign) call, overseas (continental) call *(Br.)*, ~**guthaben** foeign assets (deposits).

Auslandshilfe foreign aid (assistance);
amerikanische ~ US-financed foreign aid.

Auslandshilfs|abkommen foreign-aid program(me); ~**projekt** foreign-aid project.

Auslands|investitionen capital invested abroad; ~**kapital** foreign (outside) capital; ~**käufe** *(Kriegsmaterial)* offshore purchases *(US)*; ~**korrespondent** *(Bank)* foreign correspondence clerk; ~**markt** export (foreign) market; ~**nachrichten** foreign news; ~**niederlassung** overseas branch; ~**postanweisung** international (foreign) money order; ~**reise** foreign voyage (journey, travel); ~**scheck** foreign check *(US)* (cheque, *Br.)*; ~**schuldendienst** foreign-debts service; ~**schuldverschreibungen** external bonds; ~**stimmen** *(Zeitung)* extracts of foreign newspapers; **mindestreservepflichtige** ~**verbindlichkeiten** reserve-carrying foreign liabilities; ~**vermögen** external assets (property), assets held abroad; ~**wechsel** foreign bill of exchange, bill in foreign currency; ~**werbung** foreign advertising; ~**wert** *(beim Zoll)* foreign valuation; ~**werte** *(Börse)* external assets; ~**wohnsitz haben** to be resident abroad; ~**zulage** foreign service (expatriation) allowance.

Auslastung *(Betrieb)* working to capacity.

Auslaufen *(Investition)* fade-out, *(Produktion)* phasing out, *(Schiff)* sailing, leaving a port.

auslaufen *(Investition)* to fade out, *(Patent)* to expire, *(Produktion)* to phase out, *(Schiff)* to sail, to put forth (off) to sea, *(Tank)* to run dry, *(Vertrag)* to run out, to expire;
fahrplanmäßig ~ to sail to schedule *(US)*.

auslaufende Termingelder maturing time deposits.

Auslauf|hafen port of departure; ~**modell** discontinued line.

auslegen *(Ware)* to exhibit, to dispose, to display for sale;
für j. etw. ~ to pay for s. o..

Auslegung, einschränkende restrictive interpretation.

Ausleihbücherei lending library.

ausleihen, Geld auf Zinsen to lend money on (at) interest; **sich Geld** ~ to borrow money.

Ausleihungen | am Geldmarkt short-term borrowings; ~ **an Kunden** advances to customers.

Ausleihungsbefugnis lending power.

Auslese selection, choice, flower.

Auslieferung delivery, *(Effekten)* surrender.

Auslieferungs|anweisung delivery (pickup) order; ~**gebiet** area of supply; ~**gewicht** delivered weight; ~**lager** deposit, repository, supply store, local supply station, warehouse, distributing stock, *(Buchhandel)* trade department, receiving house *(Br.)*; ~**stelle eines Versandhausunternehmens** mail-order store *(US)*.

ausliegen *(Waren)* to be exposed for sale, *(Zeitungen)* to be kept (taken in, *Br.)*.

auslosen, Staatspapiere to draw bonds.

auslösen, Pfand to redeem a pawn.

Auslosung drawing [by lot];
~**zur Rückzahlung** drawing for redemption; ~ **von Wertpapieren** raffle.

Auslösungsrecht des Hypothekenschuldners right of equity of redemption *(US)*.

Auslosungsschein letter of allotment, drawing certificate.

ausmachen to amount to, (come, run up) to, *(ausbedingen)* to stipulate, to condition, to fix *(US)*, *(bilden)* to constitute;
Preis ~ to settle (agree on) a price; **wesentlichen Teil der Produktion** ~ to form the bulk of the production.

ausmessen to [ad]measure, *(Grundstück)* to survey.

ausmustern to reject, to discard, to single out.

Ausnahme|angebot special (exceptional) offer; ~**frachtsätze** differential rates; ~**genehmigung** special licence; ~**klausel** exemption clause *(Br.)*.

ausnutzen to make use of, to utilize, *(Arbeiter)* to sweat, *(Bergwerk)*, to exploit.

Ausnutzung utilization, employment, *(Arbeiter)* sweating, *(Bergwerk)* exploitation;

rationelle ~ rational (efficient) employment; ~ **von Betriebserfindungen durch den Firmeninhaber** shop right.

ausrangieren to sort out, to scrap, to cast [out], *(Betriebseinheit)* to discard, *(Schiff)* to disrate.

ausrechnen to compute, to calculate, to count out; **falsch** ~ to miscalculate.

ausreichend|es Guthaben sufficient funds; **~e Sicherheit** ample bail.

Ausreise departure, leaving, *(Schiff)* exit, outward voyage (passage, journey); **~bewilligung** exit permit; **~genehmigung** exit visa.

ausrufen, Streik to call a strike.

Ausrufer, öffentlicher common crier, bellman.

ausschalten, Zwischenhandel to eliminate the middlemen.

Ausschank public house, tavern, dispense; **konzessionierter** ~ licensed premises; ~ **über die Straße** off-licence *(Br.)*.

Ausscheiden | ungeeigneter Bewerber screening of candidates; ~ **aus einer Firma** withdrawal from a company; ~ **der besseren Risiken** adverse selection.

ausscheiden, aus einer Firma to retire from (leave) a company; **turnusgemäß** ~ to retire by rotation.

Ausscheidetafel decrement table.

ausschiffen to debark, to disembark, to land.

ausschlachten *(Betrieb, Kraftfahrzeug)* to cut up for sale, to break up, to scrap, to cannibalize *(US)*.

Ausschlachtung von Anlagen asset stripping.

ausschlagen, Angebot to decline (reject) an offer; **Erbschaft** ~ to disclaim an estate.

ausschlaggebender Kapitalanteil controlling interest.

ausschließen to exclude, to seclude, to preclude, *(Arbeiter)* to lock out, *(ausstoßen)* to expel, *(Teilhaber)* to freeze out; **Haftung** ~ to exonerate o. s. from liability; **Öffentlichkeit** ~ to order the case to be heard in closed session (camera); **von der Zuteilung** ~ to preclude from allotment.

ausschließliche Beschäftigung sole occupation.

Ausschließlichkeits|abkommen tying agreement; **~aufhänger** *(Werbung)* exclusive angle; **~geschäft** exclusive dealing *(US)*; **~vertrag** tying agreement, *(Vertreter)* exclusive agency contract (dealer arrangement, *(US)*.

Ausschluß exclusion, *(Ausnahme)* exception, *(Disqualifikation)* disqualification, *(Einrede)* estoppage, estoppel; **unter** ~ **der Konkurrenz** noncompetitive; **unter** ~ **der Öffentlichkeit** in camera *(Br.)* (closed session); **unter** ~ **des Rechtsweges** disbarring legal actions; ~ **der Haftbarkeit** nonliability; ~ **des Wettbewerbs** restraint of trade.

Ausschlußklausel *(Versicherung)* memorandum clause.

Ausschnitt *(Zeitung)* cutting, cutout, clipping *(US)*.

Ausschnitts|büro, ~dienst [press] clipping bureau *(US)*, press-cutting agency, newspaper clipper *(US)*.

ausschreiben to write in full (at full length), *(Steuern)* to impose, to levy;

Auftrag ~ to invite tenders (bids, *US)*; **Rechnung** ~ to make out an invoice; **Scheck** ~ to fill (make) out a check *(US)* (cheque, *Br.);* **Stelle** ~ to advertise a vacant position (a vacancy).

Ausschreibung *(Rechnung)* making out, *(Scheck)* filling out, *(Stelle)* advertisement, *(Steuern)* imposition, *(im Subskriptionswege)* invitation to tender; **sich an staatlichen ~en beteiligen** to bid on government contracts *(US)*.

Ausschreibungs|angebot tender offer; **~bedingungen** terms of tender, specifications of work to be done; **~beteiligter** contract bidder *(US)*; **~frist** deadline for tenders; **~wettbewerb** bid competition *(US)*.

Ausschuß commission, committee, board, panel, *(Produktion)* waste, wastage, wasters, scrap; **geschäftsführender** ~ executive (managing, management) committee; ~ **zur Bekämpfung des unlauteren Wettbewerbs** Federal Trade Commission *(US)*; ~ **für Wirtschaft und Finanzen** *(UNO)* Economic and Financial Committee; ~ **der gewerblichen Wirtschaft** trade council; **~akten** committee files; ~ **bericht** committee (panel) report; **~mitglied** member of the board, committee (commission, board) member; **~stadium** committee stage; **~ware** job (damaged, rummage) goods, trumpery wares, substandard goods.

ausschütten, Börsengewinne to distribute trading profits; **Dividende** ~ to declare (strike, pay) a dividend; **außerordentliche Dividende** ~ to cut a melon *(US)*; **Konkursquote** ~ to divide a bankrupt's property (estate).

Ausschüttung | von Börsengewinnen distribution of trading profits; ~ **von Kapitalgewinnen** *(Investmentgesellschaft)* capital distribution.

Außen|anschnitt *(Anzeige)* outside bleed; **~arbeit** field (outside, outdoor) work, outdoor job.

Außenhandel foreign (external) trade, export trade; **sichtbarer** ~ visible trade.

Außenhandels|abteilung export department; **~bank** export bank; **~bilanz** balance of payments; **~defizit** foreign-trade deficit; **~finanzierung** foreign-trade financing; **~förderung** export promotion; **~monopol** export monopoly; **~passivsaldo** adverse foreign-trade balance; **~statistik** export statistics; **~ziffern** export (foreign sales) figures.

Außenorganisation field staff (organization).

Außenstände outstanding (active) debts, outstandings, outs, debts receivables *(US)*; **abgetretene** ~ accounts receivable discounted *(US)*, pledged accounts receivable *(US)*; **nach der Fälligkeit sortierte** ~ aging accounts receivable *(US)*; **unsichere (zweifelhafte)** ~ bad *(Br.),* (doubtful, *US)* debts.

Außen|stelle branch [office], field office; **~umsatz** external turnover.

außer|beruflich outside, extraprofessional; **~e Ausbildung** outside training.

Außerbetrieb|nahme von Anlagegütern retirement (removal) of fixed assets.

außerbörslich on the curb (kerb, *Br.);*
~**er Kurs** curb (kerb, *Br.)* rate.

außer|dienstlich off-duty, unofficial, private; ~**etatsmäßig** extrabudgetary; ~**planmäßig** off-schedule, not as scheduled *(US)*; ~**gerichtlich** | **beilegen** to settle.

Außerkurssetzung withdrawal from circulation.

außerordentliche | **und betriebsfremde Aufwendungen** extraordinary and outside expense; ~ **Erträge** extra profits; ~ **Reserve** *(Versicherungswesen)* catastrophe reserve; ~ **Rücklage** surplus reserve.

außer|planmäßig supernumerary, extracurricular, noncommissioned, *(Zug)* off-schedule *(US)*; ~**tarifliche Zahlungen** payments over and above.

aussetzen *(Flugzeugmotor)* to pack up *(sl.)*, *(Motor)* to fail, to misfire, to conk out;
Belohnung ~ to offer (hold out) a reward; **jem. eine Leibrente** ~ to settle a life annuity on s. o.; **Zahlung** ~ to suspend payment; **Zwangsvollstreckung** ~ to stay execution.

Aussetzung *(Preis)* offer, promise, *(Zahlung)* suspension, moratorium;
~ **einer Belohnung** offering a reward; ~ **einer Rente** settlement of an annuity.

Aussicht view, prospect, outlook, expectation;
mit der ~ **späterer Beteiligung** with a view to partnership;
wirtschaftliche ~**en** propects of the economy;
gute ~**en im Beruf** a job with good prospects.

aussondern *(abtrennen)* to separate, to set apart, *(ausmustern)* to cast off, to reject, *(im Konkurs)* to parcel (sort) out.

Aussonderung *(Geldbeträge)* appropriation, earmarking, *(Konkurs)* parcelling (sorting) out; ~ **ungeeigneter Bewerber** screening of candidates.

aussonderungsberechtigte Forderung colo(u)rable claim.

Aussperrung lockout.

Ausstand [labo(u)r] strike, standout, tie-up, turnout *(Br.)*, walkout *(US)*;
sich im ~ **befinden** to be on strike; **in** ~ **treten** to [go on] strike, to come (walk, *US*) out.

ausstatten, mit Kapital to endow with capital, to capitalize; **mit Vollmachten** ~ to vest (clothe) with authority.

Ausstattung fitting out, outfitting, rig, equipment, *(Aussteuer)* dowry, marriage portion;
in feiner ~ fancy-packed;
erste ~ *(Bankwesen)* initial allocation;
~ **einer Anleihe** terms of a loan; ~ **eines Hotels** appointments for a hotel;
Laden mit gesamter ~ **erwerben** to buy a shop with all fixtures.

Ausstattungs|film feature (costume) film; ~**kosten** cost of equipment, outfit.

ausstehend|e Forderungen outstanding debts, outs, account receivables *(US)*.

ausstellen to make out, to issue, *(auf einer Ausstellung)* to exhibit, to expose, *(im Schaufenster)* to [set on] show, to display;

etw. blanko ~ to make out in blank; **auf den Inhaber** ~ to make out to bearer; **Kreditbrief** ~ to issue a letter of credit; **Waren auf einer Messe** ~ to exhibit goods at a fair; **Reitwechsel** ~ to fly a kite *(Br.)*; **Scheck** ~ to draw (write out, make out) a check *(US)* (cheque, *Br.); **Wechsel an Order** ~ to make out to order.

ausstellende Behörde issuing authority.

Aussteller *(Emittent)* issuer, emitter, *(Kreditbrief)* issuing bank, *(Messe)* exhibitor, shower, *(Wechsel, Scheck)* drawer, maker, writer;
an den ~ **zurück** refer to drawer;
~**verzeichnis** list of exhibitors, fair directory.

Ausstellung making out, drawing, *(Akkreditiv)* issue, issuing, *(Messe)* fair, exhibition, exposure, exposition *(US)*, *(Schau)* show;
~ **eines Frachtbriefes** memorandum billing; ~ **von Gefälligkeitswechseln** kiteflying *(Br.);* ~ **eines Kreditbriefes** issue of a letter of credit; ~ **einer Rechnung** invoicing, making out a bill, billing; ~ **eines Schecks** making out (drawing) a check *(US)* (cheque, *Br.);*
~ **besuchen** to attend a fair.

Ausstellungs|datum date of issue; ~**fläche** [stand]-space, exhibition (floor) space; ~**gebäude** fair (exhibition) buildings; ~**gegenstand** show piece; ~**halle** exhibit hall; ~**material zum Selbstkostenpreis** self-liquidating display; ~**raum** showroom, exhibition (display) room, salon, *(Hotel)* stock (sample) room; ~**stand** exhibition stand; ~**ware** goods displayed.

aussteuern *(Tochter)* to portion off, to endow.

Aussteuerversicherung endowment insurance.

Ausstiegluke *(Raumschiff)* espace hatch.

Ausstoß output, outturn production, run;
~ **pro Arbeitsstunde** manhour output;
~**zahlen** output (production) figures.

ausstrahlen *(Rundfunk)* to transmit, to flash.

Austausch | **von Fertigprodukten gegen Rohstoffe** exchange of finished goods against raw materials; ~ **von Vorstandsmitgliedern** management switch.

Austausch|abkommen two-way agreement; ~**programm** exchange program(me); ~**werkstoff** alternative (alternate, *US*) material, substitute.

Austritts|erklärung resignation, retirement; ~**klausel** escape clause.

ausüben *(berufsmäßig)* to practise, *(Kontrolle)* to exercise, *(Tätigkeit)* to follow, to pursue, to conduct, to perform, to carry on, to exert;
Beruf ~ to pursue an occupation; **Bezugsrecht** ~ to exercise subscription rights; **Handwerk** ~ to ply a trade.

Ausübung | **eines Geschäftsbetriebes** doing business; ~ **eines Gewerbes** carrying on a trade; ~ **des Prämienrechtes** exercise of options.

Ausverkauf selling off (out), winding-up sale;
vollständiger ~ clearance sale, closeout *(US)*; ~ **von Beteiligungen** sell-off of holdings.

Ausverkaufs|abteilung im Erdgeschoß bargain basement; ~ **ware** reduced goods.

ausverkauft cleared, sold (closed, *US*) out, *(Theater)* filled to capacity;

Auswahl choice, assortment, *(Musterkollektion)* assortment;
~ eines repräsentativen Querschnitts sampling; ~ der besseren Risiken *(Versicherung)* selection by the company.

auswählen, stichprobenweise to select at random.

Auswahl|einheit *(Statistik)* sampling unit; ~lehrgang selective course.

Auswanderer emigrant, emigree, migrant;
~büro emigration office.

auswandern to emigrate, to migrate, to expatriate.

Auswanderungs|agent emigrant agent; ~steuer emigration tax.

auswärtiger Vertreter agent in the field.

Ausweich|beruf alternate job; ~betrieb emergency operating center; ~flughafen alternative (satellite) airport.

Ausweis permit, identity card, identification, *(Bank)* return, statement;
monatlicher ~ *(Bank)* monthly statement (return); ~ über die Verwendung von Barmitteln capital reconciliation statement *(Br.)*; ~ über die Verwendung des Grundkapitals statement of [source and] application of funds, summary of balance sheet changes.

ausweisen *(Ausländer)* to deport, to expel, *(in Büchern)* to give account of;
Saldo ~ to turn out (show) a balance.

Ausweispapiere document (identification) papers, credentials.

ausweiten, Notenumlauf to expand the currency.

Ausweitung | des Abzahlungsgeschäftes instalment credit extension; ~ des Fremdumsatzes external turnover expansion; ~ des Produktionsprogramms diversification in manufacturing.

auswerfen *(Gehalt)* to fix, to appoint;
Betrag ~ to allocate a sum.

auswerten to exploit, *(verwerten)* to utilize;
kommerziell ~ to commercialize.

Auswertung einer Meinungsbefragung opinion rating.

Auswirkungen, steuerliche tax effects; kostenmäßige ~ auf den Haushalt budgetary costs.

auszahlen to pay off (out, away), to disburse;
sich ~ to pay, to be worth-while; jem. seinen Gewinnanteil ~ to pay out s. one's share; Teilhaber ~ to buy out a partner.

Auszahlung payout, payment, *(Gläubiger)* reimbursement, *(Überbringer)* remittance;
briefliche ~ remittance by mail *(US)*, payment by letter, mail transfer *(US)*;
~en nur im Erlebensfall payment conditional to survival; ~ der Gehälter salary disbursements; ~ der Schadenssumme loss payment;
~ sperren to stop payment.

Auszahlungs|belege vouchers payable; ~bescheinigung pay voucher; ~ermächtigung authorization to pay, withdrawal warrant; ~kurs *(Anleihe)* percentage; ~postamt money-order office, office

of payment *(Br.)*; ~schalter paying counter; ~sperre stop payment; ~wert *(Anleihe)* net proceeds.

auszeichnen to tag, to label, to ticket;
mit einem Preis ~ to award a prize.

Auszeichnung *(Preis)* award, prize, *(von Waren)* labelling, marking, ticketing, pricing;
höhere ~ *(Preise)* markup; niedrigere ~ *(Preise)* markdown.

ausziehen *(Auszüge machen)* to extract, to docket, to abstract from, *(umziehen)* to move [out];
Konto ~ to make a statement (abstract, *Br.*) of account.

Auszubildender apprentice.

Auszug extract, excerpt, *(Konto)* statement, abstract *(Br.)*, *(Wohnung)* removal, move;
beglaubigter ~ duly certified extract;
~ anfertigen (machen) to make (take) an extract from, *(Konto)* to make a statement (abstract, *Br.*).

Autarkie autarchy, economic (national) self-sufficiency.

Auto [motor]car *(Br.)*, motor vehicle, auto *(US)*, automobile *(US)*;
billiges ~ low-priced car, flivver *(sl.)*;
~ für gehobenere Ansprüche executive-class car; ~ der Mittelklasse intermediate-sized car;
~ abschleppen to pick up a (tow a broken) car;
~ polizeilich anmelden to take a car's number.

Autoausstellung motor exhibition (show), auto (automobile) show *(US)*.

Autobahn freeway *(US)*, motorway *(Br.)*, [automobile] expressway *(US)*;
ähnliche Qualität near motorway standard *(Br.)*; ~ausfahrt exit point; ~gebühr *(US)* turnpike money, intermediate toll.

Autobus omnibus, autobus *(US)*, bus *(fam.)*, *(Überlandfahrt)* [motor] coach.

Auto|empfänger car radio; ~fahrer [car] driver, motorist; ~garage [automobile] garage; ~haftpflichtversicherung motorcar (automobile collision, public liability motor) insuracne; ~industrie motor (automotive, auto, automobile, *US*) industry; ~inspektion durchführen to inspect a car.

Automatenrestaurant self-service restaurant, cafeteria *(US)*, automat.

automatischer Ausgleich *(Lohnklausel)* excalator adjustment.

Auto|mietverleih rent-a-car, car-hire service; ~montagewerk auto assembly; ~nummer car (licence) number; ~reiseführer roadbook, motoring guide.

Autoren|anteil royalty, seigniorage, author's fee, copy money; ~korrektur author's proof (corrections).

Auto|reparatur car (motor, auto) repairs; ~schalter *(Bank)* drive-in windows; ~schlosser motor (automobile, *US*) mechanic, motor fitter, grease monkey *(US sl.)*; ~zubehör automotive components *(US)*.

Aval surety, guarantee *(Br.)*;
~akzept collateral acceptance; ~konto guarantee account; ~wechsel guaranteed bill of exchange.

Avis advice, letter of advice.

B

Babyaktien savings (premium treasury, baby, *US*) bonds.

Bagatell|betrag drab; ~**schulden** small (petty) debts.

Bahn *(Eisenbahn)* rail, railway *(Br.)* railroad *(US)*.

bahnamtliches Rollfuhrunternehmen contract carrier, regular cartage company, goods agent *(Br.)*.

Bahn|anschluß siding, industrial track; ~**fracht** railway *(Br.)* (railroad, *US*) freight; ~**frachtbrief** bill of carriage, waybill.

bahnfrei carriage paid, [delivered] free of station.

Bahnhof [train] station, railway (railroad, *US*) station, depot *(US)*; **frei** ~ free station.

Bahnhofs|anlagen station premises; ~**halle** waiting hall, concourse *(US)*; ~**restaurant** station restaurant.

Bahn|knotenpunkt junction; ≗**lagernd** to be called for at station office; ≗**mäßig verpackt** packed for railway transport; ~**station** railway station; ~**steig** platform; ~**überführung** subway, dry bridge *(US)*; **beschrankter** ~**übergang** crossing with gates; ~**zustellung** rail delivery.

Baisse decline [in prices], depression, fall, drop, slump;

erwartete ~ **im Voraus berücksichtigen** to undersell *(Br.)* (underdiscount, *US*) the market; **auf** ~ **spekulieren** to operate (gamble) for a fall, to speculate on (for) a fall, to [go a] bear *(Br.)*, to sell short *(US)*;

~**angebot** short offer *(US)*; ~**angriff** bearish operation (demonstration, *US*); ~**clique** operators for a fall; ~**engagements** bear accounts *(Br.)*, short stock (position) *(US)*; ~**klausel** slump clause; ~**markt** bear[ish] (falling, short, *US*) market; ~**spekulation** bear[ish] speculation, bear transaction, selling a bear *(Br.)*, going short *(US)*; ~**stimmung** bearish mood, depression of the market; ~**strömung**, ~**tendenz** bearish tendency (tone); ~**termingeschäfte** trading on the short side *(US)*.

Ballast | abwerfen to discharge ballast; ~**fracht** dead freight.

Ballen bale, pack, package, parcel, bundle; **Waren in** ~ **verkaufen** to sell in bale.

Ballungs|gebiet, ~**raum** congested (overcrowded) area.

Band *(Bandgerät)* tape, *(Schreibmaschine)* ribbon; **am laufenden** ~ on the assembly line; **aufs** ~ **sprechen** to record one's voice; ~**aufnahme** tape recording, ~**breite** *(Kursschwankungen)* band, spread, *(Vorhersage)* prediction interval; ~**breitensatz** *(Währungen)* floating rate.

Banderole revenue stamp.

Banderolensteuer stamp duty (tax).

Bank bank[ing house], banker, banking firm; **ohne Angabe einer bestimmten** ~ *(Scheck)* crossed generally; **dem Abrechnungsverkehr angeschlossene** ~ clearing bank; **auswärtige** ~ out-of-town bank; **bezogene** ~ drawee bank; **halbstaatliche** ~ semi-private bank; **konsortialführende** ~ originating banker, syndicate manager; **korrespondierende** ~ reporting bank; **zahlungsunfähige** ~ insolvent bank; ~ **für internationalen Zahlungsausgleich** Bank for International Settlements; **von der** ~ **abheben** to withdraw from a bank; **seine** ~ **anweisen** to instruct one's bank; ~ **einschalten** to interpolate a bank; **Geld bei der** ~ **einzahlen** to put money in (pay into) a bank; **Kredit bei der** ~ **in erhöhtem Maße in Anspruch nehmen** to increase the borrowings at the bank; **bei der** ~ **in Debet sein** to be overdrawn at the bank.

Bank|abhebungen bank withdrawals; ~**abschluß** bank return *(Br.)* (statement); **erstklassiges** ~**akzept** fine bank acceptance *(Br.)*, prime banker's acceptance *(US)*; ~**anweisung** bank check (cheque, *Br.*, bill, draft), registered check; ~**aufsichtsbehörde** bank supervisory commission, state superintendence of banks *(US)*; ~**auskunft** banker's reference; ~**ausleihungen** bank lending; ~**ausweis** balance of a bank, bank report (return, *Br.*, statement); ~**belege** bank receipts (records); ~**bilanz** bank balance sheet; ~**bote** bank messenger; ~**depot** bank deposit, deposit in a bank; ~**direktor** bank manager; ~**diskont** bank (banker's) discount, bank *(Br.)* (discount) rate.

Banken|abrechnung bank clearing; ~**apparat** banking system; ~**fusion** bank merger; ~**intervention** *(Börse)* banking support; ~**konsortium** banking syndicate, bank consortium; ~**liquidität** easy money market *(US)*; ~**privileg** free banking system; ~**zentrum** financial center *(US)* (centre, *Br.*).

Bankfach *(Gewerbe)* banking [business], banking field;

~**mann** financial expert.

bankfähig bankable, negotiable.

Bank|fazilitäten banking accommodation (facilities); ~**feiertag** bank holiday.

bankfremd|es Geschäft nonbanking business (activity); ~**e Interessen** nonbanking interests.

Bank|garantie bank guarantee (guaranty, *US*); ~**geheimnis** bank (banking) secrecy.

Bankgeschäft banking, business of banking, *(Bankfirma)* banking house (establishment); **irreguläre** ~**e** supplementary banking functions; **sämtliche** ~**e ausführen** to transact all types of banking.

Bank|grundstück bank premises; ~**guthaben** balance (sum) at the bank, bank balance (funds, holdings); ~**haus** bank, banking house.

Bankier sein to bank, to do business as a banker.

Bank|indossament bank stamp *(US)*; ~**inhaber** proprietor of a bank; ~**institut** banking institution, bank establishment.

Bankkonto bank[ing] account, checking account *(US)*;

überzogenes ~ [bank] overdraft, overdraught *(Br.)*; ~ eröffnen to open a bank account; ~pfänden to garnish a bank account; ~überziehen to overdraw one's account.

Bank|konzern banking concern; ~konzession bank charter.

Bankkredit bank (commercial) credit, banker's advance;

~ aufnehmen to take up money at a bank; ~e revolvierend einsetzen to roll over bank loans on a continuing basis.

Bank|krise banking crisis; ~kunde bank's client, customer (depositor) of a bank; ~liquidität liquidity of a bank.

bankmäßige Sicherheit collateral security *(US)*.

Bank|monopol note-issuing monopoly; ~note bank note *(US)* (bill, *Br.*), note, paper, bill *(US)*.

Banknoten|ausgabe note issue *(Br.)*; ~druck banknote printing; ~fälscher note forger, forger (counterfeiter) of bank notes, greengoods dealer *(US sl.)*; ~fälschung bill forgery, forgery of bank notes; ~ monopol note-issuing monopoly; ~umlauf circulation (currency) of bank notes.

Bank|platz banking centre (place); ~räuber bank robber; goldene ~regel banker's rule; ~revisor bank inspector (auditor, examiner, *US*).

Bankrott bankruptcy, smash, smashup, burst-up, bust, blowup *(US)*, failure;

am Rande des ~s verging on bankruptcy; betrügerischer ~ fraudulent bankruptcy; unverschuldeter ~ casual (simple) bankruptcy; seinen ~ anmelden to file a petition in bankruptcy.

bankrott bankrupt, bust, in chancery;

gänzlich ~ dead broke *(US)*; j. öffentlich ~ erklären to declare (adjudicate) s. o. judicially to be a bankrupt; ~ machen to become (go) bankrupt, to smash (wind, *US*) up, to fold *(Br.)*

Bank|saldo bank balance; ~schalter window *(US)*; ~scheck bank check *(US)* (cheque, *Br.*), check drawn on a bank, bank[er's] draft, cashier's check *(US)* (cheque, *Br.)*; ~schließfach safe [deposit box]; nach ~schluß after banking hours; mit den ~schulden hinter den Lieferantenschulden zurücktreten to subordinate bank debt to trade debt; ~spesen bank charges, service and activity charge; ~tätigkeit banking activity (activities).

banktechnische Einrichtungen banking facilities.

Bank|transaktion banking transaction (operation); ~tratte bank draft; ~tresor safe deposit, strong room, vault; ~unterschlagung bank embezzlement; ~usance banking custom (practice); ~valuta bank money; ~verbindung banker, bank *(einer Bank)* correspondent; ~verpflichtungen *(Bilanz)* due to banks; kurzfristige ~vorschüsse day-to-day advances from banks; ~wechsel bank acceptance (bill, draft); ~zinsen interest on deposits, *(Sollzinsen)* interest on loan capital (bank loans).

bar cash [down], cash in hand, prompt, ready;

Verkauf nur gegen ~ cash sales only;

in ~ oder in Sachleistungen in cash or in kind; ~ auf den Tisch bezahlen to pay [cash] down (in cash), to pay in cash (ready money); ~e Ausgaben cash expenditure; ~er Rückkaufwert *(Lebensversicherung)* cash surrender value.

Bar|abfindung settlement in cash; ~abhebung cash withdrawal; ~abschluß cash transaction; ~anschaffung remittance (payment) in cash; ~auslagen actual (out-of-pocket, *Br.)* expenses; ~auszahlung payment in cash; ~bestand amount of cash, cash on (in) hand; ~deckung anschaffen to deposit a margin in cash *(US)*; ~depot cash deposit; ~einlage cash investment; ~einschuß leisten to deposit a margin in cash *(US)*.

Bargeld cash [in (on) hand], ready cash;

so gut wie ~ as good as ready money; knapp an ~ sein to be short of cash; ~bestand cash balance.

bargeldlos without ready money, paid by check (cheque, *Br.*), cashless *(US)*;

~es Verkaufssystem credit-coupon plan; ~er Zahlungsverkehr clearing system, *(Kaufhaus)* drawback system.

Bar|geldverkehr trade on cash terms, cash transactions; ~guthaben balance in cash, cash balance (assets); ~lohn wage paid in cash; ~mittel cash [funds], *(Investmentfonds)* cash reserve; kurzfristige ~mittelanlage short-term harbo(u)r for one's cash.

Barren bar, ingot, *(Gold, Silber)* bullion;

~gold [gold] bullion; ~silber bar silver.

Bar|reserve money reserve, *(Bank)* minimum cash reserve; ~scheck open check (cheque, *Br.*), cash cheque *(Br.)*, uncrossed check *(US)* (cheque, *Br.),* customer's check; ~sendung cash remittance; ~vergütung money allowance, *(Lebensversicherung)* cash bonus; ~verkaufswert cash value; ~vorrat der Bank bullion at the bank.

Barzahlung cash [payment], cash downpayment;

gegen ~ for prompt cash; bei ~ 5 % Rabatt five per cent discount for cash; sofortige ~ prompt cash payment, spot cash; auf ~ berechnen to base on cash; sofortige ~ verlangen to demand cash on the barrelhead.

Barzahlungs|basis cash basis; ~bedingungen cash terms, *(Börse)* spot conditions; ~preis cash price; ~rabatt cash discount, discount for cash.

Batzen Geld kosten to cost a pretty penny.

Bau *(Bauart)* fabric, fabrication, structure, *(Maschinen)* manufacture, construction;

~abnahme [quantity, *Br.*] surveying; ~arbeiten *(Straßenarbeiten)* road repairs; ~auftrag im Submissionswege vergeben to job a building contract; ~ausnahmegenehmigung exception, *(für Geschäftshäuser)* spot zoning *(US)*; ~beschränkungen building (zoning, *US*) restriction; ~bewilligung building permit *(US)*.

Bauern|gut farm, farmhold, farmyard; durch die Familie bewirtschafteter ~hof family-sized farm *(US)*.

baufähiges Land building estate (site).
baufällig dilapidated, derelict, ramshackle, tumble-down, crazy, ruinous, in bad repair.
Bau|finanzierung constructional financing; ~**firma** building constructor; **nicht erschlossenes** ~**gelände** undeveloped land *(Br.)*; ~**geldhypothek** development (construction) mortgage; ~**gewerbe** building line; ~**grundstück** plot of land, building plot; ~**industrie** building trade, building (construction) industry; ~**jahr** year of construction (manufacture); ~**jahr 1978** 1978 model; ~**konjunktur** building boom.
Baukosten building expenses, builder's price, construction costs (prices), cost of construction (building);
  ~**index** construction cost index; ~**voranschlag** building estimate, bill of quantities *(Br.)*; **verlorener** ~**zuschuß** *(Mieter)* key money *(Br.)*
Baukredit building loan.
Bauland building ground (plot, site, land);
  ~**beschaffung** assembling of plots.
Bauplatz building ground (site, yard, lot).
baureif ripe for development, developed;
Bausch, in ~ **und Bogen** in bulk (blocks), in the gross (lump), wholesale;
  in ~ **und Bogen verkaufen** to sell by bulk.
Bau|sparer investing member *(Br.)*; **zugeteilter** ~**sparer** advanced (borrowing) member *(Br.)*; ~**sparkasse** building society *(Br.)*, house owner's loan corporation *(US)*, home building and loan (homestead-aid benefit) association *(US)*.
Bau|unternehmer [master] builder, house builder; **schlüsselfertiger** ~**vertrag** turnkey contract *(US)*; ~**wirtschaft** building trade (business), construction industry.
Beamter official, officer, officeholder, executive *(US)*, *(höherer)* functionary, executive, magistrate, *(Staatsbeamter)* civil servant *(Br.)*, government official *(US)*, public servant *(US)*;
  festangestellter ~ permanent (salaried) officer;
  ~ **des gehobeneren Dienstes** higher-echelon official.
Beamtenpension service pension.
beanspruchen, öffentliche Mittel to have recourse to public money.
Beanspruchung *(Maschine)* stress, strain;
  steuerliche ~ tax demands.
beanstanden, Rechnungsposten to query the items of an account.
Beanstandung von Waren rejection of goods delivered.
beantragen, Bezugsschein to apply for a purchasing permit; **Schadensersatz** ~ to make a claim for damages.
bearbeiten *(Akten)* to treat, to deal with, *(Kunden)* to canvass, *(maschinell)* to tool;
  Bezirk ~ *(Vertreter)* to work a district.
Bearbeitung handling, preparation, *(Akten)* treatment, handling, *(Kunden)* canvassing;
  ~ **von Steuerunterlagen** tax work; ~ **von Versicherungsansprüchen** claim administration.

Bearbeitungs|gebühr handling (processing) fee (charge), *(Bank)* service charge; ~**verbot** processing prohibition.
Beauftragter mandatary, commissioner, assign, *(persönlicher Vertreter)* private attorney.
bebaute | **Fläche** built-up area; ~ **und unbebaute Grundstücke** *(Bilanz)* real estate.
Bebauungsplan zoning ordinance *(US)*, development plan *(Br.)*.
Bedarf need, want, supply, requisition, demand; **nach** ~ when required;
  aufgestauter ~ pent-up (replacement) demand; **lebensnotwendiger** ~ necessaries of life; **öffentlicher** ~ public needs; **persönlicher** ~ personal use (requirements, wants); **gesamter volkswirtschaftlicher** ~ schedule demand;
  täglicher ~ **an Lebensmitteln** daily supply of food; ~ **der Verbraucher** consumer needs;
  nur für den eigenen ~ **arbeiten** to produce only for its own requirements; ~ **decken** to cover (comply with) the requirements, to meet the demands; **nach** ~ **halten** *(Zug)* to stop when required; ~ **hervorrufen (schaffen)** to create a demand.
Bedarfs|anflughafen flag station (stop, *US*); ~**artikel** necessaries, requisites, consumer goods; ~**deckung** commodity coverage; ~**elastizität** elasticity of demand; ~**frage einer Lizenz prüfen** to examine the need for granting a licence; **gehobene** ~**güter** luxuries and semiluxuries; ~**haltestelle** flag station (stop, *US*), halt *(Br.)*, request (whistle, *US*) stop; ~**lenkung** consumption control; ~**nachweis** certificate of convenience and necessity; ~**spitze im Saisonverkauf** peak of demand; ~**träger** user, consumer.
bedienen to wait upon, to serve, to attend, *(Maschine)* to operate, to work.
Bedienung attendance, service, serving, *(Laden)* shop assistant[s], *(Maschinen)* operation;
  einschließlich ~ attendance included;
Bedienungs|anleitung, -anweisung operation (working, service) instructions; ~**zuschlag** service charge.
bedingt | **arbeitsfähig** partially disabled;
  ~**e Annahme** *(Wechsel)* qualified acceptance.
Bedingung condition, clause, provision, proviso;
  Kurzschrift erwünscht, aber nicht ~ shorthand an advantage but not essential.
Bedingungen, kulante liberal settlement;
  ~ **für Kundenkonten** charge account terms;
  jem. vorteilhafte ~ **gewähren** to make good terms with s. o..
Bedrängnis, finanzielle embarrassment, narrow straits.
bedrängt, in ~**en Verhältnissen leben** to live in cramped conditions.
Bedürfnis need, want, necessity, requirement;
  öffentliches ~ public necessity, reasonable public demand.
Bedürfnisse | **des Einzelhandels** retail [trade] demands;
  auf jds. ~ **abstellen** to tailor to s. one's specific needs.

Bedürftigkeitsnachweis means (needs) test *(Br.)*.

beeidigter | Bücherrevisor chartered (certified, *US*) accountant; ~ **Makler** sworn broker.

Beeinflussung | der Börsenkurse durch Konzertzeichnungen stagging the market; ~ **des Lohnniveaus** wage leadership.

beeinträchtigen, jds. Interessen to affect (prejudice) s. one's interest.

Beeinträchtigung impairment, infringement, interference.

Befähigungsnachweis qualifying certificate, certificate of convenience and necessity *(US)*.

befahrbar passable, carriageable, vehicular, trafficable *(US)*, *(Gewässer)* navigable.

befördern to carry, to transfer, to convey, *(absenden)* to dispatch, to forward, to consign, *(Angestellte, Beamte)* to promote, to advance, to prefer, to upgrade;
mit der Bahn ~ to transport (send) by rail, to rail goods; **bevorzugt** ~ to promote with priority; **als Eilgut** ~ to forward by express train; **Post mit dem Flugzeug** ~ to transport post (mail, *US*) by airplane; **Telegramm** ~ to transmit (handle) a telegram.

Beförderung carriage, carrying, conveyance, *(Güter)* haul, haulage, freightage, shipment *(US)*, *(Telegramm)* handling;
~ **per Achse** road transport; ~ **per Bahn** transportation by rail; ~ **nach dem Dienstalter** promotion by seniority; ~ **als Drucksache** book post *(Br.)*; ~ **als Eilgut** carrying express; ~ **mit dem Lastkraftwagen** motor-truck transport; ~ **auf dem Luftwege** air transport; ~ **auf dem Seewege** marine transport, carriage by sea;~ **durch öffentliche Verkehrsmittel** common carrier transportation.

Beförderungs|alter seniority; ~**aussichten** *(Stellung)* promotional status; ~**gebühr** carriage, *(Post)* postage; ~**gesellschaft** highway carrier *(US)*; ~**liste** *(Stellung)* advancement, (promotion) roster; **öffentliche** ~**mittel** public conveyance; ~**richtlinien** *(Stellung)* lines of promotion; ~**steuer** transport tax, railway passenger duty *(Br.)*; ~**tabelle** opportunity chart; ~**unternehmen** haulage contractor, carrier, forwarding (shipping, *US*) agent; ~**vertrag** contract of carriage, shipping contract *(US)*; ~**zulage** *(Stellung)* seniority pay.

befrachten to charter, to freight, to load.

Befrachtung nach dem Wert freighting ad valorem.

Befrachtungsvertrag contract of affreightment, charterparty.

Befragung poll, survey;
~ **eines beschränkten Personenkreises** sample testing; ~ **auf dem Postwege** mail survey.

befreien, von Gemeindesteuern to derate of local taxes; **von einer Steuer** ~ to exempt from a tax.

Befreiung | von der Doppelbesteuerung double taxation relief; ~ **von der Zollrevision des Gepäcks** courtesy of the port *(US)*.

befriedigen to satisfy, *(bezahlen)* to pay off, *(Nachfrage)* to meet;
seine Gläubiger im Vergleichswege ~ to compound with one's creditors.

Befriedigung satisfaction, gratification;
abgesonderte ~ preferential treatment (payment).

befristet|e Einlage *(bei Bank)* time deposit; ~**er Scheck** memorandum check *(US)*.

befürworten to recommend, to advocate;
Antrag ~ to second a motion.

Befürwortungsschreiben letter of recommendation, letters recommendatory.

begebbar negotiable, endorsable, transferable;
~**es Wertpapier** negotiable instrument.

begeben, Aktien to market securities; **Anleihe** ~ to issue (float) a loan; **Wechsel** ~ to negotiate a bill.

Begebung | einer Anleihe issue (floating, flotation) of a loan; ~ **von Wertpapieren** sale of securities.

Begebungs|kosten issuing expenses; ~**preis** issue price; ~**tag** day of issue.

begehrt requested, inquired for, in demand (request), in favo(u)r, *(Geld)* scarce;
~**er Artikel** popular line.

Beginn | des Entladens breaking bulk; ~ **der Laufzeit einer Police** commencement of a policy.

beglaubigen *(Kontoauszug)* to verify, *(Unterschrift)* to certify.

beglaubigt|e Abschrift attested (exemplified) copy; ~**er Scheck** certified (guaranteed) check (cheque, *Br.*).

Beglaubigung authentication, verification, certification, caption, acknowledgement, attestation;
~ **der Unterschrift** verification of signature.

begleichen, Rechnung to meet a bill, to settle an account.

Begleichung payment, settlement, clearance;
~ **von Schulden** liquidation of debts.

Begleit|adresse accompanying address, declaration form, dispatch note *(Br.)*; ~**papiere** accompanying documents; ~**schiff** escort vessel, convoy ship.

begrenzter Absatzmarkt limited market.

begründeter Anspruch legitimate claim.

Begründung eines Vertreterverhältnisses creation of agency.

Begrüßungs|ansprache, ~rede salutatory, welcome (salutational) address.

begünstigen to favo(u)r, to aid, to benefit, *(Gläubiger)* to give a preference, to prefer.

Begünstigter beneficiary, accommodated party, *(Akkreditiv)* payee, *(Gläubiger)* preferred creditor;
~ **eines Vertrages zugunsten Dritter** third-party beneficiary (creditor, donee).

Begünstigungstarif preferential tariff.

Behälter, mehrfach verwendbarer container premium; ~**frachtversand** container shipment; ~**zug** container train.

behandeln, unterschiedlich *(Zollgüter)* to discriminate; **beim Transport vorsichtig** ~ to handle with care in carriage.

Behandlung treatment, manipulation, handling;
diskriminierende ~ discrimination; **sachgemäße** ~ proper usage; **zollrechtliche** ~ customs treatment.

behaupten, sich *(Kurse)* to hold one's ground, to keep (remain) steady, to remain firm.

Behebung | der Arbeitslosigkeit alleviation of unemployment; **~ einer Verkehrsschwierigkeit** relief of a traffic jam.

Behelfs|flugplatz emergency landing field, airstrip; **~garage** carport; **~heim** makeshift home.

behelfsmäßig makeshift[y], picknicky, in a rough-and-ready manner, by way of expedient; **j. ~ unterbringen** to put s. o. up.

Behörden|kundschaft institutional user; **~vermittler** contact man.

Beibehaltung langjähriger Angestellter bei Entlassungen bumping *(US)*, backtracking *(US)*.

Beihilfe benefit, assistance, *(Gemeinde)* grants in aid.

Beilage inclosure, enclosure, subjunction, exhibit, supplement, *(Reklame)* stuffer *(US)*, inset; **lose ~** loose inset; **~material** stuffer; **~prospekt** insert.

Beirat advisory board (group), board of trustees, superintending committee, prudential committee *(US)*, *(Einzelperson)* counsel, adviser.

Beirats|empfehlung council recommendation; **~mitglied** member of a council.

beiseite bringen, Geld to misappropriate funds.

beisteuern, zur Deckung der Unkosten to contribute towards the expenses.

Beitrag contribution, *(Anteil)* share, quota, portion, scot, *(Mitglied)* subscription, [membership] dues *(US)*, *(Umlage)* assessment *(US)*, dues *(US)*, *(Versicherung)* premium; **eingesammelter ~** whip[-round]; **laufender ~** periodical contribution; **steuerabzugsfähiger ~** deductible subscription; **wissenschaftlicher ~** contribution to a paper; **~ zu wohltätigen Zwecken** charitable contribution, contribution of alms; **~ zu den Unterhaltungskosten leisten** to make contributions towards the costs of maintenance; **seinen ~ zahlen** to pay one's subscription (contribution, dues, *US*).

Beiträge, freiwillige voluntary contributions; **~ zur Altersversorgung** *(Bilanz)* contribution to pension trust; **durch ~ aufbringen** to subscribe; **~ zur Pensionskasse leisten** to make contributions to the pension trust.

Beitrags|anteil subscription quota; **~bemessung** rating, assessment, tariffing *(US)*; **~befreiung** *(Versicherung)* waiver of premium; **~erhöhung** increased contributions, dues increase *(US)*.

beitragsfreies Pensionssystem company-financed pension plan (scheme).

Beitragsleistung subscriptions, contribution, dues *(US)*; **mit seinen ~en im Rückstand sein** to be in arrears with the payment of one's contributions.

beitragspflichtig contributory, liable to contribution (subscription); **~e Pension** contributory pension.

Beitrags|pflichtiger contributory; **~rückerstattung** return of contribution, policy dividend; **~staffelung** *(Versicherung)* scale (grading) of premiums.

beitragszahlendes Mitglied subscribing member.

Beitreibung von Steuern collection of taxes.

Beitritt adhesion, adherence, *(Vertrag)* accedence, **~zum Gemeinsamen Markt** entry into the Common Market.

bekanntgeben to notify, to make known; **amtlich ~** to gazette, to bulletin; **durch Aushang ~** to post up.

Bekanntmachung notification, *(Anschlag)* notice, *(Verlautbarung)* communiqué, bulletin; **geschäftliche ~** trade publication; **~ über die Einlösung und Tilgung von Wertpapieren** notice of redemption, sinking-fund notice *(US)*.

Beköstigungsgeld quarters allowance, allowance for board.

Beladungsgrenze load limit.

belasten *(anrechnen)* to charge, to debit, to count, to note down, to bill *(US)*; **Eisenbahnverkehr ~** to make demands on railway lines; **Etat mit etw. ~** to burden the budget; **Grundstück mit einer Hypothek ~** to mortgage a piece of real estate; **dem Kunden Porto ~** to charge the postage to the customer; **Zinsen ~** to charge interest.

belastet charged with, debited, *(Grundstück)* servient, *(mit Hypothek)* mortgaged, *(Telefonnetz)* busy; **abends am stärksten ~ sein** *(Straßen)* to have its peak hours in the evening.

Belastung charge, burden, drag, incidence, *(Konto)* debiting, debit entry, charge, charging; **finanzielle ~** financial strain (beating, burden, load), money charge; **übermäßige steuerliche ~** overtaxation; **~ für das Geschäft darstellen** to be a dead weight (drain) on the business; **~en des Schuldentilgungsdienstes erfüllen** to meet debt-service charges.

Belastungs|anzeige advice of debit, debit note (advice, memorandum, *US*); **~fähigkeit** *(Maschine)* carrying capacity; **~spitze** *(Bahn)* peak load.

belaufen, sich to amount (come, mount up, run) to.

Beleg *(Akte)* record, *(Beweisstück)* evidence, proof, *(für Buchung)* voucher, slip, *(Quittung)* receipt; **abgestempelter ~** voucher stamp; **~ abheften** to file a voucher.

Beleg|buch slip book; **~buchhaltung** voucher system (bookkeeping); **vollständiges ~doppel, ~duplikat** complete voucher copy.

Belegen | von Frachtraum freight bookings; **~ von Sendezeiten** time buying.

belegen, mit Abgaben to tax, to levy taxes (duties); **Abrechnung mit Quittungen ~** to accompany an account with receipts; **Frachtraum ~** to book freight; **Sendezeit ~** to buy time.

Beleg|exemplar checking (voucher, specimen) copy, tear sheet (ticket, *US*); **~inventur** cost-voucher inventory; **~nummer** checking copy; **~sammlung** voucher register.

Belegschaft [shop] staff, workroom staff, workforce, [operating] personnel, [production] force *(US)*; ~ **reduzieren (verringern)** to pare the workforce.

Belegschaft|abbau personnel cutback; ~**abgänge** labo(u)r-force dropouts; ~**aktien** staff shares *(Br.)*, employee stock *(US)*; **langjähriges** ~**mitglied** company old-timer; **völlige** ~**umschichtung** thorough turnover of the operational force; ~**wechsel** staff turnover.

Beleg|seite tear sheet (ticket, *US*); ~**stück** voucher (checking) copy.

Belegung *(Platz)* booking, reservation *(US)*.

beleihbar pledgeable, *(Wertpapier)* eligible to serve as collateral.

beleihen to lend, to [grant a] loan, to borrow, *(Grundstücke)* to hypothecate, to mortgage; **Effekten** ~ **[lassen]** to advance money on securities, to lodge stock as security *(US)*, to collateral securities.

Beleihung lending, borrowing, granting a loan; ~ **einer Versicherung** policy loan.

Beleihungs|grenze credit line; ~**wert** loan (collateral) value, *(mit Hypothek)* hypothecary value *(US)*.

beliebt in request (favo(u)r, (demand), *(Mode)* in vogue, fashionable, *(Wertpapiere)* in demand.

beliefern to provide, to supply, to stock, to furnish; **mit einem Sortiment** ~ to furnish with an assortment.

Belohnung reward, rewarding, remuneration.

bemessen to rate, to assess, to measure; **Zuteilung knappstens** ~ to cut an allocation as fine as possible.

bemittelt well-to-do *(Br.)*, well off.

Bemühungen, j. für seine ~ **entschädigen** to remunerate (pay) s. o. for his trouble.

bemustern to pattern, to sample.

Benachrichtigung notice, notification, information, *(Handelssprache)* advice [note], aviso; **ohne vorherige** ~ **zahlbar** payable on demand; **sofortige** ~ *(vom Eintritt des Versicherungsfalles)* immediate notice; ~ **über die Nichteinlösung** *(Wechsel)* notice of dishono(u)r.

Benachrichtigungsschreiben letter of advice.

benachteiligen, Gläubiger to prefer one creditor over the others.

benachteiligende Zollsätze discriminating duties.

Benachteiligung handicap, damage, injury, *(Gläubiger)* prejudice, *(Zoll)* discrimination; ~ **im Arbeitsleben** job discrimination *(US)*.

Benutzung appropriation, usage, use, user; ~ **öffentlicher Verkehrsmittel** commutation *(US)*; **für die öffentliche** ~ **freigeben** to throw open to the public.

Benutzungs|gebühren, ~**kosten** user fee (tax).

Benzin petrol *(Br.)*, motor spirit, fuel, gas, gasoline *(US)*, juice *(US sl.)*; **kein** ~ **mehr haben** to be short of petrol *(Br.)*, to run out of gasoline *(US)*; ~**kanister** gasoline container *(US)*; ~**tank** petrol

(Br.) (gas) tank; ~**verbrauch** petrol *(Br.)* (fuel) consumption; ~**zuteilung** petrol allowance (ration) *(Br.)*.

Beobachtungszeit *(Zeitstudie)* attention time.

bequem | zu bewirtschaften built for convenience; ~**e Raten** easy terms.

Berater | des Vorstands staff officer, outside director; ~**gruppe** advisory group.

Beratung counsel *(US)*, council, consultation, *(Beratschlagung)* deliberation, meeting, conference; **finanzielle** ~ financial advice; ~ **auf allen Gebieten** full service; ~ **in Steuerangelegenheiten** tax service.

Beratungs|firma consulting organization; ~**gremium** advisory board (body); ~**raum** *(Hotel)* customers' room.

berechnen *(abschätzen)* to estimate, to evaluate, to assess, to appraise, to rate, to bring [in]to account, to charge, to bill; **Fracht** ~ to charge freight; **Frist** ~ to compute a period; **Gebühr** ~ to charge a fee; **dem Kunden das Porto** ~ to put (charge) the postage to the consumer; **jem. etw. zum Selbstkostenpreis** ~ to let s. o. have s. th. at cost price; **Tara** ~ to rate the tare.

berechnet charged, billed; **nach dem Tageskurs von . . .** ~ **werden** to be calculated at the rate of exchange ruling on . . .; **auf Basis von 360 Tagen** ~**e Zinsen** ordinary (exact) interest.

Berechnung reckoning, *(Belastung)* charge, charging, *(Fakturieren)* billing, invoicing, *(Preisstellung)* pricing, quotation *(Rechnung)* calculation, computation; **bei billigster (niedrigster)** ~ on most moderate terms, at the lowest price (calculation); ~ **der Produktionskosten** process costing; ~ **der Selbstkosten** costing, cost accounting; ~ **von Zinsen** computation of interest.

Berechnungs|einheit work unit; ~**fehler** computational error; ~**methode** method of computation, *(Preis)* pricing method; ~**tabelle** *(Lebensversicherung)* experience table; ~**zeitraum** period of computation.

berechtigt|er Anspruch legitimate claim; ~**es Interesse** lawful interest.

Berechtigter party entitled, *(Eigentümer)* rightful owner, *(Lebensversicherung)* beneficiary.

Berechtigung justification, *(Eignung)* qualification, *(Rechtsanspruch)* right, title, claim, validity; ~ **zum freien Eintritt** free admission.

Berechtigungsschein voucher, written authorization, certificate, scrip, *(Dividende)* warrant; ~ **zum Erwerb (Bezug) neuer Aktien** subscription warrant *(Br.)*, stock allotment *(US)*, stock scrip *(US)*; ~ **auf bevorzugte Lieferung** certificate of priority.

Bereich reach, realm, precinct, beat, *(Einflußsphäre)* orbit, *(Gebiet)* sphere, field, domain, province, purview; **im industriellen** ~ in the industrial field.

bereichern, sich to line one's pockets.
Bereichsleiter area director.
bereinigen to settle, *(Statistik)* to adjust, *(Wertpapiere)* to revalidate, to reassess.
Bereinigung settlement, regularization, *(Bilanz)* verification, *(Wertpapiere)* reassessment.
bereisen, Bezirk ~ to work on (cover) a district.
bereitstehen, zur Abholung to be ready for collection.
bereitstellen, Geld to provide (appropriate) money; **Geld für einen bestimmten Zweck** ~ to earmark funds; **für Steuern** ~ to allow (make provision) for taxation.
Bereitstellung setting apart, provision, *(Gelder)* appropriation;
~ **von Arbeitsplätzen** job availability; ~ **für Einkommensteuererzahlungen** provision for income tax; ~ **von Geldbeträgen für bestimmte Zwecke** earmarking of funds.
Bereitstellungs|konto appropriation account; ~**kosten** stand-by charges; ~**kredit** commitment credit.
Bergarbeiter mineworker, coal miner, collier, pitman.
Bergbau mining, working of mines, mine work;
~ **betreiben** to work minerals;
~**gesellschaft** mining company (partnership);
~**konzession** mining licence (concession).
Bergegeld salvage money.
bergen, Bruchladung to make salvage of a shipwrecked cargo.
Bergungs|arbeiten salvage operations; ~**gebühren** salvage dues; ~**mannschaft** rescue party (squad); ~**schaden** salvage loss.
Bergwerk mine;
~ **ausbeuten (betreiben)** to work a mine at a profit.
Bergwerksunternehmen mining venture.
Bericht report, account, story, statement, notice; **laut** ~ as per advice, advised, as advised by; **offizieller** ~ official bulletin;
~ **einer Kreditauskunftei** mercantile (agency business, *US)* report; ~ **des Wirtschaftsministeriums** Commerce Department Report *(US)*;
~ **einreichen** to submit (file) a report.
Berichterstatter referee, *(Rundfunk)* commentator, *(Zeitung)* [newspaper] correspondent, writer, reporter, item man *(US)*.
berichtigen, Buchung to adjust an entry; **Preisliste** ~ to revise a price list.
Berichtigung rectification, *(Ausgleich)* settlement;
~ **des Aktienkapitals** readjustment of capital stock;
~ **der Vorjahresbilanz** prior-year adjustment.
Berichtigungs|aktie scrip issue *(Br.)*, stock dividend *(US)*; ~**buchung** adjustment entry, adjusting journal (correcting, rectifying) entry; ~**spalte** adjustment column; ~**veranlagung** *(Steuern)* reassessment.
Berichts|abfassung report writing; ~**familie einer Haushaltsbefragung** household budget survey participant; ~**zeitraum** given (covered) period.
Berücksichtigung des billigsten Angebots allocation to the lowest tender.

Beruf profession [of business], occupation, job, *(Fach)* line, department, *(Gewerbe)* trade, craft, walk, *(Geschäft)* business, shop, *(Stellung)* employment, position, post, situation, station; **ohne** ~ no occupation, without a trade; **akademischer** ~ learned profession; **hoch bezahlter** ~ top-paying job; **gefährlicher** ~ hazardous employment; **handwerklicher** ~ handicraft pursuits; **freie oder sonstige selbständige** ~**e** *(Einkommensteuererklärung)* profession or vocation; ~ **ohne Aufstiegsmöglichkeiten** terminal (blind-alley) job;
seinen ~ **als Berufung auffassen** to think of one's vocation in terms of professional status; ~ **ausüben** to carry (ply, follow) a trade; **keinen festen** ~ **ausüben** to have no regular profession; ~ **ergreifen** to take up (go in for, enter) a profession; **sich nur für seinen** ~ **interessieren** to smell of the shop; **keinem bestimmten** ~ **nachgehen** to be without any particular profession; **in seinen** ~ **erfolgreich sein** to do one's job well; **seinen** ~ **wechseln** to change one's vocation, *(häufig)* to job-hop, to switch a job.
beruflich | verreist away on business;
j. ~ **in Anspruch nehmen** to take professional advice from s. o.; ~ **ausgebildet sein** to have learned a trade; ~ **verhindert sein** to be detained by work;
~**e Ausbildung** occupational training; ~**er Werdegang eines Bewerbers** candidate career.
Berufs|analyse vocational analysis; ~**arfgaben** vocational data; ~**ausbildung** vocational (professional) *education;* ~**aussichten** professional (job) prospects; **hochqualifizierter** ~**beamter** high-career civil service officer; ~**beratung** vocational (job) counseling *(US)*; ~**bezeichnung** occupational name, job identification, business title; **innerbetriebliche** ~**förderung** in-service training *(US)*; ~**geheimnis** professional secrecy (confidence); ~**konsul** professional (career) consul; ~**krankheit** occupational disease *(Br.)*; ~**laufbahn** career, walk of life; ~**leben** occupation, professional (working) life.
berufsmäßig ausüben to professionalize.
Berufs|risiko occupational hazard (risk), job hazard, risk incident to employment; ~**schule** professional (vocational, trade, training, day continuation) school; **alle** ~**sparten** all walks of life; ~**stand** specialized vocation.
berufstätig working, having a job, employed, occupied, engaged;
~**e Frau** professional (career) woman.
Berufs|tätigkeit professional activity (employment); ~**umschulung** vocational rehabilitation, occupational retraining; ~**unfall** occupational (industrial) accident; ~**verband** functional (professional) organization; ~**verkehr** business traffic, commuting *(US)*; ~**verkehrsteilnehmer** season-ticket holder *(Br.)*, commuter *(US)*; ~**verlust** job loss; ~**wechsel** occupational shift; ~**zugehörigkeit** professional (job) classification; **überfüllte** ~**zweige** overcrowded vocations.

beschädigt damaged, in a damaged state, defective, *(Lebensmittel)* spoilt, spoiled;
unterwegs ~ damaged in transit.
Beschädigung, für vorsätzliche ~ haften to be liable for voluntary waste.
beschaffen to procure, to provide, to supply, *(Geld)* to find, to raise;
Deckung ~ to provide for cover.
Beschaffenheit, gleiche ~ und Güte like grade and quality.
Beschaffung procurement, procuring, provision, *(Deckung)* providing;
~ **von Geld** finding the means, supply of funds.
Beschaffungs|abteilung store department; ~**amt** supply office; ~**kosten** cost of acquisition; ~**liste** list of supplies; ~**preis** supply price; ~**stelle** procurement office (agency, *US*); **staatliches** ~**wesen** government procurement.
beschäftigen to employ, to occupy, to give employment, *(sich abgeben)* to deal, to concern.
beschäftigt *(angestellt)* employed, in employ, engaged, *(tätig)* busy, occupied;
ganzzeitig ~ all-time, employed on a full-time basis;
nicht mehr bei jem. ~ sein to be no longer on s. one's payroll.
Beschäftigten|stand labo(u)r force; ~**zahl** numbers of employed, labo(u)r force.
Beschäftigter employed person, employee;
ganztägig ~ whole (full) -timer; **nebenberuflich** ~ sideliner.
Beschäftigung employ[ment], egagement, appointment, *(Arbeit)* work;
ohne ~ unemployed, out of work (employ); **einträgliche** ~ gainful occupation; **ganztägige** ~ full (whole) -time job (employment); **kaufmännische** ~ commercial appointment; **nebenberufliche** ~ occupation outside the office work; **stundenweise** ~ part-time employment; **überwiegende** ~ paramount occupation;
~ **auf der Baustelle** on-site employment; ~ **in der Dienstleistungsindustrie** service employment; ~ **von Kindern** child labo(u)r; ~ **in Kurzarbeit** *(zwecks Vermeidung von Entlassungen)* work sharing; ~ **im Staatsdienst** government job, state employment.
jem. ~ **geben** to employ s. o.; **geregelter** ~ **nachgehen** to go about one's lawful business; **ohne regelmäßige** ~ **sein** to be at a loose end.
Beschäftigungs|anstieg pickup in employment; ~**bild** employment (labo(u)r) picture; ~**grad** level of employment, *(Industrie)* operating rate.
beschäftigungslos [thrown] out of employment, unemployed, unoccupied, without occupation.
Beschäftigungs|nachweis employment bureau; ~**rückgang** employment decline; ~**stand** employment picture; ~**therapie** occupational therapy; **außerhalb des** ~**verhältnisses** outside the scope of employment; ~**zeit** hours (period) of employment, appointive term.
Bescheid answer, reply, *(Anweisung)* instruction,

direction, *(Auskunft)* information, *(Beschluß)* decree, decision, ruling;
bis auf weiteren ~ until further orders;
schriftlicher ~ notice in writing;
abschlägigen ~ **erhalten** to get a rebuff; **in seinem Fach gut** ~ **wissen** to know one's trade.
bescheiden, Gesuch abfällig to refuse (turn down) a request;
~**e Ansprüche stellen** to be modest in one's requirements; ~**e Mittel** limited means; ~**es Vermögen** modest fortune.
bescheinigen to attest, to certify, to warrant;
amtlich ~ to authenticate.
Bescheinigung certificate, certification, attestation;
ohne amtliche ~ uncertificated;
zollamtliche ~ customhouse certificate;
~ **über einbehaltene Lohnsteuer** withholding statement; ~ **für zollfreie Wiederausfuhr** custom-house certificate; ~ **über abgabenfreie Verbringung ins Zollgebiet** duty-free entry certificate.
beschicken, Märkte to supply a market; **Messe** ~ to exhibit at a fair.
Beschlagnahme arrest, arrestment, levy, distress, *(Schiff)* seizure, embargo;
~ **ausländischen Eigentums** foreign attachment;
~ **von Konterbande** impounding of contraband goods;
~ **eines Vermögens anordnen** to award sequestration of an estate.
beschlagnahmefähig seizable, attachable.
beschlagnahmen to attach, to arrest, to seize, to levy, to distress, to distrain, to appropriate, *(Schiff)* to lay an embargo on, to seize;
Ware ~ to confiscate goods.
Beschluß *(Gericht)* decision, decree, act, *(Entschliessung)* determination, resolution, resolve *(US)*;
einstimmig gefaßter ~ unanimous vote.
beschlußfähig sein to constitute a quorum.
beschlußunfähig sein to lack a quorum.
Beschneiden des Spesenetats expenditure account cutback.
beschneiden *(Ausgaben)* to curtail, to scale down.
beschränkt | geschäftsfähig of limited capacity; ~ **steuerpflichtig** subject to limited taxation;
~**e Absatzmöglichkeiten** limited (narrow) market; ~**e Geschäftsfähigkeit** limited capacity; ~**es Giro** restrictive endorsement; ~**e Haftung** limited liability.
Beschränkung limitation, restraining, restraint;
ohne ~ *(Seeversicherung)* with average;
~ **des Verteilerkreises** distribution classification; **sich in den Ausgaben** ~**en auferlegen** to show spending forbearance.
Beschreibung description, account, narration;
~ **eines Autos** particulars of a car; ~ **eines Musters** design data.
Beschriftung direction, address, *(Kiste)* marking.
Beseitigung | von Elendsgebieten redemption of slums, slum clearance; ~ **von Höchstpreisbestimmungen** removal of price ceilings.

besetzen, Stelle to fill a vacancy.
besetzt *(belegt)* occupied, taken, *(Hotel)* full, *(Stellung)* filled, *(Straßenbahn, Bus)* packed, crammed, full up *(Br.)*, *(Taxe)* hired, *(Telefon)* engaged, busy *(US)*, *(vorbestellt)* reserved; **[zeitlich] sehr ~ sein** to have many demands on one's time.
Besetzung | von Schlüsselpositionen key appointments; **~ von Stellen** filling in of vacancies.
besichern *(Kredit)* to furnish security, to collaterate *(US)*.
besichtigen, Schaden to inspect [the extent of] a damage.
Besichtigung inspection, examination, visit, visitation *(Grundstück, Schiff)* survey; **bei ~ der Waren** on examination of the goods; **zur ~ aufliegen** to be exposed (exhibited).
Besichtigungs|fahrt tour of inspection; **~genehmigung** order to view; **kostenlose ~reise** all-expense tour *(US)*; **~tour** sight-seeing tour.
Besitz possession, possessorship, hand, occupancy, *(Effektenpaket)* holding, *(Vermögen)* fortune, interests; **in ausländischem ~** foreign-owned; **mein persönlicher ~** my personal belongings; **ungestörter ~** *(Grundstück)* quiet enjoyment; **~ von Aktien** shareholding *(Br.)*, stockholding *(US)*; **~ der öffentlichen Hand** government ownership; **seinen ganzen ~ abstoßen** *(Wertpapiere)* to unload one's stock.
besitzen, Aktien to hold shares *(Br.)* (stock, *US*).
Besitzer possessor, occupant, occupier; **böswilliger ~** mala-fide holder, holder in bad faith; **ehrlicher (gutgläubiger) ~** bona-fide possessor, holder in due course (in good faith).
Besitz|nachweis erbringen to prove possession; **~stand** user, *(Bilanz)* assets.
besoldet salaried, stipendiary.
Besoldung salary, *(Gehaltszahlung)* salary payment.
Besoldungs|gruppe salary group (bracket, scale), pay brackets (grade); **~ordnung** salary scale, pay plan *(US)*.
besorgen to provide, to procure, to supply; **das Abladen ~** to do the unloading; **Deckung ~** to provide funds; **Geld ~** to raise (find) money; **einem Freund eine gute Stellung ~** to manoeuvre a friend into a good job.
Besorgung *(Auftrag)* commission, *(Beschaffung)* procurement, provision, *(Botengang)* errand, *(Erledigung)* performance, handling; **~ von Aufträgen** execution of orders; **seine ~en in Wohnungsnähe erledigen** to shop near one's home; **einige kleine ~en für j. zu erledigen haben** to have two or three commission for s. o..
Besorgungszettel shopping list.
Besprechung, geschäftliche business conference.
Besprechungs|teilnehmer conferee *(US)*; **~zimmer** conference (briefing) room, *(Hotel)* commercial room.

bessern, sich *(Kurse)* to improve, to make improvements.
Besserung *(Konjunktur)* recovery, upturn, *(Kurse)* rise, improvement, upturn; **leichte ~ aufweisen** to show signs of improvement.
Besserungsschein income and adjustment bond.
Bestallungsurkunde letter of appointment.
Bestand *(Bank)* cash assets, *(Besitz)* possession, *(Bilanz)* inventory, *(Effekten)* holdings, portfolio, *(Kasse)* balance (cash) in hand, *(Vorräte)* supply stores; **eiserner ~** *(Geld)* permanent funds; **geschlossener ~** *(Abschreibungsmethode)* closed-end account; **offener ~** *(Abschreibungsmethode)* open-end account; **~ an eigenen Aktien** treasury stock *(US)*; **~ an Diskonten** discount holdings, bills discounted; **~ in Halbfabrikaten** *(Bilanz)* work in process inventory *(US)*; **~ an Wechseln, Schuldscheinen und Akzepten** *(Bilanz)* notes (bills) receivable *(US)*; **über den ~ verkaufen** *(Börse)* to oversell.
Bestände supply; **alte ~ abstoßen** to get rid of old stock; **~ räumen** to clear shop.
Bestandsauffüllung inventory accumulation.
Bestandsaufnahme stocktaking, shop check, inventory [taking] *(US)*, *(Bibliothek)* check; **~ machen** to take stock, to [take] inventory *(US)*.
Bestands|beleg stock voucher; **~buch** inventory, warehouse book; **laufende ~kartei** perpetual inventory file *(US)*; **~konto** asset account; **~liste** inventory, stock sheet; **~veränderung** *(Anlagegüter)* change in book value; **~verlust** inventory shrinkage.
bestätigen to confirm, to affirm, to vouch, to endorse; **amtlich ~** to attest, to certify, to authenticate; **Auftrag ~** to confirm an order; **Richtigkeit eines Kontoauszuges ~** to verify an account; **Scheck ~** to confirm a cheque *(Br.)*, to certify a check *(US)*.
bestätigter Scheck marked cheque *(Br.)*, certified check *(US)*.
Bestätigung affirmation, confirmation, endorsement, *(Genehmigung)* approval, ratification sanction; **um ~ des Empfangs wird gebeten** please acknowledge receipt; **amtliche ~** attestation, certification; **vorbehaltlose ~** *(Prüfer)* positive confirmation; **~ eines Kontoauszuges** verification of an account, bank confirmation.
Bestätigungs|brief letter of acknowledgement; **~formular** confirmation blank; **~vermerk erteilen** *(Buchprüfer)* to certify a financial statement.
Bestechung bribe, bribery, suborning, corruption, corrupt practices, gratification, graft *(US)*.
Bestechungsgeld bribe, golden (silver) key, graft, sook *(US sl.)*, sweetener, baksheesh, *(US)*.
bestehen *(Gültigkeit haben)* to be in force; **im wesentlichen aus Aktien ~** *(Vermögen)* to consist

mainly of shares; auf höheren Löhnen ~ to stand for more wages; **weiter** ~ *(Firma)* to remain in existence; **auf Zahlung** ~ to insist on payment.

Bestell|bezirk postal district; **~eingang** incoming orders.

bestellen to [give an] order, to commission, *(Botengänge erledigen)* to do errands, *(Hotelzimmer)* to book, to reserve *(US)*, *(im Restaurant)* to order; **Anwalt** ~ to brief (retain) a lawyer; **zu seinem Bevollmächtigten** ~ to give s. o. power of attorney; **Sicherheiten** ~ to surrender securities; **telegrafisch** ~ to order by cable.

Bestell|formular *(Einkäufer)* purchase order form; **~karte** *(Reklame)* return card; **~liste** docket *(Br.)*, order form, want list *(US)*; **~nummer** order (purchase, requisition, supply) number; **~zettel** order blank (sheet, form).

Bestellung [purchase] order, commission, *(Hotelzimmer)* booking, reservation *(US)*, *(Wertpapiere)* application;
auf ~ to (on) order, at command; **auf** ~ **angefertigt** turned out (made, *US*) to order, custom-made (built, *US*); **telefonisch aufgegebene** ~ telephone order; **nicht ausgeführte** **~en** unfilled orders; **neuer** ~ repeat [order]; **terminierte** ~ en time ordering;
~ **einer Hypothek** creation of a mortgage contract; ~ **zur Lageraufüllung** fill-in reorder; ~ **von Sicherheiten** surrender of securities; ~ **eines Vertreters (Vormunds)** appointment of an agent (a guardian);
~ **annehmen** to take (book) an order; ~ **annullieren** to cancel an order.

Bestell|ungstermin purchase date; **~zettel** order form (sheet, slip), requisition form *(Br.)*.

bestens *(Börse)* at best, at the best price (figure), at the market *(US)*, (Devisenkauf) at the best possible rate, *(beim Kauf)* at the best possible bid, *(beim Verkauf)* at the best possible offer.

Bestensorder order at best, market order *(US)*.

besteuern to tax, to burden with taxes, to impose (levy) a tax on, to assess, *(Zoll)* to impose duty on; **Grundbesitz** ~ to levy on land.

Besteuerung taxation, tax, imposition of taxes, assessment, *(Gemeinde)* rating;
von der ~ **ausgenommen** tax-exempt;
degressive ~ graduated taxation; **direkte** ~ direct taxation; **gestaffelte** ~ graduated taxation; **indirekte** ~ indirect taxation; **kommunale** ~ rating; **verschärfte** ~ **größerer Vermögen** conscription of wealth;
größeren Teil des Erwerbseinkommens der normalen ~ **unterwerfen** to shove more of the earned income into the ordinary tax brackets.

bestimmen *(anordnen)* to direct, to order, to ordain, to rule, *(ausbedingen)* to stipulate;
j. zu seinem Erben ~ to appoint s. o. as one's heir; **Geldbeträge für einen Zweck** ~ to earmark funds; **Preis** ~ to fix (state) a price; **zu seinem Vertreter** ~ to make s. o. one's deputy.

bestimmt fixed, settled, *(festgestellt)* ascertained; ~ **nach** *(Schiff)* bound for; **nicht zur Veröffentlichung** ~ off the record *(US)*;
~er Betrag given amount (sum); **vom Hersteller ~e Preise** prices laid down by the manufacturer; **~e Ware** specified goods.

Bestimmung *(Verfügung)* disposition, decree, *(Vertrag)* clause, stipulation;
einschränkende ~ *(Konkurrenzklausel)* restraining clause;
~ **über Barzahlung und Transport auf eigenen Schiffen** cash-and-carry clause *(US)*; ~ **des Einzelhandelspreises** setting the retail price;
unter eine ~ **fallen** to come within the scope of (be covered by) a clause.

Bestimmungen, laut steuerrechtlichen under tax law; **gewerbepolizeiliche** ~ inspection laws; **postalische** ~ postal regulations; **zollamtliche** ~ customs regulations;
~ **über die Einbehaltung von Lohnsteuern** withholding regulations *(US)*; ~ **über die steuerliche Behandlung von Kapitalgewinnen** capital gains provisions; **einleitende** ~ **eines Vertrages** preliminary articles of a treaty;
unter die gesetzlichen ~ **fallen** to come within the provisions (scope) of a law; **den** ~ **zuwiderhandeln** to contravene the terms.

Bestimmungsland state (country) of destination.

Bestpreis highest (best) price.

bestreiten, Ausgaben to bear (defray) the expenses; **seinen Lebensunterhalt daraus** ~ to make a living out of it.

Bestreitung der Kosten defrayal of expenses;
zur ~ **der Kosten beitragen** to contribute towards the costs.

Besuch, nachfassender *(Vertreter)* follow-up visit; ~ **einer Ausstellung** visit to an exhibition.

besuchen, Kunden to call on a client.

Besucher visitor, caller, spectator, *(Kunde)* customer, *(pl.)* turnout;
~gruppe visiting group; **~liste** visiting book.

besucht, stark frequented, numerously attended.

beteiligen, sich to take part, to participate, to share in; **j.** ~ to give s. o. a share, to interest s. o.; **sich finanziell** ~ to become financially interested; **j. am Gewinn** ~ to give s. o. a share in profits; **sich an den Kosten** ~ to contribute towards the costs.

beteiligt concerned, conjunct, interested in;
an einem Unfall ~ involved in an accident;
~ **sein** to have a hand in, to be sharer in, *(kapitalmäßig)* to have an interest.

Beteiligte eines Vertrages parties to an agreement.

Beteiligung participation, sharing, *(Anlage)* investment, *(Anteil)* share, interest, *(Teilnehmerzahl)* attendance;
mit der Aussicht späterer ~ with a view to partnership; **mit** ~ **am Gewinn** participating;
~en holdings, shareholdings, stockholdings *(US)*; **ausländische ~en** foreign interests; **kommanditische** ~ limited partnership interest; **staatliche**

~ government participation; **stille** ~ secret partnership; **verschiedene ~en** *(Bilanz)* sundry investments and interests; ~ **der Arbeiter und Angestellten am Gewinn** industrial partnership, profit sharing; ~ **an einem Konsortium** underwriting participation;

jem. eine ~ an seinem Geschäft anbieten to offer s. o. an interes in one's business; **unter lebhafter ~ der Bevölkerung stattfinden** to be accompanied by demonstrations of public sympathy.

Beteiligungs|dauer life of partnership; **fünfzigprozentiger ~erwerb** acquisition of a 50 per cent interest; **~kapital** equity capital, contribution to capital; **~konto** syndicate (joint, *US*) account; **~umstellungen** shuffle of holdings.

beträchtliches Vermögen handsome fortune.

Betrag amount, *(Buchungsposten)* item, *(Gesamtbetrag)* total, *(Satz)* rate;

gut für jeden ~ good for any amount;

~ **bar erhalten** cash received;

von der Bank abgehobener ~ sum withdrawn from the bank; **nicht abgehobener** ~ unexpended portion; **abzugsfähiger** ~ *(Einkommensteuer)* personal allowance *(Br.)* (credit, *US)*; **von der Versicherung gedeckter** ~ amount of insurance carried; **geschuldeter** ~ sum (owing); **pro forma angesetzter** ~ nominal sum; **steuerpflichtiger** ~ taxable portion; **aus der Rücklage zu tragender** ~ sum chargeable to reserve; **überschießender** ~ exceeding amount, surplus, *(Saldo)* unpaid balance; ~ **in Worten** sum in words; ~ **in Zahlen** amount in figures;

~ **abrunden** to make up an amount, to round off a sum; **bestimmten** ~ **für Abnutzung absetzen** to write off so much for wear and tear; **erheblichen** ~ **ausmachen** to run to a respectable figure; **jds. Konto mit einem** ~ **belasten** to carry (place) a sum to s. one's debit; ~ **bei einer Bank einzahlen** to bank an amount; **sich für den** ~ **seiner Spesen erholen** to recover expenses; ~ **für etw. hinterlegen** to leave a deposit on s. th.; ~ **für wohltätige Zwecke zur Verfügung stellen** to subscribe a sum to charity; ~ **auf neue Rechnung vortragen** to bring forward an amount; ~ **dem Reservefonds zuführen** to allocate an amount to the reserve fund.

Beträge, anfallende accruing amounts; **im voraus eingegangene** ~ deferred revenue; **offenstehende** ~ open items;

steuerlich absetzbare ~ **für die Bewirtung von Geschäftsfreunden** travel and entertainment expense deductions;

~ **für etw. bereitstellen** to earmark funds.

Betreff angeben to quote a reference number.

betreffendes Geschäft business in question.

betreiben, Bankgeschäft ~ to do business as a banker; **alle Arten des Finanzierungsgeschäftes** ~ to diversify into the nonbanking fields; **Gewerbe** ~ to follow (ply) a trade.

betreuen to have the care of, to look after, to maintain, *(Vertreter)* to cover.

Betreuung caretaking, care, *(Vertreter)* cover.

Betreuungs|aufgaben service functions; **~tätigkeit** custodial service.

Betrieb *(Arbeitsgang)* service, *(Betreiben)* working, running, operating, operation *(US)*, *(Betriebsanlage)* factory, [manufacturing] plant, works, mill *(Br.)*, *(Maschine)* working, operation, running; **außer** ~ standing idle, *(Bahn)* out of service (action), *(Maschine)* out of blast, idle, *(nicht in Ordnung)* not working, defunct; **nicht im** ~ inoperative, nonoperating;

billig arbeitender ~ low-cost plant; **bestreikter** ~ struck shop; **durcharbeitender** ~ all-night service; **durchgehender** ~ continuous process, continuity of operations; **einträglicher** ~ profitable enterprise; **an Preisabsprachen nicht gebundener** ~ outsider; **gefährlicher** ~ dangerous premises; **gesundheitsschädlicher** ~ offensive trade; **gewerbepolizeipflichtiger** ~ trade subject to licence; **kriegswichtiger** ~ essential industry; **landwirtschaftlicher** ~ agricultural enterprise, farm; **reibungslos laufender** ~ smooth-running entity; **lebenswichtiger** ~ vitally important establishment; **staatlich subventionierter** ~ taxeater; **stillgelegter** ~ mill out of work *(Br.)*, nonoperating property (factory) *(US)*; **wissenschaftlich geführter** ~ scientific management; ~ **eines Bergwerks** exploitation of a mine; ~ **an der Grenze der Rentabilität** marginal producer; ~ **mit geringem Lohnniveau** low-wage unit; ~ **eines Unternehmens** working of a business;

~ **anlaufen lassen** to put in (go into) operation; **im** ~ **seines Vaters arbeiten** to work in one's father's firm; ~ **wieder aufnehmen** to resume work; **ganzen** ~ **kostenmäßig durchforsten** to cut costs throughout a company; ~ **einstellen** to stop a factory (business), to cease operations (working); ~ **vorübergehend einstellen** to close down temporarily; ~ **aus den roten Zahlen herausbringen** to administer a company from red to black; ~ **schließen** to close down; **außer** ~ **sein** *(Fabrik)* to be out of operation; **billig im** ~ **sein** *(Auto)* to be run at small cost; **in** ~ **sein** *(Bahnlinie)* to be in operation (running), *(Fabrik)* to work, *(Maschine)* to run, to operate; **das ganze Jahr in** ~ **sein** *(Auto)* to be in commission all the year; **wieder im** ~ **sein** *(Hotel)* to be running (working) again; **in** ~ **setzen** to put (set) into operation (action), to start [running]; ~ **völlig umkrempeln** to turn around a company; ~ **in Vorstadtgebiete verlagern** to go suburban; **in** ~ **genommen werden** to go into operation, *(Bahnlinie, Straße)* to be opened to traffic; **Omnibus aus dem** ~ **ziehen** to take a bus off the road.

betriebliche Eignungsprüfung employment test; **~e Leistungsfähigkeit** plant capacity, operating efficiency; ~ **Ruhegeldverpflichtungen** pension liabilities.

Betriebs|ablauf operational procedure; **~abrechnung** manufacturing cost sheet.

Betriebsabteilung staff (business) department; **kaufmännische** ~ commercial department.

Betriebs|analyse operation analysis; ~angaben shop data; ~ angehörige work (working) force.

Betriebsanlage factory, working (fixed) plant, asset, *(Betriebseinheit)* productive unit;
nicht ausgenutzte ~n idle equipment;
~ außer Dienst (Betrieb) setzen to discard an asset.

Betriebs|anleitung operating instructions, shop rules *(US);* ~anteil management share; ~archiv company archives; ~arzt company (plant) physician; ~atmosphäre working atmosphere; ~aufseher works manager, *(Bahn)* traffic manager; ~aufsicht plant inspection, factory supervision; ~ausbildung industrial education, in-service training *(US);* ~ausflug works outing; allgemeine ~ausgaben general operating expense, overhead; ~ausstattung [factory] equipment; ~ausweis company identification card.

betriebsbedingte Notwendigkeiten shopfloor necessities.

Betriebs|bedingungen shop conditions; ~belegenheit plant location; ~berater management consultant, industrial relations counsellor; ≈bereit ready for operation; ~besichtigung plant visit (tour); ~bilanz operating statement; ~blindheit operational (plant) blindness; ~buchhaltung cost (manufacturing, industrial) accounting; ~defizit operational deficit; ~dezernent works (plant, *US)* manager; ~disziplin industrial (shop) discipline.

betriebseigener Prüfer internal auditor.

Betriebs|einheit business entity, operating (business) unit; ~einnahmen operating revenues *(Bahn)* traffic receipts, railway (railroad, *US)* earnings; ~einrichtungen und Maschinen *(Bilanz)* plant and machinery; ~einstellungskosten shutdown costs; ~erfahrung operating experience, *(praktische)* industrial know-how; ~ergebnis operating (working, company, trading) result; ~ergebnisrechnung operating performance income statement; ~ertrag business (working) proceeds; ~erweiterung plant addition (expansion), factory extension; ~erweiterungsfonds plant fund; ~erweiterungskosten cost of plant addition; ~fachmann operating executive.

betriebsfähig operative, in operation, in working condition (order), in running order, *(Bahn)* serviceable;
nicht ~ out of order, not working (operating);
~er Zustand operating condition.

Betriebs|fahrzeug fleet car; ~fahrzeuge factory fleet; ~ferien works holidays, staff vacations; ~ferien machen to close down for holidays.

betriebsfertig ready for operation (working, service), in running (working) order.

Betriebs|fest staff party; landwirtschaftliche ~fläche farm land, agricultural area; ~flotte operating fleet; ~fonds business (working) fund.

betriebsfremde Erträge nonoperating revenues.

Betriebsführer works *(Br.)* (plant, *US)* manager, managing operator;
eigener ~ owner-manager.

Betriebsführung operational (industrial, working, plant) management;
oberste ~ top management *(US);* wissenschaftliche ~ scientific management;
~ nur in Ausnahmefällen management by exception *(US);* ~ durch Informierung und Anhörung der Mitarbeiter management by communication and participation; ~ durch ständiges Streben nach Systemerneuerung management by innovation; ~ durch Zielvorgabe management by objectives.

Betriebsführungs|fragen management problems; ~grundsätze management principles; ~politik management policy.

Betriebs|gebäude company premises; ~geheimnisse verraten to divulge trade secrets; ~gemeinkosten indirect cost, factory overhead; ~genehmigung authorized operation, factory order; ~gewerkschaft industrial (shopcraft, company, puppet, *US)* union.

Betriebsgewinn trading (operating) profit, profit from (on) operations, earned (company's) surplus;
nicht verteilter ~ earned unappropriated surplus.

Betriebs|gleis industrial line (track); ~grundstück business (factory) property, company property (premises), plant site; ~haftpflichtversicherung manufacturer's public liability insurance *(US);* ~handbuch employee handbook (manual); ~hauptbuch property (factory) ledger; ~ingenieur industrial (operation, production, plant, manufacturing, operating) engineer.

betriebsinterne Prüfung internal auditing.

Betriebs|inventar business (plant) inventory, implements of trade; ~investitionen erhöhen to increase its spending on plant; ~jahr business (trading, operating, working, financial) year; ~kalkulator cost accountant (clerk); ~kantine industrial canteen, catering department; ~kapazität beinahe voll ausnutzen to operate close to capacity; knapp 2/3 der ~kapazität ausnutzen to operate at below two thirds of capacity.

Betriebskapital current (working, trading, business, liquid) capital, stock-in-trade, working funds, *(Bank)* fund;
~ nach Abzug der Verbindlichkeiten net working capital (current assets);
~ verstärken to beef up working capital.

Betriebs|kapitalverhältnis working capital ratio; ~kasino company cafeteria; angenehmes ~klima pleasant office atmosphere; ~kontingent production quota; ~konzession operating concession.

Betriebskosten operating cost (expenses), working expense (cost, charges), *(Unterhaltungskosten)* carrying charges;
~ bei voller Kapazitätsausnutzung capacity costs.

Betriebs|krankenkasse company sichness benefit fund; ~küche industrial canteen; ~laden company store *(US);* ~leistung operating efficiency, run; ~leiter acting (works, *Br.,* operating, operations, *US,* factory, plant, *US)* manager, *(Eisenbahn)* traffic manager.

Betriebsmaterial stock-in-trade, working stock *(Eisenbahn)* rolling stock.

Betriebsmittel employed funds, operating (working) funds, stock [in trade];
   werbende ~ revenue assets;
   ~**bedarf** working capital needs; ~**kredit** working (operational) credit; **sich ~kredit durch Debitorenabtretung verschaffen** to factor one's accounts; ~**moral** employee morale; ~**obmann** works (shop, union, *US*) steward; ~**optimum** ideal capacity; ~**pause** rest pause (period); ~**pension** company financed pension; ~**personal** [shop (company)] staff , operating staff *(US), (Eisenbahn)* maintenance team; ~**planspiel** management game; ~**planung** management (operational) planning; ~**politik** management policy, company [labo(u)r] policies; ~**prüfer** public accountant, *(Revisionsabteilung)* [internal] auditor; ~**prüfung haben** to have the auditors in; ~**psychologe** industrial psychologist; ~**rat** factory (shop) committee, factory *(Br.)* (shop, workers) council; ~**rationalisierung** plant rationalization.

Betriebsrats|mitglied union steward (committeeman); ~**versammlung** congress of factory councils *(US)*; ~**vorsitzender** shop chairmann (deputy).

Betriebs|reingewinn net operating income; ~**reserve** operating (general) reserve; ~**richtlinien** plant rules; **heute ~ruhe** *(Hotel)* closed today; **saisonbedingte ~schließung** seasonal shutdown.

betriebssicher safe to operate, reliable in operation, *(Flugzeug, Maschine)* fool-proof.

Betriebs|siedlung company town *(US)*; ~**sparen** industrial savings; ~**sparkasse** mutual benefit association; ~**stätte** permanent establishment, regular place of business, business premises; ~**stillegung** closing down, close-down, *(vorübergehende)* shutdown *(US)*; ~**stillstandsversicherung** business interruption (use and occupancy, *US*) insurance; ~**stockung** shutdown, *(Eisenbahn)* breakdown.

Betriebsstoff fuel, petrol *(Br.)*, gasoline *(US)*;
   Roh-, Hilfs- und ~e *(Bilanz)* raw materials and supplies;
   ~**verbrauch** fuel consumption.

Betriebs|störung interruption, shutdown, *(Eisenbahn)* breakdown, holdup; ~**stunden** *(Arbeiter)* factory hours; ~**umfrage** employee attitude survey; **komplette ~umstellung** thorough turnover of the operating force.

Betriebsunfall industrial (on-the-job) accident, industrial injury;
   ~**verhütung** industrial accident prevention; ~**versicherung** industrial accident insurance.

Betriebs|unkosten operating cost (expenses), operational (maintenance, *US*, plant) costs; ~**unterbrechungsschaden** use and occupancy loss; ~**versicherung** use and occupancy *(US)* (business interruption) insurance; ~**unterlagen** plant (factory) records; ~**untersuchung** operation analysis; ~**vereinbarung** single-plant bargaining, shop agreement; ~**verfassung** shop rules; ~**vergrößerung**

plant extension; ~**verlagerung durchführen** to move a plant to another locality; ~**verlust** operating deficit (loss), business (manufacturing, operational, trading) loss; ~**vermögen** working (operating, business) assets, *(AG)* company property; ~**versammlung** factory meeting; ~**verwaltung** management; ~**vorrat** stock-in-trade; ~**vorschriften** plant (working) regulations, *(Eisenbahn)* service regulations; ~**wert** going [concern] value; ~**wirt** business administrator *(US)*; ~**wirtschaft** business administration *(US)* (economics, *Br.*).

betriebswirtschaftliche | Angaben business data; ~ **Untersuchung** operation analysis.

Betriebs|wohnungen company housing; ~**zählung** industrial census; ~**zeitschrift** house organ, company magazine; ~**zugehörigkeitsdauer** period of employment, seniority *(US)*; ~**zusammenlegung** amalgamation of industries; ~**zuschuß** company contribution; **zustand** *(Maschine)* working condition (order); ~**zweck** business use.

Bettplatz berth.

beurkunden to acknowledge, to verify, *(Behörde)* to authenticate, to certify, to legalize.

Beurkundung verification, *(Behörde)* authentication, legalization, certification.

Beurlaubung mit vollem Gehalt full-pay leave.

Beurteilung | von Angestellten employee (performance, personnel) rating *(US)*; ~**der finanziellen Entwicklung** financial forecasting; ~**der Vermögenslage einer Kapitalgesellschaft** capital rating.

Beurteilungs|blatt eines Angestellten employee rating chart; ~**zeitraum** *[für Gehaltseinstufungen]* rating period.

Bevölkerung, arbeitende working-class (employed) population.

Bevölkerungs|anstieg increase (swell) in population; **alle ~gruppen** great and small; - **schicht** population stratum.

bevollmächtigen to authorize, to empower, to warrant, to constitute, to confer powers, to fiat.

Bevollmächtigte|r authorized person (commissioner), [authorized] agent;
   durch einen ~n abstimmen lassen to vote by proxy.

Bevollmächtigungsschreiben letter of authorization (attorney).

bevorrechtigt *(Forderung)* privileged, preferred, preferential, senior, *(Gläubiger)* preferred.

Bevorschussung | von Verschiffungsdokumenten advance against shipping documents; ~ **von Wertpapieren** loan against securities, collateral loan *(US)*.

bevorzugen, Gläubiger to prefer one creditor over others.

bevorzugt *(Forderung)* privileged, preferred *(US)*, preferential *(Br.)* senior;
   ~ **abgefertigt werden** to receive priority;
   ~**e Behandlung** preferential treatment; ~**e Marke** favo(u)rite brand; ~**e Stellung einnehmen** to have a privileged position.

Bevorzugung preference, preferment.
bewachter Parkplatz car park with attendant.
bewegen sich *(Preise)* to range (vary) from . . . to . . . .;
sich abwärts ~ to be on the downgrade.
bewegliche Preise flexible prices.
bewegt *(Börse)* agitated, brisk, lively.
Bewegung *(Preise, Kurse)* tendency, trend, movement;
rückgängige (rückläufige) ~ *(Börse, Konjunktur)*
downward (retrograde) movement;
~ **auf Bankkonten** fluctuation on bank accounts.
bewerben, sich to apply for, to stand, to run, to
candidate, to seek, to go up *(Br.)*;
sich um einen Auftrag ~ to make a tender; **sich um
eine Stelle** ~ to apply for a position, to put in for a
post, to compete for a job.
Bewerber applicant, aspirant, candidate, registrant,
(US), *(Lieferungen)* bidder.
Bewerbung application, competition, *(Gesuch)* petition, suit, *(Kandidatur)* candidateship;
handschriftliche ~ handwritten application;
~ **mit vollständigem Lebenslauf** application with
full career details;
~ **einreichen** to send in an application.
Bewerbungs|antrag employment application; **~for-
mular** application form; **~frist** filing period, *(Ausschreibungen)* tender period; **~unterlagen** application papers (files).
bewerten to evaluate, to value, to appreciate, *(abschätzen)* to appraise, to estimate;
mit 100 % ~ *(Bilanz)* to value at 100 per cent; **j.
nach seinen Fähigkeiten** ~ to rate s. o.; **neu** ~ to
reprice, to transvalue; **niedrig** ~ to set a low
valuation; **nach Punkten** ~ to rate on points.
Bewertung estimate, valuation, evaluation, pricing,
rating, *(Grundstück)* assessment;
zu hohe ~ overappraisal, overassessment; **steuerliche** ~ assessment, assessed valuation *(US)*;
~ **landwirtschaftlich genutzten Geländes** appraisal
of agricultural land; **berufliche** ~ **nach dem Punkt-
system** job rating; ~ **des Vorratsvermögens zu
Durchschnittspreisen** periodic average inventory
plan.
Bewertungs|durchschnitt weighted average; **~form-
blatt** operation analysis chart; **~freiheit** valuation
privilege; **~grundlage** valuation basis, *(Rentabili-
tätsrechnung)* cost basis; **schwacher ~maßstab** poor
criterion; **~richtlinien** assessment principles;
~stichtag valuation date.
bewilligen, Betrag to allocate a sum; **Haushalt** ~ to
vote the appropriation (estimates); **Kredit** ~ to
grant a loan; **Zahlungsaufschub** ~ to grant a
respite.
bewilligte Etatansätze budgetary appropriations.
Bewilligung grant, granting, permission, allowance,
allocation, *(Parl.)* vote, appropriation;
globale ~ block vote;
~ **eines Vorschusses** grant of an advance.
Bewilligungs|ausschuß allocation committee, *(Parl.)*
appropriation (budget) committee.

bewirkte Gegenleistung executed consideration.
bewirtschaften to administer, to manage, *(Acker)* to
till, to cultivate;
Wohnungsmarkt ~ to control housing.
bewirtschaftet rationed, controlled, administered,
restricted, *(Hotel)* open;
~e Waren quota goods.
Bewirtschaftung management, planning, *(Acker)*
husbanding, tillage, cultivation, farming, *(Mangelwaren)* economic control, rationing;
ordnungsgemäße ~ proper management;
~ **von Lebensmitteln** food rationing; ~ **des Woh-
nungsmarktes** housing control.
Bewirtschaftungs|maßnahmen aufheben to lift a
control; **~programm** rationing program(me);
~stelle control office; **~wesen** rationing system.
Bewirtung von Geschäftsfreunden business entertainment.
bezahlen to pay, to cash *(US)*, *(entlohnen)* to pay,
to remunerate *(Schulden)* to discharge, to settle, to
liquidate;
bei Ablieferung ~ to pay on delivery; **auf
Heller und Pfennig** ~ to pay scot and lot; **vollen
Fahrpreis** ~ to pay the full fare; **in Monatsraten** ~
to pay by monthly instalments; **postnumerando** ~
to pay on receipt; **pränumerando** ~ to make payment in advance; **sofort (auf der Stelle)** ~ to pay
down (on the nail); **j. stundenweise** ~ to pay s. o. by
the hour; **seinen Spaß teuer** ~ to pay for one's
whistle; **im voraus** ~ to prepay; **Zeche** ~ to foot the
bill.
bezahlt paid for, settled, payment received, *(ge-
dungen)* hired, *(Scheck, Wechsel)* hono(u)red;
in bar ~ paid out-of-pocket; **schlecht** ~ underpaid, penny-a-line;
sich ~ **machen** to yield, to pay in the long run; **vierteljährlich** ~ **werden** to be paid by the quarter;
schlecht ~e Stelle badly paid job.
Bezahlung pay, payment, *(Gehalt)* salary, *(Honorar)*
fee, remuneration, *(Lohn)* wages, *(Schulden)*
discharge, settlement;
als ~ **für Ihre Dienste** as remuneration for your
services;
getrennte ~ Dutch treat; **pünktliche** ~ readiness
in payment; **ungenügende** ~ insufficient pay;
~ **der Kosten** defrayal of expenses; **~in Waren** payment in goods, bartering, truck system, store pay
(US); ~ **eines Wechsels** protection of a bill;
Gäste gegen ~ **aufnehmen** to take paying guests;
mit der ~ **hinhalten** to keep s. o. out of money;
Geld für die ~ **von Schulden verwenden** to apply
money to the payment of debts.
bezeichnen *(Waren)* to label, to ticket, to mark.
Bezeichnung *(Waren)*, labelling, marking, branding;
~ **von Waren als Markenartikel** misbranding of
commodities.
beziehbar obtainable, to be had, *(Haus)* ready to
move in, inhabitable.
beziehen *(Aktien)* to subscribe, *(Geld)* to draw, *(Waren)* to obtain, to buy, to get, to procure;

junge Aktien ~ to exercise the right to subscribe to new shares (stock, *US)*; **Arbeitslosenunterstützung** ~ to receive unemployment compensation, to draw the dole *(Br.)*; **Markt** ~ to frequent a market; **Wartestandsgeld** ~ to be on half-pay; **Wohnung** ~ to move into a flat.

Beziehungen relations, affinities;
  geschäftliche ~ business relations (intercourse); ~**zur Kundschaft** customer realtions;
  seine ~ **spielen lassen** to pull wires (strings); **seine Stellung seinen** ~ **verdanken** to owe one's position to one's influence; **über gute** ~ **verfügen** to be well connected.

Beziehungskauf industrial (direct-to-customer) selling.

beziffern to [mark by a] number, to estimate;
  sich ~ **auf** to amount (run up) to, to figure at.

Bezirk district, region, confine, zone, section, sector, division, area, land, side;
  ~ **bearbeiten** *(Vertreter)* to work a district, to cover a territory.

Bezirks|agentur district office *(US)*; ~**direktor** area (local) manager; ~**geschäftsstelle** area headquarters; ~**vertreter** district (regional) representative, local agent.

Bezogener *(Wechsel)* drawee, acceptor, payer.

Bezug relation, *(im Brief)* reference;
  bei ~ **durch die Post** if delivered by post; **bei** ~ **von 100 Stück Sonderrabatt** on orders for 100 special discount;
  ~ **von jungen Aktien** subscription of new shares; **bei** ~ **von 100 Stück 5 % Rabatt gewähren** to allow a discount of 5 % with orders of 100.

Bezüge emoluments, earnings, income, *(Gehalt)* salary, remuneration, pay;
  augenblickliche ~ present salary level.

Bezugs|anweisung delivery order; ~**ausweis** buying permit; ~**bedingungen** terms (conditions) of delivery, *(Subskription)* terms of subscription; ~**berechtigung** *(Aktien)* subscription privilege (right); ~**berechtigungsschein** *(Aktien)* warrant [to stock owner].

bezugsfertig *(Haus)* ready to move in.

Bezugs|kurs issue price; ~**quelle** market, supplier, buying resource *(US)*; **eingedruckter** ~**quellennachweis** dealer imprint.

Bezugsrecht *(Aktien)* subscription privilege, right's issue *(Br.)*, preemption *(US)*;
  mit ~**en** cum rights, rights on; **mit** ~ **auf junge Aktien** cum new;
  ~ **ausüben** to exercise rights; ~ **auf junge Aktien ausüben** to subscribe to (for) new shares (stock, *US)*.

Bezugsrechts|angebot rights offering; ~**formular** application form *(Br.)*.

Bezugschein *(auf Aktien)* subscription (stock allotment, *US)* warrant, *(Berechtigungsschein)* scrip, *(Materialien)* materials requisition slip, *(Warenbewirtschaftung)* coupon, docket.

Bezugsscheinberechtigter priority permit holder.

bezugsschein|frei coupon-free, on free sale; ~**pflichtig** rationed.

Bezugs|spesen delivery cost (expenses); ~**zeichen** reference mark.

bieten to offer, to tender, *(Auktion)* to bid.

Bilanz balance [of accounts], *(Bilanzformular)* balance sheet, statement [of assets and liabilities] *(US)*;
  ausführliche ~ detailed balance sheet; **berichtigte** ~ post-closing balance sheet; **fiktive** ~ proforma balance sheet (statement, *US)*; **geprüfte** ~ certified balance, audited balance sheet; **passive** ~ adverse balance; **zusammengefaßte** ~ consolidated balance sheet;
  ~ **der gesamten Volkswirtschaft** net results of overall economic activity;
  in der ~ **unter langfristigen Schulden aufführen** to place on the balance sheet among the long-term liabilities; ~ **aufstellen** to strike a balance; ~ **fälschen** to fake a balance sheet; ~ **frisieren** to cook (doctor) a balance sheet; ~**prüfen** to audit a balance sheet; ~ **zergliedern** to analyse (break down, *US)* a balance.

Bilanz|analyse analysis sheet; ~**aufstellung** [making up a] balance sheet; ~**auszug** condensed (summarized) balance sheet; ~**buchhaltung** auditing department; ~**fälschung** window dressing; ~**gewinn** profit as shown in the balance; ~**gliederung** balance-sheet structure.

bilanzieren to [strike a] balance, to show in the balance sheet.

Bilanzierungs|arbeiten accounting work; ~**fachmann** accounting practitioner; ~**schema** sample balance sheet; ~**tag** balance-sheet (accounting, statement, *US)* date.

Bilanz|jahr financial (audit) year; ~**muster** sample balance sheet; ~**posten** heading of a balance sheet; ~**posten einer Konzerngesellschaft** inter-company items; ~**prüfer** chartered *(Br.)* (certified public, *US)* accountant, auditor; ~**prüfung**, ~**revision** balance-sheet audit, auditing; ~**sicherer Buchhalter** accountant; ~**veröffentlichung** publication of a balance-sheet; ~**zahlen** balance-sheet figures (data).

Bild **des Arbeitslosenmarktes** jobless picture;
  uneinheitliches ~ **bieten** *(Börse)* to make a mixed showing.

~**berichterstatter** press photographer, news cameraman (photographer); ~**funk** wireless picture telegraphy, picture transmission; ~**schirm** picture screen; ~**telefon** video telephone, picturephone.

Bildung | **eines Ausschusses** constitution of a committee; ~ **von Durchschnittsprämien** levelling of premiums.

Bildungsurlaub study leave, day-release training.

Bildwerbung illustrated advertisement *(Br.)*, pictorial advertising.

billig cheap, low-priced, inexpensive, low, at a low price, at little (small) cost, easy, at a moderate charge (low figure), penny-a-line, threepenny *(Br.)*;

außergewöhnlich ~ dirt-cheap;
~ **zu haben sein** *(Aktien)* to be in the dumps (down);
~es **Ermessen** discretion; ~e **Forderung** reasonable demand; ~es **Geld** easy money; ~er **Jakob** *(fam.)* cheap-Jack.

Billigpreisländer low-price countries.

Billigstauftrag market order.

Bindung, kapitalmäßige financial relationship;
~ **der Preise** freezing of prices; ~ **einer Währung an den Dollar** linking of a currency to the dollar.

Binnen|frachtführer inland carrier; ~**hafen** close (inland) port, inner (landlocked) harbo(u)r, basin; ~**handel** country (home, interior, internal, inward, *US)* trade, domestic (interstate) commerce *(US)*; **rückläufige** ~**konjunktur** domestic business slowdown; ~**konnossement** inland-waterway bill of lading; ~**schiffahrt** inland waters navigation; ~**schiffahrtsverkehr** inland water transportation.

Binnentransport inland transportation;
~**versicherung** inland transportation (marine, *US)* insurance.

Binnen|währung internal currency; ~**zoll** inland (internal, inward, *Br.)* duty.

Blankett *(Formular)* blank form.

Blankett|ausfüllbefugnis authorization to fill in a blank; ~**versicherungsschein** *(gegen Versicherungsdelikte von Betriebsangehörigen)* commercial blanket bond *(US)*.

blanko blank, short, not filled in, *(Kredit)* uncovered, unsecured;
in ~ **giriert** indorsed in blank;
~ **abgeben** to bear *(Br.)*, to sell (go) short *(US)*;
~ **ausstellen** to make out in blank; ~ **trassieren** to draw in blank; ~ **verkaufen** to sell ahead (a bear).

Blanko|abgaben uncovered sales, selling stocks short *(US)*; ~**akzept** acceptance in blank; ~**auftrag** blank engagement, carte blanche order; ~**indossament** assignment in blank, blank transfer; ~**kredit** blank credit, credit in blank, open (unsecured) credit, uncovered loan; ~**kredite gewähren** to lend money without security (collateral, *US)*; ~**offerte** offer in blank; ~**scheck** blank cheque *(Br.)* (check, *US)*; ~**unterschrift** blank signature, signature in blank; ~**verkäufe** bearish operations *(Br.)*, short selling *(US)*; ~**vollmacht** full power of attorney, dormant warrant, unlimited powers (authority); ~**zession** blank transfer.

Blickfang|preis charm price; ~**zeile** headline.

Blind|anzeige blind advertisement.

Blitz|funktelegramm priority radiotelegram; ~**gespräch** *(tel.)* lightning call.

Blockade blockade, embargo, investment;
unwirksame ~ paper blockade;
~ **aufheben** to raise (call off, remove, lift) a blockade.

Blockade|brecher blockade runner; ~**freischein** navicert.

blockieren to block [up], to jam, to blockade, *(Kapital)* to freeze, to lock (tie) up;
Konto ~ to block an account.

Blütezeit *(Konjunktur)* boom, prosperity [era]; **konjunkturelle** ~ boomtime.

Boden ground, land, soil, *(Schiff)* bottom; **fruchtbarer** ~ fertile soil, rank land; **gemeinsamen** ~ **für Verhandlungen finden** to find common ground for negotiations; **aus dem** ~ **schießen** to mushroom.

Bodenkredit mortgage loan, agricultural credit; ~**institut** mortgage loan and investment company *(US)*, mortgage bank.

Bodensatz der Arbeitslosen hard core of the unemployed.

Bodenschätze natural resources;
~ **eines Landes ausbeuten** to exploit the national resources of a country.

Bodmerei bottomry, gross adventure;
~ **auf die Schiffsladung** respondentia;
auf ~ **nehmen** to take on bottomry.
~**brief** bottomry bond, bill of bottomry; ~**darlehen** maritime (marine) loan; ~**geber** lender on bottomry; ~**kredit** bottomry (maritime) loan; ~**kredit auf Schiff und Ladung** respondentia bond; ~**versicherung** bottomry insurance.

Bogen sheet, *(Kupon)* coupon sheet;
in Bausch und ~ wholesale, in the lump; ~**anschlagsunternehmen** bill posting agency.

Bombengeschäfte machen to drive a roaring trade.

Bon voucher, coupon, check, [club] chit, *(Gutschein)* credit slip.

Bonifikation *(Bankwesen)* rebate, commission, *(Wertpapier)* bonus.

Bonität soundness, solidity, credit solvency, credit standing (status).

Bonitätsprüfung credit rating *(US)*.

Bonus bonus, premium, *(Dividende)* additional (super, surplus, *US)* dividend, superdividend, plum *(US sl.)*.

Bord shelf, rack, stand, *(mar.)* board;
frei [an] ~ delivered (free) on board, f. o. b.; **an** ~ **gebracht und gestaut** free on board and trimmed; **an** ~ **gehen** to embark, to go (put) on board; **von** ~ **gehen** to leave the ship; **an** ~ **verladen** to ship on board; **Ladung über** ~ **werfen** to jettison.

Borderauverzeichnis bill of specie, specification.

Bord|flugzeug carrier-borne aircraft; ~**funker** wireless operator; ~**funkstelle** wireless room; ~**konnossement** ship's bill; ~ **station** radio station, *(Flugzeug)* aircraft radio room.

Borg, auf on credit (tick, cuff, *US)*.

borgen *(entleihen)* to borrow, *(verleihen)* to loan out, to lend, *(vorschießen)* to advance;
auf Gefälligkeitswechsel ~ to fly a kite *(Br.)*.

Börse [stock] exchange, [stock] market;
an der ~ **gehandelt** obtainable in the market; **auf der** ~ on change *(Br.)*; **an der** ~ **zugelassen** quoted (listed, *US)* on the stock exchange;
abgeschwächte ~ down market; **stürmisch bewegte** ~ greatly agitated market; **feste** ~ firm (strong, steady, undepressed) market; **gedrückte** ~ depressed market; **lebhafte** ~ brisk (cheerful) market;

ruhige ~ featureless market; fast umsatzlose ~ nominal market; wohlgespickte ~ heavy (long, well-lined) purse;
der ~ Auftrieb geben to give a fillip to the market; auf die ~ gehen to visit the stock exchange; an der ~ spekulieren to gamble (operate) on the stock exchange; sich von der ~ zurückziehen to waddle out of the alley (Br. sl.).

Börsen|abrechnungszettel broker's ticket; ~abschlüsse stock-exchange transactions, business; ~aufsicht supervision of the stock exchange; ~auftrag stock-exchange order; ~aufträge für den gleichzeitigen Kauf und Verkauf eines Wertpapiers matched orders; bei ~beginn when the market opens; ~bericht stock-exchange news; ~blatt financial paper; ~brief market letter (US); ~coup deal on the stock exchange; ~einführung admittance to (listing on, US) the stock exchange, stock-exchange introduction (Br.); ~engagement commitment (US); ~fachmann trading specialist. brösenfähig admitted to (negotiable, quoted) on the stock exchange, on exchange, listed (US).

Börsen|fernschreiber ticker [service], quotation (stock) ticker (US); ~freiverkehr curb (kerb, Br., over-the-counter, US) market.
börsengängige Effekten stock-exchange (listed, US) securities.

Börsen|gerücht market rumo(u)r; ~geschäft [stock-] exchange business, stock (market) transaction, bargain; ~gewinn stock-market gain; ~handel jobbing, stock-exchange dealings; ~händler stock operator; ~hausse stock market boom; ~index stockexchange (price) average.

Börsen|kommissionsfirma commissiosn broker; ~geschäft stockbroking [transaction], broker's business; ~konsortium price ring, corner, pool; ~kurs [stock-exchange] quotation; ~kurszettel market report, stock list; ~makler exchange broker, insider (Br.) jobber, floor broker (US), ticker firm (US); ~manipulation manipulation on the stock exchange; ~mann stockjobber.

Börsenmanöver stockjobbery, rigging [the market], demonstration (US);
~ der Baissepartei gunning for stocks (US);
~ durchführen to wash sales of stock (US).

Börsen|mitglied member of the stock exchange, exchange (floor) member; ~nachrichten financial (stock-exchange, city) news; ~notierung market (exchange) quotation; amtliche ~notierung official list; ~ordnung stock-exchange regulation; ~panik panic; ~papiere künstlich in die Höhe treiben to balloon securities (US); ~platz exchange center US) (centre, Br.); ~saal [board] room, exchange hall, floor; ~scheinverkauf wash sale (US), washing (US).

Börsenschluß closing of the exchange, final hour of trading, (Abschlußeinheit) trading unit, full lot (board, US);
nach ~ after official hours, street (Br.);
bei ~ 2 sh höher stehen to clos 2-up.

Börsen|schwankungen exchange fluctuations; ~spekulant gambler, bargain hunter, stockjobber; ~spekulation stockjobbing, jobbery, gambling on the [stock] exchange; ~stempel stamp duty; ~stimmung stock-market sentiment; ~teil (Zeitung) city (commercial) news; ~telegraf ticker, stock ticker (indicator, printer); ~tendenz stock trend; ~termingeschäft option, trading in futures (US), forward operation; ~umsätze stock-exchange transactions; ~umsatzsteuer stock-transfer tax; ~vertreter stock-exchange agent, boardman; ~werte stock-exchange (listed, US) securities; ~zeitung financial paper, gazette (Br.); ~zettel stock-exchange list, list of [market] quotations, the list; ~zulassung beantragen to qualify with the US Securities and Exchange Commission (US).
bösgläubiger Erwerber purchaser in bad faith.
Bote messenger, runner, delivery man, carrier.
Boten|dienst messenger service; ~inkassi collection by hand, walk collections (Br.).
Boulevardblatt tabloid (US), yellow paper.
Boykott, mittelbarer secondary boycott; unmittelbarer ~ primary boycott;
~ aufheben to call off a boycott;
~feldzug boycott campaign.
boykottieren, Laden to put a shop under a boycott.
Boykottliste black (stop) list.
brachliegend unemployed, unused, (Kapital) idle, uninvested.
Branche branch [of industry], business line, line of business, trade, walk, department, lay (sl.).
Branchen|adreßbuch classified (mercantile, trade, professional, commercial) directory; ~bevollmächtigter walking delegate; ~konjunktur particular business trend; ~werbung trade advertising.
Brand|brief (fam.) dunning letter; ~kasse fire insurance office (fund); ~schaden loss by fire; ~versicherungsgesellschaft fire insurance company.
Brennstoff fuel, gasoline (US);
~bedarf fuel requirements; ~verbrauch fuel consumption; ~versorgung fuel supply (allocation).
Brett, Schwarzes notice (bulletin, US) board, newsboard (Br.).
Brief letter, (Börse) paper, asked [price], sellers only, on offer;
~ angeboten (Börse) mainly sellers; vorwiegend ~ (Börse) sellers over;
nicht abgeholter ~ unclaimed letter; persönlicher ~ personal (private) letter; postlagernder ~ letter to be called for, caller's (post-office box) letter; unbestellbarer ~ dead (returned, blind) letter; unfrankierter ~ unpaid letter;
~ folgt letter to follow (following);
~ und Geld (Börse) bills and money (offers), sellers and buyers (Br.), asked and bid;
~ abheften to file a letter away; ~ abschließen to bring a letter to a close; ~ aufsetzen to draw up (build) a letter; ~ ausfindig machen to trace (track down) a letter; ~ bestätigen to acknowledge [receipt of] a letter, to confirm a letter; ~ frei-

machen (frankieren) to pay the postage; ~e **nachsenden** to forward letters to a new address; ~ **per Luftpost schicken** to send a letter by airmail; ~ **als Eilbrief schicken** to express a letter; ~ **unterschlagen** to suppress a letter; ~ **vordatieren** to date a letter ahead; ~ **zustellen** to deliver a letter.

Brief|abfertigung dispatch of mail *(US)*, mail distribution *(US)*; ~**ablage** letter file, filing of letters; ~**annahme[stelle]** *(Post)* receiving counter, mail drop *(US)*; ~**aufgabe per Einschreiben** registration of a letter; ~**ausgangsbuch** letters dispatched book *(Br.)*; ~**durchschlag behalten** to keep a copy of a letter; ~**eingangsbuch** letters received book; ~**einwurf** letter (pillar, *Br.)* box, *(Postamt)* mailbox *(US)*, letter drop; ~**geheimnis verletzen** to break the secrecy of a letter; ~**hülle** envelope, cover, wrapper; ~**hülle mit Breitbandklappe** open side; ~**karte** letter *(Br.)* (folding, postal) card; ~**kasten** letter box, drop box *(US)*, mailbox *(US)*, postbox *(Br.)*, post *(Br.)*; ~**klammer** paper clip; ~**kopf** letterhead; ~**korb** desk tray; ~**kurs** *(Börse)* asked price (rate, quotation), selling rate, offer (selling) price; ~**kuvert** envelope, cover, wrapper.

brieflich in writing, by letter (mail, *US)*; ~ **bestätigen** to confirm by letter; ~ **überweisen** to remit by mail *(US)*.

Briefmarke [postage] stamp; **aufgeklebte** ~ affixed stamp; **entwertete** ~ defaced stamp; **ungültige** ~ spoilt stamp; ~ **aufkleben** to stick on (affix) a stamp.

Briefmarken|ausgabe issue of stamps; ~**automat** stamp machine; ~**stempel** postage stamp, postmark.

Brief|muster form (model) letter; ~**notierung** *(Börse)* asked quotations; ~**ordner** letter file; ~**papier** note (letter, writing) paper, stationery; ~**porto** postage, letter rate *(Br.)*; ~**post** letter post *(Br.)*, first-class mail *(US)*; ~**schulden** arrears of (outstanding) correspondence; ~**sortierer** letter sorter (carrier, *Br.)*; ~**tagebuch** letter book, daily mail ledger *(US)*; ~**tasche** wallet, letter (note) case, pocket book, billfold *(US)*; ~**telegramm** letter (deferred) telegram, telegram delivered by mail *(Br.)*, cable (day, night) letter *(US)*, lettergram *(US)*.

Briefumschlag envelope, cover, wrapper; **abgestempelter** ~ postage envelope; **gummierter** ~ adhesive envelope; ~ **frei durch Ablösung** on Her Majesty's service *(Br.)*, O.H.M.S., penalty envelope *(US)*.

Brief|verkehr exchange of letters, correspondence; ~**vorlage** model letter; ~**waage** letter scales *(US)*.

Briefwechsel correspondence, exchange of letters; **vertraulicher** ~ close correspondence; **im** ~ **stehen** to correspond, to be in correspondence with.

Brief|zensur postal censorship, censorship of the mail *(US)*; ~**zustellung** delivery of letters.

bringen, in Abrechnung to deduct, to make a deduction; **zum Abschluß** ~ to make a deal (bargain); **Gewinn** ~ to be profitable; **auf den Markt** ~ to [put on

the] market; **auf neue Rechnung** ~ to place to new account; **Falschgeld in Umlauf** ~ to utter counterfeit notes; **zur Versteigerung** ~ to put up for auction; **Zinsen** ~ to yield (bear) interest.

broschiert [wire-] stitched, unbound, in loose cover.

Brot, jem. Lohn und ~ **geben** to keep s. o. in one's pay; **sich sein** ~ **selbst verdienen** to earn one's bread and butter.

Brotverdiener breadwinner.

Bruch breach, rupture, *(Waren)* breakage, break; **keine Gewähr für** ~ no risk for breakage; ~ **eines Vertrages** infringement (violation) of a contract.

Bruch|gefahr risk of breakage; ~**klausel** breakage clause; ~**kohle** broken coal; ~**landung** crash [landing], smashup; ~**schaden** breakage; ~**teilsaktie** fractional share.

brutto [in the] gross, overall; ~ **erbringen** to gross; ~ **wiegen** to weigh in the gross.

Brutto|anlageninvestitionen gross investment in fixed assets; ~**betrag** gross amount; ~**durchschnittsverdienst** gross average earnings; ~**einnahmen** gross receipts (earnings, returns); ~**erlös** gross sales; ~**ertrag abwerfen** to gross; ~**ertragsanalyse** cashflow statement; ~**ertragswert** *(Haus)* gross estimated rental; ~**gewicht** gross (invoiced) weight.

Bruttogewinn gross profit (margin); ~**spanne** marginal income, gross margin; ~**zuschlag** markup percentage *(US)*.

Brutto|inlandsprodukt gross domestic product; ~**lohn** gross wage (pay), pay before stoppage *(Br.)*; ~**marge** marginal income; ~**prämie einschließlich Verwaltungskostenzuschlag** office premium; ~**preis** gross (long) price; ~**registertonne** registered ton; ~**registertonnage** gross (registered) tonnage; ~**rendite** gross yield; ~**sozialprodukt** gross national product, GNP; ~**stundenverdienste** gross hourly wages; ~**tara** percentage tare; ~**umsatz** gross sale (turnover); ~**verdienst** gross earnings (compensation), standard profit; ~**wert** gross value; **durchschnittlicher** ~**wochenverdienst** gross average weekly earnings.

Buch book, work, *(Band)* volume, *(Exemplar)* copy, *(Hauptbuch)* ledger; **zu** ~ **stehend mit** at a book value of; **über Ausgaben [genau]** ~ **führen** to keep an [a strict] account of expenses; **zu** ~ **schlagen** to be profitable; ~**ausschnittsdienst** abstract service; ~**beleg** voucher; ~**einlagen** *(Bankwesen)* time deposits and saving accounts.

buchen to [bring to] book, to enter, to note down, to make an entry, to [place to] account, *(ins Journal eintragen)* to journalize, *(reservieren)* to book, to reserve *(US)*; **jeden Posten einzeln** ~ to post each entry singly; **auf Gewinn- und Verlustkonto** ~ to pass to profit and loss account; **gleichlautend** ~ to book (enter, pass an entry) in conformity; **nachträglich** ~ to make a subsequent entry; **ins Soll** ~ to debit.

Bücher, bei Abschluß unserer in closing our books; **frisierte** ~ cooked accounts; ~ **abschließen** to balance (close) the books.

Bücher|abschluß balancing (closing) the books, rest; ~**fälschung** falsification of accounts; ~**liste** book list, list of books.

Bücherrevisor auditor, accountant; **beeidigter** ~ chartered *(Br.)* (certified public, *US)* accountant.

Bücher|sendung *(Post)* printed papers at reduced rates; ~**stand** bookstall, bookstand *(US)*.

Buchforderungen *(Bilanz)* book accounts, accounts receivable *(US)*, *(gegen Konzerngesellschaften* intercompany deposits.

Buchführer bookkeeper, accountant.

Buchführung accounting, the accounts, bookkeeping; **amerikanische** ~ columnar [system of] bookkeeping, tabular bookkeeping *(US)*; **doppelte** ~ double-entry (duplicate) bookkeeping; **kameralistische** ~ government accounting; ~ **nach angefallenen Istkosten** historical accounting; ~ **in Loseblattform** loose-leaf ledger; **doppelte** ~ **haben** to keep books by double entry.

Buchführungs|belege accounting (bookkeeping) records; ~**methode** accounting method.

Buchführungssystem accounting system; **Einnahmen-Ausgaben-~** cost-book principle.

Buchführungsunterlagen [business] records.

Buch|geld credit money (currency), fiduciary (fiat, *US)* money, money in account *(Br.);* ~**gewinn** book profit, *(Lagererhöhung)* inventory profit; ~**gläubiger** book creditor.

Buchhalter [book]keeper, accountant, ledger (entry, entering, bookkeeping) clerk; **leitender** ~ senior accountant.

Buchhaltung bookkeeping, accountancy, accounting [setup], *(Abteilung)* countinghouse *(Br.)*.

Buchhaltungs|abteilung accounting (bookkeeping) department (division); ~**beleg** bookkeeping voucher; ~**unterlagen für selbständige Bilanzierung** self-balancing accounting records.

Buch|handelspreis trade price; ~**händler** bookseller, bookdealer *(US)*.

Buch|kredit book credit; **offene ~e der Bundesnotenbank an die Regierung** ways advances *(Br.)*.

Buch|laden bookshop, bookstall, bookstore *(US)*; ~**macher** bookmaker, ringman *(Br.)*.

buchmäßig as shown by the books.

Buchprüfer accountant, auditor; **beeidigter (öffentlich zugelassener)** ~ chartered accountant *(Br.)*, certified public accountant *(US)*.

Buchprüfung, betriebseigene internal audit; ~ **auf Grund mitgenommener Belege** desk audit; ~ **und Betriebsprüfung** business auditing service.

Buch|sachverständiger auditor, auditing expert; ~**schulden** ordinary debts, stated liabilities, accounts payable *(US)*.

Buchung booking, entering [up], posting, *(einzeln)* entry, item, *(Reservierung)* booking, reservation *(US)*; **falsche** ~ misentry, covering entry; **nachträgliche** ~ postentry, subsequent entry; **für den Rückflug vorgenommene** ~ return plane reservation; ~ **auf einer Chartermaschine** charter booking; ~ **abändern** to alter an entry; ~ **aufgeben** to book, to make a reservation *(US)*; ~ **stornieren** to reverse an entry.

Buchungs|aufgabe booking note; ~**bestätigung** reconfirmation of reservation; ~**formular** bookkeeping form; ~**nummer** number of entry; ~**posten** [booking] item, [bookkeeping] entry (item); ~**stelle** accounting office; ~**unterlage** voucher accounting record; ~**verfahren** bookkeeping method; ~**vermerk** *(Flugzeug)* reconfirmation notice; ~**zyklus** bookkeeping cycle.

Buchwert book (accounting, carrying) value, book (depreciated) cost; **börsenmäßig gehandelte ~e** inscribed stocks *(Br.)*; ~ **vor Abschreibungen** gross book value; ~ **herabsetzen (heraufsetzen)** to write down (up) the book value.

Budget budget, estimates; ~ **vorlegen** to bring in the estimates, to open (introduce) the budget; ~**aufstellung** budgeting, *(Privathaushalt)* income engineering *(US)*; ~**jahr** budget (fiscal) year.

bummeln, bei der Arbeit ~ to slack at one's work.

Bummel|streik slowdown *(US)*, go-slow [strike] *(Br.);* ~**zug** *(fam.)* omnibus (way, stopping, parliamentary, *Br.,* accommodation, *US)* train.

Bündel | Banknoten wad of banknotes, bankroll; **ganzes** ~ **geldmarktpolitischer Maßnahmen** package of monetary relief.

Bundes|amt, Statistisches National Bureau of Economic Research *(US)*; ~**anzeiger** Gazette *(Br.)*, Federal Register *(US)*; ~**bank** Federal Reserve Bank *(US)*; ~**behörde** federal agency; ~**finanzhof** *[etwa]* Income Tax Appeal Tribunal; ~**haushalt** Federal Budget; ~**schuldenverwaltung** [etwa] National Debt Commissioner *(Br.)*, Debt Management *(US)*; ~**straße 51 folgen** to pick up route 51; ~**zuschuß** grant-in-aid *(US)*.

Bürge bail, bailsman, surety, bond, bondsman; **in Anspruch genommener** ~ vouchee; **selbstschuldnerischer** ~ absolute guarantor; **als** ~ **für j. haften** to stand bail (surety) for s. o.

bürgen to [stand] bail, to become surety; **für die Echtheit einer Ware** ~ to guarantee the genuineness of goods; **für einen Wechsel** ~ to guarantee a bill.

Bürgschaft pledge, assurance, caution, gage *(Br.), (Garantie)* bond, guarantee, guaranty *(US)*; warranty, *(für Wechsel)* del credere *(Br.)*; **selbstschuldnerische** ~ absolute guaranty *(US)*, guaranty of payment *(US)*; ~ **leisten** to bail, to give (furnish, stand) bail; ~ **übernehmen** to undertake a guarantee, to go (stand) surety; **selbstschuldnerische ~ übernehmen** to be liable as principal debtor.

Bürgschafts|erklärung guarantee *(Br.)*, guaranty *(US)*, surety [bond], warrant, warranty; **~nehmer** guarantee, bailer; **~schein** deed of suretyship, security, warranty, surety, guarantee, guaranty *(US)*; **~versprechen, ~vertrag** [contract of] suretyship, contract of guaranty, security.

Büro office, bureau *(US)*, *(Kontor)* countinghouse *(Br.);*
fliegendes ~ airborne traffic;
sein ~ unterbringen to locate one's office; **eigene ~s in der ganzen Welt unterhalten** to operate own offices throughout the world.

Büro|adresse business address, *(AG)* statutory office *(US);* **gehobene ~arbeit,** black-coated *(Br.),* (white-collar, *US*) job; **~ausstattung** office appliances; **~betrieb** office routine (procedure); **~chef** bureau chief; **~einrichtung** office fittings, *(Bilanz)* furniture and office equipment; **~gebäude** office building; **~gemeinschaft mit jem. haben** to share an office with s. o.; **~klammer** paper clip; **~kratismus** red tape (tapism), red-tapedom (-tapery); **~leiter** office manager, managing clerk; **~miete** office rent; **~mitbenutzung** secretarial facilities; (business) hours; **~personal** [office] personel, clerical force (staff), office staff (force), hands *(US);* **~raum zur Verfügung stellen** to furnish office room; **~schluß** closing time; **~stunden** office (business) hours; **seine ~stunden pünktlich einhalten** to be regular in one's attendance (at one's office); **~tätigkeit** secretarial (clerical) service desk work; **~verwaltung** office management; **~vorsteher** office keeper (manager), head clerk; **~zeit** office hours, meeting time; **für ~zwecke** for office use.

Bürstenabzug *(drucktechn.)* galley (stone) proof.

Bus für den Pendelverkehr commuter (shuttle) bus.

Buße exemplary damages, forfeit, fine;
~ für Nichterfüllung eines Vertrages liquidaed damages;
~geld festsetzen to assess a fine.

C

Carnet international customs pass.

Charter charter, *(Schiff)* charter, charterage; **~flug** charter flight; **~fluggesellschaft** supplemental [carrier], air charterer; **~flugzeug** hired aircraft, charter[ed] plane; **~geschäft** charter operation; **~gesellschaft** charter carrier (airline); **~maschine benutzen** to fly on a nonscheduled trip.

chartern to [take on] charter.

Charter|partie charterparty; **~vertrag** charter [party].

Chef *(Prinzipal)* employer, head, chief, principal, master, old man;
~ vom Dienst desk (news, *US*) editor;
~redakteur editor in chief, managing editor.

Chiffre cipher, key, *(Anzeige)* box number;
~anzeige box-number advertisement; **~nummer** *(Anzeige)* box (key) number; **~werbung** keyed advertising, keying of advertisements.

chiffriert in code (cipher);
~er Brief coded letter.

chronische Arbeitslosigkeit hard core.

Clearing, auswärtiges out clearings *(US);*
~abkommen clearing agree

D

D-Zug corridor ¯(express, fast, long-distance, through, vestibule, *US*) train;

Dach|gesellschaft controlling (holding, overhead, parent) establishment; ~**marke** family brand; ~**verband** umbrella organization.

Dampferlinie steamship line.

Dämpfung | der Investitionstätigkeit dampening (curbing) of business spending; ~ **der Konjunktur** compensatory fiscal policy.

Darlehn loan, credit, advance accommodation; **befristetes** ~ time (term) loan; **eingefrorenes** ~ dead loan *(Br.)*, frozen credit (loan) *(US)*; **hypothekarisch gesichertes** ~ mortgage loan; **jederzeit kündbares** ~ precarious (demand) loan; **langfristiges** ~ long-sighted (time, *US*) loan; **verzinsliches** ~ interestbearing loan; **zinsloses** ~ advance free of interest;
~ **der Landeszentralbank** reserve bank credit *(US)*;
~ **auf Grund börsengängiger Wertpapiere** advance against marketable securities *(Br.)*, collateral loan *(US)*;
~ **aufnehmen** to borrow money, to take up (raise) a loan; **gegen Lombardierung von Wertpapieren** ~ **aufnehmen** to borrow on the collateral of securities *(US)*; **kurzfristiges** ~ **gewähren** to lend at short interest; ~ **kündigen** to call in (recall) a loan.

Darlehns|antrag loan |application; ~**bank** loan bank; ~**geschäft** loan business, lending operation; ~**gesellschaft** credit corporation, loan society *(Br.)*; ~**gesuch** loan request; ~**kasse** loan association (office, society, *Br.*); ~**kassenverein** small-loan company *(US)*; ~**konto** loan account; ~**nehmer** borrower, loanee; ~**schuldner** *(Bilanz)* loans payable *(US)*; ²**weise** as a loan.

Daten data, facts;
~**bank** data bank; ~**plan der Anzeigen** advertising schedule; ~**speicherung** data storage.

Datowechsel bill [drawn] after date.

Datum| der Antragstellung date of application; ~ **des Poststempels** date of postmark, postal date.

Datums|angabe dating, date *(Lebensmittelpackung)* code date; ~**stempel** dater, date stamp, *(Poststempel)* postmark.

Dauer|akkreditiv permanent credit; ~**arbeitslosigkeit** chronic (permanent, hard-core) unemployment; ~**auftrag** permanent (standing)ʼ order, *(an die Bank)* banker's order; ~**betrieb** continuous operation; ~**fahrkarte** season *(Br.)* (commutation, *US*) ticket; ~**güter** durable manufactures, durables; ~**karteninhaber** season-ticket holder *(Br.)*, commutation passenger *(US)*, commuter *(US)*.

Debet debit, debtor, *(fam.)* tick;
~ **und Kredit** debit and credit;
im ~ **stehen** to be on the debit (debtor) side.

Debet|buchung debit entry; ~**konto** debit (debtor) account; **als** ~**posten buchen** to debit; ~**saldo** debit (debt, debtor) balance; ~**saldo aufweisen** to show a

debit balance; ~**seite** debtor [side], debit [side]; ~**zinsen** interest on debit balances.

Debitoren *(Bilanz)* debtors, debts *(Br.)*, accounts (bills) receivable *(US)*, receivables *(US)*; **sichere** ~ good debts; **verschiedene** ~ sundry debtors;
~ **aus Schuldverschreibungen** bond subscription receivables *(US)*.

Debitoren|abtretung assignment of accounts receivable *(US)*; ~**aufstellung nach Fälligkeit** aging accounts receivable *(US)*; ~**buchhaltung** accounts receivable department (borrowing) rates; **[offener]** ~**verkauf** selling accounts receivable outright *(US)*, factoring; ~**verzeichnis** schedule of accounts receivable *(US)*.

debitorisch werden to run into debt.

Deck, an verladen to ship on deck;
~**adresse** code (accommodation, cover) address; ~**blatt** backer, flyleaf.

decken, Akzept ~ to provide for acceptance; **Bedarf** ~ to meet the requirements, to supply the needs; **Kosten** ~ to defray the costs; **Leerabgaben einer Position** ~ to repurchase short sales *(US)*; **durch Hinterlegung einer Sicherheitssumme** ~ to margin.

Deck|güter deck cargo; ~**ladung** deckload; ~**name** pseudonym, assumed (cover, fictitious) name; ~**passagier** deck passenger.

Deckung cover, covering, coverage, provision of funds, *(Banknoten)* backing, *(Geldsendung)* remittance, *(Kapital)* funds, *(Wechsel)* protection, hono(u)ring;
~ **angeschafft** cover afloat (in transit); **zur** ~ **unserer Unkosten** to cover our expenses; **genügende** ~ ample security, sufficient funds; **keine** ~ not sufficient [funds] *(n. s.)*, not provided for, *(Konto)* no funds, *(Scheckvermerk)* no effects; **vorgeschriebene** ~ *(Lebensversicherung)* legal reserve; **weitere (zusätzliche)** ~ additional cover, collateral security *(US)*;
~ **des Bedarfs** meeting the requirements; ~ **eines Verlustes** covering of a loss;
~ **ablehnen** *(Versicherung)* to disclaim liability;
~ **anschaffen** to cover, to make (send, provide for) remittance; ~ **für einen Wechsel anschaffen** make provision for cover of a bill; **für** ~ **sorgen** to provide for payment (with funds); ~ **für Kursverluste stellen** *(Makler)* to margin up; **ohne** ~ **verkaufen** *(Börse)* to sell a bear (short, *US*); **als** ~ **verwenden** to apply shares as security (stock as collateral, *US*).

Deckungs|auftrag covering order, order to cover; ~**beitrag** contribution margin, marginal (variable gross) income; ~**beitragsrechnung** contribution margin; ~**betrag** margin, *(Versicherung)* insured sum; ²**fähig** eligible to serve as collateral *(US)*; ~**geschäft unterbringen** to [place a] hedge; ~**kapital** legal capital, *(Bausparkasse)* guarantee stock, *(Versicherung)* unearned premium (insurance) reserve; ~**kauf** cover[ing] purchase, *(von Effekten bei Lieferverzug)* buying in, short covering *(US)*; zu ~**käufen zwingen** *(Börse)* to squeeze the shorts *(US) (bears);* ~**mittel** cover, covering resources, ungeeignete ~**mittel** *(Versicherung)* nonadmitted assets; ~**rücklage** *(Versicherung)* insurance reserve; ~ **stock** *(Bausparkasse)* guarantee stock, *(Versicherung)* unearned premium (insurance) reserve.

deckungsstockfähig eligible to serve as collateral *(US).*

Deckungs|verhältnis *(Banknoten)* reserve ratio *(US)*; **gesetzlich vorgeschriebenes** ~**verhältnis** *(Versicherung)* legal reserve requirements; ~**zusage** *(Versicherung)* binder, binding (conditional) receipt.

Defizit deficit, deficiency, shortage, short, wantage, *(Bilanz)* adverse balance, red; ~ **abdecken** to cover a deficit; ~ **aufweisen** to show a deficit; **ins** ~ **geraten** to slip into deficit; **mit dem** ~ **fertigwerden** to cope with the red ink; ~**vorschlag** deficit projection; ~**wirtschaft** compensatory spending, deficit financing.

Deflation deflation.

deflationäre Maßnahmen deflationary measures.

Deflations|bewegung deflationary movement; ~**maßnahmen** deflationary measures; ~**politik treiben** to deflate the currency.

Degression *(Steuer)* degression.

degressive Abschreibungsmethode reducing-fraction method of depreciation.

Deklaration für zollfreie Waren entry for duty-free goods.

deklarieren to declare, to enter, to make a bill of entry, to report; **zu hoch** ~ to declare (value) too high; **zollamtlich** ~ to enter at the customhouse.

Dekoration *(Schaufenster)* window display (dressing).

Dekorations|arbeit display work; ~**fenster** display window; ~**material** window display material.

dekorieren, Fenster to dress a window.

Delkredere guarantee, surety, del credere *(Br.)*; ~ **stehen** to stand surety, to insure a debt, to give guarantee.

Delkredere|fonds contingent fund; ~**konto** contingent (contingency, reserve, del credere, *Br.)* account; ~**rückstellung** contingency reserve, reserve for contingencies; ~**versicherung** credit insurance.

Depeschenformular message (telegraph) form.

deponieren to deposit, to lodge, to bail.

Deportgeschäft backwardation business.

Depositen [time] deposits, deposited funds; **durch effektive Einlagen geschaffene** ~ primary deposits; **sofort fällige** ~ demand deposits; ~**abteilung** deposit department (division); ~**bank** deposit bank, depositary [bank] *(US)*; ~**gelder** time *(US)* (fixed-term) deposits; ~**gutha-ben** bank deposit; ~**inhaber** depositor; ~**kasse** deposit and consignment office, *(Bankfiliale)* branch [office]; ~**schein** deposit receipt (slip, *US)* safe custody receipt.

Depot depository, *(Bank)* safe, strongroom, safe custody *(Br.)*, safe deposit *(US)*; **gemeinschaftliches** ~ joint deposit; **gesperrtes** ~ blocked (frozen, *US)* deposit; **lebendes** ~ register of securities *(Br.)*, securities book *(Br.)* (register, *US)*; ~ **für unverzollte Ware** bonded warehouse; **Wertpapiere ins** ~ **einliefern** to deposit securities for safe custody *(Br.)* (custodianship, *US)*; **etw. bei einer Bank in** ~ **geben** to deposit s. th. with a bank; ~**abteilung** *(Bank)* safe custody department *(Br.)*; securities department *(US)*; ~**aufbewahrung** safe custody (keeping); ~**auszug** statement of deposited securities (custodiansship account, *US)*; ~**bank** deposit (custodian, *US)* company; ~**geschäft** deposit banking; ~**miete** safe deposit rent; ~**quittung**, ~**schein** certificate of deposit *(US)*, deposit slip *(US)*; ~**steuer** bank deposit tax *(US)*; ~**stimmrecht** proxy rights; ~**unterschlagung** embezzlement of trust money; ~**versicherung** deposit (safe-deposit box) insurance; ~**verwaltungsgebühren** safe-custody *(Br.)* (custodianship, *US)* charges; ~**wechsel** deposited (collateral, *US)* bill.

Deputatentlohnung product sharing.

Deputatwohnung tied cottage *(Br.)*.

Devisen foreign currency (exchanges, *Br.)*, international exchange *(US)*; ~ **zu Tageskursen** bills at the day's quotation; ~ **anmelden** to declare foreign exchange; ~ **beantragen** to apply for foreign exchange; ~ **umrechnen** to reduce money.

Devisen|abkommen foreign exchange (offset) agreement; ~**abrechnung** exchange statement (settlement); ~**arbitrage** arbitration [of exchange]; ~**ausländer** nonresident *(US)*; ~**bank** exchange bank; ~**beschränkungen** currency restrictions; ~**bestände** foreign exchange funds, currency (exchange) holdings; ~**bestimmungen** currency regulations; **nicht ausgenutzte** ~**beträge** remaining foreign exchange; ~**bewirtschaftung abbauen** to dismantle exchange controls; ~**bringer** foreign exchange earner; ~**forderung** foreign currency claim; ~**freibetrag** foreign exchange allowance; ~**gebühren** exchange fees; ~**genehmigung** foreign exchange permit; ~**geschäft** foreign exchange transaction (dealings); ~**guthaben** currency assets; ~**händler** cambist, currency (money) dealer; ~**inländer** resident *(US)*; ~**kontingent** foreign exchange quota; ~**konto** foreign currency account.

Devisenkurs exchange rate, rate of exchange; **in Penny notierte** ~**e** pence rates *(Br.)*; ~ **für kurzfristige Wechsel** short rate.

Devisen|kurszettel foreign exchange list; ~**makler** exchange broker (dealer); ~**notierung** quotation of [foreign] exchange [rates]; ~**plafond** foreign exchange limit; ~**polster** [foreign] exchange reserve; ᵒ**rechtliche Bestimmungen** foreign exchange regulations; ~**reserven** foreign exchange reserves; ~**schiebung** currency racket; ~**schmuggel** currency smuggling; ~**termingeschäft** forward exchange transaction; **~terminhandel** forward exchange deals *(Br.)*, forward exchange operations *(US)*, futures exchange *(US)*; **~terminkurs** forward exchange rate; **~terminmarkt** forward exchange market; **~transaktion** exchange operation (transaction); **freier ~verkehr** freedom of exchange operations; **~verrechnungskonto** foreign exchange clearing account; **langfristiger ~wechsel** long exchange *(Br.)*; **~werte** [foreign-] exchange assets, foreign securities *(US)*; **~zuteilungen** foreign exchange allotments *(Br.)* (allocation); **~zwangswirtschaft** rationing of foreign exchanges.

dezentralisieren to decentralize, to regionalize *(Betrieb)* to departmentalize.

Diäten *(Tagegeld)* emoluments, per diem, daily (sessional expense) allowance, *(Sitzungsgelder)* attendance fee.

Diebstahls|klausel theft clause; **Haftpflicht- und ~versicherung** *(Auto)* comprehensive liability and property damage insurance.

Dienst office, service, attendance, *(Amtsleistung)* duty, function;
außer ~ out [of office], retired from service, *(dienstfrei)* off-duty;
gehobener ~ higher grade, classified service *(US)*; **langjähriger ~** veteran service;
~ nach Vorschrift work-to-rule (according to the book, *US*), go-slow strike *(Br.)*;
seinen ~ antreten to enter the employ of; **jds. ~e in Anspruch nehmen** to make use of s. one's services; **Schiff in ~ stellen** to put a ship into commission; **Schiff außer ~ stellen** to take a ship off the active list;
~abteil *(Bahn)* service compartment, caboose *(US)*; **~alter** years of service, job, seniority *(US)*; **~antritt** entering upon service; **~aufwandsentschädigung** office (expense) allowance; **~auto** service vehicle; **~betrieb** daily routine; **~enthebung** discharge, dismissal, *(vorübergehende)* suspension.

dienstfrei exempt from service, at leisure, off-duty.

Dienstleistungs|abkommen service agreement; **~bereich** service sector; **~betrieb** public service company (corporation, enterprise, *US*); **~gebühr** *(Agentur)* service fee (charge); **~geschäft** service business *(US)*, *(Agentur)* agency services.

dienstlich official, on official business, functional, in the course of duty;
~ unterwegs sein to be out on official business; **~ verhindert sein** to be detained by business.

Dienst|mann street porter, outporter *(Br.)*, jobber, messenger, expressmann *(US)*; **~marke** revenue stamp, fiscal; **~obliegenheiten** official duties; **~post** official business *(Br.)*; **~reise** official tour (journey, trip); **gebührenpflichtige ~sache** *(auf Bei-Briefen)* on Her Majesty's service *(Br.)*, O.H.M.S.; **~schluß** closing hours; **~sitz** residence, registered office.

Dienststelle agency, board, department, [government] office;

ausführende ~ implementing agency; **nachgeordnete ~** subsidiary office; **zuständige ~** proper department.

Dienst|stellenleiter department head; **~stunden** hours of attendance, office (official, business) hours; **~umschlag** penalty envelope *(US)*, **~verhältnis** employment [service], employment contract *(US)*.

dienstverpflichten to press into service, to conscript, to draft.

Dienst|verpflichteter conscripted employee, enlisted specialist *(US)*; **~verpflichtung** conscription of labo(u)r, industrial (labo[u]r) conscription; **~vertrag** service (employment) agreement; **~vorgesetzter** superior (ranking) officer; **~wagen** service vehicle.

Dienstweg official channels, routine;
~ benützen to go through channels.

Dienst|wohnung residence; **~zeit** period of service, service period.

Differential|tarif differential tariff; **~zoll** discriminating duty.

Differenz|betrag balance, residual quantity; **~geschäft** call, gambling in futures, margin business.

Diktat| aufnehmen to take dictation; **~ auf die Schreibmaschine übertragen** to transcribe dictation.

Diplom|dolmetscher certified interpreter; **~ingenieur** certified engineer; **~kaufmann** Bachelor of Commerce *(Br.)*.

direkt | beziehen to buy first hand, to obtain goods straight from the factory; **~ senden** *(Radio, Fernsehen)* to broadcast live;
~er Absatz direct marketing (selling); **~e Besteuerung** direct taxation; **~e Fahrkarte** through ticket.

Direktabsatz direct marketing (selling).

Direktion board, direction, directorate, management, *(Büro)* director's (manager's) office.

Direktions|assistent company (corporate, management) secretary; **~beschluß** board decision; **~sitzung** board meeting, meeting of directors.

Direktkredite der Wirtschaft direct financing.

Direktor director, manager, conductor, master;
ausscheidender ~ retiring director; **geschäftsführender ~** acting director; **technischer ~** managing engineer, technical manager.

Direktoren|gehälter directors' fees; **~versammlung** board meeting.

direktorial oder kollegial one-man or committe (collegiate, *US*).

Direktorium board of directors (governors), *(EG)* Management Committee.

Direktoriumsmitglied executive director, member of the directorate, board member.

Direkt|sendung *(Rundfunk)* live broadcast (program(me); **~verbindung zu A erhalten** *(Bahn)* to get nonstop to A; **~verkauf** direct sale (selling), direct-to-customer selling; **~verkauf an der Haustür (durch Vertreter)** house-to-house selling; **~werbung** direct-mail promotion.

Dirigismus, staatlicher planned economy.
dirigistische Maßnahmen planning measures.
Disagio disagio, discount;
   mit ~ kaufen to buy a discount;
   ~gewinn unamortized debt (bond) discount.
Diskont discount [rate], rate of discount (rediscount,
   US), bank rate *(Br.)*, rediscount rate *(US)*, *(Ab-*
   zug) deduction, discount, rebate;
   nicht in Anspruch genommener ~ discount lost;
   handelsüblicher ~ commercial discount;
   ~ erhöhen to raise the bank rate *(Br.)*, to raise the
   discount (rediscount, *US*) rate; ~ herabsetzen to
   cut the [rate of] discount (rediscount, *US*), to
   mark down (reduce) the discount; Wechsel zum ~
   hereinnehmen to accept bills for discount.
   ~änderung discount (rediscount, *US*) rate change;
   ~bank acceptance house *(Br.)*, discount bank.
Diskonten *(Wechsel)* discounts, investment bills,
   (Wechsel in der Bilanz) discounted bills.
Diskont|erhöhung discount rate rise; ~erträge dis-
   count earned; ~ermäßigung bank rate reduction
   (Br.), lowering of (reduction in) the discount (rediscount, *US*) rate.
diskontfähig discountable, bankable *(Br.)*, eligible
   for discount (rediscount, *US*).
Diskont|geschäft cut-price shop, ~gutschrift discount
   note; ~herabsetzung bank rate reduction *(Br.)*,
   lowering of the rate of rediscount *(US)*, reduction
   of the discount (bank, rediscount, *US*) rate.
diskontierbar discountable, bankable *(Br.)*, eligible
   for discount (rediscount, *US*).
diskontieren to [take on] discount, to rediscount
   (US).
Diskontierung von Buchforderungen assignment of
   accounts receivable *(US)*.
Diskont|kasse discount office; ~kredit discount (re-
   discount, *US*) credit; ~markt discount (bill, *Br.*,
   rediscount, *US*) market; ~politik bank rate *(Br.)*
   (discount, rediscount, *US*) policy.
Diskontsatz discount, discount (bank, *Br.)* rate, rate
   of discount (rediscount, *US*);
   ~ der Bundesnotenbank bank *(Br.)* (rediscount,
   US) rate;
   ~ erhöhen to raise (increase) the bank *(Br.)* (discount, rediscount, *US*) rate.
Diskont|senkung lowering (reduction) of the bank
   (Br.) (discount, rediscount *US*) rate, fall in the
   bank rate *(Br.)*; ~spesen discount charges; ~tage
   discount days; ~wechsel discounted (investment)
   bill.
Dispache | aufnehmen to state (make up) the average;
   ~kosten adjustment charges.
Disponent chief clerk, factor, managing clerk.
disponieren to dispose, to make over, *(Aufträge er-*
   teilen) to place orders;
   entsprechend ~ to make arrangements to the effect.
Disposition disposal, disposition, *(Auftragserteilung)*
   placing orders.
Dispositions|fonds general revenue fund; ~reserve
   general (operating) reserve.

Distanz|fracht distance (pro rata, ratable) freight,
   freight pro rata; ~geschäft option business;
   ~scheck out-of-town check *(US)* (cheque, *Br.)*;
   ~tarif proportional (distance) rate.
Disziplinar|bestimmungen disciplinary regulations;
   ~fall disciplinary case; ~maßnahmen disciplinary
   action; ~verfahren disciplinary trial (proceedings).
Diverses miscellaneous, sundries, sundry goods.
Dividende dividend, share, *(Lebensversicherung)*
   bonus, dividend;
   ausschließlich ~ dividend off ex dividend *(Br.)*;
   einschließlich (mit) ~ *(US)* cum dividend *(Br.)*,
   including dividend *(US)*, dividend on;
   außerordentliche ~ bonus, extraordinary (special, surplus, *US*) dividend, superdividend, melon
   (US), plum *(US)*; fällige ~ dividend due; garantierte ~ guaranteed dividend; aus dem Kapital gezahlte ~ dividend paid out of the capital; rückständige ~ accumulated dividend; unbehobene ~
   unclaimed dividend;
   ~ in bar oder in Form einer Gratisaktie optional
   dividend; ~ in Form von Aktien stock dividend
   (US), dividend in stock *(US)*; ~ abzüglich Steuern
   dividend net *(Br.)*;
   ~ ausfallen lassen to default (omit, pass, *US*) a
   dividend; ~ ausschütten to declare (disburse, *US*,
   distribute, strike) a dividend; ~ von 14 % bringen
   to yield 14 per cent dividend; ~ herabsetzen to cut
   its dividend.
Dividenden|abschlag reduction in dividends; ~ab-
   schnitt dividend warrant; ~ausfall dividend omission; ~ausschüttung declaration (distribution,
   payment) of dividend; ~ausschüttung zuzüglich
   Abschreibung cashflow; Geschäftsjahr ohne ~aus-
 · schüttung abschließen to pass a dividend *(US)*;
   schon im Juli an der ~ausschüttung teilnehmen to
   rank for the July dividend *(Br.)*.
dividendenberechtigt entitled to a (ranking for)
   dividend.
Dividendenberechtigung dividend rights.
Dividenden|bevorrechtigung preference as to divi-
   dends; ~erhöhung dividend increase; ~erklärung
   declaration of dividends, dividend announcement;
   ~ertrag dividend yield; ~garantie dividend
   guarantee; ~guthaben *(Lebensversicherung)* divisible (life insurance) surplus; ~kupon dividend
   warrant, coupon; ~papiere dividend-paying
   stocks, dividend payers *(US)*, equity (ownership)
   securities, equities; gleichbleibende ~politik conformity in dividend politics; ~rücklage dividend
   reserve fund; ~steuer tax on dividends; ~vorschlag
   recommendation on dividends, dividend recommendation.
dividendenbevorzugsberechtigt sein to rank first with
   dividend rights.
Dividenden|werte, börsengängige dividend-paying se-
   curities; ~zahlung dividend payment.
Dock dock, quay, wharf, navy yard *(US)*;
   Schiff aus dem ~ bringen to take a ship out of
   dock.

Dock|anlagen dock (docking) facilities, docks; ~**arbeiter** dock labo(u)rer, docker *(Br.)*; ~**lagermiete** dock-rent; ~**lagerschein** dock warrant *(Br.)*.

Dokument deed, document, instrument, paper, record, title, voucher, writing; ~**e gegen Akzept** documents against acceptance; ~**e aufnehmen** to list documents; ~ **beglaubigen lassen** to have a document authenticated.

Dokumenten|akkreditiv documentary [letter of] credit; **vollständiger** ~**satz** full set of documents; ~**wechsel** documentary (acceptance) bill (draft).

Dollar|abhebung dollar drawings; ~**anleihe** dollar loan (bonds); **schwindende** ~**reserven** dwindling dollar resources.

Domäne demesne, Crown land *(Br.)*, domain, *(Sondergebiet)* domain, province.

Domänen|einnahmen land revenue of the Crown *(Br.)*; ~**pächter** tenant of a domain.

Domizil|akzept domiciled acceptance; ~**gebühr** domiciliation provision.

domiziliert|es Akzept domiciled acceptance; ~**er Wechsel** domiciled bill of exchange.

Domizilwechsel addressed (domiciled, domiciliated, indirect) bill.

Doppel|besteuerung double taxation; ~**brief** overweight; ~**preissystem** dual pricing.

doppelseitige Anzeige double-page spread.

doppelt| ausgefertigt [delivered] in duplicate; ~**e Buchführung** bookkeeping by double entry; ~**er Preis** *(Anzeige)* double rate; ~**e Quittung** receipt in duplicate.

Doppel|verdiener double earner, two-job worker (man, *US*), moonlighter *(US)*, dualist, pluralist; ~**währung** bimetallic (double) standard, gold-and-silver currency, bimetallism; ~**zimmer** double room.

Dose, auf ~ **aufgenommen** *(Rundfunk)* prerecorded, *(Fernsehen)* videotaped.

Dossierinformation credit report on file.

dotieren to endow, to allocate, to appropriate, to earmark; **Fonds** ~ to increase a reserve fund; **Konto** ~ to place an account in funds.

dotiert allocated, endowed.

Dotierung dotation, endowment, *(Fonds)* allocation, appropriation, earmarking; ~ **eines Kontos** alimentation of an account.

Draht|akzept telegraphic acceptance; ~**anschrift** cable address; ~**antwort** telegraphic answer, wire reply; ~**funk** wired radio *(US)*, ²**los** wireless, radio *(US)*; ~**überweisung** cable transfer.

drängen, seine Kunden mit der Begleichung der Rechnung to push one's clients to pay.

Draufgeld bargain (forfeit) money (penny), earnest money, deposit.

Drei|farbendruck three-colo(u)r printing; ~**meilengrenze** three-mile limit.

Dreimonats|akzept three months' acceptance; ~**geld** ninety days loan.

Dreißigster *(Witwen-Anteil)* household assets.

Dreiviertel|mehrheit three-fourth majority; ~**wertklausel** three-fourth value clause.

dringend|e Geschäfte pressure of business; ~**es Gespräch** *(tel.)* emergency (priority) call; ~**e Nachfrage** pressing demand; ~**es Telegram** priority telegram.

Dringlichkeit, von höchster of top priority.

Dringlichkeits|auftrag priority order; ~**stufe** priority degree of urgency; ~**vermerk** urgent note (memorandum).

Dritt|ausfertigung triplicate, third copy, *(Wechsel)* third of exchange; ~**begünstigter** third-party beneficiary.

Dritter, gutgläubiger bona fide (innocent) third party, *(Wechsel)* holder in due course.

Drittschuldner garnishee, third party debtor, factor *(US)*, *(Faktorei)* customer.

drosseln, Ausgaben to curb expenditure; **Geldversorgung** ~ to tighten the supply of money; **Produktion** ~ to restrain (curb) production.

Drosselung | der Ausgaben expenditure cut; ~ **der Betriebsausstattung** equipment curtailment; ~ **der Produktion** production cut.

Druck *(Abzug)* impression, *(Kurse)* depressed state of the market, low level of prices; **angeschnittener** ~ *(Anzeige)* bleed; **finanzieller** ~ squeeze; ~ **auf die Preise** forcing down the prices; **wirtschaftlichen** ~ **ausüben** to exert economic pressure; ~ **auf den Geldmarkt verursachen** to place pressure on the money market.

Druck|auflage print run; ~**bogen** proof, news (printed) sheet.

drucken to print, to imprint; **druckangeschnitten** ~ to bleed; **gesperrt** ~ to space (blank) out; **kursiv** ~ to print in italics.

drücken, Markt to depress the market; **auf die Preise** ~ to force down the prices.

drückende, Armut pressure of poverty; ~ **Steuern** pressure of taxation.

Druck|erlaubnis imprimatur; ~**fahne** galley proof, advance sheet.

Druckkosten printing expenses (cost); ~**voranschlag** printing estimate.

Druckposten *(fig.)* soft (desk, cushy) job, snap, gravy train *(US sl.)*.

Drucksache printed matter (paper, *Br.*), insert, leaflet; **als** ~ **verschicken** to send by bookpost *(Br.)*.

Drucksachen|bezugspreis subscription rate by surface mail; ~**porto** printed paper rate, rate for printed matter; ~**post** bookpost *(Br.)*, newspaper post, second-class mail *(US)*.

Dumping, verschleiertes hidden dumping; ~**preis** dumping price; ~**verfahren** dumping charge; ~**waren** dumped goods.

Duplikat tally, duplication, duplicate [copy], counterpart, double; **Wechsel im** ~ **ausstellen** to draw bills in sets.

durchbrechen, Blockade to run the blockade.

durchbringen, sich ehrlich to make an honest living; sich kümmerlich ~ to scrape a living; sein ganzes Vermögen ~ to run through one's fortune.

durch|buchen to book through; Waren ~deklarieren to enter goods as transit; ~finanzieren to finance permanently; Betrieb ~forsten to weed the garden.

Durch|forstung *(Betrieb)* garden weeding; ~fracht through shipment *(US)*, transit freight; ~frachtkonnossement through bill of lading, waybill *(US)*.

Durchfuhr|bescheinigung transit certificate (pass); ~deklaration transit declaration; ~erklärung transit entry; ~erlaubnis transit pass; ~gut transit goods; ~land transit country; ~spediteur forwarding agent.

Durchführungs|behörde regulatory agency; ~bestimmungen regulations, implementation clauses.

Durch|fuhrzoll transit duty; ~gang verboten no thoroughfare (passage).

Durchgangs|abgabe transit duty; ~bahnhof through (express, way, *US*) station; ~frachtbrief through bill of lading, waybill *(US)*; ~handel transit trade, transient business; ~hotel commercial (transient, *US*) hotel; ~lager transit camp; ~posten suspense (transitory) item, item (remittance) in transit; ~sendung through shipment; ~straße thoroughfare, throughroad, transit (cross-town) route, arterial highway *(US)*; ~strecke through route; ~tarif transit (through, *US*) rate; ~verkehr through route; traffic, transit, *(Telefon)* through communication; ~wagen corridor (through) car (coach, *Br.)*, Pullmann car *(US)*, transit (vestibule, *US)*; car.

durchgehen *(Antrag, Gesetz)* to be carried (adopted), to pass, *(Ware)* to be in transit, *(Zug)* to go right (straight) through;
Faktura ~ to check the invoice; seine Konten ~ to run over one's accounts.

durchgehend| geöffnet open throughout;
~e Arbeitszeit continuous operation (process); ~e Waren transit goods; ~er Zug nonstop (through) train.

durchgeleiteter Kredit loan passed on, transmitted credit.

Durchkonnossement through bill of lading.

durchkreuzen, Scheck to cross a cheque *(Br.)*.

durchlaufender Posten transitory item.

Durchreise|erlaubnis transit certificate (pass); ~-visum transit visa.

Durch|sage *(Rundfunk)* announcement, message, spot *(US)*; telefonische ~sage [telephone] message.

durchsagen, Telegramm telefonisch to deliver a telegram over the telephone.

Durchschlag [carbon] copy, manifold, flimsy *(Br.)*; ~papier onionskin, flimsy, carbon (bank, copying) paper.

Durchschnitt average, standard, *(Menschen)* ordinary run, *(Statistik)* arithmetic mean;
im ~ verkaufen to sell on an average.

durchschnittlich average, normal, *(gewöhnlich)* common, ordinary, *(mittelmäßig)* middling, secondrate, medium;
~e Einnahmen normal proceeds; ~e Qualität medium quality.

Durchschnitts|aufwand average cost; jährlicher ~bruttoumsatz average annual net sales; ~einkommen average income (earnings); ~kosten average cost; ~kostenverminderung *(Börse)* averaging down (up); ~kurs average price, *(Devisen)* average rate; ~lohn straight-time pay; ~qualität fai average (standard) quality; ~steuersatz average rate, *(Umsatzsteuer)* composite rate; ~stundenverdienst average hourly earnings; ~verbraucher average consumer; ~verdienst average earnings (earned rate); ~verfallzeit average [term of] maturity; ~wert average (mean, standard) value; ~zinsen average interest.

Durchschreibebuchführung multiple-copy (duplicating bookeeping, mechanical) system.

Durchsetzung von Lohnforderungen wage push.

Durchsicht auditing, examination, inspection;
bei ~ unserer Bücher on looking over our books; zur gefälligen ~ for your kind inspection.

durchstarten, sofort wieder *(Konjunkturpolitik)* to rush the economy back to full employment levels.

durchsuchen, zollamtlich to search, to rummage *(Br.)*.

Durchsuchung und Beschlagnahme search and seizure.

Durchwahlnummer direct dial number.

Düsenflugzeug jet [plane], jet cargo (propulsion) plane, jet aircraft (airliner), straight jet.

Dutzend|preis price by the dozen; ~ware articles sold by the dozen.

E

echt genuine, bona fide, real, *(rein)* pure, *(unverfälscht)* inadulterated;
~es Gold real gold.
Eck|laden corner shop (grocery, *US*); ~**lohn** basic wage (hourly rate).
Edelmetall, ungemünztes bullion.
Effekten papers, securities, negotiable instruments, *(Aktien)* shares, stocks;
abhanden gekommene ~ lost securities; **börsengängige** ~ marketable securities (stocks, *US*); **erstklassige** ~ high-grade (gilt-edged, *Br.)* securities, blue chips *(US)*; **hochspekulative** ~ wildcat securities; **lombardierte** ~ pledged securities, securities held as collateral *(US)*, stocks loaned *(US)*, pawned stocks *(US)*;
~ **mit Dividendenberechtigung** securities entitled to a dividend;
in Kost gegebene ~ auswechseln to commute securities; ~ **an der Börse einführen** to introduce (list, *[US]*, market) securities on the stock exchange; ~ **lombardieren** to advance (lend, borrow) money on securities, to collaterate (hypothecate) securities *(US)*; **aus dem Depot nehmen** to withdraw securities from a deposit; **mit ~ sehr stark eingedeckt sein** to be loaded up with securities.
Effekten|abrechnung clearinghouse; ~**abrechnungsstelle** clearinghouse; ~**angebot** securities offerings; **risikoschwächere ~anlage** *(Investmentfonds)* defensive portion *(US)*; ~**arbitrage** arbitrage in securities (funds), stock arbitrage (arbitration, *US)*; ~**austausch** *(Kapitalgesellschaftanlage)* portfolio switch; ~**bank** issuing house *(Br.)*, investment bank (banker) *(US)*; ~**bankgeschäft** investment banking; ~**berater** investment adviser, security (stock, *US)* analyst; ~**besitz** paper holdings, stockholdings *(US)*, stock ownership *(US)*; ~**besitzer** shareholder, stockholder *(US)*; ~**bewertung** securities rating *(US)*; ~**depot** securities (safe custody) account; ~**differenzgeschäft** marginal trading, margin business (buying, trading, *US)*; ~**emission** securities (underwriting) issue, issue of securities; ~**engagements** commitments; ~**gattung** description of securities.
Effektengeschäft dealing in stocks, stock-exchange (securities) business, stockbroking [transaction], [stock]brokerage, stockjobbing *(Br.)*;
~**e auf Provisionsbasis durchführen** to execute orders in quoted (listed) *(US)* securities on commission basis.
Effekten|giro transferring of stock; ~**handel** stockbrokerage, stockbroking, brokerage, [stock]jobbing, stockjobbery *(Br.)*; ~**händler** securities (investment) dealer, jobber *(Br.)*; ~**inhaber** stockholder, bondholder; ~**kassierer** securities teller; ~**kommission** underwriting commission; ~**konto** stock account, *(lebendes Depotkonto)* securities book *(Br.)* (register, *US)*, *(totes Depotkonto)* se-

curities ledger; ~**makler** stockbroker, stockjobber, *(Br.)* securities broker, salesman *(US)*; ~**markt** stock (security) market, market for stocks *(Br.)*; ~**notierungen** [securities] quotations; ~**paket** block [of shares (bonds)], lot *(US)*; ~**parität** parity of stocks; ~**portefeuille** securities on hand, holdings, investments portfolio; ~**sammeldepot** omnibus deposit; ~**schalter** bargain counter; ~**spekulant** stock adventurer *(Br.)*, [stock]jobber; ~**stempel** stamp duty (tax), *(Schlußnotenstempel)* contract (transfer, *US)* stamp; **spekulative ~transaktion durchführen** to take a flier *(US)*; ~**termingeschäfte** forward operations in securities; ~**verkauf an Kapitalsammelstellen** institutional selling; ~**verkäufer** giver, securities salesman; **stückeloser ~verkehr** stock-market trading without transfer; ~**verwalter** portfolio manager.
effektiv effective, real, actual;
~ **ausgegebenes Aktienkapital** issued stock *(US)*; ~**es Einkommen** real income; ~**e Verzinsung** net yield.
Effektiv|bestand actual amount (balance), realizable assets; ~**preis** cash price; ~**verzinsung** effective interest yield *(Wertpapier)* [true] yield; ~**wert** cash value, *(Versicherung)* actual cash value.
Ehren|akzept collateral acceptance, acceptance for (upon) hono(u)r *(Br.)* (supra protest, *US)*; ~**akzeptant** acceptor for hono(u)r; ~**annahme** collateral acceptance, acceptance for (upon) hono(u)r *(Br.)* (supra protest, *US)*; ~**karte** complimentary ticket; ~**tage** *(Wechsel)* days of grace.
Eich|gewicht standard weight; ~**schein** gauger's certificate.
eigen|e Aktien reacquired bonds, own shares *(Br.)*, treasury stock *(US)*; **auf ~e Gefahr** *(Transport)* at owner's risk; **für ~e Rechnung** for one's own account; ~**er Wechsel** note of hand, promissory note.
Eigen|bedarf personal requirements, *(eines Landes)* home requirements; **nur für den ~bedarf** captive *(US)*; **landwirtschaftlicher ~betrieb** home (owner-operated, *US)* farm; ~**fabrikat** own make, self-produced article; ~**finanzierung** self-financing; ~**gefahr** *(Flurversicherung)* individual risk; ~**geschäft** business for own account; ~**gewicht** net (dead) weight, *(Flugzeug)* empty weight; ~**händler** **principal**, *(Börse)* jobber *(Br.)*, floor trader *(US)*.
Eigenheim own home, owner-occupied house *(Br.)*, homecroft *(Br.)*, homestead *(US)*;
~**besitzer** home dweller (builder), owner occupier, homecrofter *(Br.)*, homeowner *(US)*, homesteader *(US)*; ~**hypothek** residential (home, private housing) mortgage.
Eigenkapital equity [capital], owned (ownership) capital, net worth *(US)*;
~ **ansparen** to build equity;
~**verzinsung** return on net worth *(US)*.

Eigen|marke private (house, own) brand; **~mittel** resources, *(Bauherr)* building capital.

Eigentum property, proprietorship, ownership; **im öffentlichen ~** publicly owned; **nach der Heirat erworbenes ~** after acquired property; **fiskalisches ~** government (crown, *(Br.)* property; **gewerbliches ~** industrial property; **konkursfreies (pfändungsfreies) ~** exempt property; **wirtschaftliches ~** business (beneficial, equitable) ownership; **~ belasten** to charge property; **~ konkretisieren** to appropriate goods to the contract; **in öffentlichem ~ stehen** to be under public ownership (publicly owned); **sich das ~ vorbehalten** to reserve the right of property, to retain (reserve) title.

Eigentümer owner, proprietor, proprietary, master; **materieller ~** beneficial owner; **rechtmäßiger ~** lawful (true) owner, *(Effekten)* holder in due course; **enteigneten ~ entschädigen** to indemnify the owner of property taken for public use.

Eigentums|anteil stake in ownership, ownership interest; **~erwerb** ownership purchase, acquisition of property (title); **~nachweis** property qualification, brief; **~recht** ownership, property right; **~recht vorbehalten** to reserve the right of property to reserve (retain) title; **~übergang** transfer, passing of property (title); **~übertragung** transfer of ownership (property, title); **~vorbehalt** secret lien, title retention, *(Spediteur)* shipper's order; **~vorbehaltsklausel** retention-of-title clause; **~wohnung** freehold flat *(Br.)*, condominium apartment *(US)*.

Eigen|verbrauch home (private, own, self-) consumption; **~versorgung** national self-sufficiency; **~werbung** institutional advertising.

Eignungsgarantie warranty of fitness; **~karte** *(Betrieb)* qualification card; **~prüfung** qualifying examination, probation, aptitude (screening, qualification) test.

Eil|auftrag rush job; **~beförderung** express, special delivery *(US)*.

Eilbote express [messenger] *(Br.)*, special messenger *(US)*, poster, expressman *(US)*; **Brief per ~n schicken** to express a letter.

Eilbotenzustellung high-speed delivery service.

Eil|brief express *(Br.)* (special delivery, *US*) letter, express *(Br.)*; **~briefzustellung** express delivery *(Br.)*, special delivery service *(US)*; **~fracht** express *(Br.)* (dispatch, fast, *US*) goods; **~gebühr bezahlt** express paid.

Eilgeld dispatch money *(Br.)*; **~ in Höhe des halben Liegegeldes** dispatch half demurrage all time saved; **~ nur im Löschhafen** dispatch discharging only.

Eilgut railway express, fast (express) freight *(US)*; **als ~ befördern** to [forward by] express, to ship by express [train] *(US)*.

Eilgüterzug fast goods *(Br.)* (express freight, *US*) train.

Eilgut|ladeschein express bill of lading; **~tarif** express (fast goods, *Br.*) tariff; **~verkehr** express business, special delivery service *(US)*, fast goods traffic *(Br.)*.

Eilpostzustellung express delivery *(Br.)*, special delivery service *(US)*.

Eil|zug express (fast)train; **~zustellgebühr** expressage *(Br.)*, special delivery fee *(US)*; **~zustellungsdienst** express (special delivery, *US*) service.

einarbeiten, jem. to train s. o. [for a job]; **sich in einer neuen Stellung ~** to settle down in a new job.

Einarbeitungszeit break-in period, period of vocational (professional) adjustment.

Einbahn|straße one-way street (only, *Br.*); **~strecke** *(Eisenbahn)* single track; **~verkehr** one-way traffic.

einbehalten to keep (hold) back, to retain, *(Steuer)* to deduct, to withhold.

Einbehaltung | des Lohns stoppage of pay; **~ der Lohnsteuer** withholding of tax from wage payment.

einberufen, Aktionäre zur Hauptversammlung to summon shareholders.

Einberufung der Hauptversammlung notice of meeting, call meeting *(US)*.

Einbeziehung in die Arbeitslosenfürsorge coverage by unemployment relief.

einbringen, Antrag to put a motion to the vote, to table a motion *(Br.)*; **seine Arbeitskraft ~** to contribute one's services; **schönen Gewinn ~** to yield a handsome profit.

einbringliches Geschäft lucrative business.

Einbringung | seiner Arbeitskraft contribution of one's services; **~ nach Prisenrecht** military salvage.

Einbruch *(Kursniveau)* setback, slump, drop, fall.

Einbruchsversicherung residence and outside theft (burglary) insurance; **~ von Warenlagern** mercantile open stock insurance.

einbuchen *(Schecks)* to give the value date.

Einbuße an Kundschaft loss of custom.

einbüßen, Kursverlust to suffer a decline.

eindecken, sich to provide o. s. with, to stock up, to buy heavily *(in)*, to lay in a stock; **sich mit Vorräten für den Winter ~** to lay in stores (stock up) for the winter; **zwangsweise ~** to buy in under the rule *(US)* (against s. o., *Br.)*.

Eindeckung *(Börse)* buying back (short, *US*), covering.

einfache | Buchführung bookkeeping by single entry; **~ Havarie** particular (simple) average.

Einfacharbitrage direct arbitration.

Einfahr|gleis arrival track; **~zeit** *(Auto)* running-in (breaking in, *US*) period.

Einfamilienhaus self-contained house, single-family home, residence *(US)*.

einflußreiche Stellung post of authority.

Einflußsphäre orbit, sphere of influence.

einfordern, Einzahlung auf Aktien to make a call on shares; **Außenstände ~** to collect outstanding debts; **Kapital ~** to call in funds.

Einfrierung ausländischer Guthaben freezing of foreign property.

Einfuhr import[ation], imports, import trade; **ausländische ~en** imports from abroad; **sichtbare ~** visible imports; **zeitweilige zollfreie ~** temporary admission; **zollfreie ~** free import; **~ zum eigenen Gebrauch** home-use entry; **~ auf Partizipationsrechnung** import on joint account; **~ unter Zollvermerkschein** entry under bond; **~ liberalisieren** to decontrol imports.

Enfuhr|abgabe import levy, surcharge on imports, countervailing excise (import) duty; **~antrag** import application; **~artikel** articles of importation, imported articles, importations; **nicht kontingentierte ~artikel** nonquota imports; **~aufschlag** import markup; **~-Ausfuhrbank** Export-Import Bank of Washington; **~ausgleichsabgabe** import equalization tax *(US)*; **~bescheinigung** import clearance, clearance inward; **~beschränkungen** import restrictions (restraints), curbs on imports; **verschärfte ~bestimmungen erlassen** to tighten import regulations; **~bewilligung** import licence (authorization, permit); **~deklaration** bill of entry, entry (declaration) inwards.

einführen *(Waren)* to import, to bring in; **in ein Amt ~** to install into an office; **an der Börse ~** to obtain quotation *(Br.)*, to list on the stock exchange *(US)*; **Verbesserungen ~** to adopt improvements; **Waren in ein Land ~** to import goods into a country; **Waren zum freien Verkauf ~** to enter goods for consumption.

Einfuhr|erklärung bill of entry, declaration inwards; **~erlaubnis**, **~freigabe**, **~genehmigung** import licence (permit); **~geschäft** import transaction; **~güter** imports; **~hafen** port of entry; **~kommissionär** import commission agent; **~kontingent** import quota; **~kredit** import (domestic, *US)* credit; **~prämie** bounty on importation; **~schein** bill of entry; **~steuer** import excise tax *(US)*; **~stopp** cessation of (embargo on) imports; **~überschuß** excess of imports over exports.

Einführung introduction, grounding, *(in Betrieb)* orientation, induction, *(an der Börse)* introduction, listing *(US)*; **~ einer neuen Steuer** establishment of a new tax; **schrittweise ~ eines gemeinsamen Zolltarifs** progressive introduction of a common customs tariff.

Einführungs|anzeige launch ad *(US)*; **~brief** letter of introduction; **~feldzug** initial (announcement) campaign; **~kursus** course of training; **~schreiben** introductory (recommendatory) letter, letter of introduction; **~traif** introductory rate.

Einfuhr|verbrauchsabgabe import excise tax *(US)*; **~waren** imported goods.

Einfuhrzoll customs inwards, duty on importation *(US)*, external taxes, impost; **etw. mit ~ belegen** to clap import duties on s. th.; **~erklärung** duty-paid entry.

Eingabe petition, presentation, address, request.

Eingang entrance, gate[way], door[way], *(Aktenkorb)* in *(Einnahmen)* receipts, *(Gelder)* accrual, *(Waren)* coming in, arrival, entry, goods received; **nach ~** when in cash (paid); **vorbehaltlich des richtigen ~s** reserving due payment; **langsamer ~ von Außenständen** delay in receipt of outstanding debts; **~ für Lieferanten** tradesmen's entrance; **~ eines Briefes bestätigen** to acknowledge [the] receipt of a letter.

Eingänge *(Briefkorb)* in, *(von Kunden)* receipts from customers, *(von Waren)* arrivals, incoming goods.

Eingangs|abfertigung *(Zoll)* clearance inwards; **~bestätigung** notice of arrival; **~datum** date of receipt, *(Scheck)* value date; **~fakturenbuch** invoice book; **~halle** entrance hall; **~preis** threshold price; **~stempel** receipt (received) stamp; **~vermerk** file mark; **~zoll** duty of entry, entrance (inward, *Br.)* duty; **~zollschein** jerque note *(Br.)*.

eingedeckt stocked, provided, *(Börse)* bought back; **mit Aktien ~ sein** to be long of stock; **nicht ~ sein** *(Börse)* to be short.

eingefrorene Guthaben frozen assets.

eingeführt, an der Börse quoted *(Br.)* (listed, *US)* on the stock exchange; **neu ~e Artikel** novelties; **gut ~ Waren** well-introduced articles.

eingegangene| Beträge amounts collected; **~ Spenden** contributions which came in.

Eingehen| auf ein Angebot accepting an offer; **~ eines Risikos** taking a risk.

eingehen *(Aufträge)* to come in (to hand), to drop in, *(Firma)* to go under, to close down, to cease to exist, *(Geld)* to be paid (received), to come in (to hand); **auf ein Angebot ~** to accept an offer; **Kosten ~** to incur expenses; **Risiko ~** to undertake (run) a risk; **schleppend ~** to come in slowly; **Schulden ~** to assume (incur) debts; **Verbindlichkeiten ~** to contract liabilities; **auf Verhandlungen ~** to enter into negotiations; **auf einen Vorschlag näher ~** to consider the details of a proposal.

eingehend *(Geld, Ware)* incoming; **sich ~ mit einer Sache beschäftigen** to go closely into a matter; **~e Gelder** receipts, takings, money coming in; **~e Waren** arrivals; **~e Zahlungen** receipts, takings.

eingelagerte Waren stored (warehouse) goods.

eingelöst, nicht *(Wechsel)* dishono(u)red.

eingerechnet, alles all things considered; **Verpackung ist nicht ~** package is not allowed for.

eingeschränkter Prüfungsvermerk qualified approval.

eingeschrieben *(Brief)* registered, special handling *(US)*.

eingetragen registered, booked, on record, inscripted *(Br.)*, *(Aktiengesellschaft)* incorporated; **~es Mitglied** enrolled member; **~e Schutzmarke** registered trademark.

eingezahlt *(Konto)* paid in; **voll ~e Aktie** [fully] paid-up share.

eingezogen *(konfisziert)* confiscated, seized.

einhalten, Fahrplan to stick to a timetable; Frist ~ to keep within time, to meet the deadline *(US)*; Limit ~ to observe a price limit.

Einhaltung | eines Vertrages adherence to a contract; ~ von Wiederverkaufspreisen resale price maintaining.

einheimisch|es Fabrikat home (inland, native) product; ~er Verbrauch home consumption.

Einheit *(Börse)* unit of trade, full (board) lot *(US)*; ~ der ersten Auswahlstufe primary unit.

einheitlich *(Börse)* regular, *(genormt)* standardized.

Einheits|buchführung job order cost accounting; ~erzeugnis standardized product; ~format standard size; - gewicht standard weight; ~kontoblatt standard account form; ~kosten unit (standard) cost; ~lohn single rate, union wage; ~mietvertrag standard form of rent agreement; ~police standard policy.

Einheitspreis flat price (rate), uniform (unit, all-at-one) price, *(Auktion)* reserve price; ~auszeichnung unit-price labelling; ~geschäft chain *(Br.)* one-price, *(Br., US)*, five and dime, *US*, unit-pricing, *US*) store; ~ware one-price articles, dime-store products *(US)*.

Einheits|rechnung *(Kostenrechnung)* job order cost system; ~stücklohn standard piece rate; ~tarif single-schedule (general, flat, unilinear) tariff; ~versicherung all-risks insurance; ~waren utility (standardized) goods.

Einheitswert standard value, *(Grundstück)* basic (site, assessed, ratable) value; ~ eines Grundstücks festsetzen to assess (value) a building (an estate); ~tabelle valuation list *(Br.)*.

Einheitszolltarif single-schedule tariff.

einholen, Akzept to present for (procure) acceptance.

einigen, sich mit seinen Gläubigern to compound with one's creditors; sich auf einen bestimmten Preis ~ to agree on a certain price.

einkassieren, ausstehende Schulden to recover outstanding debts.

Einkauf buying, purchase, purchasing, *(Abteilung)* purchasing department, *(gekaufter Gegenstand)* buy, acquisition, *(Hausfrau)* shopping; zentraler ~ central buying, centralized purchasing; über den ~ entscheiden to make a buying decision.

Einkäufe | eines Kunden einpacken to parcel a customer's purchase; seine ~ in der Stadt erledigen to do one's shopping in town.

einkaufen to buy, to purchase, to make purchases, to shop, to go shopping; sich in ein Altersheim ~ to buy a place in a home for the aged; regelmäßig in einem Laden ~ to patronize a shop; sich in eine Lebensversicherung ~ to take out a life insurance policy; neue Vorräte ~ to lay in fresh stock.

Einkäufer buyer for a firm, purchasing (buying) agent, *(Käufer)* buyer, customer, shopper; ~ für die Industrie industrial buyer.

Einkaufs|abrechnung *(Einkaufskommissionär)* account purchases; ~anweisung purchase requisition; ~bedingungen buying conditions, purchase (merchandise) terms; ~beleg purchase voucher (record); ~bummel buying spree; telefonische ~erledigung shop-by-phone; ~ermächtigung commission to buy; ~etat purchase budget; ~genossenschaft cooperative society, *(Großeinkauf)* cooperative wholesale society; staatliche ~gesellschaft state-buying organization; ~kommissionär buying (purchasing) agent; ~kontingent buying (purchase) quota; ~kraft einer Familie family buying power; ~leiter *(Einkaufsabteilung)* purchasing manager; ~organisation buying organization; ~preis cost (cost-plus, purchase, original, first, invoice, base, sterling) price; ~rechnung invoice; ~retouren purchase returns; ~retourenjournal purchase returns journal; staatliche ~stelle state-buying agency; zurückhaltendes ~verhalten go-slow buying pattern; ~wagen shopping (basket) cart.

Einkaufswert cost value, acquisition cost; zum ~ einsetzen to value at cost.

Einkaufs|zeit shopping hours; ~zentrum shopping center (mall, precinct), *(außerhalb der Stadt)* exurban shopping center *(US)* (centre, *Br.*).

einklarieren to enter, to invoice from a country.

Einkommen income, earnings, revenue, penny, rent, *(Einkünfte)* emoluments, perquisites; im Rechnungsabschnitt anfallendes ~ current income; berufliches ~ professional earnings; effektives ~ real income; festes ~ regular (settled, permanent, steady, assured, fixed) income; garantiertes ~ guaranteed income; gewerbliches ~ industrial income; steuerfreies ~ tax-exempt (nontaxable) income, income exempt from taxation; steuerpflichtiges ~ taxable (chargeable, assessable, *US*) income; unversteuertes ~ pretax income; verfügbares ~ spendable (disposable) income; ~ aus selbständiger Arbeit income arising from any office or employment of profit; ~ aus unselbständiger Arbeit wage income; ~ zwischen 15000 und 20000 Dollar income in the $ 15000-20000 brackets *(US)*; ~ vor Abzug der Steuern pretax income; ~ aus Vermögen[sanlage] unearned (investment) income, income-yielding property; mit seinem ~ auskommen to live within one's income, to suit one's expenditure to one's means; als in diesem Jahr angefallenes ~ behandeln to report as income for year; ~ besteuern to tax income; ~ an der Quelle besteuern to tax revenue at the source; geringes ~ [zu versteuern] haben to be in low income brackets *(US)*; als normales ~ versteuerbar sein to be taxable as ordinary income; zum ~ in keinem Verhältnis stehen to be out of proportion to one's income; als ~ versteuern to report as taxable income; Teil seines ~s zurücklegen to set aside a part of one's income.

einkommen *(Beträge)* to come in, to be paid.

Einkommens|anstieg earnings advancement, upgrading of income; ~**aufstellung** income (earnings) statement; ~**begünstigter** income beneficiary; ~**berechnung** computation of income; ~**besteuerung** taxation of income; **hohe** ~**bezieher** high-income people.

Einkommensgruppe income group (bracket); **zu den hohen** ~**n gehören** to be in high income brackets.

Einkommens|niveau level of income; **steuerlich begünstigte** ~**positionen** tax preference items; ~**schicht** income group (class); ~**steigerung** increase (rise) of income, income increment.

Einkommensteuer [federal (individual), *US*] income tax;
hinterzogene ~ evaded income tax; **nachgezahlte** ~ conscience money; **veranlagte** ~ assessed (individual, *US*) income tax;
~ **erheben** to tax income; ~ **festsetzen** to value an income; ~ **hinterziehen** to cheat on one's income tax; **zur** ~ **veranlagen** to make an income-tax assessment.

Einkommensteuer|abzug income-tax deduction; ~**aufkommen** income-tax receipts, internal revenue *(US)*; ~**berichtigung** amended return; ~**bescheid** income-tax (assessment, *US*) bill.

Einkommensteuererklärung income-tax return (statement, *US*), return (declaration, *Br.*) of income, income-tax declaration *(Br.)*;
~ **abgeben** to file one's income-tax return (statement, *US*), to declare one's income *(Br.)*; **getrennte** ~**en abgeben** to file separate returns.

Einkommensteuer|ermäßigung income-tax reduction; ~**formular** income-tax form (return, blank, *US*); ~**freibetrag** income-tax relief; **altersbedingte** ~**freigrenze** income-tax age exemption; ~**herabsetzung** income-tax cut; ~**hinterziehung** income-tax evasion, evasion of income-tax; ~**klassen** income group (brackets, schedule, *(Br.)*; ~**novelle** income-tax amendment; ~**progression** income-tax progression; ~**richtlinien erlassen** to fix the income tax; ~**rückerstattung** refunding of income tax; ~**sätze um 10 % heraufsetzen** to increase (scale up) income tax 10 per cent; ~**tabelle** income-tax schedule; ~**zahler** taxpayer; ~**zuschlag** income-tax surcharge.

Einkommens|stufe income group (class, bracket *Br.*); ~**überschuß** revenue surplus; ~**umverteilung** redistribution of income; **über seine** ~**verhältnisse leben** to live beyond one's income; ~**verteilung auf mehrere Jahre** income averaging; ~**zusatzsteuer** income tax surcharge; ~**zuwachs** growth of income.

Einkünfte emoluments, revenue, income, incomings, earnings, receipts, takings, gains;
in Rechnungsabschnitt anfallende ~ current revenue; **steuerlich begünstigte** ~ [tax] preference income; **freiberufliche** ~ earned income, income from profession or vocation *(Br.)*; **sonstige** ~ *(Einkommensteuerformular)* income not-charged under any other heading *(Br.)*; **steuerfreie** ~ tax-exempt income;

~ **aus nichtselbständiger Arbeit** wage income; ~ **aus selbständiger Arbeit** self-employment (earned) income; ~ **aus selbständiger und nichtselbständiger Arbeit** mixed income; ~ **aus Gewerbebetrieb** industrial income (earnings), business (trading) income; ~**aus Kapitalvermögen** income from interest (capital), unearned income, income from investment; ~ **aus Land- und Forstwirtschaft** income derived from landed property, property (farm) income; ~ **aus freiberuflicher Tätigkeit** professional (occupational) income;
~ **an der Quelle steuerlich erfassen** to tax income at the source; **seine** ~ **über mehrere Jahre verteilen** to average one's income.

einladen *(Gast)* to invite, to ask, *(beladen)* to load, to freight, *(Flugzeug)* to emplane, *(Schiff)* to ship.

Einlage *(Bankkonto)* deposit, *(Geldanlage)* investment, capital invested, *(Kapital)* put-in (contribution to) capital, assets brought in, stake;
befristete (feste) ~ fixed (time, *US)* deposit; **kurzfristige** ~ short-term deposit;
~ **in gleicher Höhe machen** to pay in an equal sum.

Einlagen, ausstehende auf das Grundkapital subscribed capital stock; **täglich fällige (kurzfristige)** ~ short deposits, deposits at short notice; **gegen Kündigung rückzahlbare** ~ demand deposits; **verzinsliche** ~ interest-bearing deposits;
~ **auf gebührenfreier Rechnung und sonstige Gläubiger** *(Bankbilanz)* current deposit and other accounts; ~ **mit 7tägiger Kündigung** deposits subject to (at) seven days notice.

Einlage|buch passbook, deposit book; ~**kapital** paid-in (invested, advanced) capital.

Einlagen|garantie bank guaranty *(US)*; **landeszentralbankfreie** ~**summe** reserve-free base figure.

einlagern to put in store, to store [in, away], to [deposit in a] warehouse *(US)*, to stockpile;
Vorräte ~ to lay in provisions; **unter Zollverschluß** ~ to bond, to warehouse *(US)*.

Einlagerung storage, storing, warehousing *(US)*, stockpiling.

Einlagerungs|gebühren storage, warehouse charges *(US)*; ~**schein** warehouse receipt *(US)*.

Einlaß|geld door (gate) money, entrance fee; ~**karte** admission card (ticket), ticket.

Einlaufen und Auslaufen eines Schiffes entry and departure of a vessel.

einlaufen to arrive, to come (get) in, *(Aufträge)* to drop (come) in, *(Schiff)* to put in;
fahrplanmäßig ~ to arrive on time (as scheduled).

einlaufende | **Bestellungen** incoming orders; ~ **Gelder** receipts.

Einleger [bank] depositor, *(Kapital)* investor.

Einleitung eines Konkursverfahrens beantragen to make application for receivership *(Br.)*, to petition for the appointment of a receiver *(US)*.

einliefern *(Briefe)* to post, to mail *(US)*;
Wertpapiere ins Depot ~ to deposit securities for safe custody *(Br.)* (custodianship, *US)*.

Einlieferung von Postsendungen posting of items *(Br.)*.

Einlieferungs|schein certificate of posting, receipt, *(Effekten)* deposit slip; ~**zeit** time of delivery.
einlösbar *(einziehbar)* collectible, *(fällig)* due, *(rück-zahlbar)* redeemable;
[in Gold] ~**es Papiergeld** convertible money.
einlösen *(Akzept, Wechsel)* to meet, *(eintauschen)* to convert, *(Rechnungen)* to pay, to discharge, *(Sicht-wechsel, Schecks)* to hono(u)r, to turn into cash, *(tilgen)* to redeem;
Kupons ~ to cash coupons; **Pfand ~** to take out of pawn; **Police ~** to pay (take up) a policy; **Scheck ~** to cash (collect) a check (cheque, *Br.*); **seine Ver-pflichtungen ~** to meet one's engagements (commitments).
Einlösung *(Akzept)* discharge, *(Banknoten)* with-drawal, *(Bankzahlung)* payment, *(Pfand)* redemp-tion, *(Police)* payment, *(Scheck)* cashing;
~ vor Fälligkeit anticipated repayment; **~ von In-vestmentanteilen** repurchase of units *(Br.)*; **~ vor Verfall** mandatory redemption;
einer Bank einen Scheck zur ~ vorlegen to cash a check *(US)* (cheque, *Br.*) at a bank.
Einlösungs|frist time of redemption; ~**kosten** redemp-tion fee; ~**kurs** rate of redemption, redemption price *(US)*; ~**schein** redemption voucher; ~**stelle** redemption office, *(Bank)* coupon paying depart-ment; ~**termin** date of maturity, *(Effekten)* date of redemption; ~**wert** redemption (surrender) value.
einmalig|e Abfindung lumpsum payment; ~**e Aus-gaben** nonrecurring expenses.
Einmaltarif *(Werbung)* one-time rate.
Einmann|betrieb one-man establishment; ~**gesell-schaft** one-man company *(US)*, corporation sole.
Einnahmen receipts, takings, earnings, income, in-comings, revenue, returns, *(Erlöse)* proceeds;
nicht aus Steuereingängen herrührende ~ nontax revenues; **jährliche ~** annual receipts; **ordentliche ~** *(Staat)* ordinary receipts; **zweckgebundene ~** restricted receipts;
~ aus dem Fremdenverkehr tourist receipts; **aus dem Güterverkehr** goods traffics *(Br.)*.
Einnahmen|anstieg increase in revenue; **unvorherge-sehener ~ausfall** casual deficiency of revenue; **~-Ausgaben-Buchführungssystem** costbook prin-ciple; **~- und Ausgabenrechnung** bill of receipts and expenditures; ~**seite** *(Gewinn- und Verlustrech-nung)* income account.
Einnahme|quelle source of revenue (income); ~**tag** date of receipt; ~**überschuß** surplus receipts (reve-nues).
einnehmen *(Geld)* to receive, to collect, *(verdienen)* to earn, to have as income;
Ladung ~ to take in cargo; **vier Spalten ~** *(Zei-tungsartikel)* to take up (go over) four columns; **jds. Stelle ~** to replace s. o., to take s. one's place; **Steuern ~** to collect (receive) taxes.
einräumen, Diskont to allow a discount; **sich einen Kredit ~ lassen** to open a credit account with s. o.
einreichen, Antrag to file an application; **Kupons ~** to present coupons; **Scheck zur Bezahlung ~** to

present a check (cheque, *Br.*) for payment; **Wech-sel zum Diskont ~** to remit (offer) a bill for dis-count.
Einreichung eines Konkursantrages filing of a bank-ruptcy petition.
Einreichungs|datum filing date; ~**frist** tender period; ~**termin** filing date, *(Patent)* date of patent.
Einreise|bewilligung, ~**erlaubnis,** ~**genehmigung** entry permit, visa.
einrichten, Geschäft to fit out a shop; **Wohnung ~** to furnish an apartment.
Einrichtung *(Laden)* fittings;
arbeitssparende ~en labo(u)r-saving appliances; **gemeinnützige ~** public utility; **soziale ~** welfare organization, charitable institution.
einrücken, in die öffentlichen Blätter to print s. th. publicly.
Einsatz *(Arbeitsverwendung)* use, employment, ap-pointment, assignment, *(von Kapital)* employ-ment;
seinen ~ zurückziehen to withdraw one's stake.
Einsatz|preis reserve price, *(Auktion)* starting (upset) price; ~**zug** relief train.
einschätzen, sich selbst to make a self-assessment.
einschießen *(Kapital)* to contribute, to invest, to put (pay) in, *(Teilzahlung auf Aktien)* to pay a call.
Einschiffungshafen port of embarkation.
einschlagende Artikel salable articles, hit.
einschlägig|e, Bestimmungen governing regulations; **in allen ~en Geschäften zu haben** obtainable from all stockists *(Br.)*.
einschleusen to let (channel) in, *(in Arbeitsprozeß)* to direct;
Geld in den Wirtschaftskreislauf ~ to put money into circulation, to pump money into the economy.
einschließlich inclusive, included, overall;
~ Bedienung inclusive of service; **~ Dividende** cum dividend, dividend on *(US)*; **~ der Spesen** adding charges; **~ Verpackung** package included.
Einschluß, unter sämtlicher Kosten all costs included.
einschränken *(Ausgaben)* to diminish, to reduce, to retrench, to cut down, to curb;
sich ~ to economize, to reduce one's standard of living; **sich sehr ~ müssen** to live in narrow circum-stances, to confine o. s.; **Produktion ~** to curb pro-duction.
Einschränkung restriction, restraint, diminution, *(Kürzung)* cut, curtailment, reduction;
ohne jede ~ without any qualification;
~ von Ausgaben cutting down of expenses, re-trenchment; **~ der Ausgabenwirtschaft** restraint of spending; **~ des freien Wettbewerbs** restraint of trade.
Einschränkungsmaßnahmen economy measures.
Einschreibe|brief registered letter; ~**gebühr** registra-tion (entrance, entrolment, booking) fee, *(Post)* registration (registry, *US*) fee.
Einschreiben registered, special handling *(US)*, by registered mail *(US)*.

einschreiben *(Brief)* to register, *(buchen)* to enter, to record;
sich in eine Liste ~ to put down one's name on a list.
Einschreibpäckchen registered parcel.
Einschuß *(Differenzgeschäft)* margin, *(Kapital)* capital invested, share, stake;
~ **leisten** to pay down (on account), *(Differenzgeschäft)* to [put up a] margin;
~**zahlung leisten** to [put up a] margin.
einsenden, Geld to remit money; **Rechnung** ~ to send in a bill.
Einsender sender, *(Geldbetrag)* remitter;
~**kartei** card file of writers; ~**termin** copy date.
einsetzen, Ausschuß to appoint (set up) a committee;
Begünstigten ~ *(Lebensversicherung)* to nominate a beneficiary; **zusätzlichen Omnibus** ~ to put on a relief bus.
Einsetzung appointment, nomination, installation;
~ **eines Begünstigten** *(Lebensversicherung)* nomination of a beneficiary.
Einsicht| in die Bücher inspection of the books;
zur öffentlichen ~ **ausliegen** to be open to inspection.
Einsichtnahme | in die Geschäftsbücher inspection of the books; ~ **in Urkunden** consultation of documents.
einsparen to economize, to make economies, to cut down, to save;
Stelle ~ to abolish an office.
Einsparung | von Arbeitskräften saving of labo(u)r; ~**en im Staatshaushalt** budget restrictions; ~ **in der öffentlichen Verwaltung** civil service cut.
einspielen *(Film)* to take, to bring in.
Einspruch objection, veto, negative, caveat;
~ **beim Finanzamt gegen zu hohe Veranlagung einlegen** to make representations to the Inspector of Taxes about an excessive assessment.
Einspruchs|einlegung *(Patentrecht)* notice of opposition; ~**frist** term of preclusion; ~**patent** opposition patent.
einstampfen *(Akten)* to pulp.
Einstand, seinen bezahlen to pay one's footing.
Einstands|berechnung cost accounting; ~**geld** entrance money, footing; ~**preis** cost (delivery) price.
Einstandswert cost value;
bewertet zum ~ **oder Marktwert** *(Bilanz)* valued at the lower of cost or market.
einsteigen, in ein Geschäft to become a partner of a firm.
einstellen *(Arbeiter)* to engage, to take on, to employ, to recruit *(US)*, to hire *(US)*, *(Betrieb)* to shut down;
Arbeit ~ to stop working, to leave off work, *(streiken)* to [come out on] strike, to lay down tools, to walk out *(US)*; **Briefverkehr** ~ to drop a correspondence; **Verkauf** ~ to discontinue selling; **Verkehr** ~ to stopp traffic; **Zahlungen** ~ to suspend (stop) payment, to fail; **Zwangsvollstreckung** ~ to stay execution.

Einstellung *(Arbeitskräfte)* engagement, enlistment, employment, placement, signing on, hire *(US)*, hiring *(US)*, recruitment *(US)*, recruiting *(US)*, *(Betrieb)* shutdown, suspension of operations, *(Verkauf, Verkehr)* discontinuance;
~ **zur Arbeit** work attitude; ~ **der Auslandshilfe** cutoff of foreign aid; ~ **einer Fertigung** line shutup; ~ **des Flugverkehrs** suspension of air service; ~ **der Öffentlichkeit** public attitude; ~ **der Zahlungen** stoppage, suspension of payments, failure; ~ **der Zwangsvollstreckung** stay of execution.
Einstellungs|alter hiring age *(US)*; ~**befragung** *(Betrieb)* main interview; ~**quote** hiring quota *(US)*; ~**stop verfügen** to put a freeze on employment (hirings, *US*); ~**termin** starting date; ~**verfahren** employment procedure, recruitment technique *(US)*.
einstufen to classify, to group, to grade, to categorize, *(steuerlich)* to graduate, to assess;
j. höher ~ *(Versicherung)* to rate s. o. up; **gehaltlich neu** ~ to regrade.
Einstufung *(steuerlich)* assessment, rating, graduation;
berufliche ~ job grading, service rating;
~ **in eine höhere Lohngruppe** promotional classification change.
Einstufungs|programm rating program(me); ~**system** rating system *(US)*.
einstweilig|er Ruhestand half-pay; ~**e Verfügung** restraining (interlocutory) order, injunction.
einteilen, Stadt in Bezirke to divide a town into wards; **seine Vorräte für die ganze Woche** ~ to deal out one's provisions for the whole week.
Einteilung | in Gefahrenklassen *(Versicherung)* classification of risks; ~ **in Zonen** zoning, zonation; **keine** ~ **haben** to have no sense of planning, *(in finanziellen Dingen)* to be a bad manager.
Eintrag entering, entry, registration, register, item.
eintragen *(amtlich)* to register, to incorporate, to list, to docket, to record, *(buchen)* to book, to enter, to post, to make an entry;
sich ~ to enter one's name; **auf dem Führerschein** ~ to endorse a licence; **Hypothek in Grundbuch** ~ to register a mortage; **Posten ins Hauptbuch** ~ to enter an item into the ledger.
einträglich remunerative, profitable;
~**e Beschäftigung** gainful occupation.
Eintragung posting, *(amtlich)* registry, register, registration, incorporation, recording *(US)*;
falsche ~ mis-entry; **handelsgerichtliche** ~ registration of business name, incorporation *(US)*;
~ **ins Grundbuch** recording of title, land registration *(Br.)*; ~ **eines Patents** issue of a patent; ~ **im Schiffsregister** registry of a ship, marine registry *(Br.)*;
~ **eines Warenzeichens löschen** to expunge the registration of a trademark; ~ **auf dem Führerschein vornehmen** to endorse a licence.
Eintragungs|antrag application for registration; ~**bewilligung** *(Grundbuch)* recording consent *(US)*.

eintragungsfähig registrable, capable of being registered, recordable.

Eintragungs|gebühr booking (filing, recording, registration, incorporation) fee; ~**nummer** registered (registration) number; ~**vermerk** registration, note of entry; ~**vorgang** recording act.

eintreffen, rechtzeitig am Bestimmungsort to reach one's destination in good time.

eintreiben, Außenstände to make collectons, to recover debts; **Steuer** ~ to collect (exact, levy) a tax.

Eintreibung ausstehender Schulden recovery of amounts outstanding.

eintreten *(gesetzliche Folgen)* to attach, *(Haftpflicht)* to accrue, *(als Partner)* to join, to associate;
in das Geschäft seines Vaters ~ to join one's father's firm; **in die Tagesordnung** ~ to proceed to the order of the day; **in eine Firma als Teilhaber** ~ to join a firm as partner.

Eintritt entrance, entry, entering, entrée;
beim ~ **eines Schadensfalles** at the time (upon the occurrence) of a loss;
~ **frei** admission free; ~**verboten!** no admittance!;
~ **in ein Geschäft** initiation into a business, joining of a firm;
~ **erlangen** to get admission to; **sich gewaltsam** ~ **verschaffen** to force one's entry.

Eintritts|alter entry age, age-at-entry; ~**gebühr** [entrance] fee, charge of admittance, door money; ~**karte** admission card (ticket); ~**preis** admission [fee], price of admission, cost of entry, entrance fee.

Einverständnis, stillschweigendes tacit understanding.

Einwand reclamation, objection;
~ **der Minderjährigkeit** plea for infancy (of the Baby Act, *US*).
~ **der Verjährung vorbringen** to plead the statute of limitations.

einwandfrei faultless, flawless, *(Bilanz)* uncooked, *(unanfechtbar)* incontestable;
in ~em Zustand in perfect condition.

einwechseln *(Banknoten)* to convert, *(einlösen)* to cash.

Einweg|behälter one-trip container *(US)*; ~**flasche** nonreturnable bottle; ~**packung** one-way (nonreturnable, expendable) package.

einweisen *(Angestellten in Betrieb)* to escort, to brief.

Einwickelpapier wrapping (brown, *Br.*, kraft, *US*) paper.

einzahlen, Kapital to pay in capital; **20 $ per Postanweisung** ~ to take out a post-office order for $ 20 *(US)*; **voll** ~ *(Aktien)* to pay up.

Einzahlung payment, paying in, inpayment, lodgment, consignation, *(eingezahlter Betrag)* deposit;
erste ~ *(auf Aktien)* apllication call;
~ **bei Gericht** payment into court; ~ **auf das Grundkapital** assessment of stock; ~**en in die Pensionskasse** pension deposits;
~ **auf Aktien leisten** to pay a call on shares.

Einzahlungs|beleg credit voucher, paying-in slip *(Br.)*, pay-in slip *(Br.)*;

~**buch** passbook, bankbook *(US)*, paying-in book *(Br.)*; ~**formular** application (paying-in) form; ~**schalter** collection window.

Einzel|abkommen *(mit Gläubigern)* separate compromise; ~**abnehmer** individual purchaser; ~**anfertigung** individual (single part) production; ~**aufstellung** specification, itemized schedule *(US)*; ~**aufträge** piecemeal contracts; ~**bett** single bed; ~**fahrpreis** single fare; ~**fertigung** job production, individual construction *(US)*; ~**firma** single firm, one-man business *(US)*, individual proprietorship (enterprise) *(US)*; ~**garage** one-car garage; ~**genehmigung** exclusive licence; ~**gewerbetreibender** sole trader (proprietor, *US*); ~**handel** retail[ing], [retail] trade.

Einzelhandels|betrieb retail enterprise (establishment, operation); ~**geschäft** retail shop (store, line, house, business), marketing outlet; ~**gewerbe** retail industry (trade); ~**gewinnspanne** retail margin; ~**index** retail price index; ~**konjunktur** retail spending boom; ~**kunde** retail customer (account); ~**nettoverdienst** retail net profit; ~**organisation** retail sales organization; ~**preis** retail [selling] (resale) price; ~**preisindex** index of commodity prices in retail markets; ~**umsatz** retail [trade] turnover, retail [store] sales; ~**unternehmen** retail enterprise (establishment, operation); ~**verkaufsorganisation** retail sales organization.

Einzelhändler retailer, retail dealer (merchant);
~**befragung** retailer survey; ~**rabatt** retail discount; ~**sortiment** retail line.

Einzelheiten details, data, particulars;
nähere ~ further particulars;
~ **über die finanziellen Abmachungen** financial details.

Einzel|inhaber sole proprietor *(US)*; ~**insertionstarif** transient rate; ~**kalkulationsaufschlag** individual markup *(US)*; **selbständiger** ~**kaufmann** independent retailer; ~**liste** *(Produktion)* sectional price list.

einzeln single, solitary, parcelled, odd, several, *(abgetrennt)* detached, separate;
Besucher ~ **einlassen** to admit visitors one at a time;
nur ~e Bewerbungen only a few applications.

Einzel|nachweis specification; ~**police** specific policy; ~**posten** item; ~**projekt** single project; ~**schuldner** sole (several) debtor; ~**tarifvertrag** single-plant (-employer, individual) bargaining; ~**teilfertigung** manufacture of single parts; ~**unternehmen** single enterprise, one-man business *(US)*, sole (single, individual) proprietorship *(US)*; ~**unternehmer** individual entrepreneur, sole proprietor *(US)*; ~**verkaufspreis** retail [selling] price; ~**versicherung** individual insurance; ~**vorstand** governing director; ~**zimmer** separate room, *(Hotel)* single bedroom, *(Krankenhaus)* private room.

einziehen *(beschlagnahmen)* to confiscate, to seize, to forfeit, to condemn, *(Kapital)* to call in, *(Steuern)* to collect, *(aus dem Verkehr ziehen)* to recall;

bei jem. ~ to take lodging with s. o.; **Außenstände** ~ to make collections; **Banknoten** ~ to withdraw [bank] notes; **Erkundigungen** ~ to make inquiries; **Mieten** ~ to collect rents; **Vermögen** ~ to confiscate property.

Einziehung *(Außenstände)* collecting, collection, *(Banknoten)* calling in, withdrawal, *(Beschlagnahme)* seizure, condemnation, confiscation, *(Wechsel)* cashing, retirement;
~ **von Auskünften** making inquiries; ~ **des Führerscheins** withdrawal of the driving licence; ~ **eines Passes** withdrawal of a passport; ~ **von Steuern** collection of taxes;
~ **eines Wechsels besorgen** to encash a bill.

Einziehungs\benachrichtigung advice of collection; ~**kosten** collection expense, walking charges *(Br.)*; ~**provision** collecting commission.

Einzug entry, entrance, *(Gelder)* collecting, collection, encashment, *(in Haus)* moving in;
Wechsel zum ~ **hereinnehmen** to accept bills for collection.

Einzugs\gebiet trading (buying) area, *(Arbeitskräfte)* labo(u)r market area, *(Nahverkehr)* commuter zone *(US)*; ~**gebühren, ~spesen** collection (collecting, encashment) charges.

Eisenbahn railway *(Br.)*, railroad *(US)*;
einspurige ~ single-line (-track) railway; **stillgelegte** ~ defunct railway;
mit der ~ **befördern** to send (consign, forward) by rail, to railroad *(US)*; ~ **verstaatlichen** to take over the railway;
~**abrechnungsstelle** railway clearinghouse; ~**abstellgleis** siding; ~**ausbesserungswerk** railway repair (railroad, *US*) shop, carshop; ~**beförderung** rail transport; ~**behälterverkehr** train container service; ~**betrieb** train (railroad, *US*) service; ~**betriebsmaterial, ~betriebsmittel** rolling stock; ~**endstation** terminus; ~**fahrkarte** [train] ticket, railway ticket *(Br.)*, railroad ticket *(US)*; ~**fahrplan** timetable of trains, train sheet, schedule of trains *(US)*.

Eisenbahnfracht railway (railroad, *US*) freight;
~**brief** waybill; ~**kosten** railway charges, carrying cost; ~**linie** railway (railroad, *US*) freight line; ~**tarif** railway (railroad, *US*) freight charge.

Eisenbahn\gelände railway property; ~**gleis** railway (railroad, *US*) line (track); ~**verkehr** railway (goods) traffic *(Br.)* freight traffic *(US)*, rail transportation *(US)*; ~**hotel** terminus hotel; ~**knotenpunkt** [railway (railroad, *US*)] junction; ~**kreuzung** crossover; ~**kursbuch** railway guide *(Br.)*; ~**linie** [railway (rail)] line, railroad line *(US)*; ~**netz** railway system *(Br.)*, network of railroads *(US)* (railways, *Br.*) US), railroad net *(US)*; ~**schaffner** railway guard *(Br.)*, railroad conductor *(US)*; ~**tarif** rate (schedule) of fares, railway (railroad, *US*) rates; ~**transport** conveyance by rail; ~**überführung** railway *(Br.)* (railroad, *US*) bridge, bridge over a line; ~**unterhaltung** maintenance of way; ~**verbindung** railway connection; **schlechte ~ver-**

bindungen poor railroad service *(US)*; ~**wagen** railway (passenger) carriage, coach; ~**waggon** [railroad] car *(US)*, railway carriage, goods van *(Br.)*, freight car *(US)*; ~**wärter** linekeeper; ~**zustellungskosten** hauling costs.

eisenschaffende Industrie iron and steel producing industry.

eiserner Bestand reserve stock.

elastisch\er Bedarf elastic demand; ~**e Geldmarktsteuerung** flexible control of the money market; ~**e Währung** elastic currency.

Elektrizitäts\industrie electricity industry; ~**versorgung** electricity supply.

Elektronenbuchführung electronic accounting.

Elends\bezirk, ~gebiet slum (distressed, *Br.)* area.

Embargo embargo, restraint of princes.
völkerrechtliches ~ hostile embargo;
~ **aufheben** to lift the embargo; ~ **verhängen** to embargo;
~**frage** embargo issue; ~**liste** embargo list.

Emission emission, capital flotation, issue;
junge ~ junior stock;
~ **begeben** to dispose of an issue; **fällige ~en** **zurückkaufen** to retire outstanding issues.

Emissions\bank issuing house *(Br.)*, bank of issue, investment (wholesale) banker *(US)*; ~**betrieb** nuisance industry; ~**firma** underwriting house, investment banking house *(US)*; ~**garantie** underwriting; ~**geschäft** investment banking [business]; ~**haus** issuing house (company), underwriter, investment banker (banking house, *US)*; ~**kapital** issued capital; ~**konsortium** underwriting group (syndicate), underwriters *(Br.)*; ~**kurs** issue price rate of issue; ~**markt** capital market; ~**prospekt** underwriting prospectus; ~**sperre** capital issue restrictions; ~**spitze** portion of an issue.

Empfang receipt, *(Aufnahme)* reception, *(Entree)* receptionist, *(gesellschaftlich)* reception;
zahlbar bei ~ cash on delivery;
einer Tratte guten ~ **bereiten** to meet a bill with due hono(u)r.

empfangen, in Gegenrechnung received on account.

Empfänger getter, receiver, recipient, party receiving, *(Brief)* addressee, *(Erwerber von Wertpapieren)* transferee;
am Wohnsitz des ~**s zahlbar** payable at address of payee;
~**land** recipient country.

Empfangs\abteilung receiving department; ~**bahnhof** destination; ~**berechtigter** recipient, authorized (rightful) beneficiary; ~**bescheinigung** certificate (notice, acknowledgement) of receipt; ~**chef** receptionist, reception (room, *US)* clerk, *(Laden)* shopwalker; ~**quittung** [accountable] receipt; ~**schalter** reception desk.

Empfehlung recommendation, suggestion, plug;
geschäftliche ~ business reference;
gute ~en haben to be highly recommended.

Empfehlungs\brief letter of recommendation, letter recommendatory.

emporarbeiten, sich to work one's way up.

emporschnellen *(Kurse)* to jump [up], to surge upward, to soar, to shoot up, to skyrocket *(US)*.

End|alter *(Versicherung)* maturity age; **~montage** final assembly; **~preis** final price, price to consumer; **~produkt** end-product, end-item; **~station** railhead, terminus; **~verbraucher** ultimate (final, last) consumer; **~wert** final amount, accumulated value, *(Rente)* amount of annuity.

Energie|bedarf demand for energy, power demand; **~versorgung** electric power (energy) supply; **~wirtschaft** electric power industry, energy business.

Engagement engagement, employment, undertaking,, (Börse) commitment, engagement *(Br.)*, *(Verpflichtung)* obligation;
~ der Baissepartei bear accounts (engagements) *(Br.)*, short interests *(US)*; **~s der Haussepartei** bull accounts (engagements) *(Br.)*, long accounts *(US)*, long interests *(US)*.

engagieren to take on, to engage, to enlist, to employ, to hire *(US)*, to recruit *(US)*.

Engpaßbeseitigung removal of a bottleneck.

engros verkaufen to wholesale, to sell in [the] gross.

Engros|abnehmer wholesale buyer (receiver, *US*); **~bezug** bulk buying, wholesale purchase; **~geschäft** wholesale business, *(Firma)* wholesale house; **~händler ohne eigenes Lager** wholesale peddler, waggon (truck) distributor *(US)*; **~kauf** wholesale purchase; **~preis** wholesale price (cost), trade price.

enteignen to expropriate, to disappropriate.

enteignete Gesellschaft condemned company.

Enteignung eminent domain, compulsory surrender (purchase, *Br.)*, condemnation.

Enteignungs|entschädigung special benefit, indemnity for expropriation; **~verfahren** eminent domain proceedings.

entflechten *(Kartell)* to disentangle, to decartelize, to dissolve *(US)*, to break up.

Entflechtung *(Kartell)* disentanglement, deconcentration, decartelization, trust-busting *(US coll.)*.

Entgegennahme | eines Auftrages taking an order.

Entgelt payment, pay, fee, *(Belohnung)* remuneration, reward, *(Ersatz)* recompense, *(Vertragsleistung)* consideration, onerous cause;
als ~ für Ihre Dienste (Tätigkeit) as payment (in return) for your services.

entgeltlich for a valuable consideration;
~er Vertrag onerous contract.

Entlade|beginn breaking bulk; **~frist** unloading time; **~gebühr** unloading charge; **~mannschaft** dock crew.

entladen to unload, to discharge, *(Flugzeug)* to deplane, *(Schiff)* to unlade, to discharge.

Entlade|rampe ramp, platform; **~stelle** unloading point; **~zeit** unloading time (period).

Entladungskosten discharging expenses (fees).

entlassen to dismiss, to send off, *(Arbeiter)* to discharge, to discard, to pay off, to put out; **fristlos ~** to dismiss without notice (summarily);

sofort ~ to dismiss summarily; **vorübergehend ~** to stand off;
~ sein to be off the payroll; **~ werden** to be (get) dismissed, to receive notice, to get sacked *(sl.)*.

Entlassung discharge, dismissal, discard;
begründete ~ discharge for cause; **fristlose ~** removal, summary (instant) dismissal, dismissal without notice; **vorübergehende ~** suspension, *(Arbeitskräfte)* layoff;
~ von Arbeitskräften labo(u)r separation; **~en bei der Stahlindustrie** steel layoffs; **~en während der Urlaubszeit** holiday layoffs;
jem. mit der ~ drohen to threaten s. o. with the sack; **seine ~ einreichen** to surrender one's office, to hand in (tender, submit) one's resignation.

Entlassungs|abfindung severance pay, terminal wage *(US)*; **~bescheid** notice of dismissal; **~gehalt** dismissal pay; **~grund** grounds for removal (discharge); **berechtigter ~ grund** good (sufficient) cause; **~papiere** walking *(US sl.)*(discharge) papers, walking ticket *(US sl.)*; **~zahlung** dismissal wage; **~zeugnis** testimonial, certificate of discharge.

entlasten to relieve, to discharge, to credit, to exonerate, *(Geldmarkt)* to ease;
Aufsichtsrat ~ to ratify the board of directors' acts; **Konkursschuldner ~** to discharge a bankrupt; **Schatzmeister ~** to accept (pass) the treasurer's account.

Entlastung discharge, release, credit;
liquiditätsmäßige ~ ease in money rates; **verweigerte ~** *(Konkursverfahren)* opposition;
~ des Aufsichtsrates ratification of the board of directors' acts;
dem Schatzmeister ~ erteilen to accept the treasurer's account.

Entlastungs|antrag *(Gemeinschuldner)* petition of discharge; **~erteilung** *(Aufsichtsrat, Vorstand)* approval, ratification; **~zug** extra (relief) train.

entlohnen, j. für seine Dienste to remunerate s. o. for his services.

Entnahme *(Konto)* taking off, withdrawal, drawing from an account;
~satz *(Konto)* rate of withdrawal.

entnehmen to withdraw, *(Kredit)* to borrow;
aus einem Brief ~ to learn (understand) from a letter; **Proben ~** to draw simples; **einer Zeitung ~** to see from a newspaper.

entnommener Gewinn distributed profit.

entrichten, Steuern to pay taxes; **Zoll auf etw. ~** to pay duty on s. th.

entschädigen to compensate, to indemnify, to make amends (up for), to redeem, to recoup;
j. für seine Bemühungen ~ to pay (remunerate) s. o. for his trouble.

Entschädigung indemnification, indemnity, compensation, consideration [money], compensatory damages, pay, recompense, remuneration;
zur ~ by way of requital;
großzügige ~ fair damages, fair and reasonable

compensation; **über den verursachten Schaden hinausgehende** ~ exemplary damages;
~ **in bar** compensation in cash; ~ **für entgangenen Gewinn** consequential damges;
gegen ~ beilegen to compound; **für seine Verluste keine ~ erhalten** to get no redress for one's losses; ~ **festsetzen** to lay (fix) damages, to assess compensation; ~ **verlangen** to claim damages.

Entschädigungs|anspruch claim for loss (damages), compensation claim; ⁰**berechtigt** entitled to damages; ~**festsetzung** assessments of damages; ~**summe** indemnity, compensatory damages, *(Angestellter)* dismissal pay (compensation); ~**verfahren** condemnation proceedings; **jem. etw. im ~wege zahlen** to pay s. o. a sum by way of indemnification; ~**zahlung** compensatory payment.

entschlüsseln to decode, to decipher, to unscramble, to break a code.

entschulden to disencumber, to free of debts.

entspannen, sich *(Geldmarkt)* to ease.

Entspannung escape, relaxation, resource; ~ **am Geldmarkt** ease in money rates.

entstanden *(Zinsen)* accrued; ~ **sein** *(Anspruch)* to have been perfected; ~**er Schaden** resulting damage.

entstehen *(Anspruch, Kosten, Zinsen)* to accrue.

Entstehung *(Zinsen)* accrual; ~ **eines Anspruchs** arisal of a claim; ~ **neuer Industrien** coming into being of new industries.

Entstehungszeit *(Forderung)* time of inception.

entwerten *(abwerten)* to devalue, to devaluate, *(Stempelmarken)* to cancel, to deface, to obliterate; **mit dem Datumstempel** ~ to date-cancel.

entwertete Briefmarke used stamp.

Entwertung reduction in value, *(Abwertung)* depreciation, devaluation, *(Anlagegut)* lost usefulness, *(Stempel)* obliteration, cancellation, defacement.

Entwertungs|klausel depreciation clause; ~**rücklage** allowance (reserve, provision) for depreciation.

entwickeln to develop, *(Handel)* to grow up; **sich schnell ~** *(Konjunktur)* to advance with a rush, to boom.

Entwicklung, berufliche professional growth, career development; **konjunkturelle ~** cyclical trend; **marktbestimmende ~en** governing market trends; ~ **des Einkommens** growth in income; ~ **des Fremdenverkehrs** tourist development; ~ **eines Produkts im Markt** product history.

Entwicklungs|anleihe development loan; ~**bank für die lateinamerikanischen Länder** Inter-American Development Bank; ~**gebiet** less developed (developing) area; ~**gesellschaft** development company, Overseas Private Investment Corporation *(US)*; ~**helfer** aid official, development-aid man; ~**hilfe** development assistance, aid; ~**länder** developing (undeveloped, less developed) countries; **geschäftliche ~möglichkeiten** business development possibilities; ~**programm** development program(me) (policy); **konjunktureller ~verlauf** economic trend; ~**vorhaben** development project (operation).

Entwurf eines Vertrages draft agreement.

Entwurfs|grafiker layout man, layouter; ~**skizze einer Werbesendung** story board; ~**stadium** planning (blueprint, *US*) stage.

entziehen, sich seinen Gläubigern to evade one's creditors; **Konzession** ~ to revoke (cancel) a licence; **jem. seine Vollmachten** ~ to divest (strip) s. o. of his powers.

Entziehung des Führerscheins forfeiture of s. one's driving licence.

Erbanfall hereditary succession, inheritance *(US)*; ~ **[für unbewegliches Vermögen]** succession duty (tax).

Erbauseinandersetzung family settlement (contract).

Erbbau|berechtigter leaseholder; ~**recht**, ~**vertrag** building lease, land use, lease in perpetuity, rental right *(Br.)*, mixed estate *(US)*.

Erbe heir, inheritor *(US)*, natural (real) representative; **pflichtteilsberechtigter** ~ forced heir.

Erblasser testator, bequeather, deceased.

Erbpachtvertrag copyhold, building lease, lease in perpetuity, rental right *(Br.)*.

Erbschaft inheritance *(US)*, heritage, hereditament.

Erbschafts|steuer death (estate) duty *(Br.)*, transfer (inheritance, *US*, succesion, death, *US)* tax; ~**steuerbelastung** estate-duty charge *(Br.)*; ~**steuerfreibetrag** lifetime exemption.

Erb|schein heir's certificate *(US)*, *(Testamentsvollstrecker)* letters testamentary.

Erdöl mineral (crude) oil, petroleum; ~**aktien** oil shares (stocks, *US)*; ~**industrie** oil industry; ~**leitung** pipeline.

Erfahrungen | im Anlagengeschäft investment experience; **erste ~ mit dem Kunden hinter sich haben** to have had its initial fling with the customers.

Erfahrungsbericht progress report, case history.

erfassen *(statistisch)* to cover, to register, to record; **Einkünfte an der Quelle** ~ to tax income at the source.

Erfassung *(amtlich)* registration, *(Arbeitslosenfürsorge)* coverage.

Erfinder|anteil royalty; ~**prämie** award to inventor.

Erfindung invention, origination, *(Fälschung)* fabrication, *(Patent)* patent, *(Vorrichtung)* device, gadget; **patentfähige ~** patentable invention; ~ **zum Patent anmelden** to patent an invention; ~ **praktisch verwerten** to reduce an invention to practice.

Erfindungs|gegenstand herstellen to produce an invention; **unzureichende ~höhe** insufficient subject matter; ~**höhe verneinen** to deny the inventive step.

Erfolg, geschäftlicher business success (winner), money winner; ~ **haben** *(Waren)* to go off well.

Erfolgsanteil bonus, profit sharing, royalty.

Erfolgs|ausweis trading report; **auf ~basis** on a contingent basis; ~**honorar** contingent (success,

result, *Br.)* fee, quota litis *(US), (Autor)* royalty;
~**jahr** bonanza year; ~**kontrolle** *(Werbung)* result
testing; **volkswirtschaftliche** ~**rechnung** national
income accounting; ~**träger** profit-yielding product.

erforderlich|es Alter required age; ~**e Deckung** re-
quisite cover.

Erfrischungskiosk refreshment stand.

erfüllen to discharge, to perform, to satisfy, *(abzahlen)* to acquit, *(Vertrag)* to perform, to satisfy,
(Br.), to fulfill *(US)*;
alle vorgeschriebenen Formalitäten ~ to comply
with all the necessary formalities.

Erfüllung *(Verpflichtung)* discharge, feasance, acquittal, *(Vertrag)* fulfil(l)ment, performance,
completion, accomplishment, accomplished delivery;
an ~**s Statt** in lieu of [specific] performance;
teilweise ~ part performance; **unmögliche** ~ im-
possibility of performance;
~ **einer Garantiepflicht** implementation of guarantee; ~ **Zug um Zug** (simultaneous) performance.

Erfüllungs|gehilfe vicarious agent; ~**interesse** general
damages; ~**ort** *(Börse)* settling place, *(Lieferort)*
delivery place; ~**tag** *(Börse)* settling (name) day.

ergänzen to fill up, *(Lager)* to replenish, to assort,
(Summe) to make up.

Ergänzungs|abgabe special levy, surtax; ~**lager** re-
plenishing stock; ~**versicherung** complementary
insurance.

ergeben, im Durchschnitt to average; **Gewinn** ~ to
yield (leave) a profit; **Verlust** ~ to result in (show)
a loss.

Ergebnis issue, result, outcome, *(Ertrag)* returns,
receipts, yield, *(Erzeugnis)* product;
finanzielles ~ financial result;
~ **fünfjähriger Arbeit** product of five years' work;
~ **unserer Bemühungen** effect of our labo(u)r;
mit einem besseren ~ **abschließen** to close with a
better result;
~**aufstellung** earnings statement; ~**rechnung** statement of operating results *(US).*

ergiebig *(ertragreich)* paying, profitable, lucrative,
remunerative, *(Land)* yielding, rich, fertile, fat.

ergreifen, Beruf to enter a profession.

erhalten, Betrag payment received; **Wert** ~ *(auf
Wechseln)* value received.

erhältlich, Prospekte hier prospectuses sold here.

Erhaltung von Vermögenswerten conservation of
assets.

Erhaltungs|aufwand maintenance cost (charges);
kombinierte Abschreibungs- und ~**methode** combined depreciation and maintenance method.

erheben *(Beitrag)* to collect, to levy, *(Steuern)* to
collect, to exact, to impose;
Anspruch ~ **auf** to lay (lodge) claim to; **per Nachnahme** ~ to collect on delivery; **Wechselprotest** ~
to protest a bill.

erheblich|er Schaden serious (heavy) loss; ~**e Schul-
den** heavy debts; ~**es Vermögen** sizable fortune.

Erhebung|en, amtliche official inquiry;
~ **von Kampfzöllen** fiscal retaliation;
~**en an Ort und Stelle durchführen** to make investigations on the spot.

Erhebungs|auswahl sample; ~**fehler** *(Statistik)* ascer-
tainment error; ~**termin** *(Steuer)* tax payment
date; ~**zeitraum** *(Steuer)* period of collection.

erhöhen to advance, to increase, to raise;
sich ~ *(Kurse)* to advance, to increase, to rise;
Grundkapital ~ to increase the share capital *(Br.)*
(capital stock, *US*); **Löhne** ~ to put up wages;
Preise sprunghaft ~ to jump prices.

erhöht|e Geschwindigkeit accelerated (increased)
speed; ~**er Grundpreis** raised standard rate; ~**e
Lebenshaltungskosten** advanced (increased) cost
of living; ~**er Umsatz** increased turnover.

Erhöhung | des Aktienkapitals increase of share capi-
tal; ~ **der Aktienkurse** improvement in stocks; ~
der Freibetragsgrenze *(Einkommensteuer)* personal exemption increase; ~ **des Lebensstandards**
rise in the standard of living; ~ **der Sondervergünstigungen** fringe increase;
~ **im Kurs erfahren** to experience a rise in prices.

erholen, sich to recreate, to convalesce, to recuperate, to pick up, *(Kurse)* to look (pick, prick) up, to
recover, to revive, to rally, to improve;
sich für den Betrag seiner Spesen ~ to recover expenses; **sich finanziell wieder** ~ to recover one's
strength, to recuperate.

Erholung resource, distraction, play, *(Markt)* improvement, recovery, recuperation, revival;
rasche ~ speedy recovery; **schnelle** ~ *(Kurse)* rally;
~ **der Weltwirtschaft** world economic recoery.

Erholungs|anlagen recreation facilities; ~**aufenthalt**
holiday, rest cure, vacation *(US)*; ~**gebiet**
recreation area; ~**heim** sanatorium, holiday camp,
rest center *(US)* (centre, *Br.)*; ~**reise machen** to
travel for one's health; ~**suchender** holidaymaker,
holidayer, vacationist *(US)*, vacationer *(US)*; ~**urlaub** holiday, vacation *(US)*, *(Krankheitsurlaub)*
sick leave; ~**zeit** recreation time, vacancy; ~**zentrum** rest center *(US)* (centre, *(Br.).*

Erinnerungs|brief reminder (follow-up) letter; ~**po-
sten** *(Buchführung)* nominal value *(US)*; ~**test**
(Anzeige) aided-recall (recognition) test; ~**wert**
(Bilanz) promemoria figure, nominal value *(US).*

Erkennungs|marke identity disk; ~**melodie** *(Rund-
funkstation)* signature tune; **polizeiliches** ~**zeichen**
(Auto) registration plate.

erklären to explain, *(auslegen)* to interpret, *(zollamtlich deklarieren)* to declare, to enter at the
customs;
j. bankrott ~ to adjudge s. o. bankrupt; **Dividende**
~ to declare a dividend; **Schiff für seeuntüchtig**
~ to condemn a ship; **sich für zahlungsunfähig** ~
to declare o. s. insolvent, to file a petition in bankruptcy.

Erklärung declaration, statement, representation,
(Erläuterung) explanation, legend;
amtliche ~ official statement;

~ der üblichen **Dividende** regular dividend announcement; ~ **über die Entwicklung des Eigenkapitals** statement of stockholders' equity; ~ **auf dem Sterbebett** dying declaration, deathbed deed; ~ **abgeben** to declare, to give (make) a declaration; ~ **in Wahrnehmung berechtigter Interessen abgeben** to make a statement on a privileged occasion.

Erlaß *(Rabatt)* reduction, deduction, *(Schulden)* release, remission, cancellation, *(Steuer)* abatement, remission, *(Verordnung)* act, decree, order, ordinance, issue, issuance;
ministerieller ~ ministerial act, departmental order;
~ **von Schulden** release from debts, acquittance; ~ **einer Verfügung** issue (issuance) of an order.

erlassen to make an allowance, to abate, to deduct, *(Schuld)* to remit, to release, *(Verordnung)* to issue; **Gebühren** ~ to waive (cancel) charges.

Erlaubnis licence, permit, permission, grant *(US)*; **mit obrigkeitlicher** ~ by authority;
~ **zollfreier Warenausfuhr von Hafen zu Hafen** bill of sufferance.

Erlaubnisschein licence, permit, permission.

Erlebensfallversicherung pure endowment assurance *(Br.)*.

erledigen to execute, to settle, to effect;
Auftrag ~ to carry out an order; **Formalitäten** ~ to comply with formalities.

Erledigung disposal, dispatch, handling, settlement, execution;
in ~ **dienstlicher Angelegenheiten** in discharge of official duty;
~ **eines Auftrags** execution of an order.

erleichtern, Zahlung to facilitate payment.

Erleichterung | **bei Auslandsinvestitionen** easing upon foreign investments; ~ **des Geldmarktes** ease (easing) in (relaxation of) money rates; ~ **der Zahlungsbedingungen** payment facilities;
sich für ~**en des Geldverkehrs einsetzen** to favo(u)r easier money.

erleiden, starken Einbruch *(Börse)* to break sharply; **Rückgang** ~ *(Börse)* to suffer a decline; **Veränderungen** ~ *(Preise)* to undergo changes; **Verlust** ~ to sustain (suffer) a loss.

Erlös proceeds, returns, earnings, profit, avails *(US)*, *(Reingewinn)* net profits;
~ **aus Diskontierung** net avails *(US)*; ~ **für begebene Obligationen** debenture capital;
einen den Buchwert übersteigenden ~ **abwerten** to yield a profit over the book value;
~**anteil** profit share; ~**bild** earnings picture.

Erlöschen expiration, expiry, *(Versicherung)* expiration, lapse;
~ **eines Patents** expiry (lapse) of a patent; ~ **der Vollmacht** termination of authority.

erlöschen to expire, to abate, *(Angebot)* to terminate.

Erlös|**druck** pinch of profits, earnings squeeze; ~**schmälerungen** nonoperating expense, income deductions.

ermächtigen to authorize, to commission, to enable.

Ermächtigung faculty, power, authority;
~ **der Einkaufsabteilung** purchase requisition; ~ **zur Kreditaufnahme** borrowing authorization.

ermäßigen to reduce, to mark down, to abate;
Diskontsatz ~ to lower the discount (bank, *Br.*, rediscount, *US*) rate; **Preis eines Artikels** ~ to reduce (lower, cut, cut down, *US*) the price of an article.

ermäßigt|**er Anzeigenpreis** reduced (short) rate; **zu** ~**en Preisen** at reduced (cut) prices.

Ermäßigung reduction, allowance, abatement;
~ **des Diskontsatzes** lowering of the rediscount *(US)* (bank, *Br.*) rate; ~ **der Geldmarktsätze** relaxation of (ease in) money rates; ~ **bei Mengenabnahme** quantity discount.

ermitteln to trace, to find out, to discover, *(Aufenthaltsort)* to locate;
Wert ~ to ascertain the value.

Ermittlung, polizeiliche investigations by the police.

ernähren, seine Familie to maintain one's family; **sich von seiner Hände Arbeit** ~ to live by the sweat of one's brow.

Ernährungs|**fachmann** nutrition expert; ~**industrie** food-processing industry; ~- **und Landwirtschaftsorganisation** (FAO) Food and Agricultural Organization; ~**minister** Minister of Supply (Agriculture, Fisheries and Food, *Br.*).

erneuern *(Patentrecht, Vertrag)* to renew, to revive;
Auftrag ~ to repeat an order; **Laufzeit eines Vertrages** ~ to prolong a contract; **Vorräte** ~ to replenish with fresh supplies.

Erneuerung, laufende subsequent renewals;
~ **des Maschinenparks** machinery replacement;
an einem Hause ~**en durchführen** to repair (renovate) a house.

Erneuerungs|**auftrag** reorder, renewal order; ~**bedarf** replacement demand; ~**fonds** renewal (depreciation) reserve; ~**konto** renewal (depreciation reserve) account; ~**rücklage** reserve for renewals and replacements, replacement (renewal) fund; ~**schein** renewal certificate, talon.

ernst|**gemeintes Angebot** serious offer; ~**hafter Käufer** genuine buyer.

Ernte auf dem Halm standing crop.

Ernte|**aussichten** crop (harvest) prospects; ~**finanzierungskredit** crop (agricultural, *US*) loan; ~**vorschau** crop forecast.

eröffnen, Geschäft to set up shop, to open a business; **Konto** ~ to open (set up) an account; **Kredit zu jds. Gunsten** ~ to lodge a credit in favo(u)r of s. o.; **leicht abgeschwächt** ~ *(Börse)* to open at a slight discount; **Verhandlungen** ~ to set negotiations on foot.

Eröffnung | **eines Geschäftes** setting up shop; ~ **des Konkursverfahrens** adjudication of bankruptcy; ~ **eines Kontos** opening of an account; ~ **des Vergleichsverfahrens** decree of insolvency;
nach fester ~ **schwach werden** *(Börse)* to turn weak after a firm opening.

Eröffnungs|**beschluß** *(Konkursverfahren)* adjudication of bankruptcy, receiving' order *(Br.)*; ~**be-**

stand opening stock; **~bilanz** initial (opening) balance sheet; **~buchung** opening entry; **~kurs** starting (opening) price, opening quotation (rate).

Erpresserbrief blackmailing letter.

Erpressung exortion, blackmail, squeeze.

Erprobung auf dem Prüfstand shop trial.

errechneter Wert computed value.

Errechnung | **des Fondswertes** *(Kapitalanlagegesellschaft)* validation of a fund *(Br.)*; **~ der Zinsen** working out the interest.

erreichen, seinen Anschluß to get (make) one's connexion; **vom Bahnhof leicht zu ~** within easy reach of the station.

errichten, Gebäude to erect a building; **Konto ~ to** open an account.

Ersatz replacing, substitution *(Ersatzmittel)* surrogate, substitute, stopgap, ersatz, *(Schadloshaltung)* compensation, indemnification, damages, reimbursement, recompense;
als ~ in exchange, in return for, *(Entschädigung für)* by way of compensation;
~ für werterhöhende Aufwendungen compensation for improvements; **~ immateriellen Schadens** special damages;
als ~ für j. einspringen to step in as a substitute for s. o.; **~ fordern** to claim damages; **~ leisten** to compensate, to make restitutions (amends);
~anschaffungen replacements; **~anspruch** [claim for] damages, damages claim, recourse; **~bedarf** replacement needs (demand); **~berechtigt** entitled to damages; **~beschaffung** replacement; **kostenlose ~einschaltung** *(Anzeige)* make-good; **~erbe** substituted *(US)* (representative, alternative, *US)* heir; **~investitionen** replacement capital assets; **~konnossement** exchange bill of lading; **~leistung** substitute performance, replacement, *(Schadenersatz)* indemnification, compensation; **~lieferung** replacement delivery.

ersatzpflichtig liable to pay damages.

Ersatz|reifen spare tyre (tire, *US)*; **~stück** spare part.

Ersatzteil spare [part], reserve part (unit, piece);
~dienst spare-part service; **~lager** depot for spares, stock of spare parts, spare parts warehouse, parts depot.

Ersatz|wert replacement (reproduction cost) value *(Versicherung)* full value; **~wohnung** replacement housing.

Erscheinen appearance, *(Buch)* publication;
bei ~ *(Börse)* when issued.

erscheinen *(Börse)* to be issued, *(Buch)* to come out, to be published, to appear in print;
in Lieferungen ~ to be published in instal(l)ments; **auf der Passivseite der Bilanz ~** to appear on the debit side of the balance sheet.

Erscheinungs|bild in der Öffentlichkeit public image; **~datum** *(Buch)* publication date; **~plan** *(Anzeige)* advertising schedule; **~tag** day (date) of publication, publication date; **~termin** publication date, *(Anleihe)* issue date.

erschließen, neue Absatzmärkte to find new outlets, to

open up new markets; **für den Fremdenverkehr ~** to open up to the tourist trade.

Erschließung, industrielle industrial development; **~ von Baugelände** land development; **~ neuer Hilfsquellen** creation of new resources.

Erschließungs|genehmigung, industrielle industrial development certificate *(Br.)*; **~gesellschaft** industrial development company; **~kosten** development expenses.

erschöpfen, Kontingent to use up a quota; **seine Mittel ~** to exhaust one's resources.

erschöpft, exhausted, *(Vorräte)* running low (out); **~ werden** *(Kredit)* to run out.

Erschöpfung der natürlichen Hilfsquellen depletion of resources; **~ der Reserven** exhaustion of reserves.

erschwinglich, finanziell within the reach of everybody's pocket[book].

ersetzen *(Auslagen)* to repay, to refund, to reimburse, *(Schadenersatz leisten)* to make good (up), to pay compensation, to recompensate, to make amends, to compensate;
drei Arbeitskräfte ~ *(Maschine)* to do the work of three men; **jem. seinen Verdienstausfall ~** to compensate s. o. for his broken time.

Ersparnisse savings, economies;
noch nicht wieder angelegte ~ fluid savings;
seine ~ abheben to draw on one's savings; **auf ~ zurückgreifen können** to have a sum put by to fall back upon.

erst|es Gebot *(Auktion)* opening bid; **aus ~er Hand** first-hand; **~e Hypothek** senior (first) mortgage; **~e Wahl** top-grade (choice) quality.

Erst| absatz von Wertpapieren initial placing of securities: **~anmeldung beanspruchen** *(Patentrecht)* to claim priority for an application.

erstatten, Auslagen to reimburse (refund) expenses; **Gutachten ~** to render an opinion.

Erstattung remission, *(Kosten)* reimbursement, repayment;
~ einer Anzeige reporting to the police; **~ von Auslagen** compensation for expenses incurred.

erstattungs|fähig repayable; **~pflichtig** taxable, *(Kosten)* reimbursable.

Erst| ausfertigung original; **~ausstattung** *(Auto)* original equipment.

erstehen to purchase, to buy, to acquire;
billig ~ to get cheap.

Ersteigerer purchaser, highest bidder.

ersteigern to purchase at *(US)* (by, *Br.)* auction.

Erst| einlage original investment; **~erwerb** original acquisition, initial purchase; **~erwerber** first purchaser, original subscriber; **~gebot** first bid; **~hypothek** senior mortgage.

erstklassig top, topflight, crack, classic, tiptop, excellent, first-rate, first-shop *(Br.)*, high-grade (-class), of first rate (make), box *(US)*, *(Schiff)* A 1; **~e Arbeit** excellent piece of work; **~es Hotel** first-class hotel; **~e Kapitalanlage** gilt-edged *(Br.)* (high-grade, choice) investment.

Erstmeldung exclusive story, scoop *(sl.)*, beat *(US)*.

erstrangig, erststellig ranking first, top-rate, *(Hypothek)* first-mortgage, prior.

Erst|versicherer direct insurer, leading underwriter, direct-working carrier.

erteilen, Abrechnung to render an account; **Auftrag** ~ to [place an] order; *(Behörde)* to confer (award) a contract; **Gutschrift** ~ to credit; **Zuschlag** ~ to allocate, to adjudicate.

Ertrag *(Bergbau)* output, get *(Br.)*, *(Einkünfte)* earnings, receipts, gainings, *(Ernte)* harvest, yield, outturn, *(aus Geldanlage)* investment, *(Produktionsergebnis)* yield, produce;
abnehmender ~ diminishing return;
~ **vor Abzug der Steuern** *(Gewinn- und Verlustrechnung)* profits before taxation;
guten ~ **abwerfen** to pay well; **keinen** ~ **bringen** to yield no return.

Erträge, außerordentliche extra profits, nonrecurrent income *(Br.)*; **periodenfremde** ~ periodic income; ~ **aus Beteiligungen** income from investments; ~ **wieder im Geschäft anlegen** to plough (plow, *US)* back earnings into the business; ~ **lediglich buchungstechnisch erzielen** to show earnings by mere bookkeeping devices.

ertraglos nonproductive, *(Aktie)* nonpaying.

Erträgnisse earnings, proceeds, profits, returns;
betriebsfremde ~ nonoperating income;
~ **des Amortisationsfonds** sinking-fund income.

ertragreich profit-yielding, [rent-]paying;
~ **sein** *(Geschäft)* to show a good profit;

Ertrags|anteil royalty; ~**ausschüttung** *(Investmentfond)* distribution of income *(Br.)*; ~**aussichten** earning prospects, profit outlook; ~**bild** profit picture; ~**einbuße** dent in earnings.

Ertragsfähigkeit profit-earning (productive, yield) capacity, earning power, productivity;
~ **einer Gesellschaft herstellen** to turn a company into a winner.

Ertrags|grenze margin of profit; ~**kraft** earnings capacity; **gesunde** ~**lage** health of earnings; ~**leistung** earnings performance; ~**miete** break-even rent; ~**rechnung** profit-and-loss account, earnings statement; **beträchtlichen** ~**rückgang aufweisen** to show considerable profit diminution; ~**rücklage** revenue reserve *(Br.)*; ~**schwelle** break-even point; **Kurs-** ~-**Verhältnis** earnings-to-sales ratio; ~**verlust** loss of profits (earnings); ~**vorschau** earnings projection (estimate); ~**wert** income value; ~**zahlen** *(Geschäftsbericht)* trading figures.

Erwartungs|kauf sale by expectancy; ~**struktur** *(Marketing)* anticipation.

erweitern, sein Geschäft to expand one's business.

Erweiterungen auf dem Fabrikgelände vornehmen to extend the works.

Erweiterungs|bauten enlargements; ~**kosten** cost of addition; ~**rücklagen** reserve for extension.

Erwerb acquisition, purchase, *(Verdienst)* earnings, gain, getting;
nicht auf ~ **gerichtet** nonprofitable;

gutgläubiger ~ innocent (bona-fide) purchase for value of notice;
~ **von Anlagegütern im Leasingverfahren** sale-lease back *(US)*.

erwerben, Beteiligung to secure an interest; **billig** ~ to buy at a low figure; **Fachkenntnisse** ~ to gain expert knowledge; **käuflich** ~ to purchase for value.

Erwerber acquirer, acquisitor, purchaser, purchasing party, buyer, vendee, alienee;
bösgläubiger ~ purchaser in bad faith; **gutgläubiger** ~ bona-fide holder (purchaser) for value.

Erwerbs|betrieb business enterprise; ~**einkommen** business income.

erwerbsfähig able to earn a livelihood.

Erwerbs|fähigkeit ability to earn a livelihood, earning power; ~**genossenschaft** industrial society *(US)*.

erwerbslos unemployed, unoccupied, out [of work], out of employ, idle, jobless, *(US)*;
~ **werden** to lose one's job.

Erwerbslosen|quote unemployment ratio; ~**unterstützung** unemployment benefit (relief), dole *(Br.)*; ~**versicherung** unemployment insurance.

Erwerbs|loser unemployed; **unselbständige** ~**personen** wage and salary earners; **unsichere** ~**quelle** precarious living.

erwerbstätig sein to be gainfully employed.

Erwerbstätiger gainful worker;
selbständiger ~ self-employer.

erwerbsunfähig disabled, unable to earn a living.

Erwerbsunfähiger disabled [person], incapacitated worker.

Erwerbsunfähigkeit disability, disablement, inability to support o. s.; **zeitweilige** ~ temporary disability, incapacity.

Erzeuger manufacturer, maker, producer;
~**genossenschaft** producer cooperative; ~**großmarkt** central market; **landwirtschaftliche** ~**preise** farm-product prices; ~**verband** producer organization.

Erzeugnis product, produce, production, manufacture, merchandise, turnout, make, work;
ausländische ~**se** foreign-made products; **unser eigenes** ~ domestic (home) produce; **hochqualifizierte** ~**se** high-quality (-class) goods, big-ticket items; **ladeneigenes** ~ store-brand item; **landwirtschaftliche** ~**se** agricultural commodities (produce); **preisgebundene** ~**se** price-bound merchandise; **preisstabile** ~ price-maintained goods *(US)*; **veredelte** ~ improved goods;
~**se aller Art** goods, wares, and merchandise; ~**se in der Fabrikation** *(Bilanz)* work in progress *(Br.)* (process, *US)*; ~**se mit gleichbleibenden Preisen** price-maintained articles *(US)*;
~**se aller Preisklassen führen** to carry full-price range.

Erzeugung, industrielle economic production; **mengenmäßige** ~ output in volume;;
~ **beschränken** to curtail production.

Erzeugungs|beschränkung output restriction; ~**kosten**

production (prime) cost; ~**quote** production quota.

erzielen, Abkommen to reach an agreement; **Gewinne** ~ to realize (make, secure) profits; **in rascher Steigerung neue Höchstkurse** ~ to shoot into new high ground.

Essensbon, ~**marke** meal (bread, *US*) ticket, meal (luncheon) voucher.

Etage, erste first floor *(Br.)*, second story *(US)*.

Etagenwohnung [self-contained] flat *(Br.)*, apartment *(US)*;

Etat budget, estimates, supplies;
  ausgeglichener ~ balanced budget; **außerordentlicher** ~ extraordinary budget; **genehmigter** ~ approved budget; **unausgeglichener** ~ adverse (unbalanced) budget;
  ~ **aufstellen** to draw up the budget; **regelrechten** ~ **aufstellen und danach leben** to keep an actual budget; ~ **beschneiden** to prune a budget; ~ **bewilligen** to vote the appropriation (supplies); **angespannten** ~ **entlasten** to ease the stress on the budget; ~ **auf Streichungsmöglichkeiten überprüfen** to scan the budget for possible cutbacks; ~ **überschreiten** to exceed the budget; ~ **vorlegen** to introduce (present) the budget; ~ **zusammenstreichen** to slash a budget;
  ~**abstrich** budget cut; ~**anforderung** budget request; ~**ansatz** forward projection budget; ~**aufschlüsselung** breakdown of a budget; ~**ausgleich** bugetary balance; ~**bewilligung** supply vote; ~**beschränkungen** budgetary restraints; ~**defizit** adverse budget, budget deficit; ~**jahr** budgetary year, *(Statistik)* fiscal (financial) year; ~**kürzung** budget cut (slash); ~**mittel** budgetary means, voted (budget) fund; ~**posten** item included in the budget; ~**streichungen durchführen** to cut public expenditures; ~**titel** budget item (heading); ~**überschuß** budget surplus; ~**voranschlag** budgetary estimate; ~**vorlage** application request; ~**vorschlag annehmen** to approve the budget; ~**zuweisung** budgetary allocation.

Etikett label, tally, ticket, docket, *(Anhänger) (Warenzeichen)* trademark, stamp, brand.

Euro|dollar Eurodollar; ~**dollarverschuldung** Eurodollar borrowings.

Europäisch|e Freihandelszone European Free Trade Association, EFTA; ~**e Gemeinschaft** European Community; ~**e Investitionsbank** European Investment Bank; ~**es Niederlassungsabkommen** European Convention on Establishment; ~**es Währungsabkommen** European Monetary Agreement; ~**e Wirtschaftsgemeinschaft** European Economic Community.

Eventualanspruch contingent claim.

Exedentenvertrag *(Rückversicherung)* excess of loss.

exekutieren *(Börse)* to sell out against s. o.

Exekutions|kauf *(Börse)* forced realization, buying in *(Br.)*, buying in (under the rules *US)*;
  ~**verkauf** forced sale, selling out *(Br.)*.

Exemplar copy, *(Muster)* pattern, sample, specimen, *(Urkunde)* set, *(Zeitung)* number;
  in drei ~**en ausgestellt sein** *(Wechsel)* to be drawn in sets of three.

Existenzlohn subsistence (living) wages.

Existenzminimum minimum of existence, daily subsistence allowance, subsistence level;
  ~ **sicherstellen** to procure the bare necessities.

Exklusivvertrag exclusive agreement, tying contract.

Expansionspolitik expansionism, expansionary (expansionist) policy.

Expedient copying (forwarding, dispatching, shipping, *US*, cargo *US)* clerk, [post] dispatcher.

Expedition expediting, dispatching, forwarding, shipping *(US)*, *(Abteilung)* dispatching office.

Expeditionsgebühren forwarding (mailing, shipping *US)* charges.

Experte expert, dabster *(Br.)*, dab.

Expertise expertise, expert's report.

Export exportation, export [trade].

Export|abgabe export duty, tax on exports; ~**akkreditiv** export letter of credit; ~**artikel** export (exported) article (item), *(pl.)* exports; ~**auftrag** export order; ~**beschränkungen** export restrictions; ~**bewilligung** export licence (permit); ~**dokumente** export documents; ~**erlösverlust** loss on export income; ~**finanzierung** export financing; ~**finanzierungsgesellschaft** export-financing concern; ~**firma** export house (firm, company); ~**förderung** export promotion (drive, subsidy), boost to exports; ~**genehmigung** export licence (authorization); ~**geschäft** export house (merchant), *(einzelnes)* export transaction (business); ~**handel** export trade; ~**industrie** export industry; ~**katalog** export catalog(ue); ~**kaufmann** export merchant, exporter; ~**kreditversicherung** export credit insurance; ~**land** exporting country; ~**leiter** export manager; ~**markt** export market; ~**messe** export exhibition; ~**monopol** export monopoly; ~**orientiert sein** to be geared to exprot; ~**prämie** export bounty, bonus; ~**quote** export quota; ~**rückgang** decline (cut) in exports, export fall; ~**sachbearbeiter** export clerk; ~**steigerung** increased exports; ~**subvention** subsidy to exports, bounty; ~**valutaerklärung** declaration of export value; ~**ziffern** export figures; ~**zuteilung** export allocation.

Expreß, per [versandt] shipped by express, express *(Br.)*;
  ~**dienst** expedited service; ~**gebühr** express.

Expreßgut [railway] express, expedite[d] freight, fast freight *(US)*;
  ~**spedition** express business.

Expreß|zug express [train] flier; ~**zustellung** express (special, *US)* delivery; ~**zustellungsgebühr** expressage, special delivery fee *(US)*.

Extra|ausgabe extra *(Br.)*; ~**ausgaben** sundry expenses, sundries; ~**liegetage** days of demurrage; ~**zug** special train.

F

Fabrik factory, [manufacturing] plant, works, shop, workshop, mill *(Br.)*;
ab ~ ex (loco) factory (works, mill, *Br.)*;
stillgelegte ~ nonoperating factory;
~ zur Verarbeitung von Waren unter Zollaufsicht bonded factory;
in einer ~ arbeiten to work in a factory (mill, *Br.)*;
in einer ~ mit Verlust arbeiten to run a factory at a loss; ~ mit den notwendigen Maschinen ausstatten to tool a factory; ~ betreiben (besitzen) to operate (run) a factory; ~ stillegen to tie up a factory.

Fabrik│abgabepreis factory price; ~anlage factory, works, installation, manufacturing establishment; ~arbeit factory work; ~arbeiter industrial worker (labo(u)rer), factory hand, mill hand *(Br.)*.

Fabrikat make, product, manufacture;
erstklassiges ~ first-class brand; minderwertiges ~ inferior make.

Fabrikation production, manufacture, manufacturing, fabrication, making, run;
in die ~ geben to put into production.

Fabrikations│auftrag factory (production, special, job) order; ~betrieb manufacturing enterprise (establishment); ~erfahrung productive experience; ~fehler manufacturing defect, flaw; ~geheimnis letters (trade, manufacturing) secret; ~gemeinkosten factory overhead; ~jahr year of manufacture; ~kosten cost of production, manufacturing (processing) cost; ~lizenz production permit. ~monopol production (manufacturing) monopoly; ~preis production cost (price); ~prozeß manufacturing process; ~rechte manufacturing (shop) rights; ~reife finished-product stage; ~teil production part; ~verbot production prohibition; ~vorhaben manufacturing project; ~zweig [line of] manufacture, manufacturing branch.

Fabrik│ausbau factory extension; ~ausstoß manufacturing output; ~ausweitung plant (factory) expansion; ~bahn factory (works) railway; ~besitzer manufacturer, owner of a factory, millowner *(Br.)*; ~betrieb factory, works, industrial unit, mill *(Br.)*; ~erzeugnis manufactured article, product; ~gebäude manufactory, factory building; ~gegend industrial district (area); ~gleis industrial line, siding, sidetrack *(US)*; ~grundstück factory (industrial) property, industrial site; in der ~halle on the floor; ~komplex manufacturing complex; ~kosten shop cost; ~marke trademark, brand.

fabrikmäßig hergestellt factored, factory-made, mass-produced, manufactured.

Fabrik│nähe vicinity of a factory; ~name style, brand.

fabrikneu brand-new.

Fabrik│nummer factory (serial, maker's) number; ~preis factory cost (price), cost-plus price; ~tor factory (plant) gate; ~unfall industrial accident; ~verlagerung transfer of a factory; ~viertel manufacturing quarter; ~ware manufactured articles

(goods, commodities), machine-made goods; eingetragenes ~zeichen registered trademark.

fabrizieren to make, to manufacture, to produce, to fabricate.

Fach *(Arbeitsgebiet)* field, department, line, sphere of business (action), province, beat, *(Geschäftszweig)* trade, profession;
sich in einem ~ spezialisieren to specialize (major, *US)* in a subject.

Fachanwalt │ für Grundstückssachen conveyancing lawyer; ~ für Steuerrecht tax lawyer.

Facharbeiter skilled (qualified) worker (operative), expert (skilled) workman;
~beruf skilled factory job; ~lohn occupational wage.

Fach│ausbildung industrial (occupational, professional, vocational, special) training; ~blatt trade journal; ~buch technical book, textbook; ~einzelhändler dealer, stockist *(Br.)*, limited-line retailer *(US)*.

Fach│gebiet field, line, province, department; ~geschäft speciality shop (store), one-line shop (business), dealer, stockist *(Br.)*, limited-line retailer *(US)*; ~gewerkschaft craft (vertical, horizontal) union; ~handel dealers, specialized trade; ~katalog form catalog(ue).

fachlich qualiziert sein to be qualified in one's subject.

Fach│literatur trade (specialized) literature, literary tools; ~mann master hand, practitioner, specialist, professional; ~messe trade exhibition, specialized fair; ~minister minister with portfolio; ~presse technical (trade) press; ~schule vocational (technical, industrial, professional) school; ~verband subassociation, industrial (trade) association; ~wörterbuch special (technical) dictionary; ~zeitschrift trade (business) paper, technical publication.

Fahndungsdienst *(Zoll)* preventive service.

Fahrausweis travel voucher, ticket.

Fahrbahn roadway, runway, trackway, lane;
verengte ~ narrow road;
~ für Langsamfahrzeuge deceleration lane;
vorschriftswidriger ~wechsel lane straddling.

Fahr│bereitschaft roadworthiness, *(Betrieb)* factory fleet, motor pool, carpool *(US)*; ~dienstleiter [train] dispatcher, starter, traffic manager; ~eigenschaften *(Auto)* handling qualities, roadability.

Fahren driving, riding, travel(l)ing;
~ ohne Führerschein driving without licence; ~ ohne Haftpflichtversicherung driving while uninsured.

fahren to go, *(im Auto)* to drive, to motor, *(in Verkehrsmitteln)* to travel, to ride, to go, *(Zug)* to run; mit der Eisenbahn ~ to go by train, to railroad *(US)*; mit dem Omnibus ~ to go by (ride in a) bus; mit dem Taxi ~ to take a taxi.

Fahrer driver, runner *(US), (Chauffeur)* chauffeur, driver, *(Motorrad)* rider;
flüchtiger ~ hit-and-run driver; **rücksichtsloser** ~ road hog, reckless driver;
~**flucht begehen** to be a hit-and-run driver.

Fahrgastschiff passenger boat, liner.

Fahrgeld passage, fare, *(Autobus, Straßenbahn)* carfare *(US), (Boot)* boatage;
~ **abgezählt bereithalten** please tender [the] exact fare.

Fahr|geldzuschuß assisted passage; ~**gelegenheit** transport facilities, [means of] conveyance.

Fahrkarte [passenger] ticket, *(Eisenbahn)* [railway (railroad, *US*)] ticket, pasteboard *(sl.)*;
verbilligte ~ limited (cheap) ticket;
~ **zum halben Preis** half-fare ticket.

Fahrkarten|schalter booking *(Br.)* (ticket, *US*) office (window); ~**sperre** ticket gate.

Fahrkostenzuschuß transportation (travel) allowance.

Fahrlässigkeit, grobe recklessness, gross fault (carelessness, negligence), crash negligence;
mitwirkende ~ contributory negligence.

Fahrplan timetable, time bill *(Br.)*, list of trains, railway guide, train sheet, [train]schedule *(US), (Flughafen)* flight list, *(Bus)* bus guide;
~**änderung** rearrangement of the timetable, schedule change *(US)*.

fahrplanmäßig regular, on time, according to schedule *(US)*, as scheduled *(US)*;
~**e Abfahrt** scheduled time *(US)*.

Fahrpreis passage, [rate of] fare, *(Bus, Straßenbahn)* carfare, *(Eisenbahn)* railroad fare *(US)*;
zu ermäßigtem ~ at reduced fare;
verbilligter ~ bargain-tour fare, *(außerhalb der Saison)* low seasonal fare;
~ **für die Hin- und Rückfahrt** return (round-trip, *US*) fare;
~**anzeiger** fare schedule *(US)*, clock; ~**ermäßigung** fare reduction; ~**zone** fare stage *(Br.)*; ~**zuschlag** excess (supplementary) fare.

FAhrschein, ungültiger ticket no longer available;
vergünstigter ~ privilege ticket;
~**automat** ticket-vending machine; ~**heft für Bahn, Bus und Schiff** combined ticket.

Fahr|schule motor (driving) school; ~**sicherheit** safe driving.

Fahrt drive, ride *(US), (Bahnsignal)* clear, *(Reise)* journey, tour, trip, *(zur See)* voyage, passage;
freie ~ green light, road clear *(US)*;
~ **ins Blaue** mystery tour; ~ **ins Grüne** summer outing.

Fahrt|auslagen travelling expenses; ~**ausweis** ticket, *(Führerschein)* driving (driver's *US*) licence.

Fahrten|buch, ~**nachweis** logbook; ~**schreiber** speed recorder.

Fahrt|entschädigung milage; ~**kosten** travelling expenses, fares; ~**route** lane; ~**richtungsanzeiger** direction indicator; ~**unterbrechung** break, stopover *(US), (Flugbesatzung)* layover.

Fahr|verbot driving ban; ~**vorschriften** traffic regulations; ~**weg** [carriage] road; ~**zeit** running time.

Fahrzeug conveyance, craft, vehicle, machine, *(Schiff)* vessel, ship;
gesperrt für ~ **aller Art** no entry, closed to traffic;
~**beleuchtung** lighting of a vehicle; ~**industrie** motor industry, vehicle business; ~**papiere** registration papers, claim check *(US)*.

Faksimile facsimile, *(Wertpapiere)* specimen;
~**abschrift** copy in facsimile; ~**stempel** signature (facsimile) stamp.

Faktor, preiserhöhender price-raising factor; **wertsteigernder** ~ *(Grundstück)* corner influence.

Faktura invoice, bill, account;
laut ~ as per invoice, as invoiced;
beglaubigte ~ legalized invoice;
~ **ausstellen** to [make out an] invoice;
~**betrag** invoiced amount; ~**wert** invoice value.

Fakturen|buch invoice book; ~**datum** date of invoice, billing date *(US)*.

fakturieren to bill, to invoice.

Fakturiermaschine billing machine.

Fallen *(Kurse)* fall, decline, drop, slump, easing off, *(Preise)* decline, downward movement, depression;
~ **und Steigen der Preise** fluctuation of prices.

fallen *(Kurse)* to drop, to fall, to decline, to go down, to plummet, *(Preise)* to be on the decline (fall, on the downgrade);
in jds. Aufgabenbereich ~ to come within s. one's province; **der Gemeinde zur Last** ~ to come upon the parish; **nur um 5/8 Prozent** ~ to drop a meagre 5/8 *(Br.)*; **im Wert** ~ to depreciate.

fallende | Kosten decreasing costs; ~ **Preise** falling prices; ~ **Tendenz** downward (bearish) tendency.

fällig mature, matured, due, *(Kupon)* collectible, *(zahlbar)* payable, dischargeable, outstanding;
täglich ~ due at call;
~ **stellen** to fix a due date; ~ **werden** to grow (become, fall) due, *(Bezugsrecht)* to expire, *(Wechsel)* to run off, to mature, *(Zinsen)* to accrue.

Fälligkeit maturity, due date, payability, *(Bezugsrecht)* expiration;
zahlbar bei ~ cash at maturity;
vor ~ **bezahlen** to prepay, to pay before maturity; **Wechsel bei** ~ **einlösen** to take up a draft when due; **vor** ~ **zahlen** to pay in advance (anticipation).

Fälligkeits|aufstellung aging statement; ~**buchführung** accrual accounting; ~**datum** due (accrual, maturity) date; ~**liste** aging schedule, expiration list; ~**tag**, ~**termin** due (accrual, maturity) date.

falsch *(gefälscht)* forged, falsified, feigned, fraudulent, *(Münze)* false, base, *(nachgemacht)* counterfeit, *(unecht)* spurious, bogus, mock, sham;
Brief ~ **adressieren** to misaddress a letter;
~**e Angabe in Subskriptionsanzeigen** misstatement in a prospectus; ~**e Banknote** forged (counterfeit) note; ~**e Buchung** wrong entry; ~**e Nummer wählen** to dial a wrong number.

Falsch|beurkundung falsification of a registry;

~bezeichnung **von Waren** misbranding of goods; ~buchung false (fraudulent) entry.

fälschen to falsify, to feign, *(Geld)* to counterfeit, *(Nahrungsmittel)* to adulterate;
  Bilanz ~ to cook (fake, doctor, tamper) a balance sheet.

Fälscher counterfeiter, forger, fabricator, imitator; ~bande counterfeiting ring.

Falschgeld counterfeit (bad, base, white, bogus, *US*, queer, *US*) money;
  ~ **in Umlauf bringen (setzen)** to pass (publish) counterfeit money (forged coins);
  ~druckerei bogus (forging) press; ~**note** counterfeit note.

Falschmünzer [false] coiner *(Br.)*, counterfeiter.

Fälschung falsification, counterfeiting, fabrication, fake, phony *(US sl.)*, *(Nahrungsmittel)* adulteration, *(Urkunden)* forgery;
  ~ **von Warenzeichen** imitation of trademarks.

Falt|blatt, ~prospekt leaflet, pull-out, folder *(US)*.

Familie, Fürsorgeunterstützung beziehende public-aid family, family on relief;
  große ~ **unterhalten** to provide for a large family.

Familien|abzüge *(Einkommensteuer)* allowance (credit) for dependants, personal allowance; ~betrieb family business (enterprise); **landwirtschaftlicher** ~betrieb agricultural family enterprise; ~haushaltsplan household (family) budget; ~hotel family (residential) hotel; ~standslohn family wage; ~zulage family allowance (benefit).

Farb|anzeige colo(u)r advertising (unit); ~fernsehen colo(u)r television.

Fassung tenor, version, wording, drafting;
  ungültig wegen unklarer ~ void for uncertainty.

fauler Zahler slow payer.

Faulfracht dead freight.

Favoriten *(Börsenwerte)* standard (special, *US)* stock, seasoned securities.

Fehl|anlage misemployment; ~anzeige **erforderlich** nil return requested; ~bestand deficiency.

Fehlbetrag | im Staatshaushalt deficit of the budget;
  ~ **ausgleichen** to make up a shortage.

fehlende Gegenleistung want of consideration.

Fehler, stichprobenfremder nonsampling error; **versteckter** ~ latent defect.

Fehlergrenze margin of error, tolerance.

fehlerhaft bad, false, faulty, defective, deficient, all abroad, incorrect, *(beschädigt)* damaged.

Fehler|spanne, ~spielraum margin of error, error margin.

Fehl|fabrikat defective article; ~fracht dead freight; ~geld *(Kassierer)* risk money; ~gewicht false (short) weight; ~investition misemployment, investment failure, misappropriated capital; ~kalkulation miscomputation; ~konstruktion faulty construction (design).

fehlleiten, Brief to misdirect a letter; **Kapital** ~ to misappropriate (misapply) funds.

Fehl|lenkung von Kapital misapplication of funds; ~meldung false report; ~schicht dropped shift;

~spekulation wrong (unlucky, bad) speculation; **zugelassene** ~stücke allowable defects; ~verbindung *(Tel.)* wrong connection (connexion, *Br.)*.

Feierabend leisure time;
  ~ **machen** to call it a day, to cease working, to knock off, to shut up shop.

Feierschicht dropped shift, *(Bergbau)* idle shift.

feilhalten, an einem Stand to keep a stall.

Feingehalt assayed value, standard fineness, alloy;
  ~ **feststellen** to assay.

Feingehalts|wert assay office value; ~stempel hallmark, standard, mark, touch.

Feingold fine (pure) gold.

Feldbestellung cultivation, tillage.

Fenster|aufkleber *(Werbung)* window streamer; ~briefumschlag window (panel) envelope.

Ferien holiday(s), vacation *(US)*, leave, recess;
  ~ **machen** to take (go for) a holiday, to vacation *(US)*, to go vacationing *(US)*;
  ~arbeit holiday (vacation, *US)* work; ~bedingte **Schließung** holiday (vacation, *US)* shutdown; ~geld holiday pay, vacation payment *(US)*; ~haus holiday (vacation, *US)* home, holiday chalet; ~industrie holiday trade; **billige** ~reise low-cost vacation tour *(US)*; ~reservierung holiday booking; ~zuschlag vacation bonus (time allotment) *US)*.

fernbleiben, unentschuldigt to be absent without leave.

Fern|-D-Zug long-distance train, limited express *(US)*; ~fahrer lorry (truck, *US)* driver, trucker *(US)*.

Ferngespräch trunk call *(Br.)*, toll call *(US)*, long-distance telephone call *(US)*;
  ~ **[zu jem.] anmelden** to give in a call, to book a trunk call *(Br.)*, to call s. o. long-distance *(US)*.

Fern|heizung district heating; ~kabel trunk (long-distance, *US)* cable; ~kurs correspondence course; ~lastzug, ~laster long-distance road train, industrial truck; ~leitung trunk *(Br.)* (long-distance, toll, *US)* line, *(Ölleitung)* pipe line; ~leitungswähler long-distance connector, trunk offering (toll, *US)* final selector; ~licht *(Auto)* distance light, headlight; ~meldenetz telecommunication network.

fernmündlich zugestelltes Telegramm telephoned telegram.

Fernschnellzug express train.

Fernschreib|anlage teleprinter (teletype, telex, *US)* connection, ~en teletype, telex [message].

fernschreiben to teleprint, to teletype, to telex.

Fernschreiber *(Gerät)* simplex printer, type-writing (printing) telegraph, teletypewriter *(US)*, [tele]printer *(Br.)*, teletyper *(US)*.

Fernschreib|gebühr telex call charge, line cost; ~netz teleprinter network; ~stelle teleprinter (teletype, telex, *US)* unit; ~teilnehmer teleprinter (teletype, telex, *US)* user; ~verkehr teleprinter (telex, *US)* communication; ~vermittlung telex exchange.

fernschriftlich by teleprinter (teletype, telex, *US*).

Fernseh|ansager[in] television (video, *US*) announcer; ~apparat television receiver (set); ~band-gerät video-tape recorder *(US)*; ~bildschirm [television] screen.

Fernsehen television, video *(US)*;
innerbetriebliches ~ closed-circuit television; kommerzielles ~ commercial (independent) television.

fernsehen to teleview, to watch television.

Fernseh|gebühr television expenses; ~gerät television set, box, telly *(Br.)*; ~industrie television (video, *US*) industry; ~kassette electronic video recording cartridge *(US)*; ~koffergerät portable television; ~lehrgang abhalten to teleteach; ~leitung television broadcasting circuit; beliebtes ~programm high-rated program(me); ~publikum television (viewing) audience; ~sendung television broadcasting, video[cast] *(US)*, telecast; ~tonbandgerät videotape recorder *(US)*; direkte ~übertragung live television coverage; ~werbegesellschaft television advertiser; ~werbesendung television commercial, *(kurze)* television spot commercial.

Fernspediteur long-distance mover, land (highway) carrier, haulage contractor *(US)*.

Fernsprech|amt [telephone] exchange, central *(US)*; ~anlage telephone installation (facilities); ~ansagedienst telephone information service; ~anschluß subscriber's line, telephone connection (connexion, *Br.*); ~auftragsdienst automatic telephone answering service; ~automat telephone booth (kiosk), public call box *(Br.)*, pay station *(US)*; ~buch telephone book (directory).

Fernsprecher, öffentlicher telephone booth (kiosk), public telephone, public call box *(Br.)*.

Fernsprech|gebühren telephone charges; ~grundgebühr line charge; ~nebenstelle telephone extension; öffentliche ~stelle public telephone, telephone booth (kiosk), public call box *(Br.)*, pay station *(US)*.

Fern|straße, sechsbahnige six-lane highway *(US)*; ~straßenverkehrsnetz highway network.

Fernverkehr long-distance (-hauls) transport (traffic); *(tel.)* trunk (toll-, *US*) line service.

Fernverkehrs|bereich *(tel.)* trunk zone; ~omnibus cross-country (long-distance) bus, motor coach ~straße arterial road, trunk road *(Br.)*, highway *(US)*.

Fern|vermittlung long-distance telephone connection; ~versorgung long-distance supply; ~wahl *(Telefon)* trunk (direct, long-distance, toll-line *US*) dialling.

Fertig|anzug ready-made suit, *(fam.)* hand-(reach-)me-down; ~bauweise prefabricated construction; ~bearbeitung finishing [operation]; ~erzeugnisse finished products (goods); ~haus prefabricated (precut) house (building); ~montage final assembly; ~stellung accomplishment, completion, perfection, *(Produktionsvorgang)* finishing, processing.

Fertigungs|anlage, ~betrieb factory, plant, manufacturing establishment; ~aufgabe line shutup, ~einheit production unit; ~gemeinkosten indirect (factory, production) cost, overhead costs; ~ingenieur production engineer; ~leiter production manager; ~löhne direct labo(u)r [cost], productive wages (labo(u)r); ~reif ready to go into production; betriebseigene ~stätten owned facilitiess; ~steuerung production control; ~straße production line, conveyor system; ~stufe stage of production; ~teil production part; auftragsloser ~zweig empty production.

Fertigwaren finished goods (products), manufactures;
~bestand finished-goods inventory; ~lager stock of finished goods.

fest *(Börse)* firm, stiff, *(dauerhaft)* durable, *(Kurs)* firm, *(sicher)* fast, fixed;
sehr ~ *(Börse)* strong, buoyant; ~ angelegt *(Kapital)* tied (locked, *Br.*) up; ~ angestellt permanently appointed, on the establishment; ~ anbieten to offer firm; ~ bleiben *(Börse)* to maintain a firm attitude; ~ eröffnen *(Börse)* to open steady; ~ angestellt sein to be in regular work, to draw a fixed salary;
~er Akkordlohnsatz permanent piece rate; ~es Angebot firm offer; ~er Auftrag standing order; ~e Börse firm (steady) market; ~es Einkommen assured (regular, settled) income; ~ angelegtes Geld tied (locked-up, *Br.*) money; ~e Kundschaft regular (steady) customers; ~e Preise set (fixed) prices, *(Schaufenster)* no reductions; ~er Umrechnungskurs direct exchange; ohne ~en Wohnsitz of no fixed abode.

Festgeld consolidated money, time deposit *(US)*;
~hypothek fixed mortgage; ~konto time deposit *(US)*, deposit account *(US)*, fixed deposit.

festgesetzt fixed, settled, set, determined, determinate, vested;
vertraglich ~ stipulated;
zur ~en Stunde at the appointed time.

festigen, sich to firm, to steady, to stiffen, to harden, *(Preise)* to stabilize.

Festigkeit *(Börse)* strength;
~ der Sätze für tägliches Geld firmness in calls.

Fest|kauf firm purchase; ~kurs fixed rate.

festlegen, Bedingungen to lay down conditions; Guthaben auf zwei Monate ~ to fix a deposit for two months; Quote ~ to determine a quota.

Festlegung| von Bankgeldern immobilization of bank funds; ~ der Firmenpolitik policy formation; ~ von Kapitalbeiträgen accumulation of capital, lockup *(Br.)*; ~ der Parität expression of par value; ~ der Verkaufstournee routing plan.

festliegendes Kapital frozen capital, lockup *(Br.)*.

Festpreis fixed (set, one-) price, price fixed by the government;
~auftrag straight (fixed)-price contract *(US)*; ~vertrag mit Leistungszuschlägen fixed-price incentive fee contract.

festsetzen *(ausbedingen)* to stipulate, to lay down, *(bestimmen)* to fix, to determine, to decide; **anteilsmäßig** ~ to prorate; **Dividende** ~ to declare a dividend; **Schadenersatz** ~ to assess (ascertain, award) the damages.

Festsetzung | **der Dividende** declaration of dividend; ~ **des Fluchtlinienplanes** zoning; ~ **höherer Prämien** rating up.

feststehende Abschreibungssätze fixed depreciation.

feststellen, aktenmäßig to place (take) on record; **jds. Aufenthalt** ~ to trace s. one's whereabouts; **Valutierung** ~ to fix a value date.

Feststellung | **der Aktiva** marshalling the assets; ~ **der Konkursbilanz** filing of a schedule; ~ **der Personalien** identification; ~ **des mittleren Zahlungstermins** equation of payments.

Feststellungsbescheid *(Steuer)* [notice of] assessment.

festverzinsliche Werte fixed-income investment.

Festzeitgespräch fixed-time-call.

feuerfester Geldschrank fireproof strongbox.

feuern, j. to sack (fire, *US sl.)* s. o., to give s. o. his cards (the order of the boot), to brush s. o. off *(US).*

Feuerschaden loss (damage caused) by fire, fire loss.

Feuer|schadensabteilung fire department; ~**versicherung** fire insurance.

Feuerversicherungs|gesellschaft fire office *(Br.)* (underwriter), fire insurance company, fire-casualty insurer; ~**police** fire [insurance] policy; ~**risiko** fire-insurance risk.

fiktiv|e Bilanz pro-forma balance sheet; ~**er Preis** fictitious price; ~**er Wechsel** accommodation bill.

Filial|abschlüsse branch transactions; ~**avis** branch advice; ~**bank** branch bank; ~**betrieb** ancillary undertaking, branch establishment, chain; ~**buchführung** branch accounting (ledger).

Filiale branch [house], local branch, branch establishment (office), *(Bank)* agency, branch bank; ~**n im ganzen Land unterhalten** to operate a statewide system of branches.

Filial|geschäft branch office, multiple shop; ~**leiter** manager of a branch office, branch manager, *(Bank)* bank agent; ~**unkosten** branch expenses; ~**unternehmen** branch establishment, *(Einzelhandel)* multiple chain; ~**vorsteher** branch manager; ~**wechsel** house bill.

Film film, *(Lichtspielfilm)* motion (moving) picture, film, movies *(US),* the screen; **niedrig kalkulierter** ~ low-budget film; ~ **zum Verleih freigeben** to release a film; ~**finanzierung** film (movie, *US)* financing; ~**industrie** film (motion-picture, *US)* industry; ~**rechte** screen (film) rights; ~**regisseur** film director, producer; ~**verleih** distribution of a film, film distribution.

Finanz|abkommen monetary convention; ~**abteilung** finance department (division), financial (fiscal, *US)* division; ~**amt** tax and revenue (tax, *US)* office; ~**anzeigen** financial advertisements; ~**ausgleich** tax (revenue) sharing, Exchequer

Equalization Grant *(Br.);* ~**ausschuß** finance committee; ~**ausweis** financial statement (status) *(US);* ~**bedarf** financial (monetary) requirements; ~**buchhalter** financial accountant; ~**chef,** ~**direktor** director of finance.

Finanzen finance, financial policy; **öffentliche** ~ public finances, home finance *(Br.);* ~ **einer Firma** exchequer of a firm; ~ **eines Landes in Ordnung bringen** to purge the finances of a country; ~ **einer Gesellschaft sanieren** to rehabilitate a company financially.

Finanz|fachmann financial specialist (executive), financier; ~**flußrechnung** cashflow statement; ~**gebahrung** finance, financial management; ~**haushalt** financial budget; ~**hof** fiscal (tax) court, Court of Exchequer *(Br.),* Court of Claims *(US);* ~**hoheit** financial sovereignty.

finanziell financial, fiscal, pecuniary, monetary; ~ **gesund** [financially] sound; ~ **gut dran sein** to be in funds (well off, fixed, *US);* ~ **schlecht gestellt sein** to be badly situated (in a poor, weak financial situation); ~ **interessiert sein** to be financially interested in; ~**e Angaben** financial data; ~**e Ansprüche** money claims; ~ **Belastung** financial burden (drain); ~**e Lage** pecuniary circumstances, financial status; *(US),* **gute** ~**e Lage** strong finances; ~**e Misere** financial hardship; **in ernsthafte** ~**e Schwierigkeiten geraten** to slide into deep financial troubles; ~**e Unterstützung** financial backing; ~**er Verlust** pecuniary loss.

finanzieren to [furnish with] finance, to financier, to bankroll, to fund, *(Anleihen)* to float, *(Rundfunkprogramm)* to sponsor.

Finanzierung financing, *(von Anleihen)* floating, *(Bergbau)* habilitaton *(US),* *(Unterstützung)* subsidizing; **kurzfristige** ~ short-term financing; ~ **durch Abtretung der Debitoren (mittels Forderungsabtretung)** debt (accounts receivable, *US)* financing; ~ **von Abzahlungsgeschäften** hire-purchase finance *(Br.);* ~ **durch Ausgabe von Wandelschuldverschreibungen** convertible financing; ~ **von Wohnungen** home financing; **für die** ~ **eines Projektes geradestehen** to underwrite the cost of a project.

Finanzierungs|abkommen financing agreement; **gebündeltes** ~**angebot** financing package; ~**aufschlag** financing charge; ~**dienst** financing service; ~**gebühr** finance charge; ~**geschäft** financial transaction; ~**gesellschaft** commercial (sales) finance company, financial company; ~**hilfe** pecuniary (financing) assistance; ~**institut** financing institution; ~**kosten** cost of financing; ~**lücke** financial (money) gap; ~**mittel** credit instrument; ~**mittel einsetzen** to be trading on the equity; **günstige** ~**möglichkeiten beschaffen** to find favo(u)rable financing; ~**nachweis** *(pol. Partei)* financing statement *(US);* **sich anderweitig** ~**rück-**

halt beschaffen to switch financing; ~**träger** commercial finance company; ~**zusage** promise of finance.

Finanz|institut financial enterprise; ~**jahr** financial year *(Br.)*, fiscal year *(US)*; ~**kapital** moneyed capital; ~**kontrolle** budgetary (financial) control; **mit einer ~krise fertig werden** to ride out a fiscal crisis; ~**lage** financial standing (rating, condition, position, status *US*, state), finances; ~**makler** loan agent, loanmonger, money broker, moneylender; ~**miete beweglicher Wirtschaftsgüter** finance equipment leasing; ~**minister** Chancellor of the Exchequer *(Br.)*, Secretary of the Treasury Department *(US)*, Treasury Secretary *(US)*; ~**ministerium** Finance Ministry, Ministry of Finance, Lords of the Treasury *(Br.)*, Board of Exchequer *(Br.)*, Treasury Department *(US)*; ~**politik** financial (fiscal) policy; ~**programm** financial program(me); ~**projekt** financial project; ~**reform** fiscal reform; ~**resort** finance office; ~**sachverständiger sein** to be versed in questions of finance.

finanzschwach financially weak.

Finanz|status financial condition (statement, status, *US); ~**teil** *(Zeitung)* financial page (columns); ~**transaktion** monetary transaction (operation); ~**verhältnisse** financial conditions (position); ~**verwaltung** finance (fiscal) administration, Board of Inland Revenue *(Br.)*, Bureau of Internal Revenue *(US)*; ~**vorstand** finance officer, financial executive, corporate treasurer *(US)*; ~**wechsel** revenue bonds *(US)*; ~**wirtschaft** financial policy (system, market); ~**zeitung** financial paper; ~**zoll** tariff of revenue, revenue tariff, fiscal tax.

fingierte|s Geschäft sham (fictitious) transaction; ~**e Rechnung** pro-forma account; ~**er Wechsel** bogus bill.

Firma firm, business, concern, commercial house, enterprise, establishment, company;

unter der ~ under the firm (style) of;

alte ~ old trading house; **weltweit bekannte ~** world-renowned firm; **eingetragene ~** registered company; **solide ~** reliable (solid business) firm, sound business house; **zahlungsunfähige ~** failed firm *(US)*;

Geschäftsbeziehungen zu einer ~ aufnehmen to get in with a firm; **aus einer ~ ausscheiden** to withdraw from a company; **Inkassodienst für eine ~ besorgen** to effect the collection of a firm; **~ unter seinem eigenen Namen betreiben** to trade under one's own name; **~ herunterwirtschaften** to let a firm down; **~ im Handelsregister löschen** to take a company off the books; **an einer ~ hälftig beteiligt sein** to have a half interest in a firm; **~ in eine Aktiengesellschaft umwandeln** to turn a firm into a joint stock company; **für eine ~ zeichnen** to sign on behalf of a firm.

Firmen|aktiven corporate assets; ~**angehöriger**, ~**angestellter** company official (employee); ~**anteil**

business (partnership) interest; ~**archiv** company archives; ~**aufdruck** *(Brief)* letterhead; ~**bankrott** company bankruptcy; ~**briefbogen** company stationery; ~**eindruck** corner card; ~**finanzen** company finances; ~**flugzeug** company plane, corporate aircraft; ~**gelände** company property (premises); ~**guthaben** commercial deposit; ~**image** business image; ~**inhaber** owner (head) of a firm, company head; ~**kunde** business client, corporate customer; ~**lieferant** company supplier; ~**mantel** shell; ~**marke** trademark; ~**praktikant** industrial (on-the-job, *US*) trainee; ~**register** register of companies, register general, Companies Registration Office; ~**rendite erzielen** to put a company in the black; ~**siegel** signet, common seal; ~**unterschrift** signature of a firm, corporate signature *(US)*; ~**verlust** partnership (corporate, *US)* loss; ~**vermögen** firm property; ~**verzeichnis** [trade] directory; ~**wagen** business car; **~ wert** goodwill, enterprise value; ~**zusammenschluß** coming together of firms; ~**zuschuß** company contribution.

firmieren to trade under the style, *(Firma zeichnen)* to sign a firm.

Fischverarbeitungsschiff factory vessel.

fiskalisch|es Eigentum government property; ~**es Vermögen** state property.

Fiskus fisc, Treasury, King's (Queen's) Treasury *(Br.)*, crown *(Br.)*, Exchequer.

fix|e Anlagen fixed assets; ~**e Kosten** fixed charges, overhead expenses, overheads.

fixen *(Börse)* to sell short *(US)*, to [sell a] bear *(Br.)*, to buy on (operate for) a fall.

Fix|geschäft time bargain, future deal, operation for a fall, short sale (selling) *(US)*, selling stocks short *(US)*; ~**kauf** time purchase, future deal.

Fixum basic salary, fixed allowance.

Flächen|bedarf floor space required; ~**nutzungsplan** plan for zoning *(US)*; ~**nutzungsplan aufstellen** to plan a city, to zone *(US)*.

Flagge der Handelsmarine Red Ensign *(Br.)*.

Flaggenattest certificate of registry.

flau *(Börse)* dull, dead, lifeless, sluggish, stale, slack, stagnant, depressed, quiet, inactive;

~ schließen to leave off flat; **anfangs ~ sein** to open flat *(Br.)*;

~e Stimmung auf dem Aktienmarkt dull tone (dullness) in the stock market.

Flaute *(Börse)* dullness, deadness, dead calm, stagnation, dull (inactive) market, slackness of the market, bearish tone, dull time;

sommerliche ~ seasonal slack.

Flautezeit, konjunkturelle economic downturn.

fliegender Händler pedlar, street trader, door-to-door trader.

Fließarbeit serial (flow, standardized) production.

Fließband band (belt) conveyor, assembly line; ~**arbeit** flow (conveyor belt) production; ~**arbeiter** assembly-line worker; ~**fertigung** assembly-line (conveyor-belt) production.

fließender Verkehr moving traffic.
florierendes Geschäft rattling trade.
Flucht| aus der Währung flight from the currency;
~**geld** hot (crisis) money; ~**linienplan** building
code, zoning ordinance *(US)*.
Flug flight, fly, flying, air travel (trip);
planmäßiger ~ scheduled flight;
~ **in der Touristenklasse** economy-class travel;
~**abfertigung** handling of flights; ~**blatt** throw-
away, leaflet, fly (loose) sheet, flyleaf, handbill,
pamphlet, broadsheet, flier *(US)*.
Fluggast airline (air) passenger;
beim Abflug nicht erschienener ~ no-show *(US sl.)*;
~**annahme** [passenger] check-in; ~**gebühr** airport
(passenger) service charge; ~**gepäck** passenger
luggage *(Br.)* (baggage, *US)*; ~**gesellschaft** airline,
carrier.
Flughafen airport, airdrome, airfield, aerodrome;
~ **anfliegen** to call at a port;
~**abfertigungsgebäude** air (airport) terminal; ~**gebühr** airport tax.
Flug| karte airline ticket, air fare; ~**kilometer**
aircraft kilometer; ~**linie** airline; ~**linienfestlegung**
route planning; ~**lizenz** air carrier permit; ~**plan**
airline timetable, schedule [of plans] *(US)*.
Flugplatz airfield, airdrome, aerodrome, airport;
häufig angeflogener ~ heavy-traffic airport;
~ **im Linienverkehr anfliegen** to serve an airport
commercially;
~**abholdienst** door-to-airport limousine service;
~**gebäude** terminal building; ~**hotel** hotel at an
airport.
Flug| preis plane (airline) fare, airline charge; ~**reisen-
der** air travel(l)er; ~**reservierung** passenger reservation; ~**schein** [airplane] ticket, air fare (ticket),
flight coupon; ~**sicherheit** flying (air) safety.
Flugsicherungszentrale air traffic control center *(US)*
(centre, *Br.)*.
Flug| sicht visibility; ~**steig** apron, gate, channel;
~**stunde** flying hour; ~**taxe** taxi aircraft, taxiplane;
~**verkehrsindustrie** airline industry; ~**verkehrslinie**
airline; ~**warndienst** airraid warning service;
~**zettel** flysheet, handbill, leaflet.
Flugzeug aircraft, craft, aeroplane, plane, airplane,
flier, ship;
~**e auf Wartebahn** stack;
~ **abfertigen** to handle a flight; ~ **kapern** to hi[gh]-
jack an airplane; **mit dem** ~ **transportieren** to
transport by airplane, to flight-deliver *(US)*;
~**abstellplatz** hardstand; ~**anschluß erreichen** to
catch a plane; ~**entführung** hi[gh]jacking, aerial
piracy; ~**industrie** aircraft industry (manufacturers), air (airline, aviation) industry, aircraft
business; ~**park** aircraft fleet; ~**versicherung** aviation insurance; ~**werte** *(Börse)* aircrafts.
Fluktuieren der Preise price fluctuations.
Fluß, schiffbarer navigable river.
flüssig *(Bank, Firma)* liquid, cash-rich, financial,
fluid *(US)*, ready, *(Geldmarkt)* easy;
sehr ~ cash-heavy;

~**e Gelder (Mittel)** cash, ready money, available
funds, liquid resources, funds in hand.
Flüssigkeit *(Bank)* cash (current) position, *(Bilanz)*
liquidity, liquid position, *(Geldmarkt)* ease of
money rates.
Flüssigkeits| grad degree of liquidity; ~**koeffizient**
current position ratio, *(Zentralbank)* reserve ratio
(US); ~**verhältnis** *(Bilanz)* current position (acid
test, quick assets, *US)* ratio.
flüssigmachen, Geld to mobilize money.
Flußladeschein river (inland) bill of lading.
Fobklausel free-on-board clause.
Folge| prämie renewal (current) premium; ~**schäden**
consequential damages (loss).
Fonds fund, box, *(Kapital)* capital, funds, purse;
sich stets erneuernder ~ revolving fund; **konsolidierte** ~ consols; **liquider** ~ cash-heavy fund;
~ **zur Finanzierung von Sonderaufgaben** special
revenue fund; ~ **einer Kapitalanlagegesellschaft** investment fund;
~ **auffüllen** to reestablish a fund; ~ **für seine priva-
ten Zwecke mißbrauchen** to funnel funds to one's
own use.
Fonds| anteil share in a fund; ~**auflösung** liquidation
of a fund; ~**bestände** stockholdings, fundholdings;
~**händler** stockbroker, jobber *(Br.)*; ~**vermögen**
fund assets, assets of a fund, *(Kapitalanlagegesellschaft)* asset value.
Förder| abgabe mining royalities; ~**band** conveyer
belt, band conveyor, production line; ~**kreis für A.**
group of the common cause of A.; ~**leistung** [de-
livery] output, production.
fördern to further, to promote, to advance, *(Rundfunksendung)* to sponsor;
Absatz ~ to increase (promote); **jds. Interessen** ~
to further s. one's interests; **steuerlich** ~ to assist by
fiscal policy.
Forderung call, demand, requirement, *(Anspruch)*
claim, debt;
abgetretene ~ assigned claim; **im Feststellungsver-
fahren anerkannte** ~ debt on record, judgment
debt; **anmeldefähige** ~ provable claim (debt); **vertraglich begründete** ~ debt founded on contract;
bevorrechtigte ~ *(Konkursverfahren)* secured (preferential, preferred) debt; **nicht bevorrechtigte** ~
simple contract (unsecured) debt; **buchmäßige** ~
book claim; **festgestellte** ~ liquidated demand,
(Konkurs) proved debt; **fingierte** ~ simulated debt,
bogus claim; **geldähnliche** ~ near money *(US sl.)*,
quasi money *(US)*; **strittige** ~ disputed claim; **unbegründete** ~ false claim, nonprovable debt; **verjährte** ~ statute-barred claim, outlawed obligation
(claim, *US)*, stale debt (demand, *US)*;
~ **nach Lohnerhöhung** wage demand;
~ **abbuchen** to wipe off a debit balance; **zweifelhafte** ~ **abschreiben** to write off a doubtful claim
(Br.) (bad debt, *US)*; ~ **anmelden** to lodge a proof
of (report a) debt, to lodge (prove) a claim; ~ **einklagen** to litigate (prosecute) a claim, to take legal
proceedings for the recovery of a debt; ~ **beim**

Konkursverwalter einreichen to lodge a proof of debt with the official receiver; **Verjährungseinwand gegen eine ~ erheben** to bar a debt by the Statute of Limitations; **von einer ~ Abstand nehmen** to relinquish a claim; **~ pfänden** to arrest a debt, to trustee *(US)*; **~ zurückweisen** to turn down a claim.

Forderungen *(Bilanz)* debts *(Br.)*, accounts receivable *(US)*, receivables *(US)*;
zum Ausgleich aller ~ in full settlement;
ausstehende ~ active (outstanding) debts; **diverse ~** *(Bilanz)* sundry debtors, sundries; **hochgeschraubte ~** exaggerated claims; **lohnfremde ~** nonwage demands; **uneinbringliche ~** irrecoverable (bad) debts;
~ an Kunden trade-account receivables *(US)*; **~ aus laufender Rechnung** debts founded on open account; **~ auf Grund von Warenlieferungen** debts founded on merchantable goods, trade receivables *(US)*;
~ einklagen to sue for debts; **seine ~ ermäßigen** to moderate one's claims; **groteske ~ stellen** to set up ridiculous pretensions; **~ zedieren** to assign claims.

Forderungsabtretung assignation (assignment) of claim;
~ in stiller Form nonnotification plan;
~ offenlegen to operate on a notification basis.

Forderungs|anmeldung filing of claim, *(im Konkursverfahren)* proof of claim (debts); **~aufkauf** purchase of accounts receivable *(US)*; **~berechtigter** claimant, creditor, *(Versicherungspolice)* beneficiary; **~nachweis** proving (proof of) a debt; **~nachweis im Konkursverfahren** proof in bankruptcy; **~pfändung** equitable garnishment, arrest of a debt; **~übergang kraft Gesetzes** legal subrogation.

Förderung promotion, furtherance, advancement; **berufliche ~** carrer advancement; **wirtschaftliche ~** business promotion;
~ steigern to increase the production (output).

Förderungs|kursus upgrading course *(US)*; **~programm** promotional program(me).

Form form, design, mode, fashion;
in notarieller ~ before a notary.

Formblatt [printed] form, blank *(US)*, schedule.

Formfehler defect of form, flaw, formal defect;
~ in der Ausstellung irregularly drawn.

förmliche Quittung formal receipt.

Formular [set] form, printed form, blank *(US)*, schedule;
unausgefülltes ~ blank, printed form, *(Wechsel)* skeleton bill;
~ für die Einkommensteuererklärung income-tax return blank *(US)*;
~ ausfüllen to fill in (up, to complete) a form, to fill out a blank *(US)*;
~brief form letter; **vollständiger ~satz** *(Konossement)* full set.

Forschung, außerbetriebliche external research.

Forschungs|auftrag research assignment (contract); **~aufwand** research expenditure (effort); **~etat**

research budget; **~kredit** fellowship; **~stipendium** [research] scholarship.

Fortbildung, berufliche adulteducation, advanced vocational training.

Fortbildungs|kursus extension (advanced training, placement, improvement) course, *(Abendschule)* evening class; **~schule** continuation (finishing) school.

fortfallen *(Zahlungen)* to cease, to be discontinued.

Fortkommen *(Existenz)* livelihood, living;
berufliches ~ getting on in one's career.

fortlaufend | notiert werden *(Börse)* to be quoted (listed, *US*) consecutively.

fortschreiben *(Grundstückswert)* to adjust.

Fortschritt, technologischer technological progress;
~e im Wohnungsbau improvements in house-building.

fortsetzen *(Geschäft)* to carry on, to continue.

Fortsetzung des Mietverhältnisses attornment of tenancy.

Fortsetzungsanzeige following-on.

Fotokopie photocopy, photoprint, photostat, xerox.

fotokopieren to photostat, to xerox.

Fracht freight, cargo, charge, *(Güter)* goods, *(Kosten)* freightage, portage, carriage;
als ~ by goods train *(Br.)*; **unter Vorauszahlung der ~** carriage prepaid;
von mehreren Spediteuren beförderte ~ interline freight; **zu viel berechnete ~** overcharge of freight; **durchgehende ~** through freight; **gestundete ~en** respited freight;
Kosten, Versicherung und ~ cost, insurance and freight, cif;
~ gegen Nachnahme freight forward;
~ bedingen to settle the term of a (to engage the) freight; **~ einnehmen** to take a lading; **~nehmen** to charter a ship.

Fracht|abnahme acceptance of shipment *(US)*; **~annahmeschein** shipping note *(Br.)*; **~annahmestelle** freight (goods, *Br.*) office; **~aufschlag** additional freight; **~ausgangspunktsystem** single basic point system *(US)*; **~benachrichtigung** arrival (landing) notice.

Frachtbrief waybill, bill of freight (lading, *US*), freight bill *(US)* (note, *Br.*, warrant, *US*);
durchgehender ~ through waybill;
~duplikat, ~doppel counterfoil waybill, duplicate [of] waybill, duplicate consignment; **~nummer** waybill number.

Fracht|buch book of cargo (loading); **~duplikat** duplicate of waybill, duplicate consignment; **~empfänger** consignee.

Frachten|ausgleich equalization of freight rates, freight equalization; **~ausschuß** committee for merchandise traffic; **~makler** freight canvasser (broker, salesman, agent), ship broker *(US)*.

Frachter [transport] freighter, cargo boat (vessel), transport ship (vessel), *(Verfrachter)* freighter;
~ umleiten to divert a cargo vessel.

Fracht|ermäßigung reduction in the freight rate;

~**flughafen** freight airport; ~**flugzeug** freight airplane (aircraft), airfreighter.

frachtfrei free of freight, carraige prepaid (paid, *Br.)*, carriage-free, freight free (paid);
~ **verzollt** free of freight and duty.

Frachtführer carrier [by land], conveyer, conveyor, *(Rollfuhrunternehmer)* haulage contractor;
~**pfandrecht** carrier's (cargo) lien.

Frachtfuhrunternehmen carrier's business.

Frachtgebühr cartage, carriage, freight, freight rates *(US)*, freightage;
vorausbezahlte ~ advance freight.

Fracht|genehmigung freight authorization; ~ **und Liegegeld** freight and demurrage; ~**geschäft** carrying trade, *(See)* chartering business.

Frachtgut cargo, freight, load, package, slow (shipped, *US)* goods, shipment *(US)*;
als ~ **registriert** received in shipment *(US)*;
leicht verderbliches ~ perishable freight;
als ~ **schicken** to send by freight (goods train, *Br.)*.

Fracht|gutsendung consignment; ~**gutverkehr** slow-goods traffic; ~**konjunktur** trend in freights.

Frachtkosten freight[age], carriage [expenses], charges for freight, freight charges (expenses),
~ **per Nachnahme** carriage forward;
~ **um 20 % kürzen** to wash out costs in freight; ~ **übernehmen** to absorb freight charge;
~**ausgleich** freight equalization, equalization of freight rates; ~**übernahme** freight absorption.

Fracht|liste package list, memorandum note, [cargo] manifest; ~**makler** freight broker; ~**nachlaß** freight absorption; ~**nachnahme** memorandum collection, carriage forward, collect shipment *(US)*;
~**niederlage** depot; ~**papiere** shipping documents; ~**police** cargo (freight) policy; ~**rabatt** freight absorption, rebate[ment]; ~**rate** carriage (freight) rate.

Frachtraum freight, freight space (room), freight capacity, shipping *(US)* (cargo) space;
~**belegen** to book freight.

Fracht|rechnung freight bill (note, *Br.)*, freight account; ~**satz** freight (transportation, shipping, *US)* rate; **verbilligter** ~**satz fr Leergut** returned freight (shipment, *US)* rate; ~**schiff** cargo boat (carrier, steamer, vessel, ship), freighter, freight steamer; **teure** ~**sendungen in Spitzenzeiten** high-cost peak shipments *(US)*; ~**senkung** reduction in the freight rate; ~**spediteur** freight forwarder (shipper), carrier, cargo (freight) agent; ~**stück** package.

Frachttarif freight rates (tariff, *US)* transportation rate, cargo tariff, rate of shipping *(US)*, schedule of rates *(US)*, *(Eisenbahn)* railway tariff;
nach Kilometern berechneter ~ freight mil(e)age; **kombinierter** ~ comination mil(e)age and rate prorate *(US)*; ~ **für Expreßversand** spot rate.

Fracht|tonne ton weight; ~**unkosten** transportation cost; ~**verkehr** goods *(Br.)* (freight, *US)* traffic; ~**versicherung** insurance on cargo (of merchandise), freight insurance; ~**vorschuß** advance[d]

freight; ~**zettel** waybill, freight (dispatch) bill *(US)*, freight note *(Br.)*; ~**zuschlag** additional (extra) carriage, additional freight, privilege; ~**zustellung** freight delivery.

Fragebogen [inquiry] form, questionary, questionnaire, *(Statistik)* schedule;
~ **mit vorgedruckten Antworten** aided-recall survey.

frankieren to prepay, to pay the postage, to send postpaid, to frank, to stamp.

Frankiermaschine postage meter (machine, *US)*.

frankiert, nicht genügend (ungenügend) more to pay, insufficiently stamped (prepaid).

Frankierung, ungenügende insufficient prepayment.

franko postage free, post-paid, prepaid, free of charges, delivered free of charge, uncharged for, *(Fracht bezahlt)* freight free (paid), flat *(US)*;
~ **Bahnhof** free station; ~ **Bord** free on board (f. o. b.); ~ **Courtage** free of broker's commission; ~ **Zinsen** flat.

Frankovermerk frank, note of prepayment.

frei *(Eisenbahn)* free on rail(s), *(franko)* prepaid, post-free, *(Leitung)* disengaged, not busy *(US)*, *(Paket)* carriage-paid, *(von Steuern)* exempt, *(Straße)* clear, *(Taxi)* for hire, *(unbewirtschaftet)* without control, unrationed, nonrationed;
~ **durch Ablösung** on Her (His) Majesty's Service *(Br.)*; ~ **für Anlieger** open to residents only; ~ **an Bord** free on board, fob, free of steamer; ~ **von Bruch und Beschädigung** free from break and damage; ~ **ein und aus und gestaut** free in and out and stowed; ~ **[ins] Haus** free to the door, carriage-free; ~ **konvertierbar** [freely] convertible; ~ **Schiff** free of steamer, free overside (overboard); ~ **von Schulden** clear of debt, unencumbered;
Tag ~**geben** to give a day off; **sich einen Tag** ~**geben lassen** to take a day off; **20 Pfund Gepäck** ~ **haben** to be allowed 20 pounds luggage *(Br.)* (baggage, *US)*; ~ **werden** *(Posten)* to fall void (vacant); ~ **Bahnsteig geliefert werden** to be delivered free railway station;
~**verfügbares Einkommen** free income; ~**er Eintritt** free admission; **nach** ~**em Ermessen** at one's own discretion; ~**es Geleit** safe conduct; ~**e Hand lassen** to give free run; ~**e Kost und Station** free food and accommodation; ~**e Marktwirtschaft** free-enterprise system; ~**es Meer** open sea; ~**er Mitarbeiter** *(Werbung)* outside artist, *(Zeitung)* freelancer; ~**e Rücklage** available reserve; ~**e Stücke** *(Börse)* negotiable securities; **im Wege** ~**er Vereinbarung** by private treaty; ~**es Vermögen** unencumbered assets; ~**konvertierbare Währung** free currency; ~**e Warenausfuhr** free import of goods; ~**e Wechselkurse** fluctuating exchange rates; ~**er Wettbewerb** free competition; ~**finanzierter Wohnungsbau** privately financed dwellings.

freiberuflich professional, *(Journalist)* free-lance; ~**e Arbeitskraft** professional worker; ~**e Tätigkeit** profession, occupation of a professional nature.

Freibetrag *(Einkommensteuer)* [income tax] relief *(Br.)* (credit, *US)*, *(Lohnsteuer)* withholding

exemption, *(Steuer)* exempted amount, exemption, tax allowance, basic abatement;
pauschaler ~ flat exemption; **persönlicher** ~ personal allowance (exemption, *US);*
~ **für die Ehefrau** *(Erbschaftssteuer)* marital deduction; **zusätzlicher** ~ **für das Arbeitseinkommen der Ehefrau** additional allowance; ~ **für niedriges Einkommen** small-income allowance *(Br.);* ~ **für Einkünfte aus freiberuflicher Tätigkeit** earned-income allowance; ~ **für Beschäftigung einer Haushaltshilfe** housekeeper relief *(Br.);* ~ **für einen doppelten Wohnsitz** temporary living-quarters allowance; ~ **für über 65jährige** age relief *(Br.).*
freibleibend, anbieten to offer without engagement; **Preise** ~ **aufgeben** to quote prices conditionally.
Frei\|börse curb, kerb, *(Br.);* ~**exemplar** presentation (gratis, free) copy; ~**fahrschein** free (complimentary) ticket; ~**flug** free ride; ~**flughafen** customs-free airport.
Freigabe release, *(Bewirtschaftung)* decontrol, *(Flugzeug)* clearance, *(Konto)* unblocking;
~ **für die Presse** press release; ~ **der Wechselkurse** floating of the exchange rate.
freigeben to release, *(im Betrieb)* to give time off, *(Bewirtschaftung aufheben)* to decontrol, to free, *(Konto)* to unblock, to deblock, to unlock, *(Wechselkurse)* to float;
für den Verkehr ~ to open to traffic; **aus der treuhänderischen Verwahrung** ~ to release from custody; **jem. eine Woche** ~ to give s. o. a. week off;
freigemacht prepaid, postage paid, postage-free.
Frei\|gepäck free luggage *(Br.)* (baggage, *US)* allowance; ~**gewicht** weight allowed free, baggage allowance *(US);* ~**grenze** free quota, *(Steuer)* exemption; ~**gut** *(Zoll)* bonded manifest, goods free of duty.
Freihafen free (bonded, open) port;
~**gebiet** free zone, free port area; ~**niederlage** sufferance wharf, free port store.
Freihandels\|gemeinschaft, Europäische European Free Trade Association (EFTA); ~**zone** free-trade area (zone, *US).*
freihändig \| **verkaufen** to sell by private contract;
~**er Verkauf** sale on the open market, *(Effekten)* direct sale, over-the-counter trade *(US).*
freiheitliche Wirtschaftsordnung free economic system.
Frei\|jahr year of grace; ~**karte** free ticket (pass), order *(Br.);* ~**kuvert** stamped (addressed, return, business, reply, *US)* envelope; ~**lager** bonded warehouse *(US)* (store, *Br.);* ~**liste** *(zollfreier Gegenstände)* free list; ~**los** free ticket; ~**machung** prepayment of postage.
Freimachungs\|gebühr prepayment fee; ~**zwang** compulsory prepayment.
Frei\|platz *(Stipendium)* foundation, prize, scholarship; ~**raumklausel** clear space clause; -**schaffend** free-lance; ~**schicht** extra shift; ~**sprechung** *(Lehrlinge)* release; ~**stelle** foundation, prize, scholarship, free place *(Br.).*

Freistellung \| **zur beruflichen Fortbildung** day release; ~ **von einer Steuer** exemption from a tax.
Frei\|stempler postage meter; ~**umschlag** stamped (addressed, return, business, reply *US)* envelope; ~**verkehr** *(Börse)* inofficial dealings, curb (kerb, *Br.)* market, open (outside, street, *Br.,* unofficial, *Br.)* market, listless trading *(US).*
Freiverkehrs\|börse curb *(US)* (kerb, *Br.)* exchange, unofficial market *(Br.),* outside (over-the-counter) market *(US);* ~**kurs** sidewalk (kerb[stone], *Br.,* curb[market, *US]* price, free-market price; ~**markt** outside (unofficial, kerb, *Br.)* market, curb, (over-the-counter) market *(US);* ~**werte** outside *(Br.)* (unlisted, *US)* securities, curb stocks *(US).*
freiwillig\|e Liquidation voluntary bankruptcy; ~**e Versicherung** optional insurance; ~**e Versteigerung** private auction.
freizeichnen, sich to exempt o. s. from a liability.
Freizeichnung exoneration.
Freizeichnungsklausel *(Abrechnung)* saving errors and omissions (S.E.A.O.), *(Havarie)* average clause.
Freizeit leisure (free, off, spare) time, leisure;
~**artikel** leisure items (products); ~**industrie** leisure industry (business), recreation market.
Freizone free zone.
fremd\|e Gelder trust money; **in** ~**e Hände übergehen** to change hands; ~**e Mittel** outside (borrowed) funds; **für** ~**e Rechnung** for third account.
Fremd\|arbeiter foreign labo(u)r (worker), alien employee; ~**aufwendungen** extraneous expenses.
Fremden\|bett tourist bed; ~**liste** list of arrivals; ~**pension** boarding house, private hotel; ~**verkehr** tourism. tourist trade.
Fremdenverkehrs\|abgabe nonresident tax; ~**büro** tourist office; ~**gewerbe** tourist trade (industry); ~**ort** tourist center *(US)* (centre, *Br.),* tourist resort; ~**verband** tourist association.
Fremd\|erträge extraneous (extraordinary) income; ~**finanzierung** outside financing; ~**kapital** outside (borrowed) capital; ~**mittel** borrowed funds.
Fremdsprachen\|korrespondent foreign correspondence; ~**sekretärin** foreign-correspondence secretary.
Fremd\|versicherung third-party insurance; ~**währungsschuldverschreibungen** foreign exchange bonds.
friedensmäßig\|e Preise prices at peacetime level; ~ **Qualität** pre-war quality.
Friedens\|miete pre-war rent; **Wirtschaft wieder auf** ~**produktion umstellen** to reconvert industry.
frisieren *(Bericht)* to cook;
Bilanz ~ to fake (cook, doctor) a balance sheet; **Einkommensteuererklärung** ~ to fiddle an income-tax return; **Konten** ~ to wangle accounts.
Frist time [allowed], [prescribed] period, *(Aufschub)* extension, prolongation, *(Kündigungsfrist)* notice, *(Termin)* time limit, date, [set, fixed] term, deadline *(US);*

in angemessener ~ within a reasonable period of time; **innerhalb der gesetzlichen** ~ within the time allowed by the law;

~ **abkürzen** to shorten a period; ~ **berechnen** to compute a period; ~ **einräumen** to allow time; **dem Schuldner eine** ~ **von einer Woche gewähren** to give a debtor a week's grace; **j. mit einer** ~ **von einem Monat kündigen** to give s. o. a. month's notice; ~ **verstreichen lassen** to let the appointed time pass.

Frist|ablauf expiration (expiry) of a period; ~**einlagen** time *(US)* (fixed-term) deposits.

fristgerecht in due time, timely.

Fristgewährung delay in payment.

fristlos | entlassen werden to be dismissed without notice; ~**e Entlassung** dismissal without notice.

Frist|setzung appointment of a date; ~**überschreitung** noncompliance with a time limit; ~**verlängerung** extension of time.

Front, grüne *(Parl.)* agricultural (farm) bloc.

fruchtlose Pfändung unsatisfied execution.

früher|e Firma old firm; ~ **Ladenschluß** early closing.

Frühjahrsartikel spring merchandise.

Früh|kapitalismus early capitalism; ~**schicht** morning shift; ~**stücksraum** *(Hotel)* breakfast room, coffee room (shop) *(US)*.

führen, Artikel ~ to have (keep) an article in stock; **Artikel nicht mehr** ~ to be out of an article; **Briefwechsel** ~ to correspond; **Bücher** ~ to keep the books; **zu Kurssteigerungen** ~ to carry to higher prices (levels).

Führerschein driving licence, (driver's) license *(US)*; ~**eintragung** endorsement of licence; ~**entzug** driving ban, disqualification (forfeiture) of licence.

Fuhr|geld carriage, cartage; ~**geschäft** carriage, haulage; ~**lohn** [charges of] carriage, cartage, wag(g)onage, freight; ~**park** transport (car) park.

Führung lead, leading, leadership, *(Besichtigung)* guided tour;
~ **der Bücher** bookkeeping;
~ **übernehmen** *(Börse)* to forge ahead; ~ **eines Unternehmens übernehmen** to get operational responsibilities.

Führungs|apparat modernisieren to update its management techniques; ~**gremium** governing body; ~**kraft** executive [employee, officer]; **mittlere ~kraft** middle-management executive; ~**kräfte** executive officers (personnel) *(US)*; ~**nachwuchs** *(Industrie)* management trainee, prospective managers; **mittlere ~schicht** advanced (middle) management; ~**zeugnis** good conduct certificate.

Fuhr|unternehmen carrier, carter, trucking (carloading) company *(US)*, haulage-contracting

business *(US)*, hauler *(US)*; ~**werk** cart, wag(g)on, conveyance, vehicle.

Füllanzeige stopgap advertising, filler.

Fund|abteilung lost-property office; ~**büro** lost-property office.

fundieren, Anleihe neu to refund a loan; **Staatsschuld** ~ to consolidate the public debt.

fundiert|es Einkommen unearned income; ~**e Staatspapiere** funds, consols *(Br.)*.

Fundierung einer Anleihe consolidation of a loan.

fündig|werden to strike oil.

Fund|ort find place (spot), habitat; ~**sache** object found, lost property.

Fünfsternehotel five-star hotel.

Funk|bild radio picture, photoradiogram; ~**fernschreiber** radio teletyper, teletypewriter *(US)*; ~**lotterie** radio lottery; ~**sprechkanal** radio telephone channel; ~**sprechgerät** radiophone, radiotelephone; ~**taxi** radio taxi, call car; ~**verbindung** radio contact, (communication, link); ~**verkehr** radio traffic (communications); ~**wagen** radio patrol (squad, *US*) car, cruiser.

Fürsorge *(Wohlfahrt)* [poor] relief *(Br.)*, social service, welfare work, plug *(coll.)*;
soziale ~ national *(Br.)* (public, *US*) assistance, public relief *(Br.)*, social welfare (service).

Fürsorge|ausgaben welfare expenditure; ~**beamter** welfare worker (officer).

fürsorge|bedürftig in need of assistance *(Br.)*; ~**berechtigt** eligible for relief (welfare).

Fürsorge|empfänger welfare recipient (beneficiary, client), assisted person *(Br.)*, recipient of relief; ~**staat** welfare state; ~**tätigkeit** social [case] work, social service, welfare work; ~**unterstützung** welfare check (payment), out[door] relief *(Br.)*, national assistance *(Br.)*; ~**unterstützung beziehen (empfangen)** to be on relief *(US)* (the parish, *Br.*), to be on welfare *(US)*.

Fusion merger, merging, fusion, tie-up;
~ **von Aktiengesellschaften** corporate consolidation *(US)*; ~ **branchenfremder Unternehmen** conglomerate merger.

Fusions|abkommen merger arrangement; ~**bilanz** consolidated balance sheet *(US)*; **für ~genehmigungen zuständig sein** to rule on mergers; ~**gewinn** consolidation profit *(US)*; ~**überschuß** negative goodwill, consolidation excess *(US)*; ~**vertrag** merger arrangement, agreement of consolidation.

Fußgänger|ampel beacon, pedestrian crossing light; ~**überweg** crosswalk, pedestrian crossing (platform, lines).

Futterkrippenwirtschaft placemanship *(Br.)*, spoils system *(US)*.

G

gängige Ware darstellen to find a ready sale.
ganz all, whole, entire, full, round, complete, total;
im ~en kaufen to buy in bulk (wholesale, in the lump).
Ganzfabrikat finished product.
ganzseitige Anzeige full-page advertisement.
Ganzstahlkarosserie all-steel body.
Garant guarantor, guarantee *(Br.)*, guaranty *(US)*, warrantor, surety, *(Effektenemission)* underwriter.
Garantie guarantee *(Br.)*, guaranty *(US)*, *(Bürgschaft)* suretyship;
    mit ~ warranted;
    abgelaufene ~ expired guarantee *(Br.)*; **vertragliche ~** warranty in the contract;
    ~ eines Bauunternehmens construction bond; **~ des Direktabsatzes** *(Emissionskonsortium)* standby guarantee *(Br.)*; **~ der Herstellerfirma** maintenance bond, warranty for fitness;
    ~ annullieren to cancel a guarantee *(Br.)*; **ein Jahr ~ haben** to be guaranteed for one year *(Br.)*; **~ in Anspruch nehmen** to raise claims under a guarantee *(Br.)*.
Garantie|abkommen covenant of warranty; **~ansprüche** warranty claims; **~ansprüche erheben** to raise a claim under a guarantee *(Br.)*; **~betrag** amount guaranteed *(Br.)*; **~depot** collateral security (guaranty, *US*); **~erklärung** guarantee *(Br.)*, guaranty *(US)*, warranty, *(Freistellung)* bond, *(Scheck)* certification *(US)*; **~fonds** guarantee *(Br.)* (guaranty, *US*) fund; **Verletzung der ~haftung** break of warranty; **~konsortium** underwriters *(Br.)*, underwriting syndicate *(US)*; **~leistung** guarantee *(Br.)*, guaranty *(US)*, surety, suretyship; **~provision** underwriting commission.
garantieren to guarantee, to guaranty, to warrant, to undertake, to furnish (give) security, to insure, to avouch, *(Effektenemission)* to underwrite;
    Wechsel ~ to guarantee a bill of exchange.
Garantiereparaturen *(Autohändler)* warranty work.
garantiertes Grundgehalt guaranteed rate, base pay.
Garantieschein [guarantee] bond *(Br.)*, guaranty *(US)*, fidelity (del credere, *Br.*) bond, surety bond *(US)*, *(für Effekten)* letter of indemnity *(Br.)*, indemnity bond *(US)*;
    kaufmännischer ~ maintenance bond *(US)*, warrant of merchantability *(US)*.
Garantie|umfang extent of warranty; **~vereinbarung** indemnity contract, del credere agreement *(Br.)*; **~verpflichtung** caution obligation, [security] bond, quality warrant, warranty of fitness *(US)*; **~versicherung** guaranty (fidelity) insurance *(US)*, fidelity guarantee *(Br.)*; **~versprechen** warranty promise, security contract; **~vertrag** contract of indemnity (suretyship, *Br.*), indemnity contract, guaranty [agreement (contract, *US*)], contract of warranty *(US)*.

Garantie|vertragsletzung breach of warranty; **~vertreter** *(Kommissionär)* del credere agent *(Br.)*; **~zeit** [period of] guarantee *(Br.)*, guaranteed period; **~zusage erfüllen** to hono(u)r a guaranty *(US)*.
Garderoben|aufbewahrung cloakroom *(Br.)*, checkroom *(US)*; **~marke** cloakroom ticket *(Br.)*, check *(US)*.
Gast guest, visitor, caller, *(Fremdenheim)* boarder, *(Hotel)* travel(l)er, tourist;
    regelmäßiger ~ regular [customer], frequenter; **~arbeiter** foreign worker, alien employee.
Gäste|haus guesthouse; **~zimmer** guest chamber, spare room (bedroom).
Gasthaus public (eating) house, stop, tavern, saloon *(US)*, restaurant, refreshment house *(Br.)*;
    in einem ~ absteigen to put up at an inn.
Gast|land host country (government); **~stätte** public (eating) house, inn, eatery, refreshment house *(Br.)*, tavern, saloon *(US)*, restaurant.
Gaststätten|besitzer restaurant owner; **~gewerbe** catering trade (industry), restaurant business.
Gastwirt innkeeper, landlord, hotelkeeper, restaurant keeper (proprietor), host, publican *(Br.)*;
    konzessionierter ~ licensed victualler *(Br.)*.
Gastwirtschaft betreiben to keep an inn (saloon, *US*).
Gattungs|kauf quantity contract, sale of unascertained goods; **~schuld** indeterminate obligation; **~waren** unascertained goods.
Gebäude, baufälliges dilapidated building;
    ~ abschätzen to assess a building; **~ für Versicherungszwecke schätzen lassen** to rate a building for insurance purposes.
Gebäude|abnahme final architect's certificate; **~abschätzung** quantity surveying *(Br.);* **~versicherung** residence insurance.
Geben und Nehmen *(Prämiengeschäft)* put and call *(Br.)*, straddle *(US)*, spread *(US)*.
geben, in Auftrag to order; **jem. etw. fest an die Hand ~** to make a firm offer to s. o.; **in Prolongation ~** *(Prämiengeschäft)* to give on stock *(Br.)*.
Geber und Nehmer *(Börse)* givers and receivers.
Gebiet district, area, ground, region, territory, *(Wirkungskreis)* field, domain, province, line;
    bebautes ~ built-up area; **im Stadtzentrum gelegenes ~** midtown area; **assoziierte überseeische ~e** *(EG)* associated overseas territories;
    Fachmann auf einem ~ sein to be an authority on a subject.
Gebiets|kartell localized cartel; **~körperschaft** political corporation (subdivision, *US*).
Gebot offer, call, *(Versteigerung)* bid, bidding;
    ohne ~e no offers;
    erstes ~ opening bid; **geringstes ~** put-up price.
Gebrauch use, usage, employment, exercise;
    zum öffentlichen ~ bestimmen to devote to the public use, to dedicate *(coll.)*.

Gebrauchs|abnahme *(Gebäude)* final architect's certificate; ~**anweisung** directions for use, instruction booklet, fly sheet; ~**fahrzeug** commercial vehicle; **persönliche ~gegenstände, ~güter** personal effects, convenience goods.

Gebrauchsmuster design (utility, petty, *US)* patent, discovery;
~**gesetz** Protection of Inventions Act *(US)*; **eingetragener ~inhaber** registered proprietor.

Gebrauchs|überlassung loan for use; ~**wert** value in use, use (going, service) value.

gebrauchte Sachen secondhand goods.

Gebrauchtwagen used (secondhand) car.

Gebühr charge, fee, due, duty, indirect tax *(US)*, subscription, *(Postanweisung)* poundage *(Br.)*, *(Straßenbenutzung)* toll, turnpike money, road tax *(Br.)*, *(Tarif)* rate, scale, *(Zoll)* duty;
zu ermäßigter ~ at a reduced rate;
doppelte ~ double rate; **notarielle ~en** notarial charges (fees);
~ **für bevorzugte Abfertigung** priority fee;
~**berechnen (erheben)** to charge a fee.

Gebühren charges, fees, dues, *(Tarif)* rates;
gegen Zahlung der ~ upon payment of charges;
fiskalische ~ fiscal dues (fees);
~ **und Abgaben** rates and taxes;
~ **erheben** to exact fees, to levy dues; ~**niederschlagen** to abate fees;
~ **zahlt der Empfänger** postage will be paid by licensee, reverse charge.

Gebühren|abkommen fee arrangement; ~**ansage** *(Telefon)* advice duration and charge call; ~**aufstellung** table of charges; ~**berechnung** calculation of fees; ~**einheit** tariff unit, *(tel.)* unit charge; ~**erlaß** remission of (abatement in, waiver of) fees; ~**festsetzung** rate making.

gebührenfrei free of charge, all charges paid, *(steuerfrei)* tax-exempt (-free, *US)*, exempt from taxes (taxation), *(tel.)* toll-free, *(zollfrei)* duty-free.

Gebühren|herabsetzung fee cut; ~**minuten** *(Telefon)* chargeable time; ~**ordnung** scale of charges (fees), schedule of commissions (fees, *US)*, tariff.

gebührenpflichtig taxable, liable to charges, subject to a fee, chargeable, *(Post)* subject to postage, postage to be charged, *(Zoll)* customable;
~**e Dienstsache** official communication.

Gebühren|rechnung note of fees, *(Anwalt)* bill of costs; ~**rückerstattung** return of duties; ~**satz** [tariff] rate; ~**stempel** tax stamp; ~**übernahme** absorption of charges; ~**verzeichnis** tariff, table of charges, charge book; ~**zuschlag** additional charge, excess fee (charge), surcharge.

gebundene | Preise controlled prices; ~ **Zinsbeträge** amounts of interest set aside.

Gedeck cover, plate, *(Gebühr hierfür)* cover charge.

gedeckt | sein to be held covered, *(im Konkurs)* to hold security; **gegen einen Verlust ~ sein** to be insured against a loss.

gediegene | Arbeit solid workmanship, able work; ~ **Waren** sterling goods.

gedrückt *(Börse)* depressed, *(Kurs)* low;
auf Verkäufe hin ~ liegen to be under selling pressure; ~ **sein** to drag.

Gefahr danger, peril, *(Risiko)* risk, hazard;
auf ~ des Absenders to consigner's (sender's) risk; **versicherte ~** risk run, peril insured against.

Gefährdungshaftung strict (absolute) liability.

Gefahren|anzeige *(Versicherung)* representation; ~**einteilung** *(Versicherung)* classification of risks; ~**geld** danger money; ~**industrie** hazardous industry; ~**klasse** accident branch; ~**klassifitierung** classification of risks; ~**stelle** danger (accident black) spot; ~**übergang** passing of risk; ~**umfang** degree of risk; ~**zulage** *(Angestellter)* hazard (danger) zone, hazardous work bonus, danger money, *(Versicherung)* penalty rates *(US)*.

gefährlicher Beruf hazardous employment (occupation).

Gefahrtragung risk of loss, risk taking.

Gefälle *(Löhne)* differential, *(Preise)* price gap, *(Steuer)* revenues, imposts.

Gefälligkeits|adresse accommodation address; ~**akzept** accommodation acceptance (bill, paper, note, *US)*; ~**giro, ~indossament** accommodation (collateral) endorsement (indorsement); ~**unterschrift** bogus signature; ~**wechsel** accommodation (proforma, nonvalue) bill, windbill *(Br.)*, windmill *(Br.)*, kite *(Br.)*.

gefälscht|e Banknote falsified (dud, *sl.)* note; ~**e Bilanz** cooked (doctored, faked) balance sheet; ~**er Scheck** forged check *(US)* (cheque, *Br.)*.

gefeuert werden to get the sack *(sl.)*, to be fired *(US sl.)*, to go down the line *(US)*.

Gefolgschaft *(Betrieb)* personnel, workers, employees, staff *(Br.)*.

gefragt in request (demand, favo(u)r), asked for, sought after, inquired for;
~ **sein** to have a ready market; **wenig ~ sein** to be in little demand, *(Börse)* to be neglected.

gegen | bar for cash (ready money); ~ **Quittung** on receipt.

Gegen|akkreditiv countervailing (secondary, *US*, back-to-back, *US*, dos-a-dos, *US)* credit; ~**buch** *(Bank)* passbook, *(Kunde)* tally; ~**deckung** countersecurity, counterremittance, *(Börse)* hedging; ~**forderung** cross demand, counterclaim, *(Wertberichtigung)* setoff *(Br.)*, offset *(US)*; ~**gebot** counterbid, counteroffer; ~**geschäft unterbringen** to [place a] hedge.

Gegenleistung consideration, equivalent;
angemessene ~ good consideration; **geldwerte ~** valuable consideration; **vereinbarte ~** consideration bargained for.

Gegen|mine legen *(Börse)* to make a market; ~**posten** contra, counterentry, *(Bilanz)* contra asset; ~**quittung** receipt in return; ~**rechnung** counterreckoning, check *(Br.)* (controlling, *US)* account.

gegenseitige | Bankguthaben interbank deposits; ~**e Forderungen ausgleichen** to counterbalance.

Gegenseitigkeit der Zolltarife reciprocity in trade.

Gegenseitigkeits|abkommen reciprocal trade agreement; **~geschäft** barter transaction; **~prinzip** reciprocity principle; **~versicherung** mutual insurance company; **~vertrag** reciprocity treaty.

Gegenstand object, article, item, thing; **gepfändeter ~** distress, object seized; **versicherter ~** insured matter, risk; **~ [erneuter] Verhandlungen** subject of [renewed] negotiations.

Gegenstände des persönlichen Gebrauchs personal effects, chattels personal.

Gegen|transaktion *(Börse)* straddle *(US)*; **~verkehr** oncoming (cross, two-way) traffic; **~versicherung** mutual (reciprocal) insurance.

Gegen|wert worth, equivalent, value, valuable consideration, countervalue, *(Ausgleich)* compensation, setoff *(Br.)*, offset *(US)*; **entsprechender ~** adequate (valuable) consideration; **~ in Geld** money equivalent; **~ für sein Geld** run for one's money; **~ anschaffen** to remit the proceeds; **entsprechenden ~ leisten** to give value for; **~ überweisen** to transmit the return; **~konto** *(ECA)* counterpart account; **~mittel** *(ECA)* counterpart funds.

Gehalt salary, earnings, pay, compensation, emoluments, stipend, *(Münze)* alloy, *(Schiff)* tonnage; **~ Nebensache** *(Anzeige)* salary secondary consideration (no object); **~ ist Verhandlungsgegenstand** salary open; **dickes ~** *(fam.)* fat salary; **festes ~** standing wages, straight (fixed, stated, regular) salary; **rückständiges ~** overdue pay; **steuerfreies ~** tax-free salary; **~ leitender Angestellter** wages of management, executive salaries; **~ nach Vereinbarung** salary by agreement; **sein ~ abheben** to draw one's salary; **~ aufbessern** to raise a salary; **schönes ~ haben** to earn good wages; **mit vollem ~ pensioniert werden** to be retired on full pay.

gehalten sein *(Kurse)* to be maintained.

Gehälterliste payroll [records], pay (payment, *Br.*) sheet, salary list.

Gehalts|abbau salary reduction; **~abzug** reduction from (retrenchment of) salary, stoppage *(Br.)*; **~angaben** *(Anzeige)* stating salary, *(Lohnliste)* payroll data; **~ansprüche** *(Anzeige)* salary required (expected); **~anstieg** pay boost; **~aufbesserung** salary increase; **~auszahlung** wage paying, payroll servicing (disbursement); **~bogen** payroll; **~einbehaltung** detention of wages; **~eingruppierung** salary classification; **~empfänger** salary (wage) earner, salaried employee (worker).

Gehaltserhöhung salary advance (hike, increase, increment), pay increase (rise, raise, *Br.*), rise *(US)* (raise, *Br.*) in (of) wages; **mit einer Beförderung verbundene ~** promotional salary increase;

Gehalts|festsetzung wage fixing; **~fortzahlung im Krankheitsfall** payment during illness; **~gruppe** salary group (bracket, class, range, scale); **~konto** salary account; **~kürzung** salary decrease (cut); **~liste** payroll [ledger], list of salaries; **~rahmen** salary range (structure); **~rückstand, ~rückstände** accrued salaries, back pay *(US)*; **jährliche ~steigerung** yearly (annual) increment; **~vorgriff** anticipation of salary; **~vorschuß** advance[d] salary; **~zulage** addition to s. one's salary, extra pay.

gehandelt *(Börse)* done, traded, quoted (listed, *US*) on the stock exchange; **an der Börse ~ werden** to be dealt in on the stock exchange; **im Telefonverkehr ~ werden** to be dealt in after hours *(Br.)*.

Geheim|anschluß ex-directory (unlisted, *US*) telephone; **~fonds** secret [service] fund; **~konto** private account; **~nummer** *(Telefon)* ex-directory (unlisted, *US*) number; **~telefon** scramber [telephone]; **~verfahren** *(Produktion)* secret process, letters of secret.

gehen *(Angestellter)* to leave, to quit, *(Maschine)* to run, to operate, to work; **nach A ~** *(Schiff)* to be bound for A.; **bankrott ~** to fail, to flutter, to smash; **flau ~** to drag; **gewaltig ins Geld ~** to make a big hole in one's capital; **glänzend ~** to sell like hot cakes (dogs) *(US)*.

gekreuzt *(Scheck)* crossed.

gekündigt *(Anleihe)* called; **~ sein** to be under notice to quit.

Gelände, bebautes built-up area; **erschlossenes ~** development, developed land, improved site.

Geld money, furniture of one's pocket *(coll.)*, gold, dimes, scales *(US)*, *(Bargeld)* cash, *(Börse)* buyers, bid, prices negotiated, *(Hartgeld)* coin, *(Kleingeld)* small change, *(Papiergeld)* paper money (currency, notes), *(Wechselgeld)* change; **hinter dem ~ her** on the make *(sl.)*; **keinen Pfennig ~** not a shot in the locker; **ohne jedes ~** out of cash, penniless, broke *(sl.)*; **so gut wie bares ~** as good as (equal to) cash; **auf ~ wird nicht gesehen** *(Anzeige)* money is no object; **angelegtes ~** money put up; **anvertrautes ~** consigned money held on trust; **billiges ~** cheap (easy, easy-terms) money; **erspartes (erübrigtes) ~** savings, spare money; **täglich fälliges ~** money at (on) call; **festgelegtes ~** immobilized money; **gepumptes ~** touch *(sl.)*; **heißes ~** hot money; **restliches ~** odd money; **überschüssiges ~** surplus money; **leicht verdientes ~** easy money; **sauer (schwer) verdientes ~** hard earnings, hard-earned wages; **schnell verdientes ~** fast buck *(US sl.)*; **sehr viel ~** no end of money; **Brief und ~** *(Börse)* bills and money, bids and offers, sellers and buyers; **~ auf Abruf (auf tägliche Kündigung)** call loan (money, *US*), day-to-day loan (money) *(Br.)*, street (demand, *US*) loan; **~ auf eine Woche** weekly fixtures;

~ **von der Bank abheben** to draw money from the bank; **jem.** ~ **abknöpfen** to squeeze money out of s. o.; ~ **abzweigen** to divert money; **j. fortlaufend um** ~ **angehen** to keep at s. o. with appeals for money; **sein** ~ **in Aktien anlegen** to invest one's money in stocks and shares; ~ **gut anlegen** to invest one's money to good account; ~ **in Rentenwerten anlegen** to sink money in an annuity; ~ **in Staatspapieren anlegen** to fund *(Br.)*; **um** ~ **anpumpen** *(fam.)* to touch (pump) for money *(sl.)*; **sein** ~ **arbeiten lassen** to put one's money out at interest; ~ **aufbringen** to put up funds, to raise cash; ~ **gegen hypothekarische Sicherheiten aufnehmen** to borrow on a mortgage; ~ **für ein Unternehmen auftreiben** to finance an institution; ~ **mit vollen Händen ausgeben** to be off on a spending spree, to spend money like water; **jem. mit** ~ **aushelfen** to aid s. o. with money; ~ **gegen Sicherheiten ausleihen** to lend money on security; **von jem. keinen Pfennig** ~ **bekommen** not to see the colo(u)r of one's money from s. o.; ~ **abgezählt bereithalten** no change given; ~ **einkassieren** to pocket cash; ~ **einschießen** to give in, to put into, to contribute capital; **sich sein** ~ **sehr genau einteilen** to make a penny go a long way; **im** ~ **ersticken** to be rolling in money; **ins** ~ **gehen** to run into money (up into large amounts); **etw.** ~ **beiseite gelegt haben** to have a little money in reserve; **haufenweise** ~ **(**~ **wie Heu, Mist) haben** to have scads (lots, piles) of money; ~ **im Überfluß haben** to have scads (lots, piles) of money; to have money to burn; **am** ~ **hängen** to be a slave to money; ~ **aus jem. herauspressen** to wring money out of s. o.; ~ **aus etw. herausschlagen** to make money out of s. th.; ~ **zum Fenster hinauswerfen** to throw money down the drain; ~ **bei Gericht hinterlegen** to bring money into the court; **plötzlich zu viel** ~ **kommen** to come into the big money; **Haufen** ~ **kosten** to cost a packet of money; ~ **auf die hohe Kante legen** to put money by; ~ **locker machen** to spring money *(Br. coll.)*; **gutes** ~ **schlechtem** ~ **nachwerfen** *(fam.)* to throw good money after bad; ~ **reinbuttern** *(fam.)* to kick in *(US sl.)*; **monatlich** ~ **nach Hause schicken** to remit money home each month; **viel** ~ **schulden** to be involved in debts; **im** ~ **schwimmen** to be rolling in cash (money, wealth); **völlig ohne** ~ **sein** to be penniless (broke); ~ **in ein Geschäft stecken** to put capital into a business; ~ **bei einer Bank stehen haben** to keep money at a bank; **sich** ~ **in die Taschen stopfen** to shove money into one's pocket; **jem.** ~ **überweisen** to put s. o. in cash, to send s. o. a remittance; **telegrafisch** ~ **überweisen** to transfer money by cable; **sein** ~ **dreimal jährlich umsetzen** to turn one's money three times a year; ~ **verauslagen** to disburse; **Haufen** ~ **verdienen** to make stacks of money; **eine Stange** ~ **verdienen** to make a pile of money; **sein** ~ **auf anständige Art und Weise (ehrlich) verdienen** to turn an honest penny; **jem. sein ganzes** ~ **vermachen** to leave one's money to s. o.; **sich das nötige** ~ **ver-**

schaffen to raise the wind *(fam.)*; ~ **vorschießen (vorstrecken)** to advance money; **jem.** ~ **vorzählen** to count money before s. o.; **sein** ~ **zurückbekommen** to recover one's money; **zuviel gezahltes** ~ **zurückgeben** to return an overpaid amount; ~ **zusammenkratzen** to scrape up a sum of money, to scratch together; ~ **zuschießen** to contribute money.

Geld|abfindung pecuniary compensation (satisfaction), cash settlement; ~**abwertung** devaluation, devalorization; ~**anforderung** requisition for money, *(Geldmarkt)* currency demands; **in** ~**angelegenheiten großzügig sein** to be liberal of money; **todsichere** ~**anlage** perfectly safe investment of capital; ~**anweisung** remittance, draft, money (post-office, *Br.)* order, postal [money] order *(US)*; ~**aufnahme** raising of money, borrowing; ~**ausfuhr** exportation of money; ~**ausgabe** expenditure disbursement; ~**ausgänge** withdrawals; ~**bedarf** need (want) of money, borrowing demand, reqisite money, monetary needs, *(Geldmarkt)* currency demands; ~**bedarfszunahme** run-up in the money supply; ~**belohnung** pecuniary reward; ~**beschaffung** raising of money; ~**beschaffungskosten** cost of money, money costs.

Geldbetrag money [amount], amount (sum) of money, monetary contribution, purse; **für Vergnügungszwecke vorgesehener** ~ happy money; ~ **abheben** to withdraw a sum of money; **bestimmten** ~ **für Forschungszwecke zur Verfügung stellen** to earmark a sum of money for research; **geliehenen** ~ **zurückgeben** to repay a sum of money borrowed.

Geldbeutel moneybag, purse, pocket, wallet, bag; **magerer** ~ a light purse; **Daumen auf den** ~ **halten** to tighten the purse strings.

Geld|bewegung fluctuation of money; ~**bewilligung** appropriation of funds, grant of money; ~**bewilligungsklausel** *(Parl.)* money clause *(Br.)*; ~**brief** money *(US)* (insured, *Br.,* cash) letter; ~**eingang** money received, money paid in; ~**einlage** deposit, money paid in; ~**einziehung durch die Post** postal collection; ~**entschädigung** money relief, pecuniary compensation; ~**entwertung** fall (depreciation) of the currency.

Gelder means, sum of money, purse, funds; **langfristig angelegte** ~ long-term (funded) capital; **unterwegs befindliche** ~ money in the post *(Br.)* (mail, *US)*; **durchlaufende** ~ cash in transit; **täglich fällige** ~ sight deposits; **festgelegte** ~ tied-up funds, lockup *(Br.)*; **kurzfristige** ~ money at short notice *(Br.),* short-term loans *(US)*; **langfristige** ~ time money, long-term loans *(US)*, deposit accounts *(US)*.

Geld|ersatz token money, auxiliary currency; ~**fälscher** counterfeiter, smasher *(Br.)*; ~**flüssigkeit** *(Geldmarkt)* glut (ease) of money; ~**forderung** money claim (demand); ~**geber** moneylender, advancer; ~**geschenk** gift of money, pecuniary present; ~**hahn aufdrehen** to turn on the money tap; ~**handel** money trade, stockbrokerage; ~**händler** moneylender, money jobber *(Br.)*; ~**heirat** money match, marriage of interest; ~**hilfe** pecuniary aid; ~**institut** financial institution; ~**kassette** till, money chest, cashbox; ~**klemme** financial straits, pecuniary difficulty (embarrassment); ~**knappheit** dear money, money pinch (scarcity, stringency, *US,* tightness); ~**kosten** cost of money; ~**kurs** demand (money) rate, demand price, bid quotations (price), *(Devisen)* bankers' buying rate; ~**legat** pecuniary legacy; ~**leitsätze** key-money rates; ~**makler** money (bill) broker; ~**mangel** impecuniosity, lack of funds (money).

Geldmarkt money (cash) market;
angespannter ~ tightness of the money market; gespaltener ~ two-tier money market;
auf dem ~ aktiv sein to be a creditor in the money market.

Geldmarkt|anlage financial investment; ~**bedingungen** money-market conditions; ~**bericht** money article; ~**erleichterungen** monetary ease; ~**instrumentarium** monetary and fiscal techniques; ~**papiere** money-market securities (instruments).

geldmarktpolitische | Änderungen shift in monetary policies; ~ **Erleichterungen zulassen** to relax monetary policy.

Geldmarkt|sätze, leichte easy money rates; ~**schwankungen** fluctuations in the money market; ~**verknappung** money scarcity; ~**verschuldung** money-market indebtedness; ~**versteifung** stiffening of prices.

Geldmittel funds on hand, [money] means, pecuniary (financial) resources, purse, finances;
öffentliche ~ public means; verfügbare ~ available funds;
~ beschaffen to raise funds; ~ bewilligen *(Parl.)* to vote the supplies; ~ zur Verfügung stellen to ladle out funds; j. mit ~n versehen to set s. o. up in funds.

Geld|nachfrage money demand; ~**nehmer** borrower, *(Hypothekarkredit)* mortgagor; ~**onkel** sugar daddy; ≗**politische Maßnahmen** monetary policy devices; ~**preis gewinnen** to win the purse; ~**protz** moneybag; ~**rente** money payment; ~**sack** moneybag, pouch for money; ~**sammlung** collection, gathering, purse, drive to raise funds.

Geldsätze money (loan) rates, rates for money on loan, market rates;
billige ~ cheap money;
~ am offenen Markt open-market rates.

Geld|schein bank note *(Br.)*, bank bill *(US)*; ~**schneiderei** usury, extortionate charge, extortion; ~**schöpfung** creation of money.

Geldschrank money chest, strongbox, safe [deposit]; feuer- und diebessicherer ~ fire and burglar resisting safe;
~**knacker** safeblower, safebreaker, safecracker.

Geld|schraube fester anziehen to tighten the monetary screw; ~**schwierigkeiten haben, in ~schwierig**

keiten sein to be in embarrassed circumstances (pushed for money); ~**sorgen** money troubles, financial straits; **ausländische ~sorten** foreign coins and notes; ~**sortenzettel** specie list; ~**spende** money gift.

Geldstrafe fine, pecuniary penalty, money bote (penalty), amercement, amends, mulct, forfeit;
dem richterlichen Ermessen überlassene ~ fine left to the discretion of the judge;
mit einer ~ belegen to fine, to surcharge; ~ **festsetzen** to assess a fine.

Geldstück coin, piece of money, bean *(sl.)*;
jem. ein falsches ~ andrehen to palm off (foist) a bad coin on s. o.

Geld|summe aussetzen to subscribe an amount; ~**theorie** theory of money; ~**theoretiker** money-supply economist; ~**überhang, ~überschuß** surplus (excess) money, abundance (backlog, superfluity) of money.

Geldüberweisung remission (transmission) of money, remittance, [money] transfer;
telegrafische ~ express money order, wire transfer *(US)*.

Geldumlauf currency, circulation (flux) of money;
gesamter ~ total money in circulation;
~ künstlich steigern to inflate the currency.

Geld|umtausch exchange of currency; ~**unterstützung** money relief, pecuniary aid; ~ **verdienen** moneymaking, earning; ~**verkehr** money transfer, currency; ~**verknappung** scarcity of money, monetary restraint.

Geldverlegenheit pecuniary difficulty (embarrassment), involvement;
sich in ~ befinden, in ~ sein to be hard up [for money], to be at a loss (pushed, embarrassed, pressed) for money (in pecuniary embarrassment).

Geld|verleiher moneylender, moneymonger; ~**verlust** pecuniary loss, loss of money; ~**versorgung** money supply; ~**vorrat** cash reserve (in vaults); ~**waage** coin balance; ~**wechsler** money dealer (changer).

Geldwert value of money, monetary value;
dem ~ nach in terms of money;
~**korrektur** monetary correction.

Geld|wirtschaft money economy; ~**zuschuß** money allowance; ~**zuwachsrate** rate of money growth.

Gelegenheits|arbeit odd job, char *(Br.)*, jobbing, chore *(US)*; ~**arbeiter** casual, casual worker (labo[u]rer); ~**beschäftigung** casual employment, odd job, char *(Br.)*; ~**spediteur** special (private) carrier.

Geleit|fahrzeug escort vessel, convoy ship; ~**schein** pass, navicert.

gelten to be in force (effective, valid, operative;
nicht mehr ~ *(Paß)* to be no longer valid.

geltend machen, Verjährung to plead the statute of limitations.

Geltendmachung des Unterhaltsanspruches recovery of maintenance.

Gemeinde community, body corporate, [civil] parish, borough *(Br.)*;

~abgaben local (county, *Br.)* rates; ~betrieb municipal enterprise; ~finanzen local finance; ~steuern local (municipal) taxes *(US)*, municipal (borough, local, *Br.)* rates; ~umlage municipal (borough, *Br.)* rates.

Gemein|gläubiger *(Konkurs)* creditor at large, general creditor; ~kosten fixed (general, apportionable, indirect) costs, overhead [expenses].

Gemeinkosten|anteil overhead rate, share of overheads; ~löhne indirect labo(u)r costs; ~verrechnungssatz burden absorption rate.

gemeinnützig nonprofit-making;
~er Betrieb nonprofit (public-service) enterprise *(US)*; ~es Unternehmen public-utility undertaking.

gemeinsam | haften to be jointly and severally liable; ~es Konto joint account.

gemeinschaftlich common, joint[ly], conjointly.

Gemeinschafts|anschluß *(Telefon)* party line; ~depot joint deposit, alternative safe-custody *(Br.)* (custodianship, *US)* account; ~eigentum community of goods, collective ownership; ~einkauf group (combine) buying; ~sekretariat typing (secretarial, typists') pool; ~versicherung group insurance; ~vorhaben *(ENEA)* joint services.

Gemeinschuldner *(Konkurs)* common debtor, insolvent, certificated (adjudicated) bankrupt; entlasteter ~ discharged bankrupt.

Gemeinwirtschaftsbank trade-union bank.

gemischt|er Ausschuß joint committee *(Br.)*; ~e Ladung mixed cargo.

Gemischt|waren groceries, general merchandize *(US)*; ~warengeschäft, ~warenhandlung, ~warenladen grocery [business], grocery store.

gemischtwirtschaftliches Unternehmen semi-public enterprise, mixed ownership property *(US)*.

genaue Abschrift true copy; ~er Betrag exact amount.

genehmigen, Bilanz to approve [of] a balance sheet.

genehmigtes | Anleihekapital authorized bonds; ~ Grundkapital authorized capital (capital stock, *(US)*.

Genehmigung approval, *(Behörde)* licence, permit, *(Erlaubnis)* permit, permission;
baupolizeiliche ~ building permit *(US)*; gebührenpflichtige ~ local taxation licence.

Genehmigungs|antrag application for a permit; ~behörde approving authority; ~gebühr licence fee (tax).

genehmigungspflichtig subject to approval (authorization).

Genehmigungsvermerk approved stamp, *(Paß)* visa.

General|agent general agent; ~bebauungsplan zoning code *(US)*; ~bevollmächtigter general (managing, universal) agent; ~direktor director general, general manager, president; ~klausel blanket (basket, *US)* clause, *(Tarif)* dragnet clause; ~konsul consul general; ~konsulat consulate general; ~police comprehensive insurance, blanket (compound, floating, block) policy; ~quittung ausstellen to receipt in full; ~streik general (mass)

strike; ~überholung overall examination, *(Auto)* overhaul, turnaround; ~unkosten [general] overheads, indirect (undistributed) cost; ~unternehmer main (general) contractor.

Generalversammlung *(AG)* general (corporate) meeting;
außerordentliche ~ called extraordinary general meeting of shareholders (stockholders, *US)*; ~ abhalten to hold a general meeting; ~einberufen to summon a general meeting.

General|vertreter head (general, universal, principal, general-commission) agent; ~vertretung general (head) agency; ~vollmacht general power (authority, proxy), full power of attorney.

generelle Preiserhöhung overall increase of prices.

Genossenschaft cooperative association *(US)*, co-operative [society];
gewerbliche ~ industrial cooperative society; landwirtschaftliche ~ agricultural cooperative society.

genossenschaftliches Kreditinstitut cooperative bank.

Genossenschafts|bank cooperative bank; ~laden co-operative store; ~vertrieb cooperative marketing.

Genuß|aktie bonus share (stock, *US)*; ~schein participating certificate.

Gepäck luggage *(Br.)*, baggage *(US)*;
aufgegebenes ~ registered luggage *(Br.)*; zur Aufbewahrung gegebenes ~ left luggage *(Br.)*; zuschlagpflichtiges ~ extra luggage *(Br.)*, excess baggage *(US)*;
~ mit Übergewicht overweight luggage *(Br.)*;
sein ~ aufgeben to check one's luggage, to send one's luggage in advance *(Br.)*, to check (one's baggage, *US)*.

Gepäck|abfertigung dispatch of luggage *(Br.)*, baggage dispatch *(US)*; ~abgabe cloakroom, checkroom *(US)*; ~annahme left-luggage *(Br.)* (baggage, booking, *US)* office; ~aufbewahrung luggage (parcel) office *(Br.)*, [baggage] checkroom *(US)*; ~aufbewahrungsschein left-luggage ticket *(Br.)* luggage receipt *(Br.)*, cloakroom check (ticket) *(US)*; zollamtliche ~revision luggage *(Br.)* (baggage, *US)* examination; ~schalter registration window, luggage *(Br.)* (baggage, *US)* counter (office); ~schließfach luggage locker *(Br.)*; ~selbstbedienung self-claim baggage system *(US)*.

Gerätekonto equipment account.

gerichtliche | Beschlagnahme attachment, judicial sequestration; ~ Hinterlegung bail; ~ Versteigerung judicial sale.

geringer | Lohn low wages; ~ Ölverbrauch low oil consumption.

geringwertige| Anlagegüter *(Einkommensteuer)* inadmitted assets; ~ Waren inferior (low-quality) goods.

Gesamt|abschluß *(Rundfunkwerbung)* blanket contract; ~aufkommen total yield; ~ausgaben outright expense; ~bedarf total demand (requirements); ~betriebswert going-concern value; ~einnahme total receipts; ~ergebnisrechnung statement of income and accumulated earnings; ~gläubiger joint and several creditors; **~haftung** joint liability, joint guaranty; **~herstellungskosten** total cost price; **~hypothek** blanket (general, consolidated, *US*) mortgage; **~kosten** total cost (expense, outlay), overall costs; **volkswirtschaftliche ~leistung** gross national product; **~mieteinnahmen** total rentroll; **~preis** allround (overhead, lump) price; **~produktion** total output (production); **~produktionskosten** total production costs; **~schuld** entire (total, gross *US*), debt, *(gemeinsame Schuld)* community debt, joint liability; **~schuldner** joint and several debtor.

gesamtschuldnerisch haftbar liable jointly and severally.

Gesamt|summe der Abzahlungskredite instal(l)ment credits outstanding; **~tarifvertrag** area-wide bargaining; **~umsatz** aggregate (overall) sales, global turnover; **~verbrauch** overal consumption; **~vergütung** compensation package; **~verkäufe** aggregate sales; **~verlust** overall loss, *(Versicherung)* total loss; **steuerpflichtiges ~vermögen** aggregate taxable property; **~wert der Aktiva** total assets; **~zeichnungsberechtigung** joint signature.

Geschäft business, *(Börse)* trading, *(Beruf)* shop, vocation, occupation, business, *(Büro)* office, *(Firma)* enterprise, commercial house, concern, establishment, undertaking, *(Geschäftsabschluß)* bargain, deal, dealing, transaction, operation, *(Gewerbe)* occupation, trade, job, calling, employment, *(Laden)* shop *(Br.)*, store *(US)*; **abgeschlossenes ~** completed (executed) transaction; **anrüchiges ~** hole-and-corner business; **betriebseigenes ~** captive shop, company store *(US)*; **dickes ~** big deal; **dunkles ~** shady deal, racket *(sl.)*; **einträgliches ~** remunerative (lucrative) business; **fingiertes ~** bogus transaction; **in der Hauptgeschäftsgegend gelegenes ~** downtown store *(US)*; **glänzend gehendes (glänzendes) ~** booming (roaring) business, gold mine; **glattes ~** *(Börse)* swimming market; **lebhaftes ~** *(Börse)* brisk trading; **nachbörsliches ~** interoffice deal, after-hours dealing *(Br.)*, business in the street *(Br.)*; **reelles ~** fair-dealing firm; **ruhiges ~** slack business; **steuerpflichtiges ~** taxable transaction; **unbedeutendes ~** picayune business; **unrentables ~** business that does not pay; **verbotene ~e** illegal sales; **verlustbringendes ~** losing business; **~ mit erstklassiger Bedienung** high-class service store *(US)*; **~ auf Geben und Nehmen** put and call; **~ unter dem Ladentisch** under-the-counter trading; **~ für Produkte des täglichen Bedarfs** neighbo(u)rhood shop; **~ für eigene Rechnung** transaction for own account; **~ abschließen** to drive (strike, conclude) a bargain; **~ mit Gewinn abschließen** to make a profit out of a transaction; **wieder im ~ anlagen** to plough (plow, *US*) back in business; **~aufgeben** to go out of business, to give up trade; **~ aufmachen** to set up shop (a business); **aus einem ~ ausstoigen** to fold up *(US)*; **bankmäßige ~e be-**

sorgen to supply banking facilities; **j. an einem ~ beteiligen** to give s. o. a financial interest in a business; **eigenes ~ betreiben** to be one's own master; **vorteilhaftes ~ zum Abschluß bringen** to drive a good bargain; **immer ans ~ denken** to always have an eye to business; **sich auf gewagte ~e einlassen** to dabble in speculative conerns; **~ eröffnen** to open a trade (business), to set up shop; **~ fortführen** to continue a business; **neues ~ gründen** to launch a new venture (enterprise); **gutgehendes ~ haben** to drive a good trade; **Nase für [gute] ~e haben** to have a keen eye for a bargain; **~ in Bausch und Bogen kaufen** to buy the whole stock [of a business]; **~ leiten** to be at the head of the business; **~e machen** to transact business, to merchandise, to deal, to monger; **gewagte ~e machen** to speculate; **~ rückgängig machen** to break off an engagement; **seinen ~en nachgehen** to attend to one's business, to ply a trade; **nach dem Krieg groß ins ~ gekommen sein** to boom after the war; **in ~en unterwegs sein** to be on one's tour (away, out); **Geld in ein ~ stecken** to invest money in a business; **~ übernehmen** to take over (succeed to) a business; **~ um die Hälfte verkleinern** to reduce a business one half; **sich vom (aus dem) ~ zurückziehen** to give up one's (withdraw, quit) business.

geschäftehalber on business.

Geschäftemacher profiteer, jobber, racketeer.

geschäftlich commercial, mercantile, businesslike, business-wise, on business;

~ verhindert prevented (held up) by business;

~ mit jem. zu tun haben to do business with s. o.;

~ unterwegs sein to be away (out on one's tour), to travel on business;

~es Ansehen credit, [business] reputation; **~e Besprechung** business conference (conversation); **~e Beziehungen** business relations; **~e Empfehlung** business reference; **~e Verabredung** business appointment; **vor dem ~en Zusammenbruch stehen** to face the collapse of one's business, to steer near receivership.

Geschäfts|ablauf course of business; **~abschluß** business transaction, making a deal (bargain), *(fürs laufende Jahr)* annual report (balance sheet); **~abwicklung** windup of a business; **~anbahnung** introduction of business; **~ankündigung** trade publication.

Geschäftsanteil interest in a firm (business), business interest, [partnership] share;

jem. einen ~ überlassen to give s. o. a partnership in one's business; **~ übernehmen** to buy an interest in a firm.

Geschäfts|anzug lounge *(Br.)* (business, *US*) suit; **~aufgabe** (abandonment of) business; **wegen ~aufgabe zu verkaufen** for sale, owner retiring from business; **~aufschwung** boom, upturn, brisk trade; **~aufsicht** *(Konkursverfahren)* receivership, *(im Laden)* shop walker, store superintendant *(US)*, floorwalker *(US)*; **~ausdehnung** expansion (extension) of business; **~aussichten** business outlook;

~ausstattung *(Bilanz)* furniture and equipment; ~bedingungen terms of trade (business), trading (trade) conditions; vor ~beginn before commencing business; allmähliche ~belebung gradual pickup in activity; ~bereich business line, scope (sphere) of activity (business); ~bericht business record (report), operating (financial, annual, *Br.)* report; ~besitzer shop *(Br.)* (store, *US)* owner; ~besorgung business errand, *(für Dritten)* commission; ~besprechung business conference.

Geschäftsbetrieb commercial pursuit, transacting (transaction of) business, *(Firma)* business [establishment], business enterprise; unbefugter ~ unauthorized business; ~ unterhalten to do business.

Geschäftsbeziehungen business (commercial) relations, transactions; ~ mit einer Firma aufnehmen to open up a business connection with a firm.

Geschäfts|bilanz balance sheet (statement, *US)* of a business enterprise; ~branche line of business; ~brief business (commercial) letter.

Geschäftsbücher books, shopbooks *(US)*, ledgers, business records, account (commercial, office) books, *(Aktiengesellschaft)* corporate books; ~ frisieren to salt the books.

Geschäfts|eigentümer principal, shop (store, *US)* owner; ~einlage contribution to capital, partnership share; ~einrichtungen office equipment, business arrangement, *(Laden)* shop (store, *US)* equipment; ~einstellung discontinuance of business; ~empfehlung business (trade) reference; ~erfahrung experience in business (trade); ~ergebnis trading (operating) result, company result; ~erlaubnis erteilen to accord permission to transact business; ~eröffnung Anfang November shop will open at the beginning of November; ~erweiterung expansion (extension) of business.

geschäftsfähig legally competent (responsible), of sound mind, capable to act in law (of contracting); beschränkt ~ reponsible to a limited extent.

Geschäftsfähigkeit business (legal) capacity, capacity to contract, competence; bedingte (beschränkte) ~ limited competence.

Geschäfts|frau woman dealer (trader); 2freier Nachmittag earlyclosing day; ~freund [business] correspondent, business friend (guest).

geschäftsführend|er Ausschuß managing (executive) committee, board of management; ~er Gesellschafter managing partner; ~e Regierung caretaker government.

Geschäftsführer [business] manager, director, factor, managing agent, *(im Sinn des BGB)* agent, executive *(US)*, runner *(US)*, *(Hotel)* hotel manager; ~ ohne Auftrag agent of necessity, volunter; ~abberufen to remove a manager; ~tätigkeit managership.

Geschäftsführung conduct of business, [business] management, administration, direction;

alleinige ~ sole management; schlechte ~ mismanagement; ~ ohne Auftrag agency of necessity; voll in die ~ eingeschaltet sein to be given full swing in the conduct of business.

Geschäfts|gang [run (course) of] business, trend of business, course of trade.

Geschäftsgebaren dealing, business policy (manners), *(Anlagegesellschaft)* performance; korrektes (lauteres) ~ straight (plain) dealings.

Geschäfts|gebäude office building, business premises; ~gegend business district (quarter, section), the City *(Br.)*, downtown district *(US)*, trading center *(US)*, location *(US)*; ~geheimnis trade (business) secret; ~gewinn business gain, commercial (business, operating trading) profit; ~grundsätze operating princi- ~s; ~grundstück business property (premises); ~haus business enterprise (house); ~inhaber proprietor, business owner, head of the firm, shopkeeper; ~interesse interest in a business, business interest; ~inventar business inventory *(Bilanz)* furniture and equipment, (OHG) partnership personalty *(US)*; ~irrtum *(jur.)* mistake as to the existence of the subject matter.

Geschäftsjahr business (commercial, trading, official) year, *(Regierung)* financial year *(Br.)*, fiscal year (period) *(US)*; vom Kalenderjahr abweichendes ~ natural business year *(US)*.

Geschäfts|kapital [firm's] capital, trading (share) capital, stock in trade; ~karte business (trade, calling) card; ~konto business (overhead-charges) account; ~kosten business (office, overhead) expenses; auf ~kosten laufen *(Auto)* to run on expenses; ~kredit credit of a firm; ~lage state of business, business standing; teure ~ high-rent location *(US)*.

Geschäftsleben business [life], business movement (world), mercantile affairs; Privatdinge das ~ beeinflussen lassen to let pleasure interfere with business; im ~ stehen to be in business; sich aus dem ~ zurückziehen to retire from (bail out of public) business.

Geschäfts|leiter managing clerk (director, *Br.)* [general-office] manager, director; ~leitung conduct of business, *(Geschäftsführer)* [store, *US]* management, *(AG)* board of directors; führende ~leute business executives (leaders), key businessmen.

Geschäftsmann businessman, man of business, commercial (city, *Br.)* man; gewiegter ~ shrewd businessman; kleiner ~ petty trader; ausgezeichneter ~ sein to have excellent business capacity.

geschäftsmäßig businesslike, commercial, merchantlike, *(rein mechanisch)* routine.

Geschäftsmethoden business practice (policy); unlautere ~ unfair [methods of] competition, unfair [business] practices, improper practices.

Geschäfts|miete shop rent; ~**moral** business morality.
Geschäftsordnung routine orders, business rules *(US), (Tagesordnung)* agenda;
~ **einhalten** to observe the rules of procedure; **das Wort zur ~ verlangen** to raise a point of order.
Geschäfts|papiere commercial documents (papers), business records; ~**partner** [business] associate, partner; ~**politik** business (corporate) policy; ~**prinzip** business principle; ~**räume** office, business premises, chambers *(Br.)*; ~**reise** business tour (travel, trip, round), journey on business, itineration, industrial tour *(US)*; ~**reise unternehmen** to travel for the (on) business; ~**reklame** business advertising, goodwill propaganda; ~**risiko** commercial (mercantile, trade, business) risk; ~**rückgang** decline in (falling off of) business, business contraction, dip; **saisonbedingter ~rückgang** seasonal slump; ~**schließung** shutdown, closing of business; ~**schluß** closing time (hours); ~**sinn** business acumen.
Geschäftssitz establishment, office, place of business, business location *(US)*;
eingetragener ~ principal establishment (place of business), registered office *(Br.)*; **steuerlicher ~** location for tax purpose *(US)*, business situs.
Geschäfts|sparte **aufgeben** to diversify away from a business; ~**sprache** commercial language (parlance), business language (slang).
Geschäftsstelle agency, branch, office, *(Gericht)* registrar's office *(Br.)*;
eingetragene ~ principal establishment, registered office *(Br.)*;
~ **unterhalten** to maintain an office.
Geschäfts|stellenleiter *(Gericht)* county clerk *(US)*, clerk of the court, *(US)*; ~**stockung** business stagnation, slackness (slump) in trade; ~**straße** business (shopping) street; ~**stunden** business (office) hours, *(Bank)* banking hours; ~**tag** business day.
Geschäftstätigkeit business activity (operations), continuous operation;
normale ~ ordinary course of business;
~ **aufnehmen** to begin operations.
Geschäftsteilhaber associate, partner;
abwickelnder ~ liquidating partner.
Geschäfts|transaktion transaction; ~**trick** business trick.
geschäftstüchtig efficient, skilled in trade, well versed in business, smart.
Geschäfts|tüchtigkeit business acumen; ~**übergabe** transfer of a business; ~**übernahme** taking over a business, takeover; ~**umfang** volume of business; ~**umschlag** *(Brief)* commercial envelope.
geschäftsunfähig incompetent, not responsible, disable, unable, incapacitated.
Geschäfts|unkosten business (office) expenses, *(Gemeinkosten)* burden, overhead [expenses], oncost *(Br.)*; ~**unterhaltungskosten** office-operating costs; ~**unterlagen** business records, office files; ~**unternehmen** [commercial] enterprise, business concern.

Geschäftsverbindung business connection (connexion, *(Br.)*, *(Bank)* correspondence;
[neue] ~ anbahnen (anknüpfen) to enter (open) new business connections (relations); **mit jem. in ~ stehen** to have dealings (business connections), (deal with) s. o.; ~**verkauf** sale of business ~**verkehr** dealings, commercial intercourse, course of business; ~**verlauf** business trend; ~**verlegung** removal of business *(Br.)*.
Geschäftsverlust business (trading, operating) loss, loss of profits (earnings);
~ **infolge leerstehender Räume** vacancy loss.
Geschäfts|vermögen business (firm) property, ordinary assets, stock in trade, *(Betriebskapital)* working (trading) capital; ~**verpflichtungen** commitments; ~**viertel** business quarter (section, zone), downtown *(US), (Läden)* shopping area (district), city *(Br.)*; ~**volumen** volume of business; ~**vorfall** business case, piece of business, transaction; ~**vorgänger[in]** predecessor [company]; ~**vorhaben** business project (plan); ~**wagen** commercial (fleet) car, *(Lieferwagen)* delivery van; ~**welt** business community (front, interests), financial men; ~**wert** goodwill, enterprise (firm's) value; ~**zeichen** reference (file) number, file reference; ~**zeit** business (office, official) hours; ~**zentrum** chief seat of commerce, business center *(US), (Läden)* shopping center *(US)* (centre, *Br.)*; ~**zimmer** office, bureau; ~**zweck** business purpose (edge), *(Firma)* corporate object; **nur zu ~zwecken** strictly for business; ~**zweig** line (branch, way) of business, business line, trade [section].
Geschenk|abonnement gift subscription; ~**artikel** giftware, gift articles, fancy goods; ~**sendung** gift parcel.
geschlossen closed, defunct, *(Kurszettel)* sales transacted, paid;
wegen Auftragsmangels ~ closed down because of lack of orders; **am Nachmittag ~** early closing day, closed for a half holiday;
~**er Bestand** *(Abschreibungsmethode)* closed-end account; ~**es Depot** trust deposit.
geschwächt *(Börse)* weak, low, depressed.
Geschwindigkeit, zulässige permissible speed.
Geschwindigkeits|beschränkung speed restriction (limit); ~**überschreitung** exceeding speed limit.
Geselle journeyman, little master *(Br.)*.
Gesellen|lohn approved journeyman's rate; ~**prüfung** journeyman's examination; ~**stück** diploma piece.
Gesellschaft *(Handelsgesellschaft)* company, corporation *(US)*, body, *(Teilhaberschaft)* [co]-partnership, *(Vereinigung)* society, association, union, fellowship;
angegliederte ~ associated company; **aufgelöste ~** company wound up; **handelsgerichtlich eingetragene ~** incorporated company *(Br.)*, registered corporation *(US)*; **aus Steuergründen vorübergehend gegründete ~** collapsible corporation *(US)*; **gemeinnützige ~** nonprofitmaking company, (public-service, utility, *US)* corporation; **staat-**

lich kontrollierte ~ publicly-owned corporation *(US)*; öffentlich-rechtliche ~ public company (corporation, *US*), stille ~ dormant (secret, silent, *US*) partnership; **vorgeschobene** ~ dummy corporation *(US)*;

~ mit öffentlich-rechtlichen Befugnissen quasi-public company; ~ **zur Finanzierung von Warenkrediten** commercial credit company; ~ **mit beschränkter Haftung** *[etwa]* exempt private (limited) company *(Br.)*, a type of close corporation *(US)* under German law; ~ **des bürgerlichen Rechts** [etwa] partnership at will, nontrading partnership;

~ **auflösen** to liquidate a company; **einer** ~ **als Mitglied beitreten** to affiliate o. s. to (with) a society; **seine Arbeitskraft in eine** ~ **einbringen** to contribute one's services to a company; ~ **gründen** to establish a partnership, to incorporate (float, *Br.*, found, form, promote, set up, start) a company; ~ **liquidieren** to dissolve a business company; **an verschiedenen ~en beteiligt sein** to have holdings in several companies.

Gesellschafter member of a company *(Br.)*, partner, associate, corporate member;

abwickelnder ~ liquidating partner; **neu eintretender** ~ incoming partner; **geschäftsführender** ~ active (managing, working) partner; **scheinbarer** ~ ostensible partner;

als ~ **aufnehmen** to introduce as partner; **als** ~ **ausscheiden** to withdraw from a partnership; ~**anteil** share, partnership interest; ~**versammlung** company (corporate, *US*) meeting; ~**vertrag** articles of partnership, partnership agreement.

Gesellschaftsanteil share, partnership interest, *(AG)* share, stock *(US)*; ~**e übernehmen** to subscribe for shares in a company.

Gesellschafts|bericht company (corporate earnings, *US*) report; ~**beschluß** *(AG)* corporate resolution *(US)*; ~**eigentum** company ownership, partnership property; **in eine öffentlich rechtliche ~form umwandeln** to go public; ~**gewinn** company profit (earnings), *(AG)* corporation earnings; ~**gläubiger** creditor of a firm (partnership); ~**gründung** company promotion; ~**jahr** company's financial year.

Gesellschaftskapital capital of a partnership, a company's resources, partnership's funds, funds of a company, *(Eigenkapital einer AG)* capital stock *(US)*, capitalization, net worth *(US)*, stockholders' equity *(US)*;

ausgewiesenes (satzungsmäßiges) ~ stated (nominal, *Br.*, authorized, *US*) capital.

Gesellschafts|leitung corporate management; ~**räume** reception room, recreational space; ~**recht** company law *(Br.)*; ~**reingewinn** corporate surplus; ~**sanierung** corporate reorganization; ~**satzung** *(AG)* articles of association *(Br.)* (incorporation, *US*); ~**siegel** common *(Br.)* (corporate, *US*) seal; ~**sitz** registered office *(Br.)*; ~**verhältnis** partnership; ~**verlust** partnership loss;

~**vermögen** *(AG)* corporate assets, company (corporate) property, *(OHG)* partnership assets (property); ~**vertrag** *(AG)* articles (memorandum) of association *(Br.)*, articles of incorporation *(US)*; ~**zweck** partnership purpose.

Gesetz|e, gewerbepolizeiliche labo(u)r laws, factory acts *(Br.)*;

~ **von Angebot und Nachfrage** law of supply and demand.

gesichert secure[d], coverd, *(garantiert)* guaranteed, warranted *(US)*;

~**e Forderung** privileged debt; ~**er Gläubiger** secured (catholic) creditor.

gesperrtes Konto blocked account.

Gespräch, dienstliches *(Telefon)* business (official) call; **gebührenpflichtiges** ~ *(Telefon)* call charged for;

~ **abmelden** *(Telefon)* to cancel a call; ~ **anmelden** *(Telefon)* to book (place, *US*) a call.

Gesprächs|belegzettel *(Hotel)* traffic sheet; ~**uhr** *(Telefon)* speaking clock.

gestaffelt graduated, graded, differential, *(Arbeitszeit)* staggered, *(Steuern)* progressive; ~**er Preis** graduated price.

Gestehungs|kosten first (prime, original, producing, production) cost; ~**kosten plus Gewinnspanne** cost-plus *(US)*; **unter dem ~preis verkaufen** to sell below cost price.

gestreut, risikomäßig diversified.

gestrichen *(Kurs)* no quotation.

Gesuch| aufsetzen to draw up a request; **einem** ~ **stattgeben** to accord a petition.

gesucht wanted, *(Börse)* asked, in demand, *(Ware)* wanted, in vogue; **für sofort** ~ wanted immediately.

gesunde Finanzgebarung sound finance.

Gesundheitsattest *(Schiff)* bill of health.

gesundstoßen, sich *(fam.)* to make a packet.

Gesundung, finanzielle reorganization.

Getränke| ausschank counter, bar, refreshment kiosk (counter); ~**automat** drink dispenser; ~**steuer** tax on alcohol, excise on liquors *(US)*, beverage tax.

Getreide | auf dem Halm standing grain, crop; ~**börse** corn (grain) exchange, grain pit, ~**termingeschäfte** grain futures trade *(US)*.

getrennte Rechnung separate bill, Dutch treat.

Gewähr guarantee *(Br.)*, guaranty *(US)*, warranty, warrant;

ohne ~ without engagement;

~ **für zugesicherte Eigenschaften** warranty of fitness.

gewähren, Anleihe to grant a loan; **Diskont** ~ to allow a discount; **Entschädigung** ~ to pay compensation; **jem. eine Konzession** to license s. o.

Gewährleistung guarantee *(Br.)*, guaranty *(US)*, warrant of merchantability;

unter Ausschluß der ~ without guarantee *(Br.)*, with all faults, caveat emptor;

vertragliche ~ express warranty *(US)*.

Gewährleistungs|ansprüche erfüllen to stand behind a

guarantee *(Br.)*; ~**bruch** breach of warranty;
~**frist** period of warranty; ~**pflicht** guarantee
(Br.), guaranty *(US)*, warranty; ~**versicherung des
Produzenten** producer's liability insurance *(US)*.
Gewährsmangel redhibitory defect *(US)*.
Gewässer, schiffbare navigable (public) waters.
Gewerbe business, trade, *(Beruf)* calling, profession,
occupation, vocation, job *(US)*, *(Industrie)* industry, *(Industriezweig)* line of business;
in Ausübung eines ~s in pursuance of a trade;
ambulantes ~ itinerant trade; **dunkles** ~ shady
business; **konzessioniertes** ~ licensed trade;
unterentlohntes ~ sweatshop industry;
~ **im Umherziehen** itinerant trade, pedlary,
runaway shop;
~ **anmelden** to register a trade (business); ~ **ausüben (betreiben)** to carry (drive, exercise, ply,
pursue, follow) a trade.
Gewerbe|anmeldung registration of business; ~**auf-
seher** factory inspector, industrial executive *(US)*;
~**ausschuß** trade committee; ~**ausstellung** industrial (trade) exhibition, trade show (fair) *(Br.)*;
~**berechtigung** [business (trade) licence; ~**betrieb**
business, factory, trade, industrial (business)
enterprise, manufacturing establishment; ~**betrieb
ausüben** to carry on a trade; ~**genehmigung** trade
licence, commercial privilege, letters of business
(Br.), concession *(US)*; ~**konzession** [business
(trade)] licence, letters of business *(Br.)*, commercial privilege, concession *(US)*; ~**lehrer** trade
master, technical instructor; ~**lizenz** [business]
licence, letters of business *(Br.)*; ~**ordnung** factory
act (law), statute of labo(u)rers *(Br.)*; ~**polizei**
factory inspection.
gewerbepolizeiliche Anordnung factory regulations.
Gewerbe|schein [business] licence, trading certificate,
letters of business *(Br.)*; ~**schule** industrial (vocational, technical, trade) school; ~**steuer** license
(industrial, earned-income, *US)* tax.
gewerbesteuerpflichtig subject to licence.
Gewerbe|steuerpflichtiger recognized merchant; ~**tä-
tigkeit** industrial employment (work).
gewerbetreibend manufacturing, trading.
Gewerbe|treibender industrial[ist], manufacturer;
~**unfallversicherung** industrial accident insurance;
~**zweig** line of] industry.
gewerblich industrial, commercial, business;
~ **tätig sein** to follow (carry on, ply) a trade;
~**er Betrieb** manufacturing (industrial, business)
enterprise; ~**es Einkommen** business income; ~**e
Kreditgenossenschaft** industrial finance company,
cooperative bank; ~**e Niederlassung** commercial
establishment; ~**er Verbraucher** industrial user;
~**e Wirtschaft** trade and industry.
gewerbsmäßig business, professional, on a commercial scale.
Gewerkschaft trade *(Br.)* (lab(u)r, *US)* union;
betriebsfremde ~ outside union; **gelbe** ~ peaceful
(yellow, *US)* union;
einer ~ **als Mitglied beitreten** to join a union.

gewerkschaftlich organisiert unionized.
Gewerkschafts|abkommen union contract; ~**ange-
stellter** union official (officer, *US)*; ~**bank** union
(labour, *Br.)* bank; ~**beitrag** labo(u)r-union due.
gewerkschafts|feindlich antiunion, antilabo(u)r;
~**freundlich** pro-union, pro-labor *(US)*.
Gewerkschafts|führer [trade] union (labo(u)r) leader;
~**gelder** union funds; ~**institut** labo(u)r research
association; ~**mitglied** union member (man),
unionist; ~**organisation** labo(u)r organization.
gewerkschaftpflichtiger Betrieb closed (union) shop.
Gewerkschafts|sekretär trade-union secretary; ~**um-
lagen** union assessments; ~**vertreter** trade-union
delegate, union representative (agent), walking
(business) delegate, business manager (agent)
(US); ~**vertretung** labo(u)r representation; ~**zeitung** trade union paper.
Gewicht weight, *(Handelsgewicht)* avoirdupois;
ausgeliefertes ~ delivered weight; **knappes** ~
underweight;
~ **eichen** to gauge a weight; **nach** ~ **verkaufen** to
[sell by] weight.
Gewichts|abgang loss in weight; ~**angabe** declara-
tion; **falsche** ~**angabe** *(Spediteur)* false billing;
~**nota** weight note; ~**zoll** specific duty; ~**zugabe**, ~**zuschlag** makeweight, additional weight,
(Gepäck) excess luggage charge *(Br.)*.
Gewinn profit, gain, gainings, getting, increment,
(Einkünfte) emolument, spoil, *(Ertrag)* receipts,
proceeds, return, yield, produce, avails *(US)*, *(Gewinnspanne)* [profit] margin, *(Kursgewinn)* increase, advance, gains, *(Lotterie)* prize;
auf gemeinschaftlichen ~ **und Verlust** on joint
profit and loss; **nicht auf** ~ **gerichtet** nonprofit
[-making];
im Geschäft angelegter ~ earnings ploughed *(Br.)*
(plowed, *US)* back; **ausgeschüttete** ~**e** distributed
profits; **ausgezahlter** ~ *(Versicherung)* bonus in
cash; **besteuerungsfähiger** ~ taxable gain; **buchmäßiger** ~ book profit; **nicht entnommener** ~
retained income (earnings, *US)*, donated surplus,
paid-in surplus *(US)*; **leicht erzielter** ~ *(Börse)*
velvet *(US)*; **gewerblicher** ~ operating (industrial)
profit; **mitgenommener** ~ take-home pay; **noch
nicht realisierbarer** ~ contingent profit; **realisierter**
~ realized profit (revenue); **steuerpflichtiger** ~
taxable profit; **theasaurierter** ~ retained income
(earnings, *US)*, accumulated earnings *(US)*; **unrealisierte** ~**e** paper profits; **unverteilter** ~ unappropriated [earned, *US]* surplus, undistributed
(nondistributed) net profit *(Br.)*; **zwecks Rückstellung auf Reservekonto verfügbarer** ~ net surplus *(US)*; **verteilter** ~ appropriated surplus;
nicht verteilter ~ accumulated profit;
einbehaltene ~**e und Abschreibungen** retained cashflow; ~ **vor Berücksichtigung der Steuern** pretax
profit; ~ **aus Beteiligungen** investment profit; ~
aus Buchwerterhöhungen surplus of appreciation;
~ **aus Gewerbebetrieb** business profit; ~ **nach
Abzug von Steuern** after-tax earnings (profit); ~

und Verlust profit and loss;

mit ~ abschließen to show a profit; ~e abschöpfen to siphon off profits; ~ abwerfen to leave (bring in, render, yield, return) profit; ~e aktivieren to capitalize profits; mit ~ arbeiten to operate at a profit (in the black); ~ und Verlust durchschnittlich ausgleichen to average; ~ ausschütten to distribute a surplus, to divide profits; gewaltige ~e einstreichen to make huge profits; ~ nicht entnehmen to plough (plow, US) back earnings; bisher noch keinen ~ gemacht haben to have produced zero profit to date; ~e realisieren to reap (realize, take) profits, to cash in; am ~ beteiligt sein to have an interest (share) in profits, to share in the profits; ~e transferieren to repatriate profits; mit ~ verkaufen to sell to advantage (at a profit), (Wertpapiere) to sell a premium; kleine ~e verzeichnen to register (show) small gains; ~e steuerlich zurechnen to attribute profits.

Gewinn|abführung surrender of profits; ~abführungsvertrag surrender-of-profits agreement; ~abschöpfung taxing away (skimming off) excess profits; ~aktivierung capitalization of profits; ~ansammlung (Lebensversicherung) surplus accumulation.

Gewinnanteil [profit] share, share of profits, percentage (share, quota, portion, slice) of profits, (Rückversicherung) profit commission; rückständiger ~ reversionary dividend; ~plan profit-sharing plan.

Gewinn|aufschlag markup; ~ausfall und Verlust loss of earnings; ~ausschüttung division (distribution) of profit; gute ~aussichten nap hand; große ~aussichten haben to be (play) on velvet (US).

gewinnberechtigte Aktien participating shares (stocks, US).

Gewinnberichtigung reconciliation of surplus, surplus adjustment.

gewinnbeteiligte Versicherungspolice participating policy.

Gewinnbeteiligung profit (gain) sharing, share (interest) in profits, participation;
ohne ~ (Lebensversicherung) nonparticipating;
~ der Arbeitnehmer employee profit sharing.

Gewinnbeteiligungs|fonds profit-sharing fund (trust); ~plan profit-sharing plan; ~vereinbarung profit agreement (arrangement).

Gewinn|betrieb profitable operation; ~bonus bonus.

gewinnbringend| anlegen to invest advantageously (one's money) to good account);
~e Anlage paying investment; in ~er Weise productive.

Gewinn|chance fighting chance, (Erträgnisse) profit opportunity (chance).

gewinnen (Bergbau) to mine, to acquire, to obtain, (verdienen) to earn, to make, to net;
jds. Mitarbeit ~ to enlist s. o.; am Kurs ~ to benefit by the exchange; Preis ~ to win a prize; 10 Punkte ~ (Kurs) to gain 10 points.

Gewinnentnahme withdrawal of profits; sich in

~erhöhungen niederschlagen to pay off in increased profits; ~ermittlung calculation of profits; ~ermittlungen durch Betriebsvermögensvergleich accrual method; ~erwartungen profit expectations; ~feststellung ascertainment of profits; ~konto profit account, (Betriebsgewinn) earned-surplus account (US); ~ und Verlustkonto revenue (profit and loss) account; ~liste list of awards, prize list; ~los winnig (drawing) number; ~marge profit margin, margin of profit; ~mitnahme (Börse) profit taking; ~nummer (Lotterie) winning number; ~obligationen participating (income, US, reorganization, US) bonds; ~plan (Lebensversicherung) bonus system; ~posten surplus item; ~prognose profit forecast; ~realisierung realization of profit, (Börse) profit taking; ~ und Verlustrechnung profit and loss account, operating account (statement, US); ~rückgang drop-off in profits (earnings); ~rücklage, ~rückstellung surplus reserve, ploughing (plowing, US) back of earnings, unappropriated [earned, US] surplus, earned income (US); ~schrumpfung profit shrinkage; ~schuldverschiebungen participating (income, US) bonds, participating debentures, reorganization bonds (US).

Gewinnschwelle pay-off stage, break-even point, profitability level, profitable basis;
~ erreichen to be on a profitable basis, to break even, to come out of the red (US); ~ überschreiten to turn the profit corner;
~schwellendiagramm break-even chart; verbesserte ~situation improvement in profits.

Gewinnspanne margin of profit, profit margin;
~ nach Begleichung der Steuern post-tax margin.

Gewinn|streben, ~sucht profit motive; ~teile steuerlich auf ein bestimmtes Jahr aufteilen to apportion part of profits to a particular tax year; ~transfer repatriation (remittance) of profits; ~überschuß surplus, surplus profit (US).

Gewinnung von Nebenprodukten recovery of by-products.

Gewinn|verband (Pensionsplan) experience rating; ~verdeckung profit squeeze; ~verlustversicherung loss of profits insurance; ~verteilung division (distribution) of profits; ~verwendung appropriation of funds (profits); ~verwendungsrücklage retained income (US), unappropriated [earned, US] surplus; ~vorschau earnings estimate; ~vortrag undistributed (undivided) profits, reserved surplus, unappropriated earned surplus (US), surplus brought forward (US); ~zone (Bilanz) black; ~zurechnung (Einkommensteuer) allocation of profits, bonus distribution; ~zuschlag markup.

gewogener Mittelwert mean average.

Giralgeld credit currency (money), fiduciary (fiat, US) money, money in account (Br.).

Girant, späterer subsequent endorser (indorser).

girieren to endorse, to indorse;
blanko ~ to endorse (indorse) in blank.

giriert, blanko endorsed (indorsed) in blank.

Giro endorsement, indorsement;
~ **bestätigt** endorsement (indorsement) confirmed; ~ **fehlt** endorsement (indorsement) required;
beschränktes ~ restrictive endorsement (indorsement); **unbeschränktes** ~ absolute endorsement (indorsement);
~ **ohne Verbindlichkeit** endorsement(indorsement) without recourse, qualified indorsement;
durch ~ **übertragen** to transfer by endorsement (indorsement).
Giro|abschnitt bank slip; ~**abteilung** check *(US)* (cheque, *Br.)* department; ~**bank** deposit bank, bank of circulation, clearing (cheque) bank *(Br.)*;
~**einlagen** deposits; ~**geschäft** [business of] clearing; ~**kasse** clearinghouse; ~**konto** drawing (checking) account; ~**konto bei der Landeszentralbank** Federal Reserve Bank account *(US)*; ~**kunde** checking account depositor, current account [customer]; ~**sammeldepot** collective (omnibus) deposit; ~**schuldner** bill debtor; ~**verbindlichkeiten** contingent liabilities on bills discounted; ~**zahlung** bank transfer; ~**zentrale** clearinghouse.
glatt|es Geschäft clear profit; ~**e tausend Mark** a cool thousand.
Glattstellung *(Börse)* realization, liquidation, evening up, *(US)*, *(Konto)* liquidation, settlement; **umfangreichen ~en unterworfen sein** to come in for heavy liquidations.
Glattstellungs|geschäft evening-up transaction *(US)*; ~**konto** realization (liquidation) account; ~**verkauf** realization (realizing) sale, sell-off.
Glaube, guter good faith, bona fides.
Glaubhaftmachung substantiation.
Gläubiger creditor, demander, debtee, obligee;
absonderungsberechtigter ~ secured creditor *(US)*; **bevorrechtigter** ~ prior (preferential, *Br.*, preferred, *US*) creditor; **gleichrangiger** ~ creditor ranking equally; **erstklassig gesicherter** ~ catholic creditor; **nachrangiger** ~ subsequent creditor; **nicht vorzugsberechtigter** ~ general creditor;
~ **aus Kontokorrentgeschäften** trade creditor;
seine ~ abfinden to settle with one's creditors; **seine ~ voll auszahlen** to pay one's creditors in full; ~ **begünstigen** to favo(u)r a creditor; **seine ~ hinhalten** to delay (put off) one's creditors; **Vergleich mit seinen ~n schließen** to come to terms (compound) with one's creditors; **sich mit seinen ~n wegen eines Zahlungsaufschubs verständigen** to arrange with one's creditors for an extension of time; ~ **vertrösten** to put off creditors.
Gläubiger|anspruch creditor's claim; **auf ~antrag** upon the application of a creditor; ~**ausschuß** body of creditiros, committee in a winding up*(Br.)*; ~**befriedigung** satisfaction of (paying off) a creditor; ~**begünstigung** fraudulent (undue) preference; ~**gefährdung** jeopardizing a creditor's interest; ~**liste** list of creditors, schedule of a bankrupt's creditors *(US)*; ~**rang** ranking of a creditor; ~**rang-**

ordnung feststellen to marshal creditors; ~**schutzverband** trade protection society; ~**stellung erhalten** to enter into the rights of a creditor; ~**vergleich** settlement (agreement) with one's creditors; ~**versammlung** creditors' meeting; ~**verzeichnis** list of creditors, schedule of a bankrupt's estate *(US)*.
gleich|er Lohn für ~e Leistung equal pay for equal work.
gleichberechtigt having equal rights, on equal terms, equally ranking, on an equal footing.
gleichbleibende | Kosten constant costs; ~ **Nachfrage** steady demand.
Gleichgewicht von Angebot und Nachfrage equation of demand and supply.
gleichlautend | buchen to enter (pass) in conformity; **e Abschrift** duplicate, true (exact) copy.
gleichrangig equally ranking, of equal rank, *(mit neuen Aktien)* pari passu.
Gleis|anlagen erneuern to rebuild tracks; **privater ~anschluß** private siding.
gleitend|er Lohn sliding wage; ~**e Skala** sliding scale.
Gleit|klausel escalator clause; ~**lohntarif** sliding wage scale; ~**zoll** slid1ng-scale tariff.
Gliedertaxe *(Versicherung)* dismemberment schedule.
Gliederung *(Gläubigeransprüche)* marshalling;
~ **nach Sachgebieten** funtional classification.
global | bewilligen to vote as a lump sum;
~**er Lohnanstieg** round (across-the-bord) wage increase; ~**e Wirtschaftsprobleme** global economic problems.
Global|aktie multiple certificate *(Br.)*; ~**betrag** inclusive (global, round) sum; ~**kontingent** overall (global) quota; ~**versicherung** comprehensive (allloss, *US*) insurance.
Glückwunschtelegramm congratulatory telegram, greetings telegram.
Gold, in rückzahlbar redeemable in gold;
18karätiges ~ common gold; **24karätiges** ~ twenty-four carat gold; **ungemünztes** ~ bullion, bar gold;
~ **von gesetzlicher Feinheit** standard gold;
mit ~ aufwiegen to pay a heavy price.
Gold|abfluß gold outflow; ~**abzüge** gold withdrawals; ~**ankauf** gold buying (purchase); ~**ausfuhr** gold export; ~**barren** gold bar (ingot), bullion, ingot of gold; ~**barrenwährung** gold bullion standard; **auf ~basis** on gold; ~**bestände** gold coin and bullion; ~**blockländer** gold-bloc countries; ~**deckung** gold backing (cover, coverage); ~**devisenwährung** gold exchange standard; ~**embargo** gold embargo; ~**gewicht** troy weight; ~**klausel** gold clause; ~**land** gold-producing country; ~**parität** gold parity; ~**pfandbriefe** gold bonds *(US)*; **gespaltener ~preis** two-tier gold price; ~**punkt** gold (specie, bullion) point; ~**reserve bei ausländischen Noteninstituten** earmarked gold; ~**schatz** treasure of gold; ~**standard abschaffen** to go off the gold standard; ~**stück** gold coin (piece), goldfinch*(Br.)*, yellow boy *(Br. sl.)*, shiner *(sl.)*; ~**umlaufwährung**

gold specie standard; ~**versendung** shipment of gold; ~**vorkommen** occurrence of gold; ~**währung** gold standard (currency); ~**währungsland** gold-standard country; ~**zahlung** gold payment; ~**zertifikat** gold certificate *(US)*.

graphischer Betrieb printing establishment.

Gratifikation bonus, gratuity.

gratis gratis, without payment (cost), gratuitous, as a free gift, free of charge (costs).

Gratisaktie free share, bonus share *(Br.)* (stock, *US*), stock dividend *(US)*;
~ **mit Wahlrecht der Barabfindung** optional dividend.

Gratis|aktienausgabe bonus (scrip, *Br.)* issue; ~**beilage** free supplement; ~**muster** free sample.

greifbare Vermögenswerte tangible assets.

Gremium body, group, committee, panel.

Grenz|abfertigung customs clearance; ~**betrieb** marginal company.

Grenze der Rentabilität break-even point.

Grenz|ertrag marginal revenue (profit); ~**kontrolle** *(Zoll)* customs inspection; ~**kosten** marginal (incremental, terminal) costs; ~**kostenkalkulation** marginal costing.

Grenznutzen marginal profit (utility, desirability), dimishing utiliy, margin of profitableness; ~**schule** marginal utiliy school.

Grenz|plankostenrechnung direct *(US)* (marginal, *Br.)* costing; ~**produktivität** marginal productivity (productiveness); ~**schein** frontier pass; ~**station** frontier (border) station; **[kleiner]** ~**verkehr** [local] frontier (border) traffic; ~**zollamt** customhouse, customs office.

Groschen, seine paar zusammenhalten to look after one's money;
~**automat** penny-in-the-slot (coin) machine;

Groß|abnahme industrial consumption, quantity (heavy) buying; ~**abnehmer** bulk (heavy, quantity) buyer; ~**aktionär** principal (controlling) shareholder (stockholder, *US*); ~**auftrag** *(Börse)* big-ticket order; ~**bank** big banking house; ~**betrieb** large establishment, large-scale enterprise (industry).

Größe, in allen ~**n und Ausführungen** in all sizes and styles;
nicht gängige ~ odd size; **handelbare** ~ *(Börse)* regular lot; **lagergängige** ~ stock size.

Groß|einkauf bulk buying (purchasing), quantity (bulk, volume, *US)* purchase; ~**einkäufer** wholesale (quantity, heavy) buyer; ~**einkaufsgenossenschaft** cooperative wholesale society *(Br.)*.

Größen|angaben statement of size; ~**klasse** size.

Groß|familie *(Soziologie)* extended family; ~**finanz** high finance, moneyed interest; ~**format** *(Briefumschlag)* commercial size; ~**gepäck** registered luggage *(Br.)* checked baggage *(US)*; ~**grundbesitz** landed aristocracy; ~**grundbesitzer** [many-acred] landlord.

Großhandel wholesale [trade], wholesale dealing, merchant trading, jobbing *(US)*, service center;

nur den ~ **beliefern** to supply only to wholesalers.

Großhandels|artikel wholesale goods; ~**filiale** wholesale branch; ~**geschäft** wholesale business (shop, store); ~**gewerbe** jobber's trade *(US)*; ~**index** wholesale price index; ~**preis** wholesale (trade) price, wholesale cost; ~**rabatt** quantity (wholesale) discount, trade allowance; ~**spanne** wholesale margin; ~**zentrum** wholesale center (centre, *Br.*).

Großhändler wholesale merchant (dealer), wholesaler, distributor, jobber *(US)*, large merchant; **auftragsvermittelnder** ~ drop shipper;
~ **ohne eigenes Lager** waggon jobber *(US)*, truck wholesaler *(US)*.

Groß|hersteller large-scale (mass) producer; ~**industrie** large-scale (big) industry; ~**industrieller** magnate of industry, big industrialist.

Grossist wholesale (quantity) buyer;
~ **ohne eigenes Lager** desk jobber *(US)*.

Grossistenpreis wholesale cost (price).

Groß|kapitalist capitalist, tycoon *(US)*; ~**kaufmann** wholesaler, warehouseman; ~**kunde** big customer; ~**lebensversicherung** ordinary life insurance *(US)*; ~**markt** supermarket; **in** ~**packung** economy-sized; ~**raumtransporter** bulk carrier; ~**stadt** large town, city, *(Weltstadt)* metropolis; ~**stadtbezirk** metropolitan district (territory); ~**stadtgebiet** metropolitan (big-city) area (region), urban center *(US)* (centre, *Br.)*; ~**verkehr** big-city traffic.

Groß|unternehmen large-scale (big) enterprise, big business *(US)*; ~**verbraucher** bulk (heavy, large-scale) consumer; ~**verdiener sein** to make lots of money.

Gruben|abbau mining; ~**anteil** royalty; ~**schließung** mine shutdown (closing).

Grund|abgabe ground rent, land tax; **nicht einmal die** ~**begriffe des Finanzwesens begreifen** not to know the ABC of finance; ~**beitrag** basic fee.

Grundbesitz ground, land, [landed] property (estate), ownership of land, landholding;
ausgedehnter ~ vast estate; **freier** ~ free tenement, freehold [property] *(Br.)*; **gewerblich genutzter** ~ commercial property; **öffentlicher** ~ public land (domain, *US)*; **unveräußerlicher** ~ entailed property;
erheblichen ~ **haben** to own acres of land (large estates); ~ **parzellieren** to break up an estate.

Grundbesitzer landowner, landed proprietor.

Grundbuch land register *(Br.)*, register of deeds *(US)*; ~**einsehen lassen** to have the title searched; **Hypothek ins** ~ **eintragen lassen** to register a mortgage, to have a mortgage recorded in the office of the register of deeds *(US)*; **jem. im** ~ **[im Range] vorgehen** to have priority over s. o. in claim on mortgaged property.

Grundbuch|amt Land Registry *(Br.)*, registry of deeds *(US)*; ~**auszug** abstract of title, land certificate *(Br.)*; ~**blatt** real-estate map *(US)*; ~**eintragung** registration of land (title, deeds), entry made

in the register *(Br.)*, real-estate rerecording *(US)*.
Grund|dienstbarkeit rent charge, landed (real, *US)* servitude, [right of] easement; **~eigentum** landed property (estate).
gründen to ground, *(einrichten)* to establish, *(einsetzen)* to set up, to institute, *(Geschäft)* to open, to establish, *(Gesellschaft)* to found, to float, to promote;
Filiale ~ to establish a branch office.
Gründer|aktien promoter's shares (stocks, *US)*; **~anteil erhalten** to be let in on the ground floor; **~konsortium** promoting syndicate *(Br.)*.
Grunderwerb purchase (acquisition) of land.
Grunderwerbs|bescheinigung *(Zwangsversteigerung)* certificate of purchase; **~kosten** purchase cost of real estate; **~steuer** realty transfer tax *(US)*.
Grund|freibetrag *(Einkommensteuerformular)* basic abatement; **~gebühr** base fee, *(Telefon)* telephone subscription (rate), line charge; **~haltung beibehalten** *(Börse)* to maintain the tone.
Grundkapital *(AG)* share capital *(Br.)*, capital stock *(US)* (fund), nominal capital *(Br.)*, first stock; **genehmigtes ~** authorized capital stock *(US)*.
Grundlage, gesunde wirtschaftliche sound economic basis;
auf eine bessere finanzielle ~ stellen to put on a better financial footing; **~ eines Unternehmens verbreitern** to spread its business base.
Grundlohn basic wage (pay), base wage rate; **~tarif** base wage rate.
Grund|pfandbrief mortgage bond; **~pfandrecht** encumbrance, mortgage lien; **~preis** standard [purchase] (basic) price; **~produkte** primary (basic) products; **~rente** annual (economic, net, pure, true) rent; **~satz von Treu und Glauben** expectation of good faith in business dealings; **~schuld** [etwa] land charge.
Grundsteuer land *(US)* (real estate, *US*, property *Br.)* tax;
~ablösung redemption of land tax *(US)*; **~pflichtiger** ratepayer; **~veranlagung** assessment on landed property *(Br.)*.
Grundstoff|industrie primary (basic) industries; **~preis** raw-material price.
Grundstück plot [of land], land, property, premises, piece of land, *(Bauplatz)* building site, location *(US)*;
abgeschlossenes ~ enclosure; **angrenzendes ~** adjoining property; **baureifes ~** building estate; **enteignetes ~** condemned property; **genutztes ~** seated (used) land; **gewerblich genutztes ~** industrial property; **im Wert gestiegenes ~** improved real estate; **unbebautes ~** idle (undeveloped) land; **unbebaute und bebaute ~e** *(Bilanz)* land and buildings;
~e und Gebäude *(Bilanz)* land and buildings; **~ in gleicher Lage** similarly located property;
~ abschreiben to write down property; **~ auflassen** to transfer (convey, assure, surrender) land; **~ hypothekarisch belasten** to mortgage a piece of

real estate, to charge land; **~ im Grundbuch eintragen** to enter an estate at the Register of Deeds Office *(US)*; **~ lastenfrei erwerben** to get a property free from all encumbrances; **~ lastenfrei machen** to disencumber an estate; **~ parzellieren** to parcel (divide) an estate; **~e zusammenschreiben** to assemble two parcels of land.
Grundstücks|abschätzung valuation of an estate; **~abschreibung** allowance on premises; **~anzeigen** *(Zeitung)* real-estate column; **~areal aufkaufen** to buy land on a large scale; **~auflassung** transfer of title to land; **~belastung** mortgage of land; **~besitzer** real-estate owner; **~bewertung** assessment on landed property *(Br.)*, survey; **~eigentum** proprietorship, landed (real) estate, landed property; **~eigentümer** [real] estate owner, owner of land, property owner; **~erschließung** land (property) development; **~erschließungsgesellschaft** development agency; **~finanzierung** real-estate financing; **~kauf** land purchase; **~kaufvertrag** real covenant, real-estate closing, warranty deed *(US)*; **~komplex aufteilen** to slice a piece of property; **~makler** land agent *(Br.)*, real-estate agent (broker, dealer, operator); **einem ~makler an die Hand geben** to list with (place in the hands of) a real-estate broker; **~markt** real-estate (property) market, *(Zeitungsspalte)* real-estate columns (section); **~nachbar** adjoining landowner; **~pacht** land tenure, ground lease (rent); **~parzelle** lot, plot (portion) of land, parcel, allotment *(Br.)*; **~parzellierung** breaking up an estate; **~preis** real-estate price, land cost; **~spekulation** realty (property, land) speculation; **~taxe** real-estate appraisal; **~übertragung**, **~umschreibung** alienation (conveyance) of an estate; **~unterhaltungskosten** cost of carrying real estate *(US)*; **~verkauf** sale of land, property sale, real-estate dealing (selling); **~verkäufer** real-estate salesman *(US)*; **~verkaufsvertrag** estate contract, warranty deed *(US)*; **~verwalter** estate (property) manager, steward, bailiff; **~verwertungsgesellschaft** development company; **~wert** land (plottage, real-estate, property) value, value of land.
Grund|tarif base (basic) rate, class basis (rate), *(Feuerversicherung)* basis rate; **~ton** *(Börse)* prevailing tone.
Gründung foundation, creation, *(Aktiengesellschaft)* formation, promotion, flotation;
schwindelhafte ~ bogus concern, bubble company *(Br.)*; **~ von Tochterunternehmen** founding of subsidiaries.
Gründungs|akten organization files *(US)*; **~aufwand** organization expenses (cost) *(US)*; **~bericht** statutory report; **~bilanz** reigstration statement; **~jahr** year of foundation (organization, *US)*; **~konsortium** underlying syndicate *(US)*; **~mitglied** charter (founder) member; **~versammlung** founders' (organization, *US)* meeting; **~zeugnis** *(AG)* certificate of organization *(US)*.
Grundvergütung basic compensation (pay).

Grundvermögen [landed (fixed)] property, real estate; **sein ~ flüssigmachen (realisieren)** to turn one's land into money, to convert realty into personaly.
Grund|zins annual rent; **~zuteilung** basic ration.
Grünkramladen greengrocery.
Gruppe body, group, *(Arbeiter)* team, crew, gang, section, band, *(Steuer)* bracket; **~ von Banken** group of banks, banking syndicate; **~ landwirtschaftlicher Interessenvertreter im Parlament** farm bloc *(US)*.
Gruppen|abschreibung group depreciation; **~akkordlohn** group piece rate; **~disziplin** *(Kartellwesen)* quasi agreement *(US)*; **~lebensversicherung** group-term life insurance; **~leistungslohnsystem** group piecework system; **~reise** organized (packaged, *US)* tour, group trip; **~rentenversicherung** group annuity insurance; **pauschalierter ~tarif** *(Versicherung)* wholesale group rate; **~verkauf** *(Kraftfahrzeuge)* fleet sale; **~versicherung** group (collective) insurance, *(Kraftfahrzeuge)* fleet insurance.
gültig *(Fahrkarte)* available, valid, *(Gesetz)* active, in force, effective, *(Münze)* current; **nicht mehr ~ sein** to be no longer current (out of circulation), *(Paß)* to have expired; **unwiderruflich ~es und bestätigtes Akkreditiv** irrevocable and confirmed letter of credit.
Gültigkeit validity, force, effect, *(Fahrkarte)* availability, *(Gesetzlichkeit)* legality; **~ eines Testaments bestreiten** to contest (dispute) a will.
Gültigkeitsdauer validity, run, *(Fahrschein)* period for which a ticket is available.
gummierter Briefumschlag adhesive envelope.
Gunsten, zu ~ von *(Buchhaltung)* to the benefit of, in favo(u)r of; **Saldo zu Ihren ~ aufweisen** to show a balance to your credit.
günstig, zu ~en Bedingungen on easy terms.
Gut *(Besitz)* property, possessions, *(Land)* estate, farm, *(Rittergut)* manor, *(Vermögen)* property; **herrenloses ~** abandoned property; **seetriftiges ~** flotsam; **sperriges ~** bulky goods; **eingebrachtes ~ der Ehefrau** separate (dotal) property.
gut, ziemlich ~ bis mittelmäßig fair to middling; **~ erhalten** well-preserved, in good condition; **~ situiert** well-off, well-to-do; **~ gehen** *(Absatz)* to meet with ready sale; **~ gehalten sein** *(Kurse)* to maintain a good tone; **~e Qualität** high quality.
Gutachten [expert] opinion, expertise, survey.
Gutachter expert, advisor, *(Schätzer)* appraiser; **~ausschuß** panel of experts; **~gruppe** expert group.
Güte *(Beschaffenheit)* quality, grade, class, sort; **von gleichmäßiger Art und ~** of uniform kind and quality; **von mittlerer Art und ~** of medium kind and quality; **handelsübliche ~ und Beschaffenheit** good merchantable quality and condition.
Güte|bestimmung quality designation (description);

~einteilung grade labelling; **~klasse** grade, class, quality category; **~klasseneinteilung** grading.
Güter merchandise, commodities, goods, articles; **aufgeopferte ~** *(Havarie)* sacrificed goods; **bahnlagernde ~** goods at the railway depot *(Br.)*; **eingelagerte ~** stored goods; **feuergefährliche ~** combustibles; **im Inland hergestellte ~** home-produced goods; **immaterielle ~** *(Bilanz)* intangible assets; **lebenswichtige ~** essential goods, essentials; **sperrige (lose verladene) ~** measured (bulky) goods, goods shipped in bulk; **vertretbare ~** fungible things; **zollpflichtige ~** dutiable goods; **~ löschen** to unload (discharge) goods, to wharf; **~ über Bord werfen** to [make] jettison.
Güter|abfertigung dispatch, goods office (department) *(Br.)*, freight service (agency) *(US)*; **~annahme** receiving (goods, *Br.)* office; **~bahnhof** goods yard (station) *(Br.)*, freight depot (yard) *(US)*; **~bahnsteig** goods platform *(Br.)*; **~expedition** dispatch, forwarding agency; **~fernverkehr** long-distance goods traffic *(Br.)*, long-haul freight traffic *(US)*; **~frachttarif** rail tariff; **~gemeinschaft** goods in communion, communal estate (tenure); **~halle** goods depot *(Br.)*, freight shed *(US)*; **~kraftverkehr** truckage *(Br.)*, road haulage (transport); **~makler** estate (land) agent *(Br.)*, land jobber *(US)*; **~nahverkehr** short-distance freight traffic, short-haul freight traffic *(US)*; **~schuppen** goods depot (loft) *(Br.)*, freight shed *(US)*; **~spediteur** freight forwarder, common carrier; **~speicher** goods loft (shed, *US)*, depot, warehouse *(Br.)*; **gesetzlicher ~stand** *(Ehe)* legal community *(US)*, separate property; **~tarif** freight (goods, *Br.)* rates; **~tonnage** freight tonnage; **~transport** freight transportation *(US)*, conveyance of goods; **~transportversicherung** freight insurance; **~trennung** *(Eheleute)* separation of property *(Br.)*; **~umschlag** goods turnover; **~umschlagstelle** rail and water terminal; **~verkehr** merchandise (freight, *US*, goods, *Br.)* traffic; **~verlader** loader, shipper *(US)*, shipping agent *(US)*; **~versand** dispatch, shipping of goods *(US)*; **~versorgung** supply of goods.
Güterwagen, ~waggon waggon *(Br.)*, box (goods) waggon *(Br.)*, freight car (waggon) *(US)*; **gedeckter (geschlossener) ~** closed freight car *(US)*, goods van *(Br.)*, covered waggon *(Br.)*, house car, box waggon *(Br.)*, boxcar *(US)*; **offener ~** flat car, platform carriage (car) *(US)*; **~ladung** carlot *(US)*, carload *(US)*, truckload, waggonload *(Br.)*.
Güterzug goods train *(Br.)*, freight train *(US)*.
Güte|schutz quality protection; **statistische ~überwachung** quality control; **~zeichen** quality label, brand, trademark.
Gutgewicht tret, tare.
gutgläubig bona fide, in good faith; **~er Dritter** innocent [third] party.
Guthaben *(Anlagevermögen)* assets, *(Bilanz)* money owing to us, accounts receivable *(US)*, receiv-

ables *(US), (Konto)* credit [balance], money on account, balance in s. one's favo(u)r;
eingefrorene ~ frozen assets; **täglich fälliges** ~ current (demand, *US)* deposit; **gesperrtes** ~ blocked credit balance; **kein** ~ no assets (effects, funds); **verfügbares** ~ amount standing to the credit; **jederzeit verfügbares** ~ money at call, call money;
~ **im Ausland** foreign deposits; ~ **bei [anderen] Banken** *(Bilanz)* due from banks; ~ **der öffentlichen Hände** public deposits; **freie** ~ **bei der Landeszentralbank** free reserves *(US);*
~ **auf zwei Monate festlegen** to fix a deposit for two months; ~**pfänden** to garnish an account; ~**abzug** outflow of funds; ~**konto** credit [balance], deposit account (balance).

Gutsbesitzer gentleman farmer, landowner, landed proprietor, squire *(Br.),* farmer *(US).*
Gutschein *(Bezugsschein)* coupon, ticket, *(Einzahlungsbeleg)* credit slip, *(Prämie)* free-gift coupon, gift voucher, giveaway; ~**heft** coupon book; ~**system** credit-coupon plan.
gutschreiben, jem. to pass to s. one's credit, to enter to the credit of s. o.; **Gegenwert einem Konto** ~ to place the proceeds to the credit of an account.
Gutschrift crediting, credit entry;
~ **Eingang vorbehalten** entering short;
~ **erteilen** to pass to the credit.
Gutschrifts|anzeige credit advice (memorandum, note, *US);* ~**beleg** *(im internen Bankverkehr)* credit slip *(Br.)* (ticket, *US).*
Gutsverwalter managing man, land steward, bailiff *(Br.).*

H

Habe having, effects, belongings, possessions;
persönliche ~ personal things (belongings).
Haben credit [side], *(Bilanz)* creditors;
im ~ **buchen** to [place to the] credit;
~**buchung** credit entry; ~**zinsen** credit interest; ~**zinsabkommen** agreement on creditor interest rates.
Hafen, eisfreier ice-free port (harbo(u)r; **offener** ~ open harbo(u)r; ~ **mit Zollager** bonded port;
~ **buchen** to put into (stop at, touch, call at) a port; **aus einem Hafen** ~ **auslaufen** to leave harbo(u)r; ~ **sperren** to shut up (blockade) a port; ~**abgaben** harbo(u)r (dock) dues; **sich beim** ~**amt melden** to report to the port authority; ~**arbeiter** docker *(Br.),* dock labo(u)rer (worker), wharf worker; ~**seher** harbo(u)r master, port warden *(US);* ~**becken** basin, dock; ~**behörde** port (dock) authority, harbo(u)r board; ~**einfahrt** entrance to a harbo(u)r, inlet; ~**gebühren** [port] toll, port charges (dues), ~**kommissar,** ~**meister** harbo(u)r master, dockmaster; ~**polizei** harbo(u)r (dock) police; ~**sperre** harbo(u)r barrage; ~**viertel** dockland, dock area; ~**zoll** harbo(u)r dues (charges).
haftbar responsible, answerable, [legally] liable;
insgesamt und einzeln ~ jointly and severally liable; **sekundär** ~ secondarily liable; **selbstschuldnerisch (unmittelbar)** ~ primarily liable *(US);*

persönlich ~ **sein** to be personally answerable (liable); **für den Erfüllungsgehilfen** ~ **sein** to be vicariously liable.
haften to be liable (answer, be answerable) for;
aus Gefährdung ~ to be strictly and absolutely liable; **für einen Schaden** ~ to be liable (responsible); **selbstschuldnerisch** ~ to be liable as principal debtor; **unbeschränkt** ~ to be liable without limitation;
Haftpflicht liability, responsibility, accountability;
mit beschränkter ~ with limited liability;
gesetzliche ~ legal liability, liability created by statute; **unbeschränkte** ~ absolute (unlimited) liability;
~ **ablehnen** *(Versicherung)* to decline the responsibility; **sich gegen** ~ **versichern** to insure against third-party risk *(Br.);*
~**ausschluß** nonliability.
haftpflichtig [legally] liable [for damages], answerable for a debt, bound, responsible;
mittelbar ~ secondarily liable *(US);* **unmittelbar** ~ liable at once, primarily liable *(US);*
Haftpflicht|police third-party risk policy *(Br.);* ~**umfang** liability coverage; ~**versicherung** liability (third-party) insurance; ~**versicherungspolice** general liability (third-party risk, *Br.)* policy.
Haftung liability, obligation, responsibility;
mit Ausschluß der ~ nonliable;

selbstschuldnerische ~ primary liability; **gesetzliche** ~ *(Betriebsprüfer)* legal liability; **vertragliche** ~ contractual obligation;
~ **des Erfüllungsgehilfes** accountability of a vicarious agent; ~ **für den Erfüllungsgehilfen** vicarious liability; ~ **aus unerlaubter Handlung** tortuous liability;
~ **ablehnen** to decline responsibility; ~ **ausschließen** to exclude (negative) liability; ~ **übernehmen** to undertake a liability, to underwrite.

Haftungs|ausschluß nonliability, nonwarranty, exemption from liability; ~**beschränkung auf eigenes Verschulden der Beamten** risk note; ~**grenze** limit of indemnity; ~**übernahme** assumption of liability; ~**umfang** accountability, accounting unit.

halber Fahrpreis half rate.

halbamtlich semiofficial, quasi-official.

Halb|fabrikate semimanufacture, semifinished articles (products), work in process *(US)* (progress, *Br.);* ~**jahresabschluß** midyear settlement; ~**pacht** sharecrop system *(US);* ~**part** half share, fifty-fifty.

halbseitig gesperrt *(Straße)* closed on one side.

Halbtags|arbeit part-time employment; ~**arbeiter** half-timer, half-time worker; ~**bezahlung** part-time worker rate; ~**stelle** part-time job.

Haldenbestände dump (pithead) stocks.

halten, sich *(Kurs)* to remain firm, to keep their ground, to rule steady; **Preise auf dem gleichen Niveau** ~ to maintain the same level of prices; **sich an seinen Vormann** ~ to have recourse against the preceding party.

Halte|platz *(Taxi)* taxi rank *(Br.)* (stand); ~**stelle** station, stop; ~**verbot** *(Schild)* no waiting; ~**verbotsstraße** clearway *(Br.);* ~**verbotszone** no-waiting area, no-stopping zone.

Haltung attitude, posture, deportment, post, *(Ansicht)* ground, *(Börse)* tone, tendency;
abwartende ~ look-(wait-and-see) position; **auf Spezialwerte beschränkte feste** ~ *(Börse)* selective strength; **unentschlossene** ~ straddle;
feste ~ **zeigen** *(Börse)* to show a bold front.

hamstern gehen to go shopcrawling *(Br.).*

Hand, aus zweiter secondhand, at second hand; **im Besitz der öffentlichen** ~ public-owned;
an die ~ **geben** *(Grundstück einem Makler)* to list; **unter der** ~ **verkaufen** to sell privately (by private bargain); **von der öffentlichen** ~ **unterstützt werden** to live upon the parish.

Hand|akten reference files; ~**buch für Verkäufer** sales manual.

Handel commerce, trade, *(Einzelgeschäft)* bargain, business, deal, dealing, transaction;
im ~ on the market;
ambulanter ~ peddlery, pedlary *(Br.),* peddling; **darniederliegender** ~ languishing trade; **konzessionierter** ~ licensed traffic, lawful trade; **zwischenstaatlicher** ~ interstate commerce;
~ **mit dem Ausland** export trade, foreign commerce; ~ **in Bezugsrechten** rights dealing *(US);* ~ **und Gewerbe** trade and industry; ~ **mit nicht**

notierten Wertpapieren over-the-counter trading *(US);*
~ **aufgeben** to quit business; ~ **aufkündigen** to break a bargain; **in den** ~ **bringen** to commercialize; ~ **rückgängig machen** to rescind a contract; **nicht mehr im** ~ **sein** to be no longer on the market; ~ **treiben** to [carry on (follow) a] trade.

handelbar salable, *(Wertpapiere)* negotiable.

Handeln | auf eigene Gefahr assumption of risk; ~ **im guten Glauben** bona-fide operation.

handeln to act, to take action, to proceed, *(feilschen)* to haggle, *(Geschäft treiben)* to be in business, to carry on a trade, to negotiate;
mit Aktien ~ to job; **an der Börse** ~ to quote (list, *US)* on the stock exchange; **innerhalb seiner Vertretungsmacht** ~ to act within the scope of one's authority.

Handelsabkommen commercial treaty (accord, convention), treaty of commerce, trade agreement; **allgemeines Zoll- und** ~ General Agreement on Tarrifs and Trade (GATT).

Handels|abordnung trade delegation; ~**- und Wirtschaftsabteilung** *(Auswärtiges Amt)* trade service; ~**adreßbuch** trade (business) directory; ~**akademie** commercial (business, *US)* school; ~**attaché** commercial attaché (counsellor), trade-service diplomat; ~**- und Gewerbebank** commercial bank, merchant bank[er] *(Br.);* ~**beschränkung** impediment to (restraint of) trade; ~**besprechungen** commercial negotiations, trade talks; ~**bestimmungen** economic clauses; ~**bevollmächtigter** commercial agent; ~**bezeichnung** trade name, brand; ~**beziehungen** trade relations.

Handelsbilanz trade balance *(Firma)* balance sheet; **aktive** ~ favo(u)rable balance of trade; **passive** ~ unfavo(u)rable balance of trade;
~ **ausgleichen** to redress the balance of trade; ~**bilanzüberschüsse** surpluses of balance of payments.

Handels|bräuche trade usage, custom of merchants; ~**delegation** trade mission (delegation); ~**erzeugnis** trading item; ~**firma** business firm, commercial house; ~**flagge** merchant flag, Red ensign *(Br.);* ~**flotte** merchant fleet; ~**frau** feme-sole-trader; ~**gericht [etwa]** commercial court.

handelsgerichtliche Eintragung registration, incorporation *(US).*

Handels|geschäft commercial establishment (house); ~**gesellschaft** [trading (registered), *Br.*] company, trading corporation; **Offene** ~ general (ordinary, *US)* partnership; **Offene** ~ **in eine GmbH umwandeln** to turn a partnership into a limited company; ~**gesetz** commercial law, law merchant; ~**gewicht** avoirdupois; ~**gut mittlerer Art und Güte** fair average quality; ~**hafen** trading port; ~**haus** commercial estabishment (house); ~**hochschule** commercial college, business school; ~**kammer** chamber of commerce, board of trade *(US);* ~**konferenz** trade conference; ~**konzession** licence; ~**korrespondent** business correspondent;

~korrespondenz commercial (business) correspondence; ~kreise merchants, business circles; ~krieg commerce destroying, tariff (trade) war; ~marine mercantile (merchant) marine; ~messe trade fair; ~minister President of the Board of Trade *(Br.)*, Secretary of Commerce *(US)*; ~ministerium Board of Trade *(Br.)*, Department of Commerce *(US)*; ~mission trade mission; ~monopol trade (commercial) monopoly; ~nachrichten financial columns, city article *(Br.)*; ~name trade (business) name; ~niederlassung trading post (station), trade settlement; kurzfristiges ~papier commercial paper; ~platz trading post (town).

handelspolitische Abmachungen trade agreement; ~er Graben trade policy moat.

Handels|preis market price; unter dem normalen ~preis verkaufen to sell below dealer costs; ~produkt trading item; ~recht law merchant.

Handelsregister register of companies (corporations, *US*);
ins ~ eintragen to register *(Br.)*, to incorporate *(US)*; im ~ löschen to deregister *(Br.)*, to disincorporate *(US)*;
~auszug extract of a registered statement.

Handels|rückgang loss of trade; ~sache *(Gericht)* commercial case; ~schiff merchant vessel (ship), merchantman; ~schiffahrt maritime commerce.

Handels|schranken impediment to (barriers of) trade; ~schule commercial school (college), trade school; ~sorte merchantable quality; ~spanne [profit] margin; ~stadt mercantile (business) town; ~statistik Board of Trade returns (figures); ~teil *(Zeitung)* commercial supplement, financial columns, city article *(Br.)*.

handelsübliche | Bezeichnung trade name, brand, description; ~e Qualität merchantable quality.

Handels|unkosten trade expenses; ~unternehmen commercial establishment; ~usance custom of merchants; ~verkehr commerce, traffic, trade; ~verkehr mit dem Ausland untersagen to interdict trade with foreign nations; ~vertrag commercial treaty, trade agreement (treaty, pact); ~vertragspartner trade partner; ~vertreter commercial (travel(l)er), drummer *(US)*; ~vertretung commercial (mercantile) agency; ~vorrat stock-in-trade; ~ware article of merchandise; ~wechsel commercial paper, mercantile (trade) paper; ~wert commercial (market, economic) value, trade-in-value; ~zeitschrift trade magazine; ~zentrum center *(US)* (centre, *Br.*) of commerce, trading center *(US)*; ~zone trading area.

Handeltreibender trader, tradesman, merchant.

Handgeld imprest (earnest, bargain) money.

Handgepäck personal luggage *(Br.)* (baggage, *US*), hand baggage *(US)*, grip *(US)*;
sein ~ aufbewahren lassen to leave one's luggage *(Br.)* (baggage, *US*) in the cloakroom;
~aufbewahrung left-luggage office *(Br.)*, cloakroom, baggage room *(US)*.

Händler trader, tradesman, merchant;

fliegender ~ itinerant trader, pedlar *(Br.)*; ~ in kleinen Effektenabschnitten odd-lot dealer *(US)*;
~analyse dealer research; ~befragung dealer survey (research); ~lager dealer inventory; ~rabatt distributor's (trade) discount, dealer's rebate (allowance); ~stand pitch.

Handlungs|beauftragter agent; ~bevollmächtigter proxy, attorney in fact; ~gehilfe [merchant's (office)] clerk; ~reisender commercial travel(l)er, travel(l)ing (sales) agent (salesman, *US*), commercial *(Br.)*, traveller *(Br.)*, bagman *(Br.)*, drummer *(US)*; ~unkosten [general] overhead, overhead charges (cost, expenses), cost, burden, oncost *(Br.)*; ~vollmacht power [of attorney], authority to act, proxy.

Handschrift handwriting, [writing] hand; kaufmännische ~ commercial hand.

Handwerk [handi]craft, small trade;
sein ~ restlos beherrschen to be a consummate master of one's craft.

Handwerker craftsman, handicraftsman, artificier, artisan, tradesman, mechanic, operative, workman.

handwerklicher Betrieb hnadicraft, craftsman's establishment.

Handwerks|beruf skilled trade, handicraft pursuits; ~betrieb handicraft, crafsman's establishment.

Handzettel handbill, throw-away leaflet.

harte Währung hard currency.

Härte|ausgleich *(Dienstentlassung)* severance pay *(US)*, dismissal compensation; ~zulage hardship allowance.

Hartgeld specie, coin, coined money, coinage.

Haufen | Geld pots (pile, sight) of money; ~ Rechnungen swarm of bills.

Haupt|absatzgebiet prime market area; ~aktionär leading (principal) shareholder *(Br.)* (stockholder, *US*); ~anschluß *(Telefon)* direct [exchange] line; ~bahnhof main (railroad, *US*) station, depot *(US)*; ~beruf main profession.

hauptberuflich as a regular (permanent) occupation, professional, full-time.

Haupt|buch ledger [book], shopbook *(US)*, general ledger;
~ abschließen to balance the ledger; Posten ins ~ eintragen to post an item in the ledger;
~auszug ledger abstract (report); ~führer ledger clerk (keeper); ~halter senior clerk (cashier).

Haupt|büro chief (head, home) office, headquarters; ~einnahmequelle major means of income; ~geschäft head office, parent store, headquarters.

Hauptgeschäfts|führer general manager; ~sitz principal place of business; ~zeit rush (peak) hours.

Haupt|kassierer chief (head) cashier; ~lieferant original (prime, main) contractor; ~motiv *(Werbung)* keynote idea; ~niederlassung main office, principal establishment; ~postamt head (general, *Br.*) post office; ~schuldner principal [debtor]; ~sendezeit prime time; seinen ~sitz haben to headquarter; ~**straße** principal street, main street, high street; ~**strecke** artery, arterial highway, *(Eisenbahn)* main road; ~**umschlagplatz** staple place; ~**verkaufszeit** peak season, peak hours.

Hauptverkehrs|**linie** heavy traffic (trunk, *US*) line, main stem *(US)*; ~**straße** thoroughfare, highway; ~**zeit** rush (busy) hours, peak time.

Hauptversammlung general (company, stockholders', *US*) meeting, regular meeting *(US)*; außerordentliche ~ special (extraordinary, *Br.)* meeting; ~ **einberufen** to call a meeting of shareholders *(Br.)* (stockholders, *US*).

Haupt|**versammlungsbeschluß** corporate resolution *(US)*; ~**versorgungsbasis** key supply; ~**zollamt** Excise Office *(Br.)*.

Haus house, building, premises, dwelling, home; **zum Verkauf angebotenes** ~ house advertised for sale; **bezugsfertiges** ~ vacant possession; **zahlungsfähiges** ~ solvent merchant; ~**feuerversichern** to insure one's house against fire; ~ **ganzjährig voll vermietet haben** to have a property 100 per cent rented at all times; ~ **mit Vorkaufsrecht mieten** to rent a building with the option of purchase; ~ **in Einzelwohnungen vermieten** to let off (rent) a house into flats; ~**angestellte** [domestic] servant; ~**bank** borrower's bank; ~**besitzer** householder, owner of a house; ~**einweihung** house warming party.

Häuserkomplex set of houses, block of buildings *(US)*.

Haushalt household, *(Budget)* budget, estimates; **ausgeglichener** ~ balanced budget; **getrennter** ~ separate establishment; **seinen** ~ **auflösen** to break up one's household; ~ **einbringen** to bring in (introduce) the estimates.

Haushalts|**abstriche** budget cuts; ~**anforderungen** budget request; ~**ansatz** estimates, budget; ~**ausgleich** budget equilibrium; ~**ausschuß** budget (appropriation, *US*) committee, Committee of Supply (Ways and Means, *Br.*), House Ways and Means Committee *(US)*; ~**ausweis** budget statement; ~**bewilligung** budget grant, voting the estimates; ~**defizit** budget[ary] deficit; ~**defizit herbeiführen** to put the budget in the red; ~**experte** budget specialist (analyst); ~**jahr** budgetary (financial, *Br.*, fiscal, *US*) year; ~**kürzungen vornehmen** to prune a budget; ~**mittel** budgetary appropriation (means), budget funds; ~**nachtrag** supplementary budget (estimate); ~**packung** family size, giant package; ~**plan** budget, the Estimates *(Br.)*; ~**plan aufstellen** to draw up the Estimates *(Br.)*; **langfristige** ~**politik** long-range budgeting.

haushaltsrechtliche Bestimmungen budgetary regulations.

Haushalts|**rede** budget message; ~**titel** budget item (heading); ~**titel auflösen** to deobligate.

Haushaltsvoranschlag estimate of expenditure, budgetary estimate, the Estimates *(Br.)*;

~ **bewilligen** to vote the appropriation (Estimates, *Br.*, funds).

Haushalts|**vorgriff** advances on the succeeding budget, credit *(Br.)*; ~**vorlage** appropriation (budget, *US*) bill, budget document;

Haushaltungs|**buch** housekeeping account; ~**fragebogen** census paper; ~**vorstand** household head.

Hausieren hawking, peddling, peddlery; ~ **verboten!** No canvassing allowed!

Hausierer peddler, pedlar *(Br.)*, hawker, canvasser, itinerant vendor (dealer, trader); ~**gewerbe** hawking business, itinerant trade.

Hausierhandel house-to-house selling, itinerant peddling (trade), peddlery, pedlary *(Br.)*.

Haus|**industrie** domestic industry (system); ~**instandhaltungskosten** occupancy expenses; ~**marke** private (own) brand, *(Händler)* dealer's brand; ~**meister** doorkeeper, custodian, concierge, caretaker, janitor *(US)*; ~**number** street number; ~**ordnung** *(Hotel)* hotel regulations.

Hausse rise, bull movement, bullish demonstration; **auf** ~ **spekulieren** to speculate on a rise; ~**bewegung** bull movement, bullish demonstration (performance); ~**engagements** bull account, the long interest (account, *US*); ~**kauf** purchase for a rise, bull purchase; ~**partei** bull clique; ~**position** bull account (position); ~**spekulant** bull, infalter, operator (speculator) for a rise; ~**stimmung** bullish tendency (tone); ~**tendenz** bullishness.

Haussier bull, long, inflator.

haussieren to feel bullish, to be all bulls.

Haus|**stand** household; **genormte** ~**teile vorfertigen** to prefabricate; ~**versicherung** home insurance; ~**verwalter** property manager; ~**wart** caretaker, porter, concierge, janitor *(US)*; ~**zeitschrift** company magazine, house organ; ~**zinssteuer** inhabitated house duty, rent tax.

Havarie average, ship damage, damage by sea; **nicht gegen große und besondere** ~ **versichert** free of all average; **einfache** ~ partial (simple, common) average; ~ **aufmachen** to assess the damage, to settle the average; ~**aufmachung** assessment (statement) of damage; ~**beitrag** average contribution; ~**gelder** average charges (expenses, money); ~**gutachten** damage survey; ~**kommissar** claims (average) agent; ~**rechnung** average account; ~**schaden** average loss, damage by sea water; ~**vertreter** average adjuster (stater, agent); ~**zertifikat** survey report.

Hebe|**liste** assesment roll, tax book; ~**satz** collection rate.

Hebung des Lebensstandards improvement of the standard of living.

Heft|**klammer** [paper] clip, staple; ~**zwecke** drawing pin *(Br.)*, thumbtack *(US)*.

Heim|**arbeit** indoor work, outwork; ~**arbeiter** taker-in, outside worker, outworker.

Heimat|**anschrift** home address; ~**hafen** home port, port of registry.

Heim|industrie cottage (home, domestic) industry; **auf der ~reise begriffen** homeward bound.

Heimstätten|besitzer homecrofter *(Br.)*, homesteader *(US)*; **~grundstück** homecroft *(Br.)* homestead *(US)* lot.

Helfer in Steuersachen tax counsel[(l)or] (preparer).

Heller, keinen roten wert not worth a rap (picayune, cent, whoop).

herabdrücken, Kurse to bear the market; **Preise ~ to** force down the prices.

herabgesetztes Kapital reduced capital.

herabsetzen to lower, to reduce, to make a reduction, to depress, to bring down, *(Konkurrenzerzeugnisse)* to disparage; **Diskont[satz] ~** to lower (reduce, cut) the discount (bank, *Br.,* rediscount, *US)* rate; **Kapital ~** to reduce (write down) capital; **Tarif ~** to cut the rates.

herabsetzende Werbung knocking *(Br.)* (competitive, US) copy.

Herabsetzung lowering, reduction, cut, cutting [down], bringing (levelling) down, *(Kapital)* cut, reduction, *(Konkurrenzerzeugnisse)* disparagement; **~ des Grundkapitals** reduction of share capital *(Br.)* (capital stock, *US)*; **~ der Qualität von Waren** slander of goods.

heranziehen *(Fachkraft)* to consult, to call in; **j. zur Beitragsleistung ~** to collect dues from s. o.; **Kapital ~** to attract (mobilize) capital.

heraufsetzen, Diskontsatz to increase the discount (bank, *Br.,* rediscount, *US)* rate; **Höchstkurs ~** to lift the top; **Zinsfuß ~** to increase the rate of interest.

herausbringen *(Buch)* to bring (get) out, to publish, *(Fabrikat)* to turn (get) out; **Nachricht groß ~** to splash a piece of news.

Herausgabe *(Bücher, Zeitungen)* publishing, publication, issue; **~anspruch** revindication, claiming back.

herausgeben *(Bücher)* to publish, to edit, to issue; **Wechselgeld ~** to give change for.

herauskommen *(mit einem Artikel)* to come (bring) out, to put on the market; **in Lieferungen ~** to be issued in instal(l)ments.

heraus|wirtschaften to earn, to obtain, to make a profit; **jem. seinen Anteil ~zahlen** to pay s. o. out.

hereingeben *(Wertpapiere)* to deposit, to give on.

Hereinholung von Aufträgen soliciation of orders.

hereinkommen *(Aufträge)* to come in, to perk up.

Hereinnahme von Wechseln discounting of bills.

hereinnehmen *(Börse)* to carry over, to take in *(Br.)*; **zum Diskont ~** to discount; **Ware ~** to take in stock.

Herkunft, ausländischer of foreign origin.

Herkunfts|bescheinigung certificate of origin; **~bezeichnung** informative labelling; **~ort** point of origin *(US)*.

Hermes|bürgschaft *[etwa]* Export Credit Guarantee; **~gesellschaft** *[etwa]* Export Credits Guarantee

Department *(Br.)*, Foreign Credit Insurance Association *(US)*.

herrenlos vacant, unappropriated, unowned; **~e Aktie** unclaimed share (stock, *US)*.

herrschend|e Mode leading fashion; **~es Unternehmen** controlling company.

herstellen to make, to fabricate, to manufacture; **fabrikmäßig ~** to manufacture, *(Hausteile)* to prefabricate; **lagermäßig ~** to make for stock; **maschinell ~** to machine; **serienmäßig ~** to serialize.

Hersteller maker, fabricator, fabricant, producer, operator, manufacturing man, manufacturer; **mit geringen Selbstkosten arbeitender ~** low-cost-operator; **~firma** manufacturer, manufacturing firm; **~land** manufacturing (producer) country; **~marke** producer's (manufacturer's) mark; **~zeichen** trademark.

Herstellung making, fabrication, manufacture, manufacturing, producing, production; **fabrikmäßige ~** wholesale manufacture; **serienmäßige ~** serialization, mass (volume) production; **~ am laufenden Band** standardized mass production; **~ einstellen** to discontinue the manufacture; **in der ~ begriffen sein** to be in process of production.

Herstellungs|abteilung manufacturing division, *(Verlag)* production department (division); **~aufwand** original cost; **~beschränkungen** production restrictions; **billigster ~betrieb** lowest-cost manufacturer; **~dauer** production time; **~firma** manufacturing company; **~jahr** year of manufacture; **~kosten** cost of manufacturing (goods manufactured), manufacturing cost (expenses); **~land** producing country; **~preis** cost of manufacture, manufacturing (manufacture's, production) price; **~programm** manufacturing (production) program(me); **~prozeß** manufacturing (industrial) process, productive technique; **alleiniges ~recht haben** to have the exclusive rights in a production; **~verbot** production prohibition; **~verfahren** manufacturing (production) process; **~vorschriften** production prescriptions; **~wert** production (productive) value, *(Selbstkosten)* cost value.

herunter|gehen, etw. *(Kurse)* to ease a fraction; **mit dem Preis ~** to reduce (lower) the price; **~gekommen** down at heel, in reduced circumstances; **in ~gekommenem Zustand** *(Geschäft)* in a run-down condition; **~handeln** to beat down, to knock off; **Ausgaben ~schrauben** to cut down expenses; **Gehalt stark ~setzen** to slash a salary; **~wirtschaften** to run down, to bring low.

Heuerbüro shipping office *(Br.)*.

heuern to hire, to recruit, to engage, to ship.

Heuervertrag ship's articles, company service contract *(Br.)*, *(Schiff)* charterparty.

Hilfe, finanzielle grant, financial aid.

Hilfs|abkommen auf Gegenseitigkeit mutual aid plan; **~aktion** provident scheme, relief work; **~anlage**

(Betrieb) emergency set; ~**arbeiter** unskilled (subsidiary) worker; ~**betrieb** service department *(US)*; ~**buchhalter** assistant bookkeeper; ~**fonds** relief (aid, emergency) fund; ~**gelder zahlen** to subsidize; ~**kasse** relief (provident) fund; ~**kostenstelle** nonproductive department; ~**kräfte im Büro** secretarial help; ~**landeplatz** emergency landing field; ~**mittel** resources, purse, auxiliary means, *(Notbehelf)* expedient, makeshift; ~**organisation** relief organization (agency), welfare association; ~**organisationen der Vereinten Nationen** specialized agencies of the United Nations; ~**quellen** resources, potential, purse; ~**schicht** relief (swing, *US*) shift; ~**schiff** relief ship; ~**stelle** aid center *(US)* (centre, *Br.)*; Roh-, ~- **und Betriebsstoffe** *(Bilanz)* raw materials and supplies; ~**werk** relief organization (agency); ~**zug** relief (emergency, supply, breakdown) train.

Hin- und Rück|fahrkarte return, return (round trip, *US*) ticket.

hinauftreiben *(Preise)* to run (push, send, force) up.

hinausschieben, Fälligkeit eines Wechsels to prolong (renew) a bill of exchange.

Hin|flug outgoing flight; ~**fracht** freight out.

hinhalten, seine Gläubiger mit Versprechungen to feed one's creditors with empty promises.

Hinhaltungstaktik delaying tactics, stall *(US sl.)*.

hinkende Währung limping standard.

hintenherum | ergattern to wangle, to get under the counter; ~ **verkaufen** to sell on the quiet.

Hinterbliebenen|bezüge widow's benefit *(Br.)*; ~**pension** [war] pension, *(Eheleute)* survivor's pension; ~**rente** death benefit, [war] pension.

Hinterland hinterland, back country, upstate *(US)*.

hinterlassen *(Erbschaft)* to leave, *(Grundbesitz)* to devise, *(Vermächtnis)* to give and to bequeath.

hinterlegen, Betrag to deposit an amount; **bei Gericht** ~ to pay into the court; **Kaution für j.** ~ to put up bail for s. o..

hinterlegt|e Aktie deposited share (stock, *US*); ~**er Betrag** deposit; ~**es Geld** trust money.

Hinterlegung deposit, deposition, depositation, bailment;
gegen ~ **von** on depositing of;
öffentliche ~ custody of the law;
~ **von Geld** lodging of money; ~ **von Wertpapieren** deposit of securities;

Hinterlegungs|abteilung *(Bank)* escrow department; ~**bescheid** notice of deposit *(Br.)*; ~**kosten** costs of deposit; ~**schein** depository (trust) receipt, certificate of deposit, trustee's certificate; ~**summe** money deposited, *(Börse)* margin; ~**stelle** prosimple (bare, *US*) trust; ~**vertrag** deposit, escrow agreement, delivery in escrow, *(entgeltlich)* ~ lucrative hire, *(unentgeltlicher)* gratuitous bailment.

Hintermann backer, bottleholder;
einflußreicher ~ agent of influence, fat cat *(sl.)*.

hinterziehen, Einkommensteuer to defraud the revenue, to evade paying taxes.

Hinweis indication, reference, hint, tipoff, lead;
~ **am schwarzen Brett anbringen** to post an announcement on the notice board.

Hinzuschlagen der Zinsen zum Kapital capitalization of interest.

hoch high, *(im Kurs)* up, stiff, *(im Preis)* high, hard;
zu ~ **versichert** overinsured;
sich dauernd ~**halten** *(Kurse)* to continue high;
~ **zu stehen kommen** to cost dear.

Hochachtung, mit vorzüglicher yours faithfully, very respectfully yours, yours very truly *(US)*.

Hochfinanz haute (high, *US*) finance, world of high finance.

hoch|gehen *(Preise)* to go up, to rise; ~**geschraubte Forderungen** exaggerated demands.

Hochhaus multi-story *(US)* (high-rise) building, skyscraper *(US)*;
~**garage** parking garage, autosilo.

Hochkonjunktur cyclical boom, boom times, peak season, booming economy;
~ **bremsen** to curb the boom;
~**niveau** boom-time level.

hochqualifiziert highly qualified, high-calibre(-level).

Hochsaison peak (high, height of the) season.

Hochschul|absolvent [university] graduate; ~**ausbildung** university training; ~**bildung** university (tertiary, college, higher) education (level); ~**lehrgang** college course, university extension.

Hochsee|dampfer ocean-going ship; ~**fischerei** deep-sea fishing; ~**schiffahrt** high-seas navigation.

Höchst|alter maximum age; ~**bedarf** peak of the demand; ~**betrag** maximum [amount], *(Preisgrenze)* limit, *(Versicherung)* office limit; ~**bietender** best bidder; ~**gebot** closing (highest, last) bid, best offer; ~**gehalt** maximum salary, ceiling; ~**geschwindigkeit** maximum (top, permissible) speed; ~**gewicht** maximum weight, working load; ~**grenze** maximum, *(Versicherungen)* gross line; ~**kredit** line of credit.

Höchstkurs top (maximum, peak, highest) price, maximum rate, high record;
~**e erreichen** to reach peak levels; **in rascher Steigerung neue** ~**e erzielen** to shoot into new high ground *(US)*; **zu** ~**en verkaufen** to sell at best.

Höchst|leistung top (maximum, peak) output; **gesetzliche** ~**miete** rent ceiling.

Höchstpreis highest (outside, peak, maximum, top) price, peak maximum [rate];
festgesetzter (gesetzlicher) ~ ceiling [price];
~ **erzielen** to secure the best value; ~**e festsetzen** to clamp ceilings on prices.

Höchststand high, highest (peak) level, *(Kurse)* top price;
absoluter (einmaliger) ~ all-time high *(US)*;
auf seinen wirtschaftlichen ~ **bringen** to upgrade economically.

Höchst|verkaufspreis maximum selling price; ~**wert** maximum (top, peak) value.

hochtreiben to force up, to boost, *(US)*;
Kurse ~ to bull the market.

hochwertige Anlagewerte high-grade investments, blue chips *(US)*.

Höflichkeits|besuch courtesy visit; **~floskeln** forms of address.

hoh|e Anforderungen stellen to make great demands; **ᵉe Behörde** *(EG)* High Authority; **auf die ~e Kante legen** to put away for a rainy day.

Höhe *(Ausmaß)* extent, measure, *(Preise)* level; **durchschnittliche ~ des Diskontkredits** line of discount; **~ des Schadens** measure of damage; **Geschäft wieder in die ~ bringen** to put a business back on its feet again; **plötzlich in die ~ gehen** to [go up with a] jump; **j. bis zur ~ von . . . für kreditwürdig halten** to consider s. o. trustworthy to the extent of . . .; **Aktie um 44 Punkte auf 640 in die ~ treiben** to bid up a stock 44 points to 640.

Hoheits|abzeichen *(Flugzeug)* national marking; **~akt** act of state; **~gewässer** territorial sea (waters).

höher | bewertet of higher value, *(Effekten)* high-priced; **~ denn je stehen** *(Kurse)* to be at an all-time high *(US)*; **~e Schulbildung** secondary education.

Höher|bewertung write-up, writing up; **~gebot** higher bid.

Holdinggesellschaft holding (controlling, proprietary, *US,* parent) company.

Honorar [retaining] fee, honorarium, terms; **festes ~** salary compensation, general retainer.

Honorar|konsul honorary consul; **~rechnung** bill of costs *(Br.)*.

honorieren to fee, *(Wechsel)* to hono(u)r; **nicht ~** to refuse payment; **Wechsel nicht ~** to dishono(u)r a bill of exchange.

Hörer|analyse listener (audience, *Br.)* research; **~publikum** [listening] audience.

Hörfunkwerbung radio advertising.

Hortung von Arbeitskräften labo(u)r hoarding.

Hortungskäufe panic buying (purchase).

Hotel hotel; **Ia ~** high-class hotel; **erst[klassig]es ~** first (high) -class hotel; **~garni** residential hotel, apartment hotel *(US)*; **~ der gehobenen Mittelklasse** upper-bracket hotel; **~ nach Rechnungsbegleichung verlassen** to check out of a hotel *(US)*; **~angestellter** hotel clerk (employee); **~anzeiger** hotel directory; **~betrieb** hotel operation; **~bett** hotel bed; **~direktor** hotel manager; **~halle** entrance hall, lobby, foyer, lounge; **~nachweis** hotel broker; **~rechnung** [hotel] bill; **~reservierung** hotel booking; **~restaurant** hotel dining room; **~unterbringung,** **~unterkunft** hotel (sleeping) accommodation; **vom ~zimmer aus seiner Arbeit nachgehen** to work from a hotel room.

Hubschrauberlandeplatz heliport, helicopter terminal.

Huckepackverkehr roll-on (roll-off) service.

Hypothek [real estate] mortgage, landed security, dead pledge, hypothec; **aufgewertete ~** revalorized mortgage; **erst[stellig]e ~** first *(Br.)* (senior) mortgage; **mit einer Lebensversicherung gekoppelte ~** insured mortgage; **nachrangige ~** overlying (subsequent, junior, puisne, *Br.)* mortgage; **verfallene ~** default (foreclosed) mortgage; **~ über einen festen Betrag** fixed mortgage; **~ ablösen** to redeem (pay off, satisfy) a mortgage; **~ amortisieren** to pay off (extinguish) a mortgage; **~ auf ein Haus aufnehmen** to raise a mortgage on a house; **aus einer ~ die Zwangsvollstreckung betreiben** to foreclose a mortgage [deed], to levy an execution; **~ kündigen** *(Gläubiger)* to foreclose a mortgage, *(Schuldner)* to give notice of redemption; **~ im Grundbuch löschen** to release a mortagage; **~en verschiedenen Ranges zusammenschreiben** to tack mortgages.

Hypothekar|darlehen mortgage loan; **~gläubiger** mortgage creditor.

hypothekarisch| belasten to borrow money on the security of an estate, to [encumber with a] mortgage; **~e Beleihung eines Grundstücks** raising of a mortgage on an estate; **~e Forderung** mortgage claim.

Hypothekar|kredit mortgage (real-estate) loan; **~schuldverschreibungen** [corporate] mortgage bonds *(US)* (debentures, *Br.)*.

Hypotheken|ablösung redemption of a mortgage; **~abtretung** assignment of a mortgage; **~angebot** mortgage facility; **~ausleihungen** mortgage lending; **~bank** mortgage (land) bank; **~belastung** mortgage charge, encumbrance, incumbrance; **~bestellung** delivery (creation) of a mortgage.

Hypotheken|darlehn mortgage loan; **~eigentümer** mortgagee; **~eintragung** registration *(Br.)* (recording, *US)* of a mortgage; **~forderung** mortgage debt (claim); **~geschäft** mortgage business (investments); **~gläubiger** mortgage creditor; **~klausel** *(Feuerversicherung)* mortgage clause; **~kredit** mortgage broker; **~markt** mortgage market; **~pfandbrief** mortgage note (debenture, *Br.)*; **mit einer ~rate in Verzug kommen** to miss a payment on one's home.

Hypothekenschuld hypothecary (mortgage) debt; **~ bezahlen** to satisfy (pay off, cancel, wipe off) a mortgage.

Hypotheken|schuldner mortgager, mortgagor; **~tilgung** extinguishment of a mortgage; **~übernahme** assumption of a mortgage; **~valuta** mortgage money; **~zinsen** mortgage interest.

I

Ideen|anreger *(Werbung)* ideas man; ~**sitzung** brainstorming.

Identitäts|karte identification (identity) card; ~**nachweis** identity certificate, *(Zoll)* certificate of orgin.

illiquide nonliquid, illiquid, insolvent.

Imagewerbung prestige (goodwill, indirect-action) advertising.

immateriell|e Anlagewerte *(Patente, Firmenwert)* fixed (intangible) assets, incorporeal chattels; ~**er Wert** *(Firma)* goodwill.

Immobiliar|kredit real-estate credit; ~**vermögen** real estate, realty, landed property.

Immobilien real things (estate), realty, immovables; ~**anlageberater** real-estate investment counsellor; ~**büro** real-estate office (agency), land agency; ~**fonds** real-estate investment trust; ~**geschäft** real-estate business; ~**makler** real-estate dealer (broker) *(US)*, house agent, land agent (broker, *Br.)*, realtor *(US)*; ~**markt** real-estate market (section).

Import|e, billige cut-price (low-price) imports; ~**abgabe** import surcharge; ~**artikel** imported stocks, imports; ~**erklärung** bill of entry *(Br.)*; ~**firma** importing firm, importer; ~**geschäft** import business (trade), *(einzelnes)* import transaction; ~**haus** importing firm; ~**industrie** importing industry; ~**kaufmann** import merchant, importer; ~**konnossement** inward bill of lading; ~**kontingent** import quota; ~**kredit** import credit; ~**lizenz** import licence; ~**monopol** import monopoly; ~**ware** imported stocks (goods), imports.

Impulskäufe impulse buying.

Inanspruchnahme use, utilization, availment; **ohne ~ öffentlicher Mittel** without recourse to public funds; **übermäßige ~ von Geldmitteln** drain on financial resources; **~ der Landeszentralbankfazilitäten** *[etwa]* memberbank borrowings *(US)*.

Inbetriebnahme opening, putting into operation.

Index index, *(Inhaltsverzeichnis)* register, table of contents; **gewogener ~** weighted index [number]; **unbewerteter ~** unweighted index; **~ der Großhandelspreise** wholesale-price index; **~ der industriellen Nettoproduktion** national production index; **~, dem der Durchschnitt von 1914 mit 100 zugrunde liegt** index based on 1914 averages as 100; **²gebunden** tied to the index; ~**währung** multiple (tabulator) standard, commodity (neutral) money; ~**ziffer** index number; ~**ziffern der Börsenkurse** Standard and poor's indices *(US)*.

indirekte Arbitrage indirect (triangular, *US)* arbitration.

Indossament indorsement, endorsement; **beschränktes ~** conditional (qualified, restrictive) indorsement;

~ ohne Obligo (Rückkehr) indorsement (endorsement) without resource; **Wechsel durch ~ übertragen** to indorse (endorse) a bill of exchange.

Indossant indorser, endorser.

indossieren to indorse, to endorse, to place an indorsement (endorsement), to negotiate.

industrialisieren to industrialize.

Industrialisierungsprozeß process of industrialization.

Industrie [manufacturing] industry; **mit geringen Unkosten (niedrigen Selbstkosten) arbeitende ~** low-cost production; **bodenständige ~n** stable industries; **zollpolitisch geschützte ~** sheltered (protected, *US)* industry; **lebenswichtige ~** vital industry; **saisonbedingte ~** seasonal industry; **staatlich subventionierte ~** subsidized industry; **durch Staatsaufträge unterstützte ~** sheltered (bounty-fed) industry *(Br.)*; **verarbeitende ~** manufacturing (finishing, processing, process) industry; **~ für Güter des gehobenen Bedarfs** sophisticated industry; **einheimische ~ steuerlich begünstigen** to benefit local industry; **Wachstum der ~ verlangsamen** to slow down industrial expansion.

Industrie|abnehmer industrial customer; ~**aktien** industrial equities (shares, *Br.*, stocks, *US)*; ~**anlagen** industrial installations, *(Investitionen)* industrial investments; ~**arbeiter** industrial labo(u)rer (worker), factory (production) worker; ~**artikel** manufactured goods; ~**ausstellung** industrial exhibition; ~**ausstoß** industrial output; **in einem anderen ~bereich Fuß fassen** to gain a foothold in another industry; ~**betrieb** manufacturing establishment (plant); ~**bezirk** industrial area (district); ~**dunst** smog; ~**erfahrung** industrial experience; ~**erwartungsland** industrial estate; *(Br.)* ~**erzeugnis** industrial product; ~**führer** captain of industry; ~**gebiet** industrial area (community); ~**gelände** industrial sites (estate); ~**und Handelskammer der USA** United States Chamber of Commerce *(US)*; ~**komplex** industry complex; ~**kredit** industrial credit (loan); ~**kundschaft** *(Werbeagentur)* industrial accounts.

industriell|es Erzeugnis industrial (manufactured) product; ~**e Kapazität** industrial capacity; ~**es Wachstum** industrial growth.

Industrieller industrialist, industrial [producer].

Industrie|markt *(Börse)* industrial market (list), *(Börsenbericht)* „industrials"; ~**messe** industries fair; ~**nation** industrial nation (power); ~**organisation** industrial machine *(US)*; ~**produkte** industrial (maufactured) goods; ~**siedlung** industrial (trading, *Br.)* estate; ~**spionage** industrial espionage; ~**stadt** industrial city, manufacturing town; ~**unternehmen** industrial concern (establishment, cor-

poration, undertaking; ~**verband** industrial organization (association); ~**verlagerung** translocation (relocation) of industry; ~**viertel** industrial area (district, estate); ~**werte** *(Börse)* industrial equities (issues, features), industrials.

Industriezweig manufacturing branch, manufacture, industry, line (group, branch) of industry; **devisenschwache** ~**e** soft-goods industries; **dienstleistungsorientere** ~**e** service-oriented industries; **zollpolitisch nicht geschützte** ~ unsheltered *(Br.)* (unprotected, *US)* industries; **unterbezahlte** ~**e** sweated industries; **ganze** ~ **stillegen** to shut down whole industries.

Inflation, durch Lohnsteigerung bedingte wage-push inflation; **kostentreibende** ~ cost-push inflation; **schleichende** ~ creeping inflation; **zügellose** ~ runaway inflation; ~ **anheizen** to kindle (prime) inflation; ~ **in den Griff bekommen** to bring inflation under control; ~ **zurückdrängen** to hold the line on inflation.

inflationärer Preisanstieg inflationary hike.

inflationistischer Druck inflationary pressure.

inflationsbedingt inflation induced.

Inflations|bekämpfung inflation fighting; ~**faktor** inflationary factor; ~**gewinn** inflationary profit (gain); ~**maßnahmen** protection against inflation; ~**orientiert sein** to tend to inflation; ~**politik** inflationary policy; ~**rate** rate of inflation; **verlangsamtes** ~**tempo** slowdown of inflation; ~**währung** inflated currency; ~**wirkungen** effects of inflation; **rasante** ~**zunahme** inflationary upsurge.

Informations|brief newsletter; ~**lücke** communication gap; ~**material** information, research (handout) material; ~**quelle** source (repository) of information; ~**stelle** information bureau.

Infrastruktur infrastructure.

Inhaber *(Besitzer)* possessor, *(Eigentümter)* proprietor, owner, *(Gasthof)* innkeeper, *(Geschäft)* principal, proprietor, head; **auf den** ~ **lautend** in bearer form; **zahlbar an den** ~ payable to bearer; **gutgläubiger** ~ bona-fide holder; **rechtmäßiger** ~ lawful (legitimate) owner; ~ **eines Bankkontos** owner of a banking account; ~ **einer Schuldverschreibung** debenture holder; ~ **eines Spezialgeschäfts** limited-line retailer, stockist *(Br.);* **auf den** ~ **ausstellen** to issue (make out) to bearer.

Inhaber|aktie bearer share, share payable to bearer, bearer stock *(US);* ~**indossament** endorsement made out to bearer; ~**obligation** bearer bond, bond (debenture) to bearer, *(ohne Giro)* clean bond, *(mit Zinsschein)* coupon bond *(US);* ~**papier** bearer instrument, instrument (certificate) payable to bearer; ~**schuldverschreibung** bearer (registered) debenture (bond, *Br.);* ~**zertifikat** bearer certificate, depositary receipt.

Inkassi, ausländische foreign collections; **spesenfreie** ~ free items *(US);* ~ **besorgen** to effect collections.

Inkasso encashment, debt collecting, collection; ~ **zum Pariwert** par collection; ~ **von Wechseln zum Pariwert ohne Abzug der Spesen** par collection of checks *(US);* ~ **eines Wechsels besorgen** to attend to the collection of a bill; **zum** ~ **vorlegen** (vorzeigen) to present for collection; ~**abschnitt** collection item; ~**auftrag** encashment (collection) order; ~**auskunftsabteilung** tracer department *(US);* ~**bearbeiter** collection manager, collector; ~**bote** *(Bank)* walk clerk *(Br.);* ~**formular** collection form; ~**gebühr** collection fee (commission); ~**geschäft** collection work, collecting (collection) business; ~**kosten** collection expense; ~**provision** collection commission, *(Versicherung)* renewal commission; ~**scheck** collection check *(US)* (cheque, *Br.);* ~**spesen** collection charges (expense); ~**vollmacht** letter of delegation, power to collect; ~**wechsel** short (country) bill, bill for collection, collection item.

Inland, im within the country (realm); **im** ~ **aufgenommen werden** *(Produktion)* to be absorbed by'the internal market.

inländisch inland, domestic, native, internal, home, inward, home-made; ~**er Bedarf** domestic (internal) demands; ~**er Verbrauch** home consumption.

Inlands|abgabe inland duty; ~**bedarf,** ~**bedürfnisse** domestic needs, internal (domestic, home) consumption (demand); ~**erzeugnisse** home-produced (homemade) goods; ~**fluglinie** internal air route; ~**investitionen** domestic investments; ~**markt** domestic (home, inland) market; ~**porto** inland (domestic) postage; ~**post** inland mail *(Br.),* (domestic) mail *(US);* ~**preis** domestic (home-market) price, home rate; ~**produkte** home-made goods; ~**schuldverschreibungen** internal bonds; ~**spediteur** inland carrier, country shipper *(US);* ~**tarif** inland tariff, domestic rates; ~**verbrauch** home use (consumption); ~**währung** internal currency; ~**wechsel** domestic (inland, *Br.)* bill of exchange.

Innen|abschnitt *(Anzeige)* gutter bleed; ~**dienst** office work, indoor service; ~**stadt** center *(US)* (centre, *Br.)* of a town.

Insassenunfallversicherung motor vehicle passenger insurance.

Inserat insertion, insert, advertisement, ad *(US);* ~ **aufgeben** to put in (insert) an advertisement.

Inseraten|annahme advertisement department, advertising office; ~**werber** canvasser.

inserieren to insert, to advertise for; **in einer Zeitung** ~ to put an advertisement in a newspaper.

Insertions|auftrag space order; ~**gebühren** advertising fees (charges).

Insichgeschäft *(jur.)* agent and patient.

Insolventenliste black list.

Inspektion inspection, visit, survey, examination; **sein Auto regelmäßig zur** ~ **bringen** to have one's car serviced regularly.

Instandhaltungs|konto maintenance expense account; ~**kosten** cost[s] of maintenance, maintenance charges; ~**verpflichtung** *(Pächter)* impeachment of waste; ~**vertrag** maintenance contract.

Instandsetzungs|arbeiten repairs; ~**konto** maintenance-expense account; ~**kosten** maintenance expenses (costs).

institutionelle Werbung institutional advertising.

Instrumentarium, konjunkturpolitisches economic policy tools.

Interesse, gegen das öffentliche contrary to public policy; **im öffentlichen** ~ for the public benefit; **berechtigtes** ~ legitimate interest; **finanzielles** ~ moneyed (pecuniary) interest; **versicherbares** ~ insurable interest;
sich auf Wahrnehmung berechtigter ~**n berufen** to plead justification; **jds.** ~**n gefährden** to jeopardize s. one's interests; **im öffentlichen** ~ **liegen** to benefit public welfare; ~**n wahren** *(Börsenmakler)* to protect (guard) interests; **jds.** ~ **wahrnehmen** to protect (safeguard) s. one's interests.

Interessen|abstimmung agreement of interests; ~**gebiet** sphere of influence (interests); ~**gemeinschaft** community of interest, *(Arbeitsgemeinschaft)* working agreement, *(Bank)* combination, *(Kartell)* syndicate, combine; ~**käufe** *(Börse)* support buying.

Interessent party interested (concerned), *(potentieller Käufer)* prospective purchaser, *(Lobbyist)* lobbyist, pressure group.

Interessen|verpflechtung interlocking interests; **bezahlter** ~**vertreter** bendable lobbyist.

Interims|abkommen temporary agreement; ~**dividende** interim dividend, dividend on account; ~**konto** suspense (interim) account.

Interimschein *(Aktie)* scrip, scrip (provisional) certificate *(Br.)*, interim (temporary) [stock] certificate *(US)*.

international|er Devisenmarkt international exchange market; ~**e Handelskammer** International Chamber of Commerce; ~ **geschütztes Warenzeichen** international trademark.

Intervenient intervening party, intervenient, intervenant, intervener, *(Prozeß)* interpleader.

intervenieren to intervene, to intermediate; **am Effektenmarkt** ~ to give supporting orders; **als Notadressat** ~ to accept for hono(u)r.

Intervention intervention, intercession, *(Kursstützung)* supporting order, banking support, *(Wechsel)* acceptance (payment) for hono(u)r; **staatliche** ~ *(in der Wirtschaft)* direct intervention in the economy.

Interventions|akzept, ~**annahme** acceptance for (upon) hono(u)r (supra protest); ~**käufe** *(Börse)* supporting orders, *(Währungsfonds)* intervention buying; ~**kurs** *(Währungsfonds)* intervention price; ~**syndikat** supporting syndicate.

Interzonen|abkommen interzonal agreement; ~**handel** interzonal trade.

Intimsphäre privacy.

Invaliden|marke insurance stamp; ~**rente** *(Altersrente)* old-age annuity (pension), retirement pension, primary benefit *(US)*, *(Arbeitsunfähigkeit)* disablement (dependant's, *Br.)* benefit; ~**rentner** old-age pensioner, annuity holder; ~**versicherung** *(Altersversicherung)* social security tax, *(Arbeitsunfähigkeit)* disablement (disability, *US)* insurance.

Invalidität disablement, permanent incapacity; **dauernde** ~ permanent disability *(US)*.

Invaliditäts|grad degree of disablement.

Inventar inventory, stock on hand, accountable (expendable, *US)* stores, *(Landwirt)* furnishings and fixtures;
tatsächlich aufgenommenes ~ physical inventory; **buchmäßiges** ~ book inventory; **totes** ~ dead stock; ~ **aufnehmen** to [make up] inventory.

Inventar|abschreibung inventory writedown; ~**aufnahme** inventory [taking] *(US)*, stocktaking *(Br.)*; ~**blatt** inventory sheet; ~**buch** inventory (balance-sheet) book.

inventarisieren to [make] inventory, to take inventory (stock, *Br.),* to catalog(ue).

Inventar|konto inventory (furniture and fixture) account; ~**liste** inventory; ~**preis** inventory price; ~**verlust** inventory loss; ~**verzeichnis** inventory, inventory record (schedule); ~**wert** inventory value, value of inventory, *(Investmentfonds)* net asset value.

Inventur stocktaking *(Br.)*, inventory [taking] *(US)*; **laufende** ~ book inventory *(US)*; **tatsächliche** ~ physical inventory *(US)*;

Inventur|arbeiten inventory proceedings *(US)*; ~**aufnahme** stocktaking *(Br.),* inventory [taking] *(US)*; ~**ausverkauf** clearance (inventory, *US)* sale, stocktaking sale *(Br.)*; ~**preis** inventory price *(US)*.

investieren to invest [capital] *(US)* to place (make) investments;
seine Ersparnisse in einem Geschäft ~ to invest one's savings in a business enterprise; **vorteilhaft** ~ to make a good investment.

investiertes Kapital capital invested.

Investition investment, investing, placement, capital spending;
durchgeführte ~**en** capital expenditure; **soziale** ~**en** social investments;
~**en im Immobiliensektor** real-estate investments; **für** ~**en im Ausland auswerfen** to dole out in overseas investments; ~**vornehmen** to place, to effect investments, to invest.

Investitions|abschreibungen investment allowance; ~**anleihe** investment loan; ~**aufwand** capital expenditure; ~**ausschuß** investment committee; **Europäische** ~**bank** European Investment Bank; ~**beihilfe** investment aid; ~**drosselung** capital expenditure cutback.

Investitionsgüter capital (industrial) goods; ~**aufwand** capital-goods outlay; ~**konjunktur** boom in the capital-goods industry.

Investitions|hilfe investment assistance (aid); **~ka-pital** capital investment (invested), investment capital; **~klima** investment climate; **nicht ab-schreibungsfähige ~kosten** uncoverable cost; **~pro-gramm** capital [expenditure] program(me), capital investment plan, program(me) of investment; **~project** investment project; **~risiko** investment risk; **~tempo** pace of investment; **~verbot** investment ban; **~vorhaben** investment plan (project), capital budget; **~zuschuß** investment grant; **für ~zwecke bestimmen** to earmark for investment.
Investmentanteil certificate of participation (interest, *US*), unit *(Br.)* collateral trust certificate *(US)*.
Investmentfonds investment fund (trust), unit trust *(Br.)*, mutual fund *(US)*;
thesaurierender ~ cumulative fund; **versicherungs-eigener** ~ in-house fund;
~ **mit unbeschränkter Anteilzahl** open-end investment fund *(US)*, nondiscretionary trust *(Br.)*; ~ **mit strengen Anlagevorschriften** nondiscretionary trust *(Br.)*; ~ **mit beliebiger Emissionshöhe** open-end fund *(US)*; ~ **mit auswechselbarem Portefeuille** flexible fund *(US)*; ~

mit veränderlichem Portefeuille managed fund *(US)*.
Investmentgesellschaft investment company (trust); ~ **mit breitgestreutem Aktienportefeuille** discretionary trust *(Br.)*.
Investment|sparen investment saving; **~zertifikat** certificate of participation (interest, *US*), unit *(Br.)*, collateral trust certificate *(US)*, mutual investment share.
irreführende Werbung deceptive advertising.
Irrtum | über die Bedeutung einer abgegebenen Willenserklärung mistake in expression of true agreement; ~ **über wesentliche Eigenschaften** mistake as to the quality of the subject matter; ~ **über die Geschäftsgrundlage** mistake as to the existence of the subject matter;
sich im ~ befinden to stand in error, to labo(u)r under a mistake (misapprehension).
Ist|ausgabe actual expenditure; **~bestand** real amount; **~kosten** actual costs; **~stärke** *(Betrieb)* manpower, total (effective, actual) strength; **~wert** true value; **~zeit** time taken, *(Zeitstudie)* clock (actual) hours.

J

Jagd nach Arbeitskräften raiding manpower.
Jahr, anrechnungsfähiges *(Sozialversicherung)* year of coverage; **steuerpflichtiges** ~ taxable (financial, fiscal, *US*) year.
Jahres|abonnement annual ticket; **~abschluß** [annual] accounts, annual balance [sheet], year-end closing; **~ausweis** annual report (return, statement *US*); **~auszug** [annual] accounts; **~beitrag** yearly (annual) subscription; **~bericht** financial (annual, *Br.*) report (return); **~bilanz** annual balance [sheet]; **~durchschnittsverdienst** annual average earnings; **~einkommen** annual income, yearly income (revenue); **~einnahme** annual receipts (revenue); **~ertrag** annual receipts (proceeds), *(Haus)* annual value *(Br.)*, purchase; **~fahrkarte** annual season ticket; **~gehalt beziehen** to be hired on a yearly basis; **~karte** annual ticket; **garantierter ~lohn** annual wage guarantee *(Br.)*; **~miete** annual rent, year's rental; **~prämie** *(Versicherung)* annual rate; **~produktion** annual production (output); **~rendite** annual return; **~rente** annuity.

Jahresschluß close of the year;
~bericht year-end report *(US)*; **~bilanz** postclosing balance sheet; **~vergütung** year-end compensation *(US)*.
Jahres|ultimo end off the year, year end; **~umsatz** annual turnover (sales); **mit den besten Wünschen zum ~wechsel** with the compliments of the season.
jahreszeitliche Belebung seasonal increase.
jährlich|e Abrechnung annual balance; ~ **erscheinende Zeitschrift** annual magazine.
Jahrmarkt fair, mart, market.
Journal journal [book], daybook, shop book *(US)*, diary, register;
amerikanisches ~ ledger-type journal;
~ **für einfache Buchführung** simple journal;
ins ~ **eintragen** to journalize.
Journalbuchung journal entry.
Journalistenausweis press credentials.
Jungfern|fahrt maiden trip (voyage); **~rede** maiden speek.
Juwelenversicherung jewelry insurance.

K

Kabel, transatlantisches transatlantic cable.
Kabel| adresse cable address; **~anweisung** cable money order; **~auszahlungssätze** cable rates; **~notierung** tape price (quotation); **~satz für Termingeschäfte** futures cable rate *(US)*.
Kabine cabin, *(Abteil)* compartment.
Kabinen| dampfer cabin cruiser; **~klasse** cabin class.
kaduzieren *(Aktien)* to declare forfeited, to forfeit.
Kai dock, pier, quay, wharf;
ab ~ ex wharf (quay); **längsseits ~** alongside the quay, berthed;
am ~ löschen to discharge at the quay;
~ablieferungsbescheinigung dock receipt, wharfinger's certificate *(Br.)*; **~arbeiter** stevedore, longshoreman *(US)*; **~gebühren** wharfage, berthage, pierage; **~lagerschein** wharfinger's warrant *(Br.)*.
Kalkulation calculation, computation;
knappe ~ close calculation;
~ aufstellen (vornehmen) to make a calculation, to work out the figures.
Kalkulationsaufschlag markup, markon *(US)*;
~ auf den Einstandspreis markup on cost.
Kalkulations| basis calculation basis; **~buch** cost ledger; **~fehler** miscalculation; **~tabelle** pricing schedule.
kalkulieren to calculate, to compute, to reckon, to estimate;
Preis sehr vorsichtig ~ to establish a price at a low level.
kaltgestellt werden to be left out in the cold.
Kammer für Handelssachen commercial court *(Br.)*.
Kampf| fonds *(Gewerkschaft)* strike fund; **~marke** fighting brand; **~preis** competitive (cut-rate) price; **~zoll** retaliatory duty.
Kanal| abgaben canal tolls; **~dampfer** cross-channel steamer.
Kannvorschrift discretionary clause.
Kantine canteen, company (industrial retail) store, factory snack shop *(US)*.
Kantinenwirt canteen keeper.
Kanzleipapier foolscap, briefpaper.
Kapazität, voll ausgenutzte full operating capacity; **ungenützte ~** idle *(US)* (spare, *Br.)* capacity.
Kapazitäts| ausnutzung use of (employment to) [plant] capacity; **unterhalb der ~grenze laufen** to operate below its potentiality.
Kapital capital *(Eigenkapital von Kapital- und Personengesellschaft)* proprietorship, capital net worth *(US)*, *(Geldmittel)* funds, means, resources, *(Kapitalmacht)* moneyed interest, capitalists, *(Stammkapital einer AG)* authorized capital stock *(US)*, share capital *(Br.)*;
mit herabgesetztem ~ and reduced;
amortisiertes ~ sunk capital; **im Ausland angelegtes ~** capital invested abroad; **arbeitendes ~** productive (employed, active, net working) capital; **aus-**

gegebenes ~ issued capital (stock, *US)*; **ausgewiesenes ~** declared capital; **betriebsnotwendiges ~** fixed (permanent) working capital; **dividendenberechtigtes ~** capital entitled to a dividend; **voll eingezahltes ~** paid-up capital; **fehlgeleitetes ~** misappropriated capital; **flüssiges ~** liquid (circulation) capital; **geringfügiges ~** nominal capital *(US)*; **produktives ~** employed (engaged) capital; **registriertes ~** registered (authorized, *Br.)* capital, authorized capital stock *(US)*; **totes ~** unemployed (unused, unapplied) funds; **unkündbares ~** irredeemable capital; **verfügbares ~** capital that can be made available, expendable (available) funds; **verwässertes ~** watered stock; **werbendes ~** interest bearing (working, quick) capital; **zurückgezahltes ~** redeemed capital;
~ einer Bank bank's capital, bank assets; **~ nebst Zinsen** principal and interest;
~ abschreiben to write off capital; **~ anlegen** to embark money, to invest capital; **mit fremdem ~ arbeiten** to trade with borrowed money (òn the equity); **~ aufnehmen** to raise capital (funds); **sein ~ aufzehren** to eat up one's capital; **mit ~ ausstatten** to furnish (endow, provide) with capital; **~ beschaffen** to finance, to raise the money; **Geschäft mit geliehenem ~ betreiben** to trade on the equity; **~ einbringen** to contribute capital; **~ erhöhen** to raise the capital [stock, *US]*; **~ flüssigmachen** to liberate (mobilize) capital; **~ herabsetzen** to reduce the share capital (capital [stock, *US])*; **vom ~ leben** to live on *(Br.)* (off) the capital; **~ der staatlichen Zwangswirtschaft unterwerfen** to conscript capital; **Dividende vom ~ zahlen** to pay a dividend out of capital; **~ zeichnen** to subscribe capital, *(Übernahmekonsortium)* to underwrite; **~ zusammenlegen** to reduce the capital stock *(US)*.
Kapital| abfindung lump-sum settlement; **~abschöpfung** depletion, capital depreciation; **~abwanderung** exodus (migration) of capital.
Kapitalanlage [capital] investment, capital assets, *(Anlage von Kapital)* employment (investment, placement) of capital;
bestimmungswidrige ~ unproper investment; **erstklassige ~** high-grade (prime, gilt-edged, *Br.)* investment; **kurzfristige ~n** temporary investments; **langfristige ~n** long-dated (long-term) capital investment (spending); **mündelsichere ~** gilt-edged *(Br.)* (trustee, trust fund, *US)* investments; **verzinsliche ~** interest-bearing investment;
~ in Wertpapieren portfolio investment;
im ~geschäft erfolgreich tätig sein to prosper on institutional business.
Kapitalanlagegesellschaft investment company (trust, *US)* unit trust *(Br.)*;
nach eigenem Ermessen anlegende ~ management trust;

~ **mit breitgestreutem Aktienportefeuille** diseretionary trust *(Br.);* ~ **mit freizügiger Anlageverwaltung** management trust (investment company); ~ **mit wechselndem Portefeuille** flexible trust.

Kapitalanlage|**güter** capital assets; ~**konto** capital asset account.

Kapitalanlagen|**berater** investment adviser, security analyst *(US);* ~**beratung** investment advice; ~**bewertung** appreciation of assets, security analysis *(US).*

Kapitalanteil [capital] share, share of stock, stock share, *(Beteiligung)* ownership interest;
ausschlaggebender ~ control in ownership interest, controlling [stock] interst; ~**schein** stock certificate.

kapitalarm short of funds, lacking capital.

Kapital|**aufbringung** raising (contribution) of capital; ~**aufstockung** capital appreciation (reequipment, increase).

Kapitalaufwand capital expenditure (outlay, spending, cost), financial expense;
aktivierungspflichtiger ~ capital charges;
~ **der Wirtschaft** industry spending.

Kapital|**ausfuhr** capital export; ~**ausstattung** capitalization, capital equipment; ~**auszahlung** capital payment (distribution); ~**basis** capital (financial) requirements, capital demand (needs); ~**beitrag** contribution to capital; ~**bereitstellungskonto** capital adjustment account; ~**beteiligung** [financial] interest, [equity] participation; ~**betrag** amount of capital, capital [amount]; **über Gewinn- und Verlustkonto abgebuchte** ~**beträge** capital items charged against profits; **bewegung** capital movement; ~**bewertung** capital valuation (rating, *US);* ~**bewertungsziffern** capital-rating figures *(US);* ~**bildung** capital accumulation (formation); ~ **unzureichende (knappe)** ~**decke haben** to lack the requisite (be strapped for) capital; ~**dienst sicherstellen** to service its capital investment; ~**einlage** contribution to capital; **ausländische** ~**einfuhr abbremsen** to stem the inflow of foreign funds; ~**einkünfte** unearned (investment, *US)* capital receipts; ~**einlage** contribution to capital, invested capital, money sunk *(US);* ~**einsatz** capital appropriation; ~**emission** capital issue; ~**entwertung** capital depreciation; ~**entwertungsrücklage** provision for depreciation of investments; ~**erhöhung** capital appreciation, stock appreciation; ~**ertrag** unearned income, return on capital (stock, investment), investment return; ~**ertragsteuer** capital-yield tax *(Br.),* capital-gains tax *(US);* ~**export** capital export; ~**fehlbetrag** stock shortage; ~**fehlleitung** misappropriation of capital funds; ~**flucht** exodus (flight) of capital; ~**geber** capital-giver, moneylender; ~**gesellschaft** [joint] stock company, stock corporation *(US).*

Kapitalgewinn capital gain (surplus, *US);*
der Behandlung als ~ **unterworfen sein** to qualify for capital-gains treatment;
~**konto** capital-gains (surplus, *US)* account.

Kapitalgüter | **dauerhafte** capital (durable) goods; ~**bereich** capital-goods area; ~**industrie** capital-goods industries; ~**konjunktur** capital-goods boom.

Kapital|**herabsetzung** writing off, reduction of share capital *(Br.)* (capital stock, *US);* ~**hilfe** capital aid.

Kapitalien, brachliegende unapplied funds; **reichliche** ~ ample means.

Kapital|**import** import of capital; ~**intensität** high gearing.

kapitalintensiv capital-intensive.

Kapitalinteresse financial (moneyed) interest.

Kapital|**investierung,** ~**investition** capital (equity) investment;
steuerbegünstigte ~ tax investment;
übermäßige ~**en in Warenständen** overinvestment in inventories.

kapitalisieren to capitalize, to finance, to fund.

kapitalisiert|**er Aufwand** capitalized expenses; ~**er Wert** capitalized value.

Kapitalisierungs|**aufwand** capitalization unit; ~**satz** rate of capitalization.

Kapitalismus capitalism.

kapitalistisches System capitalistic system.

kapitalknapp capital-short, low geared.

Kapital|**koeffizient** *(volkswirtschaftliche Erfolgsrechnung)* capital output ratio, capital coefficient; ~**konto** capital [stock] (proprietary, proprietorship) account; ~**kosten** capital expenditure (cost); ~**kraft** sound financial position, financial strength (standing).

kapitalkräftig financially sound, in good financial standing, substantial.

Kapital|**lenkung** investment control; ~**lücke** capital gap.

Kapitalmarkt capital market;
privater ~ private placement market;
~**publikum** investing public, investors; ~**zins** price of money.

kapitalmäßig, sich ~ **beteiligen** to take up a financial interest;
~**e Bindung** financial relationship.

Kapital|**mehrheit** controlling interest, *(AG)* majority shareholding (stockholding, *US);* ~**mittel** capital [equipment] means, funds, resources; ~**nachfrage** demand for capital; ~**nettoverlust** net capital loss; ~**rendite** return on capital employed, investment income (revenue); ~**reserven** capital (investment, revenue, *Br.)* reserve; ~**rückdauer** payback (payoff) period; ~**rückzahlung** repayment of principal; ~**sammelstelle** institutional investor (buyer, lender); ~**schmälerungen** [capital]impairments.

kapitalschwach capital-poor, financially weak.

Kapital|**schwund** dwindling assets; ~**spritze** injection of capital; ~**steuer** capital levy, tax on capital, capital-stock tax *(US);* ~**struktur** capital (financial) structure; ~**transaktion** capital transaction; ~**umschichtung** capital movement; ~**umschlag** capital turnover (sales); ~**umstellung** *(AG)* reorganization; ~**verflechtung** capital (financial) interrelation; ~verhältnis capital ratio; ~verkehr capital movement (transactions); ~verlust capital loss, leakage; ~vermögen property of a capital nature, funded property, *(Kapitalanlagegesellschaft)* investment estate; ~verschulden capital liability; ~versicherung auf den Erlebensfall pure endowment insurance; ~verwässerung watering of stocks; ~verwendung capital appropriation, employment of funds (capital); ~verwendungsnachweis statement of application of funds, capital reconciliation statement *(Br.)*; ~verzinsung investment return (revenue); ~wert capital value, *(Police)* cash value; ~zahlung oder Rentenzahlung insurance option; ~zeichnung [stock] subscription; ~zufluß capital flow, influx of capital; ~zusammenlegung writing off, capital reduction; ~zuwachs capital gain (appreciation), *(Investmentfonds)* capital growth.

Kapitän captain, master, skipper;
~ auf großer Fahrt master mariner.

Karenzzeit *(Versicherung)* waiting period.

Karte card, *(Bewirtschaftungssystem)* ration card, coupon, *(Restaurant)* bill of fare;
~ abstempeln *(nach Arbeitsschluß)* to check out *(Br.)*; ~ stempeln to check in *(Br.)*.

Kartei card index [file], card catalog(ue);
in ~form erfassen to card-index; ~karte index (record, file) card; ~kasten filing box; ~reiter top, signal; ~schrank filing cabinet.

Kartell cartel, pool, industrial combine (monopoly), ring *(Br.)*, trust *(US)*;
horizontales ~ horizontal combine;
~auflösen to break up a cartel; ~bilden to pool, to cartelize.

Kartell|abkommen restrictive trading agreement *(Br.)*, pooling agreement in restraint of trade *(US)*; ~abteilung antitrust division *(US)*; ~amt cartel office, Federal Trade Commission *(US)*; ~anwalt antitrust lawyer; ~aufsichtsbehörde monopoly commission (commissioner, *Br.)*; ~bestimmungen cartel regulations; ~entflechtungsbehörde decartelization agency.

kartellfeindlich anti-trust, anticartel.

Kartell|gericht cartel court, Restrictive Practice Court *(Br.)*; ~gesetz Restrictive Trade Practice Act *(Br.)*, Statute of Monopolies *(Br.)*, Sherman Act *(US)*.

Kartellisierung cartelization, pooling.

Kartell|kontrolle cartel control; ~mitglied member of a cartel; ~preis cartel price; ~verbot ban on cartelization, cartel ban; ~vereinbarung cartel (restrictive trade, *Br.)* agreement; gegen eine ~vereinbarung verstoßen to break the rules of a cartel; ~verkauf pool selling; ~vertrag cartel agreement (arrangement).

Kartenausgabe booking office *(Br.)*, ticket window *(US)*.

kartenpflichtig sein to go on points, to be rationed.

Kartenverkauf booking (ticket, *US)* office.

Karton cardboard, pasteboard, paper box.

kartoniert *(Buch)* [bound] in boards.

Kartothek card index [file], card catalog(ue).

Kasino casino, *(Betrieb)* catering department;
~ für leitende Angestellte executive dining room.

Kasko|police comprehensive insurance policy; ~versicherer hull underwriter; ~versicherung automobile personal liability and property-damage insurance *(US)*, *(Schiff)* hull insurance.

Kassa|buch cashbook; ~geschäft cash (ready money) business, cash operation (sale), *(Devisen)* spot transaction; ~konto petty cash account; ~kurs cash price, *(Devisen)* spot quotation; ~markt cash market, *(Devisen)* spot market (outlet, *US)*; ~papiere securities dealt in for cash, *(Devisen)* securities quoted on the spot market; ~ware *(Devisen)* spot commodities; ~werte *(Devisen)* securities dealt with (quoted) on the spot market.

Kasse cash, *(Bahnhof)* booking office *(Br.)*, ticket window *(US)*, *(Bank)* cashier's (teller's, *US)* department, *(Barangebot)* cash offer, *(Börse)* spot cash, *(Kassenschalter)* cash (paying) office, pay desk, *(Ladenkasse)* cashbox, till, money chest, *(Registrierkasse)* cash register, *(Theater)* box (booking) office, ticket window *(US)*, *(Unterstützungskasse)* relief fund;
an der ~ *(Bank)* over the counter (window); knapp bei ~ short of cash; nur gegen ~ for cash only; ~ *(Devisen)* on spot terms, *(Wertpapiere)* for cash, payable cash down;
auszahlende ~ paying office; getrennte ~ Dutch treat;
~ gegen Dokumente cash against documents; ~ bei Lieferung cash on delivery;
~ abstimmen to tally (count, *US,* make up) the cash; mit der ~ durchbrennen to make (run) off with money (cash), to shoot the moon *(sl.)*; in die ~ greifen to rob (dip into) the till; per ~ kaufen to buy for cash (spot cash, outright, *US)*; gemeinsame ~ machen to put one's funds in common; bei ~ sein to be in funds (cash, stock, flush of money); nicht gut (schlecht) bei ~ sein to be in low funds (water); an der ~ zahlen to pay at the desk.

Kassen|abschluß cash settlement; ~abstimmung cash reconciliation; ~anweisung cash note, pay *(Br.)* (cash) voucher, *(Bank)* bank bill *(US)*; ~arzt panel doctor *(Br.)*; ~ausgangsbuch cash disbursements book; ~beleg journal (cash) voucher; ~bestand balance in (cash on) hand, cash balance (assets); schwache ~bestände haben to run short of cash; ~bon receipt; ~buchhalter cash accountant; ~defizit adverse cash balance *(Br.)*, cash deficit; ~disposition cash arrangements; ~eingang cash receipts; ~einnahme cash (box-office, *US,* gate) receipts; ~einnahmen box-office takings *(US)*; ~erfolg box-office success *(US)*; ~führer cashier, treasurer, teller *(US)*; ~gebarung cash management; ~guthaben cash assets, cash in hand (vault, *US)*; ~journal cash journal; ~kladde rough cash book; ~kredit *(Notenbank)* cash advance; ~magnet *(Film)* boxoffice draw *(US)*.

kassenmäßig| durchleiten *(Bank)* to pass through one's books;
~e Entwicklung cash position.
Kassen|**mitglied** *(Krankenkasse)* health-service (panel, *Br.)* patient; **zur ~praxis zugelassen sein** to be working under the panel system *(Br.)*; ~**prüfer** cash auditor; ~**prüfung** cash check, proving cash, *(Revision)* cash audit[ing]; ~**quittung** cash (cashier's) receipt; ~**raub** payroll robbery; ~**raum** cash office, *(Kino)* paybox; ~**revision** cash audit[ing], checkup (verificaton) of the cash; ~**revisor** cash auditor; ~**schalter** paybox, pay (cash, cashier's) desk, *(Bank)* [teller's, *US*] counter, bank counter; ~**schein** *(Anweisung)* cash order, slip, check, *(Krankenkasse)* sickness certificate, *(Schatzanweisung)* treasury bill (note) *(US)*; ~**schlager** jackpot winner, box-office success *(US)*; ~**stand** cash position; ~**sturz machen** to tally (count, *US*) up, to make up (balance) the cash; ~**überschuß** surplus [in cash], cash surplus; ~**verkehr** cash transactions over-the-counter business; ~**verwalter** treasurer, cashier, cash clerk; ~**vorschuß** cash advance; ~**zugänge** inflow of cash.
Kassette strong box, *(Buch)* box, clipcase, *(Fernsehen)* cartridge, *(Film)* magazine, plateholder.
Kassetten|**fernsehen** electronic video recording, cartridge television; ~**gerät** cassette recorder.
kassieren to cash, to collect, *(Beamter)* to supersede; **Bombengehalt** ~ to earn a packet of money.
Kassierer cashier, cash clerk, cashkeeper, bank teller *(US)*, *(Geldeinnehmer)* money taker, collector, *(Geldzähler)* money teller;
~ **für Auszahlungen** first (paying, *US*) teller, disbursing officer *(US)*; ~ **für Einzahlungen** second (receiving, *US*) teller.
Kastenlieferwagen box truck.
Katalog, alphabetischer alphabetical catalog(ue);
~ **mit Preisangaben** price list;
nur nach ~ **verkaufen** to sell from its catalog(ue).
~**nummer** catalog(ue) (index) number; ~**preis** catalog(ue) (list[ing]) price.
Kataster cadaster, cadastre *(Br.)*, land register *(Br.)*, cadastral survey (map, plan);
~**nummer** tract (cadastral) number.
Katastrophen|**rücklage** *(Versicherung)* catastrophe reserve; ~**rückversicherung** catastrophe reinsurance.
Kauf buying, purchase, purchasing, acquisition;
zum ~ **angeboten** on offer;
fingierter ~ sham purchase; **günstiger** ~ good bargain (buy), find;
~ **zur Ansicht** purchase on approval (subject to inspection); ~ **in Bausch und Bogen** purchase in the lump; ~ **nach Beschreibung** sale by description; ~ **auf Grund von Erinnerungswerbung** repeat sale *(US)*; ~ **unter Eigentumsvorbehalt** conditional (executory, qualified) sale; ~ **auf Lieferung** purchase for future delivery *(US)*;~ **auf Probe** purchase on approval (trial), approval sale; ~ **auf feste Rechnung** purchase on account; ~ **auf**

Zeit time bargain, forward (future, *US*) purchase;
~ **abschließen** to effect a sale; **durch** ~ **erwerben** to acquire by purchase; ~**rückgängig machen** to rescind a sale; **von einem** ~ **zurücktreten** to repudiate a purchase;
~**andrang** pressure to buy; ~**anlaß** buying motive; ~**anreiz** sales inducement; **abschließender Appell** *(Anzeige)* rider, close; ~**auftrag für Abschnitte zu verschiedenen Kursen** split order *(US)*; ~ **aus dem Ausland** indent; ~**bereitschaft** animation among buyers; ~**bindungspolitik** buy-American policy.
Käufe *(Börse)* buying orders;
auf Grund von Warenproben getätigte ~ sales made on the basis of samples;
~ **am offenen Markt** open-market purchases;
auf eine Hausse hin ~ **tätigen** to buy for a rise.
kaufen to buy, to [make a (acquire by)] purchase, *(bestechen)* to bribe, to subsidize, to corrupt;
auf Abzahlung ~ to buy on the instal(l)ment (hire-purchase, *Br.,* deferred-payment, *US*) system; **billig** ~ to make a bargain; **billig ~ und teuer verkaufen** *(Börse)* to reload; **auf Lieferung ~** to buy forward (future delivery, *US*); **auf Pump** ~ to buy on the sleeve *(US)* (tick, *Br.)*; **für fremde Rechnung** ~ to buy for third account; **spottbillig** ~ to buy for a mere song; **von der Stange** ~ to buy ready-made; **Ware lose oder verpackt** ~ to buy bulk or packed goods.
Kaufentschluß buying impulse.
Käufer purchaser, purchasing party, buyer, vendee, salegoer, prospect, bargainee;
ohne ~ no buyers; **Risiko beim** ~ caveat emptor; **nach ~s Wahl** optional with the buyer;
gutgläubiger ~ purchaser in good faith; **preisempfindlicher** ~ price-finicky customer; **ungenannter** ~ undisclosed buyer;
~ **einer Vorprämie** giver for a call *(Br.)*;
als ~ **auftreten** to be in the market; **zur Verfügung des ~s halten** to hold subject to the seller's order; ~**liste** buyer's list; ~**markt** buyer's market; ~**ring** sales ring; ~**schicht** spending group; ~**verhalten** purchase pattern.
Kauf|**fahrteischiff** trading vessel, merchantman, merchant ship (vessel); ~**frau** feme-sole trader.
Kaufgeld purchase money (price);
~**finanzierung** purchase-money financing; ~**hypothek** purchase-money mortgage.
Kauf|**gewohnheiten** *(Kundschaft)* custom,. buying habits; ~**haus** [variety chain] store, departmental *(Br.)* (general department, *US*) store, stores *(US)*, universal providers *(Br.)*, warehouse *(Br.)*; ~**interesse** inclination (desire) to buy; ~**interessent** intending purchaser, prospective (would-be, potential) buyer, prospect *(US)*.
Kaufkraft purchasing (buying) power;
überschüssige ~ surplus of spending power;
~ **des Geldes** purchasing power of money;
überschüssige ~ **abschöpfen** to absorb buying power;

~lenkung control of purchasing power; **~überhang** excessive (backlog of) purchasing power; **~wert** purchasing value of money.

käuflich for (on) sale, purchasable, by purchase; **~ erwerben** to acquire by purchase.

Kauflust inclination (disposition, propensity) to buy animation among buyers, buying desire; **abnehmende ~ der Verbraucher** consumer spending slowdown.

Kaufmann merchant, *(Gemischtwarenhändler)* grocer, *(Geschäftsinhaber)* shopkeeper, storekeeper *(US)*, businessman, *(Händler)* dealer, trader, tradesman;
selbständiger ~ established merchant;
~ mit offenem Ladengeschäft tradesman;
sich als ~ niederlassen to set up shop, to open a trade; **~ werden** to go into business.

kaufmännisch commercial, mercantile, trading, businesslike;
~ geschult brought up in business;
~er Angestellter clerk, employee; **~er Beruf** mercantile profession; **~er Betrieb** business enterprise, commercial establishment; **nach ~en Gesichtspunkten** from a commercial point of view, businesslike; **~e Lehre** apprenticeship.

Kaufmanns|beruf commercial profession; **~gehilfe** shop assistant; **~kreise** commercial circles, businessmen.

Kauf|motiv buying motive; **~option** buying (buyer's, *Br.*) option, call; **~orgie** buying binge.

Kaufpreis purchase money (price), [sales] price;
~ erlegen to pay the sales price; **~ herabsetzen** to abate the purchase price;
~rate instal(l)ment.

Kauf|reflektant prospective (would-be, potential) buyer, prospect *(US)*; **~unlust** sales (consumer) resistance; **~verhalten** buying behavio(u)r.

Kaufvertrag [contract of] sale, sales (purchase) contract, purchase deed;
notarieller ~ special contract under seal;
~ unter Eigentumsvorbehalt conditional sales contract;
vom ~ zurücktreten to rescind a sales contract.

Kauf|wert purchasing (market) value; **~zentrum** shopping center *(US)* (centre, *Br.*); **kein ~zwang** free inspection invited.

Kaution bail [bond], bailment, caution, risk money, financial bond, surety, guarantee *(Br.)*;
~ eines Bauunternehmens construction bond; **~ gegen Veruntreuung** fidelity bond;
~ stellen to give (furnish, stand) bail, to [post a] bond.

Kautionseffekten guarantee securities.

Kautions|höhe caution money, security; **~leistung** bailment.

kautionspflichtig liable to give security.

Kautions|verpflichtung fiduciary bond; **~versicherung** surety (fidelity, *US* guarantee, *Br.*) insurance.

kein|e Deckung no funds; **~ Konto** no account.

Keller|lokal underground bistro, beer cellar, dive bar;

~wechsel accommoadtion (fictitious, *Br.*, bogus, pro-forma) bill, spurious note, kite *(Br.)*.

Kenn|buchstabe code letter; **~karte** identity card.

Kenntlichmachung abgetretener Konten bookmarking of assigned accounts.

Kennzahl code number, indicative figure, *(Fernschreiber)* dialling code, *(Telefon)* area code prefix.

Kennzeichen sign, (distinctive, distinguishing) mark, symbol, distinctive feature;
polizeiliches ~ *(Auto)* registered (licence, *US*) number, identification (number) plate;
~mißbrauch *(Markenartikel)* passing off one's goods as those of another make *(US)*.

kennzeichen to identify, to mark, to hallmark, to feature, *(Geldbeträge)* to earmark, *(Waren)* to label, to ticket.

Kennzeichnungsbestimmungen labelling provisions, marketing instructions.

Kennziffer index, code (index, key) number, key, *(Fernschreiber)* dialling code, exchange, *(Insertion)* box number;
~anschrift keyed address; **~anzeige** box-number advertisment, keyed advertising.

Kernbestandteil *(Anzeige)* body.

Ketten|bankwesen chain banking; **~geschäft**, **~laden**, **~unternehmen** chainstore business, multiple shop *(Br.)*.

Kilometer|berechnungsgrundlage milage basis; **~geld** milage allowance, *(Eisenbahn)* car milage; **~pauschalsatz** flat milage rate.

Kinder|arbeit employment of children; **~beihilfe** dependency allowance, allowance for dependants; **~fahrkarte** half ticket; **~freibetrag** child relief *(Br.)* (exemption, *US*).

Kino cinema *(Br.)*, picture [theater], film, motion picture *(US)*, movies *(US, sl.)*;
~besucher cinema (movie, *US*) goer; **~reklame** screen (movie, *US*) advertisement.

Kiosk [concession] stand, kiosk, outlet, newsstand *(US)*.

Kladde notebook, rough (auxiliary) book, petty journal, memorandum book, daybook.

Klage | eines Aktionärs gegen seine Gesellschaft shareholder's bill; **~ aus ungerechtfertigter Bereicherung** action for money had and received *(Br.)*; **~ auf Rechnungslegung** action of accounts; **~ auf Schadenersatz** damages suit; **~ auf Unterhalt** maintenance suit; **~ auf Zahlung des Kaufpreises** action for payment;
Kläger mit seiner ~ abweisen to nonsuit the plaintiff;
~antrag motion in court (for judgement, *Br.*).

klagen to institute an (take legal) action, to go to law, to sue in court, to declare;
unter seinem handelsgerichtlichen Namen ~ to sue in its corporate name.

Klarierungsschein bill of clearance.

Klarsicht|folie transparent foil; **~hülle** window envelope.

Klasse class, category, rate, *(Qualität)* class, quality, sort, brand, *(Schiff)* rating;
erster ~ *(Abteil)* first-class, *(Krankenhaus)* private; **erster ~ fahren** to go first; **erster ~ liegen** *(Krankenhaus)* to have a private room.
Klassenlotterie class (serial, Dutch) lottery.
Klausel [contract] clause, article, reserved power, *(Bedingung)* condition, stipulation;
übliche Haus-zu-Haus ~ *(Spediteur)* standard warehouse-to-warehouse coverage;
~ über Haftung für versteckte Mängel latent-defect clause; **~n für Seewarenversicherung** institute-cargo clauses *(Br.)*; **~für beiderseitiges Verschulden** both-to-blame collision clause.
Klebestreifen adhesive (gummed) tape, sticker *(US)*;
klein | anfangen *(Unternehmen)* to start from scratch;
Kosten ~ halten to keep down the expenses;
~e Anzeigen classified advertisements, smalls; **~e Steuerreform** minor tax reform; **~es Vermögen** small fortune; **~e Wohnung** small flat.
Klein|aktie baby share, penny stock *(US)*; **~anzeigen** classified advertisements, smalls, want ads *(US)*; **~bahn** light (narrow-gauge, branch) railway (railroad, *US*); **~betrieb** splinter operation, small establishment, small-scale operator.
Kleingeld small change, small (fractional, broken) money, loose cash, fractional currency *(US)*.
kleingestückelt of low denomination.
Kleingewerbe small-scale trade (service, business).
Kleinhandels|betrieb small-scale operator, small merchandising unit *(US)*; **~preis** retail [selling] price, resale price; **~rabatt** retail discount; **~verkauf** sale by (at, *US*) retail; **~verkaufspreis** retail [selling] price, retail value, resale price.
Klein|kredit small loan; **~landwirt** peasant proprietor; **~lebensversicherung** industrial life (low-rate) insurance; **~lieferwagen** pickup [car]; **~omnibus** minibus; **~rentner** pensioner.
Kleinstbetrieb small infant business, hole in the wall.
Klemme *(finanziell)* squeeze, tightness [of money].
Klientele cliency, goodwill, custom, customers.
knapp short, narrow, *(Geldmarkt)* tight, close, stringent, *(Ware)* scarce, scant, scanty;
~ an Arbeitskräften short-handed; **~ bei Kasse** short of cash, in low water;
~ disponieren to show caution in the placing of orders;
~s Angebot scanty supply; **~e Mittel** narrow means.
Knappheit shortage, scantiness, deficiency, lack;
~ an Arbeitskräften shortage of manpower.
Knappheits|erscheinung tightness, shortage, scarceness, scarcity; **~kurs** scarcity price.
Knappschafts|kasse miners' provident (benefit) fund, miners' insurance.
Knoten|amt *(Telefon)* tandem office; **~bahnhof** junction.
Kode benutzen to write a dispatch in code.
Kofferraum *(Auto)* luggage (baggage, *US*) compartment, boot *(Br.)*, trunk *(US)*.

Kohlen|abbau coal mining; **~bergwerk** coal mine, pit, colliery; **~förderung** coal output; **~grube** coal pit; **~halden** pithead stocks; **~zeche** coal mine, colliery.
Kollektion collection, assortment, selection, set.
Kollektiv|arbeitsvertrag collective labo(u)r agreement; **~frachtbrief** blanket waybill; **~versicherung** blanket (group, blanket-clause) insurance.
Kollision von Interessen clash of interests.
Kollisionsversicherung collision insurance.
Kolonialwaren colonial produce (products, wares); **~geschäft** grocer's shop (store, *US*), grocery.
Kolumnen|schreiber syndicated (newspaper) columnist; **~titel** headline, running title.
Kolonnenarbeit gang work.
Kombi|nationstarif combination rate; **~wagen** carry all *(US)*, beach wag(g)on *(US)*, estate car *(Br.)*, station wagon *(US)*.
Komfortwohnung luxury flat.
Kommandit|anteil limited partnership interest; **~gesellschaft** limited partnership; **~ist** special (dormant, silent, sleeping, *Br.)* partner; **~vertrag** articles of partnership.
Kommission commission, committee, board, *(Entgeld)* commission [fee], brokerage;
~ aus Beteiligungen underwriting commission; **Waren in ~ nehmen** to take goods on consignment; **gegen ~ verkaufen** to sell on commission.
Kommissionär commission agent (merchant), middleman, mercantile agent *(Br.)*;
unselbständiger ~ agent middleman;
Kommissions|artikel goods on commission (in trust), memorandum goods *(US)*; **auf ~basis [verkauft]** on sale or return, factored; **~buch** order book; **~firma** commission merchant; **~gebühr** commission, factorage; **~geschäft** agency (agent's) business, factorage, *(einzelnes)* commission dealing; **~handel** agency (agent's) business, commission marketing; **~lager** stock on consignment (commission); **~makler** commission broker; **~nummer** order number; **~reisender** commercial travel(l)er, travelling salesman; **~verkauf** consignment sale, sale and return; **~vertreter** consignment agent; **~ware** goods on commission (in consignment) memorandum goods *(US)*.
kommissionsweise on consignment, on (by way of) commission (memorandum, *US*).
kommunal|es Rechnungswesen municipal accounting; **~e Steuern** municipal rates (taxes); **~e Wirtschaftstätigkeit** municipal trading.
Kommunal|abgaben local (municipal) taxes *(US)*; **~anleihe** municipal loan, local authority loan *(Br.)*, advances to local authorities; **~schuldschein** municipal (county) warrant, municipal negotiable bond; **~schuldverschreibungen** municipals, local bonds *(Br.)*, municipal bonds *(US)* (stocks) *(Br.)*, corporation stocks *(Br.)*.
kommunalsteuerpflichtig ratable, ratepaying.
Kommunalsteuer|pflichtiger, **~zahler** ratepayer; **~steuersatz** ratal *(Br.)*.
Kompensations|abkommen barter agreement; **~ge-**

schäft barter transaction; ~konto clearing account; ~zoll countervailing duty.
kompensieren to compensate, to set off, to offset.
Komplementär general (unlimited) partner.
komplementäre Güter *(Volkswirtschaft)* complementary (joint demand, *US*) goods.
Komplettierungsanzeige rate holder.
Konfektionär ready-made clothier, slop dealer.
Konfektions|anzug ready-made-suit, reach-me-down, hand-me-down *(US)*; ~geschäft ready-made shop; ~ware ready-to-wear (made-up) clothes, slop
· work.
Konferenz| am runden Tisch round-table conference; ~ablauf conference proceedings; ~schaltung *(Rundfunk)* hookup; ~zimmer conference room, *(Hotel)* commercial room.
konfiszieren to condemn, to confiscate, to make seizure, to seize, to sequester, to forfeit.
konform buchen to enter (book) in conformity.
Kongreß congress, assembly, meeting, conference.
Konjunktur market conditions (prospects), state of the economy, economic (upward) trend, [business] boom, business outlook (activity);
glänzende ~ booming economy; rückläufige ~ business (economic) slump, slowing economy; überhitzte ~ overheated boom;
[überhitzte] ~ abkühlen to cool off an [overheated] economy; ~ ankurbeln to enliven business; ~ wieder zum Anlauf bringen to get the economy back on the tracks; ~stützen to underpin the economy; ~ überhitzen to overtake the boom; ~ zügeln to curb the boom.
konjunkturabhängige Industrie cyclical industry.
Konjunktur|ablauf business cycle; ~abschwung downward swing, [cyclical] downturn, cyclical downswing; ~analyse business-cycle analysis; ~anstieg upward business trend, cyclical recovery; ~aufschwung business revival, upward business trend, upswing, upturn in the business cycle; ~ausgleich levelling out of business fluctuations, seasonal adjustment; ~ausgleichsrücklage countercyclical reserve; ~aussichten business outlook (prospects), cyclical prospects; ~barometer trade (business) barometer, indicator of business.
konjunkturbedingte Arbeitslosigkeit cyclical unemployment.
Konjunktur|belebung economic recovery (revival); rückläufige ~bewegung business downturn; ~bremse zurückhaltend anwenden to ease the economic brakes; ~dämpfung auf einzelnen Gebieten rolling adjustment; ~einflüsse cyclical influence.
konjunkturell cyclical, economic;
~er Anstieg upward trend; ~e Auftriebstendenz upward (boom) trend; ~e Belebung economic recovery (revival); ~e Erholung booming recovery; ~e Flautenbewegung sluggish pace of business; ~e Preissteigerung cyclical rise in prices; ~e Strömungen trends in the economy; ~e Verschlechterung economic downturn; ~er Wendepunkt business cycle turning point.

konjunkturempfindlich sensitive to business movements (business fluctuations).
Konjunktur|entwicklung economic development (trend); der ~entwicklung entgehen to buck the trend; ~erholung pickup *(US sl.)*; ~faktoren cyclical factors; ~flaute slack in the economy; ~forscher market research worker; ~institut institute for business cycle research, business research institute; ~kurve cyclical (economic) trend; ~mulde depression low, dip in business; abgeschwächte ~periode period of decline in economic activity; rückläufige ~phase economic downswing;
Konjunkturpolitik cyclical (economic) policy;
antizyklische ~ compensatory fiscal policy; ausgeglichene ~ treiben to remain on an even keel.
konjunkturpolitisch|e Erwägungen cyclical considerations; ~es Ziel economic policy goal.
Konjunktur|prognose business forecast, outlook for the economy; ~prognostiker business forecaster; ~regulativ economic regulator; ~rückgang business slump, downtrend, economic downturn; ~rhythmus business cycle; ~steuerung cycle riding; ~stockung economic slowdown; ~studie business-cycle study; ~tief depression low (level); ~umschwung market (cyclical) swing *(US)*; ~verlangsamung business slowdown; ~verlauf economic trend (course); ~zuschlag cyclical surtax; ~zyklus trade (economic, business) cycle.
Konkurrenten ausstechen to flog a competitor.
Konkurrenz competition, rivalry, emulation, *(Konkurrenten)* competitors, rivals in business;
meine ~ my competitors in trade; preisdrückende ~ cut-price competition; unlautere ~ unfair competition in trade;
keine ~ aufkommen lassen to defy competition; ausländische ~ eindämmern to curb foreign competition; der ~ immer um eine Nasenlänge voraus sein to be one jump ahead of one's competitors; ~ aus dem Markt verdrängen to put competitors out of business;
~angebot competitive bid (quotation); ~ausschreibung invitation to tender, bid invitation *(US)*; ~beschränkung restraint of trade; ~betrieb eröffnen to set up a business in competition; ~erzeugnisse competing (competitive) products.
konkurrenzfähig able to compete (to meet competition), competitive, *(Ware)* marketable; ~er Preis competitive price.
Konkurrenz|firma competitor, competing (competitive) firm; ~geschäft rival business; ~kampf competition, trade rivalry.
konkurrenzlos dastehen to be far ahead of one's competitors.
Konkurrenz|preis competitor's (competitive) price; ~tarif competitive rate; ~unternehmen business rival; ~verbot restraint of trade, exclusivity stipulation *(Br.)*; ~vereinbarung restrictive covenant; ~ware anschwärzen to run down the goods of a competitor.
konkurrieren to compete, to rival.

konkurrierendes Verschulden contributory negligence.

Konkurs bankruptcy, [business] failure;
~ **auf Gläubigerantrag** involuntary bankruptcy;
~ **abwenden** to avoid bankruptcy proceedings;
seinen ~ anmelden to file one's petition (a declaration of bankruptcy); **seine Forderung zum ~ anmelden** to prove one's claim; **über jds. Vermögen den ~ erklären** to declare (adjudicate) s. o. judicially to be a bankrupt; **in der Liste der ~ stehen** to have one's name (appear) in the gazette.

Konkurs|abwendung avoidance of bankruptcy proceedings; ~**abwicklungsbilanz** realization and liquidation statement, schedule of a bankrupt's debts *(US)*; ~**anmeldung vornehmen** to file one's schedule *(US)* (a declaration of bankruptcy).

Konkursantrag bankruptcy petition;
~ **gegen j. stellen** to throw s. o. in bankruptcy, to bring bankruptcy proceedings against s. o.

Konkurs|aufhebung discharge of a bankrupt; ~**ausschüttung** division of a bankrupt's estate; ~**bilanz** realization and liquidation statement, statement of affairs *(Br.)*, schedule of a bankrupt's debts *(US)*; ~**erklärung** [filing of a] petiton in bankruptcy, declaration of bankruptcy; ~**eröffnung** adjudication in bankruptcy, receiving order *(Br.)*; **Antrag auf ~ gegen j. stellen** to bring bankruptcy proceedings against s. o.; ~**eröffnungsbeschluß** adjudication in (decree of) bankruptcy, receiving order *(Br.)*.

Konkursforderung claim provable in bankruptcy;
anerkannte ~ proved debt (claim); **anmeldungsfähige ~** provable claim (debt);
~ **anerkennen** to allow a claim.

konkursfreies Vermögen unattachable property.

Konkursgläubiger petitioning creditor;
bevorrechtigter ~ preferential (preferred, *US*) creditor;
~ **benachteiligen** to make a fraudulent conveyance.

Konkurs|masse assets of a bankrupt, bankrupt's estate; ~**eröffnungsbeschluß zustellen** to serve with a bankruptcy notice; ~**ordnung** National Bankruptcy Act *(US)*, Bankruptcy Act *(Br.)*; ~**quote** dividend of a bankrupt's estate, liquidation dividend; ~**schuldner** bankrupt [merchant], insolvent debtor; ~**tabelle** realization and liquidation statement, statement of affairs; **zur ~tabelle anmelden** to lodge a proof in bankruptcy; ~**verbrechen begehen** to commit an act of bankruptcy.

Konkursverfahren bankruptcy proceedings;
~ **aufheben** to discharge a bankrupt; ~ **einleiten** to initiate bankruptcy proceedings.

Konkurs|vergehen bankruptcy offence; ~**vergleich** composition in bankruptcy; ~**verschleppung** obstructing proceedings of bankruptcy.

Konkursverwalter receiver, liquidator of an estate;
~ **bestellen** to appoint a receiver for the bankrupt's estate;
~**zeugnis** receiver's certificate.

Konkurs|verwaltung administration of a bankrupt's estate, receivership *(Br.)*; ~**voraussetzung** act of bankruptcy.

Konnossement bill of lading, *(Original)* original bill of lading *(B/L)*;
auf den Namen ausgestelltes ~ straight bill of lading *(US)*; **an Order ausgestelltes ~** order bill of lading;

Konnossements|klausel bill-of-lading clause; ~**vermerk** remark endorsed on a bill of lading.

Konserven tinned (canned, *US*) foods (provisions);
~**fabrik** tinning factory, packing company, packhouse *(US)*; ~**fabrikant** packer *(US)*, tinner *(Br.)*; ~**industrie** tin (can, *US*) industry.

Konsignations|buch order book; ~**geschäft** consignment marketing (sale); ~**konto** commission account; ~**lager** consignment stock; ~**verkauf** consignment sale.

konsignationsweise on consignment (commission, memorandum, *US*).

konsolidierte | Bilanz consolidated balance sheet (statement); ~ **Schuld** funded debt; ~ **Staatspapiere** consols *(Br.)*, consolidated funds (stocks, *US*).

Konsolidierungs|anleihe funding loan; ~**gewinn** surplus from consolidation.

Konsols consols *(Br.)*, consolidated funds (stocks).

Konsortial|anteil underwriting share, share in a syndicate; ~**bank** underwriting (member) bank; ~**beteiligung** underwriting share, syndicate participation *(US)*; ~**führer[in]** leading underwriter, *(Bank)* originating banker (house); ~**konto** joint (syndicate, underwriting, participation, *US*) account; ~**provision** spread, underwriter's commission; ~**vertrag** underwriting contract, syndicate agreement.

Konsortium consortium, syndicate, underwriting group, *(Emissionen)* purchase (selling) syndicate;
Anleihe an ein ~ geben to put a loan into the hands of a syndicate.

Konsortiumsmitglied syndicate member, purchaser, underwriter.

Konstruktions|büro drawing (drafting) office; ~**fehler** structural defect (error).

Konsular|abkommen consular convention; ~**dienst** consular service.

konsularisch|er Dienst consular service; ~**es Korps** consular corps; ~**e Tätigkeit** activities of a consul; ~**e Vertretung** consular agency.

Konsular|papiere consular documents; ~**vertreter** consular agent (representative).

Konsulats|bescheinigung consular certificate; ~**faktura** consular invoice; ~**gebühren** consular charge (fees).

Konsum consumption, *(Konsumladen)* cooperative store (shop, *Br.*).

Konsum|artikel consumer goods (items); **frei verfügbares ~einkommen** discretionary income.

Konsument consumer, user.

Konsumenten|befragung consumer research (survey);

~kaufkraft consumer purchasing power.

Konsum|finanzierung consumer financing; ~**genossenschaft** retail cooperative (industrial and provident, *Br.*) society.

Konsumgüter consumer (consumption) goods, (first-order shopping) goods *(US)*;
kurzlebige ~ perishable consumer goods, perishables;
~**industrie** consumer-goods industry; ~**konjunktur** consumer boom; ~**markt** consumer market.

Konsum|knappheit consumer shortage; ~**kredit** consumer (instalment) credit; ~**steigerung** increased (growth in) consumption; ~**steuer** excise (consumption) tax; ~**verein** cooperative purchasing (industrial and provident, *Br.*) society, cooperative store *(US)*, the stores *(Br.)*; ~**verzicht** deferred demand; ~**waren** consumer (consumption) goods.

Kontakter contact man, *(Werbeagentur)* account executive.

Kontakt|kosten calling costs; ~**pflege** human (public) relations.

Konten, debitorische accounts having a debit balance, accounts receivable *(US)*; **kreditorische** ~ accounts having a credit balance, accounts payable *(US)*; **tote (unbewegte)** ~ dead accounts;
~ **nach ihrer Fälligkeit aufgliedern** to age accounts; ~ **auf den neuesten Stand bringen** to bring accounts up to date, to post accounts; ~ **glattstellen** to settle accounts; ~ **zusammenlegen** to merge (pool) accounts.

Konten|abrechnung settlement of accounts; ~**abschluß** reconciliation (balancing) of accounts; ~**aufgliederung** account classification; ~**ausgleich** squaring of accounts; **bei der ~führung Unregelmäßigkeiten begehen** to tamper with (cook) the accounts; ~**rahmen** accounting system; ~**sperre aufheben** to release blocked accounts; ~**zergliederung** account classification (analysis); ~**zusammenlegung** pooling (merger) of accounts.

Konterbande contraband [articles], prohibited goods (articles);
bedingte ~ conditional contraband.

Kontermine *(Börse)* bear speculation, the bears.

konterminieren *(Börse)* to sell a bear, to speculate for a fall, to be short of the market *(US)*.

Kontingent quota, share, allocation, allotment;
erschöpftes ~ exhausted quota;
~ **erhöhen** to increase a quota; ~ **erschöpfen** to exhaust (use up) a quota.

kontingentfreie Einfuhren nonquota imports.

kontingentieren to fix by quotas, to quota, to allocate *(Währung)* to ration; **Banknoten** ~ to limit the fiduciary issue.

Kontingentierung der Notenausgabe limitation of the fiduciary issue.

Kontingentierungs|system quota system; ~**zuweisung** allocation of quotas.

Kontingents|anteil quota share; ~**festsetzung** fixing of quotas; ~**träger** quota agent.

Konto account, *(Guthaben)* balance;

zum Ausgleich eines ~s to settle an account; **abgeschlossenes** ~ closed account; **ausgeglichenes** ~ balanced account; **eingefrorenes** ~ frozen account; **fingiertes** ~ pro-forma (fictitious) account; **laufendes** ~ account current, working (personal, running, continuing, checking, *US*, drawing, *US*, open, *US*) account; **tägliches** ~ account current, checking account *(US)*; **totes** ~ *(Sachkonto)* nominal (impersonal, *Br.*) account; **überzogenes** ~ overdrawn account; **verzinsliches** ~ interest-bearing account;
~ **der Anlagewerte** fixed-assets (capital) account; ~ **Beteiligungen** investment (syndicate) account; ~ **für Privatentnahmen** drawings account; ~**zweifelhafte Zinseingänge** reserve (suspense, *Br.*) interest account;
vom ~ **abheben** to draw on an account; ~ **abschließen** to balance an account; ~ **alimentieren** to place an account in funds; ~ **auflösen** to eliminate an account; ~ **debitieren** to pass (place) to the debit of (debit) an account; ~ **dotieren** to place an account in funds; ~ **mit dem Gegenwert erkennen** to credit the proceeds to an account; ~ **für j. errichten** to open an account in s. one's name; ~ **glattstellen** to discharge an account; ~ **überzogen haben** to have an overdraft; ~**pfänden** to garnish (attach, *US*) an account; ~ **schließen** to close an account; **sein** ~ **überschreiten (überziehen)** to overdraw (overcheck, *US*) one's account, to make an overdraft *(US)*; ~ **bei der Landeszentralbank unterhalten** to have a deposit account with the Federal Reserve Bank *(US)*;
~**abrechnung** bank reconciliation statement; ~**abschluß** closing an account, rest *(Br.)*; ~**ausgleich** account balance.

Kontoauszug statement (abstract, extract) of account, customer's (bank) statement;
bestätigter ~ account stated;
Richtigkeit eines ~ bestätigen to verify an account.

Konto|auszugsbestätigung verification form *(Br.)* account stated *(US)*; ~**belastung** debit; ~**blatt** account form; ~**freigabe** unblocking of an account; ~**führer** account manager; ~**inhaber** holder of an account.

Kontokorrent current (open, *US*, running) account, account current;
~**auszug** statement of account; ~**bestätigung** account stated *(US)*, verification form *(Br.)*, reconcilement (statement) blank *(US)*; ~**einlagen** call deposits, demand (current) deposits *(US)*; ~**geschäft** deposit banking; ~**konto** book (current, running, continuing, open, *US*, checking, *US*) account, account current, demand deposit *(US)*; ~**kredit** current account advance; ~**kunde** current account customer; ~**verkehr** current account business, deposit banking *(US)*; ~**zinsen** interest rates for a current account credit, demand deposit rates *(US)*.

Konto|nummer account number; ~**rist** clerk; ~**sperre** blocking of account; ~**spesen** account-carrying charges; ~**stand** balance; ~**überziehung** [bank] overdraft.

kontrahieren, mit sich selbst to act as principal and agent; **Anleihe** ~ to negotiate a loan.

Kontroll|**abschnitt** checking form, counterfoil *(Br.)*, stub *(US)*; ~**befugnis** authority, power to control; ~**blatt** counterfoil *(Br.)*, stub *(US)*; ~**buch** check book *(Br.)*, *(Kunde)* passbook, bankbook.

Kontrolle des Außendienstes field control.

Kontrolleur controller, supervisor, *(Fracht)* tally clerk (keeper), check taker, *(Schaffner)* guard.

kontrollieren to control, *(abstreichen)* to tick off, *(Bücher)* to audit, *(nachprüfen)* to verify; **Preise** ~ to administer prices.

Kontroll|**karte** *(Arbeitszeitkontrolle)* time card; ~**kasse** cash register; ~**organ** controlling (supervisory) body; ~**recht** *(Bücher)* audit privilege; ~**turm** *(Flugplatz)* control tower; ~**uhr** timeclock, journeyman (master) clock; ~**vermerk** stamp, check, mark; ~**zeichen** tick, tally, [check]mark.

Konversions|**anleihe** conversion loan; ~**guthaben** conversion balance; ~**kasse** clearinghouse; ~**kurs** conversion price.

konvertierbare Papiere convertible securities.

Konvertierbarkeit, beschränkte restricted convertibility.

Konzentration concentration, integration; ~ **einer Industrie** localization of an industry.

Konzentrationsgenehmigung merger clearance *(US)*.

Konzept foul paper (copy), rough copy, first draft; ~**papier** scribbling paper, common foolscap.

Konzern combination, combine, [business] concern, conglomerate, group, trust *(US)*; **vertikaler** ~ lateral combination; ~**absatz** intercompany sale; ~**abschluß** group accounts; ~**ausgleich** *(konsolidierte Bilanz)* intercompany elimination (squaring); ~**betrieb** affiliated company (organization); ~**bilanz** consolidated balance sheet, combined financial statement *(US)*; ~**forderungen** intercompany claims (equities); ~**gesellschaft** affiliated (associated) company, affiliated (consolidated) corporation *(US)*; ~**guthaben** intercompany assets; ~**leitung** central management of a combine; ~**umsatz** external (group) turnover (sales); ~**verflechtung** interlocking combine; ~**vorstand** group's board.

Konzertzeichner *(Börse)* stag *(Br.)*.

Konzession concession, *(Bank)* charter, [commercial] privilege, *(Erlaubnis)* permit *(Br.)*, *(Verkaufsrecht)* licence [to operate], franchise *(US)*; ~ **beantragen** to apply for a licence; ~ **entziehen** to withdraw a concession, to revoke a licence; ~ **erteilen** to grant a charter (privilege).

konzessioniertes Gewerbe licensed (licenced, *US)* trade.

Konzessions|**abgabe** municipal compensation *(US)*; ~**entzug** revocation of a licence; ~**gebiet** franchise field *(US)*; ~**gebühr** charter (licence, concession) fee; ~**inhaber** concessio(n)aire, holder of a licence, franchisee *(US)*, concessionary *(US)*; ~**rück**-

nahmeklausel escape clause *(US)*; ~**steuer** licence tax, franchise (privilege) tax *(US)*; ~**urkunde** *(Bank)* charter, organization certificate *(US)*; ~**vertrag** licensing (franchise, *US)* agreement; ~**zeit** chartered time, permitted hours *(Br.)*.

Kopf | **eines Briefes** letterhead; ~ **einer Rechnung** billhead; **maßgebender** ~ **eines Unternehmens sein** to be the ruling spirit in a firm; ~**arbeiter** headworker, blackcoated worker *(Br.)*, white-collar man (worker) *(US)*; ~**bahnhof** loop station, terminus *(Br.)*, terminal *(US)*; ~**filiale** principal branch; ~**geld** allowance per head.

Kopie copy, counterpart, *(Durchschlag)* carbon [copy], tracing, flimsy *(Br.)*, transcript; **beglaubigte** ~ certified copy; **zusätzliche** ~ blind carbon copy.

Kopier|**anstalt** printing establishment; ~**einrichtung** copying equipment.

kopieren to [make a] copy, to print off, *(nachahmen)* to imitate, *(vervielfältigen)* to duplicate.

Kopier|**gerät** photostat, copying equipment; ~**papier** printing-out paper, flimsy.

Kopplungs|**geschäft** package (tie-in, *US)* deal, tying agreement *(US)*; ~**klausel** tying (tie-in, *US)* clause.

Körperschaft [organized] body, organization, corporate (incorporate) body.

Körperschaftssteuer corporation income *(US)* corporate, *Br.)* tax, income tax on corporations *(US)*.

Körperschaftssteuersatz corporate *(Br.)* (corporation, *US)* tax-rate.

Korrektur|**abzug** copy (first) proof, impress copy, proof sheet.

Korrespondent *(Berichterstatter)* [newspaper] correspondent, press agent (correspondent), stringer, *(Bank)* out-of-town correspondent, correspondent bank *(US)*, *(Geschäftsfreund)* business friend.

Korrespondenz *(Papiere)* papers, *(Post)* letters, post *(Br.)*, mail *(US)*; **frühere** ~ letters exchanged; ~ **mit jem. abbrechen** to cut off one's correspondence with s. o.; ~ **führen** to conduct a correspondence.

Korrespondenz|**bank** out-of-town correspondent, banker's correspondence, correspondent bank *(US)*; ~**büro** news (press) agency; ~**versicherung** home-foreign insurance *(Br.)*.

Kost | **und Logis** room and board; **in** ~ **geben** to board out, *(Börse)* to give on *(Br.)*; **in** ~ **nehmen** to take as a boarder, to board, *(Börse)* to take in.

Kosten cost, costs, expense[s], *(Auslagen)* outlay, *(Gebühren)* charges, fees, *(Preis)* price, cost; **abzüglich der** ~ charges deducted; **auf gemeinsame** ~ at joint expense; **auf** ~ **der Qualität** at the expense of quality; **mit großen** ~ **verbunden** at great cost; **unter Auferlegung der** ~ awarding the costs; **unter Nachnahme der** ~ charges forwarded; **abschreibungsfähige** ~ service cost; **aktivierte** ~

capitalized expenses; **direkte** ~ direct cost (expenses), traceable cost; **kalkulatorische** ~ imputed cost; **nachkalkulierte** ~ post-mortem cost; **pauschalierte** ~ bunched cost; **auf den Tageswert umgerechnete** ~ adjusted costs; **vorkalkulierte** ~ standard costs; **zusätzliche** ~ additional charges (expense), added costs;

~ **zuzüglich Verdienstspanne** cost plus; ~ **nach Abschreibungen** amortized cost; ~ **vor Abzug des Bardiskonts** billed cost; ~ **des Konkursverfahrens** cost of preserving and administrating the bankrupt's estate; ~ **der Lebenshaltung** cost of living; ~, **Versicherung und Fracht** cost, insurance and freight, c. i. f.; ~ **der Wiederbeschaffung** replacement cost; ~ **absetzen** to deduct costs; ~ **auferlegen** to allocate (order to bear) the costs; ~ **aufschlüsseln** to break down expenses; **sich auf jds.** ~ **bereichern** to get rich at s. one's expense; **sich an den** ~ **schlüsselmäßig beteiligen** to pool expenses; ~ **niedrig halten** to hold down costs, to keep costs in line; ~ **kalkulieren** to cost-account; ~ **nachgehen** to keep track of costs; ~**scheuen** *(fam.)* to balk at an expense; **entstandene** ~ **übernehmen** to pay the costs incurred from; ~ **umlegen** to apportion the costs; ~ **veranschlagen** to figure up the costs; ~ **nach sich ziehen** to carry costs.

kosten, etw. **100 $** to cost a matter of $ 100; **kleines Vermögen** ~ to cost the earth.

Kosten|abrechnung cost sheet; ~**abschreibung** cost recovery; ~**abwälzung** cost pass-alongs; ~**anschlag** cost account, estimate of costs; ~**anteil** cost fraction, share of the expense; ~**aufschlüsselung** expense classification; ~**aufstellung** statement of expenses, cost schedule.

Kostenaufwand expenditure, expense, cost, outlay; ~ **zu Marktpreisen** current cost; ~ **berechnen** to cost a job.

Kosten|begrenzung cost limit; ~**belastung** burden of costs; ~**berechnung** computation of costs, calculation of expenses; ~**blatt** *(Produktionsauftrag)* cost sheet; ~**buchhaltung** cost [book] keeping; ~**deckung sicherstellen** to cover production costs; ~**einsparung** economy, cost cutting (saving); ~**entwicklung** cost trend; ~**ersparnis von 30 % gegenüber den Konkurrenzfirmen erzielen** to save 30 % on costs versus competitors; ~**fachmann** cost accountant.

kostenfrei free of charge, off all (clear of) charges, cost-free, expenses covered.

Kosten|index standard cost system; ~**kalkulation** cost estimate; ~**kontrolle** cost control.

kostenlos gratuitous, gratis, cost-free, costless; **sonnabends** ~ **zugänglich sein** to be open free on Saturdays.

kostenmäßig, sich auswirken to make a showing on cost.

Kosten|miete minimum rent; ~**niveau halten** to hold the line on costs; ~**orientierung** cost orientation

Kostenpreis cost price, prime cost;
unter dem ~ **verkaufen** to sell below cost price.

Kosten|punkt factor cost, ~**rechnung** account of charges, statement of costs; ~**rechnungsblatt** job-order cost sheet; ~**rechnungssystem für auftragsweise Fertigung** job-order costing, specific order cost method; ~**rückstand** recoverable (residual) costs; ~**seite** cost side; ~**senkungsprogramm** cost-reduction program(me); ~**spirale** spiral(l)ing of costs; ~**stellenrechnung** cost centre accounting *(Br.)*, cost location accounting *(US)*; ~**tabelle** cost chart; ~**teilung** cost sharing; ~**träger** unit of cost; ~**überschreitung** cost overrun; ~**umlegung** apportionment of costs, cost allocation; ~**vergleich** comparison of costs; ~**verteilung** cost distribution; ~**voranschlag** estimate of costs, cost prediction (estimate); ~**vorschuß** [charges paid in] advance, advanced expense; ~**zuschlag** oncost.

Kost|gänger boarder, lodger; ~**geber** *(Börse)* giver on *(Br.)*; ~**geld** boarding money, pension allowance; ~**geld zahlen** to put on board wages; ~**geschäft** *(Börse)* contango *(Br.)*, backwardation business *(Br.)*; ~**probe** sample.

kostspielig costly, expensive, high-priced.

Kraftfahrer driver, motorist, automobilist.

Kraftfahrzeug motor vehicle, [motor] car, automobile;

zugelassenes ~ legally operating automobile; ~ **anmelden** to register a motor vehicle; ~**anhänger** trailer; ~**brief** car licence, motor vehicle registration certificate *(US)*; **allgemeine** ~**haftpflichtversicherung** standard automobile public liability policy; ~**industrie** motorcar (automobile) industry; ~**papiere** automobile ownership documents, car licence; ~**produktion** auto production; ~**steuer** automobile (motor vehicle) tax *(US)* (duty, *Br.*); ~**verkehr** vehicular (motor-vehicle) traffic, motor transportation; ~**zulassung** motorvehicle licence.

kraftlos inefficient, *(Markt)* languid; **für** ~ **erklären** to invalidate, to declare null and void, *(Wechsel)* to cancel.

Kraftstoff fuel, motor spirity, gasoline *(US)*, petrol *(Br.)*, gas *(coll)*;
wenig ~ **verbrauchen** to be good on fuel economy; ~**zuteilung** petrol ration *(Br.)* gasoline allowance *(US)*.

Kraftwagen [motor]car, automobile, motor, vehicle; ~**park** motor pool.

Kranken|hausbeihilfe in-hospital benefit; ~**kasse** sick-benefit (sickness) fund; ~**kassenmitglied sein** to subscribe to a health insurance *(Br.)*; ~**kassensystem** health-insurance plan *(US)*, panel system *(Br.)*; ~**versicherung** health *(Br.)* (medical, sickness, *US)* insurance.

Kredit credit, loan, advance, *(Ansehen)* public (general) credit, business reputation;
abgelehnter ~ declined credit; **beanspruchter** ~ used credit; **besicherter** ~ secured (covered) credit, collateral loan *(US)*; **bestätigter** ~ guaranteed (confirmed, *Br.*) credit; **durchgeleiteter** ~ transmitted credit; **genehmigter** ~ authorized loan;

gesicherter ~ secured loan (advance), collateral credit *(US)*; **von einem Konsortium gewährter** ~ syndicate credit; **zinslos gewährter** ~ credit given flat; **mittelfristiger** ~ medium-term credit; **projektgebundener** ~ tied credit; **überzogener** ~ overdraft, overdrawn credit; **ungedeckter** ~ open (unsecured, uncovered) credit, blank advance; **nicht zweckgebundener** ~ no-purpose (untied) loan; ~ **in laufender Rechnung** credit in current account; ~ **gegen Sicherungsübereignung** field warehouse loan; ~ **gegen Wertpapierlombard** lending on security, collateral loan *(US)*; ~ **abdecken** to repay a credit; ~ **aufbrauchen** to eat up (use) a credit; ~ **aufnehmen** to borrow money; ~ **beantragen** to request a loan; ~ **bewilligen** to grant a loan; **auf** ~ **geben** to [give on] credit, to chalk up, to [give upon] trust; **nur begrenzten** ~ **genießen** to enjoy very restricted credit; **abgesicherten** ~ **gewähren** to lend on security, to loan on collateral *(US)*; **zinslosen** ~ **gewähren** to give a flat credit; **j. für einen** ~ **von 4000 $ für gut (sicher) halten** to consider s. o. safe for a credit of $ 4000; ~ **kündigen** to draw in a loan; ~ **in Anspruch nehmen** to run a line of credit; ~ **refinanzieren** to refinance a loan; ~ **untergraben** to undermine credit; ~ **verlängern** to extend [the term of] a credit; ~ **mit 12 % verzinsen** to pay 12 per cent interest on a loan; **fälligen** ~ **zurückzahlen** to meet a loan when due; ~**anfrage ablehnen** to turn thumbs down on a loan; **umfassendes** ~**angebot sicherstellen** to arrange for a credit package; ~**anstalt für Wiederaufbau** Reconstruction Loan Corporation; ~**antrag** application for credit, loan (credit) application.
Kreditaufnahme borrowing, raising of credit; ~ **durch Abtretung von Debitoren** borrowing on accounts receivable *(US)*.
Kredit|auskunft credit information *(Report)*, trade reference, special rating *(US)*; ~**ausschuß** credit (loan) committee; ~**bearbeiter** credit man, loan officer; **erhebliches** ~**bedarf auslösen** to build up a lot of loan demand; ~**bedingungen** credit terms; ~**bereitstellung** allocation of funds; ~**bestätigung** confirmed credit; ~**bewilligung** credit vote; ~**brief** letter (bill) of credit, credit [letter]; ~**bürgschaft** continuing (special) guaranty *(US)*, credit guarantee *(Br.)*; ~**erhöhung** credit expansion, further advance; ~**erleichterungen** easing of (ease in, relaxion in) credit; ~**fachmann** credit manager.
kreditfähig good, [financially] sound, solvent.
Kredit|fähigkeit credit standing (status), creditability, borrowing power; ~**fazilitäten** credit (borrowing, overdraft) facilities; ~**geber** lender, borrower, creditor.
Kreditgenossenschaft credit cooperative (union), mutual loan society *(Br.)*; **landwirtschaftliche** ~ production credit association *(US)*.
Kredit|geschäft credit transaction (operation); ~**gesuch** application for a credit; ~**gewährung**

borrowing, lending; ~**gewährung mit offengelegter Forderungsabtretung** notification type of a loan; ~**grenze** limit of credit *(Br.)*, credit limit *(Br.)*, credit line *(US)*; ~**höhe** amount (extent) of a loan.
kreditieren *(gutschreiben)* to [pass (place) to the] credit, *(Kredit gewähren)* to sell (give) on credit.
Kredit|inflation credit inflation; ~**institut** credit (financial) institution; ~**kapital** borrowed capital; ~**karte** credit card; ~**kasse** loan (credit, *Br.)* bank; ~**kontingent** portion of a credit; ~**konto** loan (personal) account; ~**kosten** borrowing costs; ~**kündigung** notice of withdrawal; ~**laufzeit** period of credit.
Kreditlinie credit limit *(Br.)*, limit of credit *(Br.)*, credit (cash) line *(US)*;
einjährige ~ **eingeräumt erhalten** to obtain a line of credit to run for one year *(US)*; ~ **überschreiten** to exceed a credit, to run over the credit limit *(Br.)*.
Kredit|marge limit of credit *(Br.)*, credit line (margin) *(US)*; ~**mittel** credit instrument (resources); ~**möglichkeiten einschränken** to contract credit; ~**nachfrage** demand for credit; ~**nehmerin** borrowing company (corporation).
Kreditoren creditors, *(Bilanz)* accounts due (payable, *US)*, account payables *(US)*; ~ **in laufender Rechnung** account current creditors; ~**buchhalter** voucher (accounts payable, *US)* clerk; ~**buchhaltung** accounts payable department *(US)*.
kreditorisch, mit seiner Bank nur ~ **arbeiten** to maintain cash balances at a bank on a nonborrowing account.
Kredit|plafond *(Betrieb)* borrowing limit, *(Bankdirektor)* lona portfolio; ~**politik** credit (loan, lending) policy.
kreditpolitisches Instrumentarium credit instrument, measures of credit policy.
Kredit|prolongation extension (renewal) of a credit; ~**prüfung** means test *(Br.)*, credit rating *(US)*; ~**rahmen** credit limit *(Br.)* (line, *US)*; ~**richtlinien** credit rules (standards).
Kreditsaldo credit (loan) balance; ~ **zu meinen Gunsten ausweisen** to present (show) a balance to my favo(u)r.
Kredit|schädigung discredit; ~**schwindel** obtaining money by false pretences; **Aktien als** ~**sicherheit verwenden** to apply shares as collateral security *(US)*; **nicht in Anspruch genommener** ~**teil** credit reserves, unused credit; ~**überschreitung** overdrawing of an account, overdraft; ~**verhandlungen** loan talks; ~**verkäufe in offener Rechnung** credit sales on open accounts; ~**verknappung** credit restriction (tightness, crunch); ~**versorgung** credit supply; ~**vertrag** credit agreement (arrangement); ~**volumen** credit volume; **auf dem** ~**wege** by raising a credit.
kreditwürdig good, [financially] sound, solvent, creditable, credit-worthy.
Kredit|würdigkeitsprüfung credit standing (rating, *US)*; ~**zinsen** interest due (receivable, *US)*; ~**zusage** standby credit.

Kreis circle, quarter, *(Bezirk)* borough *(Br.)* parish *(Br.)*, county *(US)*, district *(US)*;
aus ~en der Industrie according to industry sources;
~lauf der Wirtschaft trade (business, *US)* cycle.
Kreuzung crossing, crossover, crossroads, *(Bahn)* junction, *(Scheck)* crossing.
Kriegs|anleihe war loan, national war (defence) bonds; ~beschädigtenrente war pension; ~gewinnsteuer express profit duty *(Br.)*, war profits tax *(US)*; ~risikopolice war-risk policy; ~versehrtenrente disability pension; ~versicherung war-risk insurance.
kriegswichtig|en Beruf ausüben to be in a reserved occupation; ~e Güter strategic goods.
krisen|anfällig prone to crisis; ~fest panic-(crisis-) proof, *(Konjunktur)* depression- (slump-) proof.
Kühl|schiff refrigerated (cold-storage) vessel; ~waggon *(Bahn)* reefer.
kulante Bedingungen accommodating terms.
Kulisse *(Börse)* coulisse, curb (kerb, *Br.)* market.
kündbar callable, *(Anleihe)* redeemable, redemandable, *(Kapital)* subject to call (notice);
jederzeit ~ at (on) call;
täglich ~es Geld call money, demand deposits.
Kunde customer, purchaser, consumer, demander, *(Anwalt)* client, *(Werbeagentur)* account;
bar bezahlender ~ cash customer; fester ~ regular customer, patron; sparsamer ~ economy-minded customer; voraussichtlicher ~ sales prospect; zahlungsfähiger ~ solvent client; ~ in laufender Rechnung checking-account depositor;
~n abziehen to entice away (drum up, *US)* customers; ~n anschreiben lassen to carry a customer; ~n besuchen to canvass customers; regelmäßiger ~ sein to patronize; ~n werben to acquire (canvass, drum) customers, to bring business.
Kunden|akte *(Werbeagentur)* account folder; ~auftrag customer's order; ~bedienung serving of customers; ~berater *(Werbeagentur)* account executive; ~beschwerden customer's complaint; ~besuch business (sales) call, calling on customers; ~beurteilung durch die Bank customer's position at the bank.
Kundendienst service [to the customer], servicing of consumers, repair (after-sales) service;
guten ~ haben to provide with intelligent service; ~abteilung service department.
Kunden|etat *(Werbeagentur)* account; ≙feindlich against the interest of customers; ~forderungen *(Bilanz)* uncollected debts, receivables from customers *(US)*, receivables *(US)*; ~guthaben consumer deposit; ~kartei list of customers; ~konto customer's ledger, charge account.
Kundenkredit consumer credit, customer's loan, retail credit *(US)*;
~bank hire-purchase finance house *(Br.)*, consumer credit agency, instalment house *(US)*, personal loan company *(US)*; ~karte charge card.
Kunden|kreis [range of] customers, goodwill; ~liste list of customers, client list, customer register;
sich in eine ~liste eintragen lassen to register with a tradesman; ~skonti discounts granted; ~stamm customers, custom, connection; ~wechsel trade bill (paper), customer's acceptance (bill), *(Bilanz)* customer's notes, trade receivables *(US)*, bills receivable *(US)*; ~werbung canvassing of orders, acquiring (getting) business; auf die ~wünsche abstellen to aim at the needs of customers; ~zeitschrift external house organ, sales bulletin, shopping news.
kündigen *(Anleihe)* to give notice of withdrawal (redemption), *(Arbeitgeber)* to give notice (warning), *(Arbeitnehmer)* to sign off, to quit one's job *(US)*, *(Kapital)* to call in, to recall, to demand repayment, *(Mieter)* to give notice to quit, to vacate, *(Obligationen)* to call in;
zum nächsten Ersten ~ to give a month's notice; jem. fristlos ~ to dismiss s. o. without notice (summarily); Hypothek ~ to foreclose a mortgage; Kredit ~ to demand repayment of a loan; seinem Vermieter ~ to give one's landlord notice [of leave]; Vertrag ~ to cancel (revoke) a contract.
Kündigung notice [to quit (to leave)], *(Abkommen)* denunciation, *(Anleihe)* notice of redemption, *(Kapital)* calling in, recalling, *(Mieter)* warning, notice to quit, *(Vermieter)* notice to leave;
mit monatlicher ~ subject to a month's notice; außerordentliche ~ dismissal for exceptional reasons; fristgemäße ~ dismissal with notice; kurzfristige ~ short-term cancellation; nahegelegte ~ *(Beamter)* involuntary resignation; unberechtigte ~ unjust discharge;
~ eines Angestelltenverhältnisses loss of service; ~ einer Anleihe call for redemption of a loan; ~ einer Hypothek foreclosure; ~ eines Vertrages termination (cancellation) of a contract;
einem Angestellten mit der ~ drohen to threaten an employee with dismissal; einem Mieter die ~ zustellen to give a tenant notice to quit.
Kündigungsbenachrichtigung notice of dismissal.
Kündigungsfrist term (period) of notice;
unter Einhaltung einer ~ observing a term of notice;
gesetzliche ~ legal (statutory) notice;
auf Einhaltung der ~ verzichten to waive notice.
Kündigungs|grund ground for giving notice; ~recht *(Anleihe)* redeemable feature, *(Vertrag)* cancellation privilege; ~schreiben written notice, *(Bank)* letter of withdrawal.
Kundschaft custom, patronage *(coll.)*, clientele, business, buyers, connection, connexion *(Br.)*;
ausgedehnte ~ wide connection; gut verdienende ~ upper-income customers;
wenig ~ haben to have little custom; sich die Aufmerksamkeit seiner ~ sichern to key one's publicity; ~ übernehmen to acquire the goodwill.
Kunst|auktion art sale; ~stoff plastics, synthetic (plastic) material; ≙stoffverarbeitende Industrie plastics-processing industry.

Kupon [dividend] coupon, *(scheck)* block slip, counterfeit *(Br.)*, stub *(US)*;
ohne ~ coupon off, ex coupon;
ausstehende ~s outstanding coupons;
~ in Form einer Bestellkarte return coupon.
Kupon|abschlag einbringen to recover the coupon;
~inhaber coupon holder; ~scheck coupon check *(US)* (cheque, *Br.)*; ~steuer tax on coupons (dividend).
Kupplungsangebot combination offer.
Kurator curator, trustee, warden, guardian.
Kuratorium board of trustees (regents, *US).*
Kurs price, market rate (price), market, *(Lehrgang)* course, *(Notierung)* quotation, value, *(Schiff)* course, *(Termingeschäft)* forward (future, *US)* rate, *(Wechselkurs)* rate of exchange;
bei sinkenden ~ at reduced prices;zu verschiedenen ~en limitiert on a scale; zum ersten ~ at the opening [price]; zum höchsten ~ at the highest rate of exchange;
amtlicher ~ market (official) rate, official quotation; außerbörslicher ~ curb [market] price, inofficial quotation; fester ~ fixed (established) rate, fixed (firm) price; gedrückte ~e depressed (slackening, low level of) prices; gestützter ~ pegged price, günstiger ~ favo(u)rable exchange (rate); nachgebende ~e sagging (receding) prices; rückläufige ~e dropping rates; steigende ~e soaring prices, rising market; variabler ~ variable exchange, consecutively quoted price;
~ für Sichtpapiere sight rate; ~e mit großer Spanne zwischen Geld- und Briefkurs wide prices;
~ des Pfundes an den Dollar anhängen to peg the value of the pound to the dollar; ~e unzulässig beeinflussen to rig the market *(Br.)*; ~e auf einen neuen Tiefstand bringen to carry the price to a new low level; ~ drücken to depress the market; ~e durch Verkäufe drücken to raid the market; plötzlich im ~ fallen to break; am ~ gewinnen to benefit by the exchange; sich auf dem gestrigen ~ halten to remain stationary at yesterday's price; schlechtes Geld außer ~ setzen to call in clipped money; hoch im ~ stehen to be in great demand, *(Börse)* to rule (be) high; plötzlich im ~ steigen to have a sudden rise, to skyrocket *(US)*; Abschlüsse auf New York zum ~ von ... tätigen to effect exchange deals on New York at . . .; ~ von 480 überschreiten to cross 480; ~ stützen to peg the market;
~e bröckeln ab prices are easing off (crumble [off]);
~e gingen sprunghaft höher prices jumped; ~e liegen gebessert prices have improved; ~e mangels Nachfrage gestrichen no quotation, only sellers; ~e sind abgeschwächt prices have eased, market off *(US)*; ~ sind unverändert prices have remained unchanged; ~e zeigen eine rückläufige Bewegung prices show a downward tendency; ~e zogen an prices have hardened.
Kurs|abschlag decline, drop (fall, decline) in prices;
~abschwächung weaker tendency in prices; ~angabe quotation; ~anstieg improvement in prices

(rates); leichter ~anstieg moderate rise; ~anstieg auf breiter Front widely spread improvement (rise); ~anzeigetafel exchange board; mit kleinen ~aufbesserungen schließen to close with small advances; ~aufschlag price increase, improvement; ~auftrieb upward movement; ~befestigung stronger tendency in prices; amtlicher ~bericht official quotation, stock-exchange list; heftige ~bewegungen pyrotechnics *(US)*; rückgängige ~bewegung retrograde movement of prices; ~blatt stock-market report *(US)*, stock-exchange list *(Br.)*; ~blatt für Freiverkehrswerte over-the-counter report *(US)*; ~druck pressure of prices, raid; ~einbruch break [in prices], stock-market slump; ~einbuße bis zu 10 % erleiden to suffer a loss in exchange up to 10 per cent; ~ertragskraftverhältnis price-earnings ratio; ~festsetzung [price] quotation, rate-fixing mark *(US)*; ~garantie exchange-rate guarantee; ~gefälle price differential; ~gewinn *(Börsengewinn)* turn of the market *(Br.)*, market profit, *(Devisengeschäft)* exchange profit.
kursieren to circulate, to be in circulation, to be current (in circulation).
Kurs|index price (stock-exchange) index; ~intervention price (exchange) intervention; ~limit limited price; ~makler stockbroker, exchange broker; ~manipulation manipulation of the market.
Kursniveau price level;
~ künstlich beeinflussen to boom (rig, *Br.)* the market; hohes ~ haben to rule high.
Kursnotierung exchange list (advice), prices p{uo}ted, price quotation, marking;
erste ~ first board; letzte ~en latest prices.
Kurs|notiz market quotation; ~parität exchange parity; ~risiko risk of exchange; ~rückgang, ~rückschlag decline [in prices], receding (sagging, dropping) prices; ~schwankungen fluctuations in the exchange; ~sicherung foreign exchange guaranty; ~spanne exchange difference, turn of the market.
Kursstand price level, level of prices;
hoher ~ high rate;
. niedrigsten ~ erreichen to touch the bottom; ~ halten to hold the level.
Kurssteigerung price advance, improvement, rise [in prices], appreciation in (run-up of, *US)* prices; ~en in Spezialwerten advances in special shares (stocks, *US)*;
erhebliche ~ aufweisen to show great improvement.
Kurs|stützung price support, peg, pegging the exchange (of prices); ~tafel quotation board; ~telegramm telegraphic exchange quotation; ~treiber market maker (rigger, *Br.)*; ~umschwung price swing.
Kursus course, class, school, lecture;
vollständiger ~ full-credit course;
sich zu einem ~ anmelden to sign up for a course;
~leiter instructor; ~teilnehmer enrollee, trainee.

Kurs|verbesserung [price] improvement; ~**verhältnis** rate of exchange; ~**verlust** shrinkage in the price of stocks; ~**wert** market price (value), quoted value, *(Devisen)* market rate; ~**zettel** exchange (price) list, printed exchange; ~**zuschlag** *(Report)* contango (continuation, carrying-over) rate *(Br.)*.

Kurtage brokerage.

Kurtaxe nonresident tax.

Kurzarbeit part time [work], short hours, *(zwecks Bekämpfung der Arbeitslosigkeit)* staggering short.

kurzarbeiten to be on part (short) time.

Kurzarbeiter short- (part-) time worker.

Kurzarbeitsvereinbarung share-the-work plan *(US)*.

kürzen to reduce, to abate, *(Ausgaben, Gehälter)* to cut down, to curtail;
Arbeitszeit ~ to reduce working time.

Kurzfilm short subject, filmlet, short *(Br.)*, quickie.

kurzfristig short, at short date (notice);
j. ~ **beschäftigen** to employ s. o. temporarily;
als ganz ~ **Anlage** for a turn; ~**e Anleihe** short-term loan; ~**e Einlagen** deposits at short notice; ~**e Finanzierung** short-term financing; ~**er Kredit** short-term loan (credit); ~**er Schatzwechsel** trasury bill.

kurzlebige Konsumgüter perishable consumer goods.

Kurz|nachrichten news summary, news item (in brief), wrapup of the news, newsflash *(US)*; ~**parkzone** limited parking zone; ~**schrift** stenography, shorthand; ~**streckenfrachtgeschäft** short-haul business; ~**streik** quickie strike *(US)*.

Kürzung deduction, diminution, decrease, *(Ausgaben, Gehälter)* cut, cutting down, curtailment.

Kurz|versicherung term insurance; ~**waren** petty wares (goods), narrow goods, haberdashery *(Br.)*, dry goods *(US)*.

Küsten|dampfer coasting steamer (trader); ~**fracht** coasting cargo; ~**schiffahrt** coastal navigation.

Kux mining share (stock, *US);*
~**buch** cost book.

L

Lade|bühne ledge, platform, loading jack *(US)*; ~**fähigkeit** cargo (carrying) capacity, *(Schiff)* tonnage, load [displacement]; ~**fläche** loading space; ~**frist** loading time; ~**linie** load line.

Laden shop *(Br.)*, store *(US)*, outfit;
betriebseigener ~ industrial store *(US)*; **vermieteter** ~ store for rent *(US)*; **zollfreier** ~ duty-free shop;
~ **und Löschen zu Lasten des Schiffs** gross terms; **seinen** ~ **aufmachen** to open one's shop; ~ **führen (haben)** to keep [a] shop, to storekeep *(US)*; ~ **vermieten** to rent (lease) a shop.

laden to load, to lade, *(Fracht)* to [take in] freight, to embark cargo, *(Schiff)* to ship;
Aktionäre zur Hauptversammlung ~ to summon shareholders to a general meeting *(Br.)*; **Stückgüter** ~ to freight (ship, *US*) by parcel.

Laden|aufseher shopwalker *(Br.)*, floor walker *(US)*; ~**besitzer** merchant, shopkeeper *(Br.)* storekeeper *(US)*; **j. zu einem ~bummel mitnehmen** to trot s. o. round; ~**dekoration** store decoration *(US)*; ~**diebstahl** shoplifting, shopbreaking; ~**front** shop front, storefront *(US)*; ~**geschäft** shop *(Br.)*, store *(US)*, business; ~**hüter** shelf warmer, old stock, back number, drug in the market, sticker *(US)*; ~**inhaber** occupier of a shop, shopkeeper *(Br.)*, storekeeper *(US)*; ~**kasse** cash drawer, stand, [shop] till, *(Registrierkasse)* cash register; ~**miete** shop rent, store lease (rental) *(US)*; ~**schild** [shop] sign, facia; ~**schluß** closing time, shutting up shop; **nach ~schluß** after hours; **früher ~schluß** early (half-day, *Br.)* closing; ~**straße** shopping (shoppy) street, promenade street; ~**tisch** counter, desk, shopboard; ~**verkauf am Sonntag** Sunday store openings *(US)*; ~**verkaufspreis** selling (retail, resale) price.

Lade|papiere shipping documents; ~**platz** wharf, loading place; ~**rampe** ramp, loading platform, dock *(US)*; ~**raum** stowage, freight (cargo, loading) space, *(Schiff)* hold.

Ladeschein bill of lading, carrier's receipt, receiving note, consignment, shipping bill (note) *(US)*; **abgestempelter** ~ backed note;
~ **an Order ausstellen** to prepare an order bill of lading.

Lade|spesen loading charges; ~**tage** running days; ~**tonnage** load displacement; ~**verzeichnis** freight (cargo) list, *(Zoll)* shipper's manifest; **gebührenfreie ~zeit** free time.

Ladung load, loading, lading, burden, portage, *(voller Waggon)* truckload, wag(g)onload, *(Warensendung)* consument shipment *(US)*;
abgehende ~ outward cargo (freight); **durchgehende** ~ through shipment; **gemischte** ~ general (mixed, *Br.)* cargo; **sperrige** ~ measurement (bulky) cargo;
~ **zur Hauptverhandlung** originating summons; ~ **brechen** to break bulk; ~ **einnehmen** to load [up], *(Schiff)* to take in freight (cargo); ~ **löschen** to discharge (land) a cargo, to clear a ship of her cargo, to unload; ~ **versichern** to take a risk on a cargo; ~ **verstauen** to stow freight.

Ladungs|fähigkeit carrying capacity, *(Schiff)* tonnage, load displacement; ~**manifest** captain's (shipper's, ocean, *US*) manifest.

Lage state, position, situation, condition, *(Belegenheit)* site, locality, situs, location *(US)*;
meine finanzielle ~ my worldly circumstances;
sich finanziell in einer schlimmen ~ **befinden** to be at one's beam-ends;

~**bericht** background (situation) report; ~**plan** layout, groundplan, site plan.

Lager *(Flüchtlinge)* camp, encampment, *(Gebäude)* storehouse, warehouse *(US)*, depot, *(Vorrat)* store, stock, stockpile, inventory;
ab ~ ex store (warehouse, *US)*; **nicht am** ~ out-of-stock;
beweglich geführtes ~ buffer stock; **reich sortiertes** ~ well-assorted stock;
~ **in allen Sorten** stock of all kinds;
~ **abbauen** to reduce (cut) an inventory, to run down stocks; **auf** ~ **arbeiten** to work on stock; ~ **wieder auffüllen** to stock up, to restock *(US)*; ~ **ausverkaufen** to clear out; **zu großes** ~ **führen** to be overstocked; **auf** ~ **haben** to [hold in] store, to keep in (have on, *US)* stock; **nur gängige Sorten auf** ~ **haben** to have only conventional designs in stock; ~ **knapp halten** to keep down an inventory; ~ **räumen** to unstock a store, to clear off old stock; **ganzes** ~ **verbrauchen** to work up all the stock;
~**abbau** inventory cutting (reduction); ~**abnahme** stock shrinkage; ~**anforderung** stores (stock, purchase) requisition; ~**anstieg** growth of inventories; ~**auffüllung** inventory buildup; ~**aufseher** storeman, storer, storekeeper *(Br.)*, warehouseman *(US)*; ~**aufstockung** stockpiling; ~**aufwertung** writeup of stock value.

Lagerbestand stock [in (on) hand], unsold inventory, leftover stocks, statement of goods;
höchster ~ stock peak; **zu hoher** ~ inflated stocks;
~ **aufnehmen** to [make up an] inventory, to take stock; ~ **ergänzen** to refill the stock.

Lagerbestands|auffüllung replacement of inventories, inventory building; ~**wert** inventory value.

Lager|bewertung inventory (merchandise) valuation; ~**bezugsschein** stores (stock, purchase) requisition; ~**buch** warehouse (store, inventory, stock) book; ~**buchhalter** stores ledger's clerk; ~**empfangsbescheinigung** warehouse receipt *(US)*; ~**ergänzung vornehmen** to replenish one's inventory (stock); ~**fläche** floor space; ~**gebühren** storing (warehouse, *US)* charges; ~**geschäft** storage (storing) business, warehousing *(US)*.

Lagerhalter storekeeper *(Br.)*, store clerk *(Br.)*, stockkeeper;
~**konossement** custody bill of lading.

Lagerhaltung stockkeeping, storing, warehousing *(US)*.

Lagerhaus staple house, storehouse, storage, depot, packhouse, warehouse *(US)*;
~ **für unverzollte Waren** bonding warehouse *(US)*;
~ **für zollpflichtige Güter** licensed warehouse *(US)*;
~ **für nicht zollpflichtige Güter** wharf;
~**gewerbe** storage business, warehousing *(US)*.

Lager|herstellung production for stock; **hohe** ~**investitionen** heavy stock; ~**ist** store (warehouse, *US)* clerk, warehouseman *(US)*; ~**kartei** stock recorder; ~**kontrolle** stock (inventory) control; ~**kosten** cost of storage, yardage, carrying (warehousing, warehouse, *US)* charges.

lagermäßig herstellen to make for stock.

Lagermiete storage, store (warehouse, *US)* rent, store hire.

lagern to store, to stockpile, to deposit, to [put in] warehouse *(US)*, *(im Freien stapeln)* to dump; **unter Zollverschluß** ~ to bond.

Lager|nummer store (storing) number; ~**pfandschein** deposit warrant, warehouse receipt *(US)*; ~**platz** depot, entrêpot, storing place; **vorsichtige** ~**politik betreiben** to keep down an inventory; ~**rabatt** stock rebate; ~**raum** storage, stowage, storeroom; ~**restbestand** leftover, residue of stocks.

Lagerschein warrant for goods *(Br.)*, storage check, wharfinger's receipt, warehouse receipt (certificate, warrant) *(US)*;
für sicherungsübereignete, beim Eigentümer verbliebene Waren field warehouse receipt *(US)*;
~**inhaber** warehouse receipt holder, *(US)*.

Lager|schrumpfung dwindling of stocks; ~**schuppen** shed; ~**umschlag** inventory (stock, merchandise) turnover.

Lagerung storing, storage, stowage, housing, warehousing *(US)*;
~**sicherungsübereigneter Waren** field warehousing *(US)*.

Lagerungs|gebühren cost of storage, stowage, warehousing expenses *(US)*; ~**geschäft** storage business, warehousing [business] *(US)*.

Lager|veralterung obsolescence of stock; ~**verwalter** store-room (stock) clerk, stockman *(US)*, warehouse keeper *(US)*.

Lagervorräte, geringe low inventory;
~ **abbauen** to liquidate an inventory; **auf** ~**n festsitzen** to sit on stockpiles.

Lager|wirtschaft updating of inventory, stockpiling; ~**zeit** time of storing, storing time; ~**zugänge** addition to stocks; ~zyklischer Aufschwung step-up in inventory growth *(US)*.

lahmlegen *(Handel)* to paralyse, to cripple.

lancieren, j. to start s. o. on a career, to carve out a carrer for (launch) s. o.; **Anleihe** ~ to float a loan.

Land country, land, *(Ackerboden)* ground, soil, *(Grund und Boden)* [piece of] land, landed property, plot, lot;
am Verrechnungsabkommen [nicht] beteiligtes ~ [non]clearing country; **brachliegendes** ~ fallow; **valutaschwaches** ~ country with a low monetary standard;
~ **mit stabiler Währung** hard-currency country;
~ **parzellieren** to divide (parcel out) land into smallholdings;
~**aufkäufer** landgrabber.

Lande|bahn *(Flugzeug)* airstrip, landing strip; ~**einrichtungen** landing facilities; **auf** ~**erlaubnis warten** *(Flugzeug)* to stoppe around; ~**genehmigung** landing permit; ~**platz** landing, landing place (platform, site), quay, wharf, pier, *(Flugzeug)* landing field.

Länder, devisenschwache soft-currency countries;
~ **des Sterlingblocks** scheduled territories *(Br.)*.

Landes|arbeitsamt regional labo(u)r office; **~auf-sichtsmat für das Kreditwesen** bank commissioner *(US)*; **~bedarf** home consumption; **~produkte** home (inland) commodities, inland produce; **~währung** home (legal, local, domestic) currency.

Landeszentralbank *[etwa]* Federal Reserve Bank *(US)*, Bank of England *(Br.)*; **Konto bei der ~ unterhalten** to have a deposit account with the Federal Reserve Bank *(US)*.

Landhaus country house, country seat, chalet.

ländliche Kreditgenossenschaft agricultural credit corporation.

Landstraße country (local, parish, public, main) road, public way; **~ erster Ordnung** highway, classified *(Br.)* (primary) road.

Landung landing, *(Ausschiffung)* debarkation, disembarkation, *(Flugzeug)* landing, descent.

Landungsgewicht *(Flugzeug)* landing weight.

Landwirt peasant [proprietor], farmer.

Landwirtschaft agriculture, rural economy; **industriell betriebene ~** factory farm.

landwirtschaftlich|er Betrieb farm, agricultural enterprise; **~e Genossenschaft** agricultural cooperation; **~er Verlustbetrieb** submarginal farm.

Landwirtschafts|bank land (farmer's) bank, farm loan bank; **vollmechanisierter und völlig durchorganisierter ~betrieb** highly mechanized and intensively cultivated farm.

längerfristige Kredite medium-term loans.

langfristig long-term (-dated, -range); **~e Anleihe** long-term loan; **~ angelegte Kapitalien** capital investments; **~e Verschuldung** long-term indebtedness.

lang|jähriger Mietvertrag long-term lease; **~lebige [Wirtschafts]güter** durable goods.

Langstreckenflugzeug long-range airplane.

Last burden, *(Belastung)* encumbrance, charge; **zu ~en der Gemeinde** chargeable to the parish; **zu ~en des Käufers** to be paid by the buyer; **finanzielle ~en** financial burden, charge; **soziale ~en** social contribution; **Saldo zu Ihren ~en aufweisen** to show a balance to your debit; **zu jds. ~en gehen** to fall on (be borne by) s. o.

lastenfrei free of charges (from encumbrances); **~es Grundstück** unencumbered estate.

Lastschrift debit entry (item), debit [advice]; **~anzeige** debit note; **~beleg** debit voucher; **~verfahren** direct debiting method.

Lastwagen [motor] lorry *(Br.)*, automobile] truck; **schneller ~** pickup truck; **schwerer ~** heavy lorry *(Br.)* (truck); **mit ~ befördern** to lorry *(Br.)*, to [ship by] truck *(US)*; **~beförderung** road haulage (transport), motor transport, truckage *(US)*; **~fahrer** lorry *(Br.)* (truck, *US)* driver, trucker *(US)*, truckman *(US)*; **~kolonne** trucking fleet *(US)*; **~transport** motor transport, road haulage, truckage *(US)*.

Laufbahn career, walk, race.

Laufbursche footboy, pageboy, caddie, runner, shopboy, delivery (messenger, errand), boy;

laufen *(gültig sein)* to run, *(Maschine)* to go, to operate, to run, *(Verhandlungen)* to be in progress.

laufend | ergänzen to keep up to date; **~ notieren** to quote consecutively; **~e Ausgaben** fixed expenses; **~er Bedarf** current demand; **~es Konto** account current; **~e Notierung** consecutive quotation; **in ~er Rechnung stehen** to have a current account.

Laufkunde change (street) customer (purchaser).

Laufzeit period to run, running, run, validity, duration, life, *(Fälligkeit)* maturity, due date, *(Wechsel)* term, currency, tenor; **~ eines Akkreditivs** life of a letter of credit; **~ einer Hypothek** mortgage term *(Br.)*; **dreißig Tage ~ haben** to have thirty days to run.

Laufzettel tracer, clearance chit, routing slip.

laut | Aufstellung as per statement; **~ beiliegender Rechnung** as indicated in enclosed invoice.

lauten to read, to run; **auf den Inhaber ~** to be payable to bearer; **auf den Namen ~** to be registered, *(Wechsel)* to be payable to bearer; **an Order ~** to be payable to order.

Lauterkeit des Wettbewerbs fair trade *(US)*.

Leben life, existence, *(Handel)* activity; **verbundene ~** *(Versicherung)* joint lives; **sein ganzes ~ mit finanzwirtschaftlichen Fragen beschäftigt sein** to spend one's entire career on the financial side; **sein ~ versichern** to insure one's life.

leben, au pair to get food and lodging in requital of one's services; **im Ausland ~** to stay abroad; **von den Einkünften seiner Frau ~** to live on one's wife; **auf großem Fuße ~** to live on a large scale (in a lavish style); **getrennt ~** *(Eheleute)* to live apart; **von seinem Kapital ~** to live on one's capital; **von staatlicher Unterstützung ~** to live off government checks; **über seine Verhältnisse ~** to overrun the constable.

lebendig live, *(Börse)* brisk, animated.

Lebens|bedarf livelihood, subsistence; **in jds. privaten ~bereich eindringen** to violate s. one's privacy.

Lebensdauer age, life, length (duration, span) of life, *(Anlagegut)* mortality, service life; **mutmaßliche ~** probable life, life expectancy; **wirtschaftliche ~** economic life.

Lebens|erwartung life expectancy; **~haltung** cost of living.

Lebenshaltungsindex index number of cost of living, cost-of-living (consumer's price) index.

Lebenshaltungskosten living costs, cost of living; **preistreibend für die ~ sein** to pace the general increase of living cost; **~anstieg** cost-of-living rise; **~ausgleichsformel** cost-of-living adjustment formula; **~[gleit]klausel** cost-of-living [escalator] clause.

lebenslänglich|er Nießbrauch life interest; **~e Rente** life annuity.

Lebenslauf course of life, career, *(schriftlich)* personal record, curriculum vitae.

Lebensmittel provisions, victuals *(Br.)*, food [supplies], foodstuffs;
~ **rationieren** to ration food;
kostenloser ~**abschnitt** food stamp benefit; ~**geschäft** food shop (store, *US*), grocery shop *(Br.)* (store, outlet) *(US)*; ~**paket** food parcel; ~**preise** food prices; ~**versorgung** food supply.

Lebens|standard standard (level, *US*, scale, rate) of living, living standard; ~**stellung** walk of (place in) life, establishment.

Lebensunterhalt livelihood, living [costs], sustenance, necessaries, bread, support, subsistence;
seinen ~ **finden** to pick up a livelihood *(Br.)*.

Lebensunterhalt[ung]s|kosten cost of living, living expenses; ~**zuschuß** cost-of-living allowance.

Lebensversicherung life insurance (assurance, *Br.*), *(auf den Todesfall)* whole-life assurance *(Br.)*, ordinary life insurance *(US)*;
~ **mit laufender Beitragszahlung** life insurance in force; **gemischte** ~ **auf den Erlebnis- und Todesfall** combined endowment and whole-life insurance;
~ **mit abgekürzter Prämienzahlung** limited payment insurance.

Lebensversicherungsgesellschaft life [-insurance (-assurance, *Br.*)] company.

Lebensversicherungspolice life [insurance, assurance, *Br.*] policy, life,
~**zeitlich befristete** ~**police** term policy; **umwandelbare** ~**police** convertible term policy;
~ **mit Gewinnbeteiligung** life insurance with profits;
~ **mit gleichbleibenden Prämien** ordinary life policy.

Lebensversicherungs|prämie life-insurance (-assurance, *Br.)* premium; ~**vertrag** life-insurance (assurance, *Br.)* contract.

lebenswichtige | Betriebe key industries; ~ **Güter** essential goods.

lebhaft *(Börse)* animated, brisk, cheerful, active;
~ **und fest** *(Börse)* active and strong;
~**e Nachfrage** strong (brisk, active) demand; ~**er Verkehr** heavy traffic.

Leckage, Leckwerden leakage, ullage.

leer empty, *(Formular)* blank, *(Haus)* vacant, unoccupied;
~**e Stelle** vacancy.

Leer|abgabe *(Börse)* bearish sale *(Br.)*, short selling *(US)*; ~**aufmachung** dummy; ~**gewicht** deadweight; ~**gut** empties; ~**laufzeit** idle time; ~**taste** space bar; ~**tonnage** dead-weight tonnage, light displacement; ~**verkauf** short sale *(US)*; ~**verkauf tätigen** to write a call naked; ~**zimmer** vacant (empty) room, unfurnished lodging.

Legat legacy, bequest, gift by will, devise.

Legitimationspapiere identification papers.

Lehr|beruf teaching profession (job); ~**brief** indenture; ~**gang** [training] course, class school; **teures** ~**geld zahlen** to pay dearly for one's experience; ~**jahre** apprenticeship.

Lehrling apprentice, learner.

Lehrlings|ausbilder apprentice teacher, apprentice-

ship; **im** ~**verhältnis** indented, apprenticed, articled, indentured.

Lehr|stelle apprenticeship; ~**werkstätte** shop-training department, vestibule school *(US)*; ~**zeit** [period of] apprenticeship.

Leibrente life annuity (rent, interest).

Leibrentenempfänger life annuitant, annuity holder.

leicht light, *(geringfügig)* slight, *(Markt)* easy
am Schluß ~ **sein** *(Geldmarkt)* to be an easy finish;
~ **Absatz finden** to meet with a ready market.

Leichtgut light cargo (goods, freight).

leihen to lend, to loan, to advance, *(von jem.)* to borrow, to take on hire;
Geld auf Hypotheken ~ to lend on mortgages.

Leih|gebühr lending fee; ~**haus** pawnshop, pawnbroker's shop; ~**kapital** loan (borrowed, hire of) money; ~**wagen** rented car; ~**wagengeschäft** car rental business, rent-a-car.

leisten to perform, to do, *(ausführen)* to carry out, to execute, to effect, to realize, *(erfüllen)* to fulfil(l), to accomplish, *(Maschine)* to render service;
Anzahlung ~ to make a deposit, to pay an account;
Nachzahlung ~ to make a subsequent payment;
Schadenersatz ~ to respond in (pay) damages.

Leistung performance, effort, *(geleistete Arbeit)* job, piece of work, work done, flow, stroke, *(Dienst)* service, *(Fähigkeit)* efficiency, ability, *(Gebrauchsgüter)* serviceableness, *(Maschine)* power, capacity, efficiency, performance, rating, *(Sozialversicherung)* benefit;
während des Bezuges der ~**en** while drawing benefits;
vertraglich geschuldete ~ contract debt; **vermögenswirksame** ~**en** property-creating performance;
~**en im Krankheitsfall** *(Versicherung)* sickness benefit *(Br.)* (allowance, *US*); ~ **der Sozialhilfe** public *(US)* (national, *Br.*) assistance benefits;
nach ~ **bezahlen** to pay by results; **mit den** ~**en in Verzug kommen** to get behind with the performance of a contract.

Leistungs|angaben performance data; ~**anspruch** *(Sozialversicherung)* right to draw benefits; ~**berechtigter beneficiary**; ~**beurteilung** performance (service, experinece, efficiency) rating; ~**empfänger** recipient of services; ~**entgelt** rate.

leistungsfähig able, capable, efficient, *(Gebrauchsgüter)* serviceable.

Leistungsfähigkeit ability, capability, functional capacity, efficiency, proficiency, form;
berufliche ~ job efficiency; **betriebliche** ~ productive (plant, operating) efficiency; **finanzielle** ~ financial capacity;
~ **bei voller Kapazitätsausnützung** full operating capacity.

Leistungs|grenze marginal productivity; ~**hindernis** *(Vertrag)* frustration; ~**höhe** *(Versicherung)* rates of benefit; ~**kurve** performance graph; ~**lohn** payment by results, incentive pay, efficiency wage *(US)*; ~**norm** standard of performance.

leistungspflichtig liable for service, contributory.
Leistungs|pflichtiger contributor; ~**prämie** production (performance, merit, *US*, step) bonus; ~**rückgang** decrease in performance; ~**steigerung** increased performance; ~**verlust** loss of efficiency; ~**verzeichnis** bill of quantities; ~**verzug** failure to meet obligations; ~**zulage** merit salary increase *(US)*, production (incentive) bonus.
Leit|artikel leader, leading (editorial) article; ~**bild eines Unternehmens** *(Werbung)* corporate image.
leiten to lead, to guide, to master, to head, to steer, *(Betrieb)* to manage, to run, to conduct, to operate, to be in charge, to direct.
leitend|er Angestellter executive [employee]; ~**e Stellung** leading (key, managerial) position.
Leiter leader, guider, manager, head, director; ~**kaufmännischer** ~ business manager; **technischer** ~ technical director (manager);
~ **der Exportabteilung** export manager; **alleiniger** ~ **einer Firma** sole proprietor; ~ **der Verkaufsabteilung** sales manager; ~ **der Versandabteilung** shipping clerk.
Leitfaden guide, handbook, textbook, manual.
Leitung lead, leading, conduct, carriage, *(Betrieb)* governing body, management, direction, operation *(US)*, *(Telefon)* line, wire;
unter der ~ von A. with A. in the chair; **unter neuer** ~ under new management;
~ **einer Gesellschaft** direction of a company, *(AG)* corporate management;
in der ~ bleiben *(Telefon)* to hold the line; **in der ~ mitzureden haben** to have a voice in the management.
Leitungs|störung *(Telefon)* line fault; ~**vermerk** *(auf Briefen)* routing; ~**währung** key currency; ~**zahl** code number.
Leser|analyse readership (circulation) analysis; ~**briefspalte** correspondence column; ~**prozentsatz** *(einer Anzeige)* noting advertising.
letzt|es Gebot highest bid; ~**e Nachrichten** *(Zeitung)* latest (stop press) news; ~**e Notierung** previous quotation.
Letztverbraucher ultimate user (consumer).
Leuchtreklame neon light (electric sign) advertising, translight.
Leumundszeugnis certificate of good behavio(u)r.
Liberalisierung liberalization, *(Importe)* decontrol; ~ **aufheben** to deliberalize.
Liberalisierungsliste free list.
Licht|pause blueprint, photocopy; ~**reklame** illuminated (electric sign) advertising; ~**spielhauswerbung** picture (movie, *US*) advertisement.
Liebhaber|preis fancy price; ~**wert** sentimental (fancy) value.
Liefer|abkommen supply contract, contract for [future] delivery; ~**annahme** taking delivery.
Lieferant supplier, contractor, deliverer, deliveryman, dealer, trade creditor, undertaker, vendor.
Lieferanten|eingang tradesmen's entrance; ~**kredit** supplier's (trade) credit; ~**skonti** trade discounts.

Liefer|anweisung delivery order; ~**auftrag** delivery (purchase) order.
lieferbar deliverable, available, ready for delivery, *(begebbar)* negotiable, *(auf Lager)* on stock, carried in stock, available;
in allen Größen ~ available in all sizes; **kurzfristig** ~ for short delivery; **sofort** ~ *(Börse)* spot; **beschränkt** ~ **sein** to be in short supply; **sofort** ~ **Waren** prompts *(Br.)*, *(Börse)* spots.
Liefer|bedingungen terms (conditions) of delivery, delivery terms; ~**bewilligung** delivery order, docket *(Br.)*; ~**datum** delivery date.
lieferfähig deliverable, available, carried on stock.
Liefer|firma supplier, purveyor [firm], deliverer; ~**frist** term of delivery; ~**garantie** performance guarantee; ~**gewicht** delivery weight; ~**geschäft** *(Börse)* time bargain, futures *(US)*; ~**klauseln** commercial (trade) terms.
liefern to supply, to deliver, to furnish, to provide, to procure, to place, *(Prämiengeschäft)* to put;
auf Bestellung ~ to supply to order; **sofort zu** ~ *(Börse)* spot; **Ware längsseits Schiff** ~ to deliver the goods alongside the ship.
Liefer|ort point (place) of delivery; ~**posten** lot; ~**preis** delivered price; ~**schein** bill of delivery (sale), delivery note (slip, receipt, ticket), docket *(Br.)*, supply note, shipping ticket *(US)*; ~**schwierigkeiten** delivery failures; ~**sperre** refusal to deal *(US)*; ~**termin** time (date, day) of delivery, delivery date.
Lieferung delivery, deliverance, supply, supplying, furnishing, *(Effekten)* delivery, *(Lebensmittel)* purveyance, catering, *(Schiffsladng)* cargo, *(Sendung)* consignment, *(Waggon)* carload;
bei ~ **zahlbar** payable (cash) on delivery;
vertraglich ausbedungene ~**en** contract supplies;
mangelhafte ~ bad delivery; **prompte** ~ *(Börse)* spot delivery; **unvollständige** ~ short delivery; **verspätete** ~ delayed delivery;
~ **am gleichen Tag des Abschlusses** *(Börse)* cash; ~ **frei Bahnhof** delivered at station; ~ **frei Haus** delivered (free) at residence; ~ **gegen Nachnahme** payment on delivery; ~ **nach Wahl des Käufers oder Verkäufers** buyer's or seller's option *(US)*; ~ **nur an Wiederverkäufer** supplied to trade only;
~ **anbieten** to tender delivery; **in** ~**en erscheinen** *(Buch)* to be published (appear) in instal(l)ments (parts); **auf** ~ **kaufen** *(Börse)* to buy forward (for future delivery, *US*, for settlement); **auf zukünftige** ~ **verkaufen** to sell on delivery (by anticipation), to sell forward (ahead).
Lieferungs|angebot tender, bid, proposal; ~**annahme** acceptance; ~**bedingungen** terms of delivery; ~**frist** term of delivery; ~**geschäft** *(Börse)* time bargain (purchase), *(Prämiengeschäft)* option deal *(Br.)* trading in puts and calls *(US)*; ~**preis** price agreed upon (of delivery); ~**schein** delivery order; ~**tag** *(Börse)* settling day, payday *(Br.)*; ~**verkäufe** *(Börse)* forward sales (selling), futures *(US)*.

~**verweigerung** withholding supply of goods from a dealer; ~**verzug** deferred (delayed) delivery; **im** ~**verzug sein** to be in default (late) in delivery; ~**vorschriften** delivery instructions; ~**wagen** delivery truck, van *(Br.)*, pickup; ~**zeit** delivery time.

Liege|bett couch; ~**gebühren** demurrage; ~**geld** *(Waggon)* demurrage, car service.

liegen *(Grundstück)* to be situated (located, *US*); **fest** ~ *(Kurs)* to hold, to be a hard spot; **gedrückt** ~ *(Kurse)* to be under pressure;
~ **bleiben** *(Waren)* to remain on stock.

Liegenschaften possession, immovables, immovable (real) estate, landed property.

Liegenschaftskonto real-estate (premises) account.

Liege|platz berth, moorage; ~**sltz** *(Schlafwagen)* sleeperette; ~**zeit** lay days.

Limit limit, stop order;
~ **erhöhen** to extend (raise) a limit.

limitierter Auftrag limited order.

Linie line *(Eisenbahn)* [railway, railroad, *US*] line, branch, leg, *(Straßenbahn)* number;
offene ~ *(Kredit)* unused portion.

Linien|abschluß *(Werbung)* package; ~**flug** scheduled *(US)* (commercial, one-line) flight; ~**flugzeug** commercial (scheduled, *US*) airliner; ~**gesellschaft** national flag (commercial) airline, sked *(US sl.)*; ~**verkehr** liner (stage) service, *(Flugzeug)* scheduled airliner service *(US)*, *(Frachtgeschäft)* linehaul movement.

Liquidation liquidation, dissolution, winding-up, *(Anwaltshonorar)* bill of costs *(Br.)*, fee;
~ **unter Aufsicht des Gerichts** liquidation (winding-up) subject to the supervision of the court; ~ **einer Bank** suspension of a bank's charter;
in ~ **gehen (treten)** to wind up, to liquidate.

Liquidations|anteil [liquidating] dividend; ~**bedingungen** *(Börse)* settlement terms; ~**bilanz aufstellen** to submit a statement of one's affairs; ~**erlös** proceeds of a liquidation; ~**guthaben** clearing balance; ~**masse** liquidating trust; ~**rate** [liquidating] dividend; ~**vergleich** scheme of arrangement *(Br.)*; ~**vorschlag** liquidation plan; ~**wert** liquidating value, *(Börse)* realization value, *(Investmentfonds)* net asset value.

Liquidator liquidator.

liquide liquid, cash-rich, (zahlungsfähig) solvent; **nicht** ~ illiquid, not liquid.

liquidieren to liquidate, to dissolve, to wind up *(Honorar)* to charge, to fee;
Gesellschaft ~ to wind up the affairs of a partnership.

Liquidität liquidity, liquid position;
mangelnde ~ liquidity shortage;
~ **ersten Grades** acid test, liquid ratio; ~ **zweiten Grades** current (working-capital) ratio;
für wirtschaftliche ~ **sorgen** to put the economy on a richer monetary diet.

Liquiditäts|abschöpfung absorption of liquidity; **kurzfristige** ~**anhäufung** *(Bankausweis)* window dressing; ~**anspannung** pressure on liquidity;

~**beengt** short of liquid assets (funds); ~**bestimmungen verschärfen** to clamp down on liquidity; ~**bilanz** liquid position; **für eine ausreichende** ~**decke sorgen** to establish enough liquidity; ~**grad** *(Bank)* current position, acid-test (quick-assets, *US*) ratio; **hoher** ~**grad** liquid strength; ~**kredit** liquid loan; ~**lage** liquid (cash) position, *(Bank)* current position.

liquiditätspolitisch|e Maßnahmen policy of active ease;
~**neutral sein** to have no effect on liquidity.

Liquiditäts|prüfung acid (liquidity) test; ~**spielraum** liquidity margin, reserve ratio *(US)*; ~**status** liquid (current) position; ~**umschwung** reversal in the money market; ~**verbesserungen für den Bankenapparat** easing of the monetary policy; ~**wirkung** liquidity-creating effect.

Liste list, calendar, schedule, scheme, bill, account, *(detaillierte Aufstellung)* specification, *(Inventarverzeichnis)* inventory;
schwarze ~ black (stop, unfair, *US*) list; ~ **der stimmberechtigten Aktionäre** voting list of shareholders *(Br.)* (stockholders, *US*); ~ **empfohlener Börsenwerte** stockbroker's list of recommendation; ~ **fauler Kunden** black book; ~ **übernommener Risiken** *(Versicherung)* risks book; ~ **geführter Telefongespräche** *(Hotel)* traffic sheet; ~ **börsengägniger Wertpapiere** the list;
~ **anführen** to top (head) a list; **in eine** ~ **eintragen** to enrol(l) (enter) in a list; **auf die schwarze** ~ **kommen** to be blacklisted.

Listenpreis catalog(ue) (scheduled, list[ing]) price, *(Werbung)* scale price;
empfohlener ~ suggested list price; **festgesetzter** ~ posted price.

Lizenz licence, license *(US)*, permit, royalty, franchise *(US)*;
~ **erteilen** to [issue (grant) a] licence, *(Gewerbe)* to accord permission to transact business;
~**abgaben** licence fees, royalty; ~**anteil** royalty interest; ~**betrieb** franchise *(US)*; ~**einkünfte** licensing income; ~**geber** licenser, grantor [of patent]; ~**gebühr** royalty, licence fees.

lizensieren to approbate, to license, to franchise *(US)*.

Lizenz|inhaber licence (claim) holder; ~**makler** franchise broker *(US)*; ~**verfahren** licence proceedings; ~**vertrag** licensing agreement.

Lobby lobbying group, lobby.

Lockartikel bait, lure, [loss] leader *(US)*.

Logis, Kost und board and lodging.

Lohn wage, hire, rate, *(Bezahlung)* pay, payment, *(Entgelt)* compensation, consideration, return;
auskömmlicher ~ living wage; **geringer** ~ chickenfeed *(sl.)*; **überdurchschnittlich hoher** ~ loose (runaway) rate; **ortsüblicher** ~ local wage; **übertariflicher** ~ out-of-line rate; **untertariflicher** ~ superannuated wage, subminimum rate;
gleicher ~ **für gleiche Arbeit** equal pay for equal work; ~ **unter dem Existenzminimum** below poverty wage;

vom ~ **abziehen** to deduct from the wage; **j. um ~ und Brot bringen** to deprive s. o. of his livelihood; ~ **pfänden** to garnishee (attach, US) the wages; **bei jem. im ~ stehen** to be in s. one's service (pay). **Löhne, außertarifliche** bootleg wages; **fällige ~** *(Bilanz)* accrued payrolls; ~ **und Gehälter** cost of labo(u)r, *(Bilanz)* payrolls *(US)*; ~ **angleichen** to equalize (realign) wages; ~ **auszahlen** to pay (hand) out wages.

Lohn|abkommen mit garantierter Mindestbeschäftigungszeit guaranteed wage plan; ~**abrechnung** earnings statement, pay slip; ~**abzug** stoppage *(Br.)*, dockage, payroll deduction, deduction of wages; **gebündeltes** ~**angebot** pay package; ~**angleichung an den Lebenshaltungsindex** cost-of-living adjustment.

Lohnanstieg wage increase (rise, hike, boost, US); **gnereller (umfassender) ~** across-the-board wage increase; **produktivitätsgebundener ~** productivity-related pay hike.

Lohn|arbeit wage (paid) labo(u)r, wage-earning work; ~**aufbesserung** wage increase (rise); ~**aufwand** cost of labo(u)r, wage costs (expenses); ~**auseinandersetzung** labo(u)r dispute; ~**ausgleich** wage stabilization.

Lohnbuch salary (wages) book; ~**halter** wage (payroll, US) clerk; ~**haltung** personnel (payroll, US) accounting.

Lohn|diener daily (hired) servant; ~**einbehaltung** detention (stoppage, Br.) of (withholding from) wages; ~**einstufung** wage classification; ~**empfänger** wage earner; ~**empfehlungen** wage recommendations.

lohnend paying, payable, payoff, remunerative.

Lohn|erhöhungen auf den Verbraucher abwälzen to pass on wage increases to the consumer; ~**faktor** wage factor in costs; ~**festsetzung** wage determination (fixing); ~**forderungen** wage claims (demands); ~**- und Gehaltsfortzahlung im Krankheitsfall** short-term disability benefits; ~**- Preis-Gefüge** wage-price structure; **einbehaltene** ~**gelder** holdback pay *(US)*; ~**gleitformel** escalator formula; ~**gruppe** wage scale (bracket); ~**index** wage index; ~**konto** payroll (wage) account.

Lohnkosten labo(u)r, cost of labo(u)r, payload *(US)*; **unmittelbare ~** direct wages (labo[u]r cost); ~ **je Produktionseinheit** unit wage costs; ~**anteil** payload *(US)*, labo(u)r charge; **inflationsbereinigter** ~**index** national wage index corrected to take out inflationary effects.

Lohn|leitsätze wage guidelines; ~**liste** payroll [ledger (book, US], pay bill (sheet).

Lohnniveau wage (pay) level, standard of wages; ~ **einfrieren** to peg the wage rates.

Lohn|pfändung wage garnishment *(US)*; ~ **- Preiskontrolle** wage-price control; ~**-Preis-Spirale** wage-price spiral; ~**quote** wage share; **gleitende** ~**regelung** wage escalation; ~**scheck** wage check

US) (cheque, Br.); **Staatliche ~schlichtungsstelle** National Wages Board *(Br.)*.

Lohnskala scale of wages, wage scale; **gleitende ~** sliding scale, escalator clause.

Lohn|spanne wage (rate) range (spread); ~**steigerung** wage increase (raise).

Lohnsteuer witholding (wage) tax; **einbehaltene ~** personal withholding tax *(US)*; ~**abzüge** payroll deductions *(US)*; ~**abzugsverfahren** payroll deduction plan *(US)*, pay-as-you-earn system (plan) *(Br.)*; ~**freibetrag** employee's withholding exemption *(US)*; ~**pflichtiger Beruf** payroll employment *(US)* (tax) table; ~**tabelle** withholding *(US)* (tax) table.

Lohnstopp wage freeze (stop); ~ **und Preisstopp** freeze of pay and prices; ~**- und Preissenkungspolitik** wage-freezing and price-lowering policy.

Lohn|streifen wage (pay) slip; ~**summensteuer** selective employment tax *(Br.)*, payroll tax *(US)*; ~**tabelle** wage schedule, pay scale *(US)*.

Lohntarif wage (compensation) rate (schedule); ~**änderung** wage rates changes.

Lohn|tüte wage packet (envelope), pay packet; ~**unterschied** wage differential; ~**veredelung** job (contract) processing; **betriebliche ~vereinbarung** labo(u)r-management contract; ~**verhandlungen** wage talks (negotiations); ~**verrechnungskonto** payroll clearing account *(US)*; ~**vorauszahlung** wage advance; ~**zahlung** wage payment; ~**zettel** payroll voucher *(US)*, pay slip; ~**zulage** wage increase, supplementary wage.

Lokal rstaurant, public [eating] house, premises, pub *(fam.)*, saloon *(US)*.

Lokal|interessen local interest; ~**markt** spot market; ~**umschreibungen** interbank clearings.

loko verkaufen to sell for spot delivery.

Loko|geschäft spot (cash) business (transaction); ~**preis** price loco, spot price; ~**waren** spot goods, spots.

Lombard|bestände collateral holdings (deposits) *(US)*; ~**darlehn** loan on securities, collateral loan *(US)*; **als ~deckung fungieren** to serve as security (collateral, US); ~**depot** derivative (collateral, US) deposit.

lombardfähig suitable for loans, pawnable, eligible to serve as collateral *(US)*.

Lombardgeschäft lending on securities, collateral loan business *(US)*.

lombardieren to advance (lend) money on securities, to pawn *(Br.)*, to collaterate *(US)*, to hypothecate *(US)*.

Lombardierung von Wertpapieren pledging of securities, borrowing on collateral security *(US)*.

Lombardkredit secured advance, lombard (collateral, US) loan; ~ **aufnehmen** to pledge securities, to borrow on collateral *(US)*.

Lombard|satz lombard margin (lending, US) rate; ~**schein** qualifying agreement, hypothecation certificate *(US);* als ~**unterlage nicht gewertet werden** to be thrown out of loans, to be ineligible to serve as security (collateral, *US).*

Los lot, *(Anleihe)* lottery bond, *(Anteil)* share, lot, portion, *(Lotterie)* [lottery]ticket, *(Warenpartie)* lot, parcel.

Löscharbeiten unloading.

Löschen der Ladung breaking bulk.

löschen *(Waren)* to discharge, to land, to unload, to unship;
Firma im Handelsregister ~ to remove a firm from the register; **Konto** ~ to close an account.

Lösch|erlaubnis discharging (landing) permit; ~**platz** discharging port (berth), unloading berth; ~**tage** laying days.

Löschung *(Auflösung einer Firma)* dissolution, extinguishment, *(Entladen)* discharge, unloading, landing, unshipping;
franko ~ landed terms;
~ **eines Eintrags** cancellation of an entry; ~ **im Handelsregister** deregistration; ~ **durch Leichter** lighterage;
~ **einer Hypothek im Grundbuch eintragen lassen** to enter satisfaction *(Br.).*

Löschungs|antrag *(Grundbuchrecht)* memorandum of satisfaction *(Br.), (Patentrecht)* application for revocation; ~**bewilligung** *(Grundbuchrecht)* satisfaction (release, *US)* of mortgage; ~**fähige Quittung** *(Grundbuch)* satisfaction piece *(US);* ~**gebühren** unloading (landing) charges; ~**hafen** port of discharge (delivery); ~**kosten** unloading (landing) charges; ~**schein** landing certificate.

lose loose, unpacked, in bulk, *(Öl)* naked;
~ **verladene Güter** bulk goods.

Loseblattbuchführung loose-leaf ledger (accounts).

lösen, Fahrkarte to take (buy) a ticket.

Losnummer ticket (lottery) number.

Lotse, amtlich angestellter branch pilot; **seeamtlich befähigter** ~ licensed pilot.

Lotsen|boot pilot craft (cutter); ~**dienst** pilot service; ~**gebühr** pilotage; ~**zwang** compulsory pilotage.

Lotterie lottery, drawing of prizes (lots);
in der ~ setzen to put in the lottery;
~**anleihe** lottery loan; ~**einnahme** lottery office; ~**klasse** class; ~**los** [lottery] ticket; ~**steuer** lottery tax; ~**ziehung** drawing lots.

Lotto lotto, policy *(US),* pools, number lottery;

~**annahmestelle** policy shop *(US);* ~**schein** policy slip (ticket) *(US).*

Luft|brücke airlift, sky lift; ~**eilfrachttarif** air express rates *(US).*

Luftfahrt aviation, aerial (air) navigation;
~**abkommen** aviation agreement; ~**industrie** aircraft industry.

Luftfracht air freight *(Vorzugssatz)* commodity rate; ~**bahnhof** aircargo terminus; ~**dienst** airfreight service; ~**geschäft** airfreight forwarding, air cargo business; ermäßigte ~**rate** commodity rate; ~**sendung** air shipment.

Luft|kissenfahrzeug air-cushion vehicle; ~**korridor** air-cushion vehicle; ~**korridor** air lane (corridor); ~**linie** airline, beeline; ~**paketpost** air-[mail] parcel post; ~**pirat** hi[gh]jacker.

Luftpost airmail, aerial (air) post *(Br.);*
per ~ schicken to transport mail (post) by airplane, to airmail;
~**bezugspreis** airmail rate; ~**brief** airmail letter; ~**gebühr** airmail fee; ~**papier** onionskin, foreign paper; ~**verkehr** airmail service; ~**zustellung** delivery by air.

Lufttransport air transport[ation] (shipment, commerce, conveyance), movement by air;
~**gesellschaft** airline (air-cargo) carrier; planmäßig gewerblicher ~**verkehr** commercially scheduled air transport.

Luftverkehrs|abkommen air transport convention (travel agreement); ~**gesellschaft** airline (airways) company (corporation, *US);* ~**ordnung** rules of the air; ~**strecke** airline.

Luft|verschmutzung pollution of the air; ~**weg** air route, airway; ~**werbung** sky writing, aerial advertising.

Lumpen|händler rag-and-bone man, dealer in rags; ~**sammler** rubbish hunter, *(letzter Zug)* flying fornicator.

Lustbarkeitssteuer entertainment (admission, *US)* tax.

lustlos *(Börse)* flat, dull, lifeless, sluggish, quiet, easy, slack, inactive, featureless, lackluster.

Lustlosigkeit des Marktes market inactivity.

Luxus|artikel luxury (fancy) goods, luxuries, fancy article(s); ~**dampfer** luxury liner; ~**güter** luxury goods, luxuries; ~**hotel** luxurious (luxury, exclusive) hotel; ~**packung** fancy packaging; ~**waren** luxuries, fancy (luxury) goods; ~**wohnung** luxury apartment (flat).

M

Macherlohn make, maker's wage, manufacturing price.

Magazin store, storehouse, magazine, depot *(Zeitschrift)* periodical, magazine;
~verwalter storekeeper *(Br.)*, warehouse keeper *(US)*.

Mahnbrief dunning (monitory, collection, *US)* letter.

mahnen, Schuldner brieflich to claim one's debts from s. o., to dun a debtor.

Mahnschreiben dunning (monitory, collection, *US)* letter.

Mahnung monition, demand, *(Zahlungsaufforderung)* dunning [screw], request for payment;
schriftliche ~ monitory (follow-up, dunning) letter.

Mahnzettel prompt note, reminder.

Majorität, anteilmäßige majoritiy in interests; **kapitalsmäßige** ~ majority in amounts; **qualifizierte** ~ qualified majority; **zahlenmäßige** ~ majority in numbers.

Majoritäts besitzer controlling shareholder *(Br.)* (stockholder, *US)*; ~**kauf** *(Börse)* nontaxable exchange.

Makler [merchandise] broker, go-between, middleman, agent, factor, negotiator, *(Börse)* [stock]-broker, jobber *(Br.)*, stockjobber *(Br.)*, dealer *(US)*, *(Immobilien)* real-estate broker, land jobber; **selbständiger** ~ associate broker, floor broker (trader); **vereidigter** ~ sworn broker;
~ **in kleinen Effektenabschnitten** odd-lot broker (dealer, *US)*;
als ~ **tätig sein** to be in the stockbroking line;
~ **verbeten** no agents *(Br.)*;
~**büro** broker's office, *(Immobilien)* [real] estate office, land agency; ~**courtage** broker's fee; ~**firma** brokerage, broker's firm, firm of stockbrokers, *(Immobilien)* land agency *(US)*, estate agency *(Br.)*; ~**gebühr** broker's charge, brokerage; ~**geschäft betreiben** to job, to deal in stocks; ~**gewerbe** brokerage industry; ~**provision** brokerage, broker's commission (fee), *(Finanzmakler)* finder's fee; ~**stand** broker's board, trading (stock, *US)* post, pitch *(Br.)*.

Makulatur surplus sheets, waste (spoil) sheet;
~**bogen** sheet of waste paper.

Mangel *(Fehlbetrag)* deficiency, deficit, *(Knappheit)* shortage, scarcity, penury, need;
aus ~ **an Mitteln** for lack of funds;
innewohnender ~ inherent defect (vice); **versteckter (verborgener)** ~ latent (hidden) defect;
~ **des Erfüllungsgeschäftes** lack (want) of delivery;
~ **an Schiffsraum** scarcity of tonnage; ~ **der im Verkehr erforderlichen Sorgfalt** ordinary negligence;
für einen ~ **haften** to be liable for a defect.

Mängel shortcomings;
~**anzeige** demonstration (notice) of defect; ~**aus-**

schuß caveat emptor; ~**gewähr** warranty of fitness, express warranty.

mangelhafter Zustand defectiveness, faultiness.

Mängelhaftung warranty of fitness, express warranty.

mangelnde | Gegenleistung failure of consideration; ~ **Vertretungsmacht** absence of authority.

Mängelrüge notice (demonstration) of defect, customer's complaint;
~ **berücksichtigen** to consider a complaint.

mangels | Akzeptes protestiert protested for non-acceptance; ~ **Nachfrage** owing to lack of demand;
~ **Zahlung** for want of payment.

Mangelware scarce (deficiency) goods, goods in short supply.

Manipulation handling, *(Börse)* manœuvre, manipulation, *(Währung)* management.

Manipulationsgebühr handling charge.

manipulieren *(Währung)* to manage, to manipulate.

manipuliert *(Börse)* manipulated, technical;
~**e Währung** managed currency.

Manko deficit, deficiency, defect, shortage, short; ~**geld** cashier's allowance, cash indemnity.

Mannschaft team, *(Schiff)* company, crew.

Mantel *(Firma)* shelter, cover, *(Wertpapier)* stock certificate;
~**gesetz** omnibus bill; ~**tarif[abkommen]** industry-wide (skeleton) agreement; ~**zession** general assignment.

Manuskript mansucript, MS, matter, copy, handwriting, *(Film)* scenario, script;
~ **durchsehen** to revise the copy.

Marge margin [of profit], spread *(US)*, *(Unterschied zwischen Brief- und Geldkurs)* turn of the market.

Marke *(Bezugsscheinwesen)* coupon *(Br.)*, *(Briefmarke)* [postage] stamp, *(Fabrikat)* brand, make, type, *(Kontrollmarke)* check, pass;
auf ~n rationed, couponed;
gut eingeführte ~ popular brand.

Marken artikel proprietary (patented, genuine, branded) article, speciality goods, branded merchandise; ~**betreuer** product (brand) manager; ~**bezeichnung** description, *(Einzelhandelsgesellschaft)* private brand; ~**erzeugnisse** trademarked commodities (goods), branded merchandise.

marken frei ration-(coupon)free, off ration, unrationed, uncouponed.

Marken index brand trend survey, brand barometer; ~**lieferant** brand supplier; ~**name** brand (distinctive) name, trade[mark] name.

markenpflichtige Waren coupon (rationed) goods.

Marken produkt make, brand; ~**treue** brand loyalty, consumer insistence; ~**werbung** brand advertising; **unerlaubtes** ~**zeichen** wildcat brand.

markieren to mark, *(kennzeichnen)* to earmark, to label, *(Ware)* to brand.

Markt market *(Absatz)* outlet, market, *(Börse)* stock exchange, *(Geschäft)* bargain, business, sale, *(Handelsplatz)* emporium, mart, *(Messe)* fair.

günstig auf dem ~ zu haben in season; **nicht für den ~ bestimmt** captive;

abgeschwächter ~ sagging market; **aufnahmefähiger ~** broad (ready) market; **schlecht befahrener ~** scanty market; **gut beschickter ~** market well stocked with goods; **sehr fester ~** buoyant market; **grauer ~** (grey) market; **uneinheitlicher und lustloser ~** sick market *(US)*; **auf umfangreiche Glattstellungen hin schwacher ~** liquidating market *(US)*; **schwarzer ~** black market; **mit Waren überschwemmter ~** glutted (overstocked) market; **unerschlossener ~** untapped market;

~ für Anlagewerte investment market; **~ für Industriewerte** industrial market; **~ für Kommunalpapiere** municipal market; **~ mit steigendem Preisniveau** advancing market; **~ für Staatspapiere (Staatsanleihen)** consols market; **~ mit großem Warenangebot** easy market; **für mündelsichere Wertpapiere** gilt-edged market *(Br.)*; **~ für nicht notierte Werte** off-board market *(US)*, over-the-counter market *(US)*, kerb market *(Br.)*.

~ abhalten to hold a market; **~ aufteilen** to apportion a market; **~ durch Konzertzeichnungen beeinflussen** to stag the market; **~ beleben** to stimulate the market; **~ beschicken** to [send goods on the] market; **Aktienpaket auf den ~ bringen** to market one's block of shares; **~ erschließen** to tap a market; **am offenen ~ kaufen** to purchase in the open market; **~ stützen** to rescue the market; **~ mit Aktien überschwemmen** to unload stocks on the market; **auf den ~ werfen** *(Effekten)* to unload.

Markt|absprache marketing arrangement (agreement); **~analyse** market analysis (survey); **größeren ~anteil erobern** to get a bigger foot in the market; **~aufteilung** allocation of markets; **~aussichten** market prospects; **⌐beherrschend** market-dominating; **~belieferung** supplying of the market; **~beobachter** *(Börse)* security analyst *(US)*; **~bericht** market report, *(Kurse)* market price list; **rückläufige ~bewegung** downturn in the market.

Märkte beziehen to frequent fairs (markets).

Markt|enge narrow market; **~entwicklung** market development (trend); **~erholung** rally.

marktfähig marketable, salable.

Marktforschung market research, field survey; **~ für ein neues Erzeugnis** product research; **~ an Ort und Stelle** field survey.

marktgängig marketable, merchantable, current; **~e Preise** usual market prices.

Marktgeld stallage *(Br.)*, toll.

marktgerecht verzinst werden to carry a rate of interest in conformity with the market.

Markthalle covered market, market house *(Br.)*.

marktkonform in keeping with the market; **sich nicht ~ entwickeln** to run against the market's favo(u)r; **~e Mittel** [anti]cyclical measures.

Markt|lage market position (situation), market condition[s], course; **~lücke** market hole (gap); **~nachfrage** seller's market; **~ordnung** *(EG)* marketing regulation; **⌐orientiertes Verhalten** marketing behavio(u)r; **~pflege betreiben** to cultivate the market; **~platz** market place (square), market.

Marktpreis market price (rate), today's rate; **im freien Kräftespiel entstandener ~** commercial price; **freier ~** open-market price; **gegenwärtiger ~** ruling price; **~e durch Zurückhaltung beeinflussen** to wait out the market *(sl.)*.

Markt|regulierung regulation of the market; **~reifgestaltung** product planning; **~sättigung** saturation of consumer demands.

marktschreierische Ankündigung puffing advertisement, noisy advertising, ballyhoo *(US)*.

Markt|schwäche weakness in the market; **~schwankungen** market swing, fluctuating market; **~stellung** position in the market; **~studie** market-trend analysis; **~untersuchung** market research (analysis, audit), [market] survey, trade research; **~verhalten** market behavio(u)r; **~versorgung** supply of the market; **~vorrat** stock in the market.

Marktwert market, market (marketable, commercial) value, *(Börse)* exchange value; **führende ~e** *(Börse)* stalwarts of the market, leaders.

Marktwirtschaft, freie free enterprise (market) system.

marktwirtschaftliche Ordnung free enterprise system.

Maschine|n, arbeitssparende labo(u)r-saving machines; **betriebsbereite ~** machine in operating condition.

maschinelle Arbeit shopwork.

Maschinen|anlage machinery, plant, *(Schiff)* engine room; **~belegungsplan** jobshop sequencing *(Br.)*; **~benutzung abschreiben** to write off for depreciation of machinery; **~buchhaltung** mechanical bookkeeping, machine accounting; **~miete** machine rental; **~pachtvertrag ohne Wartung** financial lease; **~park** machinery, equipment; **~stundensatz** machine-hour rate.

Maß measure[ment], *(Eichmaß)* gauge, gage *(Br.)*, standard;

~ nach gemacht made to measure, bespoke *(Br.)*, custom-made *(US)*;

nach ~ anfertigen to make to order.

Masse mass, body, lump, *(Konkurs)* assets, debtor's property, *(Menge)* quantity, volume; **mangels ~** *(Konkurs)* return unsatisfied; **~n von Arbeitslosen** large bodies of unemployed men; **~ eines Vermögens** the bulk of a property; **mangels ~ einstellen** *(Konkursverfahren)* to stop bankruptcy proceedings for lack of funds; **in ~n herstellen** to mass-produce, to volume-produce; **~anspruch** *(Konkurs)* unsecured claim; **~gläubiger** general (unsecured, *US*, nonprivileged) creditor.

Massen|absatz mass marketing (selling); **~anreiz**

mass appeal; ~artikel staple articles (commodities, goods) ~aussperrung general lockout; ~beförderung transport in bulk; ~drucksachen bulk mail; ~einkommen mass income; ~entlassungen mass dismissals; ~fabrikation mass (volume, bulk, large-scale) production; ~güter bulk articles (commodities, goods); ~kaufkraft mass purchasing power; ~media mass-circulation media; ~produktion volume (serial, large-scale, mass, lot, quantity, bulk) production; ~publikum *(bei Werbesendungen)* admass; ~publikum anziehen to pull in the crowds; ~verbrauch mass (general, bulk) consumption; ~verhalten crowd (group) behavio(u)r; ~vertrieb mass selling.

Masse|schuldner debtor of a bankrupt's estate; ~verwalter *(auf Antrag der Konkursgläubiger)* receiver [and manager]; ~verzeichnis *(Konkurs)* statement of affairs, list of assets and liabilities, inventory of property.

Maß|geschäft bespoke business *(Br.)*, custom tailor *(US).*

Maßnahmen, finanzielle financial measures; marktwirtschaftliche ~ marketing operations; wirtschaftliche ~ economic regulations; ~ gegen den Höchstverbrauch treffen to cope with peak consumption; ~n zur konjunkturellen Belebung treffen to boost the stagnant economy.

Material material, matter, equipment, *(Börse)* supply, offerings; heute angebotenes ~ *(Börse)* offerings of stock today; fehlerhaftes ~ defective material; kriegswichtiges ~ strategic goods; rollendes ~ *(Eisenbahn)* rolling stock, equipment; ~ in Verarbeitung stock (work) in process; aus schlechtem ~ herstellen to fake; nur bestes ~ verarbeiten to employ the best workmanship only; ~anforderung requisition of materials; unmittelbarer ~aufwand direct material costs; ~ausgabeschein property-issue form; ~behandlung materials handling *(US);* ~bestandskonten direct goods accounts; ~empfangsbescheinigung material-received report *(US);* ~gemeinkosten indirect material costs; ~gemeinkostenzuschlag material cost burden rate; ~knappheit shortage of material.

Materialkosten material costs, costs of materials; indirekte ~ indirect materials, Löhne und ~ labo(u)r and material.

Material|lager contractor's store; ~probe specimen; ~prüfung material control; ~verbrauch material consumption; geschätzter ~verbrauch direct materials budget; ~verwalter storekeeper; ~vorrat stores, material supplies.

materielle Hilfe pecuniary aid.

Matern|dienst mat service; ~klischee pattern (boiler, *US)* plate.

matt *(Börse)* dull, stagnant, lifeless, inanimate.

Maximalpreis ceiling [price], limit, top price, peak.

Media|auswahl media selection; ~planung media planning.

Medio|abrechnung fortnightly (midmonth) settlement; ~liquidation fortnightly (midmonth) settlement.

Mehr|arbeit extra work, overtime; ~arbeitszuschlag overtime [premium] pay; ~ausgaben additional (increased) expenditure; ~bedarf additional (increased) demand; ~ertrag surplus, increment, excess profits.

mehrfaches Wechselkurssystem multiple currency.

Mehrfach|arbitrage compound arbitrage (arbitration); ~besteuerung double (multiple) taxation; ~stimmrecht multiple voting.

Mehr|familienhaus cooperative apartment house *(US)*, multiple-family dwelling; ~gebot advance, higher (further) bid; ~gepäck excess luggage *(Br.)* (baggage, *US);* ~gewinnsteuer supertax *(Br.),* excess profits tax *(US).*

Mehrheit majority, plurality *(US);* anteilmäßige ~ proportionate majority; beschlußfähige ~ quorum; einfache ~ bare (clear) majority; qualifizierte ~ qualified (special) majority; ~ nach der Höhe der angemeldeten Forderungen *(Konkursverfahren)* majority in amount of claims.

Mehrheits|aktionär majority stockholder *(US)* (shareholder, *Br.);* ~beschluß majority vote (decision, resolution); qualifizierter ~beschluß extraordinary resolution.

Mehr|kosten additional costs (expense, charges); ~phasensystem *(Besteuerung)* cumulative multistage system; ~preis higher (surplus) price; ~schichtbetrieb multiple-shift operation.

mehr|spaltig *(Anzeige)* spread; ~stellig of several places.

Mehr|verbrauch additional (excess) consumption; ~wegpackung dual-use (reusable) package.

Mehrwert surplus (added, excess) value; ~besteuerung value-added taxation; ~steuer value-added tax.

Mehrzweck|bauten multiple-unit housing; ~waggon general-purpose wag(g)on.

Meinung | der Schriftleitung editorial view; öffentliche ~ abschätzen to gauge public opinion.

Meinungs|befragung public-opinion poll; ~forscher public-opinion analyst, Gallup (research) man; ~forschung opinion poll (survey); ~käufe *(Börse)* speculation (speculative) purchases; ~verkäufe *(Börse)* speculative selling (sales).

Meistbegünstigung *(Zoll)* imperial preference *(Br.),* most favoured-nation treatment.

Meistbegünstigungs|klausel most-favo(u)red-nation clause; ~tarif most-favo(u)red-nation (preferential, *Br.)* tariff, preference *(Br.).*

meistbietend verkaufen to sell by (at, *US)* auction.

Meister master [of a trade], dabster *(Br. coll.), (Industrie)* foreman, master, overseer.

Meistgebot highest (last) bid, best offer.

melden *(amtlich)* to return, *(dienstlich mitteilen)* to report; sich ~ *(Gläubiger)* to come forward; sich auf ein Inserat hin ~ to answer an advertisement.

Meldeschein registration form.
Meldung registration, notification, *(Bewerbung)* application;
letzte ~en *(Zeitung)* stop-press news;
rechtzeitige ~ am Abfertigungsschalter *(Flugplatz)* check-in time.
Meliorations|darlehn loan for the purpose of improvement; ~gewinn *(Grundstück)* general benefit; ~kosten cost of improvement.
Menge quantity, amount, volume, deal, bulk, parcel, host, posse, wag(g)onload;
der ~ nach quantitative, by volume; in ungenügender ~ verladen short-shipped *(US)*;
nicht zum Handel geeignete ~n noncommercial quantities;
große ~ Geld loads (a mint, scads, *US)* of money;
in großen ~n eingehen *(Aufträge)* to pour in.
Mengen|absatz quantitative sales; ~abweichung quantity variance; ~auftrag volume (quantity) order; ~diskont space (volume) discount ; ~index quantum (quantity, quantitative) index; ~konjunktur quantitative market tendencies; ~notierung fixed exchange; ~produktion quantity production; ~rabatt quantity rate (rebate, reduction), space (volume) discount; ~staffel quantity scale; ~umsatz bulk sales; ~vorgabe quantity standard; ~zoll specific duty.
Merkmal, qualitatives *(Marketing)* attribute.
Merkposten *(Bilanz)* monitory item.
Meß|betrag *(Steuer)* ratal, rate; ~brief bill of admeasurement (tonnage).
Messe [industries] fair, show, exhibition, market, *(Fachmesse)* dealer show;
~ im Freigelände outdoor fair;
~ abhalten to hold a fair; sich zu einer ~ anmelden to register for a fair; ~ aufziehen to organize a fair; ~n besuchen to frequent (attend) fairs;
~ausweis fair pass; ~besucher fair goer (dealer); ~gelände fair site, exhibition grounds (site); ~gut goods sent to a fair; ~katalog fair catalog[ue]; ~stand exhibition (fair) stand; ~teilnehmer exhibitor.
Metageschäft *(Bankwesen)* deal on joint account, joint venture.
Metall|bestand *(Notenbank)* bullion reserve; ~warenindustrie ironmongery *(Br.)*, hardware industry *(US)*.
Miet|anzahlung key money; ~aufkündigung notice to quit; ~ausfall rental loss; ~bringschuld rent lying in prender *(Br.)*.
Miete rent, *(Entgelt für bewegliche Sachen und persönliche Dienste)* hire, *(Grundstück)* lease;
fällige ~ rent due; dem Mieterschutz unterliegende ~ controlled rent; jahresübliche ~ rackrent *(Br.)*;
rückständige ~ rent arrear;
~ für ein Zimmer lodging money;
~ abwerfen to yield a rent; ~ heraufsetzen to put up the rent; mit der ~ im Rückstand sein to be behindhand with one's rent; zur ~ wohnen to lodge, to live as lodger.

Miet|einkommen rental income, rent-roll; ~einkünfte abwerfen to produce rental income.
mieten to rent, to [take a (on)] lease, *(Arbeitskräfte, Sachen)* to [take on] hire;
Haus ~ to take a house on lease; Zimmer ~ to engage a room.
Mietentschädigung lodging allowance.
Mieter tenant, lessee, lodger, renter *(US)*, *(Einzelzimmer)* roomer *(US)*, *(Gegenstände)* hirer;
ausziehender ~ outgoing tenant; exmittierter ~ evicted tenant; unter Kündigungsschutz stehender ~ statutory tenant *(Br.)*;
~ hinaussetzen to turn s. o. out of a lodging, to evict a tenant; einem ~ kündigen to give s. o. warning (notice to quit).
Miet|erhöhung increase in rent; ~ermäßigung re mission of rent.
Mieterschutz rent control *(Br.)*;
~ in Anspruch nehmen to claim the protection of the Rent Acts *(Br.)*;
~bestimmungen rent restrictions *(Br.)*; ~gesetz Landlord and Tenant Act *(Br.)*.
Miet|ertrag rental, rent-roll; ~ertragstabelle rent schedule.
mietfrei wohnen to live rent-free in a house.
Miet|gegenstand leased (rental) property; ~höhe schiedsgerichtlich festsetzen lassen to refer the amount of rent to arbitration; ~kündigung notice to quit; ~pfändung distress for nonpayment of rent; ~preisentwicklung rental development; ~rückstände accrued rent; ~schuldner defaulting tenant; ~senkung reduction of rent.
Mietshaus apartment (lodging, tenement, flat, flat-ted) house, multiple dwelling, mansions *(Br.)*; ~besitzer apartment-house owner *(US)*;
Mietverhältnis tenancy, lease, landlord and tenant relationship;
gewerbliches ~ business tenancy;
~ aufheben to terminate a lease.
Mietvertrag lease [contract], [general] tenancy, *(Sache)* [contract for] hire;
monatlich kündbarer ~ tenancy from month to month;
~ für gewerblich genutzte Räume commercial lease;
~ abschließen to sign a lease; ~ kündigen to terminate a lease.
Miet|vorauszahlung forehand rent, advance rental, key money *(Br.)*; ~wagen hired (rented) car.
mietweise on hire (lease).
Mietwert, steuerlicher assessed rental;
~ der eigengenutzten Wohnung imputed rent.
Mietwohnung lodgings, lodgement, tenement;
abgeschlossene ~ self-contained flat.
Miet|zins, wirtschaftlich berechtigter commercial rent; ~zuschuß lodging allowance, rent subsidy.
Mikroökonomie microeconomics.
Minder|aufkommen deficit in taxes; ~betrag *(Kassendefizit)* cash shortage; ~erlös short proceeds, diminishing returns, *(Wertpapier)* discount; ~heitsbeteiligung minority interest (holding, share);

~**kaufmann** tradesman; ~**lieferung** short shipment.
Minderung des Kaufpreises abatement of purchase price.
minderwertig inferior, of inferior value, base, second-rate, trashy, off, low-class, low-grade; ~**e Ware** inferior goods, trash.
Mindest|anforderungen minimum requirements; ~**angebot** lowest tender; ~**beschäftigungszeit** minimum period of employment; ~**einkommen** minimum income; ~**einlage** *(Bank)* minium deposit; ~**frachtsatz** minimum freight rate; ~**freibetrag** *(Steuer)* exemption minimum; ~**gebot** *(Auktion)* put-up price, lowest bid; ~**grenze** *(Selbstbehalt)* franchise *(Br.)*; ~**guthaben** compensating balance; ~**leistung** *(Akkordlohn)* task, *(Versicherung)* minimum term period; ~**lohn** minimum wage (rate), base pay; **handelsübliche** ~**menge** minimum commercial quantity; ~**prämie zur Fortsetzung der Versicherung** natural premium; ~**preis** minimum (lowest possible, reserve, floor) price, *(Anzeigen)* minimum rate; ~**preise für den Einzelhandel festlegen** to establish minimum retail prices; ~**preishöhe** floor; **unter der gesetzlich festgelegten** ~**qualität** substandard *(US)*.
Mindestreserve statutory (bank, *US*) reserve, minimum reserve;
vorgeschriebene ~**n** fractional reserves;
~**n bei der Bundesnotenbank erhöhen** to increase the minimum reserve requirements *(US)* (their special deposits with the Bank of England, *Br.*).
mindestreservepflichtig reserve-carrying.
Mindest|reservesätze minimum reserve *(US)* (special deposits, *Br.*) requirements; ~**satz** minimum rate, *(Spediteur)* minimum charge; ~**stückgutgewicht** minimum carload weight; ~**stundenlöhne** minimum hourly rates of pay; ~**tarif** minimum rate (wage); ~**verdienst** minimum pay; ~**verkaufspreis** *(Auktion)* reserve (reservation) price; ~**wiederverkaufspreis** minimum resale price; ~**zeichnungsbetrag** minimum [amount of] subscription.
Mineralöl|steuer mineral-oil tax; ~**vorkommen** mineral deposit, prospect.
Minister Minister of the Crown *(Br.)*, Cabinet officer, Secretary of State *(Br.)*, Secretary *(US)*; ~ **ohne Geschäftsbereich** Minister without Portfolio.
Ministerium board *(Br.)*, ministry, office *(Br.)*, department *(US)*;
~ **für Arbeit** Ministry of Labour *(Br.)*, Labor Department *(US)*; ~ **für Wirtschaft** Commerce Department *(US)*.
Minoritätsbeteiligung minority interest.
Minutenpreis *(Rundfunkwerbung)* rate.
Misch|preis mixed price; ~**zoll** compound duty.
Miß|stimmung *(Börse)* depressed state, depression; ~**wirtschaft** maladministration, mismanagement, poor management.
Mitarbeit cooperation, collaboration, assistance.
Mitarbeiter colleague, cooperator, fellow worker, workfellow;

freier (freiberuflicher) ~ *(Zeitung)* contributing editor, stringer, free lance.
Mit|aussteller *(Wechsel)* fellow drawer; ~**besitzer** joint occupant (holder); **betriebliche** ~**bestimmung** management partition, codetermination; ~**bewohner** cohabitant, flatsharer *(Br.)*; ~**eigentum** common ownership; ~**eigentümer** joint owner (holder).
Mitglied, beitragspflichtiges contributory, dues payer *(US)*; **geschäftsführendes** ~ *(Aufsichtsrat)* managing director;
~ **eines Ausschusses sein** to sit on a committee.
Mitglieder|staat member country; ~**währung** *(OECD)* member's currency; ~**zahl** membership.
Mitglieds|beitrag membership contribution (dues, fee); ~**firma** member firm (corporation); ~**karte** membership card, ticket.
Mit|inhaber [co]partner, co-owner, joint partner, member of a firm; ~**nahme von Aktien** picking up of shares; **entscheidendes** ~**spracherecht haben** to have a say in the matter.
Mittags|pause lunch break, noon interval; **geschäftliche** ~**verabredung** business lunch.
Mitteilung information, communication, intelligence, *(amtliche Bekanntgabe)* notice, notification; **amtliche** ~**en** official news; **geschäftliche** ~ business press; **telefonische** ~ telephone message (communication);
~ **über die Einberufung zur Hauptversammlung** special notice.
Mittel instrument, means, vehicle, *(Geldmittel)* means, funds, resources;
aus eigenen ~**n** out of one's resources; **mit reichlichen** ~**n ausgestattet** well-financed; **ohne** ~ penniless, destitute, stranded;
bereitgestellte ~ appropriated funds; **flüssige** ~ available funds, funds on hand; **langfristige** ~ long-term funds; **die mir zur Verfügung stehenden** ~ the money at my command; **zweckbestimmte (zweckgebundene)** ~ earmarked (appropriated) funds;
~ **der Verkaufsförderung** sales-promotion aids; ~ **für den Wohnungsbau** funds for housing;
~ **abschöpfen** to siphon off funds; ~ **bewilligen** to grant the money; **bereitgestellte** ~ **um 4 % kürzen** to trim one's appropriations by 4 per cent; **über bedeutende** ~ **verfügen** to have large resources; ~**aufbringung** fund raising, mobilization (procurement) of funds.
mittelbar| haftpflichtig secondarily liable *(US)*; ~**er Boykott** secondary boycott.
Mittel|betrieb medium-sized (small, *US*) business; ~- **und Kleinbetriebe** medium and small-scale enterprises, small business *(US)*.
mittellos needy, impecunious, destitute, penniless; ~ **zurückbleiben** to be left unprovided for.
Mittel|qualität middle quality; **gehobene** ~**schicht** middle-upper class.
Mittelsmann middleman, intermediary, broker.
Mittelsorte medium quality.

Mittelstand middle class[es];
   gewerblicher ~ medium and small-scale enterprises, small business *(US)*.
mittelständisches Unternehmen medium-sized business, small business *(US)*.
Mittelverwendung allocation of resources; **~wert** mean [value], mean number; **~zuweisung** appropriation.
mittlere Qualität middling, medium quality; **~er Verfalltag** average due date.
Mitverschulden contributory (comparative, *US)* negligence; **~versicherung** coinsurance.
Möbelspediteur remover *(Br.)*, removal contractor *(Br.)*, mover *(US)*; **~speicher** pantechnicon *(Br.)*, [furniture] warehouse *(US)*.
Mobiliar furniture, furnishings, appointment, movables, household goods;
   ~pfändung distress, distraint.
mobilisieren to realize, to convert into cash.
möbliert | wohnen to live in furnished lodgings (apartments, rooms), to stay at private lodgings; **~es Zimmer** furnished room (apartment, *US)*.
Mode fashion, style, mode, vogue, go, kick;
   ~ aufbringen to set up (create) a fashion; **aus der ~ kommen** to get (go) out of fashion;
   ~artikel fancy article; **~geschäft** outfitter, fancygoods business.
Modell model, pattern, form, *(Maschine)* type;
   billiges ~ economy model;
   ~flugzeug model aircraft; **~haus** show house.
modern fashionable, modern, up-to-date, stylish.
modernisieren to modernize, to bring up to date, to streamline *(US)*.
Modernisierungskredit modernization loan.
Modesalon fashion bureau; **~warengeschäft** fancygoods business, millinery *(Br.)*.
Monatsabonnement monthly ticket; **~abstimmung** *(Konto)* monthly reconciliation; **~bedarf** monthly requirements; **~fahrkarte** monthly return (season, *Br.*, commutation, *US)* ticket; **~geld** time loan; **letzter ~umsatz** this month's trading.
Moneten *(fam.)* chink, tin, dibs, spondulicks, beans, gingerbread *(sl.)*, dingbat *(sl.)*, shiners *(sl.)*.
Monopol, gesetzliches artifical (special privilege) monopoly;
   ~e auflösen to break up monopolies; **~errichten (fördern)** to foster a monopoly;
   ~abgabe monopoly tax.
Monopolartikel proprietary article; **~gewinn** monopoly profit; **~industrie** monopolistic (monopolized) industry.
monopolisieren, Markt to engross (monopolize) the market.
Monopolkapitalismus monopoly capitalism; **~preis** monopoly price; **~stellung** monopoly, monopoly status; **~wirtschaft** monopolism.
Montage fitting, mounting assembly, assemblage.

~arbeit assembly work; **~betrieb** assembling (assembly) shop; **~halle** erecting (assembly) shop; **~werk** assembly plant; **~zeichnung** erection blue print.
Montanaktie mining share (stock, *US)*, steel stock *(US)*; **~industrie** mining (coal, iron and steel) industry; **~markt** mining market; **~union** European Coal and Steel Community; **~werte** mines.
Moratorium moratorium, moratory.
Morgenausgabe early-morning edition; **~schicht** first shift.
Mühewaltung, für Ihre as recompense for your trouble.
Müllabfuhr refuse (garbage, *US)* disposal (collection), *(Gesellschaft)* cesspool clearing company.
Mündelgelder unterschlagen to embezzle the funds of a ward.
mündelsicher gilt-edged *(Br.)*, eligible *(US)*;
   ~e Anlagewerte gilt-edged securities *(Br.)*, trustee stocks *(Br.)*, trust (savings bank) investments *(US)*; **~e Sparkasse** trustee savings bank *(US)*.
mündliches Angebot verbal offer.
Münzautomat penny-in-the-slot machine.
Münze coin, money, bean;
   in klingender ~ in hard coin (cash, good money); **~n aus dem Verkehr ziehen** to retire coins from circulation.
Münzfernsprecher coin (public call) box, pay station (telephone) *(US)*.
Mußvorschrift mandatory clause.
Muster *(Form)* pattern, set form, device, shape, *(Gebrauchsmuster)* design, pattern [sample], *(Modell)* model, copy, prototype, *(Warenprobe)* sample, trial piece, specimen;
   als ~ ohne Wert by sample post; **nach ~** according to pattern (sample);
   auf Bestellung angefertigtes ~ custom design; **beigefügtes ~** attached sample; **ungeschütztes ~** open pattern;
   ~ ohne Wert *(Postversand)* samples, no commercial value *(US)*, samples only, sample post;
   dem ~ entsprechen to correspond to pattern; **~ zusammenstellen** to make a collection of samples; **~anforderungskarte** sample request card; **~bestellung** sample offer; **~betrieb** model enterprise (plant, workshop), pilot plant; **~buch** specimen (pattern, sample, design) book; **~entnahme** sampling; **~karte** show (sample) card; **~kollektion** set (variety, range, collection) ot patterns, sample stock (assortment); **~lager unterhalten** to keep a stock of samples; **~messe** sample fair; **~-ohne-Wert-Sendung** parcel shipment, sample packet; **~wohnung** housing prototype; **~ziehung** taking samples.
Muttergesellschaft parent company (establishment, corporation).
Mutung claim, prospect, mining concession.

N

nachaktivieren to revalue assets.
Nacharbeit refinishing, retouching.
nacharbeiten to repeat, to [re]finish, to retouch.
Nacharbeitungskosten rework expense.
Nachbar|gefahr *(Versicherung)* exposure hazard, surrounding risk; **~schaftsladen** neighbo(u)rhood shop.
Nach|bearbeitung dressing, finishing, finish; **~belastung** additional charge.
nachbestellen to [give a] recorder, to place a repeat order, to repeat an article.
Nach|bestellung reorder, subsequent (second, repeat) order; **~besteuerung** supplementary taxation.
nachbezahlen to make an additional (further) payment, *(Zuschlag)* to pay extra.
Nachbörse afterhours, *(Freiverkehr)* outside (street, unofficial, *Br.*, curb, *US*) market.
nachbörslich after [official] hours;
 ~e Preise street (kerb) prices *(Br.)*.
Nachbuchung *(ergänzend)* supplementary entry, *(zeitlich)* subsequent entry, postentry.
nachdatieren to postdate, to afterdate.
Nach|erhebung additional assessment; **~faßbrief** follow-up letter; **~finanzierung** supplementary financial assistance; **~folgegesellschaft** successor company; **~folger** successor, follower, *(Miet-, Pachtverhältnis)* incomer.
nachfordern *(Aktieneinzahlung)* to call for additional payment.
Nachforderung supplemental claim, extra charge.
Nachfrage demand, request, call, requisition, market, *(Bedarf)* need, *(Erkundigung)* inquiry;
 anhaltende ~ steady demand; **gesamtwirtschaftliche ~** overall demand; **lebhafte ~** active (brisk, lively, keen, strong) demand;
 Angebot und ~ supply and demand;
 ~ nach Gütern des gehobenen Bedarfs demand for luxuries; **ungeheure ~ nach Ölaktien** run on oil stocks;
 ~ befriedigen to meet (supply) the demand;
 ~anstieg growth of demand; **~druck** pressur (pull) of demand; **~konjunktur** booming demand; **~monopol** buyer's monopoly; **~schwäche** softness in demand; **~stau** pent-up demand *(US)*; **~steuerung** demand management.
Nachfrist period of grant, respite.
Nachgeben| der Kurse decline in prices; **~ der Preise** slowdown in prices.
nachgeben *(Kurse)* to [be on the] decline, to recede.
Nachgebühr surcharge, excess (additional) postage.
nachgemachte Waren imitations, imitation goods.
nachgeordnete Dienststelle subordinate authority.
nachgiebig *(Kurse)* receeding, yielding, declining.
Nachholbedarf pent-up *(US)* (replacement, backlog) demand.
Nachkriegs|bedürfnisse postwar demands; **~konjunktur** postwar boom.

Nachlaß estate of [general] inheritance *(US)*, deceased (decedent's, *US*) estate, *(Preisnachlaß)* allowance, abatement, rebate[ment], reduction, deduction;
 liquidierter ~ solvent estate;
 reiner ~ nach Auszahlung aller Legate net estate;
 ~ bewilligen to allow an abatement;
 ~abwicklung administration of decedent's estate.
Nachlassen der Konjunktur economic slowdown.
nachlassen *(Börse)* to ease off, to slacken, *(Konjunktur)* to move backwards, to wane, to soften, to slow down, *(Verkaufsziffern)* to fall off;
 Forderung ~ to remit a claim.
Nachlaß|gläubiger creditor of an estate; **~staffel** scale of discounts; **~steuer** succession (death) *(US)* (probate, estate) *(Br.)* duty; **~verbindlichkeit** liability attaching to the inheritance; **~verteilung** distribution of an estate; **~verwalter** testamentary trustee, trustee of an estate; **~verwaltung** administration of an estate; **~verzeichnis** inventory.
Nachlieferung verlangen to demand goods in replacement.
Nachmann *(Wechsel)* subsequent endorser (indorser).
Nachnahme cash (collect, *US*) on delivery *(C.O.D.)*;
 unter ~ der Spesen charges forward;
 ~ einlösen to meet a cash delivery;
 ~betrag amount to be collected on delivery, trade charge *(Br.)*; **~postanweisung** trade-charge money order *(Br.)*; **eingeschriebene ~sendung** registered C.O.D. mail *(US)*, cash-on-delivery shipment.
Nach|porto surcharge, extra (additional) postage; **~prüfung von Forderungen** reconsideration of claims.
nachrangige Hypothek junior mortgage.
Nachricht news, advice, intelligence, item, *(Bericht)* report, account;
 ~ telefonisch übermitteln to send a message by telephone.
Nachrichten, geschäftliche business news;
 ~ in Kurzfassung news summary; **~ aus dem Wirtschaftsleben** industrial news service;
 ~dienst news bulletin (service); **~sprecher** newscaster.
Nachsaison afterseason, off-season, late season.
nach|schicken *(Brief)* to reforward, to redirect; **~schießen** to make an additional payment, *(Effektendifferenzgeschäft)* to put up more margin.
Nachschuß supplementary (additional) payment, *(Effektenlombard)* additional (further) cover; **~pflicht** *(Aktienmission)* reserve liability *(Br.)*, *(Effektenlombard)* call for additional cover; **~pflichtiger** *(Gesellschaftskonkurs)* contributory *(Br.)*; **~zahlung** *(Effektenlombard)* additional cover (margin).
Nachsende|anschrift forwarding address; **~gebühr** forwarding charges.
nachsenden to send on, to forward, to readdress.

Nachsichts|tage days of respite; ~**wechsel** time bill (draft), after-sight bill.

Nacht|arbeit nightwork, night employment; ~**ausgabe** late night final.

Nachteil disadvantage, drawback, *(Schaden)* detriment, prejudice, damage, injury; **steuerpolitische** ~e fiscal deficiencies.

Nachtrag addendum, supplement, additional clause, *(im Brief)* postscript (P. S.).

nachträglich|e Buchung subsequent entry, postentry; ~**e Zahlung** additional payment.

Nachtrags|anschlag supplementary estimate; ~**buchung** subsequent entry; ~**kreditbewilligung** supsupplementary vote; ~**zahlung** payment of arrears.

Nacht|safe night safe; ~**schicht** night shift; ~**stromtarif** off-peak (time-of-the-day, *Br.)* tariff; ~**zeitgespräch** *(Telefon)* night call.

Nachveranlagung additional assessment.

nachversichern to reinsure.

Nach|versicherung additional (subsequent) insurance; ~**versteuerung** subsequent taxation.

Nachweis proof, evidence; **als** ~ **des Anspruchs genügt die Police** policy proof of interest.

nachweispflichtig accountable.

Nachwuchs|ausbildung executive training; ~**kraft** junior executive, trainee *(US).*

nachzahlen to pay in addition, to make an additional (supplementary) payment, to supply; **auf Aktien** ~ to pay a further call on shares.

Nachzahlung supplementary (extra) payment.

nachzahlungspflichtig contributory.

Näherungswert approximate value, approximation.

Nahgüterverkehr short-distance goods traffic.

Nahrungsmittel food[stuffs], provisions, victuals; ~**bedarf** food requirements; ~**betrieb** food plant; ~**zuschußgebiet** food deficit area.

Nah|schnellverkehr rapid transit *(US)*; ~**verkehr** short distance transport, local (suburban, way, *US)* traffic, commuting *(US).*

Nahverkehrs|amt *(tel.)* toll exchange *(US)*; ~**betrieb** commuter service *(US)*; ~**netz** commuter lines *(US).*

Name name, style, *(Fabrikmarke)* trademark name, brand, *(Wertpapier)* title; **auf den** ~**n lautend** registered, *(Wechsel)* payable to order; ~ **in eine Liste eintragen** to enter a name on a list; **an der Börse einen guten** ~ **haben** to have a blue eye in the city *(US)*; **unter seinem handelsgerichtlichen** ~ **klagen** to sue in its corporate name.

Namens|aktie registered share *(Br.)* (stock, *US)*; ~**frachtbrief** straight bill of lading *(US)*; ~**lagerschein** nonnegotiable warehouse receipt; ~**papier** registered share *(Br.)* (stock, *US)*, straight note *(US)*; ~**schuldverschreibung** registered debenture *(Br.)* (coupon, bond, *US)*; ~**unterschrift** signature; ~**verzeichnis** list of names, nominal register, roll.

Nämlichkeits|zeichen identification mark; ~**zeugnis** proof of identity.

National|bank National Bank *(US)*; ~**einkommen** national income (dividend, revenue, *US)*; ~**ökonomie** national (political) economy, economics; ~**vermögen** national property.

Natural|abgabe tax (levy) in kind; ~**lohn** allowance in kind, store pay *(US).*

Neben|abrede collateral covenant; ~**adresse** *(Notadresse)* reference in case of need; ~**anschluß-[stelle]** *(Telefon)* extension [line]; ~**beruf** bywork, avocation, sideline; ~**beschäftigung** spare time work, sideline; **landwirtschaftlicher** ~**betrieb** part-time farm, small farming; **landwirtschaftliche** ~**erwerbssiedlung** homecroft *(Br.)*, homestead *(US)*; ~**leistung** secondary obligation; ~**stelle** *(Bank)* branch, suboffice, *(Post)* substation; ~**strecke** byroute, *(Bahn)* loop [line], branch line; ~**verdienst** incidental (subsidiary) source of income, perquisites *(Br.)*; ~**werte** *(Kurszettel)* sundry securities.

Negativverpflichtung covenant against encumbrances.

Nehmer *(Börse)* taker, buyer, purchaser, *(Kurszettel)* money, bid.

Nenn|betrag einer Schuld face of debt; ~**wert** nominal (face) value.

nennwertlose Aktie no-par-value share (stock, *US).*

Neonwerbung neon sign.

netto net, neat, clear, *(ohne Verpackung)* without packing; ~ **erbringen** to net.

Netto|anteil net worth *(US)*, equity; ~**ausweis** *(Bank)* net return; ~**bestandsveränderung** *(Volkswirtschaft)* net change in business inventories; ~**bilanz** net balance; ~**einkommen** net income (receipts, earnings); ~**erlös** net yield (proceeds, avails, *US)*; ~**gehalt** take-home pay, pay after stoppage *(Br.)*; ~**gewicht** net (shuttle) weight; ~**kapitalgewinn** net capital gain; ~**preis** *(Zoll)* short price; ~**registertonne** net ton; ~**umsatz** net sales (return); ~**verdienst** net earnings; ~**verlust** net (clear, dead) loss; ~**verzinsung** net yield; ~**wert** net value, proprietary interest, *(Unternehmen)* book value.

Netz|gruppenwähler *(tel.)* code selector; ~**karte** *(Eisenbahn)* runabout *(Br.)* (rover, go-as-you please) ticket.

neu new, fresh, *(Patentrecht)* novel; ~ **für alt** *(Versicherungswesen)* new for old; ~ **bewerten** to reappraise; ~ **veranlangen** to reassess; ~**e Aufträge** reorders, repeat orders; ~**es Kapital** fresh capital.

Neu|abschlüsse new orders (business); ~**anlagengeschäft** drosseln to hold down investment in new facilities; ~**ausgabe** *(Aktien)* junior issue; ~**bauten** housing starts; ~**bauwohnung** newly built flat (apartment, *US).*

Neubewertung des Anlagevermögens revaluation of assets; ~ **von Effekten** markdown (markup) of securities.

Neu|einstellungen replacements, new hiring *(US)*;

~einstufung ohne Gehaltsänderung ingrade classification change; ~festsetzung des Einheitswertes reassessment of real property; ~festsetzung der Währungsparitäten realignment of parities; ~gründung reconstruction, reorganization.

Neuheit novelty [item], latest fashion, *(Patentrecht)* novelty.

neuheitsschädlich *(Patentrecht)* anticipatory.

Neu|kalkulation vornehmen to revise one's estimates; ~landgewinnung reclamation of land;~ordnung des Geldwesens monetary (currency) reform; ~orientierung *(Wirtschaft)* readjustment; ~veranlagung reassessment; ~wagengarantie new-car warranty.

Neuwert original value, value as new; gleitende ~versicherung *(Feuerversicherung)* floating policy.

Neu|zugänge *(Belegschaft)* accessions; ~zulassung von Kraftfahrzeugen new-car registration.

nicht | bewirtschaftet nonrationed; ~ notiert *(Börse)* unquoted, unlisted *(US)*; ~ mitarbeitende Ehefrau *(Steuer)* nonworking wife; ~ entnommener Gewinn undistributed (paid-in, US) profit.

Nicht|annahme nonacceptance; ~anzeige *(Versicherung)* nondisclosure; ~ausschüttung von Gewinnen ploughing (plowing, US) back of profits; ~diskriminierung *(im Außenhandel)* fair trade *(US)*, *(Zoll)* nondiscrimination; ~erfüllung failure to perform (comply), nonperformance, nonfulfil(l)ment; ~genehmigung *(Gesuch)* refusal.

nichtig void, invalid, null, insufficient.

Nicht|kaufmann nontrader; schuldhafte ~kenntnis constructive notice, voluntary ignorance *(US)*; ~mitgliedsland *(EG)* nonmember country; ~unterzeichner *(Preisvereinbarung)* nonsigner; ~zulassung nonadmission, exclusion.

Niedergang, wirtschaftlicher economic downturn.

Niederlage storehouse, warehouse *(US)*, depot.

niederlassen, sich to settle, to establish o. s. as a business man, to take up one's abode.

Niederlassung establishment, branch, location, *(Bank)* branch, agency; gewerbliche ~ commercial establishment.

Niederlassungsfreiheit freedom of establishment.

niederlegen| Arbeit to [lay] down tools, to stop work, to walk out *(US)*; Waren unter Zollverschluß ~ to bond goods.

Niederschrift, stenografische stenographic record; vereinbarte ~ minutes agreed upon.

Niederstwertprinzip *(Bilanz)* cost of market value, whichever-is-lower method.

niedrig low, *(Preis)* cheap, moderate, down; ~ Preise berechnen to ask moderate prices.

niedriger, beträchtlich sein *(Kurse)* to be appreciably lower.

niedrignotierend *(Kurse)* low-priced.

niedrigster | Kurs lowest quotation; ~ Stand bottom (lowest) price.

Nießbrauch usufruct, beneficial interest, *(Grundstück)* lifehold, life estate; ~ bestellen to create a life estate.

Nießbrauchberechtigter beneficial occupant.

Niete *(Lotterie)* blank.

Nochgeschäft *(Börse)* call of more *(Br.)*.

Nominal|einkommen nominal income (wages); ~kapital nominal (subscribed, registered) capital, authorized capital *(US)*; ~verzinsung nominal interest; ~wert nominal (face) value, face, *(Aktie)* par value.

Non|stopflug nonstop flight; ~stopvorstellung continuous performance.

normale | Ausführung standard design; ~ Berufsgefahr ordinary hazard of occupation.

Normal|abweichung *(Statistik)* standard deviation; ~arbeitsstunden nominal (regular) hours; ~ausführung standard design (make), regular model; ~bezug regular supply; ~einheit *(Börse)* regular lot; ~kosten standard (predicted) cost; ~leistung standard output (production), *(Maschine)* standard machine time; ~lohnsatz, ~tarif general tariff, regular rate; ~zuteilung basic rations.

Nostro|geschäft business done for own account; ~guthaben *(Bilanz)* due from (credit with other) banks, nostro balance, our account *(US)*; ~verpflichtungen *(Bilanz)* due to banks.

Not need, want, *(Armut)* indigence, destitution, *(Bedrängnis)* distress, trouble; Wechsel ~ leiden lassen to dishono(u)r a bill.

Not|abgabe capital levy; ~adressat referee in case of need; ~akzept acceptance in case of need; ~anzeige *(Wechsel)* notice of dishono(u)r.

Notariatsgebühren notarial fees (ticket), conveyancing costs.

notariell beglaubigt attested by a notary, certified, notarized.

notdürftiger Unterhalt bare existence.

Note *(Banknote)* bank note *(Br.)* (bill, US).

Notenausgabe [new] issue of bank notes; ~recht note-issuing privilege.

Notenbank bank of circulation (issue); ~ausweis bank return *(Br.)* (statement, US); ~liquuidität liquidity of the Federal Reserve System *(US)*.

Noten|druck printing of notes; ~kontingent note issue *(Br.)*; ~presse printing press; ~umlauf circulation of bank notes.

Not|flagge distress flag; ~geld emergency currency; ~groschen nest egg; ~groschen zurücklegen to put aside for a rainy day; ~hafen port of refuge; Technische ~hilfe Organization for the Maintenance of Supplies *(Br.)*, Salvage Corps *(US)*.

notieren to [make a] note, to take a note of, *(Börsenkurse)* to quote, to list *(US)*; fortlaufend ~ to quote consecutively; hoch ~ *(Wertpapiere)* to rule high; bei Börsenschluß höher ~ to close dearer; Posten ~ to enter an item in the books.

notiert marketable, quoted, listed *(US)*; amtlich ~ officially quoted, listed *(US)*; fortlaufend ~ consecutively quoted, bunched *(US)*; niedriger ~ werden to be marked down *(Br.)*.

Notierung *(Buchung)* booking, entry, *(Effekten)* [market] quotation, mark, listing *(US)*;
unter der letzten ~ **angeboten** offered down *(US)*;
amtliche ~ official quotation *(Br.)*, listing *(US)*;
uneinheitliche ~ split quotation;
~ **für Industriewerte** industrial share prices.

Notiz note, memorandum, memo, *(Börse)* quotation, listing *(US)*;
~ **ohne Umsätze** *(Börse)* nominal quotation.

Notlage [state of] need, calamitiy, distress, *(Geldverlegenheit)* embarrassment.

Not|landeplatz emergency landing field; ~**landung** forced (emergency) landing.

notleidend *(Wechsel)* dishono(u)red, overdue;
~**e Aktie** nondividend-paying stock; - **e Gesellschaft** company in default.

Notprogramm austerity program(me).

Notstands|anleihe relief loan; ~**arbeiten** relief (remedial) works; ~**darlehn** emergency loan; ~**hilfe** depressed-area aid *(Br.)*; ~**programm** relief (emergency-aid, crash) program(me).

Not|strom emergency current; ~**unterkunft** shelter; ~**verkäufe** forced sales; ~**währung** emergency currency.

null und nichtig null and void, absolutely void.

Null|serie pilot lot; **auf den ~wert setzen** to reduce to zero.

Nummer number, mark, *(Fabriknummer)* serial, *(Größe)* size, *(Lotterie)* ticket;
~**n** *(Zinsnummern)* decimals *(Br.)*;
nächstgrößere ~ next in size; **rote** ~ *(Autohändler)*

dealer's licence number; **schwarze ~n** *(Zinszahlen)* black products;
~ **des statistischen Warenverzeichnisses** statistical code number.

Nummern|bezeichnung numbering; ~**konto** *(Bank)* numbered account; ~**schild** *(Auto)* number (licence, *US)* plate.

Nutzbarmachung einer Erfindung industrial application of an invention.

nutzbringend anlegen to turn to account.

Nutzen use, *(Ertrag)* emolument, yield, proceeds, return, *(Gewinn)* capital, gain, profit, *(Nützlichkeit)* usefulness, utility, good, *(Vorteil)* interest, advantage *(US)*;
mit einem ~ **von** leaving a margin of;
~ **bringen** to benefit, to [yield a] profit.

Nutz|ertrag, steigender improved value; ~**fahrzeug** commercial vehicle; **landwirtschaftliche ~fläche verpachten** to rent a field to a farmer; ~**leistung** *(Maschine)* duty, mechanical effect; ~**nießer** usufructuary; ~**nießung** use, usufruct; ~**nießungsrecht des Ehemannes am eingebrachten Gut** apronstring tenure.

Nutzung use, *(Einkommen)* revenue, *(Ertrag)* profit, yield, proceeds;
wiederkehrende ~en recurring returns.

Nutzungs|berechtigter beniciary; ~**dauer** useful (expected, economic) life; ~**entgelt** hire.

Nutzungswert amount of revenue, value in use;
~ **des eigengenutzten Einfamilienhauses** *(Steuererklärung)* net annual value *(Br.)*.

Nutzungszeit *(Maschine)* machine time.

O

obdachlos unhoused, homeless, houseless.

Obdach|losenasyl casual ward, pauper asylum; ~**loser** casual [pauper].

Ober|buchhalter chief accountant; ~**finanzdirektion** Regional Office *(US)*; ~**schicht** top drawer, the upper classes.

Objekte, beliehene mortgaged properties.

Obligationen bonds, stocks *(Br.)*, debentures, debenture bonds *(US)*, obligations;
aufgerufene ~ called bonds; **mit Dividendenberechtigung ausgestattete** ~ dividend bonds *(US)*; **mit attraktiven Steuervorteilen ausgestattete** ~ bonds with attractive tax feature; **durch Effektenlombard gesicherte** ~ collateral trust bonds; **durch Vorranghypothek gesicherte** ~ prior-lien (underlying, *US)* bonds; **auf den Inhaber lautende** ~ bearer (coupon, *US)* bonds; **steuerfreie** ~ tax-exempt bonds, tax-free obligations; **unverzinsliche** ~ noninterest-bearing bonds;
~ **mit Gewinnbeteiligungsrecht** participating bonds *(US)*; ~ **öffentlicher Versorgungsbetriebe** publicutility bonds;

~ **ausgeben** to issue bonds; ~ **einlösen** to pay off bonds.

Obligationen|agio bond premium; ~**ausgabe** bond (debenture) issue; ~**inhaber** bondholder; ~**zinsen** interest upon bonds, debenture interest *(US)*.

Obligationszinsen bond interest.

Obligo liability, engagement, commitment;
ohne ~ *(Wechsel)* without resourse.

offen open, unclosed, unlocked, running, clear, overt, *(Ausschreibung)* unlimited, *(Stelle)* vacant, running;
~**es Depot** safe custody *(Br.)* (custodianship, *US)* account; ~ **Handelsgesellschaft** general (ordinary, *US)* partnership; ~**e Kreditlinie** unused credit line; ~**er Posten** unpaid item; ~**e Rechnung** current (running) account, *(nicht bezahlt)* unsettled account; ~**e Reserven** declared reserve.

Offen|barungseid poor debtor's oath *(US)*, affidavit of means; ~**halten am Sonntag** Sunday opening; ~**legung** *(Revisionsbericht)* disclosure; ~**legungspflicht** duty to disclose.

Offenmarkt|geschäft open-market operation; ~**politik** open-market policy.

offenstehend *(Rechnung)* open, unliquidated, unsettled, outstanding.

öffentlich public, in public, open;
~ **beglaubigt** certified, notarized, legalized;
~ **ausschreiben** to advertise; ~ **versteigern** to sell at (by, put up for, *US)* auction;
~**e Abgaben** rates and taxes; ~**e Bekanntmachung** public notice; ~**e Fernsprechstelle** public call box; ~**e Fürsorge** national *(Br.)* (public, social, *US)* assistance; ~**e Hand** mortmain.

Öffentlichkeitsarbeit public relations, publicity.

offerieren, unverbindlich to offer without commitment.

Offerte bid, offer, tender;
unverbindliche ~ offer without commitment, flat offer *(US)*;
~**n unterbreiten** to submit tenders (offers).

offiziell notiert werden *(Börsenwerte)* to be quoted (listed, *US)* on the stock exchange;
~**es Organ** bulletin, gazette.

Öffnungszeiten business (opening) hours.

Ökonomie economy, *(Landwirtschaft)* agriculture.

Oktanzahl octane number.

Oel| aktien oil shares (stocks, *US)*; ~**heizung** oil heater; ~**konzession** oil concession; ~**vorkommen** oil field (reservoir, basin).

Omnibus omnibus, autobus, [motor] coach;
mit Liegemöglichkeiten ausgestatteter ~ restroom-equipped bus;
~**bahnhof** bus terminal *(US)*; ~**fahrplan** omnibus timetable, bus schedule *(US)*; ~**fahrschein** bus fare (ticket); ~**werbung** bus advertising.

optimale Ertragsfähigkeit maximum output.

Option optation, option [to put], *(Vorkaufsrecht)* right of preemption;
~ **ausüben** to exercise an option.

Options|anleihe optional bond; ~**ausübung** option exercise; ~**geschäft in Termindevisen** option forward *(Br.)*; ~**klausel** optional clause; ~**nehmer** taker of an option; ~**recht** option, right to opt, optional right, *(Bezugsrecht)* subscription right.

Order order, commission;
an fremde ~ to order of a third party; **an** ~ **ausgestellt** made out to order; **auf** ~ **und Rechnung von** by order and on account of;
freibleibende ~ conditional order; **bis auf Widerruf gültige** ~ open order; **limitierte** ~ limited (stop-loss) order;

Wechsel an ~ **ausstellen** to make a bill payable to order;
~**frachtbrief, ~konnossement** order [-notify] bill of lading; ~**papier** negotiable instrument; ~**scheck** check to order.

Ordnung order, *(Anlage)* pattern, setup *(US)*, *(Reihenfolge)* succession, rank, order;
in ~ in good working order, in key, okay, *(Paß)* valid, *(Scheck)* covered, *(Wechsel)* good.

ordnungsgemäße| Kündigung due notice; ~ **Quittung** formal receipt.

Organ organ, body, *(Behörde)* authority, agency, *(Blatt)*, publication, medium, organ;
beratendes ~ advisory body;
~**e der Europäischen Gemeinschaften** Institution of the European Communities;
~**gesellschaft** subsidiary company (corporation, *US)*, organ company *(US)*.

Organisation | für wirtschaftliche Zusammenarbeit und Entwicklung Organization for Economic Cooperation and Development (OECD);
~ **ins Leben rufen** to call an organization into existence.

Organisations|abteilung administration department (division); ~**fehler** faulty organization; ~**schaubild** organization diagram.

organisiert organized, organic;
genossenschaftlich ~ cooperative[ly]; **gewerkschaftlich nicht** ~ nonunion, unorganized.

Orientierungsdaten *(Konjunkturpolitik)* wage-price guideposts.

Original einer Rechnung original invoice;
~ **ausfertigen** concurrent writs; ~**faktura** original invoice; ~**verpackung** original package (wrapping).

Ort | der Lieferung place of delivery;
an einem ~ **wohnen** to dwell in a place.

örtliche Werbung local campaign (advertising).

Orts|angabe address, indication of place; ~**ansässiger** resident, local man, home towner *(US)*; ~**brief** local (drop, *US)* letter; ~**gebühr** *(tel.)* local charge; ~**gespräch** local call; ~**klassen-[lohn]ausgleich** intercity wage differential; ~**statut** local statute (act, byelaws, *Br.)*, *(Baupolizei)* zoning law (act) *(US)*, building byelaw; ~**teilnehmer** *(Telefon)* local subscriber; ~**zuschlag** residential allowance, local bonus.

Ozean|dampfer ocean liner, ocean-going steamer; ~**transport** sea transport.

P

Pacht lease, leasehold, tenancy, tenure;
  vertraglich ausbedungene ~ contract rent; **jederzeit
  kündbare** ~ tenancy at will; **von Jahr zu Jahr
  verlängerte** estate from year to year; **in Naturalien
  zahlbare** ~ share tenancy;
  in ~ **geben** to let on (put out to) lease, to farm out;
  in ~ **nehmen** to take on lease, to farm.
Pacht|ablauf expiration of a lease; **~bedingungen**
  terms of a lease; **~dauer** tenancy, [life of] lease.
pachten to lease [out], to take on lease (at rent);
  Lotterieunternehmen ~ to farm a lottery.
Pächter tenant, lessee, leaseholder, renter, farmer,
  holder, *(Deputant)* sharecropper *(US)*;
  jederzeit kündbarer ~ tenant at will.
Pacht|einnahmen rental; **~gebühr** [land] rent, rental;
  ~grundstück leasehold, leased property; **~hof**
  farm, barton.
Pachtung leasehold, holding, tenement, tenancy.
Pachtvertrag [covenant of] lease, lease contract, farm
  (farming) lease;
  ~ **für gewerblich genutzte Räume** commercial lease.
Pachtzins rental, [land] rent.
Päckchen parcel, [small] packet *(Br.)*, package.
packen to pack, to do one's packing *(coll.)* to wrap up;
  in Bündeln ~ to bundle; **in Pakete** ~ to package.
Packerlohn package, charge for packing.
Pack|leinwand packcloth, canvas; **~material** packing,
  wrappage; **~papier** packing sheet, parcel (cap,
  packing, brown) paper; **~zettel** packing slip
  (ticket), docket.
Paket parcel, packet, pack, bundle, *(Aktien)* block
  [of shares];
  kleines ~ packet *(Br.)*; **postlagerndes** ~ parcel to be
  called for; **zusammenhängendes** ~ *(Wertpapiere)*
  considered package;
  ~ **aufgeben** to send by parcel post, to dispatch
  (send off) a parcel; **~e numerieren** to put numbers
  on packages; ~ **per Nachnahme schicken** to send a
  package on delivery *(US)* (c. o. D., *Br.*).
Paket|adresse label, facing slip *(US)*; **~annahme-und
  ~ausgabestelle** parcel-post office *(US)*; **~aufklebe-
  adresse** parcel sticker; **~dienst** parcel service *(Br.)*;
  ~gebühren parcel-post (parcels) rates; **~händler**
  large-lot (big-block) trader; **~karte** parcel mailing
  form, dispatch note *(Br.)*.
Paketpost parcel post, fourth-class mail *(US)*;
  ~schalter parcel-post window *(US)*; **~zustellung**
  parcel delivery, parcels cartage *(Br.)*
Paket|wert ersetzen to reinstate the contents of a
  parcel; **~zettel** label.
Panzerschrank safe, strongbox;
  feuersicherer ~ fire-protection steel filing safe.
Papier paper, *(Aktie)* share *(Br.)*, stock *(US)*,
  (Wertpapier) instrument, paper, stock;
  auf den Namen ausgestelltes ~ straight note *(US)*;
  bankfähiges ~ bank paper (bill), bankable paper;
  börsengängige **~e** realizable stock, quoted (listed,

US) securities; **festverzinsliche** **~e** fixed-interest
  securities; **mündelsichere** **~e** gilt-edged securities
  (stock) *(Br.)*, trust stock *(US)*, trustee's bonds
  (US); **wertloses** ~ instrument of no effect;
  ~e auslosen to draw securities by lot; **seine ~e
  mitbringen** to bring one's qualifications with one.
Papier|blockade paper blockade; **~bogen** sheet of
  paper; **~fabrikant** paper manufacturer; **~geld**
  paper money (currency), notes *(Br.)*, bills *(US)*;
  ~geldinflation paper-money inflation; **~geldum-
  lauf** credit (note) circulation; **~geldwährung** paper
  currency; **~handlung** stationer's shop; **~krieg** red
  tape, paper warfare (work); **~zeichen** watermark.
Pappkarton cardboard box.
Parallel|buchung parallel posting; **~versammlung**
  overflow meeting.
paraphieren to paraph, to initial.
Pari par [value]; •
  al ~ at par (parity); **über** ~ above par, at a
  premium; **unter** ~ below par, at a discount;
  ~stehen to be at par (at a parity); **unter ~ gehandelt
  werden** to stand (sell, be) at a discount;
  ~emission issue at par; **~kurs** par of exchange,
  parity price.
Parität par value, parity, equality.
Paritätentafel table of parities, parity table.
Paritäts|wechsel bill at par (on a par point, *US*);
  ~wert par value, parity.
Parken parking;
  auf eine Seite beschränktes ~ unilateral parking;
  ~ **im Parkverbot** parking in dangerous position.
Park|gebühr parking fee; **~[hoch]haus** multistor(e)y
  garage (car park, *Br.)*; **~möglichkeit** parking
  facilities; **~platz** parking site *(Br.)* car park *(Br.)*,
  stall *(US)*, parking space (spot, lot, *US)*; **~scheibe**
  parking disk; **~uhrbereich** parking-meter zone;
  ~verbotszone noparking area (zone), *(absolut)*
  pink zone *(Br.)*; **~zeit** parking time; **verbotene
  ~zeit** restricted hours.
Partie *(Buch)* passage, *(Fest)* party, *(Menge)* quantity,
  (Teil) part, *(Ware)* parcel, lot;
  ~handel spot business.
partienweise verkaufen to sell in lots.
Partie|preis wholesale price; **~ware** job goods (line,
  lot), dead stock.
Partizipations|geschäft joint venture (adventure).
Partner partner, copartner, party, *(pl.)* associates in
  office, companions.
  geschäftsführender ~ acting partner.
Parzelle plot [of land], parcel, lot *(US)*, allotment
  (Br.)
  in ~n aufteilen to plot, to separate into small fields,
  to lot out *(US)*.
Parzellierung parcellation, parcel[l]ing out of land
  into small holdings.
Parzellierungs|gesellschaft freehold land society,
  homestead corporation *(US)*.

Paß passport, *(Durchlaßschein)* pass, permit;
~ **abstempeln** to stamp a passport; ~**vorübergehend außer Kraft setzen** to withhold tentatively passport privileges; ~ **mit Sichtvermerk versehen** to visa.

Passagier passenger, fare;
blinder ~ deadhead, stowaway, blind baggage; ~ **der Touristenklasse** tourist passenger;
als blinder ~ **mitfahren** to hop the freight, to stow away.

Passagier|dampfer ocean liner, passenger; steamer; ~**geld** fare; ~**gut** luggage [in advance] *(Br.)*.

Paß|antrag passport application; ~**ausstellung** issuance of a passport; ~**einziehung** withdrawal of a passport.

Passierschein [free] pass, pass check *(US)*, permit, *(Zollbegleitschein)* transire, *(Zollplombe)* docket.

passiv passive, *(Bilanz)* unfavo(u)rable, adverse;
~**e Handelsbilanz** unfavo(u)rable balance of trade, adverse trade balance.

Passiva liabilities, accounts payable *(US)*;
als ~ **behandeln** to carry as liabilities.

Passiv|geschäft *(Bankwesen)* deposit function; ~**handel** import trade.

Passiv|posten der Rechnungsabgrenzung deferred credits [to income], prepaid (unearned) income; ~**saldo der Handelsbilanz** balance-of-payments deficit; ~**seite** left[-hand] side, liability; ~**zinsen** interest cost (due).

Paß|kontrolle passport control, examination of passports; ~**verlängerung** extension (renewal) of passport.

Patent, angemeldet patent pending; **abgelaufenes** ~ patent lapsed;
~ **anfechten** to attack a patent; ~**anmelden** to file an application (apply, put up) for a patent; ~ **praktisch verwertbar machen** to reduce a patent to practice.

Patent|anmeldung application for a patent, copyright notice; ~**einspruch** interference, opposition; ~**beschreibung** patent specification.

patentierter Artikel proprietary article.

Patent|schrift letters patent; ~**umgehung** colo(u)rable alteration; ~**verletzung** patent infringement.

Patronatssendung sponsored broadcast (program) *(US)*, commercial.

Pauschal|abfindung lump-sum settlement; ~**abschluß** bulk bargain; ~**abschreibung** overall depreciation; **abzugsfähiger** ~**betrag** *(Einkommensteuer)* standard deduction *(US)*; ~**fracht** lump-sum (lump, flat-rate) freight; ~**freibetrag** *(Steuer)* flat exemption *(US)*; ~**police** floating (blanket) policy, unvalued policy *(US)*; ~**preis** flat rate (price), price in the lump; ~**reise** package (packing, bulk, all-expense, *US)* tour; ~**tarif** *(Versicherung)* blanket rate; ~**versicherung** floater; ~**zahlung** lump-sum payment.

Pauschbetrag lump (average) sum, flat yield.

Pendelbus shuttle bus.

pendeln *(Verkehrsteilnehmer)* to shuttle, to commute *(US)*, to have a season ticket.

Pendelverkehr shuttle [service], commutation *(US)*, commuting business *(US)*.

Pension *(Altersrente)* pension, retiring (gratuitous, superannuation) allowance, *(Fremdenheim)* boarding (rooming, *US)* house, *(Kostgeld)* board, pension, *(Kostschule)* boarding school;
in ~ retired [from service];
auf das Einkommen angerechnete ~ pension charged on an income; **staatliche** ~ government pension;
~ **auf Lebenszeit** life pension, pension for life; ~ **bewilligen** to grant a pension; **in** ~ **gehen** to retire on a pension; **in** ~ **gehen, aber noch beratend tätig bleiben** to retire to consultant status; **zu seiner** ~ **hinzuverdienen** to supplement one's pension.

Pensionär pensioner, retiree, pensionary *(Br.)*, *(Fremdenheim)* boarder, lodger, paying guest.

pensionieren to pension [off], to superannuate, to put on the retired list, to retire;
sich ~ **lassen** to retire [on a pension, from active service]; **sich aus Altersgründen** ~ **lassen** to retire under the age limit.

Pensionierung retirement, retiring, pensioning off;
~ **wegen Erreichung der Altersgrenze** superannuation; ~ **mit vollem Ruhegehalt** retirement on full pension; ~ **auf eigenen Wunsch** optional (voluntary) retirement.

Pensionierungsalter pensionable (retirement, retiring) age, age of retirement.

Pensions|alter pensionable (retirement, retiring) age; ~**anspruch** retirement credit, pension claim; ~**beitrag** superannuation money.

pensionsberechtigt pensionable, entitled to (eligible for) a pension.

Pensions|berechtigter pensioner, pensionary *(Br.)*; ~**berechtigung** pension claim, retirement eligibility; ~**bezüge** pensionable emoluments, retirement income (benefit, *US)*; ~**empfänger** pensioner, pensionary *(Br.)*, holder (recipient) of a pension, stipendiary.

pensionsfähig pensionable, entitled to a pension.

Pensionsfonds [old-age] pension fund, pension trust, provident (superannuation) fund; ~**gäste haben** to take in visitors; ~**jahre** retirement years.

Pensionskasse [old-age] pension, superannuation (staff pension, *Br.)* fund;
beitragsfreie ~ noncontributory pension plan; **allein vom Unternehmen finanzierte** ~ company-financed pension plan.

Pensions|leistung pension payment, retirement (fringe) benefit; ~**ordnung** pension (retirement) plan; ~**preis** *(Fremdenheim)* board; ~**rückstellung** pension reserve; ~**vereinbarung** pension-scheme arrangement; ~**wechsel** bill on deposit; ~**zahlung** retirement (retired) pay, pension payment; ~**zusage** pensionning warrant; ~**zuschüsse** *(Bilanz)* pension payments, service apportionments *(US)*.

Periode erhöhter Gefahr apprehensive period.

Periodenreingewinn *(Bilanz)* net profit for the year, surplus net profit *(US)*.

Person person, individual, man;
  juristische ~ juristic (juridical, artificial, fictitious) person; **versicherte** ~ *(Versicherungswesen)* risk.
Personal personnel, staff, crew, employees, *(Haushalt)* domestic staff, servants, attendants;
  geschultes ~ *(Hotel)* good valeting service;
  ~ **abbauen** to reduce the staff.
Personal|abbau reduction of staff, personnel cutback; ~**abteilung** personnel (appointments, staff) department; ~**akte** case history, personnel files (folder, jacket); ~**ausbildung** staff training; **zahlbar gegen Vorlage des** ~**ausweises** payable upon submission of proof of identity; ~**bearbeiter** personnel assistant (technician); ~**bedarf** manpower (staff, personnel) requirements; ~**berater** personnel counselor *(US)*; ~**beratung** employee counselling; ~**beurteilung** personnel (merit) rating; ~**buchhaltung** personnel accounting; ~**chef** personnel manager (chief, director, officer); ~**etat** manpower budget.
Personalien [name and] description, particulars, personal data, personalia.
Personal|knappheit shortage of personnel (staff); ~**kosten** personnel (staff) expenses; ~**kredit** personal (private) credit, open (uncovered, personal, unsecured) loan; ~**mangel haben** to be understaffed (short of staff); **betriebliche** ~**politik** labo(u)r management; ~**umbesetzung** shifting of personnel; ~**union bei Verwaltungen verschiedener Gesellschaften** interlocking directorates; ~**wechsel** changes in the staff.
Personen|bahnhof passenger station (depot, *US);* ~**beförderung** passenger transportation; ~**beschreibung** description, descriptive signalment; ~**kraftwagen** [passenger] car, private motorcar, automobile; **befragter** ~**kreis** panel, persons reviewed; ~**verkehr** *(Eisenbahn)* passenger transport, coaching traffic *(Br.);* **beförderte** ~**zahl** traffic; ~**zug** stopping (passenger, omnibus, *Br.,* way, *US,* accommodation, *US)* train.
persönlich personal, in person, intimate, direct, private;
  ~ **haftbar** personally liable (answerable);
  ~**haftender Gesellschafter** active (general) partner;
  ~**es Konto** private (personal) account.
Persönliches *(Zeitung)* personals *(US).*
Persönlichkeiten des Wirtschaftslebens policy-makers of business.
Pfand pledge pledged property, pawn, gage *(Br.),* charge, *(Pfandrecht)* lien, *(Sicherheit)* collateral security;
  uneingelöstes ~ unredeemed pledge; **verfallenes** ~ forfeited pledge;
  ~ **auslösen** to redeem a pawn, to replevin.
Pfandauslösung redemption of a pledge, replevin.
pfändbar attachable, distrainable, seizable;
  ohne ~**es Vermögen sein** to be judgment-(mace-, *US)* proof.
Pfand|besitzer pawnee, pledgee; ~**bestellung** pawning, pledging, charge.

Pfandbrief debenture *(Br.),* [mortage] bond, mortage deed;
  zur Rückzahlung gekündigte ~**e** bonds under notice of redemption; **durch erststellige Hypothek gesicherte** ~**e** first mortgage bonds *(US).*
Pfandbrief|agio bond discount, issue of debentures *(Br.);* ~**ausgabe** bond issue; ~**emission** bond issue, issue of debentures *(Br.);* ~**inhaber** bond creditor, bondholder, debenture holder *(Br.);* ~**rendite** bond yieldings.
pfänden to levy, to attach, to lay attachment, to distress, to distrain, to extend, to affix the seal;
  jds. Sachen wegen Mietschulden ~ to distrain upon s. one's goods for rent.
Pfand|gebühr pawn money; ~**gegenstand** pawn, pledge, pledged property; ~**geschäft** pawnbroking, pawnbrokery; ~**inhaber** pawnee, bailee, lien creditor, lienor; ~**leihanstalt** pawnbrokery, pawn (loan, *US)* office, pawnshop; **auf der** ~**leihe sein** to be up the spout (in pop, *Br. sl.).*
Pfandrecht, bevorrechtigtes prior lien; **gesetzliches** ~ statutory lien; **vorgehendes** ~ prior lien;
  ~ **begründen** to constitute a lien.
Pfand|sache pledged property; ~**schein** pawn ticket.
Pfändung levy, attachment, seizure, distraint, distress, distrainment, execution;
  ~ **einer Forderung** arrest (attachment) of a debt, garnishment *(US);* ~ **wegen Mietschulden (Mietrückstands)** distress for [nonpayment of] rent;
  ~ **aufheben** to remove the seals, to vacate an attachment; ~ **betreiben** to levy a distraint; ~ **vornehmen** to put in an execution.
Pfändungs|beamter broker, executioner; ~**befehl** warrant of distress (attachment); ~**bericht** return of writ; ~**beschluß** distress warrant, order of attachment, garnishee order.
pfändungsfrei exempt from execution, judgment-proof, mace-proof *(US).*
Pfändungs|freibetrag exempted amount; ~**gläubiger** attaching (judgment) creditor; ~**kosten** costs of levy; ~**schuldner** judgment debtor.
Pfand|untergang extinguishment of a lien; ~**verkauf** distress sale; ~**verleiher** pawnbroker, pawnee, pledgee; ~**verwertung** enforcement of a lien.
Pfennig penny, farthing, stiver;
  ~**e** chickenfeed *(sl.);*
  mit dem ~ **rechnen** to think of pennies; **jeden** ~ **zweimal umdrehen** to look at every penny twice.
Pflaster, teures *(fig.)* high cost-of-living region.
Pflege| und Wartung maintenance;
  ~**geld** guardian's allowance.
Pfleger *(Nachlaß)* administrator, testamentary guardian, *(Vermögen)* trustee, curator, custodian.
Pflicht|beitrag compulsory contribution; ~**exemplar** presentation copy; ~**reserve** *(Bankwesen)* legal *(Br.)* (lawful, *US)* reserve; ~**teil** *(Erbe)* legal (lawful, statutory-forced, *US)* share, legitimate (legal, hereditary) portion; ~**teilsrecht** forced heirship *(US),* *(Witwe)* widow-bench *(Br.);* ~**versicherung** compulsory insurance.

placieren to place, to site, to invest;
Anleihe ~ to place (negotiate) a loan.
Placierung *(Anzeige)* position, location, *(Gelder)* investment, placement, *(Wertpapiere)* negotiation;
bevorzugte ~ *(Anzeige)* preferred (full) position; vorgeschriebene ~ *(Anzeige)* stated position;
~ einer Anleihe negotiation of a loan; ~ einer Anzeige position of an advertisement.
Placierungs|aufschlag *(Anzeige)* position charge; ~kosten position costs; ~vorschrift prescribed position.
Plafond [upper] limit, ceiling.
Plakat poster, placard, affiche, posting bill;
~ ankleben (anschlagen) to stick a bill, to post a placard;
~anschlag billposting, billsticking; wilder ~anschlag sniping *(US)*; ~anschlagunternehmen poster plant, billposting agency; ~fläche hoarding *(Br.)*.
Plan plan, arrangement, device, *(Entwurf)* draft, blueprint *(US)*, *(Lageplan)* groundplan, layout;
Grüner ~ farm program(me);
~festsetzung zoning *(US)*; ~feststellungsverfahren zoning case *(US)*; ~kostenrechnung budget accounting, budgeting.
planmäßig|e Absatzförderung sales drive; ~er Beamter regular official, established civil servant *(Br.)*; ~er Luftverkehrsdienst scheduled airline service.
Plan|stelle establishment; freie ~stelle vacancy; ~stelleninhaber established civil servant *(Br.)*, fixture.
Planung plan, planning, projection, blueprint *(US)*, *(Anlage)* layout;
langfristige ~ long-range planning;
optimale ~ einer Wertpapieranlage portfolio selection.
Planungs|abteilung planning (layout) department;
an den ~arbeiten beteiligt sein to be in on the planning; ~instanz planning board; ~stab planning board; ~verfahren planning process.
Planwirtschaft planned (managed, draft, directed) economy, statism.
Plan|zahl standard; ~ziel target [area], *(Produktion)* planned output.
Platz place, spot, point *(US)*, *(Grundstück)*, site, plot, lot, location, *(Schiff, Schlafwagen)* berth, *(Sitzplatz)* seat;
reservierter ~ reservation, reserved seat;
~ belegen (bestellen) to book space (a place), to secure (reserve, US) a seat.
Platz|agent local agent; ~anweiser usher; ~aufschlag extra charge; ~bedarf space required; ~bedingungen *(Schiffsverkehr)* berth terms; ~belegung booking [space], seat reservation *(US)*; nicht ausgenutzte ~buchung *(Flugzeug)* no-show.
Plätze zu volkstümlichen Preisen cheap seats.
Platz|gebrauch local custom; ~geschäfte machen to deal with the supplier on the spot; ~inkasso walk bills *(US)*; ~kartenschalter reservation office; ~käufe local (spot) purchase; ~kurs spot-market

price, spot rate; ~reisender town travel(l)er; ~spesen local expenses (charges); ~verlust loss on the spot; ~vertreter local agent, agent on the spot, town travel(l)er; mit beschränkter ~zahl *(Bahn)* limited.
Pleite smash, washout, failure, bankruptcy, burst-up, bust, blowup *(US)*, flop;
~ machen to go to the wall *(Br.)* (bust).
pleite bankrupt, broke, bust, on the nut *(US sl.)*, gone up *(s.)*, stonybroke *(sl.)*.
~ sein to be on the rocks (beam-ends, cracked).
Police policy, *(Lebensversicherung)* life policy;
abgelaufene ~ expired policy; auf den Namen ausgestellte ~ registered policy; beitragsfreie ~ free policy; gewinnberechtigte ~ participating policy; auf den Tag der Antragstellung vordatierte ~ antedated policy;
~ mit Wertangabe valued policy; ~ ohne Wertangabe open (unvalued) policy *(Br.)*;
~ ausfertigen to issue (effect) a policy; ~ beleihen to lend money on a policy.
Policen|ausfertigung issue of policy, policy drafting; ~datum date of policy; ~inhaber policyholder; ~nummer policy number; ~vordruck policy form.
Politik politics, policy, polity, deal *(coll.)*;
auf Lohnstabilisierung und Preissenkung gerichtete ~ wage-freezing and price-lowering policy;
~ des billigen Geldes cheap-money policy;
~ der offenen Tür betreiben to open a door to agreements on international affairs.
Portefeuille portfolio;
~ eigener Aktien reacquired capital stock, treasury securities (stock, *US*), donated surplus *(US)*; ~ an Wechseln billholding;
~wechsel portfolio bill.
Porto postage, postal rate, *(Pakete)* carriage;
~ für Kontoauszüge statement postage;
~auslagen postal expenses; ~einnahmen postage and postal revenue; ~ermäßigung reduction of the postal tariff.
portofrei postpaid, postage paid (free), prepaid, post-free, free of postage *(US)*;
Porto|gebühren postal (postage, Br.) rates; ~kasse petty cash, imprest fund, office stamp-book; ~kassenbeleg petty-cash voucher; ~kosten expense for postage, postal charges, postage *(Br.)* charges; ~nachnahme postage to be collected.
portopflichtig liable (subject) to postage.
Porto|rückvergütung refunding of postage; ~vergünstigung mail privilege *(Br.)*; ~zuschlag extra (additional) postage, surcharge.
Position position, post, employment, job, *(in Aufstellung)* item, *(Buchung)* entry;
einflußreiche ~ position of influence, purchase; leitende ~ policy-making position;
~ des Zolltarifs tariff heading;
gute ~ bekommen to drop into a position; hohe ~ innehaben to be high up the stick.
Positionslichter *(Flugzeug)* position (navigation, running, *US*) lights, *(Schiff)* top light.

Post post *(Br.)*, mail *(US)*, *(Postamt)* post office, *(Postdienst)* postal service, *(Postsachen)* letters, mail *(US)*;
mit der ersten ~ by the first mail *(US)* (delivery, *Br.)*;
abgehende ~ outgoing post (mail, *US)*; **durch Freistempler freigemachte** ~ metered mail *(US)*; **noch nicht zugestellte** ~ undelivered mail *(US)*;
~ **abfertigen** to dispatch the post (mail, *US)*; **Brief bei der** ~ **aufgeben** to post (mail, *US)* a letter at the post office; **eingegangene** ~ **erledigen (durchsehen)** to attend to (go through) the correspondence; **mit der** ~ **zustellen** to deliver by mail *(US)*;
~**abfertigung** dispatch of mail *(US)*; ~**ablage** postal rack; ~**abschnitt** postal receipt.
postalische Bestimmungen postal regulations.
Postamt post, post (letter) office, mail station *(US)*;
betriebseigenes ~ self-service postal unit.
Post|angestellter postal worker (employee, clerk, *US)*, post-office servant *(Br.)*; ~**anschrift** mailing *(US)* (post-office, postal) address; ~**antwortschein** reply coupon *(US)*; ~**anweisung** money order, post-office order, postal order *(Br.)*, postal money order *(US)*, postal note *(US)*; ~**aufbewahrungsstelle** post restante *(Br.)*; ~**auftrag** mail order *(US)*; ~**auslieferung** mail delivery *(US)*; ~**beförderung** postalt transport, transport of mail *(US)*; ~**begleitschein** post bill; **bei** ~**bezug** if delivered by post *(Br.)* (mail, *US)*; ~**bezugspreis** postal subscription rate; ~**bote** postman, postboy, letter (mail, *US)* carrier, mailman *(US)*.
Pöstchen, fettes fat living, snug berth; **ruhiges** ~ snap, soft job;
~**inhaber** placeman; ~**jäger** pie (place) hunter.
Post|diebstahl mail robbery *(US)*; ~**einlieferung** posting, mailing *(US)*.
Posten post, place, station, *(Betrag)* sum, amount, *(Buchhaltung)* entry, item, *(Effektenpaket)* block, lot, *(Stellung)* position, situation, job, berth;
in kleinen ~ by (in) parcels;
ausstehender ~ receivable item, outstander; **der**

debitorischer ~ receivable item; **durchlaufender** ~ suspense (transitory) item; **einträglicher** ~ snug berth; **offener** ~ unpaid item; **unbeglichener** ~ item not squared; **unbesetzter** ~ unfilled post, vacancy, vacant position; **verauslagte** ~ *(Spediteur)* advanced charges;
~ **auf der Aktivseite** asset; ~ **der Rechnungsabgrenzung** deferred charges [to expense] *(US)*, deferred (prepaid) assets (expenses); **unsichtbare** ~ **der Zahlungsbilanz** invisible items of trade;
~ **abstreichen** to deduct an item; ~ **einzeln aufführen** to specify items; **verantwortungsvollen** ~ **bekommen** to move to a position of greater responsibility; ~ **neu besetzen** to fill a vacancy; **sich um einen** ~ **bewerben** to run for a position; ~ **im Hauptbuch eintragen** to enter an item in the ledger; ~ **nachtragen** to book an omitted item; ~

stornieren to cancel an item; **von seinem** ~ **zurücktreten** to relinquish one's appointment; ~**jäger** office seeker (hunter), job jockey, carpetbagger *(US)*.
Post|entwertungsstempel postmark cancellation; ~**fach** post-office box; ~**fachnummer** boxnumber; ~**karte** postcard *(Br.)*, postal card *(US)*, *(fam.)* postal *(US)*; ~**karte mit Rückantwort** replypaid postcard *(Br.)*, double card *(US)*; ~**kartenautomat** postcard automatic supply *(Br.)*; ~**kasten** letterbox, pillar box *(Br.)*, mailbox *(US)*.
postlagernd to be left till called for, general delivery *(US)*, poste restante.
Post|laufkredit mail credit *(US)*; ~**leitvermerk** post route; ~**leitzahlgebiet** zip code area *(US)*; ~**minister** Postmaster General; ~**ministerium** General Post Office *(Br.)*, Post Office Department *(US)*; ~**nachnahme** postal collection order *(US)*, cash (collect, *US)* on delivery, C.O.D.; ~**paket** parcel, postal packet *(Br.)*, package *(US)*; ~**quittung** certificate of posting *(Br.)*, post-office receipt; ~**sack** postbag, mailbarg *(US)*, ~**schalter** counter position, window.
Postscheck postal check *(US)*, postal giro *(Br.)*;
~**amt** National Giro Centre *(Br.)*; ~**dienst** National Giro Service *(Br.)*; ~**guthaben**, ~**konto** giro *(Br.)* (postal check, *US)* account.
Postschließfach post-office box.
Postsendung post, mail *(US)*, item, postal packet *(Br.)*;
unzustellbare ~ undeliverable mail *(US)*, nix *(US sl.)*, dead letter *(Br.)*.
Postspar|buch post-office (postal, *US)* savings book; ~**einlagen** post-office (postal, *US)* savings deposits, postal savings *(US)*; ~**kasse** post-office (postal, *US)* savings bank; ~**kassenbuch** post-office *(Br.)* (postal, *US)* savings book.
Poststempel postmark, date stamp; ~**tarif** postal tariff *(US)*, rates of postage *(Br.)*; ~**umschlagstelle** schedule point *(US)*; ~**verkehr einstellen** to suspend postal (mail, *US)* service.
Postversand mail order;
~**artikel** postal items, mailings, wrap-up; ~**geschäft** mail-order business (concern, establishment, house, selling); ~**katalog** mail-order catalog(ue).
postwendend by return of post (mail, *US)*.
Post|werbung direct-mail (mail-order) advertising; ~**wertzeichen** [postage] stamp; ~**wurfprospekt** direct-mail literature; ~**wurfsendung** bulk mail, unaddressed mailing *(US)*; ~**zensur** postal censorship; ~**zug** mail [train]; ~**zustellungsadresse** post-office address; ~**zustellung** mail (postal) delivery, post.
Präferenz preference, *(Zoll)* preferential *(Br.)* (most-favo(u)red-nation) treatment;
~**abmachung** (GATT) preferential arrangement; ~**spanne** margin of preference; ~**zoll** preferential tariff; ~**zollsatz** preferential (most-favo(u)red-nation) rate.

Präge|anstalt mint; ~gebühr coinage.
Praktikant practitioner, learner, improver, probationer, nonapprentice, trainee *(US)*.
Prämie premium [pay], consideration, *(Anreiz)* bonus, bounty, *(Belohnung)* reward, *(Kaufmann)* giveaway, goody, *(Prämiengeschäft)* premium, option, privilege *(US)*, *(Zollvergütung)* drawback; **einheitliche** ~ flat bonus; **noch nicht fällige** ~ *(Versicherung)* deferred premium; **höchstmögliche** ~ highest possible award; **[nicht] produktionsgebundene** ~ [non]production bonus; **nicht verdiente** ~ unearned premium; ~ **für langjährige Betriebszugehörigkeit** longevity pay; ~ **für unfallfreies Fahren** no-claim bonus *(Br.)*; ~ **abwerfen** to yield a premium; ~ **erklären** to declare an option; **auf** ~ **verkaufen** to sell at option.
Prämien|akkordsystem task and bonus system; ~**anleihe** lottery (premium) loan; ~**aufkommen** *(Lebensversicherung)* premium income, earned premium; ~**aufschlag** loading; **auf** ~**basis arbeiten** to go on a bonus, to work on a bonus system; ~**berechnungsstelle** rating office; ~**bon** *(Sparen)* premium savings bond; ~**brief** confirmation of an option deal; ~**erklärung** *(Börse)* declaration of options *(US)*; ~**erklärungstag** *(Börse)* carrying-over *(Br.)* (contango, *Br.,* making-up, *Br.,* option, *US)* day; ~**festsetzung** rate making (setting); ~**geber** *(Börse)* giver of option money; ~**geld** *(Börse)* option money; ~**geschäft** *(Börse)* option business (deal), optional (time) bargain, trading in puts and calls (privileges, *US)*, spread *(US)*; **in eine höhere** ~**gruppe einstufen** to rate higher (up); ~**handel** option business, *(Börse)* trading in puts and calls (in privileges, *US)*; ~**händler** *(Börse)* option dealer; ~**käufer** *(Börse)* option buyer; ~**kurs** *(Börse)* option price; ~**lohn** premium (incentive) pay; ~**los** lottery bond; ~**makler** *(Börse)* privilege broker *(US)*; ~**plan** premium (savings) plan; ~**rechnung** *(Versicherung)* premium note, renewal notice; ~**recht ausüben** *(Börse)* to exercise an option; ~**reserve** unearned premium reserve, *(Deckungsstock)* premium stock, *(Lebensversicherung)* reserve fund, insurance reserve; ~**rückerstattung** reimbursement of premium; ~**satz** premium rate, rate of consideration, *(Börse)* option rate (price) *(Br.)*; ~**staffelung** scale of premiums; ~**system** *(Betrieb)* premium (bonus, wage-incentive) plan, *(Exportförderung)* system of bounties; ~**tarif** insurance tariff; ~**überhang** reserve for unearned premium; ~**vergütung** bonus payment; ~**verkäufer** *(Börse)* taker of option money *(US)*; ~**verteilung** bonus distribution; ~**werte** *(Börse)* securities dealt on the option market, option stock *(Br.)*; ~**zahlung** premium payment; ~**ziehung** prize drawing; ~**zuschlag** extra (additional) premium, *(Gefahrenzuschlag)* hazard bonus, *(Verwaltungskosten)* load.
pränumerando zahlen to prepay, to pay in advance (by anticipation).
Präsidialsitzung board meeting.

Präsidium presidency, chair, *(Direktorium)* board of directors, *(Verein)* house committee.
Praxis *(Anwalt)* clientele, *(Anwalt, Arzt)* practice; **langjährige** ~ long personal experience.
Preis price, *(Belohnung)* reward, premium, *(Kosten)* cost, *(Satz)* rate, figure, *(Wert)* value, *(im Wettbewerb)* prize, award;
bei sinkenden ~**en** at prices dropping; **zu bedeutend ermäßigten** ~**en** at a sweeping reduction; **zu überhöhten** ~**en eingekauft** bought at excessive cost; **zum amtlich festgesetzten** ~ at the established price;
~ **freibleibend** price subject to change without notice;
abgemachter ~ price agreed upon; **nicht amtlicher** ~ *(Börse)* sidewalk price *(US)*; **angegebener** ~ quoted price; **äußerster** ~ rock-bottom (close) price, cut rate; **ausgezeichneter** ~ marked price; **billiger** ~ budget price; **nicht die Selbstkosten deckender** ~ losing price; **fakturierter** ~ invoiced price; **fallende** ~**e** dropping (sagging) prices; **feste** ~**e** steady prices, *(Schaufenster)* no abatement (discount, reduction); **amtlich festgesetzter** ~ administered (controlled) price; **gebundener** ~ fixed (fixed-selling, maintained) price; **genehmigter** ~ approved price; **gestützter** ~ pegged price; **handelsüblicher** ~ market (ruling) price; **niedrigst kalkulierter** ~ bargain level; **kostendeckender** ~ price covering the costs of production; **mörderischer** ~ cutthroat price; **optischer** ~ charm price; **ganz schöner** ~ smart price; **subventionierter** ~ subsidized (support, pegged) price; **unerschwinglicher** ~ prohibitive price; **unverschämter** ~ steep (outrageous) price; **volkstümlicher** ~ popular price; **zivile** ~**e** moderate (reasonable) prices;
~ **bei der Anlieferung** landed cost; ~ **bei Barzahlung** cash price; ~ **einschließlich Bedienung** terms inclusive of service; ~ **ab Erzeuger** factory price; ~ **für Güter und Dienstleistungen** cost of goods and services; ~ **frei Haus** in-the-mail price; ~ **bei sofortiger Lieferung** spot quotation; ~ **bei Ratenzahlung** hire-purchase (time, deferred-payment, *US)* price; ~ **ab Versandbahnhof** at-station price; ~ **ab Werk** price at works, factory price;
vom ~ **abhandeln** to obtain a reduction; ~**e schrittweise angleichen** *(EG)* to approximate prices progressively; ~ **aushandeln** to negotiate a price; **mit einem höheren** ~ **auszeichnen** to mark up; **niedrige** ~**e berechnen** to ask moderate prices; ~**e drücken** to bring (run) down (bang, *sl.)* prices; ~ **empfehlen** to recommend (suggest) a price; **sich nach dem** ~ **erkundigen** to ask (inquire about) the price; **enorme** ~ **erzielen** to fetch huge prices; ~ **festsetzen** to price, to quote (make, arrive at, fix, lay down) a price; **höchste** ~**e bei einem Wettbewerb gewinnen** to win the top hono(u)rs in a competition; ~ **herabsetzen** to abate (cut, sink) a price; **mit dem** ~ **heruntergehen** to reduce the price; ~ **hochschrauben** to screw up (lift) prices; ~**e hochtreiben** to boost (puff up) prices, to bull (rig, *Br.)* the market; ~**e schärf-**

stens kalkulieren to cut prices to a minimum;
~ sehr vorsichtig kalkulieren to establish a price at
a low level; unter dem ~ losschlagen to sell under
value; nicht auf den ~ sehen not to consider the
price; ~ senken to lower (reduce) a price; ~e stützen
to peg (buttress, valorize) prices; ~e unterbieten
to undercut (cut s. one's) prices; zu höheren als den
amtlich festgesetzten ~en verkaufen to sell above
the established price; etw. zum halben ~ verkaufen
to sell s. th. half-price; während der Saison enorm
hohe ~e verlangen to stick it on during the busy
season; vollen ~ zahlen to pay full fare;
der ~ spielt keine Rolle price is no object.

Preis|abkommen, ~abrede price-fixing agreement;
~abschlag discount, allowance, price deduction,
abatement; ~änderungen price changes; ~änderun-
gen vorbehalten subject to alterations; ~anfrage
inquiry for a price; unverbindliches ~angebot prices
without commitment; ~anhebung price increase;
beschleunigter ~anstieg price acceleration; ~auf-
schlag markup, mark-on, (Zuschlag) extra cost
(charge), surcharge; ~auftrieb enhancement in prices, price-raising tendency; ~ausschreiben competition, prize contest; ~auszeichnung price marking
(ticket), shopmark, tag, (Tätigkeit) pricing, marking, labelling; ~berechnungsmethode pricing formula; ~berechnungsverfahren auf einheitlicher
Frachtbasis basing-point system (US); ²bereinigt
adjusted for price; ~bewegung price range; ~be-
wertungsmethode pricing method; ~bewußtsein
price consciousness; ~bildung formation of prices;
~bildung im freien Wettbewerb competitive determination of prices.

preisbindend price-fixing.

Preisbindung| der zweiten Hand resale (retail) price
maintenance (Br.), maintenance of resale prices,
vertical price-fixing contract;
der ~ unterliegen to be subject to a condition as to
the price.

Preisbindungs| abkommen fair trade agreement (US)
(Einzelhandel) resale price (price maintenance)
agreement (Br.); ~klausel tying clause; ~verein-
barungen price arrangement scheme.

Preis| brechergruppe anführen to lead the price-
cutting wave; ~diskriminierung price discrimination (US); ~einbruch depression of prices,
slump; ~elastizität des Angebots elastic supply;
~empfehlung price recommendation; ~entzerrun-
gen vornehmen to straighten out foundered prices;
~erhöhung price advance (increase, climb),
markup on prices, (Grundstück) improvement
appreciation; ~erholung comeback in prices;
~ermäßigung reduction in prices, allowance; ~fä-
cher scale of prices; ~faktoren cost (pricing) factors; ~festsetzung pricing; ~festsetzung von Fall zu
Fall piecemeal price fixing (US); ~forderung asked
price, charge; ~führer price leader (US).

preisgebunden price-controlled, price-bound, price-
fixed, frozen;
~e Artikel price-maintained goods.

Preis|gefälle price gap; Lohn- ~-Gefüge wage-price
structure; ~gleitformel escalator formula; ~grenze
price limit.

preisgünstig cheap, well-(economy-)priced, budget
(thrift)-priced (US).

Preis|herabsetzung price reduction, abatement,
markdown (US); ~index für die Lebenserhaltung
cost-of-living (consumer) price index; ~kalkula-
tion price calculation; ~kalkulation durch Gewinn-
zuschlag auf Herstellungskosten costplus pricing;
~karussel price merry-go-round; ~katalog price
list, priced catalog(ue); ~klasse range of prices;
~kommissar price administrator (US); rückläufige
~konjunktur price slowdown; ~korrektur (Anzeigenwesen) short-rate adjustment.

Preislage range of prices, price bracket;
in niedriger ~ low-priced;
in der ~ von 3000,— DM aufwärts liegen to be in the
DM 3000,— plus range.

preislich richtig liegen to be priced right.

Preis|liste price current (list, schedule, catalog[ue];
~manipulierung manipulating of prices; ~nachlaß
price deduction (reduction), discount, abatement;
~notierung quotation [of prices]; ~ortssystem
multiple basing point system (US); zurückhaltende
~politik price restraint; ~prüfer regulator of
market prices, pricer (Br.); ~rückgang fall (drop,
dip) in prices; ~schere price scissors; ~schwankun-
gen price fluctuations (oscillations); ~senkung
price cut (cutting, fall, reduction); staatliche
~senkungsaktion rollback (US); angespannte ~si-
tuation pricetight situation; ~skala scale (range) of
prices.

preisstabil stable in price.

Preis|stabilisierungsabkommen price stabilization
pact; ~stand level of prices; ~steigerung price
advance (increase, improvement, rise); ~steige-
rungsrate price-increase rate; ~stopp price stop
(freeze, ceiling); ~sturz slump [in prices], break
(fall) in prices; ~stützung price support (relief
maintenance); ~stützungsmaßnahmen price-sup-
port activities; ~subventionierung price subsidy;
rückläufige ~tendenz price recession.

preistreibend price-enhancing (-raising).

Preis|treiberei boost (US coll.), rigging the market
(Br.) ~überprüfung [durch staatliche Stellen]
[government] price review; ~überwachung price
control (administration US); ~unterbietung price
cutting, underselling; ~unterbietung im Ausland
dumping; ~unterschied price difference; ~ver-
gleich price comparison; ~verteilung distribution
of prizes; ~verzeichnis price current (catalog[ue],
statement (schedule) of prices, price list, (Restaurant) tariff (Br.).

preiswert cheap, moderately priced, good value,
worth the money, at a cheap (low) rate;
~ kaufen to get good value for one's money.

Preis|wucher profiteering; ~zettel price tag (mark,
ticket, US, label); ~zugeständnis price concession; ~zuschlag supplemental cost, markup.

Presse press, papers, journalism, newspaperdom; **regierungsfeindliche** ~ papers opposed to the government;
~**ausschnitt** press clipping *(Br.)* (cutting, *US)*; ~**dienst** news (press) service; **vertrauliche** ~**information** inside dope *(sl.)*.

Prestige|artikel prestige merchandise; ~**werbung** indirect-action (corporate-image) advertising.

Prima|disksonten prime banker's acceptances *(US)*; ~**wechsel** first of exchange.

Priorität priority, precedence, preference, ranking.

Prioritäts|aktie priority (preference, *Br.* share (stock), preferred share (stock) *(US); ~***anspruch** priority claim; ~**liste** priority table.

Prise prize, capture.

Prisen|geld prize bounty (money); ~**gut** prize goods.

Privat|anschluß private line, *(Bahn)* private siding; ~**bank[haus]** private bank, individual banker *(US); ~***diskontsatz** market rate of discount *(Br.)*, private rate of discount *(Br.)*; **nur zum ~gebrauch** for private use; ~**haftpflichtversicherung** personal liability insurance; **in ~hand übergehen** to pass into private hands; ~**konto** private (personal) account; **sich ins ~leben zurückziehen** to go into retirement; ~**sekretär[in]** private (confidential) secretary; ~**wirtschaft** private business (sector, enterprises, economy, industry); ~**wohnung** private dwelling (quarters).

Probe test, trial, tryout, *(Muster)* sample, pattern, *(Probezeit)* probation;
auf ~ on approbation, *(Warensendung)* on approval; **der** ~ **entsprechend** answering the (to) pattern, up to sample;
unsortierte, nicht ausgewählte ~n unpicked samples;
j. auf ~ **anstellen** to engage s. o. on probation; ~ **entnehmen** to [take a] sample;
~**abonnement** trial subscription; ~**abschluß** *(Bilanz)* [preclosing] trial balance; ~**anstellung** probationary employment, trial engagement; ~**auftrag** trial (sample) order; ~**bilanz** rough (preclosing trial) balance; ~**entnahme** sampling; ~**erhebung** *(Statistik)* pilot study; ~**fahrt** *(Auto)* trial run (trip, drive), road test; ~**heft** specimen; ~**lauf einer Fabrik** trial run of a plant; ~**packung** trial package; ~**stück** specimen, pattern [sample], trial [piece], sample.

Probezeit probation[ary term], qualifying period;
j. mit ~ **anstellen** to engage s. o. on probation.

Produkt produce, product[ion], making, *(Handelsware)* commodity;
gewerbliches ~ industrial (manufactured) product; **hochqualifizierte ~e des gehobeneren Bedarfs** high-quality (sophisticated) products;
~**analyse** product analysis.

Produkten|börse produce (goods) exchange; ~**handel** produce trade; ~**makler** produce (merchandise, commercial) broker.

Produktion production, producing, output, manufacture, manufacturing, outturn;
mit hohen Kosten arbeitende ~ high-cost production; **gewerbliche** ~ factory production; **stetige** ~ settled production;
~ **am laufenden Band** moving-band production, assembly-line technique; ~ **von Massengütern** large-scale (wholesale) production;
~ **ankurbeln** to crank up production; **bei geringer** ~ **wirtschaftlich arbeiten** to work economically at a lower output; **mit der** ~ **beginnen** to go on stream *(US)*; ~ **drosseln** to reduce the output, to restrain (curb, cut, check, restrict) production; ~ **künstlich einschränken** to ca'canny; ~ **programmieren** to scale production.

Produktions|ablauf festlegen to schedule production *(US)*; ~**anlage** plant, manufacturing establishment; ~**anlauf** starting up of production; ~**aufgabe** *(Stillegung)* closing down, shakeout; ~**aufnahme** going into production; ~**auftrag** production order (contract); ~**aufträge erst nach positiv verlaufenen Modellversuchen erteilen** to fly before you buy; ~**ausstoß** output; ~**bedingungen** manufacturing conditions; ~**beginn sofort aufnehmen** to rush into production; ~**beschränkung** output restriction; ~**betrieb** productive enterprise, manufacturing enterprise (establishment); ~**bilanz** production (manufacturing) statement; ~**drosselung** production cutback; ~**einschränkung** restriction of production, *(Volkswirtschaft)* disinvestment *(US)*, diminution of capital goods; **industrielle** ~**erfahrungen** manufacturing know-how; ~**erlaubnis** production permit; ~**faktoren** production agents; ~**gebiet** production (producing) area, *(Herstellungszweig)* product line; **unrentable ~gebiete aufgeben** to eliminate unprofitable operations; **landwirtschaftliche ~genossenschaft** collective farm.

Produktionsgüter production (producers', industrial) goods;
~**betrieb** manufacturing establishment; ~**industrie** producer-goods industry.

Produktions|index index of industrial production; **betriebliche ~kapazität voll ausfahren** to gear production to the capacity of a plant; ~**kapital** productive capital; ~**kennziffer** index of industrial production; ~**kontrolle** production control.

Produktionskosten cost of manufacturing (goods manufactured, production costs;
einmalige ~ sunk cost;
~**aufstellung** manufacturing cost sheet.

Produktions|kredit production (productive) credit; ~**leistung** production rate (capacity), manufacturing efficiency, output; ~**leitung** plant management; ~**löhne** productive labo(u)r; ~**material** direct material; ~**mittel** productive equipment, capital goods; ~**mittelindustrie** capital-goods industry; ~**planung** planning of production; ~**prämie** production (piece-rate) bonus, production grant *(Br.)*; ~**preis** cost of production.

Produktionsprogramm prodcution budget (plan, schedule), manufacturing program(me);

reichhaltiges (weitgestreutes) ~ product diversification, diversification program(me);
sein ~ abrunden to round off one's production; seinen Erfolg einem breitgefächerten ~ verdanken to owe one's performance to diversification.
Produktions|prozeß manufacturing (production, productive) process; alleinige ~rechte haben to have the exclusive production right; ~risiko producer's risk; ~rückgang falling (setback, decline in, drop in) production; ~schwerpunkt verlagern to shift product emphasis; ~stätte manufacturing establishment (plant, factory); ~steuerung production control (planning); vorübergehende ~stillegung shutdown in production; ~stufen stages of production; termin production date; ~überschuß production surplus; ~verbot prohibition to produce; ~verfahren technique of production, production (manufacturing) method; günstige ~verhältnisse low-cost facilities; ~vorschau production outlook; ~vorschriften manufacturing directions; ~wert production (cost) value; ~zahlen output (production) figures; schwankende ~ziffern unsteady output; ~zweig product line, branch.
produktive Anlage paying investment.
Produktivgenossenschaft producer cooperative.
Produktivität productivity, productiveness.
Produktivitäts|abnahme diminishing productivity; erstklassige ~ergebnisse aufweisen to turn in the best porductivity performance; ~grenze marginal productivity; ~rate rate of productivity; ~theorie marginal productivity theory of wages; tarifliche ~vereinbarung productivity agreement; ~zuwachs productivity gain (increase).
Produktiv|kapital productive (auxiliary) capital; ~kredit production credit.
Produktmanager brand (product) manager.
Produzent producer, manufacturer, maker, operator, outputter (US), (Film) producer;
mit geringen Selbstkosten arbeitender ~ low-cost operator.
produzieren to produce, to manufacture, to make; in Massen ~ to massproduce.
Profit profit, gain, advantage, turn, makings.
profitieren to profit by, to gain;
an einem Geschäft ~ to profit by a bargain; steuerlich ~ to benefit tax-wise; von einem Streik ~ to capitalize on a strike.
Profitjäger profiteer[er], profitmanager.
Proforma|bilanz pro-forma balance sheet; ~rechnung pro-forma (simulated) account.
Prognose forecast, forecasting.
Programm program(me), plan, (Unternehmen) product line.
Progressions|satz rate of progression; ~steuer progressive (graduated) tax.
Progressivlohn progressive wage rate.
Projekt project, scheme, design, plan;
aus Steuermitteln finanziertes ~ project supported by taxes;
~auswahl project identification.

Projekt|ingenieur project engineer; ~leiter project leader; ~mittel project funds; ~studie feasibility study, blueprint (US).
Prokura procuration, agency, proxy;
~ erteilen to confer (give) procuration; per ~ zeichnen to sign by (per) procuration (p. proc.);
~indossament indorsement by procuration.
Prokurist [etwa] proxy, authorized (confidential, managing) clerk.
Prolongation renewal, extension, prolongation, (Reportgeschäft) carryover, carrying over;
in ~ geben to give on (Br.), to give on stock (US); in ~ nehmen to carry over (Br.), to take in (Br.), to continue, to take in stock (US).
Prolongations|gebühr contango (carrying-over, continuation, Br.) rate, (Tagesgeld) renewal rate; ~geschäft contango (continuation, Br., carrying-over, Br.) business; ~preis making-up price; ~wechsel renewal (continuation, Br.) bill.
prolongieren to extend, to renew, to prolong, (Effektenengagement) to carry forward (over, Br.), to continue (Br.);
Zahlungstermin ~ to extend the time of payment.
Promesse promissory note, due bill.
prompt| bezahlen to make ready payment;
~e Bedienung prompt service.
Proportionalbesteuerung proportional taxation.
Propregeschäft business for own account.
proratarisch pro rata, in proportion, proratable (US).
Prospekt catalog(ue), brochure, pamphlet, leaflet, literature, circular, booklet, handout;
eingelegter ~ cover folder;
~ für den Handel trade folder;
~ wird zugeschickt literature on request.
Prospektversand circularization.
Protektionswirtschaft favo(u)ritism, protectionism, spoils system (US).
Protest protest[ation];
mangels ~s in the absence of protest; sofort zum ~ to be protested at once;
~ wegen Nichtannahme protest for nonacceptance;
~ aufnehmen to draw up a protest; ~ aufnehmen lassen to have a bill noted; mit ~ zurückgehen lassen to return under protest.
Protest|anzeige note (notice) of protest; ~gebühr protest fees (charges); ~gläubiger protester.
protestieren to [enter a] protest, to object.
protestierter Wechsel dishono(u)red bill.
Protest|spesen (Wechsel) protest fees; ~verzichtserklärung waiver of protest.
Protokoll record, register, minutes, (Verkehrsteilnehmer) ticket (US), warning and fee (Br.);
~ abfassen to draft the minutes; im ~ vermerkt sein to stand on record;
~aufnahme recording, entry in the minutes; ~eintragung entry, minute (Br.).
protokollieren to enter in (keep) the minute book, to take down [the minutes].
Proviant|lager supply depot; ~schiff supply (victualling, Br.) ship, storeship, victualler (Br.).

Provision commission, compensation, *(Makler)* brokerage, *(Prozentsatz)* percentage; **franko** ~ free of commission; **unter Abzug Ihrer** ~ deducting your commission; ~ **aus Konsortialbeteiligungen** underwriting commission; **3 %** ~ **berechnen** to charge 3 per cent commission; ~ **sparen** to save middlemen's profit.
Provisions|agent commission merchant (agent); ~**anspruch** accrued commission.
Provisionsbasis commission basis; **j. auf** ~ **anstellen** to appoint s. o. as buyer on commission.
Provisionsbeleg commission note.
provisionsberechtigt sein to have earned one's (be entitled to a) commission.
Provisions|einkünfte commission earnings (income); ~**gebühr** commission, factorage *(US)*, compensation, *(Finanzmakler)* brokerage; ~**geschäfte machen** to go marketing, to sell goods for a commission; **auf** ~**grundlage arbeiten** to operate on a commission basis; ~**gutschrift** commission note; ~**nachlaß** *(Versicherungswesen)* rebate.
provisionspflichtig commissionable.
Provisions|rechnung commission note (account); ~**satz** commission rate; ~**tabelle** commission schedule.
Provisionsvertreter commission (del-credere) agent, travelling salesman, factor *(US)*; **als** ~ **arbeiten** to be paid on a commission basis.
provisorisch provisional, provisory, temporary, make-shift, ad interim; ~**es Konto** interim account.
Prozent per cent, percentage; ~**gewinn** per cent gain; ~**notierung** quotation in percentage.
prozentualer Anstieg percentage of increase.
Prozeß action at law, [law] case, lawsuit *(US)*, suit at law *(US)*; ~ **gegen j. anstrengen** to initiate proceedings (institute legal proceedings) against s. o.; ~**bevollmächtigter** pleader, attorney of record *(US)*, plaintiff's counsel.
prozessieren to maintain an action, to sue, to carry on a lawsuit *(US)*.
Prozeßkosten [law] costs, cost of an action.
prüfen to prove, *(besichtigen)* to inspect, to survey, *(Maschine)* to overhaul, *(überprüfen)* to control, to look over, to review; **Bücher** ~ to audit the books; **Rechnung** ~ to audit (check) an account; **Unterschrift auf ihre Echtheit** ~ to authenticate a signature.
Prüfer examiner, searcher, *(Abnahme)* inspector.
Prüf|liste check list; ~**stück** specimen.
Prüfung examination, *(Abnahme)* inspection, *(Bi-*

lanz) audit[ing], *(Erprobung)* trial, test, *(Konto)* verification, reconcilement, check[ing], *(Kontrolle)* supervision, checkup *(US)*; **bei** ~ **Ihres Kontoauszuges** upon reconcilement of your abstract of account; **betriebseigene** ~ internal audit; ~ **der Auszahlungsbelege** voucher audit; ~ **der Kasse** cash audit; ~ **am Versandort** shipping-point inspection *(US)*; ~ **abschließen** *(Revisor)* to conclude an audit; **sich zur Teilnahme an einer** ~ **melden** to enter for an examination.
Prüfungs|abschnitt *(Revision)* period under audit; ~**auftrag** *(Abnahme)* inspecting order, *(Revision)* auditing order (engagement); ~**beamter** *(Abnahme)* inspecting officer, test clerk, *(Revisor)* auditor; ~**bescheinigung** *(Abnahme)* inspection certificate, *(Revision)* accountant's (audit) certificate; ~**gebühr** *(Abnahme)* inspection fee, *(Revision)* audit fee; ~**gesellschaft** auditing company, auditor; ~**kommission** *(Abnahme)* inspection committee; ~**personal** *(Buchprüfer)* auditing staff; ~**posten** *(Abnahme)* inspection lot; ~**richtlinien** *(Revision)* audit standards; ~**schein** *(Lagerei)* certificate of inspection; ~**termin** *(im Konkurs)* public examination, *(Revision)* audit date.
Prüfungsvermerk test note, *(Revisor)* accountant's (audit) certificate; **einschränkender** ~ qualified report.
Prüfungsvorschriften *(Revision)* audit standards.
Publikum public, *(Hörer)* audience, *(Leser)* readers; **Anlage suchendes** ~ prospective (capital-seeking) investors, general investing public.
Publikums|gesellschaft publicly-owned corporation *(US)*; ~**zeitschrift** consumer publication.
Pump *(fam.)* touch, tick *(Br.)*, cuff *(US)*; **auf** ~ **kaufen** to buy on credit (tick, *Br., mace, sl.)*, to take on cuff *(US)*.
Punkt *(Bewirtschaftung)* point, ration coupon, *(Börsennotierung)* point, *(Posten)* item, article; **unerledigte** ~**e [der Geschäftsordnung]** unfinished business; ~**e auf der Tagesordnung** items on the agenda; ~ **erledigen** *(Tagesordnung)* to discuss a point; **zehn** ~ **fallen** *(Kurs)* to drop (slump, decline) ten points; **auf** ~**e freigeben** *(Bewirtschaftung)* to release on points; **um 13** ~**e auf 567 steigen** *(Kurs)* to forge ahead 13 points to 567; ~**bewertungssystem** *(Angestellte)* point [rating] system.
pünktlich punctual, on the nose, prompt, sharp; **in seinen Zahlungen** ~ **sein** to be punctual in one's payments.
Punktlohnsystem point wage system.

Q

Qualifikation qualification, capacity, eligibility.
qualifizierte Mehrheit qualified majority.
Qualität *(Art)* kind, *(Güte)* quality, class, *(Marke)* brand, description, mark, *(Sorte)* sort, type; **erster** ~ first-rate, of finest grade; **von geringer (minderer)** ~ low-class (-grade), poor, third-rate; **allererste** ~ sterling quality; **ausreichende** ~ acceptable quality level; **durchschnittliche** ~ standard quality; **gangbare** ~en fair assortment; **marktgängige** ~ merchantable quality; **mittlere** ~ medium goods (sorts); **zugesicherte** ~ warrant of merchantability; **gute** ~ **und Beschaffenheit** good merchantable quality and condition; **mehr auf Quantität als auf** ~ **gehen** to seek size rather than quality; ~ **steigern** to enrich (upgrade) a quality.
Qualitäts|abweichung deviation of quality; **hohe ~ansprüche stellen** to promote high standards; **für ~arbeit garantieren** to guarantee the finest workmanship; ~**artikel** branded goods; ~**bestimmung** quality grading; ~**erzeugnisse** high-quality products, high-grade goods; ~**klasse** grade; ~**kontrolle** process (statistical quality) control; ~**marke** brand; ~**probe** sample, pattern; ~**prüfung** quality control; ~**rüge** quality complaint; ~**verschlechterung** deterioration in quality; ~**zeichen** quality mark, kite mark *(Br.)*.
Quantität quantity, bulk, lot; **in kleinen** ~**en** in small lots.
Quarantäne | **aufheben** to remove the quarantine; ~**flagge** quarantine (sick, yellow) flag, flag of quarantine; ~**zeit** quarantine period.

Quartals|abrechnung quarterly account; ~**dividende** quarterly dividend; ~**miete** quarter's rent.
Quelle source, origin, *(Auskunft)* source, authority, spring, *(Einkommen)* source of income, *(Gewährsmann)* informant, mother, parent; **an der** ~ **kaufen** to buy at first hand.
Quellenbesteuerung collection at source, pay-as-you-go-system *(US)*.
Querschnitt cross section, sample.
quittieren to receipt, to acknowledge receipt of; **per Saldo** ~ to give receipt in full.
Quittung receipt, acknowledgment, acquittance, quittance, bill, discharge, *(Beleg)* voucher; **laut beiliegender** ~ as per receipt enclosed; **löschungsfähige** ~ *(Grundbuchrecht)* satisfaction piece; **unvollständige** ~ receipt that is not in order; ~ **über eingelagerte Güter** warehouse-keeper's certificate; ~ **ausstellen** to [give (make out) a] receipt.
Quittungs|blankett receipt form; ~**heft** *(Bank)* receipt book, chequelet *(Br.)*; **mit ~stempel versehen** to receipt; ~**vordruck** receipt form.
Quote quota, proportional allotment (share), *(Anteil)* share, proportion, *(Konkurs)* liquidation dividend, *(Rückversicherung)* quota share; **anteilsmäßige** ~ pro-rata share; **seine** ~ **aufbringen** to pay one's share; **unausgenutzte ~n ins nächste Jahr übertragen** to allow unfilled quotas to carry into next year.
Quoten|aktie no-par value share *(Br.)* (stock, *US)*; ~**erhöhung** quota increase; ~**rückversicherung** reinsurance by quota cession; ~**vertrag** quota treaty.

R

R-Gespräch *(Telefon)* reverse (transfer, *Br.)* charge call, call-collect *(US)*.
Rabatt abatement, rebate[ment], allowance, deduction, reduction, *(Skonto)* discount; **von der Gesamtabnahme abhängiger** ~ deferred discount *(US)*; **dem Händler eingeräumter** ~ dealer's discount; **Retouren und** ~**e** returns and allowances; **besonderer** ~ **bei Belegung mehrerer Regionalausgaben desselben Blattes** combined edition discount; ~**bei Mengenabnahme** quantitiy discount; ~ **geben** to allow an abatement, to grant a reduction; **mit** ~ **kaufen** to buy at market discount; ~**gewährung bei Inzahlungnahme** trade-in allowance; ~**preis** discount price; ~**staffel** *(Anzeigenwesen)* sliding scale (discount).
Radarblindlandung ground-controlled approach.
Radio wireless, broadcasting, radio *(US)*; ~**durchsage** spot announcement, spot *(US)*; ~**programm finanzieren** to sponsor a program(me);

~**werbung** broadcast advertising; ~**werbesendung** commercial *(US)*.
Rahmen frame, scope, limits, *(Zeitung)* box; **außerhalb des ~s von jds. Vertretungsmacht** beyond the scope of s. one's express authority; **im** ~ **des üblichen Geschäftsverkehrs** in the course of business; ~**abkommen** skeleton agreement; ~**police** master policy; ~**tarif** skeleton wage agreement.
Rampe platform, ascent, elevated approach.
Ramsch trumpery, junk (job) goods, refuse, rubbish; ~**geschäft** junk shop; ~**partie** job lot, trumpery.
Rand|bezirk fringe; ~**geschäfte aufgeben** to sell off one's peripheral activities.
Rang rank, degree, *(Besoldungsskala)* rate, rating, grade, *(Güte)* quality, grade, *(Stellung)* rank, standing, status, state, position, station; ~ **der Gläubiger** ranking of creditors.
Rangfolge order of preference, sequence, priority; ~ **von Sicherheiten** marshalling of securities.

Rangierbahnhof shunting station, switchyard *(US)*.
rangieren *(Eisenbahn)* to marshal, to shunt, to switch *(US)*, *(Gläubigerforderungen)* to rank, to marshal.
Rangliste list of precedents, ranking list.
Rangordnung ranking, order of ranks, rank order.
~ **der Gläubiger** ranking of creditors; ~ **der Sicherheiten** *(Konkursverfahren)* marshalling of assets.
Rat für gegenseitige Wirtschaftshilfe Council of Mutual Economic Aid (COMECON).
Rate instal(l)ment, part payment, *(Konkurs)* dividend;
in vierteljährlichen ~n paid quarterly;
erste ~ *(Anzahlung)* deposit, first instalment, downpay *(US)*;
in ~n abzahlen to clear off by instal(l)ments, to buy (pay) on the instal(l)ment (hire-purchase, *Br.*, deferred-payment, *US)* system.
Raten|kauf instal(l)ment business, hire-purchase *(Br.)*, purchase on deferred terms *(US); ~zahlung* instal(l)ment [payment], payment by instal(l)ments, part (deferred, *US*, spaced) payment.
Ration ration, *(Anteil)* portion, *(Schiff)* allowance.
rationalisieren to rationalize.
Rationalisierung rationalization.
Rationalisierungs|fachmann efficiency engineer (expert); ~**konjunktur** rationalization boom.
rationell efficient, *(sparsam)* economical.
rationieren to ration, to allocate, to allowance.
rationierter Artikel rationed item.
Rationierung rationing, allocation, alottment, points scheme.
Rationierungs|system rationing system; ~**vorschriften** rationing regulations.
Raubbau exhaustion, exhaustive cultivation.
Raumbedarf room (space) required.
räumen *(Wohnung)* to quit, to evacuate, to vacate;
Lager ~ to sell off, to clear (push off) old stock.
Räumung *(Lager)* clearance, clearing, *(Wohnung)* evacuation, removal, *(zwangsweise)* eviction.
Räumungs|ausverkauf clearance (closing-down) sale; ~**klage erheben** to sue for possession *(Br.)*, to take legal proceedings for ejectment *(US)*.
Reaktivierung *(Bilanz)* revaluation of assets.
Realeinkommen real income.
Realisationsprinzip *(Bilanz)* retail method of valuation; ~**wert** salvage value.
realisierbar realizable, liquidatable, convertible, *(Effekten)* marketable;
sofort ~ **Aktiva** liquid (fluid, *US*) assets.
realisiert|er Gewinn realized revenue (profit); **noch nicht ~e Gewinne** paper profits *(US)*.
Realisierungsverkäufe profit-taking sales.
Real|kreditinstitut mortgage (land) bank; ~**lohn** actual (real) wages.
Rechenmaschine calculator, calculating (computing, counting) machine.
Rechenschaftsbericht statement, account rendered, *(AG)* report and accounts, director's report; **vorläufiger** ~ flash report.
Rechenschaftslegung rendering an account.

rechenschaftspflichtig accountable, responsible.
rechnen to reckon, to compute, to calculate, *(anrechnen)* to charge, to debit;
zu seiner Kundschaft ~ to number among one's customers; **mit Mark und Pfennig** ~ to stretch one's money. to think of pennies.
Rechnung account, note, tally, *(Waren)* invoice, *(Zeche)* reckoning, bill, check *(US)*, score;
auf ~ on account, to be carried; **auf** ~ **und Gefahr** for account and risk; **auf neue** ~ **vorgetragen** carried forward to new account; **für fremde** ~ for third account; **zum Ausgleich unserer** ~ in full discharge of our accounts;
ausstehende ~en *(Bilanz)* accounts receivable *(US) nicht bezahlte)* accounts payable *(US)*; **detaillierte** ~ specified account; **längst fällige** ~ past-due account; **fingierte** ~ simulated (pro-forma) account; **gepfefferte** ~ *(fam.)* swinging bill, salt account; **laufende** ~ current (continuing, running, open book, *US)* account; **offene** ~ running account;
~ **ablegen** to [render] account; **für eigene** ~ **abschließen** to trade for own account; ~**ausstellen (ausschreiben)** to [make out an] invoice (an account); ~ **begleichen** to pay the reckoning, to settle (balance) an account, to settle a bill; **mit ~en belegen** to verify by invoices; **in einem Geschäft auf** ~ **einkaufen** to run an account with a shop; ~ **legen** to render account; ~ **quittieren** to receipt a bill; **jem. eine** ~ **schicken** to bill s. o.; ~ **spezifizieren** to state an account, to itemize a bill *(US)*; **in** ~ **stellen** to bill, to charge, to invoice; **Arbeit auf feste** ~ **übernehmen** to job; **spezifizierte** ~ **verlangen** to demand an itemized bill; **auf neue** ~ **vortragen** to bring (carry forward, place) to new account.
Rechnungsabgrenzung *(Bilanz)* deferral, deferred liability *(US)*, accrued expenses and deferred income *(US)*;
aktive ~en prepaid expenses, deferred charges [to expense] *(US)*; **passive ~en** prepaid income, deferred credits [to income] *(US)*;
Rechnungs|ablage invoice filing; ~**abschluß** final settlement, rest *(Br.)*, balancing (closing) an account; ~**betrag** face (amount) of invoice; ~**datum** billing date *(US)*; ~**erteilung** rendering an account; ~**führer** accountant, bookkeeper; ~**führung** accountancy, accounting, keeping of accounts; ~**gewicht** billed weight; **Oberster ~hof** General Accounting Office *(US)*, Commissioner of Audits *(Br.)*; **staatliches ~jahr** financial *(Br.)* (fiscal, *US)* year; **beglaubigte ~kopie** certified copy of invoice; ~**legung** rendering of account; ~**nummer** invoice number.
rechnungspflichtig accountable, liable to account, responsible.
Rechnungsposten accounting unit, head, billed cost; ~ **abhaken** to tick off items in an account; **einzelne** ~ **angeben** to itemize an account.
Rechnungs|preis invoiced amount, invoice price; ~**prüfer** auditor, comptroller, controller, ac-

countant; ~**prüfung** audit, auditing [of accounts]; ~**rückstand** account in arrears; ~**saldo** balance, rest; ~**übertrag** invoice continued; ~**vordruck** billhead; ~**vorgang** accounting operation.

Rechnungswesen accountancy, accounting; **betriebliches** ~ cost (manufacturing) accounting, costing.

Recht law, *(Anspruch)* right, claim, interest, title; ~ **auf Arbeit** right to work; ~ **auf vorzugsweise Befriedigung im Konkursverfahren** priority, preference claim; ~ **auf den Bezug junger Aktien ausüben** to exercise the right to subscribe for new shares (stocks, *US).*

Rechts|anspruch claim, [legal] right; ~**anwalt** lawyer, solicitor *(Br.),* barrister [at law *(Br)],* attorney at law *(US),* counsel *(Br.),* counsel(l)or *(US);* ~**anwalt beauftragen** to engage the service of a lawyer, to brief a barrister *(Br.);* ~**anwaltsbüro** barrister's [writing] chamber *(Br.),* law office *(US);* ~**beratung** legal advice; ~**geschäft** legal act (transaction).

rechtsgültig valid, legal, sufficient (good) in law, lawful, in force, *(Unterschrift)* authentic, genuine.

rechtzeitige Kündigung legal notice to quit.

Redakteur des Wirtschaftsteiles city (financial, *US)* editor.

Redaktion editorial staff (board), editors, desk *(US).*

Rediskont rediscount.

Rediskont|kontingent rediscount quota; ~**kredit** rediscount credit.

Reede roads, roadstead; **auf der** ~ **ankern** to remain off the harbo(u)r.

Reeder shipowner, shipper, freighter; ~ **und Befrachter** owner and charterer.

Reederei shipping business, freighting, *(Firma)* shipping company (house, office, *Br.);* ~**flagge** house (merchant) flag; ~**vertreter** shipping agent.

reell fair, fair-dealing, *(finanziell gesund) (Preis)* reasonable, *(Ware)* genuine, good, sound; ~**es Gewicht** full weight; ~**e Preise** fair (moderate) prices; ~**e Qualität** sound quality.

Referent referee, reporter, *(Behördenleiter)* department head.

Referenz reference, credentials; **persönliche** ~**en** character reference; ~**en angeben** to quote (furnish) references; **über j.** ~**en einholen** to take up s. one's references.

refinanzieren to refinance.

Refinanzierung refinancing.

Refinanzierungs|kredit *(Landeszentralbank)* rediscount credit.

Reflektant prospective (potential) buyer, prospect *(US).*

reflektieren to intend to purchase, to be interested.

Regalgroßhändler rack jobber.

regellos *(Markt)* irregular, unsettled.

regelmäßiger Besucher regular customer.

regeln, seine Finanzen to adjust one's finances; **Rechnung** ~ to meet (pay) a bill.

Regelung settlement, arrangement, adjustment, *(Geschäftsabwicklung)* winding up; ~ **eines Versicherungsfalles** claim settlement.

Regie management, administration, *(Film)* direction, stage managership, *(Staatsmonopol)* state monopoly; **in eigener** ~ **betreiben** to operate for one's own account; ~**auslagen** overhead, oncost *(Br.);* ~**betrieb** quasi-public corporation.

Regional|abkommen area agreement; ~**bank** country (interior, *US)* bank; ~**streik** sectional strike; ~**zeitungen** provincial press *(Br.).*

Register register, registry, list, schedule; **in ein** ~ **eintragen** to [make an entry in the] register; **im** ~ **löschen** to strike off the register (roll); ~**abschrift** certificate of incorporation (registration); ~**führer** recorder, keeper of the records, registrar; ~**hafen** port of register; ~**tonnage** registered (register, net) tonnage; ~**tonne** register ton.

Registrator registrar, recorder, filing clerk *(Br.).*

Registratur filing, registry, register (registration, enrol(l)ment) office; ~ **nach Orten** geographical filing; ~ **nach Sachgebieten** subject filing; ~**system** filing system.

registrieren to [enter in the] register, to record, to bill, to calendar, to tally *(Br.);* **Arbeitsbeginn** ~ to clock in.

Registrierkasse cash register, damper *(US sl.).*

Registrierung registry, register, registration; ~ **von Ausländern** aliens' registration.

Regreß recourse, regress, *(Schadenersatz)* recovery of damages; ~ **nehmen** to recover [over, *US],* to seek recovery, to go back; ~**anspruch** recourse, right of relief; ~**ansprüche stellen** to seek recourse; ~**haftung** liability to recourse.

regreßpflichtig liable to recourse.

Regreß|risiko third-party risk; ~**schuldner** party to recourse; **auf dem** ~**wege** by way of recovery.

regulieren to regulate, to regularize, *(Ansprüche)* to settle, *(an der Börse)* to even up, to liquidate; **Versicherungsanspruch** ~ to settle an insurance claim.

Regulierung regulation, regularization, *(Börse)* evening up, liquidation, settlement; ~ **eines überzogenen Kontos** remittance of cover; ~ **eines Versicherungsfalles** adjustment of an insurance claim.

Regulierungskosten *(Versicherung)* claim costs.

reiche Auswahl wide selection.

Reichhaltigkeit des Produktionsprogramms diversification of products.

reichliche Mittel ample means.

Reihenfolge | der Eintragung order of registration; ~ **der Pfandrechte** marshalling of liens.

rein | netto Kasse net cash; ~**er Verlust** dead loss.

Rein|erlös net proceeds, *(Diskontierung)* net avails *(US)*; ~ertrag net (clear, clean, pure) profit, net income; ~ertragsverwendung disposition of net profit (income).

Reingewinn clear (clean, pure, net) profit, clear (net) gain, net proceeds (earnings); unverteilter ~ undivided profits, undistributed profit; verfügbarer ~ surplus available; ~ einschließlich Vortrags net profit including balance; ~ abwerfen (erzielen) to net, to clear a profit; ~verwendung distribution of profit, disposition of net income (profit).

Rein|verlust net loss; ~vermögen financial worth, net (actual) assets.

Reise journey, course, *(kurze Fahrt)* trip, walk, tour, excursion, *(längere Fahrt)* travel; auf ~n *(Vertreter)* on the road.

Reise|agentur travel agent (agency); ~auslagen travel(l)ing expenses; ~devision tourist expenditure; ~führer travel book (guide), guidebook; ~genehmigung travel permit, clearance.

Reisegepäck luggage *(Br.)*, baggage *(US)*; ~versicherung luggage insurance *(Br.)*, tourist baggage insurance *(US)*, personal floater *(US)*.

Reisegesellschaft touring company (party), coach party.

Reisekosten travel (tourist) expenses, travel(l)ing charges (expenses); ~abrechnung travel-expense report *(US)*; ~erstattung refund of travel expenses; ~zuschuß travel(l)ing allowance.

reisen to travel, to make (go on) a journey, to go, *(mit Auto)* to be touring.

Reisender travel(l)er, voyager, tourist, journeyer, *(Vertreter)* travel(l)ing salesman *(US)*, sales representative, commercial travel(l)er;

Reise|paß passport; ~prospekt [travel] folder, tourist pamphlet; ~scheck travel(l)er's check *(US)* (cheque, *Br.*), circular cheque *(Br.)*; ~spesen travel expenses (cost, allowance), travel(l)ing charges (expenses); ~unfallversicherung travel(l)er's accident insurance; ~ziel destination.

reißend abgehen (Absatz finden) to have a quick draft, to be of quick sale, to sell rapidly (like hot cakes, dogs, *US).*

Reklamation reclamation, claim, *(Einspruch)* protest, objection, *(Mängelrüge)* complaint; ~ annehmen to admit a claim; ~ zurückweisen to reject a claim.

Reklamations|abteilung claim (complaint) department; ~schreiben complaint letter.

Reklame advertisement, advertising, publicity, propaganda, puff *(Br.)*, claptrap, boost *(US)*; ausgefallene ~ off-beat advertising; irreführende ~ misleading advertisement; marktschreierische ~ flaming (puffing, *Br.*) advertisement, puff *(Br.)*, puffery *(Br.)*; mit ~ übersät sein to be covered with advertisements;

wilder ~anschlag fly posting; ~beigabe dealer help; ~fläche advertising space, hoarding, billboard *(US)*; ~kärtchen [zur Beschreibung der Ware] store sign (card); ~preis knockdown (early-bird, cutrate) price, loss leader; ~rummel ballyhoo; ~schlager stunt; ~verkauf bargain sale; ~zettel handbill, throwaway, leaflet, dodger *(US).*

reklamieren to complain, to object.

Rekord|gewinn record profit; ~preis record price.

Rekta|giro, ~indossament restrictive endorsement (indorsement); ~klausel restrictive clause; ~papier nonnegotiable instrument; ~wechsel nonnegotiable bill.

Rembours|bank commercial bank, merchant bank[er]; ~geschäft bill-of-lading financing.

Remittenden unsold (surplus) copies.

Rendite revenue, investment (net) return, *(Wertpapier)* [interest] yield, income basis; effektive ~ net yield; gute ~ good rate of return; geringe ~ abwerfen to yield little; hohe ~ abwerfen (bringen) to yield high interest; hochverzinsliches ~objekt high-rent building; ~verhältnis bond-stock ratio.

rentabel lucrative, profitable, paying, remunerative, payoff, profit-earning, payable; sein Geld ~ anlegen to invest one's money to good account.

Rentabilität earnings (profit-earning) capacity, earning power.

Rentabilitäts|bild survey of productiveness; ~grenze marginal profit, break-even point; ~schwelle erreichen to break even.

rentables Geschäft paying (profitable) business.

Rente [retiring] pension, *(Einkommen)* income, revenue, *(Kapitalertrag)* yield, unearned (investment) income; ~n *(Staatsanleihen)* funds, governmental bonds; aufgeschobene ~ deferred annuity; festverzinsliche ~n *(Börse)* fixed-interest bearing securities; lebenslängliche ~ life pension (annuity); steuerfreie ~ clear annuity; ~ mit bestimmter Laufzeit annuity certain; ~ auf den Überlebensfall reversionary annuity; ~ ablösen to redeem an annuity; in ~n anlegen *(Börse)* to place in funds; lebenslängliche ~ aussetzen to liferent; ~beziehen to hold an annuity *(Pension)*, to draw a pension; von einer ~ leben to live on a pension.

Renten|ablösung commutation of an annuity; ~anstalt life-annuity company; ~basis annuity basis; ~berechtigter, ~empfänger annuitant, annuity holder; ~markt bond market; ~papiere bonds, annuities; ~versicherung annuity insurance *(US)*; ~zahlung annuity [benefit] payment.

Rentier annuitant, pensoner, gentleman of independent means.

rentieren, sich to pay [one's way, for costs], to give good returns, *(Betrieb)* to be profitable, to yield good profits.

Rentner annuitant, annuity holder, pensioner.
Reparations|abkommen reparation agreement; ~**zahlungen** reparations.
Reparaturen, normal anfallende ordinary repairs.
Reparatur|abteilung repair department; **während der** ~**arbeiten geschlossen sein** to be closed during repair; ~**werkstatt** repair (repairing, repairman) shop.
repartieren *(Aktien)* to apportion, to realloı.
Report *(Kursabschlag)* contango rate *(Br.)*, over spot *(Br.)*, *(Prolongationsgebühr)* continuation *(Br.)* (carrying-over) rate;
in ~ **geben** to give in continuation *(Br.)* (pension); ~**geber** person carried over *(Br.)*; ~**geschäft** continuation business *(Br.)*, carrying over; ~**nehmer** giver *(Br.)*; ~**satz** *(Kursabschlag)* contango rate *(Br.)*, *(Prolongation)* continuation *(Br.)* (carrying-over) rate.
Repräsentations|anzeige prestige announcement; ~**erhebung** sample statistic; ~**fonds** representation (office, entertainment) allowance; ~**werbung** image (prestige) advertising; ~**zulage** extra pay (sums) for entertainment, allowance for professional expenditure.
Repressalien, wirtschaftliche economic reprisals.
reprivatisieren, Staatsbetriebe to hive off state industries.
Reproduktions|vorlage *(Werbeagentur)* copy; ~**wert** reproduction cost value.
Reptilienfonds secret service (slush, *US*) fund.
Reserve reserve[s], reserve fund, *(Bank)* reserve, rest *(Br.)*;
abnehmende ~**n** reserve running short; **ausgewiesene** ~ declared reserve; **außerordentliche** excess (surplus, *US*, true, *US*) reserve; **gesetzliche** ~ statutory (legal, *Br.*, lawful, *US*) reserve; **stille** ~**n** secret (latent, undisclosed, inner, passive) reserve;
~ **an Arbeitskräften** labo(u)r reserve; ~**n für zweifelhafte Forderungen** bad-debt reserve *(US)*; ~**n angreifen** to raid (draw on) the reserves; ~ **auflösen** to release a reserve; ~**n unterhalten** to maintain reserves; **Betrag den** ~**n zuweisen** to carry an amount to reserve.
Reservefonds guarantee *(Br.)* (guaranty, contingent, reserve, emergency) fund;
~ **für mögliche Verluste** surplus contingency reserve;
dem ~ **zufließen** to go to the reserve fund.
Reserve|kapazität industrial plant reserve; ~**lager** reserve (buffer) stock.
Reserven|berechnung nach dem Nettowert der Prämien net valuation; ~**bildung** accumulation of reserves; ~**zunahme** growth of reserves.
Reserve|posten reserve position, surplus item; ~**tank** *(Auto)* storage tank.
reservieren to book [in advance], to make reservations *(US)*.
reservierter Platz reserved-seat ticket.
Reservierungsgebühr reservation *(US)* (booking) fee.

Ressort department, division, *(im Vorstand)* group, desk;
kein besonderes ~ **haben** to be without portfolio; ~**bearbeiter** desk officer; ~**leiter** group executive; ~**minister** holder of a portfolio.
est rest, remainder, residual, rump, remanet, *(Saldo)* balance, remainder, *(Überschuß)* surplus, *(Ware)* remnant;
~ **eines großen Vermögens** overplus of a great fortune.
Restanten leavings, odd lots, *(Buchhaltung)* suspense items, *(Effekten)* leftovers.
Restaurant restaurant, tavern, refreshment house; ~ **mit Selbstbedienung** self-service restaurant, cafeteria; ~**kette** restaurant chain.
Rest|bestand balance, remaining stock, remainder [of stock], *(Arbeitslosigkeit)* hard core; ~**betrag** remainder, remaining (residual) amount; ~**buchwert** residual cost, depreciated cost, net book value.
Reste|händler piece broker; ~**lager aus Konkursen** bankrupt stocks.
Restitutionsanspruch claiming back.
Restkaufgeld balance of purchase price.
restliches Guthaben remaining credit balance.
Rest|nutzungswert scrap value *(US)*; ~**posten** closed (remaining) stock; ~**vermögen** remaining property, residual assets.
Retorsionszoll retaliatory duty.
Retourenkonto purchase returns account.
Retour|fracht cargo homeward; ~**rechnung** banker's ticket; ~**spesen** back charges; ~**waren** sales return, goods returned.
Reugeld atonement (forfeit, smart) money, *(Prämiengeschäft)* option money.
Revers [counter]bond, *(Garantieerklärung)* undertaking, *(Münze)* reverse.
revidieren, Kasse to verify the cash.
Revision audit[ing];
außerbetriebliche ~ external audit; **zollamtliche** ~ customs examination.
Revisions|abteilung auditing department (division); ~**arbeiten** audit work; ~**bericht** accountant's report, audit (auditor's) certificate (report); ~**firma** auditing company, accounting firm, auditors; ~**jahr** audit year; ~**leiter** accountant in charge; ~**richtlinien** audit standards; ~**zeitraum** auditing period.
Revisor auditor, auditing expert, visitor, examiner; **betriebseigener** ~ private accountant *(US)*, internal auditor.
Rezession recession, business decline;
industrielle ~ industrial slump;
sich mit allen Mitteln gegen eine ~ **stemmen** to buck the recession.
rezessions|bedingt recessional; ²**gesteuert** recessionborne; ²**phase** stage of a recession.
Richtbetrieb consulting (fact-finding, guiding) establishment.
Richtigkeit der Abschrift wird beglaubigt certified true copy.

Richt|kosten standard cost; ~**preis** standard [purchase] price, administered (guiding, leading) price; **empfohlener** ~**preis** suggested (recommended) price.

Richtungsverkehr one-way traffic.

Richtwerte *(Zeitstudie)* standard time data.

Rikambio|nota, ~**rechnung** account of re-exchange, cross account *(Br.)*.

Rimesse remittance, *(Wechsel)* bills receivable *(US)*.

Ring ring, syndicate, corner, pool, combine, combination, trust *(US)*;
~**buch** loose-leaf (ring) binder; ~**sendung** *(Rundfunk)* chain broadcast, hookup.

Risiko risk, hazard, jeopardy, peril;
wohl abgewogenes ~ calculated risk; **ausgeschlossenes** ~ excluded risk; **erhöhtes** ~ abnormal (substantial, aggravated) risk; **nicht gedecktes** ~ uncovered risk; **subjektives** ~ *(Versicherung)* moral hazard; **versicherbares** ~ hazard;
~ **trägt der Käufer** let the buyer beware;
sein Geld mit verteiltem ~ **anlegen** to diversify one's investments;
~**abwälzung** shifting (passing) of risk; ~**auslese** selection of risks; ~**beginn** attachment of risk; ~**häufung** accumulation of risks; ~**kapital** risk (venture) capital; ~**klasse** *(Transportversicherung)* rate; ~**streuung betreiben** *(Kapitalanlage)* to diversify; ~**träger** risk bearer (taker); ~**übernahme** (assumption of) risk; ~**versicherung** hazardous insurance; ~**verteilung** diversification (spread, distribution) of risk.

riskantes Geschäft touch-and-go business.

roh *(brutto)* gross, *(Entwurf)* rough, *(unbearbeitet)* raw, in native state.

Roh|bilanz trial (rough) balance; ~**ertrag** gross proceeds (receipts); ~**gewinn** gross profit.

Rohgewinnaufschlag gross profit extra, *(auf den Einkaufspreis)* markup;
~ **auf das Warenlager** inventory markup.

Roh|material raw material (produce); ~**produkte** raw produce (products).

Rohrpost blow post *(Br.)*, pneumatic dispatch (post, *Br.)*.

Rohstoffe raw materials (products), primary materials (commodities, products).

rohstoffarm poor in raw materials.

Rohstoff|bedarf raw-material requirements; ~**bestände** raw-materials inventory; ~**ersparnis** economy in raw materials; ~**mangel** scarcity of raw materials; ~**verbrauch** raw materials used.

Rollbahn *(Flugplatz)* runway, airstrip, lead.

Rollfuhr|dienst cartage service, pick-up [and delivery] service; **bahnamtlicher** ~**dienst** door-to-door service, rail express agency *(US)*; ~**geschäft** carrier's business.

Roll|geld cartage, carriage, portage, porterage *(Br.)*; ~**gut** carted goods, cases and casks; ~**treppe** moving (travelling) staircase.

Routinebesuch routine visit.

Rubrik rubric, column, *(Steuerklasse)* bracket.

Rück|abtretung reconveyance, recession; ~**antwortkarte** business reply (self-addressed) card, reply-paid postcard *(Br.)*; ~**belastung** return debit.

rückbuchen to write back, to reverse an entry.

Rück|buchung reversal, reverse entry, storno; ~**bürgschaft** backdown, backbond, surety for a surety; ~**datierung** dating back, postdating.

rückerstatten to restitute, to refund.

Rückerstattung reimbursement, refunding, drawback;
~ **in bar** cash refund; ~ **des Kaufpreises** restitution of money paid.

rückerstattungspflichtig sein to be liable to make restitution.

Rückfahrkarte return [ticket, fare], round-trip ticket *(US)*.

Rückfahrt belegen to book the return ticket.

Rück|fall *(Heimfall)* reversion; ~**flug** flight (plane, trip) home; ~**fracht** cargo homeward, return cargo, reshipment *(US)*; ~**gaberecht** *(Investmentfonds)* repurchase privilege.

Rückgang fall, falling off, decline, drop, downward movement, letdown, *(Kurse)* decline, recession;
~ **der Aktienkurse** stock-market decline; ~ **der Produktion** production decrease; ~ **des Touristenstroms** dropoff in tourists;
leichten ~ **erfahren** to suffer a slight reaction.

rückgängig machen to countermand, to annul, to cancel.

Rückgängigmachung von Bestellungen withdrawal of orders.

Rückgriff | auf die Hilfesquellen hold on the resources; ~ **auf den Indossanten** recourse to the endorser.

Rück|gut returns, goods returned; **finanzieller** ~**halt** financial background; ~**kauf** repurchase, buy-back, buying back.

Rückkaufs|preis redemption price; ~**recht** right (equity, option, power) of redemption; ~**wert** redemption (repurchase, nonforfeiture) value, *(Lebensversicherung)* cash [surrender] value.

Rückkehr zum Goldstandard return to the gold standard.

Rücklage|n provisions *(Br.)*, reserve[s], appropriations *(US)*, surplus *(US)*;
allgemeine ~ general purpose contingency reserve, unappropriated surplus *(US)*; **freie** ~**n** available reserve, discretionary appropriations; **stille** ~**n** undisclosed reserves;
~ **für Abschreibungen** reserve for wear, tear, obsolescence or inadequacy; ~ **für Betriebsneuerungen** reserve for additions; ~ **für zweifelhafte Forderungen** bad-debts reserve *(US)*; ~ **für laufende Risiken** *(Versicherungsgesellschaft)* loss reserve; **seine** ~ **aufzehren** to overrun one's reserves; ~**n bilden** to create (build up) reserves; **den** ~**n zuführen (zuweisen)** to add (transfer, place) to the reserve fund.

Rücklagenbildung creation of reserves, appropriation of surplus *(US)*.

rückläufig on the decrease, *(Konjunktur)* recessional, *(Kurse)* declining, falling off, drooping; ~e **Bewegung der industriellen Fertigung** decline in industry; ~e **Tendenz** downward tendency.

Rücklieferungen der Kundschaft property returns.

Rücknahme | *eines Auftrags* withdrawal of an order; ~preis *(Investmentgesellschaft)* redemption price.

Rück|porto return postage; ~prämie kaufen to take for the put; ~prämiengeschäft option deal for the put; ~rechnung *(Wechsel)* reaccount; ~reisefahrkarte return (round trip, US) ticket; ~schein counterbond, *(Post)* return receipt; leichten ~schlag erleiden *(Börse)* to suffer a slight reaction; ~sendung der Verpackung return of empties; ~spesen return (back) charges.

Rückstand arrears, arrearage, lag, *(Aufträge)* backlog, *(Rest)* remainder, remnant, *(Saldo)* balance; **technischer ~** technological gap; **mit der Zahlung im ~ bleiben** to default .n payment; **mit der Miete im ~ sein** to be behind [hand] with one's rent.

Rückstände aufarbeiten to make up (clear off) arrears [of work].

rückständig residuary, *(altmodisch)* not up-to-date, obsolete, old-fashioned, *(Land)* back, backward, undeveloped; **mit den Zahlungen ~ sein** to be behind[hand] with one's payment; ~e **Beträge** arrears; ~es **Gehalt** back salary; ~e **Miete** rent in arrears; ~e **Zinsen** arrears of interest.

rückstellen *(Reserven)* to allow, to make allowance (provision), to set aside as reserve.

Rückstellung provision, reserve[s], transfer to reserve, reservation, deduction; **besondere ~** special (provident) reserve; **~ für Abschreibungen** allowance (provision) for depreciation, depreciation reserve; **~ für Abschreibung langfristiger Anlagegüter** reserve for amortization; **~ für unvorhergesehene Ausgaben** reserve (provision) for contingencies; **~ für Devisenschwankungen** allowance for exchange fluctuations; **~ für Dividendenausschüttungen** reserve for dividends voted; **~ für Ersatzbeschaffungen** replacement reserve; **~ für Grundstücksentwertungen** reserve for depreciation of real-estate owned; **~ für mögliche Inventarverluste** reserve for possible inventory losses; **~ für Neubewertungen** revaluation reserve; **~ für erforderliche Reparaturen** reserve for repairs; **~ für noch nicht feststehende Risiken** *(Bilanz)* contingencies; **~en für Steuern** deduction (reserve) for taxes, provision for taxation, taxation reserve; **~ für Substanzverminderung** reserve for depletion; **~ für Verluste** loss reserve; **~ für schwebende Versicherungsfälle** reserve for claims pending; **~ für Wertberichtigungen** revaluation reserve; **~en vornehmen** to set aside as (create) reserves.

Rückstellungs|betrag sum reserved, reserve item; ~zuweisung reserve allocation.

Rücktritt retirement, resignation, rescission, demission, vacating of office; **seinen ~ erklären** to hand in (send in, tender) one's resignation.

Rücktritts|alter retiring age; ~bestimmung escape clause; ~gesuch [letter of] resignation.

Rück|übereignung reconveyance; ~überweisung return remittance.

rückvergüten to refund, to reimburse, to replace.

Rückvergütung refund, reimbursement, drawback; **~ von Steuern** refunding of taxes.

Rückversicherer reinsurer, reinsurance (direct-working) carrier, accepting company.

Rückversicherung reinsurance, counterinsurance; **~ für einen Spitzenbetrag** excess reinsurance; **~ abschließen** to lay off a risk.

Rückversicherungs|geschäft reinsurance business; ~gesellschaft direct-working carrier, reinsurance company; ~vertrag reinsurance agreement.

Rück|waren returns, return goods, returned goods *(US)*; ~wechsel redraft, unpaid (returned) bill.

rückwirkend retroactive, with retroactive effect; ~es Gesetz ex-post-facto law.

rückzahlbar repayable, reimbursable, returnable; **in Gold ~** to be redeemed (redeemable) in gold; **innerhalb 24 Stunden ~er Kredit** overnight loan *(US)*.

rückzahlen to repay, to refund, to reimburse.

Rückzahlung paying back (off), repayment, reimbursement, return, *(Einlösung von Anleihen)* redemption; **~ in voller Höhe** full repayment; **~ zum Nennwert** redemption at par; **~ eines Kredits verlangen** to ask for the return of a loan.

Rückzahlungs|bedingungen terms of repayment (redemption); ~termin redemption date; ~wert redemption value.

Rück|zinsen interest returned; ~zoll drawback, rebate[ment], long duty; ~zollschein debenture.

Ruf repute, reputation, character; **kaufmännischer ~** credit standing (status); **guten ~ genießen** to enjoy a good reputation; ~nummer telephone number; ~schädigung detraction, defamatory statement.

rügen *(Mängelanzeige)* to make a claim.

Rügefrist period (time limit) for claims.

Ruhegehalt pension, retiring (retirement) pension; **~ aussetzen** to settle a pension.

Ruhegehalts|ansprüche haben to be entitled to a pension; ~bezüge retirement income; ~empfänger pensioner, retiree, recipient of a pension, pensionary *(Br.)*.

Ruhegeld retirement benefit *(US)*, benefit pension.

ruhen *(basieren)* to be based on, *(Geschäft)* to be at a standstill, *(Verhandlungen)* to have been interrupted, *(Versicherung)* to be suspended.

Ruhestand retirement; **im ~ sein** to be on the retired list; **j. in den ~ versetzen** to pension s. o. off.

Ruhe|störung noisemaking, *(der öffentlichen Ordnung)* disturbance (breach) of the peace; ~**stunde** leisure hour.
ruhig *(Markt)* quite, lifeless, flat, easy, at ease.
ruiniert lost, broken, down, smashed up.
Rund|fahrt circular (sightseeing) tour, round trip; ~**flugkarte mit variablem Endflugplatz** openjaw.
Rundfunk broadcast[ing], wireless, radio *(US)*; ~ **hören** to listen in; **im ~ sprechen** to talk over the radio *(US)*;
~**ansage** broadcast announcement; ~**ansprache** broadcast (radio, *US)* address; ~**anstalt** broadcasting corporation; ~**empfang stören** to black out, to jam; ~**empfänger** [wireless] set, broadcast;

~**gebühr** radio receiver fee *(US)*, radio (wireless, *Br.)* tax; ~**genehmigung** wireless licence; ~**hörer** listener; ~**nachrichten** broadcast news; ~**programm** broadcast (wireless, radio, *US)* program(me); ~**reporter** broadcast journalist *(US)*; ~**sendung, übertragung** radio broadcast, broadcasting; ~**werbung betreiben** to go on the air.
Rundreise [circular] tour, round trip (voyage, *US)*; ~**flugkarte** roundtrip air fare, point-to-point ticket; ~**schreiben verfassen** to issue a circular.
Rüstungs|anleihe defence loan (bonds), armament credit *(Br.)*; ~**betrieb** defence plant (contractor, factory); ~**güter** war goods, armament supplies.
Rüstzeug zur Berufsausbildung tools of trade.

S

Sabotage im Betrieb plant wrecking.
Sachanlage|n fixed assets, investment, *(Bilanz)* land, buildings, plant and machinery *(Br.)*; ~**vermögen** physical (tangible) assets.
Sach|bearbeiter official (officer) in charge; ~**bezüge** payment (allowance) in kind, perquisites *(Br.)*.
Sachen things, belongings, effects, chattels, goods, *(Gepäck)* luggage *(Br.)*, baggage *(US)*; **von Natur aus gefährliche ~** things dangerous in themselves; **leicht verderbliche ~** perishable goods.
Sach|einlage contribution in kind; **nach ~gebieten ablegen** to file by subject matter; ~**katalog** subject catalog(ue) (index); ~**mängelgewähr** express warranty, *(für besonderen Zweck)* warranty of fitness; ~**schaden** material damage; ~**schadensversicherung** property damage liability insurance; ~**vermögen** tangible property (assets).
Sachverständiger expert, authority, competent judge (party), specialist, official referee; **amtlich bestellter ~** qualified expert.
Sachverständigen|beirat committee (panel) of experts; ~**gutachten** expert opinion, expertise.
Sackbahnhof terminus *(Br.)*, terminal *(US)*.
Safe safe, strongbox;
~**klausel** iron-safe clause; ~**miete** hire of a safe.
Saison, außerhalb der in the off-season;
stille (tote) ~ dead (dull) season, off-season; ~**arbeiter** seasonal labo(u)r (worker); ~**artikel** seasonal goods (articles); ~**ausgleich** seasonal ad-

justment; ~**ausverkauf** [seasonal] sale, clearance sale.
saisonbedingt|er Anstieg seasonal upturn; ~**e Arbeitslosigkeit** seasonal unemployment.
saisonbereinigt seasonally adjusted.
Saison|geschäft seasonal trade (business); ~**schlußverkauf** seasonal closing-out (end-of-season) sale, seasonal clearance sale *(US)*; ~**schwankungen** seasonal fluctuations (variations).
Saldenbestätigung verification statement.
saldieren to balance, to square, to settle, to clear.
Saldo balance, *(Rest)* remainder;
täglicher ~ daily balance; **ungedeckter ~** uncovered balance; **vorgetragener ~** balance carried forward, carryforward;
~ zu Ihren Gunsten balance in your favo(u)r; **~ zu ihren Lasten** your debit balance;
~ auszahlen to pay over the balance; **per ~ quittieren** to receipt (give receipt) in full; ~ **auf neue Rechnung vortragen** to carry a balance forward to new account;
~**auszug** balance, extract (statement) of account; ~**übertrag** balance brought (carried) forward, carryforward.
Salon|dampfer saloon steamer; ~**wagen** salon carriage *(Br.)* (car, *US)*, state (pullman, *US)* car.
Sammelaktion drive [to raise funds];
~ **für Altmaterial** salvage campaign.
Sammel|anschluß *(Telefon)* party line, collective

number *(US)*; ~**aufgabe** *(Versicherung)* bordereau; ~**bestellung** omnibus order; ~**büchse** collecting box; ~**depot** irregular deposit; ~**fracht** carload freight *(US)*; ~**klausel** *(Tarifwesen)* dragnet clause; ~**konnossement** omnibus (grouped) bill of lading; ~**ladung** general cargo (commodity) shipment, truckload, (consolidated) shipment *(US)*; ~**ladungstarif** general commodity rate, carload rate *(US)*.

sammeln to collect, *(Geld)* to gather (raise) a subscription (funds).

Sammel|nummer *(Telefon)* party line, collective call (number, *US)*; ~**police** group policy; ~**transport** collective transport, full truckload shipment, carloading *(US)*; ~**wertberichtigung** global value adjustment.

Sammlung gathering, collecting, *(Geld)* collection, subscription, fundraising, drive to raise a fund, whip-round *(Br. coll.)*;
im Wege einer öffentlichen ~ by public subscription.

sanieren to reorganize, to reconstruct *(Br.)*, to refloat, to rehabilitate;
j. ~ **to put** s. one's finances on a healthy basis; **Elendsgebiete** ~ to clear slums; **Währung** ~ to restore the currency.

Sanierung reconstruction *(Br.)*, reorganization, reorganizing, readjustment, financial recovery, rehabilitation;
~ **von Elendsgebieten** slum clearance; ~ **einer Firma** company reorganization; **versuchsweise** ~ **eines Kontos** nursing an account.

Sanierungs|bericht reorganization report; ~**maßnahmen** reconstruction (austerity, reorganization) measures; ~**plan** reorganization (rehabilitation) plan; **staatliches** ~**programm durchführen** to put the finances of a country on a healthy footing.

Sanktionen, wirtschaftliche economic sanctions.

sättigen *(Markt)* to saturate, to satiate.

Sättigungspunkt *(Markt)* absorption (saturation) point.

Satz *(Betrag)* amount, rate, *(Dokumente)* set, file, *(Garnitur)* suit, set, *(festgesetzte Menge)* limit, rate, *(Preis)* price, rate, *(Waren)* lot, parcel, assortment;
zu einem ermäßigten ~ at a reduced rate; **gestaffelter** ~ graduated rate; **stufenförmiger** ~ step rate;
~ **für briefliche Auszahlung** rate for mail transfer *(US)*; **voller** ~ **Dokumente** full set of documents; ~ **für Sichtwechsel** sight rate; ~ **für Tagesgeld** call money rate;
~ **für tägliches Geld heraufsetzen** to mark up call money.

Satzung statute, charter, byelaw, bylaw, *(Gesellschaft)* memorandum (articles) of association, articles of corporation;
~ **verleihen** to grant a charter; ~ **zurücknehmen** to vacate a charter.

Satzungsänderung alteration in the articles of an association, charter amendment.

satzungsmäßig| bestellt appointed by the articles; ~**vorgeschriebene Reserve** statutory reserve.

Satzungszweck statutory object.

Saugpapier mimeograph (manifold, absorbent) paper.

säumiger Schuldner (Zahler) slow (defaulting) debtor, defaulter.

Säumniszuschlag *(Einkommensteuer)* delinquent tax due.

Schachtel *(Beteiligung)* interlocking interest, intercorporate stockholdings *(US)*;
~**gesellschaft** subsidiary (interrelated) company, consolidated corporation; ~**privileg** interlocking rights, intercorporate privilege *(US)*.

Schaden damage, loss, *(jur.)* tort, *(Nachteil)* prejudice, detriment, disadvantage, mischief, *(Verletzung)* injury, harm, *(Versicherung)* loss, casualty;
auf Brandstiftung beruhender ~ incendiary loss; **bereits eingetretener** ~ detriment already incurred; **erlittener** ~ damage suffered; **festgestellter** ~ ascertained (observed) damage; **fingierter** ~ constructive injury; **durch die Versicherung voll gedeckter** ~ loss fully covered by insurance; **mittelbarer** ~ indirect (prospective, consequential) damage; **regulierter** ~ *(Versicherung)* settled claim; **von Ihnen zu vertretender** ~ damage chargeable to you;
~ **abschätzen** to estimate (assess, value) the damage; **für einen** ~ **aufkommen müssen** to be liable for a loss; ~ **ersetzen** to repair damage, to make good a loss, to settle a loss.

Schadenersatz amends, indemnification, indemnity, reimbursement, *(in Geld)* damages, compensation;
vertraglich festgesetzter ~ liquidated damages; **der Höhe nach noch nicht feststehender** ~ unliquidated damages;
~ **für entgangenen Gewinn** consequential damages; ~ **beanspruchen** to claim damages; **auf** ~ **erkennen** to award damages against; ~ **leisten** to pay (respond in) damages, to make amends, to pay compensation; ~ **wegen Nichterfüllung verlangen** to sue in tort for conversion.

Schadenersatzanspruch damage (compensation) claim, right of recovery (indemnity);
anerkannter ~ liquidated damages; **bedingt zuerkannter** ~ contingent damages *(US)*;
~ **aus unerlaubter Handlung** claim founded in tort, tort claim;
~ **begründen** to sound in damages; ~**leistung** indemnification, compensation; ~**pflicht** liability for damages.

schadenersatzpflichtig answerable (held, liable) for damages;
j. ~ **machen** to recoup s. o. for injury.

Schadenfeuer *(Versicherung)* unfriendly fire.

Schadens| abfindung indemnification, compensation; ~**abschätzung** appraisal (adjustment) of damge, loss assessment; **sofortige ~anzeige** immediate notice; **der Höhe nach nicht festgestellter ~betrag** unliquidated damages; **im ~fall** in case (the event) of loss; **~fälle bearbeiten** to handle claims; **~forderung** claim for damages; **~formular** claim form; **~freiheitsrabatt** *(Autoversicherung)* no claim bonus *(Br.)*, preferred risk plan *(US)*; **~häufigkeit** loss frequency; **~höhe festsetzen** to assess the damage; **~meldung** damage report; **~nachweis** proof of loss; **~quote** loss ratio; **~regulierung** loss adjustment (settlement); **~sachverständiger** [claim] adjuster; **~verhütung** loss prevention.

schädliche Immissionen noxious air.

Schadlos|bürgschaft collateral guaranty, guaranty of collection *(US)*, indemnity bond.

Schalter counter, desk, window, *(Eisenbahn)* booking (ticket, *US)* office, *(Theaterkasse)* box office; **~ geschlossen** *(Postamt)* position closed; **~ schließen** to close the doors; **~beamter** booking (window, *US)* clerk, *(Bank)* cashier, teller *(US)*; **~dienst** counter service, window delivery *(US)*; **~stunden** *(Bank)* banking hours, *(Post)* post-office hours.

Schankkonzession excise (liquor, publican's, justice's, *Br.)* licence.

Schatz, aufgefundener treasure trove.

Schatz|anleihe treasury loan; **~anweisung** [treasury] warrant *(Br.)*, reasury note *(US)*, Exchequer bill (bond) *(Br.)*, treasury certificate *(US)*.

schätzen *(bewerten)* to rate, to value, to evaluate, *(steuerlich)* to assess, to rate, *(Versicherung)* to appraise, to prize; **zu hoch ~** to overvalue, to overrate.

Schätzer appraiser, appreciator, valuer, valuator, *(Steuerwesen)* assessor, *(Zoll)* merchant appraiser; **beeidigter ~** sworn appraiser, licensed valuer *(Br.)*.

Schätzpreis assessed value (price).

Schätzung estimate, estimation, valuation, pricing, *(Steuerwesen)* rating, assessment, *(Versicherung)* appraisal, appraisement, *(steuerlicher Wert)* assessed value (valuation, *US)*; **bei vorläufiger ~** at a venture (rough estimate); **annähernde ~** approximation; **zu hohe ~** overestimation, overvaluation; **zu niedrige ~** low estimate, undervaluation; **~ des Nettowertes** *(Effekten)* bond rating.

Schätzungs|beamter *(Zoll)* merchant appraiser, liquidator *(US)*; **~kosten** appraiser's fees; **~wert** *(Steuer)* assessed value (valuation, *US)*, *(Versicherung)* appraisement.

Schatzwechsel government note *(Br.)*, treasury bill *(Br.)*, (note *US)*, *(kurzfristig)* treasury certificate; **~ einlösen** to fund government notes; **~finanzierung** treasury financing.

Schätzwert valuation, appraised value.

Schau|bild chart, graph, flowsheet; **~budenbesitzer** [itinerant] showman.

Schaufenster shopwindow, shopfront *(Br.)*, show (store, *US)* window; **~ dekorieren** to dress a [shop] window.

Schaufenster|auslage [window]display; **~dekoration** window dressing (display); **~reklame** [shop-]window display (advertising).

Schau|kasten showcase, display case; **~packung** dummy [pack], sham (display) package.

Scheck cheque *(Br.)*, check *(US)*; **abhanden gekommener ~** lost check; **im Einzug befindliche ~s** checks in process of collection, float *(US)*; **beglaubigter (bestätigter) ~** marked cheque *(Br.)*, certified check *(US)*; **eigener ~** house item *(Br.)*, own check *(US)*; **durch Erhöhung des Betrages gefälschter ~** raised check *(US)*; **gesperrter ~** stopped (blocked) check; **girierter ~** endorsed check; **auf den Namen lautender ~** nonnegotiable check; **auf den Überbringer lautender ~** check [payable] to bearer; **ungedeckter ~** flash (dud, bad, uncovered) check, check without provision, kite *(Br.)*; **~ mit Rechnungsvermerk** check voucher *(US)*; **~ auf sich selbst** cashier's check *(US)*; **~ nur zur Verrechnung** nonnegotiable check, crossed cheque *(Br.)*, clearinghouse check *(US)*; **~ ausschreiben** to write out a check; **~ auf j. ausstellen** to make out a check to s. o.; **~ bestätigen** to mark a cheque *(Br.)*, to certify a check *(US)*; **~ zur Gutschrift einreichen** to deposit a check; **~ stornieren** to cancel a check; **~ einer Bank zum Einzug übergeben** to lodge a check with a bank for collection; **~ mit Verrechnungsvermerk versehen** to cross a cheque *(Br.)*; **sich einen ~ vom Konto auszahlen lassen** to draw a check upon an account; **~ platzen lassen** to bounce a check.

Scheck|abrechnung check (cheque, *Br.)* clearing; **~aussteller** drawer (maker) of a check; **~bestand** checks in hand; **~betrug** cheque fraud *(Br.)*, issuing bad checks *(US)*; **~buch** cheque book *(Br.)*, checkbook *(US)*; **~fälschung** check alteration; **~formular** blank check, check form; **~heft** cheque book *(Br.)*, checkbook *(US)*; **~karte** banker's card; **~nummer** number of a check; **~verrechnung** clearing of checks; **~versicherung** check alteration and forgery insurance.

Schein certificate, bill, *(Formular)* form, blank, *(Quittung)* receipt, *(Zettel)* slip, *(Zeugnis)* certificate, attestation; **~auktion** mock (sham) auction; **~bieter** mock (straw, *US)* bidder, by-bidder; **~firma** bogus firm, bubble company *(Br.)*, dummy concern; **~gebot abgeben** to puff; **~gewinn** apparent (imaginary, illusory) profit; **~kauf** mock (feigned, pro-forma, fictitious, sham) purchase; **~verkauf von Börsenpapieren** wash sale *(US)*, washing *(US)*; **~vollmacht** apparent authority.

Schenkung donation, gift, charitable disposition; **steuerpflichtige ~** taxable gift.

Schenkungssteuerfreibetrag gift-tax exemption *(US)*.

Schicht shift, spell, bout, *(Arbeitskolonne)* shift, gang, *(Arbeitszeit)* shift, turn, work period; **verlorene ~en** men shifts lost;

breite ~en der Bevölkerung wide sections (great masses) of the population;
~ machen to close down, to knock off.

Schicht|arbeit daywork, shift [operation (work)]; ~betrieb [multiple] shift operation; ~lohn shift (basic) wage (pay); ~verkürzung *[Arbeitslosigkeitsbekämpfung]* staggering shift; ~zuschlag shift allowance.

schicken to send, to dispatch, to forward, *(Brief)* to post *(Br.)*, to mail *(US)*;
mit der Bahn ~ to rail, to transporty by railroad *(US)*; als Drucksache ~ to send s. th. by book post *(Br.)* (book rate, *US)*; per Nachnahme ~ to send cash (collect, *US)* on delivery.

schieben *(Börse)* to carry over *(Br.)*, to continue *(Br.)*, *(Schwarzhandel treiben)* to sell on the black market.

Schieber profiteer, trafficker, wangler, grafter *(US)*, racketeer *(US)*, shyster *(US)*.

Schiebung sharp practices, underhand dealing, profiteering, wangling, put-up job, graft *(US)*.

Schiebungsgeschäft *(Börse)* carrying over *(Br.)*, continuation *(Br.)*.

Schieds|abkommen arbitration agreement; ~gericht arbitration [board, tribunal], board (court) of arbitration.

Schiedsgerichtbarkeit, betriebliche labo(u)r arbitration; gewerbliche ~ industrial arbitration.

Schieds|klausel arbitration clause; ~[ob]mann umpire, arbiter, arbitrator.

schiedsrichterlich beilegen to settle by arbitration; ~e Entscheidung arbitrator's award (finding).

Schiedsspruch arbitrament, arbitration [award]; staatlicher ~ state award.

schief liegen *(Börse)* to be on the wrong side.

Schiff ship, vessel, steamer, steamship; frei ~ free on board;
aufgebrachtes ~ prize; aufgegebenes ~ derelict (abandoned) ship; beladenes ~ laden vessel; eingelaufene ~e arrivals; außer Dienst gestelltes ~ laid-up vessel; havariertes ~ ship under average; seetüchtiges ~ seaworthy vessel;
~ in Seenot ship in distress;
~ abwracken to break up (dismantle) a ship; ~ befrachten to take a ship to freight; ~ mit Stückgütern befrachten to load a ship on the berth; ~ einklarieren to clear inwards; ~ vom Stapel laufen lassen to launch a ship; ~ auf Kiel legen to lay a ship on the keel; ~ in Dienst stellen to put a ship into service (in commission); ~ den Versicherern überlassen to abandon the property covered by a policy.

Schiffahrts|abgaben navigation dues; ~aktien shipping shares (stocks, *US)*; ~ interessen the shipping interest.

schiffbares Gewässer navigable waters.

Schiff|bauauftrag shipbuilding order; ~bruch wreck, shipwreck.

schiffbrüchig wrecked, shipwrecked.

Schiffs|anteil interest in a vessel; ~ausschlachtung

shipbreaking; ~bedarfsgeschäft marine store *(Br.)*; ~beladung shiploading; gesamte ~besatzung ship's company, crew; ~eigner shipowner; ~hypothek ship mortgage; ~kaskoversicherung hull insurance; ~ladung shipload, cargo, freight, loading, shipment *(US)*; ~ladung deklarieren to enter a cargo; ~liegeplatz loading berth; ~makler ship broker, ship's agent (husband), shipping agent (master, *Br.)*; ~musterrolle muster roll, ship's articles; ~paß ship's passport; ~pfandbrief bottomry bond; ~raum *(Laderaum)* hold, shipping space; ~reeder shipowner; ~register register of shipping, Lloyd's register *(Br.)*; ~reise sea journey (trip); ~tagebuch logbook; ~tonnage tonnage; ~untergang mit der gesamten Besatzung loss of a ship with all hands; ~verpfändung bottomry; ~vorräte naval (ship's) stores; ~werft shipbuilding yard, shipyard, dockyard.

Schirmherr protector, patron, *(Geldgeber)* sponsor.

Schirmherrschaft patronage, sponsorship.

Schlaf|koje sleeping cabin, *(Schlafwagen)* sleeperette; *(Schiff)* bunk; ~sitz *(Flugzeug)* slumberette.

Schlafwagen sleeping car *(US)*, (carriage, *Br.)*, compartment (Pullman, *US)* car, sleeper *(US)*; ~abteil sleeping compartment; ~gesellschaft sleeping-car company; ~karte berth (sleeping-car) ticket.

Schlange *(beim Anstehen)* queue, line *(US)*;
~ stehen to form (stand in) a queue, to stand in line *(US)*, to queue up, to line up *(US)*.

schlecht *(Aktie)* inferior, dubious, *(Markt)* poor, *(verdorben)* rotten, spoilt;
~ dran badly off; ~ verkäuflich slow of sale;
~ gehen *(Artikel)* to drag, *(Geschäft)* to be in a bad way (on the downgrade);
~e Finanzlage financial embarrassment; ~e Geschäftsführung poor management.

Schleich|handel illegal (illicit, clandestine) trade, *(Schmuggel)* smuggling, contrabandism; ~werbung masked (camouflaged) advertisement.

schleppend *(Geschäft)* dragging, slow;
~ eingehen to come in slowly.

Schlepper motor tractor, mule, hauler, haulier.

Schlepp|gebühr towage; ~schiffahrt towage.

Schleuder|ausfuhr dumping; ~geschäft cutting trade. ~preis giveaway (cutting, cutthroat, wretched, ruinous, slaughtered) price; ~ware job line (goods).

Schleusengeld lockage, lock dues.

Schlicht|er arbiter, arbitrator, conciliator; ~tung reconciliation, reconcilement, adjustment, *(durch Schiedsspruch)* arbitration.

Schlichtungs|amt *(Gewerbe)* industrial court *(Br.)*; ~ausschuß council (court) of conciliation *(Br.)*; ~verfahren grievance procedure, *(gewerblicher Streitigkeiten)* [industrial] arbitration.

schließen *(Abkommen)* to negotiate, *(Betrieb)* to shut down, *(Börse)* to close, to finish;
mit 185 1/2 gegen 185 ~ *(Börse)* to close 185 1/2 against 185; behördlich ~ to interdict the use of,

to padlock; **flau** ~ *(Börse)* to leave off; **Konto** ~ to close an account; **Laden** ~ to shut up (close a) shop.

Schließfach *(Bank)* safe [deposit box (vault, *US)*], locker, *(Post)* post-office (private) box; ~**aufbewahrung** safe-deposit keeping *(US)*; ~**gebühr** safe-deposit fee; ~**vermietung** renting of safes.

Schließung closing, closure, *(Betrieb)* shutdown; ~ **in der Ferienzeit** holiday (vacation, *US)* shutdown.

Schluß close, closure, *(Börsengeschäft)* unit of trade, board (full) lot *(US)*; ~**fest** *(Börse)* close (closing) firm; ~ **geordnet** *(Börse)* transaction noted; ~**abrechnung** final account; ~**alter** *(Versicherung)* final age; ~**bestand** closing inventory (stock); ~**börse** terminal market.

Schlüssel *(für Telegramm)* cable code, cipher; **schlüsselfertig** on a turnkey basis;

Schlüssel|gemeinkosten prorated expenses; ~**gewalt** *(Ehefrau)* agency of necessity; ~**gewalt ausüben** to pledge the husaband's credit for necessaries *(Br.)*; ~**industrie** key (pivotal) industry, basic trade; ~**kraft** key aid (man, executive); ~**position** key [position], leading position; **wirtschaftliche** ~**stellung** key industrial emporium; ~**unterlagen** encoding and decoding chart.

Schluß|formel *(Brief)* [formal] ending, complimentary close; ~**haltung** *(Börse)* final tone; ~**note** *(Kauf)* bought (sold) note *(Br.)*, *(Makler)* call, contract note *(Br.)*; ~**notenstempel** contract stamp *(Br.)*, transfer tax *(US)*; ~**notierung** *(Börse)*, closing (last, final, terminal) quotation; ~**quittung** receipt in full; ~**quote** *(Konkursverfahren)* liquidation dividend; ~**schein** *(Makler)* broker's note, contract note *(Br.)*; ~**verkauf** close-out (clearance) sale, *(Räumungsverkauf)* closing-down sale, *(Saisonausverkauf)* seasonal sale; ~**verteilung** *(Konkurs)* distribution of assets of the bankrupt's estate; ~**zettel** broker's (contract, *Br., sales, US)* note.

Schmälerung curtailment, cut, retrenchment.

Schmerzensgeld damages for pain and suffering *(Br.)*, compensation for pain and suffering *(US)*.

Schmiergelder palm oil, grease, sop. sweetener, payola *(sl.)*, soak *(US sl.)*.

Schmuggel smuggling, illegal (contraband) trade.

schmuggeln to smuggle, to contraband.

Schmuggler smuggler, contrabandist, runner; ~**schiff** smuggler, runner, contraband vessel.

Schmutz|konkurrenz sharp practices, mean (cutthroat) competition; ~**zulage** dirty money *(Br.)*.

Schnell|abschreibung rapid depreciation; ~**bahnverkehr** rapid transit; ~**dampfer** clipper, ocean greyhound, express liner *(US)*; ~**gaststätte** luncheonette, cafeteria; ~**kurs** blitz training *(US)*; accelerated (crash, *US)* course; ~**paket** special handling parcel *(US)*; ~**straße** expressway, speedway *(US)*; ~**verkehr** rapid transit, *(Telefon)* no-delay service, toll traffic *(US)*.

Schnellverkehrs|amt *(Telefon)* no-delay traffic office; ~**linie** express (rapid-transit) line; ~**weg** express lane, expressway, speedway *(US)*.

Schnellzug express [train], quick (fast) train.

Schreib|arbeit clerical (paper, desk) work; ~**büro** typewriting bureau.

Schreiben, amtliches official letter, writ; **Ihr geschätztes** ~ your esteemed lines.

schreiben, nach Diktat to write from dictation; **mit der Maschine** ~ to type; **Rechnung** ~ to make out a bill.

Schreib|gebühren clerk's (copying) fee; ~**kräfte** clerical staff (force); ~**maschine** typewriter.

Schreibmaschinen|büro typewriting office; ~**manuskript** typescript, typewritten matter.

Schreibtisch|arbeit desk work; ~**einkäufer** armchair shopper.

Schrift|führer secretary, clerk, reporter, recorder; ~**leiter** editor; ~**leitung** editorial staff (management, board), editors.

schriftliche Kündigung written notice.

Schrift|probe specimen (sample) of one's handwriting; ~**sachverständiger** handwriting (graphological) expert;'~**satz** writ *(US)*, bill, declaration, statement of claim *(Br.)*; ~**stück** writing, writ, paper, *(Urkunde)* deed, document, instrument; ~**wechsel** correspondence, exchange of letters.

Schrittmacher abgeben *(Börse)* to pace the market.

Schrott scrap [iron]; ~**angebot** supply of scrap; ~**auto** junked car (auto); ~**preis** scrap price; ~**wert** scrap (junk) value.

schrumpfen *(Umsätze)* to diminish, to shrink.

Schuld debt, claim, *(geschuldeter Betrag)* sum due, money owing; **abgetragene** ~ paid-up debt; **drückende** ~ pressing (heavy-weighing) debt; **sofort fällige** ~ liquid debt, debt owing; **konsolidierte** ~ funded (consolidated) debt; **verjährte** ~ barred (prescriptive, stale) debt; ~ **abarbeiten** to work off (out) a debt; **seine** ~ **auf Heller und Pfennig bezahlen** to pay twenty shillings in the pound *(Br.)*; ~ **erlassen** to release from a debt; **j. für die ganze** ~ **haftbar machen** to hold s. o. liable for the whole debt.

Schuld|anerkenntnis debtor's acknowledgement, I. O. U. (I owe you), *(beim Kontoauszug)* account stated confession; ~**aufnahme** borrowing; **verschiedene** ~**beträge** *(Bilanz)* sundry money owing.

Schuldbuch|forderungen registered debt, inscribed stock *(Br.)*.

Schulden debts, liabilities, *(Aktivschulden)* due from customers, accounts receivable *(US)*; **bis über die Ohren in** ~ over head and ears (up to the eyes) in debt. **aufgenommene** ~ debts incurred; **vor Fälligkeit bezahlte** ~ dues paid in advance; **längerfristige** ~ *(Bilanz)* long-term debts; **kurzfristig rückzahlbare** ~ quick liabilities; **zweifelhafte** ~ **abschreiben** to write off doubtful *(Br.)* (bad, *US)* debts; **seine** ~ **bezahlen** to pay one's debts, to discharge one's liabilities; ~ **decken** *(Nachlaß)* to be solvent; ~ **eingehen** to contract (make) debts; **sich seinen** ~ **entziehen** to escape one's liabilities; ~ **haben** to be indebted (in the red, *US);* **hohe** ~ **haben** to be deep in the books; ~ **machen** to contract (incur, make, run into) debt, to run up a score *(Br.).*

schulden, aus Giroverbindlichkeiten to be contingently indebted.

Schulden|annullierung abolition of debts; **~aufnahme** borrowing; **~berg** mountain of debts; **~dienst** debt service.

schuldenfrei debtless, clear, even, free from debt, *(Grundstück)* unencumbered, unincumbered.

Schulden|konsolidierung debt consolidation; **~macher sein** to have a propensity for running into debt; **~tilgung** extinction (sale, liquidation, sinking) of debts.

Schuldentilgungs|fonds sinking (redemption) fund; **~reserve** sinking-fund (debt-redemption) reserve.

Schulden|verwaltung debt administration (management); **~zahlung** payment of debts.

Schulderlaß debt relief, release from (remission of) debts, acquittance.

Schuldforderungen *(Bilanz)* debt due, debts receivable *(US).*

schuldhafte Nichtkenntnis constructive notice.

Schuldkonto anwachsen lassen to run up a score *(Br.).*

Schuldner debtor, party liable, *(Hypothekenschuldner)* mortgagor, *(säumige Zahler)* defaulter; **flüchtiger** ~ absconding debtor; ~ **in laufender Rechnung** debtor in account current, *(Bilanz)* advance to customers and other accounts; **einem** ~ **Zahlungsfrist gewähren** to allow a debtor time to pay; **gegen einen** ~ **zwangsvollstrecken** to distrain upon a debtor. **~land** debtor nation; **Gläubiger-~-Verhältnis** creditor-debtor relation.

Schuldschein I.O.U. (I owe you), note [of hand], hand bill, promissory note, recognizance, *(Aktiengesellschaft)* corporate bond, *(Kommunalschuldschein)* municipal bond; **erstklassig abgesicherter** ~ iron-clad note; ~ **mit Zwangsvollstreckungsklausel)** judgment (instalment, *US)* note; ~ **ausstellen** to sign a bond; **~darlehn** loan against borrower's note, open-market credit; **kommunales ~darlehn** registered warrant; **~inhaber** noteholder, *(Kommunalwesen)* warrant (certificate) creditor.

Schuld|übernahme assumption of indebtedness; **~verhältnis** contractual obligation; **~verpflichtung** liability, [contractual] obligation.

Schuldverschreibungen debenture bonds   *(US)* (stocks, obligations); **in verschiedenen Serien ausgegebene** ~ classified (class) bonds; **ertragssteuerfreie** ~ tax-exempt bonds; **durch Ersthypothek gesicherte** ~ first-mortgage bonds; **kommunale** ~ local bonds *(Br.),* municipal (special assessment) bonds *(US);* **auf den In-**

haber lautende ~ bearer bonds, debentures (bonds) to bearer; **auf den Namen lautende** ~ registered bonds; **unverzinsliche** ~ passive bonds, noninterest bearing obligations *(US);* ~ **mit Gewinnbeteiligung** participating (profit, profit-sharing) bonds; ~ **der öffentlichen Hand** civil stocks (bonds, *US);* ~ **öffentlicher Versorgungseinrichtungen** public-utility bonds; ~ **einlösen** to retire bonds.

Schuldversprechen promise, common assumpsit.

Schuld|wechsel *(Bilanz)* notes (bills) payable *(US);* **~zinsen** interest due (costs).

Schulungskurs [training] course.

Schundware trash, trashery, catchpenny article *(Br.),* slopmade goods, waste.

Schürf|rechte prospect, royalty, prospecting licence; **~stelle** prospect, location.

Schütt|gut bulk materials (goods, cargo); **~platz** dump.

Schutz, konsularischer consular protection; ~ **gutgläubiger Dritter** protection of third parties acting in good faith; **~ablauf** *(Patent)* expiration; **~frist** copyright period; **~marke** trademark, mark, brand, label.

Schutzmarken|inhaber trademark owner; **~verletzung** infringement of trademark.

Schutz|verband *(Gläubiger)* trade protection society; **~zeichen** trademark, brand; **~zoll** protective tariff, prohibitive tax.

Schutzzölle, durch ~ **abgesichert** tariff-protected; ~ **für einen Industriezweig festsetzen** to safeguard an industry.

schwach *(Börse)* poor, weak, feeble, infirm; **weiterhin** ~ **liegen** *(Börse)* to continue to rule low; **~er Besuch** poor attendance; **~e Nachfrage** slack demand.

Schwäche | des Pfundes weakness in sterling; **zur** ~ **neigen** *(Börse)* to be likely to fall.

schwächer werden *(Börse)* to fade, to decrease.

Schwanken der Kurse fluctuation of the market.

schwanken *(Börse)* to move irregularly, to range between, *(Preise)* to vary, to fluctuate.

schwankend *(Börse)* irregular, fluctuating, variable, unsettled, unsteady, unstable; **in ~er Haltung verkehren** to fluctuate.

Schwankungen, konjunkturelle cyclical fluctuations in business; ~ **der Beschäftigungsziffer** ups and downs of employment; ~ **im Handelsverkehr** leads and lags in trade.

Schwänze *(Börse)* corner.

Schwarz|arbeit illicit (scab) work; **~fahrt** joy ride (riding); **~handel** illicit (clandestine, underhand) trade, black-market operations; **~händler** black-market operator; **~marktpreis** black-market price; **~weißanzeige** black-and-white advertising.

schwebend *(unfundiert)* floating, unfunded; **~es Engagement** forward deal not yet completed.

schweres Geld kosten to cost a lot (pot) of money.

Schwer|arbeit hard work, heavy work; **~gut** heavy weight; **~industrie** heavy industries.

Schwerpunkt|e der Nachfrage chief demands; **~verlagerung** *(Betrieb)* diversification step.

Schwierigkeiten, finanzielle financial difficulties (pressure, straits), pecuniary difficulties.

schwimmen, im Gelde to be rolling in cash.

schwimmend|e Ladung cargo afloat; **~es Material** *(Börse)* floating supply.

Schwindel|auktion mock auction; **~firma** bogus (bubble, long, *Br.)* firm; **~geschäft** (bogus) transactions, monkey business.

Schwund shrinkage, reduction, wearing away, *(Gewicht)* loss in weight, *(Lager)* inventory shrinkage, *(durch Lecken)* leakage; **~ des Eigenkapitals** dwindling assets; **~geld** scalage, scrip money *(US).*

See|assekuranz marine (maritime) insurance; **~blockade** naval blockade; **~fracht** ocean freight, cargo, freight *(Br.)*; **~gefahr** marine peril (risk, adventure); **~hafen** seaport; **~handel** seaborne (maritime, marine) trade; **~konossement** ocean bill of lading.

Seele des Geschäfts soul of the enterprise, life and soul of a company.

Seelenmassage *(Konjunkturpolitik)* moral suasion.

See|mannsberuf ergreifen to use (follow) the sea; **~not** distress; **~pfandrecht** maritime hypothecation *(US)*; **~police** marine-insurance policy (certificate, *US)*; **~rückbehaltungsrecht** maritime lien; **~schaden** damage by sea water; **~schadensberechnung** average adjustment.

Seetransport shipment (carriage) by sea; **~gefahr** maritime perils; **~versicherer** marine [insurance] underwriter.

see|tüchtige Verpackung seaworthy packing; **~verpackt** packed for ocean shipment.

Seeversicherungs|geschäft underwriting; **~police** marine insurance policy.

Seeweg sea route, ocean lane; **~ benutzen (nehmen)** to travel by sea, to voyage.

Seite, [druck]angeschnittene *(Anzeigen)* bleed-off page.

seitenbeherrschende Anzeige page dominance.

Sekretariat, straff organisiertes professional secretariat; **im ~ tätig sein** to perform the office of a (act as) secretary.

Sekretariatarbeit secretarial work.

Sekretärin [lady] secretary; **deutschsprachige ~** German-language secretary.

Sekunda *(Wechsel)* second [of exchange].

Sekundärliquidität *(Banken)* secondary reserve.

selbständig independent, in an independent capacity, free, on one's own, self-employed; **sich ~ machen** to set up (go into business) for o. s.; **~es Einzelhandelsgeschäft** independent retail shop (store, *US)*; **~er Unternehmer** independent contractor, self-employer.

Selbst|bedarf personal requirements; **~bedienung** self-service.

Selbstbedienungs|geschäft self-service shop (store,

US), groceteria *(US)*, supermarket *(US)*; **~restaurant** cafeteria.

Selbst|behalt *(Autoversicherung)* own risk, *(Rückversicherung)* coinsurance, *(Versicherung)* franchise, net retention; **~beschränkung bei Lohnforderungen** voluntary wage restraint; **~beschränkungsabkommen** *(internationaler Handel)* orderly marketing; **~fahrer** owner-driver; **~hilfeverkauf** intromission, resale, replevin.

selbstkontrahieren to contract with o. s.

Selbstkostenpreis prime (first, net) cost, cost price; **unter dem ~ verkaufen** to sell under cost price.

Selbst|mordklausel *(Lebensversicherung)* suicide clause; **~reflektanten** no agents need apply; **~schuldner** primary obligor.

selbstschuldnerisch|er Bürge absolute guarantor, primary obligor; **~e Bürgschaft** guaranty of payment.

Selbst|veranlagung self-assessment; **~verbrauch** private (internal) consumption; **~verbraucher** private consumer; **~ im Verlag des Verfassers** published by the author; **~versorger sein** to be self-sufficient (-supporting); **~verwaltung der Wirtschaft** industrial self-government; **~wählfernverkehr** *(Telefon)* intercity (subscriber-trunk, *Br.)* dialling, toll-line dialling *(US).*

Seminar seminar, lecture with discussion.

sende|fertig *(Tonkonserve)* pre-recorded; **~freie Zeiten** nonbroadcasting hours.

senden to send, to dispatch, *(expedieren)* to consign, to forward, *(Fernsehen)* to telecast, to transmit, *(mit der Post)* to post *(Br.)*, to mail *(US)*; **etw. als Frachtgut ~** to send by goods train *(Br.).*

Sende|pause ansagen to sign off *(US)*; **~programm finanzieren** to sponsor a program(me).

Sendergruppe basic (broadcast, broadcasting) network.

Sendezeit air (station) time; **~ belegen** *(Werbung)* to buy time.

Sendung sending, forwarding, dispatch, *(Fernsehen)* telecast, *(Postversand)* posting *(Br.)*, mailing *(US)*, *(Waren)* consignment, invoice, lot; **eingeschriebene ~** registered letter (item); **Muster-ohne-Wert-~** parcel shipment; **portofreie ~** prepaid remittance; **zugkräftige ~** audience builder; **~ von Belegexemplaren** sending of vouchers; **~ als Nachnahme** cash (collect, *US)* on-delivery; **~ abrufen** to call forward a shipment.

Senkung | der Ausgaben retrenchment of expenses; **~ des Diskontsatzes** lowering of the discount (bank, *Br.)* rate, lowering of the rate of rediscount *(US).*

sensationelle Werbung stunt advertising, gimmick *(US, sl.).*

Serie series, line, run, set, cycle, *(Ausgabe)* issue; **in ~ hergestellt** mass-produced, manufactured.

Serien|anleihe serial bonds; **~ausführung** standard model; **~herstellung** repetition work, mass (multiple, machine) production; **~lotterie** serial lottery.

serienmäßig herstellen to mass-(volume-)produce.

Serien|modell standard (stock, *US)* model, *(Auto)* mass-production car, stock car (model, *US)*;

~nummer serial number; ~obligation serial bond; ~rabatt frequency discount; ~ziehung serial drawing.

sicher *(Anlage)* safe, *(kreditwürdig)* reliable, trustworthy, sound, good;
~ angelegtes Geld safely invested money.

sichergestellter Kredit secured credit.

Sicherheit security, *(Bürgschaft)* bail, surety, guarantee *(Br.)*, guaranty, warranty, *(Kreditdeckung)* security, collateral *(US)*;
nur zur ~ *(auf Wechseln)* for deposit only;
auswechselbare ~ floating (shifting) security; erstklassige ~en first-class (gilt-edged, *Br.* trustee, *US)* securities; nicht realisierbare ~ dead security;
~ des Flugverkehrs airline security; ~ durch Hinterlegung von Industrieaktien industrial collateral *(US)*;
~ bestellen to register a (give) security, to collaterate *(US)*; als ~ dienen to serve as cover (collateral, *US)*; ~ für verfallen erklären to forfeit security; als ~ hinterlegen to post a bond, to deposit as underlying security *(US)*; ~ stellen *(Bürgschaft)* to offer bail, to post a bond *(US)*; gegen ~ verkaufen *(Effektengeschäft)* to sell on margin.

Sicherheitenmappe *(Kreditakte)* loan envelope.

Sicherheits|betrag für unvorhergesehene Fälle working margin; ~depot, ~fonds guarantee *(Br.)* (contingency) fund; ~klausel safeguard, escape clause; ~leistung lodging of security, *(Bürgschaft)* bail, *(Kreditunterlage)* [collateral] security; ~marge safety margin; ~risiko safety hazard; ~wechsel geben to deposit a bill as collateral *(US)*; ~zuschlag *(Lebensversicherung)* loading.

sicherstellen to secure, to safeguard, *(durch Deckung)* to cover, to impound;
gegen Verluste ~ to safeguard (protect) against losses.

Sicherstellung safeguard, *(durch Deckung)* cover, *(Garantie)* guarantee *(Br.)*, guaranty *(US)*, *(Kredit)* security, collateral *(US)*.

Sicherung des Arbeitsplatzes employee security.

Sicherungs|eigentum purchase-money chattel mortgage *(US)*, *(am Warenlager mit wechselndem Bestand)* statutory factor's lien *(US)*; ~geschäft hedge; ~gut equitable lien, pledged goods; ~schein trust letter *(Br.)*; ~übereignung chattel mortgage, *(Warenlager)* field warehousing; ~übereignungsvertrag *[etwa]* bill of sale by way of security *(Br.)*, trust receipt *(US)*.

Sicht sight, *(Flugwetter)* visibility;
auf kurze ~ at short sight, short-dated; auf lange ~ at a long date, long-dated;
bei ~ fällig werden to mature by presentation.

sichtbare Reserve open (declared) reserves.

Sicht|einlagen demand *(US)* (sight) deposits; ~kurs sight (demand) rate; ~verbindlichkeiten liabilities due on presentation; ~vermerk *(Paß)* visa; ~wechsel draft payable at sight, sight (demand, *US)* bill.

Siedlung settlement, colony, housing project.

Siedlungs|bau housing estate; neuentstandenes ~gebiet built-up area; ~gesellschaft land settlement (building) society, homestead-aid benefit association *(US)*.

Siegel abnehmen to take off the seals.

Silber|kleingeld loose silver; ~währung silver currency (standard, basis).

Simultankauf und -verkauf *(Börse)* wash sale *(US)*.

Sinken *(Kurse)* fall, decline, easing off, drop;
~ der Beschäftigung reduction of employment;
~ der Preise falling of prices, price decline.

sinken *(Kurs, Preise)* to fall, to drop, to go down, to ease off (down);
allmählich ~ *(Kurse)* to shade.

situiert, gut wealthy, well-to-do, well-off, on one's legs, well-fixed *(US)*; schlecht ~ badly off.

Sitz *(Geschäftsleitung)* headquarters, head òffice, location, seat;
~ im Aufsichtsrat seat on the board; ~ einer Industrie site of an industry; ~ der gewerblichen Niederlassung commercial domicile;
~streik sit-down strike.

Sitzung meeting, conference;
in öffentlicher ~ in full session; in nicht öffentlicher ~ in chambers;
turnusmäßige ~ regular session;
~ des Aufsichtsrates board meeting;
~ abhalten to hold a meeting (conference); ~ ansetzen to fix a date for a meeting; ~ leiten to preside at a conference; ~ unterbrechen to adjourn a meeting.

Sitzungsbericht minutes, protocol, conference paper;
dem ~ zustimmen to vote for approval of the minutes.

Sitzungs|leiter conference leader; ~pause einlegen to take a recess; ~protokoll record (minutes) of a meeting, *(AG)* corporate minutes; ~saal meeting room; ~teilnehmer meeting participant; ~termin festlegen to settle a day for a meeting; ~unterlagen documentation for a meeting; ~zimmer committee (board, conference, cabinet) room.

Skonto [trade] discount;
3 % ~ für Barzahlung 3 % for cash;
~schinderei discount piracy; ~verlust lost discounts.

Skontrierungstag settling day, ticket (name) day *(Br.)*.

Sockelbetrag basic allowance.

sofort lieferbar spot.

Sofort|auftrag crash job; ~hilfsprogramm emergency-aid (crash) programy(me).

Solawechsel promissory note, single bill.

Solidarbürge joint surety (warrantor).

solidarisch joint and several, jointly and severally;
~ haften to be jointly and severally liable.

Solidaritätsstreik sympathetic strike.

solide *(finanziell gesund)* good, substantial, solvent, solid, sound, *(Preis)* reasonable, moderate, fair, *(in gutem Ruf stehend)* respectable, trustworthy, of good standing;
~ Finanzgebarung sound finance; ~ Firma house of good standing.

Soll debit [account], *(Produktion)* target;
im ~ buchen to enter on (carry to) the debit side, to debit.

Soll|aufkommen budgeted yield; **~etat** budget; **~kostenrechnung** budget accounting; **~posten** debit item; **~saldo abdecken** to cover a short account; **~- und Habenzinsen** interest pro and contra.

solvent solvent, sound, good, able to pay.

Sommer|fahrplan summer timetable; **~schlußverkauf** summer sale *(US)*; **~zeit einführen** to alter the time to the summer.

Sonder|abgabe special levy (assessment); **erhöhte ~abschreibung** initial allowance *(Br.)*; **~anfertigung** special make, *(Auto)* private (custom) car-[riage]; **~angebot** special (introductory) offer, *(günstiges Angebot)* bargain, premium; **~ausgabenpauschale** standard deduction *(US)*; **~ausstattung** *(Auto)* optional equipment; **~flugzeug** special plane; **~freibetrag** *(Einkommensteuer)* excess deduction; **~genehmigung** special licence (permit); **~honorar** special retainer; **~konto** separate (segregated, *US*, special bank) account; **~nummer** special edition; **~preis** special (exceptional, out) price; **~provision** overriding commission; **~rücklage** contingency (provident, special) reserve; **~tarif** *(Bahn)* special service tariff, *(Versicherung)* specially favo(u)rable rate, *(Werbung)* special rate, *(Zoll)* specific tariff; **~vergütung** extra allowance, *(Angestellter)* fringe, perquisite; **~verkauf** bargain sale; **~vermögen der Ehefrau** paraphernalia, paraphernal property; **~ziehungsrechte** *(Weltwährungsfonds)* special drawing rights; **~züge einsetzen** to run (put on) extra trains; **~zulage** *(Leistungszulage)* merit increase; *(Produktionsprämie)* bonus payment.

Sondierungsgespräche talks about talks *(US)*.

Sonntags|arbeit Sunday working; **~ruhe** *(Geschäfte)* Sunday closing.

Sorgeberechtigter tutor, curator, guardian.

Sorgfalt care, carefulness, diligence;
im Verkehr erforderliche ~ ordinary care and prudence, due diligence;
~ eines ordentlichen Kaufmanns attention of a conscientious businessman.

Sorte *(Art)* sort, kind, description, denomination, class, order, *(Güte)* quality, grade, run;
von feinster ~ of first (prime) quality;
ausländische ~n foreign coins and notes; **feinste ~** choicest brand; **vorzügliche ~** choice brand; **nur eine ~ führen** to stock only one quality.

Sorten|handel dealings in foreign coins and notes; **~konto** specie account; **~kurszettel** bill of specie, bordereau.

sortieren to sort, assort, *(nach Größen)* to size, *(nach Qualitäten)* to grade.

Sortiment assortment, collection, choice, range of goods, product line, sales mix *(US)*, *(Satz)* set;
weit gestreutes ~ wide variety of product lines;
~ des Einzelhandels retail line.

Sortimentsausweitung increase in range of goods.

sozial|e Abgaben old-age benefit taxes, social [security] contributions; **~e Leistungen** *(freiwillige)* fringe benefits *(payments)*, welfare expenditure *(US)*, *(gesetzliche)* social-security contributions; **~e Marktwirtschaft** free-enterprise system.

Sozial|abgaben old-age benefit taxes, social [security] contributions (payments); **betriebliche ~beihilfen** company benefits; **~einrichtungen** welfare institutions (facilities, services); **~hilfe** [social] welfare, public (social) *(US)* (national, *Br.*) assistance, parish relief *(Br.)*.

sozialisieren to socialize, to nationalize *(US)*.

Sozialleistungen social service (security) payments.

Sozial|produkt national product (dividend); **Wirtschafts- und ~rat der Vereinten Nationen** United Nations Economic and Social Council; **~rentner** social-security recipient, annuity holder, pensioner; **~versicherung** social insurance *(US)*, old age and survivor's insurance *(US)*, national insurance *(Br.)*.

Sozialversicherungs|anteil des Arbeitnehmers emloyee benefit; **~beiträge** social insurance (security, *US*), (national insurance, *Br.*) contributions; **~karte** national insurance *(Br.)* (social security, *US*) card; **~leistungen** social security (insurance, *US*, national insurance, *Br.*) benefits; **~träger** social *(US)* (national, *Br.*) insurance institution.

Sozial|wohnung council home (flat) *(Br.)*; **~zulage** family allowance (benefit).

Spanne margin, spread *(US)*.

Spar|anlage savings account; **~buch** savings bank [deposit] book, passbook; **~büchse** thrift box.

Spareinlagen savings [deposits];
~bestand bei Bausparkassen savings put into building and loan associations.

Sparen, kollektives social savings.

sparen to save, to spare, *(Einsparungen machen)* to practise economy, to economize, *(knausern)* to be stingy, to skimp;
für sein Alter ~ to save up for one's old age; **keine Kosten ~** to spare no expenses; **für Notfälle ~** to put away for a rainy day.

Sparer [money] saver, depositor.

Spar|förderung *(Betrieb)* company saving plan; **~groschen** savings, nest egg; **~guthaben** savings account, thrift deposit *(US)*.

Sparkasse, gemeinnützige trustee bank (savings bank, *US*).

Sparkassen|buch savings bank [deposit] book, passbook; **~geschäft** savings banking (business); **~leiter** savings-bank manager.

Sparkonten annehmen to accept savings accounts.

spärliche Nachfrage slack demand.

Spar|maßnahmen measures of economy; **~pfennig** nest egg, money put by for a rainy day; **~prämienversicherung** salary deduction (savings) insurance; **~programm** cost-cutting drive; **volkswirtschaftliche ~quote** rate of saving.

sparsam saving, sparing, thrifty, provident, near; ~ **leben** to economize; **äußerst ~ wirtschaften** to be careful of one's small savings.

Spar|schwein piggy bank; **~- und Darlehnskassenverein** savings and loan association; **~vertrag** savings plan; **~vorgang** saving [process].

Spät|ausgabe evening edition, final; **~einlieferungsgebühr** late fee *(Br.)*; **~schicht** night (swing, *US)* shift.

Spediteur carrier [and forwarding agent], motor carrier,hauler, haulier *(Br.)*, shipping agent (clerk); **bahnamtlicher ~** railway express agency *(Br.),* common carrier *(US)*; **~haftung** carrier's liability; **~übernahmebescheinigung** forwarder's receipt.

Spedition forwarding, carrying, dispatch, conveyance, haulage *(US)*, shipment *(US)*.

Speditions|auftrag dispatch (shipping, *US)* order; **~betrieb** forwarding house, haulage firm; **~firma** forwarding house, transportation agency, haulage firm, trucking company, shipper *(US)*; **~gebühren** forwarding charges, shipping charges *(US)*, haulage *(US)*; **~geschäft** carrying (carrier's, freight) business, carrying and forwarding trade, shipping trade (agency) *(US)*; **~gewerbe** road haulage industry, carrying (shipping, *US)* trade; **~tarif** transportation rates; **~vertrag** contract fo carriage, shipping contract *(US)*.

Speicher store, storehouse, warehouse *(US)*, magazine, depot, entrepot, *(Möbel)* furniture depository (repository), storage, warehouse; **öffentlicher ~** public warehouse (store); **~gebäude** loft building *(US)*; **~gebühren** warehouse rates; **~miete** warehouse rent.

Speisewagen luncheon (refreshment, buffet) car.

Spekulant speculator, speculative dealer, gambler, *(Baisse)* bear *(Br.) (Hausse)* bull *(Br.);* **berufsmäßiger ~** market operator; **unerfahrener ~** lamb; **wilder ~** wildcatter *(US)*; **~ in Staatspapieren** fund monger.

Spekulation speculation, jobbing, gamble, venture; **gewagte ~** hazardous speculation, flier *(US sl.)*; **zügellose ~** unbridled speculation; **~ auf Baisse** speculation for a fall, bearish operation *(Br.)*; **~ mit Grundstücken** speculation in real estate; **~ auf Hausse** bull[ish] operation *(Br.)*.

Spekulations|aktie speculative share (stock, *US)*; **~geschäft** adventure, speculative business (transaction); **~kapital** venture (risk-bearing) capital; **unsichere ~papiere** fancy stocks *(US)*; **~ring** corner; **~verkäufe** speculative selling; **zu ~zwecken aufkaufen** to corner the market.

spekulative Kapitalanlagen speculative investments.

spekulieren, in Aktien to play the stock market; **auf Baisse ~** to operate (speculate) for a fall, to bear *(Br.)*, to sell short *(US)*; **ein bißchen an der Börse ~** to dabble on the stock exchange; **auf Hausse ~** to buy (operate) for a rise, to bull *(Br.)*.

Spende charitable disposition (distribution), subscription (contribution) to charity;

freiwillige ~ unasked contribution; **~ für wohltätige Zwecke** charitable subscription; **~n sammeln** to whip round for subscriptions, to go round with the hat.

Spenden|aktion gift-parcel program(me); **~gelder persönlich verwenden** to divert campaign funds to one's personal use.

Spender subscriber to charity, contributor, giver, donor.

Sperr|betrag blocked amount; **~depot** blocked account (deposit).

Sperre blocking, *(Hafen)* closing, *(Handel)* embargo, *(Zoll)* toll bar; **~ eines Kontos** blocking of (freezing) an account; **~ aufheben** to lift an embargo.

sperren to block, *(Grenze)* to shut, *(Hafen)* to blockade, to lock, *(Konto)* to block, to freeze, *(Warenverkehr)* to embargo, to blockade; **Scheck ~** to stop payment of a check; **offene Stellen ~** to freeze vacancies.

Sperr|frist period of embargo, blocking period; *(Versicherung)* waiting period; **~gut** bulky (encumbering) goods, goods shipped in bulk, measurement cargo, heavy or bulky articles; **~guthaben** blocked account (balance); **~majorität** vetoing stock; **~markguthaben** blocked-mark account; **~minorität** blocking minority.

Sperrung | eines Kontos blocking of an account; **~ eines Schecks** stop payment of a check.

Sperrvermerk *(Wertpapier)* nonnegotiability notice.

Spesen charges, expenses [incurred]; **ab an ~** charges to be deducted; **franko ~** free of charges; **unter Nachnahme der ~** expenses to be collected; **fremde ~** *(Bank)* cost of our correspondent; **vereinbarte ~** agreed costs; **seine ~ abrechnen** to account for one's expenses; **jem. 40 $ und den Ersatz der ~ anbieten** to offer s. o. 40 $ and expenses; **jem. seine ~ ersetzen** to reimburse s. o. for his costs; **doppelte ~ in Rechnung stellen** to double-bill.

Spesen|abrechnung expense sheet; **~aufgliederung** breakdown of expenses; **~belastung** expense loading; **gefälschter ~beleg** swindle sheet; **~belege sammeln** to keep a record of one's expenses; **seinen ~etat vergrößern** to increase one's expenditure.

spesenfrei free of charge (charges, expenses).

Spesen|konto expense (imprest, *Br.)* account; **zu Lasten des ~kontos verreisen** to travel on expense account; **~ritter** expense-account travel(l)er; **~richtlinien** expense-account rules; **~vergütung** reimbursement of expenses; **~vorschuß** advanced expense, imprest *(Br.)*; **~zettel** cost record, expense voucher.

Spezial|anfertigung *(Auto)* custom car; **~[artikel]geschäft** one-line business, speciality store, stockist *(Br.)*; **~fach** special line (subject), major subject *(US)*.

spezialisieren, sich auf etw. to specialize in (on) s. th., to major in a subject *(US)*.

Spezialitätenmakler privilege broker *(US)*, specialist *(US)*.

Spezial|karosserie *(Auto)* custom body; **~versandkatalog** flyer; **~werte** specialities *(Br.)*, special stocks *(US)*; **~wörterbuch** technical dictionary.

Speziessachen ascertained (specified) goods.

Spezifikation specification, detailed statement, statement of particulars, itemization *(US)*.

spezifisches Gewicht specific weight.

spezifizierte Rechnung detailed (itemized, *US)* account.

Spielschuld gambling (play) debt.

Spirituosen|geschäft liquor store *(US)*; **~handel** traffic in liquors, the trade *(Br.)*.

Spitze *(Börse)* fractional amount, remainder, odd twert) top, peak, summit, *(Rückversicherung)* excess, surplus;

~n der Behörden top-ranking officials, the leading authorities, heads of the government;

an der ~ eines Unternehmens stehen to have control of an undertaking.

Spitzen|ausgleich clearing transfer, *(Börse)* evening up; **~bedarf** peak [of the] demand **~belastung** peak load; **~einkommen haben** to be in the highest income brackets; **~erzeugnis der Markenindustrie** top-selling brand; **~gremium** top-management team *(US)*; **~kräfte** top management (executives, officials) *(US)*; **~marke** brand leader; **~modell** top-of-the-line model; **~positionen** top echelons; **~qualität** prime, top (star) quality; **~reiter unter den Investmentfonds** top-performing mutual funds; **~verband** head (umbrella, top, summit) organization; **~verdiener** top earner; **~verkehr** peak hours, rush hours traffic; **~werte** *(Aktien)* gilt-edged (leading) shares *(Br.)*, favourites, blue chips *(US)*.

Split *(Börse)* split, splitup, share bonus.

Spontankauf impulse buying.

Sporteln emoluments, appointments, fees.

spottbillig dirt-cheap, dog-cheap, dead bargain.

Spottgeld, um ein for a (an old) song.

Sprachen|dienst language department; **~zulage** language allowance.

Sprecher [public] speaker, spokesman.

sprunghaft *(Kurse)* erratic, by leaps and bounds, by fits and starts, jerky;

Preise ~ erhöhen to jump prices.

Staat, vom finanziert state-financed;

vom ~ unterhalten werden to live at the common expense.

staatlich| gefördert government-sponsored;

~e Beihilfe state grant.

Staatsanleihe public loan, government *(US)* (public, *Br.)* bonds, funds *(Br.)*, state securities *(US)*;

Geld in ~ anlegen to invest money in funds *(Br.)*;

~n kaufen to buy funds *(Br.)*.

Staats|aufträge government orders (business); **~ausgaben** national (public, state) expenditure; **~bankrott** national bankruptcy; **~betrieb** public business (ownership), state (government) enterprise (cor-

poration); **~einkünfte** inland *(Br.)* (internal, *US)* revenue; **nicht aus Steuern herrührende ~einnahmen** nontax revenue *(US)*; **~finanzen sanieren** to put the finances of a country on a healthy footing; **~hilfe** government help, state aid *(US)*, grant-in-aid *(US)*; **~kasse** Treasury, Exchequer *(Br.)*, Federal Treasury *(US)*; **auf ~kosten** at public expense; **~obligationen** public stocks *(Br.)* (securities, *US)*, government bonds.

Staatspapiere government bonds *(US)* (stocks, *Br., securities, US)*;

konsolidierte ~ consolidated stocks funds *(Br.)*, consolidated government bonds *(US)*; **in ausländischer Währung zahlbare ~** external bonds.

Staatsschuld public *(US)* (state, national) debt; **fundierte ~** stocks *(Br.)*; **kurzfristige ~** floating debt;

~ konsolidieren to fund the floating debt.

Staatsschuldbuch National Debt Register, Great Ledger *(Br.)*.

Staatsschulden|aufnahme state borrowing; **~dienst** servicing of the national debt; **~verwaltung** administration (management) of the national debt.

Staats|subvention subsidy; **~unternehmen** government business (corporation); **~verschuldung** state indebtedness; **~wirtschaft** national economy; **~zuschuß** state (government) grant (subsidy), grant-in-aid *(US)*.

stabil stable, *(Kurs)* steady, *(im Wert)* standard;

Preise ~ halten to keep prices on an even keel; **~e Währung** stable currency.

Stabilisierungsanleihe stabilization loan.

Stabspersonal front-office personnel.

Stadt, auf Kosten der at city expense.

Stadt|abgaben town dues, municipal taxes (rates); **~anleihe** municipal (corporation, *Br.)* loan; **~autobahn** urban freeway (motorway, *Br.)*.

städtische Abgaben town dues, rates, municipal taxes; **~e Sparkasse** municipal savings bank.

Stadt|kasse city branch; **~zentrum** urban (town, city) center *(US)* centre *(Br.)*, town.

Staffel|auszug equated abstract of account; **~preis** sliding-scale (graduated) price; **~tarif** sliding scale, flexible (differential, graduated) tariff.

Staffelung| der Arbeitszeit staggering of hours; **~ der Steuersätze** progressive rates of taxation.

Staffelzinsen compensatory (compound) interest.

stagnierender Markt stagnant (trading, *US)* market.

Stamm|aktie ordinary share *(Br.)* (stock, *US)*, common share *(Br.)* (stock, *US)*; **~arbeiter** permanent labo(u)rer; **~betrieb** parent plant; **~einlage** original share; **~gast** regular (standing, steady) customer; **~haus** parent company (establishment); **~kapital** *(Aktiengesellschaft)* joint stock, *(Bank)* fund *(Br.)*, *(Grundkapital)* authorized (nominal, *Br.* share) capital, *(ohne Vorrechte)* ordinary capital; **~kunde** regular (registered, standing, steady) customer; **~kundschaft** steady customers, goodwill; **~personal** permanent staff, skeleton [crew].

Stand rank, standing, order, *(Gewerbe)* calling, profession, vocation, *(Stellung)* position, standing;
höchster ~ highest (peak) level; **niedrigster** ~ bottom, lowest (bargain, *US*) level.
Standard|abweichung standard deviation, *(Statistik)* variance; **~aktien** representative shares (stocks, *US*), gilt-edged shares *(Br.)*, blue chips *(US)*; **~ausführung** standard, conventional type, *(Auto)* standard car, stock model *(US)*; **~größe** stock size.
Standgeld toll, stallage *(Br.)*, demurrage.
standgeldfreie Ladezeit free time.
ständige Adresse permanent address; **~e Nachfrage** steady demand.
Stand|inhaber stall holder; **~ortpolitik** industrial location policy, *(EG)* regional economic policy.
Stapel, vom laufen to be launched;
~güter staple commodity, staples; **~lauf** *(Schiff)* launch[ing]; **~platz** staple, entrepot, emporium.
Stärke der Belegschaft personnel strength.
Start|hilfe initial aid; **~kapital** startup money.
Station station, *(Teilstrecke)* stage;
gegen freie ~ arbeiten to work for one's keep.
statistisch|es Bundesamt National Bureau of Economic Research *(US)*; **~e Erhebung** statistical inquiry.
Status financial status (statement);
~gewinn status-plus.
stauen *(Fracht)* to stow;
sich ~ *(Verkehr)* to be jammed (congested).
Stauerlohn [rate of] stowage.
Steck|karte timecard, time ticket; **~uhr** time clock.
stehen *(Kurse)* to rule, to remain;
in Arbeit ~ to be employed; **vor dem Bankrott ~** to be on the verge of bankruptcy; **in Geschäftsbeziehungen mit jem. ~** to transact business with s. o.; **sehr niedrig ~** *(Kurse)* to stand at a minimum; **über Pari ~** *(Anleihe)* to sell at a premium; **unter Pari ~** to sell at a discount.
Steigen *(Börse, Preise)* improvement, advance, rise, rising, upward movement, recovery;
~ und Fallen up and down; **~ der Preise** price advance;
auf das ~ der Kurse spekulieren to buy for a rise, to bull *(Br.)*.
steigen *(Kurse)* to rise, to advance, to improve, to move up;
immer noch ~ to go on increasing; **langsam ~** *(Preise)* to creep; **sprunghaft ~** *(Hausse)* to surge forward; **raketenartig in die Höhe ~** to skyrocket.
steigende | Ausgaben growing expenditure; **~ Kurse** rising market; **~ Preise** rising prices; **~ Unkosten** increasing costs.
steigern *(Auktion)* to bid, to outbid;
Ausstoß ~ to increase the output; **Kurse ~** to bill the market; **Produktion ~** to step up production.
Steigerung progression, *(Kurse, Preise)* rise, increase, advance, improvement, enhancement;
sprunghafte ~ rise by leaps and bounds; **~ des Sozialprodukts** economic growth;

in rascher ~ neue Höchstkurse erzielen to shoot into new high ground; **der ~ der Lebenshaltungskosten Einhalt gebieten** to control the rise in the cost of living; **schnellen ~en unterworfen sein** to move briskly ahead.
Stellagegeschäft put and call, pac, spread *(US)*.
Stelle place, spot, stead, *(Beruf)* position, post;
von amtlichen ~n from official quarters;
offene ~ vacancy, *(Inserat)* help wanted; **öffentliche ~** public authority; **zuständige ~** proper quarter, competent office;
~ ausschreiben to advertise a post (vacancy); **nicht von der ~ kommen** *(Verhandlung)* to be at a deadlock.
stellen, sich *(Kurse)* to rule; **sich [im Preis auf] ~** to amount (come) to; **in Dienst ~** *(Schiff)* to put into commission; **Kaution ~** to put up bail; **jem. hinreichende Deckung zur Verfügung ~** to furnish s. o. with funds; **zum Verkauf ~** to expose for sale, *(Grundstück)* to list.
Stellen|angebot situation vacant, position offered; **~anzeigen** help-wanted ads *(US)*; **~besetzung** filling of vacancies; **~besetzungsplan** organizational chart, manning table, employee roster; **~bewerber** [employment (job)] applicant; **~bewerbung** application for a position; **~gesuche kostenlos veröffentlichen** to run free ads for job seekers *(US)*; **~nachweis, ~vermittlung** employment (domestic) agency; **amtliche ~vermittlung für Führungskräfte** appointments board *(Br.)*; **~vermittlungsdienst** placement *(US)* (employment) service.
Stellung position, post, place, job, employ[ment], engagement, station, occupation, level, berth;
in angesehener ~ of good position; **in führender ~** at executive level, in the highest flight; **in einer guten ~** well-positioned, in good bread; **in einer hohen ~** in a high position; **in leitender ~** in managerial capacity; **in ungekündigter ~** not under notice; **unter Mißbrauch seiner amtlichen ~** under colo(u)r of one's office;
~ gesucht *(Zeitung)* [situation] wanted;
beruflich bedeutsame ~ career position; **schlecht bezahlte ~** badly paid situation; **einflußreiche ~** post of authority; **gehobenere ~** elevated position, higher-level job *(US)*; **leitende ~** key position, policy-making (senior, executive) position; **pensionsberechtigte ~** pensionable post;
~ ohne Aufstiegsmöglichkeiten blind-alley-job; **~ ablehnen** to turn down a job; **~ annehmen** to accept (take) a position; **~ antreten** to take up one's post; **~ aufgeben** to leave (give up) one's position; **hohe ~ bekleiden** to be high in office; **~ durch Beziehungen bekommen** to secure an office through one's pull; **~ finden** to land a job; **für j. finden** to fix s. o. up with a job; **gute ~ haben** to have a good berth *(Br.)*; **in untergeordneter ~ sein** to be in an inferior position; **sich nach einer ~ umsehen** to look for a job; **seine ~ wechseln** to change one's position.
Stellungnahme *(Antwort)* answer, *(Beurteilung)* en-

dorsement, *(Entscheidung)* decision, *(Meinung)* [advisory] opinion, comment.
Stellungsgesuch application for a position.
stellungslos out of a job (employ), unemployed.
stellvertretend representative, vicarious, deputy; ~**er Vorsitzender** vice-chairman (president).
Stellvertreter *(Aktienstimmrecht)* proxy [holder], *(Bevollmächtigter)* agent, representative, attorney in fact.
Stempel impress, imprint, *(Datum)* [dated] stamp, *(Stempelsteuer)* stamp duty *(Br.)* (tax, *US);* ~**bruder** dole drawer *(Br.);* ~**gebühr** stamp duty *(Br.)* (tax, *US), (Aktien)* transfer duty; ~**kissen** stamp (ink) pad; ~**marke** inland-revenue stamp.
stempeln gehen to be on (draw) the dole *(Br.)*
Stempelsteuer stamp duty *(Br.)* (tax, *US).*
Stenogramm aufnehmen to take dictation in shorthand.
Stenograph stenographer *(US)*, shorthand writer.
stenographieren to write (take down in) shorthand.
Steno|kontoristin shorthand clerk; ~**typist** stenotypist, [shorthand] typist.
Sterbe|hilfe death benefit, funeral allowance; ~**fallversicherung** funeral-cost insurance.
Steuer tax, *(Abgabe)* impost, assessment, lot *(Br.),* rate *(Br.), (Zoll)* customsduty, lot *(Br.);*
nach Abzug der ~ tax deducted; **vor Berücksichtigung der** ~**n** prior to deduction of taxes, less tax; **direkte** ~**n** direct taxation; **einbehaltene** ~**n** withheld taxes; **fällige** ~**n** *(Bilanz)* taxes payable; **gestundete** ~ deferred tax; **hinterzogene** ~ defrauded tax; **progressive** ~ progressive (graduated, graded) tax; **rückständige** ~**n** tax [in] arrears; **veranlagte** ~ assessed (scheduled) tax; **versteckte** ~ hidden tax; ~**n und Umlagen** rates and taxes;
~ **gleich vom Ertrag abführen** to pay a tax at the source; ~**n ausschreiben** to levy taxes; ~**n nach dem Vermögen bezahlen** to pay scot and lot *(Br.);* ~**ermäßigen** to reduce a tax; ~ **erstatten** to repay a tax; ~ **niederschlagen** to drop a tax; ~**n sparen** to save on [income] taxes; ~ **umgehen** to dodge a tax, to avoid payment of a tax; **für** ~**n zurückstellen** to allow (make provisions) for taxation.
steuerabgabepflichtig taxable, assessable.
Steuerabschluß machen to close its fiscal books.
Steuerabzug tax deduction, *(Einkommensteuer)* income-tax relief *(Br.),* tax credit *(US);*
~ **für das Büro im eigenen Haus** office-at-home deduction.
steuerabzugsfähig tax-deductible.
Steuer|anfall tax incidence; ~**anwalt** tax attorney *(US)* (lawyer); ~**aufkommen** revenue (tax) receipts, tax yield, inland *(Br.)* (internal, *US)* revenue; **rezessionsbedingter** ~**ausfall** recession-induced loss of revenue; ~**ausgleich** *(Länder)* revenue sharing; ~**ausgleichsrücklage** *(Bilanz)* taxation equalization reserve *(Br.);* ~**beamter** fiscal officer, revenue officer (agent, *US);* ~**befreiung** tax exemption.
steuerbegünstigt tax-privileged (-supported); ~**es Geschäft** tax-shelter deal.

Steuerbehörde taxing (taxation, fiscal) authority, inland revenue office, internal revenue authority; ~*(Br.);* ~**bemessungsgrundlage** tax base; ~**berater** tax expert (adviser); ~**bereinigt** adjusted for taxation; ~**bescheid** tax demand (bill, *US),* demand note *(Br.),* tax assessment; **gegen einen ~bescheid Einspruch einlegen** to appeal against a tax assessment; ~**bilanz** statement (balance sheet, *US);* ~**defizit** revenue (fiscal) deficit; ~**delikt** revenue offence; ~**einnahmen** *(Staat)* taxation, public (inland, *Br., internal, US)* revenue; ~**einspruch** tax appeal; ~**entrichtung** payment of taxes; ~**erhöhung** tax rise (increase); ~**erklärung** tax return; ~**erleichterung** tax relief (benefit); ~**ermäßigung** abatement of a tax, tax reduction; ~**ersparnisse machen** to save on [income] taxes; ~**erstattung vornehmen** to repay a tax; ~**fahnder** tax ferret; ~**flucht** tax avoidance (evasion, *US);* **fällige** ~**forderungen** accrued taxes, tax accruals *(US).*
steuerfrei tax-exempt (-free), exempt from taxes; **vom Nettoeinkommen abzugsfähige** ~**e Beträge** credits allowed against net income; ~**er Pauschalbetrag** flat exemption *(US).*
Steuerfreibetrag basic abatement, tax-free (personal) allowance *(Br.),* tax exemption *(US),* (relief, *Br.);* **allgemein gewährter** ~ outright (flat) exemption; **zusätzlicher** ~ **für Arbeitseinkommen der Ehefrau** wife's earned-income allowance *(Br.);* ~ **für Familienangehörige** allowance for dependents, dependent relative allowance *(Br.).*
Steuer|gewinn taxable profit (gain); ~**gruppe** [income] tax bracket; ~**gutschein** tax-anticipation bond (warrant, certificate, *US);* ~**hinterziehung begehen** to defraud the revenue; ~**jahr** financial *(Br.)* (fiscal, *US,* taxable, *US)* year; ~**klasse** tax bracket.
steuerlich| absetzbar deductible from income tax; ~**begünstigt** tax-supported; ~**subventioniert** tax-eating;
~ **wie eine juristische Person behandelt werden** to be treated as a corporate body for tax purposes; **Einkommen** ~ **verteilen** to spread income over the years;
~ **zulässige Abschreibungen** capital allowances *(Br.),* tax writeoffs *(US);* ~ **subventionierter Betrieb** taxeater; ~**es Hintertürchen** tax loophole; ~**e Vergünstigungen** tax privileges (benefit, *Br.,* concession, credit, *US);* ~**es Verlustgeschäft** tax-loss selling; ~**es Zugeständnis** tax concession.
Steuer|liste assessment roll (list), *(Kommunalsteuern)* rate book; ~**meßwert** ratable value *(Br.);* ~**moral** tax morale; ~**nachlaß** tax reduction; ~**nachveranlagung** tax reappraisal; ~**paradies** tax haven; **beschränkte** ~**pflicht** limited taxability.
steuerpflichtig taxable, assessable, liable to pay taxes; ~**es Einkommen** assessable (taxable) income.
Steuer|pflichtiger taxpayer, taxable, ratepayer; ~**politik** tax practices (policies), *(Geldpolitik)* fiscal policy, fiscality; ~**progression** tax progression;

~**prüfer** tax inspector (auditor, *US*); ~**prüfung** tax inspection (audit); ~**reform** tax (fiscal) reform; ~**richtlinien** rules of taxation; ~**rückstände** back taxes, delinquent taxes, tax arrears; ~**rückstellungen** reserve (provision) for taxes; ~**rückvergütung** tax refund.

Steuersatz tax rate, rate of assessment (taxation); **ermäßigter** ~**satz** marginal relief *(Br.);* **höchster** ~ top tax rate;
~ **anwenden** to apply the tax rate.

Steuer|säumniszuschlag tax penalty; ~**schraube ansetzen** to put the tax bite (screw) on; ~**schuldner** tax debtor; ~**senkung** tax reduction; ~**strafe** tax (fiscal) penalty, surcharge, fine; ~**tarif** scale of taxation, assessment; ~**termin** tax payment (filing, *US*) (deadline); ~**umgehung** tax avoidance, *(unerlaubte)* fiscal evasion.

Steuerung | **von Engpaßwaren** channel(l)ing of scarce materials; **elastische** ~ **des Geldmarktes** flexible control of the money market.

Steuerveranlagung taxation, assessment of taxes; **um getrennte** ~ **einkommen** to apply for a separate assessment.

Steuerveranlagungs|behörde tax commissioner *(Br.);* ~**stelle** assessment office, tax assessor.

Steuer|vergünstigung tax benefit (allowance, break, *US*); ~**verlust über fünf Jahre verteilen** to spread the impact of a tax loss over five years; ~**verlustvortrag** tax-loss carryforward; ~**verwaltung** Board of Inland Revenue *(Br.),* internal revenue service *(US);* ~**vorauszahlung** prepayment of taxes, advance tax payment; ~**vorgriffsschein** tax-anticipation bond *(US);* **attraktive** ~**vorteile** attractive tax features; ~**wohnsitz** commercial domicile; ~**zahler** taxpayer, *(Gemeinde)* ratepayer; **auf Kosten des** ~**zahlers** at the public expense; ~**zahlung** tax payment; ~**zuschlag** extra duty, additional tax (duty), *(für höhere Einkommen)* surcharge, surtax.

Stich|bahn branch line; ~**probe** random sample, spot (snap, *US*) check.

Stichproben|auswahl random sample selection; ~**einheit** sample unit; ~**entnahme** bulk sampling; ~**prüfung** sampling inspection; ~**verfahren** spot-check system.

Stichtag appointed day, fixed (key, crucial, target) date, deadline *(US), (Bewertung)* value (valuation, *US)* date, *(Börse)* settling day.

stiften to found, to institute, to establish, *(dotieren)* to endow, to donate *(US).*

Stiftung *(Anstalt)* foundation, endowed institution, trust, settlement;
testamentarisch errichtete ~ testamentary trust; **milde** ~ charitable foundation; **rechtsgeschäftliche** ~ voluntary trust;
~ **zum Zwecke der Familienversorgung** sheltering (spendthrift) trust;
~ **errichten** to create a trust (foundation).

Stiftungs|berechtigter trust beneficiary, cestui que trust; ~**gelder** trust fund (money).

still *(flau)* dull, flat, dead, slack, *(ruhig)* calm, quiet; ~**e Beteiligung** silent partnership; **Forderungsabtretung in** ~**er Form vornehmen** to operate on a non-notification basis; ~**er Gesellschafter** dormant (sleeping, silent, *Br.)* partner; ~**er Vorbehalt** mental reservation.

stillegen *(Auto)* to lay up, *(Betrieb)* to shut down, to close, *(Geld)* to immobilize, to neutralize.

Stillegung shutdown, closing, cessation, *(Geld)* immobilization, neutralization;
~ **in der Ferienzeit** holiday shutdown.

stillgelegt *(Betrieb)* shut-down, closed;
~**es Geld** lockup *(Br.).*

Stillhalte|abkommen standstill agreement; ~**gläubiger** standstill creditor; ~**kredit** frozen credit; ~**vereinbarung** standstill agreement.

stilliegen *(Betrieb)* to run (stand) idle, *(Geschäft)* to be dormant.

stillschweigend|e Bedingung implied condition; ~ **gewährte Garantie** implied warranty.

Stillstand standstill *(Betrieb)* shutdown, *(Flaute)* dullness, deadness, *(Verkehr)* breakdown.

Stillstandskosten idleplant expenses.

stimmberechtigtes Aktienkapital voting capital stock.

Stimmbindungszertifikat voting-trust certificate *(US).*

Stimmrecht voting power (privilege);
sein ~ **ausüben** to vote [on, *Br.*] the stock; ~ **durch einen Vertreter ausüben lassen** to vote by proxy.

Stimmrechts|aktie voting share (stock, *US);* ~**nachweis** voting-trust record; ~**vereinbarung** voting-trust agreement.

Stimmung *(Börse)* tone, tendency, sentiment; **zurückhaltende** ~ dull (reserved) tendency.

STimmungswechsel *(Börse)* change of tendency.

Stipendium scholarship, grant, sizarship *(Br.),* foundation, stipend, studentship *(Br.).*

Stocken stagnancy, stagnation;
ins ~ **geraten** to stagnate, to slacken *(Export)* to fall off, to decline.

stocken *(Handel)* to stagnate, *(slack)* to slacken, to be slack, *(Verkehr)* to be congested (blocked).

Stockung *(Handel)* stagnation, stagnancy, *(Verkehr)* block, congestion, traffic jam.

Stockwerkseigentum condominium.

Stopp|lohn ceiling wage; ~**preis** ceiling (controlled, blocked, frozen) price.

stornieren, Auftrag ~ to revoke (countermand) an order; **Buchung** ~ to reverse an entry.

Stornierung cancellation, countermanding;
~ **eines Zahlungsauftrages** stop payment.

Storno|buchung writing back, reversing (cross) entry; ~**gebühr** counterbalance commission.

Störung, der Brotversorgung dislocation of bread supplies; ~ **der öffentlichen Ruhe und Ordnung** violation (disturbance) of peace.

Stoß, Akten bundle of files; ~ **Briefe** packet (batch) of letters;
~**aktion** one-shot promotion; ~**angebot** *(Börse)*

concentrated offer; ~**bedarf** deferred (pent-up, US) demand.

Stottern (Abzahlung) never-never (Br. sl.).

Straf|porto penalty (extra, excess) postage, surcharge; ~**zettel** ticket (US), warning and fee (Br.).

Strandgut lfoarages, flotsam and jetsam, waif, wreck.

Straße street, (breite Allee) lane, avenue, broadway (US), boulevard (US), (Landstraße) road;
befahrbare ~ vehicular road; **gebührenpflichtige** ~ toll road; **für den Autoverkehr gesperrte** ~ road closed to motor traffic;
~ **erster Ordnung** main highway, classified road (Br.);
~ **dem öffentlichen Verkehr öffnen** to dedicate a highway; **sein Geld auf die** ~ **werfen** to throw one's money out of the window.

Straßen|anlieger frontager; ~**arbeiten** road labo(u)r.

Straßenbahn tram[way], street railway (Br.), streetcar (US), trolley car (coach, US);
~**haltestelle** tram (streetcar, US) stop; ~**linie** tramway (Br.), tramline, streetcar line (US).

Straßen|benutzungsgebühr road-using (road, Br.) tax, highway-user fee (US); ~**händler** pedlar (Br.), peddler, hawker, costermonger; ~**überführung** crossover, viaduct, dry bridge (US); ~**übergang** crossover, pedestian crossing; ~**verkaufsstand** kiosk, roadside stand (US); ~**verstopfung** traffic jam.

Strecke route, road, stretch, distance, (Bahn) line.

Strecken|abschnitt fare stage, section (US); ~**ausfall** line break; ~**belastung** (Eisenbahn) load on section.

Streichen eines Auftrags cancellation of an order.

streichen, Auftrag to cancel (countermand) an order.

Streifband [newspaper] wrapper;
unter ~ by book post;
~**depot** general deposit.

Streik strike, tie-up, work stoppage, turnout (Br.) walkout (US);
von der Gewerkschaft nicht anerkannter ~ outlaw strike; **schwerpunktartig durchgeführter** ~ selective strike; ~ **innerhalb eines ganzen Industriezweiges** industry-wide strike; ~ **der öffentlichen Versorgungsbetriebe** public-utility strike; ~ **zwecks Wiedereinstellung eines entlassenen Arbeiters** one-man strike;
~ **abblasen (abbrechen, absagen)** to call off a strike; ~ **ausrufen** to call a strike; **in den** ~ **treten** to [go on] strike, to come out on strike;
~**abkommen,** ~**abstimmung** strike vote; ~**ankündigung** strike notice; ~**brecher** strikebreaker, nonstriker, blackleg (Br. sl.), rat, scab (US).

streiken to [be (go) on] strike, to come out on strike, to down tools (Br.).

Streik|fonds strike (fighter) fund; ~**leitung** strike committee.

Streikposten picket;
betriebsfremde ~ secondary picketing (US);
durch ~ **absperren** to picket; ~ **aufstellen** to throw a picket line.

Streikunterstützung strike benefit.

Streu|abdeckung coverage; ~**bereich** (Werbefeldzug) dispersion area.

streuen (Risiko) to spread, (Werbewesen) to distribute, to disperse.

Streuplan spreadover, space (media) schedule.

Streuung (Risiko) spread, (Werbung) coverage, frequency, distribution, dispersion, spread.

Strich, unter dem (Bilanz) below the line.

Strohmann man of straw, stalking horse, front, (Effektentransfer) nominee, (Repräsentationsfigur) figurehead, pawn.

Strom|abnehmer consumer of electricity; ~**ausfall** [power] blackout; ²-**linienförmig** streamline; ~**versorgung** power (current) supply.

strukturelle Arbeitslosigkeit structural unemployment.

Strukturkrise structural crisis.

Stück piece, unit, (Teil) part, portion, article;
nach dem ~ by the tally; **pro** ~ a (by the) piece, each;
fehlerhaftes ~ defective unit; **sofort lieferbare** ~**e** (Börse) spot parcels;
hübsches ~ **Geld** nice little sum; ~ **Land** plot, lot, tract, parcel, slice (piece) of land;
nach dem ~ **verkaufen** to sell by the piece;
~**akkord** job work, piece price; ~**arbeit** piecework, taskwork, job work; ~**arbeiter** pieceworker, taskworker, job worker.

Stückekonto stock (securities) account, safe-deposit (Br.) (custodianship, US) account.

Stückelung (Aktien, Anleihen) denomination.

Stückeverzeichnis dispatch note, (Sortenzettel) bill of specie.

Stück|fracht mixed (general) cargo, less-than-carload freight (US); ~**gut** mixed (general) cargo, astray freight; **als** ~**gut [versandt]** freighted by parcels, less-than carload (US).

Stückgüter mixed (general) cargo, parcels, less-than carload (truckload) freight (US);
~**auftrag** less-than-carload order (US); ~**ladung** mixed (general) cargo, astray freight, less-than-carload shipment (US).

Stückgut|tarif all-commodity rate, less-than-carload (US) (mixed cargo) rate, less-than-truckload rate (US); ~**verkehr** berth freighting, less-than-carload business (traffic) (US); ~**versand** less-than-carload (truckload) shipment (US), packed parcels.

Stück|kosten, niedrigere lower per-unit costs; ~**liste** piece list, specification.

Stücklohn task wages, piece (unit) wage, piecework pay;
im ~ by the job;
im ~ **arbeiten** to [work by the] job; **j. im** ~ **beschäftigen** to put s. o. on piecework;
~**arbeiter** jobber, job worker, pieceworker; ~**berechnungsformel** piece-rate formula; ~**richtsatz** job (piece) rate.

Stück|preis piece (unit) price; ~**verkauf** retail sale.

stückweise | einkaufen to buy piecemeal; ~ nachzählen to tally.

Stück|zahl, rationelle economic lot size; ~zeitakkord job-work, taskwork, piecework; ~zinsen accrued interest, additional interest; ~zoll specific duty (tariff).

Stufen|akkord step bonus; ~plan *(Werbung)* cream plan; ~rabatt chain discount; ~tarif graded (flexible) tariff.

stunden, Zahlung to extend the term of (allow a respite in) payment.

Stunden|durchschnittslöhne average hourly earnings; ~leistung *(Maschine)* hourly output, *(Mensch)* output per man-hour.

Stundenlohn hourly wage (rate), wage per hour;
garantierter ~ clock card rate;
garantierter ~tarif guaranteed hourly rate.

stundenweise bezahlt werden to be paid by time.

Stundung respite [for payment], delay of payment, forbearance, *(Wechsel)* indulgence.

Stundungsgesuch request for respite.

stürmisch|er Aufschwung boom; ~er Kursanstieg skyrocketing *(US)*.

Sturz *(Kurse)* slump, crash, collapse, decline.

stürzen *(Kurse, Preise)* to tumble, to drop, to collapse, to plunge downward, to plummet;
sich in Schulden ~ to plunge into debt; sich in Unkosten ~ to spend a lot of money.

Sturzgüter bulk (loose) goods;
~laden *(Schiff)* to load in bulk;
~sendung bulk shipment.

stützen, Preise to maintain (peg, uphold) prices.

Stützkurs pegged price.

Stützung der Währung backing of currency.

Stützungs|aktion durch die Banken banking support; ~käufe supporting orders (purchases); ~kredit emergency credit; ~kurs des Frankens rate at which the franc has been established; ~-syndikat supporting syndicate.

Submission invitation for tenders, bid invitation *(US)*;
~ ausschreiben to invite tenders (bids, *US*) for a subscription.

Submissions|angebot tender; ~bedingungen terms of tender; ~bewerber contractor; ~preis contract price; ~verfahren competitive bidding; ~vergebung allocation by tenders; auf dem ~wege by tender.

Subskription subscription.

Subskriptions|ankündigung prospectus; ~dauer period of subscription; ~gebühr subscription fee; ~liste subscription list; ~preis subscription price (fee); ~schein subscripton warrant *(US)*; im ~wege subscriptive.

Substanz substance, material, body, *(Kapital)* principal;
in der ~ abschreibbar depletable;
vorsätzliche ~schädigung voluntary waste;
~schwund dwindling assets; ~verzehr consumption; ~wert assets value, *(Wertpapiere)* breakdown value.

Subvention subvention, subsidy, grant;
~ für die Exportindustrie export bounty.

subventionieren to subvention, to subventionize, to subsidize, to bonus, to pay (give) a subsidy.

subventioniert, staatlich state-fed(-aided), bounty-fed, taxeating.

Subventionierung von Preisen price subsidy.

Such|anzeige wanted, want ad *(US)*; ~kartei tracing file (index).

Sukzessivlieferung multiple delivery.

Summe sum, amount, stock, value, total;
in einer runden ~ in round figures;
ausgesetzte ~ amount allowed; fehlende ~ deficit, deficiency; veranschlagte ~ estimated amount;
~ abrunden to round off a sum; ~ auswerfen to allow an amount; fehlende ~ ergänzen to make up the requisite sum; ~ validieren to place a sum against; ~ der Rechnungsspalten ziehen to extend an invoice.

Summenversicherungspolice valued policy.

Super|dividende super (surplus, *US*) dividend, bonus, melon *(US)*, *(Bardividende)* cash surplus; ~markt supermarket *(US)*.

Swap|abkommen swap arrangement; ~geschäft swap; ~satz swap rate.

Swinggeschäft *(Devisen)* swing.

Switchgeschäft switch.

Sympathiestreik sympathetic strike.

Syndikus syndic, trustee, general (standing) counsel *(US)*, corporation lawyer.

System, kapitalistisches capitalistic (profits) system;
~ der differenzierten Preisfestsetzung für Auslieferungsstellen basing-point pricing system; ~ gespaltener Preise two-price system; ~ betrieblicher Sozialzulagen employee-benefit plan; ~ flexibler Wechselkurse flexible exchange-rate system.

Tabelle   178

T

Tabelle table, scale, schedule *(US)*, *(Zusammenstellung)* tabulation, tabularization;
~ **zur Berechnung der Lohnsteuer** pay-as-you-earn schedule *(Br.)*, wage-tax table *(US)*;
in ~**n anordnen** to tabulate; ~**n aufstellen** to compile (dress) tables.
Tabellen|form tabular form; ~satz tabular composition.
Tafel| **der ankommenden und abfahrenden Züge** timetable of trains, schedule of arrivals and departures *(US)*;
~geschäft over-the-window business *(Br.)* (counter trade, *US)*.
Tag | **und Nacht geöffnet** open day and night;
freier ~ free (open) day, day off, holiday *(US7*;
~ **der Rechnungsausstellung** date of invoice; ~ **der offenen Tür** open-door invitation;
sich einen ~ **freinehmen** to arrange to take a day off, to take a holiday *(US)*.
Tag- | **und Nachtarbeit** double shift; **durchgehender** ~~ **und Nachtbetrieb** continuous operation.
Tage|geld attendence fee, per diem (daily travelling) allowance;
im ~ **arbeiten** to work by the day;
~löhner dayman, jack, hackney, hired man *(US)*.
Tages|abschluß daily balance; ~auszug bank deposit, ~auszug bank deposit, statement of account; ~einnahme[n] daily sales (receipts, takings); ~geld *(Bankwesen)* call money *(Br.)* (loan), overnight loan *(US)*, day-to-day money *(Br.)*; ~hilfe day servant, daily; ~karte day ticket; ~kasse *(Theater)* box office [receipts]; ~kurs *(Devisen)* current rate [of exchange], rate (quotation) of the day, *(Wertpapiere)* market price (quotation); ~leistung daily output (produce).
Tagesordnung order of the day, agenda [paper];
konjunkturpolitische ~ economic-policy agenda;
schriftliche ~ order paper;
auf die ~ **setzen** to place on the agenda.
Tages|preis market (going, current, today's) price, *(Börse)* latest price, last quotation; ~produktion daily output; ~satz *(Spesen)* travel allowance, per diem charges; ~schau television news show.
Tagewerk *(Bergbau)* stint, *(Schicht)* shift.
täglich|es Angebot floating supply; **auf** ~e **Kündigung** at call.
Tagung conference, meeting, congress, sitting;
geschäftspolitische ~ policy meeting;
~ **leiten** to preside at a conference; ~ **veranstalten** to arrange a meeting.
Tagungs|bericht conference paper (report); ~ort meeting place; ~raum conference room; ~zentrum convention center *(US)*.
Talon talon, apron, stub, countertally, counterfoil;
~buch counterfoil book; ~steuer coupon tax.
Tank|stelle petrol *(Br.)* (filing, gasoline, service, *US)* station; ~wagen *(Bahn)* tank truck (car).

Tante Emma Laden pop and mom shop.
Tantieme *(Autor)* royalty, *(Gewinnanteil)* share, bonus, premium, *(Vorstand)* bonus, director's fee;
produktionsgebundene ~ production bonus;
~ **des Aufsichtsrates** director's royalty;
Tantiemen|einkünfte bonus income; ~regelung für **leitende Angestellte** management cash-incentive scheme; ~vergütung payment of a royalty.
Tara, **am Empfangsort umgerechnete** converted tare;
~ **und Gutgewicht** tare and tret;
~rechnung tare account (note).
Tarif tariff, scale, rates, statement, *(Anzeigenwesen)* advertising charges, space (advertisement, *Br.)* rate, rate card *(US)*, *(Gebührenordnung)* scale (list, schedule) of charges, *(Transportgewerbe)* freight tariff, transportation;
den Lebenshaltungskosten angepaßter ~ cost-of-living sliding scale; **autonomer** ~ *(Zoll)* single tariff; **geltender** ~ rates in force; **gestaffelter** ~ differential tariff, rate scale *(US)*; **gleitender** ~ *(Löhne)* sliding wage scale;
~ **für Einzelinsertion ohne Rabatt** transient rate;
~ **für Expreßgüter** spot rate; ~ **für Stückgüter** all-commodity rate, mixed carload rate *(US)*;
~ **festsetzen** to [fix the] tariff; ~ *(nach Teilstrecken)* to zone;
~abkommen trade (industrial) agreement, wage settlement, union contract, bargaining agreement, *(Zollwesen)* tariff treaty; ~abschluß *(Gewerkschaft)* bargaining; ~abschlußvollmacht *(Gewerkschaft)* bargaining power; ~angestellter standard wage earner; ~angleichung *(Zoll)* standardization of tariffs; ~ausgangspunkt *(Spediteur)* common point; ~bevollmächtigter *(Löhne)* [collective] bargaining agent; ~differenzierung discrimination in rates; ~einstufung *(Angestellter)* wage classification; ~erhöhungen **auf Produktivitätszunahmesätze abstellen** to settle for rises based on a productivity rate; ~ermäßigung rate (tariff) reduction; ~festsetzung tariff (rate) making; ~formel *(Löhne)* wage formula; ~gebiet *(Eisenbahn)* zone; ~gehalt flat rate of pay.
Tarifgruppe bargaining unit, wage class (group);
~n **bei der Einkommensteuer** income brackets;
in eine niedrigere ~ **einstufen** to downgrade.
tarifieren to [fix the] tariff, to fix rates.
Tarif|klasse wage class, *(Zoll)* tariff category; ~klausel wage clause; ~kommission *(Gewerkschaft)* collective bargaining commission, *(Zoll)* tariff commission *(US)*.
tariflich | **geschützt** tariff-protected; ~ **subventioniert** tariffed;
~ **aushandeln** *(Löhne)* to bargain collectively;
~er **Stundenlohn** standard hourly wage.
Tariflohn standard wages, union rate.
Tarif|mauern **gegen ausländische Produkte errichten**

to raise tariff walls against foreign goods; ~**nummer** position, *(GATT)* item; ~**ordnung** wage pattern; ~**partner** bargaining agent, collective bargainor; ~**position** tariff item (heading); ~**prämie** tabular premium, premium pay; ~**satz** *(Löhne)* standard rate [of wages], *(Zoll)* tariff rate; ~**senkung** *(Löhne)* rate cutting, downshift in rates, *(Zoll)* tariff reduction; ~**spanne** rate range; ~**stunden** standard hours; ~**tabelle** class tariff, scale of wages; ~**unterschied** *(Löhne)* wage differential; ~**verbilligung** rate decrease; ~**vereinbarung** collective bargaining agreement, *(Frachtsätze)* rating agreement; ~**verhandlungen** collective bargaining, wage negotiations.

Tarifvertrag trade agreement, *(Löhne)* collective (bargaining) agreement, *(Zoll)* tariff treaty;
~ mit Lohngleitklausel open-end wage contract.

Tarifvertrags\bestimmung collective agreement provision; ~**bevollmächtigter** [collective] bargaining unit; ~**vollmacht** *(Gewerkschaftsvertreter)* bargaining power.

Tarif\vorschriften tariff regulations; ~**vorteil** *(Zoll)* tariff advantage; ~**vorzug** tariff preference; ~**wert** *(Zoll)* tariff value; ~**zugeständnis** tariff concession.

Tasche, aus eigener out of one's own purse;
jem. auf der ~ liegen to live on s. one's income.

tätig active, acting, operative, busy;
freiberuflich ~ professional;
nicht mehr geschäftliche ~ sein to be out of business; amtlich ~ werden to officialize.

tätigen, Abschluß to conclude a bargain; Devisenabschlüsse ~ to effect foreign exchange transactions; Effektengeschäfte auf Provisionsbasis ~ to execute orders in quoted (listed, *US*) securities on a commission basis.

Tätigkeit activity, *(Beschäftigung)* occupation, business, employment, pursuits;
außerberufliche ~ outside activities; bisherige ~ previous career; kaufmännische ~ mercantile pursuits; pflichtversicherte ~ covered job *(US)*; selbständige ~ self-employment; unselbständige ~ payroll employment.

Tätigkeits\bereich way, field (radius) of activity, purvies.

tatsächlicher | Bedarf effective demand; ~ Gesamtverlust actual total loss; ~**e Kosten** actual costs.

Tauglichkeitszeugnis qualifying certificate.

Tausch barter, truck *(US)*, *(Börse)* swap;
im ~ weggeben to barter away;
~**abkommen** barter agreement (deal); ~**gegenstand** exchange, barter; ~**geschäfte machen** to barter, to trade, to dicker *(US)*, to truck *(US)*.

Tauschhandels\geschäft barter transaction; ~**mittel** circulating medium.

Tauschwert exchange (exchangeable) value.

Tausendsatz permillage, *(Anzeigenwesen)* cost-per-thousand, milline *(US)*.

Taxator appraiser, valuer, valuator, appreciator;
vereidigter ~ sworn valuer.

Taxe valuation, appraisement, appraisal, rate, *(Ge-*

bühr) charge, fee *(Tarif)* tariff, *(Taxi)* cab, taxicab, motorcab, hack *(US)*;
~ **aufstellen** to draw up a valuation; unter der ~ **verkaufen** to sell at a reduced price (discount).

Taxi cab, taxicab, motorcab, hack *(US)*;
freies ~ empty taxi, taxi with the flag up, crawler *(Br.)*;
~**chauffeur** taxi driver, cabbey *(Br.)*, cabman *(Br.)*.

taxieren to appraise, to appreciate, to value, *(steuerlich)* to assess, to rate;
zu niedrig ~ to undervalue, to underrate.

taxiert | auf valuted at;
zu hoch ~ rated too high.

Taxi\fahrer cab (taxi) driver, cabby *(Br.)*, cabman *(Br.)*; ~**haltestelle** taxi rank *(Br.)* (stand), cabstand, taxistand.

Tax\ordnung scale of fees; ~**preis** appraised (assessed) value, set-up (assessed) price, *(Auktion)* put-up-price; ~**wert** appraised (assessed, estimated) value.

technisch\e Betriebsabteilung technical (engineering) department; ~**er Betriebsleiter** chief engineer; ~**e Nothilfe** Organization for the Maintenance of Supplies *(Br.)*, Office of Emergency Preparedness *(US)*.

Teil *(Abschnitt)* section, segment, *(Anteil)* lot, share, portion, quota;
innerhalb eines Jahres fälliger ~ *(Obligation)* current maturity; risikoreicher ~ *(Kapitalanlagegesellschaft)* aggressive portion *(US)*; überlebender ~ *(Versicherung)* surviving party;
zu gleichen ~**en beteiligt sein** to go shares; ~**abrechnung** partial account; ~**betrag** fractional amount, *(Anleihe)* part.

teilen to divide, to halve, *(Aktien)* to split, *(Gewinne)* to pool;
Gewinne und Verluste zu gleichen Teilen ~ to share and share alike; sich mit jem. in die Kosten ~ to share (go shares) with s. o. in the costs.

Teilerhebung *(Statistik)* sample statistics.

Teilhaber [joint] partner, copartner, [business] associate, *(Beteiligter)* participant, participator, sharer, shareholder;
abwickelnder ~ liquidating partner; ausscheidender ~ retiring partner; geschäftsführender ~ active (acting, managing) partner; persönlich haftender ~ responsible (associated, ordinary, *Br.*) partner; stiller ~ sleeping *(Br.)* (dormant, latent, secret) partner;
[als] ~ **aufnehmen** to take in a (admit as) partner;

Teilhaber\verhältnis partnership relation; ~**versicherung** partnership (business life) insurance.

Teil\indossament partial endorsement; ~**kasko** comprehensive coverage; ~**kaskoversicherung** comprehensive motorcar insurance *(Br.)*; in ~**ladungen verschiffen** to ship goods by instal(l)ments; ~**lieferung** short (part) delivery, consignment in parts.

Teilnehmer participant, partaker, partner, participator, *(Lehrgang)* student, *(Telefon)* [telephone] subscriber, *(Wettbewerb)* competitor;

angerufener ~ *(Telefon)* called subscriber; ~**liste** list of participants; ~**verzeichnis** attendance list, *(Telefon)* telephone directory.

Teil|privatisierung hive-off of parts; ~**quittung** receipt in part; ~**schaden** partial loss; ~**sendung** consignment in part; ~**strecke** *(Eisenbahn)* zone, fare stage.

Teilung der Kosten distribution of costs (expenses).

Teil|verkauf less-than-lots sale; ~**verladung** partial shipment; ~**verlust** *(Seeversicherung)* partial loss.

Teilzahlung partial payment, *(Rate)* instal(l)ment; ~**en einhalten** to meet the payments; **auf** ~ **kaufen** to buy on the instal(l)ment plan.

Teilzahlungs|aktie partly paid stock; ~**bank** hire-purchase finance house *(Br.)*; ~**geschäft** instal(l)ment buying, hire purchase [transaction] *(Br.)*, deferred-payment sale *(US)*; ~**vertrag** instal(l)ment contract, hire-purchase agreement *(Br.)*.

Teilzeitbeschäftigung part-time employment.

Telefon|annahme telephone desk; **gebührenfreier** ~**anruf** toll-free number; ~**anschluß** subscriber's telephone (line), *(auf dem Zimmer)* room telephone; **umsteckbarer** ~**apparat** plug-in telephone; ~**buch** telephone directory.

Telefongespräch [telephone] call, conversation by telephone; ~ **abhören** to listen in, to intercept a telephone call; ~ **brieflich bestätigen** to confirm a telephone message by letter.

Telefonhandel *(Börse)* telephone trade.

telefonisch | **anmelden** to telephone ahead; ~ **aufgegebene Bestellung** telephone order; ~**e Erreichbarkeit** telephone contact.

Telefon|konferenz conference telephone call; **gebührenfreie** ~**nummer** toll-free number; ~**rechnung** telephone bill; ~**verbindung** telephone connection (connexion, *Br.)*; ~**verkehr** *(Börsenverkehr)* interoffice dealings; **im** ~**verkehr gehandelt werden** to be dealt with after hours.

Telegrafen|amt telegraph office; ~**dienst der Wirtschaft** commercial telegraph service.

telegrafisch | **Geld auszahlen** to transfer money by cable; ~**e Geldanweisung** telegraphic money order.

Telegramm telegram, message, wire *(US)*; **vom Empfänger bezahltes** ~ telegram sent collect *(US)*; **dringendes** ~ urgent telegram; **gebührenfreies** ~ deadhead; **verschlüsseltes** ~ cipher (code) telegram; ~ **zu Lasten des Empfängers** cash-on-delivery telegram; ~ **mit bezahlter Rückantwort** reply-paid telegram, wire collect *(US)*; ~ **aufgeben** to send [off] (deliver) a telegram.

Telegramm|adresse telegraphic (telegram, cable) address; ~**formular** telegraph (message) form; ~**gebühr** telegram rate, cable expenses.

Telquelkurs *(Börse)* tel quel rate *(Br.)*.

Tendenz trend, drift, direction, leanding, *(Börse, Konjunktur)* tendency, trend, movement, *(Zeitung)* political (colo(u)r);

abschwächende ~ sagging tendency; **zum Umsatz disproportionale** ~ leverage; **preissteigernde** ~ upward surge of prices; **saisonbedingte** ~ seasonal trend; **zurückhaltende** ~ tone of restraint; ~ **der Aktienkurse** stock trend.

tendieren to tend, to lean, to show a tendency; **fest** ~ to show a stronger tendency; **schwächer** ~ to edge down.

Termin date, day, *(Verfallzeit)* term, maturity, *(Zahlungstermin)* respite; **mittlerer** ~ average date; **auf** ~ **kaufen** to purchase forward *(Br.)* (for future delivery, *US)*; ~**abschluß** forward (future, *US)* contract (deal), time bargain; ~**auftrag** *(Börse)* order for the account (settlement, *Br.)*; ~**börse** forward market, market for future [delivery, *US]*, futures market *(US)*; ~**devisen** forward exchanges (currency); ~**gelder** time (fixed) deposits, restricted cash; ~**geschäft** forward business (transaction *Br.)*, time bargain (purchase), futures dealing (contract) *(US)*; ~**handel** option business, forward operations *(Br.)*, [trading in] futures *(US)*.

Terminkalender tickler *(US coll.)*, letter (desk) calendar *(US)*, appointments schedule *(US)*, engagement book; ~ **abstimmen** to coordinate one's schedule *(US)*; **vollbesetzten** ~ **haben** to have numerous engagements for the next week.

Termin|kauf put and call, forward purchase; ~**kontrolle** *(Anzeigen)* progress control; ~**kurs** *(Devisen)* forward rate, futures price *(US)*; ~**markt** forward (option, settlement, *Br.,* contract, *US)* market, futures market *(US)*; ~**notierung** forward quotation *(Br.)*, quotations for futures *(US)*; ~**sätze** *(Devisen)* forward (futures, *US)* rates; ~**überwacher** expediter, *(Werbeagentur)* traffic manager; ~**verkauf** seller's option, time (forward, futures, *US,* short *US)* sale; ~**werte** forward securities *(Br.)*, futures *(US)*.

Terraingesellschaft real-estate trust (company).

Tesafilm cellulose transparent, adhesive tape, Scotch tape.

Testament will, last will and testament, devise; **notariell beglaubigtes** ~ notarial will; **eigenhändiges** ~ holographic will; **widerrufliches** ~ ambulatory will; ~ **anfechten** to dispute (contest, oppose) a will; ~ **für kraftlos erklären** to invalidate a will; ~ **durch das Nachlaßgericht öffnen lassen** to have a will proved.

Testaments|eröffnung opening (reading) of a will; ~**nachtrag** codicil, label; ~**vollstrecker** executor of a will.

testieren to make (write) a will.

testierfähig of sound and disposing mind *(US)*.

Testmarktaktion sales test.

teuer dear, expensive, costly, high-priced, at a high cost (figure, rate); **schamlos** ~ shockingly expensive;

sehr ~ **sein** to cost money, *(Hotel)* to have steep prices; **sehr** ~ **werden** to run into a lot of money.

Teuerung dearness, high prices, general price increase, *(Knappheit)* dearth, scarcity.

Teuerungs|welle wave of high prices; ~**zulage** cost-of-living (high-cost) bonus, dearness allowance.

Text text, tenor, matter;
~ **und Kontext stimmen nicht überein** *(Wechsel)* words and figures differ;
verschlüsselter ~ coded text;
~ **frei auslegen** to take liberties with a text;
~**analyse** copy research; ~**anzeige** *(im redaktionellen Teil)* reading notice, reader advertisement.

Texter *(Werbeagentur)* copywriter.

Textil|industrie textile industry; ~**messe** textile goods **nach dem Stück verkaufte** ~**waren** piece goods; ~**waren nach dem Meter** dry goods *(US)*.

thesaurieren to store up, *(Gewinn)* to retain.

Thesaurierungsfonds nonexpendable fund.

Tickerdienst ticker service.

Tiefkühl|industrie refrigeration industry; ~**schiff** reefer; ~**truhe** food (home) freezer.

Tiefpunkt der Konjunktur depression low.

Tiefstand *(Kurse)* low level (point), bottom;
absoluter ~ *(Börse)* all-time low;
zu einem neuen ~ **der Kurse führen** to carry the prices to a new low level.

tilgen to amortize, *(Buchung stornieren)* to reverse, to cancel, *(Schuld)* to cancel, to acquit, to clear off, to compound, to discharge, to liquidate;
Anleihe ~ to retire a loan.

Tilgung amortization, *(Hypothek)* extinction, satisfaction, *(Schulden)* discharge, acquittal, paying off, repayment;
vorzeitige ~ previous (priority) redemption;
~ **der öffentlichen Schuld** retirement of the public debt.

Tilgungs|anleihe redemption (sinking-fund) loan; ~**bestimmungen** terms of redemption; ~**betrag** redemption money (capital); ~**darlehen** redemption loan; ~**fonds** sinking (liquidation, redemption, *US)* fund; ~**klausel** redemption clause; ~**kurs** redemption price (rate); ~**rücklage** redemption (sinking-fund) reserve; ~**zeitraum** time of redemption, payoff period *(US)*.

Titel *(Wertpapiere)* securities, *(Wertpapiername)* title, *(Zoll)* position, item;
vollstreckbarer ~ enforceable judgment;
~ **des Haushaltsplans** item of the budget.

Tochtergesellschaft affiliate, affiliate company (corporation), subsidiary, subsidiary company (corporation);
abhängige ~ underlying company *(US)*.

Todes|nachrichten obituary notice; **gleichzeitige** ~**vermutungsklausel** *(Versicherung)* common disaster clause.

Tonnage tonnage, *(Schiff)* displacement;
aufgelegte ~ idle shipping.

Tonne tun, cask, *(Boje)* buoy *(Faß)* barrel, vat, *(Gewicht)* ton, short ton *(US)*.

Tonnen|fracht freight by the ton, ton freight; ~**geld** tonnage, tonnage rent *(US)*, beaconage.

tot *(nicht angelegt)* uninvested, idle, dormant;
~**e Hand** mortmain; ~**es Kapital** idle money (funds), unemployed capital.

Total|ausverkauf clearance (going-out-of-business, winding-up) sale; ~**schaden** *(Auto)* worthless wreck, *(fingierter, Schiff)* constructive total loss.

Toto *[etwa]* pools, policy *(US)*, sweepstake;
~**schein** sweepstake card, policy slip *(US)*; ~**spieler** pool filler.

Tour tour, trip, round, *(Kundenbesuch)* business round;
auf ~ **gehen** *(Vertreter)* to go out on business (commerce-destroying, on the road); **auf niedrigen** ~**en laufen** *(Konjunktur)* to run flat.

Tourist tourist, travel(l)er, excursionist.

Touristen|attraktion hot spot; **positive** ~**bilanz** favo(u)rable balance of payments in tourism; ~**flugschein** economy fare; ~**hotel** travel(l)er's hotel; ~**kabine** deck cabin; ~**klasse** *(Schiff)* tourist (cabin, deck) class, *(Flugzeug)* economy class; ~**visum** tourist visa.

träge Nachfrage sluggish demand.

tragen, sich [selbst] to pay its way; **Kosten** ~ to defray (meet the) expense; **Zinsen** ~ to yield interest.

Trajektschiff train ferry, steam ferryboat.

Tranche einer Anleihe portion (slice) of loan.

Transaktion transaction, operation, bargain, deal;
~**en in verschiedenen Effekten** spreading operations *(Br.)*; ~**en am offenen Markt** open-market credit transactions;
ungedeckte ~**en vornehmen** to operate without cover.

Transatlantikfracht ocean freight.

Transfer|abkommen transfer agreement; ~**gebühr** *(Wertpapiere)* transfer (registration) fee.

Transit|abgabe transit duty; ~**güter** transit goods, goods in transit; ~**hafen** intermediate port; ~**konnossement** through bill of lading; ~**lager** bonded warehouse, transit storehouse.

transitorisch|e Buchungen suspense entries; ~ **Posten** *(Bilanz)* prepaid expenses, deferred charges [to expenses] *(US)*, suspense (transitory, *US)* items.

Transit|sendung through shipment; ~**tarif** transit rate; ~**verkehr** transit, through traffic.

Transport transport, carriage, carrying, conveyance, portage, haul, transportation *(US)*;
auf dem ~ **verlorengegangen** lost in transit;
~ **per Bahn** rail (railway, railroad *US)* transport;
~ **per Flugzeug (auf dem Luftwege)** aircraft (air) transport, transportation by air *(US)*; ~ **auf dem Seewege** sea transport;
auf dem ~ **beschädigt werden** to be damaged in transit.

Transport|agentur transport agent (agency), transportation agency *(US)*; ~**anweisungen** forwarding (shipping, *US)* instructions; ~**einrichtungen** transportation means; ~**fahrzeug** vehicle, transportation, means of conveyance; ~**firma** haulage firm, common *(US)* (land) carrier, forwarding agency; ~**gefahren** marine perils, transport risk; ~**gesellschaft** forwarding (shipping, *US,* transport) company, common carrier *(US)*; ~**gewerbe** carrying trade, transport industries.

Transportkosten carriage, carriage (running, transport) expenses, transportation (shipping) charges *(US)*;
überhöhte ~ phantom freight;
~ **gehen zu Lasten des Empfängers** carriage forward; ~ **trägt der Absender** carriage paid home; ~**rechnung** freight account.

Transport|makler forwarding (shipping, *US,* transport) agent; ~**mittel** means of transport (conveyance), transportation *(US)*.

Transportmöglichkeiten means (facilities) of transport, transport (facilities);
mangelnde ~ shortage of transport.

Transport|raum shipping (transportation) space *(US)*; ~**risiko** risks of carriage, transport risk; ~**schaden** damage (loss) in transit; ~**spesen** carriage, transport charges; ~**unternehmer** [common] carrier *(US)*, land carrier, haulage (road) contractor; ~**versicherung** transport (transportation, *US,* shipping, *US*) insurance.

Transportversicherungs|formular *(Seeversicherung)* marine-insurance form; ~**police** marine policy *(US)*.

Transport|verzögerung delay in transit; ~**vorschriften** forwarding (shipping, *US*) instructions; **öffentliches** ~**wesen** public transportation *(US)*.

trassieren, in blanko to make out in blank; **Wechsel al pari** ~ to draw a bill at par.

Trassierungskredit drawing (acceptance) credit.

Tratte draft, bill [(letter) of exchange];
domizilierte ~ domiciled (domiciliated) bill;
~ **mit Dokumenten** documentary bill (draft); ~ **ohne Dokumente** clean draft;
~ **akzeptieren** to give a draft due protection; ~ **nicht akzeptieren** to show dishono(u)r to a draft; ~ **einlösen** to discharge a bill; ~ **mit Akzept versehen** to provide a bill with acceptance.

Tratten|ankauf negotiation of a draft; ~**kopierbuch** bill register, *(nach Kunden geordnet)* bill book (ledger).

Treibgut flotsam, driftage.

Treibstoff fuel, petrol *(Br.)*, gasoline *(US)*, gas *(coll.)*;
~ **einnehmen** to fuel [up], to bunker;
~**lager** fuel dump (depot); ~**verbrauch** fuel consumption; ~**versorgung** fuel supply.

Trennungsentschädigung severance (separation) allowance.

Tresor safe [deposit], strong room, vault *(US)*;

~**fach** safe [deposit], strongbox, vault *(US)*; ~**miete** safe-deposit fee; ~**versicherung** safe deposit insurance.

Treu und Glauben im Geschäftsleben good faith in business policy.

Treu|geber trustor, donor, grantor *(US)*, *(Sicherungsübereignungsvertrag)* beneficial owner; ~**geber und** ~**nehmer** trustee and beneficiary; ~**gut** *(Sicherungsübereignungsvertrag)* equitable lien.

Treuhand|abkommen trust engagement (agreement); ~**bericht** trust report; ~**eigentum** beneficial interest, equitable lien.

Treuhänder trustee, custodian, fiduciary [agent], trust officer, holder on trust, escrow holder;
behördlich bestellter ~ conventional (official) trustee;
~ **von Mündelvermögen** custodian trustee;
~ **einsetzen** to appoint a custodian; **als** ~ **fungieren** to [serve as] trustee; **auf einen** ~ **übertragen** to vest in a trustee;
~**depot** trust deposit; ~**eigenschaft** fiduciary capacity; ~**funktionen wahrnehmen** to serve as custodian; ~**gremium** board of trustees.

treuhänderisch fiduciary, in trust;
~ **verwalten** to act as trustee, to hold in trust (escrow);
~ **verwaltetes Vermögen** trust estate; ~**e Verwaltung** trusteeship. *

Treuhänder|konto trust (trustee's) account; **unter** ~**schaft stellen** to place under trusteeship; ~**vertrag** trust agreement, custodian's contract.

Treuhand|gelder trust fund; ~**gesellschaft** trust institution (company); ~**gut verwalten** to administer a trust; ~**konto** trust (fiduciary, escrow) account; ~**sondervermögen** trust-and-agency fund; ~**verhältnis** trust, trust (fiduciary) relationship; ~**vermögen** trust, trust estate (property, assets, fund); ~**vertrag** escrow (trust) agreement; ~**verwaltung** trusteeship, assigneeship, trust administration.

Treu|nehmer trustee, fiduciary debtor, bailee; ~**rabatt** *(Ladengeschäft)* patronage discount.

Triebwagen rail car, *(Straßenbahn)* shuttle car, tramcar *(Br.)*.

Trinkgeld fee, tip, perquisite, drink money.

trockener Wechsel promissory note.

Trockendock dry (graving) dock.

Trödel|geschäft, ~**laden** marine stores *(Br.)*, junk (jumble) shop, swagshop; ~**markt** rag fair, broker's row *(Br.)*.

Tumultversicherung civil commotion insurance.

turnusmäßig ausscheiden to retire by rotation.

TÜV-Bescheinigung roadworthiness test certificate.

Typen|muster sample; ~**schild** name plate.

U

U-Bahn metropolitan railway *(Br.),* underground, *(Br.),* tube *(Br. coll.),* Metro *(Br. coll.),* underground railroad *(US),* subway *(US);*
~**station** subway station *(US);* ~**zug** underground train.
Überangebot glut, oversupply, surplus stocks;
~ **an Arbeitskräften** surplus manpower, overcrowded labo(u)r market.
Über|besetzung mit Arbeitskräften featherbedding *(US);* ~**bewertung** overvaluation, overestimate, *(Wertpapiere)* top-heaviness.
überbieten to overbid, to outbid, to bid higher (in).
Überbringer bearer, deliverer, carrier, bringer, *(Scheck)* bearer, *(Wechsel)* presenter;
~**klausel** bearer clause.
Überbrückungs|hilfe stopgap (interim) aid; ~**kredit** accommodation (stopgap, holdover) loan.
Überdeckung excess cover (coverage).
übereignen to make over, to transfer;
Grundstück ~ to convey land to a purchaser.
Übereinkommen mit seinen Gläubigern treffen to arrange (compound) with one's creditors.
übereinstimmen to agree, *(Bücher)* to [be] conform, to run with, to tally *(Br.);*
nicht ~ *(Debet- und Krediteintragungen)* to be out of balance.
übereinstimmend| gebucht booked in conformity;
mit dem Muster ~ matching the sample;
~**e Buchung** corresponding entry.
Übereinstimmung | mit dem Markenbild brand identity; ~ **der Willenserklärungen** meeting of minds.
Überfahrt passage, [channel] crossing *(Br.).*
überfällig overdue, past-due *(Schiff)* out of time.
Überfallversicherung personal holdup insurance.
Überfluß abundance, overflow, glut;
~**gesellschaft** affluent society.
überfluten *(Markt)* to flood.
überfremden to bring under foreign control.
überführen, in Gemeineigentum to nationalize *(Br.),* to socialize.
Überführung, kreuzungsfreie overpass; **schienengleiche** ~ level *(Br.)* (grade, *US)* crossing;
~ **in städtischen Besitz** municipalization.
Überführungskosten *(Auto)* destination charges.
überfüllt *(Markt)* glutted, overstocked, *(Straße)* crowded, jammed, *(Versammlung)* stuffed.
Übergabe delivery, deliverance, surrender, turning in, *(Einreichung)* filing, handing in;
~ **zu treuen Händen** delivery in escrow *(US).*
Übergabe|bescheinigung delivery receipt; ~**klausel** delivery clause; ~**wert** transfer value.
Übergang *(Rechte)* transition, change, transfer;
schienengleicher ~ level *(Br.)* (grade, *US)* crossing;
~ **des Eigentums** devolution of title.
Übergangs|abkommen transitory treaty; ~**beschäftigung** changeover employment; ~**bestimmungen** provisional regulations; ~**phase** intervening

(transitional) period; **sich in einem** ~**stadium befinden** to be in a state of transition; ~**station** junction, transit station; ~**wirtschaft der Nachkriegszeit** postwar transitional period.
übergeben, jem. etw. zu treuen Händen to entrust to the care of (confide) s. th. to s. o.; **Geschäft seinem Nachfolger** ~ to turn over a business to one's successor; **dem Verkehr** ~ to open for traffic.
übergehen, in andere Hände to change hands; **zur Tagesordnung** ~ to pass (proceed) to the order of the day.
Über|gewicht overweight, overload, extra (surplus) weight, *(Gepäck)* excess luggage *(Br.)* (baggage, *US);* ~**größe** oversize, outsize, giant package.
Überhang | der Aktiva excess of assets; ~ **an Aufträgen** backlog of orders.
überhäuft, mit Anträgen snowed under with applications.
überhitzte Konjunktur overtaxed boom.
Überkapazität overcapacity, excess capacity.
überkapitalisieren to overcapitalize.
Überland|bahn transcontinental railway; ~**frachtsatz** truck rates *(US);* ~**omnibus** cross-country bus, motor coach; ~**transport** long-distance transport.
überlassen, entgeltlich to sell for value (a consideration; **Schiff der Versicherungsgesellschaft** ~ to abandon a ship covered by a policy.
Überlebens|rente two-life (joint and survivor, survivorship) annuity, annuity on the last survivor; ~**vermutung** presumption of survival; ~**versicherung** survivors' (survivorship) insurance.
Überleitungsbestimmungen provisional regulations, transition provisions.
überliegen lassen to allow on demurrage.
Überliege|geld demurrage; ~**tage** extra lay days.
Über|mittlungsgebühr remittance fee; ~**nachtung** overnight [stop (stay)].
Übernahme assumption, undertaking, *(Amt)* taking over (up), takeover, *(Effekten)* takeover;
~ **in das Angestelltenverhältnis** transfer to the salary payroll; ~ **von Dokumenten gegen Bezahlung** lifting of documents against payment; ~ **auf dem Konsortialwege** outright purchase; ~ **eines Versicherungsrisikos** underwriting a risk.
Übernahme|angebot takeover offer (bid); ~**bedingungen** *(Konsortium)* underwriting conditions; ~**betrag** *(Börse)* subscription quota; ~**konsortium** [underwriting] syndicate, underwriters; ~**kurs** negotiation (underwriting) price, transfer price (rate) *(Br.);* ~**spesen** underwriting fee.
übernehmen *(abnehmen)* to accept, to receive, *(Arbeit)* to undertake, *(Schiff)* to hoist in;
Aktiva und Passiva ~ to take over the assets and liabilities; **Anleihe** ~ to subscribe to a loan; **zusätzliche Arbeiten** ~ to take on extra work; **neuen Aufgabenbereich** ~ to enter upon new duties; **Hypothek [unter Anrechnung auf den Kaufpreis]** ~ to

assume a mortgage; **Inkasso von Wechseln** ~ **to** attend to the collection of bills; **Präsidium** ~ **to** take the chair; **Vertretung** ~ **to** take up an agency.

Über|nehmer *(Empfänger)* receiver, party receiving, *(Warensendung)* consignee; **~pariausgabe** issue above par; **~produktion** surplus production.

überprüfen *(Bücher, Konten)* to audit, to examine.

Überprüfung *(Bücher, Konten)* auditing, re-examination, checking, verification, *(Maschine)* overhaul;
gewerbepolizeiliche ~ factory inspection; **stichprobenartige** ~ snap check, spot checking; ~ **von Frachtrechnungen** rate check; ~ **einer Kostenrechnung** review of costs; ~ **des finanziellen Status** means test *(Br.)*.

überschäumen *(Konjunktur)* to boil over.

Überschlag computation, estimation, estimate, rough calculation, sketch.

überschreiben, dem Käufer ein Grundstück to convey land to the purchaser.

überschreiten, seinen Auftrag to override one's commission; **sein Konto** ~ to overdraw one's account (the badger, *Br.)*, to make an overdraft; **Limit** ~ to exceed a prescribed amount.

Überschreitung der Höchstgeschwindigkeit exceeding the speed limit *(Br.)*, speeding violation *(US)*.

überschuldet deep[ly involved] in debts, *(Grundstück)* encumbered.

Überschuß surplus, redundancy, *(Differenz)* margin, *(Ernte)* carryover, *(Kasse)* over;
buchmäßiger ~ book surplus; ~ **der Aktiva über die Passiva** surplus of assets over liabilities.

Überschüsse | und Fehlbeträge shorts and overs; **haushaltsrechtliche** ~ budget surpluses; ~ **in der Exportwirtschaft** overbalance of exports.

Überschuß| ernte surplus crop; [wirtschaftliches] **~gebiet** surplus area.

überschüssig| er Betrag balance, surplus; **~e Kaufkraft abschöpfen** to mop up excess spending power.

Überschuß| produkte surplus products (goods); **~wirtschaft** economy of abundance.

Überschwemmung overflow, flow, *(Markt)* glut; ~ **durch Touristen** inundation of tourists.

Übersee| auftrag overseas order; **~bank** oversea[s] bank; **~handel** ocean (oversea, foreign) trade, maritime commerce.

überseeische Besitzungen overseas possessions.

Übersee| koffer steamer trunk; **~produkte** overseas products.

übersenden to send, to forward, *(Geld)* to transmit, to remit, *(Waren)* to consign, to ship *(US)*.

Übersender *(Geld)* transmitter, remitter, *(Waren)* consignor, forwarder.

übersetzt| er Arbeitsmarkt overcrowded labo(u)r market; **~e Forderungen** exaggerated claims; **~er Preis** exorbitant price.

Übersetzungs| büro translation agency, translating bureau *(US)*; **~gebühr** translation charge.

Übersicht survey, scheme, statement, review, *(Abriß)* sketch, outline, account.

Übersichtsplan *(Betriebsanlage)* plan of the installation (site).

überspitzte Forderungen overcharged claims, exaggerated demands (claims).

übersteigen, Bedarf to be in excess of demand.

Überstunde overtime, extra (excess) hour; **~n ablehnen** to jib at working overtime; **~n machen** to do (make) overtime.

Überstunden| bezahlung overtime [premium] pay, time and one-half pay; **~genehmigung** overtime authorization; **~satz** overtime rate; **~zulage** overtime bonus (pay).

Übertagebau surface mining (working).

übertarifliche Leistungszulage merit increase.

Übertrag carryover, holdover, carry (brought) forward, amount carried over; ~ **machen** to carry over, to pass a transfer *(Br.)*.

übertragbar transferable, assignable, alienable, *(begehbar)* negotiable; **einfach** ~ negotiable without endorsement; **nicht** ~ nontransferable, nonassignable;

übertragen to transfer, to assign, to make an assignment, to alienate, *(Buchführung)* to carry forward (over, up), to post (bring) forward, *(Kurzschrift)* to transcribe;
jem. eine Angelegenheit ~ to place a matter into the hands of s. o.; **seiner Bank die laufende Bezahlung seiner Steuern** ~ to commission one's bank to pay one's taxes; **blanko** ~ to assign in blank; **durch Giro** ~ to endorse; **im Hauptbuch** ~ to post up the ledger; **Vollmacht auf j.** ~ to delegate authority to s. o..

Übertragung transfer, assignment, alienation, delivery, *(Buchung)* transfer, entry, *(Grundbesitz)* conveyance, *(Übersetzung)* translation, rendering; **ungültige** ~ improper transfer; **unwiderrufliche** ~ irrevocable assignment;
~ **von Befugnissen** delegation of powers; ~ **einer Forderung** assignation of a claim; ~ **in das Hauptbuch** posting up the ledger; ~ **der beweglichen Sachwerte** *(Unternehmen)* bulk transfer *(US)*; ~ **in den Büchern vornehmen** to effect a transfer in the books.

Übertragungs| beleg transfer voucher; **~formular** transfer form; **~spesen** transfer expense; **~urkunde** [deed of] assignment, escrow, *(über Effektenverkäufe)* instrument of transfer, *(Namensaktie)* transfer deed.

überversichern to overinsure.

Überversicherung overinsurance, excess insurance.

Überwachung | der Buchhaltung accounting control; ~ **eingehender Rechnungen** invoice supervision.

Überwachungs| ausschuß supervisory (watchdog) committee; **~organ** supervisory organ; **~tätigkeit** regulatory job, control.

überwälzen *(Steuer)* to shift, to pass.

überweisen to remit, to transfer; **durch eine Bank** ~ to pay through a bank;

Gegenwert ~ to remit the proceeds; **telegrafisch** ~ to cable.

Überweisung remittance, remittal, transfer, transmission;
briefliche ~ mail transfer (payment) *(US)*;
~ **zu Lasten des Kreditkontos** credit transfer;
~ **eines Geldbetrages verzögern** to postpone the payment of an amount.

Überweisungs|abschnitt transfer slip, *(Post)* postal check; ~**auftrag** remittance order; **Pfändungs- und** ~**beschluß** attachment (garnishee) order; ~**formular** remittance form, *(im Clearingverfahren)* transfer ticket (slip); ~**träger** transfer voucher (ticket); ~**verkehr** clearing system.

überzeichnen *(Anleihe)* to oversubscribe, to cover a loan.

überziehen *(Konto)* to overdraw, to make overdrafts, to overcheck *(US)*.

Überziehung overdraft, overdraught *(US)*.

Überziehungs|kredit overdraft facilities; ~**provision** overdraft commission (fee).

überzogenes Konto overdraft, overdrawn account.

üblich general, customary, usual;
im ordentlichen kaufmännischen Leben ~ **sein** to be consistent with sound commercial practice;
~**e Zahlungsbedingungen** standard payment clauses, usual terms of payment; ~**er Zinsfluß** standard interest.

Ultimo end of the month;
~**abrechnung** monthly settlement; ~**ausgleich** year-end adjustment; ~**fälligkeiten** monthly accruals; ~**gelder** last-day money.

umadressieren to readdress, to redirect.

umarbeiten to work over, to remake.

Umbesetzung der Schlüsselpositionen in der Vorstandsspitze reshuffling of top management, executive shuffle.

Umbruchredakteur copy editor, copyreader.

umbuchen to transfer from one account to another; to rebook, to make cross entries.

Umbuchung transfer, cross entry, rebooking;
~ **im Hauptbuch** ledger transfer.

Umfang *(Ausdehnung)* extent, scope, size, measure, *(Größe)* size, dimensions;
~ **des Fertigungsprogramms** range of products; ~ **einer Garantie** extent of warranty; ~ **der Sorgfaltspflicht** degree of care; ~ **der Vertretungsmacht** scope of an agent's authority.

Umfrage poll, survey, field investigation.

umgehen to evade, to avoid, to get round *(US)*;
leichtsinnig mit Vaters Geld ~ to play fast and loose with father's money.

Umgehung | von Devisengesetzen evasion of currency laws; ~ **einer Steuer** tax evasion (avoidance).

Umgehungsstraße by-pass, by-road, sliproad.

umgesetzt werden mit *(Börse)* to change hands at . . .

umgründen, Gesellschaft to reorganize a company.

umherziehendes Gewerbe itinerant trade, pedlary.

Umlade|gebühren transfer (reloading) charges; ~**hafen** tran(s)shipping port; ~**konnossement** tran(s)-

shipment bill of lading; ~**spesen** transfer (reloading) charges.

Umlage levy, contribution, allocation, encumbrance;
städtische ~ assessment, rating, county rate *(Br.)*;
~ **für Anlieger** special assessment;
j. zu einer ~ **heranziehen** to rate (assess) s. o.

Umlage|behörde assessment office, rating authority; ~**ermäßigung** rate reduction; ~**liste** assessment roll (list).

umlagepflichtig ratable, assessable.

Umlage|pflichtiger ratepayer; ~**veranlagung** rating, assessment of property; ~**zeitraum** assessment period.

Umlagerung shift, *(Quoten)* redistribution.

Umlagerungskaution *(Zoll)* removal bond.

Umlauf *(Geld)* circulation, currency, *(Kapital)* flotation, *(Rundschreiben)* circular [order], *(Waggon)* transit time, turn-round;
in ~ **bringen** *(Geld)* to issue, to circulate, *(Kapital durch Effektenausgabe)* to float, to set afloat; **falsches Geld in** ~ **bringen** to utter forge'd money;
außer ~ **setzen** *(Banknoten)* to withdraw from circulation; **in** ~ **setzen** *(Geld)* to circulate; ~**geschwindigkeit** *(Geld)* velocity of circulation; ~**kapital** circulating (floating, liquid, fluid, *US)* capital; ~**mittel** current funds (assets); ~**vermögen** current funds, liquid (current, circulating, *Br.*, fluid, *US*, quick, *US)* assets.

Umlegemappe flip-flop *(US)*.

umlegen, Kosten to apportion the cost.

umleiten, umlenken *(Kapitalströme)* to switch, *(Verkehr)* to divert *(Br.)*, to deroute *(US)*.

Ummeldegebühr registration fee.

umorganisieren, Unternehmen to reshape a company (corporation).

umrechenbar convertible, reducible.

umrechnen, Pfunde in Schilling to reduce pounds to shillings.

Umrechnungskurs rate of exchange;
zum ~ **von** at the parity (the current exchange) of; **amtlicher** ~ official exchange rate.

Umrechnungs|satz *(Devisen)* conversion rate; ~**schlüssel** conversion key; ~**tabelle** ready reckoner, *(Börse)* cambist.

Umsatz turnover, sales, *(Börse)* business, transactions, trading, *(Werbeagentur)* billing;
kein ~ nothing doing; **ohne** ~ no sales;
fakturierter ~ invoiced sales; **geringer** ~ *(Börse)* thin (narrow, quiet) market; **schneller** ~ quick turnover, early returns; **steuerpflichtiger** ~ taxable turnover;
~ **des Betriebskapitals** working-capital turnover;
~ **an die Kundschaft** *(Konzernbilanz)* consolidated outside sales;
~ **steigern** to roll up the sales *(coll.)*;
~**anstieg** upsurge in sales; ~**ausgleichssteuer** countervailing duty, import equalization tax; ~**belebung** increase in sales.

Umsätze sales, dealings, transactions;
bei guten ~**n** with a brisk market;

geringe ~ in Ölaktien not much move in oil shares; hohe ~ durch die Vertreter im Außendienst large returns from agents isn the field; bei der Börseneröffnung mit lebhaften ~n beginnen to advance from the start in brisk dealings; große ~ in . . . tätigen to deal in big volume.

Umsatz|entwicklung sales trend; ~geschwindigkeit rate (speed) of turnover; ~kurve in graphischer Darstellung sales chart.

umsatzlos without sales, (Börse) featureless; ~es Konto dead (inoperative) account (Br.).

Umsatz|provision commission on sales effected; ~rückgang decrease in (drop of) turnover, falling off of sales; ~schwankungen sales fluctuations; sich ≙steigernd auswirken to help sales; ~steigerung erzielen to roll up (boost) the sales.

Umsatzsteuer turnover tax (Br.), tax on turnover (Br.) business receipts (sales) tax (US); ~rückvergütung sales (US) (turnover, Br.) tax refund.

Umsatz|tantieme (Vertreter) bonus; ~ziffern turnover rate, sales figures; ~zuwachs increase in turnover.

Umschlag (Brief) envelope, (Buch) cover, dust jacket, (Kreuzband) wrapper, (Umladung) tran(s)-shipment, reloading, (Umsatz) [rate of] turnover; ~ des Kapitals capital turnover.

umschlagen (Konjunktur) to reach the turning point, (umladen) to reload, to tran(s)ship.

Umschlag|kosten reloading (tran(s)shipment) charges; ~platz tran(s)shipment point, rail and water terminal.

Umschlagsgeschwindigkeit rate of turnover.

Umschlagshäufigkeit | des Eigenkapitals capital turnover ratio (Br.), sales volume rate (US); ~ des Rohstofflagers raw-materials turnover.

Umschlagszeit turnover period.

umschreiben (Aktien) to transfer, (Grundstück) to convey, to surrender.

Umschreibungs|gebühr registration fee, (Aktien) transfer tax (US).

umschulden to refund debts, to convert, to fund.

Umschuldung debt refunding, conversion, funding.

Umschuldungs|aktion funding operation; ~anleihe conversion loan; ~kasse conversion office.

Umschulung reeducation, reconditioning; berufliche ~ vocational reeducation (rehabilitation).

Umschulungsbeihilfe rehabilitation relief.

Umschwung (Börse) sudden change, turn; ~ in den Lagerpositionen reversal in stockpiling; ~ verzeichnen (Börse) to turn the corner (US).

umsetzbar realizable, salable, marketable; gut ~ (lieferbar) good delivery.

umsetzen to sell, to dispose, (Arbeitskräfte) to transfer, to dislocate, (Umsatz haben) to turn over; in bares Geld ~ to convert into cash.

Umsetzung, innerbetriebliche production transfer.

umsonst free of (without) cost, cost-free, costless, gratis, gratuitous.

Umsteigefahrschein detour (through, correspondence) ticket, transfer (US).

umsteigen, in Wachstumswerte to switch into growth stock.

umstellen to regroup, to reorganize, to readjust, (Außenhandelsgeschäft) to switch, (Betrieb) to convert, to shift; auf Friedensproduktion ~ to reconvert to peacetime production.

Umstellung regrouping, reorganization, (Betrieb) change-over; ~en im Wertpapierbesitz changes in holding.

Umstellungs|betrag conversion amount; ~betrieb plant in process of conversion; ~guthaben conversion balance.

Umtausch exchange, barter, (Börse) swap; kein ~ all sales final, no goods exchange; ~angebot exchange offer.

umtauschen to change, to exchange (Börse) to swap, (Wertpapiere) to commute, to convert.

Umtausch|frist conversion period; ~kosten costs of exchange; ~satz (Devisen) cross (firm) rate; ~verhältnis eins zu eins share-for-share exchange.

umwandeln to transform, (Rente) to commute, (Wertpapiere) to convert, to reconvert; Gesellschaft ~ to reorganize a company; schwebende Schuld ~ to fund a debt.

Umwandlung rearrangement, (Rente) commutation, (Wertpapiere) conversion; ~ einer offenen Handelsgesellschaft in eine Aktiengesellschaft conversion of a partnership into a company (corporation).

Umwandlungs|klausel convertibility clause; ~recht (Anleihe) right of conversion; ~wert (Lebensversicherung) paid-up value.

umwechseln to change, to exchange.

Umwechslungskurs rate of exchange.

Umwelt|einflüsse (Anlagegeschäft) investment environment; ~schäden environmental damage; ~verschmutzung environmental pollution.

Umzug shift, change of residence, remove (Br.), removal [of furniture], move (US).

Umzugs|anzeige notice off removal; ~beihilfe moving allowance; ~gewerbe household-moving industry; ~kosten removal expenses; ~kostenbeihilfe removal allowance (Br.), transfer allowance (US); ~spediteur remover, moving man (US).

unabhängig independent, self-reliant, on one's own; wirtschaftlich ~ autarchic, autonomous, self-supporting; finanziell ~ sein to be of independent means.

unabkömmlich nonvailable, indispensable, (mil.) exempt from military service, deferred.

Unabkömmlichkeit, berufliche occupational deferment.

unablösbare Rente irredeemable (perpetual) annuity.

unangemeldetes Vermögen property not returned.

unausgefülltes | Formular blank form; ~ Wechselformular skeleton bill.

un|ausgeglichen (Etat) unbalanced, out of balance;

~ **bearbeitet** natural, in the native state, raw *(US),* unmanufactured, unfinished.

unbebaut *(Feld)* uncultivated, *(Gelände)* unimproved, *(Grundstück)* vacant; ~**e und bebaute Grundstücke** *(Bilanz)* real estate.

unbedingte Verpflichtung absolute liability.

unbefugt unauthorized, incompetent; ~**es Betreten eines Grundstücks** trespass.

Unbefugten ist der Eintritt verboten no admittance except on business.

un|beglichen *(Rechnung)* unsettled, unpaid; ~**behobene Dividende** unclaimed dividend; ~**belastet** *(Grundstück)* clear, unembarrased, *(Haus)* unmortgaged; ~**bemittelt** without means; ~**benutzt** *(Kapital)* unemployed, dormant, idle; ~**unberechtigte Entlassung** wrongful dismissal; ~**beschadet irgendwelcher Ansprüche** without prejudice to any claims; ~**beschädigt** not damaged, sound.

unbeschränkt|es Eigentumsrecht absolute ownership; ~**e Vollmacht** unlimited power, blank check (cheque, *Br.*).

unbeständig *(Markt)* unsteady, unsettled.

un|bestätigtes Akkreditiv unconfirmed letter of credit; ~**bestellbar** undeliverable, *(Brief)* unclaimed; ~**bewegliches Vermögen** real property, realty; ~**bewertet** *(nicht steuerlich abgeschätzt)* unassessed.

unbezahlt unsettled, not settled, unsatisfied; ~**e Rechnungen** outstanding bills; ~**er Urlaub** leave without pay.

un|brauchbar *(Maschine)* unserviceable; ~**deklariert** *(Zoll)* unentered, undeclared.

unein|bringlicher Verlust irretrievable loss; ~**geschränkt** unreserved, entire, all-out, *(Revisionsvermerk)* unqualified; ~**heitlich sein** *(Börse)* to make an irregular showing.

unentgeltlich gratis, gratuitous, free of charge, without return (consideration, remuneration); ~**e Beratung** free consultation; ~**er Vertrag** gratuitous contract; ~**er Verwahrer** gratuitous bailee; ~**e Zuwendung** free gift, transfer payment *(US).*

unerlaubte | Gewinne illicit profits; ~ **Handlung begehen** to commit a tort.

uner|ledigt|e Aufträge backlog of orders, unfilled orders; ~**schlossen** *(Gelände)* undeveloped; ~**schwingliche Kosten** enormous costs; ~**warteter Gewinn** windfall profit.

Unfall accident, casualty, misadventure; **außerdienstlicher** ~ off-the-job accident; ~ **mit Arbeitsausfall** lost-time accident; ~**innerhalb der Arbeitszeit** on-the-job (industrial, occupational) accident.

Unfall|anfälligkeit accident proneness; ~**anzeige** notification of an accident, *(bei Versicherung)* immediate notice; ~**entschädigung** accident benefit (indemnity), *(Arbeiter)* workers' *(US)* (workmen's, *Br.)* compensation.

unfall|freier Fahrrekord spotless accident record; ~**gefährdet** accident-prone.

Unfall|haftpflicht der Arbeitgeber employers' liability; ~**haftpflichtversicherung** third-party accident insurance *(Br.),* casualty insurance *(US);* ~**meldung** accident report; ~**rente** accident (injury, *Br.)* benefit; ~**schaden** accident damage; ~**station** ambulance station, first-aid post (station), casualty ward; ~**tod** casualty, death by misadventure; ~**verhütung** accident prevention; ~**versicherung** accident insurance.

Unfallversicherungs|gesellschaft provident society; ~**gesetz** workmen's compensation law *(Br.);* ~**leistung** accident benefit, *(Arbeiter)* compensation.

Unfall|zeitverlust accident severity; **freiwillige** ~**zulage** accident benefit; ~**zusatzversicherung** double indemnity clause.

un|frankiert unstamped, [postage] unpaid, without prepayment, *(Fracht)* carriage forward *(Br.);* ~**förmig** *(sperrig)* bulky; ~**gebundener Preis** free price.

ungedeckt|er Kredit insecured credit; ~**e Notenausgabe** fiduciary limit (issue, *Br.);* ~**er Scheck** rubber check *(US),* bouncing cheque *(Br.);* ~**er Wechsel** uncovered note, kite *(Br.).*

ungefährer Kostenüberschlag rough estimate.

ungelernter Arbeiter unskilled workman.

ungemünztes Edelmetall bullion.

ungenannter Auftraggeber undisclosed principal.

ungenügende Deckung insufficient funds.

ungeordnete Verhältnisse scattered finances.

ungesichertes Darlehen unsecured (personal) loan.

ungültig invalid, [null and] void, cancelled; **Garantieversprechen für** ~ **erklären** to rescind a guaranty; **Scheck durch Streichungen** ~ **machen** to obliterate the writing of a check *(US)* (cheque); ~**es Akkreditiv** invalid letter of credit.

Ungültigkeitsvereinbarung backletters *(US).*

Universalversicherung all-in (comprehensive) insurance, *(Auto)* all-risks policy.

Unkosten cost[s], expenses, expenditure, charges; **abzüglich** ~ less charges; **abzugsfähige** ~ permissible expenses; **allgemeine** ~ overhead [charges], factory overhead, cost, burden, oncost *(Br.);* **entstandene** ~ expenses accrued; **laufende** ~ current expense, running costs; **steigende** ~ rising costs; ~ **der Fabrikation** work-in-process burden *(US);* ~ **abwälzen** to pass costs on; ~ **aufschlüsseln** to break down expenses; ~ **bestreiten** to defray the expense; ~**niedrig halten** to control the expenditure; **sich in** ~ **stürzen** to launch out [into expense]; ~ **auf die Vereinsmitglieder umlegen** to assess members of a society for expenses; ~ **über drei Jahre verteilen** to amortize costs over a period of three years.

Unkosten|anteil cost (overhead) rate; ~**aufgliederung** expense classification; ~**aufteilung** burden adjustment; ~**beitrag** contribution to the expenses; ~**berechnung** cost accounting, costing; ~**erstattung** reimbursement of expenses; ~**faktor** expense (cost) factor; ~**konto belasten** to charge to expense; ~**schätzung** estimated cost.

unkulant unaccommodating.

unkündbar irrevocable, binding, *(Anleihe)* irredeemable, *(Hypothek)* not to be foreclosed, *(Rente)* perpetual;
~**e Stellung** permanent appointment.

unlauterer Wettbewerb unfair [methods of] competition, unreasonable restraint of trade.

unlustig *(Börse)* dull, slack, dead, flat.

unmittelbar | haftbar sein to be personally (individually, primarily) liable;
~**er Arbeitsaufwand** direct labo(u)r costs; ~**er Materialaufwand** direct material costs.

unnotierte Werte securities not quoted (listed, *US*) on the stock exchange.

un|organisierter Streik wildcat strike; ~**pfändbar** exempt [from execution], privileged from distress; ~**pünktliche Zahlungen** irregular payments; ~**rentabel** unprofitable, unremunerative, not paying.

unrichtig | adressieren to misdirect;
~**e Angaben** *(Versicherung)* misrepresentations.

un|sachgemäße Lagerung careless storage; ~**schädlich** *(Industrie)* innoxious.

unselbständige | Arbeit wagework; ~ **Erwerbsperson** salary (wage) earner.

unsichere Kapitalanlage insecure investment.

unsichtbare Reserven hidden (latent, secret) reserves.

unsolide | Finanzverhältnisse unsound finances; ~ **Firma** unreliable firm.

unter | dem Strich *(Bilanz)* below the line; ~ **Tag** underground; ~ **der Hand verkaufen** to sell privately.

Unter|beteiligung subpartnership; ~**bewertung** underestimation, undervaluation, depreciation.

unterbieten to undersell, to undercut, *(Auktion)* to underbid, *(Weltmarkt)* to dump;
j. preislich ~ to cut s. one's prices.

Unterbilanz adverse (short) balance.

unterbrechen, Verjährung to interrupt prescription, to toll the statute of limitations *(US)*.

Unterbrechung der Handelsbeziehungen interruption of the flow of commerce.

unterbringen, Anliehe zum Kurs von 98 % to place a loan at 98 per cent; **am offenen Markt** ~ to sell in the open market; **j. in einer Stellung** ~ to find a situation for s. o.; **Wechsel** ~ to discount a bill.

Unterbringung *(Anleihe)* negotiation, placement; ~ **in Werkswohnungen** company housing.

Unterdrückung von Vermögenswerten concealment of assets.

unterentwickelte Gebiete underdeveloped areas.

Untergang *(Schiff)* shipwreck;
~ **von Sachen** destruction of goods.

untergebracht, fest *(Börse)* digested.

untergehen *(Forderungen, Rechte)* to extinguish, *(Schiff)* to sink, to founder;
mit der gesamten Besatzung ~ to be lost with all hands; **durch Vermischung** ~ to merge.

untergeordnet|er Angestellter nonpolicy-making

funtionary, subordinate officer; ~**e Dienste** inferior services.

Untergewicht short (shortage in) weight, underweight.

Unterhalt maintenance, support, subsistence, sustenance, sufficiency, livelihood, living, keep, *(an geschiedene Ehefrau)* alimony;
notdürftiger ~ bare necessaries of life;
~ **bei Getrenntleben** separate maintenance;
~ **gewähren** to provide maintenance, *(Ehefrau)* to pay alimony; ~ **für seine Familie sicherstellen** to support one's family.

unterhalten to maintain, to support, to keep, *(Betrieb)* to operate;
Bankkonto bei jem. ~ to bank with s. o.; **Filiale** ~ to maintain a branch; **Gebäude** ~ to keep a building in repair; **Geschäftsbeziehungen** ~ to entertain business connections;
aus öffentlichen Mitteln ~ **werden** to be maintained at public expense, to live on the parish (town, *US*);

Unterhalts|anspruch right of support, *(Ehefrau)* claim of (right to) alimony, *(Kind)* maintenance claim; ~**beihilfe** subsistence (maintenance) allowance (grant); ~**berechtigter** dependant, beneficiary; ~**kosten** living expenses, *(Betrieb)* maintenance charges; ~**leistung** maintenance allowance *(an getrennt lebende Ehefrau)* separate maintenance *(US)*, alimony.

unterhaltspflichtig liable to maintain (support).

Unterhalts|zahlung alimony (support) payment; ~**zusage** maintenance bond; ~**zuschuß** living allowance, subsistence [money], maintenance grant.

Unterhaltung *(Betrieb)* maintenance, *(Unterstützung)* maintenance, support, upkeep;
~ **von Gebäuden** building maintenance.

Unterhaltungs|aufwand current maintenance; ~**industrie** show business; ~**kosten** maintenance cost (expense); ~**teil** *(Zeitung)* feuilleton, column *(US)*.

unterkapitalisiert undercapitalized, low geared.

Unterkommen accommodation, lodging.

Unterkunft lodging, place, bed, accommodation; **einschließlich ~ und Verpflegung** found *(US)*.

Unterlage *(Aufzeichnung)* record, *(Beleg)* voucher.

Unterlagen data, information, material, *(Urkunden)* [supporting] documents, records, dossier;
einem Bericht beigefügte ~ documents joined to a report; **buchungstechnische** ~ bookkeeping records; **technische** ~ technical data;
~ **aufbewahren** to keep one's records; **keine ~ haben** to have nothing to go upon.

Unterlagenprüfung voucher audit.

unterlassen *(Wettbewerb)* to cease and desist *(US)*.

Unterlassung omission, forbearance, failure, neglect, nonperformance, *(jur.)* default;
fahrlässige ~ passive negligence *(US)*.

Unterlieferant subcontractor, little master.

unterliegen, der Verjährung to be barred by the statute of limitations.

Unter|lizenznehmer sublicensee; ~**mieter** lettee, subtenant, lodger, roomer *(US)*.

Unternehmen enterprise, establishment, firm, concern, outfit, business, business undertaking;
beherrschtes ~ controlled company (concern); **selbständig bilanzierendes** ~ accounting entity; **fortschrittliches** ~ forward-looking company; **breit gefächertes** ~ diversified corporation; **gemeinnütziges** ~ public institution, nonprofit corporation (enterprise); **gemischtwirtschaftliches** ~ quasi-public corporation; **gewerbliches** ~ manufacturing (commercial) establishment; **gewerkschaftseigenes** ~ union enterprise; **gewinnbringendes** ~ profitable enterprise, paying concern; **konzessioniertes** ~ licensed undertaking; **marktbeherrschendes** ~ monopoly enterprise; **mittleres** ~ mediumsized business;
~ **mit breit gestreuten Absatzmärkten** multimarket company; ~ **im Eigentum der Arbeitnehmer** employee-owned corporation; ~ **der öffentlichen Hand** publicly-owned enterprise;
~ **aufgeben** to shut the books; **sich an einem neugegründeten** ~ **beteiligen** to embark on a new business undertaking; **Kapitalmehrheit in einem** ~ **erwerben** to acquire a controlling interest in a concern; ~ **leiten** to control an undertaking, to conduct a (manage the) business; **an einem** ~ **finanziell nicht beteiligt sein** to have no money interest in a concern; **sein ganzes Geld in ein** ~ **stecken** to sink all one's money in a concern.
unternehmen, Stützungsaktion *(Börse)* to rescue (hold) the market.
Unternehmens|berater management counsel(l)or (consultant); ~**beratung** management consulting firm; ~**formen des Handelsrechts** business organization; ~**forschung** operations *(US)* (operational, *Br.)* research; ~**leitung** company's (top executive, *US)* management; ~**zweck** object of an enterprise.
Unternehmer entrepreneur, contractor, industrialist, owner;
selbständiger ~ private trader, independent contractor;
~**funktionen** managerial (entrepreneurial) functions; ~**garantie** contract bond; ~**gewinn** producer's rent, producer profit; ~**haftpflicht- und Sachschadenversicherung** contractors' (manufacturers') public liability and property damage liability insurance.
unternehmerisch enterprising, managerial, managemental, entrepreneurial;
~**es Risiko** entrepreneurial (business) venture.
Unternehmer|kaution contract bond; ~**tätigkeit** entrepreneurial activity; **freies** ~**tum** free-enterprise industry; ~**verband** contractor association; ~**wagnis** business hazard, entrepreneurial business risk; ~**wirtschaft** enterprise economy *(US)*.
Unter|pacht subtenancy, sublease; ~**pariausgabe** inferior issue, issue below par; ~**schied zwischen Einkaufs- und Verkaufspreis** margin.
unterschiedliche | Behandlung discriminating treatment; ~ **Sätze** differential rates.

unterschlagen to embezzle, to defalcate, to misappropriate, to peculate.
Unterschlagung embezzlement, constructive (legal) fraud, fraudulent conversion;
~ **von Bankgeldern** abstraction of bank funds; ~ **von Briefen** interception of letters; ~ **eines Testaments** suppression of a will.
unterschreiben to sign [one's name], to undersign, to subscribe, to make one's mark;
blanko ~ to sign a blank document.
unterschrieben, ordnungsgemäß duly signed.
Unterschrift signature, hand, subscription;
laut meiner ~ witness my own hand; ~ **unbekannt** signature unknown; ~ **unvollständig** incompletely signed;
gefälschte ~ forged (fictitious) signature; ~ **als Stellvertreter** proxy signature;
seine ~ **anerkennen** to acknowledge one's signature; ~ **beglaubigen** to attest the signature of a document.
Unterschriften|karthotek signature card file; ~**liste** signature book; ~**mappe** blotting book.
Unterschrifts|beglaubigung attestation (verification) of signature; ~**berechtigter** authorized signer; ~**probe** facsimile (specimen) signature; ~**stempel** facsimile signature.
unterstehen, unmittelbar dem Vorstand to report directly to the board of directors.
unterstützen to [give] support, to back, to help, *(begünstigen)* to favo(u)r, to patronize, to patron, to nourish, *(fördern)* to further, to promote, *(Wohlfahrt)* to relieve;
Antrag ~ to second (support, carry, speak in support of) a motion; **Bewerber** ~ to back a candidate; **mit staatlichen Zuschüssen** ~ to subsidize, to subvention, to subventionize.
unterstützt, staatlich government, sponsored, statefed, bounty-fed;
finanziell ~ **werden** to receive financial support.
Unterstützung support, *(Förderung)* furtherance, patronization, boost, *(Sozialversicherungsleistung)* benefit;
auf städtische ~ **angewiesen** on the parish (town, *US)*; **mit kommunaler** ~ rate-aided;
finanzielle ~ pecuniary assistance, financial help (backing), *(durch kommunale Stellen)* municipal aid; **öffentliche** ~ pauper relief, public welfare (aid), outdoor relief;
~ **eines Bewerbers** backing up of a candidate; **werbliche** ~ **des Händlers** dealer-aid advertising; ~ **bei der Wohnungsbeschaffung** subsidized housing; **seine Freunde um finanzielle** ~ **angehen** to lay one's friends under contribution; ~ **beziehen** to obtain (receive) state relief; **mit der vollen** ~ **eines Ausschusses rechnen können** to be solid with a committee; **auf öffentliche** ~ **angewiesen sein** to be thrown upon the parish (on the town, *US)*, to be a public charge.
Unterstützungsanspruch *(Angehöriger)* right of support, *(Fürsorgeempfänger)* claim for benefit.

unterstützungs|bedürftig needy, poor; ~berechtigt eligible (entitled) for relief, relievable. Unterstützungs|berechtigter pauper *(US)*, rate-aided person; ~fonds aid (sustentation, benefit, benevolent) fund; ~kasse provident (charity) fund, *(Fürsorge)* relief (public, poor) fund; ~leistungen *(Fürsorge)* benefits, *(Sozialversicherung)* social security contributions; ~programm aid (relief) program(me); ~zahlungen maintenance payments, grants, allowances; ~zeitraum benefit period, *(Betriebsunfall)* compensation period.

Untersuchung investigation, inquiry, inspection, quest, *(Abhandlung)* treatise, paper; betriebswissenschaftliche ~ industrial research; stichprobenartige ~ accidental sampling; ~ von Verbrauchergewohnheiten habit survey; Kassierer während der ~ beurlauben to suspend a cashier pending investigation.

Untertage|arbeiter underground worker; ~bau underground mining (working).

untervermieten to sublease, to sublet, to underlet.

Untervermieter sublessor, subletter, underlessor.

unterversichern to underinsure.

Unter|versicherung underinsurance; ~vollmacht substitute power, subagency.

unterwegs on the way (go, *US*), *(Güter)* in transit, *(Vertreter)* on tour, en route; geschäftlich ~ on the road; Drittel des Jahres ~ sein to be on the road about a third of the time.

unterzeichnen to sign, to undersign, to subscribe, *(Versicherungspolice)* to underwrite; blanko ~ to sign in blank; Vertrag ~ to sign an agreement.

Unterzeichner subscriber, *(Effektenemission)* underwriter; ~staat signatory power, signatory *(Br.)*.

un|tilgbar *(Anleihe)* irredeemable, *(Rente)* perpetual, ~übertragbar unassignable, inalienable, non-transferable; ~veränderliche Kosten constant costs.

unverändert *(Börse)* unchanged, firm; ziemlich ~ schließen *(Börse)* to leave off without material alteration.

un|verbraucht *(Kredit)* unconsumed; ~verjährbar imprescriptible; ~verjährt still valid.

unverkäufliche Ladenhüter drug on (in) the market.

un|vermietet untenanted, unlet, unoccupied, vacant, void; ~verpackt unpacked, in bulk, bulk, loose;

~versichert uninsured, unassured, uncovered; ~versteuert duty off (unpaid); ~verteilter Reingewinn undistributed net profit, unappropriated earned surplus *(US)*; ~verwendete Etatsmittel unexpended appropriation; ~verwertbar unsalable, unrealizable; ~verzinsliches Darlehen free loan; ~verzollt duty off (not paid), unpaid, unentered, *(unter Zollverschluß)* bonded, in bond; ~vorteilhaftes Geschäft losing bargain; ~widerrufliches Akkreditiv irrevocable letter of credit; ~wirtschaftlich uneconomical, unproductive, unthrifty, wasteful; ~zulängliche Mittel inadequate means; ~zulässige Bevorzugung von Konkursgläubigern preference of one debtor over the others; ~zustellbarer Brief dead letter.

Urabstimmung *(Lohnkämpfe)* ballot (strike) vote.

Urheberrechtsschutz copyright protection.

Urkunde *(Beleg)* record, voucher, *(Beweisurkunde)* written instrument, writing, title deed, *(Dokument)* document, deed, copy, paper, certificate; begebbare ~ negotiable instrument; öffentliche (öffentlich-rechtliche) ~ official document; ~ aufsetzen to engross a document; ~ hinterlegen to place an instrument in escrow.

Urkunden|fälschung falsification of documents; ~stempel documentary (deed) stamp.

urkundlich belegen to support by documents.

Urlaub holiday, leave, vacation *(US)*; bezahlter ~ paid holiday (vacation, *US*); genehmigter ~ leave of absence; noch zustehender ~ terminal leave; um einen dreitägigen ~ bitten to put in for three days' leave (holiday); jedesmal um seinen ~ kommen to be done out of one's leave every time; ~ verlängern to extend a leave.

Urlauber holidaymaker, vacationer *(US)*.

Urlaubs|abgeltung vacation allowance *(US)*; ~anspruch vacation privilege (right) *(US)*; durchschnittliche ~dauer average length of a holiday; ~geld leave (holiday, vacation, *US*) pay; ~gesuch vacation request *(US)*; ~liste leave book; ~vertretung holiday replacement *(Br.)*, vacation replacement *(US)*; ~zeit holiday season (time), vacation period *(US)*.

Ursprungs|bezeichnung informative labelling; ~land country of origin; ~zeugnis certificate of origin.

Usancen, kaufmännische usage of trade, custom of merchants.

V

validieren to validate, to make valid.

Valorenversicherung registered mail insurance *(US).*

Valuta *(Devisen)* foreign exchange, *(Devisenkurs)* exchange rate, *(Hypothek)* mortgage money, *(Währung)* [monetary] standard, *(Wertstellung)* value (availability, *US)* date;
  ausländische ~ foreign currency (exchange); ~**abschluß** currency transaction; ~**forderung** currency claim; ~**guthaben** *(Bilanz)* balances with foreign bankers; ~**klausel** currency (value-given) clause; ~**kredit** foreign currency loan; ~**notierung** quotation of [foreign] exchange [rates]; ~**risiko** exchange risk; ~**schuld** currency claim.

valuta|schwaches Land soft-currency country; ~**starkes Land** hard-currency country.

valutieren, Buchungsposten to fix the value of an entry.

variabel notiert werden to be quoted consecutively.

variabl|e Kosten variable expenses (cost); ~**e Notierung** consecutive quotation.

Verächtlichmachung der Konkurrenz disparagement of competitors.

veraltet antiquated, obsolete, old-fashioned, superannuated, out-of-use (-date).

veränderlich|es Agio fluctuating premium; ~**e Kosten** running (variable) costs.

verändern, sich to drop one's work.

Veränderung *(Börse)* turn, fluctuation; **geringfügige** ~**en** *(Kurs)* fractional changes; ~**en im Vorstand** management changes.

veranlagen to assess, to rate; **sich getrennt** ~ **lassen** to file separate returns; **zur Vermögenssteuer** ~ to assess property for taxation.

veranlagte Einkommensteuer assessed (individual, *US)* income tax.

Veranlagung assessment, taxation, rating; **gemeinsame** ~ *(Ehegatten)* joint return; **getrennte** ~ separate assessment, splitting *(US);* ~ **zur Einkommensteuer** assessment of income tax, *(sofortige wegen befürchteten Steuerausfalls)* jeopardy assessment.

Veranlagungs|bescheid tax assessment; ~**jahr** year of assessment, taxable year; ~**pflicht begründen** to make taxable.

veranlagungspflichtig ratable, assessable, taxable, subject to taxation.

Veranlagungs|richtlinien assessment directives; ~**stelle** tax assessor, taxation authority, special commissioner *(Br.);* ~**zeitraum** period of assessment.

veranschlagen to [make an] estimate, to appraise, to evaluate, *(bewerten)* to value, to rate; **hoch** ~ to value at a high rate *(US);* **zu niedrig** ~ to underrate.

veranschlagt|er Betrag estimated amount; ~**e Kosten** estimated cost; ~**e Zuschüsse** budgeted provisions.

Veranschlagung der Baukosten building estimate.

verantwortlicher Teilhaber general (associated) partner.

Verantwortungsbereich area of responsibility.

verarbeiten to process into, to convert, to finish.

verarbeitende Industrie processing (finishing) industry.

Verarbeitung processing, finishing, manufacturing, manufacture, conversion.

Verarbeitungs|betrieb processing plant; ~**genehmigung** processing permit; ~**industrie** processing (finishing) industry; ~**stufe** processing stage.

Veräußerer seller, disposer, alienor, alienator.

veräußerlich salable, alienable.

veräußern to alienate, to dispose of, to sell.

Veräußerung von Grundbesitz mobilization, conveyance of real estate.

Veräußerungs|befugnis power of sale; ~**beschränkung** *(Grundbesitz)* restriction *(Br.);* ~**genehmigung** sales permit; ~**gewinn** sales profit; ~**verbot** restraint on alienation (on anticipation, *US).*

Verband association, federation, organization; **gemeinnütziger** ~ public utility; ~ **der Europäischen Landwirtschaft** European Confederation of Agriculture; ~ **der Steuerzahler** National Tax Association *(US);* **sich einem** ~ **anschließen** to affiliate with an association.

Verbands|abkommen association agreement; ~**land** convention country; ~**mitglied** syndicate (trade) member; ~**organ** trade paper *(Br.);* ~**priorität** convention priority.

verbessern, sich *(Kurse)* to improve, to experience an advance, *(Markt)* to look up; **sich finanziell** ~ to get a raise *(Br.)* (rise, *US);* **sich um 3 Punkte** ~ *(Kurs)* to gain 3 points.

Verbesserung progress, advance, improvement, *(Berichtigung)* correction, rectification, *(Grundstück)* improvement, betterment; ~ **des Lebensstandards** rise in the standard of living; ~ **im Pfundkurs** improvement in sterling exchange.

Verbesserungsinvestition capital deepening.

verbilligte Fahrkarte cheap (reduced, reduced-rate, *Br.)* ticket.

Verbilligung der Geldmarktsätze cheapening of money.

verbindlich binding, obligatory, mandatory *(US).*

Verbindlichkeit obligation, liability, engagement; **ohne** ~ without prejudice, *(Giro)* without recourse.

Verbindlichkeiten indebtedness, liabilities, *(Bilanz)* debts due, creditors, accounts payable *(US),* payables *(US);* **ausstehende** ~ outstanding liabilities; **befristete** ~ time liabilities; **sofort fällige** ~ sight liabilities; **kurzfristige** ~ short-term liabilities (obligations); **langfristige** ~ long-term (fixed) liabilities; **rück-**

lagepflichtige ~ liabilities subject to reserve requirements;
~ gegenüber Banken *(Bilanz)* accounts due to banks; ~ aus Depositenkonten deposit liabilities; ~ aus Giroverpflichtungen liablities on account of endorsements; ~ aus noch nicht eingelösten Wechseln liabilities upon bills, bills payable *(US)*; kurzfristige ~ abdecken to meet short-term liabilities; seinen ~ nachkommen to pay one's way, to meet one's obligation; seinen ~ nicht nachkommen to make default.

Verbindung relation, connexion *(Br.)*, connection *(US)*, *(Personenvereinigung)* association, society, *(pol.)*;
direkte ~ *(Bahn)* direct communication; durchgehende ~ *(Bahn)* through connection;
~ von Warenzeichen association of trademarks; geschäftliche ~ mit einer Firma aufnehmen to open up a business connection with a firm.

Verbindungs|ausschuß liaison committee; ~stelle liaison office.

Verbrauch consumption, expenditure;
gewerblicher ~ industrial consumption; sparsamer ~ *(Auto)* economy run;
~ pro Kopf per-capita consumption;
~ steigern to predispose (increase) consumption.

verbrauchen to consume, to use up, *(abnutzen)* to wear [out], *(ausgeben)* to spend, to expend; viel Öl ~ *(Motor)* to be heavy on oil.

Verbraucher consumer, user, expender;
gewerblicher ~ business (industrial) user;
Lohnkostenerhöhung auf die ~ abwälzen to pass increased labo(u)r costs on to consumers;
~analyse consumer research; ~aufnahmebereitschaft propensity to consume; ~ausschuß panel of consumers; ~bewußt consumer-conscious; ~erzeugnis consumer product; ~genossenschaft consumer cooperative; ~gewohnheiten consumer (buying) habits; ~index consumer price index; ~konjunktur consumer prosperity; ~markt consumption market; ~nachfrage consumer purchasing (demand); ~preis consumer[s'] price, price to consumers; ~schaft consuming public, usership; ländliche ~schaft agricultural clientele; ~schutz consumer protection; ~umfrage consumer survey; ~verhalten consumer behavio(u)r; ~wünsche consumer wants (desires); ~zeitschrift consumer magazine.

Verbrauchs|artikel articles of consumption; ~gewohnheiten consuming habits.

Verbrauchsgüter consumption (consumer, convenience *US*, current) goods, goods of the first order;
kurzlebige ~ soft (nondurable consumer) goods; ~industrie consumption goods industry.

Verbrauchs|land consuming country; ~lenkung consumption control; ~rückgang decreased (decrease, cut in) consumption; ~steigerung induced (increase in) consumption; ~steuer consumption (indirect) tax, use tax *(US)*.

verbrauchssteuerpflichtig excisable.

Verbrauchs|werbung consumer advertising; ~wirtschaft consumer economics.

verbriefte | Forderung bonded debt; ~ Rechte vested rights.

verbuchen to post, to book, to enter, to record;
als Ausgabe (Betrag über Handlungsunkosten) ~ to enter an amount in the expenditure; neuen Höchstkurs ~ to reach (register, establish) a new high, to rise into new high ground *(US)*; Kursverbesserung ~ to secure an advance; jeden Posten einzeln ~ to post each entry singly; auf Reservekonto ~ to put to reserve.

Verbuchungsdatum value (availability, *US*) date.

verbundene | Kosten composite cost; ~ Leben *(Lebensversicherung)* joint lives; ~ Warenzeichen associated trademarks.

Verbundwirtschaft integrated economy, vertical trust, *(el.)* compound arrangement.

Verderb spoilage, decay, ruin, deterioration.

verderblich injurious, destructive, perishable.

verdienen to earn, to gain, to get, to make, to win;
sein Brot ehrlich ~ to turn an honest penny; viel Geld ~ to earn big money; seinen Lebensunterhalt ~ to make a living; netto 10 000 £ jährlich ~ to clear ten thousand a year.

Verdienst *(Gewinn)* gain, profit, gains, gainings, makings, *(Lohneinkommen)* earnings, wages; mein ganzer ~ all I make by it.

Verdienst|ausfall broken time, loss of trade; ~spanne profit margin; kaufmännische ~spanne dealer markup.

verdingen, sich to engage o. s. [as a servant], to go into (enter, take) service, to bind o. s..

verdeltes Erzeugnis finished product.

Veredelung finishing, processing, refining, improvement, aging.

Veredelungs|betrieb processing (finishing) plant; ~industrie processing (finishing, refining) industry; ~kosten processing expenses; ~stufe processing stage.

Verein, eingetragener registered (incorporated, *US*) society, membership corporation *(US)*.

vereinbaren to agree, to come to an agreement;
Bedingungen ~ to stipulate conditions; Gehalt ~ to appoint a salary; Preis ~ to agree about a price; vierteljährliche Zahlungen ~ to stipulate that the payment should be quarterly.

vereinbart|er Preis price agreed upon; ~e Schiedsgerichtsbarkeit voluntary arbitration; ~er Zolltarif conventional tariff.

Vereinbarung agreement, arrangement, stipulation, settlement, memorandum;
aufgrund mündlicher ~ by parol; mangels ~ failing agreement;
entgegenstehende ~en agreements not in accordance with; lockere ~ *(Firmen)* loose combination *(US)*; stillschweigende ~ implicit (silent, tacit) agreement;
~ über die Freistellung von Schadensersatzver-

verpflichtungen hold-harmless agreement; ~ **einer Konventionalstrafe** penal bond; ~ **über die Zahlungsmodalitäten** stipulations of payment; ~ **bestätigen** to confirm an agreement; **schriftliche** ~ **treffen** to enter into a written agreement.

Vereinigung *(Körperschaft)* body, corporation, *(Verein)* association, society, club; **gemeinnützige** ~ nonprofit corporation.

vereinzelte Geschäfte casual (spasmodic) transactions.

Verfahren *(Arbeitsvorgang)* operation, *(Gericht)* procedure, proceeding(s), process, suit at law *(US)*, *(Herstellung)* process, treatment, technique; **kostspieliges** ~ costly proceeding; **patentfähiges** ~ patentable process; **sich einem schiedsrichterlichen** ~ **unterwerfen** to submit to arbitration.

Verfall *(Anspruch)* lapse, forfeiture, *(Fälligwerden)* maturity, *(Gebäude)* dilapidation, decay, *(Hypothek)* foreclosure, *(Pfand)* forfeiture; **bei** ~ **zahlbar** payable at expiration (maturity); **Wechsel bei** ~ **einlösen** to hono(u)r a bill when due; **vor** ~ **zahlen** to pay (make payments) in advance, to pay in anticipation.

Verfall|buch debt book, maturity tickler *(US)*, tickler diary *(Br.)*; **datum** *(Ablaufdatum)* expiring date, *(Fälligkeit)* due (maturity) date.

verfallen *(Fahrkarte)* to expire, *(fällig sein)* to be due, *(fällig werden)* to become (fall) due, *(Optionsrecht, Versicherungspolice)* to expire, *(Pfand)* to become forfeited; ~ *(a.)* *(abgelaufen)* expired, lapsed, *(fällig)* matured, due, overdue, *(Haus)* decayed, dilapidated, *(Hypothek)* foreclosed, *(Patent)* void, *(Pfand)* forfeited; **Kaution** ~ **lassen** to forfeit a bond; **Patent** ~ **lassen** to drop (abandon) a patent.

Verfallsklausel acceleration clause; ~**liste** aging schedule; ~**tag** date of expiration (expiry); ~**zeit** time of payment, *(Wechsel)* maturity.

Verflechtung, produktionsmäßige interlocking arrangements of production.

Verflüssigungspolitik *(Geldmarkt)* policy of active ease.

verfrachten to freight, to charter, to ship *(US)*.

Verfrachter freighter, carrier, forwarding agent.

Verfrachtung freighting, freightage, forwarding, shipping *(US)*, *(Schiff)* charter;

verfügbar available, disposable, on tap; **am Platz** ~ delivery spot; ~**es Bargeld** cash in hand; **frei** ~**es Einkommen** disposable income.

verfügen to dispose, *(anordnen)* to arrange, to direct, *(Behörde)* to order, to decree; **über einen Betrag bei jem.** ~ to draw value on s. o. for an account; **über große Kapitalbeträge** ~ to have large capital at one's disposal; **letztwillig** ~ to make one's will; **j. über ein Konto** ~ **lassen** to authorize s. o. to operate on an account.

Verfügung disposition, disposal, *(Anordnung)* direction, regulation, provision, act, mandate; **auf Grund gerichtlicher** ~ by order of the court; **im Wege letztwilliger** ~ by will; **einstweilige** ~ restraining order, interim (provisional, temporary, *US)* injunction; **ministerielle** ~ departmental order; ~ **von hoher Hand** restraint of princes and rulers; **einstweilige** ~ **beantragen** to file an application (ask for, seek) an injunction; **jem. finanziell zur** ~ **stehen** to put one's purse at s. one's disposal; **ohne letztwillige** ~ **zu hinterlassen sterben** to die intestate.

verfügungsberechtigt entitled (authorized) to dispose.

Verfügungs|recht disposing capacity (mind), *(Abhebungsbefugnis)* drawing right, *(Veräußerungsrecht)* power of sale; ~**verbot** restraint on alienation, *(gerichtliche Verfügung)* restraining order *(US)*.

Vergabe |von Aufträgen placing of orders; ~ **öffentlicher Aufträge** awarding of contracts; ~ **im Submissionswege** allocation by tenders. ~**verfahren** bidding (contract-awarding) procedure.

vergeben, Auftrag to place an order.

Vergebung von Arbeiten und Lieferungen letting of works and supplies.

Vergesellschaftung municiplaization, *(Verstaatlichung)* communization, socialization, nationalization *(Br.)*.

Vergleich settlement, composition, compromise, reorganization *(US)*; **mit den Konkursgläubigern abgeschlossener** ~ composition in bankruptcy; **außergerichtlicher** ~ out-of-court composition (settlement); **mit seinen Gläubigern einen** ~ **abschließen** to compound (compose) with one's creditors.

vergleichen to compare, *(schlichten)* to settle, to adjust; **sich** ~ to compromise, to compound with, to come to an arrangement (terms); **sich außergerichtlich** ~ to settle an affair out of court; **Kontoauszug** ~ to audit an abstract of account; **postenweise** ~ *(Buchführung)* to prick up items.

Vergleichs|antrag reorganization petition *(US)*, *petition for arrangement;* ~**bilanz** liquidating balance sheet; ~**ordnung** Insolvent Law, Insolvency Laws, Deed of Arrangement Act *(Br.)*; ~ **und Sanierungsverfahren** insolvency (equity, composition, reorganization, *US)* proceedings; ~**verfahren beantragen** to file a petition for an arrangement (Chapter X proceedings, *US)*; ~**verwalter** estate manager, reorganization trustee *(US)*; ~**vorschlag** proposal for a settlement.

vergleichsweise Forderungsbefriedigung compounding of claims.

Vergnügungs|dampfer cruise ship, cruiser; ~**fahrt** joy (thrill) ride, junket; ~**industrie** entertainment industry.

vergreifen, sich an anvertrautem Geld to embezzle

trust funds; **sich an der Kasse** ~ to tamper with the cash.

vergrößern, sein Geschäft to expand one's business.

Vergünstigung *(Erlaubnis)* permit, permission, licence, indulgence, *(Ermäßigung)* allowance, abtement, *(Vorteil)* benefit, advantage, *(Vorzugsbehandlung)* preferential treatment; **betriebliche ~en** fringe benefits; **steuerliche** ~ tax privilege.

vergüten to remunerate, to pay; **jds. Auslagen** ~ to reimburse s. o. for his costs; **Schaden** ~ to make amends; **für Tara** ~ to allow for tare.

Vergütung remuneration, payment, requital, *(besondere Bezüge)* emoluments, fringe, perquisites *(Br.)*, *(Honorar)* fee; **angemessene** ~ fair and reasonable compensation; ~ **für leitende Angestellte** executive compensation (bonus); ~ **für schnelle Entladung** dispatch money; ~ **von Spesen** reimbursement of charges; ~ **für Tara gewähren** to make allowance for the tare.

Verhalten, aufeinander abgestimmtes *(Kartellrecht)* quasi agreement; **gleichartiges** ~ *(Kartellrecht)* conscious parallelism *(US)*; **standeswidriges** ~ malpractice, professional misconduct; **unzumutbares** ~ **des Mieters** misconduct of a tenant.

Verhältnis relation[ship], condition, *(Quote)* quota, dividend, *(Vergleich)* proportion, rate; **im** ~ **1 : 2** *(Bezug neuer Aktien)* in the proportion of one new share against every two old shares held; **vertragsähnliches** ~ quasi-contractual realtionship; ~ **der Aktiva zu den Passiva** equity ratio; ~ **der finanziellen Mittel** financial ratio; ~ **von Nettoumsatz zu Betriebskapital** working-capital turnover; ~ **zwischen Umlaufvermögen und kurzfristigen Schulden** current ratio; **nach dem** ~ **beitragen** to contribute proportionally; **nach dem** ~ **der Beträge kürzen** to reduce pro rata.

verhältnismäßiger Anteil comparative (proportional) share.

Verhältnisse *(persönliche Lage)* situation, *(Vermögenslage)* status, circumstances; **aus kleinen ~n** from a humble cottage; **in guten ~n** of good position, well circumstanced; **unter den derzeitigen steuerlichen ~n** with taxes as they now are; **in bedrängten ~n leben** to live in close quarters, to be in straitened (narrow) circumstances; **über seine** ~ **leben** to live (above) one's means, *(fam.)* to outrun the constable.

verhandeln to confer, to hold a conference, to negotiate; **über einen Tarifvertrag** ~ to bargain collectively.

Verhandlung counsel, deliberation, conference, talk; **bevorstehende ~en** forthcoming negotiations; **~en über eine Anleihe** negotiations for a loan.

Verhandlungs|angebot bargaining offer; **~basis** ne-

gotiation basis; **~delegation** negotiating group; **~gegenstände** [items on the] agenda; **~leitung** übernehmen to assume the chair; **~protokoll** minute book; **~spielraum** negotiating room, *(Tarifverhandlungen)* bargaining room; **am ~tisch vertreten sein** to have representatives at the bargaining table; **~vollmacht** power to negotiate, *(Tarif)* bargaining power.

verheimlichen, ausländische Vermögenswerte to conceal foreign assets.

verjähren to become barred by the statute of limitations (statute-barred).

verjährt prespective, statute-barred; **~e Forderung** barred (unenforceable, outlawed, US) claim.

Verjährung statute of limitations; ~ **ausschließen** to bar prescription; ~ **unterbrechen** to toll *(US)* (save) the statute of limitations.

Verjährungs|bestimmungen statutory limitations; **~zeitraum** statutory period, period of limitations.

Verkauf sale, selling, vending, disposal; **zum** ~ for sale, on the market; **freihändiger** ~ voluntary (private) sale *(Effekten)* sale in the open market; **langsamer** ~ *(Börse)* dull sales; ~ **auf Abzahlungsbasis** instal(l)ment sale, hire purchase *(Br.)*, deferred-payment sale *(US)*; ~ **auf Baisse** bear sale (selling, *Br.)*, short sale *(US)*, going short *(US)*; ~ **in Bausch und Bogen** sale in gross (by the bulk); ~ **ohne Deckung** uncovered sale, [selling] short *(US)*; ~ **unter Eigentumsvorbehalt** executory (conditional) sale; ~ **zwecks GEwinnrealisierung** profit-taking sale; ~ **auf Grund übersandten Katalogs** catalog(ue) (mail order, *US)* sale; ~ **über den Ladentisch** over-thecounter sale; ~ **auf Lieferung** *(Börse)* forward sale, sale for forward (future, *US)* delivery; ~ **am offenen Markt**sale by sample (to pattern); ~ **durch Postversand** direct-mail selling *(US)*; ~ **zur Probe** sale on approval; ~ **mit Rückgaberecht** sale and return; ~ **unter Selbstkosten** selling below cost price; ~ **am Sonntag** Sunday trading; ~ **wie es steht und liegt** sale with all faults; ~ **unter Vorbehalt** conditional sales contract; ~ **unter dem Wert** sacrifice sale; ~ **ab Zollager** sale ex bond; ~ **ohne Zwischenhandel** direct selling, sale to the market; ~ **abschließen** to effect (negotiate) a sale; **zum** ~ **anbieten** to put up for sale; ~ **rückgängig machen** to rescind a sale; **zum** ~ **angeboten sein** to be in the market.

Verkäufe selling, *(Börse)* sales, transactions; **vereinzelte** ~ scattered sellings; ~ **gegen sofortige Kasse und Lieferung** spot trading *(US)*; ~ **zum Selbstkostenpreis** marginal sales; ~ **gut (glatt) aufnehmen** to take sales well; **seine** ~ **über eine Hausseperiode verteilen** to sell on a slice.

verkaufen to sell, to dispose, to vend, to value, *(absetzen)* to market, *(Börse)* to unload, to negotiate, *(Verkäufer sein)* to be behind the counter; **nicht zu** ~ *(Effekten)* not to float; **zu** ~ for (on) sale, *(Anzeige)* to be sold;

mit Abschlag ~ to sell at reduced prices; **gegen bar** ~ to sell for cash (ready money); **möglichst billig** ~ to go as low as possible; **blanko (ohne Deckung)** ~ to go to bear *(Br.)* (short, *US);* **im Freiverkehr** ~ to sell on the street (over the counter, *US);* **mit Gewinn** ~ to sell at a profit (premium, to advantage); **Ernte auf dem Halm** ~ to sell the crop standing; **auf Kommissionsbasis** ~ to sell on commission; **lastenfrei** ~ to sell free from encumbrances; **meistbietend** ~ to sell to the highest bidder; **nach modernsten Methoden** ~ to streamline one's sales representation; **an der Nachbörse** ~ to sell on the street (kerb market, *Br.);* **in kleinen Partien** ~ to sell in dribs and drabs; **zu einem festen Preis** ~ to sell outright; **mit Rabatt** ~ to sell at a reduction; **im Ramsch** ~ to sell as a job lot; **gegen Sicherheitsleistung** ~ *(Effektendifferenzgeschäft)* to sell on margin; **mit Verlust** ~ to [sell at a] sacrific; **Effekten mit Verlust** ~ to slaughter stocks; **unter Wert** ~ to sell below cost price;

sich schlecht ~ **lassen** to come to a bad market.
Verkäufer seller, vendor, vender, bargainer, *(Angestellter)* salesman, shop assistant, sales clerk *(US),* *(Einzelhändler)* retailer;
hochqualifizierter ~ high-cost-(powered) salesman;
zusätzliche ~ **einstellen** to hire extra sales people; **der geborene** ~ **sein** to be a born salesman.
Verkäufer|markt seller's market; **~schulung** sales meeting.
verkäuflich salable, vendible, on (for) sale, *(absatzfähig)* marketable, merchantable, *(Börse)* on offer; **frei** ~ free on sale; **leicht** ~ easy to sell; **schwer** ~ **sein** to go off slowly;
Verkaufs|abrechnung *(Kommissionär)* account sales *(US);* **~aktion** sales representation; **~angebot** sales offer; **~anreiz** pull, selling appeal; **seine** ~**anstrengungen verstärken** to beef up one's sales operations; **~argumente** selling points, sales talk; **teurer** ~**artikel** big ticket; **~auftrag an mehrere Grundstücksmakler** open listing *(US);* **~ausrüstung** sales kit *(US);* **~bude** stand, stall, sales booth, concession stand; **~datum** date sold *(US);* **hervorragende** ~**ergebnisse** sales records; **~erlös** proceeds of sale; **~feldzug** selling campaign; **betriebseigene** ~**filiale** manufacturer's own shop (outlet); **~förderung** sales promotion; **~mittel** point-of-purchase display; **~gebiet** sales area, trading (selling) territory; **~gesichtspunkt** sales approach (angle); **~hilfe** selling (display, dealer) aid; **~katalog** sale catalog(ue); **~kommission** commission; **~kommissionär** selling agent, factor; **~-, Verwaltungs- und allgemeine Kosten** *(Bilanz)* administrative and general selling expenses *(US);* **werkseigener** ~**laden** own (industrial) retail store (shop); **~lager** stock, depot; **~leiter** sales executive (supervisor), director of sales; **anschauliche** ~**methode** direct-to-point selling; **unaufdringliche** ~**methode** low-pressure selling; **~monopol** sales monopoly; **~- und Kundendienstnetz** sales and service forces; **~niederlassung**

sales branch; **Kauf- und** ~**orders zu verschiedenen Zeiten geben** *(Börse)* to scale *(US);* **~pavillon** kiosk, display stand; **~politik** merchandising (sales, selling) policy; **aggressive** ~**politik** hard (high-pressure) selling; **unfaire** ~**praktiken** unfair salesmanship.
Verkaufspreis sales (selling, disposal) price *(Börse)* asked (selling, realization) price, *(für Investmentanteile)* offering price;
vom Hersteller festgesetzte ~e prices laid down by the manufacturer;
~ **ab Fabrik** manufacturer's sales price;
~ **für ein Grundstück festsetzen** to price a property;
sich den ~ **eines Hauses vorhalten** to put a reserve price on a house.
Verkaufs|programm, globales overall selling plan; **sein** ~**programm darauf abstellen** to tailor one's sales representation; **~provision** selling brokerage, commission, *(Kapitalanlagegesellschaft)* underwriting provision; **fingierte** ~**rechnung** proforma account sales; **~schlager** big seller, article of quick sale, hit *(US);* **~spanne** margin on sales; **~stand** stall, stand, sales booth; **~stelle** sales agency (outlet), *(Einzelhandel)* retail outlet; **~stunden** selling (shopping) hours; **~technik** salesmanship; **~tisch für Sonderangebote** bargain counter; **feste** ~**tourneen festlegen** to build regular routes; **bildliche** ~**unterstützung** visual aid; **~vertrag** agreement for sale, sales contract; **~wettbewerb** sales contest; **~wirkung** sale; **~woche** white sale.
verkauft sold, disposed of;
freihändig ~ over the counter; **unter der Hand** ~ at private sale.
Verkehr traffic, *(Bahn)* service, *(Beförderung)* transport, transportation *(US), (Börse)* trading, market, doing, dealings, *(Handel)* trade, commerce, *(Umsätze)* business, dealings;
für den öffentlichen ~ **freigegeben** open to the public; **im freien** ~ *(Börse)* on the curb (kerb, *Br.)* market, in outside (unofficial, *Br.)* trading; **bargeldloser** ~ clearing system; **lebhafter** ~ *(Börse)* lively dealings;
Waren aus dem Zollager zum freien ~ **abfertigen** to withdraw goods from warehouse for consumptions; **Effekten in** ~ **bringen** to issue (market, *US)* securities; **in den freien** ~ **überführen** *(Zollwaren)* to enter into the channels of distribution; **Obligationen aus dem** ~ **ziehen** to retire bonds.
verkehren *(Bahn, Bus)* to go, to run, to ply, to be operated, *(Handel treiben)* to trade, to traffic.
Verkehrs|abkommen traffic arrangement; **~ampel** traffic lights, beacon *(Br.);* **~bedürfnisse** traffic requirements, transportation needs; **~betrieb** transport service, transportation; **~einnahmen** traffic receipts.
verkehrsfähig marketable, *(begebbar)* negotiable.
Verkehrs|flughafen [commercial] airport; **~flugzeug** airliner, transporter, commercial plane; **~gesellschaft** transit company, transportation agency *(US).*

verkehrsgünstig gelgen in a desirable location.
Verkehrs|hypothek common-law mortgage; **~insel** safety island (isle), street (traffic) island; **~kreisel** rotary; **~minister** Minister of Transport *(Br.)*, Transportation Minister *(US)*; **~ministerium** Ministry of Transport *(Br.)*, Transportation Department *(US)*.
Verkehrsmittel vehicle, [means of] communication, conveyance;
öffentliches ~ public (transit) vehicle, public conveyance, transportation *(US)*.
Verkehrs|netz communications (road) system *(Br.)*, transportation network *(US)*; **~polizist** traffic policeman (constable, officer, cop); **~regelung** [road] traffic control.
verkehrsreiche Straße congested street.
Verkehrs|schild traffic (highway) sign; **≗schwache Zeit** slack period, off-peak hours; **~spitze** peak hours.
verkehrsstarke Zeit rush (heavy, *US*) hours, busy (peak) period.
Verkehrs|statistik traffic return (statistics); **~stau-[ung]** traffic jam (tangle, holdup, block), block in the traffic; **~strafe** traffic fine; **~streife** traffic (courtesy) patrol, traffic squad, cruiser *US)*; **~teilnehmer** road user; **~träger** carrier; **~übertretung** driving (motoring) offence; **~umleitung** diversion of traffic *(Br.)*, detour *(US)*.
verkehrsunfähig unmarketable, *(nicht begebbar)* nonnegotiable.
Verkehrs|unfall street (road) accident; **öffentliches ~unternehmen** public transport company, common carrier *(US)*; **~verstopfung** tie-up *(US)*, traffic jam (tangle, holdup); **~wacht** scout [car], *(ADAC)* Automobile Association patrol.
Verkehrsweg, öffentlicher public highway (thoroughfare); **~werbung** tourist advertising; **~wert** market (sound, salable, trade, attached-business) value; **~wirtschaft** transport economics, transportation industry; **~zählung** traffic census; **~zeichen** traffic signal (beacon, *Br.*, post, sign); **schwache ~zeit** slack hours; **starke ~zeit** rush hours.
verklagen, wegen Nichterfüllung eines Vertrages to sue for nonperformance.
Verklarung ship's (extended) protest.
Verknappung shortage, scarcity, shortcoming;
~ an Arbeitskräften labo(u)r shortage; **~ am Geldmarkt** money stringency.
verkürzen, Arbeitszeit to shorten one's working time;
Legat ~ to abate a legacy.
verkürzt curtailed, *(Rente)*, curtate;
~e Arbeitszeit part-time employment.
Verkürzung, der Arbeitszeit shortening of working hours.
Verlade|anlage loading plant; **~aufseher** loading officer; **~bahnhof** loading station; **~gebühr** loading (shipping, *US*) charges; **~hafen** loading (lading, shipping, *US*) port; **~liste** freight list, shipping note *US)*.

verladen to lade, to load, to freight, to embark, to ship *(US)*, *(versenden)* to consign;
auf Deck ~ to ship on deck; **lose ~** to ship in bulk; **Stückgüter ~** to load in (freight by) parcels.
Verlade|ort place of loading, loading place (point); **~rampe** loading platform; **~schein** bill of lading; **~vorschrift** loading pamphlet; **~zeit** loading days.
Verladung loading, lading, *(Versendung)* consignment, shipping *(US)*;
~ mehrerer Stückgutladungen multiple loading.
verlagern to displace, *(Betrieb)* to evacuate, to remove, to dislocate, *(Industrie)* to relocate; **Aufträge ~** to shift orders.
Verlagerung evacuation, removal, dislocation; **~ einer Industrie** relocation of an industry.
Verlags|geschäft publishing trade (business); **~katalog** list of publications; **~preis** publishing price.
Verlangen, auf by request, on demand (on application); **auf ~ zahlen** to pay on demand.
verlängern, Abonnement to renew a subscription; **Paß ~** to renew a passport; **Zahlungsfrist ~** to grant a respite.
Verlängerung | der Abgabefrist filing extension; **~ eines Mietvertrages** renewal of a lease; **~ seines Urlaubs** extension of one's holidays (leave); **~en zum Satz von 2 % tätigen** to put through renewals at 2 per cent.
Verlängerungs|antrag application for renewal; **~frist** period of extension; **~police** renewal policy; **~prämie** renewal premium; **~stück** *(Wechsel)* allonge; **~zettel** rider.
verlangsamen, Konjunktur to slow down the economy.
Verlangsamung des Preisanstiegs price slow-down.
verlegen *(Geschäft)* to relocate, to dislocate; **Bankinstitut ~** to transfer a bank; **Sitzung ~** to adjourn (postpone) a meeting; **seinen Wohnsitz ~** to change one's address, to shift one's quarters.
Verleih, Film für den ~ freigeben to release a film.
verleihen to lend, to loan, to let out, to rent; **Geld auf Zinsen ~** to lend money at interest.
Verleihfirma *(Film)* catering firm.
verletzen, jds. Interessen to injure (interfere with) s. one's interests; **Vertrag ~** to break (violate) a contract.
Verletzung | der vorvertraglichen Anzeigepflicht *(Versicherung)* nondisclosure; **~ des Berufsgeheimnisses** breaking of professional secrecy; **~ der Unterhaltspflicht** wilful neglect to provide reasonable maintenance *(Br.)*; **~ von Warenzeichenrechten** infringement of trademarks; **~ einer vertraglichen Zusicherung** breach of warranty.
verlorener Zuschuß lost contribution.
verlosen to allot, to draw by lot, to lot out, to cast lots, *(Wertpapiere)* to raffle.
Verlosung lottery, allotment, prize drawing.
Verlust loss, sacrifice, *(Abgang)* wastage, *(Defizit)* deficit, red, *(Konfiskation)* forfeiture, *(Leckage)* leakage, *(Nachteil)* disadvantage, detriment, *(Schaden)* damage, detriment, cost;

bei Eintritt eines ~es in the event of a loss; nach Abschreibung aller ~e after charging off all losses; steuerlich abzugsfähiger ~ deductible loss; buchmäßiger ~ accounting (book) loss; von der Versicherung voll gedeckter ~ loss fully covered by insurance;

Gewinn und ~ profit and loss;

~ der Arbeitskraft der Ehefrau loss of services of the spouse *(Br.)*; ~ aus zweifelhaften Forderungen bad-debt losses *(US)*, loss from doubtful debts *(Br.)*; ~ aus Kursschwankungen exchange loss; ~ an Zeit und Lohn broken time; ~ in Höhe des Zeitwertes [des versicherten Gegenstandes] actual loss;

mit ~ abschließen to show (result in) a loss; mit ~ arbeiten to operate (run) at a loss; ~e auffangen to absorb losses; j. für einen ~ entschädigen to indemnify (compensate) s. o. for a loss; ~e an der Börse erleiden to meet with losses on the stock exchange; ~e durch Börsenspekulationen wieder hereinholen to recoup one's losses in gaining on the stock market; am ~ beteiligt sein to participate in a loss; jds. ~e übernehmen to reimburse s. o. for his losses; mit ~ verkaufen to sell at a loss (discount, sacrifice); ~e gleichmäßig über ein Jahr verteilen to apportion losses evenly over a year.

Verlust|abschluß *(Bilanz)* balance sheet that shows a deficit, deficiency statement *(US)*; ~anrechnung *(Einkommensteuer)* loss relief; ~anzeige *(Versicherung)* immediate notice; ~artikel loss leader; ~ausgleich *(Einkommensteuer)* carryback *(US)*; ~betrieb plant working with a deficit, money-losing operation; ~eintragung red-ink entry; wirtschaftliches ~gebiet deficit area; steuerliches ~geschäft tax-loss selling; ~höhe amount of loss; ~kalkulation estimable loss; Gewinn- und ~konto revenue (profit and loss) account; ~nachweis proof of loss; Gewinn- und ~rechnung profit and loss account (statement); Gewinn- und ~rechnung in Staffelform report form; ~rücktrag *(Einkommensteuer)* carryback *(US)*; ~verkauf ruinous (sacrifice, losing) sale; ~vortrag *(Einkommensteuererklärung)* carryover, debt balance (loss, *Br.)* carried forward; ~zahlen loss figures; betriebsbedingte ~zeit delay (down, *US)* time; plötzlich in die ~zone geraten to spurt (plunge) into red ink.

Vermächtnis|kürzung abatement of legacy; ~nehmer legatee.

Vermerk note, notice, notation, mention, memorandum, *(Buchung)* entry.

vermessen, Grundstück to survey.

vermieten to let [out to tenants (on hire)], to let on (put out to) lease, to lease [out], to hire out;

Haus ~ to rent a house; Zimmer ~ to take in lodgers, to let rooms;

bezugsfertig zu ~ to be let with immediate possession.

Vermieter und Mieter landlord and tenant.

Vermieterpfandrecht lessor's warrant.

vermietet rented, leased, let, hired, for hire.

Vermietung | der Ausrüstung equipment leasing;

~ von Schrankfächern safe-deposit facilities; ~ von Zimmern letting of rooms.

Vermietungsgeschäft flat-letting business, rental deal.

vermindern to diminish, to lessen, *(beeinträchtigen)* to impair, *(beschränken)* to curtail;

seine Ausgaben ~ to retrench one's expenses.

Verminderung der Gewinnspanne profit squeeze.

Vermischtes *(Zeitung)* miscellaneous.

Vermittler middleman, mediator, intermediator, intermediary, intermeddler, go-between, *(Anleihen)* negotiator, *(Makler)* broker;

~ verbeten *(Zeitung)* only principals will be dealt with.

Vermittlung mediation, intermediation, intercession, interposition, interagency, *(Telefon)* telephone exchange, operator;

mit freundlicher ~ through the kind offices;

~ einer Anleihe negotiation of a loan.

Vermittlungs|ausschuß mediation (arbitration) committee; ~gebühr commission, *(Bank)* service charge, *(Makler)* brokerage; ~geschäft agency business, brokerage.

Vermögen property, fortune, *(Aktiva)* assets, *(Gesellschaft)* treasury, *(Kapital)* funds, means, *(Reichtum)* wealth, riches, money, substance; abgesondertes ~ *(Ehefrau)* separate property; anmeldepflichtiges ~ property to be reported; beschlagnahmtes ~ confiscated property; bewegliches ~ personal chattels (property), goods and chattels; gesperrtes ~ blocked property; kein nennenswertes ~ no property worth mentioning; persönliches ~ private property, *(Gemeinschuldner)* personal assets; pfändungsfreies ~ exempt (unattachable) property; unbewegliches ~ landed (immovable, *US)* property; zweckgebundenes ~ restricted property;

~ der öffentlichen Hand social wealth;

sein ~ angreifen to make a dent in one's fortune; sein ~ aufzehren to get through one's fortune; gesamtes ~ beschlagnahmen to levy on the entire property; sein ganzes ~ für wohltätige Zwecke bestimmen to dispose of one's fortune in charity; sein ~ flüssigmachen to realize one's property; eigenes kleines ~ haben to have a little independence of one's own; mit seinem ganzen ~ haften to be liable without limitation; gut von seinem ~ leben können to have plenty to live upon; jds. ~ auf ... taxieren to rate s. one's fortune at ...; sein ~ auf seine Gläubiger übertragen to surrender one's goods to one's creditors; ~ vergeuden to dilapidate (run through) a fortune; jem. ein ~ vermachen to will a fortune upon s. o.; sein verlorenes ~ wiederbekommen to recover one's fallen fortunes.

vermögend rich, wealthy, well-off, moneyed, possessed of property, opulent, well-to-do *(Br.)*.

Vermögensabgabe capital (property) levy.

Vermögensanlage investment of one's capital;

~ in Industriewerten industrial investment.

Vermögens|anmeldung declaration of property; ~anteil proprietary (ownership) interest; ~aufstellung property statement, statement of assets and liabilities; **~auseinandersetzung** partition of an estate; ~berater property finance consultant; **~beschlagnahme** seizure (attachment) of property; **~bilanz** *(Gemeinschuldner)* statement of affairs; ~bildung accumulation of capital; **~erklärung** property statement; **~freigabe** release of property; ~lage financial condition (position), pecuniary circumstances; **~masse** *(Konkurs)* assets of a bankrupt's estate, *(Nachlaß)* estate; **~regelung** property settlement; ~rückgabe restitution of property.

Vermögenssteuer tax on capital, wealth tax; **~ auf bewegliches Vermögen** personal property tax *(US);* **~ auf Grundbesitz** general property tax *(US);* **~ auf Kapitalvermögen** capital-stock tax; ~erklärung listing of property for taxation.

Vermögens|stück portion of property, asset; **testierfähiger (frei verfügbarer) ~teil** disposable portion of property; ~übertragung alienation (assignment, transfer) of property; **~verfügung** disposal of property.

Vermögensverhältnisse pecuniary circumstances; **gute ~** good (flourishing, easy) circumstances, good position; **zerrüttete ~** decayed (broken) fortune; **seine ~ offenbaren** *(Gemeinschuldner)* to discover one's assets.

Vermögens|verlust pecuniary loss; ~verschiebung *(Gemeinschuldner)* fraudulent alienation; **~verschleierung** concealment of assets; ~verwalter estate manager, receiver, fund adminsitrator (manager), *(Kapitalanlagegesellschaft)* portfolio manager.

Vermögensverwaltung administration (custody, management) of property; **ausländische ~** alien property custodian *(US);* **~ anordnen** to appoint an adminstrator.

Vermögensvorteil capital gain, pecuniary benefit.

Vermögenswerte assets, effects, resources *(coll.),* property holdings; **abschreibungsfähige ~** depreciable property; **aussonderungsfähige ~** equitable assets; **blockierte ~** frozen assets; **kurzfristig realisierbare ~** liquid strength; **zweckgebundene ~** earmarked assets; ~ flüssigmachen to realize assets.

vermögenswirksame Leistung property-creating performance.

Vernachlässigung | notwendiger Gebäudereparaturen permissive waste; **~ der Unterhaltspflicht** wilful neglect of reasonable maintenance *(Br.),* nonsupport *(US).*

Veröffentlichung *(Ankündigung)* announcement, *(Anzeige)* advertisement, insertion, *(Buch)* publication, published work, *(Pressenotiz)* release; **nicht zur ~ bestimmt** off the record *(US);* **~ von Informationsmaterial** information disclosure.

Veröffentlichungs|datum *(Presse)* release date; **~rechte in Zeitschriften** magazine rights.

Verordnung decree, order, ordinance, enactment,

(Vorschrift) institute, regulation, rule, provision, directive.

Verordnungsblatt official gazette.

verpachten to let [out to tenants], to let on (put out to, grant a) lease.

Verpächter lessor, leaser, locator *(US),* landlord.

Verpachtung von Industrieanlagen plant leasing.

verpacken to pack, to package, to wrap up.

verpackt, seemäßig packed for exportation by sea; **lose oder ~** loose or in packages.

Verpackung package, packaging, packing; **~ wird besonders berechnet** packing extra; **~ wird nicht berechnet** no charge is made for packing; **mangelhafte ~** defective (insufficient) packing; **verlorene ~** nonreturnable packing, one-trip container *(US).*

Verpackungs|bestimmungen packaging regulations; ~betrieb packing plant; **~gewicht** tare; ~leinwand balecloth; **schlechter ~zustand** bad (poor) packing.

verpfänden to [put in] pawn, to pledge, to put in pledge, to bond, to gage, to hock, to pop *(Br.).*

verpfändete | Gegenstände pledged chattel; **als Sicherheit ~e Wertpapiere** pledged securities, pawned stock *(US),* collateral securities *(US).*

Verpfändung pawn, pawnage, pawning, pledge; **~ von Sicherheiten** pledging of securities.

Verpfändungsurkunde bond, *(Hypothek)* mortgage deed, *(Warenrembours)* letter of hypothecation.

Verpflegung board, keep, subsistence; **freie ~ und Wohnung** free food and accommodation.

Verpflegungsgeld allowance for board, meal allowance.

verpflichtet, zum Schadenersatz liable to respond in damage; **vertraglich ~ sein** to be under contract.

Verpflichtung obligation, liability, bond, responsibility, commitment, engagement, sponsion; **finanzielle ~** commitment; **gesamtschuldnerische ~** joint and several liability; **~ eingehen** to incur a liability.

Verpflichtungen, geschäftliche business commitments; **kurzfristige ~** current liabilities; **langfristige ~** long-term obligations; **~ aus abgetretenen Debitoren** accounts receivable discounted *(US);* **~ der Kundschaft** customers' liabilities; **~ aus diskontierten Wechseln** contingent liability on account of endorsements on bills discounted; **seinen ~ nicht nachkommen** to fail to meet one's obligations (commitments); **finanzielle ~ übernehmen** to enter into pecuniary obligations.

Verpflichtungs|erklärung bond, undertaking; ~schein surety bond.

verplant budgeted; **noch nicht ausgegebene, jedoch ~e Etatsmittel** unexpended appropriations.

verrechnen *(im Clearingwege abrechnen)* to clear, *(ausgleichen)* to balance, *(in Gegenrechnung bringen)* to compensate, to set off *(Br.),* to offset *(US);*

jeden Posten ~ to put to account every single item.

Verrechnung settlement, *(Buchung)* placing to account, *(Gegenrechnung)* compensation, setoff *(Br.)* offset *(US)*, *(im Verrechnungswege)* clearing.

Verrechnungs|abkommen clearing (offset, *US*) agreement; ~**bank** clearinghouse agent (bank); ~**geschäft** *(im Konzern)* intercompany operation; ~**guthaben** clearing balance; ~**kasse** clearing fund; ~**land** agreement (clearing) country; ~**preis** internal (intercompany) price; **nicht übertragbarer** ~**scheck** clearinghouse (nonnegotiable) check *(US)*, crossed cheque *(Br.)*, voucher check *(US)*; ~**system** clearing system; ~**währung** agreement currency; ~**wert** trade-in-value.

verreist, geschäftlich away on business.

verringern, Ausgaben to cut down expenses.

Verringerung | des **Geschäftsvolumens** business contraction, ~ des **Personalbestands** reduction in (axe of, *Br.)* staff.

Versammlung assembly, meeting, gathering, convention;
Resolution in einer ~ **einbringen** to bring up a conclusion at a meeting.

Versammlungs|leiter conference leader; ~**raum** assembly (common) room.

Versand forwarding, dispatch, dispatching, shipment *(US)*, shipping *(US)*, *(durch Post)* posting *(Br.)*, mailing *(US)*;
sofortiger ~ prompt forwarding; **verzögerter** ~ delay in dispatch;
~ **per Bahn** dispatch (delivery, transport) by rail; ~ **ab Fabrik** factory shipment; ~ **auf eigene Rechnung** shipped on consignment *(US)*;
als Stückgüter zum ~ **bringen** to ship in carloads *(US)*.

Versand|abteilung delivery (forwarding) department; ~**anschrift** forwarding address; ~**anzeige** dispatch *(Br.)* (consignment, receiving) note; ~**bahnhof** forwarding (dispatch) station; ~**behälter** shipping container *(US)*; ~**betrieb** shipment operation, dispatch [service].

versandfertig ready for dispatch (shipment, *US*).

Versand|gebühren mailing expenses *(US)*, forwarding (shipping, *US*) charges; ~**geschäft** catalog(ue) (mail-order, *US*) sale, direct-mail selling, mail-order business *(US)*; ~**hafen** lading (shipping) port; ~**handel** catalog(ue) sale, direct-mail selling.

Versandhaus catalog(ue) house, mail-order firm (house);
~**betrieb** catalog(ue) distribution plant; ~**katalog** trade (mail-order) catalog(ue).

Versandkosten forwarding (mailing, dispatch, transport) expenses, shipping costs (expenses, charges) *(US)*;
niedrige ~ low-cost transportation *(US)*.

Versand|lager catalog(ue) distribution plant; ~**liste** packing (freight) list, shipping bill *(US)*; ~**muster** shipping sample *(US)*; ~**papiere** shipping documents (papers) *(US)*; ~**prospekt ohne Umschlag**

selfmailer *(US)*; ~**rechnung** expense (shipping, *US*, shipment, *US*) invoice; ~**spesen** forwarding expenses (charges); ~**tasche** American envelope; ~**vorschriften** forwarding (shipping, *US*) instructions.

verschachteln to pyramid, *(Kapital)* to interlock.

Verschachtelung pyramiding, interlocking;
~ des **Aktienkapitals** interlocking stock ownership.

verschaffen, Deckung to provide for payment; **Geld** ~ to raise funds.

Verschiebe|bahnhof marshalling yard; ~**gleis** shunting track.

verschiedene Schuldbeträge *(Bilanz)* sundry moneys owing.

verschiffen to ship, to freight, to send by water.

Verschiffung shipping, shipment, water carriage.

Verschiffungs|anzeige advice of shipment; **zahlbar gegen Aushändigung der** ~**dokumente** payable against surrender of shipping documents.

Verschlechterung der Kaufkraft deterioration of purchasing value of money.

verschleiern, Bilanz to cook (doctor, fake, tamper with) a balance sheet.

verschleierte Vermögenswerte concealed assets.

Verschleiß attrition, wear and tear, deterioration.

verschleudern to undersell, to sell under the value (dirt-cheap), to barter away, *(Vermögen)* to waste, to squander.

Verschluß *(Zoll)* seal, bond;
unter zollamtlichem ~ bonded, in bond.

verschlüsseln to code, to cipher, *(tel.)* to scramble.

Verschmelzung amalgamation, fusion, confusion.

Verschmutzungsschaden pollution damage.

Verschönerungsarbeiten *(Wohnung)* voluntary improvements.

verschrotten *(Schiff)* to scrap, to break up.

Verschulden, mitwirkendes contributory negligence.

verschulden, sich to run into debt, to take on debts, to run up a score *(Br.)*; **sich kurzfristig erheblich** ~ to borrow heavily on a short-term basis.

verschuldet indebted, in debt in[to] arrear[s];
bis über die Ohren ~ over head and ears in debt.

Verschuldung, kommunale indebtedness of local authorities; **langfristige** ~ fixed (long-term) indebtedness.

Verschwender waster, squanderer, dissipator, spendthrift.

verschwenderisch leben to live in lavish style.

Verschwendung waste, wastage, dissipation.

versehen, mit Akzept to provide with acceptance; **mit Deckung** ~ to furnish with cover (funds); **mit Geld** ~ to keep in money; **mit Vollmacht** ~ to invest (clothe) with power.

versenden, ins Ausland to export; **mit der Bahn** ~ to dispatch (send) goods by rail; **als Eilgut** ~ to forward by express train.

Versendung sending [off], forwarding, dispatch;
~ **von Rundschreiben** circularization.

Versendungs|kosten transport (shipping, *US*) charges; ~**ort** place of consignment.

Versetzung, innerbetriebliche interplant transfer; **turnusmäßige ~ leitender Angestellter** executive rotation; **~ in den Ruhestand** retirement.
versicherbares Interesse insurable interest.
Versicherer insurer, underwriter.
versichern to insure, to underwrite, to write; **sich mit Abkürzung auf das 70. Jahr ~** to take out an endowment policy maturing at the age of 70; **höher ~** to rate up; **zu niedrig ~** to insure below value;
sich ~ lassen to take out an insurance [policy].
versichert, unter dem Wert underinsured; **nicht gegen Havarie ~** free from average;
~e Gefahr risk subscribed.
Versicherung insurance, assurance *(Br.)*, *(Erklärung)* declaration, statement;
abgekürzte ~ term insurance; **aufgestockte ~** extended insurance; **beitragsfreie ~** paid-up insurance; **eidesstattliche ~** affidavit, statutory declaration *(Br.)*; **nicht gewinnbeteiligte ~** non-participating insurance; **~ mit ermäßigten Prämiensätzen** low-premium insurance;
~ abschließen to effect an insurance; **~ unterhalten** to carry insurance *(US)*.
Versicherungs|agent insurance broker (agent), policy broker, writer; **~alter** insured's age; **~angestellter** insurance clerk; **~anspruch** insurance claim; **~anstalt** insurance company; **~antrag** [insurance] application; **~anzeige** immediate notice; **~aufsichtsbehörde** Bureau of Old-Age and Survivors Insurance *(US)*, State Insurance Commission **allgemeine ~bedingungen** standard provisions; **~beginn** commencement of an insurance; **~beitrag** insurance premium; **~bestand** *(Versicherungsgesellschaft)* business in force; **~betrug** insurance fraud; **vorläufige ~deckung** binder; **~fall** insurance case; **~formular** insurance slip, covering form; **~geschäfte aller Art betreiben** to write all lines of insurance.
Versicherungsgesellschaft insurance company (corporation, *US*), insurers, office *(Br.)*;
~ auf Gegenseitigkeit mutual insurance corporation (office, *Br.*).
Versicherungs|gewerbe insurance trade (industry); **~höchstgrenze** line; **~inspektor** claim adjuster; **~kalkulator** actuary; **~karte** ticket; **~klausel** insurance clause; **~kosten** insurance charges (costs); **~leistung** insurance benefit (payment); **~makler** insurance (policy) broker; **~mathematiker** actuary; **~nachlaß für unfallfreies Fahren** selective driver plan *(US)*, no-claim bonus *(Br.)* **~nehmer** insured [person], assured *(Br.)*, policyholder; **~pflicht** compulsory insurance.
Versicherungspolice [insurance] policy, policy of assurance *(Br.)*;
kurzfristige ~ für ein besonderes Risiko special-risk policy; **laufende ~** floating policy; **prolongierte ~** extended-term policy;
~ aufrechterhalten to keep a policy alive; **~ erwerben** to take out an insurance policy.

Versicherungs|prämie insurance premium, rate of insurance *(US)*; **~provision** commission; **~rate** insurance instalment (rate, *US*); **~risiko** insurable risk, hazard; **~sachverständiger** claim adjuster, appraiser.
Versicherungsschaden loss;
~ aufnehmen to assess the damage.
Versicherungsschein insurance certificate, ticket; **vorläufiger ~** cover note, binder.
Versicherungsschutz insurance protection (cover-[age]);
kostenloser ~ free insurance; **zusätzlicher ~** *(Feuerversicherung)* extended coverage;
~ gegen Naturkatastrophen natural-disaster coverage.
versicherungsstatistisch actuarial.
Versicherungs|stempel plicy stamp; **~steuer** premium tax, policy duty; **erhöhte ~summe** increased limit; **~tarif** insurance rates (tariff); **~träger** insurer, assurer *(Br.)*, underwriter, insurance carrier; **~unterlagen** insurance papers; **~verein auf Gegenseitigkeit** mutal life insurance, benefit (friendly, *Br.*, benevolent, *US)* society; **~verlust** underwriting deficit; **~vertrag** insurance contract; **~vertrag abschließen** to take out a policy; **~vertreter** insurance canvasser (traveller, salesman, writer, agent); **~wirtschaft** insurance industry (business); **~zweig** insurance line (branch).
versilbern *(fam.)* to convert into cash (money).
versorgen to provide, to supply, to furnish, *(mit Lebensmitteln)* to purvey, to cater, to victual *(Br.)*;
Markt mit Waren ~ to supply the market.
Versorgung supply, supplying, furnishing, procuration, provision, *(Familienunterhalt)* maintenance, *(mit Lebensmitteln)* catering, purveyance, victualling *(Br.)*;
der öffentlichen ~ dienen to constitute a public utility.
Versorgungs|aktien public utilities; **~anspruch** claim to maintenance, *(Beamter)* pension claim.
versorgungsberechtigt entitled to maintenance, *(Beamter)* eligible for (entitled to) a pension.
Versorgungs|betrieb public utility [agency]; **~bezüge** pensionable emoluments, retirement income; **~engpaß** bottleneck in supplies; **~gebiet** supply area, *(el., Gas)* service area; **~schwierigkeiten** difficulties of supply; **öffentliches ~unternehmen** public utility company; **~wirtschaft** utility service.
verspätete Lieferung late delivery.
Verspätungszuschlag default fine.
verstaatlichen to nationalize *(Br.)*, to transfer to state ownership, to put under government control, to socialize.
Verstaatlichung nationalization *(Br.)*, socialization.
verständig|es Alter age of discretion; **~er und umsichtiger Kaufmann** reasonable and prudent businessman.
verstauen, etw. to stow s. th. away; **seine Einkäufe im Auto ~** to fill one's car with one's purchases.

versteckt|er Mangel hidden (latent) defect; **~e Reserven** secret (hidden) reserves.
Versteifung | des Geldmarktes tightening of money conditions (market), pressure in the money market; **~ der Kurse** stiffening prices.
versteigern, [öffentlich] to sell (put up) at *(US)* (by, *Br.)* auction, to sell by public sale (publicly).
Versteigerung auction [sales], auctioneering; **zur ~ anstehend** on the block; **gerichtliche ~** judicial sale *(US)*.
Versteigerungs|bedingungen terms of auction; **~erlös** proceeds of an auction; **~liste** auction bill, catalog(ue) of sale; **~saal** auction room.
verstempelt stamped.
versteuern to pay duty (taxes) on; **als Einkommen ~** to report as income.
Verstoß gegen die Betriebsordnung shop infraction.
verstümmeltes Telegramm mutilated telegram.
Versuchs|anlage research (pilot) plant; **auftrag** trial order; **~gelände** proving ground, test site; **~objekt** test object; **noch in einem ~stadium sein** to be in a tentative stage.
verteilen, Abzahlungsraten über mehrere Monate to spread instal(l)ments over several months; **Dividende ~** to declare a dividend; **Konkursmasse ~** to marshal the assets; **Verluste gleichmäßig ~** to apportion losses evenly.
Verteiler distributor, *(Gewerbe)* retail trade, dealer, *(Liste)* distribution list; **~gewerbe** distributive trade; **~netz** distribution network; **~postamt** post-distributing (-separating) office; **~schlüssel** key of distribution; **fester ~schlüssel** specified formula; **~stelle** marketing board.
Verteilung distribution, dispensation, share-out, *(Streuung)* dispersal, *(Zuteilung)* allotment, allocation, partition; **anteilsmäßige ~** pro-rata distribution; **~ der Geschäftsunkosten** overhead allocation; **~ des Gesellschaftergewinns** distribution of partnership profit; **~ eines Nachlasses** distribution of an estate; **~ des Risikos** spread of risk.
Verteilungs|apparat *(Firma)* distributive facilities; **~plan aufstellen** to marshal the assets; **~schlüssel** distribution ratio (coefficient).
verteuern to raise (increase, enhance) the price.
Vertikalkonzern vertical combination.
Vertrag contract, covenant, *(Urkunde)* deed, instrument, document, indenture; **mit Preisgleitklausel ausgestatteter ~** cost-of-living escalator contract; **objektiv unmöglich gewordener ~** frustrated contract; **notarieller ~** contract under seal; **~ zugunsten Dritter** third-party beneficiary contract; **~ mit Preisfestsetzung nach den Kosten zuzüglich Verrechnung fester Zuschläge (einer Leistungsprämie)** cost-plus-a-fixed-fee contract; **~ abschließen** to conclude (enter into) an agreement; **~ anfechten** to rescind (void) a contract; **~ bis in die kleinsten Kleinigkeiten aushandeln** to

negotiate a contract in exhausting detail; **von einem ~ zurücktreten** to recede (withdraw) from an agreement.
vertraglich verpflichtet sein to be under bond.
vertragsähnliches Verhältnis quasi-contract.
Vertrags|auslegung construction of a contract; **~bestimmungen** articles (terms) of an agreement.
vertragsbrüchig werden to break a contract.
Vertrags|haftung contractual liability; **~händler** appointed (recognized, authorized) dealer; **~land** member country; **~leistung** consideration; **~preis** contract (target) price; **~restaurant** *(Bierverlag)* tied house *(Br.)*; **~teilnehmer** party to an agreement; **~verhandlungen** contract negotiations (talks); **~verletzung** contract violation; **~währung** currency of a contract.
Vertrauen des Anlagepublikums investor confidence.
Vertrauensmann private (confidential) agent; **~ der Belegschaft** shop deputy *(US)*.
Vertrauens|posten position of trust; **~schaden** loss incurred from breach of contract; **~werbung** institutional advertising.
vertretbare Sachen fungibles, fungible things.
vertreten, j. anwaltlich to plead s. one's cause; **Firma allein ~** to be sole agent for a firm; **im Aufsichtsrat ~ sein** to be represented on the board.
Vertreter [authorized] agent, business agent, proxy, representative, attorney [in fact], *(Erfüllungsgehilfe)* vicarious agent, *(Ersatzmann)* deputy, substitute, *(einer Firma)* selling agent, factor, *(Reisender)* commercial travel(l)er, travelling salesman, drummer *(US)*, runner *(US)*; **amtlicher ~** official representative; **ordnungsgemäß bestellter ~** duly appointed agent; **gesetzlicher ~** statutory guardian; **konsularischer ~** consular agent; **~ der Anteilseignerseite** representative of ownership; **~ der Arbeitnehmerseite** labo(u)r representative; **~ ohne Vertretungsmacht** apparent (ostensible) agent; **~ abberufen** to recall an agent; **~ beschäftigen** to retain an agent; **~bericht** sales report, call slip; **~besuch** sales call; **~bezirk** sales (travelling) territory; **~tagung** sales meeting.
Vertretung agency, representation, *(Geschäft)* agency business; **in ~** by proxy, acting as deputy; **ausschließliche ~** exclusive agency; **gewinnbeteiligte ~** agency coupled with an interest; **konsularische ~** consular agency; **~ seiner Interessen** safeguarding of one's interests; **mit seiner ~ einen erfahrenen Anwalt betrauen** to trust one's affairs to an experienced lawyer; **~ einer Firma übernehmen** to accept the agency of a firm.
Vertretungsbefugnis power of attorney, authority; **außerhalb seiner ~se handeln** to act beyond the scope of one's authority (ultra vires, *Br.)*.

Vertretungsmacht [scope of] authority, power of an agent, procuration;
im Rahmen seiner ~ within one's power;
mangelnde ~ absence of authority; **scheinbare** ~ colo(u)r of (apparent, ostensible) authority, holding out;
seine ~ **überschreiten** to exceed one's power (authority).

Vertrieb sale, selling, marketing, distribution, run;
~ **landwirtschaftlicher Erzeugnisse** agricultural market;
~ **verschiedener Erzeugnisse übernehmen** to take up a line of goods.

Vertriebs|abkommen marketing agreement; ~**apparat** marketing organization (machinery); ~**bedingungen** sales terms *(US)*; ~**berater** sales consultant; ~**erfahrungen** marketing know-how; ~**fachmann** marketing specialist; ~**gebiet** sales territory; **verrechnete** ~**gemeinkosten** allocated sales overhead expenses; ~**genossenschaft** marketing association; ~**gesellschaft** trading (marketing) company, distributing agency; ~**kennzahlen** distribution indices; ~**kontrolle** sales progress (marketing) control; ~**kosten** marketing cost distribution (selling) costs; ~**leiter** sales (distribution) manager, marketing director; ~**monopol** sales monopoly; ~**produkt** marketing product; **alleiniges** ~**recht** sole right to sell; ~**wege** channels of distribution, sales channels; ~**zahlen** sales figures.

veruntreuen, öffentliche Gelder to misappropriate public funds.

Veruntreuungsversicherung fidelity insurance.

vervielfältigen *(hektographieren)* to mimeograph.

vervielfältigter Brief process letter.

Vervielfältigungsapparat duplicating machine, copying apparatus, manifold writer.

vervollständigen, sein Lager to replenish one's (lay in fresh) stock.

verwahren *(Wertpapiere)* to hold in [safe] custody.

Verwahrstück vault deposit.

Verwahrung keeping, trust, custody, bailment, charge, *(Effekten)* safekeeping, safe custody *(Br.)*, custodianship *(US)*;
unentgeltliche ~ gratuitous bailment, naked deposit.

Verwahrungs|gebühr custody fee; ~**vertrag** *(Effekten)* safe custody *(Br.)* (custodianship, *US)* contract.

verwalten to administer, to administrate, *(Betrieb)* to manage, to conduct, to direct, to operate;
Effekten ~ to assume safe custody *(Br.)* (custodianship, *US)*; **Geld** ~ to appropriate money; **Konto** ~ to carry an account; **jds. Vermögen** ~ to act as trustee for s. one's property.

Verwalter person in charge, sequester, curator, *(Nachlaß)* administrator, executor, *(Treuhänder)* trustee;
gerichtlich eingesetzter ~ judicial factor.

Verwaltung administration, *(AG)* managing board, *(Leitung)* management, dispensation, charge, conduct;

aufwendige ~ wasteful administration; **treuhänderische** ~ trusteeship;
~ **von Effekten** safe deposit keeping, custodianship *(US)*; ~ **öffentlicher Gelder** handling of public funds;
in der ~ **mitzureden haben** to have a voice in the management.

Verwaltungs|apparat administration [machinery]; ~**beirat** advisory (administrative) board; ~**gebäude** *(AG)* business premises; ~**gebühr** *(Bank)* account-carrying (administrative) charge, *(Investmentfonds)* management fee, service charge *(Br.)*; ~**gemeinkosten** administrative overhead; ~**kosten** administrative cost *(US)* (charges, expenditure, expense), handling costs; ~**rat** board of governors (directors), governing body.

Verwarnung warning, reprimand, caution *(Br.)*;
gebührenpflichtige ~ warning and fee, [parcking] ticket *(US)*.

Verwässerung des Aktienkapitals watering of stock *(US)*.

verweigern, Annahme to decline (refuse) acceptance;
Lieferung ~ to withhold delivery; **Annahme eines Wechsels** ~ to dishono(u)r a draft by nonacceptance.

verwenden to employ, to use, to dispose (make use) of, *(ausgeben)* to appropriate;
für sich ~ to take for one's own use;
Aktien als Deckung ~ to apply shares as a collateral security *(US)*; **für sich persönlich** ~ to divert to one's personal use.

Verwendung employment, application, use, utilization, *(als Anlage)* investment;
unrechtmäßige ~ misappropriation;
~ **des Gegenwertes** application of proceeds; ~ **des Gewinns** appropriation of profit (funds); ~ **im öffentlichen Interesse** public use *(US)*.

Verwendungs|nachweis statement of application of funds, source and disposition statement *(US)*; **vorgesehener** ~**zweck** intended use.

verwertbar exploitable, utilizable, *(einlösbar)* convertible, *(verkäuflich)* realizable, salable.

verwerten to make use of, to use, to employ, *(ausbeuten)* to exploit, *(auswerten)* to evaluate, *(Effekten)* to realize;
Patent ~ to work a patent;
sich gut ~ **lassen** to fetch a good price.

Verwertung *(Abfall)* salvage, recovery of waste, *(Gebrauch)* employment, use;
gewerbliche ~ industrial use;
~ **eines Patents** working a patent.

Verwertungs|klausel realization clause; ~**kosten** exploitation cost.

verzeichnen, Gewinne to record gains; **Kursgewinn** ~ to score an advance; **neuen Tiefstand** ~ to establish a new low level.

Verzeichnis register, registry, record, *(Aufstellung)* specification, schedule, *(Katalog)* catalog(ue), *(Liste)* list, file, docket, account;
~ **der Aktiva und Passiva** schedule of assets and

liabilities; ~ **der Aussteller** list of exhibitors; ~ **empfohlener Börsenwerte** list of recommendation, official list *(US);* ~ **zollfreier Gegenstände** free list; ~ **kreditfähiger Kunden** credit list; ~ **unsicherer Kunden** black book; ~ **der abzulehnenden Risiken** *(Versicherung)* decline list; ~ **nicht eingelöster Schecks** unpaid register; ~ **der Zollverschlußwaren** register of goods in bond; ~ **anlegen** to draw up (take) an inventory; **in ein ~ aufnehmen** to enter (enrol(l), put onto) a list.

Verzicht waiver, release, renunciation, relinquishment, resignation, renouncement; ~ **auf alle gegenwärtigen und zukünftigen Ansprüche** general release.

verzichten to waive, to release, to renounce, to relinquish, to resign, to abnegate; **auf eine Forderung** ~ to release a claim.

Verzicht|erklärungsformular renunciation form *(Br.);* ~leistung waiver, release, resignation, renunciation; ~**urkunde** quitclaim deed.

verzinsen, sich to yield (bear, carry) interest; **Einlagen mit 4 %** ~ to allow 4 per cent interest on deposits; **sich nicht** ~ to lie dormant.

verzinslich paying (bearing, yielding) interest; **Geld** ~ **anlegen** to put out money at interest; ~**es Kapital** interest-bearing capital; ~**e Schatzanweisungen** treasury bills *(Br.)* (bonds, *US*).

Verzinsung *(Ertrag)* interest, yield, return *(Zinssatz)* rate of interest, interest rate; **effektive** ~ net return (yield); **laufende** ~ flat (running, *Br.*) yield; ~ **des Eigenkapitals** return on net worth.

verzogen, unbekannt gone away, no address.

verzollen to pay duty on, to custom, to declare, *(Güter, Schiff)* to clear through the customs; **zu niedrig** ~ to enter short.

verzollter Wert declared value.

Verzollung customhouse entry, clearance [through the customs], payment of duties; **nachträgliche** ~ post entry; ~ **am Bestimmungsort** bonded to destination; ~ **vornehmen** to effect customs clearance; **vorläufige** ~ **vornehmen** to lodge a prime entry.

Verzollungspapiere clearance papers.

Verzug default, laches, *(Verzögerung)* delay; **mit den Leistungen in** ~ **kommen** to fail to complete within contract time.

Verzugs|kosten *(Schiff)* demurrage; ~**tage** *(Wechsel)* days of grace; ~**zinsen** accumulated (penal, default) interest.

Vetternwirtschaft nepotism, partisanship, patronage system, favo(u)ritism, spoils system *(US).*

Vierteljahres|abrechnung *(Börse)* term settlement; ~**ausweis** *(Bank)* quarterly return *(Br.).*

Visitenkarte visiting *(Br.)* (calling, *US)* card.

Visum | **ausstellen** to issue a visa; ~**gebühr** visa fee; ~**zwang aufheben** to abolish visas.

Volks|einkommen national dividend (income); ~**vermögensrechnung** national income accounting; ~**wirtschaft** national (political) economy.

volkswirtschaftlich|e Entwicklung economic process; ~**es Gesamtprodukt** gross national product; ~**e Gesamtrechnung** national income accounting.

Volkswirtschafts|lehre social (political) economy, economic science *(US),* economics; ~**theorie** pure (political) economy.

voll | **beschäftigt** fully occupied; ~ **eingezahlt** *(Kapital)* fully paid [up]; ~**e Risikoübernahme** *(Versicherung)* full risk; ~**er Satz Verschiffungspapiere** complete set of shipping documents.

Vollbeschäftigung full employment, full-time job; **vom Status der** ~ **zur Kurzarbeit übergehen** to shift from full-time schedules to part-time.

Vollbeschäftigungspolitik full employment policy (economy).

Voll|eigentümer sole and unconditonal owner; ~**giro** full (direct, *US*) indorsement.

volljährig sein to be of [full] age.

Voll|kaskoversicherung comprehensive automobile and property damage (motorcar, *Br.)* insurance; ~**konvertibilität** full convertibility.

Vollmacht power, full powers, authority, *(Urkunde)* power of attorney; **im Rahmen seiner** ~**en** within the scope of one's authority; **unbeschränkte (unumschränkte)** ~ unlimited (discretionary, full) power of attorney, plenary powers, carte blanche; ~ **unter Ausschluß des Selbstkontrahierens** power coupled with an interest; **j. mit** ~ **ausstatten** to vest (clothe) s. o. with power; ~ **für die Verhandlungen mitbringen** to be authorized to negotiate; **seine** ~**en überschreiten** to exceed one's powers.

Vollmacht|geber mandator, constituent, principal; ~**nehmer** appointee, donee, proxy, mandatary.

Vollmachts|formular mandate (authorization, proxy) form; ~**urkunde** power (letter) of attorney.

Vollständigkeitserklärung *(Vorstand für Prüfer)* liability certificate.

vollstreckbar|e Ausfertigung special execution, authority to execute a deed; ~**en Schuldtitel haben** to have a writ of execution for service.

vollstrecken, gegen einen Schuldner to distrain upon a debtor.

Vollstreckung | **wegen Mietschulden** distress for nonpayment of rent; ~ **betreiben** to levy a distraint, to enforce a judgment by execution.

Vollstreckungs|anordnung writ of execution (delivery); ~**gläubiger** execution (executing) creditor; ~**schuldner** judgment debtor.

Volontär unsalaried clerk, improver, supernumerary, apprentice, volunteer, trainee *(US).*

voran|kommen, beruflich to grow, to get along, to make one's way; **Projekt** ~**treiben** to push (promote) a scheme.

Vor|ankündigung einr Emission [red-herring, *US*] prospectus; ~**anmeldung** [previous] announcement, notice in advance, *(Patentrecht)* prior (previous) application, *(Telefon)* personal (person-to-person, *US)* call.

Voranschlag estimate, rough (preliminary) calculation;

~ **für die Lohn- und Gehaltskosten** labo(u)r [budget] estimate;

seinen ~ **überschreiten** to exceed one's estimate.

Vor|anzeige previous (advance) notice; ~**arbeiter** foreman, overseer, master mechanic.

vorausbestellen to order in advance, *(Karten)* to book in advance;

Zimmer ~ to book (reserve, *US)* rooms at a hotel.

voraus|bezahlen to pay in advance (by anticipation, *US); ~***datieren** to foredate, to antedate.

Voraus|frachten im Ortsverkehr prepaid local freights; ~**kasse** cash before delivery; ~**sage** *(Marktforschung)* forecast, forecasting.

Voraussetzung | für Unterstützungsleistungen qualification for benefits;

berufliche ~en erfüllen to qualify [o. s.] for a job; ~**en für die Gewährung einer Pension erfüllen** to be eligible for a pension.

voraussichtlich|er Bedarf potential demand; ~ **er Käufer** prospective buyer.

Vorauszahlung advance (advanced, anticipated, *US)* payment, prepayment, payment in advance.

Vorbehalt exception clause, reservation, caveat;

ohne ~ without reservation; **unter dem üblichem** ~ under the usual proviso; **unter** ~ **des Eingangs** reserving due payment; **unter** ~ **sämtlicher Rechte** all rights reserved.

vorbehalten, Regreßansprüche to reserve the right of recourse.

Vorbehalts|gut *(Ehefrau)* extradotal property, separate estate; ~**preis** reserve price.

vorbelastet sein *(Grundstück)* to carry prior encumbrances.

Vorbenutzer previous (prior) user.

Vorbereitungs|kurs preparatory course; ~**zeit** *(Produktion)* make-ready time.

vorbestellen to order (book) in advance, to make reservations *(US).*

Vorbestellung advance order, booking in advance, reservation *(US).*

vordatieren, Scheck to date a check (cheque, *Br.)* ahead, to antedate a check (cheque, *Br.).*

Vordermann predecessor, *(Wechsel)* prior (previous) endorser, preceding indorser.

Vordruck [printed] form, [application] form, blank *(US);*

~ **ausfüllen** to fill in (up, out, *US)* a form.

vorfabriziert prefabricated, prefab.

Vorfahrts|recht right of way, yield *(US);* ~**straße** major road.

vorfinanzieren to prefinance.

Vorfinanzierung preliminary (advance) financing, prefinancing.

Vorführ|gerät projection machine, projector; ~**raum** projection room; ~**wagen** demonstration car.

Vorgabe|leistung standard [performance]; ~**zeiten** *(Zeitstudie)* time standards.

Vorgang zu seinen Akten nehmen to place a report on one's files.

vorgehen *(Hypothek)* to have priority, *(Konkursforderung)* to have precedence.

vorgehender Hypothekengläubiger prior mortgagor.

vorgeschrieben|es Alter statutory age; ~**e Höhe** *(Mindestreserven)* prescribed level; ~**e Mindestreserven** fractional reserve.

Vorgriff anticipatory expenditure, anticipation; **steuerliche ~e** anticipation of tax payments.

Vorgründungsgewinn profit prior to incorporation.

Vorhaben intention, plan, design, counsel, project.

vorhanden *(auf Lager)* in (on) stock, on hand, on tap, *(auf dem Markt)* on the market, *(verfügbar)* available;

nicht ~ *(Ware)* out of stock;

nicht mehr ~ **sein** *(Firma)* to have ceased to exist; ~**es Kapital** effective capital; ~**e Vorräte** supplies on hand.

Vorherrschen des Kleinbesitzes small-holdings system.

Vorjahres|dividende last year's dividend; ~**modell** previous year's model; ~**zahlen** year-ago figures.

vorkalkulieren, Kosten hoch to establish standard cost at a high level.

Vorkaufs|berechtigter preemption claimant, preemptioner; ~**recht** preemption [right], preferment; ~**recht haben** sto have [the] first refusal.

Vorkommen, bei *(Wechsel)* on presentation.

Vorkriegs|anliehe prewar loan; ~**preis** prewar price.

Vorlage *(Einrichtung)* filing, *(Kredit)* advance, *Muster* model, sample, pattern, *(Parl.)* bill, motion, *(Wechsel)* presentation;

bei ~ **zahlbar** payable on presentation;

reproduktionsreife ~ *(Anzeige)* finished art;

~ **zur Annahme** presentment for acceptance; ~ **des Jahresabschlusses** presentation of the annual balance sheet;

~ **einbringen** to bring in (table, *US)* a bill; **mit einem Betrag in** ~ **treten** to advance an amount; **auf Grund der** ~ **von Mustern verhandeln** to negotiate on the strength of samples;

~**provision** overdraft commission.

Vorlasten haben to carry prior encumbrances.

vorläufig|er Abschluß provisional booking; ~**e Bilanz** interim balance sheet; ~**e Deckungszusage** binding slip, cover note; ~**e Quittung** interim receipt.

vorlegen, zur Ansicht to display, to exhibit; **Betrag** ~ to advance an amount (a sum); **Wechsel zur Annahme** ~ to present a bill for acceptance.

Vormann prior party, previous (preceding) indorser (endorser).

vormerken, Plätze to book seats, to make reservations *(US).*

Vormerkgebühr booking (reservation, *US)* fee.

Vormund guardian, custodian, parent, warden.

vornehmen, Buchung to effect an entry; **Inkasso eines Wechsels** ~ to undertake the collection of a bill.

Vorort|bahn suburban line, surburban (local, district, *Br.*) railway; ~**verkehr** suburban (local) traffic.

Vorprämie, kaufen to buy a call option, to give for the call; ~ **verkaufen** to take for the call.

Vorprämien|geschäft option deal for the call, trading in calls *(Br.)*; ~**kurs** price of a call.

Vor|rang *(Gläubiger)* priority [of rank], ranking, *(Hypothek)* precedence.

Vorrangs|aktie classified stock; ~**behandlung** priority treatment.

Vorrat provision, supply, stock, stockpile, bank, repertory, fund, store *(US)*, *(Reserve)* reserve; **geringer** ~ scanty supply; **jem. den ganzen** ~ **abkaufen** to clear off s. one's stock; ~ **ergänzen** to stockpile, to restock *(US)*.

Vorräte supplies, provisions, *(Bilanz)* inventories *(US)*; ~ **anlegen** to lay in supplies; **knapp an** ~**n werden** to run short of provisions.

vorrätig stocked, stock, on stock, in (on) hand; **nicht mehr** ~ sold out; **Ware im Augenblick nicht** ~ **haben** to be short of an article; **stets** ~**e Größe** stock size.

Vorrats|aktie reserved share (stock, *US)*; ~**anstieg** inventory buildup; ~**bildung** stockpiling; ~**gelände erwerben** to acquire land in advance of development; ~**käufe** advance (stockpiling) purchases; ~**lager** stock of provisions, warehouse *(US)*; ~**raum** stock room, magazine; ~**vermögen** stock-in-trade.

Vorrecht preference, privilege, benefit, indulgence, *(Gläubiger)* preferential right; ~**e genießen** to hold special privileges.

Vorrechts|aktien preference shares *(Br.)*, preferred stock *(US)*; ~**anleihe** preference loan.

Vorsaisongeschäft early-season business.

vorschießen, Geld to advance money.

Vorschrift *(Anweisung)* direction, instruction, order, charge, injunction, *(Verordnung)* decree, prescript, provision, regulation; **nach** ~ as prescribed; **steuerrechtliche** ~**en** fiscal provisions; ~**en über den Versand** shipping instructions *(US)*; ~ **zu weit auslegen** to stretch a rule.

vorschriftsmäßig|e Größe regulation size; ~**e Kündigung** due and proper notice.

Vorschuß advance, advanced money, *(Anwalt)* retainer, retaining fee, *(aus öffentlichen Mitteln)* imprest *(Br.)*; ~ **in bar** cash advance; **auf** ~ **arbeiten** to go in advance; ~ **genehmigen** to grant an advance, to imprest *(Br.)*.

Vorschußanweisung advance note, bill of imprest *(Br.)*.

Vorschüsse, geleistete advances made.

Vorschuß|kasse loan office; ~**klausel** *(Konnossement)* red clause; ~**konto** advance (imprest, *Br.)* account; ~**zahlung** payment in advance (by anticipation, *US)*.

vorsehen, zur Beförderung to mark out for promotion; **im Etat** ~ to budget for; **Gelder für einen bestimmten Zweck** ~ to earmark funds; **für Steuern** ~ to make provisions for taxation.

Vorsitz führen to be in (occupy, preside over, fill) the [speaker's] chair.

Vorsitzende|r chairman, president, principal; **geschäftsführender** ~**r** executive vice-president; **j. zum** ~**n wählen** to call s. o. to the chair.

Vor|spalte preceding column; ~**spiegelung falscher Tatsachen** cheat, fraudulent representation.

Vorstadt|bewohner suburban inhabitant, suburbanite; ~**wohngegend** residential suburb.

Vorstand executive board (management), management, officers, *(AG)* top executive management *(US)*; **geschäftsführender** ~ managing committee; ~ **entlasten** to discharge the directors from their responsibilities; **im** ~ **vertreten sein** to have a voice in the management.

Vorstands|anwärter board candidate; ~**berater** management adviser (consultant); ~**bericht** directors' report; ~**beschluß** corporate resolution; ~**bezüge** directors' fees, mamagement fee; ~**genehmigung** board approval; ~**kasino** private dining room.

Vorstandsmitglied board member, member of the executive board, top-management official; **ausscheidendes** ~ retiring director; **geschäftsführendes** ~ acting (managing) director *(Br.)*, executive president *(US)*; ~ **für Absatz und Vertrieb** marketing executive.

Vorstands|protokoll board minutes; ~**ressort** executive department; ~**sitzung** meeting of the [executive] board, board meeting; ~**vergütung** management fee, remuneration of directors; ~**vorsitz** managing directorship; ~**vorsitzender** board chairman, chairman of the [executive] board; **dem** ~**vorsitzer unmittelbar unterstehen** to report directly to the president; **an** ~**weisungen gebunden sein** to serve at the pleasure of the board.

vorteil, preislicher price advantage.

vorteilhaft advantageous[ly], profitable, profitably, reumunerative, beneficial to business; **sein Geld** ~ **anlegen** to lay out one's money to advantage; ~**es Geschäft** paying business, bargain; ~**e Kapitalanlage** profitable investment.

Vortrag *(Ansprache)* address, speech, *(Buchführung)* carryforward, brought (balance carried) forward, *(Umbuchung)* transfer in the books; ~ **aus alter Rechnung** balance carried forward from last account.

vortragen *(buchen)* to carry forward (up); **Effekten** ~ to carry over stock; **auf neue Rechnung** ~ to carry forward to new account.

Vorverkauf advance sale, *(Karten)* advance booking, booking in advance, *(Theater)* ticket agent, booking office.

Vor|vertrag preliminary agreement (contract); ~**wahlnummer** call prefix.

vorwärtskommen, beruflich to improve one's position, to progress.
Vorwegentnahme preferential benefit *(US)*.
vorzeigen, seinen Paß to produce one's passport.
Vorzeigung, bei zahlbar payable at sight.
vorzügliche Qualität superior (first-rate) quality.
Vorzugsaktie preference (preferential, priority, share, *(Br.)*, preferred stock *(US)*; **kumulative ~n** noncontingent preference shares *(Br.)*, cumulative preference stock *(US)*; **stimmrechtslose ~** nonvoting preference share *(Br.)* (preferred stock, *US)*; **~ mit Dividendenbezugsrecht** cumulative preferred stock *(US)*; **~ mit Umtauschrecht** convertible preferred stock *(US)*.

Vorzugs|aktionär preference (preferential, privileged) shareholder *(Br.)*, preferred stockholder *(US)*; **~ausgabe** preference issue; **steuerliche ~behandlung** discriminatory taxation; **~dividende** participating (preference, preferential, preferred, *US)* dividend; **~obligationen** participating (senior) bonds; **~preis** bargain (exceptional, private, special, preferential) price, *(Anzeigen)* special rate; **~satz** specimen (preferential) rate; **~tarif** preferential tariff (rate).
vorzugsweise Befriedigung preferential treatment.
Vorzugs|zinssatz für erstklassige Firmen prime [lending] rate *(US)*; **~zoll** preferential tariff, differential duty, imperial preference *(Br.)*.
Vostroguthaben vostro (their, *US)* account.

W

Wachstum growth, increase, augmentation; **~ der Industrie verlangsamen** to slow down industrial expansion.
Wachstums|aussichten growth prospects; **~industrie** growth industry; **kein ~jahr** no-growth year; **zum Stillstand führende ~rate** zero growth rate; **in ~werte umsteigen** to switch into growth stocks.
Wagen carriage, vehicle, conveyance, *(Auto)* car, auto[mobile], *(Bahn)* carriage, car *(US)*, wag(g)on; **durchgehender ~** through carriage; **firmeneigener ~** company car; **in Zahlung genommener ~** traded-in car; **~ der Mittelklasse** intermediate-sized car; **seinen eigenen ~ fahren** to have a car of one's own.
Wagen|abteil compartment; **~dienst** car service; **~geld** *(Bahn)* truckage; **~mangel** *(Bahn)* shortage of rolling stock; **~ladung** waggonload, carload *(US)*; **~ladungstarif** carload rate *(US)*; **~miete** car rental; **~park** *(Firma)* fleet of cars, delivery equipment; **~standgeld** *(Bahn)* demurrage, truckage; **~vermietung** rent-a-car.
Waggon wag(g)on, [railway] carriage *(Br.)*, railroad car *(US)*, *(Güter)* goods van *(Br.)*, freight car *(US)*, box wag(g)on *(Br.)*, **leerer ~** idler, deadhead; **offener ~** platform (flat) car *(US)*, truck *(Br.)*, lorry; **~bestand** rolling stock; **~fracht** bulk (carload, *US)* freight (rate).
Waggonladung bulk cargo, truckload *(Br.)*, wag(g)onload, carload *(US)*; **Frachtsätze für ~en zur Anwendung bringen** to handle a shipment as a truckload *(Br.)* (carload, *US)*.
Waggon|ladungsfracht carload freight *(US)*, truckload freight *(Br.)*; **~liegegelder** demurrage [charges]; **²weise versandt** shipped in wag(g)onloads (carloads, *US)*, shipped by truckloads *(Br.)*.

Wahl, nach Käufers optional with the buyer; **~en zum Aufsichtsrat** board election.
Wahrnehmung | von Interessen safeguarding (protection) of interests; **~ berechtigter Interessen** justification and privilege, privilege by reason of occasion *(Br.)*.
Währung currency, exchange, [money] standard; **abgewertete ~** devalued currency; **feste ~** hard (stable) currency; **frei konvertierbare ~** free currency; **nicht frei konvertierbare und transferierbare ~** blocked currency; **staatlich regulierte ~** managed currency; **weiche ~** soft currency; **englische ~ stützen** to peg the rate of sterling exchange.
Währungs|abkommen monetary (currency) agreement; **~abwertung** currency (exchange) depreciation, devaluation; **~ausgleichsfonds** Exchange Equalization Fund *(US)*, Exchange Equalization Account *(Br.)*; **~disparitäten** currency disparities; **Internationaler ~fonds** International Monetary Fund; **~gebiet** currency (monetary) area; **~klausel** currency (exchange, standard) clause; **~parität** par value of currency; **~risiko** exchange risk.
währungsschwaches Land country with a low monetary standard (soft currency).
Währungs|standard monetary standard; **~zwangskurs** forced rate of exchange.
Wandelanleihe convertible loan.
Wanderausstellung travel(l)ing show, flying exhibition *(US)*.
Wandergewerbe itinerant (pedlar's) trade; **~schein** pedlar's licence *(US)* (certificate, *Br.)*.
Wandlung *(beim Kauf)* redhibition *(US)*; **auf ~ klagen** to maintain a redhibitory action *(US)*, to sue for conversion.
Wandlungsfehler redhibitory defect (vice) *(US)*.

Waren goods, commodities, stock, articles, products, *(Warenart)* line;
abgepackte ~ packaged goods; **anmeldepflichtige** ~ *(Zoll)* goods to declare; **im Schaufenster ausgestellte** ~ articles shown in the window; **ausgesuchte** ~ choice goods (articles); **unterwegs befindliche** ~ goods afloat; **beschädigte** ~ damaged goods; **vom Zoll beschlagnahmte** ~ goods held up at customs; **bewirtschaftete** ~ quota (rationed) goods; **devisenstarke** ~ hardgoods; **gut eingeführte** ~ popular make; **unverzollt eingeführte** ~ uncustomed merchandise; **nicht unter den Tarif fallende** ~ exempt commodities; **freigegebene** ~ derationed goods; **von Natur aus gefährliche** ~ goods dangerous in themselves; **auf Kredit gekaufte** ~ goods bought on credit; **erst nach Preisvergleich gekaufte** ~ shopping goods; **aus See-(Brand)-schäden gerettete** ~ salvage stock; **dem Kunden in Rechnung gestellte** ~ goods billed to customer; **im Preis herabgesetzte** ~ marked-down merchandise; **kontingentierte** ~ quota goods; **kriegswichtige** ~ strategic goods; **leichtverderbliche** ~ perishable goods; **markenpflichtige** ~ coupon goods; **minderwertige** ~ goods of inferior workmanship; **preisgebundene** ~ price-fixed goods; **preiswerte** ~ cheap line; **verpfändete** ~ pledged goods; **unter Eigentumsvorbehalt überlassene** ~ memorandum goods *(US);* **unbestellte** ~ goods not ordered; **unsortierte** ~ nongraded products; **unverkäufliche** ~ dead commodity (stock), dud stock, drug in the market; **schnell vergriffene** ~ goods selling like wildfire (hot dogs *US);* **nach dem Stück verkaufte** ~ piece goods; **auf Rechnung versandte** ~ goods shipped on account *(US);* **verzollte** ~ cleared goods; **wertlose** ~ trash; **zollhängige** ~ goods in the process of clearing; **zugkräftige** ~ popular articles; **zurückgesetzte** ~ as-is-merchandise;
~ **mittlerer Art und Güte** merchantable quality, seconds; ~ **für den persönlichen Gebrauch** personal exports *(Br.);* ~ **mit hoher Gewinnspanne** higher-margin merchandise; ~ **in hoher Preislage** high-cost merchandise; ~ **mittlerer Preislage** medium-priced goods; ~ **minderwertiger Qualität** thirds; ~ **mit geringer Umschlaghäufigkeit** slow-moving goods, sleeper *(US);* ~ **mit hoher Umschlaggeschwindigkeit** fast-moving goods; ~ **unter Zollverschluß** bonded goods;
~ **auf einer Liste abhaken** to keep tally of goods; ~ **abnehmen** to take delivery of goods; **seine** ~ **anpreisen** to puff one's wares; ~ **aufkaufen** to corner the market; ~ **ausklarieren** to clear goods out of bond; ~ **ausliefern** to have goods delivered; ~ **auszeichnen** to tally goods; ~ **beziehen** to obtain goods; ~ **in großer Menge billig auf den Markt bringen** to dump goods; **sich mit** ~ **eindecken** to supply o. s. with goods; ~ **einlagern** to lay in goods; ~ **nach Güteklassen einstufen** to grade goods; **Einfuhrzoll auf** ~ **erheben** to levy a duty on goods; **alle Arten von** ~ **führen** to stock varied goods;

~ **auf Lager halten** to stock an article; ~ **unter Zollverschluß lagern** to have goods bonded; ~ **auf Kredit liefern** to grant credit terms; ~ **am Kai niederlegen** to place the goods on the dock; **auf seinen** ~ **sitzenbleiben** to be left with goods, to hold the bag *(US);* ~ **in Rechnung stellen** to bill goods; ~ **in Ballen verkaufen** to sell in bales; **seine** ~ **unter falschem Warenzeichen vertreiben** to pass off one's goods as those of another make *(US);* **beschädigte** ~ **wieder zurechtmachen** to render goods marketable; ~ **zurücknehmen** to take goods back.
Waren|abkommen commodity (goods) agreement; ~**abschluß** commodity contract; ~**absender** consignor, shipper *(US);* ~**akkreditiv** commercial letter of credit; **großes** ~**angebot** wide range of items; ~**annahme** receiving of goods; ~**auftrag** buyer's order; ~**ausfuhr zu Schleuderpreisen** dumping; ~**ausgangsbuch** sales journal (register); ~**begleitschein** bill of delivery; ~**beschaffung** procurement of merchandise; ~**beschaffungskredit** purchase-money loan; ~**bestand** merchandise inventory, stock[-in-trade]; ~**bestände zum Anschaffungs- oder niedrigerem Marktpreis angesetzt** inventories at the lower-of-cost-or-market; ~**bestellung aufgeben** to put goods on order; ~**bevorschussung** warehouse loan, commodity advance; ~**bezeichnung** description of commodities; ~**bezugsprämie** trading stamp *(US);* ~**- und Dienstleistungsbilanz** balance of trade in goods and services; ~**börse** produce (commodity) exchange; ~**diskont** trade discount; ~**eingänge** goods received, incoming stocks.
Wareneingangs|bestätigung delivery verification; ~**buch** purchase journal (ledger).
Waren|einkaufsbuch goods-bought ledger; ~**einstandspreis** cost price; ~**einteilung nach Güteklassen** grading of commodities; ~**empfänger** consignor; ~**empfangsschein** delivery receipt; ~**entlohnung** truck [system], store pay *(US);* ~**handel** merchandising, mercantile business.
Warenhaus store, department *(US),* (departmental, *Br.),* multiple, general, *US)* store; **billiges** ~ limited-price variety store; **großes** ~ supermarket *(US);*
~**kette** supermarket (department-store, *US)* chain.
Waren|hortung hoarding of goods; ~**katalog** catalog(ue) of merchandise; ~**knappheit** stock shortage; ~**konto** goods account; ~**korb** *(Statistik)* basket of available commodities.
Warenkredit commercial (commodity, omnibus, *Br.,* mercantile) credit;
kurzfristiger ~ self-liquidating loan *(US).*
Warenladung commodity cargo.
Warenlager warehouse, merchandise (inventory) stock, *(Lagerhaus)* depot, repository, magazine, warehouse, storehouse, *(Vorrat)* stock-in-trade, assortment (stock) of goods;
sein ~ **absetzen** to make one's market.
Waren|lieferant supplier [of goods], contractor; ~**lieferung** goods delivery; ~**liste liberalisieren** to

liberalize a list of items; ~**mangel** *(Börse)* scarcity of (few) offerings; ~**muster** sample, pattern; ~**partie** parcel of goods, lot; ~**preis** commodity price, price of goods.

Warenprobe sample [of merchandise], specimen; **kostenlose** ~ free trial; ~ **zum Selbstkostenpreis** self-liquidator.

Waren|prüfung quality control (inspection, *Br.);* ~**qualität** qualities of merchandise; ~**rechnung** goods account, invoice; ~**retouren** goods returned, return sales; ~**rohgewinn** gross profit on sales; ~**rohgewinnaufschlag** inventory markup; ~**schulden** *(Bilanz)* trade accounts payable *(US).*

Warensendung consignment [of merchandise], package (panel, shipment, *US)* of goods; **gemischte** ~**en** miscellaneous collections of goods.

Warensortiment line (assortment) of goods; **breit gestreutes** ~ broadly diversified product line.

Waren|statistik merchandising statistics; ~**tarif** commodity tariff; ~**termingeschäft** [trading in] commodity futures *(US);* ~**umsatz, umschlag** merchandise turnover, momentum of sales *(US);* ~**verkehr** movement of freight (goods), goods trade; ~**- und Dienstleistungsverkehr** goods and service transactions, exchange of goods and services; ~**versand** consignment (shipping, *US,* sending, shipment, *US)* of goods; ~**verzeichnis** [merchandise] inventory, stock book, inventory of goods; ~**vorrat** stock-in-strade; ~**wechsel** commercial note (paper), trade paper (bill); ~**wettbewerb** commodity competition.

Warenzeichen trademark, brand, trade name; **eingetragenes** ~ registered trademark; **irreführendes** ~ deceptive mark; ~ **anmelden** to register a trademark; ~ **im Register löschen** to cancel a trademark registration; ~**fälschung** colo(u)rable imitation; ~**rechte** trademark rights; ~**rolle** registry of trademarks.

Waren|zettel docket, label, mark; ~**zufuhr** supply of goods.

Warn|blinkanlage emergency traffic signal; ~**streik** warning strike.

Warte|bahn *(Flugzeug)* holding (landing) pattern; ~**geld** *(Beamter)* half-pay, *(Schiff)* demurrage; ~**liste** waiting list; ~**schlange** queuing line *(Br.),* line-up *(US);* ~**zeit** *(für Anwartschaft)* qualifying (waiting) period, *(Streik)* cooling-off period, *(Schiff)* demurrage.

Wartungskosten maintenance costs.

Wasser|fahrzeug watercraft, vessel, boat; ~**flugzeug** seaplane, hydroplane; ~**kopf haben** *(Verwaltung)* to be top-heavy; ~**schadensversicherung** water-damage insurance; ~**straßenverkehrsordnung** Inland Rules of the Road *(US);* ~**transport** water carriage, conveyance by water; ~**weg** waterway, riverway.

Wechsel *(Bilanz)* bill holdings, bills receivable *(US), (Tratte)* bill [of exchange]; **abgelaufener** ~ bill overdue; **nicht bankfähiger** ~ nonegotiable paper, noneligible bill *(US);* **diskont-**

---

fähiger ~ bankable (discountable) bill; **diskontierter** ~ discounted bill; **eigener** ~ promissory note, note of hand; **erstklassiger** ~ fine *(Br.)* (prime, *US)* bill; **fauler** ~ worthless (query) bill; **gezogener** ~ drawn bill, draft; **honorierter** ~ hono(u)red bill; **indossierter** ~ indorsed (made, *Br.)* bill; **auf den Inhaber lautender** ~ bill made out to bearer; **auf Order lautender** ~ bill made out to order; **trockener** ~ promissory note, hand bill; **unbegebbarer** ~ nonnegotiable bill; **uneingelöster** ~ bill in suspense; **ungedeckter** ~ uncovered bill (note); **verfallener** ~ matured bill; **zentralbankfähiger** ~ eligible paper *(US);*

turnusmäßiger ~ **im Amt** rotation in office; ~ **mit Dokumenten** documentary draft; ~ **auf kurze Sicht** short (short-sighted) bill, short paper; ~ **im Vorstand** change in the management;

~ **akzeptieren** to accept a bill; **Deckung für einen** ~ **anschaffen** to provide for a bill; ~ **ausfertigen** to make out (issue) a bill; ~ **an Order ausstellen** to make a bill payable to order; **Inkasso eines** ~**s besorgen** to attend to the collection of a bill; ~ **vor Fälligkeit bezahlen** to take up a bill under rebate-[ment] *(Br.);* ~**diskontieren** to discount a bill; ~ **einlösen** to meet (cash, draw in, pay, take up, discharge) a bill; ~ **bei Verfall einlösen** to hono(u)r (protect) a bill at maturity; ~ **Eingang vorbehalten gutschreiben** to enter a bill short; ~**lombardieren** to pledge a bill as security for a loan; ~ **prolongieren** to extend (renew) a bill of exchange; ~ **protestieren** to protest a bill, to note [down] a bill (draft); ~ **zahlbar stellen** to domiciliate a bill; ~ **mit Bürgschaft versehen** to guarantee (guaranty) a bill; ~ **verstempeln** to furnish a bill with a stamp; ~ **zur Annahme vorlegen** to present a bill (draft) for acceptance; ~ **mit Akzept zurückschicken** to return a bill accepted;

~**abschrift** copy of a bill; ~**akzept** acceptance of a bill, *(Warenakzept)* trade acceptance; ~**allonge** rider; ~**arbitrage** arbitration of exchange; ~**ausfertigung** drafting of a bill; **zweite** ~**ausfertigung** second [of exchange]; ~**aussteller** drawer of a bill, notemaker *(US);* ~**begebung** negotiation of a bill; ~**bestände** bills in hand, bills receivable *(US);* ~**blankett** blank (skeleton) bill; ~**buch** bill book (ledger), notebook *(US);* ~**bürge** guarantor for a bill, backer; ~**bürgschaft** guarantee (guaranty) of a bill of exchange, bail bond; ~**courtage** bill brokerage *(Br.);* ~**debitoren** bills receivable *(US);* ~**diskont** bill discount; ~**diskontierung** bill discounting, taking up bills under rebate *(Br.);* ~**fälscher** bill forger; ~**forderungen** *(Bilanz)* notes (bills) receivable *(US);* ~**formular** blank (skeleton) bill, skeleton note; ~**geld** change, *(Kleingeld)* small coin (change), fractional money *(US);* ~**geschäft** exchange business, agiotage, bill brokerage *(Br.);* ~**gläubiger** holder of a bill, bill creditor.

Wechselinkasso draft (note) collection; ~ **besorgen** to attend to the collection of a bill.

Wechsel|intervention acceptance for hono(u)r (supra

protest); ~**kopie** second (third) of exchange; ~**kopierbuch** bill copying book; ~**kredit** acceptance (bill)

Wechselkurs rate of exchange, course [of exchange] *(Br.);*
amtlicher ~ official exchange rate; **flexibler** ~ floating exchange rate; **gestützter** ~ pegged exchange;
~**arbitrage** arbitration of exchange; ~**satz** *(Weltwährungsfonds)* par exchange rate.

Wechsel|makler bill discounter, note broker; ~**material** commercial papers; ~**nehmer** taker (payer) of a bill; ~**notierungen** foreign-exchange rates; ~**obligo** contingent liabilities, *(Bilanz)* bills payable *(US);* ~**ordnung** Bills of Exchange Act *(Br.),* Uniform Negotiable Instrument Act *(US);* **feste** ~**parität** mint par of exchange; ~**prolongation** renewal (prolongation) of a bill of exchange; ~**protest einlegen** to enter protest of a bill; ~**reiterei** drawing and redrawing, kite flying *(Br.);* ~**schicht** rotating shift; ~**schulden** *(Bilanz)* bills (notes) payable *(US);* ~**schuldner** bill debtor; ~**spesen** bill charges; ~**stube** exchange; ~**umlauf** bills in circulation, outstanding notes; ~**verbindlichkeiten** bills (notes) payable *(US);* ~**verfallbuch** bills payable journal; **unmittelbar** ~**verpflichteter** party primarily liable; ~**vordruck** bill form; ~**vorlage** presentment of a bill; ~**vormann** prior party.

Weg, auf offiziellem through channels;
öffentlicher ~ public way (road).

Wegegebühr wayleave rent, road toll, *(Notar)* mil(e)age.

Wegfall eines Vermächtnisses lapse of a testamentary bequest.

Wegwerfpackung one-way package.

weichen *(Kurse)* to decline, to drop, to ease off, to recede, to go down, to [be on the] fall.

weichende Preise falling prices.

Weichwährungsland soft-currency country.

Weisung, auf ~ und für Rechnung by order and for account of.

weisungsgebunden ministerial, subject to directions.

weiterbefördern *(Briefe)* to forward, to reforward, to send on, to redirect.

Weiter|begebung further negotiation; ~**bestand einer Firma** continuance of a firm.

weiterführen, Firma to continue a firm.

weiterverarbeiten to process, to finish.

Weiterverarbeitungsbetrieb processing company, end-processing plant, processor.

Weiterversicherung, freiwillige voluntarily continued insurance.

weitgehend|e Preissenkungen sweeping reductions in prices; ~**e Vollmachten** plenary powers.

Welt|arbeitsamt International Labo(u)r Office; ~**ausstellung** international (universal, world) exhibition; ~**bank** International Bank of Reconstruction and Development; ~**marktpreis** world (international) price; ~**währungsfonds** International Monetary Fund; ~**währungsreserven** world

monetary reserves; ~**wirtschaft** international (world, global) economics.

Weltwirtschaftskonferenz World Economic Conference.

Wende, konjunkturelle economic turnaround.

Werbe|abteilung advertising *(Br.)* (advertisement, *US,* publicity, promotion, *US)* department; ~**agentur** advertising (publicity) agency; **bezahlte** ~**ankündigung** *(Rundfunk)* paid announcement; ~**antwortkarte** business-reply card; ~**argument im Text** copy point; ~**atelier** commercial studio; ~**aufwand** publicity expenses, advertising investment; ~**auslage** display, advertising layout *(US);* ~**berater** advertising consultant; **nachfassender** ~**brief** follow-up letter; ~**broschüre** booklet, brochure; ~**drucksache** advertising matter, broadsheet, broadside; ~**durchsage** radio (spot) announcement, commercial; ~**einblendung** chain break, spot announcement *(US);* **zugkräftiges** ~**element** interest factor, ~**erfolgskontrolle** advertising control, keying of advertisements *(US);* ~**etat** advertising [expense] budget, *(Werbeagentur)* account; ~**feldzug** publicity (sales, advertising, media) campaign.

Werbefernseh|anzeige television advertisement; **privates** ~**en** independent television.

Werbefilm advertising film;
einminütiger ~ minute movie *(US);* **kurzer** ~ quickie, spotfilm;
~ **mit eingeblendeten Händleradressen** open-end commercial.

Werbe|firma advertising contractor; ~**photo** commercial photo; ~**funk** radio advertising, commercial, broadcast advertising; ~**geschenk** advertising article, free (business, specialty, goodwill) gift; ~**gesichtspunkt** advertising angle; ~**graphiker** industrial artist, art designer; ~**kampagne** advertising (marketing, sales, publicity, media) campaign; ~**kolonne** team of canvassers; ~**konzeption** media conception; ~**leiter** publicity (advertising) manager (director).

Werbematerial advertising (publicity) material, advertising article *(US),* promotion matter, *(Vertreter)* sales kit *(US);*
~ **für den Händler** dealer aids, package.

Werbe|minute *(Fernsehen)* commercial minute; ~**muster** trial sample.

werben to advertise, to campaign, to publicize, to make propaganda, to promote *(US);*
Mitglieder ~ to enlist members.

werbend|e Aktiva earning assets; ~**es Kapital** capital-bearing interest.

Werbe|neuheit advertising novelty; ~**plakat** placard, poster; ~**prospekt** booklet, handbill, [propaganda] leaflet, handout, *(Gesellschaftsgründung)* prospectus; ~**rummel** puffing publicity, ballyhoo *(US).*

Werbesendung commercial;
für ~**en gesperrt** blocked-out;
~ **für Nebenprodukte** trailer, hitchhike.

Werbe|spot spot announcement, advertising spot;

kurzer ~spot quicky, spot film; ~spruchband banner, streamer; ~streifband advertising tape.

Werbetext slogan, [advertising] copy; aggressiver ~ competitive copy; herabsetzender ~ disparaging (knocking) copy.

Werbe|texter copywriter, sloganeer; ~träger [advertising] medium; ~trommel rühren to make propaganda, to boost, to drum (US); ~unterlagen advertising matter, promotional material; ~veranstaltung publicity event; ~vorspann (Sendung) warmup; ~wirksamkeitstest association test; ~wirkung attention value; ~woche propaganda week; ~zeichner advertising artist (cartoonist); käufliche ~zeit (Rundfunk) time, availabilities.

werbliche Unterstützung advertising support.

Werbung advertising, advertisement (Br.), propaganda, publicity, promotion (US), copy; aggressive ~ disparaging copy, competitive advertising (US); redaktionell aufgemachte ~ editorial (sl.); aufklärende ~ reason-why advertising; ein-geblendete ~ tie-in advertising; auf Massenwirkung gerichtete ~ mass-emotional appeal; kostenlose redaktionelle ~ write-up (US), free puff (Br.); überzogene ~ persuasive advertising, harmless puffing (Br.); unterschwellige ~ subliminal advertising; zugkräftige ~ audience builder; ~ durch Ausgabe von Warenproben sample advertising; ~ durch Druckschanversand direct-mail advertising (US); ~ im Einzelhandeslgeschäft point-of-sale (purchase) advertising; ~ mit Kennziffern keyed advertising; ~ innerhalb eines Einzelhandelsgeschäfts inside-store advertising; ~ durch Musterverteilung sampling, free trial, free-gift (novelty) advertising; ~ für Sonderangebote bargain-sale advertising; ~ für den Verbraucher consumer advertising; ~ in öffentlichen Verkehrsmitteln travel(l)ing display; auffällige ~ betreiben to beat (thump) the drum.

Werbungs|aufwand (steuerlich) professional expenditure (outlays), business allowance (US); ~mittler publicity agent, space buyer.

Werdegang career, background, curriculum vitae; beruflicher ~ employment history.

Werft dockyard, shipyard, shipwright's wharf; ~arbeiter dock worker, docker, longshoreman (US).

Werk (Arbeit) work, labo(u)r, (Erzeugnis) piece of work, product, production, (Fabrik) works, factory, mill (Br.), plant (US); ab ~ ex(loco) factory, ex works; ~lieferungsvertrag cost-plus contract; ~meister foreman, overseer, head (master, US) workman.

Werks|angehöriger employee; ~anschluß (Bahn) private siding; ~kantine canteen, tommy shop (store), factory snackshop (US); ~leiter factory (plant, US) manager; ~leitung plant (US) (works) management; ~schutz industrial police.

Werkspionage industrial espionage.

Werkstatt workshop, workroom, shop (Br.); ~ausbildung workshop (vestibule, US, in-plant, US) training; ~montage shop assembly.

Werkswohnung company dwelling (flat, house).

werktätige Bevölkerung working-class population.

Werkvertrag contract to manufacture (for work and service).

Werkzeug tool, instrument, gear, stock in trade; ~kasten toolbox, workbox; ~miete tool rent.

Wert value, worth, (Gegenwert) equivalent, (Güte) quality, (Vermögen) asset, (Wertstellung) value (availability, US) date; dem ~ nach ad valorem; dem nominellen ~ entsprechend by tale; ~ 1. März value (due) 1st March; anerkannter ~ fair market value; angerechneter ~ imputed value; berichtigter ~ absorption value; buchmäßiger ~ accounting (book) value; deklarierter ~ declared (registered) value; gegenwärtiger ~ present (today's) value; gemeiner ~ fair market (principal, Br.) value; immaterieller ~ tangible value; realer ~ effective value; durch sofortigen Verkauf realisierbarer ~ salvage value; rechnungsmäßiger ~ (Versicherung) actuarial value; reiner ~ net worth; steuerbarer ~ ratable (Br.) (taxable) value, assessable value (Br.) (valuation, US); unverzollter ~ bonded value; ~ in Rechnung value in account; ~ bei Verfall value when due; ~ im beschädigtem Zustand damaged value; ~ [bei der Verzollung] angeben to declare the value; unter dem ~ bieten to underbid; ~ einer Anlage heraufsetzen to write up the value of assets; etw. für ein Viertel des ~es kaufen to buy s. th. at the quarter of the price; im ~ sinken to depreciate, to recede; im ~ steigen to increase (advance, improve) in value; unter dem fakturierten ~ verkaufen to sell at a loss on the invoice; ~änderungsgewinn reappraisal surplus; ~angabe declaration (statement) of value; ~ansatz nach Anschaffungskosten valuation at cost.

Wertberichtigung value adjustment, (Bilanz) qualifying (valuation) reserve; ~ des Vorratsvermögens inventory reserve.

wertbeständig|e Anlagegüter fixed capital goods; ~e Währung stable currency.

Werte (Aktiva) assets, (Anlagen) investment, (Wertpapiere) securities, stocks; an der Börse eingeführte ~ quoted (listed, US) securities; festverzinsliche ~ fixed-interest bearing securities; führende ~ [market] leaders, trading favo(u)rites; im Freiverkehr gehandelte ~ open-market papers, curb stocks (US); mündelsichere ~ gilt-edged (trustee) securities (Br.); nicht notierte ~ unquoted (unlisted, off-board, US) securities.

Wert|erhöhung (Grundstück) appreciation, improvement; ~ermittlung [assessed] valuation; ~feststellung value (valuation) assessment; ~fortschreibung adjusted basis; ~gegenstand object (item) of value, valuable thing; ~klausel devaluation clause.

wertlos worthless, valueless, of no value, catchpenny (Br.), two-bit (US).

Wertmarke ad-valorem stamp.
Wertminderung depreciation (reduction) in value, *(Grundstück)* waste;
~ **der Vorräte** *(Bilanz)* inventory price decline.
Wertpaket insured *(Br.)* (registered, numbered, sealed) parcel.
Wertpapiere securities, shares, stocks, bonds, descriptions *(Br.)*;
vom Markt aufgenommene ~ digested securities *(US);* **gut eingeführte** ~ seasoned securities; **ertragssteuerfreie** ~ tax-exempt securities; **festverzinsliche** ~ fixed-interest [bearing] securities (bonds), percents; **im Sammeldepot hinterlegte** ~ assented bonds (stock, *US);* **auf den Inhaber lautende** ~ bearer bonds; **auf den Namen lautende** ~ registered securities; **lombardfähige** ~ collateral securities *(US);* **mündelsichere** ~ gilt-edged (trustee) securities (investments) *(Br.),* trustee (widow and orphan) stock *(US),* trust investments *(US);* **[amtlich] nicht notierte** ~ outside securities *(US),* kerb (curb, *US)* stocks; **stimmrechtslose** ~ nonvoting securities; **vernachlässigte** ~ inactive (neglected) stocks; **[als Sicherheit] verpfändete** ~ pledged securities *(Br.),* hypothecated stock *(US);* **börsengängige** ~ **zum Anschaffungspreis** *(Bilanz)* quoted investments (marketable securities) at cost; ~ **mit hoher Rendite** high-yield securities; ~ **des Umlaufvermögens** *(Bilanz)* temporary investment;
~ **zur Börsenzulassung anmelden** to qualify securities for sale to the public; ~ **durchhalten** to carry securities *(US);* ~ **für kraftlos erklären** to retire securities; ~**lombardieren** to advance money on securities, to pawn stock *(Br.);* ~ **in Erwartung einer Kurssteigerung zurückhalten** to be on the long side of the market.
Wertpapier|anlage investment [in securities]; ~**bereinigung** validation of securities; ~**handel,** ~**verkehr** security trading, trading in securities; ~**verzeichnis** statement of securities deposited.
Wert|sachen valuable articles (things), valuables; ~**schöpfung** *(Sozialprodukt)* net value added; ~**steigerung** appreciation (rise, increase) in value, *(Grundstück)* betterment, valuable improvement, unearned increment; ~**stellungstermin** value (availability, *US)* date; ~**veränderungen** *(Bilanz)* additions and improvements; ~**verlust durch Abnutzung** waste; ~**zeichen** *(Post)* [postage] stamp; **kombiniertes** ~ **und Ursprungszeugnis** Combined Certificate of Value and Origin *(Br.);* ~**zoll** advalorem duty, duty charged by the weight; ~**zuschlag I** *(Luftfracht)* valuation charge; ~**zuschlag II** value surcharge; ~**zuwachs** appreciation, plus value, *(Grundbesitz)* [unearned] increment, betterment, valuable improvement; ~**zuwachssteuer** property increment tax, increment value duty.
wesentlicher Bestandteil *(Grundstück)* immovable, fixture.
Wettbewerb contest, competition, rivalry;
unter Bedingungen des freien ~**s** under fully competitive conditions;

mörderischer ~ cutthroat competition; **unlauterer** ~ fraudulent (mean, unfair, unfair methods of) competition, unreasonable restraint of trade; **öffentlichen** ~ **ausschreiben** to put up for competition, to invite tenders (public competition); **unlauteren** ~ **betreiben** to engage in unfair competition, to pass off *(US).*
Wettbewerbs|abrede, formlose hono(u)rable understanding; **ungleiche** ~**bedingungen** imperfect competition; **vertragliche** ~**beschränkung** loose-knit combinations.
wettbewerbsfähig competitive, able to comepte.
Wettbewerbs|klausel competitive (restraint) clause; **unlautere** ~**methoden** unfair methods of competition, unfair practice *(US);* ~**preis** competitive (equilibrium) price; ~**verbot** restraint of trade; ~**verzerrungen** competitive distortions (imbalance).
Wettervorhersage weather forecast.
Widerruf *(Aufträge)* countermand, cancellation, withdrawal;
~ **einer Schenkung** return of a gift.
widerrufen, Auftrag to countermand (cancel, withdraw) an order; **Konzession** ~ to revoke a licence.
Widerspruch *(Warenzeichen)* opposition *(US).*
widerstandsfähig durable, *(Börse)* resistant, strong;
~ **werden** *(Börse)* to pick up strength.
Wiederanlage des Erlöses reinvestment of proceeds, *(im internationalen Ölgeschäft)* recycling.
wiederanstellen to reengage, to reemploy, to reinstate, to reappoint, to rehire.
Wiederanziehen der Kurse recovery of the market.
Wiederaufbau | **der Betriebe** plant rehabilitation; ~ **der Wirtschaft** economic reconstruction;
~**anleihe** reconstruction (rehabilitation) loan; **Internationale** ~**bank** International Bank for Reconstruction and Development; ~**kredit** reconstruction credit (loan); **Europäisches** ~**programm** European Recovery Program(me).
wiederauffüllen, seine Vorräte to replenish one's stock.
Wiederaufleben einer Versicherung reinstatement of an insurance.
wiederaufleben *(Markt)* to revive, to recover.
Wiederaufnahme | **des Anleihezinsendienstes** resumption of service of a loan; ~ **der Arbeit** resumption of (return to) work; ~ **von Prämienzahlungen** reinstatement of an insurance policy.
Wiederausfuhr reexport[ation], reshipment.
wiederbeleben sich *(Börse)* to revive, to recover.
Wiederbelebung *(Börse)* recovery, revival; **konjunkturelle** ~ trade revival.
Wiederbeschaffung replacement, repurchase.
Wiederbeschaffungs|kosten replacement (reproduction, repurchase) cost; ~**wert** replacement-cost standard (value), market price *(US).*
wiedereinbringen, Verlust to retrieve a loss.
Wiedereinfuhr, zollfreie duty-free return;
~**schein** bill of store.
Wiedereingliederung, berufliche und soziale rehabilitation and resettlement.

Wieder|einstellung eines Angestellten reinstatement of an employee; ~**erkennungstest** recognition test.
wiedergutmachen to restitute, to repair, to recompense, to redeem, to make amends.
Wiedergutmachungs|abkommen reparations agreement, restitution treaty; ~**anspruch** restitution claim.
wiederherstellen, Gebäude to restore a [ruined] building, to rebuild a house; **Kredit eines Unternehmens** ~ to reestablish a firm's credit.
Wieder|herstellung eines verfallenen Patents restoration of a lapsed patent; ~**holungsanzeige** repeat [ad], rerun; ~**holungsrabatt** *(Anzeige)* series discount; ~**holungssendung** *(Fernsehen)* rerun, *(Rundfunk)* rebroadcast; ~**kaufsrecht** redemption right.
wiederkehrende | Ausgaben recurring expenses; ~ **Nutzungen** recurring revenues.
Wiederverkäufer reseller, dealer, *(Einzelhändler)* retailer, retail dealer;
    Lieferung nur an ~ supplied to trade only; ~**rabatt** distributor discount.
Wiederverkaufs|preis [fixed] retail (reserved, dealer's resale, trade) price; ~**wert** resale value.
Wiederverpfändung rehypothecation *(US).*
Wiegegeld weighing cost, weighage *(Br.).*
wiegen, brutto to weigh in the gross.
Wiegeschein weight note.
wild|er Anschlag fly posting, sniping; ~**er Streik** outlaw (wildcat, quickie) strike.
Willens|einigung *(Vertragsschluß)* meeting of minds; **mangelnde** ~**einigung** absence of assent.
Winkel|börse bucket shop *(US);* ~**makler** outside (street, *US)* broker, guttersnipe *(US).*
Winter|fahrplan winter schedule; ~**schlußverkauf** winter sale.
wirksam effective, operative, efficient, valid;
    ~**e Blockade** effective blockade; **automatisch** ~**e Rückversicherung** treaty reinsurance.
Wirkung, mit sofortiger effective immediately.
Wirtschaft economy, economics, economic system, *(Gastwirtschaft)* public house, inn, restaurant, tavern, pub *(Br.),* saloon *(US);*
    extensive ~ extensive agriculture; **freie** ~ private enterprise [system]; **gewerbliche** ~ industrial economy, manufacturing trade;
    ~ **ankurbeln** to foster trade, to boost business, to pep up the economy; **in die** ~ **gehen** to enter private business; ~ **umstellen** to switch production.
wirtschaften to keep house, to manage, *(Landwirt)* to farm;
    sparsam ~ to husband one's money, to cut and contrive; **in die eigene Tasche** ~ to job.
wirtschaftlich *(ertragabwerfend)* profitable, yielding a return, remunerative, paying;
    ~ **sein** to be on a profitable basis; ~ **tätig sein** to be in trade (business);
    ~**e Belange** trade concerns; ~**er Berater** economic adviser; ~**er Betrieb** profitable enterprise; ~**e Durchdringung** economic penetration; ~**e Interessen** commercial interests; ~**e Schlüsselstellung**

key industrial emporium; ~**e Struktur eines Landes** economic setup of a country; ~**e Tagesfragen** bread-and-butter economic issues; ~**e Verflechtung** web of business.
Wirtschaftlichkeit economical operation, economy, profitability, efficiency.
Wirtschaftlichkeitsprüfung efficiency audit.
Wirtschafts|abkommen trade convention (pact); ~**abordnung** trade delegation; ~**anwalt** businessman's lawyer; ~**artikel** city article *(Br.);* ~**aufschwung** upturn in business, [trade] recovery; ~ **und Sozialausschuß** *(EG)* Economic and Social Council; ~**beirat** council of economic advisers *(US);* ~**berater** business (economic, trade) consultant; ~**betrieb der öffentlichen Hand** state (government) enterprise; ~**boykott** economic boycott; ~**epoche der Rezession zurechnen** to put the recession tag on a period; ~**experte sein** to be an expert on (in) economics; ~**flaute** recession, dip; **gemischte ~form** mixed economy; ~**führer** captain of industry, business (industrial) leader; ~**gebäude** farm buildings (office); **Europäische ~gemeinschaft** Common Market Community.
Wirtschaftsgüter economic goods, *(Bilanz)* assets; **nicht buchungsfähige** ~ nonledger assets; **langlebige** ~ permanent assets; ~ **des Anlagevermögens** capital assets; ~ **mit überhöhtem Buchwert** watered assets *(US).*
Wirtschafts|hilfe economic aid (assistance); ~**hochschule** business school; ~**jahr** [company's] financial *(Br.)* (fiscal, *US)* year; ~**journalist** economic journalist; ~**kommission for Europa** Economic Commission for Europe (ECE); ~**kraft** *(Land)* economic resources (strength); ~**kreise** commercial circles, economic front; ~**kreislauf** business cycle; ~**krise** economic (commercial) crisis, economic wrench, slump; ~**leben** economic life, business [life]; ~**lenkung** controlled economy, *(Planwirtschaft)* planned economy; ~**minister** Minister of Economic Affairs *(Br.);* ~**ministerium** Department of Commerce *(US),* Department of Economic Affairs *(Br.);* ~**monopol** industrial monopoly; ~**nachrichten** industrial (commercial, business, city) news; ~**organisation** trade organization; **[anti]zyklische** ~**politik** cyclical bugeting; ~**politik mittels steuerlicher Maßnahmen** compensatory fiscal policy; ~**programm** economic (industrial) expansion program(me); ~**projekt** industrial project; **[beeidigter]** ~**prüfer** auditor, chartered (incorporated, *Br.)* accountant, [certified] public (independent) accountant *(US);* **Europäischer ~rat** Organization for European Economic Cooperation (OEEC); ~ **und Sozialrat der Vereinten Nationen** United Nations Economic and Social Council; ~**raum** trading (marketing) area; ~**redakteur** financial (economist, city, *Br.)* editor; ~**seite haben** *(Zeitung)* to carry a financial page; ~**spionage** economic (industrial) espionage; ~**tagung** industrial gathering; ~**verbrechen** white-collar crime *(US);* ~**vereinigung** trade organization

(association); ~**wissenschaft** economics, economic science; ~**wissenschaftler** economist; ~**zeitung** economic journal, trade paper; ~**zweig** industry, trade group, branch of trade.

Wirtshaus inn, pothouse, taphouse, tap room, public house, pub *(Br.)*, bush, saloon *(US)*.

Witwen|anteil jointure, dower interest; ~- **und Waisengeld** compassionate allowance.

Woche, Weiße white sale.

Wochen|abonnement *(Bahn)* season (commuter, *US*) ticket; ~**abschluß** weekly return.

Wochenend|ausgabe weekly edition; ~**fahrkarte** weekend ticket; ~**geschäft** Saturday business.

Wochen|geld *(Börse)* weekly fixtures; ~**schau** newsreel, news (topical) film (picture).

Wohlfahrt social service, poor relief *(Br.)*.

Wohlfahrts|einrichtung welfare center (centre, *Br.)*, settlement [house]; ~**empfänger** welfare recipient (beneficiary); · **küche** soup kitchen; ~**marke** semipostal; ~- **und Wiedergutmachungsorganisation der Vereinten Nationen** United Nations Relief and Rehabilitation Administration; **[öffentliche]** ~-**pflege** welfare (charity) work, district visiting *(US)*; ~**unterstützung** public (poor, *Br.)* relief, welfare check (payment).

wohlhabend affluent, pecunious, well-heeled, well-off, wealthy, well-to-do *(Br.)*.

Wohlstand der Verbraucher consumer wealth.

Wohlstandsindex prosperity index.

wohltätig|e Spende charitable contribution; ~**e Stiftung** charitable foundation.

Wohltätigkeits|anstalt charitable establishment; **auf dem ~gebiet beispielhaft sein** to subscribe liberally to charity; ~**veranstaltung** benefice (charity) performance.

Wohn|bedarf housing requirements; ~**bezirk** residential district; ~**block** apartment block.

wohnen to live, to dwell, to reside, to quarter, to home, *(als Mieter)* to room *(US)*; **möbliert** ~ to live in furnished apartments; **umsonst** ~ to have free quarters, *(Hotelgast)* to be a guest of the management.

Wohn|fläche floor space (area); ~**gebäude** rsidential premises, dwelling house; ~**gegend** residential area (district); ~**gemeinschaft** residential community, flatsharing; ~**haus** [dwelling] house; **billige ~lage** low-rent rsidential district; ~**ort** residence, domicile, abode, [dwelling] place; ~**raum** residential (housing) space.

Wohnsitz [dwelling] place, residence, seat, settlement; **ehelicher** ~ matrimonial domicile; **fester** ~ fixed (settled) abode, established place of residence; **steuerlicher** ~ ordinary residence *(Br.)*;

~ **der gewerblichen Niederlassung** commercial domicile, domicile of corporation; **seinen** ~ **aufgeben** to vacate (relinquish, abandon) one's residence; **seinen** ~ **begründen** to set (take) up one's abode, to settle down, to [establish a] domicile; ~**änderung** change of residence (abode).

Wohnung dwelling, lodging[s], quarters, housing, place, abode, home; **abgeschlossene** ~ separate dwelling, self-contained flat; **billige** ~ low-cost housing; **freifinanzierte** ~ privately financed housing unit; **leerstehende** ~ idle tenement; **möblierte** ~ furnished apartment (flat, dwelling), chambers; ~ **für gehobenere Ansprüche** higher-bracket apartment, upper-level housing; ~ **beschaffen** to procure a housing; ~ **mieten** to rent a flat (apartment); ~ **mieten und die Möbel übernehmen** to rent a flat and take over the furniture.

Wohnungs|amt housing office, National Housing Agency *(US)*; ~**anzeiger** directory.

Wohnungsbau house (home, *US*) building; **billiger** ~ low-cost home construction; **sozialer** ~ low-(moderate-) income housing, federally financed low-cost housing *(US)*; ~**darlehn** housing loan; ~**genossenschaft** housing cooperative; ~**programm** housing program(me); ~**projekt** housing development plan *(Br.)*.

Wohnungs|bedarf housing requirements; ~**beihilfe** lodging allowance (assistance); ~**beschaffungskredit** housing credit; ~**defizit** housing shortage; ~**finanzierungsgesellschaft** housing and home financing agency *(US)*; ~**geld[zuschuß]** lodging money (allowance); ~**inhaber** lodger, tenant, householder, roomer *(US)*; ~**marktlage** housing scene; ~**miete** apartment (residential) rent; ~**nachweis** accommodation registry *(Br.)*; **auf ~suche gehen** to house-hunt; to flat-hunt; ~**suchender** househunter; ~**zwangswirtschaft** housing control.

Wohn|verhältnisse housing conditions, living accommodation; ~**viertel** residential area; **vornehmes ~viertel** affluent area; ~**wagen** caravan *(Br.)*, house wag(g)on, trailer *(US)*.

Wort|führer speaker, spokesman; ~**gebühr *(Telegramm)*** telegraph (telegram) rate.

Wortlaut tenor, text, wording; ~ **einer Buchung** narration of an entry.

Wrack shipwreck, wreck, abandoned ship.

Wucher usury, extortion; ~**geschäft** usurious trade (transaction).

Wucher|miete rack rent; ~**preis** ransom (cutthroat, extortionate, usurious) price; ~**zinsen** illegal (usurious, excessive) interest.

Wurfsendungen direct mail advertising.

Z

Zahl number, figure, cipher, *(Betrag)* amount, (Stelle) digit, *(Wert)* numeral;
in runden ~en in round[ed] figures;
von der Handelskammer veröffentlichte ~en released Board-of-Trade figures;
Betrieb in die roten ~en bringen to administer a company from black to red.
zahlbar payable, *(fällig)* due, mature;
bei Auftragserteilung ~ cash with order; **in bar ~** terms cash; **bei Lieferung ~** cash on delivery (C. O. D.); **pränumerando ~** payable in advance; **bei Sicht ~** payable at sight; **sofort ~** spot [cash]; **~ bei Aushändigung der Verschiffungspapiere** payable against surrender of shipping documents;
~ stellen *(Wechsel)* to domiciliate, to make payable.
zahlen to pay, to make payment, *(Schuld voll begleichen)* to pay off, to clear, to discharge;
als Abstand ~ to pay by way of compensation; **[in] bar ~** to pay cash down; **langsam ~** to be slow in paying; **zu viel ~** to overpay.
zahlen|des Mitglied paying member; **~er Passagier** revenue passenger.
Zahlen|kode cipher code; **~material** data, figures.
Zahler, pünktlicher prompt payer; **säumiger ~** defaulter, tardy payer.
Zahl|karte money order, *(Post)* postal order; **~stelle** paying agent (office) *(Post)* office of payments *(Br.)*, *(Wechsel)* domicile, official payee.
Zahlung payment, paying, *(Schulden)* discharge, liquidation, settlement, clearance;
gegen ~ einer Lizenzgebühr on a royalty basis; **mangels ~** failing payment;
~ eingestellt payment stopped; **~ erfolgt gleichzeitig per Post** payment is in the mail *(US)*;
avisierte ~en amounts advised; **bargeldlose ~** cash transactions, cashless payment *(US)*; **fingierte ~** fictitious payments;
~ bei Auftragserteilung cash with order; **~ bei Eingang der Waren** payment must be made upon delivery of the goods; **~ gegen Nachnahme** cash *(Br.)* (collect, *US*) on delivery;
zur ~ auffordern to demand payment; **mit der ~ im Rückstand bleiben** to default on one's payment; **seine ~en einstellen** to default, to become (declare o. s.) insolvent, to suspend payments; **vierteljährliche ~en festsetzen** to stipulate that the payment should be quarterly; **mit den ~en in Verzug kommen** to default [in payment]; **~ stunden** to grant (allow) a respite; **~ Zug um Zug verlangen** to require payment on delivery; **Scheck zur ~ vorlegen** to present a check for payment; **Wechsel zur ~ vorlegen** to collect on a note.
Zahlungs|abkommen monetary agreement; **~adresse** *(Wechsel)* domicile; **~anweisung** order [to pay], pay ticket (voucher, *Br.*), payment voucher, *(Bank)* pay bill *(Br.)*, order; **~aufforderung** demand

for payment, *(Mahnschreiben)* dun; **~aufschub** indulgence, rspite [for (delay of, prolongation of, extension of) payment]; **~auftrag stornieren** to countermand a payment.
Zahlungsbedingungen terms [of payment], payment conditions;
übliche ~ standard payment clause.
Zahlungs|befehl order to pay; **~beleg** [pay] voucher.
Zahlungsbilanz balance of payments;
passive ~ adverse balance of payments; **~ausgleich** equilibrium in the balance of payments; **~lücke** payment gap; **~überschüsse** surpluses of payment balances.
Zahlungs|eingänge takings, payments received; **~einstellung** failure, suspension (stoppage) of payments; **~empfänger** payee; **~erleichterungen** easy terms.
zahlungsfähig able to pay, good, [financially] sound, solvent.
Zahlungsfrist term, time of payment, *(Wechsel)* grace period;
~ einhalten to pay at maturity.
zahlungskräftig able to purchase, sound.
Zahlungsmittel circulating (currency) medium, medium of exchange, money, currency;
bargeldlose ~ deposit currency; **gesetzliches ~** legal coin (tender, *Br.*), lawful money *(US)*.
Zahlungsmittel|aufschub forbearance; **vermehrter ~umlauf** currency expansion.
Zahlungs|modalitäten terms [of payment]; **gute ~moral haben** to be a good pay *(US)*; **~pflichtiger** debtor, assessee; **~schwierigkeiten** embarrassment, pecuniary difficulties; **~sperre über ein Konto verhängen** to block an account.
Zahlungstermin day (time) of payment, *(Verfalltag)* day of maturity;
mittlerer ~ average due date;
~ vereinbaren to agree on a date for the payment.
zahlungsu:afähig unable to pay, insolvent, defaulting *(Br.)*, bankrupt, nonsolvent, *(Bank)* failing circumstances, illiquid;
sich für ~ erklären to declare o. s. a bankrupt; **für ~ erklärt werden** to be struck from the list, to be gazetted bankrupt, to be hammered on the exchange *(Br.)*.
Zahlungs|unfähigkeit inability to pay, commercial insolvency; **Europäische ~union** European Payments Union; **~verbot** stop order, freezing of payment, *(an den Drittschuldner)* garnishment; **~vereinbarungen** payment agreements (arrangements); **bargeldloser ~verkehr** clearing system.
Zahlungsverpflichtung financial responsibility;
seine ~en einhalten to meet one's commitments; **sicher einer ~ entziehen** to evade payment.
Zahlungs|versprechen promise to pay; **~verzug** default, delay in payment; **~ziel** respite, grace period; **offenes ~ziel** open terms.

Zeche *(Bergbau)* coal mine, coalpit, colliery, *(Rechnung)* score, bill;
~ **bezahlen** to stand the treat (shot), to pay the piper.

Zechen|preis pithead price; ~**stillegung** pit closure.

zeichnen, Aktien to make an application for shares, to subscribe for shares (stock, *US*); **Kapital** ~ *(Konsortium)* to underwrite.

Zeichnung, zur aufgelegt open for subscription.

Zeichnungsangebot tender, subscription offer.

zeichnungsberechtigt authorized to sign.

Zeichnungs|berechtigung auf junge Aktien ausüben to subscribe to new shares (stock, *US*); ~**bogen** subscription list; ~**grenze** *(Rückversicherung)* writing limit; ~**liste** subscription list.

Zeilen|honorar penny-a-line payment, space fee *(US)*; ~**preis** *(Anzeige)* agate rate *(US)*.

Zeit time, *(Frist)* term, *(Zeitraum)* period;
fahrplanmäßige - scheduled time; **tote ~** dull time, off-season, *(Lohnausfall)* dead time; **verkehrsstarke ~** busy period, rush hours; **verlorene ~** *(Produktionsausfall)* idle time;
~**en wirtschaftlicher Blüte** boom years; **~ nach Börsenschluß** afterhours;
auf ~ kaufen to buy on credit (account); **auf ~ verkaufen** *(Terminverkauf)* to sell forward (for future delivery, *US*).

Zeit|ablauf expiration of time; ~**arbeit** job leasing; ~**fahrkarte** season (commutation, *US*) ticket; ~**fracht** time freight; ~**geschäft** time bargain, forward deal, dealing for the account *(Br.)*, privilege *(US)*; ~**karteninhaber** season-ticket holder *(Br.)* commuter *(US)*, daily breader *(Br.)*; ~**kontrolleur** time clerk, timekeeper; ~**lohn** task (time, *US*) wage; ~**police** time (term) policy.

Zeitpunkt, zum der Lieferung at the time of delivery;
~ des Inkrafttretens effective date;
richtigen ~ zum Verkauf verpassen to overstay one's market *(US)*.

Zeitschrift journal, periodical [newspaper], magazine, review, *(Verband)* bulletin;
wissenschaftliche ~ scientific periodical.

Zeit|schriftenabonnement magazine subscription; ~**spanne erhöhter Gefahr** apprehensive period; ~**studie** time study.-

Zeitung newspaper, paper, journal;
amtliche ~ bulletin, gazette; **eingegangene ~** defunct paper;
~ im Kleinformat tabloid; **~ im Weltformat** blanket sheet;
~ abbestellen to give up (discontinue) a newspaper; **~ abonnieren** to take in *(Br.)* (subscribe for, *US*) a newspaper; **durch alle ~en gehen** to go the round of the papers; **in einer ~ inserieren** to advertise in a newspaper; **bei einer ~ beschäftigt sein** to be on the staff of a newspaper.

Zeitungs|abonnement subscription [to a newspaper]; ~**annonce,** ~**anzeige** insertion, [press] advertisement, newspaper (news) advertisement; ~**artikel** [newspaper] article, news item; ~**ausschnittsbüro** [press-] clipping bureau, press-cutting service *(Br.)* clipping agency *(US)*, newspaper clipping *(US)*; ~**beilage** supplement, *(Reklame)* inserts, inset; ~**drucksache** newspaper post *(Br.)*, second-class mail *(US)*; ~**kiosk** kiosk *(Br.)*, newsstand *(US)*, news stall *(Br.)* bookstall; ~**korrespondent** correspondent, news reporter; **alte ~nummer** back number; ~**verkäufer** news vendor (dealer), newsboy.

Zeit- | und Reiseversicherung mixed policy *(Br.)*; ~**wertprinzip** cost method of valuation.

zentralbankfähig eligible for rediscount *(US)*.

Zentralbank|institut central bank, Federal Reserve Bank *(US)*; ~**rat** Federal Reserve Board *(US)*.

Zentrale principal establishment (office), headquarters, main (head, front) office, *(Telefon)* central switchboard, chief operator *(US)*.

Zentral|notenbank central bank, Federal Reserve Bank *(US)*; ~**registratur** master (central) file.

Zergliederung einer Bilanz analysis sheet, breakdown of a balance sheet *(US)*.

zerrütten, Finanzen to shatter finances; **Währung ~** to dislocate the currency.

Zertifikat einer Kapitalanlagegesellschaft certificate of interest *(US)*, unit *(Br.)*.

Zertifikatbesitzer unitholder *(Br.)*.

Zettel slip, *(Adressenanhänger)* label, ticket, tag.

Zeugnis certificate, attestation, record, *(Bescheinigung für Angestellte)* written character, testimonial;
~ der mittleren Reife [etwa] Ordinary General Certificate of Education *(Br.)*.

ziehen *(Lotterie)* to draw;
Bargeld eines Landes aus dem Verkehr ~ to drain a country off money; **Scheck auf j. ~** to draw upon s. one's account; **aus dem Verkehr ~** to put out of commission, *(Geld)* to withdraw from circulation.

Ziehungs|liste drawing list; ~**plan** lottery scheme.

Ziel object, target, aim, *(Zahlungsfrist)* prompt;
auf ~ on credit, *(Börse)* forward;
~**punkt** *(Spediteur)* basing point.

Ziffer cipher, figure, number, digit, *(in einem Abkommen)* item, paragraph;

Ziffern|kode code; ~**telegramm** cipher (code) telegram.

Zimmer | zu vermieten rooms (apartments) to let;
freies ~ *(Hotel)* vacant room; **möblierte ~** lodging(s);
~ in einem Hotel bestellen to book (engage, reserve, *US*) rooms at a hotel;
~**bedienung** room service; ~**preis** room rates, *(im Hotel)* hotel tariff; ~**reservierung** hotel reservation *(US)*; ~**vermietung** letting of rooms.

Zins interest, *(Miete)* rent, rental.

Zins|abkommen agreement on interest rates; ~**anpassung,** ~**ausgleich** interest rate adjustment; ~**bogen** coupon sheet; ~**eingänge** interest received.

Zinsen interest, *(Bilanz)* interest charges;
franko ~ no interest charged, flat;
aufgelaufene [noch nicht fällige] ~ accrued interest;
aufgelaufene [und fällige] ~ accumulated interest;

auf Basis von 360 Tagen berechnete ~ ordinary interest *(US)*; auf Basis von 365 Tagen berechnete ~ exact interest *(US)*; gutgeschriebene ~ credited interest; überfällige ~ past du interest; ~ aus Buchforderungen accrued accounts receivable *(US)*; ~ aus Kontokorrenten interest on fluctuating overdrafts; ~ abwerfen to yield (draw) interest; ~ belasten to charge interest; ~ zum Kapital schlagen to capitalize interest; ~ vergüten to allow interest; ~berechnung computation of interest.

Zinsendienst payment of interest; ~ einer Anleihe durchführen to service a loan.

Zinsermäßigung reduction of the interest rate.

Zinseszins compound interest.

Zins|forderungen interest due (receivable, *US*); ~fuß rate of interest, interest (bank) rate; ~garantie guaranteed interest; ²günstig at a low rate of interest; ~konditionen interest rates.

zinslos noninterest-bearing, free of interest, flat.

Zinsrückstände outstanding interest.

Zinssatz rate of interest; gesetzlicher ~ legal interest; wucherischer ~ exorbitant rate; ~ im Fixgeschäft loaning rate *(US)*; ~ für überzogene Konten overdraft rate.

Zinsschein interest coupon (ticket); notleidende ~e outstanding coupons; verfallene ~e ablösen to detach coupons due; Stücke ohne ~e handeln to sell bonds exclusive coupons.

Zins|spanne *(Bank)* margin of profit; ~tabelle table of interest, ready reckoner; ~verbilligung interest reduction; Wertpapiere ohne ~vergütung veräußern to sell stocks flat; ~verlust loss on interest; ~zahlen red (interest) numbers, products *(Br.)*.

Zivil|flugplatz commercial airport; ~luftfahrtabkommen civil aviation agreement; Internationale ~luftfahrtorganisation International Civil Aviation Organization (ICAO); ~verbrauch private use.

Zoll customs [duty], duty, tariff, toll, dues; diskriminierender ~ discriminatory tariff; nach dem Gewicht erhobener ~ poundage; sein Gepäck durch den (vom) ~ abfertigen lassen to clear one's luggage through the customs; mit ~ belegen to [rate in the] tariff; Schiff beim ~ deklarieren to clear a ship; ~ entrichten to pay duty on, to clear the customhouse; ~ hinterziehen to defraud the revenue.

Zoll|abfertigung customs examination (entry), permit, *(Schiff)* [customs] clearance.

Zollabfertigungs|antrag stellen to enter for customs clearance; ~gebühren clearance charges; ~hafen port of entry; ~schein customhouse permit, *(Schiff)* bill of sufferance *(Br.)*; ~stelle customhouse.

Zoll|abkommen tariff treaty (agreement); Allgemeines ~ und Handelsabkommen General Agreement on Tariffs and Trade *(GATT)*.

Zollager locked warehouse, *(Zolleigenlager)* bonded warehouse (store, *Br.*).

Zollamt customhouse, customs (revenue) office.

zollamtlich | erklärt declared; sich ~ abfertigen lassen to effect customs clearance; Schiff ~ durchsuchen to search (rummage, *Br.)* a ship; ~e Erlaubnis customs permission; ~er Verschluß bond.

Zoll|angabe customs declaration, customhouse entry; ~angleichung tariff adjustment; ~aufseher customs inspector, surveyor of the customs *(US)*; ~ausfuhrerklärung declaration *(Br.)* (clearance, entry) outwards; ~ausschlußgebiet free zone (trade area), foreign trade zone *(US)*; ~autonomie autonomous tariff [system]; ~beamter customs officer (official), customhouse officer, jerquer *(Br.)*, revenue agent *(US)*; ~begleitschein bond note, customs passbook; ~begünstigung preferential treatment; ~begünstigungstarif preferential tariff; ~behörde customs [authorities]; ~bescheinigung customs certificate, bond note, *(Schiff)* clearance certificate, transire *(Br.)*; ~bestimmungen customs (tariff) regulations; ~bezirk customs district; ~boot revenue cutter; ~deklaration [customs] declaration, customhouse entry (clearance), *(Schiff)* captain's (bill of, *Br.)* entry; ~depot locked warehouse, *(Zolleigenlager)* bonded warehouse; ~dokumente clearance papers; ~durchsuchung search, *(Schiff)* rummaging *(Br.)*; ~durchsuchungsbefehl search warrant, writ of assistance *(Br.)*.

Zölle, mit hohen ~n belastet tariff-ridden; ~ und Steuern customs and excise duties; ~ erheben to levy customs duties; ~ senken to lower the tariff.

Zoll|einfuhrerklärung customs bill of entry; ~einnahmen customs revenue; ~erklärung [customs] declaration, customhouse clearance (entry); ~erlaubnisschein clearance certificate, bill of sight; ~fahndung customs (preventive, *Br.)* service, Revenue Cutter Service *(US)*; ~faktura legalized (customs) invoice; ~flughafen airport of entry; ~formalitäten erledigen to clear through the customs.

zollfrei customs-exempt (-free), duty-free; ~e Einfuhr duty-free admission; ~er Hafen free port; ~e Wiedereinfuhr duty-free return.

Zoll|freibetrag duty-free allowance; ~freigabe release from bond; ~freigrenze nontariff barrier; ~freilager bonded warehouse (store, *Br.)*; ~garantie leisten to deposit the duty [repayable]; ~gebiet customs territory (area); ~gebühren customhouse fees; ~grenzstelle frontier control point; ~hafen point of entry, bonded port; ~hinterziehung begehen to defraud the revenue, to evade customs duty; ~inland customs area; ~inspektor examiner, locker *(Br.)*, surveyor *(US)*; ~kontingent tariff [-rate] quota; ~kontrolle customs examination; ~kutter revenue cutter; ~lager bonded store; ~makler customhouse broker; ~mauer tariff (trade) wall; ~niederlage locked warehouse;

(bonded, *Br.*, entrepot), store, *(Zolleigenlager)* bond, bonded warehouse (store, *Br.*); ~**papiere** clearance papers; ~**passierschein** docket, landing order *(Br.)*, bill of sufferance *(Br.)*.

zollpflichtig dutiable, leviable, customary, tariff-bound, customable, tollable;

Zoll|plombe [customhouse (lead)] seal; ~**position** heading on the customs tariff, tariff item; ~**präferenzen genießen** to enjoy preferential treatment; ~**quittung** customhouse receipt, docket *(Br.)*; ~**rechnung** customhouse note; ~**rückgabeschein** customs debenture, debenture certificate; ~**rückvergütung** drawback, customs rebate *(US)*; ~**schiff** revenue cutter; ~**schranke** turnpike, toll gate; ~**schuppen** locked warehouse, customs shed, bonded store *(Br.)*; ~**senkung** tariff reduction; ~**spediteur** customs expediter; ~**speicher** locked warehouse, bonded store *(Br.)*; ~**stempel** duty mark; ~**tariff** tariff [duty], customs tariff (regime); ~**tarifsätze** tariff charges; ~**union** customs union; ~**untersuchung** customs examination (inspection), search, *(Schiff)* rummage *(Br.)*; ~**vergünstigung** preferential tariff, sufferance *(Br.)*.

Zollverschluß bond, [customhouse] seal;
    unter ~ **bringen** to warehouse, to bond.

Zollverschluß|vorschriften bonding requirements; ~**waren** bonded goods.

Zoll|vertrag tariff treaty; ~**verwaltung** customs authorities; ~**vormerkschein** excise bond, bond note; ~**vorzugsabkommen** preferential tariff; ~**vorzugsgebiet** preferential tariff area; ~**zugeständnis** tariff concession.

Zonen|plan *(Werbung)* zone plan; ~**tarif** zone tariff (rates) *(US)*.

Zubehör accessories, appurtenance, appendix, *(Inventar)* fittings, fixtures.

Zubringer access (feeder) road, local service line; ~**dienst** feeder service; ~**kosten** hauling costs; ~**linie** *(Bahn)* feeder [line], jerkwater railroad *(US)*.

zuerkennen to adjudicate, to adjudge;
    Schadenersatz ~ to award damages.

Zuerstentnahme | der älteren Vorräte und Bilanzierung zum jeweiligen Buchwert first-in, first-out; ~ **der neueren Vorräte und Bilanzierung zum jeweiligen Buchwert** last-in, last-out.

Zufahrtsstraße accommodation (feeder) road.

zufließen *(Einkommen)* to issue.

Zufuhr supply, delivery, *(Wareneingänge)* arrivals, imports, importation.

zuführen | Kunden to introduce customers; **dem Reservefonds** ~ to carry (add) to the reserve fund.

Zug, abfahrender ~ outgoing train; **durchgehender, D-**~ nonstop (direct, through, corridor, express, vestibule, *US)* train; **fahrplanmäßiger** ~ ordinary (scheduled, *US)* train; **zuschlagspflichtiger** ~ limited train;
    ~ **ins Blaue** mystery train;
    D-~ **benutzen** to travel express; **neuen** ~ **in den Fahrplan einführen** to schedule a new train *(US)*.

Zugabe *(Gewichtsauffüllung)* makeweight, *(Prämie)* [direct] premium, giveaway, bonus, gratuitous article, free gift;
    ~**angebot [für Händler]** dealer premium offer; ~**artikel** [advertising] premium; ~**werbeplan** gift enterprise system; ~**werbung** [free] gift advertising; ~**wesen** premium promotion, gift giving.

Zugang access, admittance, approach, *(Lager)* quantity;
    zollfreier ~ tariff-free access;
    freien ~ **zum Kapitalmarkt haben** to gain access to capital.

Zugänge *(Belegschaft)* accessions, additions, *(Bilanz)* subsequent additions, accruals;
    ~ **an Bausparverträgen** investment inflow.

Zugangs- und Abgangsrate *(Belegschaft)* replacement rate.

Zugartikel draw, price leader, eye appeal (catcher).

zugelassen admitted, licensed, authorized;
    amtlich ~ certified;
    zum Handel an der Börse ~ **sein** to be quoted (listed, *US)* on the stock exchange;
    ~**es Gewerbe** lawful trade; **amtlich** ~**er Makler** certified (inside, *Br.)* broker.

zugkräftige Werbung audience builder.

Zugverkehr einschränken to cut the train service.

zukaufen to buy in addition.

zukünftiger Käufer prospective buyer.

Zulage extra pay, surplus, *(Gehaltserhöhung)* rise *(US)*, advance, increase, raise *(Br.)*.

zulassen, Auto to register a car, to take a car's number; **Bank** ~ to charter a bank; **Konkursforderung** ~ to admit (allow) a claim; **Wertpapier zur Börse** ~ to quote (list, *US)* a security.

Zulassung entrance, admission, admittance, *(Börse)* quotation, listing *(US)*, *(Konzession)* licence, approval, charter, permit;
    ~ **von Kraftfahrzeugen** licensing of motor vehicles; ~ **zur zollfreien Wiedereinfuhr** duty-free admission.

Zulassungs|antrag application for admission; ~**bescheid** *(Börseneinführung)* official listing notice *(US)*; ~**papiere** car licence.

Zulieferant, Zulieferer subcontractor.

Zulieferungs|auftrag vergeben an j. to subcontract s. th. out to s. o.; ~**betrieb** manufacturing subsidiary, feeder plant; ~**industrie** supplying (ancillary) industry; ~**teile** fabricating parts.

Zunahme increase, advance, rise, gain, step-up *(US)*; ~ **der Arbeitslosigkeit** increase in unemployment; ~ **der Spareinlagen** growth of savings deposits.

zurechnen, Gewinne [steuerlich] to allocate profits.

zurückbehalten, Ware to detain goods.

Zurückbehaltungsrecht retainer, lien on goods, charging (equitable, special) lien;
    ~ **aus Werklieferungsvertrag** material man's lien.

zurückbezahlen to pay back, to repay, to refund; **erste Hypothek** ~ to pay off the first mortgage.

zurückdatieren to antedate, to date back.

zurückerstatten, Auslagen to refund the expenses;

zuviel gezahltes Geld ~ to return an overpaid amount.

Zurückerstattung restitution, restoration;
~ des Kaufpreises refund of the purchase price.

zurückführen *(in die Heimat)* to repatriate;
Kontoüberziehung ~ to reduce an overdraft.

zurück|gehen *(Aufträge)* to go down, *(Einnahmen)* to fall off, *(Konjunktur)* to dip, to move backwards, *(Kurse, Preise)* to [be on the] decline, to fall off, to give way, to recede; ~gesetzte Waren old stock; ~haltende Stimmung *(Börse)* reserved (dull) tendency.

Zurückhaltung *(Börse)* stagnancy, stagnation, flatness, dullness, *(Käufer)* restraining, restraint;
~ bei Neuanlagen caution over new investment.

zurücklegen to lay aside (by, up), to put (set) by;
Geld für sein Alter ~ to lay aside money (be saving) for one's old age; Ware ~ to store, to lay up (away, *US).*

zurücknehmen, Antrag to revoke a motion; Auftrag ~ to cancel (countermand) an order.

zurückstellen *(Geld bereitstellen)* to earmark, *(Reservekonto)* to reserve, to set aside [as reserve] *(US);* für Steuern ~ to make provision (allow) for taxation.

Zurückstellung *(Bilanz)* allowance, provision, reserve, *(Verschiebung)* postponement, adjournment, deferment.

zurücktreten *(Minister)* to resign from the cabinet, to step down;
von einem Geschäft ~ to rescind a bargain.

zurückvergüten, Portospesen to reimburse the cost of postage.

Zurückvergütung refund, reimbursement.

zurückzahlen to pay back, tor epay, to refund, to return, to restitute, to wipe off.
Hypothek ~ to pay (wipe) off a mortgage; Kredit ~ to repay a loan; seine Schulden ~ to discharge one's debts.

zurückziehen, Akkreditiv to revoke a letter of credit;
sich völlig aus der Geschäftsführung ~ to drop all operational duties.

Zurückziehung erteilter Aufträge countermanding of orders given.

Zusammenarbeit *(zweier Firmen)* working affiliation;
~ auf dem Währungsgebiet monetary cooperation.

zusammenarbeiten, geschäftlich mit jem. to do business with s. o.

Zusammenballung congestion, conglomeration;
~ von Kapital concentration of capital.

zusammenbrechen *(fallieren)* to fail, to break down, to crash, to smash, to go bankrupt, *(Verhandlungen, Verkehr)* to collapse, to break down;
beinahe ~ *(Verkehr)* to reach near-collaps.

Zusammenbruch collapse, debacle, yield, *(Bankrott)* breakdown, failure, ruin, collapse, smash, blowup *(US), (Börse)* crash, smash;
~ des Aktienmarktes stock-market crash; ~ eines Unternehmens collapse of an enterprise;

kurz vor dem ~ stehen to be on the brink of ruin.

zusammenfassen, Bilanz to consolidate a balance.

Zusammenfassung | von Lizenzen package licensing;
~ von Sicherheiten tacking of securities.

zusammenkaufen to buy up, *(Börse)* to forestall the market, to corner.

Zusammenkunft, zwanglose informal meeting, get-together *(US).*

zusammenlegen *(Anleihe)* to consolidate, *(Firmen)* to amalgamate, to merge, to fuse;
Aktienkapital ~ to write down (off) capital.

Zusammenlegung | von Aktien reserve split-up; ~ des Aktienkapitals writing down (off) of capital; ~ des Kapitals merger of funds.

Zusammenschaltung *(Sender)* hookup, linkup.

zusammenschießen *(Geld)* to club together.

Zusammenschluß *(Firmen)* amalgamation, consolidation, combination, combine, merger, fusion;
marktpolitischer ~ concentration of powers; vertikaler ~ vertical merger (integration);
~ von Fernsehstationen television linkup.

zusammenschreiben, Grundstücksparzellen to incorporate a field into an estate; Hypotheken verschiedenen Ranges ~ to tack mortgages.

Zusammensetzung der Hörerschaft audience composition.

zusammenstellen, Ausschuß to set up (constitute, appoint) a committee; Liste ~ to make up a list;
nach Qualitäten ~ to grade.

Zusammenstellung compilation, combination, composition, arrangement, make-up;
tabellarische ~ schedule, table, summary.

Zusammenstoßklausel *(Schiffe)* collision (running-down) clause.

Zusammentritt der Gläubiger meeting of creditors.

Zusammenwirken, planvolles *(Kartellrecht)* unity by design.

Zusatz *(Abänderung)* alteration, amendment, *(Anhang)* appendage, appendix, *(zum Testament)* codicil, *(Versicherungspolice)* endorsement, rider.

Zusatz|abkommen supplementary agreement; ~artikel subsequent clause, *(Gesetz)* rider; ~ausstattung *(Auto)* optional equipment; ~dividende cumulative (extra, additional) dividend; ~fahrkarte excess fare (ticket).

zusätzlich additional, supplementary, supplemental, cumulative, extra, to boot, auciliary;
mit ~en Kosten verbunden sein to involve additional costs;
~e Lohnzahlung wage supplements; ~e Schicht relief (swing) shift *(US);* ~er Versicherungsschutz extended coverage.

Zusatz|patent improvement patent, patent of addition; ~rente *(Sozialversicherung)* supplementary pension, (benefits, *US);* ~versicherung additional (supplementary) insurance; ~vertrag *(Versicherung)* endorsement, rider.

Zuschaueranalyse audience analysis.

Zuschlag extra (supplementary) charge, surcharge,

(Auftragserteilung) acceptance of tender, awarding a contract, *(Auktion)* acceptance of a bid, *(Fahrkarte)* extra fare, *(Steuer)* late fee, surtax; ~ **zur Erzielung eines gewogenen Index** *(Statistik)* loading; ~ **an den Meistbietenden** sale to the highest bidder; ~ **erteilen** to award a contract, *(Auktion)* to knock down, to strike off.

zuschlagen, dem Meistbietenden to allot to the highest bidder.

Zuschlags|erteilung adjudication; ~**fahrkarte** excess fare (ticket); ~**frist** time of adjudication; ~**porto** excess postage, surcharge; ~**zahlung** additional (extra) payment; ~**zoll** additional duty.

Zuschuß allowance, benefit, pecuniary aid, *(Beitrag)* contribution, *(Staat)* subsidy, subvention, grant, grant-in-aid *(US)*; **nichtvermögenswirksamer** ~ nonasset-creating subsidy; **steuerabzugsfähiger** ~ tax-deductible contribution; **verlorener** ~ lost contribution; **seiner Tochter einen** ~ **zukommen lassen** to allow one's daughter a stipend; **jem. den** ~ **sperren to** stop s. one's allowances.

zuschußbedürftig subsidizable.

Zuschußbetrieb subsidized (supply) undertaking.

Zuschuß|empfänger nominee; **betriebliche** ~**kasse** pension plan trust fund.

zusenden, mit der Post to post, to mail *(US)*.

zusetzen, jedes Jahr hunderte von Dollar to be hundreds of dollars out-of-pocket each year.

Zusicherung *(Gewährleistung)* warranty, guaranty, guarantee.

Zustand | in betriebsfähigem in operating condition; **in neuwertigem** ~ as new; **in schlechtem** ~ in bad order, *(Haus)* in bad repair, *(Waren)* ill-conditioned; **bewohnbarer** ~ tenantable repair.

zuständige | Behörde competent authority; ~ **Stelle** responsible quarters.

Zuständigkeit competence, responsibility, province, sphere, *(Befugnisse)* powers.

Zuständigkeitsbereich scope, powers.

Zustell|anschrift address for service *(Br.)*, mailing address *(US)*; ~**dienst** delivery service.

zustellen *(Brief, Waren)* to deliver, to distribute; **jem. eine Kündigung** ~ to serve notice on s. o.

Zustellgebühr portage, delivery (carrier's) charge.

Zustellung consignment, delivery; **kostenlose (portofreie)** ~ free delivery; ~ **durch Eilboten** express delivery *(Br.)*; ~ **frei Haus** free (store-door) delivery.

Zustellungs|adresse address for service *(Br.)*, mailing address *(US)*; ~**bevollmächtigter** authorized recipient.

Zustellungsdienst delivery system, mail service; **Abhol- und** ~ pickup and delivery service.

Zustellungs|gebühr service fee, *(Spediteur)* cartage; ~**zeiten** times of delivery.

Zustimmung affirmation, approval, placet, consent. **stillschweigende** ~ implicit (tacit) assent;

~ **der Gläubiger zu einem Schuldenregulierungsplan** deed of accession.

zuteilen to assign, to allocate, to allot, to apportion, to deal, to measure (portion) out, *(Bausparer)* to advance; **Quoten** ~ to allocate the shares in a quota.

Zuteilung allocation, allotment, granting, assignment, *(Bausparer)* advance; **gleichmäßige** ~ apportionment; ~ **von Devisen** allocation of currency; **Antrag auf** ~ **von Aktien stellen** to make application for shares (stock, *US*).

Zuteilungs|antrag *(Börse)* application for allotment, letter of application *(Br.)*; ~**kurs** allotment rate, tender (allotment) price; ~**schein** allotment letter *(Br.)*, (certificate, *US*); ~**system** quota system.

Zuwachs accession, growth, accretion, accruement, increase, increment, *(Grundstück)* unearned increment, added value.

Zuwachs|rate growth (accession) rate; **keine** ~**rate** zero growth rate; ~**wert** *(Grundstück)* betterment, unearned increment.

zuweisen, Betrag den Reservefonds to allocate an amount to the reserve fund.

Zuweisung *(von Mitteln)* appropriation of funds; ~ **an die Pensions- und Wohlfahrtskasse** allocation to staff pension and provident fund; ~ **an den Reservefonds** allocation to reserve fund.

Zuwendung allocation, allowance, *(Fonds)* contribution, *(Geschenk)* gift, donation; **finanzielle** ~ grant; **steuerfreie** ~ tax-free gift; **unentgeltliche** ~ voluntary gift.

zuzahlen to pay in addition, to make an additional payment.

zuziehen to settle down, to take up one's abode; **Sachverständigen** ~ to call in an expert.

zuzüglich | Einzugsspesen with exchange; ~ **Stückzinsen** and interest.

Zuzugsgenehmigung residence permit.

Zwangs|abgabe compulsory contribution; ~**arbeit** hard (compulsory) labo(u)r; ~**arbeiter** displaced person; ~**beiträge zur Sozialversicherung** social security taxes *(US)*; ~**bewirtschaftung** rationing (standby) control; ~**geld** compulsory levy; ~**hypothek** judicial (distress sale) mortgage; ~**kurs** involuntary conversion, forced rate of exchange; ~**liquidation** winding up by the court; ~**pensionierung** compulsory retirement; ~**vergleich** composition agreement, *(Konkurs)* composition in bankruptcy; ~**verkauf** sale by order of the court, forced sale; ~**versteigerung** execution (compulsory, forced, judicial, *US*) sale, *(Grundstücke)* foreclosure.

Zwangsversteigerungs|beschluß foreclosure decree; ~**verfahren** foreclosure suit.

Zwangsverwalter receiver, sequester of land.

zwangsvollstrecken to levy, to issue execution, *(auf Grund einer Hypothek)* to foreclose.

Zwangsvollstreckung levy [of execution], enforcement by writ, distraint;

nicht der ~ unterliegen exempt, judgment-(mace-) proof *(US)*;
~ **in das unbewegliche Vermögen** foreclosure;
~ **aussetzen** to stay execution.
Zwangsvollstreckungs|beschluß foreclosure decree; ~**verfahren** executory process, process of distraint.
Zwangswirtschaft state-controlled economy;
~ **abbauen** to decontrol.
Zweck | einer Gesellschaft object of a company;
für einen bestimmten ~ vorsehen to appropriate, to earmark.
Zweck|abgabe special rate; ~**bestätigung** letter of charge *(Br.)*; ~**bestimmung** appropriation.
zweckentfremden, Wohnung to convert rooms to office use.
zweckgebunden|e Anleihe tied loan; ~**es Konto** earmarked account; ~**e Mittelzuweisung** itemized appropriation.

Zweck|verband county corporate, *(Versicherungswesen)* rating bureau.
zweckwidrige Verwendung öffentlicher Gelder misappropriation of public funds.
Zweig|anstalt branch establishment, affiliate; ~**betrieb** subsidiary (branch) plant, affiliated organization; ~**büro** sub-office; ~**geschäftsstelle** branch office (establishment).
Zweitausfertigung *(Wechsel)* second [of exchange].
zweite | Etage second stor(e)y *(Br.)*, third floor *(US)*; ~ **Wahl** medium quality.
Zweitwagen second car.
Zwergbetrieb small business, hole in the wall.
Zwischen|abschluß interim account; ~**beschäftigung** temporary employment; ~**bescheid** interim reply; ~**bilanz** interim balance sheet; ~**finanzierung** interim financing; ~**handel** transient (middleman's) business; ~**schein** provisional bond (certificate, scrip); ~**verkauf vorbehalten** subject to prior sale.